DOCUMENTS ON BRITISH FOREIGN POLICY
1919–1939

EDITED BY

W. N. MEDLICOTT, M.A., D.Lit., D.Litt., Litt.D.

Emeritus Professor of International History, University of London

AND

DOUGLAS DAKIN, M.A., Ph.D.

Emeritus Professor of History, University of London

ASSISTED BY

GILLIAN BENNETT, M.A.

SECOND SERIES
Volume XVII

LONDON
HER MAJESTY'S STATIONERY OFFICE

© *Crown copyright 1979*

First published 1979

HER MAJESTY'S STATIONERY OFFICE

Government Bookshops

49 High Holborn, London WC1V 6HB
13a Castle Street, Edinburgh EH2 3AR
41 The Hayes, Cardiff CF1 1JW
Brazennose Street, Manchester M60 8AS
Southey House, Wine Street, Bristol BS1 2BQ
258 Broad Street, Birmingham B1 2HE
80 Chichester Street, Belfast BT1 4JY

*Government publications are also available
through booksellers*

PRINTED IN ENGLAND
FOR HER MAJESTY'S STATIONERY OFFICE
BY ERIC BUCKLEY AT THE UNIVERSITY PRESS, OXFORD
Dd 586752 K10 8/78
ISBN 0 11 590192 2 *

DOCUMENTS ON BRITISH FOREIGN POLICY

1919–1939

Second Series, Volume XVII

Western Pact Negotiations: Outbreak of Spanish Civil War
June 23, 1936–January 2, 1937

O

PREFACE

In the autumn and winter of 1936–7 the chief concern of British policy makers was still to bring the Fascist powers into a general European settlement, although it was the civil war in Spain which captured the headlines and appeared to be the Foreign Office's main preoccupation. The war followed the revolt of the Spanish Foreign Legion in Morocco against the Spanish Government on July 18, 1936, just at the moment when the British, French, and Belgian Governments were meeting in London to inaugurate a new phase in the negotiations between the Locarno Powers. As a result three main and closely related themes can be traced in the documents printed in this volume, which covers the period from the third week in June 1936 until the beginning of January 1937. These are (1) the search for agreement with Germany on the basis of a revised 'Locarno' treaty; (2) the attempt, which at the end of the year appeared to have largely succeeded, to remove Anglo-Italian tensions following the end of the Italo-Ethiopian war; and (3) efforts, which largely failed, to localize the Spanish civil war by agreement on non-intervention. Each of the four continental great powers found it necessary to intervene in some measure in the war, in forms hardly conducive to progress towards the general settlement on which the British Government set so much store.

The documents relating to these three topics are printed chronologically in Chapters II–VII, after a brief Chapter I which prints a few Foreign Office documents on the immediate background of the Spanish struggle and of the British commercial interests involved. There are also references to such related topics as British defence policy (Nos. 35, 126, 156, 361, 386, 390), the Moscow treason trials (Nos. 129, 130), King Edward VIII's holiday travels (Nos. 31, 74, 168, 169, 175), and the visits to Germany of Sir Robert Vansittart (Nos. 53, 58, 59, 60, 63, 82, 85, 86, 87, and Appendix I), Mr. Lloyd George (Nos. 232, 288, 295, 317), and Lord Londonderry (No. 365). The British Embassy in Berlin sent some illuminating despatches on general conditions in Germany, signed by the Ambassador, Sir Eric Phipps (Nos. 318, 350), or by the Minister, Mr. B. C. Newton (Nos. 108, 138, 233).

Earlier volumes (XII, XIII, XV, XVI) in this series have shown that since 1934 the British Foreign Office had never quite abandoned hope of achieving peacefully a 'general settlement' by meeting Germany's more legitimate grievances under the Versailles treaty and otherwise. It was essentially a belief in the disposition of at least some of the German leaders to be satisfied with as powerful an international position as could be secured by negotiation, even though the 'extremists' preferred the rewards and exhilarations of war.

In January 1936 Mr. Anthony Eden, Secretary of State for Foreign Affairs, had secured the Cabinet's agreement to attempts to come to 'some modus vivendi—to put it no higher—with Hitler's Germany', pending the progress of British rearmament. After Germany's Rhineland coup of March 7, 1936, Herr Hitler's voluminous proposals of March 7 and 31 were not rejected out of hand by the Foreign Office as utterly hypocritical, and even his failure to reply to the British questionnaire of May 7 as to his intentions was not considered to have ended the dialogue, although it was undoubtedly a major disappointment. The meeting of representatives of Britain, France, and Belgium in London in July was intended to give a fresh impetus to the negotiations: a tactfully worded *communiqué* of July 23 invited Germany and Italy to negotiate at a five-power conference a new agreement which would replace the Rhine Pact of Locarno, and perhaps lead to a wider discussion facilitating a general settlement essential to the peace of Europe.

The German Government's acceptance of this invitation in principle on July 30 was on condition that the five-power conference should meet only after thorough diplomatic preparation (No. 37). The Italian Government gave the same answer on August 1 (No. 43). It was agreed that Great Britain should take the lead in the discussions. For the Cabinet and Foreign Office the ensuing exchanges were exhaustive and frustrating, and no substantial progress had been made by the end of the year. And yet there was no desire in either London or Berlin to bring the debate to an end, and negotiations continued with a careful if rather distrustful urbanity on both sides throughout 1937. The German leaders continued to refer from time to time to their desire for an Anglo-German agreement. Herr von Ribbentrop, the advocate of such an agreement, was, after some apparent hesitation on Herr Hitler's part, duly despatched to London as Ambassador (Nos. 73, 337).

It was evident that Germany, like the United Kingdom, had uses for a modus vivendi pending the completion of her rearmament, and had no intention of revealing her final objectives in the meantime. In London the Cabinet was adequately briefed as to the progress of German armaments and (when not distracted by the abdication and other domestic crises) well aware of the dangers and ambiguities of the situation as they appeared to their Foreign Office advisers. A gloomy view was usually taken in the Foreign Office of German intentions, which were, however, variously assessed. Would Germany march east? And if so, against whom? And when? Would her economic burdens hasten war or prevent it? Did she really want colonies? And if she really desired an Anglo-German agreement, on what terms? At this period a Nazi invasion and dismemberment of European Russia, as foreshadowed in *Mein Kampf,* was not regarded in the Foreign Office as very likely, mainly perhaps because Germany's plans for central Europe appeared quite grandiose enough. The peaceful turn in German policy for which the Foreign Office yearned as a basis for the 'general settlement' was indicated by Mr. Orme Sargent in a minute of December 29. If it took place, he said, 'then we may look forward to a new Locarno treaty; Germany's collaboration in clearing up the present economic and currency chaos in Germany; the limitation of armaments; the return of Germany to the League; the establishment of a real policy of non-intervention in Spain; and a *détente* with Russia and Czechoslovakia'. He evidently considered such a settlement highly unlikely but not quite impossible (No. 521).

While there was general agreement in Cabinet and official circles in London as to the need for the modus vivendi there tended to be a polarization of opinion between those who regarded it as merely a device for buying time before British rearmament reached a point of comparative safety in 1939, and those who had lingering hopes of a genuine satisfaction of totalitarian claims on terms which would be acceptable to the western powers. If the Foreign Office officials tended towards the more pessimistic alternative there was no finality of views at this stage, and they still found some difficulty in making up their minds about Adolf Hitler. There lingered the belief, or hope, that he was not 'an extremist', a label which was applied without hesitation to General Goering and Dr. Goebbels. Sir E. Phipps placed the Chancellor on October 19 along with Dr. Schacht, Herr Hess, and General von Epp among Germany's moderate leaders (No. 300); on November 4 he described him as an idealist (No. 350). Sir Robert Vansittart, Permanent Under Secretary of State to the Foreign Office, visited Berlin from July 31 to August 13 to attend the Olympic Games as the guest of his wife's brother-in-law, Sir E. Phipps, and wrote a characteristically lengthy and finely phrased report on his impressions entitled 'A Busman's Holiday' (Appendix I); but on this point he too was inconclusive.

It would certainly seem, however, and to judge from this report, that when they met he and Adolf Hitler each had difficulty in discovering anything particularly monstrous in the other. But they avoided discussion of the more controversial issues. Hitler appeared 'an amiably simple, rather shy, rotundly ascetic, *bourgeois*, a man of almost obvious *physical* integrity, very much in earnest, not humorous, not alarming, not magnetic, but convinced of a variable mission and able to impress himself so strongly that he impresses himself on those around him'. Vansittart concluded that the 'Great Man' was 'a clear case of the chameleon; and it is well that he should be so, for in that the chief, if any, hope of the future lies'. He might still, in other words, opt for peace. Much of Vansittart's memorandum was taken up with a résumé of the diagnoses of Europe's 'common and fundamental troubles' with which he endeavoured to persuade 'nearly all the important Germans whom I met, including Herr Hitler' that 'a return to normality was essential, that an economic must be preceded by a political settlement, and that the area of appeasement must be as wide as possible'. None of his interlocutors appeared convinced, but his belief in Herr Hitler's capacity for fitful moods of reasonableness remained.

In general the Foreign Office believed that Germany's economic embarrassments might be the most likely to facilitate a broad political settlement, although there should be no specific concessions without an adequate German *quid pro quo*. This partly explains the very cautious response to feelers put out by Dr. Schacht, President of the Reichsbank, who, in conversation with M. Blum late in August, asked for economic assistance and colonial concessions. He said that the Chancellor was deeply concerned about the economic and financial situation in Germany, and in return for an 'alignment' of currencies and help over raw materials supplies would go a long way to meet French views, and even discuss disarmament (No. 145). A month later, on September 20, M. Blum impressed on Mr. Eden the importance attached by Dr. Schacht to the question of colonies and raw materials and his anxiety for co-operation between the United Kingdom, France, and Germany in the colonial and economic spheres, which were now of 'vital importance to Germany'. It was evident that M. Blum was reluctant to allow a chance of agreement with Germany to slip by (No. 209). Mr. Eden's reply was cautious: he referred to his statement about the German colonies on July 27 (which had not quite closed the door on concessions) but said in effect that these matters could be considered only after a more complete appreciation of the attitude of the German Government towards a general European settlement, for which the diplomatic preliminaries of the Five-Power Conference provided the most convenient means (No. 211). This reply, as reported to Dr. Schacht by M. Blum, was taken as an uncompromising negative, although it was really evidence of distrust of Dr. Schacht's unorthodox tactics (cf. Nos. 282, 296, 300, 306, 307, 318, 319, 342). His initiative, and the problem of whether he was speaking with any authority, continued to complicate Anglo-German discussions for at least the next twelve months.

Meanwhile the Foreign Office had made an elaborate survey of elements which would be involved in the negotiation of a new Western Pact and of means to resolve the situation created by the 'German initiative of March 7'. The result was embodied in a memorandum of August 19 (No. 114) which visualized a new agreement reproducing the old Locarno treaty, with the modifications necessitated by the German action. It provides interesting evidence of the full range of British aspirations at this stage. It was anticipated that the German Government would be ready as before to agree to a non-aggression pact between Germany and France and Belgium, although she might object both to the continuance of the League Council's former role in deciding whether an aggression had taken place and to the former arbitration treaties between Germany and Poland and Czechoslovakia. It was proposed that the British Government should press for the continuance of the League Council's role in deciding about aggression, and should seek to become both a guaranteed and a guarantor power; Belgium if she so desired should not be required to continue as a guarantor power, although she should undertake to defend herself; the possibility of an air pact, the accession of Holland to the Western Pact, and staff conversations were also visualized. This programme was accepted without much alteration by the Cabinet Committee on Foreign Policy on August 25 (No. 115, note 4), and the Cabinet agreed on September 2 to approach the other four governments (of Germany, Italy, France, and Belgium) with a view to a meeting of the

Five-Power Conference at the end of October. The German Government replied promptly that the question of date must be left open until preparations had been so far advanced as to give a real promise of success (Nos. 184, 186). Although Mr. Eden thought this 'not very promising' he gave instructions for the preparation of an agenda, which was communicated as a proposal to the other four governments on September 17.

From the proposed agenda the Foreign Office thought it best to omit at this stage a number of the points which had been mentioned in the survey of August 19, including the possibility of air limitation, staff discussions, Irish and Dutch participation, and the future of Eupen and Malmédy. The agenda was in fact limited to reference to the form of the proposed agreement, provision to meet the problem of air attack, and arrangements for arbitration and conciliation. There was no direct reference to the conformity of the non-aggression arrangements with the French eastern treaties, although the document did mention (paragraph 5(1)) certain exceptions to the proposed non-aggression arrangements 'on the lines which were laid down in Article 2 of the Treaty of Locarno' (No. 206). On receiving the suggested agenda on September 18 the German Chargé, Prince Bismarck, at once remarked on the reference to 'exceptions' (No. 207).

When the comments of the four governments on the agenda had been received the Foreign Office summarized them in a long memorandum which was discussed by the Cabinet on October 28 (Nos. 321, 349). Mr. Eden referred to the German opposition to the exceptions as the vital difficulty in the negotiations; if accepted, it would make it impossible for France to assist Russia, Czechoslovakia, or Poland if attacked by Germany, and would even prevent Great Britain from assisting Egypt or Iraq if they were attacked by another party to such an arrangement. Nor would either power in those circumstances be able to assist a state attacked in violation of the League Covenant. He added that Germany was still not prepared to accept the League as the deciding body in case of aggression, and that she and Italy were opposed to the extension of the guarantee system as it existed under the Locarno Treaty. France, on the other hand, was objecting to Belgium's refusal to give her a guarantee.

The memorandum was circulated to the four governments on November 4, and was followed by a note of November 19 giving the British Government's own views on the agenda for the Five-Power Conference (No. 389). This is perhaps the most important document in this volume, for it provided the basic definition of Great Britain's attitude towards German policy and aspirations and a point of reference in negotiations for the next year or more. It reaffirmed the British desire for guarantees from France and Germany; insisted with regard to the exceptions that the British and French must carry out their obligations under the Covenant; and suggested that the basis of the exceptions should be an act of aggression by a signatory against a non-signatory violating some instrument such as the Pact of Paris by which the signatory was bound. It again suggested that the Council of the League was the best body to judge on the fact of aggression, but agreed to consider alternatives. Lastly it stressed the government's desire that other matters affecting European peace should come under discussion if progress were made with the Five Power conference. On the following day, November 20, Mr. Eden in a major speech at Leamington promised British support for Germany against unprovoked aggression if the new Western European settlement were reached (No. 400, note 1). All, however, in vain: on December 8 the new German Ambassador in London, Herr von Ribbentrop, told Mr. Eden that the memorandum of November 19 had been 'a grievous disappointment to the Chancellor' (No. 455).

It seems evident that this reaction was due to the failure to leave Germany with a free hand in Eastern Europe, even though there was no suggestion at this point that Great Britain should underwrite French treaty obligations there. This was in line with the Foreign Office's recommendation on August 19, that 'We should decline to disinterest ourselves from the East and Centre of Europe and continue to insist on the need for a general settlement, while urging France not to wreck a Western settlement by maintaining impossible demands in the East and Centre' (No. 114). The British formula about an ultimate general settlement gave an opening for German counter-proposals about economic aid and the colonies, but the German Government's objections to the 'exceptions' ruled out any such widening of the western-pact discussions. Since neither side wished at this stage for an 'impasse', and since the Foreign Office still apparently retained faint hopes of an ultimate peaceful turn in German policy, the talks went on (Nos. 420, 454, 455, 480, 485, 490). But the officials now showed increasingly an interest in 'gaining time—or not preventing others from wasting it' (No. 488, note 3).

After the calling off of sanctions against Italy on July 4 and of British defensive assurances in the Mediterranean on July 27 (No. 13), Anglo-Italian tensions were eased, but the Foreign Office continued to regard Signor Mussolini as a more imminent threat to peace than the German Chancellor. In a Cabinet paper of August 19 Mr. Eden referred to Italy's active and unsatisfied desire for dominance in the Mediterranean basin, and the likelihood that she would regard the disturbances in Spain not only as a struggle between Fascism and Communism, but as a means of weakening British sea power in the Western Mediterranean (No. 115). There was already no doubt about Italian aid to the Spanish insurgents. On the other hand, Count Ciano, the Italian Foreign Minister, gave a specific assurance on August 18 that his government did not contemplate any deal with the insurgents for the cession of Ceuta, Spanish Morocco, or the Balearic Islands (No. 159). The British Government replied on September 12 with a carefully worded statement that 'any alteration of the status quo in the Western Mediterranean must be a matter of the closest concern to His Majesty's Government' (No. 159).

However, the British Ambassador at Rome, Sir Eric Drummond, became convinced after his return from leave early in October that at the moment few things would give the Italian Government greater pleasure 'than to return to really friendly relations with His Majesty's Government' (No. 312), and on October 13 Count Grandi, the Italian Ambassador at London, spoke of Signor Mussolini's wishes in almost the same words (No. 291). Count Ciano's visit to Berlin from October 20 to 24 laid the foundation of the Rome–Berlin axis but was not regarded with any great alarm in London, and Signor Mussolini's bombastic speech of November 1 at Milan was intended, it was understood, to be conciliatory to Great Britain (Nos. 334, 353). The British decision to withdraw the Legation Guard from Addis Ababa was regarded as a friendly counter-gesture, and there were amiable references to Italy in speeches by Lord Halifax and Mr. Eden, whose distrust of Italian aims was, nevertheless, unabated (No. 352).

The result was the Anglo-Italian 'Gentleman's Agreement'—a term chosen by Signor Mussolini and rather disliked by Mr. Eden (No. 461)—which did little to remove the Foreign Office's basic doubts as to Italian intentions. In a further Cabinet Paper of December 14 Mr. Eden referred in strong terms to the build-up of Italian strength in the Balearic Islands as a potential threat to a vital British interest which, if acquiesced in, 'would be for His Majesty's Government to abdicate the responsibilities of a Great Power' (No. 471). Three days later it was known that the chief Italian trouble-maker, Signor Rossi, who had been the subject of repeated British representations, was being permanently withdrawn from Majorca (No. 477); and although the scale of Italian participation in the Spanish struggle was not diminished, the Italian Government was quite willing to agree to the British Government's main requirement, the acceptance without qualification of the territorial status quo in the Mediterranean (No. 376). A joint declaration was signed in Rome on January 2, 1937, affirming the desire of the two powers to better relations between themselves and all the Mediterranean Powers, to disclaim any desire to modify or see modified the national sovereignty of territories in the area, to maintain freedom of transit there as a vital interest of the British Empire and Italy, and generally to further the ends of peace. In an attached exchange of letters dated December 31, 1936, Sir E. Drummond referred to Italy's assurances that as far as she was concerned the integrity of 'the present territories of Spain' should 'in all circumstances remain intact and unmodified'. Count Ciano confirmed this statement (No. 530).

The Spanish civil war had, however, presented the British Government with problems apart from the possibility of a direct Italian challenge to British interests in the Western Mediteranean. There was, on the one hand, the difficulty of deciding 'whether the victory of the Right or of the Left in Spain would be the more undesirable from the point of view of British interests'. A Foreign Office minute of September 1, elaborating this baffling formulation, could only suggest that it was highly desirable to ensure that 'the government which does emerge should not enter upon its inheritance with any grudge against His Majesty's Government' (No. 157). There was, on the other hand, concern for the embarrassments of M. Blum, whose government faced the same predicaments as the British in a more acute form, that is, with a stronger apprehension as to Italian and German intentions and a stronger internal ideological movement for and against aid to the Spanish Government.

M. Blum was thought indeed to face the possibility of civil war if he responded to the appeal of the Spanish Government on July 20 and on subsequent occasions for arms, munitions, and bombers. It was known in Paris on July 25 that the first request had been refused. A long footnote to document No. 19 discusses the suggestion that this refusal was influenced by British pressure on M. Blum, who was in London on July 23 for the three-power conference. There is no evidence in the Foreign Office archives to support this assertion. On a number of subsequent occasions Mr. Eden denied it, while saying that he thought the French decision a wise one (Nos. 113, 136, 147). The decisive word on the British side against French intervention seems in fact to have been spoken by the British Ambassador at Paris, Sir George Clerk, to the French Foreign Minister, M. Delbos, on August 7 in remarks 'entirely personal and on my own responsibility' (No. 67). It was believed at the British Embassy that this intervention might well have tilted the scale in the Council of Ministers in favour of a policy of non-intervention, which it announced on August 8 (Nos. 72, 81).

In this situation, which was upsetting both his sleep and his digestion (No. 80), M. Blum looked to the British Government for backing. He failed to get it when two French admirals, Darlan and Decoux, came to London on August 5 to enlist British naval support against a suspected Italian seizure of the Balearic Islands and a German seizure of the Canaries (No. 56). But a French proposal of August 1, addressed to the British and Italian Governments, for an agreement by the three 'Mediterranean powers' on non-intervention was welcomed by Mr. Eden with the suggestion that it should be extended to include Germany and Portugal. On August 6 proposals were telegraphed from Paris to sixteen governments for agreement on non-intervention in Spanish affairs (Nos. 46, 52, 64). The general response was neither hostile nor prompt, and to strengthen M. Blum's hand an exchange of letters on August 14 affirmed the devotion of Britain and France to the principle of non-intervention (No. 94). Soon MM. Blum and Delbos were reported to be 'near the end of their tether' owing mainly to Germany's delay in accepting the French proposals, but this was done on August 24, and the British Government accepted at once the French proposal for a committee which would sit in London and deal with the many technical details that would arise over the implementation of the agreement (No. 128).

The committee's business was essentially to deal with complaints submitted on behalf of any participating government alleging that the non-intervention agreement had been breached. As the meetings and secretariat were in London it fell to the British Government to take the lead in efforts to make the work of the committee a success. With the German and Italian Governments helping the Spanish insurgents in the first phase of the war, and the Soviet Union aiding the Spanish Government's forces a little later, allegations were frequent and inconclusive, while the French border, whatever the government's intentions, could not be effectively closed. The documentation relating to Spain which is printed in this volume in Chapters IV to VII does not attempt to tell the whole story of the war, which would be outside the purpose of this Collection. It does, however, include some representative samples of the information reaching the Foreign Office about the problems of the British diplomatic agents at Hendaye, Madrid, and elsewhere (e.g. Nos. 8, 9, 38, 40, 42, 75, 97–100, 137, 150, 213, 236, 304, 383, 493, 510) and about Spanish conditions resulting from the war (Nos. 46, 120, 123, 183, 247, 252). The 'Introductory Note' to Chapter IV comments further on the printing of material from the records of the Non-Intervention Committee.

The first meeting of the Committee was on September 9, 1936 (No. 178); its early deliberations did not stem either the flow of arms and manpower into Spain or the flow of criticism inside the Committee, and at the twelfth meeting on December 2 a new phase began with proposals for the supervision of the import of war material at the principal points of entry, with the co-operation of the two parties in Spain (No. 427). When it became clear in the new year that this co-operation would not be forthcoming, alternative arrangements had to be made; these came into operation in the following April, 1937, and will be referred to in Volume XVIII.

Surveying the whole field of foreign policy on December 31, 1936, in one of his lengthy memoranda (Appendix II), Sir R. Vansittart was pessimistic: since the 'truce' of the Olympic Games the general trend of world events had been 'almost uniformly unfavourable to our interests'. The country had 'entered upon a period of emergency'. Germany was 'admittedly the cause of our rearmament, just as she is the focus of disquiet in Central Europe'; British attempts to meet and divert the coming crisis since 1934, first by a comprehensive European settlement, then by a Five-Power agreement confined to Western and then Central Europe, had not succeeded; 'on any showing Germany will be ready for big mischief at least a year—and probably more—before we are ready to look after ourselves'. It was a 'complacent assumption' that 'the Germans are *necessarily* going—and staying—East'. In fact, perhaps swayed unduly by his secret advisers, he thought a Russo-German war unlikely: the 'German and Russian armies do not contemplate the geographical impossibility of attacking each other'. The real purpose of German expansion was the control of the Baltic–Adriatic–Black Sea block, but there were many indications that some of the German leaders now looked on Great Britain as the greatest obstacle to German expansion and to the 'heroic conception' of life and German destiny. He believed that the year 1939 was the first 'in which we shall be able to breathe with even comparative relief' and time was therefore the principal preoccupation of the Foreign Office 'since time is the very material commodity which the Foreign Office is expected to provide in the same way as other departments have to provide *other* material'. This sombre and wide-ranging review extended over the whole field of contemporary world politics, and ended with sixteen listed recommendations, which offered guide lines for British foreign policy during the next two years. He thought that the aim of British foreign policy should be to stabilize the position until 1939, and that, in order to make this possible, the cession of a colony as part of a political settlement should not be ruled out.

We may also note that in the period covered by this volume various important organizational changes within the Foreign Office took place or were foreshadowed. The Abyssinian Department, set up in August 1935, was disbanded, and responsibility for Abyssinian affairs returned to the Egyptian Department. Mr. M. Peterson, who had been head of the Abyssinian Department, was appointed H.M. Minister at Sofia in October, 1936. Mr. W. Roberts succeeded Mr. H. Seymour as head of the League of Nations and Western Department on the latter's appointment as H.M. Minister at Tehran in October. In accordance with Mr. Eden's wishes, Sir Alexander Cadogan returned to the Foreign Office from Peking in the summer of 1936 and succeeded Sir Victor Wellesley on October 1 as one of the two Deputy Under Secretaries of State (with Sir L. Oliphant). On December 31, 1936, with the death of the head of the Central Department, Mr. R. F. Wigram, the Foreign Office lost its chief adviser on German affairs: he was succeeded by Mr. W. Strang. We learn from Mr. Eden's memoirs that Sir R. Vansittart's position, which had been somewhat shaken by the Ethiopian crisis, was again in doubt at the end of 1936, when both the Prime Minister and Mr. Eden urged his retirement on grounds of health. It was proposed that he should go to Paris as Ambassador to finish off his career, but he felt that he could be of more use in London, and his memorandum of December 31 was a furthur demonstration of his preoccupation with German affairs and his continued authority.

The conditions under which the Editors accepted the task of producing this Collection, namely, access to all papers in the Foreign Office archives and freedom in the selection and arrangement of documents, continue to be fulfilled. Use has been made of the private papers of Lord Gladwyn in the Foreign Office, of Sir Anthony Eden (Series A) when they were deposited in the Foreign Office, and those of Sir Robert Vansittart in the Archive Centre, Churchill College, Cambridge. I have to thank Mr. B. Cheeseman, O.B.E., the Head of the Library and Records Department of the Foreign and Commonwealth Office, and his staff for all necessary facilities. Mrs. Gillian Bennett, M.A., the Assistant Editor, has given me valuable help at every stage of work on this volume.

W. N. MEDLICOTT

December 1977

CONTENTS

LIST OF ABBREVIATIONS

A.T.B.	Advisory (Committee) on Trade and Blockade Questions in Time of War.
B.F.S.P.	*British and Foreign State Papers* (London).
Cmd.	Command Paper (London).
D.A.P.E.	*Dez Anos de Política Externa (1936–1947)* (Lisbon).
D.D.B.	*Documents Diplomatiques Belges 1920–40* (Brussels).
D.D.F.	*Documents Diplomatiques Français 1932–1939* (Paris).
D.G.F.P.	*Documents on German Foreign Policy 1918–1945* (London).
D.R.C.	Defence Requirements Committee.
D.V.P.S.	*Dokumenty Vneshney Politiki SSSR* (Moscow).
F.R.U.S.	*Papers relating to the Foreign Relations of the United States (Washington).*
H.C. Deb. 5 s.	*Parliamentary Debates (Hansard), Official Report, 5th Series,* House of Commons (London).
H.L. Deb. 5 s.	*Parliamentary Debates (Hansard), Official Report, 5th Series,* House of Lords (London).
L/N.O.J.	*League of Nations Official Journal* (Geneva).
L/N.O.J., S.S.	*League of Nations Official Journal, Special Supplement* (Geneva).

An asterisk following the file number of a document indicates that the text has been taken from Confidential Print.

CHAPTER SUMMARIES

CHAPTER I

The beginning of the Spanish Civil War
June 23–July 23, 1936

Conversations in Berlin: French proposal for non-intervention in Spain

July 24–August 15, 1936

CHAPTER III

Establishment of the Non-Intervention Committee: Dr. Schacht's conversations in Paris: Moscow treason trials

August 16–September 8, 1936

CHAPTER IV

Non-Intervention Committee starts work: League reform: British note of September 17 proposes Five Power Meeting

September 9–30, 1936

CHAPTER V

Western Pact proposals: replies to British note of September 17: breaches of non-intervention agreement

October 1–31, 1936

CHAPTER VI

British memorandum of November 19 on Five Power Conference: search for Anglo-Italian rapprochement: plans for supervision of Spanish imports

November 2–30, 1936

CHAPTER VII

Western Pact proposals hang fire: conclusion of Anglo-Italian Gentleman's Agreement: discussion of supervisory schemes for Spain

December 1, 1936–January 2, 1937

1

CHAPTER I

The beginning of the Spanish Civil War

June 23–July 23, 1936

No. 1

*Note by Mr. W. H. Montagu-Pollock[1] on recent
developments in Spain*

[*W 5693/62/41*]

FOREIGN OFFICE, *June 23, 1936*

The third General Election held under the Republican régime,[2] which took place last February, resulted unexpectedly in an overwhelming victory for the parties of the Left.[3] This was due not to any violent swing of the pendulum of popular feeling in the direction of socialism so much as to the fact that the parties of the Left Centre, realising the unpopularity which the previous government of Señor Lerroux[4] had incurred through its dependence upon the clerical right-wing parties, had concluded an electoral pact with all the parties of the Left.

After the election a government was formed under the leadership of Señor Azaña, which consisted entirely of members of the Left Centre parties, as the Socialists refused to participate. This Government was committed to the ambitious programme which had been laid down in loose terms in the election pact, and it was also dependent for its existence upon the support of the parties of the Left, including the Socialists, Communists and Syndicalists, with whom its members had little or nothing in common beyond a hatred of Fascism and Clericalism. (Shortly afterwards the President, Señor Alcala Zamora, was removed from office by a vote of the Cortes and his place was taken by the Prime Minister, Señor Azaña, who was succeeded by his close friend Señor Quiroga.[5] The political complexion of Señor Quiroga's government is the same as that of its predecessor).

---

[1] A Second Secretary in the League of Nations and Western Department of the Foreign Office. The filed copy of this note stated that it was prepared for the use of the Secretary of State for Foreign Affairs, Mr. Anthony Eden.

[2] The second Spanish republic had been set up in 1931 following the decision of King Alfonso XIII to leave Spain, although without formal abdication, on April 14.

[3] At the elections held on February 16, 1936, the so-called Popular Front, led by Señor Manuel Azaña, had secured 256 seats, the Centre 52, and the Right 165.

[4] Señor Alejandro Lerroux, leader of the Radical party, had headed four governments from 1933 to 1935.

[5] Señor Santiago Casares Quiroga.

Since the election the situation throughout the country has steadily deteriorated. The Government, in a well-meaning attempt to carry out its election promises and under strong pressure from the Left, has passed by decree a number of laws which have resulted in a state of chronic strikes and lockouts and in the virtual paralysis of a great deal of the country's business. Prominent amongst these decrees are the Labour Decree of February 29th last, under which employers are compelled to reinstate and compensate all workmen dismissed for political reasons since the end of 1934 and to reconstitute their establishment[s] as they existed in October 1934, and a decree of May 7th providing for enormous increases of wages of ships' crews, since the passing of which the whole of Spanish shipping has been at a standstill owing to the refusal of the employers to agree to the enforcement of its provisions in full. The election results were also generally regarded by the working classes as a victory for the revolution, and to such an extent did popular feeling get out of hand that 140 churches were burnt during the first six weeks after the election. In view of their weak Parliamentary position and of the revolutionary feeling in the air, which has affected also the civil and armed services, the Government has been either afraid or powerless to maintain order; and in many places, owing to the feeling of fear and confusion resulting from the disappearance of authority, control of the local government, the law courts etc. has fallen into the hands of the Extreme Left minority. Similarly the effective control of the Socialist Party has virtually passed into the hands of its extremist leader Señor Caballero;[6] and Señor Prieto,[7] its moderate 'official' leader, is now shouted down if he tries to speak in public. The Communists have at the same time been busy arming themselves and strengthening their organisation.

In spite of repeated assertions by the Government that it intends to 'defend the Republic and suppress disorder', there is no sign of an improvement in the situation. Various developments have been prophesied, such as the taking over of power by the Communists, a Fascist putsch, and a military putsch. There is no doubt that Fascism has gained many recruits as a result of the disorders and the anti-clerical excesses, but its leader, young de Rivera,[8] is in prison and the movement seems hardly powerful enough to take such a drastic step at present. Similarly the army is a very uncertain element as Left Wing feeling is very strong among the lower ranks and no forceful leader has made his appearance. At all events the feeling is widespread that, with things developing as they are, the chances of Parliamentary government surviving are becoming very slight (except perhaps in Catalonia, where there is comparative order under the autonomous Government of Señor Companys).[9] The financial position is also deteriorating rapidly, and a black rate for the peseta has made its appearance.

[6] Señor Francisco Largo Caballero.　　　　　[7] Señor Indalecio Prieto y Tuero.
[8] Señor José Antonio Primo de Rivera (1903–36) was the son of the former Spanish general and dictator (1870–1930).
[9] Señor Luis Companys had been president of the *generalidad* or government of Catalonia since 1933.

British firms in Spain have had their full share of the difficulties resulting from the labour unrest and from the recent Government legislation, and our Embassy has been active in protesting to the Spanish Government against the application to British firms of the provisions of the Decree of February 29th, the enforcement of which has been placed in the hands of popularly elected local commissions, from whose decision there is no appeal. Our protests have been based not on grounds of discrimination against British firms, but on the contention that an order whereby firms are being penalised for having dismissed employees at the order of a previous government is contrary to international standards of justice and equity. So long as the Spanish Government fails to put its own house in order and to regain its authority, there is little hope of obtaining any real satisfaction for British interests, and the best we can do is to continue our protests and to hope that the legislation will quickly prove itself unworkable. Apart from the injustices of the legislation there have also been considerable fears for the safety of British life and property owing to the workers getting out of hand. Prominent among firms on behalf of whom strong protests have been made is the Rio Tinto Company, of which Sir Auckland Geddes is chairman, and His Majesty's Chargé d'Affaires informed the Spanish Government that His Majesty's Government had grounds for believing that an organized attempt was being made by the workers' representatives to force this concern out of business.[10]

Anti-foreign feeling has also shown signs of developing in official circles, and a book entitled 'Spain, to whom does she belong?', containing a violent attack on British enterprise in Spain, was published a few months ago by a member of the Spanish Foreign Service.[11] The Government has also recently imposed without any warning heavy surcharges on nearly all imports into Spain, and His Majesty's Government have protested against this measure on the grounds that it constitutes a serious breach of the standstill agreement concluded in August last.[12] The Embassy reports, however, that Members of

[10] Mr. G. A. D. Ogilvie-Forbes, Counsellor in H.M. Embassy at Madrid and Acting Chargé d'Affaires, made a strong protest on these lines to the Spanish Government on June 12, 1936. The Rio Tinto Company owned nearly all the large Spanish deposits of copper. Other companies adversely affected by the legislation of February 29 were Messrs. Yeoward Bros., owners of banana-growing estates in the Canary Islands, and the Alquife Mining Company, the British directors of which were said to be contemplating the closing down of the concern owing to the deterioration of labour conditions: cf. W 5533/62/41.

[11] La España . . . de quien?, written by Señor Virgilio Sevillano Carbajal, a First Secretary in the Spanish Foreign Service and head of the Press Department of the Ministry of State, was published on February 29, 1936. Sir H. Chilton, H.M. Ambassador at Madrid, transmitted a copy of the book and a covering memorandum to the Foreign Office in his despatch No. 244 of April 9.

[12] The standstill agreement of August 29, 1935, followed preliminary discussions in London between Spanish and United Kingdom delegations regarding possible trade concessions on both sides. These talks were suspended when it became evident 'that the Spanish offers in respect of the United Kingdom desiderata would not materially improve the position of British exports to Spain, and would certainly not justify the granting of the important concessions Spain required from the United Kingdom'. The negotiations were

the Government and of the Ministry of State (Foreign Ministry) with whom it has been in contact have shown every desire to be as accommodating as is within their power.

The declared foreign policy of the Spanish Government follows traditional lines.

suspended on the understanding that each country would treat the commerce of the other benevolently until conversations were resumed (cf. W 2276/1164/41, para. 133). On Mr. Eden's instructions, Mr. Ogilvie-Forbes sent a note on June 8, 1936, to the Spanish Government expressing grave concern at the customs surcharges of May 29 as a serious breach of the standstill agreement; if maintained it would make it impossible for His Majesty's Government to 'resist further the demand for an extension of the high duty period on tomatoes' (W 5252/359/41). Remonstrances on this point were discontinued after the outbreak of the Civil War on July 18.

No. 2

Mr. C. A. Edmond[1] *(Geneva) to Foreign Office*[2] *(Received June 30)*
No. 37 Saving: Telegraphic [W 5894/626/41]

GENEVA, *June 29, 1936*

Following from Secretary of State.

The Spanish Foreign Minister[3] and Señor de Madariaga[4] called upon me this afternoon when we had a conversation about the international situation. Both were agreed upon the immense difficulties attendant upon attempting any amendment of the Covenant itself, but they indicated that they regarded an amendment of the 1921 resolutions[5] as both possible and desirable.

We spoke of the difficulty of securing agreement upon any such amendment at short notice, and the Spanish representatives indicated that they thought that the rate at which we should work was dependent upon the extent to which the French Government could establish itself at home. If, as they feared was unlikely, the French Government could show itself to have a strong internal backing, then probably we had two years in which to work, but if the authority of France was to be vitiated by internal strife, then maybe we had no more than six months in which to save the peace of Europe. We agreed that it was desirable that every attempt should be made

[1] H.M. Consul at Geneva.
[2] Mr. Eden was in Geneva from June 25 to July 4 to attend meetings of the League Council and Assembly: cf. Volume XVI, Nos. 383, note 2 and 395, note 2.
[3] Señor Augusto Barcia.   [4] Spanish delegate to the League of Nations.
[5] The reference is to resolutions adopted by the League Assembly on October 4, 1921, during a debate on the Economic Weapon of the League, and following a report by the International Blockade Committee. They embodied modifications and interpretations of Article 16 of the Covenant which were to be used as guidelines in the future application of that Article, recognizing the special role of the League Council in the organization of economic action under Article 16 and providing for the substitution of progressive economic sanctions in place of total severance of economic relations: see *L/N. Records of the Second Assembly*, 1921, pp. 796–814.

to come to a decision on the League's future at the September meeting of the Assembly.[6]

I then drew the attention of the Spanish Minister for Foreign Affairs to the internal condition of Spain, and stated that I had received certain reports from our Embassy in Madrid which made me very anxious. The position of important British companies, such as Rio Tinto and Messrs. Yeoward, were disquieting examples of what I had in mind.[7] While I admitted that there had been no discrimination against British companies, I must draw the Minister's attention to the conditions in which those companies were attempting to carry on their business. If a company were instructed by one Government to discharge a certain number of its employees it made its situation extremely difficult if it were instructed by the next Government not only to take these same men back, but to pay them compensation.

The Minister replied that he appreciated the difficulties, but so far as the Rio Tinto company was concerned he had during the last 24 hours received reports which were definitely more reassuring. As a result of this conversation he would certainly make further enquiries and speak to me again on the matter tomorrow. In the meanwhile he pointed out in justification of the attitude of the present Government that when in opposition it had always contested the authority of the edicts of its predecessors. I replied that while this might be so there remained the fact that under the legislation of February 29th there was no appeal. This placed the companies in a position of great difficulty. M. Barcia, however, contested my statement. He admitted that there might be no juridical appeal, but there was under the Spanish constitution an appeal against the acts of any Government, and he felt sure that it would be wise, if necessity arose, for the British companies to have recourse to such appeal before resorting to international arbitration.[8] M. Barcia insisted that the Spanish Government were steadily regaining control of the local situation, and expressed himself as most confident of its ability to establish its authority throughout the country within a short time.

The Spanish Foreign Minister was throughout extremely conciliatory in his attitude, and was clearly anxious to show, so far as he was concerned, an intention to meet all legitimate complaints.

Repeated to Madrid No. 2 Saving.

[6] Cf. Volume XVI, No. 385, note 4.

[7] Cf. No. 1.

[8] After discussion in the Foreign Office it was agreed that an appeal against the acts of the Spanish Government or the constitutionality of the decree of February 29 appeared hardly practicable. Instead, Mr. Ogilvie-Forbes was instructed in telegram No. 107 of July 3 to press for reasonable treatment for British companies without directly calling in question decrees which the government were not in a position to repeal for the present (W 5825/626/41).

No. 3

Mr. Ogilvie-Forbes (San Sebastian[1]) to Mr. Eden (Received July 16)
No. 568 [W 6458/62/41]

SAN SEBASTIAN, *July 14, 1936*

Sir,

With reference to my despatch No. 531[2] of July 3rd, regarding political developments, I have the honour to report that at 3 a.m. on the morning of the 13th July Don José Calvo Sotelo, the Monarchist leader, was kidnapped from his home in Madrid. Some hours later his dead body was found in a cemetery, with bullet wounds in the head and the heart.

2. Although the formal head of the 'Renovacion Española', the orthodox Monarchist party, is Sr. Goicoechea, Sr. Calvo Sotelo—a former Minister of Finance, a brilliant debater and a slashing speaker—was easily the most prominent Monarchist personality in Spain. His assassination must therefore cause extreme indignation (not only among Monarchists but also among the Fascists with whom he was much in sympathy) and newspaper reports of the affair are being censored with severity. Interest centres on the question whether or not his abductors were what they were dressed as, viz. Assault Guards, and all discussion of the point has been ruthlessly cut out of the newspapers.

3. The impression in Monarchist circles is that Assault Guards were indeed the murderers and that this crime is the latest in a chain of reprisals which began with the shooting by police on April 16th of a relative of Sr. Primo de Rivera, the Fascist leader (Sir Henry Chilton's despatch No. 268 of the 17th April[3]). In revenge for this, a Captain of the 'Asaltos' was shot in Madrid on the night of July 12th/13th apparently by members of the 'Renovacion Española' fourteen of whom are reported to have been arrested. The counterstroke by the 'Asaltos' followed quickly enough and I am told they meant to include Señores Gil Robles[4] and Goicoechea in their revenge. These two, however, were not in Madrid although the former—rashly perhaps—returned to the capital to-day.

4. The Government have issued a *communiqué* in which, after expressing their horror at these assassinations, they once more assert their determination to maintain order and they appeal to all peace-loving Spaniards for support. It is too early to say whether this time the Government will do any more to

[1] It was the custom in Spain for the leading members of the diplomatic corps to leave Madrid about this time for the summer capital of San Sebastian. Sir H. G. Chilton, H.M. Ambassador at Madrid, who had gone on leave on June 2 leaving Mr. Ogilvie-Forbes in charge of the Embassy, returned to San Sebastian on July 15.
[2] Not printed. He reported signs of 'certain elements of disintegration in the [Spanish] Socialist Party', in particular the defeat of Señor Largo Caballero by Señor Ramón González Peña in the elections to the executive committee of the party. He also reported that the 'internal situation of the country, although outwardly quiet, still gives cause for anxiety'.
[3] Not printed.
[4] Señor José María Gil Robles was leader of CEDA, the Catholic party.

6

preserve order than they have in the past. Now that political leaders have begun to fall under the gunman's bullets they have a strong inducement to act: but the prospects cannot be gauged until it can be seen whether the disorders they must contend with are seriously intensified through the passions let loose by this latest crime.

I have, &c.,

GEORGE OGILVIE-FORBES

No. 4

Sir H. Chilton (San Sebastian) to Mr. Eden (Received July 18, 7.25 p.m.)
No. 144 Telegraphic [W 6529/62/41]

SAN SEBASTIAN, *July 18, 1936, 4 p.m.*

Report has reached me which is confirmed by local military authorities, that the Foreign Legion in Morocco has revolted against the régime.

I also hear rumours of military rising at Burgos but have no confirmation. Telephonic communication to Madrid is temporarily prohibited.[1]

[1] A minute on the file read: 'H.M. Ambassador was able to get into communication with the Madrid Embassy later on in the day. W. H. M. Pollock 20/7.' Details of the military revolt and ample information concerning Spanish personalities and political developments generally are given by Professor Hugh Thomas in *The Spanish Civil War* (London, revised edn. 1965); cf. pp. 181-9 and 202-3.

No. 5

Mr. E. F. Gye[1] (Tangier) to Mr. Eden (Received July 19, 10.40 p.m.)
No. 23 Telegraphic [W 6544/62/41]

TANGIER, *July 19, 1936, 7.45 p.m.*

My telegram No. 22.[2]

Contrary to reports broadcast General Franco arrived at Tetuan this morning and left almost at once for Ceuta.[3] It is rumoured that some troops have landed at Cadiz and that Seville is in their hands.

[1] H.M. Consul-General at Tangier.
[2] Not printed; it mentioned a report that the military at Tetuan in Morocco had the situation well in hand.
[3] After the Popular Front victory in February 1936 General Francisco Franco y Bahamonde, born 1892, had been dismissed from his position in the Spanish War Office because of his part in the suppression by the Foreign Legion of the rising of miners in Asturias in 1934. He was sent to command the Spanish forces in the Canary Islands; for further details of his career and his part in the military rising see Thomas, *The Spanish Civil War*, pp. 120-4, 135-6, 141-2, 179-80, 184, and 196. He flew from Las Palmas on the morning of July 18, reaching Tetuan after stops at Agadir and Casablanca.

7

No. 6

Mr. G. E. Vaughan[1] *(Barcelona) to Mr. Eden (Received July 20, 6 p.m.)*
No. 14 Telegraphic [W 6619/62/41]

BARCELONA, *July 20, 1936, 3.30 p.m.*

Garrison rose and marched against the Generality.[2] Early yesterday morning the Government were prepared for rising and it has largely been suppressed by shock police, Civil Guards and a few loyal troops together with masses of armed workers amongst which anarchists and syndicalists were prominent. Casualties are said to be heavy and several churches have been burnt. There is a general strike and all communications inter[r]upted. Have not heard so far of any damage to British subjects and property. Firing is still going on but the situation is relatively quiet although not reassuring. Should army rebels win in other parts of Spain revolutionary workers Government may yet be the result in Catalonia. Air force and warships here were loyal to the Government.

Please repeat to San Sebastian.

[1] H.M. Vice-Consul and Acting Consul-General at Barcelona.
[2] Under the Catalan Statute of Autonomy of 1932 the Barcelona municipal government had been reorganized as the government, or *generalidad*, of Catalonia.

No. 7

Minute by Lord Cranborne[1]
[W 6753/62/41]

FOREIGN OFFICE, *July 21, 1936*

I had a visit this morning from the Spanish Ambassador,[2] who came with an urgent message from his Government. He had spoken on the telephone with his Foreign Minister, who had asked him to make a *démarche* with His Majesty's Government and enquire from them urgently whether they would be willing to sell oil from Gibraltar to the Spanish fleet. I understood from His Excellency that the main sources of oil supply normally in the possession of the Spanish Government were in Morocco and were now in the hands of the rebels. If His Majesty's Government could assist the Spanish Government in this way, it would therefore be very greatly appreciated.

After consultation with the Secretary of State, I told His Excellency that I understood that there were at Gibraltar considerable stores of privately owned oil. If the Spanish Government were wishing to buy this oil, His Majesty's Government would of course put no difficulties of any kind in their way. The Ambassador seemed not to know of the existence of this privately owned oil and said that he had understood from the Spanish Foreign

[1] Parliamentary Under Secretary of State for Foreign Affairs.
[2] Señor José López Oliván.

Minister that what he had in mind was Government owned oil. I again assured His Excellency that I understood that there was plenty of privately owned oil available and that to purchase this no authorisation would be necessary from His Majesty's Government. It would be an ordinary normal peacetime transaction.

His Excellency said that he would telephone to this effect to his Foreign Minister. If, however, he received a reply that they wished to purchase from the British Government, what would be the attitude of His Majesty's Government? I said that I could not give him an immediate answer. It would be necessary to find out what our stocks were and whether we had any to spare. If, however, he rang me up on the subject, I would make further enquiries and would give him an answer as soon as possible.[3]

C.

[3] Mr. Eden told the Cabinet on July 22 that the Spanish Ambassador had told him of the desire of the Spanish Government to purchase oil for the Spanish fleet at Tangier. The fleet could not move until it had oil. He had replied after consulting the Admiralty that the Spanish Government was entitled to purchase oil from commercial sources. In the discussion that followed it was noted that it would be undesirable for the Spanish ships to be sent into Gibraltar for refuelling by commercial firms, owing to the possibility of their being bombed there. It was also considered undesirable that a British tanker should be sent to Tangier, owing to the risk of bombing. The Cabinet agreed that no further immediate action was necessary, but the situation should be carefully watched.

No. 8

Mr. J. H. Milanes[1] (Madrid) to Mr. Eden (Received July 23, 9.30 a.m.)
No. 4 Telegraphic [W 6698/62/41]

MADRID, *July 22, 1936, 12 noon*

Unable to communicate with Embassy at San Sebastian.[2] Situation quiet at present. Have organised emergency arrangements with help of members of colony. Embassy provisioned and will in case of emergency shelter women and children. Am establishing touch as far as possible with all members of colony. Only casualties so far Mr. and Mrs. Borger with slight gun shot wounds now doing well in hospital. Rowland Winn, *Daily Telegraph* correspondent arrested. I am doing everything in my power for him. Keeping in touch with American colleague and other diplomatic missions. Please inform Embassy San Sebastian.[3]

[1] H.M. Acting Consul at Madrid.
[2] See No. 3, note 1.
[3] A note on the filed copy by Mr. Montagu-Pollock read: 'This is being communicated to the Embassy at San Sebastian via the Admiralty. W.H.M.P. 23/7.'
The situation in San Sebastian during the first days of the civil war was described in a long despatch from Sir H. Chilton, No. 585 of July 28 (W 7618/62/41). The gist of this was that on Sunday, July 19, news reached the Ambassador and Lady Chilton at Zarauz, ten miles from San Sebastian, where they were staying, that clashes had taken place between armed police and workmen, who apparently wished to prevent the soldiers from joining

the revolt. Mr. O. A. Scott, First Secretary at the Embassy, who was also staying at Zarauz, motored into San Sebastian that day, and Sir H. and Lady Chilton did so on Tuesday 21 July. On the way they encountered 'crowds of armed men and met lorries, bristling with guns, on their way to meet a rebel army'. In view of the high state of tension in San Sebastian the Ambassador decided at once to stay overnight at the Hotel Continental, where he and others were confined during the whole of July 22 owing to the heavy shooting and shelling in the town. On July 23, Mr. T. W. Dupree, Honorary Attaché at the British Embassy, 'very gallantly volunteered' to swim out to a French ship with a telegram for despatch to the Foreign Office; he did the three-quarter mile swim successfully, 'at considerable risk to himself, since he might quite easily have been mistaken for an escaping rebel and fired upon'. Two British destroyers, *Veteran* and *Verity*, arrived from Plymouth early on July 24. Some 250 British subjects and other foreign nationals had already been sent across the French frontier by road. H.M.S. *Verity* now took evacuation parties by sea to St. Jean de Luz, in French territory. All except a few British subjects had been evacuated by July 26, when H.M.S. *Keppel* replaced the two destroyers. By this stage all members of the Embassy staff had been brought into the Hotel Continental, which had been officially conceded an 'international and diplomatic character' and guarded by armed police. In view of the possibility of 'terrible excesses' in San Sebastian by both sides Sir H. Chilton decided to remove the Embassy staff and archives to Zarauz, a move successfully accomplished on the 27th. Shortly afterwards he moved to Hendaye, inside the French frontier. See Nos. 38, 40, and 42 below.

No. 9

Mr. Eden to Sir H. Chilton (San Sebastian)
No. 121 Telegraphic [W 6628/62/41]

FOREIGN OFFICE, *July 22, 1936, 10 p.m.*

French Government have instructed their Ambassador in Madrid[1] to draw the attention of the Spanish Government to the danger of retaliatory measures being used by aviation and other units of the rebel army against the Spanish Government naval forces in Tangier, if these latter use the port as a base of operation against the rebels.[2] You should immediately endeavour to concert with your French colleague and take similar action with a view to persuading the Spanish Government not to use Tangier as a base for military operations.

Repeated to Tangier.

[1] M. Herbette.
[2] An undated note by Mr. H. J. Seymour, head of the League of Nations and Western Department, on this file said that M. de Margerie, First Secretary in the French Embassy in London, had 'telephoned to me about this and urged us to telegraph to Sir H. Chilton'. Mr. Seymour saw no harm in telegraphing, although he thought it would do no good 'as (a) the Embassy at S. Sebastian appears to be in territory occupied at present by the rebels and (b) the Spanish Government will pay no attention even if they get the message'.

No. 10

Note communicated by the Italian Embassy
[*W 6748/62/41*]

ITALIAN EMBASSY, LONDON, *July 22, 1936–XIV*[1]

Following the serious riots which have broken out in Barcelona, and various attacks made by anarchist elements against the life and property of Italian subjects, the Italian Government have despatched two naval units of 10,000 and 8,000 tons respectively, which are due to arrive in front of Barcelona during the night between the 22nd and 23rd instant.

The two ships are in constant touch with the Italian Government and will await further orders before actually entering the Spanish territorial waters and the port of Barcelona. They are to take on board Italian subjects whose life may be considered in danger.

[1] This refers to the number of years of Fascist rule in Italy, dating from 1922.

No. 11

Note by Mr. Seymour
[*W 6830/62/41*]

FOREIGN OFFICE, *July 23, 1936*

Ask Admiralty to send the following to the ship which is going to San Sebastian.[1]

'Following for Embassy San Sebastian from Foreign Office.

As soon as journey to Madrid can safely be made it is desirable that representative of Embassy should return to Madrid.'[2]

Sir G. Mounsey[3] agrees.

[1] See No. 8, note 3.
[2] A note by Mr. Montagu-Pollock read: 'Done. 4.30 p.m. W.H.M.P.' Mr. Eden told the Cabinet on July 22 that at his request the Admiralty 'had moved ships to all the more important ports in Spain for the protection of British residents and visitors, and incidentally it was hoped thereby to obtain further information of what was happening'.
[3] An Assistant Under Secretary of State in the Foreign Office.

No. 12

Minute by Lord Cranborne
[*W 6776/62/41*]

FOREIGN OFFICE, *July 23, 1936*

The Spanish Ambassador came to see me this morning with regard to the situation in Spain. He first referred to the question of the attempted bombing of British ships by Spanish aeroplanes, which the Secretary of State had mentioned in his interview with him yesterday.[1] The Secretary of State had seemed uncertain as to whether these aeroplanes were under the control of the *de facto* Government or of the rebels. The Ambassador said that he had regarded this as a matter of importance and had therefore telephoned to Spain and had received an assurance from the Foreign Minister that the aeroplanes concerned had not been Government aeroplanes. Presumably they were machines belonging to the forces commanded by General Franco. I thanked the Ambassador for his assurance.

The Ambassador then turned to the question of the supply of oil to Spanish warships at present in Gibraltar Bay. He said that he had had last night an interview at the Foreign Office[2] from which he had derived a faint impression that His Majesty's Government were disinclined to allow the supply of oil even from private sources. I assured His Excellency that this was not the case. Our position was a very simple one. Since I had talked to him yesterday the situation had changed in one respect. There had been attempted bombing of British tankers apparently by the rebel forces. It must be assumed that this action had been taken because it was feared that the oil in the tankers might be used for the supply of the Spanish fleet.

In these circumstances it was obvious that the Companies concerned ran a greater risk than they had hitherto done in supplying oil to Spanish Government ships, and His Majesty's Government therefore felt that they could not under any circumstances bring pressure on them which might involve their running this extra risk. It was still open to the Spanish Government to negotiate an ordinary commercial transaction with the oil companies concerned and His Majesty's Government would certainly put no obstacles in their way. But they would regard any such transaction as an ordinary commercial one in which they were not themselves concerned, and they would put no pressure one way or the other.[3]

The Ambassador thanked me for this explanation, which he seemed fully to accept.

I asked His Excellency whether he himself had had any reports from Spain and whether in particular he had any news of the bombing of Spanish warships by rebel aeroplanes in Gibraltar Bay, or had heard that the Govern-

[1] No further details of this interview have been traced in the Foreign Office archives. A note by Mr. Seymour (W 6777/62/41) described an interview with the Ambassador late on the evening of July 22. He warned the Ambassador on Mr. Eden's instructions that any further attacks on British shipping would be resisted by force. Efforts were being made to convey this warning to the Spanish authorities in revolt in Morocco, as it was their machines which were believed to be responsible for the attacks.

[2] See note 1. Mr. Seymour wrote: 'I told M. Oliván that we had just heard that there was actually a Spanish oil-supply vessel at Gib[raltar] with enough oil on board to enable the Spanish warships now there to get to a Spanish port, such as Málaga. The action of the insurgents in bombing ships which either were, or were thought to be, tankers, showed the difficulty & possible dangers which the Oil Co. might incur if it sold supplies to the Spanish war ships.' The Ambassador seemed 'a good deal upset at the possibility of not being able to buy oil at Gibraltar'; he could not believe that his government would have wished to purchase oil if there had been enough Spanish oil there to remove the ships.

[3] Cf. No. 7, note 3.

ment warships had replied by shell fire with the result that shells had fallen within the precincts of the Fortress of Gibraltar.

The Ambassador said that he had no information on this point. Indeed so far as I could understand he had no information of any kind from his country giving an accurate account of the situation.[4]

[4] Mr. Eden noted on the filed copy of this minute: 'Lord Cranborne spoke very correctly. I hope that the B[oard] O[f] T[rade] have used similar language to oil companies. A.E. 23 July.'

CHAPTER II

Conversations in Berlin: French proposal for non-intervention in Spain

July 24–August 15, 1936

No. 13

Mr. E. M. B. Ingram[1] *(Rome) to Mr. Eden (Received July 24, 9.30 a.m.)*
No. 488 Telegraphic [R 4476/294/67]

ROME, *July 24, 1936, 1.30 a.m.*

Your telegram No. 279.[2]

I read out to Minister for Foreign Affairs this afternoon the first two paragraphs of your telegram under reference. At first His Excellency angled for a joint *communiqué* but eventually accepted an announcement in the House of Commons, where original statement had been made,[3] as reasonable. Finally he assured me that there would be no objection to course proposed in paragraph 2 of your telegram.[4]

Count Ciano seemed much elated by the course of events but I warned him that it might be a mistake to be over-optimistic and to try to move too fast. He then passed on to Abyssinian affairs on which I am reporting separately by despatch.[5] His Excellency, whom I knew intimately in China, was most cordial and assured me would always be at my disposal.

---

[1] Counsellor and Chargé d'Affaires in H.M. Embassy at Rome.

[2] This Foreign Office telegram of July 22 referred to a conversation that afternoon between Mr. Eden and Signor Vitetti, Counsellor and Chargé d'Affaires in the Italian Embassy in London, concerning the Italian aide-mémoire dated July 17 which Signor Vitetti had handed to Mr. Eden on July 21 (see Volume XVI, No. 473). After securing the approval of the Cabinet on July 22, Mr. Eden told Signor Vitetti that he proposed to tell the House of Commons on Monday, July 27, of the assurances which the Italian Government had given to the Turkish, Yugoslav, and Greek Governments that no aggressive action against them was, or had been, contemplated; he proposed to quote from the Italian memorandum and to say that in view of these very satisfactory assurances there was no need for the continuance of any assurances to the three governments on the part of His Majesty's Government. This announcement formed part of Mr. Eden's speech in the Supply Committee on July 27; see 315 *H.C. Deb. 5 s.*, cols. 1122–3, and No. 21 below.

[3] Cf. Volume XVI, No. 373, note 2.

[4] This evidently refers to the proposal 'to quote fairly fully from the [Italian] memorandum itself'.

[5] Not printed.

No. 14

Sır G. Clerk[1] (Paris) to Mr. Eden (Received July 25)
No. 215 Saving: Telegraphic [C 5471/4/18]

PARIS, *July 24, 1936*

Events in Spain have restricted the space which would otherwise no doubt have been devoted in the press to discussion of the London conversations,[2] but such preliminary comment as has appeared is almost uniformly favourable. Journals of the Right and the Left are alike delighted. Emphasis is laid with the warmest approval upon M. Blum's statement that the agreement which has been reached is whole-hearted, and not merely formal; this is not a mere agreement on paper but something which shows unity of thought and intention. These words are largely quoted in big type as headings to the various articles. The press dwells also upon the fact that the invitation to Italy and Germany has now been given and quotes the Secretary of State as saying that the invitation constitutes a touchstone of Germany's and Italy's intentions. France, says Tabouis in the 'Oeuvre' (Left Radical), by this agreement, gets everything that she considers essential, that is to say, the probable expansion of the five-Power conference. France has also ensured that the French plan will be taken into consideration side by side with the German plan. The only point on which France must maintain an absolute firmness is a refusal to sign any agreement with the five Powers which could in any way injure her alliances in Eastern Europe.

Among the few journals which are critical of the conversations are the 'Ère Nouvelle' (Left Radical: Herriot) which bewails the fact that a sponge has been passed over the German *coup de force* of March 7th, now blandly labelled an 'initiative'. The problem, it is considered, does not consist in replacing a pact or a treaty by some other arrangement; it is, on the other hand, a question of knowing what the Powers faithful to their engagements can and must do, in the presence of those who do not keep their word and by what means these engagements will be respected. On this vital problem the *communiqué*[3] is curiously vague while as to the guarantees given to France by Great Britain no one knows whether they still hold good or not.

Pertinax, 'Echo de Paris' (Centre), writes in much the same strain though he accords a certain grudging praise to the meeting as being perhaps better than nothing at all. After adducing much the same arguments against the conversations as the leader writer in the 'Ère Nouvelle', he then seeks to link up the question of the future of Europe with that of Spain. Will Rome or Berlin intervene there to bolster up the forces of fascism, he asks, and what will be the effect if they do? His Majesty's Government has been asked by the Spanish Ambassador for assistance against the rebel forces and this, it is

[1] H.M. Ambassador at Paris.
[2] See Volume XVI, Nos. 476 and 477.
[3] The text of the *communiqué* issued on July 23 was identical with that printed in Volume XVI, Annex to No. 476, subject to a minor alteration suggested by M. van Zeeland, the Belgian Prime Minister: see *ibid.*, No. 477, para. 1.

believed, has been refused.[4] France is likely to do otherwise under communist pressure and if the Left are sustained by French help France and Great Britain will be more completely divided than at any time since the war.

[4] Cf. Nos. 7 and 12.

No. 15

Mr. Eden to Mr. B. C. Newton[1] (Berlin)
No. 870 [C 5483/4/18]

FOREIGN OFFICE, *July 24, 1936*

Sir,

I asked the German Chargé d'Affaires to come and see me this afternoon when I told him that I thought it would be useful before he went on leave if we could have a conversation in respect of the *communiqué*[2] which had been issued by the French, Belgian and United Kingdom representatives as the result of yesterday's meeting in London. As Prince Bismarck would be aware, this *communiqué* had already been delivered in Berlin[3] together with a[n] invitation, the terms of which I gave to the German Chargé d'Affaires, to the German Government expressing the hope that they would be able to send an affirmative reply to the invitation contained in the *communiqué*.

2. Prince Bismarck then went through the *communiqué*. I made it clear to him that the phrase in the second sentence of paragraph 3 of the *communiqué* 'through the collaboration of all concerned' referred to our desire that a new agreement should be negotiated by the Five Powers together and not by the Three. There was no intention of inviting more than the five Powers to carry through this particular peace (? piece) of work. Prince Bismarck replied that he was grateful for my explanation for that was the very question he was about to ask me. He had not been clear as to the meaning of that phrase. Prince Bismarck went on to ask me why it was necessary to give two parts to that same sentence. Would it not have been enough to say that the first business to be undertaken would be to negotiate a new agreement to take the place of the Rhine Pact of Locarno? Why was it necessary to talk of resolving the situation created by the German initiative of 7th March? I replied that I could really see no objection to this phrase. It seemed to me to be a mere statement of fact. Prince Bismarck did not further demur. He then asked me if I could explain the meaning of the word 'natural' in the second sentence of paragraph 5 of the *communiqué*. He had noticed that there had been some question as to the validity of this point of view in the German press. I replied that if I remembered correctly this sentence had been first drafted as the point of view of the three Powers, but on reflection we thought it better to put the matter in this indefinite form

[1] H.M. Minister at Berlin. [2] See No. 14, note 3.
[3] See Volume XVI, Nos. 479 and 480.

in which it could give offence to no-one. Prince Bismarck seemed also to accept this explanation.

3. I emphasised to the German Chargé d'Affaires that this *communiqué* fully carried out the two purposes which I had expressed to him as being in our minds when agreeing to this Conference. First, that the meeting should be brief, second that it should be constructive, thereby paving the way to a five Power meeting at which alone important work could be carried through. I expressed the earnest hope of His Majesty's Government that the German Government would appreciate the great effort which now had been made to facilitate a European settlement. Much dead wood had been cut away and I could see no reason why the five Powers should not meet and collaborate. I hoped that the German Government would be able to return us a favourable answer in due course. I wished also to impress on Prince Bismarck the very great advance that had been made by the French Government in agreeing to the terms of this *communiqué*. Prince Bismarck admitted that the French Government had indeed made a real step forward—it was no use denying that. Meanwhile he understood that as far as the German Government was concerned, Herr Dieckhoff had made an interim reply.[4] Naturally he could say no more as to the views of his own Government until there had been more time for consideration in Berlin where he understood that most Ministers were away from the capital. Nonetheless, he was glad to note that the reactions of the German press which I had mentioned to him appeared to be sympathetic and satisfactory.

4. Prince Bismarck then asked me whether I could give him any views of our own as to a date or place of meeting. I replied that we had been careful not to consider either of these during the discussions so as to avoid giving any impression of imposing our views in advance on the Powers who were not present. So far as His Majesty's Government were concerned, I thought that the meeting should be held as soon as we had given time for the necessary preparation through the diplomatic channel. The German Chargé d'Affaires replied that he was glad to hear me speak of this preparation, for in conversation with Herr von Ribbentrop[5] on the telephone after his previous interview with me Herr von Ribbentrop had emphasised to him the importance the German Government attached to full and careful diplomatic preparation. In their view if the conference were to be held and failed, it would be even worse than if it were not held at all. I replied that I fully appreciated the strength of this argument, but at the same time I did not think that the Conference should be unduly delayed, since if this was, as it appeared to be, the psychological moment, this moment was not to be missed. To this Prince Bismarck assented.

[4] See *ibid.*, No 481. Herr Dieckhoff was Head of the Political Department of the German Foreign Office.

[5] Herr Joachim von Ribbentrop, appointed Ambassador on Special Mission in June 1935, had led the German Delegation to the League Council meeting in London in March 1936 (see Volume XVI, No. 136, note 1, and No. 142), and was appointed German Ambassador to Great Britain in August 1936, taking up his duties in October.

5. On his departure I again impressed on the German Chargé d'Affaires His Majesty's Government's expectation that the German Government would now send us a reply which would be helpful towards a meeting of the five Powers which we so much desired to see held.

I am, &c.,

ANTHONY EDEN

No. 16

Mr. Eden to Mr. Ingram (Rome)
No. 908 [C 5473/4/18]

FOREIGN OFFICE, July 24, 1936

Sir,

I asked the Italian Chargé d'Affaires to come and see me this afternoon when I told him that though we had already communicated the text of yesterday's *communiqué* to Rome¹ and had expressed our hope that the Italian Government would be able to return a favourable answer to our invitation, I wished to see the Italian Chargé d'Affaires today in order to speak to him further of yesterday's meeting.²

2. His Majesty's Government considered the outcome of our brief exchange of views with the representatives of the French and Belgian Governments as very satisfactory. We hoped that the Italian Government would take the same view. Signor Vitetti would observe that the two conditions which I had told him we hoped to realise in respect of this meeting had in fact resulted from it, i.e. the meeting had been short and constructive. It had led to an invitation in friendly and unequivocal terms to the two other Governments who had signed the Locarno Treaties to co-operate with us in the work of reconstruction. I wished to emphasise to the Italian Chargé d'Affaires the very helpful spirit which had been displayed by the French Government at this meeting. Those who had in mind the attitude which French Governments had so often upheld in the past would appreciate the extent of the effort which the present French Ministers had made to contribute to a solution of the problems which at present confronted Europe. In all the circumstances, I hoped that the Italian Government would soon be able to return us a favourable reply. At the same time, I did not ask that that reply should be made before Monday.³

3. Signor Vitetti at once seized upon the date and said that he had been glad to hear from Rome that all difficulties with reference to my making a statement in the House of Commons about the Italian assurances to the Mediterranean Powers had apparently been removed.⁴ This was very good news. The Italian Chargé d'Affaires appreciated that I had made it clear that no reply from the Italian Government was expected until after

¹ See Volume XVI, No. 479, note 1, and No. 482.
² See *ibid.*, Nos. 476 and 477.   ³ i.e. July 27.
⁴ See No. 13.

Monday in order that the Italian Government should not condition their reply by the reference to the assurances which they had given to the other Mediterranean Powers. Signor Vitetti undertook to transmit what I had said to him to his Government, and I understood that he had already done what he could to secure a favourable reaction in the Italian press to the outcome of yesterday's meeting.

I am, &c.,
ANTHONY EDEN

No. 17

Mr. Eden to Sir H. Chilton (Madrid)[1]
No. 358 [*W 6893/3694/41*]

Very Confidential   FOREIGN OFFICE, *July 24, 1936*

Sir,

Señor Oliván came to see me this afternoon and said he wished to speak to me not as the Spanish Ambassador, but as a friend, since we had known each other and worked together for so many years. The position in Spain was now so serious that he was compelled to consider his personal position. There were three possible outcomes of the present situation: either the rebel Government would triumph, in which case he would have to resign since he had been appointed by their predecessors; or the Communist Government would triumph, in which case Señor Oliván would be unable to continue to serve such a Government—he was not a Communist, and he was brought up for an entirely different position and would find it quite impossible to be their representative. The third alternative was the continuation in power of the present Government. It was clear from the way he spoke that Señor Oliván was inclined to regard the second alternative as the more likely. In these conditions he told me in the strictest confidence that not only he but four other members of the Spanish Embassy would resign rather than continue to serve. He had come to see me this afternoon in order to ask me whether in such conditions it would be possible for him and his colleagues to continue to remain in England for some months as private citizens and maybe ultimately to find some work here. He was sorry to speak of such matters, but after all, he had a wife and children and he must think of them. His property in Spain was in Saragossa, where fighting was still going on. He had been unable to obtain any information of any kind from there. His father, who was an old man, was in Madrid, and he had no idea even whether he was alive or not. He added parenthetically that he was anxious about Señor Madariaga's safety, as he was in Madrid and was known to be antipathetic

---

[1] The draft was so inscribed on the filed copy, although the Embassy at this date was at Zarauz (see No. 8, note 3).

to the Communists. The Ambassador concluded that he was not asking for a reply now but that he felt I would not mind these preliminary enquiries.

2. I replied that we should of course be only too pleased to do anything we could to help Señor Oliván at any time. I would at once make enquiries to ascertain what the technical position would be, but he could be sure that anything we could do within the law we would do. I thought I should perhaps utter a warning about the possibility that he and other members of the Spanish Embassy would wish to obtain employment here. That was usually a complicated question. Señor Oliván replied that this was certainly a matter which could wait. All that he wished to know for the present was whether he and his colleagues could stay on as private citizens should the need arise.

3. The Ambassador went on to speak of the situation in Paris, where his Embassy were in gravest difficulties also. The Spanish Ambassador had now left, his time being in any case shortly up, and the Chargé d'Affaires had refused point-blank to sign, on behalf of his Government, an order for the purchase of munitions from France. He could not endure to sign a document to supply materials for Spaniards to shoot down Spaniards. The general position was inconceivably wretched for anyone who loved Spain.

4. I expressed what sympathy I could, and added that I hoped that Señor Oliván would appreciate our difficulties in respect of his request for oil.[2] We had felt it impossible to put pressure upon the company either way in the existing conditions in Spain. Señor Oliván replied, speaking purely privately, that he not only appreciated our position but approved our answer. He had at once told the Spanish Government they could have the oil if they paid cash and he had since heard no more. The Ambassador hinted strongly that our answer had been a great relief. He had evidently not greatly relished his task in putting forward such a request.

I am, &c.,
ANTHONY EDEN

[2] See Nos. 7 and 12.

No. 18

Mr. Newton (Berlin) to Mr. Eden (Received July 25, 11.13 a.m.)
No. 234 Telegraphic: by telephone [C 5482/4/18]

BERLIN, *July 25, 1936*

My telegram No. 228.[1]

The general line taken in this morning's press is to give reserved approval to the London *communiqué*.[2] Emphasis is laid on the fact that Germany has not been presented with a decision reached in her absence. Secondly, the

[1] This telegram of July 24 gave a summary of German press comment on the proceedings of the Three-Power conference in London.
[2] See No. 14, note 3.

conclusion of a pact to replace the Locarno treaty represents a limited and practical objective. In regard to these two points of view the London conference marks a promising step forward. The fly in the ointment is that point five of the *communiqué*, and reports from Paris, indicate that the French Government wish to connect the Western settlement with a settlement in the East. In other words, France proposes to appear at the conference surrounded by her Russian and Little Entente allies. It will require the greatest pushfulness and firmness on the part of England if this idea is to be vetoed and the conference saved from disaster.

Attention is also drawn to the fact that if the meeting takes place, Italy will have to be squared.

A more detailed press report follows.[3]

---

[3] Not printed.

No. 19

Sir G. Clerk (Paris) to Mr. Eden (Received July 25, 2.45 p.m.)
No. 253 Telegraphic [W 6960/62/41]

Confidential   PARIS, *July 25, 1936, 1.42 p.m.*

Director of African Affairs informed the Minister[1] this morning that the French Government had now definitely decided not to furnish aeroplanes or munitions of war to the Spanish Government.[2]

---

[1] Mr. H. Lloyd Thomas.
[2] In his telegram No. 216 Saving of July 24 Sir G. Clerk had reported that considerable space had been devoted in the French press to the discussion of a request alleged to have been made to the French Government by the Spanish Republican Government to be supplied with arms and munitions with which to combat the rebels. The evening press reported a semi-official denial by the Quai d'Orsay that any such request had been made to the Foreign Ministry. However, a telegram of July 23 from M. Coulondre, Assistant Director of the Political Affairs department of the French Foreign Ministry, to M. Yvon Delbos, French Foreign Minister, who was attending the London conference, indicates that M. Cot, French Air Minister, had already received a request from the Spanish Government for 20 or 30 bombers, and that he assumed M. Léon Blum, the French Prime Minister, and M. Delbos to be favourable to the execution of this proposal (*D.D.F.*, Series 2, vol. iii, No. 17). Details of the Spanish requirements were sent to M. Delbos by the Spanish Embassy on July 24 (*ibid.*, No. 25). There is no evidence in the Foreign Office archives or in Lord Avon's memoirs (*Facing the Dictators*, London, 1962) that the Spanish request was discussed with Mr. Eden or with Foreign Office officials by M. Blum or M. Delbos during this visit to London. Later discussions and assertions on this point are examined in articles by David Carlton, 'Eden, Blum, and the Origins of Non-Intervention' (*Journal of Contemporary History*, Volume 6, No. 3, pp. 40–55), and M. D. Gallagher, 'Leon Blum and the Spanish Civil War' (*ibid.*, pp. 56–64). Nor is there any confirmation of the statement that the Prime Minister, Mr. Stanley Baldwin, had made a special request through M. Corbin that M. Blum should accompany M. Delbos to the London conference in order to discuss the supply of arms to the Spanish Republican Government by France: see P. Renouvin, *La Politique Extérieure du*

2. M. de St. Quentin added in confidence that this decision had only been arrived at after a sharp clash of opinions in the Cabinet and that the Quai d'Orsay had had to exert all their influence to prevent the contrary decision being taken.

3. The Quai d'Orsay had already had reason to think that the Italian and German Governments were assisting the 'White' forces in Spain and they had definite information that communications between Balearic Islands and Tetuan were being maintained by German aeroplanes.

premier gouvernement Léon Blum, in J. Bourdin (ed.), *Léon Blum, Chef de Gouvernement 1936–37* (Paris, 1967), pp. 373–4; cf. also p. 340.

After M. Blum's return to Paris from London a meeting of the Council of Ministers decided to forbid the export of all arms and munitions, and a *communiqué* issued to the press on July 25 stated that 'Le gouvernement français . . . a été unanime à décider de n'intervenir d'aucune manière dans le conflit intérieur d'Espagne.' See *ibid.*, p. 332. This decision did not necessarily exclude private transactions, and sales through Mexico and elsewhere. It was known that £140,000 in gold from the Spanish national gold reserve arrived at Le Bourget on July 25 as guarantee for such payment: *The Times*, July 27, p. 12.

No. 20

Mr. Eden to Sir P. Loraine[1] *(Constantinople)*
No. 47[2] *Telegraphic* [R 4513/294/67]

FOREIGN OFFICE, *July 25, 1936, 9 p.m.*

Mediterranean Assurances.

I propose in the course of a speech on foreign affairs in the House of Commons on July 27th to make the statement contained in my immediately following telegram.[3] The text of this statement will be communicated to the Turkish, Yugoslav, and Greek representatives in London on the morning of July 27th. You should make a similar communication in the early afternoon of the 27th to the Government to which you are accredited. In doing so you should explain that this return to the normal situation does not of course in any way affect the traditional friendship of the United Kingdom with Yugoslavia, Greece, and Turkey, or the enduring interest which the United Kingdom takes in the wellbeing of these three countries.

Repeated to Rome No. 290.

[1] H.M. Ambassador at Angora. Sir P. Loraine preferred to divide his time between Angora and Istanbul, and usually referred to the latter by its old name.
[2] No. 113 to Athens, No. 78 to Belgrade.
[3] No. 21 below. Cf. No. 13, note 2.

No. 21

Mr. Eden to Sir P. Loraine (Constantinople)

No. 48¹ Telegraphic [R 4513/294/67]

FOREIGN OFFICE, *July 25, 1936, 9 p.m.*

Following is statement referred to in my immediately preceding telegram.²

Another sphere in which there are signs of definite improvement in international relations is the Mediterranean. I would recall that on the occasion of the last Foreign Affairs debate in this House³ I referred to certain assurances which His Majesty's Government had given to certain Mediterranean countries in connexion with the imposition of sanctions, and I then added: 'It is the view of the Government that this assurance given by this country should not end with the raising of sanctions but should continue to cover the period of uncertainty which must necessarily follow any termination of action under Article 16.' Subsequently, on the withdrawal of sanctions, I made this declaration in a speech at the League on July 1st.⁴ I did so, as I had explained to the House, with the object of making a contribution to establishing confidence in the regions concerned. Happily, now, there are specific grounds for affirming that the position of uncertainty to which I then referred has now been brought to an end. About the middle of this month the Italian Government made to the Governments of Yugoslavia, Greece and Turkey a spontaneous declaration. The substance of these messages has been communicated to me by the Italian Chargé d'Affaires in London.⁵ From this communication it emerges clearly that the Italian Government have approached the Turkish, Yugoslav and Greek Governments and have given to each of these three Governments the most clear assurances that Italy has never contemplated, nor is contemplating, an aggressive action against any of them in retaliation for their past sanctionist policy. In expressing these views the Italian representatives in these three capitals have also emphasised that Italy considers the sanctions chapter as being completely and definitely over, and that she looks confidently ahead towards a new period of mutual co-operation amongst all nations. They have also recalled that between Italy and Greece and between Italy and Turkey, Treaties of Friendship are in existence with which Italy has never failed to comply, and which the Italian Government intend fully to respect. With Yugoslavia Italy intends no less to develop the same good relationship she enjoys with Turkey and Greece.

I think the Committee will agree that the information which I have just given to it fully justifies the conclusion that the circumstances which in the view of His Majesty's Government had made it desirable to give these

---

¹ No. 114 to Athens, No. 79 to Belgrade.

² No. 20. The statement made by Mr. Eden in the House of Commons on July 27 was in substantially the same terms as those of this telegram; see No. 13, note 2.

³ On June 18: see Volume XVI, No. 373, note 2.

⁴ See *ibid.*, No. 395.   ⁵ See *ibid.*, No. 473.

assurances no longer exist, more especially, as I stated at the time, that they were intended to operate 'only so long as in the opinion of the Government they remain appropriate to the circumstances'.[6] I am therefore glad to be able to recognise and declare that in the view of His Majesty's Government there is now no further necessity for the continuance of these assurances.

Repeated to Rome No. 291.

[6] The second half of this sentence, from 'more especially' to the end, was omitted from Mr. Eden's House of Commons statement.

No. 22

Sir P. Loraine (Constantinople) to Mr. Eden (Received July 26, 10 a.m.)
Nos. 84 & 85 Telegraphic [R 4502/294/67]

Important Immediate CONSTANTINOPLE, *July 25, 1936, 10 p.m.*
Private and Confidential.
My telegram No. 78.[1]

As a result of a long conversation with Minister for Foreign Affairs[2] may I please beg you earnestly to go very slowly as regards withdrawal of unilateral assurances to Turkey. The position here now that Turkey has given His Majesty's Government an unilateral assurance[3] is quite different to what it appears on the surface.

2. The Turks do not fear an Italian attack nor do they believe in any likelihood either of assurances being operative; although Italian assurances do not carry much conviction here Turks do not wish to belittle them or

[1] In this telegram of July 23 Sir P. Loraine referred to Foreign Office telegram No. 41 of July 21 (Volume XVI, No. 471), which had explained the position with regard to the unilateral assurances to Turkey and indicated that the British Government had declined to express an opinion as to whether the reciprocal undertakings of December 1935 had lapsed, but considered that the general situation in the Mediterranean had been radically altered by the Italian Government's pacificatory assurances (see No. 13, note 2). Sir P. Loraine said that he had seen the Acting Minister for Foreign Affairs twice on July 22 and that the situation was 'now perfectly well understood, both by Turkish Government and by myself'.
[2] M. Tewfik Rüştü Aras.
[3] In reply to an urgent request from the Turkish Embassy in London, the Foreign Office informed M. Örs, Turkish Chargé d'Affaires, in a letter of July 17 that in the view of His Majesty's Government the assurances of December 1935 still held good only in so far as they were continued by the declarations made by Mr. Eden on June 18 and July 1 (see Volume XVI, No. 373, note 2 and No. 395), and that it was 'for the Turkish Government to decide for themselves whether, in their view, the assurances which they gave in December to His Majesty's Government still continue to be or have ceased to be in force' (*ibid.*, No. 462). A Turkish note of July 23 from M. Örs to Mr. Eden stated that 'le Gouvernement de la République considère que pendant la période d'incertitude qui suivra la levée des sanctions, les mêmes obligations existent à sa charge envers la Grande Bretagne d'une façon unilatérale et dans la mesure où elles restent appropriées aux circonstances, le Gouvernement de la République étant seul juge de décider de la durée de ces assurances'. The full texts of this note and of a note of July 21 from the Turkish Government to the Italian Ambassador in Angora in the same sense are filed in R 4461/294/67.

additional value they doubtless acquired through having been officially communicated to you. Turks would neither misunderstand nor resent it if you told them that for the sake of securing Italian collaboration in Europe generally you were terminating British assurance of what is no longer appropriate to the circumstances and as being an obstacle to such collaboration; though they would actually doubt whether you would achieve your object by these means, anticipating that Italy would find other obstacles the removal of which was likewise a . . .[4] of her collaboration.

3. It is for a quite different set of reasons that the Turkish Government would regret the termination of British assurance. Its lapse would cut across their foreign policy as now determined in the light of events and results at Montreux;[5] it would leave them fully in the air as regards obtaining internal support for that policy. I do not believe they would expect even this argument to be specially influential with you, except for their conviction that their policy is inspired by the same principles as that of His Majesty's Government viz. to ensure peace and security and is designed to serve the same purpose viz. to prevent splitting up of Europe into hostile camps.

. . .[4] respective unilateral assurances hold good their mere existence gives Turkey a justification both externally vis à vis her Balkan partners and internally vis à vis Grand National Assembly for keeping outside multi-State security Pacts which in their opinion would spell danger as connoting (1) an encirclement of Germany, (2) encirclement of Italy and/or (3) division of Europe with hostile camps on pre-1914 lines.

5. French Press at least are already clamouring for a pact to include France, Little Entente, Balkan Entente and Russia i.e. a general alliance against Germany. Germans (this was news to me) have already taken soundings through Belgrade with a view to pact between Germany, Yugoslavia and Turkey; whether it is intended to cover Greece and Roumania is not yet clear to me. This would be a general alliance maybe against Italy maybe against Russia.

6. Both schemes appear to Turks to be fraught with gravest dangers and they want to avoid being confronted with a Hobson's choice. They have to some extent freed their hands vis à vis their Balkan friends by conceding absolute discretion to Greece and Yugoslavia to deal with the question of Mediterranean assurances exactly as they fit in their own individual interests. But Turkey's sheet anchor is unilateral assurances given by the United Kingdom and herself; if this drags or parts she fears she will be drawn . . .[4] into one or other vortex. Otherwise the only alternative is isolation. Isolation in company with tranquillisation would be perfectly tolerable; literal isolation unbearable.

7. Minister for Foreign Affairs entirely confirms the view I had myself formed that Italians are not put out by Turkish assurance to United Kingdom. He tells me he will exert himself to convince the Italian Ambassador here that the continuance of the British and Turkish assurance is actually

---

[4] The text was here uncertain.   [5] See Volume XVI, Chapter VI.

beneficial to Italy, for it is a guarantee that Turkey will join in no anti-Italian bloc. He would like to suggest to you that so long as these two assurances stand, His Majesty's Government may find in Turkey a very useful . . .⁴ union between themselves and Italy, not in the least an obstacle or a stumbling block.

8. Minister for Foreign Affairs seems to have returned from Montreux with distinct impression that with the exception of United Kingdom, all larger European powers and many smaller ones are working frantically and quite unscrupulously for their own hand; for this reason also he wishes to harmonise Turkey's policy more closely than ever with that of His Majesty's Government. He wants no guarantees; he asks us to undertake no commitment; the existing assurances are quite enough for him; but for the present their continuance is indispensable for reasons stated above.

9. He emphatically disbelieves in the possibility of an effective Italo-German understanding; he thinks Herr Hitler and Signor Mussolini will make our flesh creep at danger of one so long as they can; that even if there was such an agreement, it would degenerate into a . . .⁴ race; that in a battle of dictatorial wits the dice are loaded in Herr Hitler's favour; that Signor Mussolini can hardly be such a fool as not to notice this; that then, as now, his one line of salvation will be to seek an understanding with England.⁶

⁶ In a minute on file R 4479/294/67, Mr. O. G. Sargent, an Assistant Under Secretary of State in the Foreign Office, wrote on July 27: 'The upshot of all this is that [M. Aras] has got himself into an impossible position. First he went about telling everybody, including his own Government, that he had got a permanent alliance with Great Britain. When he was forced from that position he tried to get back from it by suddenly giving us a "unilateral assurance" without consulting us. Unfortunately we were too late to stop him doing this, and, having made this silly gesture, he now does not know how to withdraw it without loss of face. At present he seems to be arguing that this unilateral assurance, far from being directed against Italy, is really a contribution to a general *détente* with Italy. A more specious argument cannot be imagined. In Sir P. Loraine's subsequent telegrams Nos. 84 and 85 [M. Aras] makes his final appeal to us not to leave him in the lurch by withdrawing our own assurance today. He has been told that there is nothing doing [see No. 24 below] . . .'

No. 23

Mr. Newton (Berlin) to Mr. Eden (Received July 27)
No. 773 [R 4520/73/3]

BERLIN, *July 25, 1936*

Sir,

I have the honour to state that the leading article in the latest number of 'Die Deutsche Volkswirtschaft', a National Socialist economic newspaper, contains a strong appeal for the union of Germany with Austria.¹

¹ A minute by Mr. C. Bramwell, a Second Secretary in the Southern Department, described this as 'A very outspoken article containing many points of interest. e.g. para. 2. "might rules". paras. 4–7. Drang nach Osten, para. 8. Pan-Germanism versus Habsburgs. C. Bramwell. 28/vii.'

2. After a short preamble on the meaning of nationalism and the necessity for it, the writer comes to the point at once. 'Since we are a homogeneous people having the same ideas on civilisation, we want to be a single political nation; for might rules the world, and only by our united might can we hope to preserve the independence and freedom of the cultural life of the nation. Nobody in Austria or in Germany will dispute the unqualified truth of these words. The Austrian Government, in its declaration of 11th July,[2] has confirmed them in unmistakable form.'

3. At times, in the three years of 'bitter misunderstanding', which was more a misunderstanding between the governments than between the two peoples, it had seemed doubtful whether the Austrian Government realized that it was controlling the destinies of a German race, but gradually, 'daily and hourly', public opinion had been brought round by the sheer weight of the facts themselves. Germany on the other hand had seen all along that what was needed was simply 'the diplomatic skill and tolerance' displayed by Bismarck in 1871.[3]

4. In future, therefore, Austrian and German national policy must be based upon a community of interests. The unity of the nation must be guaranteed by the uniform policy of the respective governments, until 'another solution' should prove to be practicable. The reason for the bitter resistance which the opponents of 'German might' had ever since 1918 offered to this 'other solution' was to be found in Austria's position today on the map of Central Europe, and its great strategic significance for Germany's economic expansion in South Eastern Europe and beyond. It was the key to Germany's highway to the Near East, and this was why Germany had 'so great an interest in the independence of the Balkan States, the Turks, the Persians and the Arabs'. In a word, Austria was of capital importance to Germany's status as a world power. In addition, it was Germany's sacred mission to save Austria from herself. Austria might well 'shudder at the thought of the abyss into which, without Germany's strong helping hand, she might have plunged'.

5. It is then shown how three years of political strife could not sever the economic ties uniting Berlin and Vienna. A number of statistical returns are quoted to show how Germany, in the exchange of manufactured goods, was Austria's best customer, and vice versa. Czechoslovakia was the only serious competitor in this field, Italy's products being of a different kind. In addition, Germany took Austria's timber, and Austria Germany's coal.

6. A harmonious Austro-German understanding was an essential condition for the promotion of German trade with the Balkan countries. If Austrian commercial policy were shaped to follow Germany's with regard to Yugoslavia, Bulgaria, Greece, Roumania, these countries would realise more clearly still what economic benefits were to be derived from Central European solidarity under the modern system of preferential tariffs, quotas,

[2] A reference to the Austro-German agreement of July 11, 1936: see Volume XVI, No. 436, note 4.

[3] A reference to Bismarck's treatment of Austria in 1866 is presumably intended here.

foreign exchange and the like. For decades there had existed between Vienna and Constantinople the greatest possibilities for capital investment in industry, which would in turn find the money for the import of great quantities of raw materials and food stuffs from the Balkans.

7. The economic development of the countries lying in the centre of South-Eastern Europe would rest, not upon a policy of aggrandizement, but upon recognition of their complete freedom and autonomy. Nobody would be exploited or be expected to put up with anything of the kind. Self-determination would be the rule, and those countries would soon see in what direction their true interests lay. Austria had no revisionist claims upon her South-Eastern neighbours. She lived in peace with them, so no tension adversely affecting trade was to be expected here. Germany and Austria would not interfere with Hungary's relations with her neighbours. Thus Germany's natural high-road to the South East lay through Vienna so long as the one through Prague remained impassable. In the long run, therefore, the obstruction of trade with Austria would have meant a critical and unjustifiable loss to Germany.

8. The step of the 11th of July might have been in this or that respect tactically connected with the Locarno problem, but it really meant a return to the unswerving national policy of all Germans within or beyond the frontiers of the Reich. In time all former differences of opinion, all bitter memories would be forgotten, just as after Königgrätz.[4] What would remain was the consciousness of national unity and the lesson of the common sacrifice in the Great War. Austria's task for the past thousand years has been to be the springboard to the South-East. That this task shall be carried out by the correct use of the sovereignty accorded to Austria in the interests of Pan-Germanism and not in the interests of Habsburg egoism, is the demand of all Germans to the Austrian Government. Another necessary task was for Austria to put her financial house in order, and 'mesh by mesh' to repair the broken net of Austro-German economic co-operation.

I have, &c.,

(For His Majesty's Minister)

I. KIRKPATRICK[5]

[4] The battle in which Prussia defeated Austria on July 3, 1866.
[5] First Secretary in H.M. Embassy at Berlin.

No. 24

Mr. Eden to Sir P. Loraine (Constantinople)
No. 49 Telegraphic [R 4498/294/67]

Immediate　　　　　　　　　　FOREIGN OFFICE, *July 26, 1936, 9.30 p.m.*
Your telegram No. 86.[1]

I have given full consideration to your telegrams Nos. 84 and 85[2] but do not feel that I can now reverse or delay contemplated action. My speech however and in particular the passages relating to Montreux will contain cordial references to Anglo-Turkish friendship and collaboration.[3] These should I think be sufficient to enable the Turkish M[inister for] F[oreign] A[ffairs] to continue his present policy without hindrance. You may, however, if you think it would be helpful in this direction, arrange for the publication of the messages exchanged between M. Aras and myself in regard to Montreux.[4]

[1] In this telegram of July 26, despatched at 11.30 a.m., Sir P. Loraine referred to Foreign Office telegrams Nos. 47 and 48 (Nos. 20 and 21) which had crossed with his Nos. 84 and 85 (No. 22) and asked for instructions.
[2] No. 22.
[3] For the passages in Mr. Eden's speech of July 27 referring to Montreux see 315 *H.C. Deb. 5 s.*, cols. 1119–21.
[4] Messages exchanged between Mr. Eden and M. Aras after the Montreux Conference (see Volume XVI, Chapter VI) expressing gratification at the successful conclusion of the negotiations were published simultaneously in the British and Turkish press on July 29: see *The Times*, July 29, 1936, p. 11.

No. 25

Sir G. Clerk (Paris) to Mr. Eden (Received July 27)
No. 219 Saving: Telegraphic [W 6978/62/41]

PARIS, *July 26, 1936*

My telegram No. 216 Saving of the 24th July.[1]

Press continues to occupy itself with the question of the alleged request of the Spanish Government to be supplied with arms by the French Government. The newspapers of the Right, as might be expected, continue to show considerable indignation at the suggestion that such help should be given at such a juncture as the present to the Left Government at Madrid.

No official statement on the subject has been published. A semi-official *communiqué* given to the press last night states that the French Government, after having discussed the question at a meeting of the Council of Ministers, had decided unanimously, on the suggestion of the Minister for Foreign Affairs, to abstain from all intervention in the internal conflict in Spain.[1] The statement goes on rather cryptically, to say that as regards the requests for the supply of war material which the Spanish Government were said to

[1] Cf. No. 19, note 2.

have made, it was stated in official circles that it was entirely false that the French Government were resolved to adopt an interventionist policy.

It is reported in the press that a Spanish aeroplane, with a cargo of 19 million francs worth of gold, landed yesterday at Le Bourget. This gold is assumed to represent the quid pro quo for the munitions and aeroplanes to be sent to Spain. The position in this respect is far from clear, but today's newspapers seem to believe that so far at any rate no munitions have left France for Spain. On the other hand a Right newspaper points out that whereas the authority of the Ministry of Foreign Affairs is required before a licence can be given for the export of war material, the export of *commercial* aeroplanes is entirely free.[2]

A number of interpellations have been put down for discussion in the Chamber next week on the subject of the Government's attitude towards the civil war in Spain.

[2] A circular issued by the Quai d'Orsay on July 27 to French diplomatic posts stated that the export of unarmed aircraft to Spain by private industry was not forbidden; see *D.D.F.*, *op. cit.*, No. 36.

No. 26

Mr. Newton (Berlin) to Mr. Eden (Received July 27, 10 p.m.)
No. 236 Telegraphic [C 5522/4/18]

BERLIN, *July 27, 1936, 8.22 p.m.*

My telegram No. 231.[1]

As Sunday's 'Observer' take discouraging view of German attitude towards proposed Conference[2] I asked Herr Dieckhoff[3] today whether there had been any change. He said none. Question was no doubt being carefully and calmly considered by the Chancellor[4] and his advisers who were at present away from Berlin. Foreign Minister[5] was due back on Wednesday[6] and Herr Dieckhoff evidently did not expect any development before that date if so soon.[7]

[1] Volume XVI, No. 481.

[2] A minute of July 28 by Mr. H. A. C. Rumbold, a Third Secretary in the Central Department, remarked that the headline 'Cool Reception in Germany' to the *Observer*'s article of July 26 seemed 'only to be justified by the lack of editorial comment in the German press'.   [3] See No. 15, note 4.

[4] Herr Hitler.   [5] Baron von Neurath.   [6] July 29.

[7] In relation to the Spanish civil war, however, decisive action had just been taken by the Chancellor. There is no certain evidence of German assistance to the Spanish insurgents before the outbreak of hostilities on July 19, but on or about July 22 General Franco sent a letter to Herr Hitler asking for transport planes and other assistance. This was brought to Germany by two members of the *Auslandsorganisation* resident in Morocco. They delivered the letter to Herr Hitler at Bayreuth late on July 26; he agreed to give aid without consulting the German Foreign Office. Thirty Junkers 52 transport aircraft were immediately sent to Morocco, solving the vital problem of getting the Moroccan troops on to Spanish soil. Other help followed. See *D.G.F.P.*, Series D, vol. iii, pp. 1 and 2 and Nos. 2, 3, 4, 6, 12, and 13; Thomas, *op. cit.*, pp. 298–302; Hans-Henning Abendroth, *Hitler in der spanischen Arena* (Paderborn, 1973), pp. 23–39.

No. 27

Rear Admiral Commander-in-Chief, First Cruiser Squadron, to Admiralty[1]
(Received July 27, 10.42 p.m.)
No. 916 Telegraphic [W 7066/62/41]

July 27, 1936

Admiralty pass to Foreign Office.

Number of refugees evacuated to Marseilles from Barcelona and Catalonian ports by His Majesty's Ships under my orders up to 0800 27th July is as follows:

Nationality	Men	Women	Children	Total
British	202	262	80	544
American	15	17	8	40
Swiss	75	44	23	142
Russian	—	1	—	1
German	5	7	—	12
Belgian	—	2	—	2
Italian	1	1	1	3
Dutch	1	1	—	2
Norwegian	—	1	—	1
Peruvian	—	1	—	1
Paraguayan	—	1	—	1
Honduras	2	1	—	3
Lebanon	1	—	—	1
Danish	—	1	—	1
Finnish	—	2	—	2
French	12	—[2]	—	21
Cuban	3	1	—	4
Czech	2	2	—	4
Totals	319	354	112	785

Numbers in s.s. 'City of Hongkong' are included in above. Nominal lists are being forwarded by post via Marseilles.

[1] Also addressed to Commander-in-Chief, Mediterranean, and Rear Admiral, Gibraltar.
[2] It would seem that to produce the right totals the figure '9' should appear here.

No. 28

Mr. Ingram (Rome) to Mr. Eden (Received July 28, 9.30 a.m.)
No. 510 Telegraphic [W 7075/62/41]

ROME, *July 28, 1936, 2.15 a.m.*

French Ambassador[1] tells me he saw Count Ciano this morning and that latter once again emphasized the seriousness with which Italian Government were viewing events in Spain. According to Count Ciano the Italians

[1] M. le Comte de Chambrun.

thought that because Portugal had declared its sympathy with insurgents and as the Portuguese hardly ever came out into the open on any matter without first being assured of British support owing to long standing Anglo-Portuguese alliance, Great Britain was in favour of the rebels.

I told Count de Chambrun that this seemed to me a most dangerous assumption to make. I had no . . .[2] as to Portuguese attitude, nor indeed, beyond what I had read in the press, as to that of my own Government but I felt quite sure that on this, as on other analogous occasions, the attitude of His Majesty's Government was one of strict neutrality.[3]

Repeated to Paris No. 31.

[2] The text was here uncertain.

[3] In a further telegram, No. 513 of even date, Mr. Ingram remarked: 'Italian Government are clearly anxious lest they should be faced with governments in France and Spain in which Communist and anti-Fascist elements may predominate.'

No. 29

Sir P. Loraine (Constantinople) to Mr. Eden (Received July 28, 4.45 p.m.)
No. 91 Telegraphic [R 4538/294/67]

Important   CONSTANTINOPLE, *July 28, 1936, 2 p.m.*
Your telegrams Nos. 47 and 48.[1]

As Minister for Foreign Affairs had unexpectedly and very fortunately cancelled his journey to Angora July 26 I was able to make to him personally at 2 p.m. yesterday a written communication in the sense of your instructions. He took it very well. In subsequent discussion of the effects so far as concerns Turkey of declaration which you have now made in the House of Commons,[2] your telegram No. 49[3] was very useful to me indeed and Minister for Foreign Affairs quite appreciated that at the moment when my telegrams Nos. 84 and 85[4] reached you, it was not possible either to reverse or to retard your action. He willingly accepted that valid set of reasons which had determined your action; he much appreciated that I should have explained to you and that you should have examined attentively the different set of reasons that were influencing the Turkish point of view.

2. It would adequately summarise his attitude to say that he can manage all right with situation created by your declaration; sees his way all right to adjust his forthcoming statement in the Grand National Assembly to somewhat altered circumstances, and feels able to carry on with his policy.

3. He does not propose to withdraw unilateral Turkish assurances to the United Kingdom.

4. He has seen the Italian Ambassador, has spoken to him in the sense foreshadowed in my telegram No. 84, paragraph 7, and has sent the Turkish representative in London an account of his interview for communication to you.[5]

[1] Nos. 20 and 21.   [2] See No. 13, note 2.   [3] No. 24.   [4] No. 22.
[5] See No. 33 below.

5. Italian Ambassador admitted that he himself was convinced of the good sense of the Turkish Minister for Foreign Affairs' views and undertook to try to convince Rome. He added however that if in this connexion the statement in the Grand National Assembly were accompanied by any acid comment in the press or elsewhere it would render his task in so doing well-night [*sic*] impossible.

Repeated to Athens, Belgrade, Rome and to Bucharest Saving.

No. 30

Mr. Eden to Sir H. Chilton (Madrid)[1]
No. 359 [W 7174/62/41]

FOREIGN OFFICE, *July 28, 1936*

Sir,

In the course of my conversation with the Spanish Ambassador this evening Señor Oliván spoke of a cutting in the *Daily Herald*[2]—the information, he said, was repeated in to-night's evening papers—with reference to the alleged sale of four British aeroplanes to Portugal, apparently with the intention of their journey being continued to Spain. The Ambassador said he had as yet no instructions from his Government, but he felt sure he would receive some, and he therefore wished to call my attention to the matter at once.

2. Having read the cutting, a copy of which is enclosed,[3] I pointed out to his Excellency that the aircraft referred to were described as passenger craft. If this were so, then they were not machines over the export of which the Government had any control. While we had in this country, as I thought other countries had, a system of licensing for the export of arms and munitions, this did not apply to civil aeroplanes, and on the face of it the matter would appear to have been one in which the Government had no power to intervene.

3. The Ambassador repeated that he had no instructions as yet from his Government, and no doubt, if the position was as I had described it, then I would have to give him that reply, if and when he did receive instructions. In the meanwhile, however, he would press that I should make enquiries, since he had no doubt that the matter would cause some considerable concern in Madrid.[4]

4. The Ambassador asked me if I could tell him that the position in respect of providing supplies for the Spanish Government was that no

---

[1] Cf. No. 17, note 1.   [2] Of July 28, 1936.   [3] Not printed.
[4] Mr. Eden told the Cabinet on July 29 that the aircraft had been sold to France by British Airways and suggested that after their arrival in France the French Government became responsible for permitting or preventing their exportation to Spain. The Cabinet agreed that Mr. Eden should make it clear to the Spanish Ambassador or in Parliament if questioned that the British Government had no legal power to stop the sale of commercial aircraft.

obstacle would be put in the way of such supplies by His Majesty's Government. I said that that was certainly the position. The Ambassador then asked whether the same thing would apply to the supply of arms and munitions. He had not yet received any request from his Government to ask for the supply of such munitions, but he would be glad if I could give him any information as to our attitude in that eventuality. I replied that exports of arms and munitions from this country required a licence, and if the Spanish Government made such an application then it would certainly be considered by the normal machinery set up. The Ambassador again thanked me, and emphasised that he had received no official intimation of a request for the supply of arms and munitions and, indeed, I had the impression that he hoped no such request would be forthcoming from his Government.[5]

5. Finally, the Ambassador said that he wished to make a personal suggestion. Would it be possible for the League to do anything in this conflict? He admitted the difficulties now created by the League's loss of authority and of membership. If it could speak with the united voice of Europe in this conflict, it might be able to stop it in the name of humanity. Perhaps even now it could achieve something. He was speaking to me without instructions and would not like his Government even to know of his suggestion, he only put it forward out of love of Spain and because he feared that if left to itself this conflict would continue for many months; indeed, until one side or the other was virtually annihilated.[6]

I am, &c.,

ANTHONY EDEN

[5] In reporting this portion of the Ambassador's remarks to the Cabinet on July 29 Mr. Eden suggested that if a request should be received to purchase arms from private manufacturers he should deal with it in the ordinary way, by reference to the Board of Trade and the government departments concerned. 'The Spanish Government, he pointed out, was a recognised Government, and we could not act otherwise unless it was decided to recognise the Spanish insurgents.' The Cabinet were reminded that the Defence Departments might wish to retain the whole output for British rearmament. The Cabinet agreed that Mr. Eden 'should follow the ordinary procedure in the event of an application from the Spanish Government to purchase arms'.

A note by Mr. Seymour of July 31 stated that a report had been received to the effect that the French Government 'had informed the Spanish Government that the exportation of war material from France to Spain (except unarmed aeroplanes) was forbidden', and that Mr. Eden had written on this report: 'This may mean that we shall be asked now. I hope that we shall be able to avoid supplying, by some means or other.'

[6] With regard to the last paragraph of Señor Oliván's remarks Mr. Eden told the Cabinet, which shared his view, that it appeared impossible for the League of Nations to interfere at the present time in the affairs of Spain.

Sir G. Clerk (Paris) to Mr. Eden (Received July 30)
No. 976 [T 12027/8725/379]

PARIS, *July 28, 1936*

Sir,

The official announcement which appeared in the press yesterday that The King had felt obliged by recent events to abandon his intention to spend his holidays in the South of France, has of course been received with deep regret in this country.[1] A few of the more irresponsible writers of the Right press, such as Bailby in the 'Jour', are, as was to be expected, ready to use this event as a stick with which to beat the Government, but the decision has on the whole been received with sympathy and an unusual measure of understanding.

2. The simultaneous announcement that the Prime Minister[2] had felt constrained to renounce his yearly holiday at Aix-les-Bains was most opportune and served as a useful reminder of the seriousness with which His Majesty's Government regard recent political developments in Europe.

3. The King discussed the situation in France with me when He arrived at Calais on the morning of the 26th July and I ventured to express my entire agreement with His decision.[3]

4. At the same time I suggested that he should take advantage of His meeting with the President of the Republic at Vimy to explain to His Excellency the reasons of this change of plans. This His Majesty was able to do, and while M. Lebrun expressed his sorrow at the news I know that he much appreciated the fact that he had learnt of it from The King himself.

5. His Majesty was good enough to show me the telegram which He addressed to the President of the Republic at the moment of his departure from France on Sunday evening; and I was very glad that it had been found possible to include in it a reference to the regret which His change of plans had caused Him. This telegram would, I knew, be published immediately and would prepare the ground for the official announcement, which was

[1] The original plan of H.M. King Edward VIII, announced on July 21, had been to holiday at the Château de l'Horizon at Cannes. On July 28 it was announced that this plan had been cancelled owing to the proximity of the château to the Franco-Spanish frontier and to the King's desire not to add to the heavy responsibilities of the French Government arising from the Spanish war.

[2] Mr. Stanley Baldwin.

[3] The King had visited France to unveil Canada's War Memorial at Vimy Ridge on Sunday, July 26. The ceremony had been attended by 6,000 Canadian ex-service men, 3 Canadian ministers, the President of the French Republic and others. A minute by Mr. F. R. Hoyer Millar (Assistant Private Secretary (Diplomatic) to the Secretary of State) of May 14 noted that it had been agreed 'that as the actual ceremony at Vimy is entirely a matter concerning the Canadian Government it shall be the Canadian Minister in Paris who formally approaches the President of the French Republic and informs him of His Majesty's intentions. All other arrangements, however, except those connected with the actual ceremony will be made by Sir George Clerk who will of course be informed beforehand of all the proposals.'

shortly to be made, and which could not naturally fail to occasion keen disappointment.[4]

6. The situation in the South of France is very different today from what it was some weeks ago when the idea of a Royal visit was first mooted. It has been practically impossible for the French authorities to control the hurried flight of thousands of refugees from Spain. The usual passport formalities have of necessity in many cases been waived or evaded and there is no doubt that desperadoes and undesirables of every class and nationality have availed themselves of this opportunity to cross into French territory. Whatever the result of the present struggle in Spain this exodus will continue; and should the present Spanish Government eventually be worsted, numbers of anarchists and extremists of the most violent sort will seek in this country a refuge from the wrath to come—a refuge which a Government of the *Front Populaire* can hardly refuse to afford. I confess that this untimely reinforcement of the elements of disorder and revolution—already only too numerous in Marseilles and other seaports of the South—causes me grave concern.

I have, &c.,
GEORGE R. CLERK

[4] It was announced on July 30 that the King had chartered Lady Yule's yacht *Nahlin* for a holiday cruise along the Dalmatian coast and beyond.

No. 32

Viscount Chilston[1] (Moscow) to Mr. Eden (Received July 29, 1 p.m.)
No. 119 Telegraphic [W 7236/62/41]

MOSCOW, *July 29, 1936, 1.5 p.m.* [*sic*]

Soviet press which has shown a great though non-committal interest in Spanish war finds interest displayed by German and Italian press highly significant and indeed accuses Berlin directly and Rome less directly of having supplied 'rebel generals' in advance with material support in exchange for 'undertakings of international importance.'[2] Attention is called to presence of German and Italian warships in Spanish waters 'though Germany and Italy have no common frontiers with Spain'. Statement of General Franco that a Soviet oil tanker was present during operations on Morocco coast is categorically and indignantly denied. 'Spanish Government has never asked Soviet Union for assistance and we are convinced that they will find in their own country sufficient forces to liquidate this mutiny of Fascist generals acting on orders from foreign countries.' Soviet Union has no desire to acquire a military base against Gibraltar or submarine bases on Spanish territory.

[1] H.M. Ambassador at Moscow.   [2] See No. 26, note 7.

No. 33

Mr. Eden to Sir P. Loraine (Constantinople)

No. 53 Telegraphic [R 4538/294/67]

Most Immediate   FOREIGN OFFICE, *July 29, 1936, 2.35 p.m.*

Your telegram No. 91.[1]

The Turkish Chargé d'Affaires has now communicated to me a written account of M. Aras's views on the present state of Anglo-Turkish relations and of the latter's recent conversation with the Italian Ambassador. I gather that this account represents more or less what he proposes to say to the Grand National Assembly, and it is for this reason that I must put in a caveat in regard to two assertions contained therein.

(1) M. Aras proposes to inform the Grand Council that the Turkish Government have given a unilateral assurance to Great Britain to the effect that the undertakings given by the Turkish Government last December shall be continued without time limit and without any demand for reciprocity. The Turkish Government are of course completely free of their own volition to give any unilateral assurance they like, but before they announce their intention to do so publicly I hope that M. Aras will seriously consider the views of His Majesty's Government as set forth in my telegram No. 41.[2] The Turkish assurance now in question has indeed been communicated to me by the Turkish Chargé d'Affaires but no reply has been returned to him, and in the circumstances I do not propose to do so. Meanwhile I notice in your telegram No. 78[3] you say that this Turkish assurance is irrevocable. I do not understand why this should be the case seeing that the circumstances have so altered as to enable His Majesty's Government to withdraw the assurance they gave on June 18th.[4] If nevertheless M. Aras feels that he is constrained to continue this new Turkish assurance and to announce the fact to the Grand National Assembly, I must beg that he will say nothing to give the impression that His Majesty's Government have asked for this assurance or that they consider that it is necessary in present circumstances.

(2) In the Chargé d'Affaires' account of M. Aras's recent conversation with the Italian Ambassador, M. Aras is reported to have declared that Turkey had with Great Britain 'a bond which assured that there was consultation between the two countries with regard to every event and every proposal touching the Mediterranean either directly or indirectly'. This statement, not only does not represent the facts of the case, but it would seem to imply that the British and Turkish Governments had concluded some agreement for mutual consultation and co-operation. For this reason I cannot believe that M. Aras can have made such a statement to the Italian Ambassador, and I naturally expect that he will not say anything at the Grand National Assembly on these lines.

You should at once communicate with M. Aras to this effect, and impress

---

[1] No. 29.   [2] Volume XVI, No. 471.   [3] See No. 22, note 1.
[4] Cf. No. 21.

upon him the importance of choosing his language very carefully in referring in his speech to the cordial relations which happily exist between our two countries.[5]

Repeated to Rome, No. 298, Athens, No. 116, Belgrade, No. 81.

[5] In his telegram No. 95 of July 30, Sir P. Loraine said that early on July 30 he had read to the Secretary General of the Ministry of Foreign Affairs a letter based on Mr. Eden's instructions in telegram No. 53, and as a result M. Aras would modify his speech to the Turkish Grand National Assembly and announce the withdrawal of the Turkish unilateral guarantee. With regard to the second point of telegram No. 53 he reported the Turkish Secretary-General, M. Numan Menemençioğlu, as saying that M. Aras had never made the statement to the Italian Ambassador attributed to him, and believed that the report was due to a complete misunderstanding for which the Turkish Chargé in London was responsible. A minute by Mr. Green of the Southern Department commented: 'Good. They've done the right thing at the eleventh hour. W. R. C. Green. 31/7.'

No. 34

Sir G. Clerk (Paris) to Mr. Eden (Received July 30)
No. 228 Saving: Telegraphic [W 7264/62/41]

PARIS, *July 29, 1936*

My telegram No. 255 of July 28th.[1]

On Major McCrindle telephoning this morning he was informed that I had consulted your department and that I was not authorised to intervene on his behalf with the French authorities.

This evening's press states that the four aircraft in question are still detained at Bordeaux while investigations are being made in Paris.[2]

The evening press also announces that another British aeroplane which, piloted by Captain Ewens, arrived late last night at Bordeaux, left this morning early for Biarritz en route for Lisbon.

[1] This telegram stated that Major McCrindle, representing British Airways, had requested Sir G. Clerk to intervene with French authorities to secure permission for four British aircraft detained at Bordeaux by local authorities to proceed to Lisbon for delivery to a purchaser there. The planes were four Fokker F XII aircraft purchased by British Airways from Messrs. Koninklijke Luchtvaart Maatschappij in February 1936. Cf. No. 30.

[2] The Foreign Office had refused to take any action pending the receipt of satisfactory assurances from the Air Ministry as to the use to which the four planes were to be put. Sir G. Mounsey minuted on July 30: 'We have known from the first, confidentially, that the aim was to sell the machines *somehow* to the rebels. Let them do so at their own risk.' However, on July 31 the company gave full particulars of their negotiations with the French authorities, and Lord Swinton, Air Minister, recommended that diplomatic assistance should be given to the company as it was now anxious to bring the planes back to England. It appeared that the French authorities had not been prepared to act without a recommendation from the Foreign Office. Sir G. Clerk was authorized to give this in an unnumbered telegram of July 31 (W 7503/62/41).

No. 35

Memorandum[1] *by the Chiefs of Staff Sub-Committee on proposals for an Eastern Mediterranean understanding with Turkey and Greece*

[*R 5533/294/67*]

2 WHITEHALL GARDENS, S.W.1, *July 29, 1936*

The Cabinet, at their meeting on the 23rd June, 1936, agreed

'That the Minister for Co-ordination of Defence[2] should invite the Chiefs of Staff Sub-Committee to consider and report on the proposals in C.P. 165(36)[3] for an Eastern Mediterranean understanding with Turkey and Greece' (Cabinet 43(36), Conclusion 3(*c*)).

2. We instructed the Joint Planning Sub-Committee to make, in the first instance, a detailed study of the strategical commitments and requirements involved in such a proposal, and to submit to us an appreciation showing its advantages and disadvantages. We invited them also to include in the appreciation general considerations affecting the possible establishment of an additional naval, military and air base in Cyprus, since that was relevant to the matter under consideration, although a detailed examination of this particular question is to form the subject of a separate Report.

3. In accordance with these instructions the Joint Planning Sub-Committee have submitted an appreciation, a copy of which is attached to this Report.[4] This appreciation sets out the pros and cons of the proposal in a form which we think will be of value as a record. It was, however, prepared on the assumption an understanding with Italy was not achieved, and we believe that the international situation has developed, since the Sub-Committee were given their terms of reference, in such a way that that assumption need no longer be held as necessarily valid.

4. Our own conclusions on the broad question of the desirability of an understanding with Turkey and Greece are as follows.

(*a*) From the strategical point of view the first desideratum is a secure Mediterranean. This involves, as the primary consideration, the restoration of our former friendly relations with Italy. No action should be taken which is liable to prejudice this primary consideration.

(*b*) Subject to the above primary consideration, any step that can be taken to renew a peaceful situation in the Mediterranean will be an advantage from a strategical point of view.

(*c*) In particular, it is important to avoid an unfriendly Turkey or to throw her into the arms of a hostile Power. The maintenance of friendly relations with that country is second in importance only

---

[1] Circulated to the Cabinet as C.P. 211(36).   [2] Sir T. Inskip.
[3] Volume XVI, No. 361.
[4] Not printed. This report is briefly referred to in Volume XVI, No. 361, note 9.

to that of friendly relations with Italy. It is also important to avoid an unfriendly Greece in time of war.

(*d*) Our present circumstances are not favourable to the acceptance of fresh military commitments, since some years must elapse before we should be in a position to give effect to them. Assurances, we suggest, are only too readily taken as pledges of support.

5. In the unfortunate event of the situation vis-à-vis Italy not improving, Turkey's co-operation and support will be of great value, and certain other measures referred to in the Report for improving the strategical position will receive additional importance. Notable among these are the suggested railway between Baghdad and Haifa (paragraph 28) and the establishment of a new naval, military and air base at Cyprus (paragraph 30). In the latter connection we consider that a more accurate description of the problem of the air defence of Cyprus against a hostile Turkey would be to say that its geographical position in relation to the mainland would lay it open to a scale of attack similar to that which might have to be faced at Malta. In the former case, however, counter-attacks could be delivered from bases in Palestine as well as those on the island itself; moreover, the size of the island would permit a greater dispersion in the interests of security.

6. To summarise, therefore, we recommend that everything possible should be done to maintain the most friendly relations with Turkey, but we consider that nothing should be done that is liable to alienate Italy, and that no new military commitment should be entered into. This would not preclude some international diplomatic arrangement between all the Mediterranean Powers with a view to a maintenance in that region of the territorial status quo which would be all to our advantage.[5]

> ERNLE CHATFIELD
> E. L. ELLINGTON
> C. J. DEVERELL[6]

[5] A covering note of September 10, 1936, by Sir Maurice Hankey, Secretary to the Cabinet, states that these memoranda 'were laid before, and taken note of by, the Cabinet at a Meeting [Cabinet 56(36) Conclusion 7] on the 2nd September, 1936'.

[6] Respectively Chief of the Naval Staff, Chief of the Air Staff, and Chief of the Imperial General Staff.

No. 36

Mr. Newton (Berlin) to Mr. Eden (Received July 31)

No. 792 [R 4618/73/3]

BERLIN, *July 29, 1936*

Sir,

I have read with great interest Sir Walford Selby's despatch No. 215 of July 18th[1] in which he reviews the events leading up to the Austro-German agreement[2] and comments on possible developments.

[1] Volume XVI, Appendix IV. Sir Walford Selby was H.M. Minister at Vienna.

[2] Of July 11, 1936: see *ibid.*, No. 436, note 4.

2. In the continued absence of the Chancellor with his staff together with all the Cabinet Ministers most closely concerned it is difficult to obtain inside information in Berlin as to exactly what was in Herr Hitler's mind when at last he decided that the dispute with Austria should be brought to an end on the terms obtained by Herr von Papen. As Sir Eric Phipps wrote in his despatch No. 1305 of December 10th last,[3] opinion was gaining ground here that Germany's former policy in regard to Austria had been a mistake. On January 22nd Sir Eric Phipps reported in a letter to Sir Robert Vansittart[4] that Herr Hitler favoured the idea of a plebiscite in Austria whilst Signor Mussolini was occupied in Abyssinia. As events turned out, the predictions of all military experts were falsified and it soon became apparent that the Abyssinian campaign had by no means eliminated Italy as a factor in Europe. Austria, as Herr Hitler stated in his speech of May 21st, 1935 (page 28 of White Paper) represented the only conflict of interest with Italy.[5] This circumstance, the development of the Locarno question (see paragraph 8 of my despatch No. 773 of July 25th),[6] and strategical considerations undoubtedly had their effect. But essentially it was obviously in Germany's interest to liquidate the Austrian dispute, and this fact had no doubt long been recognised by moderate opinion and the Wilhelmstrasse. The only obstacle was the attitude of the Nazi party, who opposed the so-called betrayal of their Austrian comrades in Germany and over the border, regardless of the major national interests involved. When finally Herr Hitler decided to overrule the party, and the agreement with Austria was concluded, the general opinion abroad and also inside Germany, except amongst the more radical party elements, was that he had scored a striking success. Instead of speculating why he threw the helm over on to a new tack at that particular moment one is tempted to ask oneself why he did not decide to do so long ago.[7]

3. From the strategical point of view the General Staff are certainly glad to be relieved for the time being of the danger of military complications over Austria. It must also be borne in mind that the German Government attaches importance to the use by the Russian air force of bases in Czechoslovakia. The agreement with Austria narrows the potentially hostile front

[3] In this despatch (C 8198/134/18) Sir E. Phipps, H.M. Ambassador at Berlin, reviewed what seemed to him at the time to be the probable direction of Germany's foreign policy.
[4] Volume XV, No. 471. Sir R. Vansittart was Permanent Under Secretary of State for Foreign Affairs.
[5] See Volume XIII, No. 222; cf. No. 278 (p. 325). [6] No. 23.
[7] Addressing a deputation of distinguished Tory back benchers and others at 10 Downing Street on July 29, the Prime Minister, Mr. Baldwin, speaking of Herr Hitler, remarked that 'none of us know what goes on in that strange man's mind', but he added: 'We all know the German desire, and he has come out with it in his book, to move East, and if he should move East I should not break my heart. . .' The deputation's purpose was to voice disquiet over the progress of British rearmament, and in the opening session on July 28 Mr. Churchill made a searching and lengthy statement, to which Mr. Baldwin replied in rather general terms on the 29th. Sir Thomas Inskip promised that everything that had been said by the deputation would be 'studied and checked and considered'. There is a good summary of the discussion in M. Gilbert, *Winston Churchill* (London, 1976), vol. v, pp. 768–80.

against Germany, denies to Russia a free passage by air to France and may enable distant targets to be reached via Austria, if necessary.

4. As regards the development of economic relations, an Austrian delegation is at present in Berlin to discuss the matter. According to information obtained at the Ministry for Foreign Affairs here it is expected that an increase of mutual trade will be slow. Polish and Czech coal, for example, can only be gradually replaced by German coal. Similarly a large expansion of the tourist trade cannot take place immediately. The Minister of the Interior, Dr. Frick, in a recent public speech announced that the thousand mark visa would be abolished, but on account of currency difficulties unrestricted permission to travel to Austria could not yet be granted. He undertook, however, that the German Government would do all that lay in their power.

5. In the political as well as in the economic field the liquidation of existing problems will take time. As I indicated in my despatch No. 783 of 28th July[8] the Nazi party in Germany are disposed to make excessive demands which may cause trouble. But the average German is convinced that Herr Hitler will eventually achieve his ends. As National Socialist speakers constantly put it, tactics may have to be altered to suit the exigencies of the moment, but the goal remains the same.

6. I am sending a copy of this despatch to His Majesty's Minister at Vienna.

I have, &c.,
B. C. NEWTON

[8] Not preserved in the Foreign Office archives.

No. 37

Mr. Newton (Berlin) to Mr. Eden (Received July 30, 6.10 p.m.)
No. 240 Telegraphic [C 5628/4/18]

BERLIN, July 30, 1936, 5 p.m.

My telegram No. 236.[1]

In reply to my personal enquiry this morning Minister for Foreign Affairs said he could tell me unofficially for private information of His Majesty's Government that German Government would in principle accept the invitation to a conference. He thought that an official reply would be forthcoming in the course of the next week. This reply without making conditions would include certain observations the nature of which he did not further specify.

The necessity for most careful prior preparation and . . .[2] national and international engagements including Nuremburg party rally from September 9th to September 16th and the League of Nations meeting would in his opinion make it impossible to hold conference before the middle of October.

[1] No. 26.   [2] The text was here uncertain.

As I had been informed by British correspondents that the impression given to them at the Ministry of Foreign Affairs had been discouraging and I thought Herr Kircher's article reported in my telegram No. 195 Saving[3] might have been inspired I expressed disappointment at difficulties foreseen in this article and in particular at the unreasonable complaint that agenda for conference had not yet been defined. Baron von Neurath said that he had not read the article but could assure me that it had certainly not been inspired.

[3] Not printed: cf. No. 26.

No. 38

Sir H. Chilton (Zarauz) to Mr. Eden (Received August 6)
No. 587 [W 7812/62/41]

ZARAUZ, *July 30, 1936*

Sir,

In my despatch No. 585 of July 28th,[1] I had the honour to submit a report of the events which took place in San Sebastian and the surrounding country during the past week but I did not attempt to describe the political situation in this province which one may reasonably believe, is typical of conditions in those regions of Spain still under Government control.

2. In San Sebastian itself there was a Civil Governor and a Mayor. Their powers, however, were much restricted. The Mayor had at his disposal the municipal police, who, released from their traffic control duties, appeared to be taking a holiday and proved singularly ineffective on the one occasion on which I asked for their services. The Civil Governor's office was besieged by persons requesting every kind of facility but though safe-conducts were issued there and military staff officers were at work in an inner room the life of the city and the control of the militia forces was organised and administered by a small Committee having its office in the 'House of the People' ('Casa del Pueblo').

3. I imagine that anyone who had experience of Russian administration in the early days of the 1917 revolution would have found those conditions very faithfully reproduced in the 'Casa del Pueblo'.

4. A small group of men, unshaven and short of sleep, but fired with enthusiasm for their cause, issuing orders, which must have lacked co-ordination, by telephone and in writing, and improvising transport, commissariat and munition arrangements to meet the needs which were constantly brought to their notice by loud voiced individuals all armed with revolver, shot-gun or rifle. Such orders as they gave for the fulfilment of requests made by this Embassy were, however, carried out with an alacrity and precision not characteristic of normal times which may have been attributable in part to fear of the consequences which would attend failure

[1] See No. 8, note 3.

43

to comply with the instructions of the Committee. It was noticeable that none of the members of the Committee appeared to be Basques and this feature was also apparent among persons holding posts of responsibility outside headquarters. It applies too here where the administration is also in the hands of a Workers' Committee.

5. The control in these regions is in fact in the hands of Communists. For the present it serves their purpose to go with the Republican Government but it seems almost certain that if the latter emerge victorious from the present struggle the next problem which will confront them will be a struggle with the Communists for supreme command.

I have, &c.,

H. G. CHILTON

No. 39

Sir G. Clerk (Paris) to Mr. Eden (Received July 31, 5.20 p.m.)

No. 256 Telegraphic [W 7445/62/41]

Confidential   PARIS, *July 31, 1936, 4.20 p.m.*

Quai d'Orsai is much perturbed by forced landing on French soil of three Italian aeroplanes, destined for Spanish Morocco and apparently carrying machine guns and arms, as reported in today's 'Times'.[1] This incident will not only make things more difficult for those members of the French Government who have hitherto successfully stopped President of the Council and Air Ministry from supplying bombing aeroplanes and arms to Spanish Government but may have wider repercussion in Franco-Italian relations.

[1] The report in *The Times* of July 31 (p. 14) was from Oran, Algeria, dated July 30; it said that the planes were three out of six which were flying from Sardinia to Spanish Morocco. Cf. *D.D.F., op. cit.,* No. 46. It is now known that Italian aid to the insurgents resulted from the initiative of General Mola, who sent Antonio Goicoechea, described by Professor Hugh Thomas as 'the ageing dandy who was Monarchist leader in the Cortes', to Count Ciano. In March 1934 Goicoechea had concluded an agreement in which Signor Mussolini had promised recognition and assistance to a monarchist government in Spain after a successful uprising which would overthrow the Republic. On July 24 1936 he assured Ciano that the rebels needed only aeroplanes and some arms for speedy success. Ciano undertook that Italy would send twelve Savoia S 81 bombers to Spanish Morocco by early August, in return for an immediate cash payment of over one million pounds sterling, which was promptly supplied by the Spanish financier, Señor Juan March. The 12 planes took off from Sardinia at dawn on July 30. They were delayed by strong headwinds. In the end nine managed to land in Spanish Morocco, but one fell into the sea off French Morocco, and two others made a crash landing there. See Thomas, *op. cit.,* pp. 114, 286, and J. F. Coverdale, *Italian Intervention in the Spanish Civil War* (Princeton, 1975), pp. 3-5, 50-4, 72-4.

No. 40

Sir H. Chilton (Zarauz) to Mr. Eden (Received July 31, 5.30 p.m.)
No. 172 Telegraphic: by wireless [W 7450/62/41]

ZARAUZ, *July 31, 1936*

My telegram No. 152 of 24th July.[1] It[2] is considered desirable that member of Embassy staff should go to Madrid. Could not Mr. Ogilvie-Forbes proceed there by air? It is impossible for anyone to reach Madrid from here.

[1] This apparently refers to a code telegram from Sir H. Chilton (W 6895/62/41) despatched through H.M.S. *Veteran* (see No. 8, note 3) and received in London on July 25; it welcomed the arrival of British destroyers, said that the Embassy was so cut off that it was difficult to know what was happening in Spain, and concluded that there was 'no possibility of sending any members of Embassy to Madrid at present' (cf. No. 11).

[2] A minute of August 1 by Mr. Seymour suggested that the word 'If' had been missed out at the beginning of this sentence.

No. 41

Sir E. Phipps (Berlin) to Mr. Eden (Received July 31, 10.20 p.m.)
No. 243 Telegraphic [C 5653/4/18]

BERLIN, *July 31, 1936, 9.35 p.m.*

Mr. Newton's telegram No. 240.[1]

The Minister for Foreign Affairs received Sir R. Vansittart[2] and me this afternoon.

At the end of a friendly conversation His Excellency informed us officially that the German Government would be happy to accept the invitation to a Five Power Conference but not before the middle of October at the earliest in order to give ample time for thorough preparation diplomatically and for reasons given in paragraph 2 of telegram under reference.

Sir R. Vansittart remarked that he hoped in that case that we could be certain that meanwhile there would be no disturbing acts committed by any of the participating Powers. The Minister for Foreign Affairs declared that he could rest assured that perfect calm would prevail in the intervening period.

[1] No. 37.
[2] Sir Robert and Lady Vansittart had left London on July 30 for Berlin with Sir E. Phipps, who had just concluded his summer leave. They were to stay with him as his guests and to visit the Olympic Games, which commenced on August 1. It was explained in *The Times* of July 30 (p. 14) that Sir R. Vansittart's visit was in no sense official, and that Lady Vansittart was to be hostess for her brother-in-law, Sir E. Phipps, during the Olympic Games in place of her sister, Lady Phipps, who was staying on in England for health reasons. Cf. *D.G.F.P.*, Series C, vol. v, No. 489, notes 1, 2.

No. 42

Sir H. Chilton (Zarauz) to Mr. Eden (Received August 1, 10 a.m.)
No. 173 Telegraphic: by Admiralty wireless[1] [W 7469/62/41]

Important   ZARAUZ, *July 31, 1936*

Admiralty have instructed Captain of H.M.S. *Kempenfelt* to evacuate British Embassy early tomorrow, Saturday August 1st. I have so far no instructions from you, but am proposing to leave tomorrow Saturday afternoon. We should arrive St. Jean de Luz about 1730. Please inform Pack.[2]

[1] Through Captain of 2nd Destroyer Flotilla.
[2] Mr. A. J. Pack, Commercial Secretary, was at this time staying at Biarritz. A telegram from Sir H. Chilton, despatched at 9 a.m. on August 2 to the Foreign Office, reported that he had arrived at the Hotel Eskualduna, Hendaye Plage, with the Embassy staff.

No. 43

Mr. Ingram (Rome) to Foreign Office[1] (Received August 1, 9.30 a.m.)
No. 524 Telegraphic [C 5681/4/18]

Important   ROME, *August 1, 1936, 6 a.m.*

Minister for Foreign Affairs summoned the French Ambassador, Belgian Chargé d'Affaires[2] and myself this afternoon at 5 o'clock to communicate to us the Italian Government's reply to the invitation to a Five Power Conference conveyed to him on July 24th.[3] Count Ciano declared that his government was happy to accept 'in principle' this invitation and to participate in a conference of the Locarno Powers at some date to be fixed later. The Italian Government were anxious that the meeting should be prepared for with the greatest possible care through diplomatic channels with a view to achieving the important objectives before it. He added that he had already informed the German Ambassador of this communication.

His Excellency then handed to us a copy of the *communiqué* which had already been given to Stefani Agency and which was in the above sense.

The French Ambassador after thanking Count Ciano on our behalf asked what was the exact meaning to be attached to the word 'in principle' (this was how the Italian 'in massima' was translated by Count Ciano) and I enquired whether it was intended to cover any mental reservations. The Minister for Foreign Affairs assured us that his government's acceptance was complete and without . . .[4] The expression 'in principle' had no reference to the fact of acceptance but only to the eventual elaboration of the agenda, the fixing of the date and other details.

[1] Mr. Eden left London on the afternoon of July 31 for a fortnight's holiday in Yorkshire, during which period Lord Halifax, Lord Privy Seal, took charge of day-to-day events at the Foreign Office.
[2] M. le Comte du Chastel.   [3] See Volume XVI, No. 482.
[4] The text was here uncertain. 'Reservations' was suggested on the filed copy.

On being questioned as to the usefulness of making in the *communiqué* any reference to the German Ambassador as lending substance to the theory that Germany and Italy were in one camp and the other three Powers in another, Count Ciano replied that there was no such underlying intention and that there has been no prior agreement in the matter between Italy and Germany. He had merely felt it necessary to inform Herr von Hassell of the Italian Government's decision since he represented one of the five interested Powers. The *communiqué* was only designed to announce the facts of the situation.

No. 44

Sir G. Clerk (Paris) to Foreign Office (Received August 3, 3 p.m.)
No. 237 Saving: Telegraphic [W 7566/62/41]

PARIS, *August 2, 1936*

My telegram No. 256.[1]
Spanish situation.
Government's attitude towards civil war in Spain seems to be shifting away from the official neutrality indicated in its public pronouncements (e.g. that of the Minister for Foreign Affairs in the debate in the Chamber on July 30th—see my telegram No. 233).[2] Thus it was announced semi-officially in last night's 'Temps' and in this morning's press, that it was decided at the Council of Ministers yesterday that French and foreign volunteers should be allowed to cross the frontier into Spain, provided that such volunteers are in possession of valid *individual* passports (no collective passports admitted) and that they circulate on and leave French territory unarmed. This decision though taken ostensibly in order to emphasise the complete neutrality of the French Government would seem to be chiefly to the interest of the Madrid Government as forces favourable to that Government appear to control the regions adjoining the main routes from France into Spain. Another example of the tendency to assist the Madrid Government is no doubt to be seen in the detention of four British Airways machines at Bordeaux (see my telegram No. 255)[3] presumably on suspicion of being en route for rebel headquarters, at a time when no restriction is apparently being placed on circulation of French aeroplanes between France and Madrid. Further, a *communiqué* issued last night by the Ministry for Foreign Affairs concludes by stating that the Government have decided to invite the other principal Governments concerned to agree upon and observe certain common rules of non-intervention in the affairs of Spain. (According to the press a *démarche* in this sense has already been made both at London and at Rome.)[4] The *communiqué* goes on to say that the French

[1] No. 39. [2] Of July 31 (W 7454/62/41), not printed. [3] Cf. No. 34, note 1.
[4] Cf. No. 45 below.

47

Government have hitherto declined to authorise the export of any consignment of arms to Spain even in the fulfilment of contracts entered into before the present troubles began but that pending the reaching of an agreement on the lines indicated between all the Governments principally concerned, the fact that munitions of war are now reaching the rebels from abroad obliges the French Government to reserve to itself full freedom as regards the application of the decision already taken. (A full translation of this *communiqué* is contained in my telegram No. 238 Saving).[5] The despatch of Italian aeroplanes to Spanish Morocco and the forced landings made by several of these machines in French territory (now the subject of official enquiry) have undoubtedly strengthened the hands of those members of the Government who have always been in favour of assisting the *Frente Popular*.[6] Moreover pressure in this sense is being exerted on the Government by means of public meetings such as that at the Salle Wagram reported in my telegram No. 234 (Saving)[7] and that in memory of Jaurès which was held at the *Vélodrome d'Hiver* on July 31st. At this second meeting in the presence of 20,000 spectators (including several Ministers) stirring appeals were made by MM. Zyromski and Duclos[8] for intervention on behalf of the Madrid Government and M. Blum, on arrival after these speeches, was greeted with shouts of 'aeroplanes for Spain'. He ignored these cries however, and devoted his speech to the celebration of the virtues of Jaurès, the proper *raison d'être* of the meeting.

The press announces that several more consignments of gold have reached Paris by aeroplane from Madrid.[9]

The new Spanish Ambassador[10] presented his credentials to the President of the Republic yesterday.

[5] Not printed: see *D.D.F., op. cit.*, No. 59.

[6] Cf. No. 39.

[7] Not printed.

[8] M. Jacques Duclos was leader of the French Communist Party.

[9] See No. 19, note 2, and Thomas, *op. cit.*, p. 295. Later, when substantial Soviet supplies began to reach Republican Spain during the battles around Madrid in October, the Spanish Government took the decision to despatch the bulk of the Spanish gold reserve, valued at about £63 million sterling, to Russia, partly for safe keeping, partly as payment for supplies received and anticipated. Thomas (p. 395) estimates that about 70 per cent of the Spanish monetary gold was shipped from Cartagena to Odessa on October 25 in 7,800 boxes. Most of the rest of the reserve was already in Paris. The gold apparently stayed in Russia (*ibid.*, pp. 418–19).

[10] Señor Álvaro de Albornez. The previous Ambassador, Señor Cardenas, had resigned his post on July 22, and negotiations between the Spanish and French Governments in the interim period had been conducted by Señor Fernando de los Rios.

No. 45

Note[1] *from M. Cambon*[2] *to Mr. Eden (Received August 3)*
[*W 7504/62/41*]

AMBASSADE DE FRANCE, LONDRES, *le 2 août 1936*

M. le Secrétaire d'État,

Ainsi que j'ai eu l'occasion de le communiquer verbalement au Foreign Office, le Gouvernement français a pris la décision d'interdire l'exportation des armes à destination de l'Espagne, et cette interdiction a été jusqu'ici strictement observée.

Il est apparu, au cours de ces derniers jours, que les insurgés espagnols reçoivent maintenant des fournitures de guerre en provenance de l'étranger; le fait n'est pas sans causer de graves préoccupations au Gouvernement de la République, car une assistance de plus en plus large aux divers éléments qui se combattent actuellement en Espagne risque de provoquer des complications propres à faire tort au maintien des bonnes relations internationales.

En conséquence, le Gouvernement français, toujours attaché au principe de non-intervention, souhaiterait que ce principe pût être accepté comme une règle commune par les Gouvernements de Londres, de Paris et de Rome. Une telle entente entre les Puissances méditerranéennes les plus intéressées aux évènements d'Espagne devrait être étendue le plus tôt possible aux autres nations.

En attendant qu'un accord puisse être réalisé à cet égard, et en raison du fait que les insurgés ont dès maintenant reçu des fournitures de guerre, le Gouvernement de la République jugerait difficile d'opposer désormais un refus de principe aux demandes d'un Gouvernement régulièrement constitué et officiellement reconnu, et devrait se réserver, dans ce domaine, une liberté d'appréciation allant au delà de la règle qu'il s'est imposée jusqu'ici.

Le Gouvernement français attacherait du prix à connaître le plus tôt possible l'accueil que votre Excellence est disposée à réserver à cette proposition dont il a également saisi le Gouvernement italien.[3]

Veuillez, &c.,

ROGER CAMBON

---

[1] This note was based on instructions from M. Delbos of August 1: see *D.D.F.*, *op. cit.*, No. 56.

[2] Counsellor and Chargé d'Affaires in the French Embassy at London.

[3] This note was received in the Foreign Office on the morning of Sunday, August 2. Sir G. Mounsey, who dealt with it, sent a long memorandum to Lord Halifax the same evening, explaining that 'to-day being Sunday and all departments closed I can get hold of no papers, and cannot therefore send you a draft reply for consideration', but he sent full comments on the note as a preliminary to further discussion on Monday, August 3. He thought that the urgency of the French action was due to the news that Italian aircraft had been sent to Spanish Morocco to assist the rebels (cf. No. 39). He pointed out that the French Government reserved their full right to depart from their present policy and supply assistance to the existing Spanish Government. He then remarked: 'I think that we must be careful about our answer. The French Government would no doubt like to draw us into some commitment to support, even if only morally, the present Spanish Government, and then deter

other foreign Governments from sending arms to the rebels in face of Anglo-French opposition. We are as anxious as they can be to hold the ring, but our main object should, I think, be to be completely impartial and free to pursue the policy of non-intervention in Spain. An Anglo-Franco-Italian Agreement would not be of the slightest use (and might be very dangerous) unless other important countries, such as Germany, and also Soviet Russia, came into line; and I do not think that we should tie our hands to any agreement which is not practically universal.' See No. 52 below.

No. 46

Mr. N. King[1] (Barcelona) to Foreign Office (Received August 6) No. 76 [W 7809/62/41]

BARCELONA, August 2, 1936

Sir,

In continuation of my despatch No. 75 of July 29th,[2] I have the honour to report that there is little change in the situation. Outwardly there is a slight increase of apparent public confidence, but the intense panic-stricken apprehension amongst the bourgeois and property-owning classes continues. Most of them remain shut in their houses and their feelings can be imagined when they hear the firing at night, of which they know the meaning only too well. The common people talk openly and ignorantly of their schemes for overthrowing the well-to-do and refer in a most callous way and even with approval to the disgusting atrocities which have been and are being perpetrated. There is little doubt that the threat of a general massacre of anyone not supposed to belong to the proletariat might easily be no idle one if the anarchist extremists are not disarmed. In some towns, e.g. Tarrasa, an important manufacturing centre, I hear, although the report is unconfirmed, that practically all the property-owning class has been exterminated. In Barcelona the Government and even the anarchist committees have forbidden the murders and robberies which are carried out every night, but they are unable to check them although there does appear to be some diminution in their number. Nobody is allowed to search private houses without an authorization from the Government, but naturally this is an order which cannot be enforced and the most alarming feature of these midnight assassinations is that nobody seems to know by whom they are carried out. There is apparently as yet no systematic house-to-house search for nuns and priests and 'malignants'. In the residential quarter where I

---

[1] Mr. King, Consul-General at Barcelona since 1926, was now the doyen of the consular corps there.

[2] Not printed: cf. No. 6. Returning from leave, Mr. King had arrived at Barcelona on board H.M.S. *Douglas* from Marseilles at 7 p.m. on July 27. He immediately had conferences with Rear Admiral Horton and with the French, German, and Italian Consuls General on the 28th. On their behalf he secured the agreement of the local authorities to the use of an area in the harbour for the sole purpose of facilitating the evacuation of foreigners. His despatch No. 75 gave a graphic account of deteriorating conditions and said that he had given the order for the remaining British subjects in the district (probably 200 or 300) to leave forthwith.

live I suspect that almost all the houses are hiding one or more religious. In some cases the Government police have arrested nuns and priests for their protection, and I was asked by a Jesuit whom I know if I could do something to assist them. But I have refrained from taking any action. The most reasonable explanation of the assassinations is that the extreme anarchists and communists have had lists compiled beforehand of people who were to be murdered in case they got the upper hand, and they are now carrying out this scheme. There is probably also a good deal of private vengeance on the part of workers against unpopular employers.

A caravan of motor-cars of British subjects, armed with permits from every possible entity, left this morning for the frontier via Puigcerda, and it is intended to organize another one for Tuesday.

Trains and cars have now begun to reach the frontier, but they have to pass through districts where different committees are in control, who recognise no authority but their own. Spaniards, therefore, even if they have passports and the necessary permits from the Government of Cataluña to leave the country, are afraid to run the risk. I heard of one case of a well-known Spaniard who got as far as Port Bou only to be turned back on the frontier. At the present moment the only danger apparent to British subjects in Barcelona is from the automobiles which rush in headlong career driven by incapable chauffeurs ignoring all the rules of the road, as one of the first outward signs of the new-found freedom is the abolition of all ordinary traffic conventions. I myself had a narrow escape when my car was squeezed between two converging trams, and Mr. Vaughan was eyewitness of an accident to a car full of bombs which overturned when taking a corner too rapidly with the result that all the bombs exploded and all six of the occupants were killed.

The anarchists and communistic extremists are still *de facto* masters of Barcelona and the surrounding country. From the accounts I hear I imagine that every church in the district and many of the large houses have been sacked and fired. The destruction of private property, art treasures and historic monuments is appalling. New parties are constantly being formed and as every vehicle in the streets has to bear some letters to afford protection they are all marked with U.G.T.,[3] C.N.T.,[4] F.A.I.,[5] etc., the latest edition to this collection being P.O.U.M.[6] which has something to do with the Party of Unification of Marxist ideals. In this confused imbroglio the Government of Sr. Companys is endeavouring to maintain a semblance of authority by working with the committees of the extremists. Commissioners of public food and public amusements (*sic*) etc., have been nominated, presumably in imitation of the Russian system. Sr. Companys told me personally that he hoped to find the solution of his difficulties by appointing a new Government and he has now delegated his authority as President of the Government to

[3] Unión General de Trabajadores (Socialist Trade Union).
[4] Confederación Nacional del Trabajo (Anarcho-Syndicalist Trades Union).
[5] Federación Anarquista Ibérica (Anarchist Secret Society).
[6] Partido Obrero de Unificación Marxista (Trotskyists).

51

Sr. Casanovas, a popular Catalan figure, and he has included in the Cabinet several leaders of the extreme Left in the hope of reaching a working compromise and prevent the friction between the armed anarchists and the Government from coming to an open struggle. The Government of course rely chiefly on the disciplined Civil Guards of whom there are about 1,200 in Barcelona and 800 in the rest of Cataluña, but these men, even with the Government's shock-police and the anti-fascist militia, do not dare to try to disarm the anarchists and the armed proletariat in the capital and the provinces. A premature attempt might be fatal. It has always been the nightmare of respectable Catalans that the 'underworld' of the proletariat should break loose and obtain control, and this they are now within an ace of doing. Sr. Companys, therefore, must play for time by endeavouring to induce their leaders to work with him and making whatever concessions are necessary. In this connexion I am glad to be able to report that a very satisfactory reply from the President to my letter of 30th July protesting against the confiscation of British property, has been received. A copy of my letter of protest is attached,[7] and as will be seen from the enclosed translation of his reply,[7] Sr. Companys has given me the assurance that property has only been intervened for its protection and that no British property has been confiscated. He also promises every possible protection for the rights of British subjects. I have shown a copy of this document to Mr. Lawton of the Light and Power company and one or two other interested British subjects, to whom it has given great satisfaction as it is a definite declaration by the Government which may be of great utility later on when the question of compensation may arise. In my conversation with Sr. España[8] on the 31st. ultimo, he referred verbally to the question of intervention of the property of British subjects and stated that it was not intended to do anything without due compensation.

I imagine that time is on the side of the Government. Hand grenades and bombs are being rapidly manufactured and as it is very difficult to believe that the armed proletariat will lay down their arms at the Government's bidding without a struggle, the best that can be hoped is that the Government will win. There are articles in the newspaper today calling on the workers not to lay down their arms as this would involve the loss of all they had gained. The Government obviously regards the situation today as delicate, as the Civil Guards are confined to barracks, and the guard of four at my house has not been relieved.

Mr. Lawton informs me that the consumption of electricity indicates that factories, electric trams, etc. are working about 55–60 per cent of normal, which shows that very many of the factories are being run. Possibly many of the workers think that they have now reached Utopia but I anticipate critical times when the supply of raw materials gives out. There is also a threat of food shortage and prices of food are certainly rising.

The town of Palma[9] is now being bombed daily. Yesterday, three seaplanes

---

[7] Not printed.   [8] Councillor of Public Order.   [9] Capital of Majorca.

carrying 20 bombs each attacked central points of the city and the inhabitants are said to have fled to the mountains. I have urged British subjects to leave forthwith and Admiral Horton sent a destroyer yesterday at 5.00 a.m. to evacuate them.

A base has been established in a Yacht Club at the end of the pier where the warships are lying, kindly put at my disposal for the British Colony by the Club—no doubt to protect it—thanks to the excellent work done by Mr. George Noble and Sr. Danes. The Anarchist Association who are in control in that part have been extremely friendly and helpful; beds and provisions have been installed and members of the Colony can stay there thus keeping in touch with Barcelona and be able to evacuate at short notice if necessary. It would be practically impossible for any of the other British subjects scattered throughout the town to reach the pier if street fighting became general. A proposal has also been mooted to transfer the Consulate, or a branch of it, to this Yacht Club, but I do not think this feasible. The Admiral has pointed out, and I have emphasized this, in his name, to British subjects, that he cannot keep his ships here indefinitely until the members of the Colony may decide whether they wish to leave or not. I am therefore urging British subjects very strongly to go on board now while they have the chance, and the Admiral is sending destroyers to various ports on the coast where British subjects are still known to be.

Some criticism may be made of the fact that on my arrival at Barcelona I ordered the British subjects to leave this town and district. This step was taken after I had attended the meeting of Admirals and Consuls referred to in my despatch No. 75 of July 29th, after consultation with the most important British subjects in Barcelona, and in particular after consultation with Admiral Horton. The Consulate was crowded with refugees and the improvised staff installed by Mr. Vaughan were, in spite of their excellent work, unable to compete with the congestion. It was obvious, also, that in the case of a renewal of violent street fighting, there might be a stampede and it would be dangerous, if not impossible, to reach the ships. The order was therefore given to assist hesitating people to make up their minds to go while the opportunity presented itself. I explained personally that it was an order which I had no authority or power to carry out, and it meant simply that persons who chose to stay on might have to do so at their own risk. Spanish wives of British subjects and others technically British, but really foreign whose only interests are in Barcelona, were not urged to leave but rather the contrary, so as to avoid swelling the number of penniless refugees at Marseilles.[10]

Mr. Lawton of the Light and Power company, Mr. Gagnon of the Canadian Bank and various other gentlemen have decided to remain at their posts so long as they can afford any protection or assistance to the interests they represent, and I think their decision is very wise as the wholesale exodus of

[10] Minutes on this despatch show general agreement in the Foreign Office with Mr. Seymour's comment that 'Mr. King was absolutely right in pressing British subjects to leave'.

British subjects would have a bad effect, in more than one way. Admiral Horton has very kindly offered me the hospitality of H.M.S. *London* and I have decided to accept his invitation for a night or two and then return to my house and stay in Barcelona. I consider that both Mr. Vaughan and Mr. Amoore, who have had most trying experiences, should take a rest, but prefer to stay, as does Mr. John Witty. Mr. Everson who arrived here on the 29th., has been of very great assistance in the office, but as the official staff has been reduced by the departure of Mr. Martinez, Miss Toothill and Miss Pearson—temporary stenographer—I have engaged temporarily at a salary of Ptas. 350.—per month, Mr. P. Amoore, brother of the present member of my staff.[11]

I understand that a proposal has been made for the organization of some fund for distressed refugees from Spain who reached Marseilles or England, and if anything can be done to assist this proposal and carry it to some practical issue, it would assist a great many unfortunate people who must now be penniless and without any prospects for the immediate future.

I have, &c.,

NORMAN KING

[11] These staffing arrangements were approved by the Foreign Office.

No. 47

Sir E. Phipps (Berlin) to Foreign Office (Received August 3, 9.30 a.m.)
No. 244 Telegraphic [C 5678/4/18]

BERLIN, *August 3, 1936, 12.19 a.m.*

My telegram No. 243[1] and my despatch No. 807.[2]

The *communiqué* issued by German Government contains passage to the effect that Germany has accepted a meeting of the Five Powers for discussion of 'a Western Pact'. This phrase has been interpreted in some quarters here in a restrictive sense, i.e., as excluding the sequels. It may indeed reflect the preference or even the ultimate intention of the German Government though it is more likely that they wish at this stage to create the restrictive impression amongst their own people without actually using any definitely exclusive language. In any case I think it both right and fair to say at once that Baron von Neurath in his conversation with me and Sir R. Vansittart neither laid down nor implied any restriction [? restrictive] condition—beyond stipulation as to the date, which I have already reported —but couched his acceptance in very general terms.

[1] No. 41.
[2] This despatch of August 1 (received August 4) gave the text of a short message from the *Deutsches Nachrichten-Büro* of July 31 summarizing Baron von Neurath's communication to the British, French, and Belgian representatives on July 31 of Germany's acceptance of the invitation 'to a Five-Power Conference on the subject of a Western Pact'.

No. 48

Sir E. Phipps (Berlin) to Foreign Office (Received August 3, 2.50 p.m.)
No. 245 Telegraphic [C 5679/4/18]

BERLIN, *August 3, 1936, 11.59 a.m.*

My telegram No. 244.[1]
French Ambassador[2] tells me that Minister for Foreign Affairs did not make any restriction [? restrictive] conditions to him either. My Belgian colleague[3] on the other hand was told by Baron von Neurath that point 5 of London Conclusions of July 23rd[4] (viz. the subsequent extension of scope of discussions) would present grave difficulties.

[1] No. 47. [2] M. François-Poncet. [3] Vicomte Davignon.
[4] See No. 14, note 3.

No. 49

Sir E. Phipps (Berlin) to Foreign Office (Received August 3, 10 p.m.)
No. 247 Telegraphic [C 5680/4/18]

Immediate BERLIN, *August 3, 1936, 8.25 p.m.*

Herr Dieckhoff told me yesterday as his personal opinion that the coming conversations should open informally between Great Britain and Germany only and could of course be extended later to other Powers. As Sir R. Vansittart and I will be seeing Minister for Foreign Affairs at parties at his house during the next few days[1] it is possible he may make the same suggestion in a more official form. Should he do so we propose to reply that the invitation was issued by the three Powers and that it would be safer with a view to success of Conference to include the other Powers from the start. Unless all parties concerned keep each other informed of any preliminary conversations or correspondence suspicions may well be engendered which would prove the reverse of helpful.

[1] Cf. No. 41, note 2.

No. 50

Sir E. Phipps (Berlin) to Foreign Office (Received August 4, 9.15 p.m.)
No. 248 Telegraphic [W 7668/62/41]

BERLIN, *August 4, 1936, 7.53 p.m.*

The French Ambassador tells me that under instructions from his Government he enquired today of German Minister for Foreign Affairs whether German Government would on principle be ready to discuss with other

Governments the best means of ensuring general neutrality towards Spanish Civil War.

Baron von Neurath replied in the affirmative provided that Russia maintained neutrality also.

No. 51

Minute by Sir G. Mounsey

[W 7748/62/41]

FOREIGN OFFICE, *August 4, 1936*

M. Cambon called to see me this morning to explain that having received urgent instructions from Paris during the night[1] to see a Cabinet Minister and deliver personally to him the message contained in the annexed note,[2] he had felt bound to ring up Lord Halifax's private secretary and try and get the message conveyed to Lord Halifax through him.[3] M. Cambon said he hoped I would not misunderstand his action, and he came in fact to give me the same message for Foreign Office information.

He also desired to impress upon me the great embarrassment in which M. Blum and M. Delbos were being placed by German and Italian activities in Spain, and to urge most earnestly that our reply to the French arms note might be delivered to-day without fail, that it would support the French proposal in principle and especially that it would express approval of the French Government's policy of neutrality. Only, M. Cambon said, by the exhibition of Anglo-French solidarity on the latter point, could M. Blum resist the elements in France who are determined to support the Spanish Government. It might even now be too late to do so.

The message was later in the morning read to Lord Halifax over the telephone, and at the same time the terms of our reply were arranged with him, having been shown by him to the Secretary of State and by me to Sir W. Malkin[4] before despatch to the French Embassy in the afternoon.[5]

Later in the evening M. Cambon called, having telephoned the reply to Paris, and went through its terms with me. He said he realised that we had done what we could to help his Government, but they were distinctly de-

---

[1] Cf. *D.D.F.*, *op. cit.*, No. 72.　　　　　　　　　　[2] See Annex to this document.

[3] A note of August 4, apparently by Mr. Hendriks, Lord Halifax's private secretary at Treasury Chambers, to Sir G. Mounsey, said that he had replied to M. Cambon's request by saying that Lord Halifax, who was in Yorkshire, had made no plans to return to London that week, but was always willing to come back if events made it necessary or desirable. Shortly after, M. Cambon telephoned the text of the letter (see Annex) which he wished to have telephoned to Lord Halifax as early as possible. Mr. Hendriks added that M. Cambon had asked him to stress in any conversation with Lord Halifax the importance of a reply to the French note that day (cf. No. 45), and of 'strong approval' in the reply of 'the present attitude of the French Government'. This latter was 'particularly important in order to assist the Government to resist pressure from certain quarters in France'.

[4] Legal Adviser to the Foreign Office.　　　　　　　　　　[5] See No. 52 below.

pressed and doubted if our reply would assist them to resist the increasing pressure for them to depart from a neutral attitude.[6]

ANNEX TO NO. 51

Letter from M. Cambon to Lord Halifax

AMBASSADE DE FRANCE À LONDRES, *4 août 1936*

Cher Lord Halifax,

Je sais que la communication que nous avons remise avant-hier matin au Foreign Office[7] au sujet des affaires d'Espagne a été l'objet d'un examen sympathique et immédiat de la part du Gouvernement britannique. Je crois même que ce dernier se propose d'y répondre sans délai.

Permettez-moi néanmoins d'attirer votre attention sur des faits nouveaux qui se sont produits dans le Maroc espagnol et qui présentent une gravité particulière. Deux navires de guerre et, semble-t-il, cinq avions allemands, sont arrivés à Ceuta. Les Etats-Majors allemands auraient déja été l'objet des égards particuliers des militaires espagnols (réception de l'Amiral par le Général Franco, etc. . .)

Cette situation est pour mon Gouvernement une cause de très graves préoccupations. Il lui devient en effet de plus en plus difficile de maintenir l'attitude d'absolue correction et de neutralité qu'il a réussi à faire accepter jusqu'ici par l'opinion publique française. Après l'affaire des avions italiens, la manifestation allemande va déterminer aujourd'hui en France des réactions très vives et qui peuvent obliger M. Blum et M. Delbos à modifier complètement leur politique.

Dans ces conditions, ils m'ont chargé de vous demander de nous adresser, si possible dès aujourd'hui, une première réponse de principe qui constaterait l'accord des Gouvernements français et britannique et qui exprimerait le vœu de voir la France maintenir l'attitude si prudente qui est actuellement la sienne. Si le Gouvernement britannique croyait devoir formuler au sujet de la situation et des initiatives qu'elle comporte une suggestion quelconque, je puis vous assurer que cette suggestion serait immédiatement acceptée par le Gouvernement français.

Je m'excuse de vous adresser ainsi, par téléphone, une communication de cette nature, et vous prie, cher Lord Halifax, de bien vouloir agréer l'expression de mon respectueux dévouement.

ROGER CAMBON

[6] Cf. *D.D.F.*, *op. cit.*, No. 73.   [7] No. 45.

No. 52

Letter[1] from Mr. Eden to M. Cambon
[W 7504/62/41]

FOREIGN OFFICE, *August 4, 1936*

Sir,

I have the honour to acknowledge the receipt of your note of the 2nd August[2] regarding the export of arms and munitions of war to Spain, and to request that you will be so good as to inform the French Government that His Majesty's Government in the United Kingdom share their anxiety to avoid any risk of the complications to international relations which might arise were assistance to be afforded from outside Spain to any of the parties engaged in the present conflict.

2. As has recently been stated in Parliament,[3] the attitude of His Majesty's Government in this connexion has hitherto been to act only in strict accordance with the existing law, but His Majesty's Government would in present circumstances welcome an early agreement between all Powers who may be in a position to supply arms and munitions to refrain from doing so and to prevent the supply of arms and munitions from their territories on the principle of non-interference in Spanish affairs.

3. They are of the opinion, however, that such agreement would not have the requisite value unless simultaneously accepted at the initial stage by such Governments as those of France, Germany, Italy, Portugal and His Majesty's Government, who are primarily affected by the course of events in Spain owing to their paramount material interests in, or close geographical connexion with, that country. It would be hoped that the agreement would eventually be subscribed to by all other Powers concerned.

4. His Majesty's Government will accordingly be glad to learn the result of the enquiries which the French Government may make of other Powers as to their willingness to concur in the course which the French Government propose to adopt.

5. If pending such general agreement, the French Government as well as

---

[1] See No. 45, note 3. Sir G. Mounsey had promised to telephone Lord Halifax between 12 noon and 1 o'clock on Monday morning, August 3, and to read to him the proposed reply. A further minute of August 3 addressed to Lord Halifax after this conversation said that the draft had been revised according to his suggestions, and that it had then occurred to Sir G. Mounsey that 'to meet the difficulty about singling Germany out as a fourth party to any agreement, we could also add Portugal, who is Spain's nearest neighbour and the Power most vitally concerned in the course of events in that country'. This further revision of the draft was approved by Lord Halifax on the morning of August 4, and delivered to the French Embassy in the afternoon. See also para. 3 of No. 51.

[2] No. 45.

[3] In answer to a question in the House of Commons on July 27 regarding the policy of the British Government towards the supply of arms and munitions to Spain, Mr. Eden replied that no applications for licences to export arms to Spain had been received, but that the 'ordinary regulations governing the licensing of exports of arms destined to foreign countries are applicable to shipments of arms to Spain' (315 *H.C. Deb. 5 s.*, cols. 1071–2). Cf. also No. 30, note 5.

the Italian Government, who are understood to have been already approached by the French Government, declare that they are ready as soon as agreement between the Powers concerned has been reached to apply the principle that the supply of arms and munitions to Spain from abroad should cease, His Majesty's Government will be for their part prepared to make a similar declaration.

I have, &c.,
ANTHONY EDEN

No. 53

Sir E. Phipps (Berlin) to Foreign Office (Received August 5, 1.50 p.m.)
No. 249 Telegraphic [W 7737/62/41]

BERLIN, *August 5, 1936, 1.2 p.m.*

My telegram No. 248.¹
In conversation yesterday at lunch with Sir R. Vansittart Baron von Neurath referred to French suggestion that discussions should take place in regard to maintenance of neutrality towards the struggle in progress in Spain. Baron von Neurath said, that while international [support] might be discussed it interested him much more [? from] the side of measures adopted in regard to export of arms. He evidently realised that if Italy (and presumably therefore Germany) began any export of arms to the Spanish right the gainer would eventually be the Spanish left because export of arms from a left . . .² through France would be easier and more systematic across land frontier of the Pyr[e]nees than would be possible from any other country to Morocco.

¹ No. 50.   ² The text was here uncertain.

No. 54

Foreign Office to Sir E. Drummond¹ (Rome)
No. 308² Telegraphic [W 7808/62/41]

Immediate   FOREIGN OFFICE, *August 5, 1936, 4.30 p.m.*

French Government have instructed their representatives in Rome, Lisbon and Berlin to approach the Italian, Portuguese and German Governments with a view to cooperation in regulating arms supply to Spain.

His Majesty's Government in the United Kingdom have similarly been approached³ and have replied that they would welcome an early agreement between all Powers who may be in a position to supply arms and munitions to refrain from doing so, and to prevent the supply of arms and munitions from their territories, on the principle of non-interference in Spanish affairs.⁴

¹ H.M. Ambassador at Rome.   ² No. 88 to Lisbon.   ³ See No. 45.
⁴ See No. 52.

His Majesty's Government are, however, of opinion that such agreement should at the initial stage be simultaneously accepted by such governments as those of France, Germany, Italy, Portugal and His Majesty's Government who have paramount material interest or are in close geographical connexion with Spain. It would be hoped that agreement would eventually be subscribed to by all other Powers concerned.

Please bring sense of above reply urgently to the notice of the Italian/Portuguese Government and support the *démarche* of the French Government in Rome/Lisbon in whatever way you think most cogent.

No. 55

Sir E. Phipps (Berlin) to Foreign Office (Received August 5, 10.25 p.m.)
No. 250 Telegraphic [C 5749/3727/18]

BERLIN, *August 5, 1936, 8.40 p.m.*

Mr. Newton's telegram No. 239, July 30th.[1]

Intrigues from various quarters are being carried on to prevent Herr von Ribbentrop's appointment to London. Extreme Nazis, led by Doctor Goebbels,[2] insist that all big appointments as they fall vacant should be reserved for the party. Personal enemies of Herr von Ribbentrop on the other hand point out that his policy of Anglo-German friendship has produced no fruits and has cost Germany the Naval Agreement.[3] To send him to London now would be to continue this policy the ultimate failure of which they think inevitable and would recoil on the Chancellor. Others again point out to Herr Hitler that Herr von Ribbentrop is not up to the job.

Ministry of Foreign Affairs who naturally ardently desire to abolish Herr von Ribbentrop's rival office here[4] presumably asked for *agrément* too hastily and without obtaining Chancellor's written consent.

I have reason to believe that Herr von Ribbentrop is at time[s] even nervous about his personal safety and would be relieved to get to London.

[1] This telegram has not been preserved in the Foreign Office archives. It referred to Foreign Office telegram No. 162 of July 29, and said that Mr. Newton had informed Baron von Neurath that Herr von Ribbentrop's appointment as German Ambassador in London (cf. No. 15, note 5) would be agreeable to H.M. the King.

[2] Reich Minister for Popular Enlightenment and Propaganda.

[3] Cf. Volume XIII, No. 348.

[4] i.e. *Dienststelle Ribbentrop*, a foreign affairs advice service provided for Herr Hitler by Herr von Ribbentrop.

No. 56

Record¹ by Lord Chatfield of a conversation² with Vice-Admiral Darlan and Rear-Admiral Decoux

[*W 7781/62/41*]

ADMIRALTY, *August 5, 1936*

I interviewed this morning the following Officers of the French Ministry of Marine

Vice-Admiral Darlan
Chef de Cabinet Militaire
Rear-Admiral Decoux
Naval Staff.

They were accompanied by the French Naval Attaché³ and came specially over from the Minister of Marine to give me information as to their anxieties about the Spanish situation.

Admiral Darlan said they viewed the situation in Spain with great anxiety because of the possible action by other Powers. They did not wish either a Fascist or Communist Government in Spain, yet one or the other seemed inevitable. This meant a prolonged civil war which would exhaust Spain and whichever side won no strong Government would exist. Consequently, Spain would be in a weak position and unable to resist any predatory action by Italy or Germany. What they feared was that Italy would take advantage of the situation to seize the Balearic Islands, and Germany the Canary Islands. This would be highly dangerous both for France, in her communications with Algeria and French Morocco, and for England as regards the Mediterranean and Cape routes. What did we feel about it? The French Naval Staff were very anxious.

I said—Was what he was telling me conjecture, or was it based on information? He said 'as regards Italy and the Balearic Islands we have information, but we have no definite information as to Germany and the Canary Islands'. I asked him whether, if they had these anxieties, they had any intention of sending ships to watch the situation in both groups of Islands. He said if you will do so, we will, but we do not wish to send French ships there alone. We want to follow you in what you do; if you intend to leave ships on the coast of Spain we will do so, if you intend to withdraw them, we shall also withdraw ours.

I then informed him that the Admiralty had no policy in these matters but were merely acting under the instructions of the Foreign Office, whose policy had been explained very clearly in the Press this morning.⁴ Our ships were only round the coast of Spain for the safety of our Nationals, but

¹ This record was addressed to Sir S. Hoare, First Lord of the Admiralty, and was received in the Foreign Office on August 6. Sir S. Hoare's comments on it are printed as an Annex to this document.

² A very full French record of this meeting is printed in *D.D.F., op. cit.*, No. 87.

³ Captain du Tour.

⁴ See *The Times*, August 5, 1936, pp. 12 and 13.

we have already evacuated the great majority of these and we are therefore considering reducing our forces to a minimum for the safety of those that were left.[5] For my part, I had no information similar to that which he had conveyed to me (this is, of course, not strictly correct as we have certain information) but that if the French Ministry of Marine really considered the situation so seriously, especially as regards the Balearic Islands, I thought the proper steps would be for the Quai d'Orsay to so inform our Ambassador in Paris. I was, however, exceedingly obliged to him for having been so good as to come over to explain the situation as it was viewed by the French Ministry of Marine. I would take note of it and would communicate it to the First Lord of the Admiralty, who would probably acquaint the Foreign Office.[6]

E.C.

Admiral Darlan also suggested he should interview Sir M. Hankey— but I said I thought this was unnecessary and he was I knew on his holidays.

I have taken so far no action to inform the F.O. as I have left it to your decision.

[5] Cf. No. 57 below.
[6] A copy of Lord Chatfield's record and Sir S. Hoare's comments was sent to Sir G. Clerk in Paris with a covering letter from Sir G. Mounsey.

ANNEX TO No. 56

Note by Sir S. Hoare

ADMIRALTY, *August 5, 1936*

I have discussed the position with the First Sea Lord. He and I agree that the French information is not sufficiently definite for us to base any action upon it. Indeed, the French Ministry of Marine seems to be in something like a state of panic. What other reason can be assigned for this curious visit of two Admirals in plain clothes, at a moment's notice and apparently without the knowledge of the Quai d'Orsay?

For the present it seems clear that we should continue our existing policy of neutrality, and that when opportunity arises we should withdraw all the ships that are not actually required from the Spanish coast. I imagine that if the Italians or the Germans seem really likely to make a 'coup' we could send ships at short notice to the threatened point. I should, however, be astonished if either Government contemplates action of this kind at a moment when both have agreed to take part in the new Locarno conversations, and when Italy seems anxious to resume friendly relations with France and ourselves.

I should like to be kept regularly informed of any new developments.

The Acting Secretary of State for Foreign Affairs may like to see these minutes.

When I speak of 'neutrality' I mean strict neutrality, that is to say, a situation in which the Russians neither officially or unofficially give help to the Communists. On no account must we do anything to bolster up Communism in Spain, particularly when it is remembered that Communism in Portugal, to which it would probably spread and particularly in Lisbon, would be a grave danger to the British Empire.

S.H.

No. 57

Foreign Office memorandum on British warships in Spanish waters
[*W 7755/62/41*]

FOREIGN OFFICE, August 5, 1936

The Foreign Office offer the following comments on Admiralty memorandum[1] of the 4th August on the general position regarding British warships in Spanish waters. (The paragraphs are referred to according to the Admiralty numbers).

2.[2] This applies to all British subjects in the principal ports and in Madrid, but not at other places on the coast or in the interior.

3.[3] The number of British subjects still remaining in the principal ports and in Madrid appears to be nearly 1,000 out of a total of just over 3,000.

4.[4] At salaried Consulates clerks in charge in the absence on leave of the Consul should be treated in the same way as the Consul (e.g. at Seville and Malaga). At some unsalaried Vice-Consulates, e.g. Valencia and Palma, big British interests would necessitate the Vice-Consuls remaining as long as Consuls in the salaried Consulates.

5.[5] The Foreign Office have at present no comments to make on paragraph 5.

6.[6] It is considered that an urgent appeal to rescue British subjects during emergency could not be disregarded.

7.[7] The Foreign Office suggest, therefore, the following general line of action.

(i) It is agreed that the number of His Majesty's Ships serving in Spanish waters should now be reduced somewhat.

[1] Not printed. The Foreign Office comments are a sufficient indication of the questions asked by the Admiralty. The Admiralty noted that there were now 28 British men-of-war in Spanish waters, excluding the *Maine* hospital ship, and the *Amphion* in Canaries.

[2] The Admiralty had stated that all British subjects had been advised to leave and all who were prepared to do so had been evacuated.

[3] The Admiralty had remarked that a number of British subjects were prepared to take the risk of remaining in Spain.

[4] The Admiralty considered that as unpaid vice-consuls were being advised that their presence in Spain was no longer necessary, it would be necessary in an emergency to evacuate consular officers from only six Spanish ports.

[5] The Admiralty had remarked that the presence of so many of H.M. ships in Spanish waters might be politically undesirable.

[6] While desiring not to retain a large number of ships, the Admiralty had recognized that an urgent appeal for rescue could not be disregarded.

[7] Here the Admiralty had asked the Foreign Office to reconsider the general position, under the four headings indicated.

(ii) The remaining ships should be sufficient to lie at or near ports where there are either salaried consuls or unsalaried vice-consuls who on account of big British interests must remain at their posts as long as salaried consuls. There should also be in the vicinity of Spain sufficient ships to answer an urgent appeal to rescue British subjects from other ports.

(iii) & (iv). The Navy's responsibility having been defined as in (ii) above, the Foreign Office should immediately ascertain which unsalaried vice-consuls, on account of British interests, should remain at their posts as long as salaried consuls, and inform those who it is decided need not remain that they need not stay at their posts, and that if they do not take the opportunity of leaving by a certain date they will remain at their own risk.[8] The Foreign Office and the Admiralty should issue to all British subjects at Madrid and in the principle [sic] ports one more warning more definite than that issued by the Admiralty on the 30th July, to the effect that His Majesty's Government can take no further responsibility for the evacuation of British subjects in Spain after a certain date. Finally, endeavour might be made to reach other British subjects in the interior or at other ports by broadcasting a similar message.

It is assumed that officers commanding His Majesty's Ships in the case of evacuation in an emergency will do everything possible to refrain from drawing fire or firing in return, and will confine themselves to the work of rescue, avoiding, of course, any acts that might be provocative of reprisals.

[8] On August 6 telegraphic instructions were sent through the Admiralty to the British consular officers in charge at Barcelona, Bilbao, Malaga, Seville, Vigo, and Tetuan to report whether any vice consulates in their districts should be retained for the present.

No. 58

Sir E. Phipps (Berlin) to Foreign Office (Received August 6, 1.30 p.m.)
No. 251 Telegraphic [C 5750/4/18]

BERLIN, *August 6, 1936, 12.24 p.m.*

Sir R. Vansittart had an interview with Herr Hitler on Wednesday morning.[1] The interview was long and exceedingly friendly but contained nothing of immediate moment. Herr Hitler showed no disposition to discuss any points connected with the five Power conference; indeed when the topic inevitably occurred he preferred not to dwell on it. He seemed particularly preoccupied with events in Spain which have of course markedly strengthened his views on communism. He evidently considered the Left more likely to win temporarily than their opponents and took a gloomy view of the consequences. A fuller account will follow by despatch.[2]

[1] August 5.
[2] Sir R. Vansittart's account (dated September 10) of his visit to Berlin, including his interview with Herr Hitler, is printed as Appendix I to this Volume. See also No. 85 below.

No. 59

Sir E. Phipps (Berlin) to Foreign Office (Received August 6, 1.30 p.m.)
No. 252 Telegraphic [C 5751/3727/18]

BERLIN, *August 6, 1936, 12.25 p.m.*

My telegram No. 250.[1]

It is perhaps of interest to add, two days ago Sir R. Vansittart advised Herr von Ribbentrop to speak to Herr Hitler with a view to publication of his appointment since otherwise the news would be bound to leak out. Just before Sir R. Vansittart's interview with Herr Hitler he asked von Ribbentrop whether he had acted on this advice. Von Ribbentrop replied in the negative. Sir R. Vansittart asked von Ribbentrop whether he would like him to mention it to Herr Hitler in the course of conversation. After a moment's hesitation von Ribbentrop replied in the negative again. Sir R. Vansittart thought von Ribbentrop preoccupied and somewhat depressed.[2]

[1] No. 55.
[2] In a minute of August 8 Mr. C. W. Baxter, a First Secretary in the Central Department, remarked: 'I hope the German Govt. will soon make up their minds. Otherwise the intention to appoint Herr R. will almost certainly leak out, and *we* shall probably be blamed for not keeping the secret!'

No. 60

Foreign Office to Sir E. Phipps (Berlin)
No. 164 Telegraphic [C 5780/4/18]

FOREIGN OFFICE, *August 6, 1936, 4.15 p.m.*

Following for Sir R. Vansittart from Mr. Sargent.

We hear from a private source that the Quai d'Orsay are suspicious of your conversations with German notabilities. I have no doubt that you are keeping French and Belgian Ambassadors pretty fully informed, but you may like to do more in view of this report.

No. 61

Foreign Office to Sir E. Phipps (Berlin)
No. 165 Telegraphic [C 5680/4/18]

FOREIGN OFFICE, *August 6, 1936, 4.40 p.m.*

Your telegram No. 247.[1]

I quite agree to answer you propose to give to Dieckhoff's proposal that conversations should open between Great Britain and Germany alone. But I should like you to bear in mind the following consideration.

[1] No. 49.

At present our idea is that the exchanges of view which are to take place through the diplomatic channel must involve some centralisation, and this would probably result in our becoming a sort of clearing house for the views thus exchanged. With this object we shall try and initiate discussions by ourselves putting forward suggestions as to programme and as to the general direction which subsequent negotiations should follow. If we are successful in thus establishing London as a clearing house it is probable that we shall at certain moments and in respect of certain subjects find ourselves involved in bilateral discussions with one or other of the governments concerned. I do not think that we ought in such circumstances to object to such bilateral discussions, provided always that it is clearly understood that the other governments concerned are informed as soon and as fully as possible of their results.

No. 62

Mr. Ingram (Rome) to Foreign Office (Received August 7, 9.30 a.m.)
No. 535 Telegraphic [W 7916/62/41]

ROME, *August 6, 1936, 10 p.m.*

The following *communiqué* appears this afternoon.[1]

'The following are points of verbal reply given by the Minister for Foreign Affairs to French Ambassador to verbal proposal put forward by him concerning a preliminary agreement for non-intervention between Italy France and Great Britain with regard to present events in Spain.

(1) Italy adheres in principle to thesis of non-intervention in civil war with which Spain is afflicted.

(2) Italy asks whether moral solidarity with one of the parties to the conflict—a solidarity which finds expression and is expressed in public manifestations press campaigns financial subscriptions enlistments of volunteers etc., does not already constitute a conspicuous and dangerous form of intervention.

(3) Italy desires to know whether the undertaking of non-intervention will have a universal character or not and whether it will bind only governments or will apply also to private individuals.

(4) Italy wishes to know whether the government making the proposal has also in view measures of control as regards observance or otherwise of undertaking of non-intervention'.[2]

Repeated to Paris No. 37.

[1] An earlier *communiqué*, on the evening of August 4, stated that Count Ciano had received the French Ambassador who had informed him verbally of proposals for a preliminary Anglo-French-Italian understanding on maintenance of neutrality: cf. No. 45.

[2] According to Mr. Ingram's telegram No. 536 of August 6, despatched at 10 p.m., Count Ciano handed M. de Chambrun the text of this *communiqué* that morning at 10 a.m. The French Ambassador had at once taken exception to para. 2 as 'opening the way to profitless polemics'. Mr. Ingram reported that the French Ambassador was 'disillusioned and depressed'. Cf. *D.D.F., op. cit.,* No. 90.

Sir E. Phipps (Berlin) to Foreign Office (Received August 7, 9.30 a.m.)
No. 254 Telegraphic [C 5781/4/18]

BERLIN, *August 6, 1936, 10.42 p.m.*

Your telegram No. 164.[1]

Following for Mr. Sargent from Sir R. Vansittart.

I will certainly speak to French and Belgian representatives as you suggest, but I have had no conversations of any particular importance or interest to them and I think they are aware of this as I have already seen them frequently.

Had there been any talks of real moment I should of course have reported to the Foreign Office, but I have not sought these, and have indeed avoided any appearance of being here on business. I shall report my general impressions at length and at leisure;[2] but it may be useful for your guidance to know that I have endeavoured, when occasion offered, tactfully to dwell on need for restoration of confidence in Europe and not only locally. This has been well received. For the rest the condition of affairs in Spain and its possible consequences seems for the time being more in the front of the mind of those in authority here than October meeting. Their usual views on communism have been thereby, it appears, much strengthened and there is unceasing talk on this theme in all quarters, on lines of Herr von Ribbentrop's talks in London, but with increased volume and conviction.

[1] No. 60.   [2] See No. 58, note 2.

No. 64

Record by Sir G. Mounsey of a conversation with M. Cambon
[W 7981/62/41]

FOREIGN OFFICE, *August 6, 1936*

The French Chargé d'Affaires called this morning and, on instructions from his Government, submitted for our consideration the attached draft of the declaration which they suggest should be made by the Powers who will agree to refrain from allowing the supply of arms and munitions to Spain.[1]

The French Government desire to explain that in their view the action to be taken should be as swift and clear as possible; they are of course ready to consider any amendments or additions, such as on the question of financial help, but it is most desirable in their opinion that a simple declaration covering arms and munitions should be made as soon as possible.

I told M. Cambon that I feel sure His Majesty's Government would share these views and promised him that the draft declaration would be carefully and quickly examined.

[1] See *D.D.F.*, *op. cit.*, No. 83 and *Annexe*.

He asked whether we saw any objection to the French Government submitting this draft to the other Powers whom they were consulting, as being, of course, their own suggestion. This would save time and be of assistance to the French Government in their internal difficulties. I said I could see no objection to these procedures as it was natural that the French Government should want all other comments as well as ours on their basic proposal.

M. Cambon said his Government were very grateful for the action which we had taken at Lisbon and Rome in support of their proposal.[2] They had as yet received no replies from either post, and believed that there might be difficulty over the former, the question of financial support being a very live issue across the Portuguese–Spanish frontier. From Berlin the answer was in principle satisfactory,[3] but M. Cambon could give me no news from Moscow, nor say whether his Government wished us to support them there. His personal impression seems to be that they do not want our support. The French Government have further approached the Dutch and Belgian Governments, the latter of whom have at once agreed to support them.

The text of the French draft proposal has been examined by the Department and Sir W. Malkin, who agree that we can accept it as a general basis, except unfortunately on two points, both of some importance, which primarily concern the Board of Trade. They are

    1 *le transit à destination de l'Espagne.* Board of Trade and Customs will have to make some amendment to define transit as involving unloading and reloading of the goods in transit.

    2 *contrats en cours d'execution.* This requires legislation, which is apparently an insuperable objection.

I am having the note translated and sent over to the Board of Trade for their immediate comments and suggestions, and we must await these before we can send the French Embassy a reply.

G. M.

      [2] No. 54.   [3] Cf. No. 70 below.

No. 65

Mr. Dodd[1] (Lisbon) to Foreign Office (Received August 7, 2.40 p.m.)
No. 123 Telegraphic [W 7918/62/41]

Immediate   LISBON, *August 7, 1936, 12.54 p.m.*
Your telegram No. 88.[2]

French Minister[3] made his *démarche* on August 5th and I supported it in concert with him immediately afterwards.

Yesterday evening Portuguese Minister for Foreign Affairs[4] sent for us in succession and held similar language to us both though he seems to have spoken more fully to me.

   [1] Mr. C. E. S. Dodd was Acting Counsellor and Chargé d'Affaires in the British Embassy at Lisbon.
     [2] No. 54.   [3] M. Amé-Leroy.   [4] M. Monteiro.

To me His Excellency asserted that Portugal was observing a policy of non-intervention. But a decision to join agreement to which Portuguese Government were being invited involved vital issues for Portugal and could only be taken after maturest reflection.

Before reaching decision Portuguese Government were bound to put to His Majesty's Government the following questions.

Tangier. In the opinion of the Portuguese Government an agreement of non-intervention in Spanish civil war ought to include the maintenance of neutrality of international zone. Spanish warships navigated by crews who have murdered their officers or held them to their posts under duress are using Tangier as a base of supply. This is a dangerous precedent. Do His Majesty's Government concur?

Soviet Russia. Two ships heavily laden with arms and munitions have discharged at Barcelona and a third is expected there shortly. Russian bombs have already been dropped on Spanish army. An agreement of non-intervention cannot be contemplated by Portuguese Government if Soviet is to be free to continue these supplies. Does His Majesty's Government intend to stop them?

Recognition of belligerency. The Portuguese frontier zone is virtually all in the occupation of the Spanish army and Portuguese Government will shortly be cut off from communication with Madrid. There are important Portuguese interests over the frontier which will require protection and this involves relations with the Spanish army authorities. Will the Portuguese Government be entitled to proclaim neutrality and recognise belligerency of Spanish army? Minister for Foreign Affairs cited action of His Majesty's Government in American civil war as an [sic] precedent.

Portugal's national defence. Azaña has publicly proclaimed her [sic] intention to march on Lisbon if the Spanish Government win.[5] Portuguese would defend herself [sic] against this deadly peril. It is to avert this that Portuguese Government see national safety depending on defeat of Spanish Government. Some assistance from Portugal to Spanish army at an opportune moment might turn the balance in the army's favour. If Portuguese Government sign away their liberty to render such assistance will His Majesty's Government compensate this renunciation by an undertaking to come immediately to the defence of Portugal against a Spanish invasion. Minister for Foreign Affairs' words were: 'Will British soldiers be on Portuguese frontier and British aeroplanes be above Portugal within 24 hours?'

He recalled the declaration made at Madrid in 1873[6] and enquired

---

[5] In a minute of August 8 Mr. Seymour remarked that the Foreign Office knew nothing of this alleged public statement by President Azaña.

[6] In the same minute Mr. Seymour referred to an account of this declaration given in an 'annexed copy' (not preserved in the Foreign Office archives) of a memorandum by Sir Edward Grey. 'It was to the effect that "The Spaniards could not count upon the indifference of England to an external attack upon Portugal", the Portuguese being at the same time informed that "H.M. Government reserve to themselves to judge of the circumstances under which any appeal was made to them by Portugal for succour". Our attitude has always been, as defined by Sir Edward Grey, that while the treaties are admitted to be still

whether His Majesty's Government were prepared as a condition of Portugal joining in non-intervention agreement to take some similar action now and will His Majesty's Government guarantee the integrity of Portugal?

The French Minister informs me that Minister for Foreign Affairs also asked him for a similar guarantee of French Government.

Interest of His Majesty's Government. Minister for Foreign Affairs enlarged on general dangers of a conflict. The Soviet has chosen Spain as an important battlefield. It cannot be in the interests of His Majesty's Government that Spanish army if victorious in spite of His Majesty's Government's intervention should be full of resentment against His Majesty's Government. An Imperial fascisti régime in Spain on bad terms with His Majesty's Government would be dangerous to Portugal but equally fatal to the position of His Majesty's Government in the Mediterranean since it would inevitably fall into the orbit of Germany and Italy.

Minister for Foreign Affairs invites His Majesty's Government to weigh these considerations carefully and reply to these questions urgently in order that the Portuguese Government may take their decision.[7]

in force, H.M. Government reserve to themselves the right of judging the circumstances under which help may be given or withheld.'

[7] M. Monteiro's account of this conversation is given in the collection of Portuguese foreign policy documents published by the Ministério dos Negócios Estrangeiros, *Dez Anos de Política Externa (1936–1947)* (Imprensa Nacional de Lisboa, 1964, cited subsequently as '*D.A.P.E.*'); vol. iii, No. 111; cf. No. 112.

No. 66

Foreign Office to Mr. Milanes (Madrid)
No. 33[1] Telegraphic [W 7998/62/41]

Immediate   FOREIGN OFFICE, *August 7, 1936, 7.20 p.m.*

Please inform Spanish Government that owing to the danger which results from Spanish warships, including auxiliaries, proceeding to anchorage in the naval or commercial harbour at Gibraltar, His Majesty's Government are obliged to request that they shall refrain from doing so for any purpose whatever.

You should state clearly that firing on British ships must cease forthwith and that a British man-of-war will patrol Straits of Gibraltar to protect British shipping from interference.

You should add with reference to the previous warning communicated to Algeciras Command through Governor of Gibraltar relating to the entry of military aircraft that if such aircraft fly over the Colony they will be warned by the firing of three rounds in advance of the aircraft, and that if the warning is disregarded they will then be fired at for effect.[2]

Similar warning is being given to both sides.

[1] No. 7 to Mr. G. E. Monck-Mason, British Consul at Tetuan, with the opening words, 'Please inform General Franco'.   [2] This paragraph was marked 'to Tetuan only'.

No. 67

Sir G. Clerk (Paris) to Foreign Office (Received August 8, 8.30 a.m.)
No. 252 Saving: Telegraphic [W 7964/62/41]

PARIS, *August 7, 1936*

Your telegram No. 308 to Rome.[1]

I asked Minister for Foreign Affairs to see me this afternoon. I told him that my visit was a personal one and made because I was profoundly disturbed about the situation in Spain and hoped that he might possibly have some comfort to give me. What was his latest information from Rome, Berlin, Lisbon and Moscow in regard to the French proposal for non-intervention? M. Delbos said that the Soviet Government was favourable; that from Rome he had had nothing since the Italian *communiqué* of August 6th in regard to which he said that he was not going to be drawn into a polemical discussion on point 2;[2] Herr von Neurath had expressed a personal agreement in principle but M. Delbos had had no official reply of any sort; and Lisbon had included in its answer the conditions that the Soviet Government should also accept fully the French proposal and that the French and British Governments should guarantee the safety of Portugal if that safety was threatened by the conflict in Spain.[3] M. Delbos continued that he would be very grateful for any support that His Majesty's Government could give the French proposal in Berlin, where he felt that at the moment we carried more weight than the French Government.[4] As regards the Portuguese request, he presumed that our treaty with Portugal was a sufficient answer so far as we were concerned and France would of course act up to her obligations under the Covenant.

Turning to another aspect of the question I said that I understood that the French Government, though they were still maintaining their refusal to deliver ammunition or war material to the Madrid Government, had felt that they could not refuse to allow five Dewoitine aircraft, which it was said had been ordered before the troubles began, to be delivered and the departure of the five machines had accordingly been authorised. M. Delbos admitted that that was so. He said that in face of the already known provision of Italian aircraft to the insurgents and of the despatch of twenty-eight German aeroplanes from Hamburg to the same destination, of which information had reached the French Government though it was not known whether the machines had yet arrived, the French Government considered that it was not possible for them to maintain their embargo. But this showed the urgent need for agreement on the French proposal. I said that, while I could understand the reasoning of the French Government, there

[1] No. 54.   [2] Cf. No. 62, note 2.   [3] Cf. No. 65.
[4] Foreign Office telegram No. 168 of August 7 to Berlin had already instructed Sir E. Phipps to support his French colleague's *démarche* and to state that His Majesty's Government 'would welcome an early agreement between all powers who may be in a position to supply arms and munitions to refrain from doing so and to prevent supply from their territories, on principle of non-interference in Spanish affairs'.

were two points that occurred to me. One was, how could he reconcile the despatch of French aircraft to Spain with the holding up in France of British aircraft destined for Portugal? The other point was, was he sure that the Government in Madrid was the real Government and not the screen behind which the most extreme anarchist elements in Spain were directing events? M. Delbos made no attempt to reply to my first question, though he made a note of it. As regards my second point, he said that it might be so in Catalonia, but law and order ruled in Madrid and the Government was functioning unhampered by extremists. I asked him if he considered that the forcible entry into a foreign Legation and the dragging out and shooting of two Spanish gentlemen was an instance of law and order. He had no reply. (This incident was reported to the Embassy this morning by Captain Charles, formerly Commercial Secretary in Madrid and manager of Rio Tinto, who has just returned from the Spanish frontier. The victims were the two sons of the Conde de Casa Valencia, at one time Spanish Ambassador in London.)

I concluded the interview by expressing the hope that the French Government, even though, pending an agreement of non-intervention, they might feel themselves precluded from stopping private commercial transactions with Spain, would do what it could to limit and retard such transactions as much as possible. I asked M. Delbos to forgive me for speaking so frankly and I repeated that all I had said was entirely personal and on my own responsibility but I felt that in so critical a situation I must put before him the danger of any action which might definitely commit the French Government to one side of the conflict and make more difficult the close co-operation between our two countries which was called for by this crisis. M. Delbos said that, on the contrary, he thanked me for speaking so openly and that he and his colleagues wished for nothing more than that the two Governments should act together as closely as possible. He viewed the situation with the gravest anxiety. He had every reason to fear that General Franco had offered the bait of the Balearic Islands to Italy and the Canaries to Germany, and if that materialised, goodbye to French independence.

I realise my responsibility in speaking to the Minister for Foreign Affairs as I did without instructions, but I had reason to believe that the extremists in the Government were putting increasing pressure on M. Blum and I felt sure what I said might strengthen the hands of the moderate and sober elements.[5]

[5] Foreign Office telegram No. 51 Saving of August 10 said that Sir G. Clerk's language 'is approved and appears to have had good results'. *D.D.F.*, *op. cit.*, No. 108 appears to refer to this interview: cf. p. 159, note 1.

No. 68

Record by Mr. Norton[1] of a conversation with Mr. Arthur Greenwood[2]

[*W 8204/62/41*]

FOREIGN OFFICE, *August 7, 1936*

The Right Honourable Arthur Greenwood, M.P., left this document[3] with me this afternoon. He explained that as Mr. Attlee[4] was in Russia and Sir Walter Citrine[5] was not in London, he had thought it advisable to communicate it to us informally.

We had a general talk about the situation, and I explained the considerations which were influencing His Majesty's Government and with which Mr. Greenwood appeared to agree. He told me confidentially that the Labour Party were under considerable pressure from their rank and file, who were always demanding a campaign whether it was in favour of the Spanish Government or the Communists in Greece. The leaders realised that no good could come of adding fuel to the flames and were damping things down. They were also receiving messages from the Communist Party which however they did not answer. He said that as he was more or less 'in charge' he felt it his duty to keep in touch and was always available at Transport House.

I said that I felt sure Sir George Mounsey would be glad to see him if occasion arose, but Mr. Greenwood said he did not wish to trouble Sir George at present.

Reverting to the attached document, Mr. Greenwood said that he hoped the Portuguese Government could be induced not to do anything foolish, and I gathered that he would like Lord Halifax to be informed of his call.[6]

C. J. NORTON

[1] Mr. C. J. Norton was Private Secretary to Sir R. Vansittart.

[2] Deputy Leader of the Parliamentary Labour Party.

[3] The document was a letter dictated by Mr. H. V. Tewson, Assistant Secretary of the T.U.C. General Council, forwarding a message from a M. de Brouckère to the effect that the Portuguese Government had openly sided with the Spanish rebels, that it was 'impossible for Spain to allow the continuation of this practice' and that she had 'definitely decided to prevent it *whatever the cost*'.

[4] Leader of the Parliamentary Labour Party.

[5] General Secretary of the T.U.C. since 1926.

[6] A minute by Mr. Seymour read: 'If the Portuguese make further difficulties about the non-intervention proposal we shall have to consider whether to have another go at them. H. J. S. 13/8.'

No. 69

Mr. Ingram (Rome) to Foreign Office (Received August 12)
No. 882 [W 8315/62/41]

ROME, *August 7, 1936*

Sir,

In amplification of my telegram No. 538 of yesterday's date,[1] I have the honour to report fully on the interview which I had with the Minister of Foreign Affairs yesterday in order to carry out the instructions contained in your immediate telegram No. 308[2] regarding the *démarche* of the French Government designed to secure co-operation among various Powers in the regulation of arms supplies to Spain.

2. On receipt of that telegram, namely at 6.30 on the evening of August 5th, I at once applied for an interview with the Minister of Foreign Affairs, but unfortunately Count Ciano, whose morning was already filled with other appointments, was unable to receive me until 5 o'clock in the afternoon. I then handed him an Aide-Mémoire and spoke in the sense of your instructions. Count Ciano at once replied that the views of his Government coincided with our own, as would be seen by the perusal of the *communiqué* which was appearing in the evening papers (see my telegram No. 535).[3] He gave me the text to read. I expressed satisfaction that in principle the Italian Government thus seemed to be in general agreement with the aim of non-intervention and localisation of events in Spain. Speaking personally, however, I said that while I realised that paragraphs 2–4 of the *communiqué* were very pertinent when it came to working out the details of how effect should be given to the principle upon which we all seemed to be agreed, I could not help wondering whether the specific mention of matters such as those contained in paragraph 2 might not lead to mutual recrimination and thus hinder the main object in view. I seemed to see a vista of pots and kettles calling each other black, but as this proverb was unknown to the Minister the effect of its citation was inconsiderable. Count Ciano said that these matters were inserted with a very definite object: the Italian Government did not wish for non-intervention in principle and not in fact—they wished that the fullest possible measures should be adopted by all the Powers concerned to preserve neutrality and for this reason they had thought it opportune to point to the practical questions which would have to be faced and solved if that full neutrality were to be realised. A neutrality in spirit as well as in letter was what was required. No effort must be spared to prevent events in Spain being interpreted as, and then developing into, a conflict between two ideologies amounting almost to religions, viz. between Fascism and Bolshevism. In the eyes of the Italian Government the greatest danger to Europe lay in the disposition in certain countries to interpret what was going on in Spain in the above terms. For this reason he felt that the

---

[1] Not printed: it summarized events described in the present despatch.
[2] No. 54.   [3] No. 62.

74

five Powers mentioned in Foreign Office telegram under reference should be increased to six so as to include Soviet Russia.

3. For his part, His Excellency continued, he could assure me that Italy had observed, and would continue to observe, the completest neutrality in the matter. No public meetings had been held in Italy, and there had been no press campaign in favour of one side or the other; no volunteers were being enrolled for either side, no subscriptions were being launched to help one party or the other. If certain Italian aeroplanes had found their way to Spanish territory, that was purely a matter affecting a private firm and was now the subject of investigation. I would note, he said, that one of the questions raised in the *communiqué* was whether it was intended that private firms or individuals should be included in the commitment to non-intervention, and, if so, what were the means by which this doctrine could be enforced.

4. I assured His Excellency that I could endorse much of what he had just said from my own observations. I pointed out, however, that other Governments might not find it so easy, owing to their organisation, as the Italian Government might, to give effect to all the propositions put forward in the *communiqué*. The Italian Government controlled the press; other Governments had no machinery for this purpose. In England it was difficult to prevent meetings being held if they did not endanger the public peace. Anyhow, replied the Minister, it should be easy to prevent money being sent. Finally I said that this was not the moment, it seemed to me, to lay emphasis on the difficulties of implementing non-intervention: the essential thing was that the Governments mainly concerned should indicate their readiness to give the undertaking and to implement it.

5. Count Ciano assured me once more that it was the policy of the Italian Government in the Spanish affair to adopt an attitude of one hundred per cent neutrality.[4] They thought that they could enforce this and only hoped that other nations would be able to do likewise.

6. I had an uneasy feeling throughout this interview that Count Ciano rather resented our intervention in the matter. He was sensibly less cordial than usual.

I have, &c.,

E. M. B. Ingram

[4] Referring to this comment in telegram No. 538, Mr. C. A. E. Shuckburgh, a Third Secretary in the League of Nations and Western Department, minuted: 'Count Ciano's "100% neutrality" is a little difficult to reconcile with the aircraft incidents. C. A. E. Shuckburgh. 8/8.'

No. 70

Sir E. Phipps (Berlin) to Foreign Office (Received August 8, 2.30 p.m.)
No. 256 Telegraphic [W 8047/62/41]

Immediate   BERLIN, *August 8, 1936, 1.43 p.m.*
Your telegram No. 168.[1]

My French colleague made his *démarche* a couple of days ago. He tells me Minister for Foreign Affairs replied affirmatively *in principle* but made certain reservations, for instance regarding necessity for strict inclusion of Russia.

Yesterday French Ambassador handed to Baron von Neurath text of draft common declaration[2] in three paragraphs by the Powers concerned prohibiting export of arms etc. to Spain. Paragraph 3 stipulated that governments would exchange information as to putting these rules into practice.

Baron von Neurath whilst making no positive objections pointed out certain difficulties in the suggested procedure: for instance how would proposed measures be controlled? If by a blockade what would United States say? His Excellency further indicated that there was always the difficulty of the Russian Government who would agree to something on the one hand while it would be violated by Comintern on the other.

I have this morning strongly supported the French *démarche*. Minister for Foreign Affairs gave me a practically identic reply. He pointed out in addition that there were other things besides arms whose entry into Spain should be prevented viz. money and men. Moreover how could France be sure of preventing people passing into Spain all along her long frontier? Finally His Excellency remarked to me that it would be necessary for other countries such as United States of America, Sweden and Switzerland to sign proposed declaration.

I urged Baron von Neurath to make the considered reply of the German Government as soon as possible and pointed out that with a view to preventing a division of Europe into two groups it would be well to issue a joint declaration even though its enforcement might prove difficult to bring about completely.

His Excellency promised to see the Chancellor today and to give reply as soon as possible. He assured me the last thing German Government wished was for the Spanish trouble to spread.

[1] See No. 67, note 4.   [2] Cf. No. 64.

No. 71

Mr. Ingram (Rome) to Foreign Office (Received August 8, 7.30 p.m.)
No. 544 Telegraphic [W 8054/62/41]

ROME, *August 8, 1936, 4.50 p.m.*

My telegram No. 538.[1]
French Ambassador told me last night that he had presented French draft of neutrality [declaration] to Minister for Foreign Affairs yesterday.

[1] See No. 69, note 1.

The latter while emphasising that final decision must come from Signor Mussolini who is still away from Rome stated he did not think personally that the draft would satisfy the Italian Government in as much as it did not sufficiently underline the existence or at any rate the necessity for moral solidarity. He went so far as to hint that unless the foreign press cease to talk of events in Spain as a conflict between fascism and bolshevism Italy would not play. Mental disarmament was he said required before physical disarmament.

I am somewhat uneasy as to the manner in which this situation seems to be developing here into a doctrinal conflict. One can only hope that with his greater sense of realism Signor Mussolini will not over-play his hand in this respect; but the present Italian tactics whether consciously or unconsciously seem designed to precipitate rather than eliminate the very development which they profess to be anxious to avoid.

No. 72

Sir G. Clerk (Paris) to Foreign Office (Received August 8, 11 p.m.)
Nos. 262 & 263 Telegraphic: by telephone [W 8055/62/41]

Immediate   PARIS, *August 8, 1936*
My telegram No. 252 saving.[1]
I did not know when I asked Minister for Foreign Affairs to receive me that immediately after my interview he had to attend a Cabinet meeting but the interview seems to have been timely.

No. 263. The meeting lasted for over 3 hours. No *communiqué* was issued, but this morning's press announced that the matter discussed had been of such importance that the decisions agreed upon could only be taken officially at a formal meeting of the Council of Ministers under the presidency of Monsieur Lebrun.

It was added that as a result of the deliberations of the Cabinet yesterday it had been agreed that France should observe an attitude of strictest non-intervention in the affairs of Spain.

Council of Ministers duly met this afternoon. After a session of over 4 hours *communiqué* has been issued of which following are salient relevant points.

Monsieur Delbos gave a long account of the international situation with particular reference to the Spanish crisis.

He mentioned that on July 25th the government had decided that no exports of war material to Spain would be allowed, except that private industry might ultimately be allowed to deliver unarmed aircraft.[2] On August 1st the government, having learned that supplies from foreign sources were reaching the rebels, had appealed to the governments chiefly concerned to agree to the adoption of common rules of non-intervention in Spanish

---

[1] No. 67.   [2] See No. 25.

affairs, but had at the same time reserved France's liberty of action pending the achievement of the proposed agreement.[3] On August 6th the government, feeling that an international competition in support of the respective parties might have the most dangerous consequences, took, with the support of His Majesty's Government, a fresh initiative and submitted to all the interested Powers the text of a Convention laying down definite rules with a view to the effective application of common undertakings.[4] The almost unanimously favourable replies so far received gave hope of an early solution.

In these circumstances the government had decided to suspend exports to Spain, which in any case had up to date only comprised deliveries coming within the strict scope of the decision of July 25th. The government hopes that its attitude will facilitate the rapid conclusion of the definite agreement it had put forward in the interests of international peace.

A separate *communiqué* states that no permission is required for the export of oil to Spain.

Copies of *communiqués* by post.[5]

[3] See Nos. 44 and 45.   [4] See No. 64.   [5] Not printed.

No. 73

Sir E. Phipps (Berlin) to Foreign Office (Received August 10, 9.30 a.m.)
No. 209 Saving: Telegraphic [C 5836/3727/18]

Very Confidential   BERLIN, *August 8, 1936*
My telegrams Nos. 250[1] and 252.[2]

After conversation on other subjects with Minister for Foreign Affairs this morning I asked him when Herr von Ribbentrop's appointment to London would be definitely announced. His Excellency lifted his arms into the air and remarked that I could have no idea of his difficulties in the matter. Whilst at Bayreuth he had extracted Chancellor's consent to appointment but three days later he met Herr von Ribbentrop at Munich and latter told him that he did not wish to go to London. Herr von Ribbentrop's attitude in the matter was still very undecided but Baron von Neurath admitted it was a certain indication of party attacks on him and that he felt the danger of leaving his office in Berlin. Meanwhile decree appointing Herr von Ribbentrop is daily placed before the Chancellor, who refuses to sign it.

I pointed out the unfortunate impression that would be created in London if further delay occurred, after *agrément* being given. His Excellency realises this only too well.

I hear privately from other sources that Herr von Ribbentrop is really

[1] No. 55.   [2] No. 59.

78

most depressed at the hitch and would only be too glad to go to London as soon as possible.[3]

In view of approaching Nuremberg Party Congress, the Chancellor has to be particularly careful not to offend Nazi extremists.

[3] Herr von Ribbentrop's appointment as German Ambassador at London was announced in Berlin on August 11: *The Times*, August 12, 1936, p. 10; cf. Joachim von Ribbentrop, *Zwischen London und Moskau* (1953), pp. 88–93.

No. 74

Sir P. Loraine (Constantinople) to Foreign Office (Received August 10, 12 noon)
No. 106 Telegraphic [*T 12564/8725/379*]

Important   CONSTANTINOPLE, *August 10, 1936, 11 a.m.*

My telegram No. 102.[1]

Turkish Government are very happy to give desired authorization. It includes even fortified and prohibited zone of Smyrna. They would be very grateful however if notice could reach them at least twenty-four hours and preferably two days in advance of His Majesty's wish to visit one or more points on Turkish littoral in order that needful instructions may be sent to local authorities.

Should The King decide to go to Smyrna and wish to visit places of archaeological interest in that region e.g. Ephesus, Pergamum, etc., they would wish to ensure His Majesty's comfort and privacy by placing a special train at his disposal.

I was given to understand that a visit by His Majesty to Istanbul would be particularly welcome to the Turkish Government.

I also specifically ascertained that general authorization would cover a visit to the war graves on Gallipoli peninsula should The King desire to undertake it.

Personal and informal character of The King's cruise is fully appreciated here.[2]

[1] In this telegram of August 6, Sir P. Loraine referred to Foreign Office telegram No. 58 of August 4, which had instructed him to request permission for one of the two destroyers escorting the King on his cruise (see No. 31, note 4) to enter any harbour visited by His Majesty or any adjoining harbour. Telegram No. 58 was repeated to Mr. Walker (Chargé d'Affaires at Athens) and Mr. Balfour (Chargé d'Affaires at Belgrade). Telegram No. 313 to Mr. Ingram (Rome) of August 8 said: 'Please explain to Italian Government that His Majesty the King is undertaking cruise with his yacht, escorted by two destroyers, and request permission for a destroyer to enter Brindisi to collect mail for His Majesty.'

[2] Travelling incognito as the Duke of Lancaster the King and his party spent August 10–19 in Yugoslavia, and August 20–September 2 in Greece. He arrived in Turkish waters on September 3, and anchored in the Bosphorus on September 4.

No. 75

Foreign Office to Sir H. Chilton (Hendaye)
No. 145 Telegraphic [W 8092/62/41]

FOREIGN OFFICE, *August 10, 1936, 5 p.m.*

I understand that Secretaries of French and Belgian Embassies have returned or are returning to Madrid. Naval authorities have also recommended[1] return of a member of His Majesty's Embassy.

We have hitherto hesitated to send Mr. Ogilvie-Forbes back owing to fighting round Madrid, risk of capital being cut off altogether, apparent weakening of authority of Central Government, and desire to give no encouragement to British subjects to remain in Madrid.

In present circumstances however it appears desirable that an official of more authority than Vice Consul should be at Embassy and, unless you see any strong objection[2] Mr. Ogilvie-Forbes is being instructed to return at once.[3]

Please telegraph reply urgent.

[1] In a message of August 9, from the Rear-Admiral Commanding the First Cruiser Squadron, addressed to the Admiralty.

[2] Sir H. Chilton telephoned his agreement on August 10.

[3] Foreign Office telegram No. 41 to Mr. Milanes (Madrid) of August 12 said that Mr. Ogilvie-Forbes would leave London on the following day on his way to Madrid. The Spanish Government was to be informed and asked to provide full facilities at Valencia and for the journey to Madrid.

No. 76

Foreign Office to Mr. Dodd (Lisbon)
No. 92 Telegraphic [W 7818/62/41]

FOREIGN OFFICE, *August 10, 1936, 7.15 p.m.*

Your telegram No. 123.[1]

You may give an oral reply to the Minister for Foreign Affairs on the following lines.

Tangier. Every effort has been and is being made to secure the neutrality of Tangier.

Russia. It is understood that the French Government have every hope that the accession of Russia to the proposed non-intervention agreement will be obtained.

Recognition of Belligerency. Question of recognising existence of state of civil war in Spain will no doubt, unless situation changes rapidly, shortly come to the front. It is, however, highly desirable that the Powers principally concerned should act in agreement on this question. Recognition of the contending parties as belligerents entails conferring upon them certain

[1] No. 65.

belligerent rights, for instance, right of search, which would require careful consideration. It would be entirely premature and strongly to be deprecated for one Power closely concerned, such as Portugal, to take such a step at this stage.

Defence of Portugal. All the information at the disposal of His Majesty's Government indicates that Spanish Government are not in full control of the forces on their own side, and representations to them at present on any important subject are considered useless. His Majesty's Government have always admitted the validity of the treaties between themselves and Portugal, though they have necessarily retained the right of judging the circumstances under which these treaties should come into play. Invasion of Portugal by a foreign country would also raise question of obligations incumbent upon His Majesty's Government as on other Powers under the Covenant. His Majesty's Government do not consider that further guarantees to Portugal should be necessary as consideration for entering into an agreement which is designed to avoid the very dangers which Dr. Monteiro anticipates.

The Portuguese Government will no doubt recognise the danger that individual Powers, in the absence of any understanding, may gradually come to support, more and more openly, one side or the other in the Spanish dispute. It is of great importance to avoid any such development and for this reason His Majesty's Government have themselves welcomed the French proposal and trust that it will also commend itself to the Portuguese Government.

No. 77

Minutes by Sir G. Mounsey for Sir A. Cadogan[1]
[*W 8229/62/41*]

FOREIGN OFFICE, *August 10, 1936*

Since writing the attached minute[2] I have had conversations with the French Chargé d'Affaires, who has been charged by his Government to

---

[1] Sir A. Cadogan had returned to the Foreign Office from his post as H.M. Ambassador at Peking and became a Deputy Under Secretary of State for Foreign Affairs on October 1, 1936; cf. Volume XV, No. 437.

[2] Not printed. Dated August 9, it suggested an immediate communication by His Majesty's Government to all the Governments to whom the French Government had up to the present appealed on the question of preventing the supply of arms and munitions to Spain, affirming the willingness of His Majesty's Government to take similar action when the other Governments agreed to do so, but pointing out, in order to avoid any future misunderstanding, that the French proposals presented certain administrative and other difficulties. It was also suggested that the communication should make the condition that the 'troubled conditions in Spain' did not give rise to 'any developments which may tend to alter the existing balance of Power in the Western Mediterranean'. On this last point a minute by Sir G. Mounsey of August 11 read: 'Sir A. Cadogan and Lord Halifax were opposed to giving any such warning; and thought the presence of our ships was a more effective measure and less liable to undesirable foreign reactions.'

express their appreciation of the support that we have given them in their efforts to limit the effects of the troubles in Spain. They hope that we realise the importance of the action taken by them on August 8th[3] in prohibiting the export of war material for Spain at once, and they attach great importance to receiving our further support in regard to the declaration which they wish all Powers concerned to make.

Our reply on this declaration was somewhat reserved owing to the difficulties of the Board of Trade (see W 8040/62/41)[4] and I went through these difficulties with M. Cambon in order to show him that they were due to hard fact and not to lack of good will on our part.

I said I thought most Governments would find themselves faced with similar difficulties in adopting as it stands the French draft declaration and I said that I wondered whether it would not save time and produce more chance of a unanimous attitude if the various Governments were asked to do what we are ready to do viz: accept the draft proposal in principle, and agree to carry out at once that part of which for which [sic] we possess the requisite legal powers: and that for the remainder, for questions of interpretation or future additions to the proposed prohibition, the door should be left open for future negotiation.

M. Cambon rather jumped at this suggestion and asked if he could put it forward as coming from His Majesty's Government. I said it was purely my own idea and I had consulted no one, so he could only indicate that it was a personal suggestion if he cared to do so. He is going to put it at once to his Government on this basis.

All this of course has a bearing on my previous minute.[5]

G. M. 10.8.36

After discussion with Lord Halifax and Sir A. Cadogan I was authorised to communicate the attached version[6] of my originally suggested proposal, i.e. omitting the last paragraph. I was to give the French Government the alternatives of either themselves making a *démarche* to the other Powers on the lines shown, or, if they preferred, letting us do so, as a step in support of the action they took on August 8.

I have sent for M. Cambon and given him this revised text, which I explained was simply a rough idea and not a textual communication; and I added that if the French Government concurred in its general terms and

---

[3] See No. 72.

[4] This referred to a letter from Mr. J. J. Wills of the Board of Trade to Mr. P. Leigh Smith, a First Secretary in the League of Nations and Western Department of the Foreign Office, of August 7, 1936, setting out the steps needed to implement the French draft declaration. The control of transit was the main difficulty. The Customs considered that the practical difficulties of administering a prohibition of transit in all its forms ('whether involving transit across this country, transhipments in its ports, or the mere through-carriage of arms, etc., in vessels touching at United Kingdom ports') would be 'completely insuperable'. Cf. No. 64.

[5] See note 2.

[6] Not printed.

wished us to make the *démarche*, we would in doing so have to specify more fully our difficulties re transit, war materials etc.[7]

G. M. 10.8.36

[7] M. Cambon called on Sir G. Mounsey (W 8846/62/41) on the morning of August 12 and said that his government 'had greatly appreciated our suggestions and more particularly the spirit of co-operation which had inspired them', but they felt that 'it would be inadvisable and tend to delay matters if they agreed to adopt the somewhat different procedure which our suggestions would involve'. They were, however, 'so far ready to accept the idea inspiring our suggestions as to be willing' to ask the British and other governments to send the French Government a reply which would take the French draft proposal as a basis and 'state in as general terms as possible the interpretation which each Government will place upon the obligations which it enumerates, in undertaking to carry them out'. Sir G. Mounsey did not consider that this constituted any appreciable difference from his own proposal. It was agreed that they should reply at once in the sense desired, and then 'take up with the Board of Trade and Customs the exact wording of our proposed reply'.

No. 78

Viscount Chilston (Moscow) to Foreign Office (Received August 14)
No. 468 [W 8628/62/41]

MOSCOW, *August 10, 1936*

Sir,

Soviet reactions to the Spanish civil war have in most respects been so nearly inevitable that there is little to add to my telegrams on this subject. Although the war seems all too likely to end in the establishment of a communist régime in that country, I do not think that the news of its outbreak can have been received with any enthusiasm by the Soviet Government. Señor Quiroga's government was probably quite good enough for the Kremlin in present circumstances, and no troubling of the European waters which gives Germany a chance to fish can be very welcome here. The Soviet press, therefore, though from the outset it devoted much space to the war and displayed the inevitable bias in its selection of foreign reports, gave no sign during the early stages that anything more would be forthcoming from the U.S.S.R. than platonic sympathy for the Madrid Government.

2. This correct and neutral attitude might possibly, I think, have been maintained but for the growing weight of evidence that the two principal 'fascist' States were actively assisting the insurgents. When the Soviet Government decided to act, they acted quickly: on the 2nd August, some fifteen days after the outbreak of the revolt, not a word had yet been said about a single 'popular' demonstration; on the following day indignation meetings and 'popular' demonstrations took place by the thousand in all parts of the Soviet Union. As reported in my telegram No. 123 of the 6th August, collections were organised in all factories by the Central Council of Soviet Trade Unions in aid of the 'Spanish fighters for the Republic'; the workers displaying their unexampled solidarity by voting unanimously, in each single case, the 'voluntary' contribution of an identical proportion of

83

their wages, viz. one half per cent, deduct[i]ble at the source.[1] At this rate, as I have pointed out, the monthly contribution should have been in the neighbourhood of one million pounds, calculating on the basis of the number of trade union members and the latest statistics regarding the average wage. On the 6th August the press published a bald announcement to the effect that 12,145,000 roubles had been collected, and that the equivalent in French francs at the official rate, i.e. Fr. 36,435,000 or roughly half a million sterling, had been made over to the Spanish Prime Minister. I concluded at the time that the arrangements entailed by the collection had not been completed in the remoter districts of the Union, and that we should in due course hear of the making over of another half million (and possibly of further sums for the ensuing months). But nothing further has yet been said on the subject by the Soviet press, and I am now inclined to think that we shall hear no more from Soviet official sources, though the other half million may quite possibly have been paid to the Spanish Government. I have reason to believe that the announcement made on the 6th August was the outcome of pressing representations by the French Chargé d'Affaires, who appears to have urged the Soviet Government, in connexion with his Government's proposals regarding non-interference, to terminate as quickly as possible all publicity concerning the collection or levy. It was for this reason that the announcement of the collection and disposal of the 12,145,000 roubles appeared side by side with the statement concerning the Soviet Government's official attitude towards M. Blum's proposals. Several foreign journalists have since attempted to 'draw' the press censor, taking the line that the Soviet workman can hardly be as poor as the officially announced result of the collection suggests; but their enquiries have been received in embarrassed silence, and no explanation has been forthcoming of what one of them has described as 'the vanished half million.'

3. This is not, as you are aware, the first time that the Soviet Government have employed the tactics of an allegedly popular and spontaneous collection to assist foreign causes which they do not choose to support openly: a large sum was collected in the same way during the last general strike in England. But as stated in my telegram No. 124,[2] the Soviet Government cannot escape the charge of official intervention, since the rouble is not a medium of international exchange.

4. The Moscow newspapers have paid their usual indirect tribute to the importance of the British press, quoting from it more extensively than from any other source and displaying great indignation that the 'Times' should have thought fit to reproduce German stories of 'the hand of Moscow.' Karl Radek, in the 'Izvestiya' of the 4th August, explains that the parasites of still rotting capitalism naturally shudder when they see the popular masses of Spain cleansing themselves of the parasites of already rotten feudalism.

[1] This telegram also stated that in reply to the French representations of August 5 regarding non-interference the Soviet Government had concurred 'in principle of non-interference in Spanish internal affairs and are ready to participate in proposed agreement thereon'.   [2] Of August 6 (W 7903/62/41), not printed.

'And so this same "Times", which knows its history, and is aware of the true character of the "Spain" that has risen in mutiny against the legal democratic government,—this same "Times" is not ashamed to lie and slander, echoing the fascist press of Germany and Italy about the "hand of Moscow"!

Do not shout, gentlemen. For in the first place, however much you strain your lungs you will not drown the voice of the world, which asks you to produce your proofs. Are we then to be told that Moscow controlled that sitting at the house of Gil Robles at which, according to your own agents, it was decided to rise in revolt, and at which the signal was given for the start of the civil war? Do you imagine that 500 years of fiendish exploitation and savage oppression speak with a less convincing voice than that which Moscow could command? Apart from this, you had better not shout, gentlemen, for it prevents you from thinking and looking about you; and at this moment it would be very useful to you if you could keep your heads. For it is not only the *habitués* of the European watering-places whose skins are in danger—not only the exploiters squandering on the Riviera and in the dancing-halls of London the money bled from the Spanish workers and peasants. It is also a question of your own skins!'

and M. Radek proceeds to dilate upon the cunning smoke-tactics of the fascist press and on the certainty of a world conflagration if the Germans and Italians should succeed in gaining a foothold in Morocco, the Balearic Islands or the Iberian peninsula itself. 'The louder the German fascists shout about Bolshevik or French intervention in Spain, the plainer it becomes that they are preparing for serious action not only against Spain, but against France also.' This last sentence reveals, of course, the kernel of the Soviet Government's problem. Lenin prophesied long ago that Spain would be the first to follow in Russia's footsteps, but Spain and the world revolution can wait; meanwhile any danger to France is a danger to the Soviet Union.

I have, etc.,
CHILSTON

No. 79

Sir E. Phipps (Berlin) to Foreign Office (Received August 11, 7.30 p.m.)
No. 259 Telegraphic [W 8327/62/41]

BERLIN, *August 11, 1936, 5.50 p.m.*

Your telegram No. 169.[1]
There has been no misunderstanding. Baron von Neurath's reference to blockade was merely hypothetical and he quite understood that it was not

[1] This Foreign Office telegram of August 10 referred to No. 70 and remarked that 'M.F.A.'s reference to the possibility of a blockade shows that there must be some misunderstanding. What is proposed is a self-denying undertaking and there is no suggestion for the prevention of action by third parties. Question of blockade cannot therefore arise'.

part of the proposal. To make sure however I have so informed Herr Dieckhoff. I asked him at the same time when we might expect the German reply. (My French colleague has just informed him of Russia's unreserved acceptance[2] and has pressed for early German decision.)

Herr Dieckhoff told me that the German reply was ready and would already have been given and published had it not been for seizure of a German aeroplane by the Spanish Government who so far refuse to surrender it. He added that the reply would be to the effect that Germany agreed to the proposed common declaration provided that it were also accepted by *all* States that manufactured ammunition war material military aeroplanes etc. He hopes that the above mentioned incident will be settled without delay in which case the German reply will be given immediately afterwards.

[2] Cf. No. 78.

No. 80

Sir G. Clerk (Paris) to Foreign Office (Received August 12)
No. 258 Saving: Telegraphic [W 8321/62/41]

PARIS, *August 11, 1936*

Reliable source found M. Blum extremely depressed to-day at the situation arising out of the Civil War in Spain. M. Blum declared that he was 'in torture' at having been obliged for reasons of high international policy, to embargo the despatch of arms and munitions from France to Spain, and that the whole thing was having such an effect upon his nerves that he could neither sleep nor digest properly. M. Blum referred to the conditions made by the Italian Government for agreeing to the French suggestions for non-intervention,[1] and said that he would be prepared to prevent volunteers proceeding en masse to Spain and to prevent any regular kind of recruiting here, though it would obviously be difficult, and indeed impossible, to prevent individuals from going to Spain if they wanted to. It was, however, quite out of the question for him to attempt to prevent financial assistance being sent to the Madrid Government. As the source observed, M. Blum's career would speedily be terminated if he was to try and prevent political sympathisers in France from sending money to Madrid.

In reply to a question regarding the basis for his belief that war material was reaching the insurgents from Germany M. Blum said that the French Consul at Hamburg had reported the despatch thence to the insurgents of a number of aeroplanes, while the French Consul at Larache had reported the unloading from a German vessel for the use of insurgents of aerial bombs as well as aircraft.

Cf. No. 62.

No. 81

Letter from Mr. Lloyd Thomas (Paris) to Sir A. Cadogan
[W 8676/62/41]

Private and Confidential   PARIS, *August 11, 1936*

Dear Alec,

I think that the Ambassador's conversation with Delbos on Friday evening[1] may well have been the factor which decided the Government here to announce the policy of non-intervention in Spain. We know that the decision was only arrived at after a very sharp difference of opinion among the Ministers themselves and Bargeton,[2] whom I saw on Friday morning, had told me that the position of Delbos, Chautemps[3] and the other more reasonable members of the Government [was] very shaky and that anything that we could do to strengthen Delbos' hand would be most welcome. Bischoff, the Austrian Chargé d'Affaires, who came to see the Ambassador this morning, told him that it was his opinion and the opinion of the well-informed members of the Diplomatic Corps that the Ambassador's counsels of moderation, even though given personally and unofficially, had turned the scale. Viénot, the Under-Secretary for Foreign Affairs, who lunched with me to-day told me that he was present at the meeting and that the Ambassador's timely words had been most useful. He added, however, that they were not out of the wood yet; the somewhat equivocal answer of the Italian Government had caused great uneasiness not only in the Cabinet but among the Deputies in general. A further interpellation on the subject had been put down for this week, and Vincent-Auriol, the Minister of Finance, who had hitherto been undecided, had now come down heavily on the side of intervention on behalf of the Government of Madrid.

Yours ever,
HUGH LLOYD THOMAS

[1] See Nos. 67 and 72.
[2] Director of the Political and Commercial Affairs Department of the French Foreign Office.   [3] Minister of State.

No. 82

Sir E. Phipps (Berlin) to Foreign Office (Received August 12, 5.10 p.m.)
No. 262 Telegraphic [W 8485/62/41]

BERLIN, *August 12, 1936, 3.50 p.m.*

Your telegram No. 170.[1]

Herr Dieckhoff in conversation with Sir R. Vansittart mentioned the matter of the detained German aeroplane. He said that it had been sent for

[1] This Foreign Office telegram of August 11 reported Señor Oliván as stating that a German machine had been detained on August 10 by Spanish authorities who suspected it to be a disguised military machine. He said that the German Government had threatened to break off diplomatic relations if the aeroplane were not immediately released. Cf. No. 79, and *D.G.F.P.*, *op. cit.*, No. 37.

the bona fide purpose of evacuating German civilians and that it was a genuine civilian aircraft although the crew had been provided with two or three revolvers in case they were attacked in endeavouring to perform the purpose of their visit. He mentioned also however that the machine was a Junker and Sir R. Vansittart gathered that it was capable of transformation though there was no intention whatever that this should be done. Herr Dieckhoff made no allusion at all to possibility of breaking off relations. He said indeed that he hoped that the incident might be shortly regulated. He coupled his remarks about the detention of aeroplane with allusions to the fact that the German government had obtained no real satisfaction beyond I think an apology from Spanish Government for the recent murders of German citizens. What Sir R. Vansittart understood German Government really wanted was compensation for families of the dead and anyhow proper punishment of the guilty. Sir R. Vansittart concluded that the Chancellor himself was taking a severe line about the fate of these members of the National Socialist party and that he is probably being stimulated in this direction by men like Herr Bohler.[2]

In view of the foregoing I think to speak strongly in the sense of paragraph 2 of your telegram under reference on no stronger warrant than apprehensions of Soviet[3] Ambassador in London and despite the calm view apparently taken by Herr Dieckhoff might possibly be unwise. Even the press points too...[4] at this particular moment we may easily in view of Herr Hitler's present implied attitude create impression that we are taking Spanish Government's side and so defeat our own ends—even put into German heads an idea that is not apparently or avowedly there at present. If despite this there were indeed to be any rupture of relations, I should say that the real motive would be more likely to be murder of German subjects than detention of an aeroplane.

I will however of course take an opportunity of speaking again to-day in regard to...[4] in calming terms in continuation of conversation which Sir R. Vansittart had already had with Herr Dieckhoff before receipt of your telegram.

[2] The reference is presumably to Herr Ernst Bohle, head of the *Auslandsorganisation* of the Nazi Party. Sir E. Phipps's telegram No. 207 Saving of August 8 referred to a German press statement of August 7 concerning an 'atrocity in Barcelona' in which four German citizens had been murdered. The statement added that 'it is now not merely a question of Spaniard against Spaniard, but that German emigrés have taken upon themselves to participate in attacks on entirely unconcerned German citizens'.

[3] Corrected to 'Spanish' on the filed copy.

[4] The text was here uncertain.

No. 83

Sir G. Clerk (Paris) to Foreign Office (Received August 12, 4.10 p.m.)
No. 264 Telegraphic: by telephone [W 8379/62/41]

Immediate   PARIS, *August 12, 1936*

My telegram No. 252 Saving.[1]

Minister of Foreign Affairs asked me to come and see him this morning. He said that just as he had listened to my appeal last Friday, he hoped that His Majesty's Government would listen to appeal which he was making to me today. It was of the greatest importance that agreement should be reached on proposal for non-intervention in Spain with the utmost possible speed. He understood and appreciated considerations put forward by His Majesty's Government[2] but discussion and drafting of new texts meant the loss of precious time and gave opportunities for other Powers to make further delays. He observed that Italian and Soviet Governments had accepted French text as it stood though both governments had proposed additional clauses.

2. Monsieur Delbos therefore submitted to His Majesty's Government a most urgent plea that they too would declare their readiness to accept French text as it stood. Minister for Foreign Affairs suggested that such acceptance could be accompanied by 'texte interprétatif' or commentary setting forth the particular view of each government concerned[:] the great thing was to secure immediate and general acceptance of principle.

3. Monsieur Delbos has a further request to make of His Majesty's Government. No reply has as yet come from Berlin and he would be most grateful if His Majesty's Government could do anything to hasten the German reply. (I said I knew you had already instructed His Majesty's Ambassador in Berlin in that sense).[3]

4. Finally Minister for Foreign Affairs said that speed was also necessary on account of internal situation in France. He thought French Government could claim to have acted with a certain courage but it was growing daily, almost hourly, more difficult to withstand the pressure of their supporters who insisted that French Republic could not refuse to aid the lawful constituted government of a sister republic when the rebels were notoriously receiving help of all kinds from other countries.

5. As I had never received text of French proposal nor of reply of His Majesty's Government I was unable to attempt any discussion with Minister for Foreign Affairs and indeed I feel French Government are right in their view that the important thing is to get formal acceptance of principle of their proposal.

6. I understand that instructions have been telephoned to the French Chargé d'Affaires to speak to you at once in the sense of Monsieur Delbos' observations to me.

[1] No. 67.   [2] See No. 77.   [3] Cf. Nos. 67, note 4, 70, and 79.

No. 84

Minute by Mr. Sargent on the danger of a creation of rival ideological blocs in Europe

[*W 9331/62/41*]

FOREIGN OFFICE, *August 12, 1936*

Events in Spain are bound to have their effect on the relations of the Powers who have agreed to meet together to negotiate a Five Power Pact and to explore the possibilities of a general settlement in Europe. If the principle of non-intervention in the affairs of Spain breaks down—and I am afraid the French proposed agreement about war material is not enough to save it—it may well be that the first step will have been taken in dividing Europe from henceforth into two *blocs*, each based on a rival ideology. This would be a very different and far more horrible development than the creation of national and imperialistic *blocs* of satisfied versus dissatisfied Powers which we have hitherto foreseen and feared, for the creation of ideological *blocs* would not merely divide Governments from one another far more deeply than any political dispute, but would also cut across the domestic politics of each individual country.

This cleavage could not fail to show itself in the negotiations of the proposed Five Power Conference, and would certainly impair its prospects of reaching a successful conclusion, while rendering our own task of working for a general settlement along the present lines far more difficult and invidious than it is at present. Our natural instinct would no doubt be to try and remain neutral in this conflict between Fascism and Communism, for presumably to a parliamentary democracy both systems are almost equally abhorrent. But would pressure from abroad and public opinion at home allow us to maintian this attitude for long; and even if we were able to do so, would it do us or Europe any good?

Instead of just waiting for this dangerous cleavage to happen, ought we not—both for the purpose of the Five Power Conference and for the sake of the bigger issues of European co-operation—to be ready to take the initiative and try, before it is too late, to prevent these *blocs* from crystallising. We have contacts in both camps which ought to facilitate our task.

We ought to be able to strengthen the French Government in its efforts—or indeed bring pressure to bear to force it—to free itself from Communist domination, both domestic and Muscovite. Even though this might involve at a certain stage something very like interference in the internal affairs of France, surely it would be worth while running this risk?

As for Italy and Germany, it may be said that in both cases the chief incentive which they have to co-operate together is at present not so much a common fear of Communism as a feeling that they two stand isolated in Europe. It lies with us to remove this feeling, especially in Rome where it is most keenly felt and feared.

Moreover, in so far as the fear of the spread of Communism is bringing

Germany and Italy to co-operate, this fear is centred not so much on what is going to happen in Spain as on what is going to happen in France. Both Governments, for different reasons, dread the prospect of a France weakened or paralysed by Communistic infection. Germany dreads it because of the use that Russia would make of such a situation for the more effective encirclement of Germany; and Italy dreads it because her security lies in the even balancing of France and Germany in Western Europe, and because any further weakening of France in present circumstances would place her more or less at the mercy of Germany and make it impossible for her any longer to treat with Germany as an equal.

All these considerations seem to indicate the importance of (1) our preventing France by hook or by crook from 'going Bolshevik' under the influence of the Spanish civil war; and (2) our freeing Italy from the feeling of isolation and vulnerability which the Abyssinian affair has left her with.[1]

O. G. SARGENT

[1] In two lengthy minutes, both of August 13, Sir A. Cadogan and Sir G. Mounsey agreed that the dangers outlined by Mr. Sargent were all too obvious, and proceeded to discuss the alternative courses open to His Majesty's Government. Sir A. Cadogan did not see what could be done beyond supporting M. Blum 'in the policy which he is trying to follow in regard to the Spanish situation'. Sir G. Mounsey could only point hopefully to the formation of the non-intervention committee. 'And won't it be something still more if, once round a table, all these Powers can seriously be got to agree publicly to the principle of non-intervention?' A final comment by Mr. Sargent of August 14 suggests that he was not greatly comforted by these observations.

No. 85

Letter from Sir R. Vansittart to Mr. Eden
Ge/36/17[1]

BERLIN, *August 12, 1936*

My dear Anthony,

I expect you will begin to take your boxes again soon and you may like to have a short line from me in regard to my experiences in Berlin. I am trying to find time to write a full report, though it is difficult to find *any* time at present, and that I will send to you in due course.[2] These are only a few preliminary observations. I said that there was little time, and indeed there has been practically none, what with going to the Stadium every afternoon and lunching and dining out every day as well. Entertainment here has been prodigious and 'organised' on an overwhelming scale. Sarita[3] and I have rarely gone to bed before two and we are leaving here to-morrow to spend the next fortnight sleeping and drinking mineral water.

I have said and done nothing here which really merited any telegraphic report (the few short telegrams that I have sent you will already have seen, and seen that there is not much in them). I have of course always said that

[1] From the Private Papers of Sir Anthony Eden, Series A.
[2] See Appendix I to this Volume.   [3] Lady Vansittart.

I was here on leave and have not gone into any detailed discussions; indeed the Germans are anyhow not yet ripe for them and have been almost entirely preoccupied by the Games, troubles within the Party, preparations for the rally at Nuremberg, and with the Spanish situation. As you will see from my general report, whenever I can find a little quiet to complete it, I think that I may have been able to help matters on a little in anticipation of the October negotiations. From a general point of view and without delving into too much detail, I have been able to say a good many frank and friendly things which may prove to be of some ultimate use, but of course I cannot tell as to that now. In any case Eric[4] and I both feel that the visit has been a success and that I was right to come. One thing at least I think has been accomplished—I have succeeded in dispelling the idea that the Foreign Office is a nest of anti-German prejudices and I hope that everyone here, and I have seen pretty well everyone, will be in future more ready to believe that the Foreign Office is manned by reasonable and open-minded people who, if they do not always see eye to eye with Germans, are at least quite honest about it and are not moved by any kind of phobia. I have established very friendly personal contacts with all those in power here and I hope this may serve us in the future.

Well, this has been very much of a busman's holiday; rather a tiring if exceedingly interesting one. Sarita and I leave for Brittany to-morrow morning. I think Léger[5] will be at our seaside place (I don't know how to spell its Breton name yet) for a bit of the time, so I expect that there will be at least a touch of the bus about that too, but the sea will do us good and we shall need it, for we both thought we had better do the thing here very thoroughly while we were about it and we accepted everything and, all things considered, are remarkably fit at the end of it.

I hope you have been getting a really good rest in Yorkshire and I shall look forward to seeing you again at the beginning of next month.

Yours ever,
VAN

P.S. I have on the whole been pretty lucky with the publicity, for there has only been so far as I know one period about the middle of my stay when the press began to work me up a bit and that I should think was very likely because the British contingent to see the Games did not amount to very much. Bobby Monsell[6] was about the only other person here who had anything to do with politics. I do not count the Rodds. Camrose and his brother only turned up here at the very end. I have seen quite a lot of the French, Belgian and Czechoslovak representatives and of King Boris who is also here. I am sure that all of them are convinced of my bona fides when I tell them that I am here only for a holiday and for friendly but general contacts.

[4] Sir E. Phipps.
[5] M. Alexis Léger, Secretary General of the French Ministry for Foreign Affairs.
[6] Viscount Monsell was First Lord of the Admiralty from November 1931 to June 1936.

No. 86

Sir E. Phipps (Berlin) to Foreign Office (Received August 13, 10.40 a.m.)
No. 263 Telegraphic: by telephone [W 8482/62/41]

Immediate   BERLIN, *August 13, 1936*

My telegram No. 262.[1]

After the Chancellor's dinner last night in honour of Sir Robert and Lady Vansittart[2] I enquired of the Minister for Foreign Affairs how the matter stood. His Excellency said that the German reply was now ready and only waiting until aeroplane incident was satisfactorily settled, i.e. aeroplane and crew who were still held captive released. The Chancellor had been infuriated by the seizure of this purely civilian aeroplane which had been immediately painted red by Spaniards. Herr Hitler naturally refused to agree to common declaration until settlement of the incident.

I remarked that I had heard a rumour about a possible rupture of diplomatic relations between Germany and Spain and His Excellency admitted that this possiblity had during the first outburst of anger crossed the Chancellor's mind but he assured me that there was now no question of it. He spontaneously observed that it would not serve any useful purpose.

Baron von Neurath then suggested that with a view to rapid issue of German reply His Majesty's Government might use whatever influence they had with Spanish Government to induce them to release the aeroplane and crew. At present they only allowed one German plane to proceed to Madrid daily for evacuation purposes instead of three or four as previously. This was most inconvenient and caused unnecessary and dangerous delay.

I replied that in the present circumstances His Majesty's Government possessed little or no influence with the Spanish Government but I promised to inform you immediately of this suggestion.

From what Baron von Neurath said I derived the impression that it is more the aeroplane incident than even previous murders of Germans that now angers the Chancellor.

Meanwhile my French colleague continues to press German Government for early reply pointing out that continued delay is making the French Government uneasy and even suspicious regarding the German motives.[3]

---

[1] No. 82.

[2] Cf. Nos. 41, note 2, and 85.

[3] In his telegram No. 264 of even date Sir E. Phipps said that he had informed his French colleague of the gist of telegram No. 263, and he had agreed that further pressure by Sir E. Phipps would be useless for the present. 'We both feel that Spanish Government, realizing that effective prohibition to export arms, etc. to Spain would hit them more than their adversaries, may well be holding up settlement of aeroplane question on purpose.'

No. 87

Sir E. Phipps (Berlin) to Foreign Office (Received August 14)
No. 211 Saving: Telegraphic [C 5871/4/18]

BERLIN, *August 13, 1936*

1. Sir Robert and Lady Vansittart left Berlin this morning after a fortnight's stay at the Embassy.[1]

2. Sir Robert Vansittart had long and most friendly meetings and conversations with all the principal members of the German Government, from the Chancellor downwards, including General Goering, Baron von Neurath, Dr. Goebbels, Herr Hess, General von Blomberg, Count Schwerin von Krosigk, Dr. Frick, etc. He also met Herr von Papen, Herr von Ribbentrop, Herr Dieckhoff and others too numerous to mention, and was entertained by most of them. Many came to a dinner that I gave on August 8th to the German Government, and to the German and British Olympic Committees. An evening party followed which was attended by over 1,000 persons, including most of the members of our Empire teams. Last night the Chancellor gave a dinner of over 160 persons in honour of Sir Robert and Lady Vansittart.[2]

3. I have felt for a long time past that Sir Robert should take advantage both of his relationship with myself and of the Olympic Games to come to Berlin in order to dispel the absurd but widely held idea in Germany that he is possessed by a blind and unreasoning hatred of that country. A fortnight's personal contact with prominent Germans has more than sufficed to prick this dangerous bubble, and to convince them that Sir Robert Vansittart is a perfectly reasonable though patriotic Englishman whose great wish is to work for general peace and understanding. The future may of course unfortunately show that goal to be unattainable, but at least we on our side will have done everything possible to lighten the atmosphere in which the important coming negotiations will take place. Numbers of people have expressed to me their deep satisfaction at the visit and at the conviction acquired thereby that the violent prejudices attributed to Sir Robert were entirely imaginary.

4. At the same time I must point out that undue optimism would be out of place. I have heard privately from reliable quarters that Sir Robert Vansittart's emphasis in his conversations with Germany's leaders on the need for something more than a Western Locarno to restore European confidence has not been well received by the German Government. The Chancellor is disposed to resist with the usual arguments all attempts to bring outsiders into the discussion between the Locarno Powers. Poland, he will say, is more than satisfied with her agreement with Germany. Czechoslovakia is free at any time to negotiate a similar understanding with that Power. Russia is not Germany's neighbour unless Czechoslovakia chooses to make her so. Nobody can foresee how Russo-Japanese relations

[1] See Nos. 41, note 2, and 85.   [2] See No. 86.

94

will develop. Russia might make such sacrifices in Asia as would ensure Japanese neutrality. Germany and Europe would then be faced with fresh dangers.

5. If the preliminary discussions show that the Locarno Powers are not really anxious to conclude a Western Locarno without an Eastern pendant there will be no conference. The Chancellor will in any case never sign an instrument which would provide for the stabilisation of the 'status quo' in Europe so long as there exists no efficient machinery at Geneva or elsewhere for the revision of treaties. He remains convinced that Great Britain and Germany together constitute a stupendous force. They have no divergent aims. Acting together they could safeguard civilization and world peace more effectively than any League or any number of pacts.

6. Sir Robert Vansittart is shortly addressing to you a detailed account of his conversations here.[3]

[3] See Appendix I to this Volume. There are brief references to the Vansittarts' visit to Berlin in Ribbentrop, *op. cit.*, pp. 94–6, and Ian Colvin, *Vansittart in Office* (London, 1965), pp. 104–11.

No. 88

Sir E. Phipps (Berlin) to Foreign Office (Received August 14)
No. 854 [C 5887/4/18]

BERLIN, *August 13, 1936*

Sir,

I have the honour to report that Field-Marshal von Blomberg,[1] who continues to enjoy Herr Hitler's confidence, and frequently echoes his opinions, expressed the following views in private conversation with the Military Attaché.[2]

2. In formulating hopes for the new Locarno conference he volunteered the opinion that, from the German point of view, it could not be held in Paris as Germany mistrusted the French co-operation with Russia. London or Brussels would be acceptable, but of the two he hoped the conference would be held in London. The Field-Marshal expressed very openly the impossibility of any co-operation between Germany and Russia.

3. Although Danzig was a German town, and would no doubt eventually come back to Germany, Herr Hitler was determined not to quarrel with Poland over so small a matter. Germany and Poland, if left to themselves, would easily settle the Danzig problem.

4. Germany still despised and distrusted Italy but felt that some co-operation with Italy could in the present circumstances be turned to Germany's advantage. The Field-Marshal hinted that if Germany were really sure of Britain's friendship it would be less necessary, or desirable, to co-operate with Italy.

I have, etc.,

ERIC PHIPPS

[1] Reich War Minister and Commander in Chief of the *Wehrmacht*.
[2] Colonel F. E. Hotblack.

No. 89

Mr. Dodd (Lisbon) to Foreign Office (Received August 14, 11.20 a.m.)
No. 136 Telegraphic [W 8634/62/41]

LISBON, *August 14, 1936, 10.38 a.m.*

My telegram No. 132.[1]

Minister for Foreign Affairs sent for French Minister and myself in succession yesterday evening and gave us . . . [2] to the following effect.

In deference to view of His Majesty's Government and French Government that a policy of non-intervention would . . . [2] the dangers feared by Portuguese Government by shortening the Spanish Civil War and avoiding international complications, the Portuguese Government adhere in principle to proposed agreement.

But in the interests of sincerity in international relations the Portuguese Government feel bound to offer the following observations.

See my immediately following telegram.[3]

[1] Not preserved in the Foreign Office archives.
[2] The text was here uncertain.
[3] No. 90 below.

No. 90

Mr. Dodd (Lisbon) to Foreign Office (Received August 14, 2.35 p.m.)
No. 137 Telegraphic [W 8645/62/41]

LISBON, *August 14, 1936, 1.12 p.m.*

My immediately preceding telegram.[1]

The agreement must be executed with inexorable rigour because incomplete execution would produce mutual suspicion and disunion in international life. The necessary guarantees of execution must be provided to prove good faith and impartiality of the Governments and in order that the results may fulfil the intentions of the signatories. Such passions have been roused in different countries that its execution will not be easy. The scope of clauses will require careful consideration in order that they may be really capable of execution.

(2) The proposed agreement principally affects manufacturing countries or countries with large stocks.

Portugal falls under neither category whether as to Government or to private firms. Thus Portugal's adhesion involves the question of transit only. If country [*sic*] of categories named carry out their obligations even the question of transit will not arise. Portuguese Government consider that it is on the sale of arms in producing countries that strictest control will be required.

(3) Portuguese Government invite particular attention to the dangers

No. 89.

inherent in the Civil War for Portugal whose situation is unique. The issue of the struggle whether one way or the other will create for Portugal responsibilities such as for no other Government. The adhesion given in principle does not diminish the freedom of Portugal to judge circumstances and to take such action as may be dictated by their duty to preserve domestic peace in Portugal, the lives, property and liberties of the people and security, integrity and independence of the country.

(4) When the text of the agreement is submitted to them the Portuguese Government reserve their right to discuss it and to offer the necessary suggestions.

(5) Portuguese Government as especially interested in events in Spain cannot refrain from inviting the attention of His Majesty's Government to conditions of extreme violence of the Civil War. In so doing Portuguese Government obey an imperious duty of conscience on the grounds of humanity, in the name of fraternal bonds uniting Portugal with Spanish peoples. It is not only the fate of Spain that is at stake. It is clear that Communist and Anarchist militias are perpetrating methods of reign of terror, destroying the sacred patrimony of Spain, public and private, the accumulated riches of many generations, in obedience to a preconceived plan. They have carried out mass assassinations with cold premeditation of persons belonging to classes considered undesirable.

(6) The Portuguese Government consider agreement should be accompanied by a declaration condemning such a process of social transformation.[2]

[2] Sir G. Mounsey wrote: 'M. Cambon tells me the French are well satisfied with this Portuguese reply. But they have not apparently even begun to examine the French draft declaration! That's where the trouble begins. G.M. 15.8.36.' French and English translations of Dr. Monteiro's statement are given in *D.A.P.E.*, *op. cit.*, No. 155.

No. 91

Sir E. Phipps (Berlin) to Foreign Office (Received August 15)
No. 214 Saving: Telegraphic [C 5919/4/18]

BERLIN, *August 14, 1936*

My telegram No. 211[1] Saving of yesterday.

I called to-day on the Minister for Foreign Affairs in order to take leave of him before proceeding to England. I took this opportunity to express to him the warm thanks of Sir Robert and Lady Vansittart, as well as my own, for all the great kindness and hospitality shown to us during their visit by the Chancellor, Baron von Neurath himself and other members of the German Government.

Baron von Neurath told me that he had, when he first heard of Sir Robert Vansittart's intention to come to Berlin, strongly approved the idea. From all he had seen during the visit he was only confirmed in his

[1] No. 87.

belief that it had been most helpful. The conviction had certainly been prevalent in many quarters in Germany that Sir Robert was violently and unreasonably Germanophobe, and that conviction had certainly, as a result of his visit, been completely dispelled. The impression left upon persons here with whom Sir Robert had conversed was that he was perfectly fair-minded and unprejudiced.

His Excellency told me that the Chancellor would go to Berchtesgaden on the evening of August 16th[2] and would make that his headquarters, apart from the duration of the Nuremberg Party meeting, until about the end of September. Baron von Neurath will join Herr Hitler at Berchtesgaden from Württemberg as occasion may require.

[2] After the conclusion on that day of the Olympic Games.

No. 92

Minute by Sir G. Mounsey of a telephone conversation with Mr. Eden
[*W 8885/62/41*]

FOREIGN OFFICE, *August 14, 1936*

The Secretary of State spoke to me on the telephone this morning[1] and asked if we were really doing all that was possible to support M. Blum's Government in their Spanish policy. The press did not seem to indicate much more than an acquiescent attitude on our part. I told him that from the first we had expressed our agreement in principle with the French Government's *démarche*, that we were in daily contact with the French Embassy and supported promptly their action at other capitals when they asked us to, and that our main difficulty was that the French clung to a form of declaration to which we could not subscribe without reserves.[2] Mr. Eden suggested that we might inspire our press to emphasize our whole-hearted support of the French attitude more vigorously.

I spoke to Mr. Warner, News Department, in this sense, and found he was just preparing the annexed minute for my consideration.[3] He will do what he can to ginger up the press, but the French proposal is hanging fire so long that the press have, I suppose, got rather tired of merely repeating that His Majesty's Government support it in principle.

You will remember that the French themselves rejected our offer to support them at Moscow,[4] and we have loyally done as much as they asked of us at Lisbon, Rome, and Berlin, but naturally hesitated to do more.

[1] Mr. Eden was still on holiday in Yorkshire. He refers briefly to this conversation in his memoirs (*op. cit.*, p. 403). He returned to the Foreign Office on Tuesday, August 18.
[2] Cf. Nos. 45, 51, 52, 54, 64, 67, and 77.
[3] Not printed. Mr. C. F. A. Warner's minute of August 14 referred to signs of a growing tendency in the press 'to criticise the Government for not playing a stronger hand in regard to non-intervention in Spain'. He found 'a general feeling [among correspondents] that things might go faster if we did not leave the lead to the French'.
[4] Cf. No. 64.

I was authorised by Lord Halifax to offer the French a general *démarche* at all the capitals concerned in which we would have called attention to the French Government's decree of August 8, prohibiting the export of arms etc., declared the extent to which we could follow suit, and stated our readiness to put our measures into force as soon as other Governments would do likewise.[5]

The French rejected this on the ground that it constituted new procedure and they preferred to continue on the lines of their draft declaration.[6]

In these circumstances I do not really see what more we can do than continue to support the French as far as we possibly can on the lines which they themselves prefer to adhere to.

The Secretary of State also wondered whether we could issue some public statement which would serve to discourage sales of aircraft or aircraft flights from this country to Spain pending the conclusion of an international agreement covering this subject. He said that, if there were any such possibility, he would like Lord Halifax consulted and shown the text of our proposed announcement.

I have asked the Department and Legal Adviser to examine this subject and, if practicable, submit a draft text. I have also sounded the Air Ministry, who do not feel that they themselves could issue any notice of this kind, and think that if the Foreign Office did so, on political grounds, it would be necessary for them to obtain Lord Swinton's concurrence before agreeing to the terms.

I rather doubt whether it will be possible to agree on a step of this sort with the Air Ministry, who are of course afraid of the criticism which will be incurred in the aircraft trade and among the flying public at being asked voluntarily to refrain from activities which are freely permitted at present in other countries.

But if an agreed draft can be concerted, it might perhaps be possible to obtain Lord Halifax's views on it by telephone.[7]

G. M.

[5] See No. 77.
[6] See *ibid.*, note 7.
[7] Sir A. Cadogan sent Sir G. Mounsey's minute to Lord Halifax with the comment: 'That seems the only thing to try for at the moment. A.C. Aug. 14 1936.' Later he forwarded the draft of a communication to the press, which had been approved by the Foreign Office Legal Adviser and the Air Ministry, and remarked: 'It is not—and cannot be—very strong: it is in the form of an appeal rather than a warning. But I understand there are no threats that we can make and no "sanctions" that in fact we could apply. Such as it is, it might be helpful and I can see no harm in issuing it.' After approval by Lord Halifax it appeared in *The Times* of August 17, p. 10. It stated that the British Government were continuing to give the fullest support to the French Government's efforts to secure agreement between the Powers to refrain entirely from all interference in the fighting in Spain. It also stated that no licences had been issued since the beginning of the present troubles in Spain for the export of arms and munitions under the Arms Export Prohibition Order of 1931.

No. 93

Record by Mr. Sargent of a conversation with M. Cambon

[*C 5917/4/18*]

FOREIGN OFFICE, *August 14, 1936*

M. Cambon told me to-day that recently the Permanent Head of the Irish Free State Department of External Affairs had raised with the French Minister in Dublin[1] the question whether the Irish Free State should not collaborate in any new mutual guarantee treaty for Western Europe. The Free State Minister remarked that his Government were somewhat anxious about the defence of Ireland in view of the growing importance of military aviation, and presumably both Great Britain and other countries (meaning France) would be anxious to prevent the Irish Free State from becoming a base of hostile air operations.

The discussion does not seem to have been carried beyond this point, but M. Cambon has now been instructed by the Quai d'Orsay to report as to whether His Majesty's Government, as the Quai d'Orsay seemed to suppose, would object to the Irish Free State participating in the contemplated new Western Agreement.

I told M. Cambon that, as far as I knew, the matter had not been raised between His Majesty's Government and the Irish Free State Government. The question had, however, occurred to me personally but it had not so far been examined and discussed. However, speaking again personally, I did not see why the possibility need be altogether excluded.[2]

O. G. SARGENT

[1] M. Pierre Guerlet.

[2] In a minute, also of August 14, Mr. Sargent referred to a memorandum on the preparations for the proposed five-power conference, earlier drafts of which had included a paragraph suggesting that the position of the Irish Free State 'would appear to require special consideration'. This paragraph had been cut out 'so as not to overweight the memorandum unduly'. It was agreed that it should be reinserted in the final version of the memorandum as number (5) of the 'fundamental questions' calling for consideration. See No. 114 below.

No. 94

Foreign Office to Sir G. Clerk (Paris)

No. 1411 [*W 8597/62/41*]

FOREIGN OFFICE, *August 14, 1936*

Sir,

I have to refer to your telegram No. 265[1] of the 14th August regarding the modified procedure which the French Government wish to adopt in connexion with the proposed declaration of non-intervention in Spain.

[1] Sir G. Clerk's telegram No. 265 of August 13 has disappeared from the appropriate file (W 8597/62/41) in the Foreign Office archives. A summary reads as follows. 'In

2. I now transmit to Your Excellency a draft of the note which you are authorised to address to the French Minister for Foreign Affairs in reply to a note from His Excellency on the lines of the draft already communicated to me by you.[2] You should show this draft reply at once to the Minister for Foreign Affairs and explain that it gives a full account of the measures which His Majesty's Government, under their existing powers, are able at once to take in this respect. It is very much hoped that the French Government will not ask for any alterations in the text, which has been carefully agreed upon here after consultation with the other Government Departments concerned. You may, however, make the following observations orally to the Minister for Foreign Affairs.

(1) It will be observed that the draft reply makes no mention of warships. The conditions under which warships may be constructed in the United Kingdom to the order of foreign governments are, of course, known to the French Government. There are at present no warships on the stocks in the United Kingdom for delivery to the Spanish Government, and arrangements have been made for a careful watch to be kept at British dockyards for any ships which may in the future be built or fitted out for use in the civil war in Spain, in order that steps may, if possible, be taken to prevent their departure.

(2) His Majesty's Government hope that every effort will be made to move the remaining principal arms manufacturing countries (Czechoslovakia, Belgium and Sweden) to undertake the measures outlined in the proposed agreement as soon as possible.[3]

ENCLOSURE IN No. 94

Draft Note from Sir G. Clerk to M. Delbos

August 14, 1936

Your Excellency,
The negotiations which have taken place between His Majesty's Government in the United Kingdom and the French Government having led to

deference to wishes of H.M. Govt. French Government now propose that declaration should take form of exchange of notes between French Foreign Minister and representatives of H.M. Govt., Italy, German[y], Soviet Union and Portugal in Paris. Draft text of letter to be addressed to Ambassadors has been sent to Sir G. Mounsey by bag. French Government suggest that British, Italian, and German reservations should be added after penultimate paragraph of draft. They urge importance of exchange of notes being effected as soon as possible, reservations of each party being left to later stage when practical means of putting declaration into effect are being settled. For this purpose they suggest formation of Committee of Representatives of Powers concerned.'

[2] See Enclosure below.

[3] The concluding salutation was omitted from the filed copy. In his despatch No. 1057 of August 15, Sir G. Clerk explained that because of illness he had asked the Minister, Mr. Lloyd Thomas, to discuss the draft text with the Quai d'Orsay that morning. M. Bargeton had asked for the reinsertion in section 1 of the words 're-exportation and transit'. After telephonic discussion the Foreign Office agreed to this. Mr. Lloyd Thomas explained why the Foreign Office had been unable to extend the prohibition to the export of warships.

an agreement on the subject of a common attitude to be observed with regard to the situation in Spain, I have the honour, in conformity with the proposal of which the other European Governments have been informed, to make to Your Excellency the following declaration:

His Majesty's Government in the United Kingdom

Deploring the tragic events which are taking place in Spain, and having decided to refrain strictly from all interference, direct or indirect, in the internal affairs of that country

Animated by the desire to avoid all complications which might prejudice the maintenance of good relations between nations

Declare as follows:

1. His Majesty's Government prohibit, so far as they are concerned, the export, direct or indirect,[4] to Spain, to the Spanish possessions or to the Spanish Zone of Morocco, of all arms, munitions and war material, including aircraft assembled or dismantled, as enumerated in the Arms Export Prohibition Order 1931, of which a copy is enclosed.[5]

2. This prohibition applies both in respect of existing and future contracts.

3. His Majesty's Government will keep the other Governments participating in this understanding informed of all measures taken by them to give effect to the present declaration.

His Majesty's Government in the United Kingdom, so far as they are concerned, will put this declaration into force as soon as the French Government, the German Government, the Italian Government, the Government of the U.S.S.R. and the Portuguese Government have also acceded to it.

As regards the question of re-exportation and transit, I have to inform Your Excellency that practical difficulties would prevent the fully effective enforcement in this country of a prohibition of the transit of munitions of war and war material through the United Kingdom or of the trans-shipment of such goods in United Kingdom ports, though His Majesty's Government are prepared to take such steps as are practicable towards this end. It does not seem, however, that the question of transit in the United Kingdom should have any serious consequences in practice, since the form of transit most likely to be of importance in this respect is presumed to be land transit across the countries contiguous with Spain. Moreover, it is presumed that this difficulty will be solved as the proposed agreement is accepted by an increasing number of Powers.

M. Bargeton did not pursue this point, although the equivalent French declaration included this prohibition. The two declarations were signed later the same day. French versions of both declarations are printed in *D.D.F.*, *op. cit.*, pp. 222–3.

[4] The words 'the re-exportation and the transit' were inserted here in the signed version: see note 3.

[5] Not printed.

No. 95

Foreign Office to Sir E. Drummond (Rome)

No. 320 Telegraphic [*W 8841/62/41*]

FOREIGN OFFICE, *August 15, 1936, 6.5 p.m.*

Your telegram No. 551.[1]

French Government state that they are meeting with considerable difficulties and delays in their negotiations with the Italian Government on this question. It would appear that the latter while ready to agree to the principle of prevention of the supply of arms and munitions to Spain consider that the questions of money subscriptions and enlistment of volunteers should be included in the proposed international agreement, and that the question of enforcing the common prohibition requires further elucidation.

French Government desire the support of His Majesty's Government in Rome in their view that the first two points should form the subject of subsequent negotiation, once the principle and text of French arms declaration have been accepted by all Powers immediately concerned, and that the third point might be met by a proposal for the establishment of an International Committee of Control.

On the latter point His Majesty's Government have as yet reached no decision, but generally speaking it may be said that all three points raised by the Italian Government are deserving of further consideration at some stage of the negotiations.

The primary objective should however be the conclusion among as many interested Powers as possible of an agreement both in principle to prevent the supply of arms to Spain and in practice to take such immediate steps as may be within their power to that end. This would be a first step, which could be followed by negotiations with a view to including any other matters such as those raised by the Italian Government in the common agreement on prohibition.

You should at once communicate with your French colleague and concert with him the lines of the further representations, which, in the light of the above explanations you should address forthwith to the Italian Government.

In making these fresh representations, you should impress on the Italian Government the increasing anxiety with which His Majesty's Government regard any delay in arriving at an immediate agreement on the lines of the French Government's proposals. They feel most strongly that it is only by the speedy conclusion of such an agreement that it may be possible to avert the disastrous international complications which may at any moment arise out of the existing troubles in Spain.[2]

---

[1] In this telegram to the Foreign Office of August 12 Sir E. Drummond reported M. de Chambrun as saying that the Italian Government had accepted the French text of a non-intervention formula subject to the request that a provision should be inserted to prevent the raising of public subscriptions or recruitment of volunteers. It had also suggested that 'some kind of international machinery for checking abuses of undertakings given would be useful'. [2] Cf. No. 39, note 1.

His Majesty's Government have therefore for their part given all possible support to the French proposals, despite the difficulties which their practical application in this country must involve and Your Excellency should express their earnest hope that the Italian Government will make every endeavour to accept them in a similar spirit.

Repeated to Paris No. 54 Saving.

No. 96

Sir G. Clerk (Paris) to Foreign Office (Received August 15, 7.20 p.m.)
No. 268 Telegraphic: by telephone [W 8770/62/41]

PARIS, *August 15, 1936*

Your telegram No. 211.[1]

Minister for Foreign Affairs and I signed and exchanged notes this afternoon.[2] Fact of signature will be published at once and German, Italian, Portuguese and Soviet Governments informed immediately but Monsieur Delbos does not propose to publish texts yet.

[1] This Foreign Office telegram of even date, telephoned to Paris at 10.20 a.m., authorized the Ambassador to tell the French Government 'that H.M. Govt. would have no objection to the exchange and publication of these notes [see No. 94] at once if the French Govt. so desire'.

[2] Cf. No. 94, note 3.

CHAPTER III

Establishment of the Non-Intervention Committee: Dr. Schacht's conversations in Paris: Moscow treason trials

August 16–September 8, 1936

No. 97

Mr. Ogilvie-Forbes (Madrid) to Foreign Office (Received August 16, 2.50 p.m.)

No. 3 Telegraphic: by telephone [W 8758/62/41]

MADRID, *August 16, 1936*

Arrived and all well at the Embassy.[1] In the event of crisis we may have to take in about 200 British subjects for whom we have plenty of food for four days which no doubt could be spun out. I shall if possible accumulate an eight days' supply. We have only drinking water for two days and I am taking immediate action to increase the supply to eight days. There are 41 non-official British subjects in residence at the Embassy who are being fed from day to day without drawing on emergency stocks. While we could put up in the Embassy above-mentioned 200 Milanes and Unwin[2] have commandeered for the Embassy building of Commercial Secretariat and a building opposite the Embassy for emergency accommodation.

I am also taking immediate steps to have roofs at Embassy and Commercial Secretariat painted with Union Jacks to avoid bombing. I cannot speak too highly of the arrangements made and the foresight shown by Mr. and Mrs. Milanes and Mr. and Mrs. Unwin. I am summoning the British Colony to a meeting this afternoon when I will address them on the subject of evacuation. Please inform Admiralty and Ambassador.

[1] See No. 75. Mr. Ogilvie-Forbes was conveyed on August 14 from Marseilles to Barcelona in H.M.S. *Douglas*, and from there to Valencia on August 15 in H.M.S. *Gypsy*. He left Valencia for Madrid on the evening of August 15 with 'a small supply of stores, together with a present for our community, subscribed for by the ship's company of H.M.S. *Repulse*, which was highly appreciated'.

[2] Mr. K. Unwin was Assistant Commercial Counsellor in H.M. Embassy at Madrid.

No. 98

Mr. Ogilvie-Forbes (Madrid) to Foreign Office (Received August 17, 9.30 a.m.)

No. 4 Telegraphic [*W 8830/62/41*]

MADRID, *August 16, 1936, 9.40 p.m.*

My telegram No. 3.[1]

I urged the British colony this evening with all the force at my command to take the opportunity to go while the going was good. I appealed both to their commonsense and their higher instincts, pointing out that if as seems most likely a siege took place the presence of every unnecessary mouth to fill was not only selfish but criminal. I described the excellent arrangements made by the Navy. I invited discussion and was told that prospect of destitution after the arrival in the United Kingdom was the deterrent.[2]

I have now organised Embassy staff to cope with any sudden emergency and to run present refugee camp.

When I have had a little more time to think it over I shall furnish appreciation of the situation in Madrid which though outwardly orderly is grim, aristocrats being hunted and killed without mercy after dark. Conductor of my sleeping car burst into tears as he described entire absence of law and order and long series of murders even of men of humble origin being perpetrated in the country districts south of Madrid. Please inform Admiralty as my communications with Barcelona are uncertain.

[1] No. 97.

[2] In his telegram No. 21 of August 19 Mr. Ogilvie-Forbes reported that he had now 'more than enough reserve of food for two hundred persons for ten days and an adequate supply of water'. He then referred to Embassy residents who refused to leave through fear of destitution, and asked to be sent a 'description as attractive as possible of their treatment on arrival in the United Kingdom'. Foreign Office telegram No. 33 of August 26 to Mr. Ogilvie-Forbes stated that 'L.C.C. have in a considerable number of cases been successful in finding employment for destitute refugees. The others have been referred to the Charity Organisation Society, who are of the greatest assistance in such circumstances.'

No. 99

Mr. Ogilvie-Forbes (Madrid) to Foreign Office (Received August 17, 5.50 p.m.)

No. 7 Telegraphic: by telephone [*W 8899/62/41*]

MADRID, *August 17, 1936*

Following is appreciation of the situation.

Part I.

The British community is all well, in good spirits and not seriously molested. The Spanish Government is most anxious to be helpful in every respect. We have no reliable information regarding military situation. The streets of Madrid which in day time are otherwise normal are patrolled by armed workers and shock police. While tramways are running there are few if any private cars. Shops and hotels are controlled either by the Government or by the Workers' Union.

Part II follows.[1]

[1] No. 100 below.

No. 100

Mr. Ogilvie-Forbes (Madrid) to Mr. Eden[1] *(Received August 18, 9.30 a.m.)*
No. 9 Telegraphic [*W 8973/62/41*]

MADRID, *August 17, 1936, 10.15 p.m.*

My telegram No. 7.[2]

Part II.

There is another side to the picture. Spanish Government has no authority and law and order is in reality non-existent. Anarchists and communists and advanced socialist elements are in *de facto* charge of the situation.

For the aristocracy and right and centre there is a reign of terror. After dark when foreigners cannot see houses are raided the occupants murdered their bodies being left on the pavement for a while and also in many cases laid to rot in a public park part of which was closed for the purpose. I am informed from various independent sources which I have been careful to check that since the outbreak of the revolution about 7,000 people have been done to death in Madrid.

A reliable British informant tells me recent letter of Spanish intellectuals in 'Times' was written at the point of the pistol and that several signatories are more or less under arrest at students' residence.[3] As a further example of recent lawlessness a train load of nearly 300 prisoners from Jaen district was stopped at a Madrid suburb and its occupants murdered by local red militia quite regardless of orders from government.

Do not take notice of two recent letters to British press one from first batch of British refugees from Madrid and another addressed to you and broadcast on August 15th in refutation. Both are exaggerated and no doubt the result of nerves.

[1] Mr. Eden returned to the Foreign Office on Tuesday, August 18.
[2] No. 99.
[3] The reference is presumably to the statement in *The Times* of August 3, 1936 (p. 10) that thirteen Spanish intellectuals had signed a manifesto stating that 'in the struggle they are on the side of the Government of the Republic and of the people who, with exemplary heroism, are fighting for liberty'. Among the signatories were Don Ramón Menéndez Pidal (President of the Spanish Academy), Dr. Ramón Pérez de Ayala (late Spanish Ambassador at London), Don José Ortega y Gasset, and others. In his telegram No. 17 of August 18 Mr. Ogilvie-Forbes said that as Señor Ayala's position was 'none too safe . . . I presume I may give him asylum in Embassy if a crisis arises'. Señor Ayala 'wishes you to know that his signature to letter in the "Times" was forged and that other signatories were threatened . . .'

I saw Minister of State yesterday.[4] He had really nothing to say but be-wailed the situation.

Please acknowledge this telegram as it is important. There is moreover a traitor in the camp who has informed censor of sense of first paragraph of my telegram No. 4[5] not that that matters.

[4] i.e. Señor Augusto Barcia, the Spanish Foreign Minister.　　　　　[5] No. 98.

No. 101

Mr. Newton (Berlin) to Mr. Eden (Received August 18, 1 p.m.)
No. 217 Saving: Telegraphic [W 8974/62/41]

BERLIN, *August 17, 1936*

My telegram No. 268.[1]

At interview with Herr Dieckhoff I informed him that His Majesty's Minister in Paris had had conversation with French Foreign Minister on August 14th.[2] Monsieur Delbos had then expressed his grave apprehension at danger of delay in concluding non-intervention agreement and his fear that if matters were allowed to drift they might end in disaster. I also mentioned that French Government were using such influences as they had to induce the Spanish Government to restore the seized aeroplane and said that His Majesty's Government had taken similar action through the Spanish Ambassador in London.[3] Herr Dieckhoff here expressed his appreciation of the support given by the French Government and also by His Majesty's Government in this matter. I went on to express the strong hope that the German Government would be willing without further delay to agree to non-intervention with, if necessary, a reservation in regard to the release of the aeroplane. The idea of such a reservation was new to Herr Dieckhoff who evidently thought it hopeful.

Speaking personally, I observed that the German Government, and notably the Chancellor, were very concerned lest Communist influence should grow in France. The *Deutsche diplomatisch-politische Korrespondenz* moreover had just published an article (see my telegram Saving No. 216[4]) deploring

[1] In this telegram of August 17 Mr. Newton reported a conversation with Herr Dieckhoff regarding the incident of the German aeroplane detained in Spain (see No. 82, note 1, and No. 86). Herr Dieckhoff said that as the crew had now been released the affair was 'half settled' and Mr. Newton urged that it should not stand in the way of German adherence to a non-intervention agreement.

[2] This conversation was reported in Paris telegram No. 266 of August 14, addressed to the Foreign Office and repeated to Berlin, not printed (W 8643/62/41).

[3] Following the receipt in the Foreign Office of Sir E. Phipps's telegram No. 265 of August 14 giving the German version of the aeroplane incident, Sir G. Mounsey had an interview the same day with Señor Oliván and informed Sir E. Phipps in Foreign Office telegram No. 174 despatched at 9.50 p.m. that the Spanish Ambassador had 'undertaken to suggest at once to his Government the advisability of releasing the machine and crew'.

[4] Of August 15 (W 8868/62/41), not printed.

Monsieur Blum's apparent helplessness in face of demonstrations in aid of the Spanish Popular Front. I pointed out that these German apprehensions supplied the strongest reason why the German Government should do what they could to strengthen Monsieur Blum's hand and assist him with regard to non-intervention. I furthermore observed that Baron von Neurath had himself mentioned in informal conversation that, if intervention took place, intervention from France would for geographical reasons be of greatest effect (see Sir E. Phipps' telegram No. 249).[5] The Madrid Government might therefore wish to prevent a declaration of non-intervention. Was it not playing into their hands to allow them to delay declaration by simple means of holding up aeroplane? Herr Dieckhoff was disposed to agree with the force of these arguments, but emphasised the importance which the Chancellor attached to the release of the German aeroplane, saying that it was for him a kind of German symbol.

[5] No. 53.

No. 102

Mr. Eden to Sir H. Chilton (Hendaye)
No. 422 [W 8253/62/41]

FOREIGN OFFICE, August 17, 1936

Sir,
    The Spanish Ambassador informed Sir George Mounsey on August 8th that he was instructed by his Government to assure His Majesty's Government that they intended to do and were doing all in their power to secure the safety of British lives and property in all parts of Spain over which they have control, and that these assurances apply equally to the security of His Majesty's Embassy and other British interests in Madrid.

I am, &c.,
ANTHONY EDEN

No. 103

Mr. Ingram (Rome) to Mr. Eden (Received August 18, 9.30 a.m.)
No. 556 Telegraphic [W 8980/62/41]

ROME, August 18, 1936, 5.15 a.m.

Your telegram No. 320.[1]
    I saw Minister for Foreign Affairs at 6.30 p.m. this evening[2] and read to him an aide-mémoire on lines of your telegram under reference.
    2. I said views of His Majesty's Government might be summed up in words 'speed' and 'half a loaf is better than no bread'. So far as I understood

[1] No. 95.   [2] i.e. August 17.

the situation French proposal represents a minimum upon which it seemed likely that quick agreement could be reached and it was the attitude of the Italian Government which now appeared to be almost the only obstacle. However desirable were the ideals of one-sided neutrality[3]—and I felt sure that His Majesty's Government were as anxious as the Italian Government to achieve this—there seemed to me to be a grave danger that in delaying action on the lesser in order to obtain fuller degree of non-intervention we might all fall between two stools and end in achieving nothing but grounds of mutual recrimination and in accentuating the very conflict of ideologies which it was the Italian Government's idea to avoid.

3. Count Ciano reiterated his old thesis regarding the necessity for moral solidarity in applying any agreement for non-intervention and the full intention of the Italian Government to work for and implement one-sided neutrality.[3] Signor Mussolini had already taken into account the difference constituted in various countries and had dropped his insistence for example on an embargo on press campaigns, public meetings, etc., but the danger of recruitment and of financial subsidies was one which seemed to him of the utmost importance. If recruiting were allowed in certain centres in Paris to be held by the Reds he would find it very difficult to prevent similar centres being opened by the Fascists abroad in various places to help the Whites.

I said that I would not enter into a discussion with him over minor points. The main thing was that we seemed to be on the eve of obtaining agreement on something. That something was better than nothing. And it seemed to me that the Italian Government were the main obstacle in achieving that something. Furthermore I begged him to take into account two aspects of the matter which were more general and which I ventured to lay before him informally and entirely personally as follows:

(a) In the first place delay at present attributed to the Italian Government was giving rise to a crop of suspicions as to the motives behind the Italian policy in this respect. I for one did not believe them because logic seemed to prove their baselessness. Nevertheless every day which the Italian Government delayed caused these suspicions to increase in volume; and I emphasized the need for mutual confidence in good intentions of those outside Spanish struggle to minimise so far as lay within their power its repercussions. I was seriously afraid that the attitude of the Italian Government was slowly undermining that confidence. His Excellency warmly repudiated these suspicions and said that he could give me most formal and categorical assurance which he begged me to transmit to my Government that neither Italian Government nor any Italian had had any dealings whatsoever with General Franco[4] nor was there any truth whatsoever in suspicions that Italy had done a deal or was contemplating dealing with Whites for the cession of Ceuta, Spanish Morocco or Balearic Islands. I told His Excellency

[3] It would appear that this phrase should read '100% neutrality' as it does in Mr. Ingram's despatch No. 925 of August 18 expanding this telegram.

[4] An exclamation mark appears in the filed copy of the telegram at this point.

that I was grateful for these assurances and would communicate them to you. At the same time I would beg him seriously to consider the point that Italian Government's delay was undoubtedly increasing suspicions in the world regarding Italy's motives.

(b) Secondly, I reminded Count Ciano that Italian Government had given His Majesty's Government categorical assurances that they were animated by a desire to collaborate in the work of peace and rehabilitation in Europe. I could not conceal from him the fear that dilatory attitude of his Government in this matter which was one of supreme importance to the peace of Europe might well give rise to doubts in the minds of even Italy's well-wishers regarding the sincerity of those assurances.

5. [*sic*] I repeated to His Excellency that my observations on the above two points were purely personal but I begged that he would make them known to Signor Mussolini.

6. Finally His Excellency said that he would at once communicate the views of His Majesty's Government to Signor Mussolini who unfortunately was away from Rome and that he could promise that they would be given serious consideration. For himself, however, he was unable to give me any answer pending consultation with the head of the Government.

Repeated to Paris No. 42.

No. 104

Mr. Ingram (Rome) to Mr. Eden (Received August 18, 6 p.m.)
No. 558 Telegraphic [W 9033/62/41]

ROME, *August 18, 1936, 2.35 p.m.*

My telegram No. 556.[1]
The French Ambassador with whom I had already concerted the line upon which I should speak with the Minister for Foreign Affairs and who had seen the latter immediately after my interview told me that he found His Excellency less insistent on the subject of money subscriptions but more categorical where enlistment of volunteers was concerned. Count Ciano, however, was incensed at Monsieur Salengro's speech[2] and at the activities of Monsieur Jouhaux.[3] My French colleague attempted to persuade him that there was therefore all the more reason for Italian Government to help Monsieur Blum by a prompt adherence to French project in the task

---

[1] No. 103.
[2] M. Roger Salengro, French Minister of the Interior, made a speech at Lille in his capacity as Mayor on August 16 to the Organisation of Public Leisure, in which he expressed the hope that the Spanish Republican Government would soon triumph over its enemies.
[3] M. Léon Jouhaux, Secretary General of the *Confédération Générale du Travail*, went to Spain on August 14 as part of a delegation appointed by the 'European Conference for the Defence of the Spanish Republic and of Peace' which had met in Paris on August 13. This conference and details of the delegation were reported to the Foreign Office in Paris telegram No. 264 Saving of August 15 (W 8894/62/41), not printed.

of keeping such persons in order and of restricting their power of doing harm. He showed Minister for Foreign Affairs the text of British reply of August 15th to the French Government,[4] a copy of which he had received from Paris and he hinted that the Italian Government reserves regarding recruitment and subscriptions might be worded in some way similar to British reserves regarding, I understood, re-exportation. (It would be helpful if I could be allowed a copy of this document.)

On the whole Count de Chambrun felt an impression had been made. While he was with Count Ciano, Signor Mussolini telephoned the latter to say that he was returning to Rome last night. The Ambassador is fairly optimistic and thinks that we may get a reply within the next thirty-six hours.

Repeated to Paris telegram No. 43.

[4] See No. 94, note 3.

No. 105

Mr. Newton (Berlin) to Mr. Eden (Received August 18, 2.50 p.m.)
No. 271 Telegraphic: by telephone [W 8984/62/41]

Immediate   BERLIN, *August 18, 1936*
My telegram No. 269.[1]

German Minister for Foreign Affairs addressed a Note[2] late last night to French Ambassador expressing readiness of German Government to prohibit export and transit of arms and munitions, aeroplanes whether entire or in parts and of warships to Spain, Spanish possessions and Spanish Zone in Morocco.

The application of prohibition is subject to two conditions (a) release of German aeroplane and (b) inclusion of all other arms-producing countries of importance.

As regards (b) French Government is asked what other Government[s] besides British Government are subscribing to the declaration.

German Government also express strong hope that participating Governments will prevent departure of volunteers.

In handing me a copy of the Note of which a translation is being sent to you by air mail tonight[3] Herr Dieckhoff said that it was proposed in agreement with French Ambassador to issue an announcement on the subject to the press this evening.

Repeated to Paris.

[1] In this telegram of August 17 Mr. Newton reported that M. François-Poncet was grateful for further strong appeal for German subscription to non-intervention agreement made by Mr. Newton to Herr Dieckhoff that day, in accordance with instructions in Foreign Office telegram No. 175 of August 15 (not printed).
[2] *D.G.F.P., op. cit.*, No. 45; *D.D.F., op. cit.*, No. 157.
[3] Not printed.

No. 106

Mr. Newton (Berlin) to Mr. Eden (Received August 18, 2.50 p.m.)
No. 272 Telegraphic: by telephone [W 8985/62/41]

BERLIN, *August 18, 1936*

My immediately preceding telegram.[1]

As regards condition (a) I again alluded to arguments which I had used yesterday to the effect that Germany might be cutting off her nose to spite her face if she remained uncompromising in regard to aeroplane question. I also said that Spanish Government seemed to have some ground for their action because pilot had admittedly first lost his way and then lost his head and also because aeroplane although used for civil flying and manned by a Lufthansa crew (who are now safely back in Germany) was a Junker machine i.e. a military type. The decypher of your telegram No. 177[2] did not reach me until after interview but I have since telephoned its substance especially point about arbitration to Herr Dieckhoff. He said German Government were aware of the position and did not indicate that the Chancellor would be likely to give way.

As regards condition (b) Herr Dieckhoff explained in reply to my enquiry that German Government had not wished to mention specific countries in their note but hoped that French Government would be able to give them a satisfactory reply without delay. Herr Dieckhoff mentioned in particular Belgium and Czechoslovakia. I asked whether United States might also be meant; he did not give me a definite answer but seemed to think America might be regarded as too far off to matter.

Repeated to Paris.

[1] No. 105.
[2] This telegram, despatched at 10 p.m. on August 17, transmitted to Mr. Newton the Spanish version of the German aeroplane incident as communicated to the Foreign Office by Señor Oliván that day; cf. No. 101, note 3.

No. 107

Sir H. Chilton (Hendaye) to Mr. Eden (Received August 18, 5.25 p.m.)
No. 196 Telegraphic [W 9037/62/41]

HENDAYE, *August 18, 1936, 4.5 p.m.*

Your telegram No. 156.[1]

Question of mediation was not raised at meeting.

It was decided amongst representatives of the eleven Powers present (United States Ambassador was instructed not to attend) that they request author-

[1] Sir H. Chilton's telegram No. 195 of August 16 had reported that the Argentine Ambassador as doyen had called a meeting of the diplomatic corps at Hendaye to discuss the possibility of mediation between the Spanish combatants 'when the time comes'. Foreign Office telegram No. 156 of August 17 authorized Sir H. Chilton to attend the meeting without expressing any opinion on any suggestions put forward at it.

isation from their respective Governments to join in an endeavour by diplomatic corps to effect an exchange of civilian prisoners in the interests of humanity. Have I your authorisation to associate myself with this *démarche*?[2]

Despatch follows.[3]

[2] Foreign Office telegram No. 157 to Hendaye of August 19 read: 'You are authorized to discuss with your colleagues possible means of giving effect to this idea. Please inform me which countries are represented in putting forward this proposal. See also my telegram No. 158 of today [No. 109 below].'

[3] Not printed.

No. 108

Mr. Newton (Berlin) to Mr. Eden (Received August 20)

No. 870 [C 5983/306/18]

BERLIN, *August 18, 1936*

Sir,

I have the honour to report that the Eleventh Olympic Games were carried out in Berlin from August 1st to August 16th.

2. It is difficult for anyone in England to understand the importance attached to these Games in Germany. No trouble or expense was spared to make them an advertisement of the National Socialist régime, both as regards the organisation of the games themselves, and the performance of the German athletes. For the last six months the press, under the direction of the Ministry of Propaganda, has been engaged in fanning public interest with descriptions of the preparations. The public were admitted to view the new stadium, and the so-called Olympic village, where the competitors were housed and which is to become a military establishment. The cost of these two groups of buildings is estimated at 54 million marks. A fresh coat of paint was given to Berlin, all hoardings were compulsorily removed and house owners overlooking the railway or the road to the stadium were obliged to decorate their windows on a uniform plan. The press published every day an order by Dr. Goebbels admonishing the people to be friendly to foreigners. Triumphal receptions at the railway stations and the Town Hall were organised for all foreign teams and thousands of people stood in the gaily flagged streets to cheer them as they passed.

3. The selection and training of the German teams was undertaken by the Reich Sport Leader and his staff with a thoroughness which commands respect. For two years the country has been combed for promising athletes, who have been coached at the expense of the State. For example, the victorious military team was selected at the beginning of 1935 and has been excused all duty ever since in order to concentrate on practice for one event. Or again, the lady who represented Germany in the figure skating was trained at public expense for the whole Summer of 1935 at the ballet school of the Munich opera. Such instances could be multiplied. In the

event these prolonged and intensive methods of training were crowned by extraordinary success. Spurred on by Herr Hitler, who attended the games every day and followed his country's fortunes with the closest attention, the German athletes gained 33 gold, 26 silver and 30 bronze medals in 129 events, thus eclipsing the United States of America[1] and all other competing nations. The British team only gained 4 gold, 7 silver and 3 bronze medals. Official recognition of outstanding achievements by German athletes was immediately given. The Commissioner for Sport, Herr von Tschammer und Osten[,] was created *Staatsrat*, a position both of honour and substantial remuneration, and six competitors in the armed forces were promoted on the day of their victories.

4. The technical organisation of the games was perfect and the vast programme was carried through without a hitch. There was only one incident. In consequence of the invasion of the field of play by spectators, the International Football Association ordered the match between Austria and Peru to be replayed 'in camera'. The Peruvians, who had won the first match, declined to accept this decision and withdrew from the Games. The German Legation and Consulate in Lima were stoned by the crowd. The matter was placed in the hands of Dr. Goebbels who persuaded the Peruvian Government that Germany was not responsible and the incident was finally closed by an offer of a match between the German and Peruvian teams.

5. From the German point of view the only fly in the ointment was the success of the American negroes, who won 7 of the 22 running and field events. The 'Angriff' in a nasty article, which caused some annoyance to the American correspondents, criticised the United States authorities for persecuting negroes at home and using them abroad to win prizes for America.

6. Taken all in all, however, the Games were an extraordinary success for Germany and for National Socialism. Dr. Goebbels with shining eyes told a member of my staff that the national spirit created by this régime was responsible for the German victories and this view is widely held. The press is already beginning to discuss preparations for German participation in the Games at Tokio.

I have, &c.,
B. C. NEWTON

[1] The United States came second with 24 gold medals.

No. 109

Mr. Eden to Sir G. Clerk (Paris)
No. 214[1] Telegraphic [W 9151/62/41]

FOREIGN OFFICE, *August 19, 1936, 6.15 p.m.*

The stories of excesses which are daily reported from Spain have led me to consider whether an appeal could not be made to the contending parties to refrain from the barbarities which are being freely practised on both sides. This appeal would be made on strictly humanitarian and cultural grounds, and for the purpose of stopping, if that be possible, methods of warfare which are inconsistent with the conscience of mankind.

Please enquire unofficially of the French Government whether they see any objection to His Majesty's Government approaching them and other Powers to this end. His Majesty's Government would suggest that the appeal should be to the effect that the public opinion of the world is being deeply shocked by the reports of repeated excesses on both sides in Spain. These excesses appear to take the form of mass shootings of prisoners and of non-combatant civilians, arbitrary executions and the infliction of reprisals.

The Powers would appeal to both sides to refrain from action which could warrant these reports and to limit their operations to what is strictly necessary for the attainment of their military objective.

Your Excellency should add that His Majesty's Government have just received information that at a meeting on August 18 of representatives of eleven Powers comprising the diplomatic corps now at Hendaye it was decided to request authorisation from their respective Governments to join in an endeavour by the diplomatic corps to effect an exchange of civilian prisoners in the interests of humanity.[2] His Majesty's Ambassador is being authorised to take part in any joint efforts which can be made with this object in view,[3] and His Majesty's Government earnestly hope that the French Ambassador may receive similar instructions.[4]

[1] No. 179 to Berlin, No. 322 to Rome, No. 6 to Madrid, No. 97 to Lisbon, No. 158 to Hendaye, No. 111 to Moscow, No. 70 to Buenos Aires, *mutatis mutandis*. On Lord Halifax's instructions of August 17 (W 9151/62/41) this telegram was drafted for Mr. Eden's consideration on the following day.

[2] See No. 107.   [3] See *ibid.*, note 2.

[4] Sir G. Clerk's telegram No. 280 Saving of August 21 reported that Mr. Lloyd Thomas had been informed that the French Government had no objection whatever to the proposal but that as they had already so much on their hands they did not feel able to undertake any further initiative themselves. They were prepared to support any *démarche* that Sir H. Chilton was authorized to make.

No. 110

Mr. Eden to Mr. Dodd (Lisbon)

No. 99 Telegraphic [*W 9060/62/41*]

FOREIGN OFFICE, *August 19, 1936, 9.20 p.m.*

Your telegram No. 144 last paragraph.[1]

You should certainly act as proposed.

The French Embassy here state that one of the alleged grounds of delay by the Portuguese Government is their requirement of an assurance that other Governments will participate in the proposed agreement. On this point your French colleague will no doubt be able to satisfy them, as the French Government have received a great number of favourable replies; and there is no need for the Portuguese Government to hesitate further on that account.

As regards the question of the recognition by the Powers of a state of belligerency raised in your telegrams Nos. 140 and 141[2] you should not only request due notice of any prior intention of the Portuguese Government to grant recognition of belligerency, but you should point out that His Majesty's Government find it extremely difficult to reconcile the Portuguese Government's request for assurances of their support in the event of an attack from the Spanish Government with the tendency now becoming apparent on the part of the Portuguese Government to throw in their lot with the rebel factions.[3]

[1] In this telegram of August 18 Mr. Dodd referred to the impatience of the French Minister at Lisbon over the procrastination of the Portuguese Government in signifying acceptance of the text of the non-intervention agreement (cf. Nos. 89 and 90). He thought it might hasten the Portuguese Government's acceptance if he were 'authorized to inform them that His Majesty's Government were beginning to share the impatience of the French Minister'.

[2] These two telegrams of August 16 recorded Mr. Dodd's conversation on August 15 with the Portuguese Foreign Minister who pointed out that all Spanish territory along the Portuguese frontier was now in rebel hands, that the Portuguese Government could not entertain relations with any régime of Communist complexion in the Peninsula, and that it was clearly in their interests that the *de facto* relations with the Spanish insurgents should be put on a footing of regularity and law. They also comprehended however that there would be considerable advantage in such recognition being granted by the interested Powers in common accord.

[3] Sir C. Wingfield, H.M. Ambassador at Lisbon, returned from leave on August 19; he spoke to M. de Sampayo, Secretary General of the Portuguese Ministry of Foreign Affairs, the same day, but was not able to see the Foreign Minister until August 21.

No. 111

Mr. Newton (Berlin) to Mr. Eden (Received August 20, 9.30 a.m.)
No. 275 Telegraphic [W 9182/62/41]

BERLIN, *August 19, 1936, 10.40 p.m.*

My immediately preceding telegram.[1]

Herr Dieckhoff told me this evening that an incident which might further complicate relations between Germany and Spain had just occurred. A German ship the 'Kamerun' had been forcibly detained by a Spanish war vessel some seven miles from the coast, examined and finally diverted from Cadiz where she wished to call, to an Italian port.

Herr Dieckhoff added that the German Government had previously informed Spanish Government that they did not recognize that Government's right to close ports not under their effective control.

[1] In Berlin telegram No. 274 of August 19 Mr. Newton reported that he had read to Herr Dieckhoff the Spanish version of the aeroplane incident (cf. No. 106, note 2) and had expressed the hope that the German Government would not place such an unimportant issue before the interests of world peace.

No. 112

Minute by Mr. Seymour on exports of civil aircraft to Spain
[W 9178/62/41]

FOREIGN OFFICE, *August 19, 1936*

This[1] was discussed by the Secretary of State and Lord Halifax and subsequently with Sir W. Fisher,[2] and the Secretary of State for Air, by telephone.

The following arrangements were approved:

The open general licence for aircraft to be withdrawn in respect of Spain. The Board of Trade are doing this.

Treasury have instructed Customs that, with the open licence withdrawn, aircraft under their own power are not to be cleared for Spain.

[1] Mr. Seymour had been conducting discussions with representatives of the Air Ministry and Customs and their legal advisers about the prohibition of exports of civil aircraft to Spain, and reported on August 18 that these had proved 'profoundly unsatisfactory'. It was agreed that the first step should be the withdrawal of the existing open licence for aircraft in respect of Spain. The Customs, however, took the view that the Act under which the Arms Export Prohibition Order of 1931 was issued only gave power to prohibit the export of certain goods; that civil aircraft flown under their own power were not goods and consequently the Order only legally applied to aircraft shipped as cargo. The ramifications of argumentation around this point are set out in a minute by Mr. Seymour of August 18 on this file.

[2] Sir Warren Fisher was Permanent Secretary to the Treasury and Head of the Civil Service.

Whether this can be enforced in practice will have to be seen by experience.[3]

The Chancellor of the Exchequer[4] need not be troubled with the matter.[5]

[3] Lord Swinton approved a statement to the press on August 20 in the following terms. 'If any pilot is convicted of making a false declaration to the Customs regarding the destination of a flight from this country the question of cancelling his pilot's licence will be immediately taken into consideration by the Air Ministry. The Air Ministry will take a serious view of any attempts to deliver aircraft directly or indirectly to Spain in evasion of the prohibition.' Mr. Seymour noted on August 20 that the 'Air Ministry have played up very well over this business'.

[4] Mr. Neville Chamberlain.

[5] Meanwhile the prohibition of the export of arms and munitions from the United Kingdom to Spain had been announced on August 19 in a press statement by the Board of Trade, with details of the categories involved: *The Times*, August 20, 1936, p. 11.

No. 113

Record by Mr. Eden of a conversation with Mr. Arthur Greenwood and others

[W 9331/62/41]

FOREIGN OFFICE, *August 19, 1936*

Mr. Greenwood and Sir Walter Citrine, accompanied by Mr. Middleton and Mr. Gillies, asked to see me this afternoon when they said that they wished to speak to me about the situation in Spain and the Government's policy towards it.[1] I replied that I was glad to see them and welcomed this opportunity for a conversation which, I thought, might be useful in clearing up some misunderstandings which seemed to exist as to the Government's position. Mr. Greenwood at once concurred, adding that he too felt that there might be some misunderstanding. The deputation would therefore be glad of anything I could tell them as to the Government's position. I replied that I would do so with complete frankness on the understanding that what was said was entirely confidential. This was agreed to.

I explained that during the last few weeks the whole effort of His Majesty's Government had been concentrated on an endeavour to secure international agreements upon a policy of 'neutrality', i.e. that the principal Powers would undertake not to supply arms to either side in Spain. I said that the initiative in this matter had originally been taken by the French Government. At this one of the deputation interjected that I was perhaps aware

[1] Mr. Greenwood asked Mr. Eden in a letter of August 18 to see him for a few minutes on the afternoon of August 19. Accompanying this was a more formal typewritten letter which said that some 'of our people are worried at what appears to them to be the inactivity of His Majesty's Government, in view of the press stories of Italian and German assistance to the insurgents in Spain . . . The conclusion which is being drawn from recent events is that the democratic Powers are again weakly capitulating to aggressive measures on the part of Mussolini and Hitler'. He explained that 'Attlee is in Russia, and I am keeping an eye on things for the Labour Party'. Arrangements for the meeting were completed by telephone.

that it was being said that the initiative had been taken by the French Government under pressure from His Majesty's Government. I replied that there was no truth whatever in this suggestion, that the initiative was entirely French and that all that we had proposed was that, instead of limiting the invitation to ourselves and the Italians, it should be extended also to the Germans and the Portuguese. The deputation at once accepted this explanation, and it seemed that they had not altogether credited the rumour to which they had given expression.[2]

I then went on to explain that, in our view, M. Blum's attitude had been the correct one and, indeed, a brave one in view of the situation in France. There was the European as well as the Spanish situation to consider. The last thing we wanted, more particularly just before entering upon a five-Power conference, was the division of Europe into blocs.[3] That had been emphasised by the *communiqué* issued after our recent London Three-Power Conference.[4] It would be a real calamity if, just after the acceptance by all concerned of the invitation to a five-Power conference, Europe was to be divided over the Spanish issue and that division further emphasised by arms being supplied to each side. Moreover, if arms were so supplied, we were convinced that the risks of the Spanish conflict spreading would be greatly increased.

I emphasised to the delegation that we had not been content with quietly following the French lead. We had in fact ourselves been active in Berlin and Rome and in Lisbon, and had several times given strong support to the efforts of the French. Finally, we had today taken steps to revoke all licences for the export of arms, including aeroplanes, to Spain.[5] We had done this in advance of an international agreement in an endeavour to further progress.

In conclusion I told the deputation of the efforts which we had initiated in the humanitarian sphere in an endeavour to attempt to put a stop to some of the barbarities which were being committed at this time by both sides in Spain.

In the course of the discussion which ensued the chief complaint of the deputation was that the effect of the so-called neutrality policy was to favour the 'rebels' against the Government, since the German and Italian Governments were supplying the rebels while we and the French were withholding supplies from the Government. This, they admitted, applied more especially to the French who were the principal suppliers of arms.

In the course of the conversation Mr. Greenwood let fall the remark that he thought it possible that the outcome of this dispute would be a Communist

---

[2] In a minute of August 19, Sir G. Mounsey underlined this point with the comment that 'it was because the French Govt. perceived from the outset the dangers involved in the Spanish outbreak that they decided to approach us with a view to non-intervention, despite the natural sympathy which a democratic Govt. must have with the troubles of another Govt. constituted on similar lines . . . we at once gave the French proposal our support & have been endeavouring in concert with them ever since to bring all other Powers into the agreement'.

[3] Cf. No. 84. [4] See No. 14, note 3. [5] See No. 112.

dictatorship in Spain. This was at once vigorously challenged by the other members of the deputation.[6]

[6] A note by Mr. Hoyer Millar of August 20 read: 'I have sent a copy to No. 10.' On Mr. Eden's instructions a reply, marked 'private and confidential', was sent on August 21 to Mr. Greenwood's letter of August 18; see note 1 above. It gave reasons why the French Government 'spontaneously took the lead in an attempt to bring the Powers together on an agreement of non-intervention', and emphasized the British Government's reasons for supporting the French initiative.

No. 114

Memorandum[1] *on preparations for the proposed Five-Power Conference*
[*C 5951/4/18*]

FOREIGN OFFICE, *August 19, 1936*

The London *communiqué* of the 23rd July,[2] referring to the proposed meeting of the five Locarno Powers, described the agenda of the proposed Conference in the following terms:

'The first business to be undertaken should ... be to negotiate a new agreement to take the place of the Rhine Pact of Locarno, and to resolve, through the collaboration of all concerned, the situation created by the German initiative of the 7th March.'

After stating that it was intended to approach the German and Italian Governments with a view to obtaining their participation in the meeting thus proposed, the *communiqué* continued as follows:

'If progress can be made at this meeting, other matters affecting European peace will necessarily come under discussion. In such circumstances, it would be natural to look forward to the widening of the area of the discussion in such a manner as to facilitate, with the collaboration of the other interested Powers, the settlement of those problems the solution of which is essential to the peace of Europe.'

[1] This memorandum was circulated as F.P. (36)9 to the Cabinet Committee on Foreign Policy at its meeting on August 25 (see No. 134 below). Preparation of the memorandum had been undertaken on Lord Halifax's instructions, and there are references to several versions having been produced and circulated before August 19. These earlier drafts have not been preserved in the Foreign Office archives. On August 14 a draft was sent to Colonel H. L. Ismay, Deputy Secretary, Committee of Imperial Defence, with the request that relevant points be considered by the 'Chiefs of Staff or other competent authorities' as a matter of urgency. It was explained to him that after receiving any instructions which the Cabinet might wish to lay down the Foreign Office hoped to be in a position to approach the other four Powers through the diplomatic channel. Colonel Ismay was further informed on August 19 that Mr. Eden had now approved the final version of the memorandum, which had to be printed urgently to be in time for the meeting of the Foreign Affairs Committee on August 25. It was hoped that the comments of the Service Departments could be received within a week. [2] See No. 14, note 3.

The primary objects of the forthcoming Conference are, therefore, (1) to negotiate a new Western Pact, and (2) to resolve the situation created by the German initiative of the 7th March; it is intended, however, that the discussion of these two problems should lead to the discussion of wider problems affecting European peace.

The present paper is a first attempt to state the facts of the situation as affecting the programme of the forthcoming Conference, and to examine the wider questions which arise therefrom.

Now that the German and Italian Governments have accepted in principle the invitations for a Five-Power Conference,[3] it is a matter of considerable urgency to put in hand the preparatory work required to clear the ground before the proposed Conference can take place. As the Secretary of State said in his speech in the House of Commons on the 27th July:

'If our invitations are accepted, then there should be an agreement in general terms on our objectives. But the methods of realising them will still require much study and consultation. Much work through the diplomatic channel will be called for before the meeting of the five Powers can take place. Many obstacles yet remain to be surmounted.'[4]

As a matter of fact, before we can embark upon any such study and consultation through the diplomatic channel it will be necessary for His Majesty's Government to decide on the general lines which they themselves would wish to follow. This will involve the examination of a variety of questions, and the formulation of certain general principles. It would seem desirable that His Majesty's Government should reach the necessary decisions without delay. Otherwise, the French and Belgian Governments may be the first to lay down general principles for the coming negotiations, and thus deprive us of the initiative which it is highly desirable that we should retain.

The probable attitude of France and Germany emerges from the review of the situation which now follows. Belgium may be expected to follow on the whole the line taken by His Majesty's Government. As regards Italy, it is difficult at present to foretell what attitude she will adopt. It will largely be governed by the extent to which when the time comes she finds herself co-operating with Germany in international affairs, and thereby bound to support German policy so long as the latter does not directly conflict with Italian vital interests.

The possible reactions of the Spanish question on relations between Germany and France and Italy are impossible to estimate at the present juncture, but may have an important influence on the Five-Power negotiations.

ELEMENTS IN THE NEGOTIATION OF THE NEW WESTERN PACT

(i) *Treaty of Locarno*

Under the Treaty of Locarno, Germany and Belgium, and Germany and France, mutually undertook 'in no case to attack or invade each other or

<hr />

[3] See Nos. 41 and 43. [4] See 315 *H.C. Deb. 5 s.*, col. 1118.

resort to war against each other'; and the five Powers collectively and severally guaranteed the frontiers of Germany and Belgium and Germany and France; and, in the event of a violation of either of these frontiers, each of the five Powers undertook to come to the immediate assistance of that one of their number whose frontier had been violated. Thus, the Treaty of Locarno comprised a non-aggression undertaking by Germany as against Belgium and France, and by Belgium and France as against Germany, and a general undertaking to assist the victim of aggression in the event of a violation by Germany of the Belgian or French frontiers or by France or Belgium of the German frontier. It did not provide for any guarantee in the event of an attack on the United Kingdom or on Italy.

(ii) *The Proposed Air Pact*

The Air Pact first proposed in the Anglo-French *communiqué* of the 3rd February, 1935,[5] and of which British, French and German drafts were subsequently elaborated, was based on a different principle. Its purpose was a guarantee by each of the five contracting Powers 'immediately to give the assistance of their air forces to whichever of them might be the victim of unprovoked aerial aggression by one of the contracting parties.' The intention was to guard against sudden attack by air by providing for immediate assistance by other parties in the event of such aerial attack: this assistance to be rendered not only to France, Belgium and Germany, but also to the two guarantor Powers of the Treaty of Locarno—the United Kingdom and Italy. In the negotiations which followed the Anglo-French proposal for an Air Pact, it was agreed that arrangements would be made to provide that these mutual assistance obligations would not apply as between the United Kingdom and Italy. Thus the important distinction between the Air Pact and the Locarno Treaty was, so far as we were concerned, the guarantee of assistance which the Air Pact would have secured for us from Germany in the event of a Belgian or French attack on the United Kingdom, and from Belgium and France in the event of a German attack.

(iii) *German Proposals of March 7*[6]

On the 7th March, 1936, the German Government proposed, 'for the purpose of ensuring the sanctity and inviolability of the boundaries in the West,' a 25-year non-aggression pact between Germany, France and Belgium; the United Kingdom and Italy were to guarantee this Treaty, and the possibility of the inclusion of the Netherlands was left open. The German Government were also ready to conclude an Air Pact, presumably on the lines proposed in February 1935, thus giving the United Kingdom, as well as the other contracting parties, guarantees against unprovoked aerial attack. Further, the German Government were ready 'to enter at once into negotiations with France and Belgium with regard to the creation of a zone demilitarized on both sides, and to agree in advance to any suggestion regarding the depth and nature thereof on the basis of full parity.'

[5] See Volume XII, No. 400, note 4.   [6] Volume XVI, No. 42, Enclosure.

(iv) *Anglo-Franco-Belgian Proposals of March 19*[7]

According to the Proposals of the 19th March, it was agreed to examine the German proposals of the 7th March, to consider the future of the Rhineland and to press during the negotiations for the limitation of fortifications in the Rhineland, and to draw up mutual assistance pacts open to all the signatories of Locarno. 'So far as concerns the Four Powers represented in London, the reinforcement of their security provided for will include, in particular, obligations of mutual assistance between Belgium, France, the United Kingdom and Italy, or any of them, with suitable provisions to ensure prompt action by the signatories in case of need as well as technical arrangements for the preparation of such measures as would ensure the effective execution of the obligations undertaken.'

(v) *German Proposals of March 31*[8]

Finally, in their memorandum of the 31st March, the German Government proposed that Germany, Belgium, France, the United Kingdom and Italy should agree 'to enter into discussions, under the leadership of the British Government, for the conclusion of a twenty-five years' non-aggression pact or security pact between France and Belgium, on the one hand, and Germany on the other'; that the United Kingdom and Italy should sign this pact as guarantors; that Germany should assume such special obligations to render military assistance as should arise out of these agreements; that there should be an Air Pact; that the Netherlands should be included in the proposed Western arrangement, if desired; and that an international Court of Arbitration should be set up to ensure the observance of the above agreements. The relevant sections of the German Proposals of the 31st March are shown in Annex I.[9]

ELEMENTS IN THE NEGOTIATION OF A SETTLEMENT TO RESOLVE THE SITUATION CREATED BY THE GERMAN INITIATIVE OF MARCH 7

All that Germany has offered so far is the reciprocal and provisional arrangement for the four months which expired on the 1st August (points 2–8 of the German Proposals of the 31st March), and the declaration in point (9) of the German Proposals of the 31st March, that the German Government 'are willing, on the basis of complete reciprocity, to agree with their two Western neighbours to any military limitation on the German Western frontier.'

On the other hand, according to our letter of the 1st April to the French and Belgian Governments,[10] we stated that, if the effort of conciliation attempted in the proposals of the 19th March should fail, His Majesty's Government

'(a) Will at once consider, in consultation with your Government and the French Government, the steps to be taken to meet the new situation thus created;

[7] Volume XVI, No. 144.   [8] See *ibid.*, No. 193, note 2.   [9] Not printed.
[10] See Volume XVI, Enclosure 2 in No. 199.

(b) Will immediately come to the assistance of your Government, in accordance with the Treaty of Locarno, in respect of any measures which shall be jointly decided upon;

(c) Will, in return for reciprocal assurances from your Government, take, in consultation with your Government, all practical measures available to His Majesty's Government for the purpose of ensuring the security of your country against unprovoked aggression;

(d) Will, for this purpose, establish or continue the contact between the General Staffs of our two countries contemplated in paragraph III(2) of the said arrangement.'

Since then we have maintained, and the French and Belgian Governments have accepted, the view that, although the German Government have rejected the proposals of the 19th March for resolving the situation created by Germany's reoccupation of the Rhineland, nevertheless, the effort of conciliation should not be considered to have failed in view of the attempt now being made to call together the Five-Power Conference.

As regards the meaning of the words 'through the collaboration of all concerned,' which appear in the *communiqué* of the 23rd July, in connection with the proposal to negotiate a new agreement to resolve the situation created by the German initiative of the 7th March, it has been explained to the German Chargé d'Affaires in London that this merely means that it is our desire that the new agreement should be negotiated by the five Powers together and not by the three, and that there was no intention of inviting more than the five Powers to carry through this particular piece of work.[11]

QUESTIONS FOR DECISION

In order that the Foreign Office may make the necessary preparations for the forthcoming conference, it will be necessary for us to be clear with regard to the general line of policy which we wish to adopt in respect of the various questions which are bound to arise. The more important of these questions are enumerated below. From the preliminary explanatory comments attached to each of these questions it will be seen that at least eight, viz., questions 4, 5, 6, 7, 9, 10, 11 and 12, require examination by the Committee of Imperial Defence, and steps are being taken to refer these points to the Committee. As soon as a general line of policy has been settled, the Foreign Office will be in a position to take the initiative with the other Governments concerned, probably by communicating to them, for their consideration, a memorandum regarding the various questions at issue. It is hoped that in this way London may become a kind of clearing house for the purpose of these preliminary discussions, and that the other Governments concerned may agree to communicate their views to us in the first instance for co-ordination and circulation.

It seems as yet premature to endeavour to make any arrangements regarding the time and place of the proposed conference. These matters

[11] See No. 15.

of detail will have to be left until the preparatory discussions through the diplomatic channel have reached an advanced stage.

The following are the fundamental questions which now seem to call for consideration:

(1) Should the new agreement simply reproduce the old Locarno Treaty, with the omission of all reference to the Demilitarised Zone?

Comments. To judge by the language of the German proposals of the 31st March, it looks as though Germany wishes to reproduce the framework of the Locarno Treaty (i.e., non-aggression pact between Germany and France and Belgium, guaranteed by Great Britain and Italy), but it is equally probable that she will be opposed in the new agreement to the machinery provided for in the old Locarno Treaty (i.e., the rôle of the League Council in deciding aggression). She may even object to the renewal of the arbitration treaties with France and Belgium, at any rate in their present form, since they provide for the use of the Permanent Court of International Justice. We, on the other hand, would be in favour of altering the framework of the old agreement (as shown in the comments on the ensuing questions), and would prefer to preserve its machinery both as regards the Council of the League and the arbitration conventions (though it would not seem essential for us to insist on the use of the Permanent Court of International Justice if some other suitable tribunal were suggested as an alternative).

(2) What machinery should the new agreement contain for bringing the guarantees into operation? Should the League be employed for this purpose in the same way as in the old Locarno Treaty?

Comments. In the new agreement there must clearly be some authority to decide if and when an act of unprovoked aggression has been committed. To judge from Germany's proposals of the 31st March, this authority is to be the new international court of arbitration mentioned below, under Question (3), and would thus replace the League Council which fulfils this rôle under the old Locarno Treaty. It is a moot question whether it would be possible for us to agree to the League Council being deposed in this fashion. In any case, the proposal to create a new court will again raise the question put in paragraph 11 of our Questionnaire (Annex II).[12]

There is also the case of a flagrant violation to be considered. We would have presumably to resist any attempt by Germany to argue that, in such a case, no assistance could be given to the victim of aggression until the new 'international court of arbitration' had given its verdict.

(3) Should the new agreement contain provisions for arbitration and conciliation as does the old Locarno Treaty?

Comments. The old Locarno Treaty contained arbitration conventions between Germany and (1) Belgium, (2) France, (3) Poland, (4) Czechoslovakia. It is probable that Germany would refuse to discuss at the Five-Power Conference the renewal of (3) and (4), since this would at once bring

[12] Not printed: see Volume XVI, No. 307.

Czechoslovakia and Poland into the Conference. On the other hand, France will probably insist on such a renewal. The best line might be to endeavour to secure our aims through the acceptance of Herr Hitler's offer to conclude agreements by direct negotiation with all Germany's neighbours, instead of as part of the Western Pact. As regards (1) and (2), Germany will probably agree to renewal on condition, to quote the German proposals of the 31st March, that provision is made for the 'constitution of an international court of arbitration which shall have competence in respect of the observance of the various agreements concluded.'

(4) Do we wish in the new agreement to be guaranteed ourselves instead of being merely a guarantor? If so, against whom and by whom are we to be guaranteed?

Comments. We presumably wish in the new agreement to be guaranteed by France and possibly Belgium (and this would, for the sake of equality, involve equally a guarantee by Germany). But the fact of our being a guaranteed Power as well as a guarantor would involve considerable modification in the scheme of the old Locarno Treaty. Among other things, if we were to enjoy the advantages of guarantees, we should probably be required to conclude non-aggression pacts and arbitration treaties with France, Belgium and Germany.

The C.I.D. are being asked to consider the implications of our acceptance of a guarantee from France, Belgium and Germany.

(5) Should the Irish Free State participate in the new agreement?[13]

Comments. The position of the Irish Free State would appear to require special consideration. The Dominions are not parties to Locarno, but in view of the growing importance of military aviation the Irish Free State, on account of its geographical position, may be concerned in the new Western Pact. The counsellor of the French Embassy in London has, in fact, informed the Foreign Office that the Permanent Head of the Irish Free State Department for External Affairs has recently raised with the French Minister in Dublin the question of the Free State's collaboration in any new mutual guarantee treaty for Western Europe.

This question is being referred to the C.I.D.

(6) Is Italy to be guaranteed? If so, against whom and by whom?

Comments. Under the old Locarno Treaty we and Italy were the two guarantor Powers. If now we become a guaranteed Power it would be difficult to refuse the same advantage to Italy if she asked for it. But it may be taken for granted that in no circumstances would we or Belgium be prepared to guarantee Italy, so that in effect Italy would only be guaranteed by France against Germany, and by Germany against France. Whether France would undertake this obligation without our co-operation is a doubtful point. The whole of this question is being referred to the C.I.D.

[13] Cf. No. 93, note 2.

(7) Should Belgium be relieved of giving any guarantee and her commitments limited to an undertaking to defend her own territory?

Comments. Recent unofficial hints show that in certain quarters in Belgium there is a desire that Belgium should be relieved of the duty of guarantor in any new agreement. This feeling is prevalent in Flemish circles, and it is probably due to the fact that as long as Belgium guarantees France, the French General Staff are inclined to make plans whereby in Flemish eyes the Belgian Army is relegated to the position of fighting with the French Army in defence of French territory rather than in defence of Belgian territory. Incidentally, the old Franco-Belgian Military Agreement was terminated some months ago because it had become for these reasons unpopular in Belgium, and at present there exists only an exchange of notes providing for a restricted form of staff conversations.

It would have to be clearly understood that Belgium, if she only undertook to defend her own territory, would not be at liberty tacitly to allow foreign aircraft to cross her territory to attack a third Power.

From our point of view this question is one on which the advice of the C.I.D. is being sought in the first instance.[14]

(8) Are the non-aggression provisions to be so framed (as Locarno was) as to reserve the right of any party to come to the assistance of a non-party which has been attacked by another party?

Comments. It would seem essential that the new agreement should be so worded. We must therefore be careful to resist any attempt by Germany to interpret our guarantee as imposing upon us an obligation to use force against France in the event of her implementing her obligations to come to the assistance of her Eastern allies against Germany. Our guarantee did not have this effect in the old agreement, and it would not seem desirable that it should have it in the new agreement.

Germany might argue that in the new agreement the non-aggression provisions should be modified on the ground that the situation had been entirely altered by the conclusion of the Franco-Soviet Pact. In fact, Germany might take the following line. Although ready to acquiesce in the continuance of the Franco-Czech and Franco-Polish Agreements, since these were already in existence when the Locarno Treaty was concluded, she must insist, before concluding a new Western Mutual Assistance Pact, that France shall modify her recent Pact with Russia, since in its present form it has completely altered the balance of power to Germany's detriment. Germany might, for instance, demand that the provision should be eliminated whereby France has to come to Russia's assistance in the case of a flagrant violation without waiting for any decision by the League Council or any other body. Her argument in such a case might be that, so long as there was a possibility of such an attack by France on Germany, Germany might have, in self-defence, to take the initiative, and that Germany could not agree

[14] For the background to Belgian foreign policy at this time, see D. O. Kieft, *Belgium's Return to Neutrality* (Oxford, 1972), especially pp. 49–54 and Chapter III.

that in such circumstances the British guarantee under the new Western Pact should operate in France's favour.

As regards our position, it would clearly be useless to expect the French, and more especially the present Government of France, to modify and still less to give up their pact with Russia. It would seem equally useless to try to persuade the Germans to adhere to the Franco-Soviet Pact, for, although that pact is open to their adherence, neither the German nor the Polish Governments could reasonably be expected to welcome the idea that Russian troops should march across their territories to Germany's aid to repulse French aggression. If, therefore, we have to rule out (1) the possibility of securing the cancellation or modification of the pact, and (2) the possibility of turning it into a mutual assistance pact for Eastern Europe (with German participation), the question remains whether the present Franco-Soviet Pact can in any way be clarified to meet any reasonable objections which the German Government may put forward, more particularly with regard to the case where France and Russia claim the power to act without a League decision. The real safeguard in such cases is, of course, to be found in the fact that if France were to attack Germany in what the other parties to the Western Pact considered to be unjustifiable circumstances, the latter would have to intervene against France. This fact might possibly be reinforced in some way during the negotiations.

(9) Do we wish to make special provision in the new agreement for air attack?

Comments. So long as the Locarno Treaty existed it was quite reasonable to supplement it by a special air pact providing for mutual guarantees against air attack. But now that a new agreement is to be made, it is natural that provisions for dealing with air attack should be embodied in this new agreement. The old Locarno Treaty provided for immediate assistance (without waiting for a finding by the Council) in a case of unprovoked aggression where by reason of the crossing of the frontier, or the outbreak of hostilities, immediate action was necessary. It would seem that all that is necessary is that in the new agreement this definition should be extended so as to cover the case of attack by air, especially by bombing. The C.I.D. are being asked to consider this point.

(10) Do we wish to make special provision in the new agreement for air limitation?

Comments. The proposed air pact was always linked up with the proposal for an agreement for air limitation. It will have to be considered, in the first place by the C.I.D., whether we ought to continue in the forthcoming negotiations to press for the latter. If we do it will at once raise the problem of the Russian air force and bring us back to the question put to the Germans in paragraph 9 of our questionnaire (Annex II).[12]

(11) In view of the fact that our present liberty to hold Staff conversations with France and Belgium, without any corresponding conversations

with Germany, derives from Germany's repudiation of Locarno, and will not necessarily continue if Locarno is replaced by a fresh agreement with Germany, do we wish in the new agreement to provide for Staff conversations with France and Belgium?

Comments. The views of the C.I.D. are being obtained as to the value they attach to the continuance of the Staff conversations initiated last March, and as to whether they would like them to be repeated and their scope extended. (In this connexion the question has been raised as to whether they might not be limited to Belgium alone—see Annex III).[15] The German Government will probably try and stipulate for no Staff conversations of any kind under the new agreement. In any case they will certainly insist that if there are to be any such conversations they shall take place between all the signatories. The C.I.D. are being asked to advise how far such a stipulation would in practice render Staff conversations between ourselves and the French and Belgians valueless.

(12) Should Holland be asked to accede to the new agreement? If so, should she assume all the obligations of the agreement or only certain obligations?

Comments. There has been a good deal of discussion on this subject by the C.I.D. with special reference to the proposed Air Pact. The latest views of the Chiefs of Staff are that the advantages and disadvantages of the inclusion of Holland in an Air Pact would be about even, and that, if Holland should desire to be included in a future treaty, her wish should not be opposed.[16] Nevertheless, the Chiefs of Staff have pointed out that, as Holland in her present undefended condition is merely a temptation, we should be unwise to encourage her to become a member of an air convention unless she undertakes to take all possible measures for her own defence. (There is now evidence that she is taking certain measures to this end.)

The time has now come when we will have definitely to make up our minds whether or not we want Holland to accede to the proposed new Western Pact of Mutual Assistance, and, if we do, how best she ought to be approached. As regards the part she might play, it is probable that for much the same reasons as Belgium she would prefer not to give any guarantee beyond that of undertaking to defend her own territory. The C.I.D. are being asked whether it would be worth while our giving her a guarantee if this is all we got in exchange. (As in the case of Belgium it would have to be understood that Holland was not at liberty to acquiesce in the flight of foreign aircraft over her territory to attack a third Power.)

(13) In guaranteeing the integrity of Belgium are we prepared in all circumstances to guarantee her against all attempts by Germany to recover Eupen and Malmédy? If not, should we, before guaranteeing Belgium,

---

[15] Not printed here: this document is printed in Volume XVI, No. 353.
[16] Cf. Volume XV, Nos. 304 and 522.

require from Germany a specific assurance that for the duration of the treaty she will not raise the question of Eupen and Malmédy?

Comments. The German Government have recently, as shown in Annex IV,[17] made it clear to the Belgian Government that 'there could be no question of the German Government considering Eupen and Malmédy as permanently settled.' In these circumstances, and in view of the likelihood that the Germans will maintain troops and construct fortifications in the Rhineland opposite the Belgian frontier, the danger of a German attempt to recover those provinces will obviously be greater in future than it was when the Locarno Treaty was negotiated. The main danger, so far as this country is concerned, is that Germany might attempt a surprise occupation of Eupen and Malmédy with the assistance of the German inhabitants of that area, at the same time making it clear that there was no intention to threaten Belgian independence or integrity as existing before 1914. Such a *coup* would bring the British guarantee into play in respect of territory which does not from some points of view fall into quite the same category as the rest of Belgium.

It would seem essential that Germany should undertake as part of the new treaty some non-aggression obligation in regard to the existing frontier, and this would imply an undertaking that she would not use force to settle her claim to Eupen and Malmédy. It would, however, appear undesirable to ask Germany not to raise her claim by peaceful methods, for such a request might meet with a German refusal, and this refusal might prejudice the chances of obtaining a new European settlement on what is, to some extent, a minor point.

It would be easier to expect Germany not to use force to settle her claim if it were possible to strengthen the machinery for the peaceful revision of international disputes, i.e., if Article 19 of the Covenant could be made to function.

(14) Should the provisions for 'resolving through the collaboration of all concerned the situation created by the German initiative of the 7th March' form part of the new agreement for mutual assistance?

Comments. Germany is almost certain to refuse to allow any such provisions to figure in the Five-Power Agreement. In view of the unlikelihood of any agreement being reached on this subject, it will probably be better to keep the two subjects separate; but, in that case, the question will arise as to the relationship between negotiations for resolving the situation created by the German initiative of the 7th March, and the negotiations for the conclusion of the new agreement for mutual assistance. The French and Belgian Governments will probably argue that they are inter-dependent,

---

[17] Not printed. It gave the text of a despatch from Sir E. Phipps (No. 1266 of December 4, 1935) reporting that in October 1935 Herr Hitler had told the then Belgian Ambassador in Berlin, Count Kerchove, that he could not undertake to make a statement, as suggested by the Belgian Government, that 'Germany had no territorial claims upon Belgium and that the question of Eupen and Malmédy might be considered to be definitely settled'.

and may even ask that the negotiations regarding the German initiative shall precede any negotiations for a new Five-Power Pact. While having perhaps to agree to the two negotiations being carried on concurrently, we will presumably insist that a breakdown in one negotiation shall not affect or delay progress in the other.

(15) If there is a breakdown in the negotiations for 'resolving through the collaboration of all concerned the situation created by the German initiative of the 7th March,' shall we recognise that the effort of conciliation, referred to in our Letter of the 1st April, has failed, and that, therefore, the provisions of the above Letter shall be brought into force?

Comments. We would presumably strongly resist such a view, unless and until the concurrent negotiations for the new agreement of mutual assistance had equally failed.

(16) How far ought we to support France and Belgium in trying to obtain concessions from Germany by way of resolving 'through the collaboration of all concerned the situation created by the German initiative of the 7th March?'

Comments. Our view during the March conversations was that as regards the reoccupation of the Rhineland by German troops France and Belgium had received adequate compensation by our agreeing to Staff conversations, and by our giving them the Letter of the 1st April. Even so, France may still wish to stipulate that German troops shall continue to be limited in number and withdrawn from the actual frontier, on the lines of Germany's provisional offer. Germany would certainly not agree to this unless France was prepared to give corresponding undertakings as regards her own troops on her own territory. Although it appears unlikely that important results could be achieved through such negotiations regarding the number of troops near the frontier, the French Government might be pressed to explore the possibilities of a settlement on these lines.

As regards the refortification of the Rhineland, France and Belgium have not yet received any compensation. At the Geneva meeting on the 10th April[18] the idea was that such compensation should be obtained through Germany giving satisfactory undertakings with regard to France's allies in the East. This was the origin, in our questionnaire (Annex II[12]), of paragraphs 6, 7, and 8 regarding genuine treaties, and paragraph 10 regarding the nature of the non-aggression pacts which Germany was prepared to conclude in the East. The French will certainly raise again the question of fortifications. Germany, from what she has said, will refuse to give any one-sided undertaking in this matter and France obviously cannot discuss the destruction of her existing fortifications along the frontier. Also it is doubtful whether, in the place of any limitation as to fortifications, Germany would be ready to give France any undertakings which France would consider satisfactory regarding her Eastern allies. Thus the task of resolving the

[18] See Volume XVI, Nos. 231 and 234.

German initiative of the 7th March is likely to prove one of the crucial points in any negotiations, and we shall probably have to make it clear to the French and Belgian Governments that we will not allow a breakdown to occur on this point, and that they will have to content themselves with whatever satisfaction they can get out of our renewed guarantee of French and Belgian territory and out of any further bilateral agreements which Germany may make in the East.

(17) In the invitation it is stated that, 'if progress can be made under this head (i.e., the conclusion of a Western Agreement for Mutual Assistance and the resolution of the situation created by the German initiative of the 7th March), other matters will naturally come under discussion . . . in such a manner as to facilitate . . . the settlement of those problems the solution of which is essential to the peace of Europe.' If such an extension occurs in the field of discussion, what do we propose to work for in the further negotiations contemplated?

Comments. This question is likely to be put to us at an early stage by both France and Germany, and for diametrically opposed reasons. Germany will doubtless urge that a general settlement of Europe will be fully attained if the Conference concludes a Western Pact for Mutual Assistance. Germany may be expected to resist any attempt by France and ourselves to interfere in any further bilateral arrangements which she may be prepared to make with her Eastern neighbours, and, above all, Germany may be expected to refuse flatly to conclude any arrangement at all with Russia. France, on the other hand, may be expected to urge that, unless Germany gives guarantees satisfactory to France as regards not only her Eastern neighbours, but also and particularly as regards Russia, there can be no general settlement, and that thus the 'effort of conciliation' will have failed, thereby bringing the terms of the Letter of the 1st April into force.

This conflict of policy is likely to prove another crucial point in the negotiations and may well come to a head at a very early stage, that is to say, before 'progress has been made' with regard to the Western Pact and the settlement of the situation created by the German initiative of the 7th March. Generally speaking, it may be said that a Western Pact, unaccompanied by any general settlement, would be merely a poultice applied to one of the few parts of Europe which at present are not inflamed. As such, a Western agreement in isolation might be actually dangerous, since it would create in the West a false sense of security, while giving to Russia and to the lesser Powers of the East and Centre the feeling that they had been abandoned to their fate. In these circumstances it ought presumably to be our policy from the outset to make it clear that we decline to disinterest ourselves in the East, and that we intend to insist on the need for a general settlement, while at the same time urging France not to wreck a Western agreement, and indeed a general settlement, by maintaining impossible demands in the East.

(18) Although our invitation does not mention Germany's return to the

League, ought it to be raised during the diplomatic consultations in preparation for the Conference?

Comments. The course of negotiations will probably be such that Germany's relations with the League will inevitably have to be taken into account. It is important to note that the negotiations with Germany regarding the proposed Western Pact are closely interlocked with the discussions regarding the reform of the League, and more especially with the possibility of making some use hereafter of article 19, so as to enable treaties to be revised by peaceful means. Germany may reasonably argue that before she can implement her offer to return to the League she must know what League she is expected to return to. In these circumstances it might be worth while to explore the ground in order to discover whether it is feasible that Germany should be invited to take part in any committee which may be set up in Geneva to consider the reform of the League, so as to deprive her of the excuse that she was being expected to return to a ready-made League in the reform of which she had no voice or say.[19]

CONCLUSIONS

In the light of the above review of the situation, the following tentative conclusions are submitted. They are not intended to represent in any way a definite policy, but merely to give general indications of the direction along which His Majesty's Government should proceed during the exchange of views which it is intended to carry on through the diplomatic channel in preparation for the Conference itself.

New Western Pact

A. While not excluding altogether the possibility of accepting Germany's proposed new 'international court of arbitration,' we should prefer to use the League Council, as in the Locarno Treaty, to decide if and when an aggression has taken place. (Questions 1 and 2 above.)

B. As regards the Locarno Treaties of Arbitration, we should press for their renewal in the same form as in the Locarno Treaty; subject if necessary to provision being made for Germany's new 'international court of arbitration.' If Germany objects to the treaties with Poland and Czechoslovakia forming part of the Western Pact, we should try to secure our purpose by making use of the German offer to conclude bilateral agreements by direct negotiation with Germany's neighbours. (Questions 1 and 3 above.)

C. We should want in the new treaty to be both a guaranteed and a guarantor Power. But we should not wish either to guarantee or be guaranteed by Italy. (Questions 4 and 6 above.)

D. Subject to the views of the C.I.D., we should be prepared to consider a request by Belgium that she should not be a guarantor Power, but should merely give an undertaking to defend her own territory. (Question 7 above.)

[19] Cf. Volume XVI, Nos. 324 and 395, note 5.

E. We should resist any attempt by Germany to interpret our guarantee as compelling us to use force against France if she implemented her obligation to come to the assistance of her Eastern Allies. Similarly, we should give Germany no encouragement if she asks that France should cancel or modify her treaty with Russia. On the other hand, the implications of this treaty might be further clarified so as to reassure Germany. (Question 8 above.)

F. Subject to the views of the C.I.D., special provision should be made in the new treaty for attack by air. (Question 9 above.)

G. Subject to the views of the C.I.D., we should explore the possibility of an agreement for air limitation, bearing in mind, however, that the strength of the Russian air force is a factor which complicates the problem of securing an air limitation agreement between the Western European Powers. (Question 10 above.)

H. Subject to the views of the C.I.D., it is contemplated that Staff conversations should be provided for as part of the agreement, even though such conversations would have to take place with Germany also. (Question 11 above.)

I. Subject to the views of the C.I.D., we should be ready to consider the accession of Holland to the new Western Pact. If agreed to, the method of approaching her should in due course be discussed with the other Governments concerned. (Question 12 above.)

Negotiations to resolve the Situation created by the German Initiative of March 7

J. These negotiations might, if the French insist, be carried on concurrently with those for the new Western Pact, but a breakdown in one negotiation ought not to affect or delay progress in the other. (Question 14 above.)

K. Unless and until the negotiations for a new Western Pact have failed we should resist the view that a breakdown in the negotiations regarding the situation created by the German initiative of the 7th March must represent a failure of the 'effort of conciliation' mentioned in our letter of the 1st April, and thus bring the provisions of the above letter into force. (Question 15 above.)

L. If Germany refuses to make any concessions by way of resolving the situation created by the German initiative of the 7th March, we should urge France and Belgium to content themselves with whatever satisfaction they can get out of our renewed guarantee of French and Belgian territory and out of any further bilateral agreements which Germany may make in the East. (Question 16 above.)

General Settlement

M. We should decline to disinterest ourselves from the East and Centre of Europe and continue to insist on the need for a general settlement, while urging France not to wreck a Western settlement by maintaining impossible demands in the East and Centre. (Question 17 above.)

N. Since the question of Germany's relations with the League must react on the course of the negotiations, we ought to consider whether it would be feasible for Germany to be invited to take part in any committee which may be set up in Geneva to consider the reform of the League. (Question 18 above.)

No. 115

Note[1] by Mr. Eden

[*W 9885/9549/41*]

FOREIGN OFFICE, *August 19, 1936*

I circulate to the Foreign Policy Committee of the Cabinet a memorandum[2] drawn up in the Foreign Office on the question of Italian foreign policy in the Spanish civil war.

A. E.

Memorandum on Italian Foreign Policy in the Spanish Civil War

Italy is the only Great Power lying wholly inside the Mediterranean Basin and it is commonplace in Italian political thought that her future depends upon the relative degree of sea and air power which she can exercise there as compared with other nations. The most important limitation upon her exercise of military force (in the wide sense of the word) is the fact that of the three gates of the Mediterranean one, namely, the Dardanelles, is commanded by Turkey and the other two, namely, Suez and Gibraltar, by ourselves. These circumstances had a relatively small influence upon Italy's policy during the early period of her career as an independent nation, during which she cheerfully acquiesced in a situation which left her in a military sense at our mercy: the Great War and the Treaty of London, however, gave a powerful impulse to her ambitions which the disillusionment of the Peace Settlement did nothing to diminish. In 1922 Mussolini came into power and from this moment onwards the efforts of Italy to assert herself in one way and another rise in a steady crescendo marked, among other things, by the Fiume incident, the Corfu incident, the acquisition and fortification of the Dodecanese and the construction of a first-class military base in the Island of Leros; and terminating in the Abyssinian expedition which, we are now told, had been the subject of Mussolini's dreams for fourteen years. In parallel with these events which are matters of common knowledge an intensely active campaign of intrigue of an anti-British character has been conducted by the Italians in North Africa, Egypt, India, Arabia, Persia, Anatolia, Bulgaria, Albania and elsewhere.

[1] Circulated to the Cabinet Committee on Foreign Policy as F.P.(36)10.
[2] By Mr. O. St. C. O'Malley, Head of the Southern Department of the Foreign Office.

Taking all this into consideration we can hardly avoid the supposition that Italy will regard disturbances in Spain not only as a struggle between Fascism and Communism, but also and primarily as a field in which, by the exercise of activities in line with the policy sketched above, she might find herself at once able to strengthen her own influence and to weaken British sea power in the Western Mediterranean. Several recent Cabinet Papers on the British position in the Mediterranean make it clear that this is a supposition which should give rise to the deepest misgivings. The question is what steps, if any, can be taken to forestall the inconveniences and dangers which its realisation would open up, and the Chiefs of Staff have been requested to consider to what extent British interests would be affected and what action they advise His Majesty's Government should take in case Italy should by some means or another upset the existing balance in the Western Mediterranean.[3]

It will be recalled that towards the end of the Abyssinian affair, the Government were reproached not only by the Opposition but by the Italian Government for not having made it initially plain how strongly opposed we were to the conquest of Abyssinia by Italy. Though this reproach is unmerited, it may well be that Mussolini did not in fact properly understand the strength of our objections to his policy, and was not, unfortunately, sufficiently convinced that we meant what we said. Is it not possible that Mussolini might be tempted to take certain steps in the Western Mediterranean calculated to 'upset the balance' there against which we should be obliged to react even more strongly than we reacted against his Abyssinian policy—steps to which it would be quite impossible for us to reconcile ourselves? And if all this be even possible, is there not now an even stronger case than there was in the spring of 1935 for making it publicly plain that there are certain courses which, taken by Italy in the Western Mediterranean, might prove the source of deep and enduring antagonism with ourselves?

The expedients open to Mussolini for securing an advantage initially political but ultimately strategic in the Western Mediterranean are numerous. If a Communist Government is established intense animosity against Italy may prevail in Spain: Italians may be murdered, and the Italian Government might seize a Spanish island as security for reparation. Even if General Franco is successful his position may temporarily be very weak and he might be tempted to enter into specially intimate political relations with Italy in return for, say, military supplies or technical assistance. If the Communists are successful on the mainland and General Franco's party maintains itself for the moment in Morocco, protracted hostilities must be expected in which the latter will be particularly glad to seize any hand held out to him—at any price. Whichever party is successful, it is to be feared that the quiescence of Spain—as hitherto—in international affairs will cease, and that she will continue to be what she has now become—a focus for foreign propaganda and intrigue. It is obviously impossible as

[3] See No. 126 below.

137

yet to foresee in what manner, at what point, or by what stages the 'existing balance in the Western Mediterranean' might be threatened; but if the risk exists and we are to take any overt steps to forestall the implied danger to ourselves, it is clear that it will be better to give soon rather than late some indefinite but authoritative indication of what we consider to be the British interest in this part of the world.

The French interest is clearly the safety of their African communications, which depend in part on British sea power. There should, therefore, be no insuperable difficulty in securing French action in parallel with ours. It is difficult to suggest any useful action of the kind indicated which we could take in the near future other than a public statement by the Prime Minister or myself[4] which, though discreetly worded, would be universally understood to be a warning by this country to others that we could not remain indifferent to any alteration in the balance of sea and air power in the Western Mediterranean, which was due, not to the action of Spain within her own jurisdiction (a matter which it is not open to us to question), but to the action of some other Power which had taken advantage of civil war in Spain to enter into some kind of special relationship with either side. If the idea of making such a statement were entertained, it would be important that we should make it before Italy had committed herself to any arrangement which was objectionable from our point of view. Prevention in a case like this would have much better prospects of being successful than cure.

Whatever form be taken by the agreement for non-intervention which we are trying to achieve, it may presently become desirable that the origin, scope and purpose of such an international agreement should be briefly explained by some member of the Government in a public speech; and, in the course of doing so, an opportunity would be presented of indicating the kind of developments in the Western Mediterranean which would hardly be tolerable for us. If the Italian Government do join in this agreement, and we have reason to think they will act up to their professions, this indication might be made in comparatively gentle terms. If on the other hand, they decided to stand out or we had grounds for thinking that their professions were disingenuous, more emphasis could be lent to it. In any case, it seems not too soon to consider formulæ which we might use in either event.

It is, of course, necessary to bear in mind the necessity for not unduly antagonising Italy (or Germany) at this stage, when we are looking forward to a five-Power meeting at which their co-operation will be essential. But it should be possible to make some declaration, the sense of which will be clear enough, while its wording can give no legitimate cause of complaint or offence to any individual Government. For that purpose it might be sufficient to use even so simple and vague a formula as:

'Any alteration of the status quo in the Western Mediterranean must be a matter of the closest concern to His Majesty's Government.'[5]

[4] i.e. Mr. Eden.
[5] In minutes of August 15 Mr. Sargent and Sir G. Mounsey both supported the proposal

for a declaration of Great Britain's vital interests in the Western Mediterranean at the right moment. Sir G. Mounsey recalled that he had suggested at an earlier stage that 'our support of the French *démarche* in other capitals might include an intimation that our participation in this proposed common policy must be conditioned by the maintenance of the existing balance of power in the Western Mediterranean'. On August 17, however, Sir A. Cadogan doubted whether the declaration should be made 'in present circumstances, and we should be better advised to await some development that may not be long in coming'. At the meeting of the Foreign Policy Committee on August 25, with Mr. J. R. MacDonald, Lord President of the Council, in the chair, memorandum F.P.(36)10 was considered. Mr. Eden said that he was no longer in favour of the proposal set out in the memorandum. The Committee took note of this decision.

No. 116

Mr. Ingram (Rome) to Mr. Eden (Received August 20, 7.20 p.m.)
No. 563 Telegraphic [W 9320/62/41]

Important   ROME, *August 20, 1936, 5.30 p.m.*
Situation at this end seems to have taken a turn for the better[1] as a result of the French Ambassador's conversation last night with the Minister for Foreign Affairs.[2]

2. The latter pointed out that preamble to French project envisaged abstention from indirect as well as direct interference in the Spanish civil war whereas actual provision of project only dealt with measures to prevent direct interference. Italian Government particularly after the recent events must insist on something which would bind the parties to abstain from indirect interference and Count Ciano defined the Italian desiderata in this respect as:

(a) An embargo on despatch of money to Spain for political purposes.
(b) The prevention of departure of volunteers except for Red Cross service under customary guarantees.

Count Ciano indicated that provided substance of these two points could be agreed on it would probably be possible to reach agreement as to the form in which they should be clothed.

3. The divergence between Paris and Rome is thus sensibly narrowed down and my French colleague seems to think it might even be possible to persuade Italian Government to change existing text of French project (i.e. without mention of above two points) provided that it were accompanied by some form of undertaking which the Italians would regard as sufficiently binding on the French. Minister for Foreign Affairs quite saw the difficulty of circulating the Powers with a new French text but question whether Italian desiderata should be accepted by interested Powers other than France still seems to be an open one.

4. Much naturally depends on political situation in France on what can

---

[1] Cf. No. 104.   [2] *D.D.F., op. cit.*, No. 173.

or cannot be done by means of existing French legislation. But I cannot resist the impression that drafting stage has practically been reached and that solution of the remaining difficulties now rests quite as much with Paris as with Rome where I hardly think more progress can be made for the present.

5. Incidentally French Ambassador who has expressed to me in warmest terms his gratitude for support which intervention here of His Majesty's Government has afforded him in these negotiations, tells me that Count Ciano was quite critical of German reply to French proposal³ and assured him that there had been no collusion between Berlin and Rome in the matter.

Repeated to Paris No. 44.

³ Cf. No. 105.

No. 117

Mr. Eden to Sir H. Chilton (Hendaye)
No. 456 [W 9248/62/41]

FOREIGN OFFICE, *August 20, 1936*

Sir,

In continuation of my conversation this afternoon with the Spanish Ambassador (see my telegram No. 162 of 20 August),¹ Señor Oliván went on to speak in gloomy tones and confidentially of the Spanish situation as he saw it. I showed His Excellency a private and confidential letter which I had received from Señor de Madariaga.² Señor Oliván said that he was in general agreement with this letter. He agreed that apart from outside intervention the sides were so evenly balanced that neither could win. He also agreed with Señor de Madariaga that this was not a war of liberty and democracy against tyranny, and that neither side could be said to represent democracy and liberty. Finally, he also agreed that it was probably wrong to suppose that a régime of the Right would necessarily be very close in foreign policy to Germany and Italy, since such a régime would not be stable and the traditional foreign policy of Spain would always make itself strongly felt. Señor Oliván remarked that he did not, for instance, believe the rumours current that General Franco had entered into some agreement with Signor Mussolini in respect of either Ceuta or one of the Balearic Islands. If General Franco were to do anything of this kind, he would at once be overthrown by his own supporters, who, being of the Right, were

¹ In this telegram, a repeat of No. 11 addressed to Madrid, Mr. Eden recorded a conversation in which he told Señor Oliván that if the German ship *Kamerun* (see No. 111) had been stopped by a Spanish warship on the high seas 'then in our view the action of the Spanish ship had been incorrect'. The Ambassador promised to communicate this statement to his government.

² Not printed: cf. No. 157, note 1, below.

more nationalist and if anything therefore more determined not to surrender Spanish territory than those of the Left.

Señor Oliván did not however share Señor Madariaga's optimism that it was possible at this stage to put forward political proposals which would constitute an effective intervention. He himself would prefer to proceed by other methods. As a first step he would like to suggest, if he might do so without impertinence, that His Majesty's Government might consider taking some humanitarian initiative. They might, for instance, make an appeal to both sides to observe the rules of war, in respect more particularly of prisoners, hostages, and so forth, instead of ignoring those rules as both sides were doing at present.[3] If this were done, it might be possible that some international organisation might be set up for the exchange of prisoners, and thus a beginning could be made which might be usefully followed up later in another sphere. After some further discussion I told the Ambassador that, while I did not rule out the possibility of His Majesty's Government taking some action on purely humanitarian grounds, I must make it quite clear to him that I saw no present prospect of our being able to take any kind of initiative with a view to intervention. The Ambassador at once accepted this, and stated that he himself appreciated only too well the difficulties in the way of any action on our part.

I am, &c.,
ANTHONY EDEN

[3] Cf. No. 109.

No. 118

Sir C. Wingfield (Lisbon) to Mr. Eden (Received August 22, 9.30 a.m.)
No. 151 Telegraphic [W 9412/62/41]

LISBON, *August 21, 1936, 11.45 p.m.*

My immediately preceding telegram.[1]

Portuguese Minister for Foreign Affairs desired me to emphasize great anxiety of Portuguese Government at present situation. Spanish insurgent forces had been bombarded at Navalperal by a group of fifteen French aeroplanes some if not all of which had French flag painted on them. Tolosa and Oyarzun were yesterday bombarded by military aeroplanes coming from and returning to France and much French war material said to be used by Communists on Guipuzcoa front. He was afraid Germans would at once take strong action on the other side and then a European war would be as near as in July 1914.

Portuguese reply is not going to be published at present which is perhaps fortunate in view of paragraph attributing barbarity to Spanish Government militia alone.

[1] Telegram No. 150; see No. 119 below. This telegram and No. 119 were despatched in reverse order.

The following observations were made with regard to reserves specified:

(A) There have been numerous incidents on the frontier and incursions across it and many Portuguese live in Spain.

(D) Minister for Foreign Affairs emphasized that it was only defensive action that was contemplated such as the refusal to have any relations with a frankly Communist Government.

(E) Owing to long frontier and the fact that many Portuguese live in Spain such relations were inevitable.

(F) He did not contemplate recognition of belligerency of either party at present but reserved the right to do so.

The Minister for Foreign Affairs informed the French Minister that nothing was said as to pending contracts as there were none.

The Minister for Foreign Affairs told me that thousands of men were being openly enlisted in France nominally for work in Spain but really as combatants and that large sums were being sent to the Spanish Government from Russia.

The French Minister to whom similar written answer was subsequently given agrees with me that the Portuguese Government have done what they could to meet our wishes. Their reservations as to non-intervention being [sic] on the whole reasonable and otherwise aiming at strict enforcement of agreement.

Repeated to Paris.

No. 119

Sir C. Wingfield (Lisbon) to Mr. Eden (Received August 22, 9.30 a.m.)
No. 150 Telegraphic [W 9444/62/41]

LISBON, *August 21, 1936, 11.55 p.m.*

Your telegram No. 99.[1]

On the 19th August I spoke to Secretary-General about urgent need for an agreement as to non-intervention[2] and on 20th August after consultation with French Minister I wrote to him urging that Portuguese adhesion should be given at once.[3]

Today I was received by the Minister for Foreign Affairs who handed me memorandum and official note to the following effect.

The Portuguese Government had understood that the Powers adhering in principle were to discuss the text of ultimate agreement. The procedure actually adopted asking for adhesions to Franco-British text has the disadvantage of involving many reserves.

Official answer states that the Portuguese Government deplore the tragic events in Spain and condemn 'the barbarous manner in which Communists and Anarchist militias are treating the population residing in the zones they dominate.'

The Portuguese Government agree to limited intervention in internal

[1] No. 110.   [2] *Ibid.*, note 3.   [3] See *D.A.P.E., op. cit.*, No. 189.

affairs of Spain subject to reserve that following acts do not come under that designation:

(A) Defence of internal public order, protection of life and liberty of Portuguese citizens and defence of national territory and security.

(B) Application of international conventions and decisions called for by circumstances of existing warfare.

(C) Possible future mediation.

(D) Defence against any subversive régime established in Spain if necessary for the defence of Western civilisation.

(E) The maintenance of relations between local or central authorities exercising power in Spanish territory.

(F) Recognition of belligerencey [*sic*] of either party or of a Government and any changes of diplomatic or consular representation.

In order to avoid possible international complications the Portuguese Government agree to prohibit the exportation direct or indirect, the re-export or transit to Spain, its possessions or Spanish Morocco of arms, munitions, war-material, aeroplanes, mounted or dismounted, or warships.

The above decisions can only be of value if rigorously carried out by all Governments, the Portuguese Government will therefore communicate to the interested Governments all well-authenticated information from either side as to the violation of agreement and hopes that the French Government will make proposals for a stricter watch over the activities of armament exporting firms. They also hope that all will join in preventing any breach of the Conventions against asphyxiating gases. The Portuguese Government point out that agreement and present situation confers [*sic*] upon the belligerents no naval rights other than those enjoyed in peace time. The Portuguese Government will communicate to the other Governments the measures taken to prevent export etc. of war material and will consider agreement in force as soon as it is enforced by Germany and Italy; as soon as the British, French and Russian Governments consider themselves bound by it; and provided all observe it effectively.

The Portuguese Government consider the following facts contrary to the spirit and from [? form] intervention in internal affairs:

(A) Enlistment, even indirectly, of volunteers for Spain.

(B) Public subscriptions to carry on the war, and the transfer of sums so collected.

Consent of any Government to such acts will release the Portuguese Government from its obligations.

Translation follows by bag and my comments in my telegram immediately following.[4]

---

[4] No. 118. For a French translation of the Portuguese note and memorandum of August 21 see *D.A.P.E.*, *op. cit.*, Nos. 197, 198.

No. 120

Mr. King (Barcelona) to Mr. Eden (Received August 26)
No. 115 [W 9733/62/41]

BARCELONA, *August 21, 1936*

Sir,

I have the honour to refer to the atrocities which continue to be perpetrated in Barcelona and the surrounding districts. Reports of them are published in the English press, and no doubt received with credulity or sceptisism [*sic*] according to the standing of the papers in which the reports appear and the political sympathies of the readers, but it seems doubtful whether these atrocities meet with the attention they deserve when it is considered that they are the outcome largely of a class warfare which those responsible for it here hope to carry into other countries, including of course Great Britain, who has hitherto considered herself as immune from such calamities.

2. When one bears in mind that Spain has hitherto been regarded as a civilized European nation, it appears somewhat surprising to many people here that there has been no expression of protest or remonstrance on the part of any of the great Powers, to say nothing of the League of Nations, and that no appeal has been made to the Madrid Government to persuade the Catalan authorities to put a stop to these atrocities if not in the name of civilized humanity at least in the hope of preventing them from spreading into other countries.

3. There is no excuse for these barbarous acts on the ground that they are reprisals for similar ones on an enemy with whom the perpetrators have just been engaged in a life and death struggle, such as those which appear to have disgraced the capture of Badajoz by the Insurgents.[1] The uprising in Barcelona was suppressed immediately, and for the last month the nearest seat of fighting has been at Zaragoza, some 200 miles distant from the capital of Catalonia.

4. The Catalan Government would no doubt claim that some of the corpses exposed daily in the morgue are those of criminals summarily executed by the local militia when caught red handed in the act of pillage, but there is no doubt whatever that most of the victims have been murdered in cold blood either by the Government militia or agents of the anarcho-syndicalists with whom the Government is now working hand in glove. The Government, therefore, cannot disclaim responsibility for these atrocities which seem to be the result of a policy of deliberate and systematic elimination of all persons considered to have sympathy with political parties other than those of the extreme Left.

5. It occurred to me, therefore, that it was the duty of the local official representatives of civilized powers to adopt some attitude in the matter.

[1] The town of Badajoz on the Portuguese frontier was successfully attacked by Nationalist forces on August 14, and a large number of the disarmed defending troops were then executed. See Thomas, *The Spanish Civil War*, pp. 318–19 and fnn.

Whereas newspaper reports may be regarded as partisan and are always liable to gross exaggeration, a signed official statement from the Consuls of several of the leading nations would have some weight. Even if such a statement led to no action on the part of the Governments represented by the Consuls, a joint expression of protest might move the Catalan Government, if not to some drastic action at least to use their influence with their followers to suppress these atrocities. It must also be borne in mind that although the acts in question have hitherto almost always been committed by Spaniards on Spaniards, many well-informed persons believe that a time is not far distant when a wave of xenophobia might set in, when foreign nationality would be no protection.

6. I proposed therefore, to visit the morgue with my French, German, Italian and American colleagues. Sr. Danes, my legal adviser, informed me that he could make the necessary arrangements. The German Consul-General at once agreed with me and expressed his willingness to accompany me. The French Consul-General, as I anticipated, declined to participate without obtaining permission from his Government, which he said he felt certain would be refused as his Government 'did not wish to know the truth'. The American Acting Consul-General to whom I telephoned, expressed his willingness to accompany me, but immediately afterwards wrote a letter declining to do so. I telephoned to the Italian Consul General, but did not succeed in finding him in. Meanwhile, Sr. Danes who had promised to arrange a visit and offered to accompany me, called to express the opinion that the visit of a Consular Commission was not practicable. He pointed out that if we went officially, we should have to announce our arrival to the Authorities, who would take good care to see that nothing was visible except perhaps a few corpses which they would claim were those of criminals shot by the militia. If, on the other hand, we went incognito, there might be a certain risk for the doctors. At present the entrance to the hospital is controlled by the armed anarcho-syndicalists and the doctors who, like all decent people, are scared out of their lives, fear possible reprisals from the anarchists if they should suspect that the visit of several consuls together had been arranged with their foreknowledge, as indeed would have been the case.

7. I decided therefore, to abandon the idea of a visit of several Consular officers together and went myself this morning to the morgue, the German Consul General promising to pay a visit personally afterwards. The entrance to the hospital was controlled by an armed militiaman, little more than a boy, who demanded our names and business, and insisted on my private detective, who has been allocated to me by the Government and never leaves me except when in my office or private house or on H.M. Ships, giving up his weapon. This the detective refused to do and was allowed to have his way, as he expressed his intention of not entering the morgue.

8. This place is situated underground and is entered by a flight of steps from a large courtyard surrounded by the hospital buildings. This courtyard was full of people, a large proportion of whom were women. There were

three or four hearses, some of them carrying wreaths of flowers and coffins of those whose corpses had already been identified. A double row of people were looking down into the entrance to the morgue where the corpses, which had not been identified, were being photographed. A corpse with an electric light held over the face was visible through the narrow entrance to the morgue.

9. After entering the hospital building and meeting the chief doctor, with several of his harrassed [sic] staff, I was taken down into the morgue itself, from which the public were excluded. Apart from one or two attendants, the photographer and Sr. Danes, I was alone and I had plenty of time to make observations, but the smell was so disgusting that I could not stay long. There must have been from thirty to forty corpses in the room, of which the doctor told me that twenty-five had been brought in the night before. I pretended that I was looking for the corpse of an Englishman, who disappeared about ten days ago, and made this an excuse for examining the features of some of the corpses. Most of them appeared to have been shot through the head at close quarters. Some of them had been shot in the chest to judge by the bloodstains on their garments. In some cases the heads had been smashed almost beyond recognition, but possibly this brutality was committed after death. Practically all the corpses were dressed as workmen, although this meant nothing as most people now hiding in fear of their lives dress as work-people to escape detection. The corpses had not been washed or laid out in any way, some were lying on a table, a row of six were in one corner, others were scattered about the floor, and I had to step over pools of blood to go from one to the other. Many of the corpses appeared to me quite unrecognisable as apart from the fact that the features were distorted with fear and horror, they were covered with blood and dirt. I pointed to the corpse of a large middle-aged man whose head and face had been reduced to a jelly, in which some well-tended gold teeth were visible, and I was told by the medical officer that it was the corpse of a well known medical man, Dr. Camps, who had been the object of private vengeance. I had been told that many corpses were disfigured in this way, but this is the first actual evidence I have seen. I had no time to count the number of corpses disfigured apart from the actual shooting, as the stench in the morgue became overpowering.

10. On a balcony near the morgue there were boards on which were posted scores of photographs of unidentified corpses. These were being examined by a large crowd, presumably of people whose relatives were missing. Most of the crowd appeared to belong to the lower orders of society and most of the corpses appeared dressed as working class people. This does not, however, throw any light on their social position. Among the photographs were numerous women, and others which showed that the corpses had been disfigured, possibly after death.

11. The medical officer in charge, Dr. Canivell, informed me that about seven hundred corpses had been brought in since the beginning of the disturbances. This number, of course, only applies to Barcelona and the

neighbourhood. Reports from reliable sources indicate that conditions are much worse in parts of the country and some of the neighbouring towns, particularly Lérida, where eighty-three corpses are said to have been brought in on the night of last Monday and Tuesday alone.

12. I have of course, taken no action vis-à-vis the Catalan Government as a result of my visit to the morgue. The German Consul General has promised to give me a copy of his statement regarding his own visit.[2]

I have, etc.,

NORMAN KING

[2] A minute by Mr. H. J. Seymour of August 28 said that the 'telegram about reprisals etc. which was sent to Sir H. Chilton [No. 143, note 1 below] is being repeated to Mr. King, so he will know that all this is not being simply ignored'. Sir G. Mounsey remarked: 'The Madrid Govt. cannot stop horrors being perpetrated under their own nose. They are not in a position to have any influence with the Catalans I fear. G.M. 29.8.36.' Sir A. Cadogan wrote: 'I fear there is nothing more to be done for the moment. We can't give any publicity to this or we shd. endanger Mr. King. N.B. his warning as to a possible future outburst of xenophobia. A. C. Aug. 29, 1936.'

No. 121

Mr. Ingram (Rome) to Mr. Eden (Received August 22, 9.30 a.m.)

No. 565 Telegraphic [W 9371/62/41]

Important   ROME, *August 22, 1936, 2.20 a.m.*

My telegram No. 563.[1]

Director General of Ministry of Foreign Affairs handed me at 7.15 p.m. this evening[2] text of Italian Government's reply (see my immediately following telegram)[3] which had been communicated to French Ambassador at 7.0 p.m. by the Minister for Foreign Affairs.[4]

2. I congratulated Signor Buti on the terms of his government's reply which I said was a proof of Italian statesmanship and would ease many anxieties. I asked him whether the phrase in the final paragraph concerning Italian interpretation of indirect intervention was to be regarded as other than an expression of a point of view. He said that it must be taken in connexion with immediately following sentence which completed in a sense a kind of reserve: i.e. if experience showed that their interpretation was not followed by practice of other countries and that public subscriptions and volunteers continued to flow to Spain the situation might have to be reconsidered as the Italian Government would not abandon their point of view. He begged me however not to regard this as an official but solely as a personal observation and expression of opinion.

3. French Ambassador for whom the Italian reply is a personal triumph fully realises that it may only be a pyrrhic victory if the French Government do not take active steps to give satisfaction to Italian interpretation of

[1] No. 116.   [2] i.e. August 21.   [3] Not printed (W 9440/62/41).
[4] The Italian reply agreeing to prohibit the export of arms and munitions to Spain in accordance with the French proposals is printed in *D.D.F., op. cit.*, No. 185.

'indirect intervention'. He thinks 'Kamerun' incident[5] may not have been without its influence on Italian decision as above all else he considered Italian Government do not wish to see Germany embroiled in Mediterranean affairs.

4. My personal and preliminary reaction to this reply is that Italian[s] will 'play' for the moment but will contract out of the game if the manner in which other Powers and France in particular give practical effect of [*sic*] the agreement affords them a loophole.

Repeated to Paris No. 45.

[5] See Nos. 111 and 117, note 1.

No. 122

Mr. Eden to Mr. Ogilvie-Forbes (Madrid)
No. 20 Telegraphic [W 9349/62/41]

FOREIGN OFFICE, *August 22, 1936, 6.15 p.m.*

Your telegram No. 29.[1]

In present circumstances His Majesty's Government cannot agree officially to take charge of foreign interests in Spain. Quite apart from question of relations with Spanish Government it would place an impossible burden on His Majesty's Consular Officers if they were required to take charge of the interests of any foreigners whose official representatives choose to leave them. Nor could their protection of such interests be in any way effective.

This being the case I should not feel justified in encouraging Portuguese Government to withdraw their representative, a question which they must decide for themselves.

If you have no objection to receiving your Portuguese colleague's baggage I have none, but the normal course would be for him to destroy his archives before leaving.

[1] In this telegram of August 21 Mr. Ogilvie-Forbes reported that the Portuguese Minister had enquired whether H.M. Embassy would take his archives and personal effects and would take charge of Portuguese interests in the event of his departure.

No. 123

Mr. Ogilvie-Forbes (Madrid) to Mr. Eden (Received August 23, 10 a.m.)
No. 46 Telegraphic [W 9405/62/41]

Immediate MADRID, *August 23, 1936, 12.35 a.m.*

My telegram No. 44.[1]

At this late hour of night Spanish lawyer of Prison Officers Union who defended Socialists in 1934 made a final appeal to me as representative of

[1] In this telegram of August 22 (despatched at 10.20 p.m.) Mr. Ogilvie-Forbes reported that the Model Prison containing 1,400 political prisoners was on fire and surrounded by Red Militia.

Great Britain and as most suitable head of Mission in the circumstances to do something in the name of humanity to save the lives of at least 1,400 political prisoners in model prison who are about to be murdered.

With a full sense of responsibility of my position and in accordance with the spirit of your telegram No. 6 of August 19th[2] I have just called on the Minister of State who almost broke down, thanked me and assured me that the Spanish Government had sent all their forces but unfortunately admitted his impotence. His Excellency said that he would transmit my appeal to the Reds and I allowed him at his request to mention name of Great Britain. I hope this action may save some lives and you will approve it being taken on the spur of the moment and in firm conviction that it is in accordance with your wishes. Please acknowledge.[3]

[2] No. 109.

[3] Mr. Ogilvie-Forbes's action was approved in Foreign Office telegram No. 26 of August 24. In his telegram No. 54 of August 24 he reported that 'only forty-eight prisoners were killed at the prison last night . . . Whether this surprisingly small casualty list is due to my appeal I cannot yet tell.' This telegram was written on August 23.

No. 124

Mr. Newton (Berlin) to Mr. Eden (Received August 24, 1.30 p.m.)
No. 278 Telegraphic: by telephone [W 9531/62/41]

Immediate   BERLIN, *August 24, 1936*
My telegram No. 274.[1]

Acting Secretary of State[2] has just handed to French Ambassador a note to the following effect.

German Government have learnt with satisfaction that all other governments concerned have now also adhered to declaration proposed by French Government. They have decided to put measures therein contemplated into force immediately for Germany. In taking this decision although it has not yet been possible to conclude discussions with Spanish Government regarding release of German transport aeroplane they have been guided by the desire to do everything on their part to expedite realisation of proposed international agreement. They expect that all other participating governments will now also take necessary steps so far as they have not yet done so, to carry out effective measures agreed upon.

Translation of text follows by air mail.[3] A copy was given to me by Herr Weizsäcker the newly appointed Political Director at the same time

[1] See No. 111, note 1.

[2] Herr Dieckhoff, Director of the Political Department of the German Foreign Office, took over as Acting State Secretary after the death of Herr von Bülow on June 21, 1936, and was officially appointed to the post on August 17. Herr Ernst von Weizsäcker became Acting Director of the Political Department.

[3] Not printed: cf. *D.D.F., op. cit.*, No. 194.

as original was being handed by Herr Dieckhoff to the French Ambassador. An announcement will appear in this afternoon's press.

I expressed my warm satisfaction at the decision of the German Government.

Repeated to Paris, Rome, and Madrid.

No. 125

Sir H. Chilton (Hendaye) to Mr. Eden (Received August 24, 4.40 p.m.)
Nos. 203 & 204 Telegraphic: by telephone [W 9559/62/41]

HENDAYE, *August 24, 1936*

My telegram No. 198.[1]

My immediately succeeding telegram contains text of a telegram which representatives of Diplomatic Corps here drew up at a meeting this morning and are sending today to their respective Governments. Countries represented were Great Britain, France, Italy, Argentina, Belgium, Netherlands, Sweden, Czechoslovakia, and Finland. Mexican Ambassador has left for Madrid, Norwegian Minister was unavoidably absent and United States Ambassador did not attend.

Am I authorized to join in joint representations on this basis to be made by Argentine Ambassador by telegraph to Spanish Government in Madrid in name of Powers concerned?

Assent of Spanish Government having been obtained insurgent headquarters will be approached.

No. 204. Following is text referred to in my immediately preceding telegram.

The heads of Diplomatic Missions assembled on the initiative of their doyen the Argentine Ambassador have exchanged views which bear witness to the profound grief which they feel for the sufferings of the civil population in Spain during the course of the present events.

These sufferings consist notably in the imprisonment of hostages or other non-combatant prisoners, the danger to public health caused by lack of medicaments, water and light and the loss of human life caused by the bombardment of open towns.

With a view to diminish, so far as lies in their power, these evils the diplomatic corps would be ready to approach the Government of the Spanish Republic with an offer to intercede with both parties with a view to secure reciprocal measures and pledges which would tend, apart from any political or military intervention, to protect the civil population from the hardships enumerated above and from such others as it might seem possible to avoid.

This intervention would be made on behalf of the whole diplomatic

[1] In this telegram of August 22 Sir H. Chilton reported that he had been shown on the previous day by the Argentine Ambassador the draft of a proposed communication to be sent to the Spanish Government by the Diplomatic Corps: cf. Nos. 107 and 109.

corps by the means most appropriate in each case, notably by the despatch of commissions, *ad hoc* by the intermediary of military, naval and air attachés, by an appeal to the Red Cross, etc.

The heads of missions assembled with a view to attempt this purely humanitarian step would be glad to receive from their respective Governments authority to make the afore-mentioned *démarche* with the Spanish Government and to invite such of their colleagues as were not personally at the meeting to associate themselves with them in this step.

No. 126

Report by the Chiefs of Staff Sub-Committee on the situation in the Western Mediterranean arising from the Spanish civil war[1]

*[W 9708/62/41]**

2, WHITEHALL GARDENS, LONDON, S.W.I, *August 24, 1936*

In accordance with the request contained in the letter from the Foreign Office which is attached as Annex I[2] to this Report, we have had under consideration the extent to which British interests would be affected and what action His Majesty's Government might take in the event of Italy taking some action which might upset the existing balance in the Western Mediterranean.

British interests in the Western Mediterranean

2. The chief British interest in the Western Mediterranean is the safety of our trade and of our sea and air communications which pass through the Straits of Gibraltar and close along the southern shore of Spain. For the purpose of maintaining the required degree of security in this area, as well as for the protection of our sea communications with South America and the Cape, it is essential that Gibraltar should continue to be available to us as a secure naval base. In addition, it is hoped to establish in the comparatively near future an air base at Gibraltar which will be a key station in the 'all red' air routes from United Kingdom both to the Far East and to the Cape. Even if the air route through the Mediterranean were to be closed to us through the loss or destruction of air facilities at Malta, the Gibraltar air base would still be essential for the use of the alternative air route via the west coast of Africa.

3. For 150 miles east of Gibraltar both shores of the Mediterranean are Spanish, and are no more than one hundred miles apart at any point. In a war with a European Power it would, therefore, be essential to our interests

---

[1] Printed for the Committee of Imperial Defence and circulated as No. 1259-B.

[2] Not printed. This letter from Sir A. Cadogan to Colonel H. L. Ismay of August 12 conveyed Lord Halifax's wish that the Chiefs of Staff should consider the effect on British interests of the 'unlikely event of Italy taking some action which might upset the existing balance in the Western Mediterranean'.

that Spain should be friendly, or at worst, strictly neutral. A hostile Spain or the occupation of Spanish territory by a hostile Power would make our control of the Straits and use of Gibraltar as a naval and air base extremely difficult, if not impossible, and would thus imperil Imperial communications by way of the Mediterranean.

Similarly, apart from the situation in the Western Mediterranean itself, the possession by a hostile Power of harbours on the Atlantic seaboard in Spanish territory would imperil our communications by way of the Atlantic.

4. Our position at Gibraltar has for many years been based on a continuation of friendly relations with Spain. Apart from the risk of any foreign intervention, should a Government inimical to Britain, whether Fascist or Communist, emerge from the present struggle, the question of the security of our base at Gibraltar will require serious examination.

5. Our interests in the present Spanish crisis may therefore be summarised as

(a) the maintenance of the Territorial integrity of Spain and her possessions (Balearics, Morocco, Canaries and Rio de Oro);
(b) the maintenance of such relations with any Spanish Government that may emerge from this conflict as will ensure benevolent neutrality in the event of our being engaged in any European war.

Italy and the Morocco Treaty position

6. The Treaty position as regards fortifications and cession of territory in Morocco, so far as we have been able to assess it is explained in Annex II.[3] The effect of existing conventions seems to be briefly as follows:

(1) France, Spain and ourselves are all bound to prevent the erection of fortifications, &c., on the Spanish–Moroccan coast bordering on the Mediterranean with the exception of certain ports and islands which are under full Spanish sovereignty.
(2) With the same exceptions, Spain is under an obligation not to cede any of her rights in her sphere of influence in Morocco to another Power.

Possible Courses of Action by Italy

7. It is clear that Italy is the Power that has most to gain by upsetting the existing balance in the Western Mediterranean since her present strategic position in the Mediterranean is obviously unfavourable. Both exits are in foreign hands, and her seaborne trade with countries outside the Mediterranean is therefore at the mercy of any Power that can control the Straits of Gibraltar and the Suez Canal. Consequently, it is not impossible that Italy may try to take advantage of the present crisis in Spain to improve her position in the Mediterranean.

[3] See Annex to this document.

8. The steps which Italy might take with the above object in view may be summarised as follows:

  (i) She might openly intervene in support of the insurgents;

  (ii) She might create some pretext, such as the protection of her nationals or the infringement of her maritime rights, to occupy Spanish territory in a less conspicuous way;

  (iii) Signor Mussolini might obtain from General Franco the promise of the lease, or cession, of some Spanish territory in exchange for his effective intervention in the present struggle. Territories which might be so bartered are

      part of Spain itself, one or more of the Balearic Islands, part of Spanish Morocco, the Canary Islands, and Rio de Oro;

  (iv) In addition, or alternatively to (iii) above, Signor Mussolini might come to an understanding with General Franco that, in exchange for effective Italian intervention, the latter would conclude an offensive–defensive Italo–Spanish alliance when he came into power.

The above measures, and particularly the effect which they would have on British interests, are discussed *seriatim* in the paragraphs that follow.

9. *With regard to Paragraph 8(i) above, open Italian intervention in support of the insurgents* would precipitate a major international crisis. It would be beyond the scope of this Paper to attempt to consider in detail the situation that would arise.

10. The possibilities summarised in paragraph 8(ii) and (iii) will be considered together, since the material effect of an Italian occupation of any of the territories in question, however that occupation is brought about, is much the same.

11. *The Occupation by Italy of any land in the Spanish Peninsula* would obviously prejudice the security of our position at Gibraltar and of our communications. But the Spaniards are a people intensely proud of their own race and country, and we, therefore, consider it reasonable to rule out the possibility of any permanent Italian occupation of Spain itself. It is true that Catalonia might split away, but we do not think even this province could be dominated by foreigners for long.

12. *The Italian occupation of any part of Spanish Morocco*, and particularly of Ceuta, which is fifteen miles from Gibraltar, would bring Gibraltar within range of heavy Italian air attack, and thus deny to us its full use as a Naval Base. In addition, the possession and possible development by Italy of any of the Spanish Moroccan ports, small and undeveloped though they are at the present time, would contribute to our difficulties in controlling the Straits of Gibraltar. Accordingly, we regard the maintenance of the territorial integrity of Spanish Morocco as of vital importance to British interests. France also has an interest in this possibility, since an Italian occupation of the territory in question would menace the communications between her Mediterranean and Atlantic seaboards.

13. *An Italian occupation of any of the Balearic Islands* would probably not be acceptable to the islanders themselves, but the possibilities of their having to submit to *force majeure* cannot be ruled out.

The naval facilities in these islands are at present as follows:

Majorca, 450 miles from Gibraltar, has no harbour entirely suitable for a naval base, since Palma and Pollenza Bay, although good in some ways, are too exposed. Minorca, which is still further from Gibraltar, has in Port Mahon a small, but heavily defended, naval base.

As regards air facilities, there are, so far as is known, no military air stations in the Balearic Islands at the present time; but there is no doubt that they could be established without great difficulty. It is understood that there is a satisfactory aerodrome site at Pollenza, and that civil seaplane services were operated at Port Mahon and Palma in 1932.

In view of the foregoing an Italian occupation of any of the Balearic Islands would not vitally affect British strategical interests. At the same time it would give Italy a base for naval and air operations, 250 miles nearer Gibraltar than anything which she possesses at the present time. The menace to our control of the Straits and to Gibraltar itself would thus be increased.

14. It is to be noted in addition that an Italian occupation of any of the Balearic Islands would constitute a direct threat to French communications between France and her possessions in Northern Africa; it is, therefore, reasonable to assume that an enterprise of this kind would be most energetically opposed by France.

15. *An Italian occupation of the Canary Islands and/or Rio de Oro* would present her with a base flanking our communications to the Cape of Good Hope and South America. Since, in a war with Italy, the bulk of our eastern trade might have to use the Cape route, it is clear that an Italian occupation of either the Canary Islands or Rio de Oro would be prejudicial to our interests.

An Italo–Spanish Alliance

16. It remains to consider the possibility indicated in paragraph 8(iv), namely, the conclusion of an Italo–Spanish alliance. The effect of this would be that Spanish ports and aerodromes would be available for the use of Italian forces in time of war. This would constitute a most serious menace not only to our use of Gibraltar as a naval and air base, and to our control of the Straits, but also to our Imperial communications.

From the French point of view an Italo–Spanish alliance is equally undesirable, though obviously for different reasons.

17. It will be seen from the foregoing that the adoption by Italy of any of the courses of action which have been discussed in the preceding paragraphs would in effect be a threat, to a greater or lesser degree, to British and French interests.

We now turn to the question of what action His Majesty's Government might take to safeguard the situation.

18. The successful issue of the Abyssinian campaign in the face of League opposition, suggests that Mussolini, if determined to exploit the Spanish crisis to his own advantage, will not be deterred by threats, and only by the certainty that force, and adequate force, will be employed against him. We are, therefore, driven to the conclusion that any action, other than action in the diplomatic sphere, which His Majesty's Government might take which would effectively thwart his designs, must inevitably involve a serious risk of war between Great Britain and Italy.

19. The relative preparedness for war of these two countries has been examined so exhaustively during the past twelve months that it is unnecessary in this paper to reconsider the question in any detail. Suffice it to say that Italy is the only Power whose forces are fully mobilised and available for immediate operations.

20. We now turn to the consideration of what action, other than the threat of direct military action, might be taken by His Majesty's Government to prevent Italy from embarking upon any of the enterprises visualised at the beginning of this Report. Before setting out our views on this point we venture to suggest, with the memories of last year's events still fresh in our minds, that we should avoid at all costs the possibility of becoming involved in action which, on the one hand, fails to achieve our object, and, on the other hand, tends further to alienate Italy, i.e., we should take no action which we are not prepared to back up by all the force at our command. This statement is made on the understanding that Italy is the only enemy in contemplation.

21. With that general proviso, the courses of action that appear advisable are summarised as follows:

In the first place, we should press for the conclusion and rigid enforcement of a universal agreement of non-interference in Spain by all European Powers. If such an agreement can be reached and enforced, there would be no reason for the winning side in Spain to grant territorial concessions to, or negotiate closer military relations with, her neighbours than now exist.

22. If no general agreement of non-intervention can be reached, we should not cease to impress on France, whose strategic interests are largely identical with our own, the desirability of giving no cause for intervention by Italy. Support by France and Russia to the forces of the Spanish Left may well lead Italy to afford open support to General Franco.

23. We should endeavour to ensure that any action taken by Foreign Powers, either to protect their nationals in Spanish territory or exact reparations, is international and concerted.

Failing such agreement, every endeavour should be made locally for concerted action to be taken when occasion arises.

This applies with particular force to action by Italian ships; and we should, therefore, arrange that wherever an Italian man-of-war is berthed in Spanish waters there is also a British ship, and that at important ports the British Senior Naval Officer is, if possible, senior to the Italian.

24. Since this report was put in hand, we have seen a copy of the Foreign Office memorandum that has recently been circulated to the Cabinet Committee on Foreign Policy (Paper No. F.P.(36)10).[4] It is suggested in this Paper that it should be made publicly plain that 'any alteration of the status quo in the Western Mediterranean must be a matter of the closest concern to His Majesty's Government'. We agree that Signor Mussolini should be under no misapprehension as to the possible consequences of any action that he may take to disturb the existing balance in the Western Mediterranean; and we, therefore, desire to endorse the Foreign Office suggestion.

SUMMARY OF CONCLUSIONS

25. (i) Our interests in the present Spanish crisis are the maintenance
(a) of the territorial integrity of Spain and her possessions, and
(b) of such relations with any Spanish Government which may emerge from this conflict as will ensure benevolent neutrality in the event of our being engaged in a European war;

(ii) Open intervention by Italy in support of the insurgents in Spain would precipitate a major international crisis;

(iii) The occupation by Italy of any territory in Spain itself would be detrimental to British interests;

(iv) The Italian occupation of any part of Spanish Morocco, and particularly of Ceuta, would be a threat to vital British interests;

(v) The Italian occupation of any of the Balearic Islands, Canary Islands, and/or Rio de Oro, is highly undesirable from the point of view of British interests, but cannot be regarded as a vital menace;

(vi) Any of the contingencies specified in (ii) to (v) above would be injurious in greater or lesser degree to French interests;

(vii) The conclusion of any Italo–Spanish alliance would constitute a threat to vital British interests;

(viii) The threat of effective action, other than action in a diplomatic sphere, to thwart Italian designs would involve a grave risk of war;

(ix) Italy is the only Power whose forces are mobilised and ready for immediate action. Her preparedness for the initial phase of hostilities, vis-à-vis Great Britain, is greater than it was nine months ago.

RECOMMENDATIONS

26. Our recommendations may be summarised as follows.

(i) The principle that should govern any action on the part of His Majesty's Government should be that it is most important to avoid any measures which, while failing to achieve our object, merely tend further to alienate Italy;

(ii) We should press for the earliest possible conclusion of a non-

4 No. 115.

interference pact in Spain, embracing France, Russia, Portugal, Germany, Italy and the United Kingdom;

(iii) If no general agreement can be reached, we should impress on the French the desirability of giving no cause for intervention by Italy;

(iv) We should maintain sufficient naval forces on the Western Mediterranean and Spanish Atlantic coasts to ensure that we have at least one ship at every port where the Italians have one, and that at important ports the British S[enior] N[aval] O[fficer] is, if possible, senior to the Italian;

(v) We should, if possible, get an agreement with the other Powers that any landing or other action by armed forces to preserve order should be not only international in character, but also, wherever this is possible, preconcerted between the Powers affected;

(vi) Failing such agreement, every endeavour should be made locally for concerted action to be taken when occasion arises;

(vii) We should make it known to Signor Mussolini that, in the words of F.P.(36)10, 'any alteration of the status quo in the Western Mediterranean must be a matter of the closest concern to His Majesty's Government' in order that he may be under no misapprehension as to the consequences of any action that he may take to disturb the existing balance.[5]

E. L. ELLINGTON
C. J. DEVERELL
C. E. KENNEDY-PURVIS
(*A.C.N.S. for C.N.S.*)

ANNEX TO NO. 126

Italy and Morocco treaty position

So far as can be gathered from a cursory examination of the treaties, the position as regards fortifications in Morocco is as follows.

By Article 7 of the Declaration of the 8th April, 1904, between the United Kingdom and France, both Governments are bound not to permit the erection of any fortifications or strategic works on that portion of the coast of Morocco comprised between, but not including Melilla and the heights which command the right bank of the River Sebor. This condition

[5] In a long minute of August 28 Mr. Shuckburgh underlined the dangers from a hostile Spain to British communications as described by the Chiefs of Staff, and examined various forms of action to be undertaken in the event of the adoption of an anti-British policy by the future Spanish Government, whatever its political complexion. Both Mr. Seymour (August 28) and Sir G. Mounsey (August 29) thought that the proposed international committee for non-intervention would provide the best means of keeping in touch with other governments in order to deal with Spanish developments. Sir A. Cadogan (August 29) referred to the decision of the Foreign Policy Committee against a declaration (cf. No. 115, note 4). Mr. Eden wrote on August 29: 'I fear that, whichever side wins, the outlook for us must be anxious & we must have the ultimate position of Gibraltar constantly in mind. I am doubtful of the wisdom of the warning to Mussolini at present, but if the dept. think otherwise I shall be glad to see their views.'

does not apply to the places which were in the occupation of Spain on the Moorish Coast of the Mediterranean, i.e., Ceuta, Melilla and probably also the following islands:

Penon de Velez;
Alhucemas; and
Zafrin.

Under Article 3 of the secret portion of the Declaration of the 8th April, 1904, the two Governments also agreed that on Spain acquiring a sphere of influence in Morocco she would have to undertake not to alienate any part of that sphere.

Both of these stipulations were reproduced in the Franco-Spanish Convention respecting Morocco, signed on the 3rd October, 1904, under Article 1 of which Spain adhered to the Anglo-French Declaration of the preceding April. Under Article 7 of this Convention, Spain undertook not to alienate or to cede in any form, even temporarily, the whole or any part of her sphere of influence in Morocco.

The relations between Spain and France in Morocco were again regulated in 1912 by the Convention dated the 27th November of that year (it does not appear, however, that the Convention of the 3rd October, 1904, was abrogated). Under Article 5 of this new Convention, Spain again engaged herself not to alienate, even temporarily, her rights in any part of the territory composing her zone of influence; and under Article 6 both Governments undertook not to permit fortifications or strategic works on the coast of Morocco above mentioned.

So far as can be traced, Italy is under no obligation not to fortify any part of the coast of Morocco except at Tangier, the statute of which she acceded to in 1928.

The position in brief, therefore, seems to be as follows:

(1) France, Spain, and ourselves are all bound to prevent the erection of fortifications, &c., on the Spanish–Moroccan coast bordering on the Mediterranean, with the exception of certain ports and islands above mentioned which are under full Spanish sovereignty.

(2) With the same exceptions, Spain is under an obligation not to cede any of her rights in her sphere of influence in Morocco to another Power.

No. 127

Minute by Mr. Baxter on an invitation to Mr. Newton to attend the Nazi Party Day at Nuremberg[1]

[*C 6028/6028/18*]

FOREIGN OFFICE, *August 24, 1936*

We have hitherto always refused to allow H.M. Representative at Berlin to accept the annual invitation to the Nazi Party rally at Nuremberg in September. It is not considered desirable, in principle, that our Ambassadors, or any of our representatives abroad, should attend the meetings of political parties.

The question now for decision is whether there are any grounds for reconsidering our past attitude. The reasons which might possibly be put forward for advocating the acceptance of Herr Hitler's invitation this year are, I think, as follows:

1. Acceptance of the invitation would undoubtedly give satisfaction to Herr Hitler himself, and to the present Nazi régime in general; and from the general point of view of our relations with Germany, it is desirable at least not to go out of our way to annoy the present rulers of Germany.

2. The position of the Nazi Party in Germany is not the same as that of political parties in most other countries. According to the present German thesis, the Nazi Party *is* the State. Without going so far as to accept this doctrine, we must recognise that the Nazi Party conference is more or less a national event in Germany, and is very much more important than party conferences elsewhere. I am informed, in this connexion, that H.M. Representative in Moscow attends the Communist Party function on the 1st May (as well as the anniversary of the outbreak of the Revolution on the 7th November), but these functions take place in Moscow itself and do not involve nearly a week's absence in an obscure provincial town.

3. It may also be said that 1934 was the year of the Röhm massacre; and 1935 was the year of 'the Rally of Freedom' when the Nuremberg conference was to celebrate rearmament, 'the recovery by Germany of her military freedom'. This year, it may perhaps be said, there is no such special reason for absenting ourselves. So far as we know, there is nothing specially objectionable on the programme of the conference; (though of course there will be the usual anti-Russian and anti-Jewish speeches).

On the other hand, the reasons for refusing the invitation to the conference

---

[1] Mr. Newton's telegram No. 222 Saving of August 21 said that he had received a personal invitation from Herr Hitler as Head of the State and not as Head of the Party to attend a Party Rally at Nuremberg, from September 8 to 14. He remarked that 'it seems questionable whether it is appropriate or dignified that foreign representatives should absent themselves from their posts for nearly a week and live in a train as a kind of appendage to the Government and Party. On the other hand the presence of a British representative would be warmly appreciated.' He suggested that if a refusal was desired he should explain that the Ambassador would be away on leave and that in his absence it would 'not be possible for me to absent myself from Berlin'.

159

are fully set forth by Mr. Newton. The French, Americans and Dutch have declined the invitation; the Italians, who have accepted, went last year; it would give rise to some comment if we, who, like the French and Americans, have always refused the invitation, were to accept it this year. Again, as Mr. Newton points out, the way in which foreign diplomats have been treated at Nuremberg in the past is by no means satisfactory (see in this connexion paragraph 2 of Sir E. Phipps' despatch No. 1102[2] of September 11th, 1934). Moreover, our acceptance is merely desired in order that it may be exploited by the German Ministry of Propaganda in order to enhance the prestige of the régime. There is a considerable body of opinion in this country which would be strongly opposed to our going out of our way to bolster up the prestige of the Nazi Party. Finally, there is still, I submit, great force in the objection that it is most undesirable, in principle, for British representatives abroad to have to take part in party functions, especially as, once the precedent has been established, the practice is one which will probably have to be repeated every year, however embarrassing the situation.

Personally, I feel that, although there is perhaps something to be said on the other side, our best course will be to instruct Mr. Newton to refuse the invitation, and I submit a draft accordingly.[3]

C. W. BAXTER

[2] Not printed.

[3] A minute by Sir A. Cadogan read: 'It seems to me the weight of argument is all in favour of polite refusal, which could be given on the grounds which Mr. Newton suggests. A.C. Aug. 24. 1936.' Instructions to Mr. Newton to refuse the invitation on the grounds suggested were sent to Berlin in Foreign Office telegram No. 183 of August 24.

No. 128

Mr. Eden to Sir G. Clerk (Paris)
No. 1450 [W 9550/9549/41]

FOREIGN OFFICE, *August 24, 1936*

Sir,

The French Ambassador[1] asked to see me this afternoon, when he stated that he had originally asked for his interview in order that he might express to me the very grave anxieties of the French Government at the delay in securing agreement on non-intervention. M. Blum and M. Delbos had indeed been near the end of their tether. Happily, however, within the last hour he had received a message from Paris which radically altered the whole situation. The German Government had accepted the French invitation and the Ambassador handed me the text of the terms of the acceptance.[2] His Excellency explained that these terms were only approximate since they had been telephoned to him hurriedly, but he felt confident that I should find them in essence correct.

[1] M. Corbin.   [2] See No. 124.

2. The Ambassador went on to say that he had a request to make to me from the French Government. If this non-intervention was to work then in the view of his Government it was essential that some committee should be set up to deal with the many technical details which would inevitably arise. The question was where was that Committee to be situated? The French Government felt very strongly that London was the best place, and they much hoped that His Majesty's Government would agree.

3. I asked His Excellency how, in the view of his Government, this committee was to be constituted. Was it, for instance, to consist of the diplomatic representatives of the various countries concerned, or were special technical experts to be sent to sit on it? The Ambassador replied that that would be for the countries themselves to decide. The French Government did, however, attach great importance to the Committee meeting in London because, to be frank, they felt that our capital was more neutral than the capitals of any of the other great Powers in this difficult business.

4. Eventually, after some further discussion, I told the Ambassador that His Majesty's Government were very willing to do anything that they could to help, and that if his Government and the other Governments concerned desired it, we were quite willing to lend our aid by agreeing that the Committee should meet in London.

5. We then turned to discuss some other aspects of the situation in Spain. I told His Excellency that I had asked the French Government some days ago what were their views on intervention on purely humanitarian grounds, more especially in respect of prisoners.[3] I had gained the impression from the reply which M. Delbos had given to you[4] that the French Government felt perhaps a little hesitation about it. The Ambassador replied that he thought that if there was any hesitation it was only due to doubt as to how the invitation should be framed. The French Government would of course have to be careful not to say anything which would give the impression that they were treating both sides on an equal footing. I said that I fully appreciated this, and after further discussion we decided that the best course would be for us to endeavour to draft the terms of any appeal we might be prepared to make, and then communicate with the French Government, so that if they were in agreement they could then endorse any initiative we had taken. I made it clear, however, that I would not take that initiative until I was aware that the French Government had no actual objection to the terms of the appeal.

5. [6.] In conclusion I asked the Ambassador to congratulate the French Government on behalf of His Majesty's Government on the success of the policy they had pursued in this dispute. M. Blum had, we felt, shown great courage in taking the initiative, and nobody was happier than we were to find that courage rewarded.[5]

6. [7.] The Ambassador left with me copies of the replies[6] which the

---

[3] Cf. No. 109.　　　　　　　　　　　　　　　[4] See *ibid.*, note 4.
[5] M. Corbin's account of this interview is given in *D.D.F.*, *op. cit.*, No. 197.
[6] Not printed.

French Government had received from other Governments, on the question of non-intervention in Spain.[7]

I am, etc.,
ANTHONY EDEN

[7] Mr. Eden gave an account of this conversation to the Cabinet Committee on Foreign Policy at its meeting on August 25 (see No. 115, note 4). After describing his meeting with the Labour Party deputation on August 19 (No. 113) he said that he had agreed in principle, subject to the agreement of the Foreign Policy Committee, to the French proposals 'as he was satisfied that they would find favour with our own public opinion'. The Committee considered the whole position created by the Spanish crisis, and decided that an interdepartmental technical committee should be set up under the chairmanship of a minister to deal 'with any questions which might arise here as to the interpretation of the agreement, and . . . to be ready to deal with any questions raised by the international committee if it is established'. Mr. Eden on the same day with the agreement of the Foreign Policy Committee invited Mr. W. S. Morrison, Financial Secretary to the Treasury, to act as chairman of this technical committee.

No. 129

Viscount Chilston (Moscow) to Mr. Eden (Received August 28)
No. 493 [N 4329/565/38]

MOSCOW, *August 24, 1936*

Sir,

With reference to my telegram No. 128[1] of the 20th August, I have the honour to transmit to you herewith a summary[1] of the indictment of MM. Zinoviev, Kamenev and others on charges of having organised a terrorist association, with the aid of M. Trotski and the German Secret Police, and with the object of assassinating M. Stalin and other Soviet leaders.[2]

2. As you will observe, the indictment does not allege that any terrorist act was actually committed, with the exception of the murder of M. Kirov in December 1934[3] (as to which most people now agree that it was almost certainly non-political in origin). On the other hand, certain persons have apparently confessed to having planned terrorist acts which they failed to carry out, the most notable being one to shoot M. Stalin at the Comintern Congress a year ago.

3. In the course of the trial mention was made of one or two other alleged plans to assassinate M. Stalin, including one to which, for obvious reasons,

[1] Not printed.
[2] MM. Kamenev, Trotsky, and Zinoviev were all former high-ranking officials in the Soviet Union whose opposition to M. Josef Stalin, General Secretary of the Central Committee of the Communist Party of the Soviet Union, led to their exile and persecution. For details of these and other Soviet personalities mentioned in this despatch see No. 130 below, and the report on Personalities in the USSR for 1936 contained in Viscount Chilston's despatch No. 2 of January 1, 1936 (N 289/289/38).
[3] The murder of M. Kirov, a member of the Politburo and close associate of M. Stalin, on December 1, 1934, which was followed by a wave of arrests and executions, was later blamed by Party officials on M. Zinoviev and a supposed group of fellow conspirators.

there was but slight reference in the Soviet press: this was a plot to shoot M. Stalin in the Dorogomilovsk suburb in the course of his daily drive out to one of his country houses, which failed to materialise owing to the fact that the conspirators were alarmed by the enormous number of Ogpu agents who habitually mingle with the crowd along this route.

4. The evidence in the trial added little material to that contained in the indictment, except that it is now stated definitely that the accused Olberg obtained his Honduranean passport from that country's consul-general in Berlin, whose name is given as Lucas Parades, for the sum of 13,000 Czechoslovak crowns. There is no additional evidence of importance about the participation of the German Secret Police, and I understand from my German colleague that he has received no instructions to make a protest, the *démarche* reported in my despatch No. 487[1] of the 19th August having been made on his own initiative. The fact remains that the German police authorities, and in particular Herr Himmler, are accused of direct participation in a plot to murder M. Stalin.

5. The most remarkable feature of the evidence given at the trial was the number of prominent men in this country, not among the accused, whom it implicated: as a result, the Public Prosecutor of the U.S.S.R., M. Vyshinski, who conducted the case, announced that M. Sokolnikov, the former Ambassador in London, and M. Serebryakov were being 'held to criminal responsibility,' while he had given instructions 'to begin an investigation of the statements of the defendants with regard to MM. Tomski, Rykov, Bukharin, Uglanov, Radek and Pyatakov, and depending on the result of this investigation the Prosecutor's office will take the proper legal action with regard to this matter.' These persons will all be found in my reports on major and minor personalities in the U.S.S.R.

6. The trial concluded in the early morning of the 24th August, when sentence of death was passed on all the accused. Ordinary procedure required execution to follow immediately on sentence, but as reported in my telegram No. 129[1] of to-day it transpired that a decree had been passed on the 11th August, with special reference to this trial, permitting the accused, if condemned, to make a plea for mercy within seventy-two hours to the Central Executive Committee. At the moment of writing their fate is still in suspense.[4]

7. I am commenting in a separate despatch[5] on the general implications of this trial, and on the personalities involved in or implicated by it. Here I would only add a few comments on the conduct of the trial itself. The presiding judge was M. Ulrich (who also took the Metropolitan-Vickers case), and the prosecution was, as I have stated, conducted by M. Vyshinski with his usual ferocity. The above-mentioned decree of the 11th August permitted the accused to be represented by counsel, but none of them availed themselves of this permission. No independent evidence was called: though

[4] It was reported in *The Times* of August 26, 1936, p. 12, that all the sentenced prisoners had been executed.
[5] No. 130 below.

there were two witnesses who were not actually on trial, they were both at pains to point out that they were guiltier than any of the accused, and both are to be tried later on, together with certain other persons mentioned in the indictment. All the accused confessed and incriminated each other except MM. Smirnov and Holzman, who were consequently attacked with particular venom by the prosecutor and their fellow-defendants. The demeanour of the accused varied; M. Zinoviev appeared cowed and scarcely able to speak (he was once the party's greatest orator); M. Kamenev made a feeble attempt to maintain his dignity, which soon collapsed; the rest were either frightened and demoralised or impassive and even jaunty. The latter description applied particularly to Valentine Olberg, the two Luryes and Fritz David: these are all comparatively youthful and quite unknown Jews, who claimed all the credit for the organisation of recent terrorist acts (apart from their statements nothing later than 1934 was alleged), and on whose statements also the principal evidence against the Gestapo appears to rest. All these persons struck a British correspondent, who attended the trial, as obvious *agents provocateurs*, and he so described them in a telegram to his paper which the censor passed without demur.

8. The Soviet press, as usual, prejudged the issue by calling for the execution of the accused even before the trial opened: resolutions demanding that the 'ravening dogs' be shot continue to appear daily in large quantities. There has so far been no reference in the press to any appeal for mercy by the condemned men.

9. I am sending a copy of this despatch to His Majesty's Ambassador at Berlin.

I have, &c.,
CHILSTON

No. 130

Viscount Chilston (Moscow) to Mr. Eden (Received August 28)
No. 495 [N 4331/565/38]

MOSCOW, August 24, 1936

Sir,

The old description of revolution as a monster which devours its own children has seldom been so notably exemplified as in the witch-hunt now proceeding in the Soviet Union. With the doubtful exception of M. Stalin, no member of the present Politburo played a prominent part in the 1917 revolution. Of those who did play such a part and still survive, the most important, MM. Trotski, Zinoviev and Kamenev, have long been in exile or disgrace; most of the others, such as MM. Radek, Bukharin, Rykov, Pyatakov, Tomski and Bubnov, have had to content themselves, generally after a quarrel with the party, with administrative or other positions of relative insignificance. Except for M. Bubnov, who has never yet quarrelled with the party, all the above-mentioned persons have been involved in the trial now proceeding; and other only less important Communists have also been implicated, such as M. Sokolnikov, a former Ambassador at the Court of St. James,[1] who has been arrested, and M. Rheingold, until December 1934 a Deputy Commissar for Agriculture, who is one of the accused. It should be noted that among the persons incriminated by the evidence given since the trial opened, and whose cases are being investigated by the public prosecutor, are a member of the Government and former Prime Minister (M. Rykov), a Deputy Commissar (M. Pyatakov), the best-known journalist in the country, normally the Government's mouthpiece on foreign affairs (M. Radek), the editor of the official Government newspaper (M. Bukharin) and the head of the official publishing-house (M. Tomski).

2. The last-mentioned has been the first victim of the witch-hunt. On hearing that his case was to be investigated, he committed suicide, it was announced yesterday, at his villa near Moscow. M. Tomski, who, as you are aware, was for many years head of the trade union organisation in the U.S.S.R., was one of the less unattractive Soviet leaders, and his fall from power was chiefly due to his support of the respectable thesis that it is the duty of trade unions to protect their members against all employers, including, if necessary, the State. Since his fall, not much had been heard of him, but it transpired recently that he had become head of the Government publishing firm ('Gosizdat'), and, to judge from an interview which he had with Sir Walter Citrine last year, he appeared to have settled down happily in his new sphere of action. Most of the other actual or intended victims are less deserving of sympathy; but it is perhaps worth recalling that M. Zinoviev was Lenin's principal collaborator when the latter was in exile and in the early stages of the revolution, while M. Kamenev (who is M. Trotski's brother-in-law) was hardly less intimately associated with the founder of the régime.

3. I do not think that we shall ever know the real reasons for the holding of this trial; they can be known to only a few members of the inner circles of the party, who are unlikely to reveal them, and one cannot do more than speculate; on the whole, I think that the motive is probably to be found among the suggestions contained in my despatch No. 487[2] of the 19th August. Whatever the motive, the fact of the trial is profoundly discouraging to those who had begun to hope that the U.S.S.R. might be in process of settling down to the life of a normal and orderly State. It has probably eliminated all possibility that the introduction of the new Constitution will be followed by any increase of freedom; indeed, I am told that the population now regard the publication of the draft as having been a trap to encourage them to talk freely and betray their 'dangerous thoughts.' This is perhaps hardly probable, but it does reveal the feeling in which the inhabitants of this country will approach their promised liberties of speech and assembly,

[1] From 1929 to 1932. [2] Not printed (N 4324/565/38).

a feeling which is deepened by the constant reports of the arrests of alleged 'Trotskist cells' throughout the country; for many are convinced that the arrested persons are merely men who were deluded by the promise of free speech into expressing their genuine grievances against the régime. In the words of M. Trotski (in the statement which he is reported to have made to the Norwegian press), 'the reigning bureaucracy calls every criticism a conspiracy.' This, I think, correctly and succinctly represents the situation.

4. There remains the personal position of M. Stalin. The present Politburo consists entirely of his men, and if the result of this trial is, as seems likely, the elimination of all those who have ever at any time opposed him, his isolation from all forms of criticism will be complete. He has, I am told, recently drawn much closer to M. Yagoda,[3] and I fear that there is a danger of his falling entirely into the hands of the People's Commissariat of Internal Affairs. I should add that, to judge from his appearance in recent photographs and news-reels, he seems to be ageing somewhat.

I have, &c.,
CHILSTON

[3] People's Commissar for Internal Affairs.

No. 131

Mr. Eden to Sir C. Wingfield (Lisbon)
No. 104 Telegraphic [W 9682/9549/41]

FOREIGN OFFICE, August 25, 1936, 7 p.m.

Your telegrams Nos. 150 and 151.[1]

The French Government have communicated to me the substance of the reply which they are instructing the French Minister to return to the Portuguese note.[2]

Your Excellency should concert with your French colleague in addressing the Portuguese Government on similar lines, and you should also press them to bring into force at once the prohibition of the export of munitions of war and aircraft to Spain which is already being enforced in France, Germany and the United Kingdom.[3]

[1] Nos. 118 and 119.

[2] This French communication from M. Corbin to Mr. Eden of August 25, not printed in D.D.F., enclosed a copy of the Portuguese note of August 21 (see No. 119, note 4). The French reply pointed out that on various points 'le projet de déclaration franco-anglais lui laissait une certaine liberté d'appréciation': cf. D.D.F., op. cit., No. 201.

[3] Sir C. Wingfield's telegram No. 156 of August 26 reported that he had carried out these instructions and had been informed that a Portuguese decree prohibiting export and transit would be published on August 27: see D.A.P.E., op. cit., No. 231. A minute of August 27 by Mr. Seymour read: 'The Portuguese list of obs[ervatio]ns and reservations is far the most formidable put in by any govt. However, the main point is that they are today to bring in a prohibition of the supply of munitions. The other points, or some of them, may have to be dealt with by the international committee.'

No. 132

Mr. Newton (Berlin) to Mr. Eden (Received August 25, 10.30 p.m.)
No. 280 Telegraphic [C 6087/3790/18]

BERLIN, *August 25, 1936, 8.40 p.m.*

My telegram No. 279.[1]

Announcement of German Government has come as a great surprise.

Military Attaché was officially informed at War Ministry this afternoon that extension of period of service would not involve an increase in the strength above 36 divisions which Germany had already declared to be the future strength. It was explained that the new period of service would make a qualitative rather than a quantitative change. That is to say the total strength would not be materially increased but quality would be improved by selecting the best recruits of both classes. Conscripts now serving are to remain on for another year and sufficient of 1915 class and of remainder of 1914 class will be called up in order to create the new divisions, presumably to the total of 36, although the Ministry of War could not definitely say that this figure would be reached at once. The Military Attaché was also informed that it was unlikely men doing two years' military service would be required to do labour service as well. Those who did not do the full period of military service would probably be employed in labour service and would carry out a short period of military training (at present eight weeks in training units).

The Military Attaché is of opinion that the arrangement outlined above is in conformity with the best interests of the German army. The quality will be improved both by higher selection of recruits and by longer service. An expansion beyond the thirty-six divisions would make the present shortage of regular officers still more severely felt. As it is their task will be now somewhat lightened in that they will have two years in which to train the soldiers.

As regards the motives for this step Military Attaché learnt that the Commander-in-Chief had for some time been pressing for an extension on account of difficulty of giving adequate training in one year. Preparations for an extension of period had accordingly been made some months ago. The present moment was considered opportune for making the change firstly because of the excuse offered by the increase in the Russian army and secondly because after his peaceful gesture in regard to non-intervention in Spain the Chancellor felt he would be less open to criticism.

Although the Military Attaché was informed that it is not intended to increase German army beyond thirty-six divisions I do not think that this can be accepted as binding. It does not suit German army to expand just now but when the moment comes a decision will depend upon Herr Hitler's reading of the current political situation.[2]

[1] This telegram of August 25 referred to Herr Hitler's signature on August 24 of an order that the length of compulsory service in the three branches of the German defence forces would be uniformly 2 years. See *D.G.F.P.*, Series C, vol. v, p. 926, and No. 517.

[2] It was suggested in minutes on this telegram that it might be desirable to speak to

167

Prince Bismarck about this development in order to try to pin the German Government down to its assurance against an increase in the number of divisions beyond 36 and to reassure France and Europe. Sir A. Cadogan doubted, however, whether either object was likely to be achieved. Mr. Eden wrote: 'I share Sir A. Cadogan's doubts as to the advisability of sending for Prince Bismarck specifically on this subject. This week however we shall have to "open the ball" in connexion with Five Power meeting, and this matter could then be raised with Prince Bismarck. A.E. August 30th.'

No. 133

Mr. Eden to Sir H. Chilton (Hendaye)
No. 164 Telegraphic [W 9559/62/41]

FOREIGN OFFICE, *August 25, 1936, 10 p.m.*

Your telegrams Nos. 203 and 204.[1]

You are authorized to join in proposed representations and to do all you can to help them to a successful issue provided that a majority of your colleagues including the French representative are similarly authorized.

Until it is known whether proposals of diplomatic corps will lead to representations being made I do not propose to proceed further on the lines indicated in my telegram to Paris No. 214.[2]

[1] No. 125.   [2] No. 109.

No. 134

Extract from Draft Conclusions of the fifth meeting of the Cabinet Committee on Foreign Policy, held at No. 10 Downing Street, August 25, 1936, at 10.30 a.m.
[C 6162/4/18]

Present: The Rt. Hon. J. R. MacDonald (*in the Chair*); The Rt. Hon. N. Chamberlain; The Rt. Hon. Sir J. Simon;[1] The Rt. Hon. A. Eden; The Rt. Hon. Viscount Halifax; The Rt. Hon. Malcolm MacDonald;[2] The Rt. Hon. W. Ormsby-Gore;[3] The Rt. Hon. Sir S. Hoare; The Rt. Hon. Sir T. Inskip; Sir R. B. Howorth, *Deputy Secretary to the Cabinet*.

With reference to Cabinet 55(36) Conclusion 2, the Committee had before them a Memorandum (F.P.(36)9)[4] by the Secretary of State for Foreign Affairs, circulating a Paper prepared in the Foreign Office regarding the preparations for the proposed Conference of the five Locarno Powers.

On the suggestion of Mr. Eden, the Committee agreed to consider the questions for decision numbered (1) to (18) on pages 4 to 10 of the Draft one by one.

[1] Home Secretary.
[2] Secretary of State for Dominion Affairs.
[3] Secretary of State for the Colonies.   [4] No. 114.

The Committee accepted Conclusion A on page 10:[5]

A. While not excluding altogether the possibility of accepting Germany's proposed new 'international court of arbitration', we should prefer to use the League Council, as in the Locarno Treaty, to decide if and when an aggression has taken place. (Questions 1 and 2 above).

It was generally agreed that we should not adopt too rigid an attitude towards Germany's suggested 'international court of arbitration', while at the same time bearing in mind all the political arguments for and against that proposal and the maintenance of the existing arrangements respectively. From the point of view of the Dominions the retention of the League Council was very important.

The Committee accepted in principle Conclusion B on page 10 of F.P.(36)9:[6]

As regards C on page 11:[6]

the Committee took note that both questions 4 and 6 had been referred to the Committee of Imperial Defence.

The Committee also took note that question 5 on page 5,[6] 'Should the Irish Free State participate in the new agreement?', had been referred to the Committee of Imperial Defence.

As regards Conclusion D on page 11 of F.P.(36)9:[6]

the Committee took note that this question had been referred to the Committee of Imperial Defence.

After considerable discussion the Committee agreed in principle to Conclusion E on page 11 of F.P.(36)9:[6]

The Committee took note that Conclusions F, G, H, and I on page 11 of F.P.(36)9[6] were under consideration by the Committee of Imperial Defence:[7]

The Committee agreed that a Press Notice in the following terms should be issued forthwith:

(Official) There was a meeting of the Foreign Affairs Committee of the Cabinet today.
(Gloss) It is understood that the matters dealt with will come under further consideration with other members of the Cabinet on September 2nd.

The Committee resumed their consideration of paper F.P.(36)9.

[5] See *ibid.*, p. 134.　　　　　　　　　　　　　　[6] As in No. 114.
[7] *Note in original*: At this point the Committee adjourned for lunch, and resumed at 2.45 p.m.

Negotiations to resolve the Situation created by the German Initiative of March 7th

After some discussion the Committee accepted in principle Conclusions J, K, and L on page 11 of F.P.(36)9:[6]

General Settlement

The Committee accepted Conclusion M on page 11 of F.P.(36)9:[6]

Germany's Return to the League

The Committee accepted in principle Conclusion N on Page 11 of F.P.(36)9:[6] The Committee agreed:

(1) That Paper F.P.(36)9 should be circulated to the Cabinet for consideration at the Meeting to be held on September 2nd.

(2) That at this Meeting Mr. Eden should inform the Cabinet that the Committee on Foreign Policy were in general agreement with the political conclusions set out on Pages 10 and 11 of F.P.(36)9, subject to any modifications which may be rendered necessary as a result of the examination by the Committee of Imperial Defence of the items referred to that Committee, and that if the Committee of Imperial Defence are in general agreement with the proposals, it is intended to open negotiations on the lines proposed.

(3) Sir Thomas Inskip undertook to inform the Cabinet on September 2nd in the event of any very important questions arising out of the Committee of Imperial Defence examination of the items referred to that Committee.

No. 135

Letter from Mr. Newton (Berlin) to Mr. Baxter
[*C 6145/99/18*]

BERLIN, *August 25, 1936*

My dear Baxter,

Your letter C 5770/99/18 of August 20th, about the proposed visit of Leith-Ross here.[1]

We think that it would be an excellent idea for him to pay a visit to Berlin this autumn, but the choice of time is not altogether easy. The question of non-Reich debt held in the United Kingdom is at present regulated only

---

[1] Following a visit to Berlin from July 21 to 23, 1936, during which he had discussed Anglo-German economic relations with high officials of the Reichsbank, Mr. F. T. A. Ashton-Gwatkin, Head of the Economic Relations Section of the League of Nations and Western Department of the Foreign Office, received a letter of July 30 from Dr. Puhl of the Reichsbank referring to a suggestion that it might be a good thing if Sir F. Leith-Ross, Chief Economic Adviser to the Government, came over to Berlin to have a talk with Dr. Schacht, President of the Reichsbank and Acting Minister of Economics. Mr. Baxter in his letter of August 20 asked whether the Embassy had any observations to make on this proposal.

up to the end of next December, and there may have to be full-dress negotiations on the subject before the end of the year. We have intimated to the Germans that if any new scheme is to be adopted in place of the present issue of funding bonds they must themselves make a proposal and that they should make it as soon as possible.[2] One question is, therefore, whether it would be good tactics for Leith-Ross to come to Berlin and see Schacht before these discussions are engaged, or whether this would tend in any way to play into the hands of Schacht, who for a long time has been trying to inveigle the representatives of the British creditors to make some proposal themselves.

Even from the point of view of this particular question it would probably be an advantage if Leith-Ross came as proposed in September without waiting for the debt discussions to be engaged. Schacht would take it as a compliment—ever since the 1934 negotiations[3] he has been saying that he wanted to keep in closer personal touch with Leith-Ross—and this would put him probably in a better humour for the purpose of negotiations. A direct discussion would also clear the air and bring Dr. Schacht down nearer to realities.

The Party Rally at Nuremberg lasts from the 8th to the 14th September and *prima facie* this will not be a convenient time. But Dr. Schacht will no doubt go on holiday immediately afterwards. It is possible that he might be willing to take a day off from the Party Rally or to fit in a day either here or in the country after the Rally is over. But, as soon as you have taken a definite decision about the proposal, we could approach the Reichsbank and find out whether in fact a meeting could be arranged in the second week of September.[4]

Yours ever,

BASIL C. NEWTON

[2] Anglo-German payments were regulated by the agreement of November 1, 1934: see Volume XII, Nos. 153 and 154. After nearly a year's absence on an economic mission to the Far East, Sir F. Leith-Ross returned to London on July 25, 1936, and was told of the successful completion of the repayment of German commercial debts to the United Kingdom under this agreement. He sent Dr. Schacht a civil note on July 28 congratulating him on the results of the agreement and expressing the hope that the time might soon come when other outstanding difficulties, such as exchange control, might be disposed of. He stated that if Dr. Schacht could come to London he would like to discuss the possibilities with him. There are further details in a memorandum of October 5 by Mr. R. F. Wigram, Head of the Central Department (C 7042/99/18).

[3] See Volume XII, Nos. 23, 24, 61, 125, 153, 154.

[4] Sir R. Vansittart, who returned to the Foreign Office after his holiday apparently on August 31, was, however, strongly opposed to the visit. In a minute of September 3 he wrote: 'I am in favour of Sir F. Leith-Ross going to Germany, *but not now*. I want to get well on with the political arrangements—with which we shall have any amount of difficulty —before we embark on this other sea, on which we are not even at unity among ourselves, and which has been *quite* inadequately explored so far. In this respect we have a lever: do not let us compromise it by premature gestures. The reasons for this will be more apparent in my report on my visit to Germany [cf. Appendix I]. Briefly I got most Germans to see that a political settlement—in some respects distasteful to them by its content and extent —wd. have to precede the necessary and eventual economic one. Do not let us spoil that

effect by going off at half-cock, else we shall fail politically later in the autumn. If the Germans are uncomfortable economically, let us keep them guessing for a month or two. It will do them no harm, but much good. I hope I shall hear no more of this idea for a while. It is good in itself no doubt, but wd. be a piece of psychological mistiming. R.V. Sept. 3.'

No. 136

Record by Sir G. Mounsey of a conversation between Mr. Eden, Mr. A. Greenwood, and others

[W 9965/9549/41]

FOREIGN OFFICE, *August 26, 1936*

The Secretary of State, who was accompanied by Lord Halifax, Lord Cranborne and myself received this afternoon the deputation headed by Mr. Greenwood, M.P., and Sir W. Citrine which had previously called upon him on August 19th,[1] in order to discuss the Spanish situation.

The points raised by the deputation to-day related to:

1. The delay in arriving at an international agreement for the non-supply of arms to Spain.
2. The position of Portugal in relation to this agreement. An article was quoted from the 'News Chronicle' alleging that the Portuguese are giving all manner of assistance to the rebels including the discharge and transit across Portuguese territory of arms from the German ship 'Kamerun'. The view was strongly expressed that unless Portugal could be got to come into the agreement at once and to put it into strict force, the whole object of the non-supply of arms policy would be defeated.
3. The question of the origin of the proposed agreement for non-intervention in Spain which it was declared, upon information received from Paris, had emanated from London, and probably at the time when the Locarno discussions were taking place here i.e. about July 23–25.
4. A subsidiary point as to whether in considering under the agreement, what kind of supplies might still be allowed to go to Spain, His Majesty's Government would bear in mind the importance of coming to no understanding with the other Powers which would preclude the supply of food-stuffs and medicines by the Labour organisations in this country to their corresponding organisations in Spain.

In reply to these points the Secretary of State explained the present position as regards the proposed international agreement and told the delegation that His Majesty's Government were continuing to support the French Government in bringing pressure to bear at Rome and Lisbon to induce the Italian and Portuguese Governments to put the agreement at once into force. The Secretary of State also outlined the further steps which are in

[1] See No. 113.

contemplation for exercising control over the enforcement of the terms of the agreement, viz. the setting up of an International Committee of Control, possibly in London, which would be comprised of diplomatic or technical representatives.

As regards point 2, the Secretary of State emphasized the unique and difficult position in which Portugal is placed, both geographically and politically vis-à-vis the present troubles in Spain, but he assured the delegation that everything was being and had been done to exert pressure from here on the Portuguese Government with a view to bringing them into the proposed agreement. This was in his opinion the only practical method of overcoming the difficulties presented by the Portuguese problem; and this problem would be gradually solved, in so far as transit of arms was concerned, as and when the majority of other Powers adhered to the agreement. Portugal was not herself in a position to export any quantity of arms to Spain.

As to the origin of the proposal for an agreement, the Secretary of State again categorically denied that the initiative had come from His Majesty's Government, and remarked that he would indeed have been glad to be able to maintain that the proposal had been his, as he considered that it was the best proposal which could have been made in the circumstances.

On the question of supplies, the Secretary of State pointed out that it was premature to discuss any detailed suggestions, as the whole subject of supplies other than arms and munitions was one which still remained for consideration and would probably come before the Committee of Control if and when this body was duly established.

Mr. Eden undertook at the request of Sir W. Citrine to receive a further communication from the delegation before any decision on this question was arrived at by His Majesty's Government.

Finally the Secretary of State outlined to the delegation the nature of the humanitarian appeal which His Majesty's Government are contemplating addressing to the contending parties in Spain, in concert with other Powers, through the medium of the diplomatic corps at Hendaye.[2]

G. M.

[2] See Nos. 125 and 133.

No. 137

Mr. Eden to Sir H. Chilton (Hendaye)
No. 470 [W 8949/62/41]

FOREIGN OFFICE, *August 26, 1936*

Sir,

I have received Your Excellency's despatch No. 611[1] of August 14th recording an interview with the Marquis Merry del Val[2] and Señor José de Yanguas Messia.[3]

2. I regard any suggestion for the appointment of an unofficial agent at Burgos as being, in present circumstances, premature and unjustifiable. If approached again on the subject, I shall be glad if you will inform Señor Yanguas that His Majesty's Government do not, in present circumstances, see their way to the appointment of such an agent.

I am, etc.,
ANTHONY EDEN

[1] Not printed: see note 3 below.
[2] H.E. the Marquis de Merry del Val, born 1864, had been Spanish Ambassador at London, 1913–1931.
[3] *Chef de Cabinet Diplomatique* of the *Junta de Defensa Nacional* at Burgos; one time Minister of State in the government of Señor Primo de Rivera. The interview took place on the evening of August 13. After giving information as to the whereabouts of various British subjects believed to be in territory occupied by the forces of the Burgos administration, Señor Yanguas suggested the appointment of a British Consul at Burgos; when Sir H. Chilton pointed out that the Burgos Government had not been recognized, Señor Yanguas suggested that an unofficial agent might be sent.

No. 138

Mr. Newton (Berlin) to Mr. Eden (Received August 28)
No. 899 [E 5444/94/31]

BERLIN, *August 26, 1936*

Sir,

With reference to your despatch No. 934[1] of the 6th August I have the honour to transmit herewith a memorandum on the Jewish question in Germany, together with an annex[1] giving a very brief account of the more important regulations covering the levy of emigration tax and the transfer of property by emigrants.

2. I would also draw your attention to the memorandum by the Passport Control Office, enclosed in Sir Eric Phipps's despatch No. 103[1] of the 20th January last, summarising in convenient form the Zionist proposals for the planned emigration of Jews from Germany to Palestine.

I have, &c.,
B. C. NEWTON

[1] Not printed.

The Jewish Question in Germany

Point 4 of the National Socialist party programme reads as follows: 'None but members of the nation may be citizens of the State. None but those of German blood, whatever their creed, may be members of the nation. No Jew, therefore, may be a member of the nation.'

Before and after the war the Jewish community in Germany not only amassed wealth as bankers and financiers, but tended to monopolise the learned professions, medicine, the law, the theatre, the press and the creative arts. Excluded from the army and navy, their industry and their intellectual and artistic gifts helped them to dominate in the spheres open to them. After the war the eastern German frontier remained open for some months to Jewish immigration, and by 1925 the presence of some 10,000 immigrant Jews in Berlin had aroused serious misgivings. A number of financial-political scandals lent colour to the Nazi theory that Marxism, Judaism and corruption were synonymous terms, and from 1930 the National Socialist party found a ready response to their vigorous anti-Jewish campaign. Herr Hitler personally is fanatical in his hatred of the Jews, believing that they are a contaminating and disruptive influence in a nation. The war cry of his movement was: 'Germany awake: perish Jewry.'

A few figures will show the preponderance of 'non-Aryans' in certain professions. In 1931 out of 3,450 lawyers in Berlin, 1,925 were Jews. In Breslau the numbers were 285 and 192, and in Frankfurt 659 and 432 respectively. In Berlin the number of Jewish doctors was 52 per cent., while in most towns the average was 30 per cent. Fifteen Jewish bankers are stated to have held 718 directorships in banks and commercial undertakings. Of theatre directors 50·4 per cent. were Jews. Although the Jews formed only about 1 per cent. of the total population, there was a widespread feeling that they blocked the approaches to all the leading positions in the State, monopolising them for themselves.

When Herr Hitler became Chancellor, the Jews became the object of popular attack. The better-known Jewish politicians, pacifists and journalists had to fly for their lives. Many crossed the French, Dutch and Czech frontiers, and a great many were incarcerated in prisons and camps. Jews of the highest international reputation in the worlds of science, art, music and literature were publicly insulted or maltreated, and those in a financial position to do so left the country in great numbers. Thousands of doctors and lawyers—harmless, hard-working people for the most part—suffered personal ill-treatment. A not inconsiderable number of Jews must have lost their lives during the period of unrest.

The Nazi Government proceeded in due course to regularise the disabilities already imposed in practice. On the 7th April, 1933, a law over-riding articles 128 and 129 of the Constitution and removing 'non-Aryan' civil servants was summarily passed. (The new law furnished a very important definition by stating that a 'non-Aryan' was a person one of whose parents or grandparents was 'non-Aryan.'[)] Persons who were in the civil service before the 1st August, 1914, or who had a satisfactory war record or had lost a son or father in the war, were, however, exempted. The new law led to the dismissal of thousands of officials, including many distinguished scientists, doctors and university professors. On the other hand, the authorities had to conform to the general principle of the law and to allow those Jewish lawyers who had served in the war to practise. The definition of the term 'Aryan,' coupled with the 'Veterans' Clause,' henceforth became the more or less general criterion for the treatment of Jews throughout the country. Lawyers and doctors who were in practice before August 1914 and who had fought or lost a father or son were readmitted in theory, though in practice they met with resistance.

On the 22nd April, 1933, a law was passed restricting the number of Jewish panel doctors. On the 25th April a law curtailing the number of students to be accepted by schools, other than elementary schools, was passed. On the 15th July a law was passed authorising the revocation of naturalisation certificates issued after the 9th November, 1918.

In March 1934 the law of the 7th April, 1933, was made applicable to the armed forces, so as to bring them into line with the other public services, but the number of officers and men affected was insignificant.

At the end of 1934 and in the beginning of 1935, in view of the impending Saar plebiscite, moderation was the order of the day, and the Jews were amongst those who profited from this state of affairs. As soon as the plebiscite was over, however, the Nazi party began to show its teeth and an anti-Jewish campaign was launched which assumed even larger proportions.

By May it had become clear that a widespread anti-semitic drive was in progress. Action against the Jews was partly official and partly unofficial. The following were some of the more important official declarations and measures. According to a decree issued in February 1934 no Jewish dentist, whether a front-line fighter or not, might henceforth be admitted as a panel dentist. By a decree of the Minister of the Interior issued in February, candidates for the medical and dentistry professions must be of Aryan origin. Aryans married to non-Aryans were also barred. By decision of the president of the Literary Chamber of Culture, published in March, no non-Aryan apprentice could be admitted to the publishing trade. According to an order issued on the 27th April by the Minister of the Interior, Jews were forbidden to fly the national or swastika flags. On the 27th April in an interview to the press the Minister of the Interior stated that Jews would be excluded from German citizenship and from the holding of any public office.

Unofficial action against the Jews was intense and widespread. The *Stürmer*, Herr Streicher's[2] notorious organ, extended its sales all over the country largely by means of the support of local Nazi formations. The Franconian notice: 'Jews not wanted here,' began to appear in almost

---

[2] *Gauleiter* Julius Streicher.

every village. Jews were excluded from swimming baths, restaurants and public places of entertainment. The clients of Jewish shops were boycotted and persecuted. Pressure was exercised against the employment of Jewish doctors, lawyers and stockbrokers. Jewish hawkers and newspaper retailers were obliged to close down. The windows of Jewish shops were broken or disfigured with offensive placards. Speeches by Dr. Goebbels, the *Statthalter* Sprenger, Herr Streicher, *Gauleiter* Grohé and lesser party leaders excited the anti-Jewish passions of the masses. The Jews were members of the human race, said Dr. Goebbels, but it was equally true that the flea was an animal.

Berlin, owing to its unwieldy size and to the fact that it is the capital, is less under the influence of party bosses than any other town in Germany. It consequently was not engulfed by the anti-Jewish wave for some time, but the party was determined that it should not escape. On the 16th July and on the following days, Jewish premises and individuals were attacked by small bands of rioters. On the 15th August Herr Streicher spoke for the first time in Berlin, and in the course of a long harangue accused Queen Victoria of having ennobled the Jew Disraeli under the title of Lord Gladstone. At the end of August Herr Hinkel, the representative of Dr. Goebbels in matters relating to Jewish cultural activity, issued regulations which had the effect of confining the Jews to a cultural ghetto. On the 10th September a decree was issued by the Minister of Education designed to achieve as complete a racial separation as possible in all German schools from the school year of 1936.

By the beginning of September there were signs of a reaction against unbridled party violence and of a desire to put anti-Jewish measures on a legal basis. Not only Dr. Schacht, but even Nazi leaders such as *Gauleiter* Wagner, of Silesia, and Herr Streicher himself, pronounced themselves against isolated action. The stage was thus set for Government intervention.

This took the form of the promulgation on the 13th September, 1935, of the Nuremberg laws, which deprived the Jews of the rights of citizenship, and forbade them to marry or live with Aryans, employ Aryan servants or fly the national flag. In a public speech at Nuremberg on the 16th September Herr Hitler claimed that the new legislation would form a basis which would enable the German people to find some tolerable relationship towards the Jews. Should this hope not be fulfilled, he continued, and should the Jewish agitation in Germany and abroad continue, a further examination of the position would have to be made. If the State apparatus proved inadequate, the party would find means of solving the problem.

If the Jews thought that Herr Hitler's words meant that they would be afforded a reasonable opportunity of earning a living, events showed them to have been grievously mistaken. The promised administrative measures did not appear for over two months. Meanwhile, the effect of the Nuremberg legislation was to give the stamp of official approval to anti-Semitic agitation and to increase the pressure on the Jews. Doctors employed in hospitals were dismissed, Aryan business men were prevented from doing business with Jews, and a large number of public servants were removed from their posts.

Eventually, on the 14th November, after a delay due entirely to the difficulty of evolving an acceptable solution, the Government issued the expected regulations for the application of the Nuremberg laws. The regulations provided, *inter alia*, that, in general, Jews were persons three or more of whose grandparents were of fully Jewish blood. The German population was divided into two classes, citizens and nationals. The first were to be issued with a patent of citizenship ('Reichsbürgerbrief'), which entitled them to a citizen's rights. The Jews could not be German citizens and were relegated to the second class; they could not exercise the right to vote nor hold any public office. The conditions under which Jews or persons of mixed Jewish and Aryan blood could marry were closely defined. As a concession, it was laid down that Aryan female servants over 35 years of age already in Jewish employment could remain on, but Jews were still forbidden to engage Aryan female servants under 45 years of age.

On the 22nd November the Minister of Economics issued an order compelling Jewish official brokers to give up their appointments in all German stock exchanges.

A second executive regulation, dated the 21st December, was published on the 23rd December. It defined the word official and the public offices which Jews are not permitted to fill. As officials are regarded all Reich officials, with the exception of notaries public, all categories of officials of the States, municipalities and municipal corporations, officials of corporations in public law and employees of authorities engaged in social assurance; also teachers in State schools, professors and members of armed forces. The regulation further extends the definition of holders of public offices which Jews may not fill to all persons performing magisterial or authoritative functions. Finally, it is laid down that doctors in charge of public hospitals and consultants ('Vertrauensärzte') must leave their posts by the 31st March, 1936. An exception is made for Jewish hospitals.

Until the present time, no regulations have appeared laying down the conditions under which Jews may trade. The matter is reported to be the subject of much controversy, but, whatever the issue, experience has shown that the law lags behind realities, and every day that passes enables its amateur interpreters to win fresh ground from which it proves difficult to dislodge them. The Jews look forward to the future not only without hope, but in the conviction that further persecution, and perhaps even expropriation, is in store for them. The most serious aspect is the outlook for the children. Not only are their early years poisoned by their treatment as pariahs, but they have no prospects. The universities and the professions (armed forces, civil service, railways, municipal offices, public health, law, teaching, stockbroking, journalism, theatre, film art) are closed to them. Even in commerce and banking, although Jews have in many cases been retained, it is usually considered safer not to engage a young Jew. Moreover, the Nazis are not allowed, and the public are not encouraged, to have commercial relations with Jews; and the number of Jews in Germany is not sufficient to enable Jews to live in a Nazi-constructed Ghetto on Jewish custom alone, particularly since a large number of the richer Jews have left. Even if no further persecution is in store, and this is doubtful, the present situation is such that there is no doubt that, to the rising generation of Jews, emigration offers the only prospect of a free and useful life.

No. 139

Letter from Mr. Newton (Berlin) to Mr. Baxter
[*C 6150/4/18*]

BERLIN, *August 26, 1936*

My dear Baxter,

When we were last sent one of Wickham Steed's effusions, we said that like the poet Shadwell he might one day lapse into truth.[1]

So far he has not done so. Nor is he likely to show any better result with the papers enclosed in your slip C 5722/4/18 of August 15th.[2]

As regards his suggestion that we may expect a German coup against Danzig in September,[3] neither I nor the Military and Air Attachés know of any adequate ground for the prediction, but of course we are not prophets. One main consideration is likely to be that Germany is not ready on land and still less at sea or in the air to take a risk which might involve her with France and Russia as well as Poland.

As regards the memorandum on the 'Aims of German Policy' there is a good deal in it with which we are in general agreement, the more so if it is envisaged as a long-term estimate. At the same time it is very rambling and its point is largely spoilt by special pleading in favour of our intervention in the Danzig question. Experience has shown that the Nazis are able in due course to grind down their political opponents and it is likely to be a thankless task to try to support a German minority because their acceptance of outside support at present would be a very grave reproach against them in this country. Moreover the prospects of our being able to intervene in the Baltic in the event of war would really not be materially lessened by the absorption of Danzig[.]

The memorandum further suggests that Germany has no definite aims. With this I do not think that we agree. The aims may not be territorially

[1] Presumably an echo of John Dryden's couplet:

> 'The rest to some faint meaning make pretense,
> But Shadwell never deviates into sense.'

[2] Mr. Wickham Steed, former editor of *The Times*, had sent to Mr. O'Malley on August 4 a 19-page memorandum entitled 'The Aims of German Policy', based on communications from 'a former German officer'. Mr. O'Malley remarked that 'Mr. W. Steed's information is generally pretty poor' but agreed that copies might be sent to the D.M.I., D.N.I., and Mr. Newton, whose response seems worth printing here as a statement of the British Embassy's views. Mr. Steed's letter and memorandum are filed under C 5722/4/18.

[3] Cf. Nos. 144, 362, and 412 below.

worked out in detail (equally they may be) but it seems to us that certain German objectives are clear. The first is to unite the German-speaking peoples on the Eastern frontier. For this purpose Germany's assets are (a) the threat of her strong Army and Air Force; (b) the powerful Nazi organisations in the areas concerned; (c) a propaganda which will, when the time comes, convince Germans that the action taken is in defence of Germany and will certainly be able to confuse the issue abroad.

The second, or better perhaps the ulterior, objective, since it is necessarily more remote in time and less definite in its geographical incidence, is to find room for the expansion of the German peoples after they have been united. This would almost certainly involve war and Steed is probably correct in thinking that the Slav population would be driven out of the area annexed, for Slav the area would almost certainly be.

It is of course possible that owing to a miscalculation the attempt to gain the first objective may result in war in which case Germany, assuming she is victorious, would naturally aim at attaining both objectives at once. All this is, however, very theoretical speculation.

Yours ever,
BASIL C. NEWTON

No. 140

Mr. Eden to Sir E. Drummond (Rome)
No. 337[1] Telegraphic [W 9532/62/41]

FOREIGN OFFICE, August 27, 1936, 7 p.m.

French Government are issuing instructions by circular telegram to all European posts to urge the respective Governments to send replies, if they have not already done so, to French proposals for non-intervention in Spain, and to put the proposed measures into operation forthwith. They are also suggesting the establishment at some capital of a committee whose functions would be (1) to collate the measures already being taken by the various Governments (2) to consider other questions which may arise and the means of dealing with them.

Please give full support to your French colleague in his representations.

Prohibition of export of munitions of war to Spain is already in force in France, Germany, United Kingdom.

[1] This was a circular telegram, sent to all European posts except Paris, Berlin, Moscow, and Madrid.

No. 141

Sir G. Clerk (Paris) to Mr. Eden (Received August 28, 8.30 a.m.)
No. 292 Saving: Telegraphic [C 6109/99/18]

PARIS, *August 27, 1936*

Dr. Schacht arrived in Paris on August 25th to return the visit recently paid to him by M. Labeyrie, the new Governor of the Bank of France. He has resolutely disclaimed that his visit has any political significance, but speculation as to the reasons for his arrival in Paris at this juncture is rife throughout the Paris press. Newspaper comment this morning is confined almost entirely to embroidery on the theme of Dr. Schacht's visit, to the virtual exclusion of such matters as the German decision regarding the two years' military service[1] and the Spanish civil war.

At a luncheon given by M. Labeyrie yesterday Dr. Schacht met MM. Blum, Delbos, Vincent-Auriol, Spinasse[2] and Bastid.[3] This meeting occasioned an exchange of letters between M. Blum and M. Thorez, Secretary General of the Communist Party, in which the latter reproached M. Blum for showing honour to an emissary of Hitler by meeting him at lunch, while M. Blum has retorted that his Government will not allow any derogation from the dignity of France, of which the will to peace is a form, and that it has no intention of refusing to participate in any conference, whether economic, financial or political, which might facilitate the general settlement of European problems.

In conversation at the Ministry of Finance this afternoon His Majesty's Minister learned that though Dr. Schacht has in fact in the course of the numerous conversations he has held here so far expatiated at great length in general terms on the pacific aims of the German Government, as well as on the difficulties with which Germany is confronted by reason of her lack of colonies, he has not so far put forward a single suggestion of any practical economic or financial interest. There has, for example, been no mention of any 'alignment' between the franc and the mark. In view of the fact that Dr. Schacht had been most insistent on being allowed to return M. Labeyrie's visit at the present moment, the French Government had expected that he would be the bearer of some important communication, but they had been disappointed. This impression is confirmed by the Quai d'Orsay, the Political Director having informed the Belgian Ambassador this morning that Dr. Schacht in his talks with M. Delbos had confined himself to the most banal generalities.[4]

Dr. Schacht is to be received by M. Vincent-Auriol again this evening,

---

[1] See No. 132.   [2] Minister of National Economy.   [3] Minister of Commerce.
[4] Two documents printed in *D.D.F., op. cit.*, Nos. 196 and 211, indicate French expectations over the visit, but give no details of the discussions from August 25 to 27. The full French account of M. Blum's meetings with Dr. Schacht did not reach the Foreign Office until transmitted under a covering letter from Sir G. Clerk of February 24, 1937: this document will be printed in Volume XVIII (C 1635/78/18/1937). Cf. also No. 210 below.

and the Ministry of Finance have undertaken to inform us if anything of interest should emerge from this conversation. It is reported in the press that Dr. Schacht will return to Berlin by aeroplane tomorrow afternoon.

Copy to Berlin by bag.

No. 142

Record by Mr. Ashton-Gwatkin of a conversation with Dr. Bielfeld[1]
[C 6147/99/18]

FOREIGN OFFICE, *August 27, 1936*

I had lunch today, August 27th, with Dr. Bielfeld of the German Embassy.

As regards raw materials, he said that this is entirely a question of exchange. So long as Germany is short of free exchange, she cannot get all the raw materials which she normally and naturally requires. The more free exchange she can get, the less is her scarcity of raw materials. He did not know if there was any immediate possibility of the freeing of the exchanges. He himself would like to see the mark linked with sterling, but this would require a large credit by the Bank of England to hold the exchange. He did not think that the fact of Jewish capital escaping from Germany was any kind of reason for exchange restrictions. This would be dealt with in a different way since it is known in Germany exactly how much and what property people possess, and the German Government could easily prevent Jews or anybody else from transferring their capital. The commodities which are distressingly scarce in Germany and the acquisition of which depend on freer exchange are vegetable oils and oil seeds, soya beans (Germany is not getting as much as she wants from Manchukuo), rubber, nickel and copper. Control of a colonial territory within the mark area would be a real assistance to Germany in getting some of her supplies though it would not solve all the difficulties. Dr. Bielfeld instanced the Cameroons as a hypothetical example.

Although the armament programme is already beginning to slacken down in Germany, Dr. Bielfeld did not anticipate any difficulty as regards labour and unemployment. The men would be re-absorbed in other work; and the new military training, for example, would provide for a certain number of them.

F. A. GWATKIN

[1] Dr. H. Bielfeld was a Counsellor in the German Embassy in London.

No. 143

Sir H. Chilton (Hendaye) to Mr. Eden (Received August 28, 4.40 p.m.)
No. 207 Telegraphic [W 9961/62/41]

HENDAYE, *August 28, 1936, 2.15 p.m.*

Your telegram No. 165[1] reached me shortly after meeting convened by Argentine Ambassador yesterday. Great Britain, France, Italy, Argentina, Belgium, Sweden, Czechoslovakia, Finland and Norway were represented.

The Argentine Ambassador read over communication which formed enclosure B to my despatch No. 641[2] and meeting accepted with indifference the addition of sentence regarding preservation of monuments and works of art which Argentine Ambassador desired to include. In paragraph 2 the phrase 'villes sans défenses' was substituted after discussion for 'ouvertes villes'.

All representatives with the exception of the French Ambassador and Netherlands Minister had received authority from their Governments to associate themselves in joint representations. It was agreed that as soon as the French Ambassador received authority[3] he would inform the Argentine Ambassador who would then telegraph to the Spanish Government communication based on enclosure B with brief covering note explaining that he was acting on behalf of his colleagues.

If the Spanish Government assent steps would then be taken to approach insurgents in a manner calculated not to imply their recognition and as soon as possible military, sanitary, medical and art commissions would be formed to establish contact with both parties and cooperate in measures for alleviation of suffering etc.

Repeated to Madrid No. 8.

[1] This telegram of August 27, not printed, stated at length His Majesty's Government's desire to appeal to the contending Spanish forces on humanitarian grounds: cf. No. 133.

[2] Of August 24, not printed: enclosure B gave the French version of the text transmitted in Sir H. Chilton's telegram No. 204 (No. 125).

[3] Sir H. Chilton's telegram No. 209 of August 29, not preserved in the Foreign Office archives, apparently reported that the French Ambassador had now received authority to co-operate in the *démarche*.

No. 144

Mr. Eden to Sir G. Clerk (Paris)
No. 67 Saving: Telegraphic [C 6164/33/55]

FOREIGN OFFICE, *August 28, 1936, 6 p.m.*

My telegram No. 53 Saving.[1]

Please take suitable opportunity to speak informally at Quai d'Orsay on following lines:

It seems probable that League Council will be faced in September with

[1] This telegram of August 11 asked for the views of the French Government as to the

an acute crisis regarding Danzig. Although High Commissioner's[2] report has not yet been received, we know that position in Danzig is most unsatisfactory. Recent decrees,[3] though they have apparently not yet been fully applied, are obviously directed against the political liberties of the Opposition Parties, and would probably be declared unconstitutional if examined by an impartial legal body. All the Opposition papers have been suppressed for periods ranging from 5 to 12 months. High Commissioner may well report that his position has become impossible and that unless League can remedy matters he will have no alternative but to resign. Danzig Government probably intend to refuse all further cooperation with the League in what they regard as Danzig's internal affairs.

In such circumstances the first step to be taken at Geneva might well be to discover whether the League is in a position to insist on the integral carrying out of the Danzig Statute. This will depend mainly on the attitude of the Polish Government. The latter are naturally chiefly interested in what they regard as purely Polish interests in Danzig. They regard the League's guarantee of the Constitution as primarily the concern of the League, which is not in their opinion entitled to try to shift its responsibilities towards the Danzig minorities on to Polish shoulders alone. There may be much to be said for this view, but the fact remains that Poland is the only Power that benefits from the existing régime, and if she is unable to ensure the continued observance of the Danzig Statute in its entirety, the League may be forced to reconsider its whole position. We have, therefore, already taken steps to emphasise to the Polish Government (see my telegram No. 66[4] to Warsaw of August 2nd) that, while we appreciate that the matter of the League

necessity for a preliminary meeting of the Committee of Three, which had been appointed by the League Council on July 4, 1936, to follow developments in Danzig, and of which Mr. Eden was a member: cf. Volume XVI, No. 399, note 4. The increasingly aggressive role adopted by the German Nazi Party in the Free City of Danzig during 1936 led to considerable discussion in the Foreign Office as to whether the League would be able to continue to guarantee the Danzig constitution. Following a speech in the House of Lords by Lord Lothian on July 29 (102 *H.L. Deb. 5 s.*, cols. 370–1) in which he suggested that the connection between the League and Danzig should be severed and that Germany and Poland should make a separate agreement, Lord Halifax asked for the comments of the Central Department, and the question was raised of whether to sound out the Polish Government's reactions to the problem. It was generally agreed that it would be impossible to enforce the carrying out of the Danzig Statute, and that the alternative, to sever the connection with the League, might be unavoidable, but opinion was divided as to the approach to the Poles. Mr. Eden expressed a desire for an early discussion of the problem, and a note by Mr. Baxter of August 26 stated that the question had been discussed at a meeting with Mr. Eden, who wished to see 'whether the Quai d'Orsay had any solution in mind'.

[2] Mr. Seán Lester had been League of Nations High Commissioner for Danzig since October, 1933.

[3] On July 11 an order was issued in Danzig that all civil servants and government employees must be members of the National Socialist Party, and this was followed on July 16 by a series of legislative decrees effectively abolishing the civic rights of Danzig citizens not members of the Nazi Party. The powers of the police were also greatly increased.

[4] Not printed.

guarantee of the Constitution is not considered a vital question for Poland, the position of the Council, as guarantor of the Free City and of Poland's rights therein, will require serious consideration if it is apparent that the due observance of the letter and spirit of the Danzig Constitution can no longer be assured.

It may be desirable to speak very frankly to Polish Delegation at Geneva, and ask whether the Polish Government are in a position to insist upon the integral carrying out of the Danzig Statute, or alternatively whether they would contemplate endeavouring to negotiate with the German and Danzig Governments some modification of the existing régime, whereby Danzig problems would in future be settled direct between Germany and Poland. It would have to be explained that in the latter event the League's special obligations as regards Danzig would all have to be brought to an end. The League could not be expected to approve a suggested solution whereby the Council would disinterest itself in Danzig's internal affairs but otherwise maintain existing régime, i.e. to give up trying to protect the Danzig minorities under certain parts of the Statute, but continue to guarantee Polish rights under other parts of the Statute. If Poland and Germany could agree on some solution whereby the special connexion between the League and Danzig would be terminated, the problem of the minorities might be solved by special transitional arrangements.

The foregoing observations are purely tentative and are not to be regarded as representing a statement of policy; but it seems clear that the present situation cannot endure, and I shall be glad to learn whether the competent French officials have this or any other possible solution in mind.[5]

[5] In telegram No. 297 Saving of August 31 Sir G. Clerk reported that he had given the substance of this telegram to M. Spitzmüller, Acting Head of the League of Nations Department at the Quai d'Orsay, who stated that the French Government were in complete agreement with His Majesty's Government, and suggested that the opportunity should be taken to speak 'in the strongest terms to General Rydz-Smigly [Inspector General of the Polish Army] who arrived in Paris yesterday, and enquired whether . . . you would be prepared to instruct His Majesty's Representative at Warsaw to make a similar *démarche*'. In Foreign Office telegram No. 219 of September 2, however, Sir G. Clerk was instructed to emphasize at the Quai d'Orsay that no firm decision regarding the policy to be adopted over Danzig had been made by His Majesty's Government, and that if the French Government wished to speak to General Rydz-Smigly, His Majesty's Government did not wish to be associated with any views they might express on the subject, but considered that the matter could best be dealt with by direct discussions at Geneva.

No. 145

Sir G. Clerk (Paris) to Mr. Eden (Received August 29)
No. 294 Saving: Telegraphic [C 6156/99/18]

PARIS, *August 28, 1936*

Minister for Foreign Affairs asked His Majesty's Minister to call on him this afternoon as he wished you to have an account of the conversations which he and the President of the Council had had this week with Dr. Schacht.[1] At the two earlier meetings Dr. Schacht had confined himself to generalities, to the usual professions of Germany's peaceful intentions and disquisitions on her need of colonies. On the latter point the French Ministers had given him no encouragement whatever. They had pointed out very clearly that France had given only too many proofs of good will and love of peace, but she had now reached the limit of concessions. It was Germany's turn to make a contribution. Dr. Schacht had little to say in reply to this, and to an allusion to the League he had been particularly unresponsive.[2]

In a final conversation with the President of the Council this morning Dr. Schacht had been somewhat more explicit.[3] He had given them to understand that he had seen the Chancellor before leaving Berlin and that he would go to Berchtesgaden to report on his return. He said that the Chancellor was deeply concerned about the economic and financial situation in Germany. He was most anxious for an 'alignment' of currencies and for help as regards supplies of raw materials. Until he got them he could not afford to abandon his rearmament programme, which provided so large a volume of employment. In return for the assistance he required, the Chancellor would go a long way to meet French views, and would even be prepared to discuss disarmament.

Dr. Schacht begged that the French Government would give sympathetic consideration to his appeal and would agree to further discussions. The President of the Council had pointed out that the recent actions of the German Government had not been encouraging and that in any case he would not embark on any discussions without the participation of His Majesty's Government. The French Government fully realise that Dr. Schacht's visit was calculated to temper the wind of the German extension of military service,[4] and they have not allowed his honeyed words to arouse any false hopes. They consider that it is for Berlin to make the next move, or at least to give some official indication of their readiness to talk. On the other hand, there is no doubt that MM. Blum and Delbos are both genuinely anxious to arrive at an understanding with Germany and they consider that it would be worth while, should the opportunity occur, to pursue these conversations further. Where questions of international economics and finance are concerned, they are both convinced of the importance of a 'liberal' policy—as indeed are also M. Vincent-Auriol and M. Spinasse, the present Ministers of Finance and National Economy, and M. Delbos said that he hoped that the meeting at Geneva would give an opportunity for discussion of these questions.[5]

Copy to Berlin by bag.

[1] See No. 141.   [2] Cf. *ibid.*, note 4.
[3] Minutes of this meeting are printed in *D.D.F.*, *op. cit.*, No. 213.
[4] See No. 132.
[5] A minute by Mr. Baxter said: 'This is important, as the first indication that the Germans are beginning to need foreign economic assistance, and may be prepared to make concessions in other spheres. Hitler himself has apparently sent this message about his

"even being prepared to discuss disarmament"—though this was possibly only to counteract the effect on the French Govt. of the 2 years' service decree, and may not have been sincerely meant. But the Chancellor's concern about the economic and financial position is almost certainly genuine. C.W.B. 1/9.' Dr. Schacht's hopes of a successful outcome of this visit are stressed in his memoirs, *76 Jahre meines Lebens* (Bad Wörishofen, 1953), pp. 477–8.

No. 146

Record by Mr. Baxter of a communication from the Dominions Office
[*C 6163/4/18*]

FOREIGN OFFICE, August 28, 1936

Sir H. Batterbee[1] of the Dominions Office telephoned yesterday in the following sense:

The Secretary of State for the Dominions would like Mr. Eden to know that, having seen Mr. Sargent's recent minute of his conversation with M. Cambon,[2] he decided to 'throw a fly over' Mr. Dulanty,[3] whom he was seeing on another subject. Mr. Dulanty had just returned from Dublin, and Mr. MacDonald therefore enquired whether he had ever heard any mention of the possibility that the Irish Free State might participate in a new security pact for Western Europe. Mr. Dulanty replied that he had never heard the subject mentioned in Dublin. Mr. MacDonald thought that Mr. Dulanty would probably report his enquiry to the Irish Free State Government, and would ask to be informed of the position.

Mr. MacDonald entirely approved the line which Mr. Sargent had taken with M. Cambon, and suggested that, if the French Embassy should return to the charge, they should be told that the matter had not been raised with His Majesty's Government by the Government of the Irish Free State, and that we were not, therefore, in a position to say anything on the subject.

C. W. BAXTER

[1] An Assistant Under Secretary of State in the Dominions Office.
[2] No. 93.
[3] Mr. J. W. Dulanty had been High Commissioner for the Irish Free State in London since 1930.

No. 147

Mr. Eden to Sir G. Clerk (Paris)
No. 1490 [*W 9887/9549/41*]

FOREIGN OFFICE, August 28, 1936

Sir,

During the course of a conversation this morning the French Ambassador spoke of the non-intervention agreement in respect of Spain, and stated that he had told his Government that we were prepared to assist by having the

Committee in London.[1] The Ambassador considered that it would be some time before the French Government would receive the replies which would enable us to go ahead.

2. M. Corbin asked me whether I had any information as to the attitude of our own Labour Party in the question of Spain. He rather had the impression that they were not very much interested. I replied that I did not think that that was the case, though I had been somewhat amused at the story which one of them had brought back from Paris that the suggestion of non-intervention was not originally a French but a British initiative.[2] I had said that there was of course no truth in this, though I had always thought M. Blum's initiative a wise one. The Ambassador remarked that so far as he could recollect there had been no discussion of the Spanish problem during our Three-Power meeting.

3. Speaking of the general situation in Spain the Ambassador stated that he saw little chance of any action at present on our part to bring the fighting to an end. I had mentioned during an earlier conversation that we had been considering a humanitarian intervention, and he now saw in our press that I had definitely made such an appeal.[3] I replied that this was so, and that of course if the French Government could give that appeal their support we should greatly welcome it.

I am, &c.,
ANTHONY EDEN

[1] Cf. No. 128. [2] See No. 136.
[3] Cf. No. 133. Foreign Office telegram No. 165 of August 27 (see No. 143, note 1) was printed in *The Times*, August 28, 1936, p. 12.

No. 148

Mr. Eden to Sir G. Clerk (Paris)
No. 1491 [*C 6144/4/18*]

FOREIGN OFFICE, *August 28, 1936*

Sir,

During the course of a conversation with the French Ambassador this morning[1] M. Corbin recalled that at the end of July he had mentioned to Sir R. Vansittart and myself a phase of our conversation with French Ministers in London during which a mention had been made of the possibility of securing from the German Government some assurance that, pending the meeting of the Five Powers, no steps would be taken by them to reinforce their position in the Rhineland.[2] Though there had been no hard and fast

[1] See No. 147.
[2] In a minute on Berlin despatch No. 988 of September 16 (No. 198 below), Mr. Lawford wrote: 'There is no record of the conversation between the Secretary of State and Sir R. Vansittart and the French Ambassador at the end of July referred to in our despatch No. 1491 to Paris, but the attitude of the French Government to a possible further reoccupation

agreement on the matter in London, I had been good enough to say that I would instruct Sir E. Phipps to endeavour to obtain some assurances in Berlin. The Ambassador was all the more anxious on the subject now, since there were reports that Germany had made preparations in several towns in the Rhineland where she had previously had no troops, for their accommodation. The position was therefore now such that Germany could rapidly reinforce her troops in the Rhineland, and she might do so at any moment.

2. I replied that judging from the press Germany's eyes at the moment seemed to be turned much more to the East than to the West. So far as I recollected our conversation at the end of July it had only been suggested that some assurance should be sought from Germany in general terms. This had been done. I then read to His Excellency the last two paragraphs of Berlin telegram No. 243[3] which run as follows:

'At the end of a friendly conversation His Excellency (Baron von Neurath) informed us (Sir E. Phipps and Sir R. Vansittart) officially that the German Government would be happy to accept the invitation to a Five Power Conference but not before the middle of October at the earliest in order to give ample time for thorough preparation diplomatically and for reasons given in para. 2 of Berlin telegram No. 240.[4]

Sir R. Vansittart remarked that he hoped in that case that we could be certain that meanwhile there would be no disturbing acts committed by any of the participating Powers. The Minister for Foreign Affairs declared that he could rest assured that perfect calm would prevail in the intervening period.'

The Ambassador remarked 'and now we have the announcement of two years' service'.[5]

3. The Ambassador expressed his grave apprehension as to the use to which this continually increasing German rearmament was to be put. He did not say the German Government necessarily had any definite plan, but they would make use of any opportunity. In any event we must surely anticipate that this increased strength would be used diplomatically. Nor was the Ambassador wholly at ease about France's position in the future. He did not mean this in respect of the immediate future—say two or three months' time—but taking the longer view there was perhaps more to attract Germany in staging a difference with France, than with Russia. However much Germany and Russia might rail at each other, they had in fact no common frontier.

4. I replied that if the Ambassador's fears were justified, then there was all the more reason to make rapid progress with the preparations for the Five-Power Conference. The Ambassador assented to this, though without

---

of the demilitarised zone was explained by M. Delbos at the London Meeting on July 23rd . . . V. G. Lawford. 22nd September 1936.' Mr. Lawford was a Third Secretary in the Central Department of the Foreign Office.

[3] No. 41.   [4] No. 37.   [5] See No. 132.

enthusiasm, adding that the atmosphere for such a conference was not now very favourable.

I am, &c.,
ANTHONY EDEN

No. 149

Sir G. Clerk (Paris) to Mr. Eden (Received August 29, 9.30 a.m.)
No. 273 Telegraphic [C 6155/4/18]

PARIS, *August 29, 1936, 7.10 a.m.*

The Minister for Foreign Affairs enquired today[1] whether you had yet had time to consider preliminary procedure of the five Power meeting. Now that non-intervention agreement and Egyptian Treaty[2] were out of the way he hoped that we should be able to make some progress. As regards the date, he suggested the third week in October. As regards the place the French Government had no strong feeling; they would not object to Brussels if Belgian Government wished it to be held there. On the other hand they would be prepared to agree to a Swiss town if you considered holding of the meeting in Switzerland would be an inducement either to Herr Hitler or Signor Mussolini or both to attend in person. He would be very glad to learn views of His Majesty's Government.

[1] This telegram was drafted on August 28.
[2] See Volume XVI, No. 483 and Appendix V.

No. 150

Mr. Ogilvie-Forbes (Madrid) to Mr. Eden (Received September 1, 9.30 a.m.)
No. 102 Telegraphic [W 10193/62/41]

MADRID, *August 31, 1936, 9.25 p.m.*

Your telegram No. 54, first sentence.[1]

That is precisely the message I myself and my staff have been emphasizing but in vain. While we have some genuine and sad cases of which there will be more to come, we have also some of the less desirable elements of the British colony who prefer to be fed and lodged in Embassy at a trivial cost or for nothing rather than face evacuation or risk and discomfort of life in their homes. In my telegram 70[2] I suggested compulsory powers to evacuate because I was indignant at the selfishness of certain people who prefer to see their children needlessly suffer or who are drones who do not do their share of household duties. But I now realize that this is not practicable.

[1] The first sentence of this Foreign Office telegram of August 29 was as follows. 'While it is reasonable that British subjects should be able to take refuge at His Majesty's Embassy in the event of immediate danger and prior to their being evacuated at the earliest opportunity, I do not consider that they have any right to expect to be housed there for an indefinite period purely because they refuse to take advantage of the available facilities for their evacuation.' [2] Not printed.

The real problem is the women. I do not mind about the men. I had hoped that the bombardment would have moved them. Quite the contrary. Now owing to lack of discipline mainly on the part of the women we are having recurrent and unpleasant trouble with the drains.[3] Perhaps this may ...[4] them. All the time they are being all too well looked after by Mrs Unwin as housekeeper and waited on and protected by a small body of volunteer men, who are of admirable assistance to me.

I have already warned Embassy inmates in the sense of last sentence of your telegram under reference and result is that decent people whose lives are really in danger want to return home while the meaner sort will not budge.

Nevertheless while I think British people in their own unobtrusive flats may be just as safe as in the Embassy I certainly cannot guarantee safety for those who may be returned from the Embassy to their homes especially as many of them have gone native.

It will soon be too late for evacuation. We must therefore make the best of the situation.[5]

[3] Changed to 'drones' on the filed copy.   [4] The text was here uncertain.
[5] Foreign Office telegram No. 80 of September 5 referred to Mr. Ogilvie-Forbes's telegram No. 102 and informed him that it was 'not the desire of His Majesty's Government that you should remain at Madrid in the absence of any authority capable of affording protection, at the risk of an attack on Embassy and of a serious incident which might gravely endanger relations between H.M. Govt and the Spanish Govt.' He was also told that he should not think it necessary to place himself and his staff in excessive danger because of the presence of British subjects who had had every opportunity of leaving and had declined to do so.

No. 151

Note by Mr. Shuckburgh on Italian activity in the Balearic Islands
[*W 10452/9549/41*]

FOREIGN OFFICE, *August 31, 1936*

These telegrams[1] suggest that the Italians are attempting to establish a position in Majorca in which they may be asked to accept some sort of responsibility for the Islands, possibly in the form of a Protectorate, in the event of the insurgents being defeated on the mainland of Spain.

There are three possible lines of action to be considered in this connection.

1. The issue of a warning on the lines suggested by the Secretary of State in F.P. 10[2] that any change in the status quo in the Mediterranean will be of concern to His Majesty's Government. At the meeting of the Foreign Policy Committee recorded within the Secretary of State said that he was

[1] The reference was to six telegrams just received from naval sources in the Mediterranean, forwarded in a letter of August 31 by the First Lord of the Admiralty to the Foreign Office.
[2] No. 115.

no longer in favour of this proposal.[3] It is now understood however that he is willing to re-consider it if the Department think it advisable. It should be noted that Sir Samuel Hoare now urges that the declaration should be made (though he would favour a private communication to Mussolini rather than a public declaration in this country) and that the Chiefs of Staff in their recent memorandum also supported the proposal.[4] I think that the attitude of the Western Department would be that the evidence of Italian activities in Morocco and the Balearics justifies the fear that unless something is done to warn them off, the Italians will fish for what they can get in these areas. The Department would, I think, strongly favour the issue of some sort of warning on the lines indicated.

2. On the other hand it is understood that the Chiefs of Staff consider that the acquisition of the Balearic Islands by Italy would be more of a menace to the French than to ourselves and would not seriously endanger Gibraltar. While therefore making a general statement about the Western Mediterranean on our own behalf, it may be well to consult the French, with reference to the particular question of the Balearics, as to whether they propose to make any similar statement or communication. It would be advisable presumably that if we make a public statement we should do it *before* the French, in order not to appear to be acting in any other interests than our own.[5]

3. We have one destroyer, H.M.S. *Greyhound*, at Palma on visit, and the cruiser *Galatea* is shortly to arrive there and to remain until further notice. The *Queen Elizabeth* is at Malta. The Italians have the cruiser *Fiume* and a flotilla leader *Malo Cello* and they also appear to be landing large numbers of aircraft, including bombers, and guns. It might be advisable to increase the number of British units stationed in these waters.

[3] No. 115, note 4.
[4] See No. 126.
[5] This question came before the Cabinet at its meeting on September 2. After considering Mr. Eden's memorandum (No. 115) and a telegram of August 31 from Sir S. Hoare, recommending a statement on the lines discussed at the Foreign Policy committee on August 25 (*ibid.*, note 4), the Cabinet was reminded by Lord Cranborne (in the absence of Mr. Eden with chicken pox) of the interview between Mr. Ingram and Count Ciano on August 17 (No. 103; cf. No. 104). Lord Cranborne pointed to Count Ciano's explicit disclaimer on that occasion that his government had had any dealings with General Franco or 'was contemplating dealing with Whites for the cession of Ceuta, Spanish Morocco, or Balearic Islands', and suggested that advantage might be taken of this communication to thank Count Ciano and to add the warning that any alteration of the status quo in the Western Mediterranean must be a matter of the closest concern to His Majesty's Government. The Cabinet agreed that Mr. Eden should so act if he thought the moment appropriate. See No. 159 below.

No. 152

Mr. Newton (Berlin) to Mr. Eden (Received September 1, 2.40 p.m.)
No. 282 Telegraphic: by telephone [*W 10204/9549/41*]

Immediate   BERLIN, *September 1, 1936*
Your telegram No. 187.[1]

The French Ambassador informs me that in reply to his recent approach[2] the German Government have just stated in writing that they do not consider the establishment of proposed committee to be either necessary or useful. They suggest on the other hand that His Majesty's Government should serve as a clearing house.

Herr Dieckhoff is unable to see me before September 2nd midday but as he is in charge of Ministry of Foreign Affairs I think it preferable to see him personally in order to ascertain the reasons for German reply and do my best to secure acceptance of French proposal. In the absence of further instructions[3] and subject to any later information which French Ambassador may obtain, I propose to point out to Herr Dieckhoff first that I have no information as to whether His Majesty's Government or any other single Government would be prepared to undertake the considerable and perhaps very invidious responsibility which German counter proposal might involve; secondly that if they were so willing the other Governments might not care to entrust such a responsibility to them; and thirdly that in any event serious delay would be entailed whereas French proposal has already been approved by a large number of Governments.

[1] This Foreign Office telegram of August 31 referred to the French proposal for the establishment of a committee to collate measures taken by the various governments in pursuance of the agreement for non-intervention in Spain, and for this committee to meet in London: cf. No. 128. M. Cambon informed Sir G. Mounsey on August 31 that the German Government were 'trying to evade the question of a collating committee', and Mr. Newton was instructed 'to express to German Government the hope of His Majesty's Government that they will fall in with this proposal'.
[2] This approach had been made by M. François-Poncet following M. Delbos's circular telegram of August 25: see No. 140, and cf. *D.D.F., op. cit.*, No. 199.
[3] See No. 154 below.

No. 153

Sir C. Wingfield (Lisbon) to Mr. Eden (Received September 1, 11.20 p.m.)
No. 165 Telegraphic [*W 10281/9549/41*]

LISBON, *September 1, 1936, 8.53 p.m.*
My telegram No. 162 last paragraph.[1]

Portuguese Minister for Foreign Affairs has handed to French Minister and myself official reply which may be summarised as follows.

[1] In this telegram of September 1, received in the Foreign Office at 2.15 p.m., Sir C. Wingfield reported the Portuguese Government's view that as the non-intervention

(1) Portuguese Government consider that creation of such a committee cannot be said to be implied in agreement which was only entered into by them under essential reserves. Present proposals seem to involve renunciation of some of these.

(2) Agreement was not one previously discussed but was adhered to unilaterally by various States none of which are under any obligations towards proposed committee.

(3) But in view of their request that French Government should make proposals for efficient supervision of execution of agreement (paragraph 6 of their Note of August 21st)[2] Portuguese Government will be prepared to support a committee for the purpose of collecting information from responsible authorities, examining facts worthy of attention and transmitting its conclusions to various Governments, provided (a) that its competence is strictly limited, the reserves and conditions made by each Government being respected; (b) that committee has powers necessary to carry out its mission; and (c) that there are guarantees for impartiality of its action.

(4) It must be remembered that the devastating war in Spain is between Western civilisation and an effort to overthrow it by terrorism.

(5) Portuguese Government therefore ask, in order to avoid misunderstanding, that competence of the committee should be strictly defined and also its methods of procedure so that Portuguese Government should be able to agree beforehand as to their suitability in the existing circumstances. In particular the Portuguese Government could not agree to the committee receiving or examining information not accompanied by proofs and emanating from entities not having responsibilities of a Government. The committee must be purely an affair of Governments.

(6) There must moreover be no doubts as to the impartiality of the committee.

(7) The above observations are . . .[3] by feeling that seriousness for all of the situation in Spain makes it the more necessary to provide against difficulties beforehand rather than to find remedies for them afterwards.

Translation follows by bag.[4]

agreement was unilateral each power was the sole judge as to its obligations under it, and in the last paragraph reported Dr. Monteiro as saying that the Portuguese Cabinet would consider that evening the question of its representation on the proposed committee in London.

[2] See No. 119.
[3] The text was here uncertain.
[4] Not printed. The Portuguese text is given in *D.A.P.E.*, *op. cit.*, No. 252. Foreign Office telegram No. 116 of September 4 instructed Sir C. Wingfield to make a communication to the Portuguese Government in the sense of telegram No. 192 to Berlin (No. 164 below). After doing so he was told by Dr. Monteiro on the same day that he could not 'conceal the difficulty felt by Portugal in participating in a Committee, on which would sit a Representative of the Soviet Government' but he promised to consult the Portuguese Government as to the reply that should be returned to the British representations.

No. 154

Mr. Eden to Mr. Newton (Berlin)
No. 190 Telegraphic [W 10289/9549/41]

Immediate   FOREIGN OFFICE, September 1, 1936, 9.50 p.m.

Your telegram No. 282.[1]

In speaking to Herr Dieckhoff you should make use of following arguments and of any others which may occur to you in order to persuade German Government to agree to be represented on proposed committee.

(1) Refusal of German Government to participate at a moment when practically all other governments have agreed to do so would have the most unfortunate results on public opinion here and elsewhere and might lead many people to the conclusion that Germany did not intend strictly to enforce the prohibition.

(2) If German Government refuses other governments will certainly not be willing to participate in the meetings, and the only effective and immediate scheme for supervising the enforcement of the agreement will thus break down. This may mean the collapse of all the efforts which have been made during the last few weeks to prevent Spain becoming a battleground for opposing European interests.

(3) Proposed committee provides the best method of securing agreement on further measures of non-intervention in Spain, such for example as prohibition of volunteers mentioned in last paragraph of German Note of August 17th to French Chargé d'Affaires.[2] It is in fact only a logical consequence of the policy of non-intervention to which they have already subscribed.

(4) Alternative proposal of German Government that His Majesty's Government should act as a clearing house would not be acceptable either to His Majesty's Government or, probably, to other governments, and would in any case involve further delay which might be fatal to the success of the non-intervention agreement. Moreover it would not satisfactorily solve the problem of co-ordination and would involve much unnecessary correspondence and difficulty.

You should add that His Majesty's Government most earnestly hope that the German Government will not stand out alone against a proposal which has been accepted almost unanimously by the European powers and which will do much to allay the mutual recrimination and suspicions which are at present arising out of the Spanish situation.[3]

---

[1] No. 152.

[2] D.G.F.P., Series D, vol. iii, No. 45.

[3] The note of urgency in this telegram appears to be due to a further visit to the Foreign Office on 1 September by Messrs. Greenwood and Citrine (cf. No. 136). They told Sir G. Mounsey of press reports 'to the effect that German and British ships were loading . . . munitions for Portugal, with ultimate destination to Spain, that France had wished to summon a conference of arms-manufacturing Powers but had been prevented by H.M. Govt., and a great deal more about the supply of arms to the rebels by Germany, Portugal and Italy'.

They anticipated hostile criticism of these three Powers at the meeting of the Labour Party on the following Monday, September 7. Sir G. Mounsey minuted: 'We must telegraph to Mr. Newton at once and instruct him to put all possible pressure on the German Govt. to agree to the proposal for a Committee . . .'

No. 155

Draft telegram[1] from the Admiralty to the Commander-in-Chief, Mediterranean
[*W 10288/62/41*]

Secret   ADMIRALTY, *September 1, 1936*

Your 0003/31st August.[2] Question of Italy taking aggressive action during Spanish crisis has been considered by Chiefs of Staff Committee,[3] and following recommendations from their report are communicated for your guidance. (1) We should endeavour to maintain sufficient Naval Forces on the Western Mediterranean and Spanish Atlantic coasts to ensure that we have at least one ship at every port where the Italians have one and that, if possible, in important ports British S[enior] N[aval] O[fficer] is senior to the Italian. (2) Every endeavour should be made that any landing or other action by armed forces to preserve order should be concerted between the powers concerned.

[1] This draft telegram was forwarded to Mr. Seymour from Mr. Seal (Admiralty) on September 1. Mr. Seymour informed the Admiralty on the same day that the draft was approved for communication to the Commander-in-Chief, Mediterranean.
[2] Not printed.   [3] See No. 126.

No. 156

Report[1] by the Chiefs of Staff Sub-Committee on preparations for the proposed Five-Power Conference
[*C 6223/4/18*]

2, WHITEHALL GARDENS, S.W.1, *September 1, 1936*

1. At the request of the Secretary of State for Foreign Affairs, we have examined the attached Memorandum by the Foreign Office[2] on the subject of the general lines which should be followed by His Majesty's Government at the proposed meeting of the Five Locarno Powers.

We were particularly asked to treat this as a matter of urgency, in order that His Majesty's Government might reach the necessary decisions without delay, and thus be the first in the field with their proposals. Consequently, we have been unable to devote as much time as we should have liked to the formulation of our answers to the intricate and important questions that have been referred to us.

[1] C.I.D. Paper No. 1260–B, circulated to the Cabinet as C.P. 218(36).
[2] As in No. 114: it was circulated to the Cabinet as C.P. 220(36).

2. At the outset we desire to emphasise that we have not been asked to consider whether the conclusion of a new general agreement in Western Europe, to replace the Locarno Treaty, is, or is not, desirable from a military point of view. Accordingly, we assume that it has been decided on political grounds to attempt to negotiate such an agreement. We have, therefore, confined our attention to the questions which have been specifically referred to the Committee of Imperial Defence in the Foreign Office Memorandum, and to those other questions therein which appear to have military implications.

GENERAL PRINCIPLES

3. Before dealing with these questions in detail, we desire to formulate certain general principles which should, from the military point of view, govern our policy in negotiating any new agreement.

4. In the first place, a statement which we made in a report to the Committee of Imperial Defence in February 1935[3] bears repetition:

> 'Again, without in any way wishing to minimise the ultimate potentialities of Germany, we would urge that the broad principles on which our Empire strategy has always been based should not be forgotten nor should the lessons of history be overlooked.

> 'The greater our commitments in Europe the less will be our ability to secure our Empire and its communications . . .'

It is true that the German threat is now more formidable, and perhaps more imminent than it was when the above report was written, but the desirability of limiting our commitments in Europe is as insistent as ever.

5. Secondly, we consider that we should not undertake a liability to engage in any war in which our vital interests are not affected. We fully realise that this principle has to be reconciled with the necessity to contribute towards a general appeasement of Europe, which in turn would contribute to the security of the British Empire.

6. Thirdly, whatever our engagements may be, we should make it clear that the final decision as to whether we enter a war or stand out of it will rest with ourselves, and ourselves alone.

7. Fourthly, we consider that the form which our intervention will take should similarly be a matter for our own decision when the occasion arises.

8. Finally, we consider it of the first importance from the point of view of the full development of our Imperial war effort, that any engagements which we may undertake should command the full support of the Dominions. This, we submit, would not be assured, unless the principles set out in the preceding paragraphs are adhered to.

THE FOREIGN OFFICE MEMORANDUM

9. In the following paragraphs we deal seriatim with the questions set forth in the Foreign Office Memorandum.

[3] *Note in original*: C.I.D. Paper No. 1161–B, paragraph 17. Cf. Volume XII, No. 483.

Question 2. What machinery should the new agreement contain for bringing the guarantees into operation? Should the League be employed for this purpose in the same way as the old Locarno Treaty?

10. This question has not been specifically referred to us, but we feel that it has military implications.

11. It is immaterial, from the military point of view, what form of machinery is devised for bringing the guarantees into operation, provided that the following conditions are fulfilled:

(i) We must ensure, as already stated in paragraph 6 above, that the final decision as to whether we enter a war rests with ourselves, and ourselves alone. We should not agree to an arrangement whereby we might, for example, be automatically committed by a majority vote of some international body.

(ii) We should have the power to take instant action in case of flagrant aggression, consequently, it should be made perfectly clear in the new agreement, as is not the case in Article 4(3) of the Locarno Treaty, that the term 'flagrant aggression' includes air attack. In default of this safeguard, there is a danger that the aggressor might gain a decisive advantage during the delay which would almost inevitably ensue before the investigating authority announced its verdict.

Question 4. Do we wish in the New Agreement to be guaranteed ourselves instead of being merely a guarantor? If so, against whom and by whom are we to be guaranteed?

12. Since Great Britain is an island, no direct invasion by land forces is possible; the danger of sea-borne invasion is remote. Nor is it likely that any Power in Europe would embark upon a naval war against us alone, unless we were already engaged in hostilities in the Far East. On the other hand, we are particularly susceptible to air attack, and for this reason it would appear at first sight that it would be an advantage to have a guarantee of immediate assistance in the event of our being the victim of such a form of aggression.

13. Against this it can be argued, first, that the contingency of our being attacked by France is so remote that there would be no practical advantage in being guaranteed by Germany against France, and, secondly, that in the event of our being attacked by Germany, it is most unlikely that France would fail to come to our assistance in the interest of her own security, irrespective of any previous guarantee. If these suppositions are correct, the practical value to us of receiving a guarantee would certainly be small; but it is doubtful whether they can be taken for granted, particularly from a long range point of view.

14. The question whether our present policy of close friendship with France will endure for all time is primarily a political one, and although there is at present no particular reason for thinking that it may be otherwise,

recent events in Europe cannot but raise a shadow of apprehension as to what the future may hold, and suggest the possibility, if no more, that we may at some later date have to face the contingency of French hostility.

15. But apart from this, it is not certain, even in the existing state of our relationship, that we can rely on French assistance against Germany irrespective of the causes of the quarrel. It is quite possible, for example, that, in the event of a German air attack against ourselves owing to our refusal at some future date to surrender a Colony, France might well feel that her own security was not endangered, and might even claim that our refusal was in itself a 'provocation.' In such circumstances the absence of any guarantee of her support would result in a single-handed struggle with Germany in which our extreme vulnerability to air attack would expose us to the gravest danger; whereas, if such a guarantee existed, it might constitute a sufficient deterrent to Germany to prevent her attacking us.

16. It is true that if we consent to act as a guarantor without receiving any guarantee in return, there is a psychological advantage to be obtained from our disinterested action to preserve peace; this may be of value so far as it contributes to a general appeasement and may also put us in a stronger position for securing our interests in other directions (*vide* paragraphs 3 to 8). Nevertheless, from a defence aspect, it is felt that the considerations mentioned above lead on balance to the conclusion that we have something definite to gain from receiving a guarantee under any new Agreement, and that in view of our vulnerability to air attack, we should make every endeavour to obtain such a guarantee. This is, in fact, the view to which we inclined in our Report[4] on the French air proposals for a Treaty of mutual guarantee in the following terms:

'We note that, for the first time, a suggestion has been made to give a guarantee to us in certain eventualities, and we appreciate fully the importance of this concession.'

17. Although a political factor, and therefore outside our sphere, we feel that the above conclusion will undoubtedly accord with public opinion in this country.

18. It remains to consider against whom and by whom we should be guaranteed. From the foregoing brief review, it is apparent that we require guarantees from France against Germany, and from Germany against France. We should not, however, wish to receive any guarantee from Italy or Belgium for the reasons given in our answers to Questions 6 and 7.

Question 5. Should the Irish Free State participate in the new agreement?

19. In a recent Report[5] which we prepared at the request of the Secretary of State for Dominion Affairs, but which has not yet been presented to the Committee of Imperial Defence, we explained the strategic importance of

---

[4] *Note in original*: C.I.D. Paper No. 1161–B. [see note 3 above].
[5] *Note in original*: Paper No. C.O.S. 507 [not printed].

the Irish Free State in the following terms:

'The strategic importance of the Irish Free State to this country arises from its geographical position, across our main trade routes and less than 100 miles from the west coast of Great Britain.

The features of the greatest military importance are

(a) The naval ports and anchorages possessed by the Irish Free State.
(b) The existing and potential air bases possessed by the Irish Free State.
(c) The land frontier which separates the Irish Free State from British Territory in Northern Ireland.

If (a) or (b) are in the hands of a hostile Power, or (c) is liable to attack by a hostile Power, our strategic position obviously suffers seriously. If this were the only aspect of our interests it would be sufficient for us to ensure the neutrality of the Irish Free State in war, and a mutual guarantee between the Irish Free State and Great Britain to that effect would satisfy our needs. Our interests do not end here, however, since the use of facilities in the Irish Free State for our forces would be of great importance to us in war.'

20. In the same Report we gave the following explanation of the facilities that we should require in the event of war:

'We should require unrestricted use of all ports and anchorages in war-time. Examples of our principal requirements are as follows:

Requirements in German War—

Lough Swilly	Convoy Assembly Port: base for Auxiliary Vessels.
Queenstown ... ... Kingstown ... ... Berehaven	Bases for Auxiliary Vessels.

Requirements in French War—

Lough Swilly	Convoy Assembly Port.
Queenstown ... ... Berehaven	Bases for the Main Fleet.
Kingstown	Base for Auxiliary Vessels.

It is not practicable to define exactly where we shall require aerodromes or landing grounds in Ireland during war, but we can assume that aircraft will be needed in connection with trade protection, coast defence, and minor naval operations. It is therefore essential that in war we should have the right of unrestricted flying over Ireland, and the use of such aerodromes as we may require.'

21. The above naval base facilities are already secured to us by the Anglo-Irish Treaty of 1921; and we should presumably still enjoy them in the event of any war in which we might become engaged, irrespective of whether the Irish Free State elected to stand out.

22. Nor would the position be materially altered if, as has recently been discussed, it were decided to hand over, in time of peace, the complete responsibility for the defence of the reserved ports in the Irish Free State, provided that the conditions recommended in our Report[6] on this subject are fulfilled, i.e., we should still retain all rights that we require in time of war.

23. Accordingly, we consider that, so long as the Irish Free State remains within the British Commonwealth of Nations, no advantage is to be gained from our point of view by her participation in the new agreement.

24. Nor would there appear to be any advantage to the Irish Free State itself from any such participation for the following reasons:

(i) A guarantee by us would be redundant, as we are already under the obligation to defend the Irish Free State as a component part of the British Commonwealth.

(ii) A guarantee to the Irish Free State by the other guarantor Powers would also be superfluous, since those Powers that enter the war as our allies would thereby also become allies of the Irish Free State. It has, in any case, to be remembered that the parties to a security arrangement will not 'come to the assistance' of their fellow members by despatching forces to their aid. They merely contract to enter the war, and thereafter employ their forces in whatever way they consider most advantageous.

25. From the foregoing it will be seen that the Irish Free State stands to gain nothing by participation in the new agreement, unless, of course, there is at the back of her mind, the idea that she should be guaranteed against possible aggression by ourselves. This is an embarrassment which we would clearly be unable to accept.

26. The above arguments are based on the assumption that the Irish Free State remains within the British Commonwealth. If she should cease to be a member, we would presumably negotiate a separate treaty with her on the general lines recommended in the Report from which we have quoted in paragraph 19.

In that event the conclusions recorded in paragraphs 23–25 above, to the effect that Irish Free State participation in the new Agreement would be unnecessary and perhaps embarrassing, would continue to hold good.

Question 6. Is Italy to be guaranteed? If so, against whom, and by whom?

27. Neither Italy nor ourselves received any guarantee under Locarno; but the Foreign Office have pointed out, in their comments on question (6), that, if we now become a guaranteed Power, it would be difficult to refuse the same advantage to Italy if she asked for it.

28. The Foreign Office state that it may be taken for granted that neither we nor Belgium would be prepared to guarantee Italy, so that, in effect,

---

[6] *Note in original*: C.I.D. Paper No. 416–C [not printed].

Italy would be guaranteed only by France against Germany and vice versa. But they also say that it is doubtful whether France would undertake such an obligation without our co-operation.

29. The tentative conclusion reached by the Foreign Office is that 'We should want in the new treaty to be both a guaranteed and a guarantor Power. But we should not wish either to guarantee or be guaranteed by Italy.'

30. The first part of this conclusion has already been discussed under question 4 above.

31. As regards the second part it would be undesirable, from the military point of view, for us to give any guarantee to Italy for the following reasons:

(i) On general grounds, it would constitute an additional, and possibly a dangerous, military commitment for us; and

(ii) It is difficult to imagine circumstances in which an attack directed, in the first instance, by one of the other signatories against Italy, would also be a direct threat to ourselves.

32. As we do not wish to give a guarantee to Italy, we cannot expect to obtain a guarantee from her. It is true that such a guarantee should be of value to us if we were attacked by either France or Germany: but the disadvantages of asking for a guarantee from Italy, and, consequently, having to give her one in return, appear to outweigh the advantages of Italian assistance in the event of aggression against us.

33. We therefore agree with the Foreign Office suggestion that we should neither guarantee nor be guaranteed by Italy.

34. The question of whether Italy is to be guaranteed by any of the other signatories still remains to be considered. This must depend on the wishes of the Powers concerned, and the only comments that we desire to make are:

(i) It is to our advantage to keep a war out of North-West Europe and therefore that France should not become involved in an Italo-German war, or Germany in an Italo-French war.

(ii) France is unlikely to guarantee Italy, unless we accept a similar obligation.

Our most desirable solution, therefore, from a military point of view, would be that Italy should remain, as she was under Locarno, merely a guarantor Power.

35. We are not specifically asked to consider the question of Italy as a guarantor of countries other than ourselves; but we wish to point out that it would be extremely embarrassing if we were to decide that Germany had committed an act of unprovoked aggression against France, necessitating our armed intervention on the side of France, and Italy, swayed by her sympathies for another 'totalitarian' State, were to take a contrary view and intervene on the side of Germany. The military consequences of such a development would certainly be very serious. Whether Italy, if she were not a party to a Western Pact, might remain neutral, but, if she

were a party, might feel compelled to intervene, possibly on the opposite side to ourselves, is a political question.

Question 7. Should Belgium be relieved of giving any guarantee and her commitments limited to an understanding to defend her own territory?

36. The effect of relieving Belgium of giving any guarantee would be that, in the event of war in Western Europe, she could remain neutral for so long as her neutrality were respected by the belligerents.

37. This holds out weighty advantages. In the first place it is conceivable that Germany might make a deliberate point of scrupulously respecting Belgian neutrality—at any rate at the outset of hostilities—in order not only to lessen the chances of intervention by Great Britain, but also to ensure that her important industrial districts in the Ruhr are not subjected to close range air attack from Belgian aerodromes.

38. Secondly, it is clearly desirable to limit the area of any war so far as it is possible to do so.

39. Thirdly, from the point of view of the air defence of this country, an effective Belgian neutrality would mean that German aircraft would have to cover considerably greater distances to reach their objectives. It is true, of course, that, in these circumstances, we ourselves would be unable to use Belgian aerodromes, but the advantage which we should obtain from the decreased intensity of German air attacks outweighs this disadvantage; moreover, aerodromes in Northern France for the use of our bombing aircraft would be just as effective as those in Belgium.

40. From the above it is clear that we ourselves have most to gain by an effective Belgian neutrality.

41. At the same time, we—and more particularly the French—can feel little confidence that Germany will be any more disposed to respect Belgian neutrality in a future war than she was in 1914, for the following reasons:

(i) It appears impossible for her to deploy her vast forces within the narrow confines of the Franco-German frontier, and her best chance of turning the French defences appears to lie in an attack through Belgium.

(ii) If she should desire to develop the heaviest scale of air attack on this country, she could not do so unless she established aerodromes in the Low Countries or at least flew over them.

42. If Germany were to violate Belgium at the outset of hostilities, she would gain a tremendous military advantage; and, even if she were to respect Belgian neutrality at the outset, she would still be in a position to violate it later at the moment most suitable to herself. We would have to be constantly prepared for this contingency without ever being able to determine the precise moment at which it would arise. But clearly the longer the violation is delayed, the better prepared we should be to meet it.

43. Turning now to the alternative; the effect of insisting on Belgium

being a guarantor Power would be that she would automatically enter any war in Western Europe at its outset. We would thus know in advance exactly where we stood, and not only we, but also the French and the Belgians themselves, would be able to frame plans accordingly.

44. Moreover, the certainty that she was bound to be involved in any such war might check any tendency that there might be on the part of Belgium to neglect her defences.

45. The advantages of Belgium being a guarantor, which are set out in paragraphs 43 and 44 above, are outweighed by the disadvantages detailed in paragraphs 37 to 42. Our general conclusions are therefore as follows:

(i) An effective Belgian neutrality would be greatly to our advantage and should not deliberately be rendered impossible, even though the chances of its being maintained throughout a Western European war are remote.

(ii) We should therefore welcome a request by Belgium that she should not be a guarantor Power, but should merely give an undertaking to defend her own territory.

Question 8. Are Non-Aggression Provisions to be so framed (as Locarno was) as to reserve the right of any Party to come to the assistance of a non-Party which has been attacked by another Party?

46. This question has certain military implications upon which we desire to remark.

47. It appears that any European war involving Germany is more likely to break out upon her eastern than upon her western frontiers. It may even be argued that some rectification of Germany's eastern frontier is essential before there is any hope of lasting peace and a durable settlement in Europe.

48. We may regard it as certain that France will not cancel the Franco-Soviet Pact, unless and until there is a complete change of government in France. In addition, it appears impossible to turn the Franco-Soviet Pact into an Eastern European Pact to include Germany. This being so, it is important that we should take steps to ensure that any guarantee we give will not automatically draw us into a war which has as its origin the rectification of Germany's eastern frontiers.

49. At the present time we are not placed under an obligation to use force against France in the event of her implementing her obligations to come to the assistance of her Eastern allies; but there seems to be nothing to make it clear that, if war breaks out between France and Germany under these conditions, we are not in any circumstances obliged to come to the assistance of France, even if the latter should be invaded by Germany. In any future treaty we consider that we should reserve complete freedom to decide for ourselves whether we should intervene in any conflict arising out of German aspirations or French commitments in Eastern Europe.

Question 9. Do we wish to make special provision in the new agreement for air attack?

50. The Foreign Office comment on this question includes the following passage:

'It is natural that provision for dealing with air attack should be embodied in this new agreement.'

51. We are not altogether clear as to the precise implication of this sentence. We have on several occasions emphasised that war is not fought in one element, and that it is not possible to limit war to one particular arm of the defence forces.

52. If, therefore, the intention underlying the Foreign Office comment is that there should be some special provision for dealing with attack by air as opposed to attack by sea or land, we would deprecate it.

53. If, on the other hand—and we believe this to be the case—the intention of the comment is merely to ensure that the definition of flagrant aggression in Article 4, paragraph 3, of the Locarno Treaty, should be extended so as to cover the case of attack by air; then, as will be seen from paragraph 11 (ii) above, we are in entire agreement.

Question 10. Do we wish to make special provision in the new agreement for Air Limitation?

54. It would, of course, be extremely desirable, in view of the present air armament race throughout the world, to achieve some degree of air limitation; and we should leave no stone unturned in the forthcoming negotiations to press this point of view.

55. The principal difficulty, however, is that the new agreement is conceived on a regional basis, whereas any effective provision for air limitation cannot be so restricted. For example, as pointed out on pages 23 and 24 of the Appendix to this paper, Herr Hitler made it clear in December 1935, that the strength of the Russian Air Force, combined with the conclusion of the Franco-Soviet Pact, rendered impossible any question of air limitation on the basis of parity between the great Western Powers.[7]

56. In any case a limitation of air armaments is more difficult to achieve than is the case with land and sea armaments, owing to the fact that civil aviation resources, and the output of the aircraft industry can be so readily and rapidly converted to military use. There are also other serious difficulties which need not be detailed in this Report.

57. Consequently, we consider that it would be an almost hopeless task to attempt to incorporate any special provision for air limitation in the new agreement itself.

58. Nevertheless, we feel strongly that, in spite of the inherent difficulties of the problem, an opportunity might well occur in the course of the negotiations for ascertaining the views of the contracting parties on this important question, and possibly for initiating a separate discussion on the subject amongst all the great air Powers.

[7] See Volume XV, No. 383.

Question 11. In view of the fact that our present liberty to hold Staff conversations with France and Belgium, without any corresponding conversations with Germany, derives from Germany's repudiation of Locarno, and will not necessarily continue if Locarno is replaced by a new agreement with Germany, do we wish in the new agreement to provide for Staff conversations with France and Belgium?

59. The new agreement will presumably be on a multilateral basis. If this is so, it would be invidious to provide for Staff conversations with France and Belgium, unless provision were also made for Staff conversations with Germany.

60. Such provision would be impracticable as we have already pointed out[8] in the following terms:

' . . . Staff conversations will almost inevitably entail the disclosure of detailed war plans for the purpose of co-ordination and neither France nor Germany is in the least likely to disclose her plans to us when she knows that we are carrying on or have carried on similar conversations with other parties and there is no certainty as to the side on which we might be fighting.'

61. Apart from the practical difficulties, Staff conversations would inevitably tend to involve us in military commitments which would fetter our freedom of action as to the form that our intervention might take when the occasion arose.

62. Our conclusion therefore is that no provision should be made for Staff conversations with any Power.

Question 12. Should Holland be asked to accede to the new agreement? If so, should she assume all the obligations of the agreement, or only certain obligations?

63. In their Memorandum, the Foreign Office have summarised the views which we have recently expressed regarding the possible inclusion of Holland in an Aerial Convention, leading to the general conclusion that the advantages and disadvantages would be about even.

64. We are now asked whether we consider that Holland should be asked to accede to the proposed new Western Pact of Mutual Assistance, and, if so, whether she should be relieved of giving any guarantee, and her commitments limited to an undertaking to defend her own territory.

65. In a report dated June 1935[9] we recorded the following view:

'We stand to gain most by the effective neutrality of Holland. At present there is a chance, though not a good one, that Germany might prefer to leave Holland neutral. If, on the other hand, Holland is to be a party to the Air Pact, all chance of neutrality is removed.'

We consider that this conclusion applies with equal force to the question of her inclusion in the new agreement.

[8] *Note in original*: C.I.D. Paper No. 1224–B [not printed].
[9] *Note in original*: Paper No. C.O.S. 381; also C.I.D. Paper No. 1176–B. [Cf. Volume XIII, No. 364.]

66. Moreover, as we have stated in paragraph 38 above regarding the question of Belgian intervention, we feel that if hostilities in Western Europe should occur, it is important that the field of conflict should be kept to as narrow confines as possible.

67. We have already referred[10] to the deficiencies in the Dutch defences, and although there are indications that these are, to some extent, being remedied, it is certain that the Dutch will never be in a position to resist German invasion without greater assistance on land from ourselves and the French than we shall be able to afford. This brings us to the conclusion which we stated in a previous report,[10] 'Adherence of a weak ally, situated in an area of geographical importance, is a commitment which would add to our liabilities rather than to our resources. . .'

68. It therefore appears that it would be to our advantage if Holland were not involved in a Western War and that she should not, therefore, be included as a guarantor Power.

69. As regards the question of whether she should receive guarantees, there would be no particular advantage from our point of view, since a German invasion of Holland would constitute a direct threat to our interest in the integrity of the Low Countries and would probably involve us in war whether we had guaranteed Holland or not.

70. Consequently, we do not consider that Holland should be asked to accede to the new agreement; if, however, France or Germany wish to bring her in as a guaranteed Power, we need not oppose this; but, whether she accedes to the agreement or not, we consider that it would be valuable to obtain an undertaking from all the signatories of the agreement to respect her neutrality.

Question 17. In the invitation it is stated that, 'If progress can be made under this head (i.e., the conclusion of a western agreement for mutual assistance, and the resolution of the situation created by the German initiative of the 7th March), other matters will naturally come under discussion . . . in such a manner as to facilitate . . . the settlement of those problems the solution of which is essential to the peace of Europe.' If such an extension occurs in the field of discussion, what do we propose to ask for in the further negotiations contemplated?

71. Although we have not been asked to express an opinion on this problem, it is one that has military implications, and we therefore offer the following comments.

72. The Foreign Office comment on this question states 'we should decline to disinterest ourselves from the east and centre of Europe and continue to insist on the need for a general settlement . . .'

73. It is extremely improbable that we should be prepared to fight in a war arising out of an Eastern Europe dispute, at any rate until it had spread to Western Europe and our vital interests were threatened.

74. In urging the desirability of a general settlement, we should, as we

[10] *Note in original*: Paper No. C.O.S. 413; also D.P.R. 48.

have indicated in paragraph 5, decline to assume any commitments that would involve our intervention when our vital interests were not immediately threatened.

75. It follows that we should not support any agreement which might cause an extension of a war in Western Europe. It is fully realised that, if Germany is given a free hand in Central and Eastern Europe, there is a danger of the result recoiling ultimately on our heads. On the other hand, it would be disastrous if an appeasement in Western Europe were rendered impossible by over-consideration of Russian interests.[11]

C. J. DEVERELL

C. E. KENNEDY-PURVIS

(*A.C.N.S. for C.N.S.*)

C. L. COURTNEY

[11] The above report and the accompanying Foreign Office memorandum were considered by the Cabinet at a meeting on September 2, 1936. In the course of the discussion it was pointed out that the Chiefs of Staff had laid the greatest emphasis on the desirability from the military point of view 'of reducing our commitments to the minimum and of keeping our hands as free as possible'. It was pointed out in reply that in their paper the Foreign Office had indicated that this matter must be considered in the light of the comments of the Chiefs of Staff Sub-Committee. With regard to question 5 Mr. Malcolm MacDonald agreed generally with the conclusions contained in the Chiefs of Staff report. The Cabinet then recorded the following conclusions:

'(1) To approve the Memorandum by the Secretary of State for Foreign Affairs (C.P. 220(36)) and the Report of the Chiefs of Staff Sub-Committee (C.P. 218(36)) as the general line of policy to be followed in the preparations for the proposed Five-Power Conference and to take note that the Report of the Chiefs of Staff Sub-Committee does not involve any modifications in the recommendations set out on pages 20 and 21 of C.P. 220(36) in view of the fact that the Foreign Office have accepted the views of the Chiefs of Staff in regard to the question of Staff Conversations.

(2) That the Secretary of State for Foreign Affairs should be authorised to proceed accordingly and also approach the Governments concerned with a view to arrangements being made for a Meeting of the Five-Power Conference at the latter end of October next.'

No. 157

Note[1] by Mr. Seymour on British interests in the outcome of the Spanish struggle

[*W 10422/62/41*]

FOREIGN OFFICE, *September 1, 1936*

It is difficult to express an opinion whether the victory of the Right or of the Left in Spain would be the more undesirable from the point of view of

[1] This note resulted from a round of minuting in the Foreign Office engendered by a letter of August 24 to Mr. Eden from Señor de Madariaga, who advocated mediation by the diplomatic corps at Hendaye. There should be an Executive Committee, 'so composed as to inspire confidence to both sides', with the British Ambassador 'for political reasons,

British interests. On the whole it can be assumed that an extremist government of either complexion would be a serious embarrassment to us. A Communist Spain would mean the loss of the whole of the British invested capital in Spain and the end of British capitalist enterprise in the Peninsula, and might also favour the spreading of Communism into France. On the other hand, it is unlikely that an extreme right Government, on Fascist or closely similar lines, could establish itself on a lasting basis without some kind of foreign support, financial or other. Such a government would naturally tend to look for support to Italy and Germany. A Government in Spain under Italian influence must, under present conditions, constitute a risk to British interests.

At present it would seem that any Government which may emerge must necessarily be of one extreme or the other. It is highly desirable in either event that the government which does emerge should not enter upon its inheritance with any serious grudge against His Majesty's Government. This has been one of the objects of our non-interference policy, and we have been more or less successful so far in avoiding the accusation of partisanship from either camp. We have taken no step which could be considered as recognition of the insurgent government, and the measures which we have been compelled to take for the protection of our ships and the safety of Gibraltar have been applied equally to both Parties and based, not upon the laws of neutrality such as would have been in operation if we had recognised the belligerency of the insurgents, but upon an *ad hoc* basis for the purpose of defending our own interests. It must, of course, be recognised that if the Spanish Government are victorious, they will tend to regard our attitude of non-intervention and non-supply of arms as an unfriendly attitude towards the properly constituted government fighting rebel subjects; but this will apply to all European countries and cannot in any case be helped.

As regards the issue itself, we have no information enabling us to conclude which side is likely to win. Our reports show that during the last week, the insurgents have consolidated and concentrated their forces and are now in a position to take the offensive on a larger scale than heretofore against Madrid and against the towns of San Sebastian and Irun in the north; but their preliminary attacks have not been conspicuously successful. The morale

and in particular for reasons of "neutrality" of tendency' as its chairman. The committee should move tactfully from humanitarian to political mediation. Sir A. Cadogan summed up the debate by remarking that the plan might be useful in the future, but that at this stage 'the best procedure is to begin as we are doing, in the humanitarian tack [cf. No. 133]. Mediation cannot be imposed . . . A.C. Aug. 28 1936'. Mr. Eden wrote: 'I agree generally with these minutes . . . We must continually bear in mind in relation to this dispute that we are in a particularly strong position to intervene, because we are known to be more neutral than any other great power, & *because a compromise is in our national interest*. The victory of either extreme would be most unwelcome to us, so that we must be up & doing in favour of compromise whenever opportunity affords.

'I do not remember to have seen any appreciation of pros & cons, in our national interest, of a victory of Fascist or Communist. Should we not have this against Wednesday's Cabinet? A.E. Aug. 30th.'

of the Government supporters appears to be high in Madrid, but is reported to deteriorate progressively towards the fighting front, where there seems to be little discipline and a good deal of discouragement. Certain of the militia groups prefer to remain in and near the capital murdering suspect civilians rather than to reinforce the front line. The insurgents, on the other hand, seem to be better disciplined, though there have been few signs of any strategical skill amongst their leaders.

The factor which may, of course, be decisive in the issue will be the extent to which the various countries will evade the obligations of the non-intervention pact, and this adds to the difficulty of forecasting the result. It may depend, therefore, to a certain extent, upon the effectiveness of the work of the Committee of Control which is proposed to be set up in London.

The final issue must also depend on future events and its effects on our own interests may also be modified by considerations which cannot be foreseen. It may perhaps be suggested that an extreme right victory is likely to be embarrassing in respect of our foreign policy and interests, while an extreme left victory might be equally embarrassing, though in a different way, to any country which desires the maintenance of ordinary democratic government in those countries in which it still survives.

No. 158

Record by Lord Cranborne of a conversation with M. Corbin
[W 10395/9549/41]

FOREIGN OFFICE, September 2, 1936

1. I had a visit yesterday afternoon from the French Ambassador. He brought me a communication with regard to the recent increase in the period of German military service.[1] He had been directed by his Government to make this communication but he emphasised that it should not be regarded as an official note. The French Government realised that a formal note on this subject at the present time might well prejudice the success of the Five-Power Meeting later in the year. They were, however, anxious to put before His Majesty's Government informally their preoccupations.

2. He then turned to the subject of the Reform of the League, and asked whether His Majesty's Government had yet sent in to the Secretariat any document giving their views on this subject.[2] I said that they had not, and that, speaking personally, I thought it in the last degree improbable that they would put in any document before the Meeting of the Assembly. He said that he had noticed in the press that recent meetings of the Cabinet had been concerned with this subject. I agreed but said that they had been principally directed to an examination of the whole problem and to the

[1] See No. 132. [2] Cf. Volume XVI, No. 395, note 5, and see No. 179 below.

principles which must underlie British policy, rather than to the formulation of any definite scheme.[3]

3. He also asked whether the Secretary of State was considering forwarding to him any comments on the French proposals which had been communicated to him earlier in the year.[4] He had rather understood at the time that the Secretary of State was meditating making some reply. I said that I had no information on this subject but that I would make enquiries.

4. Finally, he said a few words about Spain. The French Government were doing all they could to obtain acceptances of their invitations to various nations. Two he understood were still outstanding, those of Portugal and Germany. The Portuguese Government had accepted in principle[5] but they had made a reservation that they claimed the right to leave the Committee if in their opinion any other nation was not operating the embargo. The French Government were not satisfied with this reservation. They considered that once a nation had joined the Committee, it would remain a member until the Committee was wound up. They were approaching the Portuguese Government further in this sense.

5. Turning to Germany, he said that an unsatisfactory reply had been received.[6] The German Government had indicated that they were opposed to the formation of the Committee and considered that His Majesty's Government could very well collate all the necessary information. He asked what was the view of His Majesty's Government on this proposal.

6. I said that I assumed that they would be opposed to it. The collation of information by one individual nation would not have by any means the same effect as a Committee of all the nations sitting round a table. I felt sure that the view of His Majesty's Government would be that they regarded the Committee as not only a better scheme but as a most material part of the operation of the non-intervention policy.

C.

[3] See No. 179, note 4 below.
[4] On June 22, 1936, at an interview with Mr. Eden (see Volume XVI, No. 377) M. Corbin had handed him a memorandum (not preserved in the Foreign Office archives) giving an 'exposé provisoire' of the French Government's views on League reform.
[5] See No. 153.   [6] See No. 152.

No. 159

Mr. Eden to Mr. Ingram (Rome)
No. 342 Telegraphic [W 10452/9549/41]

FOREIGN OFFICE, *September 3, 1936, 12.30 p.m.*

In your despatch No. 925[1] of August 18th you reported assurance given by Minister for Foreign Affairs that Italian Government had not done a deal or contemplated any deal with the Spanish insurgents for the cession of Ceuta, Spanish Morocco or the Balearic Islands.

[1] Not printed: it was an amplified version of No. 103.

You should take early opportunity of informing Minister for Foreign Affairs verbally that you reported this statement to His Majesty's Government and that you have been instructed to let His Excellency know that His Majesty's Government have received this assurance with satisfaction, as any alteration of the status quo in the Western Mediterranean must be a matter of the closest concern to His Majesty's Government.[2]

You should not ask for a special interview to make this communication, but should make it in the course of interview obtained for some other purpose. You should use the exact formula given above and you should not add to it.

[2] Cf. No. 151, note 5.

No. 160

Mr. Newton (Berlin) to Mr. Eden (Received September 3, 3.3 p.m.)
No. 286 Telegraphic: by telephone [W 10398/9549/41]

Immediate   BERLIN, *September 3, 1936*
My telegram 239 (Saving).[1]

Herr Dieckhoff has just informed me that the question of German participation in proposed committee has been further considered, but before a final answer can be given German Government wish to be more precisely informed as to committee's functions and scope, that is to say, what will be the nature of its terms of reference.

Without being able to make any definite promise, Herr Dieckhoff gave me the impression that the answer of the German Government would be favourable if they could be assured that the functions of the committee would be confined solely to matters directly concerned with Spanish arms embargo such as exchange of information regarding measures for its enforcement, views as to execution and efficacy of these measures, and consideration of suggestions for further measures, e.g. the control of volunteers.

The German misgiving's [*sic*] originally felt that the powers of committee might develop in a manner which they would think undesirable had been strongly confirmed by articles in French press by Madame Tabouis and by a leader headed 'A gap to fill' in 'Times' of September 2nd to the last three lines of which Herr Dieckhoff drew my particular attention. I gathered that if there were any question of committee developing on these lines Germany would refuse to take part.[2] Herr Dieckhoff said he noted that the Portuguese

[1] In this telegram, despatched by air mail on September 2 and received at 2.30 p.m. on September 3, Mr. Newton said he had informed Herr Dieckhoff of the extra instructions from the Foreign Office (see No. 154) and had been told that 'the German Government were not clear as to the functions of the committee and had not appreciated the importance attached to it'. He 'seemed receptive to my representations and said that after communicating with Baron von Neurath he hoped to be able to reply tomorrow or possibly tonight'.

[2] After remarking that British representatives in Berlin and Lisbon were pressing for an end to delays, the leader expressed the hope that the agreement upon non-intervention

Government seemed to entertain the same uncertainty and misgivings as the German Government. I read to him paragraph 3 of my above mentioned telegram and he said it correctly described German objection.[3]

French Ambassador has gone on leave and I understand that no similar communication is being made to French Embassy. Germany's eventual reply will presumably be addressed to French Government and would I understood be given with the least possible delay on receipt of a reply to enquiry in this telegram.

Repeated to Paris.

would 'facilitate further cooperation, first upon questions arising out of the Spanish conflict and ultimately in affairs of even wider concern'. See *The Times*, September 2, 1936, p. 11.

[3] The relevant passage in this telegram said that the main German objection was 'that the powers of the committee might grow and that its duration might also be extended to an undesirable extent. Tasks might be entrusted to it beyond the immediate issues'.

No. 161

Minutes of the first meeting of an inter-departmental committee[1] on non-intervention in Spain

[*W 10587/9549/41*]

September 3, 1936

The first meeting of the Committee was held on Thursday, the 3rd September, in the Conference Room at the Treasury.

PRESENT: Mr. W. S. Morrison, M.C., K.C., M.P. (*in the Chair*); Mr. J. H. McC. Craig (Treasury); Mr. F. Ashton-Gwatkin (Foreign Office); Mr. W. St. C. Roberts (Foreign Office); Mr. A. H. Self (Air Ministry); Brigadier D. F. Anderson (War Office); Lieutenant-Colonel M. Carr (War Office); Mr. H. B. Bain (Admiralty); Mr. E. A. Seal (Admiralty); Mr. F. A. Newsam (Home Office); Mr. L. S. Brass (Home Office); Mr. R. J. Shackle (Board of Trade); Mr. C. J. Flynn (Customs and Excise); Mr. D. K. Cherry (Customs and Excise); Mr. A. L. Innes (Lord Advocate's Department).

Secretaries: Mr. C. A. E. Shuckburgh (Foreign Office); Mr. M. T. Flett (Treasury).

The Chairman explained that the function of the Committee was to examine the necessary steps to make effective in this country the measures agreed upon internationally for non-intervention in Spain. The work of the Committee would necessarily be dependent to a great extent upon the decisions reached by the International Committee which it is proposed to set up in London.

There were, however, a number of matters on which it was already necessary for His Majesty's Government to prepare their views, and the present Committee could examine these matters at once.

[1] For the origins of this committee see No. 128, note 7.

The Committee learnt that in the view of the Foreign Office His Majesty's Government would be in a position effectively to prevent the establishment of recruiting bureaux in this country by making it clear that under Section 4 of the Foreign Enlistment Act, 1870, recruiting itself would be an offence, as would also the taking of service in the forces of either side. A number of legal points had, however, been submitted for consideration to the Home Office in a letter from the Foreign Office dated the 26th August.[2] The main points on which a decision was required were:

(*a*) Whether the Foreign Enlistment Act can be held to apply to the case of a civil war of the kind now taking place in Spain; and

(*b*) Whether Section 4 of the Act can be made applicable prior to the issue of a declaration of neutrality by His Majesty's Government.

The Home Office representative explained that these points were receiving the personal attention of the Home Secretary, and that it was not therefore possible for an opinion to be expressed at the present time.

It was agreed to await the observations of the Home Secretary, and that the view taken by the Home Office and the Foreign Office should in due course be communicated to the Committee.

MUNITIONS OF WAR

(a) *Aircraft*

The Board of Trade, Air Ministry and Customs representatives explained the present position regarding the control of the export of aircraft from this country. Aircraft assembled or dismantled and aircraft engines are prohibited to be exported under the Arms Export Prohibition Order of 1931, except under licence. Licences for such exports are not being issued for Spain. Civil aircraft are normally permitted under this Order to be exported under an open general licence, but this has now been cancelled for all aircraft whose declared destination is Spain. Moreover, certain aircraft clearing for other countries but whose destination is, in fact, suspected to be Spain have been excluded by the Board of Trade from the open general licence. *The Customs* representative explained that there is doubt whether aircraft leaving under their own power can legally be regarded as 'exports' for the purpose of clearance under the Order, but that the Board are nevertheless treating them as such under instructions from the Treasury.

The Chairman felt that the position as explained was satisfactory. The following points would, however, require further consideration:

(i) The question of aircraft flying to Spain from this country via one or more other foreign countries. It was explained that direct flights from this country to Spain would necessarily be rare and could possibly be controlled by a check being kept at airports on the amount of petrol taken on board. Any aircraft loading sufficient petrol for the 700 mile direct flight would be

[2] Not printed.

an object of suspicion and could be prevented from departing without satisfactory guarantees as to its destination. It was arranged that the Air Ministry would examine the practicability of introducing such an arrangement forthwith.

In the case of machines clearing for France or Belgium, or any other country, but whose destination was suspected as being Spain, it would become the responsibility of those countries to apply any necessary further checks if the *bona fides* of the aircraft could not be successfully challenged before leaving this country. Such an arrangement necessitates a clear understanding between the Governments concerned with the application of the Non-Intervention Agreement as to which Government is responsible for exercising control in such cases.

The Foreign Office representative said that in two cases already the French Government had been warned by His Majesty's Government that particular machines which were being flown to Le Bourget were believed to be destined for sale to persons interested in supplying aircraft to Spain.

(ii) The form of the licensing system for export of aircraft. *The Chairman* suggested that it might be desirable to abolish the system under which there is an open general licence which is suspended in particular cases, and to make it necessary for every civil aircraft leaving the country to obtain a special licence.

The Board of Trade and Air Ministry representatives thought that this would be a very cumbersome system and would seriously hamper normal civil flying, and that it would not make a more effective control than exists at present.

The Committee agreed with this view.

(b) *Gas*

The Board of Trade representative explained that gas and chemicals are not included in the Arms Export Prohibition Order. During the Italo-Abyssinian hostilities, however, the Board's Solicitor gave it as his opinion that the authorities probably have the power to add these goods to the list of articles prohibited to be exported under that Order. This, however, would be very undesirable from the point of view of the legitimate trade in industrial chemicals. An alternative system which would be equally effective and had, in fact, been used in connexion with 'sanctions' against Italy would be that the manufacturers of chemicals should be requested to submit to the War Office for approval any orders which they might receive for the sale abroad of gas or chemical substances which might be used for military purposes, and that the War Office should consult with the Foreign Office in all doubtful cases before giving authority for the goods to be exported. It was believed that all the chemical manufacturers in this country could be relied upon to fall in with the official recommendation in such cases.

This procedure was agreed to.

(c) Transport Vehicles, &c

The Board of Trade representative said that strong objection was seen to extending the prohibition to goods which did not come within the Arms Prohibition Order, and in which there was a large and legitimate export trade for industrial purposes.

In agreeing with this view, the *Chairman* said that, in the absence of international agreement to prohibit the supply of specific articles, it was very undesirable to extend the prohibition beyond such goods as could definitely be classified as military stores. Other foreign Governments would be very unlikely to adopt anything but the most narrow interpretation of military stores, and there was no reason why His Majesty's Government should damage their trade interests in going further than other participating Governments.

(d) Warships

It was explained on behalf of the *Admiralty* that there was no power to refuse licences for the export of warships unless they involved a breach of the Treaty of Washington or London Naval Treaty by being of excessive tonnage, gun calibre, &c. The only powers possessed by His Majesty's Government were under the Foreign Enlistment Act, and though these powers were ample for the purpose, there was a doubt whether the relevant section (Section 8) could be regarded as being in force until a proclamation of neutrality had been made. To meet this situation, the Admiralty had arranged for their overseers to keep a special watch on all yards, and to report any case of a vessel being fitted out for warlike purposes for the Spanish Government or insurgents. There were no warships properly so called under construction in this country for Spain.

The Home Office representative pointed out that the relevant passage of the Act, Section 8(4), would make it an offence for a person to despatch a ship in a United Kingdom port if he had reasonable cause to believe that it was to be employed in the military service of a State at war with a State with whom His Majesty is at peace. It may be argued, however, that this section does not operate before the issue of a proclamation of neutrality.

The Admiralty representative said that a case of this sort had already arisen. The British Power Boat Company had received an order from the Spanish Government for a $37\frac{1}{2}$-foot ambulance 'crash tender,' which is a motor boat intended for rescue work at sea in connexion with aircraft and having the high speed of 25 knots. This ship could be fitted with machine guns and depth charges, as could any similar motor boat, but could not carry torpedoes. It was a commercial article freely for sale on the public market, and the Admiralty felt that it would be undesirable to prohibit its supply. It was, of course, true that almost any merchant ship could be fitted with an armament, and it would probably be easier to fit an ordinary tramp steamer in this manner than the motor boat in question. This was, at any rate, the opinion of Admiral Sir R. Henderson, the Controller, with whom the matter had been discussed before the meeting.

It was agreed that, provided the Admiralty was satisfied that this craft was in all respects unarmed and not fitted with any special devices rendering it suitable for warlike purposes, and provided that the Foreign Office saw no objection on general grounds, the committee need not oppose the transaction.

(e) *Oil*

The *Foreign Office* representative drew attention to a note from the Spanish Ambassador[2] pointing out that, according to a report which had reached his Government, an order had been placed with the Ethyl Export Corporation for 500 kilog. of Ethyl spirit which were to be consigned to the insurgents.

The Committee agreed that it was neither necessary nor desirable to raise the question of oil supplies in the absence of an international agreement on the subject.

FINANCIAL ASSISTANCE

It was explained by the *Treasury* representative that the issue of loans on the United Kingdom market could definitely be prevented, and that adequate pressure could be exerted on all reputable private houses to prevent the issue of private loans to Spain.

As regards public or private subscriptions, however, the position was less easy.

In connexion with the reported intention of the Glasgow Corporation to hold a flag day in aid of 'workers distressed by the civil war' the representative of the *Lord Advocate's Department* explained that, though under the Street Collections Regulation (Scotland) Act, 1915, Scottish magistrates could refuse permits for a street collection without stating their reasons, it would be difficult to justify such refusal except for purely police motives, and that in any case other types of collection (house-to-house collections, newspaper appeals, &c.) could not be prevented.

The position in England, according to the *Home Office* representative, was that the police had not powers to prohibit street collections merely on the ground that their object was objectionable, and that it would be undesirable to entrust such powers to them.

The Chairman then asked whether it would be possible to control the transmission to Spain of sums collected in this manner. Both the *Home Office* and *Treasury* representatives said that this would not be possible in practice.

It was agreed that the measures to be taken by His Majesty's Government in this matter must depend on the attitude of other Governments. The position to be taken up at the outset would be that His Majesty's Government are doing what they can by prohibiting public and private loans, but that private subscriptions present great difficulties. It was noted that such appeals for private subscriptions as had come to notice at present were all described as for the relief of distress. If the other Governments did not regard this attitude as satisfactory, they should be asked how they themselves propose to prevent the supply of sums from private sources to Spain. In case of extreme necessity, and in order to meet a strong international demand, it might be possible to provide by special legislation some theoretical control over the export of funds, but this could not be really effective and would in any case be open to grave objections.

The *Foreign Office* representative pointed out in this connexion that the only two Governments which had referred to public subscriptions in their replies to the French Government were the Portuguese and the Italian. The former had stated that they regarded the opening of subscriptions for the continuation of the war or the despatch of sums collected publicly to this end as contrary to the spirit of the non-intervention agreement, and the latter had said that they would regard public subscriptions in countries acceding to the agreement as constituting 'indirect interference' and as being contrary to the agreement.

British Ships Trading with Spain from Foreign Ports

The *Foreign Office* representative pointed out that at a Cabinet meeting held on the 2nd September mention had been made of recent press reports to the effect that British ships had been carrying from foreign ports consignments of arms destined for Spain; that Ministers had expressed the view that it is undesirable that British ships should engage in this trade, and hoped that any steps which might be possible would be taken to prevent them doing so.

The Committee felt that it would be impossible to take effective measures to control the cargoes carried by British ships between foreign ports. This was a matter which must be controlled by the countries from whose ports the munitions are exported. In Europe the matter should not arise in the future since all countries had agreed to prohibit the export of munitions to Spain. With regard to exports from non-European countries such as Mexico or the United States, the Committee felt unable to make any recommendation in the absence of any indication as to the attitude of other Governments upon this question.

Refugees

The *Home Office* representative raised the question of admission of refugees from Spain to this country.

The *Chairman* expressed the view, with which the Committee agreed, that it would be very undesirable to alter in any way the traditional policy of His Majesty's Government, which is to provide asylum for political refugees of all complexions. The position with regard to foreigners who desired to come to this country for propaganda or recruiting purposes was different, and it was not desired to make any recommendation on the subject at the present time.

Finally the *Chairman* said that the work of this Committee and the recommendations which it would be in a position to make to the Cabinet must depend to a large extent on the instructions to be given to the international committee which was to be set up shortly in London. He felt that further discussion by the present Committee would not be of great use until the results of the preliminary negotiations of the International Committee were known. It was therefore decided not to fix the date of the next meeting of the Committee for the present. In the meanwhile a short report on the conclusions so far reached should be forwarded to the Secretary of the Cabinet for the information of the Foreign Affairs Committee of the Cabinet, which was responsible for the setting up of the inter-departmental committee.

No. 162

Mr. F. D'A. G. Osborne[1] (The Vatican) to Mr. Eden (Received September 8)
No. 108 [W 10791/62/41]

THE VATICAN, *September 3, 1936*

Sir,

I have the honour to report that before proceeding on leave I had an audience on August 31st with the Pope, to whom I presented Mr. Mallet.[2] His Holiness seemed in excellent health and has clearly benefitted [*sic*] by the stay at his magnificent summer residence at Castel Gandolfo in spite of the very great strain of the suffering and anxiety caused to him by events in Spain. On this subject he expressed himself in terms of great distress and he told me that he had that very morning been reading a long cyphered report from the Papal representative in Madrid (the newly appointed Nuncio has not proceeded to his post), which revealed a progressive deterioration in conditions, with continuing persecution of priests and destruction of Church property. He voiced his approval of the initiative supported by His Majesty's Government for the purpose of saving the lives of hostages and prisoners and generally humanizing the war, but seemed to have little confidence in its effectiveness. When I suggested that the Vatican might exert its influence to deter the nationalists from acts of violence and brutality and reminded him of the article in the 'Osservatore Romano' which asserted that, whichever party in Spain was ultimately victorious, the Government that emerged could not be recognized as an equal by other European Governments if its partisans had been guilty of atrocities, he replied with an expression of indignation at the idea that the nationalists should be put on the same level as the murderers and iconoclasts who were their opponents. In view of what the Church has suffered and of the first-hand reports that the Vatican is now receiving from the Spanish bishops and other refugees, I did not think that any arguments of mine regarding the principles governing the recognition of the respective parties would affect His Holiness' readily comprehensible partisanship, so I contented myself with a repetition of my suggestion without other comment. Shortly thereafter the atmosphere was cleared by my presentation, on behalf of Sir Stephen Gaselee,[3] of a volume

[1] H.M. Minister at the Holy See.
[2] Mr. W. I. Mallet, First Secretary in H.M. Legation at the Holy See since August 17, 1936.   [3] Librarian and Keeper of the Papers in the Foreign Office since 1920.

of Latin hexameters on the Popes. This greatly pleased him and when I subsequently presented Mr. Mallet to him he was extremely affable and kept us for about twenty minutes talking of the work of his observatory, the complications of his War-time journey from Rome to Warsaw and other non-political matters. Before we left he asked solicitously after The King's health. He was generally so very friendly that I feel sure that if there were any serious matter to be taken up with him, we could at least be sure of a sympathetic hearing and of a genuine wish to satisfy us should circumstances permit.

2. I also presented Mr. Mallet to the Secretary of State. Cardinal Pacelli was equally afflicted by events in Spain and mentioned the constant receipt at the Vatican of authoritative reports of atrocities. He expressed approval of the principle of non-intervention, but observed that it was being widely evaded. I suggested to His Eminence, too, that the Vatican might at least try to restrain the nationalists from discrediting their cause by atrocities and he expressed agreement. As regards Germany he said that there had been a lull in the persecution of the Catholics during the Olympic Games, but that it had since been renewed and he added that the immorality trials were being deliberately exploited to discredit the Church. I am interested to see that the 'Times' correspondent in Berlin, writing on August 31st, which was three days before I saw the Cardinal, expresses the belief that the Pastoral of the Catholic Bishops of Germany presages an accom[m]odation between the Government and the Church.[4] The Cardinal, on the other hand, was very explicit in his statements that there had been no improvement and in his implication that he saw no prospect of any change.

3. The Assistant Under-Secretary of State, when I saw him last week, made the interesting assertion that the Spaniards had never been a really Catholic people in the full implication of the term. They had always been, and remained, a very superstitious race and so they would flock to religious processions and demand the last sacrament when they were dying. The very Communists who were now murdering priests and nuns and burning churches were calling for the sacrament when their own time came. But, generally speaking, the Spaniards had never achieved the moral ideal and discipline that is the essential core of Catholicism for all their devotion to its outward forms and ceremonial.

I have, &c.,

D. G. OSBORNE

4 See *The Times*, September 1, 1936, p. 11.

No. 163

Sir H. Chilton (Hendaye) to Mr. Eden (Received September 4, 1.20 p.m.)

No. 216 Telegraphic [W 10509/62/41]

HENDAYE, *September 4, 1936, 11.45 a.m.*

My telegram No. 213.[1]

Following is text of reply of Spanish Government to Argentine Ambassador's communication in the name of Corps Diplomatique.

Begins. From Minister of State to the Argentine Ambassador. Having given account to Government of Your Excellency's telegraphic despatch of August 30th and repeating my personal thanks for your affectionate greeting I inform you that, while appreciating the initiative of your esteemed colleagues of the Corps Diplomatique accredited in Madrid, this Government, the only genuinely constitutional representative of the Spanish people, confines itself to subduing a military rising which has created a painful situation which the Government desires to see brought to an end in the swiftest possible way by the most humanitarian means, sparing no effort, as shown by the measures and acts which it is effecting.

[1] This telegram of September 3 reported that the Spanish Government's reply to the recent *démarche* (see No. 143) was a polite refusal.

No. 164

Mr. Eden to Mr. Newton (Berlin)

No. 192 Telegraphic [W 10398/9549/41]

Most Immediate   FOREIGN OFFICE, *September 4, 1936, 12.25 p.m.*

Your telegram No. 286.[1]

You may assure German Government that it is the intention of His Majesty's Government that the functions of the Committee should be confined to matters directly concerned with the embargo on arms for Spain, as described in paragraph 2 of your telegram under reference. His Majesty's Government fully appreciate that there would be danger in ventilating delicate questions in the Committee or in entrusting to it tasks which fall outside the immediate problem of arms embargo.

You are correct in saying that the Committee itself will be able to settle the most convenient method of working and that in any case German representative will retain full liberty to express the views of his Government as to the Committee's functions and duration. The essential thing is to secure an early preliminary meeting of the Committee at which all Governments will be represented and at which the scope of the future discussions can be amicably worked out and defined.

You should therefore express the earnest hope of His Majesty's

[1] No. 160.

221

Government that in the light of these explanations the German Government will now agree to the establishment of the proposed Committee and at once appoint their representative. See also my telegram to Paris No. 222.[2]

Repeated to Paris No. 221 and Lisbon No. 115.

[2] No. 165 below.

No. 165

Mr. Eden to Sir G. Clerk (Paris)
No. 222 Telegraphic [W 10398/9549/41]

Immediate   FOREIGN OFFICE, *September 4, 1936, 12.40 p.m.*

My telegram No. 192[1] to Berlin.

Please communicate to the French Government at once the texts of Berlin telegram No. 286[2] and my telegram under reference in so far as is necessary in order to give them the exact wording of the representation which Mr. Newton has been instructed to make.

The French Government's concurrence in this instruction was sought through the French Embassy here who stated that the French Government were generally in agreement. They were however much afraid that the words 'control of volunteers' at the end of Berlin telegram No. 286[3] might give rise to future misunderstandings and they would have preferred the use of the phrase 'recruitment of volunteers'.

It was understood however that on this point the French Government would be satisfied if they could receive the exact terms in English of the instructions which were sent to our Embassy at Berlin and would not press that any immediate elucidation of the phrase 'control of volunteers' should be sought.

In this connexion you may inform them that the question of volunteers is of course one in regard to which His Majesty's Government have as yet taken no action, as it remains for future consideration among the Powers. It would therefore appear appropriate that the views and suggestions of the various Powers on this point should be reserved for discussion in the proposed committee.

Repeated to Berlin No. 193.

[1] No. 164.   [2] No. 160.   [3] *Ibid.*, paragraph 2.

No. 166

Mr. Ogilvie-Forbes (Madrid) to Mr. Eden (Received September 5, 9.30 a.m.)
No. 138 Telegraphic [W 10612/62/41]

MADRID, *September 4, 1936, 10.10 p.m.*

My telegrams Nos. 110 and 130.[1]

Government has been reconstructed on wider basis consisting of six Socialists, two Communists, three Republicans, one Catalan Left and one

[1] Not printed.

Basque Nationalist. The latter has not yet been appointed and is destined for Ministry of Public Works.

Largo Caballero, Socialist, is Prime Minister and Minister of War. Minister of State is del Vayo[2] whom I already know and with whom I am on friendly terms. Prieto is Minister of Marine and Air.

2. The intention to include a Catholic Basque is interesting and the whole object of this reconstruction is to form a Government on the widest possible basis in order to meet the grave crisis which threatens the whole regime and of which the man in the street is at present completely ignorant.

[2] Señor Julio Álvarez del Vayo.

No. 167

Mr. Newton (Berlin) to Mr. Eden (Received September 5, 1.30 p.m.)
No. 292 Telegraphic: by telephone [W 10616/9549/41]

BERLIN, *September 5, 1936*

My telegram No. 290.[1]

Doctor Gaus has informed me that on basis of my explanation yesterday he has been authorised by Minister for Foreign Affairs to express concurrence of German Government in establishment of proposed committee. Instructions to participate will be sent to German Chargé d'Affaires today.

A brief announcement will be made through D[eutsches] N[achrichten] B[üro] on lines that French Government and subsequently British Government recently approached German Government with a suggestion that a committee should be formed in London to deal with questions concerned with Spanish arms embargo. After duties and competence of this committee had been further elucidated in the course of diplomatic conversations during the last few days German Government have declared their readiness to participate through their Chargé d'Affaires in London.

There is no objection to announcement of German decision in the English press tomorrow Sunday morning, but it is requested that until then nothing should appear abroad or be reported back to Germany.

French Chargé d'Affaires whom I have fully informed is receiving similar communication at Ministry of Foreign Affairs.[2]

Repeated to Paris.

[1] In this telegram of September 4, received in the Foreign Office by telephone at 8.15 p.m., Mr. Newton reported that he had conveyed the assurance given in Foreign Office telegram No. 192 (No. 164) to Dr. Gaus, who was in charge of the Ministry of Foreign Affairs owing to Herr Dieckhoff's departure on leave that morning. Dr. Gaus said that he must refer to Baron von Neurath, and did not expect to be able to reply that night.

[2] Cf. *D.D.F., op. cit.*, No. 234.

No. 168

Sir P. Loraine (Constantinople) to Mr. Eden (Received September 5, 6.10 p.m.)
No. 124 Telegraphic [T 13621/8725/379]

CONSTANTINOPLE, *September 5, 1936, 4.45 p.m.*

Success of the King's visit here is tremendous. Enthusiasm displayed by an habitually undemonstrative population has been very striking.[1]

[1] See No. 74. The King and his party were in Istanbul from September 4 until late on September 6; he left at 11.30 p.m. by train for Vienna. He met the Turkish President, M. Kemal Atatürk, on four occasions, two formal and two informal.

No. 169

Record by Sir A. Cadogan of a conversation with Signor Fracassi[1]
[R 5102/226/22]

FOREIGN OFFICE, *September 5, 1936*

Signor Fracassi, of the Italian Embassy, called on me this morning to ask about the projected visit of the Turkish fleet to Malta. He said that this, taken together with the suppression of the Italian language in Malta[2] and the King's avoidance of Italy,[3] must combine to produce a rather unfortunate effect.

[1] First Secretary in the Italian Embassy at London.
[2] The Governor of Malta, Sir Charles Bonham-Carter, proclaimed the coming into force on September 2, 1936, of Letters Patent establishing Crown Colony government for Malta, which he had promulgated on August 12. English and Maltese were to be the two official languages, the former of the Administration, the latter of the Law Courts. A note of September 1 by Mr. G. L. McDermott of the Southern Department included the following: 'The public confession earlier this year of a Dr. Delia, proving the Italian Consul-General and his Assistant guilty of espionage, provided the opportunity for their expulsion by the Maltese Government and the closing down of the Istituto di Cultura Italiana and the Umberto Primo School, and the withdrawal of the licence of the Casa del Fascio, the centre of all Italian penetration activities in Malta, is being contemplated.' The Rome correspondent of *The Times* reported on September 5 (p. 9) bitter comment in a section of the Fascist press, which deplored the loss of autonomy suffered by the Maltese people. Dr. Delia was a former Nationalist deputy who had been arrested in May and sentenced on June 26 to three years' imprisonment with hard labour.
[3] See Nos. 31, 74, and 168. On August 25 Signor Vitetti of the Italian Embassy had read to Sir A. Cadogan a personal letter from Count Ciano which recognized that the King's voyage 'was in the nature of a holiday trip, and had no political significance whatever'; it was nevertheless unfortunate, he thought, 'that his avoidance of Italy and his visits to Yugoslav, Greek, and apparently Turkish territory were being used in the Balkan countries as a text for propaganda and as proof of an anti-Italian policy on the part of this country'. After discussing the matter Signor Vitetti said that 'the only suggestion he could make was that, as the Italian Govt. had given certain facilities at Brindisi—for one of H.M. destroyers to collect mail etc. [cf. No. 74, note 1]—the King might, on leaving the Adriatic, send a telegram to the King of Italy thanking him for the courtesy of these facilities'. Sir A. Cadogan said that this was a matter he must think over and discuss with others.

I said that if the coincidence of these things created a wrong impression, it was most unfortunate, particularly as it was entirely fortuitous.

As regards the Turkish fleet visit, I said that, as far as I could remember, this (which of course was a matter of courtesy) had been under discussion for some time. There had at various times been British naval visits to Turkish ports, but the Admiralty had held that these could not well continue unless there was a return visit. This had been arranged some time ago, but for some reason had fallen through, and it had now been possible to arrange for a visit to Malta in the near future. (Mr. Rendel[4] confirms that this is correct.)

I did not pursue the subject of the Italian language in Malta—nor did Signor Fracassi. But he asked whether I had been able to do anything about Signor Vitetti's suggestion about a message from the King. I said that the matter was being considered but that I did not know that anything could be done about it.

I gave him, of course, all sorts of assurances that this combination of events and situations were purely fortuitous and had no significance whatever.

On leaving he asked whether, if the Turkish fleet must pay a visit, it was necessary that they should go to *Malta*. Why not Gibraltar? I could only reply that Malta was the natural venue of such a meeting, and I was not well-informed on the subject of the steaming power of the Turkish fleet.

All this shows—if that were necessary—that the Italians are in a very jumpy and suspicious mood. They have lately shown us that they are very anxious to be on good terms, and it is very necessary to keep them in that frame of mind for the 5 Power meeting. But I don't know what we can do. I should say that *now* it is all the more undesirable to recommend His Majesty to make any move—which would look almost as if it were dictated to him. When Signor Vitetti spoke to me about it, he said that the suggestion was made to him privately by Count Ciano and that *no-one* else knew about it. Now we get it repeated by his *locum tenens* in the Embassy!

It is unfortunate, but I don't quite see what we can do.[5]

A. C.

[4] Mr. G. W. Rendel was Head of the Eastern Department of the Foreign Office.

[5] A minute by Sir R. Vansittart of September 5 included the following passage: 'We can and need take no notice of Italian susceptibilities about a visit of the Turkish fleet. It is really rather an impertinence to have mentioned it in this light. But of course we have given them a tremendous pill to swallow over Malta, and we do not want them *too* much out of humour when we come to the Five Power Conference. I am therefore inclined to compromise about a message of thanks from the King to the King of Italy, particularly as it has now been twice suggested and a fresh grievance will be made of it if we turn it down altogether.' Cf. No. 175 below.

No. 170

Sir G. Clerk (Paris) to Mr. Eden (Received September 7, 3.5 p.m.)
No. 277 Telegraphic [W 10695/9549/41]

PARIS, *September 7, 1936, 1.35 p.m.*

My immediately preceding telegram.[1]

Minister for Foreign Affairs has just sent a message to me to say that instructions have been in force for some time for evacuation of Spanish refugees whether government supporters or rebels, away from the frontier, into the interior of France, for natural reasons of order, feeding, and health. On the other hand French Government consider they have no right to restrain by force refugees of either side who wish to return to Spain and the more of them who do so, the fewer mouths will remain to be filled at French expense. It is therefore to the reasonable interest of French Government to facilitate the return of such people and for this purpose goods-wagons, cattle-trucks, and all other means of conveyance have been employed and there has been no discrimination between militiamen or non-combatants or women and children. There are now some 8,000 Spanish refugees in France.

As regards arms Minister for Foreign Affairs has no definite information to give me as yet but enquiry is being pursued.[2]

[1] Foreign Office telegram No. 224 of September 5 referred to a Havas message from Hendaye published in the German press and stating that several hundred Marxist militiamen who had fled from Irun into France were being transported in special trains to Ceibere [? Cerbère] in order to enable them to rejoin the Catalan anarchists. Sir G. Clerk was instructed to enquire at once whether this report was correct. In telegram No. 276 of September 6 Sir G. Clerk reported that M. Delbos was making enquiry.

[2] On September 6 Sir G. Clerk had called M. Delbos's attention to a French newspaper report that the militiamen's arms had been collected and forwarded to the Madrid Government. Cf. No. 94.

No. 171

Mr. Eden to Sir C. Wingfield (Lisbon)
No. 119[1] Telegraphic [W 10591/9549/41]

Immediate   FOREIGN OFFICE, *September 7, 1936, 4.30 p.m.*

His Majesty's Government propose that first meeting of the Committee for supervision of embargo on exports of arms etc. to Spain shall be held at Foreign Office on 9th September under chairmanship of Mr. W. S. Morrison, Financial Secretary to the Treasury, who will represent the Secretary of State for Foreign Affairs.

2. Please request Government to which you are accredited to appoint representative if they have not already done so.

[1] This was a circular telegram which was sent, *mutatis mutandis,* for communication to other interested governments.

No. 172

Mr. Ogilvie-Forbes (Madrid) to Mr. Eden (Received September 8, 9.30 a.m.)
No. 150 Telegraphic [W 10779/9549/41]

Important   MADRID, *September 7, 1936, 9.55 p.m.*

My telegram No. 149.[1]

Minister of State[2] made to me this afternoon a moving appeal on note of fair play. He said that friendship with Great Britain had always been a cardinal feature of the foreign policy of the Spanish Left. He himself had many friends in Britain especially in journalistic circles. Spain's work for world peace and her loyalty to the League of Nations were well known. She had also during Abyssinian crisis in the face of strongest pressure from Italy supported Great Britain in her defence of League principles and now Italy was taking her revenge. The Government was the legitimate Government of Spain and present embargo on munitions was hitting the Spanish Government only. They were the victims of so called neutrality. The rebels were receiving every kind of help from Italy, Germany and Portugal, the latter buying munitions in her own name and passing them on to the rebels. He intended to raise the whole question and produce evidence at the next meeting of the League Council. He added that the fall of Irun was entirely due to lack of munitions which the French Government was rigorously denying to the Spanish Government under non-intervention pact. The rebels were advancing and Madrid was to be bombed and gassed with foreign weapons.

Spanish Government might not reasonably object to being defeated in a fair fight but they did protest against being defeated by neutrality. He appealed to the British sense of fair play.[3]

[1] This telegram of September 7 has not been preserved in the Foreign Office archives. A summary of its contents includes the statement: 'Minister of State has given fullest assurances and guarantees of protection for Embassy and has promised fullest protection to Corps Diplomatique in event of Madrid becoming untenable. He attaches greatest importance to presence of British representative in Madrid.'

[2] Signor Álvarez del Vayo: see No. 166.

[3] This telegram was rather extensively minuted in the Foreign Office, with apparently general acceptance of Mr. Shuckburgh's observation (September 10) that the 'political consequences of giving the legal government the facilities to which it is undoubtedly entitled would have been too grave to be risked'. It was agreed that the Spanish Government would be within their rights in bringing the question before the League Council under Article 11(2). Sir R. Vansittart questioned the Minister of State's remarks 'on one rather important point: the French Govt *have* been supplying the Spanish Govt, and *did* supply Irun . . . It is difficult to assess degrees of culpability: it is enough to say that we only have clean hands. We surely need not answer this individually . . . R.V. Sept. 12.' Mr. Eden wrote: 'I agree that no individual answer is called for. A. E. Sept. 15.'

No. 173

Sir C. Wingfield (Lisbon) to Mr. Eden (Received September 8, 9.30 a.m.)
No. 170 Telegraphic [W 10771/9549/41]

LISBON, *September 7, 1936, 10.35 p.m.*

Your telegram No. 119.[1]

Portuguese Government prefer that Committee should meet without a Portuguese representative. They may, if procedure gives them confidence, appoint one later; but for the present they fear accusations might there be made against them and that they would find themselves unsupported.

No arguments of mine could make Minister for Foreign Affairs move from this attitude which is due to highly nervous state of public opinion.[2]

[1] No. 171.
[2] Cf. *D.A.P.E., op. cit.*, No. 283. Sir G. Mounsey minuted on September 8: 'This Portuguese reply is childish, and I fear the absence of a Portuguese representative will have a disastrous influence on the work of the Committee . . .' Sir R. Vansittart commented: 'We have done our best on this. But who will get, and who will now consider, our request for 2nd thoughts. R. V.' See No. 174 below.

No. 174

Mr. Eden to Sir C. Wingfield (Lisbon)
No. 120 Telegraphic [W 10771/9549/41]

Immediate   FOREIGN OFFICE, *September 8, 1936, 1.55 p.m.*

Your telegram No. 170.[1]

You should make an urgent and immediate appeal to the Portuguese Government to reconsider their decision. You should emphasise the lamentable impression which will be created throughout the world and especially in this country by any unwillingness of Portugal to co-operate in the work of the Committee. If this unwillingness arises from an anxiety lest unfounded allegations should be levelled against them, you should urge that the Committee gives the best opportunity of dealing with any question of the kind, should it arise, amicably and without friction, and so of preventing the increase of such allegations which might otherwise take place. It is the view of His Majesty's Government that on the successful constitution of the Committee the policy of non-intervention materially depends. If it fails, a dangerous European situation may well develop from which Portugal cannot, any more than other nations, be immune. It is their earnest hope, therefore, that the Portuguese Government will not by any decision that they may take imperil still further an already difficult and delicate international situation.

[1] No. 173.

No. 175

Mr. Eden to Mr. Ingram (Rome)
No. 347 Telegraphic [R 5102/226/22]

FOREIGN OFFICE, *September 8, 1936, 4 p.m.*

I should be glad if you would convey orally to the Minister for Foreign Affairs an expression of the gratitude of His Majesty The King for the facilities furnished by the Italian Government at Brindisi to H.M. destroyers in connexion with the delivery and collection of mail during his recent cruise. These facilities were much appreciated by His Majesty.[1]

[1] See No. 169, notes 3 and 5. Signor Vitetti's request of August 25 for a message about the Brindisi visit was agreed to only after considerable debate and minuting in the Foreign Office. Referring to Signor Vitetti's approach, Mr. Eden wrote on August 29: 'In considering this proposal, I should like to know how the Italians are behaving now. Is their anti-British propaganda in the Near & Middle East [and] India dying down? What is the tone of their press toward us? I have seen nothing in the dep[artmen]t, but have had disquieting private reports ... If the position is unsatisfactory then requests afford an opportunity for saying so.' This elicited a comprehensive survey of September 1, signed by Mr. McDermott, showing some modifications in the anti-British Italian press and propaganda activities. It was remarked that although at Brindisi 'the Italians were very civil to the British naval officers during their visit, there was really absolutely nothing out of the ordinary which was afforded them'. Major Hardinge, Private Secretary to the King, could not agree to submit to the King the proposal that he should send a message to the King of Italy; he thought this 'would be greatly overdoing it'. Sir R. Vansittart finally decided on September 5 on a compromise: 'no message direct from H.M. but a word of recognition of the services rendered (not very remarkable ones!) through the Embassy in Rome, informing Signor Fracassi'.

No. 176

Mr. Ogilvie-Forbes (Madrid) to Mr. Eden (Received September 9, 9.30 a.m.)
No. 159 Telegraphic [W 10878/62/41]

MADRID, *September 8, 1936, 10 p.m.*

Your telegram No. 80 first paragraph.[1]

I have ordered out of the Embassy all unsuitable British subjects and they have been evacuated from Alicante this morning. Only person left whom I regard as a guest is British-born Mrs. Maeztu whose husband is in prison awaiting death and who would almost certainly herself be killed if she returned home. She is an ex-ambassadress and a friend of Lord Howard. Only other occupants of the Embassy are a volunteer typist, storekeeper, accountant, gate-keeper and servant, who stay in Madrid in all eventualities, Unwins and self.[2] But we must be prepared for a possible rush of 150.

[1] See No. 150, note 5.
[2] In telegram No. 140 of September 5 Mr. Ogilvie-Forbes had refused an offer of extra staff for the Embassy, stating that 'The present situation in Madrid where owing to increasing food shortage, absence of law and order, probability of siege and street fighting with a starving anarchist mob intent on plunder and destruction has very serious possibilities and does not justify the risk of sending here any other member of the staff.' He had already urged existing staff to leave, as he preferred to concentrate any element of personal danger on himself.

No. 177

Sir G. Clerk (Paris) to Mr. Eden (Received September 9)
No. 311 Saving: Telegraphic [W 10845/9549/41]

PARIS, *September 8, 1936*

My telegram No. 310 Saving.[1]

Difference of opinion in the *Front Populaire*, between the *Confédération Générale du Travail* and Communists on the one hand and the Socialists and Radicals on the other, with regard to the Government's policy of non-intervention in Spain, now seems to be coming to a head. It remains to be seen whether in view of the reiteration in his speech at Luna Park[2] on September 6th by Monsieur Blum of the Government's intention to stand firm by its policy, the Communists and the *Confédération Générale du Travail* will give way.

Monsieur Thorez is reported to have had an interview yesterday with Monsieur Blum, but no *communiqué* was subsequently issued. According to this evening's press the Secretary-General of the Permanent Administrative Committee of the Socialist party has now replied to the letter addressed to him by his Communist colleague on September 4th (see my telegram No. 304 Saving),[3] and has stated that he proposes to call a meeting of that Committee on September 9th to consider the suggestion that a joint Socialist and Communist delegation should make representations to the Government with regard to its Spanish policy. There can be little doubt but that the terms of the Socialists' reply will be in the negative. Meanwhile, as you will have seen from my telegram under reference, the *Confédération Générale du Travail* has been called upon to define its position with regard to the Government's policy towards Spain and it is understood that a decision may be reached today.

[1] This telegram of September 8 described the one-hour strike on September 7 of 225,000 workers in 2,500 factories in the Paris area, ostensibly against the government's Spanish policy, but with denunciations of the behaviour of employers.

[2] See *The Times*, September 7, p. 12.

[3] This telegram of September 4 referred generally to the activities of the French Communist party, but did not refer to the above-mentioned letter of September 4.

CHAPTER IV

Non-Intervention Committee starts work: League reform: British note of September 17 proposes Five Power meeting
September 9–30, 1936

INTRODUCTORY NOTE

The non-intervention committee (cf. Nos. 128, 140, 147, 161, 171, 173, and 174) held its first meeting in the Locarno Room at the Foreign Office on Wednesday, September 9, 1936, at 12 noon, with Mr. W. S. Morrison, Financial Secretary to the Treasury, in the chair (see No. 178 below). Mr. Morrison was formally elected chairman of the committee, and it was agreed that the title of the committee should be 'The International Committee for the Application of the Agreement for Non-Intervention in Spain' (usually abbreviated as 'N.I. Committee' in this volume). Mr. Francis Hemming, Secretary to the Economic Advisory Council, acted as Secretary to the committee. The Earl of Plymouth, Parliamentary Under Secretary to the Foreign Office, replaced Mr. Morrison as chairman at and after the third meeting on September 21. The committee consisted of representatives of twenty-five European countries excluding Spain. It was resolved at the first meeting that the proceedings should be treated as strictly confidential, but that an agreed *communiqué* should be issued at the conclusion of each meeting. The committee held fourteen meetings up to the end of 1936, on the following dates: September 9, 14, 21, 28; October 9 (two meetings), 23, 28; November 4 (two meetings), 12; December 2, 9, 23.

Excerpts from some of the minutes of meetings of the committee and certain key documents are printed below, but no attempt has been made to print the minutes in their entirety. They are extremely lengthy, and much of their space is taken up with verbatim discussion of the texts of the *communiqués* which usually gave a full account of the main discussions and were published promptly. The minutes and related documents are now all available in the Public Record Office under the file number W 11115/41, volumes F.O. 371/20591–20593. The more complete set used by the United Kingdom Delegation is kept under the classification F.O. 849, volumes 1–41, and also includes the minutes of a sub-committee which was appointed at the second meeting of the main committee on September 14 to assist the chairman in the day-to-day work of the committee, and which met on seventeen occasions up to the end of 1936, on the following dates: September 15, 18,

22, 28; October 5, 24, 28; November 2, 9, 10, 12, 23, 27; December 4, 7, 14, 22. This sub-committee was composed of representatives of Belgium, the United Kingdom, Czechoslovakia, France, Germany, Italy, Sweden, and the Soviet Union.

The proceedings of the committee up to the end of October 1936 are conveniently summarized as follows in the concluding paragraphs of a memorandum by Mr. Shuckburgh of October 28 (W 14499/9549/41).

'The procedure laid down by the Committee at its opening session stated that it would be the duty of the Committee to examine, with a view to ascertaining the facts, any complaints submitted on behalf of a participating government alleging that breaches of the agreement had been committed. It was provided that on receipt of such a complaint the Chairman should request the government concerned to supply "such explanations as are necessary to establish the facts", and that when these explanations arrived the Committee should "take such steps as may appear proper in each case to establish the facts".

12. During the life of the Committee the following complaints have been dealt with in accordance with this procedure.

(a) A series of complaints drawn up against Germany, Italy and Portugal by the Spanish Government which, after being raised by the Spanish representative at the League Assembly, were submitted to the Non-Intervention Committee by the United Kingdom representative on behalf of the Spanish Government. The German reply to these accusations had already been considered by the Committee and was held by the Chairman to constitute a satisfactory explanation of the incident so far as it went. At his request, however, the German representative agreed to obtain additional observations on two points. The Italian and Portuguese replies have been received by the Committee but not considered.

(b) A series of complaints against the Portuguese Government received from the Soviet Government. The reply of the Portuguese has been received but not considered.

(3)[c] A series of accusations against the Soviet Government which were contained in the German Government's reply to (1)[a] above. The Soviet representative has been asked to obtain the observations of his Government.

(4)[d] A communication from His Majesty's Government putting forward information of three cases of Soviet and one of Italian breaches. The two governments concerned have been asked to supply explanations.

13. Thus His Majesty's Government besides taking upon themselves the duty of presenting to the Committee the Spanish Government's complaint, have also presented complaints of their own, three against the Soviet and one against Italy. They have not considered it their duty to undertake an elaborate enquiry into the manner in which other countries are carrying out their obligations, but where they have received reliable and fully confirmed information they have passed it on to the Committee.

14. Other matters dealt with by the Committee are as follows.

(a) The Soviet representative submitted a proposal for the blockade of the Portuguese ports. The Chairman ruled that this was not a proposal which could properly be placed on the agenda, and he was supported in this attitude by the Committee itself.

(b) The Chairman put forward on October 24th the suggestion that the Committee might examine the possibility of establishing, subject to the concurrence of the two parties in Spain, an impartial body of persons, stationed on Spanish soil, at the principal points of entry (by sea and by land) for the purpose of reporting when called upon to do so by the Committee, any specific case. The delegates on the Sub-Committee agreed to obtain the views of their governments on this proposal.'

No. 178

Stenographic Notes of the First Meeting of the Non-Intervention Committee, held in the Locarno Room, Foreign Office, on Wednesday, September 9, 1936, at 12 noon

[*W 11115/11115/41*]*

2 WHITEHALL GARDENS, S.W.1, *September 9, 1936*

MR. W. S. MORRISON[1] (United Kingdom): Your Excellencies and Gentlemen, it is my pleasant duty to-day to welcome you in the regrettable absence of the Secretary of State, who, as you all know, is suffering from a complaint which, though not serious, renders him infectious. It is for this reason that he is not able to be with us to-day. He has, however, sent me a letter which, with your permission, I will read to you. He says:

'I am indeed sorry that I shall be prevented by my indisposition from attending the opening meetings of the International Committee which is being set up to supervise the international agreement for non-intervention in the civil disturbances in Spain. I need hardly say that I shall follow your labours with the closest attention.

I should be grateful if you would welcome the delegates warmly on my behalf and assure them that His Majesty's Government in the United Kingdom will contribute by all the means at their command to ensure a successful outcome of the work of the Committee.

His Majesty's Government attach the greatest importance to the effective application of measures which have been or may be agreed upon internationally with regard to non-intervention in the conflict in Spain. For their own part His Majesty's Government are prepared to take every step in their power to secure the rigid enforcement in this country of any measures which may be agreed upon by the Committee, and you can assure the

---

[1] Representatives of twenty-five European countries, in addition to Mr. Morrison representing the United Kingdom, attended this meeting. The names of these countries are given below in these minutes, at the beginning of the discussion of the *communiqué*.

Committee that the existing embargo on the export of arms, including aircraft, and war material, is being most strictly enforced.

Wishing the Committee every success in its most important work, and with renewed apologies for my enforced absence from the first stage of its labours.'

HIS EXCELLENCY M. CHARLES CORBIN (France): Mr. Chairman, I would wish first of all to thank His Majesty's Government in the United Kingdom warmly for the message of welcome which you have just read to us, and I would ask you to convey to the Foreign Secretary, and I am sure the whole meeting will join me in this, our thanks for his message of good wishes, and our very best wishes for a rapid recovery from his present indisposition.

This Committee, which meets for the first time here this morning, was proposed by the French Government. It was the French Government also which proposed that it should meet in London because we thought that here the conditions would be best suited to carry out the tasks which lie before the Committee. I wish, therefore, to thank His Majesty's Government warmly for agreeing to give us hospitality here, and I am sure the fact that the Committee is meeting in London will be a great help.

The French Government fully realise all the difficulties which face the Committee, but they are determined for their part that the Committee should succeed in its task. They are determined also to apply most strictly the measures designed to secure neutrality. I need only refer to the latest speech made by M. Blum in Paris on Sunday last.[2] I venture to add that I feel convinced that all of us here will bring the utmost goodwill to the achievement of the task which is before us, and before closing I should like to propose that we elect as our Chairman Mr. William Morrison, who here represents His Majesty's Government.

MR. W. S. MORRISON (*Chairman*): Has any of your Excellencies or Gentlemen any counter-proposition to make as regards the Chairmanship of this Committee?

(The French Ambassador's proposal was then adopted)

MR. W. S. MORRISON (*Chairman*): I should like to thank your Excellency for your kindness and to thank you, your Excellencies and Gentlemen, for the honour you have done me in electing me to be Chairman of this Committee. I can only say that I shall bring to the tasks which lie in front of us all the goodwill and energy that I can summon up to help me.

It seems to me that at this meeting we should be usefully employed if we could arrive at some idea of what tasks we should tackle first. One preliminary matter is the question of publicity for our proceedings. It is entirely for the Committee to decide whether we shall meet, as we are now, in private, or whether we shall meet in public. For my own part, I would suggest that we get on very well in private. Unless there is a different view expressed by any one present, may I assume that to be the wish of the Committee?

[2] See No. 177, note 2.

(Agreed)

The next question which naturally arises is the question of our relations with the Press. Meeting in private as we do we can talk frankly and freely, but it might not be equally convenient if everything that we said got into the papers. I would suggest, therefore, for the consideration of the Committee that at the conclusion of our meeting to-day we issue a *communiqué* agreed upon by us all for the purposes of the Press. If that is agreeable to the Committee, I would suggest that we exercise reticence with regard to anything that does not appear in the *communiqué*. Does that strike the Committee as sensible, or is there any counter-suggestion?

(No counter-suggestion)

Then, Gentlemen, I accept that as being agreed.

I have now to say that we miss at this Committee a representative of the Portuguese Government. They have expressed their point of view as follows. They say that for the time being, until the functions of this committee are more adequately defined, they do not wish to make up their minds whether or not they will be represented. I may say that we are still asking them to attend the subsequent meetings of this Committee, and I am sure it is the hope of us all that we may see them at our table.[3]

I have also to report the absence of any representative of Switzerland. That is, of course, due to their traditional policy of neutrality. I understand that the French Government communicated to the Swiss Government, as to all other European Governments, the draft declaration regarding non-intervention in Spain which now forms the basis of the work of this Committee. The Swiss Government in thanking the French Government for its courtesy explained that they had taken measures in accordance with the policy of non-intervention on their own initiative, but that they did not intend to participate in a common declaration, for reasons determined by the perpetual neutrality of Switzerland. The same reasons have, of course, prompted the decision of the Swiss Government not to be represented on the Committee itself.

I should like next to consult the Committee on a small point of procedure. Is it the desire of the Committee that speeches made in English should be translated into French? Is there anyone who desires that? May I leave it like this? If at any time a speech is made in English which any member of the Committee would like to hear translated into French I hope they will at once say so and it will be done at once.

Mr. J. W. Dulanty (Irish Free State): Does that mean that all the speeches will be in English, or that a speech made in French will be translated?

Mr. W. S. Morrison (*Chairman*): Any speech made in French will be translated.

One thing, if I might suggest it, which would form a very useful basis for our future work would be for the replies to the French Government's Note

[3] Cf. Nos. 173 and 174.

235

to be collated and published. I make this suggestion entirely for the Committee to decide whether they think it would be a good one to adopt or not. The reasons which prompt me to make this suggestion are that, as we are all aware, the replies from our respective countries, though they signify assent to the principle of non-intervention, have in some cases been attended with reservations judged appropriate by the countries concerned. It might therefore clear the air for us all if we had these replies to the French Government's Note brought together and published so that we know what is the attitude which each Government wishes to adopt towards the proposal. Does that suggestion commend itself to the Committee or has any of Your Excellencies any other suggestion to make?

HIS EXCELLENCY M. CHARLES CORBIN (France): Mr. Chairman, if you will allow me, I should like to say a few words on the general aspect of the task of this Committee before turning to the concrete points which you have yourself just raised.

I would repeat how glad the French Government is that this Committee is now meeting. We consider that the fact of the Committee meeting constitutes a positive result and a step forward in the effort for non-intervention which has inspired it. I need not recall the origin of the proposal for this Committee, except to say that, as soon as the French Government had made the first suggestion, it was concerned over the application of the non-intervention policy which was to be introduced. Hence this International body which now meets for the first time. Since the very beginning there have been certain fears entertained with regard to the nature of this Committee. We have done our best to sweep away those fears and we hope that now there are no doubts left in any quarter as to the proper task of the Committee. The Committee will, of course, take care to safeguard the susceptibilities of the various countries and to respect the full sovereignty which is exercised by all the participating States. The Committee should also, in our view, do everything to avoid any debates of a political nature. It will, however, welcome the very fullest exchange of all concrete information on measures taken, or to be taken, to enforce neutrality. The Committee should, in fact, centralise all the information of a practical character which is received, in order to exercise effective control of the situation. The French Government believe that the permanent contact thus established will lead to that confidence and co-operation which alone will ensure peace.

To turn now to the specific points raised by our Chairman, the French Government, of course, keenly regret the absence of a representative of Portugal at this meeting and very much hope that the difficulties will soon be overcome so as to allow Portugal to take part, since it is clear that the participation of a country adjacent to Spain is of the utmost importance.

On the point of the publicity of documents, the French Government gladly agrees to the proposal made by our Chairman and since the documents concerned were originally exchanged by the French Government and certain other Governments, the French Government has already taken action in the sense of preparing a White Book containing all those documents which, with your permission, I will ask our Secretariat to distribute this afternoon. This White Book, of course, is quite independent of the form of publication which the Chairman has proposed, but perhaps the two things might appear simultaneously.

Mr. W. S. Morrison (*Chairman*): Your Excellencies have heard what His Excellency the French Ambassador has said. It is agreed that it would be a good thing to publish from this Committee the text of the replies to the original French proposal as a basis for our work? Does anyone dissent from that?

Prince von Bismarck (Germany): Without dissenting to that proposal, Mr. Chairman, I would ask your permission to be able to consult my Government first, for I have not received any instructions on that point. That could be done very quickly, it would be a matter of a few hours.

Mr. W. S. Morrison (*Chairman*): That is, of course, a most reasonable request. I think it would be very desirable that any member of the Committee who wishes to consult his Government first should do so. If in general the idea commends itself to the Committee may we leave it like this? If those present will communicate with the Secretary of this Committee their readiness to have these replies printed, we will set about preparing them for publication. I think that I had better leave it like that. As soon as all the replies have come in we shall print them and for this purpose we would make use, as His Excellency the French Ambassador suggested, of the French publication.

His Excellency M. Charles Corbin (France): I am afraid that the French White Book will be only in French and not in both languages.

Mr. W. S. Morrison (*Chairman*): We will have it translated. We had better have it in both languages.

Bay Sedat Zeki Örs (Turkey): It seems to me that, as this publication has appeared in French and, after all, the Notes are answers given to the French Government's Note, there should really be no objection whatever to their being published here also in French.

Mr. W. S. Morrison (*Chairman*): Since the replies were replies made to the French Government, French texts have been prepared, could we not agree to their publication in French at any rate at first? We can consider later whether translation is necessary.

(Agreed)

We have a Secretary to this Committee in Mr. Hemming, whose address is 2 Whitehall Gardens, London, S.W.1, and he will undertake all the publishing arrangements that are required.

In case there should be any doubt as to the name this Committee should have, may I suggest, and it is merely a suggestion, that it should be 'The International Committee for the Application of the Agreement for Non-Intervention in Spain'. Is that a title that commends itself to the Committee?

Following that, perhaps I might bring the Committee to another point that has occurred to me. Every country has its own system of municipal and private law, and in order to give effect to the embargo on the export of arms to which we are all agreed each country has naturally expressed the embargo in terms of its own law. In our country we have an Order which we can invoke and have invoked in this case, called the Arms Export Prohibition Order, 1931, but I think it might facilitate the work of the Committee if we had before us copies of the various laws and decrees that have been issued to this end in the respective countries. It seems to me that if we all had the text of those decrees before us we should be able to see accurately what steps we have in our own respective fashions taken to give effect to the principle which we are gathered together to support. It seems to me that when we had that information we should be in a better position to judge of each other's difficulties and also to judge what has actually been done to give effect to the proposals. I was going to suggest tentatively for the consideration of the Committee that at this meeting it might be wise if we agreed, each of us, to send to the Secretary of the Committee the text of the various laws and decrees that have been enacted in our respective countries in order to give effect to this principle. Then, if the Committee agreed, we might publish these documents, or certainly in the first place we might circulate them among ourselves so that we would know what the position was. I should be very grateful indeed if any member of the Committee would comment on that proposal.

HIS EXCELLENCY BARON DE CARTIER DE MARCHIENNE[4] (Belgium): Mr. Chairman, if I may say a word on the subject, I think that it is absolutely necessary we should all know what we in our various countries have done in this matter; otherwise we shall be working in a fog. I for one have brought over here the regulations which have been passed by my Government in this matter and, if you will allow me, I will give them to the Secretary.

MR. W. S. MORRISON (*Chairman*): I am much obliged. Would any other member of the Committee like to say anything on this point?

JONKHEER R. DE MAREES VAN SWINDEREN[5] (Netherlands): These regulations are printed and published in the various national languages. Is it proposed that they should all be translated before we submit them to the Committee here[?]

MR. W. S. MORRISON (*Chairman*): I think that it would be necessary to have a translation[.] I feel myself to be in a peculiar difficulty in this Committee because I am not normally attached in any way to the Foreign Office and consequently I have not that great linguistic ability which distinguishes the representatives present. I personally would like to have them translated.

M. SAMUEL B. CAHAN[6] (U.S.S.R.): I want, Mr. Chairman, to support your suggestion about the translation of some of these languages. There are

[4] Belgian Ambassador at London.   [5] Netherlands Minister at London.
[6] Counsellor at the Soviet Embassy at London.

so many languages that no one could be expected to know them all. We ought to bring the languages down to a reasonable number, say French and English.

MR. W. S. MORRISON (*Chairman*): Gentlemen, may I leave it that they should be translated into French and English?

HIS EXCELLENCY M. CHARLES CORBIN (France): French *or* English?

MR. W. S. MORRISON (*Chairman*): French or English.

(Agreed)

JONKHEER R. DE MAREES VAN SWINDEREN (Netherlands): May I ask you something more, Mr. Chairman? We have in Holland a rather elaborate law concerning the sale and export of arms and munitions. Is it intended that the text of the whole of that law should be translated into English or French because it is upon that law that we have based the action we have taken? In other words, if an annexe is attached to a resolution taken in any of our countries, is the whole of that annexe to be translated?

MR. W. S. MORRISON (*Chairman*): That is a matter for the Committee. Personally, I would suggest that it would be sufficient if the material part of the law, in so far as it refers to the present situation in Spain and to non-intervention in the Spanish troubles, were translated. I think that that would be sufficient. Would the Committee agree with me, that there is no necessity to translate the whole law?

HIS EXCELLENCY S. DINO GRANDI[7] (Italy): Mr. Chairman, I will submit this question for the consideration of my Government.

MR. W. S. MORRISON (*Chairman*): Certainly. I think that again is a point about which naturally some members of the Committee would like to consult their Governments.

BAY SEDAT ZEKI ÖRS (Turkey): In any case, we should have to ask our Governments to send us any relevant laws.

MR. W. S. MORRISON (*Chairman*): Certainly.

HIS EXCELLENCY S. DINO GRANDI (Italy): It seemed to me that we were being asked now to agree on a proposal. I would suggest that we ask the Committee to treat this matter as a suggestion put forward by you, Mr. Chairman, and to leave the Governments to give a reply. Perhaps the proposal is quite sound, but we should reach no agreement on it now.

MR. W. S. MORRISON (*Chairman*): I do not think any of us could object to that. Shall we leave it in the same position as we left the other question about the collation of the Notes exchanged between the French and other Governments? Could Your Excellency undertake to let the Secretary know whether your Government agree?

HIS EXCELLENCY S. DINO GRANDI (Italy): As soon as possible.

MR. W. S. MORRISON (*Chairman*): We will leave it that we do not take any decision on the matter until an opportunity has been given for those members who wish to do so to consult their own Governments and to inform the Secretary.

7 Italian Ambassador at London.

JONKHEER R. DE MAREES VAN SWINDEREN (Netherlands): Mr. Chairman, in the first part of your last speech, you spoke, as many of the distinguished members around this table have done, of non-intervention. I should like simply as a remark to repeat an observation which M. Corbin knows was made by my Government to the French Chargé d'Affaires when he presented the request of the French Government. As my Government see it, there is a conflict in Spain between a legal Government—needless to repeat there is absolutely no question of our taking sides in any way—a legal Government fighting against revolutionaries. Is the sale of arms to that Government illegal, and can one say that by prohibiting it we do not intervene in the affairs of Spain? I know that the Foreign Office at The Hague suggested to the French Chargé d'Affaires that it might perhaps be better to replace the words 'conclude a non-intervention agreement' by some such phrase as '. . . adopter une attitude commune vis-à-vis les affaires d'Espagne.' I do not want any answer, Mr. Chairman, but I thought it my duty to call the attention of the Committee here to the feeling of the Netherlands Government that they do not think it right to speak about non-intervention in this case.

MR. W. S. MORRISON (*Chairman*): I am sure that the Committee have heard that with great interest. Did I understand the Netherlands representative to suggest that we should not include in the title of the Committee the word 'Non-Intervention'? Would he like to make any other suggestion?

JONKHEER R. DE MAREES VAN SWINDEREN (Netherlands): No, I do not make any other proposal; I only thought it best to tell the members of the Committee what was the view of the Netherlands Government. They do not make a formal proposal to change the title of the Committee though they think it is not quite correct. Some objection might be made to such a title from the Spanish side.

HIS EXCELLENCY M. CHARLES CORBIN (France): Mr. Chairman, I think that the point of view which has just been put forward by the Delegate for the Netherlands is based on real juridical grounds, but it seems to me that since he has just explained that in his Government's view the formula 'non-intervention' implies no sort of doubt as to the legality of the Spanish Government, we can leave the matter like that and accept the French point of view that the words 'non-intervention,' or 'non-immixtion' which we have also used in French, are valid to our purpose, now that we have heard this declaration which has been made.

MR. W. S. MORRISON (*Chairman*): Would you accept that?

JONKHEER R. DE MAREES VAN SWINDEREN (Netherlands): Yes.

MR. W. S. MORRISON (*Chairman*): Very well, we will leave it at that. Those are all the matters which have occurred to me, Gentlemen, as suitable for our first day's work. I think that if we find it convenient to adopt the course which I have suggested we shall all have the information on which to base our further deliberations. We should then be able to help each other in co-operating for this purpose. Is there any other member of the Committee who wishes to raise any matter at this time?

M. Erik Colban[8] (Norway): I should like to know whether we shall receive Minutes of this morning's meeting, and if so, whether we can have them as early as possible. I mean only the provisional minutes—there must be some slight errors or misunderstandings in the minutes, but we should not hold them up just to have everybody's agreement. Could they be sent out as provisional minutes?

Mr. Hemming (*Secretary to the Committee*): That will be done as early as possible.

M. Erik Colban (Norway): Thank you.

Mr. W. S. Morrison (*Chairman*): Is there any other point that any other member wishes to raise for our first meeting?

Prince von Bismarck (Germany): Would it be possible for the Committee to have a list of the members?

Mr. Hemming (*Secretary to the Committee*): A list of the members of the Committee will be circulated this afternoon. I hope also that the minutes of this meeting will be circulated this afternoon.

His Excellency M. Charles Corbin (France): The only remark that I wish to make, Mr. Chairman, is that in view of the great importance of the task which lies before us this preliminary task of collecting and collating certain documents should not take too long or should not retard our attacking the bigger task which lies before us. We should not lose several days waiting for certain replies or certain documents to reach the Secretariat from the various Governments.

Mr. W. S. Morrison (*Chairman*): I am sure that is an observation with which the Committee will be in entire agreement. I can say that we shall make all speed that we can on this side, and I hope that those of us who wish to consult our Governments first will do so as early as convenient, so that we shall get the information as quickly as possible. I feel, however, that we must have some sort of information before we can usefully proceed; we must know each what is the point of the other.

M. Erik Colban (Norway): I think the White Paper of the French Foreign Office contains practically the same material as our Chairman has suggested should be issued on behalf of the Committee. It is in French, but after all it will enable us to go on.

Mr. W. S. Morrison (*Chairman*): That, of course, refers to the replies.

M. Erik Colban (Norway): Yes.

Mr. W. S. Morrison (*Chairman*): We should like, however, to have the decrees as soon as possible, if that is agreeable to the Governments concerned. We shall then know the steps taken by the various Governments, and we shall be able to co-operate on the basis of that knowledge far better than we could without it.

M. Samuel B. Cahan (U.S.S.R.): May I ask a question? I understood that the French White Paper would be issued this afternoon.

Mr. W. S. Morrison (*Chairman*): I think His Excellency said so, yes.

M. Samuel B. Cahan (U.S.S.R.): Because, if that is so, we can see whether

[8] Norwegian Ambassador at London.

our particular reply is included. Otherwise, we should have to communicate with Moscow and other places to get the actual text.

Mr. W. S. Morrison (*Chairman*): Can the French Ambassador say when the White Book will be available?

His Excellency M. Charles Corbin (France): I expect it by Air Mail this afternoon. I think that it will be here this afternoon before five o'clock.

Mr. W. S. Morrison (*Chairman*): His Excellency hopes it will be here this afternoon, so it will be more convenient to wait until then.

I suggested at the opening of the meeting that we should issue a *communiqué* on which we were all agreed. May we consider that matter just for a moment before we part? Our Secretary has drafted the following which I shall read out, and I hope that the freest criticism will be made on it so that we are entirely agreed as to what is issued.

'The opening meeting of the International Committee for the Application of the Agreement regarding non-intervention in Spain was held in the Locarno Room at the Foreign Office at twelve noon this morning.

The meeting was attended by representatives of the following countries, and they are in alphabetical order: Albania, Austria, Belgium, the United Kingdom, Bulgaria, Czechoslovakia, Denmark, Estonia, Finland, France, Germany, Greece, Hungary, the Irish Free State, Italy, Latvia, Lithuania, Luxemburg, Netherlands, Norway, Poland, Roumania, U.S.S.R., Sweden, Turkey, Yugoslavia.'

I hope there is no omission there.

'On the proposal of the French Ambassador, Mr. Morrison, Financial Secretary to the Treasury, was elected Chairman of the Committee.

After a general discussion of the scope of the Committee it was proposed that the several Delegations should as soon as possible furnish the Committee with particulars regarding the legislative and other steps taken by their respective Governments to give effect to the Agreement for non-intervention. It was proposed also that the text of the Notes exchanged between the French Government and the other Governments constituting the Agreement should be published as early as possible. These proposals were adopted subject to the concurrence of the Governments represented on the Committee.'

Does that meet the reservations made?

His Excellency S. Dino Grandi (Italy): I do not think that really meets my observation when you say 'These proposals were adopted *subject* . . .' I am not in a position to agree about that. As far as the Government of my country is concerned I would beg you just to interpose some small amendment.

Mr. W. S. Morrison (*Chairman*): I will try to put it in a way that meets your difficulty. May I say: 'It was agreed that these proposals should be referred to the respective Governments for their consideration?' You see, I have said,

'It was proposed also that the text of the Notes exchanged between the French Government and the other Governments constituting the Agreement should be published as early as possible. It was agreed that these proposals should be referred to the Governments represented on the Committee for their consideration.'

HIS EXCELLENCY S. DINO GRANDI (Italy): That is quite all right.

MR. W. S. MORRISON (*Chairman*): Does that meet the views of other representatives? Would you agree to just one slight difference in the wording which has been suggested to me? 'It was agreed that these proposals should be referred to the Governments represented on the Committee for their concurrence,' or would you rather say 'for their consideration'?

HIS EXCELLENCY S. DINO GRANDI (Italy): The word 'consideration' would suit me much better than the word 'concurrence.'

MR. W. S. MORRISON (*Chairman*): Very well, I want to make it as easy for every member of the Committee to co-operate as possible. Then there is the last paragraph of the *communiqué*. Could we say 'A further announcement will be made about the date of the next meeting,' and leave it like that in the meantime?

HIS EXCELLENCY S. DINO GRANDI (ITALY): Yes, that is right.

MR. W. S. MORRISON (*Chairman*): May I address His Excellency the French Ambassador—I am not quite certain that we have it quite accurately. Do I understand that your White Book will be published in Paris this afternoon?

HIS EXCELLENCY M. CHARLES CORBIN (France): No, it will not be published.

MR. W. S. MORRISON (*Chairman*): It is a confidential print?

HIS EXCELLENCY M. CHARLES CORBIN (France): In answer to your question, Mr. Chairman, all we propose is to distribute this White Book to the members of the committee. It will only be published when the French Government itself has received the agreement of the Governments whose documents figure in that White Book to that publication. I believe that a certain number, indeed many of the Governments, have already signified to my Government their agreement that the document which concerns them should be published, but my Government is waiting till agreement about publication has been received from all the Governments before deciding on what date the White Book shall be made public in France.

LORD CRANBORNE (United Kingdom): I take it that the French Government will inform the Committee before they publish to enable the Committee to publish at the same time.

HIS EXCELLENCY M. CHARLES CORBIN (France): I understand that all the answers may arrive this afternoon or to-morrow morning. The idea of the French Government was to publish this White Book to-morrow afternoon provided, of course, that all the answers have come.

PRINCE VON BISMARCK (Germany): If the French Government is

publishing all these documents, is it then necessary that we publish the same documents again?

Lord Cranborne (United Kingdom): You mean that if the French Government's publication is at the disposal of the committee it would be a waste of money?

Prince von Bismarck (Germany): Yes.

Mr. W. S. Morrison (*Chairman*): I think that is a very sensible suggestion. If we have the French Government's White Book, why should we publish it ourselves? It would be a waste of money, which I, as representing the Treasury, am always very anxious to prevent if I can. Shall we take it that as soon as the French Government has received replies from all the Countries concerned that they see no objection to the reply being published, they will publish it then?

His Excellency M. Charles Corbin (France): Yes.

Mr. W. S. Morrison (*Chairman*): But in the meantime could we have copies for the confidential information of this committee?

His Excellency M. Charles Corbin (France): Yes, in any case.

Mr. W. S. Morrison (*Chairman*): We will leave it like that. That disposes of Your Excellency's objection, too. We need not therefore alter the *communiqué*.

Baron E. K. Palmstierna[9] (Sweden): It was a question not only of publishing the answers to the French Government, but also of publishing the laws and decrees.

Mr. W. S. Morrison (*Chairman*): Yes, that is a separate question. There are two documents which we suggested might be published. First, there are the replies with any reservations that there might be, to the French Government's proposal, and, secondly and quite distinctly, there are the decrees and laws which have been passed in order to give effect to that agreement.

His Excellency S. Dino Grandi (Italy): Mr. Chairman, does the *communiqué* speak about communication to the Committee of these laws?

Mr. W. S. Morrison (*Chairman*): No. It reads: 'It is proposed that the several delegations should as soon as possible furnish the Committee with particulars regarding the legislative and other steps . . .'

His Excellency S. Dino Grandi (Italy): It is 'Furnish' only?

Mr. W. S. Morrison (*Chairman*): Yes.

His Excellency S. Dino Grandi (Italy): Not publication?

Mr. W. S. Morrison (*Chairman*): No, I said we can deal with the question of publication later on when we get the material. Is that agreed?

His Excellency S. Dino Grandi (Italy): Yes, first publication of the notes and then consideration later on of the publication of these laws.

Mr. W. S. Morrison (*Chairman*): Certainly.

His Excellency S. Dino Grandi (Italy): Mr. Chairman, I do not know whether any part of this particular request does not involve a question of an internal character. I should therefore like it left open.

9 Swedish Ambassador at London.

Mr. W. S. Morrison (*Chairman*): Not at all, I quite appreciate your difficulty, and I hope it is adequately met.

His Excellency S. Dino Grandi (Italy): Absolutely.

His Excellency M. Charles Corbin (France): Might I ask that the *communiqué* should be read again and translated in French again?

Mr. W. S. Morrison (*Chairman*): Yes.

'After a general discussion of the scope of the work of the Committee it was proposed that the several delegations should as soon as possible furnish the Committee with particulars regarding the legislative and other steps taken by the respective Governments to give effect to the agreement for non-intervention. It was agreed that this proposal should be referred to the Governments represented on the Committee for their consideration. It was proposed also that the text of the Notes exchanged between the French Government and the other Governments constituting the agreement should be published by the French Government as early as possible.'

To make it clear that the Committee are not publishing this document would the Committee prefer to say: 'published by the French Government when the assent of the other Governments concerned has been obtained?'

His Excellency S. Dino Grandi (Italy): Yes.

Mr. W. S. Morrison (*Chairman*): I think that would be an improvement.

His Excellency M. Charles Corbin (France): Yes.

Mr. W. S. Morrison (*Chairman*): The sentence now reads: 'It is agreed that the text of the Notes exchanged between the French Government and the other Governments constituting the Agreement should be published by the French Government when the agreement of the other countries concerned has been obtained.' I think that is perfectly satisfactory.

His Excellency Count Edward Raczynski[10] (Poland): May I ask a question on a matter of style? Does 'several,' as it is employed in this *communiqué*, mean 'all'?

Mr. W. S. Morrison (*Chairman*): Yes, Your Excellency, it means all of them taken separately, 'the several.'

His Excellency Count Edward Raczynski (Poland): I am sorry, I did not hear the word 'the' before 'several.'

His Excellency M. Charles Corbin (France): I have one small comment on the last sentence in this draft *communiqué*, Mr. Chairman. My Government had decided to publish the text of the replies when agreement had been received from the various Governments, but, according to the text of the *communiqué*, as it is now, it appears as though it were this committee which is deciding that publication should be made by the French Government.

Mr. W. S. Morrison (*Chairman*): Can I make this suggestion? 'The Committee took note that the texts of the Notes exchanged between the

---

[10] Polish Ambassador at London.

French Government and the other Governments constituting the agreement would be published by the French Government when the agreement of the other countries concerned had been obtained.'

His Excellency M. Charles Corbin (France): Yes.

Mr. W. S. Morrison (*Chairman*): Is that agreed?

(Agreed)

Now, Gentlemen, the only other question which remains is the date of our next meeting. I have not consulted you about that. Perhaps the most convenient course would be to wait until we have got as much information as we can get so as not to waste our time, and express the hope that information will be forthcoming as quickly as is convenient to the members. May I, after consultation with as many as I can, suggest a convenient date later on, one that would meet with your desires? The words in the *communiqué* are: 'An announcement will be made later about the date of the next meeting.' Does that meet with the desires of the Committee?

His Excellency M. Charles Corbin (France): I am afraid, Mr. Chairman, that when the general public read that *communiqué* it would conclude that our next meeting had been postponed to a very distant date. I think that it might perhaps be wise to indicate our insistence or our hope that the next meeting will take place as soon as possible.

Mr. W. S. Morrison (*Chairman*): I think that that is probably wise.

His Excellency Baron de Cartier de Marchienne (Belgium): Do you think it might be possible to say we could have a second meeting, say, to-morrow morning or to-morrow afternoon? I think that if we give the public the impression that we are not very keen to have another meeting soon, they will be rather astonished. I agree with the remarks made by my friend M. Corbin, and I think that the public would be rather astonished if we did not follow up this meeting. To-day is Wednesday, why could we not have a meeting either to-morrow morning or to-morrow afternoon?

Mr. W. S. Morrison (*Chairman*): I feel the weight of the observations made by Their Excellencies the French and Belgian Ambassadors, and I think that it might be a good thing if we were to meet again to-morrow. I should be perfectly willing to do so myself.

His Excellency S. Dino Grandi (Italy): Mr. Chairman, I quite see the advisability of holding another meeting as soon as possible. The questions before us are very important, and my Government will be second to none in showing its goodwill and in helping to make the work of the Committee a success. I am afraid, however, that to-morrow or the day after to-morrow would be too soon. There is a risk that there would be some dissatisfaction in public opinion if we met the day after to-morrow and had very little to discuss, since by that time it would not be easy to know the points of view of all of us. I would therefore ask my friend, the Belgian Ambassador, to agree, if possible, to the formula proposed by the French Ambassador 'as soon as possible.' This would meet the wishes of everybody, and all of us would do our best, meanwhile, to secure the replies from our respective Governments.

His Excellency Baron de Cartier de Marchienne (Belgium): I am quite agreeable. All that I wish to ensure is that the impression should not gain currency with the public that we are approaching our task in a luke-warm manner. We must give the impression that we are doing our best and are working as quickly as possible. I quite realised when I said to-morrow that that would be rather early. The day after to-morrow, or at the earliest convenience would suit me perfectly.

Mr. W. S. Morrison (*Chairman*): Could we get over the difficulty by framing our announcement to the press in such a way as to explain the reason for this preliminary delay, namely, that we must have additional information at our disposal before we meet again? Could we say, 'It was agreed that the next meeting should be held as soon as the necessary pre-liminary work had been done,' or 'as soon as the necessary information and instructions had been obtained'?

M. Samuel B. Cahan (U.S.S.R.): I think that such a formula would not be any more satisfactory than the other, for there may be much preliminary work to be done. That the meeting should be postponed on that account would be the greatest calamity. I think that the formula 'as soon as possible' would be much better in the circumstances.

Mr. W. S. Morrison (*Chairman*): The proposal that seems to have gained the most acceptance in the Committee is: 'It is agreed that the next meeting should be held as soon as possible.' That is the French Ambassador's pro-posal, and it seems to me that it holds the field.

His Excellency M. Charles Corbin (France): Could the phrase 'as soon as possible' be completed by indicating that the representatives of the various countries are keeping in touch with the Secretariat for the purpose of fixing the date of the next meeting, or by some formula that would suggest that the contact established here to-day has been kept alive?

Mr. W. S. Morrison (*Chairman*): Would it meet the French Ambassador's point, if we say, 'The Committee will meet again as soon as possible. The representatives are keeping in touch with the Secretariat for that purpose'?

His Excellency Baron de Cartier de Marchienne (Belgium): Why cannot the Chairman himself call the Committee together?

Mr. W. S. Morrison (*Chairman*): Could we say: 'The Committee will meet again as soon as possible. The representatives are keeping in touch with the Secretariat on the subjects raised at to-day's meeting'; or 'It was agreed that a further meeting should be held as soon as instructions had been received regarding the subjects discussed at this morning's meeting'?

M. Erik Colban (Norway): I am a little afraid that we might then be prevented from calling a meeting until we had received information from all the Members of Committee on all the questions discussed to-day. The next meeting of the Committee should be called when we have a sufficient amount of material to discuss.

Mr. W. S. Morrison (*Chairman*): The next meeting will be called by the Chairman as soon as the latter judges that the information received, or the instructions received are sufficient for the purpose of a further meeting?

His Excellency M. Charles Corbin (France): The Committee wishes, or expresses its desire to meet as soon as may be possible. The next meeting will be called by the Chairman as soon as in his judgment sufficient information has been received without undue delay.

Mr. W. S. Morrison (*Chairman*): I think that it would be good to express the wish of the Committee to meet again as soon as possible. That is a very valuable suggestion, for which I am greatly indebted. Is that agreed? I will ask the Secretary to read it as it now stands.

Mr. Hemming (*Secretary to the Committee*): The proposed English text to the last paragraph reads: 'The Committee expressed its wish to meet again as soon as possible. The next Meeting will accordingly be summoned by the Chairman as soon as in his judgment sufficient material has been received for the purpose.'

Jonkheer R. de Marees van Swinderen (Netherlands): We can leave it to the wisdom of the Chairman to call a meeting when he thinks it necessary or possible. I do not think it is necessary to explain it in that last phrase.

His Excellency M. Charles Corbin (France): There is no question in my mind of throwing any doubt on the Chairman's goodwill, but I am thinking entirely of the reaction of public opinion and of the necessity of conveying to the public that the Committee is determined to proceed as rapidly as may be possible with its task.

Mr. W. S. Morrison (*Chairman*): I think that the words suggested make it perfectly clear that we are all anxious to get on with the work of this Committee as soon as we can, and I shall certainly undertake to call the Committee together again as soon as there is a chance that we shall do some useful work. Your Excellencies, and Gentlemen, I express my thanks to you for your attendance to-day.

(The proceedings then terminated.)[11]

[11] The text of the press *communiqué* agreed upon in the foregoing discussion is printed in *The Times*, September 10, p. 12.

No. 179

Mr. Eden to Mr. Newton (Berlin)

No. 195 Telegraphic [*W 11146/79/98*]

FOREIGN OFFICE, *September 10, 1936, 6.30 p.m.*

The question of the reform of the League of Nations will be discussed at the Assembly this month, and a number of Governments have, in response to the invitation of the Special Assembly in July, sent in to the Secretary General their observations on this subject.[1] His Majesty's Government

[1] The reform of the League had become an urgent matter for discussion by its Members during 1936. The Assembly's decision in October 1935 to apply economic sanctions against Italy (see Volume XV, No. 64, note 2) had been seen by many as a final test of the efficacy

have informed the Secretary General[2] that they do not propose to send any written observations but will be ready to make their views known when the Assembly meets.[3] One of their reasons for this decision was their anxiety to postpone as long as possible a declaration on a subject which cannot be unconnected with the proceedings of the Five Power Conference. It could not but facilitate the preparation of that Conference if the German Government could be in some way associated at an early stage with the discussions on League Reform at Geneva. His Majesty's Government for their part would cordially welcome such cooperation. Moreover, by this means it might be possible to discover what are Germany's views in regard to League reform. In any event this course would also have the advantage of demonstrating to the German Government that the last thing any of us want is to place them before [sic] a *fait accompli* by asking them to return to a League in the reform of which they had no say.

We cannot yet foresee what course the discussions will take at Geneva, but it seems likely that, after a general debate in the Assembly, the matter may be remitted for closer examination to a Committee. This might be a special Committee of the Assembly set up for this purpose.

of the Covenant in settling international disputes, and thus the decision taken on July 4, 1936, in the face of Italian military occupation of Ethiopia, to revoke those sanctions (see Volume XVI, No. 411) seemed to the critics proof of the ultimate weakness of the Covenant, a weakness which had been further underlined during the Rhineland crisis in March 1936 (see *ibid.*, Chapters I and II). The debate in the Assembly from June 30 to July 4, 1936, on the withdrawal of sanctions had developed into a discussion of the future of the League itself, and culminated in the adoption by the Assembly on July 4 of a General Committee resolution that the Council invite governments of Member States to submit proposals for the reform of the Covenant to the Secretary General of the League by September 1. See *L/N.O.J.*, *S.S. No. 151*, pp. 65–6; for the preceding debate, see *ibid.*, pp. 21–65. Cf. Volume XVI, No. 395, note 5.

[2] In a letter to M. Avenol of September 8, 1936, not printed.

[3] During the summer the question of the line to be taken by His Majesty's Government at the forthcoming Assembly meeting was widely discussed in the Cabinet and Foreign Office. At a Cabinet meeting on July 9 the question had been referred to the Cabinet Committee on Foreign Policy, and at a further Cabinet meeting on July 29 it was decided to invite Ministers to submit their views on League reform to Mr. Eden. A number of memoranda were submitted during August, including papers from the Admiralty, Dominions Office, and the Minister for the Coordination of National Defence; a collection of these memoranda is printed at W 11340/79/98. Among them was a memorandum by Mr. Neville Chamberlain, who advocated an approach to Germany to ascertain her conditions for returning to the League. All these views were considered at the meeting of the Cabinet Committee on Foreign Policy on August 25, together with the draft speech for Mr. Eden to make at the Assembly. This draft was modified by the meeting in the light of views generally expressed there that His Majesty's Government should not advocate any radical reform of the Covenant, but should stress the importance of true collective security, peaceful change, and regional pacts. They were prepared to support the separation of the Covenant from the Versailles peace treaties, and an approach to Germany was agreed upon. At the Cabinet meeting on September 2, the revised draft of Mr. Eden's speech was agreed, and it was noted that Mr. Eden 'was prepared to adopt the suggestion that an approach should be made to Germany in regard to League reform, and apart from the Five-Power Conference, in order to ascertain in advance, if possible, Germany's desiderata in regard to the reform of the League . . .'

It does not, of course, rest with His Majesty's Government alone to decide whether or not Germany should be invited to be represented by an observer or otherwise at the discussions in any committee which might consider League reform. Such an invitation would normally come from the appropriate organ of the League, and it must be recognised that all other members of the League may not share the views of His Majesty's Government as expressed above.

In the light of the above observations, which are primarily for your own information and guidance, I should be glad if you could find means to ascertain how the German Government would be likely to view such an invitation. I consider, after consulting Sir E. Phipps, that best course would be for you to sound Herr Dieckhoff informally and confidentially regarding probable German attitude to an invitation to such a committee.

It is conceivable that such an invitation might be extended to all ex-Members of the League, which would include Brazil and Japan as well as Germany.[4]

[4] In Berlin telegram No. 298 of September 16 Mr. Newton reported that he had spoken in the sense of this telegram to Herr Dieckhoff, whose personal reaction had been cautious but who had promised an official answer as soon as possible. See No. 208 below.

No. 180

Mr. Eden to Mr. Ogilvie-Forbes (Madrid)
No. 102 Telegraphic [W 11152/62/41]

FOREIGN OFFICE, *September 10, 1936, 10.30 p.m.*

My telegram No. 29.[1]

The Belgian Government have enquired whether, in view of the increasingly dangerous situation now developing at Madrid, the Belgian Chargé d'Affaires and his staff might in case of need take refuge in His Majesty's Embassy; and whether they might, in the event of evacuation, share any safe means available to you and your staff for that purpose.

The difficulties of your own situation have been explained to the Belgian Government, and they have been told that while you will no doubt be ready to maintain close contact and consultation with your Belgian colleague, it is unfortunately impossible in existing circumstances to ask you to give asylum to him and his staff or to assist them in the matter of evacuation.

[1] Of August 21, not printed.

No. 181

Sir G. Clerk (Paris) to Mr. Eden (Received September 11)
No. 317 Saving: Telegraphic [W 11035/9549/41]

PARIS, *September 10, 1936*

My telegram No. 315 Saving.¹

The crisis which was threatening yesterday seems, for the present at any rate, to have been averted and the prospect of a split in the *Front Populaire* lessened.

The Administrative Commission of the *Confédération Générale du Travail* defined its attitude towards the Government's policy of non-intervention in a *communiqué* which was issued last night. In this the Administrative Commission, after dismissing the possibility of ever securing absolute non-intervention by all Powers, and after inviting the French Government to reconsider in agreement with His Majesty's Government the policy of neutrality hitherto adopted by them, declared its fidelity to the *Front Populaire* and complete solidarity with M. Blum's Government.

From the Government's point of view the attitude of the *Confédération Générale du Travail* cannot be regarded as unsatisfactory. The influence of the trades union organisation over the working classes is greater than that of any political party and last night's declaration in no way resembled the ultimatum with which they might have faced the Government had they so desired.

Whether as a result of this or as a result of orders from Moscow, the attitude of the Communist party has also grown a great deal less intransigeant [*sic*], being now in fact not dissimilar from that of the *Confédération Générale du Travail*. At a meeting yesterday of the *Délégation des Gauches* M. Maurice Thorez, the Secretary General of the party, while refusing to approve the Cabinet's policy of 'neutrality' in Spain declared that there could be no question of a split in the *Front Populaire*, and added that if it came to a vote in the Chamber the Government could count on the support of the Communists. In a letter to the Socialist party published today, M. Thorez, after proposing that the two parties should send a joint delegation to M. Blum to urge him to raise the embargo on arms in favour of the Spanish Government, appeals to the Socialists to join with the Communists in strengthening the *Front Populaire*, and explains the Communist desire to establish a yet wider 'Front français' from which only the *deux cents familles*² and their Fascist myrmidons would be excluded. In their reply to M. Thorez the Socialists welcome the Communist offer of co-operation and declare their readiness to join the Communists in discussing with M. Blum the Government's policy in regard to Spain.

Thus both the trades unions and the Communists have now retreated from

¹ This telegram of September 9 referred to No. 177 and to the Communist Party's attitude towards the French Government's Spanish policy.
² A reference to the aristocracy of wealth and society which was believed to dominate France.

the extreme attitude, which had they persisted in it would have risked provoking a serious crisis, and it now seems likely that the Government and the more advanced elements of the *Front Populaire* will for the present, at any rate, agree to differ.

No. 182

Note by Mr. Makins[1] *on the work of the Non-Intervention Committee*
[*W 11343/9549/41*]

FOREIGN OFFICE, *September 10, 1936*

Mr. W. S. Morrison, Lord Cranborne, Sir George Mounsey and Mr. Hemming, the Secretary, met this morning to consider the work of the Committee.

The Secretary of State had suggested that the full Committee was too large to enable good progress to be made, and that it would be advisable to work through sub-committees.[2]

The meeting discussed the possibility of this procedure and came to the conclusion that it would be advisable to suggest at the next meeting the appointment of two sub-committees. The first would assist the Chairman in settling the work of the Committee, would constitute a Bureau and might be composed of the representatives of the countries adjacent to Spain (France, and Portugal if she is there) and representatives of the European arms producing countries (the United Kingdom, Germany, Italy, Belgium, Sweden, Czechoslovakia and Russia). Mr. Morrison would be Chairman of this body.[3] The second sub-committee would be given the task of collating the material supplied to the Committee and would submit its report as soon as possible to the full Committee. It was suggested that the sub-committee should be drawn from the less important members of the Committee and should number about eight. It was proposed, for example, that the Committee might be composed of Poland, the Netherlands, Norway, Roumania, Latvia, Turkey, Hungary and the Irish Free State, but that it should be open to the Committee to add any names that it wished. This committee would elect its own chairman. It would be necessary to consider the terms of reference which should be proposed for this committee.[4]

It was decided that the next meeting of the Committee should be held on

[1] Mr. R. M. Makins was a Second Secretary in the League of Nations and Western Department of the Foreign Office.

[2] Twenty-nine persons are recorded as attending the first meeting of the Committee on September 9 (see No. 178).

[3] The setting-up of this sub-committee was agreed to at the second meeting of the full Committee on September 14.

[4] After discussion at the second meeting the idea of a collating sub-committee was abandoned by the Committee, following the comment of the Polish representative, Count Raczynski, that the work involved was really secretarial and 'could be carried out quite satisfactorily by the Secretary'.

Wednesday, September 16th at 11.30 a.m. and the Secretary was instructed to send out notices convening this meeting this evening. The purpose of the meeting was to be described as 'to consider proposals by the Chairman for future procedure in the light of the documentary material furnished to the Committee'. The notice was to be accompanied by a letter to each representative signed by the Secretary on behalf of the Chairman stating the latter's desire that before its next meeting the Committee should be supplied with the legislative and other measures taken in each country to apply the agreement, and expressing the hope that this would be available.

It was further decided that it would be advisable to inform the press tomorrow that a meeting had been called for Wednesday, that the material asked for at the last meeting was already coming in, and that steps were being taken to ensure that all the documentary material would be available before the next meeting.[5]

The Chairman had been informed by the French Ambassador that it was not the intention of the French Government to publish the texts of the notes exchanged between governments as an official document but merely to issue copies to the press. The question therefore arose as to whether these texts should be published officially by the Committee. It was agreed that this point should be put to the Committee at the next meeting, and that in the meantime it might be advisable, as the documents would have to be published in English, for translations to be made.

It was agreed that it would be undesirable for the Chairman to raise the question of the examination by the Committee of breaches of the agreement. If this question was raised it would be necessary either for the Committee or the Bureau to decide whether such an examination should be undertaken, if so whether a date should be taken before which allegations of a breach should not be entertained, and thirdly what type of evidence would be accepted.

When the sub-committee appointed to collate the material had completed its work, it would be for the full Committee or for the Bureau, to consider how the information collated should be dealt with. It was suggested that any report drawn up on the basis of this information could best take the form of a statement of the measures which all governments were applying in common, together with an account of any additional measures which were being taken by individual governments. It was suggested that it was important that the report should be drafted in such a way as not to appear to be directed against any government or governments.

[5] Later, on September 11, it was decided that the meeting should be held on Monday, September 14. This was due to representations by the French Ambassador to Sir G. Mounsey that a week's delay would be too long in view of public interest in the matter; similar representations by the Belgian Ambassador; M. Corbin's desire to put a concrete case (whether gas-masks should be sent to Spain) before the Committee; and a complaint by the Italian Ambassador of press misrepresentations of the Italian attitude.

No. 183

Mr. Ogilvie-Forbes (Madrid) to Mr. Eden (Received September 12, 9.30 a.m.)
No. 181 Telegraphic [W 11208/62/41]

MADRID, *September 11, 1936, 9 p.m.*

My telegram No. 163, second paragraph.[1]

I sometimes wonder if you fully realise the tragedy that for over 50 days has been enacted in the Alcazar of Toledo when there are, or were, at least 1,500 souls including 500 women and children. The north wall has now been shot away, laying bare the interior and garrison are still holding out in cellars with now but little hope of timely release. Minister of State informed me that quarter had been offered to all concerned and reply is a refusal coupled with request for services of a priest so that the whole garrison may die as good Christians.

The intention is now to destroy the whole building and there is a disquieting notice in the press to the effect that the government has no alternative but to take certain steps repugnant to feelings of humanity.

2. When the veil of censorship is lifted I am sure that the defence of the Alcazar will be regarded as one of the most gallant in military history and of the most cruel to women and children. History will also require to know what action the British representative took in the matter.

3. I therefore went to see Minister of State, expressed my misgivings and in a private capacity offered my assistance for the women and children. His Excellency agreed that when the facts were known it would cause a sensation. He thanked me and said he would speak to the Prime Minister.

[1] Of September 9, not printed (W 10953/62/41).

No. 184

Mr. Eden to Sir G. Clerk (Paris)
No. 73[1] Saving: Telegraphic [C 6430/4/18]

FOREIGN OFFICE, *September 11, 1936*

On my instructions, Sir R. Vansittart told the French, Belgian[2] and Italian Ambassadors and the German Chargé d'Affaires[3] on September 9th that His Majesty's Government in the United Kingdom suggested that the meeting of the Five Powers should be held in London in the second half of October, the exact date being decided later.

The French and Belgian Ambassadors were told that it seemed necessary to decide this because when we began to discuss subject-matter (and we were all agreed that such preparation was necessary) we should almost

[1] No. 81 to Sir E. Ovey, H.M. Ambassador at Brussels; No. 196 to Mr. Newton (Berlin); No. 349 to Mr. Ingram (Rome).
[2] Cf. *D.D.B.*, vol. iv, No. 107.   [3] Cf. *D.G.F.P.*, *op. cit.*, Nos. 530, 532.

certainly encounter considerable difficulties: and these, unless the time and place had been already decided, might prove the source of long delays. By an early and definite decision on this point we should obviate that danger and expedite matters.

The German Chargé d'Affaires (whose Government is known to be already in favour of London) was told that the advantage of reaching agreement on London and a date between the 15th and 30th of October would be this. Baron von Neurath had told Sir R. Vansittart in Berlin that mid-October was the earliest possible date because many exchanges and preparations would be needed before the conference could safely meet.[4] With this view we had all agreed, and later Herr Dieckhoff and Sir R. Vansittart alluded to the desirability of London becoming a sort of clearing house for these preliminary exchanges. It was necessary that some such arrangement should be reached; otherwise the multilateral exchanges would tend to become chaotic. Once London was fixed as the meeting-place it would tend automatically to centralise the preparations, and this would be advantageous from every point of view.

[4] See No. 41.

No. 185

Mr. Newton (Berlin) to Mr. Eden (Received September 12)
No. 245 Saving: Telegraphic [C 6435/97/18]

Very Confidential   BERLIN, *September 11, 1936*

Dr. Jaeckh,[1] who is an old personal friend of Dr. Schacht, has given to a member of Embassy staff an account of a conversation which he had with Dr. Schacht on the 10th instant.

2. Dr. Schacht concentrated almost entirely on German demand for colonies and was in a most optimistic mood. He expressed great satisfaction with progress he had made in Paris, which he evidently regards as far greater than is indicated by Paris telegram No. 294 Saving[2] of August 28th. He went so far as to speak of his 'understanding' with M. Blum.

3. What Dr. Schacht demands is the handing over of a colony to Germany under a mandate, not from the present League of Nations, but from a reformed league or some other group of Powers. As regards the terms of the mandate Dr. Schacht would require German management and introduction of German currency; he would not accept the 'open door' in commerce.

4. As regards the particular colony desired, Dr. Schacht realised that South West Africa was impossible and Tanganyika very difficult, and returned to the Cameroons. He spoke of some broad arrangement and went on to talk rather wildly about the possibility of transfer of some Dutch colony to Germany.

[1] Former head of the German League of Nations Union, now living in England and working for the Rockefeller Peace Foundation.   [2] No. 145.

5. Dr. Schacht admitted that demand for colonies rested mainly on grounds of prestige and that the economic grounds were secondary. But he urged that Herr Hitler was a man of mutable ideas and that the handing over of a colony to Germany would enable Dr. Schacht with Herr Hitler's help to secure the support of that section of Nazi party which favoured a liberal policy in international economic affairs.

6. Dr. Schacht said that new '4 year plan' announced at Nuremburg (see my despatch No. 964 of September 10)[3] by which Germany is to be rendered independent in the highest degree of imports, was to be understood as alternative to return of a colony to Germany.

7. Dr. Schacht said that the peace of the world was in English hands, and begged Dr. Jaeckh to tell his English friends what he (Dr. Schacht) had said. He expressed his great desire to be invited to visit London, where he is confident that he could convince British Ministers as successfully as he convinced the French Ministers in Paris.

8. Dr. Schacht does not appear to have said anything specific about 'alignment' of currencies and it seems uncertain whether his present views go beyond those he expressed to Financial Adviser in June (see paragraph 9 of memorandum of National Socialists, Berlin despatch No. 553E of June 4).[4] But 'liberal policy' referred to in paragraph 5 above might include devaluation of the mark subject to some stabilisation agreement.

9. In reporting this conversation, Dr. Jaeckh said that he was unwilling to act as a semi-official emissary in this matter, though he is quite prepared to give you a first hand account of the interview if you desire it. He was openly sceptical of some of Dr. Schacht's statements and particularly of the idea referred to in paragraph 5 above, that return of a colony would enable Dr. Schacht to swing the party round to a liberal economic policy. He thought that new '4 year plan' would be more appropriately described as a threat than as an 'alternative'. He told Dr. Schacht in the course of the interview that opinion in England had lately hardened against return of a colony to Germany, largely on account of the very state of affairs which Dr Schacht requested Dr. Jaeckh to report to you last March (see Sir E. Phipp[s]' letter of April 1st to Sir R. Vansittart,[5] and record of Mr. Sargent's conversation with Dr. Jaeckh on April 6th).[6]

[3] Not printed (C 6408/6028/18).   [4] Not printed (C 4074/99/18)
[5] Not printed.
[6] In this conversation Dr. Jaeckh had passed on a personal message from Dr. Schacht to Mr. Eden expressing alarm at the development of the Nazi régime under Herr Hitler's direction, and stating that there was no hope of reaching an economic or political settlement with Germany 'until what he described as "civilisation" had been restored in Germany . . Dr. Schacht intended his message to be a warning that H.M. Government should exercise the utmost caution, should most carefully test every offer of Hitler's, and should compel him to explain himself without ambiguity on every point . . .'

No. 186

Record by Sir R. Vansittart of a conversation with Prince von Bismarck
[*C 6431/4/18*]

FOREIGN OFFICE, *September 11, 1936*

The German Chargé called upon me this afternoon with the reply of his Government to the invitation issued by His Majesty's Government to a Five Power meeting in London in the second half of October.[1]

The German Chargé d'Affaires began by saying that his Government did not interpret my communication as an invitation, but only as a suggestion.[2] I interrupted to say that it would be more correct to describe the communication as a definite invitation to London and suggestion as to the date.

The German Chargé d'Affaires then proceeded to say on behalf of his Government that they were prepared as before to take part in a conference, but in the opinion of his Government such a conference would only have a chance of success if carefully prepared diplomatically. The German Government presumed that His Majesty's Government shared this view. The German Government, however, wished to point out that no approaches or preparations at all had yet been made in the matter. They could therefore only reaffirm the principle of their preparedness to take part in the conference, while adding that it was completely impossible for them to declare or agree to any fixed date or period for the conference so long as it was not possible for them to have a conspectus of the result of the diplomatic preparations which had not yet begun. (I should add that the word used in the German note was *Termin* which can mean either date or period.) Prince Bismarck proceeded to add a personal comment from Herr von Neurath. The latter wished to say that he remembered that the second part of October was mentioned in our conversation at Berlin, and he recalled that he had said that was the earliest possible date for the conference. Herr von Neurath wished to explain now that he had assumed that between the beginning of August and mid-October there would have been some progress made in diplomatic preparations. As it was the German Government wished to leave us in no doubt that the question of date must remain open until preparations had been so far pushed forward as to give a real promise of success.

I enquired of Prince Bismarck whether his Government had made any comment in the note from which he was reading as to the place of the conference. He replied in the negative, but said that he took it for granted that London would be agreeable to his Government as a place of meeting.

In regard to the general tenor of his conversation I said to Prince Bismarck that I would report what he had said to the Secretary of State. While I understood the German point of view I thought the communication did not give much satisfaction for while we were all agreed that preparations were necessary, I should have thought that six weeks should have sufficed for

[1] See No. 184.   [2] *Ibid.*, note 3.

II. XVII   257   S

goodwill on all sides to ensure considerable progress before the tentative period that we had suggested. Unless we had some goal in front of us and were working to some timetable, however elastic, I feared that the exchanges and preparations might continue in such fashion as to relegate to a quite distant future a conference in which all here were anxious to make progress.

Prince Bismarck replied that he understood the point, but that his Government anticipated great difficulties in the course of the preparations and must meanwhile reserve their decision.[3]

R. V.

[3] A minute of September 11 by Mr. Eden said: 'Not very encouraging. We must now get down to the programme. I trust that the department will have ready for me by Tuesday of next week [September 15] procedure they propose for making progress with matter of the conference. I wish to see each of the Ambassadors before I leave for Geneva so as to make a start. The Cabinet has approved our paper [No. 156, note 11]. How do department recommend we should handle it? We will of course begin with the West, while making clear that the whole programme is that of the London *communiqué* [Volume XVI, Annex to No. 476]. A. E. Sept. 11.'

No. 187

Letter from Mr. Roberts[1] to Mr. Hemming
[*W 11044/9549/41*]

FOREIGN OFFICE, *September 11, 1936*

Sir,

I am directed by Mr. Secretary Eden to state, for the information of the International Committee for the application of the Agreement regarding non-intervention in Spain, that the measures by which His Majesty's Government in the United Kingdom have prohibited the export to Spain of arms, including aircraft, and munitions of war are based upon the Arms Export Prohibition Order, 1931, copies of which are enclosed herein for the information of the Committee.[2]

2. This Order prohibits the export from the United Kingdom of the goods enumerated in the schedule contained therein, except such as shall be expressly permitted by licence given by the Board of Trade. In accordance with the undertaking contained in the note addressed to the French Government on behalf of His Majesty's Government on the 15th August[3] no licences have been issued since that date, or will be issued in the future, for the export of such goods to Spain, the Spanish possessions, or the Spanish Zone

[1] Mr. W. Roberts was appointed Acting Counsellor and Head of the League of Nations and Western Department of the Foreign Office on October 2, 1936.

[2] Not printed.

[3] See Enclosure in No. 94.

of Morocco. Licences already issued before that date but still unused were cancelled in accordance with the undertaking regarding existing contracts.[4]

I am, &c,

WALTER ROBERTS

[4] In a minute of September 10 Mr. Shuckburgh noted that a statement might have been added to the effect that 'H.M.G. do not possess powers enabling them to prohibit the export of warships. There are, however, no warships under construction in this country for Spain.' It was agreed, however, that there was 'little point in drawing attention to the lacuna in our Reply until someone else points it out'. There seemed, also, some uncertainty as to whether it would not be possible to prohibit the fitting out of ships by means of the Foreign Enlistment Act.

No. 188

Mr. Ingram (Rome) to Mr. Eden (Received September 12, 10.20 p.m.)
No. 597 Telegraphic [W 11235/9549/41]

ROME, *September 12, 1936, 8.45 p.m.*

Your telegram No. 342.[1]

I acted upon these instructions in the course of conversation with the Minister for Foreign Affairs this afternoon using exact formula prescribed which at His Excellency's request I repeated to him.

Count Ciano took no note of it but told me that I could assure you again that neither before the revolution in Spain nor since it broke out had the Italian Government engaged in nor in future would the Italian Government engage in any negotiation with General Franco which might alter the status quo in the Western Mediterranean.[2]

[1] No. 159.
[2] Commenting on September 15, Mr. Shuckburgh noted that Mr. Ingram had been successful in obtaining a renewal of the Italian assurances 'but that does not alter the fact that Italy is helping General Franco and may well be expecting her reward later on' and he asked whether it would be 'possible to permit a discreet leakage to the press of the assurance given to H.M.G.?' Sir R. Vansittart replied: 'I think we had better not leak, anyhow not yet. R. V. Sept. 18.'

No. 189

Sir H. Chilton (Hendaye) to Mr. Eden (Received September 13, 4 p.m.)
No. 227 Telegraphic [W 11228/62/41]

HENDAYE, *September 13, 1936, 1.15 p.m.*

Madrid telegram No. 182[1] to you.

At meeting of Corps Diplomatique last night the Argentine Ambassador read out a letter[2] from Señor Castro (which I have also received) stating

[1] This telegram of September 11 from Mr. Ogilvie-Forbes, after being delayed in transmission, was not received in the Foreign Office until September 16, and has not been preserved there. It evidently communicated the Spanish Government's announcement of Señor Castro's recall. Señor Castro had been acting as liaison officer between the Spanish Government and the Diplomatic Corps at Hendaye.
[2] A copy of this letter was forwarded to the Foreign Office with Sir H. Chilton's despatch No. 675 of September 14, not printed.

that he had been relieved of his appointment here since the Spanish Government considered heads of missions could only act as such in territory of country to which they were accredited. They could of course be absent if they considered fit but their absence prevented them from carrying out their full functions. Without departing from accepted diplomatic practice the Spanish Government could not therefore recognise heads of missions living in France as having the same rights as those of members of Corps Diplomatique in residence in Madrid.

Señor Castro is remaining here though his functions ceased as from yesterday. Following are some of the views expressed by my colleagues:

1. It was considered fit that certain heads of missions should reside in France for the present.

2. Precedent had been set up in Belgium and Serbia during the Great War.

3. If we returned to Madrid we might well be cut off again as we had been for a short time at San Sebastian and be useless to our governments.

4. If Spanish Government had to leave Madrid should we be expected to follow them wherever they might go[?]

5. What advantage would it be to the Spanish Government for the Corps Diplomatique to suffer the same hardship as they[?]

6. In the event of insurgents entering Madrid what would be the position of the Corps Diplomatique pending recognition of such a government[?]

7. By appointing Señor Castro as liaison officer with the Corps Diplomatique the Spanish Government thereby recognise the latter. Why was this recognition suddenly withdrawn? It was decided no answer should be returned to Señor Castro's communication. Corps Diplomatique could not now send reply to Madrid but would be glad to know views of various governments and what reply if any they would make to Minister of State's communication which was considered by some of my colleagues to be impertinent.

Another meeting will be held on September 18th and I should be glad of your views before then if possible. I pointed out that various governments may desire to consult one and other [?another] which might take time. Belgian Ambassador left last night to consult his government; Argentine Ambassador left for Paris this morning to meet his Minister for Foreign Affairs, who is due there tomorrow. Italian Ambassador said nothing would induce him to return to Madrid.[3]

Repeated to Madrid No. 24.

[3] Having ascertained that the French Government were instructing their Ambassador to remain at Hendaye, the Foreign Office in telegram No. 183 of September 21 instructed Sir H. Chilton to do likewise.

No. 190

Mr. Eden to Mr. Ogilvie-Forbes (Madrid)
No. 105 Telegraphic[1] [W 11208/62/41]

FOREIGN OFFICE, *September 13, 1936, 7.30 p.m.*

Your telegram No. 181.[2]

I see in the press today a statement that arrangements have already been made for the evacuation of the women and children from the Alcazar at Toledo. If this however is not the case you may take any action that you prudently can to further this humanitarian cause. I approve the action reported in your telegram under reference.[3]

[1] A note in Sir R. Vansittart's handwriting on one of the two filed copies of this telegram read: 'Telephoned to F.O. on Sunday evening [September 13].'
[2] No. 183.
[3] Mr. Ogilvie-Forbes's telegram No. 197 of September 14 gave details of diplomatic moves by himself and the Chilean Ambassador, but he feared that 'nothing can be done'. The Alcazar was relieved by insurgent forces under General Varela on September 27, 1936.

No. 191

Mr. Eden to Sir C. Wingfield (Lisbon)
No. 122 Telegraphic [W 11201/9549/41]

Important　　　　　　　FOREIGN OFFICE, *September 14, 1936, 1.50 p.m.*

Your telegrams Nos. 177[1] and 179[2] (of September 11th).

You should convey to the Portuguese Government the profound disappointment of His Majesty's Government at their present decision, and express the hope that this decision will be revised at an early date.

It is nevertheless greatly feared that the non-participation of the Portuguese Government in the work of the Committee from its inception may affect the activities of that body so adversely as to undermine the whole basis of collaboration on which it must rely for any successful results.

It would be helpful in averting such a possibility if you could prevail upon the Portuguese Government at least to communicate and grant permission to the Committee to collate and publish, with similar documents from other countries, the Portuguese decrees enforcing their measures in regard to the supply of arms and munitions to Spain.

It would also be of great assistance if the Portuguese Government would

[1] In this telegram Sir C. Wingfield reported that Dr. Monteiro had told the French Minister on September 10 that the Portuguese Government were quite determined to take no part in the work of the N.I. Committee 'until they were satisfied with its working in practice'.
[2] This telegram stated that Dr. Monteiro was 'inflexible about the Committee', and that he was sailing that day (September 11) for the forthcoming meeting of the League of Nations Assembly at Geneva: cf. *D.A.P.E., op. cit.*, No. 302.

at the same time allow an assurance to be communicated to the Committee to the effect that, although they have not as yet seen their way to be represented thereon, the terms of their decree are being strictly enforced.

No. 192

Record by Sir R. Vansittart of a conversation with the Belgian Ambassador
[C 6459/4/18]

FOREIGN OFFICE, *September 14, 1936*

The Belgian Ambassador informed me today that his Government gladly accepted the British Government's invitation to a Five Power Conference to be held in London at some date in the latter half of October. I understood from the Belgian Ambassador that the acceptance of the French Government was likely to be forthcoming shortly. The Belgian Ambassador was already aware of the German refusal to agree to any date, and he was anxious to know what the next step should be.

Baron de Cartier said that he hoped that the next step might be that the British Government would address some communication to the interested Powers in regard to the Five Power meeting, making it clear in broad terms what the British Government thought (to use the Belgian Ambassador's words) 'it was all about'.

I told His Excellency that I thought his view was a sound one and I hoped that some such communication might perhaps be shortly forthcoming.

His Excellency also informed me that in his view the German Government were stalling in expectation or hope of an explosion in France in October or November.

R. V.

No. 193

Mr. Eden to Sir H. Chilton (Hendaye)
No. 522 [W 10439/62/41]

FOREIGN OFFICE, *September 14, 1936*

Sir,

I have to inform you that Señor Juan de la Cierva called on Sir George Mounsey on September 2nd in order to discuss the situation in Spain whence he has just returned.[1]

[1] Señor de la Cierva after a visit to Spain was anxious to see someone at No. 10 Downing Street, but in view of his being admittedly in touch with General Franco it was suggested by Sir Horace Wilson, Industrial Adviser to His Majesty's Government, that he should talk to someone at the Foreign Office. Here he was regarded as 'a reputable and well known person' and it was arranged that he should call on Sir G. Mounsey at 12 noon on September 2. Señor de la Cierva was the son of a former Conservative Minister in Spain, and an ardent supporter of the Nationalist cause. He lived in England and was well known as an aeronautical scientist and inventor of the Autogiro.

2. He explained that he was a private person, neither a politician nor a diplomat, that his concern was for the welfare of Spain, that his leanings were towards monarchy but of a liberal type, and that he was convinced of the necessity of good relations between Spain and this country.

3. Señor de la Cierva stated that he had gone out to Spain a few weeks previously in order, if possible, to see General Franco and give him some impression of the feelings in this country. He had succeeded in obtaining an interview with General Franco, whom he already knew, at which General Mola was also present. He had told them both about the suspicions which were harboured in England in regard to Italian and German relations with the rebel leaders and their movement. General Franco, who is perfectly straightforward and would certainly not have deceived him, had stated categorically that not only had he never made any offer of any kind to Italy or Germany in return for their help, but that their assistance had been given quite spontaneously and without any suggestion of conditions being attached thereto. This attitude he could not of course but contrast favourably with that of other countries.

4. Señor de la Cierva went on to say that he had explained to General Franco that in this country there was a general desire to remain completely impartial. General Franco had not demurred, but he had complained that in fact the actions of His Majesty's Government were not impartial, and had cited the various complicated issues with which you are familiar such as the failure at the outset to keep Tangier neutral, the facilities given to the Spanish Government war ships at Gibraltar, the practical recognition of their blockade of Spanish Morocco, the interruption of the cable services between Gibraltar and Cadiz and between Vigo, the Canary Isles and England and, above all, the impossibility of exporting agricultural goods, wines and other products from the districts in the control of the rebel forces owing to the *impasse* on the question of payments. This last question was obviously one of General Franco's major grievances.

General Franco had also complained of the attitude of the British press, and even of such papers as 'The Times' and 'The Daily Telegraph,' which bracketed the communists and rebels together in the matter of atrocities. General Franco had declared that though the rebels did admit to taking and shooting numbers of prisoners, on entry into towns etc, this was only done under the momentary provocation of witnessing the tortures, burnings and other savageries which the communists had been perpetrating without any provocation, and that he thought that no soldiers in any country would have been able to refrain from immediate retaliation on the perpetrators of the horrible cruelties which they encountered in every town and village.

5. As regards the internal position in Spain Señor de la Cierva said that six months ago there was practically no such thing as fascism in Spain. It was quite alien to the Spanish character, and perhaps 1% of the population harboured fascist ideas. On his return however to Spain he had found that fascism had spread somewhat though not yet very extensively. The more help, however, was obtained from Italy and Germany, the more fascist ideas

would take root and if the country received no assistance from elsewhere, fascism might quite conceivably come to dominate it. Much harm was being done to General Franco's cause by the irresponsible broadcasts by General Quiepo de Llano from Seville.[2] That officer had at the outbreak of the revolt behaved very gallantly with his 200 soldiers at Seville and had so merited General Franco's gratitude, but he had no real influence and his ideas were mainly his own.

6. On taking his leave Señor de la Cierva said that he was returning to Spain in a few days and enquired whether there was anything which he could do for England, adding that he wished to express his deep appreciation of all the Foreign Office had done on behalf of his family both at Madrid and Santander. Sir George Mounsey thanked him for calling and for the information which he had kindly given him. He pointed out that he did not think His Majesty's Government would wish to take advantage of Señor de la Cierva's offer of his services and in view of the nature of the conversation he reminded him that he had of course only received him as a purely private Spanish citizen and that he had no concern with his connections or sympathies in Spain. To this Señor de la Cierva entirely agreed.

I am, &c.,

ANTHONY EDEN

[2] Cf. Thomas, *op. cit.*, p. 646.

No. 194

Mr. Ogilvie-Forbes (Madrid) to Mr. Eden
(Received September 15, 9.10 p.m.)
No. 202 Telegraphic [W 11377/9549/41]

Secret   MADRID, *September 15, 1936, 5 p.m.*

Mr. Price of Labour and Socialist International, Brussels, who is known to His Majesty's Minister, Vienna, and is here to arrange supply of foodstuffs and improved press services has informed me that His Majesty's Government are becoming unpopular in certain government circles because French have put it about that they only took the initiative for non-intervention at your instance and to screen you.[1]

[1] A minute of September 17 by Mr. Roberts read: 'We are unpopular with both sides which is the best proof of our impartiality.'

No. 195

Mr. Eden to Mr. Ingram (Rome)
No. 1067 [C 6499/4/18]

FOREIGN OFFICE, *September 15, 1936*

Sir,

The Italian Ambassador came to see Sir R. Vansittart this afternoon to give him the answer of his Government to the British invitation to a meeting of the Five-Power Conference in London in the latter half of October.

2. Signor Grandi said that his Government wished to thank His Majesty's Government for the invitation and to add that before fixing the actual date they thought it necessary to proceed to a diplomatic exchange of views in order to achieve good results.[1]

3. These are the exact words of the Italian note. Signor Grandi added that he hoped that His Majesty's Government would take the initiative in setting the ball rolling, as he put it, and Sir R. Vansittart replied that he hoped that His Majesty's Government would be in a position to do so within a few days.

4. Copies of this despatch have been sent to His Majesty's Ambassador at Paris, His Majesty's Minister at Berlin and His Majesty's Chargé d'Affaires at Brussels.[2]

I am, &c.,
ANTHONY EDEN

[1] Before despatching these instructions Count Ciano had ascertained that they corresponded with the German Government's proposed reply to Mr. Eden's invitation: *D.G.F.P.*, *op. cit.*, No. 533, p. 960.
[2] Sir N. H. H. Charles.

No. 196

Mr. Newton (Berlin) to Mr. Eden (Received September 17)
No. 984 [C 6518/99/18]

BERLIN, *September 15, 1936*

Sir,

With reference to my telegram No. 245 (Saving) of September 11th,[1] I have the honour to inform you that the Roumanian Minister in Berlin, M. Comnen, mentioned to me recently certain information which he had received regarding Dr. Schacht's visit to Paris.

2. M. Comnen understood that Dr. Schacht had explained to the French Government that one reason for the increase in the period of military service was economic. Germany's campaign against unemployment, and the revival of her industry were largely based upon the growth and equipment of her military forces. She must therefore continue to increase these forces unless her economic development and the raw materials which she needed could be assured to her in other ways. He thus seems to have hinted that

[1] No. 185.

unless Germany was helped economically there would be a further increase of her armed forces in due course, but that given such help, limitation might be possible. He also raised Germany's claim to colonies, representing them, no doubt, as a partial satisfaction of her economic requirements. His account in these respects seems to tally generally with that given to His Majesty's Minister in Paris.[2] M. Comnen's information, however, was that the French attitude in regard to economic help in general, and colonies in particular, was not discouraging, and had in fact been receptive. As regards colonies there is a hint to this effect in the article by Herr Kircher reported in my despatch No. 983 of September 15th.[3] M. Comnen understood that the visit was regarded in France as a success, and from his manner it was evident that he thought the upshot of these conversations might not be altogether to the liking of His Majesty's Government.

3. From these various accounts it rather looks as though Dr. Schacht has been threatening France with a further increase of German military forces and now proposes (see paragraph 7 of my above mentioned saving-gram) to threaten Great Britain also with the responsibility for any trouble which Germany may make, unless France and Great Britain, or perhaps Great Britain alone, are prepared to buy her off. At the back of his unscrupulous mind may also lurk the thought of sowing disagreement as to who should pay the German piper.

4. This line of negotiation would indeed be an exploitation of Germany's economic situation. For her poverty so far as it genuinely exists is largely of her own making. It is due to her revolutionary upheaval, to her treatment of the Jews, to her costly social schemes and expenditure on roads, buildings and propaganda, to her unscrupulous treatment of foreign creditors and refusal to adapt her price level by normal methods to that of the outside world, and to her disregard for economic considerations in any matters even remotely concerned with military preparation. Dr. Schacht, in his present rôle, claims to be the spokesman of orthodox finance, speaking to those who stand for orthodoxy. The whole force of his argument rests on that basis. It is some inversion of normal principles when he requests that Germany, as an economic sinner, should be rewarded for her sins. His argument is hardly made more respectable when—in the vein of a highwayman rather than of an eminent economist—he threatens further misdeeds, in the form of another military increase and now also a new four years' plan of autarchy, if his demands are not met. But it is surely either infatuation or cynical effrontery when, in the name of sound finance, Dr. Schacht demands in addition that Germany should be given a colony, the development of which would (whether Dr. Schacht realises it or not) for years to come be a heavy addition to the economic burdens which he professedly wishes to lighten. Not only would Germany be burdened but expenditure on the monopolistic development of a colony would also be counter to the very policy which he ostensibly champions of a return to normal trading methods.

[2] See No. 145.   [3] Not printed.

5. In the long run an economic nemesis may be the only force, short of war, capable of putting a limit on Germany's ambitions. Germany's economic rehabilitation, much as we may desire it, can only be in the general interest provided that it furthers peace. We do not want, in giving economic help, merely to encourage Dr. Schacht and his like to prosecute a dangerous policy of expansion with all the greater vigour. If, therefore, the reckless German piper is to be paid at all, it should not only be in some other form than a transfer of colonies, but also should be in return for a general renunciation of disturbing ambitions. If this is too much to hope for, at the very least Germany, and above all the economist Dr. Schacht, should drop so completely inconsistent a claim as that to a costly colony.[4]

I have, &c.,
B. C. NEWTON

[4] In a minute of September 23 Mr. Baxter wrote: 'We hear so much about Germany's poverty, in connection with her colonial ambitions, that I think the News Dept would do well to take special note of para. 4 of this despatch. Her public expenditure, mostly military, is reckless in the extreme.' Sir R. Vansittart thought it 'a very good despatch' (September 26), and arranged for its distribution to members of the Cabinet.

No. 197

Mr. Eden to Mr. Ogilvie-Forbes (Madrid)
No. 111 Telegraphic [*W 10953/62/41*]

FOREIGN OFFICE, *September 16, 1936, 12.10 p.m.*

Your telegrams Nos. 150[1] and 163.[2]

In the difficult circumstances now prevailing I would much prefer not to send message which might be liable to misconstruction. If, however, in spite of imminence of Geneva meetings you consider this indispensable please telegraph again.[3]

[1] No. 172.
[2] This telegram of September 9 referred to No. 172 and said that it would be helpful if he could 'privately verbally convey to Minister of State some favourable reaction of yours to my telegram above mentioned'. This produced a further round of minuting in the Foreign Office, in the course of which, on September 14, Sir R. Vansittart stressed that any message might be published and made to look like a taking of sides. Mr. Eden said that he would 'much rather send no message' and he suggested the wording of this telegram No. 111.
[3] Mr. Ogilvie-Forbes's telegram No. 214 of September 16 said that the Minister of State was to leave for Geneva next morning, and that he had not reverted to the subject of a message.

No. 198

Mr. Newton (Berlin) to Mr. Eden (Received September 17)
No. 988 [C 6521/4/18]

BERLIN, *September 16, 1936*

Sir,

With reference to your despatch No. 1491[1] of August 28th, to His Majesty's Ambassador in Paris, a copy of which I have read in print, I have the honour to observe that it seems to me unlikely that Baron von Neurath would regard the words which you quoted as precluding Germany from reinforcing her position in the Rhineland up to normal strength. Presumably this was also the opinion of the French Ambassador in London when he pointed out that they had not prevented the announcement of two years' service.

2. In Herr Hitler's Peace Plan, handed to you by Herr von Ribbentrop on April 1st,[2] a proposal was made that there should be a period of four months during which the German Government undertook on a basis of reciprocity to refrain from any reinforcement of their troops in the Rhineland. As this proposal was not accepted at the time, nor during the ensuing four months, it is no doubt considered in Germany to have lapsed, or at least never to have come into force. The Military Attaché to this Embassy, however, who has just returned from the Rhineland, informs me that his impression, and that of well-informed colleagues, is that little actual work is being carried out in fortifying the Rhineland, and that there does not seem to have been any marked increase in the number of troops. Colonel Hotblack anticipates that steps will be taken in October, when it is believed that the German army will be increased to 36 divisions, to bring garrisons in the Rhineland to normal strength. For lack of new barracks it is, in his opinion, nevertheless unlikely that the Rhineland garrisons will reach that strength in the course of 1936. Colonel Hotblack points out, furthermore, that in the event of increased political tension it is always possible for Germany to move more troops into the Rhineland at very short notice. Meanwhile, it is clear that the German army wishes for time to develop on normal lines and does not wish to be harried by temporary expedients.

I have, &c.,
B. C. NEWTON

[1] No. 148.   [2] See Volume XVI, No. 193, note 2.

No. 199

Sir C. Wingfield (Lisbon) to Mr. Eden (Received September 18, 9.30 a.m.)
No. 185 Telegraphic [W 11616/9549/41]

LISBON, *September 17, 1936, 9.45 p.m.*

Portuguese Government have heard on the wireless and from other sources that it is proposed to embargo arms shipments to Portugal.

Secretary General of Ministry of Foreign Affairs who believes that French Government have made efforts in this sense enquire[s] what is the attitude of His Majesty's Government pointing out that we have not even accused Portuguese Government of sending war material to Spain and that on the contrary Portugal is herself very short of arms of all sorts.[1]

In the course of conversation he suggested that perhaps our hesitation to supply arms desired by Portugal was due to some extent to such sentiments. This I at once denied.

I have no reason for thinking that breaches of agreement are taking place here. See my letter of September 15th to Sir G. Mounsey[2] by next bag.

Such an embargo would cause deep resentment here whilst encouraging those who would like to overthrow the Government.

[1] Cf. *D.A.P.E.*, *op. cit.*, No. 330. Foreign Office telegram No. 130 of September 21 to Sir C. Wingfield said that the Portuguese Chargé d'Affaires at London had made enquiries 'on these two points' and had been told that 'His Majesty's Government were now considering the Portuguese requirements on their merits and in relation to our own needs for our defence re-organisation programme', and, on the second point, that 'there is no knowledge here of a proposal to embargo arms shipments to Portugal'.
[2] Not printed.

No. 200

Memorandum by Sir R. Vansittart

[*C 6528/4/18*]

FOREIGN OFFICE, *September 17, 1936*

It has been suggested to me that it would be useful if I placed on record the gist of conversations I had in France with M. Blum, M. Delbos and M. Léger on my return from Berlin.[1]

To the two former I had not time to speak as fully as I should have wished, but as M. Léger and I were staying in the same house in Brittany[2] I had ample opportunity of exchanging views with him and of giving him my impressions of what was possible and what was not in regard to agreement with Germany.

I found him ready to agree with my exposition of what in my view British public opinion and His Majesty's Government would regard as possible and necessary: a new Locarno, without air limitation, (which Germany would probably render impossible by excessive claims), that is a western pact with proper appendages or corollaries in Central Europe (I do not think he would be too particular as to the forms). In regard to Central Europe Germany had made offers on March 31st, and she ought *at the least* to maintain that offer. As to Russia, an Eastern Pact was no longer obtainable, and we should only wreck any prospect of negotiation by insistence on it. M. Léger agreed in thinking the latter no longer practical or desirable politics, but he said that it would take M. Blum all his time to get the abandonment past his

[1] See No. 87.　　　[2] Cf. No. 85.

Left Wing supporters. This would make it more than ever impossible for this, or any, French Government to give up at German dictation any pacts already concluded. This includes not only Russia and Czechoslovakia, but the other countries of the Little Entente and Poland. As to Italy he said that pro-Italian feeling, a growth of 1935, was rapidly disappearing in France everywhere but in the south. I replied that I thought it would be most unreasonable of Herr Hitler to claim the abandonment of the existing [?pacts], and that I did not believe he could seriously hope to induce France to isolate herself. On the other hand, I was relieved to find that he concurred in not asking the impossible of Germany; for English opinion wished to try out, with wide-open eyes, the policy of *autant croire*, and if France, at Russian instigation, blocked it, M. Blum would lose at the British swings more than he could win at the Russian roundabouts. I knew that M. Blum's chief profession and concern was collaboration with England; but M. Blum must remember, as I had told him in Paris, that the British Government was upheld by a very large Conservative majority, who were never prepared, and now probably less than ever, to make much sacrifice for red eyes. The Russian aspect of Spain could not fail to make a difference in these sections of English feeling. I begged M. Léger to repeat this to M. Blum, for I thought it would assist him in resisting undue Russian pressure or wrecking tactics; and there was something to be wrecked, for there was an undoubted possibility of limited progress. M. Léger agreed, and I am sure that we shall find him helpful; but he asked me what I thought an agreement, if obtained, would be worth. I replied that time alone could show, and that playing for time might therefore be a paying game. My known scepticism—and we had all learnt our lesson in regard to the signature of dictators—might lend weight to my advocacy of an attempt at faith. It might fail, but it would go hard with us, indeed, if we could find no faith at all even between mortals. M. Léger is ready to try the Act of Faith within reason.

On one other point I felt bound to be truthful with the French. I had preached as much as possible in Berlin the virtues and deserts of the present French régime. If that régime maintained its ground, international agreement was attainable, though with difficulty. If, however, France moved much further to the Left, we should probably find the Germans unmanageable. Moreover, I was by no means sure of the effect of such a development on my own countrymen. As the French Government well knew, there had been a strong wave of pro-German feeling in England for some time past; and it had only turned over since Germany had refused to reply to our questions.[3] Opinion had come back into focus by the end of the summer; but I thought it more than probable that any further move by France in the direction of Communism would cancel the change favourable to France that had come about, and set all this wobbling body of opinion off again in the direction of Berlin. These anticipations, especially in regard to the effect on Germany, were sufficiently probable to make it well for the French Govern-

[3] Cf. Volume XVI, No. 307.

ment to be aware of them. In some degree a fresh impetus might thus be given to that very conflict of *Weltanschauungen*, against which I had been preaching in Berlin. That was certainly the very last thing that would suit England.

No. 201

Mr. Eden to Sir G. Clerk (Paris)
No. 1578 [W 10966/9549/41]

FOREIGN OFFICE, *September 17, 1936*

Sir,

The French Ambassador came to see Sir Robert Vansittart on 7th September and spoke of the proposed international Committee for the application of the Agreement regarding non-intervention in Spain. He expressed particular anxiety regarding the attitude of the Portuguese Government in this matter.

2. Sir Robert Vansittart informed M. Corbin that His Majesty's Government sincerely hoped and felt sure that not only the Portuguese Government but all Governments concerned would live up to their obligations in regard to non-intervention and would co-operate in the work of the Committee. In this connexion he wished briefly to mention an episode which Your Excellency had already been instructed to bring to the notice of the French Government. Reports had reached His Majesty's Government that the escaped combatants from Irun had been sent back by the French authorities to Spain, where they would obviously be available for further hostilities.[1] This was exactly what the German press had been anticipating, and Sir Robert Vansittart was sorry to see that the French had fulfilled the malicious prophecy. It was to be hoped that no harm would come of this particular incident, though His Majesty's Government could only regard it as unfortunate and felt that the French Government would be well advised to avoid similar incidents in future.

3. The French Ambassador recognised the light in which the episode might be put by foreign critics animated by a desire to make capital out of it. At the same time, he said, his Government was in a very difficult position. It was impossible to prevent combatant refugees from both camps from coming across the frontier. The only way to stop it would be to shoot, and that would be impossible. His country would be in a very difficult position, quite apart from the matter of expense, if they were expected to intern people for defending what they regarded as their legitimate Government.

4. Sir Robert Vansittart did not pursue the subject as he was aware that Your Excellency was already handling it in Paris.[2]

I am, &c.,
(For the Secretary of State)
WALTER ROBERTS

[1] Cf. No. 170. [2] Cf. *D.D.F., op. cit.*, No. 243.

No. 202

Mr. Eden to Sir G. Clerk (Paris)
No. 1586 [C 6523/4/18]*[1]

FOREIGN OFFICE, *September 17, 1936*

Sir,

The French Ambassador handed the memorandum of which a copy is enclosed[2] to Sir R. Vansittart to-day. He said that it was addressed to us only and would no doubt require careful study on our part before we were in a position to reply.

2. Sir R. Vansittart told him that I should be handing to him on the 18th September a document designed to initiate the diplomatic exchanges and preparations which had been recognised as necessary before the Five-Power Conference could meet, and the Ambassador replied that there was nothing in this French memorandum which would in any way interfere with such a step on our part.

3. The Ambassador repeated that he thought that some little time might elapse before we were in a position to reply to all the points raised in the French memorandum, and he was, moreover, specifically instructed by his Government to say that these points were not exclusive or final, but that the French Government reserved full liberty to raise others at a later stage.

4. Copies of this despatch have been sent to His Majesty's Ambassador at Brussels, His Majesty's Minister at Berlin, and His Majesty's Chargé d'Affaires at Rome.

I am, &c.,
ANTHONY EDEN

[1] A note in F.O. volume 371/19912 states that the draft and flimsy copy of this despatch were 'missing at the time of weeding' (15 August 1962).

[2] Not printed: see *D.D.F.*, *op. cit.*, *Annexe* to No. 256 for the French text. This memorandum set out the French views on the basis of a new Western agreement to be discussed at the Five Power Meeting.

No. 203

Mr. Eden to Mr. Ingram (Rome)
No. 1068 [R 5401/226/22]

FOREIGN OFFICE, *September 17, 1936*

Sir,

The Italian Ambassador on his return to London came to see Sir R. Vansittart on the 8th September, and in the course of conversation referred to the prospects of the Five Power Conference.

2. Sir R. Vansittart took this occasion to say to Signor Grandi that he hoped that this would be an opportunity for the Italian Government to show that they and His Majesty's Government could now sit round a table

together and collaborate usefully and fruitfully. He added that he thought and hoped that by now the passions aroused in both countries by the Italo-Ethiopian conflict had begun to cool, and that now was the time when our two Governments could show by collaborating productively for the peace of Europe that there was really no cause for ill-feeling or strife between them. If on the other hand there were any failure to grasp this opportune moment, Sir Robert was afraid that the rift between the two countries would remain and perhaps grow, for he had heard during his absence that the press in Italy was not proving itself particularly friendly but on the contrary was tending to adopt rather a carping and contemptuous tone towards the United Kingdom which he thought was a great mistake.

3. The Ambassador replied that he was just as anxious to restore good relations between the two countries, and he was quite convinced that this desire was also shared by Signor Mussolini. The Ambassador reminded Sir Robert that before he left on his holiday he, Sir Robert, had spoken to him of the necessity of clearing the ground of all minor causes of friction in order to make it easier for the two countries to see eye to eye on the major questions. So far, however, from minor causes of friction being removed during the last month or so, they had rather tended to multiply. The Ambassador cited The King's avoidance of Italy on his recent journey, an avoidance which was made the more marked by his double visit to Yugoslavia, a direction in which the Italian Government were peculiarly sensitive. Then there was The King's visit to Turkey, and that again was shortly to be followed by a visit of the Turkish fleet to Malta, and at Malta itself there had been the practical abolition of the use of the Italian language.[1] Signor Grandi said that he himself perfectly well understood that there was nothing in particular behind any of these incidents and that they would all of course be overtaken by other events and so forgotten very shortly. The bulk of his countrymen, however, did not understand matters in this light, and the cumulative effect of these four episodes had certainly tended to create suspicion and to retard the rapprochement between the two countries.

Sir Robert expressed the opinion that Signor Grandi's countrymen were really far too susceptible for their own good. They were inclined to see something sinister behind almost anything, and such suspicions were liable to spoil people's sleep and digestion without doing them any good or corresponding with any reality. The visit of the Turkish fleet to Malta, for example, had been on the tapis for years and it seemed the most natural thing in the world that it should take place after so long a delay particularly as the Ambassador must be well aware that the recent withdrawal by His Majesty's Government of the Mediterranean assurances[2] had no doubt caused some disappointment in Turkey. But it had caused, or should have caused great satisfaction in Italy. Why grudge the Turks this small consolation? Sir Robert expressed the hope that the era of the necessity for explanations on such innocuous matters would soon really be at an end, and he repeated that the opportunity for entering upon a better era would occur not only

[1] See No. 169.   [2] See No. 13, note 2, and No. 21.

in connexion with the Five Power Conference itself but with the exchanges and preliminaries which must precede it.

5. [*sic*] The Ambassador repeated that, as Sir Robert knew, these were his sentiments too, and that he sincerely believed them also to be Signor Mussolini's. Signor Grandi himself, however, seemed to be rather dispirited and listless, and far from his former self. He said that his last eighteen months in London had taken heavy toll of him and had in some degree affected his heart, not dangerously, but enough to make him feel really ill. He had been away for two months already and had felt obliged to ask now to be allowed to go away again immediately for another month. He certainly looked far from well. Sir Robert wished him bon voyage and suggested that he should think over what he, Sir Robert, had said.

I am, &c.,
ANTHONY EDEN

No. 204

Report by Chairman's Sub-Committee of N.I. Committee on procedure to be adopted on receipt of complaints regarding alleged breaches of the agreement regarding non-intervention in Spain

[*W 10853/9549/41*]

September 18, 1936

I *Introductory*

At our meeting held on Tuesday, the 15th September, 1936,[1] we had under consideration the procedure which could most conveniently be adopted if and when the Committee receives complaints alleging that a breach of the Agreement for non-intervention in Spain has been committed by some country that is a party to that Agreement. It is the hope of us all that there will be no such complaints or at least that they will be few in number. We realise, however, that, if such complaints are received, it will be the duty of the Committee to examine them with a view to ascertaining the facts.

2. We think it important that the Committee should reach preliminary decisions on the question of procedure before any complaints are actually received as by doing so they will be able to avoid the delay which would otherwise be involved while they considered their procedure.

II *The source from which complaints may be received*

3. It would clearly be most undesirable that the Committee should place themselves in a position in which they were under an obligation to consider complaints, however flimsy, and without regard to their origin. Our view is that a complaint should only be entertained by the Committee if it is received

---

[1] The meeting referred to was the first meeting of the Chairman's sub-committee of the N.I. Committee: see No. 182, note 3.

from a responsible source and if it is regarded by the Government preferring it as being of sufficient importance and as being founded on evidence of sufficient weight to afford a reasonable presumption that in fact some breach of the Agreement has occurred.

4. We recommend that in order to secure this object the Committee should at once lay it down as a matter of principle that complaints regarding alleged breaches of the Agreement will only be entertained by them if the complaint is submitted to them on behalf of the Government of one or other of the countries that are parties to the Agreement.

5. We consider that this limitation is desirable for a number of reasons. In the first place it would ensure that the Committee, which it should always be remembered is a Committee composed not of individuals but of representatives of the participating Governments, will retain in its own hands the whole matter of complaints in exactly the same manner as it reserves to itself all other questions relating to the Agreement and its interpretation.

6. There is, however, another important reason why it is desirable that the right to submit complaints should be limited to the Governments of the countries that are parties to the Agreement. We have already referred (in paragraph 3 above) to the necessity of ensuring that complaints should only be preferred if they are accompanied by adequate supporting evidence. It would clearly be most difficult for the Committee to lay down in advance criteria by which to judge whether the evidence submitted in any particular case was of sufficient weight and importance to justify the investigation of the complaint concerned. If, however, as we propose, the right to submit complaints to the Committee is limited to the Governments which are parties to the Agreement, this difficulty will not arise, since we are confident that no Government would take it upon itself to submit such a complaint unless it had taken such steps as appeared to it reasonable to ascertain that in fact there was some substance in the complaint and that it was of sufficient importance to justify its being brought to the notice of the Committee.

7. We consider, indeed, that any Government submitting a complaint to the Committee would take upon itself a specific and moral responsibility by so doing. On the other hand, it would clearly be impossible for any Government before submitting a complaint to determine beyond all possible question whether or not the breach of the Agreement complained of had in fact taken place, for no such proof could be obtained until the Government of the country against which the complaint was made had been given an opportunity of stating the facts as known to it.

III *The procedure to be adopted by the Committee on receipt of a complaint*

8. In the peculiar circumstances in which the Committee are placed they have not available any precise precedent in the light of which to lay down the procedure to be followed upon the receipt of a complaint. In our consideration of this matter we have, however, given study to certain proposals contained in a Report (League of Nations, Conf. D. 163) dated the 13th April, 1935, drawn up by the Committee for the Regulation of the Trade in,

and Private and State Manufacture of, Arms and Implements of War appointed in connection with the Conference for the Reduction and Limitation of Armaments.[2] In that document will be found the draft of an Article (Article 29) prepared for inclusion in the projected International Disarmament Convention, which had been agreed upon by a number of delegations in the following terms:

'Should the Permanent Disarmament Commission have reason to believe that an infringement of the present Convention has occurred, or that information supplied to it under the Convention by the High Contracting Party is incomplete or inaccurate, the Commission will call upon the High Contracting Party concerned to supply it with such explanations as are necessary to establish the facts.'

9. We feel that the procedure contemplated in the draft Article quoted above provides a useful model for the procedure to be followed by the Committee on receipt of complaints regarding the non-observance of the agreement for non-intervention in Spain. We accordingly recommend that all complaints should be addressed in writing to the Secretary to the Committee, who shall immediately circulate copies to all members of the Committee. Upon the receipt of a complaint from the representative of one of the Governments that are parties to the Agreement, the Chairman should at the same time communicate the complaint to the representative of the Government of the country against which it is levelled with a request that that Government should supply the Committee 'with such explanations as are necessary to establish the facts.'

10. On receipt of the observations of the Government against which a complaint has been preferred the Committee will take such steps as may appear proper in each case to establish the facts.

IV *Summary of conclusions and recommendations*

11. We summarise our principal conclusions and recommendations as follows:

(a) It is much to be hoped that few, if any, complaints will be submitted to the Committee alleging that breaches of the Agreement for non-intervention in Spain have been committed by some country that is a party to the Agreement.

(b) If such complaints are received it will, however, be the duty of the Committee to examine them with a view to ascertaining the facts.

(c) It is important that the Committee should reach preliminary decisions on the question of procedure before any complaints are actually received as by doing so they will be able to avoid the delay which would otherwise be involved while they considered their procedure.

(d) A complaint should not be taken into consideration by the Committee unless:

(i) it is received from a responsible source; and unless

[2] Not printed.

(ii) it is regarded by the Government preferring it as being of sufficient importance and as being founded on evidence of sufficient weight to afford a reasonable presumption that in fact some breach of the agreement has occurred.

(e) In order to secure the objects laid down in (d) above, we recommend that the Committee should at once lay it down as a matter of principle that complaints regarding alleged breaches of the Agreement will only be considered by them if the complaint is submitted to them on behalf of the Government of one or other of the countries that are parties to the Agreement.

(f) We are confident that no Government would take it upon itself to submit to the Committee a complaint alleging that a breach of the Agreement had occurred unless it had taken such steps as appeared to it reasonable to ascertain that in fact there was some substance in the complaint and that the complaint was of sufficient importance to justify its being brought before the Committee, though it would clearly be impossible for such a Government to determine beyond all possible question whether or not a breach of the agreement had been made.

(g) We recommend that all complaints should be addressed in writing to the Secretary to the Committee, who shall immediately circulate copies to all members of the Committee.

(h) We recommend that upon the receipt of a complaint from the representative of one of the Governments that are parties to the Agreement the Chairman should communicate the complaint to the representative of the Government of the country against which it is levelled, with a request that that Government should supply the Committee 'with such explanations as are necessary to establish the facts.'

(i) We recommend that on receipt of the observations of the Government against which the complaint has been preferred the Committee should take such steps as may appear proper in each case to establish the facts.[3]

Signed on behalf of the Sub-Committee:

W. S. MORRISON,
Chairman

[3] These proposals were adopted *nem. con.* by the N.I. Committee at its third meeting on September 21.

No. 205

Note by Mr. Shuckburgh

[*W 12259/9549/41*]

FOREIGN OFFICE, *September 18, 1936*

The Sub-Committee of the International Spanish Committee discussed this morning[1] *inter alia* the following questions:

(1) The question of inviting certain non-European Governments to subscribe to the Agreement on Non-Intervention.

(2) The question of what action participating Governments should take in preventing the export to non-participating countries of arms which they have reason to believe are destined ultimately for Spain.

As regards question one it was agreed that the members of the Sub-Committee should obtain the views of their Governments. It will be necessary for us to supply Lord Plymouth with a note[2] on the attitude of His Majesty's Government on this matter before the next meeting of the Sub-Committee on Tuesday next, September 22nd. I would submit the following observations.

The European Governments were invited to attend the Non-Intervention Agreement [? Committee] by the French Government, supported in all necessary cases by His Majesty's Government. At first sight therefore it would seem to be open to the French Government, or to His Majesty's Government in agreement with them, to invite any other States to participate which they might think fit.

The difficulty is to decide which States to invite. It would clearly be a waste of time to invite the whole world since many countries are entirely disinterested in the matter, and there are others too remote to be of consequence in the present situation. The chief countries concerned appear in practise [*sic*] to be the Latin-American States. The French Ambassador was not able to say this morning why his Government had originally decided to limit their invitations to European countries, but he imagined it to be because a more extensive invitation would have risked refusals which might have delayed the agreement altogether. This was obviously a wise course in the early stages of the crisis, but it does not necessarily follow that no efforts should now be made to extend the area of the agreement if this appears necessary.

The Mexican Government stand in a class by themselves amongst non-participating Governments in that (1) they have openly declared their intention of shipping arms to the Spanish Government and (2) they have shown their interest in the working of the non-intervention pact by asking to be represented by an observer on the Committee (a request which was turned down). They, unlike other non-participating countries, bid fair to

[1] At the second meeting of the Sub-Committee.
[2] A note of September 24 by Mr. Roberts stated that this was being done.

278

provide a leakage in the non-intervention arrangements which may render the whole thing useless. On all these grounds it looks as if there would be an advantage in inviting them, if no one else, to join the agreement. On the other hand the likelihood of their accepting the invitation, small in any case, might be further reduced if they realised that they alone were being singled out amongst other countries.

It seems desirable that we should at once consult with the French Government (through the French Ambassador) on these points. We might suggest either (1) the selection of Mexico alone as the only country which has had sufficient interest to make enquiries about the working of the Committee, or (2) the selection of the main non-European arms exporting countries, e.g. the U.S.A. and Japan, or (3) some more arbitrary selection which would include any countries believed to have been supplying arms to Spain either direct or by re-exportation or trans-shipment from other countries. It appears fairly evident from to-day's meeting that the Committee itself will never reach a unanimous decision to invite other countries to its table, and for this reason if we and the French consider it desirable that such invitations should be issued we should do it off our own bat, as our position as originators of the pact fully entitles us to do.

As regards question two the Sub-Committee agreed to recommend that the participating Governments should approach, in a realistic manner and with the intention of making the embargo on arms really effective, the question of controlling the export from their territory to non-participating countries of arms suspected of being destined for Spain. His Majesty's Government have a good record in this respect. We have already refused licences for exports to Mexico on that suspicion and are keeping watch on all suspicious orders of a similar character. There is, however, another aspect of this matter which will require attention, namely the duties of participating Governments in the matter of orders received by them from other participating countries and which they have reasonable grounds for suspecting are ultimately destined for Spain. Portugal requires particular attention in this respect, and was indeed discussed at length, though inconclusively, this morning. So long as the Committee works on the assumption that Portugal is applying the arms embargo, it is difficult to recommend any measures restricting the supply of arms to Portugal, since such recommendations would imply a doubt of Portuguese good faith to which certain Delegations would be unwilling to subscribe, and which might indeed finally destroy all possibility of Portugal coming onto the Committee. I would venture to suggest however that some solution of this problem might be found along the lines of the control which we ourselves at present exercise with regard to the export of armaments to other participating countries. This control consists of three things: (1) the fact that we never issue export licences for armaments except to *Governments* and (2) that whenever we find an aircraft being exported to a participating country under suspicious circumstances we inform the Government of that country of its departure in order that they may supervise its destination at their end, and (3) that when we hear (by means of applications for insurances or from other sources) that a consignment of arms to Spain is about to be sent from a participating country we inform the Government of that country in order that they may take steps to prevent a breach of the agreement. It is to be considered whether we might not submit a paper to the Committee outlining our practice in this respect and suggesting that they might recommend to other Governments the adoption of a similar policy, which they would apply without distinction to each other. By this means all question of discrimination against Portugal would be avoided.[3]

[3] The topics mentioned in this paper formed the main part of the agenda of the third meeting of the sub-committee on September 22: see No. 225 below.

No. 206

Mr. Eden to Sir G. Clerk (Paris)
No. 1587 [C 6554/4/18]

FOREIGN OFFICE, September 18, 1936

Sir,

I asked the French Ambassador to come and see me this afternoon. I told him I had been considering the situation created by the replies which we had received to our suggestion of a meeting of the Powers in London towards the end of next month. It had, of course, never been our intention to have such a meeting without adequate preparation and in the circumstances I thought it would be wise to set that diplomatic preparation in motion as soon as possible. Last night the Ambassador had given Sir Robert Vansittart a copy of a paper containing the views of the French Government, but this, as I understood it, was for us alone and not for communication to other governments.[1] The Ambassador confirmed this, adding that the French paper would be found to go into the problem somewhat deeply. Meanwhile, I continued, in order to facilitate progress I wished to give the Ambassador a memorandum, which I was also handing to the other interested governments who had accepted the invitation to the Conference, containing the proposals of our Government which we thought would facilitate diplomatic progress.

2. His Excellency looked through the memorandum and noted that several of the points raised were also included in the French memorandum. On the whole he thought that the procedure we proposed was probably the best in the circumstances, but how long did I think it would take? Would it mean an indefinite postponement of the Conference? I replied that His Majesty's Government very much hoped not, that was why we had immediately followed up our suggestion of a date with an actual memorandum intended to facilitate progress through the diplomatic channel. I did not see why these questions could not be answered in say a week or ten days, during which time

[1] See No. 202.

most of us would be absent at Geneva and that on our return if we had the necessary material in the replies we could consider the next step to be taken. The Ambassador agreed.

3. I explained to the Ambassador that this document was for the confidential information of his Government and was not for publication.

I am, &c.,
ANTHONY EDEN

ENCLOSURE IN NO. 206

Memorandum[2] *by His Majesty's Government in the United Kingdom on the Agenda of the Five-Power Conference*

[*C 6259/4/18*]

FOREIGN OFFICE, *September 17, 1936*

His Majesty's Government in the United Kingdom have the honour to put forward the following suggestions as to the scope of the discussion which it is hoped to initiate in London between the Five Locarno Powers at the earliest date that may be agreed between them.

2. It will be recalled that in the words of the London *Communiqué* of July 23rd, 1936, the first business to be undertaken at such a meeting was to be the negotiation of a new agreement to take the place of the Treaty of Locarno and to resolve, through the collaboration of all concerned, the situation created by the German initiative of the 7th March. The *Communiqué* continued that if progress could be made at this meeting, other matters affecting European peace would necessarily come under discussion. In these circumstances it would be natural to look forward to the widening of the area of the discussion in such a manner as to facilitate, with the collaboration of the other interested Powers, the settlement of those problems the solution of which is essential to the peace of Europe.

---

[2] Following the Cabinet meeting of September 2 (No. 156, note 11) this memorandum was under discussion in the Foreign Office from September 11 to 17, on the basis of a draft submitted by Mr. Wigram. The draft was copiously minuted by Sir A. Cadogan, Sir R. Vansittart, and Mr. Eden. It was agreed that the agenda of the conference should be based on the London *communiqué* of July 23 (see Volume XVI, No. 476) and that there was no need at this stage to mention the Irish Free State, air limitation, staff conversations, Dutch participation, Eupen and Malmédy. With regard to these omissions Sir R. Vansittart minuted, 'not only no need—much better not', and Mr. Eden agreed. Sir A. Cadogan also wrote: 'Similarly, we should not volunteer, at this moment, anything on the "conformity of non-aggression arrangements with French eastern Treaties". (There are two sides to this question: the Germans want it to be clear that the Western Pact does not necessarily drag us into war against them as a result of hostilities arising out of the Franco-Soviet Pact, and we, for our part want to be sure that we shan't necessarily be dragged in on *either* side by such an event.)' Sir R. Vansittart commented: 'We are going to keep our hands free on this; so *we* should not bring it up. The Germans will.' Mr. Eden thought it 'a very good draft'. A note by Mr. Wigram said that the draft 'was finally discussed and approved at a meeting in the S. of S.'s room this morning. The S. of S., Sir R. Vansittart, Sir A. Cadogan, Sir W. Malkin, and I were present. R. F. W. 17/9/36.'

3. On July 31st both the German and Italian Governments pointed out[3] that this Conference would require the most careful diplomatic preparation. His Majesty's Government entirely share this view and they are inclined to think that, arising in particular out of the discussion of the proposed agreement to replace the Locarno Treaty, there are a number of points to which the attention of the five Governments might well be now directed and which might profitably be discussed by them, in advance of the meeting, through the diplomatic channel.

4. Though the following list must certainly not be regarded as in any way exhaustive, these points seem to His Majesty's Government to be as follows.

(1) What is to be the form of the new agreement to take the place of the Treaty of Locarno, i.e., will it include (a) non-aggression arrangements between certain Powers, and, if so, between which Powers, and (b) provisions guaranteeing those non-aggression arrangements, and, if so, which Powers will give and receive the guarantees and how will they operate?

(2) Will it be necessary to make special provision in the new agreement for air attack?

(3) Should the new agreement contain provisions for arbitration and conciliation as does the Treaty of Locarno?

5. On these points the views of His Majesty's Government are, generally and provisionally, as follows.

(1) His Majesty's Government assume that the new agreement will include certain non-aggression arrangements, whereby the participants would agree in no case to attack or invade each other by land, sea or air, or to resort to war against each other, subject to certain exceptions on the lines which were laid down in Article 2 of the Treaty of Locarno. His Majesty's Government would be ready to guarantee the observance of such arrangements as between Germany on the one hand and France and Belgium on the other in return for similar guarantees for the United Kingdom from France against Germany and from Germany against France. The question whether the above non-aggression undertaking has been violated should in the opinion of His Majesty's Government be submitted to the Council of the League of Nations. In the case of a flagrant violation of a frontier, the guarantees might operate immediately, as in the Treaty of Locarno, pending a final pronouncement by the Council.

(2) His Majesty's Government consider that special provision should be made in the guarantee arrangements under the new agreement for immediate assistance in the event of an air attack which constituted a violation of the non-aggression undertakings. If this is done, a separate Air Pact would not, in their opinion, be necessary.

(3) His Majesty's Government suggest that the new agreement should contain provisions for arbitration and conciliation as did the Treaty of Locarno; and for their part they would be ready to agree to such provisions.

6. His Majesty's Government would be glad to receive either in writing

[3] Cf. Nos. 41 and 43.

or orally, the observations of the French Government on these and any other points which they may think it useful to mention.

7. A similar communication has been made to the Belgian,[4] German[5] and Italian[6] Governments.

⁴ See *D.D.B.*, *op. cit.*, No. 117, for the French text.
⁵ See *D.G.F.P.*, *op. cit.*, No. 546, and No. 207 below.
⁶ In Foreign Office despatch No. 1074 to Rome, not printed (C 6554/4/18).

No. 207

Mr. Eden to Sir E. Phipps (Berlin)
No. 1081 [C 6554/4/18]

FOREIGN OFFICE, *September 18, 1936*

Sir,

I asked the German Chargé d'Affaires to come and see me this afternoon when I stated that I had been sorry to notice in the German press a tendency to regard our suggestion to fix a date for a meeting of the Conference of the Five Powers as an indication that we were not going to make adequate preparation through the diplomatic channel. This had never been our intention. On the contrary we had always realised and stated that the conference would require such preparation. I could not help feeling that there must have been some misunderstanding in Berlin about this. Prince Bismarck replied that he thought it possible that this was so, for he had reported in August after a conversation with Sir Alexander Cadogan[1] that our idea was to start the preparations through the diplomatic channel and that when the suggestion had come for the fixing of the date Berlin had apparently considered that this idea had been abandoned and that they were being asked to agree to a date in advance of any preparation.

2. I replied that in any event the matter would now be fully cleared up because I wished to give to Prince Bismarck this afternoon for his Government and for their confidential information a memorandum which we had prepared and by means of which we hoped to facilitate progress with the diplomatic preparation for the conference. A copy of this memorandum is enclosed.[2] Prince Bismarck carefully read the document through and said that he noticed that we now suggested that the meeting should be in London at the earliest date that might be agreed upon. I said that this was so and later in the conversation indicated to him that we still hoped that it might be in the latter half of October.

3. Prince Bismarck then asked whether the second paragraph contained nothing more than was in the London *communiqué*.[3] I said that this was so.

¹ Cf. *D.G.F.P.*, *op. cit.*, No. 541, note 6.   ² See Enclosure in No. 206.
³ See Volume XVI, No. 476.

He then asked what was the point of the reference in paragraph 5 sub-paragraph (1) to exceptions 'on the lines which were laid down in Article 2 of the Treaty of Locarno'. I showed Prince Bismarck Article 2 of the Treaty and pointed out that the expression used in the memorandum was 'on the lines which were laid down in Article 2 of the Treaty of Locarno'. It was therefore open to his Government to ask for a definition of these exceptions. I also pointed out that sub-paragraph 1 of Article 2 began with the definition of the right of legitimate defence that is to say resistance to a violation of the undertaking contained in the previous paragraph. Prince Bismarck pointed out that this Article 2 also referred to the demilitarised zone. I replied that it had not been our intention to specify the zone in this way in the new agreement, and again explained that if the German Government wished to know what the exceptions were then it would be of course a very proper question for them to ask in the course of the diplomatic exchanges. Prince Bismarck also showed some interest in the other exceptions in Article 2 which dealt with action in pursuance of Article 16 of the Covenant of the League and again as the result of a decision by the Assembly or the Council of the League or in pursuance of Article 15 para. 7 of the Covenant. He fully appreciated, however, that these were matters which could be further discussed in the course of the diplomatic exchanges.

4. Speaking for himself, the German Chargé d'Affaires indicated that he agreed with the view that the Air Pact could now form part of any new arrangement which would be arrived at. Finally the Chargé d'Affaires stated that he understood that we should be glad to receive a reply from his government as soon as was possible.

I am, &c.,
ANTHONY EDEN

No. 208

Mr. Newton (Berlin) to Mr. Eden (Received September 19, 3.45 p.m.)
No. 301 Telegraphic: by telephone [C 6583/4/18]

Immediate   BERLIN, *September 19, 1936*
My telegram No. 298.[1]

Herr Dieckhoff told me today, after having consulted Minister for Foreign Affairs, that German Government would not be willing at present to be represented at a League of Nations committee for discussion of League reform.

It was felt that Europe was in a state of flux and that negotiations for a Western Pact might considerably affect the situation. The League question might come up either in connexion with five Power conference or as a sequel to it and I inferred that meanwhile Germany was not prepared to be drawn into any general discussion relating solely to League reform.

[1] See No. 179, note 4.

Herr Dieckhoff told me work had already begun on proposals which you had just communicated to German Chargé d'Affaires[2] and that German Government would furnish their answer as soon as possible. He said London was of course agreeable to Germany as a meeting place and that if preliminary discussions could be completed in time there would be no objection so far as Germany was concerned to conference in fact starting October 19th, but they were not willing to fix a date in anticipation.

[2] See No. 207.

No. 209

Sir G. Clerk (Paris) to Foreign Office (Received September 21)
No. 337[1] Saving: Telegraphic [W 11797/9549/41]

PARIS, *September 20, 1936*

Following from Secretary of State, for Sir R. Vansittart.

M. Blum, who had asked me to come and see him this evening,[2] began by saying that there were three subjects about which he wished to speak to me, the first of which was the position of Portugal in relation to the non-intervention agreement.

M. Blum emphasised to me the very great difficulty in which his Government was being placed by Portugal's refusal to be represented on the committee for the organisation of non-intervention in the Spanish conflict, which was at present sitting in London.[3] There were only two countries with frontiers contiguous to Spain—Portugal and France—and if Portugal refused to play her part the position of the French Government became well-nigh intolerable. I would be aware of some of the difficulties which M. Blum had had, but these would be enormously increased if Portugal could not be persuaded to play her part with the others. He knew that His Majesty's Government had already spoken in Lisbon,[4] but he begged me to make some further effort in response to the appeal which he knew that M. Delbos would make at Geneva.

I replied that I appreciated the difficulties of the situation and that I too was anxious that Portugal should take her place in the committee in London. At the same time it would be a mistake to exaggerate the effect that Portugal's non-inclusion in the committee could have. Portugal had not vast

[1] As this telegram clearly refers to an earlier part of the conversation reported in Paris telegram No. 335 (No. 210 below) the order of these two documents has been reversed.

[2] Mr. Eden arrived in Paris on the afternoon of September 20 on his way to attend the forthcoming meetings of the League Council and Assembly in Geneva. M. Blum received him shortly after 6 p.m. Sir G. Clerk, who accompanied him, soon left, and the meeting proceeded, according to *The Times* (September 21, p. 12), *en tête à tête*. Later Mr. Eden and Lord Halifax left at 11.20 p.m. for Geneva by train.

[3] M. Corbin had already spoken to Mr. Eden on these lines in an interview at the Foreign Office on September 18, in which he said that Portugal's abstention made it doubtful whether M. Blum 'would be able to hold the situation'.

[4] Cf. No. 174.

supplies of arms which she could furnish to the rebels. She was indeed short of arms herself. Moreover, she had accepted the principle of non-intervention, and the latest information which I had had from Lisbon tended to show that no flagrant violations of this undertaking were taking place. Moreover, it must be remembered that Portugal had a very real fear of the consequences of a victory for the Extreme Left in Spain. All these conditions had to be borne in mind, and M. Blum did not appear to dispute their force. None the less, I undertook to do what I could to induce M. Monteiro to reconsider the attitude which he had hitherto taken up, when I got to Geneva.[5]

Repeated to Lisbon in cypher by Foreign Office No. 129 of September 21.

[5] Cf. *D.D.F.*, *op. cit.*, No. 269, note 4.

No. 210

Sir G. Clerk (Paris) to Foreign Office (Received September 23)
No. 335 Saving: Telegraphic [C 6636/97/18]

Immediate and personal   PARIS, *September 20, 1936*
Following for Sir R. Vansittart.

M. Blum stated that the real reason why he had wished to see me[1] in Paris this evening[2] was one that could not at present be divulged. He wished to give me a full account of the conversations which had taken place recently in Paris with Dr Schacht.[3] The first of these had been held in the presence of several Ministers including M. Delbos and the President of the Bank of France. M. Blum emphasised to me that Dr Schacht's visit to Paris was in return for a visit which M. Labeyrie had paid to Berlin at Dr Schacht's invitation solely in order that Dr Schacht might return the visit to Paris. The initiative was therefore that of Dr Schacht. At the conversation in the presence of several Ministers,[4] Dr Schacht expounded generally upon Germany's economic difficulties: her shortage of raw materials, her consequent need of colonies, the fact that though raw materials might be purchasable from abroad, Germany had no gold and no exchange wherewith to buy, the further complication that such exchange that Germany possessed she was compelled to use for the purchase of raw materials for

[1] i.e. Mr. Eden.   [2] See No. 209.
[3] See Nos. 141 and 145. Mr. Eden told a meeting of Cabinet Ministers on September 18 that he proposed to see M. Blum in Paris on his way to Geneva, and if the question of the former German colonies were raised he would refer M. Blum to his House of Commons statement of July 27, 1936, in which he had stated that 'the question of any transfer of mandated territories would inevitably raise grave difficulties—moral, political, and legal— of which His Majesty's Government must frankly say they have been unable to find any solution' (see Volume XVI, Appendix to No. 484). The meeting agreed that he should also make it clear that that statement 'was a considered declaration of policy by His Majesty's Government', who maintained that declaration. He could say if pressed on the matter that His Majesty's Government had a complete answer to various points raised by Germany with regard to the colonial question.
[4] On August 26.

her rearmament campaign, and so forth upon familiar lines. Dr Schacht also made a general appeal for co-operation between the United Kingdom, France and Germany in the colonial and economic spheres and pointed out that British Ministers, when speaking on colonial questions, had always been careful not to shut the door completely.

2. At the end of this general conversation Dr Schacht told M. Blum that before leaving Paris he wished to wait on him alone. M. Blum had no reason to suppose that this second visit would have any special importance and was therefore surprised when Dr Schacht proceeded[5] considerably to amplify what he had previously said, though without noticeably greater precision. Dr Schacht maintained that this question of colonies and of raw materials was now of vital importance to Germany. He stated that while he had no mission from the German Chancellor to discuss these matters, Herr Hitler was aware of his visit and he would report to the German Chancellor on his return to Berlin.

3. M. Blum pointed out that it hardly seemed that the possession of a colony could be of such great importance to German economy. Dr Schacht, however, would have none of this and stated that he wished to see conversations begin soon and confidentially between the French, German and British Governments (incidentally M. Blum remarked that Dr Schacht spoke several times very slightingly of the Italians) with a view to an agreement being reached which would result in Germany taking her part in giving guarantees for a European settlement and joining in an agreement for the reduction and limitation of armaments if, in return, she could obtain some satisfaction in the colonial sphere. Dr Schacht explained that it was impossible for Germany to give any direct guarantee to Soviet Russia. She was prepared to give an indirect guarantee, and after further questions M. Blum understood this to mean that Germany would give a guarantee to France and Great Britain not to attack Russia. M. Blum asked how, if it was impossible for Germany to have any dealings with Soviet Russia, was it possible for her to enter an agreement for the reduction and limitation of armaments in which Russia naturally would have to take part? Dr Schacht made it clear that in this respect he did not look for the exclusion of Russia. Dr Schacht argued that M. Blum should remember that Germany's ideology was an insuperable obstacle to direct agreement with the Soviet. M. Blum retorted that if they began to speak of ideologies then he would have something to say too. Actually, however, he was not sure that they played so great a part in international affairs as was sometimes maintained. Tzarist Russia had an alliance with pre-war Radical France and it was the Right in France that had been the authors of the present Franco-Soviet Pact. The German Chancellor had only to go back fifty years to the last Franco-Russian entente to have at least as great a shock as he had suffered from the present Franco-Soviet Pact. The cure for this state of things was the same then as now, to relieve France of the apprehensions from Germany which had brought about these policies. Dr Schacht appeared to be much

[5] On August 28: see *D.D.F.*, *op. cit.*, No. 213.

287

struck by this argument and said that he would repeat it to the Chancellor.

4. M. Blum admitted to me at a later stage of the conversation that the record which Dr Schacht had later sent him of his conversation as he had submitted it to the Chancellor gave this remark of M. Blum's a twist which the original had not justified. As reported by Dr Schacht it might have been intended to imply that were Germany to cease to be a menace to France, the Franco-Soviet Pact would lapse. M. Blum had said no such thing. In our later discussions both M. Blum and I agreed that this portion of his conversation with Dr Schacht might well have played a decisive part in the German Chancellor's mind.

5. Dr Schacht had intimated that he would like the conversations between the three Powers on this basis to start with the least possible delay, and with secrecy. He had even urged M. Blum to proceed at once to London to see Mr. Baldwin and to communicate to him the outcome of this conversation. M. Blum had explained in reply that such a method was hardly consistent with secrecy and had suggested it would be better if he were to inform me on my way through Paris of the details of what had passed between him and Dr Schacht. This could be done without attracting attention. He had emphasised to Dr Schacht the close relations between our two countries which must make it impossible for France to take any unilateral action in this matter.

6. Subsequent to this meeting Dr Schacht had returned to Berlin and had seen Herr Hitler, who had fully confirmed everything that Dr Schacht had said. More than this, he had sent for M. François-Poncet, the French Ambassador in Berlin, in order to do so officially,[6] and the letter which M. Blum had received from Dr Schacht containing his account of the interview between M. Blum and himself had been given him by the German Ambassador in Paris, which once more emphasised the official aspect of the *démarche*. Now the German Government were waiting for an answer as to whether conversations could be followed up on this basis, and they hoped for an answer both from the French Government and from His Majesty's Government.

7. What, M. Blum asked, was my reaction? I replied that I must confess to being very much astonished at the method of procedure which this interview appeared to envisage. We were at the present moment engaged in exchanges through the diplomatic channel intended to prepare the way for a European settlement. If the German Government wished to bring about such a settlement, or had conditions which they wished to attach to it, the normal way to proceed would surely have been to make this clear in the course of the confidential diplomatic exchanges which must take place in the next few weeks. At the same time I appreciated that the German Government did not make use of normal methods and that this was not the first time that feelers of this kind had been put out through Dr Schacht.

[6] This appears to be a reference to M. François-Poncet's interview with Herr Hitler on September 2: *D.D.F.*, *op. cit.*, No. 334; cf. Nos. 229, 235, 244, 255.

At the same time I thought that I ought to warn M. Blum that I had the impression that the accounts of Dr Schacht's interview with him which had reached us had indicated that the French Government had been more forthcoming in the matter of colonies than His Majesty's Government, and I thought it important that we should both guard against the dangerous possibilities that such reports foreshadowed. What, I asked, were M. Blum's own feelings as to the reply which should be made by the French Government to Dr Schacht's initiative? M. Blum replied that it was extremely difficult to decide. On the one hand he shared with me the feeling of dislike of such a method of procedure as this. On the other hand, he was very reluctant to allow such an opportunity of a European settlement, if it were one, to slip. That was why he had asked me to call, so that we could talk over the matter in all frankness.

8. I said that there seemed to me to be a certain danger in negotiations which started on a basis that our two Governments were willing to discuss Germany's desire for colonial compensation even though that basis were combined with a German intimation of a desire for a European settlement and for an agreement for the reduction and limitation of armaments. It was true that the German attitude as defined by Dr Schacht appeared to constitute a considerable advance, but when accurately defined the German proposals, both in respect of a European settlement and in respect of an arms agreement, might be found to mean a great deal or very little. Even if they only meant a very little, we should have been committed to a discussion with Germany of her desire for satisfaction in the colonial sphere. That was something that I at any rate could not agree to at present. The statement of our attitude to the colonial question which I had made to the House of Commons at the end of July had been carefully considered by the Cabinet, and I certainly could not vary it. That statement certainly would not make it possible for me to agree here and now to open conversations on the basis proposed by Dr Schacht. M. Blum at once agreed that there was force in the dangers to which I had referred. At the same time he said: 'Here is this German offer, underlined by the Chancellor. If we were to scan the last speeches at Nuremberg we might even find some echo of this offer. The German Government asked whether we were prepared to continue to explore the ground thus opened up. Were we to shut the door? Were we to offer a flat refusal? Would I, M. Blum asked, be frank with him and tell him whether I thought he had been wrong to listen to these offers from Dr Schacht.' I replied that that was far from being in my mind, but at the same time the next step, the decision as to whether we were willing to follow up these conversations, was clearly of a different character.

9. Finally, M. Blum said that he had told Dr Schacht that he would give me to-day a full account of what had passed between them;[7] and the German Ambassador would no doubt be asking to-morrow for some account of my reaction. After some discussion M. Blum and I agreed that not even an interim appreciation of my attitude, however vague, should be given

[7] Cf. No. 141, note 4.

to the German Government until I had had an opportunity to consider the situation and to communicate further with M. Blum giving him the exact terms of the interim answer which I would ask him to return. Inevitably, I warned M. Blum, it would be in the vaguest terms. Clearly no one could expect that after a communication of this kind I should be in a position to give any detailed answer until I had had an opportunity to consult the Prime Minister and my colleagues, which would not be possible, in the nature of things, for some days to come.

No. 211

Sir G. Clerk (Paris) to Foreign Office (Received September 23)
No. 338 Saving: Telegraphic [C 6637/97/18]

PARIS, *September 20, 1936*

Following from Secretary of State for Sir R. Vansittart.

My telegram No. 335 Saving.[1]

I propose that my reply to M. Blum should be on the following lines.

I am very grateful to M. Blum for having given me such full information of his conversation with Dr Schacht. He will appreciate that on a subject of this importance it is impossible for me to give him any considered opinion of the views of His Majesty's Government until I have had an opportunity of consulting the Prime Minister and my colleagues. In the meanwhile it is only fair that I should point out that while His Majesty's Government are at all times anxious to do all in their power to promote a European settlement, their attitude towards the question of colonies is governed by the statement which I made in the House of Commons at the end of July.[2] I anticipate that my colleagues will feel that they are not in a position to carry these discussions further until they are in possession of a more complete and detailed appreciation of the attitude of the German Government towards the problems that have to be solved if we are to reach a European settlement. I further anticipate that they will consider that the discussions now proceeding through the diplomatic channel to prepare for the Five Power Conference should provide the most convenient means of bringing about this result.

[1] No. 210. [2] *Ibid.*, note 3.

No. 212

Record by the Secretary of State for Dominion Affairs of an interview with Mr. Mackenzie King at Geneva[1]

[C 6797/4/18]

GENEVA, *September 20, 1936*

I had a long talk with Mr. Mackenzie King this afternoon.

He said that the Canadian people had very definite ideas about League reform. Their experience of the Italo-Abyssinian dispute had killed for them the idea of automatic sanctions under the Covenant. It would be a very long time at any rate before Canadians generally could agree to that. What they desired was a League which should not be a War Office, or be any danger of becoming a War Office, but one which maintained peace by peaceful means.

But in his view the question of League reform was at the moment of secondary importance. No doubt there would be a great deal of talk about it at the Assembly:[2] but the question which seemed to him to be of primary importance was the straightening out of the European tangle. Could we bring the European nations together, so that the danger of war in Europe was removed? He had come to Geneva to help us in any way that he could with regard to that. He was very anxious to help; was looking forward to hearing our views as to what might be done; and hoped that we would tell him of any way in which he could assist us.

I said that I knew that the Foreign Secretary and the rest of us would very much appreciate his attitude. We ourselves were principally concerned with the immediate situation in Europe. We were anxious to get agreements which would lessen the tension and restore confidence between the Powers. This aim was linked with the question of League reform. If we could get Germany back into co-operation with the other members of the League, that would be more effective than anything else that could be done in the near future to strengthen the authority of the League. The main reason why we had not sent in a written statement of our views on League reform to the Secretariat, and why our representative's speech at the Assembly would deal with general principles rather than precise proposals for reform,[3] was that we did not want to commit ourselves to any policy at this moment which might prevent Germany's return to the League. We were anxious first to explore the mind of the German Government as to the sort of League which it would be willing to return to.

Mr. Mackenzie King replied that he fully appreciated this. He himself had refrained from suggesting to his colleagues that their Government should send in any written statement, because he understood our desire and agreed with it. He had not even prepared any speech for delivery at

[1] Mr. Mackenzie King had been Prime Minister of Canada since 1935. A copy of this record of his interview with Mr. Malcolm MacDonald was sent to the Foreign Office by the Dominions Office on September 24.

[2] See No. 179, note 1.

[3] *Ibid.*, note 3.

the Assembly. He had made a speech in Parliament at Ottawa, which expressed in general terms his views about the Covenant, and no doubt in any speech which he made here he would have to repeat such general statements. But he did not propose to go further than that, and in any case he was waiting for a chance of some talks with us before making up his mind as to exactly what line he should take.

His main anxiety was to keep the Canadian nation united. There were certain forces making for disintegration. The French Canadians were difficult. There was also a very strong body of opinion throughout the Dominion in favour of following the United States' isolationist policy, and of having no commitments to the League. He had to take account of that opinion in determining his policy: at the same time he was extremely anxious to keep the British Commonwealth of Nations together. He was nervous lest, if Great Britain became involved in a European war, Canadian public opinion might not be willing to follow Great Britain. When he was leaving Canada many people had told him to give a message to us to the effect that we should keep out of the quarrel between Germany and France, wash our hands of it, and 'leave the Germans and the French to kill each other if they wanted to.'

I said that I appreciated that there was some risk that, if we became involved in a war, large sections of public opinion in one or two of the Dominions might exert themselves to keep those Dominions out of it. I thought it of very great importance to the world generally, as well as to ourselves, that the nations of the British Commonwealth should continue associated together; it would be a world disaster if we became divided. Therefore, one consideration to which we gave great weight with regard to foreign policy was to avoid, as far as possible, any situation which might result in one or other of the Dominions being divided from us in a crisis. He could rest assured that we kept the point of view of each Dominion in mind. Nevertheless, we could not cut ourselves off from Europe. There were two principal reasons for this. First, if we were to let it be known that we were washing our hands of European quarrels, that would be the signal for those quarrels to produce very quickly a war. The knowledge that if there was a war in Western Europe we should be involved in it was the greatest deterrent to a potential aggressor. Secondly, in our own interests we could not let a potentially hostile Power over-run the Low Countries and gain control of the sea ports and aerodromes there. Such a Power in such a position would be a constant threat to our security. For these reasons we were prepared to play our part in a new mutual assistance Pact for Western Europe, to take the place of the Locarno Treaty. I hoped that he did not feel that our taking a part in such an agreement would arouse strong criticism in Canada.[4]

4 A minute by Sir R. Vansittart read as follows. 'Every time I read this kind of conversation, I wish the speaker would have the courage to speak of France as well as the Low Countries. For that is the truth: we cannot afford to see either or *any* of them overrun, and it would be folly to go to war for the Low Countries if we were not even *more* concerned for

He said that he was in favour of regional pacts. After the failure of the League in the Italo-Abyssinian dispute, such regional Pacts seemed to him to be an essential part of the arrangement for securing peace. But Canada would not be able to be a party to a new Locarno, even if we were. He could not depart from the position that the Canadian Parliament should be left free to decide in case of an outbreak of war whether it should become involved in that war or not.

I said that we understood this. But I hoped that public opinion in Canada would understand clearly the motives which led us into a Western European Pact, and that these motives were not simply of concern to Great Britain alone, but to the whole Commonwealth. As I had said, our first motive was that unless we were ready to be parties to such a Pact, the peace of Europe would probably be broken very soon. But the other was that our own security required our participation. It was some assurance that a potentially hostile Power would not feel free to occupy the Low Countries. Such an occupation would be a grave threat to us. But what was a grave threat to us would also be a grave threat to the whole Commonwealth. At its present stage of development, at any rate, I could not see the Commonwealth continuing if Great Britain were overwhelmed. At some future date no doubt, when the young Dominions had gathered their strength and become great Powers, the importance of Great Britain in the Commonwealth would become proportionately less. But for a long time to come the authority of the Commonwealth would depend mainly on the power and freedom of Great Britain. I hoped that by this process of reasoning, opinion in the Dominions would realise that the independence of the Low Countries was a matter of considerable concern to them.

Mr. Mackenzie King said that this was rather a new point to him. He had not heard it mentioned much. He would like to hear more about it.

I reminded him that we had sent to all the Dominion Governments some few months ago a paper drawn up in the Foreign Office on this very question.[5] I thought that probably the paper had not gone beyond his permanent officials, as he had been so preoccupied with the heavy work of the first session of his new Parliament.

Throughout the talk he showed every sign of a genuine anxiety to help us, and a readiness to be influenced by our opinions. At the same time it was clear that he is powerfully affected by the strength of Canadian opinion in favour of keeping clear of European entanglements, and from the way in which he spoke about President Roosevelt I feel that he pays considerable

the Channel. And we cannot be sure of the Channel except by the integrity of France. But it sounds so much less alarming to talk of the Low Countries, & almost everybody succumbs to the temptation. If we were more outspoken, there would and could be none of this blither about letting France & Germany cut each other's throats. R. V. Sept. 24.'

[5] The reference is to a memorandum on England and the Low Countries, written by the late Sir J. Headlam-Morley, Historical Adviser to the Foreign Office until his death in 1929. The memorandum was originally published in 1930, but was updated and circulated to King, Cabinet, and Dominions in May 1936 (C 3811/92/62).

heed to the President's views on foreign policy. He told me that in private conversation between Lord Tweedsmuir, himself and the President the latter had thrown out the idea of calling a Conference of heads of States, including King Edward, Herr Hitler, the President of the French Republic, and others. It seems that President Roosevelt suggested that he might call such a Conference if he were successful in the American election. Mr. Mackenzie King pointed out to him the difficulty of calling a Conference of men who, however important, were in some cases not actually responsible for the conduct of government in their countries. He asked the President to keep him informed of any further ideas he had on the subject.

No. 213

Foreign Office to Sir H. Chilton (Hendaye)
No. 183 Telegraphic [W 11714/62/41]

FOREIGN OFFICE, *September 21, 1936, 6.45 p.m.*

Your telegram No. 232.[1]

You may abide by the general agreement of your diplomatic colleagues to remain at Hendaye for the present, notwithstanding the withdrawal of the Spanish Government representative.[2]

Earlier instructions were not issued to you as it was desired to know what the attitude of other Governments, especially the French Government, would be on this question before taking a decision.

[1] In this telegram of September 19 Sir H. Chilton reported that most of his colleagues, including the French, had received instructions to remain at Hendaye.
[2] See No. 189.

No. 214

Mr. Edmond (Geneva) to Foreign Office (Received September 22, 9.30 a.m.)
No. 113 L.N. Telegraphic [C 6638/97/18]

Personal   GENEVA, *September 21, 1936, 8.55 p.m.*

Following from the Secretary of State for Sir R. Vansittart.

My telegram No. 335 Saving[1] from Paris.

Monsieur Delbos in a brief reference to the same subject today said that he would be glad of an opportunity for a conversation with me on the matter. I replied that I should of course be glad to speak to him at any time but I knew that I should not for a day or two at least be in a position to carry matters any further than I had taken them with M. Blum in Paris. In the meanwhile so far as Colonies were concerned I must repeat to him what I had said to M. Blum, namely that our position had been made clear

[1] No. 210.

by statement which I had made in the House of Commons at the end of July[2] and that I was not in a position to add to that statement.

M. Delbos seemed in no way surprised at this reply and remarked that a difficulty of the situation was that whereas France and United Kingdom were being asked to give something definite and tangible the proposals on the other side were at present the reverse. I cordially agreed.

Repeated to Paris.

[2] See Volume XVI, Appendix to No. 484.

No. 215

Mr. Ogilvie-Forbes (Madrid) to Foreign Office
(Received September 22, 9.30 a.m.)

No. 233 Telegraphic [*W 11875/9549/41*]

MADRID, *September 21, 1936, 11.20 p.m.*

My telegram No. 211.[1]

I have received note dated September 15th and signed by Signor del Vayo in the following sense.

1. On September 15th Spanish Government addressed to German, Italian and Portuguese Governments notes of which copies are enclosed.[2] The facts given therein showed that non-intervention agreement is in practice a blockade of lawful Government and that rebels even after signature of the above agreement continue to receive every kind of war-like material.

2. The facts also deny the truth of the official statements of interventionist Powers one of whom for example did not hesitate to maintain that certain aviators arrested after a forced landing who belonged to the regular Air Force of their country were Spanish aviators. Moreover the attitude of certain Powers in the Control Commission has been sufficiently significant to provoke other Powers to insist on a clear statement regarding application of non-intervention agreement.

3. Any impartial observer will recognise that rebellion of Spanish officers helped solely by what remains of feudal society without any support from people would have been nipped in the bud by immense majority of the Spanish people if the rebels had not enjoyed in increasing measure the armed assistance of Germany and Italy and the cooperation of other parties. The rebellious Generals also, unable to enlist genuine Spaniards, have recruited for use against Spanish people mercenary Moorish troops notorious for their cruelty, an act which in itself should scandalize civilized world. Both recruitment of Moorish troops and importation of war materials into

[1] A reference to Mr. Ogilvie-Forbes's telegram No. 214 is apparently intended: see No. 197, note 3.

[2] Not printed.

the Spanish zone of Morocco are a flagrant violation of existing treaties from the Act of Algeciras[3] to the Franco-Spanish Treaty of 1912.[4]

4. Affairs have now reached the stage at which the constitutional Government of Spain is obliged to address His Majesty's Government as a signatory of non-intervention agreement and to enquire whether His Majesty's Government notes that embargo on exportation of arms to a lawful Government and toleration shown towards direct interference of Italy and Germany in favour of the rebels are creating a most serious precedent in international affairs and mark the initiation of a new era in Europe which permits certain States founded on a rule of force to impose with impunity and without protest their ideas of Government on another State by fomenting a civil war therein and giving armed support to the rebels.

5. The Spanish Government, convinced that His Majesty's Government will not allow such an unheard of violation of international law and custom based on a policy which would introduce into Europe the reign of force and thus gravely jeopardize the peace of the world and deal a death-blow to principle of collective security, request (1) the raising of embargo on exportation of arms destined for Spanish Government and (2) the strict prohibition of the supply of war materials to the rebels.

Repeated to Geneva No. 3.

[3] See *B.F.S.P.*, vol. 99, pp. 141–70.   [4] See *ibid.*, vol. 106, pp. 1025–42.

No. 216

Mr. Edmond (Geneva) to Foreign Office (Received September 22, 9.30 a.m.)
No. 115 L.N. Telegraphic [W 11872/9549/41]

Immediate   Strictly Confidential   GENEVA, *September 21, 1936, 11.50 p.m.*

Following from the Secretary of State.

I had a long conversation with M. Monteiro this afternoon during the course of which I did my utmost to dissipate Portuguese reluctance to serve on the Committee in London.[1] Upshot of it all was that I think it likely that we may be able to persuade Portuguese Government to come in if we can give them some small measure of satisfaction by giving them information as to scope of Committee. They are extraordinarily suspicious of that body and their attitude has no doubt been influenced in part by abuse of them by the French press of the Left. I have spoken to M. Delbos about this last difficulty and he has undertaken to counsel moderation. Towards the end of our conversation this afternoon I asked Morrison[2] to join us when he gave M. Monteiro a general description of the way in which Committee was working. This further reassured Portuguese Minister for Foreign Affairs and I am therefore hopeful that if tomorrow we can hand

[1] Cf. No. 209.   [2] Chairman of the N.I. Committee.

to M. Monteiro a letter giving him a certain amount of information on this score he can probably be induced to reply that Portuguese Government will serve on Committee.

Monteiro was anxious to help but he was also clearly perturbed by reports which are reaching him of conditions in Spain. He emphasized many times over that the objective of the Left in Spain was to overrun Portugal and to establish a Iberian Soviet Republic. In these circumstances it is not surprising that Portugal was watchful and even fearful.[3]

Repeated to Lisbon.

[3] Mr. Eden's telegram No. 116 L.N. of September 23 from Geneva described a further conversation with M. Monteiro on the afternoon of September 22 in which Mr. Morrison also took part. Mr. Eden handed M. Monteiro a letter giving the substance of the rules of procedure adopted by the N.I. Committee, and a statement was drawn up in terms which might be made public if the Portuguese Government agreed to send a representative to the committee. Mr. Eden's letter is printed in *D.A.P.E.*, *op. cit.*, No. 365; see also Nos. 361–4, and No. 368.

No. 217

Mr. Ingram (Rome) to Foreign Office (Received September 23, 9 p.m.)
No. 202 Saving: Telegraphic [C 6640/4/18]

ROME, *September 21, 1936*

In an article in this evening's 'Giornale d'Italia' Signor Gayda seeks to explain the haste with which His Majesty's Government are pushing forward the preparations for the Locarno meeting. He finds the reason for this in the desire of His Majesty's Government to share with Italy the obligations vis-à-vis France which result from the letter addressed to the French Government after the German violation of the demilitarised zone.[1]

Signor Gayda says that Italy is not in principle unwilling to collaborate, but, just as Germany is likely to ask for some clarifications in regard to the Franco-Soviet pact, so Italy will require to know more about the scheme said to be favoured by His Majesty's Government under which in the new Locarno Great Britain would receive guarantees from France and Germany but not from Italy whom she in turn would not guarantee. This proposal rather suggests that Great Britain is anxious to have her interests in the Rhine frontier guaranteed but to have a free hand in the Mediterranean, thus creating a system of alliances which might even be used against Italy if she happened to be declared the aggressor.

[1] See Volume XVI, Enclosure 2 in No. 199.

Minute by Mr. Wigram on a French memorandum of
September 16, 1936
[*C 6523/4/18*]

FOREIGN OFFICE, *September 21, 1936*

Though this French memorandum[1] was received before our memorandum[2] had been communicated to the French Ambassador, it, in fact, contains the French views on the three points raised in our memorandum.

Paragraphs 2–11 and 13, 14, 16 and 17 may be said to deal with point (1) of our memorandum (the form of the new agreement); paragraph 12 with point (2) (special provision for air attack); and paragraph 15 with point (3) (arbitration and conciliation agreements).

Paragraph 18 deals with the regularisation of the situation arising out of the German initiative of March 7th; and paragraph 19 is a general paragraph referring to the possibility of some more general settlement and some new effort for limitation or reduction of armaments, on which the French Government reserve the right to make proposals later.

As regards the paragraphs which may be said to contain the French views on point (1) of our memorandum (form of the new agreement), it may be noted

(i) that (paragraph 3) the French Government are apparently in favour of the entry of Holland into the agreement.[3] Paragraph 70 of our Chiefs of Staff Report[4] states that 'we do not consider that Holland should be asked to accede to the new agreement; if, however, France or Germany wish to bring her in as a guaranteed Power, we need not oppose this; but whether she accedes to the agreement or not, we consider that it would be valuable to obtain an undertaking from all the signatories of the agreement to respect her neutrality'.

(ii) that (paragraph 3) the French are ready to see the Irish Free State participate. One would have thought that it would have been more tactful for them to leave this matter alone.[5] The Chiefs of Staff (paragraphs 23–26 of their Report) were against Free State participation, particularly in view of the possibility that the Free State might ask for a guarantee against us; but at the Cabinet meeting on September 2nd (C 6259)[6] Mr. Malcolm

---

[1] Of September 16: see No. 202, note 2. The comments of Mr. Wigram in this minute have been printed because of the light they throw on the Foreign Office attitude. The text of the French memorandum is printed in *D.D.F.*, *op. cit.*, No. 256. It has not been reprinted here owing to its length, but the substance of those sections on which Mr. Wigram saw fit to comment will be clear from his remarks.

[2] Enclosure in No. 206.

[3] A marginal comment at this point by Sir R. Vansittart reads: 'I shd. like to see Holland in & Ireland out. So if the French press us in regard to the former, we can yield without repining. R. V.'

[4] No. 156. [5] Marginal comment: 'Yes. R. V.'

[6] Cf. No. 156, note 11.

MacDonald took the view that if the Irish Free State took the initiative, we should not discourage her in view of the possibility that she would withdraw from the British Commonwealth and that we should not be able to make a satisfactory treaty with her alone.

(iii) that as regards Luxemburg (paragraph 4 of the French note), the French Government claim that the remilitarisation of the Rhineland has created a new problem and they reserve the right to discuss the matter later with us and the Belgians. The status of Luxemburg is discussed in the annexed Foreign Office memorandum of August 21st, 1926,[7] with an Annex prepared by the Library and dated September 21st, 1936.[8] It will be seen that the position is none too clear. There is a collective guarantee of 1867 (in which this country, Austria, Belgium, France, Italy, the Netherlands, Prussia and Russia participated) which, owing to its collective nature, did not operate in 1914 (see also relevant passages in Library memorandum of August 1st, 1934, Confidential 14462),[8] and, secondly, there is the League of Nations guarantee under Article 10 of the Covenant. It will be seen from the memorandum of 1926 that Luxemburg did not take part in Locarno and that in November 1926 the C.I.D. decided that no advantage would be derived from the acceptance by this country of the further liability involved in Luxemburg's participation in Locarno. Subsequently, when in October 1929 the question of the status of Luxemburg came up again, the French took the view that the Grand Duchy having entered the League, 'her neutrality was finished'. We told the French at that time that it seemed inadvisable to raise the question.

If the French are now going to raise this question—and, in view of the remilitarisation of the Rhineland, there does seem to be a reason for so doing which had not existed in recent years—it will presumably be necessary to refer these papers to the C.I.D.[9] with a request to state what advantage, if any, (or disadvantages) would accrue to this country by any fresh guarantee for Luxemburg, or by her participation in the proposed new Western arrangement.

(iv) No comment is necessary on paragraph 5 of the French note (non-aggression arrangements between Germany and Belgium and Germany and France): though, as between Germany and Belgium, the question of Eupen and Malmédy must be borne in mind in connection with the words 'il n'existe entre les parties contractantes aucun différend territorial' (see question 13 in Foreign Office memorandum of August 19th).[10]

(v) In paragraph 6 of their note the French propose non-aggression arrangements between *all* the signatories. From the discussion in the Secretary of State's room last week it seemed that our minds were not clear

---

[7] Printed in Series IA, Volume II, No. 170.
[8] Not printed.
[9] Marginal comment: 'I agree. This shd. be set in hand at once. R. V.'
[10] Marginal comment: 'We shall have to get the matter of Eupen & Malmédy quite straight & clear, before we go far. It is a worthless but pregnant one. R. V.'

on this point: and paragraph 5(1) of our note refers only to 'certain non-aggression arrangements'.[11]

(vi) As regards paragraph 7 of the French note, we had preferred not to speak of the right of self-defence but to mention 'certain exceptions on the lines laid down in Article 2 of the Treaty of Locarno'.

(vii) We do not (sub-section 1 of paragraph 8 of the French note) want to give guarantees to Italy or to be guaranteed by her or possibly by Belgium. But, as regards Italy, this point seems to be referred to in sub-section 2 of paragraph 8.[12]

As regards the Netherlands, see comment in point (i) of this minute.

(viii) No comment seems necessary on the French paragraph 9 at the moment.[13]

(ix) The French paragraphs 10 and 11 raise the contentious question of the Franco-Russian, Franco-Czech and Franco-Polish Treaties. Here we are presumably on the French side (see question 8 in the Foreign Office memorandum of August 19th and paragraphs 46–49 of the Chiefs of Staff Report, and the comments in Cabinet Conclusions of September 2nd). But the question of when we will openly say this is evidently one of great importance.[14]

(x) It does not seem to me that the French reference (sub-section 4 of paragraph 11) to the German argument about the reoccupation of the Rhineland being necessary to re-establish the balance upset by the Franco-Soviet Treaty carries very much conviction.[15]

(xi) Paragraph 13. So far as I know, the proposal to have consultations under Article 11 is not objectionable. The proposal to admit the establishment of 'organes de constatation' in national territories, as in the Bourquin proposal, seems designed for 'window-dressing'. No one surely can take it seriously in present circumstances[16] (for text of Bourquin's proposal see Flag A[8]).

[11] Marginal comment: 'We shd. keep an open mind on this; but we can maintain our preference. R. V.'

[12] Marginal comment: 'On this it is apparently the French who have an open mind. R. V.'

[13] The French memorandum at this point stressed the need for prompt assistance against aggression, and suggested that if measures could not be devised for making it automatic the mechanism visualized in article 4 of the treaty of Locarno should at least be maintained. Sir R. Vansittart commented: 'The French view is reasonable; but it may be contested by Germany.'

[14] Marginal comment: 'We are bound to support France over this, & here we shall run into strong German resistance. But the French have an almost unanswerable case, and are unlikely to be argued out of it. R. V.'

[15] Marginal comment: 'It is quite a good debating point. The Germans can't logically claim to violate a treaty in order to redress a balance, and then claim that the cause of their illegal action must also disappear, leaving them with the double profit. Anyhow we have to support the French over this, so the argument doesn't much matter.

'Throughout paragraph 11 the French are very outspoken—so we know where we are. But we always knew it. R. V.'

[16] Marginal comment: 'I agree. This is window-dressing and will fade. R. V.'

(xii) In their paragraph 14 the French raise the question of the Staff arrangements. This question is discussed in the Foreign Office and Chiefs of Staff memoranda and again in the minutes on C 6259/4/18[6] and was further discussed in the Secretary of State's room last week. If the French want to provide for Staff discussions, they will have to apply as between the four Powers, when they are likely to have to be so limited as to be, as the Chiefs of Staff maintain, useless. Provision is made for such conversations, and we are, in fact, committed to them by the Text of Proposals of March 19th.[17] There was general agreement at the meeting in the Foreign Office last week that we should be careful to avoid in the agreement anything limiting further discussions of this nature, which would not necessarily be between the four Powers. The French might have done better, in their own interest, to let the question alone.[18]

(xiii) No comment seems necessary on the French paragraphs 16 and 17.

As regards point (2) in our note (air attack), the French paragraph 12 seems to suggest a separate arrangement, which would cover also air limitation. Presumably the French know as well as we do that air limitation is most unlikely of attainment at the moment.[19]

Paragraph 15 deals with point (3) in our note (the arbitration agreements).

No comment seems necessary on paragraph 19; it contains references to 'problèmes plus généraux' (presumably the general settlement) and some armaments agreement.[20]

[17] Volume XVI, No. 144.
[18] Marginal comment: 'They wd. have been better advised to let this alone. But we cannot have our hands tied by anyone. R. V.'
[19] Marginal comment: 'No prospect of limitation. Our proposal to cover air attack is better than theirs. R. V.'
[20] Marginal comment: 'The French are altogether inclined to talk too much about disarmament, for electoral purposes. They will get carried too far, and will embarrass us. They ought to be told soon that we won't go a step beyond budgetary publicity until we are ready. R. V.' On another part of the file Sir R. Vansittart gave his general verdict: 'My general comment is that the French postulates—some of which cannot well be challenged—are going to make agreement most unlikely on Germany's present form. R. V. Sept. 25.' On his instructions a set of these minutes and comments was sent to Mr. Eden at Geneva on September 26.

No. 219

Mr. Edmond (Geneva) to Foreign Office (Received September 23)
No. 55 [W 11928/62/41]

GENEVA, *September 21, 1936*

The United Kingdom Delegate to the League of Nations presents his compliments, and has the honour to transmit copies of the under-mentioned document.

ENCLOSURE IN No. 219

Record by Lord Cranborne of a conversation with Señor de Azcárate[1]

GENEVA, *September 19, 1936*

I had a talk this morning with M. de Azcárate, the new Spanish Ambassador, who had asked to see me. I should state that I have heard in various quarters here that his intention in coming to London as Ambassador is to remove misapprehensions with regard to the character of the Spanish Government and, if possible, to induce His Majesty's Government to reverse their policy of non-intervention and to exert their influence against the rebels.

M. de Azcárate first explained why he had not already appeared in London. He had had to go to Madrid and his government had asked him to come straight back to Geneva as the Spanish Delegation had little experience of the working of the League. He hoped to leave Geneva in the course of a week or so and would then make his way straight to England.

He then went on to talk of the Spanish situation [?government]. He said that extraordinary misconceptions seemed to exist abroad with regard to its character and composition. It was commonly reported to be of an extreme character. Nothing could be further from the truth. Indeed one of the chief Delegates at the Assembly was a Conservative and a Catholic. He added that he himself was and would remain a moderate Liberal. The government, he said, represent the vast proportion of the people of Spain. It was an administration representing all sections of opinion, who were devoted to the maintenance of democracy. In his opinion, were the generals to succeed, the cause of democracy in Spain would be thrown back for fifty years. It was the duty of every patriotic Spaniard to prevent such a catastrophe whatever the cost. He did not think that the character of the government was in the least understood in England, and he proposed to make it his business to enlighten people there as to the real facts.

I said that people in England of all shades of politics had been deeply shocked by the horrors that had marked the civil war. M. de Azcárate replied that that was unfortunately inevitable. The government had against them the whole army and they had, therefore, been obliged to press into the service of defence those who should properly have been maintaining law and order, but, were the government now to win, the authority of the law would be quickly restored and a moderate political administration set up. If, on the other hand, the conflict was prolonged, he was afraid that the gap between the two parties would grow ever greater and that the government itself would move steadily to the Left.

I asked His Excellency whether he saw any possibility of the conflict being ended by some form of compromise. He said that unfortunately he saw no prospect at the present time. The cleavage of fundamental principles

[1] Señor Pablo de Azcárate y Florez succeeded Señor Oliván as Spanish Ambassador at London, taking up his post in October, 1936.

was too great. He was evidently not particularly sanguine that the government forces would be successful, for he remarked that a military victory by the insurgents would solve nothing. The political strife would still go on under the surface.

M. de Azcárate spoke, in conclusion, shortly about the international situation, and was obviously apprehensive, like everyone else, of a cleavage of European nations between the Right and the Left. He gave me the impression of being absolutely sincere in his belief that his cause was the cause of democracy, but of being largely academic in mind and the type of man who finds it easy to ignore facts.

I expressed no opinion of any kind with regard to the attitude of His Majesty's Government towards the Spanish conflict, except to say that we were firmly wedded to the policy of non-intervention, which we regarded as essential if the conflict was not to be extended.

C.

No. 220

Letter¹ from Sir R. Vansittart to Mr. Eden
[*C 6637/97/18*]

FOREIGN OFFICE, *September 21, 1936*

My dear Anthony,
    Many thanks for your two telegrams.² I have made an appointment with the Chancellor tomorrow, and I am writing to the Prime Minister to tell him that I think your proposed answer is admirable and that if he agrees would he let me know in the course of the day.

I think your reply is excellent for the following reasons. As you know, I have always been more inclined than most people to consider the German claim for a restoration of their colonies, although in the present circumstances I know that it is not practical politics. But even I am rather horrified at the methods that the Germans now seem to be adopting. We are in fact being asked, as I said to you, to play the ace of spades the very first trick in order to take the two of clubs. If we fall into such an obvious trap we shall never take any tricks at all worth having. Nearly everybody in this country will be averse at present to playing the ace of colonial restitution at all, and I am sure that nobody would have the faintest sympathy for playing it until we were much further down the road of a European settlement, in other words until we were sure of getting something very real and tangible in return. And that is at present precisely what the opponents of colonial restitution refuse to believe possible. We cannot surely even contemplate being drawn into such a game until we are on surer ground. (And even then what would the House and the Press say?) The prospect of any real European settlement

---

¹ Addressed to Mr. Eden at Geneva.   ² Nos. 210 and 211.

will only become apparent when we have not only completed our preparations for a Five Power Conference but have actually gone far into the conference itself. At present it is still uncertain whether the Five Power Conference will materialise, and I should think that the majority of political observers would be inclined on the whole to bet against rather than for its prospects of meeting at all. I am quite sure that the Five Power Conference will never meet at all or do any good whatever if we allow ourselves to be inveigled into a surreptitious and semi-secret Three Power meeting. On the other hand I think that in the prevailing temper here, if it were known that the Germans were trying to get us into a secret deal about the colonies before they had provided any tangible earnest of their willingness to preserve European peace, there would almost certainly be a considerable explosion of feeling. To take the example nearest to my hand: I had Harcourt Johnstone[3] staying with me at Denham until this morning. We happened to get on to the colonial subject last night and he was quite remarkably and vigorously negative on the subject. The mere suggestion of any restitution made him very angry indeed. (He is still head of the Liberal Party Office.) If anybody got it into their heads that we were being solicited to start a deal on the basis described by Dr. Schacht instead of the basis described in our *communiqué*[4] and the questions now addressed to the various Governments, I feel sure that there would be a sharp anti-German reaction in all political quarters, Right and Left, and the prospects of the Five Power meeting would be still further clouded.

For all these reasons I think your proposed answer is the only prudent one. Let us proceed with the policy we are trying to press, and see how solid a return may be within our reach (the solidity is more than doubtful) before we even get on to the colonial basis at all.

The conclusion of the whole matter is really this. Ribbentrop told an acquaintance of ours some while ago that he and his were unable to understand why His Majesty's Government were quite so keen on negotiating a new agreement or agreements; but if and since they were so keen, the German Government would make them pay for it. And here you have the first attempt to make us pay without receiving any tangible goods in return.

And from a secret report which has reached me today I extract the following from a first-hand source: Hitler has been reluctant to embark on the colonial issue as opposed to German expansion in Eastern and South Eastern Europe, 'but the weakness of England has made him doubtful of the necessity of first making Germany irresistible before talking business to England regarding colonies'. I think this quotation speaks for itself.[5]

---

3 Liberal M.P. for South Shields since 1931.
4 Volume XVI, No. 476.
5 Formal concluding remarks omitted from the filed copy.

No. 221

Mr. Newton (Berlin) to Foreign Office (Received September 25)
No. 1008 [R 5655/294/67]

BERLIN, *September 22, 1936*

Sir,

I have the honour to report that The King's tour in the Eastern Mediterranean[1] has been followed daily by the press and that editorial comment while scarce, has tended to regard His Majesty's visits as inspired by anything but motives of relaxation.[2]

2. The general view ascribes His Majesty's choice of itinerary to the anxieties of the Admiralty over the British strategic position in the Eastern Mediterranean. The 'Deutsche Allgemeine Zeitung' suggests that Italo-British tension has in no way relaxed[3] and recalls that despite his much emphasised incognito The King was only following in the footsteps of His Majesty's grandfather who, on similar journeys and likewise in incognito, achieved great political successes. His Majesty certainly cannot have discussed only scenic beauties and architectural remains during his visits to Dubrovnik, Istanbul, Corfu and Sofia. There must have been 'words enough about quite real things' in connexion with the many-sided problem of the Mediterranean. The most important visit was of course to Istanbul and the paper affects to see in it a possible British initiative to prevent the accession of Turkey to the Franco-Soviet pact which is stated to be an aim of French and Russian policy.

3. The Party paper, the 'Angriff', has an article entitled 'A Paying Holiday' which is principally composed of illustrations, suitably labelled. The King's journey, it says, was not this time a trade journey but had to do with the British flag which is seeking new bases in the Eastern Mediterranean. England is not even able to take Jugoslavia's poultry exports. His Majesty was not following Dr. Schacht on his Balkan visit[4] for English commercial interests are not great there, but rather he was bent on the same errand as Sir Samuel Hoare.[5] Nevertheless what England lost last year a single summer cruise cannot win back at a stroke. Does the Mediterranean belong to England or Italy? The question is not yet decided.

4. In a later edition of the 'Deutsche Allgemeine Zeitung' Italian comment and feelings on the subject of His Majesty's voyage are prominently reproduced. Without being hostile, the tone of the German press is certainly

[1] See No. 31, note 4, and No. 74, note 2.
[2] There is nothing to justify this view in any evidence surviving in the Foreign Office archives. The relevant volume, F.O. 372/3190, has been extensively 'weeded'.
[3] Cf. No. 169.
[4] Dr. Schacht had toured the Balkan states in June 1936 in his capacity as President of the Reichsbank: see Hjalmar Schacht, *76 Jahre meines Lebens, op. cit.*, pp. 417–22; see also *D.G.F.P., op. cit.*, No. 376, note 2.
[5] Presumably a reference to Sir S. Hoare's tour of inspection of naval bases and establishments in the Mediterranean, which had just ended: see No. 226 below.

not friendly and there can be no question that Germany is again beginning to take a keen interest in Mediterranean affairs.

I have, &c.,

B. C. NEWTON

No. 222

Mr. Edmond (Geneva) to Foreign Office
(Received September 23, 9.30 a.m.)

No. 117 L.N. Telegraphic [*W 11958/9549/41*]

GENEVA, *September 23, 1936, 12.30 a.m.*[1]

Following from Secretary of State.

Following is text referred to in my immediately preceding telegram.[2]

At an interview between Portuguese Minister for Foreign Affairs and Mr. Eden, the latter urged Portuguese Government, having signified its agreement with principle of non-intervention, should now agree to participate in work of international committee for application of agreement regarding non-intervention in Spain.

In ensuing conversation Monsieur Monteiro made enquiries as to progress of committee's work.

At Mr. Eden's request chairman of Committee, Mr. Morrison, gave an account of procedure which Committee had now settled for its discussions and of lines on which it had been working.

After hearing this account Monsieur Monteiro agreed that a representative of Portuguese Government should take part in work of the Committee.

Monsieur Monteiro assured Mr. Eden that Portuguese Government had been strictly enforcing and would continue strictly to enforce agreement for non-intervention in accordance with terms of its original reply to the French Government.

Repeated to Lisbon.

---

[1] The date of despatch on the filed copy of this telegram was given as September 22, presumably in error.   [2] See No. 216, note 3.

No. 223

Mr. Edmond (Geneva) to Foreign Office (Received September 23, 1.10 p.m.)

No. 119 Telegraphic [*C 6639/97/18*]

Immediate   GENEVA, *September 23, 1936, 11 a.m.*

Following from Secretary of State for Sir R. Vansittart.

My telegram No. 113.[1]

In the course of a conversation with Lord Privy Seal and myself this evening M. Delbos and M. Spinasse referred to conversations which

[1] No. 214.

M. Blum and they had held with Dr Schacht in Paris.[2] Their account differed in no material particular from that recorded in my telegram No. 335[3] from Paris.

French Ministers were in full accord with view that it was essential to ascertain in greater detail the exact nature of German proposals. At the moment however position was that Dr Schacht was awaiting an answer from French Government ex . . .[4] ing their view and ours. M. Spinasse who was returning to tonight [sic] undertook to ask M. Blum to make no communication to Dr Schacht tomorrow in order to allow increased time for us [to] make our interim comment on information which M. Blum had given me.

In the course of conversation I told M. Delbos that report which we had received of Dr Schacht's interview with French Ministers had indicated that in German view French Government were less rigid in the matter of colonies than we. Somewhat to my surprise M. Delbos did not deny this imputation but said that as the price for instance of a settlement of the problem of the Rhineland France might be prepared to consider colonial compensation. French Government must however know exactly what it was to obtain in return and be in a position to assess the real value of any concession it was offered before it would be prepared to make any contribution in this sphere.

We thought it desirable to repeat that our own position in respect of colonies was governed by statement which I made in the House on July 27[5] and that we had no authority for departing from it. Though we had not yet received any communication from London we felt confident that so far as we were concerned the next step should be to ask German Government for some clearer definition of any proposals they might have to make. At the same time we emphasised our desire not to close the door against any possibilities which might offer.[6] French Ministers clearly shared this anxiety which was probably strengthened for both [?of] us by possible reactions in Rome of decision Assembly may be expected to make on validity of Abyssinian credentials.

Repeated to Paris.

[2] Cf. No. 141.   [3] No. 210.   [4] The text was here uncertain.
[5] See Volume XVI, Appendix to No. 484.
[6] In the course of a minute referring particularly to this and the preceding sentence, Mr. Wigram sounded a note of alarm: 'I think it would be unwise to give Germans any reason to suppose that we would enter into negotiations on colonies at present stage—and I think reply proposed would give them that reason. Surely we are not prepared to commit ourselves on basis proposed by Schacht, & we ought to make that clear. R. F. W. 23/9. Necessary action taken by Sir R. Vansittart in above sense. R. F. W. 24/9.' See No. 228 below.

No. 224

Mr. Edmond (Geneva) to Foreign Office
(Received September 23, 5.55 p.m.)

No. 120 Telegraphic [R 5630/294/67]

GENEVA, September 23, 1936, 4.35 p.m.

Following from Secretary of State.

In the course of a conversation this evening[1] with Monsieur Delbos and Monsieur Spinasse, French Ministers referred to their preoccupations about the Balearic Islands. Were we watching the situation there? It was evident that they regarded the Italian activities in this quarter in support of the insurgent forces as disturbing. Monsieur Delbos remarked that the generals in Spain seemed uncommonly like fascist governments elsewhere. They gave explicit assurances that they would not consider policies which they were in fact actively pursuing, for instance while the generals had spoken of their determination to preserve Spanish integrity, it was impossible to ignore either German activity in connexion with the Canaries or Italian activities in connexion with the Balearic Islands.[2]

In view of this situation and also of the possibility of Italy withdrawing from the League at least for the time being as the outcome of the Assembly's decision on the Abyssinian issue, it was suggested to us that the moment might be opportune to consider afresh the possibility of a Mediterranean pact. If we and the French Government were prepared jointly to propose such a pact to the Mediterranean Powers, it might have a useful steadying effect upon the Italian Government who would never be persuaded that the attitude of the Assembly in the Abyssinian affair was not due to the connivance of the Great Powers. Moreover an agreement to perpetuate the status quo in the Mediterranean if it could be reached in the near future might be of real service in the present disturbed state of Spain. French Ministers went on to give some account of their anxieties which included the possibility of an independent Catalonia applying for French protection.

So far as concerned the Mediterranean pact, we undertook to re-examine this question while admitting that so far we had not gone into it in detail because the negotiation of one important international agreement at a time seemed to be enough to occupy us. French Ministers urged that the suggestions that Monsieur Corbin had left with us some time ago should

[1] i.e. September 22.
[2] A note by Mr. Sargent dated October 5 said that papers relating to this telegram had 'just returned from Geneva without any instruction by the S. of S. as to whether we are to say anything to the French or not. You will remember that it was suggested that we might at any rate tell them of our exchange of statements with Ciano [see Nos. 103, 159, and 188] about the Balearic Is. Should we do this now?' Sir R. Vansittart's reply (undated) was: 'I see no reason at all why we shd. not tell the French about our exchanges with the Italians in regard to the Balearic islands. For the rest I wd. stall & do nothing. R. V.'

now immediately be examined.³ In our view it is well worth examining whether anything is practicable on these lines.⁴

Repeated to Paris.

³ The reference is to a memorandum dated July 22, 1936, communicated to the Foreign Office by the French Embassy, summarizing arguments in favour of a Mediterranean pact as a means of strengthening European peace. A minute by Mr. O'Malley of July 30 suggested that 'nothing whatever' should be done about this 'unless the French recur to the subject and, if they do, that it should be explained to the [French] Embassy in London verbally that though we are very glad to have this outline of their views, for purely practical reasons the subject must be put on ice for the time being'. This suggestion was evidently accepted. On August 14 in reply to a query by M. Cambon, Mr. Sargent said that 'serious discussions about a Mediterranean Pact in the present circumstances' were 'out of the question'. On his return from leave Sir R. Vansittart asked on September 5 what had been done about the French enquiry of July 22, and after being told of Mr. Sargent's reply to M. Cambon, minuted: 'I agree that for the present our line shd. be that we cannot take on the preparation of more than one large-scale pact at a time. R. V. Sept. 9.'

⁴ This recommendation led to a fresh round of minuting in the Foreign Office. Mr. Sargent wrote on September 26 that the French clearly thought that the pact would be 'a convenient way of placating Italy at the present juncture' but had probably not thought out 'the implications and difficulties of such a Pact as they are set forth in our memorandum' of June 11 (Volume XVI, No. 361). In particular he feared that the pact, to be really attractive to Italy, would probably require 'a future limitation of our naval forces in that sea'. Sir A. Cadogan also thought that the price might be too high. Sir R. Vansittart wrote: 'The weakness of the French is leading them into all sorts of feverish & thoughtless clutchings. We must be careful to give them no encouragement till they settle down. A Mediterranean agreement, in saner & cooler circumstances, might be worth while. At present it wd. bring up limitation with a bang, and we shd. have to reject it with a bang. Cui bono? Let us leave all the running to the Italians, and, rejecting the French as pacemakers, have all the appearance of the Hoggenheimer classic: "I'm not rude: I'm rich." We may then reach more profitable ground—with patience. R. V. Sept. 29. S. of S. on return.'

No. 225

Foreign Office to Mr. Edmond (Geneva)
No. 74 Telegraphic [W 12121/9549/41]

FOREIGN OFFICE, *September 23, 1936, 9.15 p.m.*

Following for British Delegation.

Committee on Non-intervention in Spain.

Chairman's Sub-Committee yesterday considered question of indirect intervention¹ raised by Italian representative. While large majority of members felt that discussion of this question would be useful, Soviet representative claimed that matter was entirely outside competence of Committee and could only be taken up directly between Governments. On his refusal to withdraw from this position, question was adjourned for further discussion at later meeting.

French Ambassador subsequently informed Lord Plymouth that he might suggest to his Government that they might sound Soviet Government discreetly with a view to fresh instructions being sent to their representative.

¹ Cf. No. 205, note 3.

Lord Plymouth proposes when this matter comes up again to urge that no advantage will be gained by further discussing question of interpretation of Committee's terms of reference, and to maintain our point of view that consideration of further measures of non-intervention is logical consequence of policy to which Governments have already subscribed and that Committee provides best method of securing agreement on such measures.

Next meeting of Sub-Committee will be held September 28th.

Repeated to Berlin No. 197, Lisbon No. 131, Moscow No. 124, Paris No. 239 and Rome No. 359.

No. 226

Mr. Ingram (Rome) to Foreign Office (Received September 25)
No. 204 Saving: Telegraphic [R 5668/294/67]

ROME, *September 23, 1936*

Sir Samuel Hoare's statement of British policy in the Mediterranean[1] is given prominence in the Italian press. In a London message to the 'Stampa' published under the headline 'The British mortgage on the Latin sea', it is stated that Sir S. Hoare's declarations confirm the intention of the Admiralty to strengthen at all costs, and whatever turn events may take in Europe, Great Britain's pre-eminent position in the Mediterranean. The 'Giornale d'Italia' London correspondent regards Sir S. Hoare's declarations as polemical in character and says that, in spite of the First Lord of the Admiralty's natural denial, Great Britain's Mediterranean policy marks a new departure.

The editor of the 'Tribuna' says that undoubtedly that part of Sir S. Hoare's statement in which he expressed a desire for friendly relations with Italy is significant, but he adds that in the present circumstances to cling to generalities is at least imprudent. There has been so far one undeniable fact: the intensification of British armaments in the Mediterranean. There should be no misunderstanding: Italy is far from questioning the naval needs of a great empire like Great Britain in the matter of communications with the Dominions. But, in the light of what has taken place during the Abyssinian conflict, the Mediterranean problem can only be considered in relation to Italian collaboration, if it is really desired to make an effective contribution to international peace. An effort to restore British prestige by a policy of strengthening Great Britain's hegemony in a sea in which Italy has such interests would inevitably exacerbate feelings which in the wider interests of European collaboration should be allowed to calm down.

[1] Sir S. Hoare returned to London from his tour of the Mediterranean (see No. 221, note 5) on September 22, and on the same day made a statement to the press stressing the determination of His Majesty's Government to maintain Britain's position in the Mediterranean and to consolidate and modernize naval defences there, while maintaining friendly relations with other Mediterranean powers: see *The Times*, September 23, 1936, p. 12.

The request for 'clarification' as regards British Mediterranean policy is fully justified if the past is recalled and if the future is considered objectively. It would be absurd as well as ingen[u]ous to expect that, after her recent experience, Italy should regard the new armaments announced by Sir Samuel Hoare as an ordinary administrative measure.[2]

Repeated to Geneva No. 9 Saving.

[2] Sir S. Hoare described his visit to the Mediterranean to the Cabinet at its meeting on October 15. He stated that he had 'discussed the defences of Malta and Gibraltar and he understood that proposals for improving the present position would shortly be submitted to the Committee of Imperial Defence. He was satisfied that, while Malta could not be made invulnerable, it could be rendered difficult for attack even by Italy. In the case of Gibraltar, the features that struck him were the lack of anti-aircraft artillery and the fact that not a single gun pointed towards Spain . . .'

No. 227

Record by Sir R. Vansittart of a conversation with M. Corbin
[*W 12074/9549/41*]

FOREIGN OFFICE, *September 23, 1936*

The French Ambassador called upon me today and read a despatch from the French Consul at Palma. From this it appeared that the Italians were not only disembarking large quantities of military supplies in the island, but had also furnished a certain number of personnel (about one hundred in all) particularly in regard to aviation and technical services, and were altogether playing a far too prominent rôle in the island. The Italian Consul was behaving as if he were a prominent person in the administration, and large numbers of the inhabitants were going about wearing Italian colours as well as the old Spanish national colours.

The Ambassador asked whether we had any information to confirm this, and I replied that I had seen nothing recent from the Balearic Islands. The Ambassador replied that we could certainly obtain information from our Consul and from our naval authorities, and he would be very grateful if we would do so, so that we might be sure how far Italian activities and pretensions were in reality being pushed. The Ambassador expressed the greatest apprehension on these scores and also on the extent to which Italian supplies were in general being furnished to Spain. He thought it likely that the Italian Government really had designs on the Balearic Islands in spite of all their denials. He repeated again that he would be glad of information both as to their activities in those islands and also on the general question of supply. He said that if our information appeared to confirm theirs, he felt sure the matter ought to be brought up in the Committee now sitting in London, but I was not quite clear from what he said whether this observation applied to the Balearic Islands only or to the question of general supplies to the mainland as well. I think that he meant the former only.

I should be grateful if we could enquire immediately[1] both from our consul and the naval authorities whether they have noticed anything abnormal of late in the conduct of the Italians in the Balearic Islands.[2]

[1] No action, however, appears to have been taken in the Foreign Office on this instruction for some days: see note 2 below.

[2] Following a request from the Foreign Office dated September 29, the Admiralty forwarded on October 3 to the British Vice-Consul at Palma, Lieutenant-Commander A. Hillgarth, a request that he should furnish the Foreign Office by telegram with any further information gained since the beginning of September on military assistance supplied to the insurgents by the Italian Government, together with any evidence of political pretensions by the latter. Cf. No. 243 below. Commenting on M. Corbin's communication of September 23, Sir G. Mounsey minuted on October 1: 'This looks to me very much as though the French are trying to manoeuvre us into the position of being the Government in possession of information about Italian assistance to the rebels, which they will then say it is our duty to put before the Committee.' He asked why the French did not themselves ever produce any evidence. Sir R. Vansittart minuted, also on October 1: 'I think I will say nothing further of this to the French Ambassador—unless he asks again . . .'

No. 228

Letter from Mr. Eden to M. Delbos
[C 6702/97/18]

GENEVA, *September 23, 1936*

My dear Minister,

M. Blum asked me when I was in Paris to let him have a view, although it were only an interim and a tentative one, upon the information which he had communicated to me when I saw him in Paris last Sunday.[1] I would therefore be grateful if you would communicate the following to him:

I am very grateful to M. Blum for having given me such full information of his conversation with Dr Schacht. He will appreciate that on a subject of this importance it is impossible for me to give him any considered opinion of the views of His Majesty's Government until I have had an opportunity of consulting the Prime Minister and my colleagues. In the meanwhile it is only fair that I should point out that while His Majesty's Government are at all times anxious to do all in their power to promote a European settlement, their attitude towards the question of colonies is governed by the statement which I made in the House of Commons at the end of July.[2] I anticipate that my colleagues will feel that they are not in a position to carry these discussions further until they are in possession of a more complete and detailed appreciation of the attitude of the German Government towards the problems that have to be solved if we are to reach a European settlement. I further anticipate that they will consider the discussions now proceeding through the diplomatic channel to prepare the Five-Power Conference should provide the most convenient means of bringing about this result.

ANTHONY EDEN

[1] See No. 210.   [2] See Volume XVI, Appendix to No. 484.

No. 229

Letter from Sir R. Vansittart to Mr. Eden (Geneva)
Ge/36/22[1]

FOREIGN OFFICE, *September 23, 1936*

My dear Anthony,

With reference to your telegrams in regard to your conversations with the French and the colonial question, I saw the Chancellor and Simon yesterday afternoon. They both agreed cordially with the terms of your proposed reply[2] and also expressed their agreement with the letter which I had written to you.[3] They both clearly felt that the Germans were raising the question prematurely and that we were not yet anything like within sight of the stage where anything in the nature of colonial retrocession could be considered in this country. Simon even expressed the view, and asked that I should repeat it to you, that he thought your reply might go rather further and indicate that this was apparently a request from the Germans for still further concessions without their having offered any counterpart at all or even indicated what counterpart they would be able to contribute. I said that I thought it would be best if he spoke to you himself when you returned, and that your interim reply had better go as it was and any more searching answer could be sent after you had discussed the matter with your colleagues on return.

I had sent a special messenger down to Blickling[4] with the telegrams and asked S.B.[5] if he would ring me up to confirm the interim reply so soon as he had got them. It was only, however, this morning that I got on to him by telephone and found that he too agreed with the course proposed.

As to the Lord President,[6] I saw him this morning and asked him to telephone to me so soon as he had read the correspondence. This he has promised to do, but I have not yet heard. In conversation he expressed himself very strongly against colonial retrocession and said that he did not believe the country would accept it in any near future.

I have told all four that the telegrams have at present only been circulated to them (they all agree with this course) and that the question of giving them a wider distribution could be discussed between you and them when you come home.

Yours ever,
VAN

P.S. Since writing the above I have had a telephone message from the Lord President. He said that he thought your answer was the only possible one in the circumstances, and he added some strong comment on the German manœuvre which he thought, to put it mildly, entirely premature.

---

[1] From the Private Papers of Sir Anthony Eden, Series A.   [2] See No. 228.
[3] No. 220.
[4] Blickling Hall, in Norfolk, was the seat of the Marquess of Lothian.
[5] i.e. the Prime Minister, Mr. Stanley Baldwin.   [6] Mr. J. R. MacDonald.

No. 230

Letter from Sir R. Vansittart to Mr. Eden (Geneva)
[C 6639/97/18]

FOREIGN OFFICE, *September 23, 1936*

My dear Anthony,

Since writing to you this afternoon[1] I have received your telegram No. 119,[2] and I confess that it makes me a little uneasy. It appears to be contemplated that we should ask the Germans for a definition of their proposals including the colonies. May not that have the effect of putting to some extent the cart before the horse? The Germans themselves always said that they hoped the colonial question could be dealt with after a European settlement and Germany's return to the Leage. The position really is that the Germans have obtained their advantage by the recovery of the demilitarized zone. What we are really after is to get into a conference whereby a substitute Locarno will be concluded without the demilitarized zone, that is the Germans will keep their profit. But it is really going rather far if in spite of their previous professions they now want some further and strong inducement before they come into a conference which is to repair and obliterate the effects of their unilateral action. To us at this end it seems rather that their own originally contemplated procedure was the right and only one, that is that we should have a European settlement (in other words that we should know exactly what we are getting) and that after that the question of further concessions and profits to Germany should be taken in hand. I have always, as you know, been an advocate of the idea that Germany would eventually have to have her colonies back, but you may remember that in my last paper on Germany[3] I suggested that we might indicate that if a European settlement were reached and worked well, and peace were maintained in Europe for an appreciable time, we might then be in a position to reconsider the colonial question. Incidentally, that procedure would also have given us time to carry out a good deal of very necessary conversion of public opinion here; but if by any action of ours we bring German colonial claims out into the open before we have got some really tangible and concrete counterpart in hand, we may have trouble.

Wigs[4] has prepared a description of the background of what has passed recently in regard to the colonial question, and I enclose a copy.[5] It does

---

[1] No. 229.

[2] No. 223. An interim reply was despatched the same day at 8.50 p.m. in telegram No. 73 to Geneva; Sir R. Vansittart explained that telegram No. 119 'seems to us in the F.O. to contemplate a reply to Dr. Schacht's *démarche* which goes beyond that foreshadowed in your telegram No. 338 [No. 211], which as I informed you on the telephone this afternoon was approved by the four Ministers . . . I am sending you by tonight's bag a letter explaining my preoccupations.' Cf. No. 223, note 6.

[3] It is not clear to which 'paper' Sir R. Vansittart was here referring; cf. however his memorandum of February 3, 1936, on 'Britain, France, and Germany': Volume XV Appendix IV (*b*).   [4] Mr. Wigram

[5] This paper, dated September 23, does not appear to have been preserved in the

not exactly increase one's confidence, for it seems clear from paragraph 3 that M. Delbos was not truthful in speaking to Hugh Thomas.[6] We have an uneasy feeling that the French may be losing their nerve and trying to go too fast. It would seem indeed very naif on the part of the French to believe that they would get the Germans to give them some guarantee in regard to the non-fortification of the Rhineland, which the Germans would keep, in return for 'colonial compensation'. This would really result in the Germans obtaining two large and concrete advantages before the rest of us had obtained even one which had proved its worth in duration.

I have written this letter in haste to catch the bag, and in consultation with Wigs and Moley.[7] We all feel that the position of M. Blum is a very weak one,[8] and such information as I have now received from the French Ambassador (I enclose a copy for your information)[9] of course does not lighten French anxiety; and in this anxiety they may be letting themselves in for a procedure which would very possibly result in our never getting a Five-Power Conference together at all.

Yours ever,

VAN

Foreign Office archives, but a copy is preserved in the Private Papers of Sir Anthony Eden (Ge/36/21). In a minute of September 23 Mr. Wigram described the paper as a memorandum on the 'recent very murky background to the French communication to S. of S. I have not been able to take memo. further back owing to only copies of recent papers being in Geneva'. This memorandum forms the first eight paragraphs, with minor alterations, of an extended memorandum dated October 29, 1936, filed under C 6701/97/18, which summarized documents printed above (Nos. 145, 185, 196, 210, 214, 223, and 228) and below (Nos. 233, 261, 282, 300, 306, 307, and 330).

[6] See No. 145.   [7] Mr. O. G. Sargent.

[8] *Note in original*: It will be weaker still if the insurgents win in Spain, as now seems probable, perhaps even imminent.

[9] Not printed: cf. No. 227.

No. 231

Mr. Newton (Berlin) to Foreign Office (Received September 25)

No. 1013 [C 6667/3790/18]

BERLIN, *September 23, 1936*

Sir,

With reference to my telegram No. 300 of 18th September[1] informing you of the German decision to increase the total number of divisions in the Army to thirty-nine all told, without including a cavalry brigade, I have the honour to transmit to you herewith a copy of the Military Attaché's note on this question.

2. It is pertinent to recall that in regard to the German construction of submarines the Naval Attaché, Captain Muirhead-Gould, had a similar experience of the unreliable and in fact misleading nature of information

[1] Not preserved in the Foreign Office archives.

315

from German official sources (see Sir Eric Phipps' telegram No. 165 of 25th April, 1935).[2] As regards the present increase of the army Herr Hitler explained to Sir John Simon and yourself on the 26th March, 1935, during your visit to Berlin that he had fixed the strength of the future German army at thirty-six divisions because the German Government's intention was to settle a figure which would not be exceeded, to whatever extent the period of military service might be raised in France.[3] Russia and the Franco-Russian alliance would doubtless be adduced as the reason for any military increases now. Nevertheless it was confirmed to the Military Attaché as recently as the 25th August last, when it was a question of tranquillising foreign opinion, that two years' military service in Germany would not involve an increase beyond the thirty-six divisions which Germany had declared to be its future strength.[4] It is clear that whatever official assurances may be given, increases in German military strength are liable to take place from time to time and will be concealed so long as practicable, partly with the help of those very assurances. It must be assumed that German military strength at any moment, both actual and prospective, is substantially greater than what is admitted.

3. The Military Attaché was also informed at the War Ministry on the 25th August that it was unlikely that men doing two years' military service would be required to do labour service as well. It is quite probable that this information will in due course also prove to be inaccurate. Although the more conservative part of the General Staff would perhaps be glad to be rid of the very strong National-Socialist element introduced by the labour service training, that institution is the expression of fundamental National-Socialist doctrines and was referred to in very eulogistic terms by Herr Hitler at the recent Party Congress at Nuremberg. Owing to the part it plays in the inculcation of the spirit of National-Socialism, it is unlikely that Herr Hitler will be willing for any substantial part of the male population to be omitted from its training. From a purely military point of view, moreover, the Military Attaché is of opinion that training in the labour service will greatly increase the future strength of the German army. There was a tendency in the past for the officer class to become a caste differentiating itself from the bulk of the nation; labour service should tend to check this tendency and increase the unity which is so important a factor in Germany's strength.

4. In a recent article in the press on the two years' service by a military writer, it was pointed out that the labour service follows immediately on school education. In other countries where no similar legal obligation exists the value of the conception of compulsory labour service has been repeatedly recognised. Training in the Hitler Youth, then in the labour service, and finally in the army constitutes an uninterrupted development which may be improved but can hardly need any fundamental alteration. The boy must be educated for ten years in advance to think of becoming a soldier—he will then act rightly when he has become a soldier and continue

[2] Cf. Volume XIII, Nos. 150, 154.   [3] Volume XII, pp. 733-7.   [4] See No. 132.

to do so long after he has left the army. The writer goes on to point out that in the two years of its existence the labour service has already shown what good work it can do for the army. Neither the school nor the vocational training nor labour service should be neglected. They should be consecutive and train a man for the army.[5]

I have, etc.,
B. C. NEWTON

ENCLOSURE IN No. 231

Note by Colonel Hotblack on the Strength of the German Army

BERLIN, *September 17, 1936*

1. Military Attachés have to-day been confidentially informed by the *Reichskriegsministerium* that in October the Army will be organized into thirty-six infantry divisions, three armoured divisions, and one cavalry Brigade. This will involve an increase of troops in the Rhineland, but can only be considered as bringing the Rhineland to normal with the rest of Germany.

2. It is interesting to note that the Law for the Fighting Services, of 16th March, 1935, states that the Army will consist of thirty-six divisions.

3. From the numbering of units and other small indications it would appear that the decision to have thirty-six infantry divisions, plus armoured divisions, was, nevertheless, made at least as early as the autumn of 1935. Rumours of this intention have been rife for about a year, but I have raised this point on three separate occasions, and on each occasion and as lately as August 26th have been informed by the *Reichskriegsministerium* that the total of the German Army would be thirty-six divisions, *including* the armoured divisions. (I reported on 25th August, however, that I did not consider this statement to be binding.[4])

4. It would appear that the normal procedure under the present régime in Germany is to issue military information, whether confidentially or to the world at large, at a moment when

(a) it has become impossible to keep the matter secret any longer,
(b) when steps are already being taken to make a further increase.

It is probable that both these factors come into play in this case.

5. The shortage of officers still remains the greatest weakness in the German Army, nevertheless I do not believe that the expansion now announced is final.

ELLIOT HOTBLACK

[5] Foreign Office minutes on this despatch reveal considerable exasperation with the broken German assurances about rearmament. Mr. Wigram suggested that some notice should be taken of the latest episode in the press, and asked whether anything should be said to the German Chargé or to Baron von Neurath (September 28). Sir R. Vansittart was at first opposed to diplomatic representations, 'We shd. get no change out of that', but subsequently on October 2 agreed that 'we had better not keep silence at Berlin'. A later note by Mr. Wigram of October 20 states that 'Sir R. Vansittart has now decided that the question of publicity can wait'.

No. 232

Mr. Newton (Berlin) to Foreign Office (Received September 25)
No. 1015 [C 6679/576/18]

BERLIN, September 23, 1936

Sir,

The National Socialist party press has not been slow to grasp the opportunities recently offered by British publicists to point to a tardy recognition in Great Britain of the achievements of National Socialism and of the good intentions of the German Government.

2. Unquestionably the first place in importance belongs to Mr. Lloyd George's article in the 'Daily Express' together with his subsequent interview to the 'News Chronicle' and a Danish Correspondent.[1] These have been reproduced at length and, in the main, accurately for there can be no doubt that the admiration of Germany's most potent enemy in the last war and of a self-styled 'life-long Liberal' is extremely welcome. Materially buttressing the impression that England is at last beginning to appreciate National Socialist Germany, have come the articles of Mr. Ward Price and Mr. Beverley Nichols in the 'Daily Mail'[2] and 'Sunday Chronicle' respectively. Special prominence has been given to Mr. Nichols' article saying that, among the writers of the letters he has received, those who have been to Germany agree with his present views and those who know the country only in theory do not.[3]

3. Hitherto the press has allowed these gentlemen to speak for themselves and has contented itself with excising anything unsuitable for German consumption, but the 'Völkischer Beobachter' of September 22nd carries a long article by its London correspondent inspired directly by Mr. Lloyd George's remarks and entitled 'Facing facts', after a passage in his contribution to the 'Daily Express'.

4. The English Cabinet, says the writer, are now back at work and it must have been with heavy sighs that they have turned to again, for things look a good deal blacker than when they dispersed for their holiday. Yet in order to understand Britain it is important to bear in mind that they have spent this troubled two months mostly in the traditional way, fishing and shooting. The mass of the nation, leaving aside a few advanced spirits such as Mr. Lloyd George, resolutely refuses to face the facts and fails

[1] Mr. Lloyd George visited Berchtesgaden from 4 to 7 September. His article in the *Daily Express* of September 17 was entitled, 'I talked to Hitler'. The interview in the *News Chronicle* was conducted by Mr. A. J. Cummings, and appeared on September 2 under the title, 'Next Step: National Reconstruction. Why Fuehrer suppressed liberty. See No. 295 below.

[2] The article by Mr. G. Ward Price appeared in the *Daily Mail* of September 21, under the title, 'This New Germany'.

[3] Mr. V. G. Lawford noted (September 30) that the Foreign Office had not acquired copy of Mr. Beverley Nichols's article, but remarked that 'no doubt it was all about "getting together"'. He also remarked that Mr. Lloyd George had quoted Herr Hitler as saying that 'the German army will not be ready for offensive action for another 15 or 20 years

signally to realise that the war and Versailles and every subsequent revolution are only steps in another vaster revolution of the spirit. That is beyond British understanding. The British public is still living in the world of the Manchester School whose democracy was so attractive that other nations thought it the road to happiness. The British themselves came to believe in their own panacea and the war was fought to make the world safe for democracy. Yet now that the Germans have a system, even though it is expressly labelled not for export, it is still suspect. It would indeed be a great step forward if other peoples could understand that their foolish fears are groundless and that there is no proselytising urge in Germany.

5. Germany is also frequently charged with forgetting realities in the enthusiasm of the moment, but it is rather the British who systematically refuse to fact [?face] facts and who strive always for a compromise in the hope that time will bring a solution of their difficulties. In times such as these compromise is of no avail. For instance British opinion affects to regard German fear of Bolshevism as illusory. Yet the same opinion is terrified that the fall of M. Blum's Government would mean Bolshevism in France. Of course England is reluctant to commit herself for she is as yet in no danger but she should at least do Germany, wedged in the middle of a distracted Europe, the justice of believing that she knows what she is about.[4]

I have, &c.,
B. C. NEWTON

[4] Minutes by Mr. Wigram and Sir R. Vansittart on this despatch were as follows. 'No wonder the Germans like this stuff. R. F. W. 30/9.' 'It is a pity that we have not got Mr. Beverley Nichols to add to this confident rubbish. He wd. have presented a bold behind to our problems. It has been entertaining to watch the effect of Mr. Lloyd George on his supporters. He has hit himself a shrewd blow,—the k.o. indeed so far as the idea of a "Popular Front" is concerned. R. V. Oct. 2.'

No. 233

Mr. Newton (Berlin) to Foreign Office (Received September 25)
No. 1017 [C 6681/6028/18]

BERLIN, *September 23, 1936*

Sir,

The Party Congress[1] which was concluded last week at Nuremberg has become an annual event at which the Führer and his Party leaders take stock of the past and point the way to the future. In Herr Hitler's own words to the uniformed Party forces, 'Every year we meet here, fighting men and brave women, to review the twelve past months and to gather strength for the future'. It may therefore be useful to draw special attention in this despatch to the chief features which emerged from the flood of oratory.

2. Last year's congress was called the Congress of Freedom, and this

[1] The annual congress of the Nazi Party had been formally opened at Nuremberg on September 8: cf. No. 127.

year's was called the Congress of Honour. In the inaugural speech on September 9th, Herr Hess[2] said that by her military reoccupation of the Rhine Germany had recovered full sovereignty and with unbounded pride could now stand once more with other nations as a nation of honour. Herr Hitler also said at the end of his manifesto that in 1936 the German nation left behind it the historical period of its loss of honour. Germany now admits therefore that in the two cardinal questions of freedom and her honour she is now a 'satisfied' Power. Unfortunately the speeches show that in other respects she is far from satisfied.

3. The most important statement at the Congress was presumably the Führer's written manifesto read out at its opening meeting.[3] He there refers to the request he made on the assumption of power for four years' time for the National Socialist Party to be justified, and he gives an account of his stewardship, which he calls a 'towering record of achievements'. At the same time he announces a further four years' programme to make Germany as economically independent as possible from the outside world. This is all according to plan. In an election appeal in February 1933 (Sir Horace Rumbold's despatch No. 113 of the 3rd February, 1933)[4] Herr Hitler said that the National Government would carry out the great work of the reorganisation of the industry of the people in two great four-year plans. Dr. Goebbels also, in a speech to Party leaders on the 24th June, 1934, said that when unemployment had been overcome a new four years' plan would be introduced for raising the standard of living of the German people. The accent now, however, is not so much on raising their standard of living as on making them militarily independent.

Economic Difficulties

4. It is significant that something like one half of Herr Hitler's manifesto, and a large part of the subsequent speeches made by himself and other leaders, dealt with Germany's economic difficulties. It is probable that Dr Schacht inspired much of what was proclaimed on this subject in the written manifesto. Herr Hitler says, for example (see page 9 of Embassy translation):

> The problem of maintaining our national economic existence is inordinately difficult.
> The 136 inhabitants on each square kilometre in Germany cannot—even with the greatest efforts and the most skilful use of the available space—obtain their full nourishment from their own resources. What the German peasant has achieved in the last few years is unique and unparalleled. What the National Socialist State has achieved in the

[2] Reich Minister and Herr Hitler's deputy.
[3] The full text of the Chancellor's statement, which was read by the Gauleiter at the inaugural meeting on September 9, was forwarded in an English translation to the Foreign Office in Mr. Newton's despatch No. 964 of September 10, not printed here: see *The Times*, September 10, 1936, p. 12.
[4] See Volume IV, No. 235, paragraph 3.

cultivation of the last patch of heather and swamp in Germany cannot be exaggerated. Nevertheless there will never be enough on our own territory for our nourishment. To cover this insufficiency by means of imports from outside is all the more difficult in that also we unfortunately do not possess in Germany a number of most important raw materials. German economy is therefore forced to cover the insufficiency in foodstuffs and raw materials by means of industrial exports which must in all circumstances be made, because it is the case, particularly as regards foodstuffs, of absolutely indispensable imports.

On page 18 he says:

The issue here is not democracy or liberty, but existence or non-existence;

and a little later:

Posterity will one day ask, not whether we were able to obtain democratic freedom, that is lack of discipline, in these critical and threatened times, but only whether we were successful in protecting a great people from economic and political collapse.

5. The Roumanian Minister who was at Nuremberg told me that the outstanding impression made upon him was the anxiety displayed in regard to the economic situation. He was convinced that the attacks against Russia were primarily intended to distract attention from causes of discontent at home, in particular the growing cost of living. I notice that in this he confirms views expressed in the French press of the Left. Similar views are held by the 'Times' correspondent, Mr. Ebbutt, who however considers that the fears genuinely entertained are probably not altogether justified and spring from a lack of perspective and sober judgment.

6. Although Herr Hitler did not announce any actual measures against the propertied classes, such as had been half expected, a reference he made in his last speech to the upper and middle classes was not reassuring. He said (page 5 of translation):

Had Communism really only meant to remove certain elements in our upper ten thousand, or in our equally worthless middle classes, we could have stood by and allowed it to continue for some time.

Towards the end of this speech he said:

We must make it clear to all our countrymen that no sacrifice is too great for this community ... The coming Winter Relief Fund will be our first opportunity of proclaiming our community spirit in a more intense form. There can be no question of leaving it to the individual to decide whether he will help or not. He must help.

Similar hints had been previously given by the leader of the Labour Front, Dr Ley, in his speech of September 12th, when he said that the National

Socialist vocabulary no longer knew the phrase 'the private individual'. At the end of that speech he said that welfare work was

> no longer charity depending on bourgeois sentimental twaddle. Our winter help is of course no charity nonsense. It is for us a holy duty to make sacrifices for the community in gratitude for what we owe it.

Bolshevik Russia

7. It had been expected that unflattering references to Bolshevism would be a feature of the Congress, but the extent of the attacks and their violent and pointed, and in fact provocative, nature exceeded all anticipations. No doubt it suited Herr Hitler both for internal and external reasons of policy to make Bolshevism into National, and so far as he could, International Enemy No. 1. In addition to economic pressure, the introduction of two years' military service has caused some grumbling. It is, however, often said by Germans that it is a cheap price to pay if the choice is between two years' service or a state of affairs such as prevails in Spain. It is therefore natural that Herr Hitler should ram this point home. Foreign observers familiar with 'Mein Kampf' and the so-called Rosenberg Plan[5] were, of course, struck by Herr Hitler's specific allusion to the Urals, Siberia and the Ukraine, in his speech to the Labour Front on September 12th, as areas which could be developed so much better by Germany than Russia. It is certainly remarkable with what insistence Herr Hitler and other speakers harped on the theme of Germany's lack of space for her existing population, her intention to increase that population, her efficiency and great deserts, as contrasted with Russia's superfluity of territory, economic incompetence, and political villainy. In the written manifesto Herr Hitler says on page 9:

> How should others talk of distress who possess perhaps fifteen or twenty times as much territory per head of population as Germany?

In a speech to the Labour Front on September 12th Herr Hitler said that:

> The real task was to raise not money incomes but real incomes, and to provide for the needs of 68 million people *who were crowded together into a hopelessly small space.*

In his final speech he said (page 13 of translation):

> Since 1917, that is to say since the victory of Bolshevism, there is no end to this misery in Russia. The Bolshevist hypocrites ought not to blame the weather, that is God, for their own sins, for this same Russia that has now been vegetating for almost twenty years was formerly one of the largest corn-growing lands in the world. There is eighteen times as much land there per head of the population as there is in Germany. What a miserable agricultural system that must be which in such circumstances is incapable of affording a people a decent existence.

[5] See Volume XVI, No. 56, note 8.

In parenthesis I might mention here that Colonel Lindberg,[6] in the course of his recent visit to Germany at the invitation of General Göring, mentioned to me the strong impression which he had derived that the Germans were, or at any rate thought that they were, short of essential space and were determined to expand. Even in the speech to 50,000 boys and girls of the Hitler Youth, Herr Hitler sought to implant in them hatred against Russia, saying:

There is another country full of cruelty, murder and arson, destruction and upheaval, filled not with life but with horror, despair, complaint and misery.

A little later in the same speech he said:

Providence gives the strong, the bold, the brave, the industrious, the orderly and disciplined man a reward for his sacrifice.

And finally he said:

We are used to conflict, for it was out of conflict that we came. We will plant our feet firmly on our soil and repel all aggression. And you will be beside me if ever that hour should come. You will stand in front of me, at my side, and behind me, and will bear our banners on high. Our old foe will then try to rise against us once more. He can carry his Soviet emblem before him—our emblem will be victorious again.

8. Dr Rosenberg was of course particularly eloquent on the subject of the Bolshevist peril. At the end of a long speech he said:

Bolshevism pretended to lead a campaign against militarism and to be the champion of world peace. Yet the Soviets were arming the world's greatest force, and were building great fortifications and works on their Western frontier in order to attack Europe with all their force when the Bolshevik revolution in the West succeeded. With the same object fifty landing grounds had been built in Czechoslovakia with Russian aid.

9. Dr Goebbels beat on the same drum in a long and extraordinarily violent speech on September 8th. He said, *inter alia*, that Jews and Bolsheviks could not be distinguished from one another, that the goal of Bolshevik propaganda was the destruction of the world, that the fight against it was a world battle begun on German soil, and that Bolshevism must be destroyed if Europe were to recover. He then described the immense strength of the Red Army which had recently been increased to two million men with a trained reserve behind it of nine to ten million men. On the declaration of war 160 to 180 infantry divisions, with 25 cavalry divisions could be set on the march, while a Russian estimate of their tank strength was 2,475. The Soviet air strength comprised 6,000 machines, with a first line consisting of 3,100 bombing and scouting machines, and 1,500 fighters, a proportion showing the aggressive character of the force. They now had 36 landing

[6] Colonel Charles Lindbergh, the American aviator.

grounds in Czechoslovakia, so that the strategically most important points of Central Europe were within one hour's flying range of this Red base. Despite the magnitude of Dr Goebbels' figures, it may be noticed that his estimate of Russian aerodromes in Czechoslovakia is less than that given by Dr. Rosenberg.

10. In the course of the many speeches made, it was claimed that National Socialist Germany wanted nothing but peace, and was building up its strength purely for defensive purposes. The passages which I have cited, and many others too numerous and lengthy to repeat, show, however, how provocative the attacks on Russia were, and how they could be used to justify 'preventive' war. In saying this I do not wish to strike any alarmist note, but merely to draw attention to the warnings given of possible eventual aggression. It may be that National Socialism requires some object of attack in order to maintain its vigour. Having destroyed all opposition at home it may now seek some object outside its own borders on which to sharpen, and then perhaps to use, its weapons. There is at least no sign that with growing experience and rapidly growing power Herr Hitler is becoming less of a fanatic and a revolutionary. In one of his speeches he himself expressly included fanaticism and contempt for death amongst the virtues which had gone to achieve the successes of the past (page 2 of the speech to the political leaders on September 11th).

Jewry and Bolshevism

11. Although no further measures against the Jews were announced, and I had been told informally on the eve of the Congress by *Reichsminister* Dr Frank,[7] who is particularly concerned with questions of legal reform, that the Jewish legislation had been virtually, if not quite, concluded, further measures were foretold in one speech. Dr. Wagner, head of the Medical Faculty and not to be confused with the better known Bavarian Gauleiter and Statthalter of that name, said (see my despatch No. 998 of 17th September, page 3)[8] that

In the opinion of the State the Nuremberg Laws had not settled the Jewish question. They would be reinforced by new legislation. It was a question of life or death for the German race. To those who might think these laws inhuman and unchristian he would say 'If the Church demanded celibacy of hundreds of thousands, surely the Party could conscientiously and before God take the responsibility in the interests of the German people in making the two hundred thousand half Jews apply for permission before they married. Prevention was better than cure, and Germany wished to be safe for centuries from the fate of Spain.

In speeches made respectively on the 8th and 11th of September Dr. Goebbels and Dr. Rosenberg made violent and insulting attacks against all Jews, saying that Bolshevism and Jewry were indistinguishable.

[7] Dr Hans Frank, Reich Minister without Portfolio and Reich Commissioner for Justice.   [8] Not printed: cf. No. 138.

'Bolshevism', said Dr. Rosenberg, 'could not be attacked unless Jewry were also attacked; and no exceptions were possible. For example, the "good Jew" cited by foreign critics was at best an occasional freak phenomenon whose existence did nothing to alter the real nature of the mighty Jewish attempt to exact vengeance on Europe and the world generally'.

'Bolshevism', said Dr. Goebbels, 'is a pathological and criminal madness clearly originating from Jewish sources and led by Jews with the object of annihilating European civilisation and the attainment of an international Jewish world domination over it'.

Later he said that Bolshevism and Jewry were bound in the closest relationship.

Colonies

12. Herr Hitler's open declaration in his written manifesto that Germany has colonial claims has naturally aroused much attention. He used very guarded language in asserting this claim, which he introduced in connection with his recital of Germany's economic difficulties. He said (page 10):

> If, therefore, an English politician declares that Germany requires no colonies, because she can buy her raw materials without them, this gentleman's expression of opinion must be regarded as on the same intellectual level as the question of the famous Bourbon princess, who in the face of the revolutionary mob shouting for bread asked in amazement why men who had no bread would not eat cake.
>
> If the German people and the German Reich had not been squeezed for fifteen years and had not lost all their international savings, if they had not lost all their capital abroad, and above all if they still possessed their own colonies, we should be in a better position to master these tasks.
>
> The objection that colonies would not help us much is unjustified. A government which under existing conditions in Germany is responsible for economic achievements which cannot be denied, would equally be able to administer colonies to economic advantage.

Then at the end of his announcement of the new four year programme (page 17) he said:

> Quite apart from this, Germany cannot renounce her colonial claims. The German people's right to live is just as great as the right of other nations.

The influence of Dr. Schacht is clearly discernible. Herr Hitler himself may in his heart of hearts still be inclined to his original belief that overseas colonies are of little use to Germany and may even be a source of weakness. He is no doubt still of the opinion that German colonial claims should not be pressed to the point of definitely alienating Great Britain. At the same time he may think that to raise German colonial claims, apart from the satisfaction it gives to some of his supporters, is no bad tactical move both in the economic and in the political spheres. Economically, if his claim is not satisfied it strengthens the case for economic concessions; politically, his reference to the colonial question may be intended as a suggestion that Germany must either get the room and raw material she needs from territory in the East or overseas, so that if we deny her colonies his case is strengthened for expansion to the East.

Miscellaneous

13. Attention may be drawn to the fact that in Dr. Ley's speech on 12th September, he gave notice that a vast building programme of five million dwelling houses would be begun in two years' time. There have been previous indications that when the expenditure on armaments came to an end and if the problem of maintaining employment became in consequence acute, large-scale State expenditure would be continued on housing and settlement schemes.

14. The Congress was, as usual, organised and staged on a vast scale, and the enthusiasm, and in fact revivalist fervour, displayed were as great as, if not greater than, on previous occasions. A special Italian delegation was present, but did not, as I have been informed from more than one source, either cut a good figure or receive a good reception. A special effort was made this year to secure as large an attendance as possible of the diplomatic representatives of foreign countries. In order to deprive missions of the excuse that they were not concerned with Party functions, the invitation was issued by Herr Hitler not as Head of the Party, but as Head of the State. Amongst those who attended the Congress for the first time were the Swedish Minister, and the representatives of the Little Entente. In the latter case I understand that pressure was actually brought to bear and that one, if not all, of the Little Entente ministers was given to understand that if he did not accept the invitation Herr Hitler would draw political conclusions from his refusal.[9]

I have, &c.,
B. C. NEWTON

[9] Minutes on this despatch included a comment by Mr. Wigram: 'This is a most important despatch . . . It is a fresh indication that we have no time to lose in our rearmament. I am afraid the Locarno negotiations, even if successful, are not likely to prove a very substantial defence against this kind of spirit about which we have had so many and such clear warnings since April 1933. R. F. Wigram. 8/10.' Mr. Eden rejoined: 'I do not think that we have any of us any illusions as to the difficulties inherent in the Locarno negotiations, but they keep the door open, should it happen that Germany's economic difficulties dispose her to talk. I agree that we have no time to lose in our re-armament & said so in Cabinet again last week. A. E. Oct. 18th.'

No. 234

Foreign Office to Mr. Edmond (Geneva)
No. 5 Saving: Telegraphic [*W 12112/9549/41*]

FOREIGN OFFICE, *September 24, 1936, 11.30 a.m.*

Following for British Delegation.

Committee on Non-Intervention in Spain.

At yesterday's meeting of Chairman's Sub-Committee[1] Italian Representative raised question of inviting one or more non-European countries to adhere to Agreement. In a note circulated to Sub-Committee, United Kingdom Representative pointed out that such extension might be considered either (1) in respect of all countries outside Europe or (2) restricted to one or more on basis to be laid down. Such basis might be either principal arms-producing countries, for example, United States and Japan, or alternatively countries believed to be sending or intending to send raw material to Spain.

As regards (1) United Kingdom Government were anxious that question should be dealt with on practical lines and from this point of view were disposed to think it would be difficult within reasonable period of time to obtain universal adherence. As regards (2) they were doubtful whether the United States Government had power to prohibit export of arms to Spain or could obtain power to do so in the near future. It seemed probable in any case that they would decline to take any positive step in associating themselves publicly with any course of action relating to question which was primary and immediate concern of only European countries. Alternative basis would seem to place on shoulders of Committee most delicate and invidious task of selection. For above reasons United Kingdom Government would in principle not favour proposal to invite non-European Governments to adhere to Agreement. They would nevertheless be willing to consider any suggestion made with regard to special cases.

Italian Representative urged interest expressed already by Mexican Legation as ground for inviting Mexico.

It was agreed that Members of Sub-Committee should consult their Governments and resume discussion of this question at later meeting.

If Mexican case is pressed, Lord Plymouth proposes to point out attitude already publicly declared by Mexican Government towards the Civil War and to deprecate despatch of invitation unless they were unofficially sounded beforehand and favourable reply seemed probable.

[1] See No. 225. This telegram was drafted on September 23.

No. 235

Mr. Edmond (Geneva) to Foreign Office (Received September 25, 9.30 a.m.)
No. 123 Telegraphic [*W 12095/9549/41*]

GENEVA, *September 24, 1936, 11.30 p.m.*

Following from Secretary of State.

My telegram No. 116.[1]

I had a further conversation with M. Monteiro this evening at which he informed me that the statement contained in my telegram No. 117[2] had encountered objections from the Portuguese Government, and though he professed to be unaware of their nature I gathered that it did not go far enough to satisfy Portuguese opinion. M. Monteiro asked whether it was not possible to authorize him to publish the ruling adopted by the Committee and communicated to him in my letter of September 22nd.

I replied that the Committee had agreed to treat its proceedings as strictly confidential and that I could not give him for publication more than was contained in the *communiqué* issued by the Committee to the Press on September 21st.

This did not appear to satisfy M. Monteiro and I put it to him strongly that the wording of the proposed statement to the Press gave the Portuguese Government all they could reasonably require.

M. Monteiro then took exception to the attitude of the French Press and to the reports of pressure which was being put on the Portuguese Government. He said that in view of my letter the Portuguese Government had no objection in principle to joining the Committee, but they must be able to make some statement which would satisfy their public opinion that they had not yielded to pressure.

I propose to reconsider the statement from this point of view but the impression made by the conversation is not encouraging.

Repeated to Lisbon.

<hr>

[1] See No. 216, note 3.   [2] No. 222.

No. 236

Mr. Ogilvie-Forbes (Madrid) to Foreign Office (Received September 24)
No. 245 Telegraphic [*W 12040/62/41*]

Important   MADRID, *September 24, 1936*

In view of the explicit instructions contained in your telegram No. 80[1] of September 5th, not to jeopardise unduly the safety of the regular staff of the Embassy and Consulate I consider that the position here in the immediate future will not justify the retention of the remaining staff namely

<hr>

[1] See No. 150, note 5: cf. No. 176.

Milanes, Unwin and Julia[2] latter of whom in case of accident would leave a wife and five children without support. I am therefore planning to evacuate them either by rail or car to Valencia or Alicante and to close the Consulate here.

As soon as the critical period in which we have already entered is over I shall have them back. Above may have some influence on the decision taken in your telegram No. 135[3] of September 23rd.

As regards the Embassy nothing has so far shaken me from the conviction expressed in my telegram No. 158[4] of September 8th. I am sure that my presence here with volunteers who in all events must stay in Madrid at their own risk will do nothing but good. See my immediately following telegram.[5]

[2] Señor Julia apparently held the rank of temporary pro-consul at Madrid.
[3] Not preserved in the Foreign Office archives.
[4] In this telegram Mr. Ogilvie-Forbes had reported on the general situation as it affected the Embassy, and concluded that for the time being the wisest and most honourable course to adopt was to stay on quietly at the Embassy if and when a storm came. Foreign Office telegram No. 106 of September 14 agreed that he should remain at Madrid 'for the present'.
[5] This telegram, No. 246 of September 24, explained that he was seeking by quiet and prudent action to forestall the dangers likely to follow a sudden bolt of the government from Madrid.

No. 237

Mr. Newton (Berlin) to Foreign Office (Received September 25)
No. 254 Saving: Telegraphic [C 6725/4/18]

BERLIN, *September 24, 1936*

My immediately preceding telegram.[1]

From conversation which the French Chargé d'Affaires had with official of Ministry of Foreign Affairs who inspired this article he understands that its main purpose was to tranquillize Italy. It was feared in Germany that Sir S. Hoare's speech and British activities in the Mediterranean might prejudice the prospect of Italian participation in the proposed conference. French Chargé d'Affaires who was at first doubtful is therefore now inclined to believe in German Government's genuine desire for Western Pact if obtainable without involving Russia.

Repeated to Geneva.

[1] Telegram No. 253 Saving of September 24 gave the substance of an article in the *Deutsche diplomatisch-politische Korrespondenz* commenting on Sir S. Hoare's speech regarding British policy in the Mediterranean (see No. 226) and welcoming his statement that 'the securing of the British position in the Mediterranean is directed against no one in particular'.

No. 238

Mr. Ogilvie-Forbes (Madrid) to Foreign Office
(Received September 25, 4.45 p.m.)
No. 249 Telegraphic [W 12167/62/41]

Important   MADRID, *September 25, 1936, 1.35 p.m.*

My telegram No. 245[1] and your telegram No. 80.[2]

Acting Consul and Mrs. Milanes have for private reasons as well as others approached me with a view to being allowed to stay on in Madrid. They understand position and have promised not to make any claim against His Majesty's Government in unlikely event of an accident. Mrs. Milanes is financially independent, a voluntary worker in the Chancery and an employee of Rio Tinto whose present employees are staying on. They have no dependants. The risk of a political incident against Acting Consul as such is very slight and I can always suspend activities of Consulate at will.

I much admire the spirit shown by Mr. and Mrs. Milanes and I am prepared to agree, against a written indenture, if you approve.

Please telegraph reply as soon as possible.[3]

[1] No. 236.
[2] See No. 150, note 5.
[3] Foreign Office telegram No. 148 of September 29 said that Mr. Eden agreed subject to the conditions laid down by Mr. Ogilvie-Forbes in the above telegram.

No. 239

Mr. Edmond (Geneva) to Foreign Office (Received September 29)
No. 72 [C 6787/4/18]

GENEVA, *September 25, 1936*

The United Kingdom delegate to the League of Nations presents his compliments, and has the honour to transmit copy of a record of a conversation between Sir W. Malkin and M. van Zuylen[1] on the 22nd September, respecting the revision of the Treaty of Locarno.

ENCLOSURE IN No. 239

Record of a conversation between Sir W. Malkin and M. van Zuylen

GENEVA, *September 23, 1936*

Monsieur van Zuylen of the Belgian Ministry of Foreign Affairs asked to see me about the French note of September 16th[2] about the revision of the Treaty of Locarno, and accordingly I had a talk with him and Monsieur van Langenhove, the Secretary-General of the Ministry, yesterday evening. The main points which emerged from our conversation were as follows.

[1] Political Director of the Belgian Ministry for Foreign Affairs.
[2] See No. 202.

They expressed considerable admiration for the note which they had received from us[3] and said that their reply would be quite short because they were in agreement with us on practically all the points mentioned. They were, I think, obviously pleased and perhaps somewhat relieved that we were not asking for a guarantee from Belgium.

As regards paragraph 3 of the French note, they said that they had been having some semi-official conversations with the Dutch Government and that the latter were disposed to come into the new arrangement, provided (a) that it was of a strictly reciprocal character so that there would be no question of Holland going into a particular camp, and (b) that Holland was not asked to give a guarantee to anybody. The Belgian Government attach great importance to getting Holland into the new arrangement on these lines, and it appeared that the French would be ready to agree. I suggested (bearing in mind that the position of Belgium under the proposed arrangement might be much the same as that of Holland) that in that case the Dutch contribution would consist of an undertaking to defend their own territories and not to allow them to be used for the purpose of an attack upon another signatory, and the Belgians agreed that this would apparently be so.

As regards paragraph 4 of the French note they said that from the strategic point of view the question of Luxemburg was of much more importance to France than to Belgium, and their attitude to this passage in the French note might be described as being a 'point d'interrogation'.

Paragraph 5 of the French note refers to a guarantee of 'l'inviolabilité des frontières de leurs possessions et dependances'. The Belgians were as puzzled as I was as to whether the French really intended that all the colonial possessions of the parties should be covered by the new arrangement, which in that case could certainly no longer be described as a Rhineland or even a Western European Pact. It is a point that will require clearing up.

The Belgians are naturally preoccupied, as indeed we are, to know what is the nature of the French proposals as regards the situation where Germany had attacked Poland, Czechoslovakia or Russia, and France went to the assistance of the country attacked under her mutual assistance arrangements with it. In such circumstances the Belgians' desire, like ours, is that we should be under no obligation to intervene on one side or the other. This was the position under Locarno and we all were disposed to agree that there was nothing in the French note which suggested that the French desired the situation to be different under the new arrangement; but it is obviously a point which will require careful watching.

It was pretty clear that the Belgians did not expect that it would be possible to make any arrangement as regards the restriction or limitation of fortifications in the demilitarised zone.

Apart from the above considerations there did not seem to the Belgians to be anything very new or startling in the French note. They however expressed some preoccupation as to what would happen in the event of the

[3] Enclosure in No. 206.

Conference breaking down on the point of France's arrangements in Eastern Europe; in that event, were we to abandon the idea of doing anything, or were we to arrange a 'second best'? Curiously enough they did not intimate that in those circumstances our letter of April 1st[4] would become operative, but it seems clear that they would wish to press in that event for some arrangements on the lines there contemplated.[5]

H. W. MALKIN

[4] See Volume XVI, Enclosure 2 in No. 199.
[5] For M. van Zuylen's account of this conversation see *D.D.B.*, *op. cit.*, No. 120.

No. 240

Mr. D. MacKillop[1] *(Moscow) to Foreign Office*
(Received September 26, 1.50 p.m.)
No. 146 Telegraphic [W 12262/9549/41]

MOSCOW, September 26, 1936, 1.43 p.m.

Geneva telegram No. 125.[2]
'Pravda' today refers critically to work of [Non-Intervention] Committee saying that its time has been mainly taken up by talk in which an attempt has been made to smother any concrete proposition tending to establish facts of intervention by Fascist Governments which are continuing to afford military help to insurgents. This inactivity is held by 'Pravda' to be the more striking in that a Committee consisting of a number of British Members of Parliament and others have, it is alleged, publicly produced material proofs which they are said to have obtained in Spain of supplies of war material to Spanish insurgents by Germany and Italy.[3]

[1] Chargé d'Affaires in H.M. Embassy at Moscow.
[2] See No. 241, note 1 below.
[3] Minutes on this telegram indicate that this 'must be Dame Eleanor Rathbone's committee' which had 'never communicated with the F.O.' but was understood to be in 'full sympathy with the Spanish Government'. See No. 270, note 5 below. Miss Rathbone was the Independent M.P. for the Combined English Universities.

No. 241

Mr. Edmond (Geneva) to Foreign Office
(Received September 27, 5.35 p.m.)
No. 128 L.N. Telegraphic [W 12272/9549/41]

GENEVA, September 27, 1936, 4.25 p.m.

Following from Secretary of State.
My telegram No. 125.[1]
In view of paramount importance of early participation of Portugal in the work of Committee on non-intervention and of assent of overwhelming

[1] In this telegram of September 26 Mr. Eden referred to No. 235, and said that after

najority of members of Committee, Mr. Morrison has today[2] decided to
ommunicate to Portuguese Government conclusions adopted by Committee
s to procedure to be followed on the receipt of complaints respecting
lleged breaches.[3]

In deciding to proceed without waiting any longer for a reply from the
talian Government Mr. Morrison has been influenced by the opinion which
ıe has formed of the desire of Italian representative on Committee to
ecure participation of Portugal in its work.[4]

Repeated to Lisbon.

eeing M. Monteiro again on September 25, Mr. Morrison had received assurances that a
'ortuguese representative would attend the next meeting of the N.I. Committee and sub-
ommittee on September 28 if Mr. Morrison would in the meantime communicate to him
ɔr publication the text of the rules adopted by the committee for dealing with alleged
ıfractions of the non-intervention agreement. The Portuguese Government must, he said,
ıave something to satisfy their public opinion'.

[2] This telegram was drafted on September 26.
[3] This was done in a letter from Mr. Morrison to M. Monteiro of September 26: the
ɔnclusions were those in Section IV of No. 204.
[4] In a letter to Mr. Morrison of September 27, M. Monteiro thanked him for his letter and
aid that as 'the rules of procedure adopted answer the doubts which I had formulated, I
ɪn happy to inform you that a representative of my country will take part in the next
ıeeting of the Committee . . .' This letter was published after being read out at the fourth
ıeeting of the N.I. Committee on September 28. The Portuguese Chargé d'Affaires in
ɔondon, Senhor Francisco de Calheiros e Menezes, was present at this meeting. Foreign
Ɔffice telegram No. 101 of September 28 to Geneva said that the N.I. Committee at its
ıeeting that evening had 'expressed satisfaction at result of negotiations in Geneva'.

No. 242

Mr. Edmond (Geneva) to Foreign Office
(Received September 29, 9.30 a.m.)
No. 131 Telegraphic [C 6785/49/55]

GENEVA, *September 29, 1936, 12.5 a.m.*

Following from Secretary of State.

I lunched with M. Beck this afternoon and in the course of conversation
vhich ensued Polish Minister for Foreign Affairs spoke at some length of
ommunity of interests of our two countries in the present day Europe.
Ie argued that we were both of us opposed to 'les guerres de religion'
vhich constituted principal peril we had to meet. Poland situated between
Nazi Germany and Communist U.S.S.R. was particularly conscious of its
eriousness.

After some further conversation M. Beck asked me whether I thought
t would be possible for him to come to London later in the autumn in order
o talk over with me Danzig affairs and European situation generally. In
view of repeated invitations which had been extended to M. Beck and as
requently postponed I felt I had no alternative but to say we should of

course be delighted to see M. Beck at any time that he cared to come One difficulty however we had to bear in mind, and that was likelihood of a meeting of Five Power Conference. We ought to consider whether it was preferable from the point of view of international relations in general for Polish visit to take place before or after the Five Power Conference. With out having deeply considered the matter myself I thought the latter would probably be safer in view of suspicions that might be aroused in certain quarters by any other order of events. M. Beck whose face fell somewhat at my observation did not however contest it and agreed that we would consider at a later conversation the problem of dates. He added that if I considered there were any international reasons why his visit should not take place he begged me to say so since because of the present serious state of Europe no personal considerations could weigh in comparison with international responsibilities we had each of us to carry. At the same time it was clear that M. Beck was anxious to pay this visit to London perhaps in part as a make-weight to General Ridz Smigley's [sic] visit to Paris.[1] It is even possible that this desire of the Polish Minister for Foreign Affairs to pay a visit to London may be of assistance to me in making progress with Danzig problem which despite many weary hours of negotiation looks at present as intractable as ever.[2]

Repeated to Warsaw.

[1] See No. 144, note 5.
[2] Cf. No. 144. Mr. Lester, League High Commissioner for Danzig, had submitted a general report on the position of the Free City to the League Council on September 12 see L/N.O.J., op. cit., pp. 1359–62. The Committee of Three (see No. 144, note 1) reported to the Council on October 5, and drawing attention to Mr. Lester's report, recommended that the Council invite the Polish Government 'to seek, on behalf of the Council, the means of putting an end to the situation described in the general report of the High Commissioner and thus of rendering fully effective the guarantee of the League of Nations'. This resolution was adopted, and negotiations were also set in motion to find a successor for Mr Lester to enable him to take up an appointment as Deputy Secretary General of the League. See L/N.O.J., op. cit., pp. 1190–2.

No. 243

Mr. Hillgarth (Palma) to Foreign Office
(Received September 30, 4.45 a.m.)

Unnumbered telegraphic: by wireless [W 12501/62/41]

Secret   PALMA, September 29, 1936

Addressed Admiralty, repeated C. in C. Mediterranean.

Following for Secretary of State.

In present condition of Spain it cannot be possible for any British Diplomatic or Consular Officer to express an authoritative opinion on more than the district under his immediate observation. Balearic Islands have a recognised strategic importance and have hitherto been distinctly anglophil. Owing to Italian intervention feeling is becoming anglophobe. When the noment comes it is imperative here that Great Britain should be if possible irst to recognise Government of insurgents. Priority over France and Italy f over no one else is essential. Theoretical considerations involving delay vill be mis-interpreted. France has already given semi-official recognition ocally[1] and according to reliable information will not wait our co-operation vhen complete recognition is inevitable.[2]

[1] In a further report of October 9 by wireless via the Admiralty Mr. Hillgarth explained his statement by saying that on September 13 the French Rear Admiral Ollive paid ·fficial calls on all insurgent authorities at Palma and gave an official luncheon on board the ˙rench cruiser *Colbert* to the authorities. This was 'interpreted by insurgents as semi-ıfficial recognition locally'.

[2] Mr. Hillgarth's reference to the possibility of the early recognition by Italy and possibly ›y France of the government of the insurgents generated a prolonged discussion in the ˙oreign Office as to the timing of, and terms of, a declaration of recognition by His Majesty's ჳovernment. In September a draft proclamation of neutrality in the war had been drawn ιp by the Foreign Office in consultation with the Law Officers of the Crown, but not issued W 11520/9549/41). Minutes on file W 12501/62/41 by Mr. Roberts (September 30), Mr. .V. E. Beckett (October 1), and Sir G. Mounsey (October 1), led to agreement that, if ›olitically desirable, the rebels could be recognized as belligerents at once, but that their ›osition was not such as to allow their recognition as the government of Spain 'either now, ·r probably for some time to come'. A further round of minuting (October 10 to 14) led o agreement on a proposal by Mr. W. E. Beckett, Second Legal Adviser, of October 13 hat the proposal to issue a proclamation of neutrality should be dropped and a statement ıssued instead 'by His Majesty's Government in the United Kingdom indicating how they ˙iew the position and what they propose to do'. The statement would recognize the fact that ĥe insurgents had succeeded in establishing their control over parts of Spain but that the ıituation did not justify recognition of General Franco's government as the government of ჳpain. It would state that this attitude was consistent with, and involved, the continuance ·f the policy of non-intervention. 'It would . . . mean our dissociating ourselves somewhat ĥarply from the attitude of Germany and Italy, but this seems unavoidable.' A marginal ·omment by Mr. Eden here read, 'and perhaps not a bad thing. A. E.' It was agreed to ·ay nothing in the statement as to whether after this degree of recognition belligerent rights ·t sea could be denied. The text of the draft statement is printed as an Appendix to No. 344 ›elow.

No. 244

Foreign Office to Mr. Edmond (Geneva)
No. 102 Telegraphic [W 12598/9549/41]

FOREIGN OFFICE, *September 29, 1936, 5 p.m.*

Following for Secretary of State from Parliamentary Under Secretary.[1]

At meeting yesterday of Chairman's sub-committee on non-intervention ong discussion, resulting in a deadlock, ranged round the question of ndirect intervention.

This question, which formed the object of precise reservations by the ჳerman, Italian and Portuguese Governments to their original acceptance ›f the non-intervention agreement, had been raised at the previous meeting[2]

[1] i.e. the Earl of Plymouth, who had succeeded Mr. Morrison as Chairman of the N.I. ჳommittee. [2] See No. 225.

by the Italian Delegate and willingness to discuss the matter was expressed by all the representatives on the sub-committee except that of the U.S.S.R. The latter maintained that indirect intervention was not within the four corners of the original non-intervention agreement and that therefore the sub-committee was not competent to discuss it. If there were a general desire to discuss it, the matter should be taken up direct between the Governments concerned.

Vigorous attempts were made by all delegates including the chairman to induce the Soviet representative to modify his attitude, but it was clear that he was bound by his instructions.

The German and Italian representatives are not likely much longer to acquiesce in delay and it is clear that, if the work and perhaps even the existence of the Committee is not to be endangered, it is of the utmost importance that some way should be found of enabling the Soviet representative to take part in a discussion of this thorny problem. I, therefore, submit for your consideration the desirability of your speaking to M. Litvinov[3] on the subject.

I understand from the French Ambassador that he is telegraphing in a similar sense to the French delegation at Geneva.

[3] Soviet Foreign Minister. See No. 251 below.

No. 245

Mr. Edmond (Geneva) to Foreign Office
(Received September 30, 9.30 a.m.)
No. 135 L.N. Telegraphic [W 12544/62/41]

GENEVA, *September 29, 1936, 11.45 p.m.*

Addressed to Madrid No. 1.
Your telegram No. 8 to Geneva.[1]
Lord Halifax spoke to Spanish Minister for Foreign Affairs on September 28th and told him that His Majesty's Government were greatly disturbed at continuance of excesses in Madrid of which they had reliable information. He asked him to do whatever he could to check such unhappy events.

Señor del Vayo evinced some surprise but did not attempt any denial. He said that he would telephone to Madrid and report to Lord Halifax any information he could obtain. Later he informed Lord Halifax that he had telephoned to Madrid and that although there might have been 'some anxiety on Sunday' his information was that now 'everything was quiet'.

Lord Halifax told him that our anxiety did not relate to the events of

[1] In this telegram of September 25 (No. 252 to the Foreign Office) Mr. Ogilvie-Forbes reported that there had been a considerable increase in the number of private murders, followed also by open robbery, during the previous two weeks. He asked whether representations could be made to the Spanish Minister of State on humanitarian grounds and in order to prevent the killing of non-combatants.

any particular day and urged him again to express to his Government how strongly British opinion felt upon the humanitarian side. He said that Minister of Home Affairs would discuss situation with you today.

Lord Halifax derived impression that Spanish Minister for Foreign Affairs was not in close touch with what was happening.

Repeated to the Foreign Office.

No. 246

Mr. Edmond (Geneva) to Foreign Office (Received October 1)
No. 65 Saving: Telegraphic [W 12667/62/41]

GENEVA, *September 29, 1936*

Following from Secretary of State.

Spanish Minister for Foreign Affairs came to see me on September 24th when he spoke at some length on the civil war in Spain. He began by assuring me of desire of Spanish Government to protect British interests. In thanking His Excellency for that assurance I added that I thought a large section of British opinion were at the moment concerned not so much for British interests in Spain in respect of which they felt sure that they could look for the full support of the Spanish Government as for the savagery of the civil war which was now being waged. This led M. del Vayo to attempt to justify the attitude of Government forces. In this respect he maintained that the executions in Madrid which he admitted had been numerous at the outset of the civil war were now comparatively rare events.[1] The difficulty at first had been that the greater part of the Army and Police had been on the side of the rebels and the Government had had to improvise militia and police.

Rest of Spanish Minister for Foreign Affairs' plea was directed to showing that a policy of non-intervention militated against the Spanish Government. I gave His Excellency however no encouragement to think that His Majesty's Government would modify their policy in this respect. In order to prove to me the extent to which the German and Italian Governments were violating non-intervention agreement M. del Vayo left with me certain documents and photographs which are enclosed in my despatch No. 85.[2]

[1] A marginal note by Mr. A. C. E. Malcolm, who had been Third Secretary in H.M. Embassy at Madrid, here read: 'i.e. about 60 a night. Two days after he spoke, 125 were killed.' Cf. No. 252 below. He also remarked in a minute of October 3: 'The Spanish Government, knowing they can't control the assassins, can only assert there are no assassins to control.' Cf. No. 245.

[2] Not printed: cf. No. 265 below.

No. 247

Sir H. Chilton (Hendaye) to Foreign Office (Received October 2)
No. 693 [W 12637/62/41]*

HENDAYE, *September 29, 1936*

Sir,

I have the honour to transmit herewith a report by Mr. Stevenson, His Majesty's consul at Bilbao, on a recent visit which he paid to Gijon, which shows the terrible conditions existing in that town.

I have, &c.,

H. G. CHILTON

ENCLOSURE IN No. 247

Mr. R. C. Stevenson to Sir H. Chilton

BILBAO, *September 25, 1936*

Sir,

I have the honour to report that yesterday, the 24th instant, I landed at Gijon, in the Province of Asturias, in the company of Captain H. M. Burrough, Royal Navy, Captain (D), Fifth Destroyer Flotilla, and Colonel G. F. Beaumont-Nesbitt, M.C., military attaché at Madrid.

2. As we approached the quay, swarms of ill-clad men, women and children ran to meet us, and we had to appeal for elbow- and leg-room to enable us to climb the steps up to the quay. Our first move was to call on the captain of the port who happened to be absent in Aviles. His assistant received us, and although somewhat taken aback at our visit, he soon recovered, and with ready tongue and in the best tradition of the Moscow 'window dressers' gave us an account of the orderly conditions and the high moral [*sic*] obtaining in his city. We, on our side, explained that we had recently come out from England via Saint-Jean-de-Luz, and feigned keen interest in all he had to say.

3. In the course of conversation he referred to the many military successes of the Government forces on all fronts in Spain. He dwelt at length on the fighting in Gijon itself after the outbreak of hostilities, and told us how, after a siege lasting a whole month, the barracks, held by a regiment of Cazadores, were stormed and 700 defenders put to the sword. The capture of these barracks had cost 600 lives on the side of the 'loyalists.' These statements, we subsequently learned from another source, were somewhat exaggerated, there having been actually over 100 survivors among the defenders, whose lives were spared on their accepting service with the Government colours.

4. The port official also discoursed on the administration of the city. He made no secret of the fact that this was based on the Soviet principle. Public affairs were being managed by a Junta of popular representatives drawn from the various parties. The recollection of the February election results and of reports of the civil disorder and of rioting in Gijon during the

six months preceding hostilities will leave no doubt in your Excellency's mind as to the composition of this body.

5. We now felt it was time to put a few questions, and, by way of a feeler, enquired after the captain of the port, in office up to the 20th July, who had been removed from his post. Replies were evasive at first, but information was eventually given that he was held in preventive custody and that he was alive. We next questioned our interlocutor about the consular corps, and were told that most consuls had left Gijon, but that the Belgian and Cuban, both Spaniards, were still in residence. As to the German, he had also left. Here we expressed a desire to call on the Belgian consul, but were told that this was unnecessary, as he could be sent for. We declined this offer and insisted on being given his address, whereupon a telephone call was put through to his office, whence information was received that he had left for his home in the village of Somo. Regrets were expressed that he could not now be reached, as his residence some miles away was not on the telephone. We pressed our point, and were eventually promised a car to take our party to Somo. An hour was lost waiting for the car, which was not surprising, having regard to the stress and chaos under which every administrative order has to be carried out. At length we set off at 7.30 p.m., accompanied by a militiaman, and after satisfying two armed control posts as to our identity, reached the Belgian consul's house half-an-hour later, only to find that he was not expected home until the following morning.

6. We interviewed his wife without gaining any information owing to her manifest fear of possible consequences. In reply to our questions she declared that she did not know where he would be spending the night. We had already taken our leave and were about to depart when she called me aside, and hesitatingly told me that her husband was persecuted and at that moment in hiding with the German consul, who was living in a village some miles away. We hurriedly conferred and decided to call on the German, and, as neither our chauffeur nor our militiaman knew the road and thought it would be difficult to find the house at night, we took her with us as guide, leaving the militiaman behind.

7. We duly reached our next objective with the help of some F.A.I. men (Federación Anarquista Ibérica), who were displaying the Anarchist colours—black and red—on their car. There we found both the German and Belgian consuls and spent nearly an hour with them listening to a tale of incredible happenings in Gijon. It appears that soon after the outbreak of hostilities hundreds of persons of both sexes and all ages, suspected of being 'Right wing' people, and in many cases guilty of no other crime than that they habitually wear collar and tie, found themselves arrested, arraigned before a popular tribunal and, after the pretence of a trial, executed.

Our informants estimated that up to date there must have been at least 500 victims, and that 1,000 might not be an exaggerated figure. They thought that the number of hostages still awaiting trial exceeded 1,000, and believed that executions were still taking place daily.

8. Another form of terror raging in Gijon is that practised by the F.A.I.

operating on the 'Cheka-cum-Chicago gangster' system. These men, representing the worst type of human specie, commit the most execrable crimes in the name of liberty and progress. Their method is to lay information against hapless members of the *bourgeoisie* obtained through, or manufactured by, spies and *agents provocateurs*, who call on their victims at dead of night, drag them from their beds, and either murder them on the spot or take them for a 'ride,' leaving their dead bodies on the roadside. In this way whole families are said to have been wiped out, either singly or together. It requires little imagination to conjure before the mind's eye a picture of the cruelty and suffering, physical and mental, to which innocent men, women and children are subjected in Gijon.

9. Economically, too, Gijon offers an interesting spectacle. Property and industry are socialised, banking is abolished, the function of capital and money is suspended, and workers receive tickets for food and services in lieu of money wages. In short, the economic system, as we conceive it, has ceased to function.

10. A cause of anxiety to the Junta and the populace generally is the acute food shortage. Oils, fats, meat and flour are strictly rationed and dispensed once a week only. Our informants anticipate that, unless this problem is solved before winter sets in, Gijon will offer another example of the revolution devouring its own children.

11. The vice-consulate at Gijon was closed early in August, since when no reports have been received from that city. I have therefore ventured to set down at some length and in considerable detail our impressions and the incidents related to us, and I trust that my account of our visit will be of interest to your Excellency.[1]

I have, &c.,
R. C. STEVENSON

[1] In minutes on this letter Mr. Roberts wrote: 'Making full allowance for exaggeration on the part of the Belgian and German consuls [cf. paragraph 7] this is a grim picture. It is just as well that Mr. Lovelace and his family are safely in this country. W. R. 6/10.' Sir R. Vansittart wrote: 'We need not boggle about figures. There is no reason to doubt the general accuracy of Mr. Stevenson's experience. It is typical of what has been going on everywhere in Spain. R. V. Oct. 9.' The appointment of Mr. J. M. R. Lovelace, acting Vice-Consul at Gijon, had been terminated on the closing of his post on August 9, 1936.

No. 248

Sir E. Phipps (Berlin) to Foreign Office (Received October 1)
No. 264 Saving: Telegraphic [C 6815/4/18]

BERLIN, September 30, 1936

I hear from an excellent source that although the Chancellor's dislike of a Conference has not been overcome, he regards our memorandum of 17th September[1] as a distinct advance. The other Nazi leaders are in no

[1] Enclosure in No. 206.

hurry, as Herr Hess puts it, to send the German fly to confer with the four spiders.

If a new Locarno Agreement can be reached without the inclusion of other Powers or extraneous matter, Herr Hitler is not disposed to make the Franco-Russian Treaty or Czech-Russian relations a stumbling block. So far he refuses to fix the date for Herr von Ribbentrop's departure.[2] The latter, for his part, is in no hurry lest on his arrival in London he may be pressed by all and sundry to bring Germany to the Conference table. He fears that his disinclination to press the Chancellor might alienate his British friends.[3]

The action of the three Governments in connection with the franc came as a severe blow. The highest Nazi circles have always been convinced that no democracy could act with secrecy and that cooperation between the three Powers in question was a thing of the past. The fact that three democratic Governments have been able to spring a surprise on the world came as a most unpleasant surprise to them.[4]

The internal situation, notably the food difficulties and the shortage of foreign currency, is preoccupying the Chancellor. His veteran supporters have been very obstreperous of late. They regard the decision to double the military service as a dangerous concession to the army. They have confidence in General von Blomberg, but in none of his colleagues.

[2] Cf. Nos. 55 and 59.

[3] This part of the telegram led to some minuting about tactics in bringing Germany to the conference table. Mr. Baxter (October 1) wrote that if 'we find that the Germans are guilty of undue delay, we shall have to take a very firm line with them . . . if the Western Pact is not going to be achieved, the sooner we know it the better'. Mr. Wigram however (October 1) was certain that 'if we go on pushing the Germans to agree to this new Locarno, we shall be asked to pay them for doing so . . . What tangible advantage, from the point of view of our interests, will the treaty represent to us? I find it difficult to see. Why then not leave the Germans to make the running from now on?' Mr. Sargent (October 2) entirely agreed with this view. The only danger he could see of a long delay was that France 'might use this as an excuse to call upon us to bring our letter of April 1st [Volume XVI, Enclosure 2 in No. 199] into force . . . But at present I see no indication of this'. He also remarked that 'Russia is working as hard as she can to prevent the conclusion of a new Locarno'. Sir R. Vansittart wrote on October 2 that any show of *empressement* would be poor tactics. 'I hope we shall *pay* nothing for an agreement that is problematical both as to signature & value: it will be worthless until it has proved its worth in practice. And I hope that we shall insist on a settlement in Central Europe.' After his return to London, Mr. Eden commented on October 8: 'But we are parties to two *communiqués*, both agreed in London, one in July [Volume XVI, No. 476] & one in April. These represent the policy of H.M.G.'

[4] It had been announced in Paris at 1.10 a.m. on September 26 that the franc was to be devalued to 107 to the pound, that an exchange stabilization fund of 10,000 m. francs was to be set up, and that the British, United States, and French Governments would use their available resources to avoid any disturbance of the exchanges that might result from the readjustment. The text of the declaration by the United Kingdom Government to this effect is printed in *L/N.O.J.*, *S.S. No. 157*, p. 101. The French crisis had arisen in part from the working of the exchange equalization systems of the British and United States Governments, which depended on a free market in gold in which the two funds could operate. There had been a flight from the franc after the German reoccupation of the

Rhineland, and again after M. Blum's accession to office in June. The value of co-operation was speedily illustrated on September 26, when the Soviet State Bank offered £1,000,000 for sale in New York and Mr. Morgenthau, U.S. Secretary of State to the Treasury, promptly bought the amount out of the U.S. stabilization fund. The Soviet aim in making the sale may have been a routine protection of its own position, but an attempt to drive down the pound sterling was suspected. Cf. *F.R.U.S.*, *1936*, vol. i, pp. 539–61; *D.D.F.*, *op. cit.*, Nos. 240, 246, 288.

No. 249

Mr. Edmond (Geneva) to Foreign Office (Received October 3)
No. 96 [C 6880/4/18]

GENEVA, *September 30, 1936*

The United Kingdom delegate to the League of Nations presents his compliments, and has the honour to transmit copies of a record of a conversation between Mr. Eden and M. Spaak on the 28th September, respecting the Locarno conversations, of which a copy has been sent to His Majesty's Ambassador, Brussels.

ENCLOSURE IN No. 249

Record of a conversation between Mr. Eden and M. Spaak

GENEVA, *September 28, 1936*

1. I had a conversation this evening with Monsieur Spaak, the Belgian Foreign Minister, who asked me whether I could give him any information as to the present position and prospects of the Five-Power meeting. He had heard some pessimistic reports which his own information did not seem to justify, and this had made him particularly anxious to obtain authentic information. I gave Monsieur Spaak some account of recent developments which I said led me to agree with him that while there were still plenty of obstacles to be overcome there seemed to me to be no grounds for excessive pessimism at present.

2. Monsieur Spaak said that he had carefully studied the memorandum[1] which we had sent to him stating our views as to the method we proposed for facilitating the progress of negotiations through the diplomatic channel. The Belgian Government were in entire agreement with those suggestions. They were, however, by no means so completely in agreement with the document submitted by the French Government,[2] and Monsieur Spaak asked me whether I intended to return any reply to this. I said that I had not yet had time to give any detailed study to the French document and that I did not expect to be able to do this until I arrived back in London. I would then consider whether the document was of a character that called for a reply. My own impression was that the French Government had stated that it was for our information, and I supposed for that of the

[1] See Enclosure in No. 206.   [2] See No. 202.

Belgian Government also, but that it had not been communicated to the other signatories of the Locarno Treaty. Monsieur Spaak said that this was so. In the circumstances I added, the document was hardly in the same category as our memorandum which had been submitted to all the signatories with a view to furthering progress, and it would perhaps be a pity if in this early stage of our diplomatic negotiations there were already two sets of proposals in existence. With this opinion Monsieur Spaak declared himself to be in complete agreement.

3. The Belgian Foreign Minister then asked me whether I had had any conversation with the Dutch Government as to their participation in a new Western Pact. I replied that I had not, whereupon Monsieur Spaak said that he had had some exchange of views with the Dutch Minister at Brussels, which had been followed up by some conversation with Monsieur de Graeff[3] himself at Geneva within the last few days. From this it appeared that the position of Holland was that she was willing to be guaranteed, but that she did not wish to be a signatory of the projected Treaty. Monsieur Spaak commented that this seemed to him to be hardly a tenable position, and he thought it likely that in due course the Dutch would move from it and be willing to sign a treaty by which their territory was guaranteed as long as they were not asked to guarantee others.

4. In this connexion the Belgian Foreign Minister expressed his gratitude that in our proposals we had not suggested that Belgium should guarantee Great Britain. As he understood our position we did not ask Belgium for such a guarantee, but we did expect her to insist upon respect of her neutrality, both by land and by air. I replied that this was the position. Monsieur Spaak expressed the earnest hope that it might be the position of the French Government also, for if Belgium had further to increase her armaments and her length of military service, both of which he feared would be necessary in the near future, it would be greatly facilitated if she were not asked to guarantee France. It was impossible to deny that unfortunately there was a certain anti-French feeling in Belgium. A graceful gesture by France, such as we had made in our proposals, while it could have no deep political significance, would be of the greatest assistance in promoting Belgian national unity in support of a national foreign policy, it would be all the better if Belgium and Holland could eventually be in the pact on the same terms.

5. I understood from Monsieur Spaak that he had made some progress with the French Government in conversation on this subject, though the latter appeared to have certain apprehensions as to the consequences of Belgium not guaranteeing France. He himself thought these misapprehensions misplaced, since France stood to gain if she only were attacked by Germany, for her own narrow frontier was heavily defended.

6. I asked Monsieur Spaak what was his view as to the problem of Luxembourg which had been raised in the French memorandum. He replied that he did not consider that the matter had any political significance.

3 Netherlands Foreign Minister.

Luxembourg's position was unchanged in this respect by the violation of the demilitarised zone. The question was purely a military one and should be considered on that basis.

7. Finally the Belgian Foreign Minister stated that he had the impression from conversations which he had had with certain members of the French delegation in the last few days that relations between France and Soviet Russia were now a little less close than they had been a month or two ago. This fact seemed to give Monsieur Spaak some satisfaction even though he is a Socialist.

ANTHONY EDEN

No. 250

Minute by Mr. Jebb on the terms of an agreement with Germany

Ge/36/23[1]

FOREIGN OFFICE, September, 1936

It is understood that the Secretary of State wishes a note to be prepared on possible ways and means of assisting Germany in the event of the latter agreeing to participate in the political settlement of Europe.

Such ways and means have been discussed on many occasions during the present year, notably in the Economic Section's memorandum of January 31st 1936[2] (see especially the conclusions) and in the Secretary of State's letter to Mr. Runciman of July 17th,[3] enclosing a copy of the Hall memorandum.[4] Both of these documents are attached. Broadly speaking, however, the possible methods whereby this country might assist Germany economically in the event of its being thought desirable to do so, may be summarised as follows.

(1) By reductions in the United Kingdom tariff designed to facilitate the importation into the United Kingdom of Central European, but chiefly German, semi-finished products.

(2) By not raising United Kingdom tariffs in the event of the devaluation of the mark.

(3) By the abolition or reduction of Imperial Preference in the Colonial Empire.

(4) By the cession to Germany of a colony or colonies in full sovereignty.

(5) By a loan or by long term credits for financing German imports of raw materials.

(6) By some debt settlement on easy terms for the Germans.

These six possible methods of assisting Germany are neither equally desirable nor capable of simultaneous adoption, however satisfactory the

---

[1] From the Private Papers of Lord Gladwyn, Volume 8. This minute was undated, but a pencilled note suggested that it was written in September, 1936. Mr. H. M. Gladwyn Jebb was a First Secretary in the Economic Relations Section of the League of Nations and Western Department.   [2] Volume XV, Appendix IV(*a*).
[3] Volume XVI, No. 463.   [4] See *ibid.*, note 2.

political situation might be. Moreover, if there was even a partial increase in world trade, the desirability of putting them forward would be correspondingly diminished. All of them may however be considered in the event of (a) the general economic situation continuing to be unsatisfactory, and (b) Germany agreeing to limit her armaments and become a peaceful member of the 'concert of Europe'.

It must however be remembered that this last pre-requisite is quite unlikely to be achieved unless Germany has some real reason to think that economic assistance would in fact be forthcoming if she 'promised to be good'; or alternatively, unless some alleviation of her difficulties in advance of a settlement made her all the more ready to agree to one.

But what the Economic Section has always advocated is that something on the lines of (2) *should be offered to the Germans here and now*, in the same way as it was offered to the French before they devalued the franc. Such action, however, could only be taken after the most careful consideration of its implications here, and as a result of direct contact with Dr. Schacht.

The Section has also consistently advised that the possibility of some tariff modifications on the lines of (1) should be examined by His Majesty's Government, not by Board of Trade experts only, but by a Committee composed of representatives of other Departments acting in full consciousness of the political issues involved. Such modifications might benefit Czechoslovakia, Switzerland and France hardly less than Germany. It is interesting and encouraging to find that these ideas have been increasingly canvassed in the press (the *Times, Economist* and *Quarterly Review*) and that they seem in general to be favoured by Sir Frederick Leith-Ross.

Both (1) and (2) are therefore things which we might, and in the view of many qualified persons, should do before a political settlement is arrived at at all.

It is scarcely necessary to add that if we did take action on such lines, it would be of great assistance if France, Czechoslovakia, Holland, Switzerland and Belgium were to increase at any rate their industrial quotas all round. Indeed, we should have considerable material for bargaining with them on this point if we were prepared to make tariff modifications ourselves. Such an enlargement of industrial quotas would naturally benefit the Germans as well as us, and in the opinion of our own Treasury at least, the countries concerned would be well advised to act accordingly; I should add that in the opinion of our own Treasury we should ourselves be well advised to give rather less protection to our own sugar beet and beef industries.

Should a real increase of triangular trade b[e] accomplished by such means as these, the possibility of a political settlement will, in the Section's view, be very considerably increased, and the time may then come to consider (4) and possibly also (3) in order to clinch a settlement.

(5) and (6) really depend on technical considerations, since it would merely hinder a general settlement to throw good money after bad. If

German credit improved, and it no doubt would if trade revived all round, it will be time enough to consider them.

On the other hand, failing any move on our part, or on that of other people, it remains the view of the Section that in all probability, the Germans will rearm until the 'blockade' forces them to call a halt to rearmament, and then embark on some military adventure, the success of which seems to be considerably less doubtful than it previously did owing to their improved relations with Italy and Japan and to the course of events in Spain.

CHAPTER V

Western Pact proposals: replies to British note of September 17: breaches of non-intervention agreement
October 1–31, 1936

No. 251

Mr. Edmond (Geneva) to Foreign Office
(Received October 1, 4.20 p.m.)
No. 139 L.N. Telegraphic [W 12654/9549/41]

Immediate   GENEVA, *October 1, 1936, 2.40 p.m.*
Following from Secretary of State.

I had a conversation with Monsieur Litvinov yesterday[1] during course of which I spoke to Soviet Commissar for Foreign Affairs about committee of non-intervention in Spain now sitting in London. I told him that I understood that Committee wished to discuss what was known as indirect intervention. This desire was agreed to by all members of the committee except Soviet representative who had resisted the proposal.[2] I begged Monsieur Litvinov to be good enough to look into the matter and I hoped that he would be able to instruct his representative to modify his attitude.

Monsieur Litvinov replied that he knew nothing of the matter himself and presumed it was being dealt with direct from Moscow.

After some further discussion during which I endeavoured to explain position to Monsieur Litvinov he undertook to look into the matter. In the circumstances if matter is still urgent it is worth considering whether it should be taken up also in Moscow.[3]

Repeated to Moscow.

[1] See No. 244.   [2] See No. 225.
[3] The question of indirect intervention was evidently discussed at the fifth meeting of the Chairman's sub-committee on October 5, the minutes of which are filed in F.O. 849/27. A minute by Lord Plymouth on the above telegram read: 'No action seems necessary on this now that the Soviet representative has met us half way. P. 6.10.76.'

No. 252

Mr. Ogilvie-Forbes (Madrid) to Foreign Office
(Received October 1, 8.20 p.m.)
No. 288 Telegraphic [*W 12655/62/41*]

MADRID, *October 1, 1936, 2.45 p.m.*

Addressed to Geneva No. 16, October 1st.

Your telegram No. 1.[1]

Rate of private murders since my telegram No. 8[2] has shown no decrease rather the contrary, for last Saturday's figure rose to 125 men and women, which includes 60 just released from prison. No wonder del Vayo admitted to Lord Halifax that there was 'some anxiety on Sunday'.

I therefore felt that under an elementary obligation of Christian charity I should take some further action.

Moreover government in its present shaken position is likely to be less resistant. Accordingly without any previous notice I yesterday visited San Anton prison and asked to see amongst others Señor Comyn, Legal Adviser to this Embassy, who is considered to be in serious danger. To my great relief I was immediately admitted, received with courtesy and given facilities. I found Comyn well, cheered him up and told him I was doing my utmost for him and his fellow prisoners. What they are all afraid of on release is the half mile from the prison gates, and unprotected homes.

Señor Maeztu, whose English wife is in this Embassy, is in another prison about to be tried on charge that his past writings were subversive to the State and which experience shows is bound to end fatally. As he had been ambassador to Argentine Republic[3] and is well known in United Kingdom I concerted with my Argentine colleague a suitable letter to Minister of State which I hope will save his life.

I am exploring possibilities of an exchange of notabilities to begin with, and better still a personal appeal to the Cabinet which will not commit you politically to protect at this critical moment the prisoners and hostages of whom there were over 7,000 a month ago.[4]

Repeated to Hendaye No. 46.

[1] No. 245.   [2] *Ibid.*, note 1.   [3] From 1928 to 1930.
[4] In his telegram No. 299 of October 3 to the Foreign Office (addressed No. 19 to Geneva) Mr. Ogilvie-Forbes described plans for a communication, drawn up with the approval of the Corps Diplomatique in Madrid, to be made to the President of the Republic concerning the safety of prisoners. In a further telegram, No. 320 of October 8, he wrote: 'Although Turkish and Japanese representatives funked it at the last moment I persuaded Mexican and Chilean Ambassadors together with French and Argentine colleagues and myself to visit Minister of State [Señor del Vayo] this morning when Mexican Ambassador read out an admirably worded memorandum on murders and on safe-guarding of prisons. Minister of State whom I had warned beforehand took it very well . . .'

No. 253

Mr. Edmond (Geneva) to Foreign Office
(Received October 2, 9.30 a.m.)
No. 140 L.N. Telegraphic [C 6868/4/18]

GENEVA, *October 1, 1936, 10.50 p.m.*

Following from Secretary of State.

M. Massigli[1] asked to see me this morning when he stated that he wished to hand to me on behalf of the French Government a memorandum which was their reply to our note of September 18th[2] (copy by bag).[3]

M. Massigli added that I would find that this memorandum was on the lines of the document which has already been sent to us privately by the French Government even before they received our note.[4] It was, however, somewhat differently worded since he understood that we might wish to communicate it to the German and Italian Governments.

I replied that communication of some reply from French Government to German, Italian and Belgian Governments would clearly be necessary if we were to make progress with our negotiations. M. Massigli said that this was exactly how he had understood the position and this memorandum was therefore definitely for communication to other Governments interested in negotiation.

M. Delbos had instructed him to ask me whether if this document would in due course be sent to German and Italian Governments we would have any objections to French Government taking this action themselves through diplomatic channel. They were, I understood, anxious to show their willingness to enter into discussions with German and Italian Governments and also to try by this method to draw the latter into general exchange of views.

I replied that I certainly saw no objection to this method. Indeed there were some advantages in it. What, however, had the French Government in mind as regards publication? Clearly this document itself must be kept confidential like our note of September 18th. It would jeopardise all our chances of meeting round a table if diplomatic preliminaries became public. M. Massigli at once agreed and after some further discussion we decided we would not at present even make it known that French Government had sent in their answer to us.

M. Massigli drew my attention to paragraph 10 of French Paper which he remarked contained the most complicated part of our negotiation. In reply to a question from me he assured me that its terms were entirely on all fours with the provisions of the original Treaty of Locarno.

Repeated to Paris.

[1] Assistant Director of the Political Department of the French Ministry for Foreign Affairs.
[2] No. 206, Enclosure.   [3] No. 263 below.   [4] See No. 202, note 2.

No. 254

Mr. Edmond (Geneva) to Foreign Office (Received October 3)
No. 68 Saving: Telegraphic [W 12789/9549/41]

GENEVA, *October 1, 193(*

Following from Secretary of State.

My telegram No. 139.[1]

M. Litvinov went on to speak of the policy of non-intervention in general. He maintained that that policy, if it had been rigidly enforced, would have been the proper one, but unfortunately, as a result of breaches of the agreement by some Powers, it had resulted in favouring the rebels.

I replied that while it was difficult to know the facts I did not altogether share M. Litvinov's view. No one could expect a system of this kind, which had been hastily improvised, to be absolutely watertight. At the early stages, indeed, there had been many criticisms of the attempt to work the agreement, and charges of sending arms had been made against many countries. Germany and Italy were accused by one side; France by the other. M. Litvinov interjected that France had never sent anything.

I replied that the important thing to consider from the point of view of the European situation was whether the agreement had resulted in a reduced supply of arms to both sides. This, I was sure, had been the result.

Repeated to Moscow No. 1 (Saving).

[1] No. 251.

No. 255

Record by Sir R. Vansittart of a conversation with M. Corbin
[R 5874/294/67]

FOREIGN OFFICE, *October 1, 193(*

The French Ambassador called on me today and asked if we were now in a position to give him any reply in regard to the question which he had raised with us in July as to the conclusion of a Mediterranean pact.[1]

I replied that I had not yet had an opportunity of discussing the matter with the Secretary of State, and that he in turn might also wish to discuss such a major question with his colleagues, of whom many were not at present in London.

The French Ambassador said that, without wishing to hurry us unduly, he would like to point out that the French Government was being pressed in the matter by other Mediterranean Governments, notably by the Government of Yugoslavia.

I said that I would take an early opportunity of speaking of the matter

[1] See No. 224, note 3.

o the Secretary of State after his return in about ten days time, but pending hat I could not say more.[2]

R. V.

[2] For M. Corbin's account of this conversation, and of a longer one on the same subject with Mr. Sargent, see *D.D.F.*, *op. cit.*, No. 314.

No. 256

Letter from Dr. Schacht to Sir F. Leith-Ross (Treasury)
[*C 7043/99/18*]*

BERLIN, October 1, 1936

Dear Sir Frederick,

I still have to thank you for your kind letter of the 28th July.[1] I did not write to you earlier because I had nothing actual to tell; but I noticed very carefully from your letter that you thought the day might come when the difficulties we suffer from might be straightened out. In the meanwhile, I have followed with the greatest interest the work you are doing, and I am glad that somebody has taken the initiative who knows economics and finance so well as you do, and who at the same time is not too far off from politics.

Whatever the reasons for the French devaluation[2] have been and whatever the results may be, I feel that the time has come nearer when something could be achieved. Enclosed I beg to hand you the wording of my yesterday's declaration,[3] from which you will see that, whilst for the moment I do not see any advantage in an adjustment of our currency, I have, nevertheless, expressed our willingness to co-operate as far as your Three-Power Declaration is in question.

Through the Anglo-German arrangement which you have made with me at the time,[1] you have successfully contributed to maintain ordinary trade between our two countries and you have enabled me to fulfil current obligations. But what is in our way are some remainders of the past which, I think, should be liquidated in a fair way to open up a peaceful future for Europe. Unfortunately, being a Minister now, there is little chance for me to come to England now, which I regret very much, because I would very much like to talk to you about all this and to make you acquainted with the possibilities which I see for peace and prosperity.

Believe me, &c.,
HJALMAR SCHACHT

[1] See No. 135, note 2.   [2] See No. 248, note 4.
[3] Not printed: it was a joint declaration on behalf of the Reich Government and the Reichsbank, read by Dr. Schacht to the central committee of the Reichsbank on the afternoon of September 30.

No. 257

Letter from Mr. Baxter to Sir M. Hankey[1]
[C 6523/4/18]

FOREIGN OFFICE, October 1, 1936

Sir,

I am directed etc. to inform you that on September 17th the French Ambassador handed to Sir R. Vansittart a memorandum[2] regarding the proposed new Western European treaty of non-aggression and mutual guarantee.

2. Paragraph 4 of this memorandum reads as follows:

'It will certainly not have escaped the attention of the British Government that the disappearance of the demilitarised zone, apart from its consequences on the security of French and Belgian territory, creates a new situation as regards Luxembourg. At the time of the signature of the Treaty of Locarno, the Grand Duchy of Luxembourg was separated from German territory on the right bank of the Rhine by the demilitarised zone. The question of the results of an invasion of the territory of the Grand Duchy did not then arise. But if the demilitarised zone is to disappear, the invasion of Luxembourg must be considered under very different conditions.

This is a grave problem which is at the moment being considered by the Government of the Republic and which that Government reserves the right at a later date to raise with the British and Belgian Governments.'

3. In connexion with this reference by the French Ambassador to the position of Luxembourg, there are enclosed in this letter three memoranda prepared in the Foreign Office in August 1926,[3] August 1934,[4] and September 1936,[4] all of which relate to discussions concerning the position of the Grand Duchy, particularly subsequent to the war of 1914–1918.

4. It will be seen from paragraph 2 of the memorandum of September 1936 that the question of the participation of the Grand Duchy in the Locarno Treaty was considered by the Committee of Imperial Defence in November 1926 and that the Committee recommended that no advantage would accrue to this country from the acceptance of the further liability which would be involved by such participation.

5. Since 1926 the position has, as the French Ambassador points out in his communication, to some extent been altered by the disappearance of the demilitarised zone.

6. If the French Government, as a result of the consideration which they are now giving to this matter, were to propose that Luxembourg should participate in the new Western Treaty, such participation would presumably involve non-aggression treaties between Luxembourg and certain of the parties to the Treaty, and guarantees of the inviolability of Luxembourg by certain of them at least against Germany and possibly also against France.

---

[1] Secretary of the Committee of Imperial Defence. [2] See No. 202.
[3] See No. 218, note 7. [4] Not printed: cf. No. 218.

Any such guarantee by this country in favour of Luxembourg would apparently involve an increase in our obligations over and above those existing under the Treaty of 1867[5] and the Covenant of the League of Nations.

7. Apart altogether from such political considerations as may arise in any subsequent discussion of this question, the Secretary of State would be grateful for an expression of opinion by the Committee of Imperial Defence as to what military advantage, if any, or disadvantage might be expected to result for this country should H.M. Government in the U.K. decide to give some fresh guarantee to Luxembourg under the proposed new Western Treaty.[6]

[5] See *B.F.S.P.*, vol. 57, pp. 32–5.
[6] Concluding salutation omitted from the filed copy of this letter. In a report of October 26 (C.I.D. 1270B) the C.O.S. Sub-Committee stated that they saw no reason to modify the conclusion reached in the 1926 C.I.D. report (see No. 218): cf. No. 332 below.

No. 258

Sir E. Phipps (Berlin) to Foreign Office (Received October 2, 7.40 p.m.)
No. 313 Telegraphic [C 6896/4/18]

BERLIN, *October 2, 1936, 6.20 p.m.*

Your despatch No. 1081.[1]

In the course of conversation today with Herr Dieckhoff I enquired what his impressions were of British memorandum of September 17th[2] regarding Five Power Conference and when we might expect a German reply thereto. Herr Dieckhoff said that our memorandum was a very useful and skilful document which was receiving close attention of German Government but to which a reply could not be made until a short time after return to Berlin on October 11th of Minister for Foreign Affairs who is at his home in the south.

Herr Dieckhoff added that he foresaw that there would be considerable difficulties in regard to the three following points:

(1) The linking of new Pact with League of Nations. Special difficulty would be met with regard to Article 16 of the Covenant.

(2) Paragraph 5 sub-paragraph (1) of British memorandum. Germany for her part was ready to renounce war on France or Belgium without any exceptions whatsoever. French on the other hand would surely claim certain exceptions to this rule. What those exceptions would be Herr Dieckhoff could not tell but this point would certainly create difficulties.

(3) The triangular guarantee proposed within the Pact between Germany, France and Great Britain had met with considerable objection in Rome and it seemed unlikely that this suggestion would be acceptable to Italy.

Herr Dieckhoff assured me that German Government had no wish to cause any undue delay in this matter but that their reply would *inter alia* probably draw attention in detail to the three above-mentioned difficulties.

[1] No. 207.   [2] Enclosure in No. 206.

I hear from another source that it has been suggested to the Chancellor that in case German reply should be fairly favourable it would be a suitable début in London for Herr von Ribbentrop to take it with him.

Repeated to Geneva.

No. 259

Mr. Edmond (Geneva) to Foreign Office (Received October 3)
No. 70 Saving: Telegraphic [C 6894/4/18]

GENEVA, *October 2, 1936*

Following from Secretary of State.

M. Litvinoff asked to see me yesterday and during the course of conversation remarked that the French Government had shown him their draft of the memorandum[1] which they had sent to us about the Locarno negotiations. Could I give him any information about their progress and prospects?

I replied that as M. Litvinoff would be aware we had submitted a short memorandum[2] to the Five Locarno Powers signature to the Locarno Treaty in an endeavour to make a start with negotiations. The document was not a complicated one, and we hoped that we might shortly receive answers to it which would better enable us to judge the prospects for the future. I could not show M. Litvinoff this document, since it concerned confidential negotiations between the five Locarno Powers. M. Litvinoff interjected that he fully appreciated that. I continued that it was in order, I hoped, further to allay his doubts about British policy towards Europe as a whole that I would read him the first two paragraphs which (apart from preliminaries which I did not quote to him) constituted, he would find, a textual reproduction of the *communiqué* already made public in London after the conference of the Three Powers at the end of July.[3]

Repeated to Moscow No. 3 Saving.

[1] See No. 202.   [2] Enclosure in No. 206.   [3] See Volume XVI, No. 476.

No. 260

Sir E. Phipps (Berlin) to Foreign Office (Received October 3)
No. 269 Saving: Telegraphic [C 6912/99/18]

BERLIN, *October 2, 1936*

My telegram No. 264 Saving.[1]

I hear from a reliable source that criticism of Dr. Schacht in leading party circles has been very outspoken. His colleagues complained to the Führer that Dr. Schacht gave the country an erroneous impression on his return from Paris and that the three power currency agreement[2] had made

[1] No. 248.   [2] See *ibid.*, note 4.

him and German Government look ridiculous. The Führer thereupon summoned Dr. Schacht to Berchtesgaden on Tuesday[3] having previously entrusted Ministry of Finance instead of Dr. Schacht with task of informing public that there would be no currency devaluation in Germany.

Dr. Schacht's head appears to have been well washed by the Führer. On his return to the Reichsbank he was occupied until a very late hour with preparation of his speech to Reichsbank though speech contained little or nothing of importance.[4]

[3] i.e. September 29.   [4] See No. 256, note 3.

No. 261

Mr. Edmond (Geneva) to Foreign Office (Received October 3, 4.20 p.m.)
No. 81 Saving: Telegraphic [C 6904/97/18]

Secret   GENEVA, *October 2, 1936*

Following from the Secretary of State for Sir R. Vansittart.

Personal and Confidential. I had a conversation with Monsieur Blum this afternoon at the outset of which the French Prime Minister remarked that he was afraid that now that the Conservative Conference had passed their resolution about mandates[1] the conversations initiated by Schacht in Paris[2] were not likely to have any sequel. I replied that I did not take the matter so tragically as that. It was even possible that that resolution would prove helpful in showing the Germans that other nations could be stiff also.

2. Monsieur Blum then remarked that in sending Dr. Schacht the interim reply which I had forwarded to him[3] he had indicated that some further reply might follow after I had consulted my colleagues. Since I was now going on a few days' holiday to the South of France he supposed that he should communicate with Dr. Schacht again explaining the circumstance to him. I replied that it was of course perfectly correct that I would report

[1] At the 63rd annual conference of the National Union of Conservative and Unionist Associations which opened at Margate on October 1, the following resolution was moved:

> 'That this conference urges His Majesty's Government, in order to dispel grave anxieties within the Empire and dangerous hopes abroad, to give an assurance that the declaration made by the then Foreign Secretary, Sir John Simon, to the German Chancellor in Berlin in March, 1935, to the effect that the cession of any British Mandated Territory was not a discussable question, still represents the unaltered attitude of His Majesty's Government.'

One member remarked that nothing created a more unhelpful attitude than a blank refusal to listen to what the other side had to say, and he proposed an amendment recognizing among other things that mandates could not be transferred 'except by the unanimous consent of the League Council as well as the present Mandatory Power'. After a speech by Sir S. Hoare, who referred to Mr. Eden's statement of July 27, 1936 (Volume XVI, Appendix to No. 484) as bringing Sir J. Simon's declaration up to date, the amendment was defeated on a show of hands and the resolution carried by a large majority amid cheers. See *The Times*, October 2, 1936, p. 8.

[2] See Nos. 141 and 145.   [3] See No. 228.

all that had passed between us to my colleagues on my return to London but that I was confident that their reply would not differ in any material degree from that which I had already sent to Monsieur Blum. I [was] sorry if Monsieur Blum thought that I was being too rigid in this matter, but I was confident that our attitude was correct. After all the Germans had entirely failed to make it plain what it was they proposed to contribute to a European settlement. In any event therefore the next move must lie with them.

Monsieur Blum at once agreed and added that he had certainly no complaint to make of our attitude, which he fully understood. At the same time he wished me to understand his. He was most anxious to let slip no opportunity which might lead to European appeasement. It was in this spirit that he had come to London, and made no difficulty about agreeing to the *communiqué* published there.[4] He wished to show the same spirit in dealing with these other problems.

I replied that there was, however, a distinction. Germans were not Englishmen. The real attitude of Germany might be one of two: Either she genuinely desired a European settlement. If this was so she certainly would not be put off in her attempts by our attitude in the matter of mandates. Or Germany might wish to lead us into a position in which we might be held to have expressed willingness to discuss mandates, in order that we might be committed while her hands remained entirely free. This was a position against which we must at all costs guard ourselves. Therefore I could only repeat that our position remained as stated in the House of Commons at the end of July, and as communicated to Monsieur Blum in the note which I had sent to Monsieur Delbos.

Monsieur Blum made no complaint at this diagnosis, and decided that on further consideration he would wait until he saw me, as he hoped to do on my way through Paris from the South of France, before holding any further communication either with Dr. Schacht or with the German Ambassador. In any case he thought it preferable that all communications should be made through the German Ambassador in Paris in future.

In the course of the conversation I dropped a word of warning in respect of Dr. Schacht, indicating that in my view he was certainly clever, if not 'malin'.

4 See Volume XVI, No. 476.

No. 262

Mr. Ingram (Rome) to Foreign Office (Received October 5)
No. 211 Saving: Telegraphic [C 6945/4/18]

ROME, *October 2, 1936*

The prominence given in the press to Sir Samuel Hoare's speech at the Conservative Conference in Margate is indicative of the importance attached to the speech itself.[1] In the words of the 'Stampa' London correspondent, Sir Samuel Hoare's statements reflect the misgivings aroused within the British Conservative Party by certain French tendencies in the matter of disarmament. Another correspondent says that the speech dispels all doubts as to Great Britain's real attitude towards the question of re-armament. 'Corriere Paduano' prints the message from London reporting the speech under the heading: 'Triumph of Great Britain's sacred egotism. Sir Samuel Hoare disavows the myth of collective security; the intangibility of territories held under British mandate solemnly re-affirmed.'

The London correspondent of 'Lavoro Fascista' says that Great Britain has been led to re-consider the old 'myths' and to modify her policy by the following events: the failure of the League of Nations on the Abyssinian question, the intensification of German re-armament, France's precarious internal situation and, finally, the Franco-Soviet agreement, which inevitably bars the way to any plans for a new Locarno. Slowly, but resolutely, as is always the case with England, attempts are being made to regain the time and prestige that for a moment were lost. Great Britain is re-arming herself both materially and morally.

In a message to the 'Tribuna', printed with the title 'Sir Samuel Hoare pre-announces Great Britain's return to the classical methods and principles of imperialism,' Signor Sansa says that the First Lord of the Admiralty, desiring not only to take full advantage of the feelings prevailing among the Conservatives, but also to complete his 'political rehabilitations', has given to his speech a tone which is reminiscent of British jingoism—a tendency which Signor Sansa considers to be the reaction of British public opinion to recent experiences, regarded as serious humiliations. 'One can easily imagine what Great Britain's attitude in international affairs would be when the absolute re-armament desired by Sir Samuel Hoare has been attained and when Great Britain thinks she no longer needed pacts of mutual assistance in the various areas and seas'.

Signor Sansa describes the vote against any surrender of mandated territories as 'another manifestation of unrestrained imperialism in contrast with the implicit promises contained in Mr. Eden's recent speech at Geneva[2] on the question of peaceful treaty revisions'.

The attitude taken by the Conservative Conference on the question of mandates is considered by the 'Giornale d'Italia' correspondent to be the

[1] See No. 261, note 1. Speaking to a motion condemning the pursuit of a policy of one-sided disarmament, Sir S. Hoare addressed the conference on October 1 and after referring to the German, French, and even United States increases in armament expenditure commented on the futility of one-sided disarmament in world conditions which left Great Britain 'with no alternative but to carry through with the least possible delay our programme of rearmament'. Mr. N. Chamberlain, speaking to the conference on October 2 in place of Mr. Baldwin, surveyed the government's record in both domestic and foreign policy, and also spoke of the need for rearmament. The full text of the two speeches is given in *The Times* of October 2 and 3 respectively.

[2] For Mr. Eden's speech of September 25 at the sixth Plenary Meeting of the League Assembly see *L/N.O.J., S.S. No. 155*, pp. 44–7.

most important feature of the congress. He also calls attention to the fact that Sir Samuel Hoare's speech contained no reference to British Mediterranean policy.

No. 263

Mr. Edmond (Geneva) to Foreign Office (Received October 5)

No. 103 [*C 6903/4/18*]

GENEVA, *October 2, 1936*

The United Kingdom delegate to the League of Nations presents his compliments and, with reference to Geneva telegram to the Foreign Office, No. 140[1] of the 1st October (repeated to Paris, No. 32), has the honour to transmit a copy of the French text of the French aide-mémoire regarding the proposed meeting in London of the five Locarno Powers, communicated by M. Massigli on the 1st October, 1936.

ENCLOSURE IN No. 263

Mémorandum[2] en Réponse à la Note anglaise du 17 septembre

30 septembre 1936

Le Gouvernement de la République a examiné avec attention les suggestions présentées par le Gouvernement britannique concernant l'objet de la discussion que l'on espère ouvrir à Londres entre les cinq Puissances signataires du Traité de Locarno.

2. Comme le Gouvernement britannique, le Gouvernement français souhaite que la discussion à ce sujet ait lieu à la date la plus rapprochée sur laquelle les Puissances signataires du Traité de Locarno pourront se mettre d'accord; quel que soit le prix qu'il attache aux garanties résultant pour lui des assurances contenues dans les lettres rendues publiques qui ont été échangées le 1 avril dernier[3] entre les deux Gouvernements, il estime en effet essentielle pour la pacification européenne la conclusion d'un nouveau traité entre les cinq Puissances.

3. Les Gouvernements allemand et italien ayant exprimé le désir, partagé par le Gouvernement britannique, que certains points, en particulier ceux qui se posent à propos de l'accord envisagé pour remplacer le Traité de Locarno, soient discutés par la voie diplomatique avant la réunion desdites Puissances, le Gouvernement de la République, pour contribuer dès maintenant à cette discussion, et sans préjudice des questions sur lesquelles il se réserve d'attirer ultérieurement l'attention, a l'honneur d'exposer les considérations suivantes qui se réfèrent aux points signalés dans le mémorandum britannique:

4. Le Gouvernement français estime que les dispositions du Traité de

---

[1] No. 253. [2] Also printed in *D.D.F., op. cit., Annexe* to No. 313.
[3] See Volume XVI, No. 199.

Locarno devraient être maintenues, sauf à y apporter les modifications et compléments que nécessitent les circonstances actuelles ou que l'expérience acquise paraît rendre désirable.

5. De même que le Traité de Locarno a pour base une garantie du statu quo territorial résultant des frontières entre l'Allemagne et la Belgique et entre l'Allemagne et la France et une garantie de l'inviolabilité de ces frontières, le nouvel accord devrait prendre pour base la constatation qu'il n'existe entre les parties contractantes aucun différend territorial avec, comme conséquence, dans leurs rapports mutuels, la garantie individuelle et collective du statu quo territorial ainsi que de l'inviolabilité des frontières de leurs possessions et dépendances.

6. Chaque signataire s'engagerait envers chacun des autres signataires à ne se livrer à aucune attaque ou invasion par terre, mer ou air, et à ne recourir en aucun cas à la force, sans que cela fasse obstacle à l'exercice, par une Puissance signataire, du droit de légitime défense, c'est-à-dire du droit de s'opposer à la violation de l'engagement ci-dessus énoncé.

7. En cas de manquement à l'engagement de non-agression, l'assistance, qui ne saurait faire l'objet d'un engagement moins étendu que celui résultant du Traité de Locarno, devrait être fournie par les autres Puissances signataires à la Puissance attaquée.

8. Pour répondre à la question posée par le Gouvernement britannique, le Gouvernement français tient dès maintenant à déclarer que, sous condition de réciprocité, il est prêt à contracter les engagements de garantie et d'assistance ci-dessus visés, à l'égard de chacune des Puissances qui seront parties au nouvel accord.

9. Les moyens d'assurer, dans des conditions satisfaisantes, l'automatisme de l'assistance devraient être recherchés. A tout le moins le mécanisme prévu par le Traité de Locarno (article 4) et qui comporte, d'une part, constatation de l'agression par le Conseil de la Société des Nations, d'autre part, en cas d'une violation flagrante du susdit engagement, entrée immédiate en application des garanties en attendant que le Conseil se soit prononcé d'une manière définitive, devrait être maintenu avec complément destiné à parer au danger d'une agression aérienne subite.

10. Le bénéfice de ce nouveau traité (et notamment l'obligation d'assistance qui en découle) ne pourrait pas être invoqué par un État signataire qui manquerait aux engagements qui y sont énoncés ou qui, en Europe, entreprendrait contre l'intégrité territoriale ou l'indépendance politique d'une autre Puissance notamment en dirigeant contre celle-ci une attaque non provoquée. L'assistance ne saurait, par voie de conséquence, jouer à l'encontre d'un État signataire qui, conformément aux principes du Pacte de la Société des Nations, s'opposerait à un acte d'agression commis par un contractant contre un État non contractant. En énonçant ce principe, le Gouvernement de la République se réfère aux dispositions figurant à l'article 2 du Traité de Locarno.

11. Le Gouvernement de la République est d'accord avec le Gouvernement britannique pour estimer qu'une attaque aérienne subite devrait être

dans tous les cas considérée comme une violation flagrante des engagements pris et entraîner ainsi une assistance immédiate de la part des autres signataires à l'État qui en serait victime. Les stipulations correspondantes pourraient, soit faire l'objet d'un protocole spécial, soit être insérées dans le traité général. Quelle que soit la solution choisie, le Gouvernement français doit attirer l'attention sur l'intérêt qu'il y aurait à compléter ces engagements par des engagements de limitation des armements aériens.

12. Ainsi qu'il est marqué dans l'arrangement fait à Londres le 19 mars 1936,[4] il serait nécessaire de prévoir la conclusion d'accords techniques d'application destinés à assurer, en cas de besoin, la prompte entrée en action des signataires et à préparer les mesures propres à rendre efficaces les engagements pris.

13. Le Gouvernement de la République reste attaché aux Traités de Locarno sur le règlement des différends par voie arbitrale ou judiciaire ou par voie de la conciliation; les conditions prévues pour que ces traités prennent fin n'ont pas été remplies: ils sont donc toujours en vigueur. Il y aurait lieu de les compléter par le moyen d'une assistance promise au cas où une Puissance signataire refuserait de suivre les procédures de règlement pacifique ainsi établies ou de donner effet aux décisions intervenues. Il est, d'autre part, désirable que des traités analogues interviennent entre celles des Puissances signataires qui n'ont pas jusqu'ici conclu des traités sur cet objet.

14. Le nouvel accord devrait être entendu comme ne portant pas atteinte aux droits et obligations résultant du Pacte de la Société des Nations, ni ne restreignant la mission de celle-ci de prendre les mesures propres à sauvegarder efficacement la paix du monde.

15. Il serait utile de le faire reconnaître par les tierces Puissances comme un acte destiné à assurer le maintien de la paix et d'obtenir qu'elles s'engagent à n'en pas gêner l'application.

16. En présentant les observations qui précèdent, le Gouvernement de la République est resté dans le cadre tracé par le mémorandum britannique où l'on a pris soin de noter que la liste des points soumis à l'attention des autres Gouvernements n'est pas limitative.

En conséquence, il lui paraît opportun de signaler dès maintenant comme devant retenir l'attention des Gouvernements les points complémentaires suivants:

(a) Suggestion faite par le Gouvernement allemand et qui ne soulève aucune objection de la part de la France, de comprendre les Pays-Bas, s'ils le désirent, dans le nouvel accord;

(b) Consultation à prévoir entre les Puissances signataires, en cas de tension politique entre elles, en vue de rendre plus efficace le jeu de l'article 11 du Pacte de la Société des Nations;

(c) Faculté pour chaque Puissance signataire d'instituer sur son territoire des organes de constatation sur la base du projet présenté à la con-

[4] See Volume XVI, No. 144.

férence pour la réduction et la limitation des armements avec un rapport de M. Bourquin (document Conf. D. CG. 108, annexe).[5]

17. Le programme ainsi tracé n'épuise pas, d'ailleurs, l'objet de la négociation à envisager en ce qui concerne le règlement de la situation créée le 7 mars 1936. En particulier et conformément aux dispositions arrêtées le 19 mars 1936, on devrait adopter des dispositions propres à interdire ou à limiter l'établissement ultérieur de fortifications dans une zone à déterminer.

A plus forte raison, n'a-t-on pas entendu viser dans le présent mémorandum toutes les questions qui se poseront au cours de la prochaine conférence et pour la solution desquelles sera indispensable la collaboration d'autres pays. On s'est volontairement limité aux principaux problèmes se rattachant directement à la négociation du traité qui devra se substituer au Traité de Locarno et qui, à ce titre, et sous réserve d'une entrée éventuelle des Pays-Bas dans la négociation, n'appelle pas la participation d'autres Puissances que celle des signataires de ce dernier traité.

Le Gouvernement de la République tient à rappeler que, dans l'esprit même de l'arrangement du 19 mars 1936 et du *communiqué* de Londres du 23 juillet,[6] cette négociation doit être le prélude d'une négociation plus vaste et qui suppose la collaboration de toutes les Puissances intéressées.[7]

---

[5] Not printed.   [6] See Volume XVI, No. 476.

[7] After an exhaustive analysis of this French memorandum by Mr. Wigram on October 5, Mr. Sargent on October 9 summed up the points of difference between the French and the British and German Governments under six heads. *'Points of difference between France and Great Britain.* (1) France wants Belgium to be a guarantor State: whereas we, on the advice of the C.I.D., are ready to guarantee her without receiving any guarantee in return. (2) France wants us (and the other signatories of the Treaty) to guarantee the inviolability of the frontiers of her 'possessions and dependencies'. (3) France wants the Treaty to provide specifically for Staff conversations; while we (on second thoughts) decided that it would be sufficient merely to resist any attempt by Germany to forbid in the Treaty any such Staff conversations . . . *Points of difference between France and Germany.* (4) France wants the guarantees of the new Treaty to be operated by the machinery provided by Article 16 of the Covenant, as was the case in Locarno . . . (5) As regards the renunciation of war between France and Germany, France wishes to preserve all the exceptions existing in the old Locarno Treaty, so as to enable her to fulfil her treaty obligations to Russia, Czechoslovakia, and Poland . . . (6) The French demand for some assurance regarding the fortification of the Rhineland.' Germany was likely to resist on each of the last three points. Mr. Eden, reviewing these papers on October 12, objected with regard to (3): 'Surely, this is not the position as agreed in London in March. A. E. Oct. 12.' Sir R. Vansittart commented with regard to (1): 'I think the French arguments in regard to Belgium remaining a guarantor are very cogent, and we shd. say so in asking the Chiefs of Staff to reconsider the point as soon as possible.' Mr. Eden, however, replied, also on October 12, that he would prefer 'that the General Staff gave us an uninfluenced opinion'. Later in the day Sir R. Vansittart pointed out to Mr. Eden that he had commented only on points (1) and (2), and had not initialled the papers. A note by Mr. O. C. Harvey (Mr. Eden's Private Secretary) in reply said that the 'S. of S. has finished with this & has no more to say for the present. O. C. H. 12/x.' Mr. Sargent had earlier pointed out that no reply could be given to the French 'until we have received the views of the Germans, Belgians, and Italians on our memorandum of September 17th'.

No. 264

Foreign Office to Mr. Ogilvie-Forbes (Madrid)
No. 158 Telegraphic [W 12282/9549/41]

FOREIGN OFFICE, *October 3, 1936, 6 p.m.*

Your telegram No. 260 (of September 26th: British subjects who enlist in Spain).[1]

A *communiqué* was issued to the press here on August 15th,[2] according to which British subjects joining the forces of either side in Spain must not expect to receive any assistance or support in difficulties which they might meet with during any enterprises which run counter to the objects with regard to non-intervention which His Majesty's Government were seeking to attain.

Foreign Enlistment Act of 1870 is to be interpreted as applicable to present circumstances in Spain, although the war is a civil one and His Majesty's Government have not recognised the insurgents as belligerents or issued a formal proclamation of neutrality. It is consequently an offence for any British subject to take service in Spain with the military forces of either side and any person so doing is liable to penalties and forfeits all *claim* to official support or assistance.

There are circumstances, however, in which on humanitarian grounds, it is left to your discretion to afford such persons assistance or support. They should not of course be afforded measure of support equal to that given to law-abiding British subjects, but you should offer assistance in event of danger to life, imprisonment, ill-treatment and risks other than those which a person who takes part in hostilities must inevitably run.

Repeated via Admiralty to Vigo No. 76, Barcelona No. 118, Valencia No. 10, Malaga No. 26, Seville No. 26, Tetuan No. 13, Santander No. 19, and Hendaye No. 13 Saving.

[1] Not printed.   [2] See *The Times*, August 17, 1936, p. 10; cf. No. 92, note 7.

No. 265

Note by Mr. Roberts
[W 12363/9549/41]

FOREIGN OFFICE, *October 3, 1936*

The Secretary of State has asked that the accuracy of the allegations made in Señor del Vayo's aide-mémoire[1] shall be checked as soon as possible from our own sources. This document is enclosed in Geneva despatch No. 85 which has not yet[2] reached the Department but from the particulars given

[1] Cf. No. 246, note 2.

[2] A marginal note by Sir G. Mounsey here stated that this despatch had been received on October 3: 'It contains further specific charges mainly against Portugal and Germany since the conclusion of the [Non-Intervention] agreement.'

in 'The Times' of October 2nd (cutting attached)[3] it is practically certain that the document is the same as that enclosed in this despatch from Mr Ogilvie-Forbes.[4]

The facts alleged by Señor del Vayo are confirmed by our own information as may easily be seen from the attached secret report.[5] But these facts alone as Mr. Pollock says do not prove a breach of the Non-Intervention Agreement by any one of the three Powers. That is not to say that the Agreement has not been broken. The same secret report proves conclusively that it has been broken at least by Italy and although the evidence does not establish a case against Germany, it is at least doubtful whether Germany has kept her undertaking. The evidence against Portugal is also not sufficient to convict her of a breach of the Agreement.

Now that the Spanish Government have officially raised this matter both in Madrid and at Geneva[6] H.M.G. must obviously consider what is their position as a member of the International Committee. The Spanish Government are not represented on it and they are therefore debarred from bringing a complaint before it under the rules of procedure adopted by the Committee. The Committee laid it down that a complaint should only be considered by it if submitted on behalf of one Government of one or other of the countries that are parties to the Agreement. The decision to debar the Spanish Government from preferring a complaint was, I think, based upon the consideration, firstly, that that Government is not a party to the Agreement and, secondly, that to do otherwise would amount to discrimination against the insurgents who have no international status at all at present. Two conditions have been laid down for the consideration of a complaint; (1) that it is received from a responsible source and (2) that it is regarded by the Government preferring it as being of sufficient importance and as being founded on evidence of sufficient weight to afford a reasonable presumption that in fact some breach has occurred. In the present case (1) is clearly fulfilled; as regards (2) it is obviously important but I am very doubtful about the evidence.

[3] Not printed. This report from Geneva in *The Times*, October 2, p. 13, stated that the Spanish Government had 'issued as a printed paper the documents they circulated to the various delegations as proof of foreign intervention on the insurgent side' (see note 4 below). These documents had been communicated to the press when the Secretary General of the League informed Señor del Vayo, who had circulated them to the Secretariat, that 'as the circumstances of these documents had not been brought before either the Council or the Assembly, he was not in a position to circulate them as League of Nations papers'.

[4] Mr. Roberts's note referred to Madrid despatch No. 30 of September 22, which transmitted a translation of the Spanish Government's note of September 15 concerning breaches of the non-intervention agreement (see No. 215), together with copies of notes to the Portuguese, German, and Italian Governments containing detailed allegations (see *ibid.*). This note of September 15 was similar, but not identical to the aide-mémoire handed to Mr. Eden in Geneva by Señor del Vayo on September 24 (see No. 246).

[5] Not printed.

[6] Señor del Vayo made a speech to the sixth plenary meeting of the League Assembly on September 25: see *L/N.O.J., S.S. No. 155*, pp. 47–50; cf. also note 3 above.

On a strict application of the rules, therefore, we should I think be quite justified in not taking the matter up. But for political reasons both internal and external it might be unwise to refuse. The Committee has been accused in many quarters of having sat for nearly a month and done nothing. This is untrue but it has certainly not got very far. This is the first important complaint which has been made and if taken up it would give the Committee a chance of showing what it can do. On the whole therefore it would seem wiser to bring the matter up but I think we should try to get at least one other government, possibly the French, to share the responsibility.

Finally and quite apart from the Agreement it should be remembered that if the Italian and German Governments as distinct from private armament firms have assisted the insurgents, they have done something against which the Spanish Government or any other government in similar circumstances have a perfect right to protest.[7]

[7] In minutes of October 4 Sir G. Mounsey and Sir R. Vansittart agreed that action must be taken on the charges levelled by the Spanish Government. Lord Plymouth was also consulted, and on his suggestion attempts were made to verify some of the statements made by the Spanish Government regarding German breaches of the non-intervention agreement. On October 5 Sir R. Vansittart telegraphed to Mr. Eden, who had stopped off at Monte Carlo on his way home from Geneva, that there was 'no doubt in our minds that we shall have to bring before the [N.I.] Committee the charges brought by Spain against Germany, Italy, and Portugal'. On October 6 Mr. Roberts forwarded to the Secretary of the N.I. Committee, Mr. Hemming, copies of both the note of September 15 and the aide-mémoire of September 24, with their enclosures.

No. 266

Message from Captain D(3) to Admiralty[1]

[W 12839/9549/41]

October 4, 1936, 11.21 p.m.

Pass to Foreign Office from Vice Consul Palma. Begins.

Part 1.

Your 1504 3rd October[2] information requested has all been reported in Confidential Memoranda 3 to 11 inclusive sent via His Majesty's Ships to Senior Naval Officer and Consul General Barcelona and to you together with local press extracts and photographs.[3] More important features were telegraphed via His Majesty's Ships. Summary follows.

By 31st August there were in Majorca 10 Italian aircraft and at least 30 officers and men and eight anti-aircraft guns and ammunition. Count Rossi[4] and Colonel Detito in practical command of operations.

[1] Repeated to Rear Admiral Commanding First Cruiser Squadron.
[2] See No. 227, note 2. [3] Not printed.
[4] The Falangist leader in Majorca, the Marqúes de Zayas, had asked the Italian Government on August 23 to send a military adviser to direct the defence of the island against Republican forces. Signor Mussolini's choice had fallen on Arconovaldo Bonaccorsi, an

On 7th September three more Italian bombers arrived and Italian merchant vessel landed rifles, bombs and six fighter aircraft that and following night. 28 Italian air mechanics and gunners also landed. Other Italians have arrived since by Italian mail plane. On 18th September Italian destroyer(s) visited Iviza in circumstances clearly showing co-operation with Majorca. On 23rd September cases of light machine guns and anti tank guns and ammunition and other material were discharged into Italian cruiser(s) and destroyer(s) by Italian *Sicillia* and landed on nights of 23rd September and 24th September. On 25th September other Italian vessels discharged cases into cruiser(s) from which many landed on nights of 29th September and 30th September. Many of these things I observed myself. Others observed from His Majesty's Ships or our Naval Signal Station on breakwater. Fullest liaison between Italian Naval Officers and Italians ashore is obvious. Local newspapers and speeches constantly refer to Italian assistance, Italians and many Spaniards wearing Italian colours. Italians prominent at all functions. Italian Consul marched in victory procession.

Part 2.

Evidence of political pretensions either indiscretions of Italians or Spaniards or was inference. Present position is that owing to insurgents' success on mainland Italians appear to have abandoned any expectation of protectorate and to be trying to gain increased influence with a view to trade advantages and probably special privileges for aircraft and harbour, in fact close treaties both commercial and military. All personnel and material paid for to date but I understand former now to be free. More Italian material and personnel expected. Hillgarth. Ends.

early member of the Fascist squads; he reached Palma on August 26. He soon let himself be known as 'Count Rossi'. See J. C. Coverdale, *Italian Intervention in the Spanish Civil War*, p. 134, where he is described as a 'Bologna-born lawyer with a great shock of reddish hair, a close trimmed beard, and fiery eyes'.

No. 267

Sir H. Chilton (Hendaye) to Foreign Office (Received October 7)
No. 698 [W 13039/62/41]

HENDAYE, *October 5, 1936*

Sir,

A statement has been issued in the Press giving the following text of a Proclamation issued by General Franco on the occasion of the assumption of his powers as Head of the State:[1]

'Spain will be reorganised according to the theory of an authoritative State while respecting the traditions and the history of Spain. This form

[1] General Francisco Franco was invested at Burgos on October 1 as *Generalissimo* of the insurgent armies and 'Head of State'. He made a brief speech. On October 2 he issued a decree providing for the establishment of a 'Technical Council of State'.

will not place obstacles in the way of the preservation of "provincial" or local rights and customs so long as the latter do not in any way impair the ideal essential to national unity.

There will be no State religion but a concordat will be signed with the Catholic Church.

We will maintain the most friendly relations with all the countries of the world, except Soviet territories, which are the enemies of civilisation.'[2]

I have, etc.,

H. G. CHILTON

[2] Foreign Office minutes on this letter were as follows. 'I don't think much can be deduced from this rather non-committal statement. The last paragraph is however engagingly definite. D. D. Maclean [a Third Secretary in the League of Nations and Western Department] 10/10.' 'I deduce a completely and poisonously Fascist mentality from this statement (reading between the lines) and from other evidence. L. C[ollier]. Oct. 15th.' 'The first paragraph will be most unwelcome to the Catalans and Basques. W. Roberts 22/10.'

No. 268

Mr. Ogilvie-Forbes (Madrid) to Foreign Office (Received October 6, 8 p.m.)
No. 312 Telegraphic: by telephone [W 13003/62/41]

Immediate   MADRID, *October 6, 1936*

Please suspend action on your telegram No. 164 last paragraph[1] until you have read my telegram No. 310[2] and my telegram No. 311[3] (Immediate) now being cabled, addressed to Geneva, repeated to Foreign Office, which reports [*sic*] my further interviews with Ministers concerned. Premature or unnecessary publication would at present be very embarrassing as the Spanish Government have received my representations with sympathy and concern. It may however be eventually necessary. In the meanwhile I will consider suitable statement for publication if necessary.

[1] This Foreign Office telegram of October 6 said that the Spanish Government seemed powerless to intervene to prevent the further massacres which seemed likely on a large scale before and after the fall of Madrid, and asked Mr. Ogilvie-Forbes to telegraph such particulars as were suitable for publication 'as only possible method of restraint left open to us'.
[2] Of October 6, addressed to Geneva No. 20. It said that Señor del Vayo had spoken of his talks with Mr. Eden and Lord Halifax (cf. Nos. 245 and 246). Mr. Ogilvie-Forbes had appealed to him as representing the lawful government to stop the increasing murder in Madrid; Señor del Vayo 'blushed to the roots of his hair' and arranged for Mr. Ogilvie-Forbes to meet 'Comrade Gallarza, Minister of the Interior' (Señor Angel Galarza y Gogo).
[3] Of October 6, addressed to Geneva No. 22. It recorded Mr. Ogilvie-Forbes's interview with the Minister of the Interior who promised that private killings would be stopped but said he could not guarantee the security of the prisons against an infuriated mob after an air raid.

No. 269

Sir E. Phipps (Berlin) to Foreign Office (Received October 8)
No. 273 Saving: Telegraphic [C 7035/4/18]

BERLIN, *October 7, 1936*

The press devotes some attention to the discussion of the armaments question at the Labour Conference in Edinburgh.[1] The frank ventilation of the Fascist peril and, in particular, the German peril by leading members of the Labour Party is naturally unwelcome.

Thus the 'Völkischer Beobachter' heads its telegram 'Labour Armaments Swindle'. After quoting Dr. Dalton,[2] the telegram says that the official justification of the attitude of the Labour Party is a conscious violation of the truth.[3] Dr. Dalton and his friends know as well as Mr. Churchill and Sir Austen Chamberlain, whose allies they have now become, that a German attack on England is quite out of the question. They know perfectly well that German policy is directed towards an understanding with England and also with France. If, therefore the English Socialists, in collusion with the reactionaries, talk of a German danger, they do it only because they dare not express their true thoughts. The real reason is the fear that the internal policy and not the external policy of the authoritarian States appears dangerous to the guardians of democracy and socialism. They fear, not German weapons, but the attraction of modern ideas.

In this matter the British Government is not free from blame, because they have to some extent justified their armaments policy by the so-called German danger and thus helped to poison the international atmosphere.

[1] The 36th annual conference of the Labour Party, meeting in the Usher Hall, Edinburgh, October 5–9, 1936.
[2] Dr. Hugh Dalton, Labour M.P. for Bishop Auckland, was elected Chairman of the Executive of the Labour Party on October 9, 1936.
[3] On October 6 Dr. H. Dalton moved a resolution stating that in view of the threatening attitude of dictatorships the armed strength of countries loyal to the League of Nations must be conditioned by the armed strength of the potential aggressors. In his supporting speech he said that the 'central brute fact in Europe was German rearmament' and that there 'could not be excluded the possibility of a direct attack upon Great Britain'.

No. 270

Note[1] from M. Cahan to Lord Plymouth
[W 13242/9549/41]

October 7, 1936

Sir,

I am instructed by the Government of the U.S.S.R. to make the following statement.

[1] Also printed in *Dokumenty Vneshney Politiki SSSR* (Moscow, 1974), hereafter cited as *D.V.P.S.*, vol. xix, No. 296.

In the Notes addressed on September 15th to the Governments of Portugal, Germany and Italy,[2] the Spanish Government protests against the continuous aid, in the shape of war equipment, given by these countries to the Spanish rebels. The Spanish Government also submitted these Notes to all the other participants in the Agreement for Non-Intervention in Spanish Affairs,[3] with a request to adopt measures for terminating a situation in which the legitimate Spanish Government finds itself in a position of virtual blockade, whilst the rebels are without hindrance receiving from various sources military aeroplanes and other kinds of arms.

In his speech delivered in the Plenary Session of the League of Nations,[4] the Spanish Minister for Foreign Affairs, M. Alvarez del Vayo, put this same question to all the Governments which are members of the League of Nations.

A long list of facts representing breaches of the Agreement for Non-Intervention and relating to the most recent period is cited by the Spanish Government in the White Paper[5] as well as in the supplementary documents published by them in Geneva on October 3rd.

It is sufficient to cite therefrom the following facts:

On September 7th there arrived in Seville from Portugal 23 railway trucks with boxes containing 14 unassembled aeroplanes, shipped from Hamburg.

On September 20th there arrived at Tetuan 12 large, German aeroplanes in which subsequently there were transported from Tetuan to Seville rebel troops from the so-called 'Foreign Legion.'

On September 29th the Spanish Government received information to the effect that on September 27th a consignment of asphyxiating gas and war materials of Italian origin left Lisbon for the Spanish frontier.

A number of eye-witnesses interrogated by the London Committee of Inquiry under the Chairmanship of Miss Eleanor Rathbone, M.P.,[6] as well as many correspondents of leading newspapers who have published their own personal observations, confirm that the supply of arms to the rebels, in the first place through Portugal, is being continued on a large scale. The rebels have at their disposal dozens of bombing and fighting 'planes of German and Italian origin which the Spanish Army did not possess when the rebellion broke out. Among the rebel aeroplanes brought down by Government forces were nine aeroplanes of German origin of the Haenkel type. Rebel troops are being transported across the Straits of Gibraltar

---

[2] See No. 215.　　[3] See No. 265.　　[4] See *ibid.*, note 6.　　[5] See *ibid.*, note 3.
[6] See No. 240, note 3. The report of this unofficial committee of inquiry into breaches of international law relating to intervention in Spain, published on Saturday, October 3, concluded that breaches of the non-intervention agreement, enabling the rebels to obtain arms denied to the Spanish Government, had placed the loyalists in a disadvantageous military position. The report was signed by Miss Eleanor Rathbone, Professor J. B. Trend, Mr. R. McKinnon Wood, Mr. E. L. Mallalieu, Lord Faringdon, Mr. J. Jagger, and the two secretaries, Mr. Geoffrey Bing and Mr. J. Langdon-Davies. Cf. *The Times*, October 5, p. 14. A copy is filed in the Foreign Office archives under the number W 13158/9549/41.

from Morocco into Spain in German and Italian aeroplanes. The frontier districts of Portugal have, from the very beginning of the rebellion, served as a base of operations for the rebels. In Portugal the rebels are organising their military units and it is from Portugal that they receive war material.

From the moment that our Committee was formed the Soviet Government has, through me, repeatedly raised the question of investigating the actions of Portugal which is openly violating the Non-Intervention Agreement, and of putting a stop to such actions.

The Soviet Government is apprehensive lest such a situation created by repeated violations of the Agreement render the Non-Intervention Agreement virtually non-existent.

The Soviet Government can in no case agree to turn the Non-Intervention Agreement into a screen shielding the military aid given to the rebels by some of the participants in the Agreement against the legitimate Spanish Government.

The Soviet Government is therefore compelled to declare that if violations of the Agreement for Non-Intervention are not immediately stopped the Soviet Government will consider itself free from the obligations arising out of the Agreement.[7]

Please accept, Sir, the expression of my high consideration and esteem.

S. CAHAN

[7] M. Cahan had already on October 6 addressed a letter to Mr. Hemming (received October 7) for circulation to the N.I. Committee drawing attention to Señor del Vayo's letter of September 15 (of which he enclosed a copy) and quoting some additional instances of active aid allegedly given by the Portuguese Government to the rebels. He suggested that the 'subject matter of this communication should take priority over all other matters under discussion by the Committee and should be urgently investigated by the Committee'. To make the investigation as exhaustive as possible he proposed that

'(a) an impartial commission be sent to the Spanish-Portuguese border to investigate on the spot the true state of affairs there, and that

(b) this commission should leave there some of its members to control the fulfilment of the Non-Intervention Agreement on that border in the future'.

No. 271

Sir E. Drummond (Rome) to Foreign Office (Received October 12)
No. 1095 [R 6015/226/22]

ROME, *October 7, 1936*

Sir,

I have the honour to report that, as stated in my telegram No. 636 of the 7th October,[1] I saw Count Ciano on that date for the first time since my return from leave.

2. I began by saying to him that I knew that the internal affairs of the United Kingdom were followed with great interest by the Head of the

[1] Not printed.

Government and I should like therefore to record certain impressions which I had formed during my visit to England. In the first place I felt that the position of the Government at the present time was strong. The Opposition was weak, both in Parliament and in the country. The country itself was distinctly prosperous and there was every sign of a continuing improvement in trade. I had had a talk with you,[2] Sir, before you left for Geneva. You had told me, and I was authorised to repeat the information, that His Majesty's Government had decided to carry through the rearmament programme. As regards air and naval rearmament the programme was proceeding in a most satisfactory way, indeed with more speed than had originally been expected. There was no lack of men or material. As regards the army, it was true that there were certain difficulties about recruiting, but these the Government intended and expected to overcome. I wanted to make it clear that the rearmament programme was not directed against any Power, and was solely for Empire defensive purposes. We could not afford to allow the safety of the Empire to depend on the goodwill of any State, however friendly that State might be to us. I felt that this position would be thoroughly appreciated by the Italian Government.

3. I could tell Count Ciano that neither you nor any member of His Majesty's Government cherished any resentment against Italy over the Abyssinian affair. There was a certain bitterness remaining in small sections of public opinion, but I did not believe that this would be of long duration. The desire of His Majesty's Government was to shake hands with Italy and be friends. The principal concern of His Majesty's Government at the present moment was to prevent Europe from becoming divided into two opposing blocs. His Majesty's Government hoped and believed that this was also the policy of the Italian Government. Here Count Ciano interrupted me to say that this certainly was Italy's policy. I went on to say that, this being so, there was every reason to think that our two countries could work together usefully as they had done in the past for European conciliation and collaboration. Count Ciano thanked me for my statement which he promised to report to the Head of the Government. He then referred to his last interview with Mr. Ingram, reported in the latter's letter of the 26th September[3] to Sir R. Vansittart, and said that the incidents which had been then mentioned, namely the visits of Sir Samuel Hoare and Sir P. Sassoon, the King's visit to Yugoslavia, the approaching visit of the Turkish fleet to Malta, the despatch of large British forces to Palestine, had been interpreted not only by the Italian press but also by the press in many other countries as proof that His Majesty's Government were adopting an anti-Italian policy. Count Ciano showed me an article on these lines which had appeared in the 'Journal de Genève' and said that other similar articles had appeared in the American press. Of course he was grateful for the assurances I had given him, but these were not known to the public. If the British press had replied to the views

---

[2] i.e. Mr. Eden.   [3] Not traced in the Foreign Office archives.

expressed by the Italian, Swiss, American and other newspapers then the position would have been made easier; but they had paid no attention to the articles in question. It was natural that when even the neutral press took such a view of British foreign policy, the Italian press should take it in an even greater degree.

I have, &c.,
ERIC DRUMMOND

No. 272

Foreign Office to Sir E. Drummond (Rome)

No. 372 Telegraphic [*W 13312/9549/41*]

Most Immediate   Personal   FOREIGN OFFICE, *October 8, 1936, 7.30 p.m.*

Following from Sir R. Vansittart.

In the course of conversation with the Italian Ambassador today His Excellency expressed the apprehension that the intention of His Majesty's Government to place before the Committee on non-intervention in Spain at tomorrow's meeting the charges preferred by the Spanish[1] and Soviet[2] Governments against Italy and other Powers will be interpreted in Italy as an act of partiality, whereby His Majesty's Government will be ranging themselves on the side of Soviet Russia and Communist Spain against Italy.

I have explained to Signor Grandi that such an interpretation would be wholly unjustifiable and that His Majesty's Government have no ulterior objects whatever in bringing these communications before the Committee. It has from the first been their view that one of the main purposes of this Committee would be to deal in a comparatively private and harmonious atmosphere with all charges of breaches of the non-intervention agreement, which would otherwise be left to be ventilated in all the acrimonious publicity of the press and public discussion.

In submitting these particular documents to the Committee His Majesty's Government are only carrying out what is their manifest duty under the terms of the agreement. The Russian documents were handed to the Chairman of the Committee and cannot of course be ignored. His Majesty's Government however are preferring no charges themselves against any Power, and they merely intend to seek the Committee's views and advice on the most suitable manner of dealing, within that body[,] with charges of this nature.

Signor Grandi expressed the view that this move on the part of the Soviet Government is deliberately aimed at breaking up the whole agreement; to which I replied that if this was in fact the case, their aim was precisely the contrary of that of His Majesty's Government who are most anxious

---

[1] See Nos. 215 and 265.   [2] See No. 270, note 6.

to keep both the agreement and the continued work of the Committee in being.

I suggest that it would be well if you saw Count Ciano or his representative at once and speak to him urgently in the same sense.

My reason for this suggestion is that I fear that if the Italian Government falsely persuade themselves of our partisan attitude in this matter, they may themselves be inclined to break up the agreement, which is apparently what they suspect the Soviet Government of desiring to do.

This would be bad enough in itself, but it would probably also affect adversely our cooperation in regard to the Five Power Conference.[3]

[3] At the fifth meeting of the N.I. Committee on Friday, October 9, at 11.30 a.m. the Chairman, Lord Plymouth, explained that he had called the meeting to consider documents received from the Spanish Government alleging breaches of the N.I. Agreement. In accordance with the rules of procedure he would communicate the documents to the Governments of Germany, Italy, and Portugal with a request for such explanations in writing as would enable the Committee to establish the facts. This procedure was agreed to after Signor Grandi had energetically repudiated every single point of the allegations as entirely fantastic. See No. 278 below.

No. 273

Foreign Office to Sir G. Warner[1] (*Berne*)
No. 24 Telegraphic [*W 12685/9549/41*]

FOREIGN OFFICE, *October 8, 1936, 8.50 p.m.*

Reliable report has been received that British s.s. 'Bramhill' reached Alicante on October 1st with a cargo of rifles, guns, explosives and bombs consigned to the Spanish Government.

In this connexion His Majesty's Government learn that an enquiry was received in the London Insurance Market early in September for the insurance of a cargo of ammunition and rifles from Zurich via Cologne and Hamburg to Hodeidah and Jedda, and a few days later a further enquiry was received for the insurance of munitions from Hamburg and Antwerp to Hodeidah by the s.s. 'Bramhill'.

Please inform the Swiss Government of the above and suggest that in view of their declared desire to cooperate with the other European Governments in preventing the export of arms to Spain, they will doubtless wish to investigate the question of the origin of these consignments which, there is strong reason to believe, were both destined for Spain. You should add that His Majesty's Government will be grateful if the Swiss Government will be good enough to inform them of the results of any enquiries which they may be able to make into this matter.[2]

[1] H.M. Minister at Berne.
[2] Sir G. Warner's despatch No. 432 of October 24 reported that the Swiss Customs authorities were unable to trace this cargo.

No. 274

Sir E. Drummond (Rome) to Foreign Office (Received October 12)
No. 1096 [R 6016/226/22]

ROME, *October 8, 1936*

Sir,

I have the honour to report that in the course of the interview which I had with the Minister for Foreign Affairs on the 7th October[1] on my return from leave I told him that I felt bound to let him know that I had been warned when I had recently been in London that there was considerable evidence which could not be ignored of anti-British propaganda inspired from Italian sources in Egypt, in Palestine and in Arab countries. His Majesty's Government felt that in Abyssinia they had played the game with regard to Italy; and they therefore confidently expected that such anti-British propaganda would cease. If the fact of such propaganda became known in England, there would be bound to be a strong public reaction with very injurious effects on Anglo-Italian relations.

2. Count Ciano replied that he was completely ignorant of any such anti-British Italian activities, in fact he did not believe that they were taking place. Such a policy would be entirely contrary to that of the Head of the Government. I said that I realised this because Signor Mussolini had several times said to me that he had no intention or wish to interfere with the British Empire. Nevertheless I felt it right to tell him that the evidence was of a character which could not be ignored. To this Count Ciano observed that if I could give him any information confirming what I had said he would be very grateful. I answered that, as he would understand, such confirmation was always difficult to give because of the sources from which the evidence came; but I remarked that I felt he might well devote his attention in this connection to Egypt, though I wanted to assure him that I believed the Italian Minister at Cairo to be perfectly innocent in this respect. Count Ciano again repeated that he had no knowledge of any such activities. He could not believe that there was any deliberate anti-British propaganda inspired by Italy, though naturally Italy, particularly during the Abyssinian crisis, had done her best to uphold her own point of view. He again pressed me for some definite indications which would enable him to pursue the matter, but I gave him no encouragement to think that I would be in a position to comply with this request.[2]

I have, &c.,
ERIC DRUMMOND

[1] Cf. No. 271.
[2] Minutes by Mr. C. Bramwell and Mr. O'Malley were as follows. 'Humbug! If the Italians keep on asking for chapter & verse and we continue to be unable to give it, they may well make it an excuse for disregarding our representations. It may be as well that Sir E. Drummond should be provided with evidence which he can quote; otherwise I fear we shall make no progress. C. Bramwell. 14 Oct.' 'I am afraid that the production of evidence would only make the Italians more careful without affecting their policy in the slightest degree. O. O'Malley, 15/10.'

No. 275

Sir E. Drummond (Rome) to Foreign Office (Received October 12)

No. 1097 [C 7145/4/18]

ROME, *October 8, 1936*

Sir,

I have the honour to report that in the course of the conversation which I had with the Minister of Foreign Affairs on the 7th October[1] on my return from leave, His Excellency informed me that he was studying the memorandum circulated by His Majesty's Government on the subject of the new Locarno Treaty.[2] He said that after having read this document he was doubtful whether any comments were required from the Italian Government because the substantive paragraph, namely No. 5, in which the views of His Majesty's Government were set out, made no mention of Italy and seemed to contemplate simply an Agreement between three Powers or, if Belgium were included, four. He implied that, as no mention was made of Italy, it was the deliberate intention of His Majesty's Government to exclude her from the new pact. I answered that I felt sure that this was a complete misunderstanding of the situation. His Majesty's Government expected and hoped that Italy as one of the guarantors of the former Locarno Pact would be equally a guarantor of the new pact. The memorandum simply had reference to the position of His Majesty's Government. Italy was on an equal footing as a guarantor and it would have been presumptuous on the part of His Majesty's Government to have made any suggestions as to what Italian policy should be.

2. This explanation, which I hope was correct, seemed considerably to relieve Count Ciano's mind and he asked me if I would have any objection to talking over the question with Signor Vitetti[3] and Signor Buti who were now examining the memorandum. I replied that although I had no official knowledge of the intentions of His Majesty's Government I should always be willing to take part in such an informal discussion. His Excellency then sent for Signor Vitetti and asked him to explain his point of view. I found that Signor Vitetti did not share the apprehensions of Count Ciano on the main point but he explained that the present view of the Italian Foreign Office, although no final conclusion had been reached, was not in favour of the changes proposed by His Majesty's Government. Signor Vitetti explained that according to his reading of the memorandum, there was to be a general pact by which Great Britain and Italy would guarantee France against attack by Germany and vice versa. But there would be an additional agreement by which Great Britain would be guaranteed by France and Germany should Great Britain be attacked by either of these Powers. Italy

---

[1] See Nos. 271 and 274.

[2] See Enclosure in No. 206.

[3] Signor Vitetti had returned to Rome from London to become head of General Affairs in the Italian Foreign Ministry from August 1, 1936.

was left out. Incidentally he asked why Belgium was omitted as a guarantor of Great Britain while Great Britain was ready to guarantee Belgium. I told him that I could not answer this question. He observed that Italy might well ask for a similar guarantee from France and Germany and then there would be one main pact and two subsidiary regional agreements. Count Ciano held that this would be a mistake. Let us assume as a hypothesis, Signor Vitetti continued, that Germany wished to attack France: if she did so directly she would be opposed by the three Powers. But supposing these regional agreements came into force, should she then attack either Great Britain or Italy instead of France she would be opposed by only two Powers instead of three. It was therefore to her advantage to do so. Italy was quite prepared to face a German–Italian quarrel, but she did not at all like the idea of being in the possible position of a State attacked by Germany because the latter really wished to fight France. He said that of course it was not the business of the Italian Government to give any advice to His Majesty's Government; but was a guarantee from France really worth running the risk which he had pointed out? If Germany intended to attack Great Britain surely the French position was such that France would in any case come to our help. He remarked that the arrangements in question seemed to him to change the whole spirit of Locarno. Instead of collaboration between the four great Powers there would be two sets of three Powers and the previous advantages of consultation between and conciliation by Italy and Great Britain would be greatly diminished. In his view the previous treaty derived special value from the disinterestedness of the two guarantors and therefore their power to keep and to promote peace between France and Germany.

3. Lastly there was a point concerning the Franco-Russian pact. Count Ciano stated that France could not move under that pact against Germany unless she had the consent of the two guarantor Powers, namely Great Britain and Italy. This ought to afford Germany considerable reassurance about that pact; but under the present system this condition would disappear and German dislike of the pact grow all the greater.

4. For all these reasons Count Ciano was inclined, although, as he had already told me, he had not yet come to any final decision, strongly to recommend that the Five Powers should revert to the general lines of the original pact. I replied that there seemed to me to be a certain force in his arguments, but might not a formula be found to cover the possibility of an attack, say, by Germany on Great Britain, because Germany wished to attack France? It was certainly important that there should be solidarity between all the guarantor Powers. To this Count Ciano replied that it might be very difficult to find any such formula. The simplest method would be a general pact of non-aggression and mutual assistance between all the signatories but he did not like such an idea which would place a completely different aspect on Locarno. Further, it would involve a British guarantee of the Italian frontiers and raise the whole question of the Mediterranean. In fact it would involve far wider questions than that of Locarno itself.

I told him that I would report his provisional views to the Foreign Office and was grateful to him for having expressed them to me.

I have, &c.,

ERIC DRUMMOND

No. 276

Sir E. Phipps (Berlin) to Foreign Office
(Received October 9, 12.15 p.m.)

No. 317 Telegraphic: by telephone [C 7082/4/18]

Immediate   BERLIN, *October 9, 1936*

A brief perusal of French reply of September 30th[1] to our memorandum[2] regarding Five Power Conference of September 17th shows that difficulties in the way of a new agreement are formidable.

Germany will almost certainly raise the question of Eupen and Malmédy with reference to paragraph 5 of French reply.

Paragraph 10 practically implies permanent stabilization of status quo and will never be accepted by Germany (see my telegram No. 313 October 2nd).[3]

Paragraph 11. Germany will never accept any air limitation that leaves Russia out of account.

Paragraph 17. Any prohibition of fortifications will have to be strictly reciprocal.

If final sentence is a *condition* viz. if new agreement is only to enter into force after 'negotiation plus vaste' it can wait for Greek Kalends . . .[4] German idea of central new Locarno is merely a renunciation of war between the Five Western Powers without any exception whatsoever.[5]

Repeated to Paris.

[1] No. 263.   [2] Enclosure in No. 206.   [3] No. 258.
[4] The text was here uncertain.
[5] Sir R. Vansittart thought that Eupen and Malmédy, air limitation, and frontier fortification were points that 'shd go in Germany's favour'. 'But that is enough, & her turn to be reasonable begins. And if she thinks she can get a simple renunciation of war between the Five Western Powers "without any exception whatsoever", she is making a mock of us & there will be no agreement. France cannot of course give up her connection with the Little Entente; nor should she be asked to do so. Germany has not a leg to stand on here, & her attitude wd. only be explicable by the intention of aggression in Central Europe—which we cannot condone in advance. R. V. Oct. 11.'

No. 277

Sir E. Phipps (Berlin) to Foreign Office (Received October 10)
No. 278 Saving: Telegraphic [W 13294/9549/41]

BERLIN, *October 9, 1936*

My telegram No. 277 Saving of October 8th.[1]

The 'Deutsche diplomatisch-politische Korrespondenz' of October 8th criticises in bitter tones the Soviet *démarche* in London[2] which must cause anxiety among all those, whatever their sympathies, who wish to avoid the sort of complications which the threatened Soviet intervention would bring about.

It is astoundingly insincere that the Soviet Union should regard itself as justified in taking up the rôle of the complainant when ample proof is not lacking that the Comintern itself has pursued a continuous policy of intervention in Spain; and the evidence of French Communists shows that this policy was in no way modified by Soviet participation in the Non-Intervention Committee. The Soviet emissaries found among the prisoners and dead of the Left forces in Spain are hardly proof of that correct behaviour which Russia now seeks to champion.

The real motives of the Soviet step are disappointment at the military set-backs of the Red Forces and the hope of still saving the 'revolutionary capital' invested in Spain by throwing the weight of Russia into the scales. This threat illustrates the close connexion between Russian diplomacy and revolutionary aspirations, and shows [that] the work begun by the Comintern is to be protected at all costs by the power of Russian diplomacy. This may, indeed, be useful in its effect upon those circles who have hitherto regarded Comintern and the Soviet Government policy as separate, and the guarantee of peace as the general object of the latter. 'Indivisible peace' is the creation of a power which has no interest in localising disturbances, and indeed wishes to miss no opportunity to generalise them: which does not shrink from pursuing its own ends by means of war and disturbances abroad. It is astounding that the civilised States of Europe should encourage such behaviour and that this Power should still be able to work to undermine peace in the guise of the altruistic friend.

[1] Not printed.   [2] See No. 270.

No. 278

Stenographic Notes of the Sixth Meeting of the Non-Intervention Committee, held in the Locarno Room, Foreign Office, on Friday, October 9, 1936, at 4 p.m.
[W 13856/11115/41]*

2, WHITEHALL GARDENS, S.W.1, *October 9, 1936*

LORD PLYMOUTH (*Chairman*):[1] Your Excellencies and Gentlemen, I should like, before we continue our discussion, to say that I have had some

[1] Representatives of twenty-six European countries, in addition to Lord Plymouth

discussion with the Portuguese Representative on this Committee since we adjourned this morning and, although, I regret to say, he feels it is not possible for him to be present during the discussion of items 2 and 3 of our agenda, he wished me to make it perfectly clear to the Committee that, in leaving the meeting, he did not wish to imply that Portugal meant to withdraw from the Committee. On the contrary, he is prepared to join our discussions once again later on.

We were discussing before our adjournment a complaint regarding certain alleged breaches of the Non-Intervention Agreement by Portugal received from the Representative of the U.S.S.R. Government.[2] It seems to me that this memorandum divides itself into two parts. The first part of it consists of a complaint against the Portuguese Government and finishes up by calling for an immediate and strict investigation into these complaints, whereas the second part consists of a proposal by the Soviet Government that a Commission should be set up to be sent to Portugal to investigate the conditions upon the spot. It seems to me that those are two entirely different questions and I suggest that we should discuss them separately. That seems to me to be the logical and the easiest way of dealing with the matter.

If there are no observations to be made by other Representatives, I propose, according to the procedure which we have laid down for ourselves, that I should address a letter to the Portuguese Representative enclosing the documents concerned and asking him to furnish this Committee with all the information that is necessary to establish the facts. That is in accordance with our rules of our procedure. There are no observations on that? Then I shall proceed accordingly.

We come now to the second point raised in the Soviet memorandum. That is the proposal that a Committee of Investigation should be sent to Portugal to examine matters on the spot. Has anybody anything to say on that? I do not know whether the Soviet Representative has anything to say in explanation of that suggestion.

M. SAMUEL B. CAHAN (U.S.S.R.): I stated at the morning session that I hardly need to say anything that would amplify the memorandum which I had submitted to the Chairman. It is now up to the Committee to discuss the suggestions contained therein. With the Portuguese Representative not here, for whatever reason that may be, it is for the other members of this Committee to say how they look upon those suggestions and subsequently to decide upon them.

JONKHEER R. DE MAREES VAN SWINDEREN (The Netherlands): If I

representing the United Kingdom, attended this meeting. Senhor Francisco de Calheiros e Menezes, the Portuguese Chargé d'Affaires in London, had attended the fifth meeting on the morning of October 9 at 11.30 a.m. (see No. 272, note 3), but announced his intention to withdraw pending his government's instructions when M. Cahan presented the Soviet Government's allegation that breaches of the non-intervention agreement had taken place in Portugal. The Committee, on Lord Plymouth's proposal, then adjourned for lunch. At 4 p.m. it reassembled without Senhor de Calheiros.

[2] See No. 270, and *ibid.*, note 6.

understand correctly, we have already decided on the first part of the Soviet communication, to send a letter to the Portuguese Representative asking him to answer those questions. Would it not be better to delay considering the question of sending out a Commission until we have had an answer from Portugal on the first question?

LORD PLYMOUTH (*Chairman*): I am in agreement with the Netherland Minister on this point. It seems to me that, according to the rules of our procedure, it is incumbent upon me as Chairman of the Committee first of all to communicate these complaints to the Representative of the Government complained against and that, before any further action can be taken, it is clearly necessary for us to await a reply from the Government concerned stating their point of view. I myself therefore look upon it as premature to consider any action such as that suggested by the Soviet Government in the last part of their memorandum. Does any other member of the Committee wish to express a view on that? I should like to get an expression of views in order to enable me to gauge the general feeling of the Committee on the matter.

HIS EXCELLENCY S. DINO GRANDI (Italy): Mr. Chairman, I entirely agree with what you have just said and I really do not think that the communication of the Soviet Representative in its present form can be acceptable by the Committee. In effect, the communication in question does not take into any account the rules of procedure which we have jointly established.

From an examination of the recommendations approved in this regard by our Committee, and in particular by an examination of paragraphs (*h*) and (*i*), it is clear and beyond all doubt that

Firstly. Complaints must be simple complaints, and cannot contain proposals by the Government presenting them, as to the measures which are eventually to be adopted on the assumption that the complaints are founded.

Secondly. The Committee cannot consider or discuss a complaint before it has been communicated to the Government concerned, and before the Government in question has furnished to the Committee 'such explanations as are necessary to establish the facts'.

Thirdly. Only after having reached this stage of the procedure, the Committee may consider 'such steps as may appear proper in each case to establish the facts'.

One may give a character of greater or minor urgency to such a procedure. But, it is not possible, for any reason whatsoever, to upset the rules agreed upon with the full approval of our Governments.

Before we begin to examine whether the proposals suggested by the Government of the U.S.S.R. are or not, in their substance, within the competence of the Committee, we must establish that our competence does not authorise the Soviet Government to set forth such proposals before that further meeting of the Committee in which the question may be discussed on the strength of the observations which might be forthcoming by the Portuguese Government.

But I would like to go beyond the establishing of this fact. Paragraph (i) of the recommendations of the Committee concerning the rules of procedure, establishes the competence of the Committee within the limits of a simple investigation aiming 'to establish facts'. An investigation which in no case considers the eventuality of sending a Commission on the spot. The examination of a proposal suggesting the despatch of a Commission of Investigation and Control (a Commission vested with powers of a precise political character) would consequently, at present, be completely beyond the competence of this Committee.

If the Soviet Government had kept in mind those very rules of procedure to which they have subscribed, they would have avoided presenting against one of the States participating in the Agreement on Non-Intervention, a complaint on the merits of which I shall abstain, for the moment, to express any opinion, but which is clearly inconsistent from the point of view of procedure clearly established by the Committee, and accepted by the Soviet Government of Russia.

His Excellency M. Charles Corbin (France): M. le Président, il est certain que l'absence du représentant du Portugal rend la discussion à l'heure actuelle extrêmement difficile. Nous ne pouvons pas aller au fond d'une question lorsque le principal intéressé fait défaut, comme c'est le cas actuel. A ce point de vue je ne puis m'empêcher de souligner ce qu'il y a de surprenant et d'anormal dans le départ du représentant du Portugal. Il est évident que si chacun de nous devait s'en aller chaque fois que son nom est prononcé et chaque fois que son pays est en cause, les discussions du Comité deviendraient extrêmement difficiles. Je crains donc qu'en quittant, comme il l'a fait, nos discussions, le représentant du Portugal n'ait créé un précédent des plus fâcheux, contre lequel il me semble que le Comité devrait se prononcer.

D'autre part, en ce qui concerne la procédure proprement dite, il nous est difficile de donner dès à présent un avis, mais j'ai écouté l'étude très détaillée qui a été exposée par le représentant de l'Italie, et je ne peux pas tout à fait me rallier à ce qu'il a dit au sujet du paragraphe (i) du sommaire des conclusions et recommandations du Comité en ce qui concerne la procédure. Dans cet alinéa en effet il est simplement indiqué que, lorsque les observations du Gouvernement contre lequel une plainte a été émise auront été reçues, le Comité prendra l'action qui peut lui paraître justifiée dans chacun des cas en vue d'établir les faits. Il est vrai que jusqu'à présent les observations du Gouvernement portugais n'ont pas été reçues, et par conséquent le Comité ne peut pas envisager l'action à prendre à la suite de ses observations. Mais lorsque ces observations auront été reçues, le Comité sera maître de décider quelle action il doit prendre, et il convient de faire toutes réserves en ce qui concerne la procédure qui devra être adoptée à ce moment.

M. Samuel B. Cahan (U.S.S.R.): I should like to make a few remarks in regard to the interpretation of the rules of procedure given by the Italian

Ambassador. I want to mention also the attitude of the Portuguese Representative. Not only has he withdrawn from the discussion of this point, but in his statement he has also said that, as the complaint emanates from a country with which Portugal has no relations, his Government consider the complaint to be in the nature of a hostile act.[3] I am not going to discuss the relations between my Government and Portugal or the absence of such relations. That is a different matter, but Portugal is a member of this Committee and is also a party to the Agreement. The complaint has been brought forward by a member of the Committee and by a participant in the Agreement. If Portugal is going to adopt such an attitude, or if any other participant is going to do so—because no doubt we shall have other complaints— and is going to consider a complaint as a hostile act, I am afraid that all those present here will have to be very careful in presenting any other complaints because such presentation is going to be construed as a hostile act. The Portuguese Representative has indicated that he cannot even be present during the discussion of this matter and, together with his attitude towards the complaint which has been preferred against Portugal, I should like to ask whether such behaviour also comes within the strict interpretation of the procedure. If such importance is attributed to every dot and comma in the procedure, I suppose that this behaviour of the Portuguese Representative and his attitude ought to call for a protest on the part of those at least who are trying to make themselves champions of that procedure.

It seems to me that there are some who are trying to squeeze the actual situation into narrower straits of a procedure which go further than the actual procedure laid down by the Committee. I fear that the question cannot be squeezed into an entirely watertight strait-jacket of a once established procedure. If I remember correctly, at the meeting when the question of procedure was discussed, there were some of the members, including the Chairman, who said it should be not a procedure of such a kind as to make it impossible for it to meet the circumstances of individual cases which might arise, but that we should make it flexible so that in each particular case it would be possible to deal with the actual situation. I think that I am right in recollecting that. Very well, that is the procedure. I do not see how, when a situation as serious as the present one comes up, it can be dismissed simply by pointing to some item in the procedure and by saying that this situation does not adjust itself to that procedure. I think that that would be to turn the table upside down and on my part I would not invite the Committee to adopt that view because I think it would be very difficult to justify.

With regard to the argument that the Soviet Government in this case and I suppose other Governments in other cases have no right, when preferring a complaint or, quite separately, to make any suggestions or proposals, that the Committee should be merely an investigating agency or something like that and restrict itself to that, I think such an argument quite wrong. I

[3] This statement was made by Senhor de Calheiros just before his withdrawal from the fifth meeting of the N.I. Committee.

think that such action must also come within the purpose of the Committee, which is to maintain the Agreement and to see that the Agreement is observed and to adopt any measures which may bring about such observance, or which may be called for the purpose of making that Agreement effective. I cannot see anything, either in the procedure or in any other document or on general grounds of principle, which would preclude any Government from making any concrete proposals as to how best to maintain an international Agreement which has been concluded between Governments. I therefore think that it is quite wrong to say that the Committee cannot hear any concrete suggestions made by any member of the Committee. It is a different question how the Committee will consider that proposal, whether they adopt the proposal or reject it, but to exclude proposals would really mean turning our Committee into a debating society.

LORD PLYMOUTH (*Chairman*): I think it only right to emphasise what the Portuguese Representative exactly said this morning. He said that he felt that he could not take part in the discussion on this item without instructions from his Government, which he had not received. Those were the words that he used, and he went on to say that he had communicated to his Government the text of the letter, and that it was only after he had received instructions that he would be in a position to make a communication to the Committee on this subject. I think that it is well to emphasise exactly what was the position that he took up. So far as the criticisms of his action are concerned, which have been referred to by one or two speakers, I might point out that he will, in the ordinary course of events, receive the minutes of this meeting, and he will from those minutes be able to judge for himself of the sense of the Committee generally on his action.

In regard to the question of procedure which has been referred to by the Soviet Representative, I understood him to say that he had on his part understood that, when these rules were adopted, it was implied that there should be a certain flexibility . . .[4]

M. SAMUEL B. CAHAN (U.S.S.R.): That was not only my statement, but the statement of other members of the Committee also. You have it in the minutes of the Committee.

LORD PLYMOUTH (*Chairman*): A statement by a number of members of the Committee?

M. SAMUEL B. CAHAN (U.S.S.R.): Yes.

LORD PLYMOUTH (*Chairman*): I can only observe on that point that, while there may have been views expressed to the effect that there should be a certain amount of flexibility in our rules, the point now under discussion is a matter of vital importance and, quite clearly, unless we are prepared to adhere to the essentials of our rules of procedure, we might just as well not have adopted them at all. It does seem to me that in a matter of this kind, where a complaint is laid against a particular Government, it is essential that that Government should be given an opportunity of stating its case from its own side before the Committee proceeds further to decide what action

---

[4] Punctuation as in the original.

it should take on the matter. That seems to me nothing more than a matter of justice and fairness. That is why I expressed the view that I considered the proposals in the last part of the Soviet memorandum premature at this stage.

M. SAMUEL B. CAHAN (U.S.S.R.): I think that you probably misunderstood my reference to the procedure. I did not refer to this part of the procedure at all. I only made my remark because there was an opinion expressed here that members, according to the procedure, are not entitled to present for the consideration of the Committee concrete proposals; and that the Committee is only to investigate complaints. It was to that part that I devoted my remarks.

HIS EXCELLENCY S. DINO GRANDI (Italy): May I make one point clear? I said 'at the present moment.' When I said that the proposals put forward by the Soviet Representative could not be discussed by the Committee, I said 'at the present moment.' I did not think that the Committee should be restrained from discussing any proposal in the future at all. I do not think that the proposal of the Soviet Representative can be discussed by the Committee until we hear the reply of the Portuguese Government.

LORD PLYMOUTH (*Chairman*): I am sure that the Soviet Representative will absolve me of any intentional desire to misinterpret what he said. Indeed, I think his further explanation clarifies the situation.

MR. J. W. DULANTY (Irish Free State): I do not want to extend this discussion about procedure; but, on that procedure, have we any authority or competence to send a commission into Portugal?

LORD PLYMOUTH (*Chairman*): I think that it is quite clear—in fact, I think it is a matter that is not subject to discussion or qualification—that it would be impossible to send a commission to Portugal as is suggested without the consent of the Portuguese Government itself. But, as I think it is generally agreed that the first step that should be taken is to request the Portuguese Government, according to our rules of procedure, to furnish us with information to enable us to establish the facts in regard to the complaints which have been made, I have proposed that I should send a letter to the Portuguese Representative on those lines. The Committee further appear to have agreed that the discussion of the last part of the Soviet memorandum would be premature. If that is the view of the Committee it seems to me that the way is clear, and in sending my message to the Portuguese Representative I will draw his attention to the fact that that was the view held by the Committee generally. It is agreed we should proceed in this way in regard to this item?

(Agreed)

We pass now to item 3 of the agenda, which is a letter, dated the 7th October, from the Representative of the U.S.S.R. Government which was addressed to me as Chairman of this Committee. I would ask the Soviet Representative if he would introduce this item on the agenda.

M. SAMUEL B. CAHAN (U.S.S.R.): Mr. Chairman, Your Excellencies and Gentlemen, the statement which I made on the instructions of my Government to the Chairman of the Committee on the 7th October, and which has been distributed to all the members of the Committee, so succinctly and precisely describes the actual situation as far as the fulfilment of the Agreement for Non-Intervention in Spain is concerned, and states the attitude of the Soviet Government so clearly, that it is hardly necessary for me to enlarge upon it.

Nevertheless, I have a few remarks which I wish to make:

There are probably some who live in bliss and think that everything is rosy. There are among us, even, some who think that the fulfilment of the obligations of the Agreement is proceeding so satisfactorily that they even suggest an extension of those obligations, and who think that all the participants so completely fulfil their obligations that they even suggest that countries at present outside the Agreement should be invited to adhere to it.

We, however, take the realistic approach and consider that the situation is so grave and serious that a stock-taking is necessitated and the unpleasant truth frankly faced. The actual situation, faced straightforwardly, is that the Agreement is not being fulfilled and that violations, on the part of some of the participants, are taking place. I am not going to cite instances; some are given in the statement made by me to the Chairman.

This state of affairs compels the Government of the U.S.S.R. to express the fear that such a situation created by repeated violations of the Agreements renders the Non-Intervention Agreement virtually non-existent. The Soviet Government, as I declared the other day in the statement made to the Chairman, can in no case agree to turn the Non-Intervention Agreement into a screen shielding the military aid given to the rebels by some of the participants in the Agreement against the legitimate Spanish Government.

What transpired at this morning's session of this meeting may, one cannot help thinking, lead to an attempt to turn the procedure also into a screen shielding the perpetuation of this unsatisfactory and impossible state of affairs.

It is because of this state of affairs that the Soviet Government is compelled to declare that if violations of the Agreement for Non-Intervention are not immediately stopped the Soviet Government will consider itself free from the obligations arising out of the Agreement.

That is all I have to say on that subject.

But before closing I would like to add only this: At the morning session of this meeting His Excellency the Italian Ambassador attempted in his declaration to brush aside any evidence by newspaper correspondents and other eye-witnesses on the spot. On the other hand, his counter-charges in regard to British airmen, &c., were based entirely on newspaper reports. He can't have it both ways. And, again, His Excellency the Italian Ambassador attempted in his declaration to dismiss summarily all the instances of violations of the Agreement by merely describing them as fantastic. But facts are stubborn things and require something more than summary dismissal to refute them.

His Excellency S. Dino Grandi (Italy): I would like to remind the Soviet Representative that in the course of a long discussion which he raised in the Sub-Committee, against the viewpoint of all other members, he stated that the competence of the Committee was extremely narrow, and that it could not, for instance, even discuss the questions relating to the sending to Spain of volunteers, political agitators and financial assistance directed to foment civil war.

To-day, on the contrary, he would like to invest our Committee with the competence of the utmost magnitude. He would like, in fact, to see our Committee examine a Note which states the political attitude of the Soviet Government towards the Agreement on Non-Intervention.

Now, if I rightly remember, in order to elude the insistence of his colleagues who wanted to discuss the question of indirect intervention, a subject apparently not so pleasant to the U.S.S.R. Government, the Soviet Representative suggested in the Sub-Committee that those Governments which wanted to include in the pledge of non-intervention the sending to Spain of volunteers, of political agitators and of funds for propaganda and war purposes should address the Soviet Government through the diplomatic channel.

This procedure, which at the time appeared to be an attempt to avoid the discussion, is instead in the present case the most logical and most suitable procedure. If the Soviet Government wish to inform us that they intend to regain their freedom of action and withdraw from the Agreement on Non-Intervention they must make known the decision direct, and through the diplomatic channel to the Governments adhering to the Agreement and not to the Committee.

If, as I believe, the object of the Soviet Government is to get themselves free from the pledges to which they are bound through the Agreement on Non-Intervention, it would be preferable that they should not invoke unfounded or insufficient pretexts in the endeavour to make others responsible for their decision.

Let us consider the situation with which we are faced. The Soviet Government threaten to leave us, unless we manage to put an immediate stop to certain alleged infractions of the Agreement on Non-Intervention. The threat has been launched, even before the Committee had an opportunity of examining, in the light of the observations and explanations which might be forthcoming, whether the complaints are actually founded and whether the infractions have actually taken place.

The Soviet Government, with a peculiar and suspicious haste, would like to force us to tear up the established rules, and go so far as to threaten us all with their immediate withdrawal if the Committee does not work miracles of speed. Why this haste? Why this sudden zeal?

The Soviet Government, which are so scrupulously vigilant of the observance by others of the Agreement on Non-Intervention, are they themselves exempt from any suspicion of interference in the affairs of Spain?

This question begs the answer. It is not necessary to read English, French, German or Italian papers: the Soviet papers are by themselves sufficient. We need only remember the public statements by Soviet leaders to realise the attitude of the U.S.S.R. in regard to the events in Spain. Only yesterday the new representative of the Madrid Government in Moscow, Señor Pasqua, extended publicly his thanks to the Russian Communist Government for the assistance of every kind which the Soviets are giving to the Spanish Government. Only a short time ago the official review of the 'Profintern' published the instructions given in Moscow by Lozovsky to the Spanish Communists for the establishment of the Soviet Republic in the territory of the Iberian Peninsula. And in the *Pravda* of the 15th September we have read an article illustrating in detail the various steps of the Communist march for the conquest of power in Spain.

The Italian Government have insistently drawn the attention of the Sub-Committee to the various forms of indirect intervention for the simple reason that, particularly on the Soviet's initiative, these interventions have acquired an importance and a gravity which are far greater than the sending of arms and munitions to Spain.

I could submit documentary evidence of these indirect interventions, but I shall restrict myself to direct interventions, that is to say, to those very interventions which cause so violent an indignation in the Soviet Government whenever they think that others are responsible for them.

I wish to point out only a few of the many instances which have come to the knowledge of the Italian Government:

(1) *September 18 and 20.*

Thirty Soviet airplanes arrived in Barcelona about the middle of September. They are machines of large build and camouflaged with Red Cross signs.

(2) *September 18 and 20.*

The Soviet Government has accepted to supply, purely on credit, the Madrid Government with the petrol already loaded on several ships.

(3) *September 19.*

Numerous airplanes have been unloaded in Barcelona from Soviet ships.

(4) *September 20.*

At the beginning of September four Soviet officers arrived in Paris from Warsaw, proceeding the following day for Toulouse, directed to Spain.

(5) *September 25.*

On the 20th and 21st September, the Russian ships *Neva* and *Volga* went through the Bosphorus in transit, directed to Alicante, and having on board about 500 tons of war materials.

(6) *September 25 and 26.*

Russian ship *Neva* arrived at Alicante on the 26th September, and unloaded cases of rifle ammunition, foodstuffs and petrol. The ship had already unloaded at Valencia.

(7) *September 25.*

The raw material for the manufacture of explosives loaded in Belgium on Mexican ship *America*, ex *Vera Cruz*, was labelled 'Soviet Union.' Russian origin evident.

(8) *September 27.*

Soviet ship, on the 19th September, unloaded wheat at Barcelona. On the following morning unloaded considerable quantity of rifles, hand grenades and machine guns. Soon after went out to sea, it would appear directed to Valencia.

(9) *September 25.*

At the Military Aerodrome of Madrid, about forty Russian Military machines are expected. Commissioned officers of the Soviet Air Force have been there the last few days so as to prepare base and quarters.

(10) *September 29.*

Russian ship *Neva* still unloading, at Alicante. Steamer unloaded an undefined number of dismantled airplanes, which have been carried on motor vans to Cartagena to be assembled by Russian officers sent there. 3,600 small cases containing rifles and 4,000 containing the relative ammunition. Part of the cargo was camouflaged as foodstuffs. Russian ship *Kuban* expected.

(11) *October 2.*

On the 27th September steamer *Kuban* left Odessa for Spain carrying nominally 2,000 tons of foodstuffs, but in reality, munitions.

(12) *September 28.*

In the afternoon of the 25th September the steamer *America*, ex *Vera Cruz*, Mexican flag, sailed from Antwerp, directed, officially, to Vera Cruz, but in reality, to a Spanish port. Has loaded 1,116 casks of Potassium Chlorate, 413 of Toluol, 1,400 of Sulphuric and 310 kilos. of Phenol, all of Soviet origin, as well as 25 tons of scrapped copper. Above goods, for the manufacture of explosives, is [*sic*] destined to the Madrid Government.

(13) *October 5.*

During the night of the 2nd October, the British ship *Bramhill*[5] unloaded at Alicante cases containing rifles, munitions, and bearing the Soviet manufacture marks.

[5] See No. 273.

(14) *October 6.*

Russian steamer *Kuban,* arrived to-day, started unloading many small cases of munitions, which have been loaded on train of fifty trucks.

(15) *October 6.*

Russian activity becomes always more intense. Ships from the Black Sea continue to arrive regularly, publicly unloading foodstuffs at Barcelona, and clandestinely arms and ammunitions often at smaller ports.

(16) *October 1.*

The steamer *Kroule* unloaded, at Barcelona, to-day, arms and ammunitions, more especially rifles.

(17) *October 6–10.*

Russia send[s] money under the form of subscriptions.

(18) *Last Week.*

At Calle Igualdad (Pueblo Nuovo, Barcelona), were installed four anti-aircraft machine guns, very powerful, of recent invention, electrically driven; Russian technicians effected their installation.

Those are the facts. This is the truth of the situation.

The Italian Government, however, do not threaten to withdraw from the Agreement because of these facts. The Italian Government have too great a sense of responsibility towards European co-operation and peace, and have adhered to the Agreement on Non-Intervention with too much loyalty to endanger its existence by showing a false zeal or invoking doubtful pretexts.

I strongly protest against these unprecedented and provocative methods of the Soviet Union.

Before publicly launching accusations against other Powers, the Soviet Government should have fulfilled the elementary duty of collecting the proofs of their allegations.

It is not only against my country and my Government that this unwarrantable action is aimed; but also against the Committee itself.

The Committee discussed very carefully at the end of each meeting the wording of the press *communiqué,* with the very wise intent of avoiding the publication of anything which might inflame the public opinion of the world and provoke regrettable polemics and conflicts.

The Russian Government in giving to the international press their note of threats and blackmail and causing the newspapers to publish this morning their allegations against the Portuguese Republic, have broken the fundamental rules of diplomatic correctness, and have violated the spirit and the letter of the Non-Intervention Agreement, which—in the words of the French Note[6]—has been promoted in order to 'avoid any complications which may prejudice the maintenance of good relations among the Nations'.

[6] Cf. No. 64, note 1.

The Soviet Government wishes to sabotage our Committee and make it impossible for it to work.

The Communist Government of Russia have not found recent events in Spain satisfactory to their wishes.

The Spanish people do not seem disposed to follow the Communist creed of destruction and upheaval of the world, preached by the Communists of Russia.

This is why, in a supreme effort to turn the tables, Soviet Russia seeks a pretext to disengage herself from the pledges she has undertaken.

These can be the morals of Soviet Communism, but these morals are not ours.

I wish to state once more that the Italian Government do not intend to share any responsibility for whatever may happen in Europe and in the world, should the Agreement—which they have faithfully applied—be annulled by the unilateral decision of one of the adhering States. It must be quite clear that such a State—whatever may be its pretexts—will have to bear the full and exclusive responsibility of its action.

LORD PLYMOUTH (*Chairman*): Your Excellencies and Gentlemen, I do not desire to intervene more than necessary, but in view of the fact that the letter now under discussion was addressed to me I feel that perhaps it is incumbent on me to make a few remarks. The letter in question was handed to me, as Chairman of the Committee, on Wednesday afternoon[7] by the Soviet Representative with the information that it would be published in Moscow the next morning, and with a request that copies should be circulated to all members of this Committee. I expressed astonishment at this course, for, according to our practice, all the proceedings of our Committee have up till now been regarded as confidential and what we have done has been to issue an agreed *communiqué* at the conclusion of each of our meetings. As this letter was handed to me specifically, as Chairman of the Committee, for circulation it appears to me to have been contrary to the rules of our procedure to have published it before this Committee had any opportunity whatsoever even to consider it. But passing for a moment to another point raised in the letter, I should like to say this. The gravamen of the complaint which it contains appears to be that the Soviet Representative had repeatedly raised the question of investigating what was going on in Portugal, but that the Committee had not done anything about it. It is certainly perfectly true that the Soviet Representative has referred to this matter on a number of occasions, but he has done so in very general terms and in such a way as to make it impossible for the Committee to take the matter up according to the rules of procedure which it has adopted. The Rules of Procedure have been fully discussed and are very well known to all of us. The Soviet Representative has had the same opportunity as any other member of laying a complaint according to those rules, but he has not, in fact, taken that opportunity until now. I merely say this because it appears to me that, on

---

[7] October 7; see No. 270.

this account, the burden of his charge that the Committee has done nothing must fall to the ground, and, indeed, that he must share responsibility fully with every member of the Committee for its past proceedings. I would, of course, strongly urge that any complaints that are to be made should be made according to the rules of that procedure, and that they should be sent in writing to the Secretary to our Committee and then dealt with in the way we have laid down in our rules. Of course, it is open to any member of the Committee to make whatever observations they would wish on the item under discussion, but, as I see it, there appears no definite action to take, and it would appear that all we can do in the end is to take note of this communication which was handed to me by the Soviet Representative, and which, by his request, was circulated to the members of the Committee. Are there any further observations? Then, if there is nothing more that anyone wishes to say, I suggest that it be . . .[4]

M. Samuel B. Cahan (U.S.S.R.): If no one else wants to make any remarks, I should like to say a few words. There is quite a popular method of constructing a defence by trying to attack, and in this instance this method has been adopted by the Representative of Italy, but the means by which he has carried out the attack do not, I think, carry much weight, and are not very convincing. First of all, I want to make a few observations on certain points that have been raised by the Italian Ambassador. The Italian Ambassador attributes to me statements to the effect that I have always insisted on the 'extremely narrow limits' of our competence. Anyone reading the proceedings of the meetings of the Committee, as well as those of the Sub-Committee, knows and will clearly see that I have always tried to point out that the competence of the Committee is *the Agreement itself*. Whether it is wide or narrow is another matter, but the fact remains that the Agreement is the limit of our Committee's competence. The statement that I made to the Chairman of the Committee deals with matters coming directly under the Agreement, therefore no insistence on the 'narrow limits of the Committee,' which was attributed to me by the Italian Ambassador, has anything to do with this matter. The statement under discussion deals with the military aid given to the rebels in Spain by certain countries, and that is exactly what is prohibited by the Agreement. The Italian Representative also tries to read my mind as to what I thought and as to what prompted my attitude towards indirect intervention, a matter which has been raised by the Italian Representative. I think that that is a futile attempt, because what I had in mind I stated in the Sub-Committee, and my statements had nothing to do with the likes or dislikes of any particular item in the Italian memorandum which had been discussed in the Sub-Committee. I have not expressed any opinion on the substance of the Italian memorandum and I have stated so, and my attitude was based entirely on the fact that it is outside the Agreement. Therefore, I said that if any Government wished to enlarge the Agreement, they would be perfectly entitled and welcome to do so, but it had nothing to do with likes and dislikes, and it is no use because of the lack of more convincing arguments to try to read people's minds. There is also the attempt of the Italian Ambassador to interpret to his own convenience the motives which prompted my Government in making the statement to the Chairman. In order to make the task easier so that some people would not have to read my mind, I can repeat again that what we had in mind was that the Agreement is not being fulfilled by some of its participants. That is what prompted my statement, and that is what prompted my Government to declare that if the Agreement is not going to be fulfilled it will have to draw certain conclusions, that it will have to consider itself freed from the obligations arising out of the Agreement, if a stop is not put to violations of the Agreement. No reading of minds is necessary to look for motives, the motive is here; violations are taking place; violations must be stopped; otherwise it is no use having an Agreement; otherwise it is no use having a Committee which acts as a screen to shield violations of the Agreement. Why, inquired the Italian Ambassador, are we in such haste? Well, no one can speak about haste. I could very well understand one saying that we are doing it rather late, that we have tolerated a situation which is quite impossible for too long. Instead of accusing me or the Government which I represent of making a hasty declaration that violations of the Agreement have to be stopped, the Italian Ambassador, who so nobly 'defended' here the Agreement, ought to have reproached us for not making such a declaration before. A great deal of his Excellency's statement again for want of better arguments was devoted to the press and speeches by some persons in the Soviet Union, &c. I will not burden the Committee with citations, but I have not mentioned anything about the Italian papers or statements by public men in Italy as to what opinions they expressed in regard to Spanish affairs, or as to what sympathy they have with one side or the other. I have not mentioned the telegram of congratulation which Herr Hess sent to Franco on the occupation of Toledo. I have not mentioned such things at all. They are outside the Agreement. What I am concerned with are guns, machine guns, ammunition, bombers, &c. That is what comes within the Agreement, and that is what we referred to when we spoke about violation, and I think that that is clear from our statement. The Italian Ambassador also mentioned a number of Russian ships that went to Spanish ports. From his description one could not avoid getting the impression that they were not ships, but three motor Caproni bombers that could make journeys from one place to another in 24 hours and come back. The dates which the Italian Ambassador mentioned I do not remember, but it looked as though these vessels made a journey from the U.S.S.R. to a Spanish port and came back with another load within a few days. That is just an illustration to show how seriously one could take such very sensational, but not too convincing stories. We heard a harrowing story about ammunition, officers, and dozens and dozens of Soviet bombers, and of other things of which we hear for the first time to-day. Where are they? I have not heard, nor had anybody else, of a single report in the press or a statement by any person who has been in Spain about a single Soviet aeroplane being shot down, about a single Soviet aeroplane being captured, about a single Soviet airman being killed or a single Soviet shell being found. Nothing of that kind has ever appeared. Is it because the whole world press is so unanimously determined to conceal the 'terrible' things that the U.S.S.R. is doing in Spain? No. *It is because there are no such things.* On the other hand, the world press is full of reports not only by newspaper men, but by public men who have been to Spain, who have been to the insurgent side of Spain, to Portugal, to the Balearic Islands, to Spanish Morocco, about Germany, Italy, Portugal. They have supplied the world with details. We know of Italian aeroplanes being shot down, we know about German aeroplanes being shot down, we know about German shells and Italian ammunition being fired. We know about Italian pilots being captured, we know about Italian pilots being lent for work with the rebels, and so on, and so on. One may try to scare little children with such 'terrible' tales about 'Soviet intervention,' but not grown-up experienced people, used to all kinds of tight corners and tight situations. On the other hand, the world press and their representatives, public men and Members of Parliament, quite impartial persons who could not be accused of any particular likes or dislikes of one side or the other, testify to the violations by the countries mentioned. And all that is apart from the documents that came from the Spanish Government, which is a Government with whom all the Governments represented here maintain normal diplomatic relations, and whose word is to be trusted just as much as the word of any Government represented here on the Committee. We have heard 'evidence' which is absolutely unfounded, especially when there are material examples to illustrate the 'value' of that 'evidence.' I would like to mention the case of the two ships which I do know went to Spain, which were mentioned here by the Italian Ambassador, the *Kuban* and *Neva*. They went to Spain; we have made no secret of it, it was published in our press. Let us take the *Neva*. It carried 30,000 pouds of butter, 95½ thousand pouds of sugar, 17,000 pouds of tinned goods, 18,000 pouds of margarine, 12,000 pouds of confectionery. The *Kuban* carried 30,000 pouds of flour, 27,000 pouds of butter, 61,000 pouds of sugar, 11,000 pouds of smoked fish, 250,000 tins of conserved goods and 1,000 boxes of eggs. Well, Your Excellencies, if the world press and other sources would report shipments of that kind from Germany, Italy and Portugal to Spain, no one would come out in the Committee and raise a question about it. His Excellency the Italian Ambassador spoke about the statement as being a threat and blackmail. I think the Ambassador had no right to use the last word at all. As to the 'threat,' is it a 'threat' to demand from one to fulfil the Agreement? I do not think anybody could call that a 'threat.' We based our statement on violations which hardly anyone will deny, except possibly the interested parties, and the 'threat' is seen in the request that measures should be taken to stop this violation. This request is quite normal and quite justified. Otherwise, what would be the use of having an international agreement if it were not observed? As you are aware, there has been adopted lately in some countries quite a new policy of violating agreements, but I do not think everyone would agree to make such a policy part of international law. I think that international law is not to be thrown overboard, and hardly anyone will accept this new maxim as to what should be the law of intercourse between Governments and Governments, between countries and countries. His Excellency the Italian Ambassador accuses us of sabotage. Well, I think the whole proceedings which we have been witnessing in the Committee so far, and the attitude adopted by some towards to-day's discussion of violations of the Agreement, indicates where sabotage is to be found. It may be that the present situation does not fit in with the procedure, but, as I said in my previous statement, you cannot adjust the actual situation to the procedure, you have to adjust the procedure to the actual situation. That is more important, and I repeat that, if there is an Agreement, *we want that Agreement to be fulfilled.* If the Committee or the countries represented on the Committee can secure that the Agreement is fulfilled to stop violation, well and good; if it cannot, let the Committee say so and everyone will draw the proper conclusions. As far as we are concerned, we say that unless the breaches are stopped we shall consider ourselves freed from the Agreement. That is all I want to say, except that I wish to make a few remarks in connection with what the Chairman has said. Would you prefer me to do that now or later?

Lord Plymouth (*Chairman*): I think now, if you will.

M. Samuel B. Cahan (U.S.S.R.): I want to remind you, Lord Plymouth, that when I handed the statement to you I made two requests, not one. I made one request that you should send copies to the members of the Committee, which was quite proper, as it dealt with the Agreement and with violations of the Agreement. It was quite proper that all members representing Governments parties to the Agreement should get a copy. On the other hand, I made a request that you should publish the statement, and I added that this statement would be published in Moscow the next day. I do not see anything improper about that. It is true that we adopted the policy in our work in the Committee that whatever took place in the Committee should not be divulged in any manner except through the *communiqués* which were issued after each meeting, but my statement did not deal with anything which was done in the Committee. It was a statement of a Government, and if that Government considered it necessary to have its own statement published, I do not see anything which could be considered as wrong or against the procedure of the Committee. In regard to Portugal, the Chairman has stated here that we should follow the procedure. Apart from the occasions referred to by the Chairman, I want to remind him of another instance when after the meeting at which I again stated that the matter of Portugal should be discussed at the next meeting from the point of view of measures to be taken to rectify the situation in Portugal, where violations were taking place, and, although that matter had been on the agenda circulated to the members, the question was taken off the agenda on the very day of the meeting. I spoke to the Chairman about this before the meeting, but the matter was not restored to the agenda, although at that meeting I wanted to raise again the matter of Portugal in its widest aspect. Finally, the Chairman has suggested that the only thing that can be done is to take note of my communication. I think that the Committee will have to do more; we in our statement proposed that measures to stop violations should be taken. It is now up to the Committee to elaborate such measures and to adopt such measures. I do not think that the question can possibly be settled by just taking note of our communication.

PRINCE VON BISMARCK (Germany): I would only like to deal with one aspect of the matter which was raised at the end of his speech by the Soviet Representative, that is, the way in which the Committee should deal with the letter of the 7th October. Whereas the Chairman proposed that we should only take note of it, the Soviet Representative asks that specific measures should be taken. I very strongly take the line that we should adopt the Chairman's proposal, as I feel that this Committee is not competent to deal with the contents of that letter, which does not demand the adoption of the normal method of procedure, but contains political threats of the Soviet Government to separate itself, under certain circumstances, from the association of the Embargo Powers and, as was apparently announced by it in Geneva, to lend its full assistance in all publicity to the Madrid Government. This Committee would surely sincerely regret a possible decision of the Soviet Government to separate itself from the association of the Embargo Powers, but, should the Soviet Government decide to take such a step as announced in its letter of the 7th October, my Government must naturally reserve its attitude as to the consequences which would follow from such decision.

LORD PLYMOUTH (*Chairman*): I should like to ask the Soviet Representative one question. He has expressed the view that my proposal that we should take note of the letter that he addressed to me was not sufficient, and that he felt that some further action should be taken. I do not think that he has suggested, either in the course of his remarks or in the letter, what kind of action he has in mind.

M. SAMUEL B. CAHAN (U.S.S.R.): I raised this matter in the statement to the Chairman and again in my remarks to-day, because the situation requires some steps to be taken by the Committee which would have the effect of immediately stopping the violations of the Agreement. I think that it is up to all the members of the Committee, if they agree with the seriousness of the situation—and I am sure that they do agree—to suggest and adopt measures which would *really* have that effect.

HIS EXCELLENCY M. CHARLES CORBIN (France): Il paraît assez difficile au point où nous sommes dans cette discussion de déterminer ce qu'on peut faire. Le représentant des Soviets a parlé des mesures à prendre par le Comité en vue de s'assurer si celui-ci remplit exactement sa tâche. Le Président de son coté a estimé qu'il convenait simplement de prendre note des observations qui ont été formulées par le délégué soviétique et de poursuivre notre tâche.

Au début de nos délibérations nous avons essayé d'indiquer les lignes générales suivant lesquelles doit se poursuivre l'activité du Comité. Nous avons adopté certaines règles de procédure. Nous avons essayé par là de trouver une commune mesure de manière à ce que notre tâche puisse être remplie conformément à l'esprit général qui inspirait l'initiative à la suite de laquelle le Comité a été créé. Si des mesures particulières doivent être prises, c'est assurément au moment où les modalités pratiques de la procédure fixées par le Comité auront été épuisées. Actuellement si ces règles doivent être changées, ou si elles doivent être complétées, il serait très utile que des propositions précises puissent être apportées. Pour éviter que de cette discussion il ne résulte dans le Comité une atmosphère de malaise, et pour répondre à l'objectif que nous poursuivons tous, il serait nécessaire d'appliquer aussi strictement que possible les principes que nous avons établis dès l'origine, et en particulier de rappeler qu'à la base de notre action doit toujours se trouver un exposé concret, appuyé sur des faits aussi précis que possible, des manquements que nous aurions à relever de la part d'un des pays adhérant à l'Accord de Non-Intervention.

Nous sommes toujours obligés d'en revenir là, et c'est lorsque nous aurons constaté des faits précis constituant des manquements, que nous pourrons déterminer si des mesures particulières doivent être prises. Je ne crois pas qu'il soit possible d'obtenir l'accord du Comité à des dispositions nouvelles, destinées à compléter celles que nous avons établies jusqu'à présent, si nous n'avons pas d'abord pu mettre sur pied l'exposé des manquements qui constituerait leur raison d'être.

Ceci dit, je m'associe, et beaucoup des membres du Comité partageront ce sentiment, au désir qui a été exprimé de voir une enquête s'engager aussi rapidement et aussi complètement que possible. Il ne faut pas que l'on puisse dire que le Comité est un écran derrière lequel on peut faire à peu près ce que l'on veut sans qu'il y ait aucune observation, ni aucune suite aux infractions qui auraient été commises, mais nous ne devons rien négliger clairement si des infractions ont été commises. Pour ma part je crois que c'est sur cette base que nous devons maintenir notre action, et que c'est à cette règle que nous devons nous tenir avant d'envisager des mesures nouvelles.

LORD PLYMOUTH (*Chairman*): Are there any other observations? We have one very formidable task before us still, I am afraid, and that is the drafting of a *communiqué* for the Press, which may require a good deal of careful consideration. As I see it, we have no actual proposal before us. I mean, no actual proposal is made in the letter which we are discussing at the present moment. I think, perhaps, that the best thing we can do is to proceed to the consideration of the question of issuing a *communiqué* to the Press, and during the course of that consideration, when we reach this item, it is possible that we shall be able to find a formula which will be satisfactory to all concerned. Does the Committee agree that it would be wise now to proceed to the drafting of the *communiqué*?

(Agreed)

Before we proceed to do that, there is just one small formal matter the Secretary wants to refer to—item 4 on the agenda.

MR. FRANCIS HEMMING (*Secretary to the Committee*): Item 4 figures on the agenda merely to bring to the notice of the members of the main Committee a supplementary request for additional information in regard to the treatment to be applied to arms and war material destined for Spain which form part of the cargo of a vessel calling at the port of a country which is a party to the Agreement, which the Chairman's Sub-Committee at their last meeting decided to put before the main Committee. A question on this subject had already been put to the main Committee, but the Sub-Committee thought that its terms were not sufficiently clear and precise. An improved formula has now been submitted to the Committee, the members of which are now asked to submit it to their respective Governments.

LORD PLYMOUTH (*Chairman*): Is that agreed?

(Agreed)

We now come to the question of the *communiqué* and I suggest that we should adjourn for ten minutes or so to enable the Secretary to grapple with this question and to produce a draft that might be placed before the Committee for their consideration.

(The Committee adjourned accordingly.)[8]

[8] The discussion of the drafting of the *communiqué* occupies a further 16 pages, and is omitted. The *communiqué* was published in *The Times*, October 10, p. 14.

No. 279

Record by Mr. Eden[1] of a conversation with M. Blum

[*C 7128/4/18*]

FOREIGN OFFICE, *October 10, 1936*

During the course of a conversation yesterday with M. Blum, at which His Majesty's Ambassador in Paris was also present, we spoke of the state of the Locarno negotiations, and I told M. Blum that my latest information indicated that I might expect a reply from Berlin in about a week's time. In the meanwhile I did not propose to take any further initiative in the matter in so far as concerned Germany. Indeed, I thought that on the whole there was considerable advantage in our not showing ourselves too much in a hurry just now. The success of the Three-Power monetary initiative,[2] upon which I once again congratulated M. Blum, had served to place the democracies in a stronger position. While, therefore, I was of course at heart as anxious as ever to promote the progress of the negotiations, I considered that as a matter of tactics we might facilitate that progress by not showing ourselves too eager.

[1] Mr. Eden had left Geneva after the meeting of the League Assembly on October 2 for a short holiday in the south of France. He stopped off in Paris to see M. Blum on his way home (cf. Avon, *op. cit.*, p. 408), and arrived in London on the evening of October 9.

[2] See No. 248, note 4.

M. Blum replied that he was in full agreement with what I had said. In the meanwhile as a result of a communication which Mr. Morrison had made to the French Delegation at Geneva,[3] conversations would be opened between the French, United Kingdom and United States Governments with regard to the possibilities of monetary economic co-operation in the future. M. Blum stated that he was sending M. Rueff[4] to London for this purpose.

On my telling the Prime Minister that owing to my absence on holiday in the South of France, I had not myself seen the text of Mr. Morrison's communication, M. Blum drew it out of his pocket, read it, and remarked that he was in entire agreement with its terms.

During the course of luncheon I had taken the opportunity to say a word to M. Delbos on what I believed to be the dangers of trying to go too fast in our negotiations with Germany. There were moments when to show a certain stiffness was the best way to promote agreement. M. Delbos, whose view generally more closely approaches to that of the Quai d'Orsay than does M. Blum's, at once assented vigorously. He added that it was under pressure from us that the French Government had shown themselves so forthcoming in the past. There would certainly be no difficulty on their part therefore in adopting a firmer attitude.

ANTHONY EDEN

[3] This referred to a French proposal for a financial conference to follow up the tripartite currency declaration of September 26: see No. 248, note 4. Mr. Morrison had been instructed to tell the French Government that His Majesty's Government could not commit themselves to a conference without full consultation beforehand between the three Powers.
[4] Assistant Director of the *Mouvement général des fonds* in the French Ministry of Finance.

No. 280

Record by Mr. Eden of a conversation with M. Blum
[C 7129/4/18]

FOREIGN OFFICE, *October 10, 1936*

During the course of a conversation yesterday with M. Blum, at which His Majesty's Ambassador in Paris was also present,[1] I told M. Blum that there was a question I wished to put to him in order to clear up certain rumours which had been current in our press and in the French press also. Was it true that in the conversation which the French Prime Minister had had with M. Litvinoff after my departure from Geneva agreement had been reached to open staff conversations between France and Soviet Russia either now or in the near future? M. Blum in reply expressed some surprise at the rumour, of which he had apparently not heard, but stated at once that it was devoid of all foundation. Some considerable time ago, he believed at the time of M. Laval's visit to Moscow,[2] the question of staff conversations had been raised by the Russians. M. Blum even thought it possible that

[1] Cf. No. 279.   [2] Cf. Volume XIII, Nos. 201 and 206.

there had been some kind of verbal understanding in the matter at that time, but nothing more. M. Blum was fully conscious of the effect that such conversations at the present time must have upon the meeting of the Five Powers. The last thing he would wish to do would be to give Germany any such pretext for not coming to the meeting. He had therefore made it plain to M. Litvinoff at Geneva that there could be no possibility of such staff conversations at present, and that the whole question must at least await the outcome of the Five-Power Meeting.

I told M. Blum that I was glad to hear that such staff conversations were not actual, for I shared with him the conviction that anything of the kind would gravely prejudice the Five-Power Meeting.

A. E.

No. 281

Record by Mr. Eden of a conversation with M. Blum
[*W 13351/9549/41*]

FOREIGN OFFICE, *October 10, 1936*

I had a conversation with M. Blum after luncheon yesterday, at which His Majesty's Ambassador in Paris was also present.[1] We began by speaking of the non-intervention agreement in respect of the Spanish Civil War. I gave the French Prime Minister some account of the proceedings which had taken place in London that morning.[2] I told M. Blum that I thought that the public intervention of the Soviet Government at this stage had been most unfortunate. We were all of us of course in possession of certain representations which the Spanish Government had made, and we had intended raising the matter at the Committee on our responsibility as a possible matter for enquiry. Now, however, that the Soviet Government had taken this initiative contrary to the rules of procedure agreed upon at the Committee, they had unnecessarily complicated matters, and I did not know what effect this might have upon the future of the Committee.

M. Blum indicated that he fully shared my preoccupations. The pressure upon him in France was growing steadily greater. As to the Soviet initiative, he understood from Geneva that M. Litvinoff had stated that this had taken place without his knowledge. M. Blum agreed as to its untimeliness.

In reply to a question the French Prime Minister made it clear however that he continued to think that the maintenance of a policy of non-intervention was the correct course to pursue. We must do all in our power to make it effective; M. Blum added that he was himself convinced that had there been no non-intervention agreement, the Spanish Government would have suffered more from that fact than would the rebels. He was going to make this clear to the Spanish Ambassador in Paris when he came to see him on Monday.

A. E.

[1] See Nos. 279 and 280.   [2] See No. 272, note 3, and No. 278, note 1.

No. 282

Record by Mr. Eden of a conversation with M. Blum
[*C 7159/97/18*]

Secret   FOREIGN OFFICE, *October 10, 1936*

In the course of my conversation with Monsieur Blum in Paris yesterday,[1] I said that my remarks as to the danger of our showing ourselves too eager for agreement applied also to the initiative of Dr. Schacht. I had nothing further to tell him about the attitude of His Majesty's Government, but I was confident that the note which I had sent him through M. Delbos[2] at Geneva accurately represented our position, and I felt confident that this was not likely to be modified.

M. Blum replied that he was in full agreement with what I had said, and that he had taken advantage of M. François-Poncet's return to Berlin to send a message by him to Dr. Schacht explaining the position.[3]

ANTHONY EDEN

[1] See Nos. 279, 280, 281.   [2] No. 228.
[3] Mr. Eden indicates in his memoirs (Avon, *op. cit.*, p. 410) that shortly after Mr. Baldwin's return to London on October 12 'I had my first talk with him for three months'. Mr. Eden was impatient to deploy the course of events 'and to take counsel with him, particularly about the Spanish civil war'. It turned out, however, that the Prime Minister was preoccupied with the first phases of the forthcoming abdication crisis, and asked Mr. Eden 'not to trouble me too much with foreign affairs just now'. His Majesty King Edward VIII signed the Instrument of Abdication on December 10. The crisis was essentially one of domestic and constitutional significance, and does not appear, from the documents preserved in the Foreign Office archives, to have had any direct bearing on foreign-policy issues of the period. See No. 465 below.

No. 283

Mr. M. MacDonald[1] (Geneva) to Mr. Eden (Received October 26)
No. 148 [*W 14377/79/98*]

GENEVA, *October 10, 1936*

Sir,

I have the honour to inform you that, as a result of the recommendation adopted at the resumption of the Sixteenth Session of the Assembly on the 4th July, 1936,[2] the Seventeenth Ordinary Session had before it a collection of replies from various Governments regarding the question of the application of the principles of the Covenant.[3] A number of other Governments made oral statements of their views during the opening debate. There were,

[1] The Secretary of State for Dominion Affairs was a member of the United Kingdom delegation to the League of Nations, and United Kingdom representative on the Special Main Committee on the Question of the Application of the Principles of the Covenant: cf. para. 2 below.   [2] See No. 179, note 1.
[3] These replies were printed in *L/N.O.J.*, *S.S. No. 154*, pp. 6–40.

moreover, several cognate questions on the agenda, such as that of bringing the Covenant of the League into harmony with the Pact of Paris, that of the Rio de Janeiro Treaty of Non-Aggression, and that of the supply of arms and war material to belligerents.

2. After some discussion the General Committee of the Assembly decided to propose to the latter that a General Commission of the kind provided for in rule 14 of the Rules of Procedure should be established for the question of the application of the principles of the Covenant and all problems connected therewith, and should report to the Assembly, submitting its recommendations on the manner in which the study of these problems should be pursued. This proposal was adopted by the Assembly, and the General Commission was duly constituted and held two meetings on the 9th October.[4]

3. Early in the discussion it became apparent that there were two currents of opinion in the commission—one in favour of the appointment of a restricted committee to study and report on the problems in question, and the other in favour of a general committee of all League members. The Chilean delegate took a prominent part in the debate. He held the view that a general committee should be appointed, and laid much emphasis on the necessity of obtaining the assistance of non-member States, in view of the importance of the principle of universality of the League. The Hungarian representative shared this view. On the other hand, the Soviet delegate, M. Litvinov, while not denying the importance of universality, considered that the task of improving the working of the Covenant should be undertaken by member States without the co-operation of Powers outside the League who had no responsibility towards it. The French delegate realised the importance of universality, but said that the French Government also attached great importance to the strengthening of the Covenant. The question of universality was not one which could be dealt with incidentally during the discussion of a matter of procedure. The United Kingdom delegate (Mr. Malcolm MacDonald) inclined to the view that a restricted committee should be appointed. Care should be taken, however, to see that the various points of view put forward in response to the Assembly resolution of the 4th July should be represented on the committee. It was eventually decided by 31 votes to 7 that the Assembly should be advised to appoint a restricted committee. The chairman of the General Commission (Mr. S. M. Bruce) was asked to act as *rapporteur*.

4. At the second meeting, which took place on the afternoon of the 9th October, Mr. Bruce's report and resolution was considered and adopted. Its general sense was that the relevant documents should be collected and classified by the Secretary-General, that they should be studied by a special committee, consisting of the fifteen States represented on the Council and thirteen other member States, with power to invite other members of the League to take part in its discussion. Special mention was made in the report of the Chilean proposal that, in the interests of universality, the views of non-member States should be ascertained, and this proposal was

4 See *L/N.O.J.*, *S.S. No. 162*, pp. 8–27.

referred to the committee itself. The committee was authorised to propose a special session of the Assembly should it consider it advisable to do so.

5. The report and resolution[5] were adopted by the Assembly on the 10th October.[6] The Special Committee thus constituted held an informal meeting on the 10th October, and decided to meet in regular session on the 7th December.[7]

I have, &c.,
MALCOLM MACDONALD

[5] Printed *ibid.*, pp. 28–30.
[6] See *L/N.O.J.*, *S.S. No. 155*, pp. 108–9.
[7] The Committee in fact met on December 14 and agreed to appoint *Rapporteurs* on the most important issues. Lord Cranborne was appointed *Rapporteur* on two questions, that of participation in the League, and of co-operation between the League and non-Member states.

No. 284

Mr. Eden to Sir E. Drummond (Rome)

No. 375 Telegraphic [*W 13080/9549/41*]

FOREIGN OFFICE, *October 11, 1936, 4.40 p.m.*

Your telegram No. 597.[1]

French Ambassador called on Sir R. Vansittart on the 6th October and the latter took occasion to tell His Excellency of the action taken by His Majesty's Government in seeking assurances from the Italian Government with regard to the Balearic Islands, and of the response of the Italian Government.

Sir Robert suggested that it might be well if the French Government at their own time and in their own way were to take similar soundings and to obtain the same response. This, he said, might be both advantageous in itself and tend to ease somewhat French suspicions on the subject.[2]

[1] No. 188.
[2] In the course of a memorandum on Italian activities in the Balearic Islands, Mr. D. F. Howard, a First Secretary in the League of Nations and Western Department, remarked that the French were understood to 'want us to submit the question to the Non-Intervention Committee. This, I submit, is another indication of the French desire to avoid any unpleasant responsibility in connexion with the working of the Committee. Not only are they endeavouring, I believe, to pass it around that it was H.M. Government who were pressing in the first place for the negotiation of a Non-Intervention Agreement, but they were, in my view, very lukewarm in their support of our action in submitting the Spanish Government's case against Italy to the Committee last week . . . I feel that the matter of Italian interest in the Islands has been given such an airing in the press that it must sooner or later be brought before the Committee, but I also feel that it would serve our purpose better for the French to do the deed this time . . . D. F. Howard. 12th October 1936.' Sir G. Mounsey agreed and suggested that the French should be told 'that if they bring the matter up in the Committee, we will support them by the production of such evidence as we can submit, to supplement their own'. Sir R. Vansittart approved of this course and wrote on October 13: 'I would much prefer that we shd not bell this cat. We have already done all the belling that has been done, & have plenty of trouble on our hands . . .'

No. 285

Mr. MacKillop (Moscow) to Mr. Eden (Received October 12, 1.10 p.m.)
No. 159 Telegraphic [W 13411/9549/41]

MOSCOW, *October 12, 1936, 2.10 p.m. [sic]*

My telegram No. 157.[1]

Press have published long Tass message from London describing dispute between Soviet and Italian representatives on Non-Intervention Committee regarding Italian charges against Soviet Government made at meeting on October 9th.[2] Message begins with 'according to information received'.

Press comment takes the line that delegates of 'the three Fascist States' had endeavour [*sic*] to obscure the issue and prevent discussion of Soviet protest by smothering the latter in formal questions of procedure and that it was regrettable that these tactics had not been resisted by the Committee. Attempts made in Committee to bury Soviet protest could only benefit 'interventionists' and reveal the hypocrisy and intentional blindness to facts on the part of those who make them. 'The attitude of the Soviet Union remains unchanged and resolute. It demands effective measures by the Committee'.

[1] This telegram of October 8 reported that the full text of M. Cahan's communication to Lord Plymouth of October 7 (see No. 270) had been published in the Soviet press, without comment.
[2] Cf. No. 278.

No. 286

Translation of a memorandum communicated by the German Chargé d'Affaires on October 14, respecting the proposed meeting of the Five Locarno Powers

[C 7247/4/18]

BERLIN, *October 12, 1936*

The German Government have the honour to express their views as follows with regard to the questions raised in the memorandum of His Majesty's Government of the 17th September,[1] so far as this is possible without knowledge of the attitude of the other Governments concerned at this stage of the present exchange of views.

1. The German Government assume, from the terms of the invitation conveyed to them on the basis of the London *communiqué* of the 23rd July last,[2] and their reply thereto,[3] that the subject to be dealt with by the conference will be the replacement of the old Rhine Pact of Locarno by a new pact between Germany, Belgium, France, Great Britain and Italy. If the *communiqué* in question contemplates the discussion later on of other problems

[1] Enclosure in No. 206.
[2] See Volume XVI, Nos. 479 and 480.
[3] See Nos. 41 and 47.

connected with the securing of European peace, a decision with regard to these problems (as indeed the *communiqué* itself indicates), can only be reached when the result of the conference of the Five Powers, with respect to the subject to be dealt with at that Conference has been arrived at. The German Government must therefore reserve till then their attitude with regard to the question whether, and if so which, other problems in given circumstances might later be discussed.

2. The structure of the new pact would naturally have to take into account the political developments which have given rise to the plan for such a pact. The German Government, as already proposed in their peace plan of the 31st March[4] last, accordingly regard obligations for non-aggression between Germany on the one hand and Belgium and France on the other, and the guaranteeing of these obligations by Great Britain and Italy, as the essential elements of the pact. The answer to the question whether these elements in the treaty should further be supplemented by non-aggression and guarantee obligations between other treaty partners will have to depend on whether such an extension of the system of the old Rhine Pact is in the general interests of peace and whether it can be introduced without upsetting the necessary balance of the treaty system. The German Government will only be able to form their final judgment on this point when they have learned the views of the other Governments concerned.

3. The German Government, in their peace plan of the 31st March last, have already declared themselves prepared for a renunciation of aggression vis-à-vis Belgium and France unrestricted by any exceptions. From their standpoint they have no motive for weakening the security for peace which lies in the conclusion of such an agreement for the renunciation of aggression by demanding exceptions of any kind whatever. In case the other Governments concerned should think it necessary to insist on making exceptions of this kind, it would be for them to put forward proposals to this end. Meanwhile, however, the German Government must indicate at once that they do not consider the method proposed by His Majesty's Government in their memorandum of the 17th September to be practicable. In article 2 of the old Rhine Pact, to which the memorandum refers, the important exceptions in practice to the provisions for the renunciation of aggression are laid down with reference to the provisions of the Covenant of the League of Nations, and in particular to article 16 thereof. The repetition of the use of this method is, in the view of the German Government, precluded by the fact that the interpretation of article 16 has led to the well-known differences of opinion between Germany and the other Locarno Powers, and, furthermore, by the fact that the discussion regarding the future of article 16 and other provisions of the Covenant of the League of Nations is at present still quite open.

4. The German Government do not consider it either necessary or appropriate to submit to the Council of the League of Nations the question of deciding whether an infringement of the obligation of non-aggression has

4 See Volume XVI, No. 193, note 2.

taken place and consequently whether the guarantee obligation has entered into force.

It will be necessary to examine whether such decisions should not be reached by a common decision of the parties to the treaty who are not, in a given case, directly parties to the conflict. A distinction between flagrant breaches of the treaty and other kinds of breaches of the treaty, such as was laid down in the old Rhine Pact, will no longer come into consideration in the new pact.

5. The obligations of non-aggression on which agreement is to be reached will, naturally, have to extend also to air attacks. Moreover, the rendering of assistance by the guarantor Powers would have to cover their air forces also. The German Government, therefore, share the view of His Majesty's Government that there is no necessity for a special air pact.

6. The German Government consider it appropriate that the parties to the treaty, especially those between whom obligations of non-aggression are agreed upon, should at the same time reach agreements for the settlement by suitable peaceful procedure, of the disputes arising between them.[5]

[5] Minutes by Sir R. Vansittart and Mr. Eden, commenting on this memorandum, were as follows. 'It is not a helpful note—in fact it is rather a bad one. I can only say that I half expected it to be worse. Points 1, 3, & 5 all seem to me very serious. In regard to 1 I doubt whether we shall be wise to go far in negotiation when there is no certainty at all "whether" there will be any extension at all. Indeed the German wording makes it quite certain that there will not. We cannot, I think, admit this prospect or attitude. 3 & 5 are also inadmissible.

We must now get the other replies, & shd ask urgently for them. I expect that the Italians & the Germans will be in together on this, particularly after the Ciano visit to Berlin. And the Belgians have also gone far to block progress by the folly of the Belgian King's speech [see No. 297 below]. All this is not helpful, but it is not hopeless [marginal comment: "I agree. A. E."] I have made a full record of my conversation with Prince Bismarck [No. 298 below]. R. V. Oct. 15.'

'Yes, let us get the other two answers as soon as possible, & then we shall be at grips with the heart of our problem. A. E. Oct. 18.'

No. 287

Letter[1] from M. Cahan to Lord Plymouth
[W 13672/9549/41]

SOVIET EMBASSY, *October 12, 1936*

Sir,

In connection with the subject matter of my statement delivered to you on the 7th instant,[2] which was under discussion at the last meeting of the Committee,[3] I have the honour, on instructions from my Government, to submit for the urgent consideration of the Committee, the following:

The bulk of the arms supply to the rebels goes through Portugal and Portuguese ports. The minimum, and at the same time the absolutely

[1] Also printed in *D.V.P.S.*, *op. cit.*, No. 303. [2] No. 270. [3] See No. 278.

immediate, measure to put an end to this supply and to violations of the Agreement for Non-Intervention must be the immediate establishment of control over Portuguese ports.

We, therefore, demand of the Committee the establishment of such control, and we suggest that this control should be entrusted to the British or French Navies—or both.

Without such measures indicated above as the minimum and immediate step against violations of the Agreement for Non-Intervention in Spanish Affairs, this Agreement not only does not serve its purpose but, on the contrary, serves as a cloak for the rebels against the legitimate government of Spain.

I have the honour to request that the proposals made above should be discussed at the next meeting of the Committee which I urge should be convened without delay.

Accept, Sir, the expression of my high consideration and esteem.

S. CAHAN

No. 288

Sir E. Phipps (Berlin) to Mr. Eden (Received October 13, 7 p.m.)
No. 322 Telegraphic: by telephone [C 7221/97/18]

Immediate   Confidential   BERLIN, *October 13, 1936*
Your telegram No. 204.[1]

1. I gather that colonial Congress has been postponed by order of the Chancellor for the following reasons.

2. During his interview with Mr. Lloyd George[2] Chancellor mentioned colonies but Mr. Lloyd George did not avail himself of this opportunity to express any view. Two days later, however, Mr. Lloyd George warned Herr Hess that it would be premature to raise colonial issue now and that it would be wiser to wait until conference of Locarno Powers had been a success before tackling British public opinion. Mr. Lloyd George also made a very wry face when Herr Hess admitted that a supply of raw materials would not satisfy Germany and that she wanted 'a re-distribution of colonies.'

3. In his conversation with Doctor Schacht French President of the Council undertook—so Dr. Schacht told Herr Hitler—to talk to his colleagues and other interested Powers about Germany's colonial needs and agreed that restoration of the Cameroons was not outside the pale of discussions.[3]

4. At present moment German organization for dealing with colonial problems is entirely a Nazi party affair under control of General von Epp. Its activities have aroused criticism in responsible German circles and in former colonies.

[1] In this Foreign Office telegram of October 12 Sir E. Phipps was asked whether he could throw any light on reports that the 'Reich Colonial Congress at Breslau has been cancelled or indefinitely postponed suddenly and without explanation'.
[2] See No. 295 below.   [3] Cf. No. 210.

5. For all these reasons Chancellor thinks the moment unsuitable for a noisy demonstration at Breslau. But it would of course be wrong to assume that there is any fundamental change in the attitude of German Government (see Herr Hess's speech which goes by air mail to-night).[4]

No. 289

Memorandum[1] on the execution of civilians and prisoners of war by adherents of either party in Spain

[*W 13623/62/41*]

FOREIGN OFFICE, *October 13, 1936*

The chief difficulty encountered in treating this subject is that the evidence relates almost exclusively to one Party, namely the Government. Our lack of information about excesses committed by the rebels is due to the paucity of reliable witnesses in the territory held by them. From the slight evidence available, however, it seems that, up to the present time, executions of civilians by the rebels have been relatively few and carried out with a certain show of justice. The Government supporters, on the other hand, have already executed several thousand civilians, self-appointed executioners, chiefly of the anarchist F.A.I. organisation, claiming far more victims than the regular tribunals. The number of killings has tended to increase as these anarchist elements have freed themselves from the control of the existing authority.

As regards the execution of prisoners of war, we are at present in possession of little useful information on the subject. No reliable witness was with the insurgent troops to describe, e.g. the massacre of captured militiamen at Badajos,[2] while on the Governmental side too few prisoners of war have been taken to permit generalisation. We know only that at San Sebastian, so H.M. Consul at Bilbao reports, in the first days of the war some 50 rebel officers and notables were despatched by Government irregulars after surrendering against a guarantee of their lives.

For the execution of civilians we have the following examples:

(1) In Madrid Mr. Ogilvie-Forbes notes on the 25th September[3] an increase in the number of private murders, followed also by open robbery, and speaks of a hunt for possible Fascist sympathisers in which women were not spared. The morgue had been closed to visitors; the entry on September 17th was 90 corpses, the daily average was estimated at 50. There were also numerous murders in the outlying villages. On the 3rd October Mr.

[1] This memorandum, the filed copy of which was unsigned, was apparently compiled by Mr. C. H. (later Sir Charles) Johnston of the League of Nations and Western Department. It is printed as a convenient summary of the wide range of reports on the treatment of prisoners and civilians which had been reaching the Foreign Office from British representatives in Spain during the preceding three months. See also Nos. 120, 123, 245, 247, and 252.

[2] See No. 120, note 1.

[3] See No. 245, note 1.

Ogilvie-Forbes reports that he has just seen horrid scenes in the University City grounds, including elderly women victims, and speaks of 'the daily harvest of corpses'. On the 7th October he reports that a press article by a Communist woman deputy known as the Passionaria,[4] deliberately inciting to the murder of all suspected of Right tendencies, led to a high record of killings. During the week-end of the 3rd, there were 200 bodies in the morgue in the same 24 hours. Bodies of other victims were being burnt, and there was an increasing tendency to kill in the outlying villages in order to avoid morgue statistics. Mr. Ogilvie-Forbes adds 'I fear that as the insurgents approach killings will increase'. In these massacres foreigners and members of the Diplomatic Corps have not been spared. Mr. Ogilvie-Forbes reports that in mid September two sisters of the Uruguayan Vice-Consul together with a nun were murdered, and a report from Lisbon of October 11th speaks of the murder of the Bolivian Minister.

(2) The record of Barcelona is even worse. Mr. King, H.M. Consul-General, reports on August 21st[5] a visit to the municipal morgue where he found between 30 and 40 corpses, 25 of which had been brought in the night before. A number of them had their heads and faces so disfigured as to be unrecognisable; that, however, had possibly been done after death. Among them were several victims of private vengence. Mr. King also describes, on the authority of the United States Consulate-General, the murder of six nuns of Vallvidrera near Barcelona on July 28th. They were taken out by car on the pretext that they were being taken to a safe place and killed in a lonely spot. Foreign nationals have not been spared in this district. A British subject, Garcia by name, was shot by an armed patrol while driving a car near Barcelona; he had apparently disregarded or failed to hear an order to stop. The Portuguese Consul-General drew the attention of Mr. King to the killing by anarchists of numerous Portuguese subjects including nuns. On the 24th July four Germans who tried to escape by car to France were murdered, and early in August four Italian subjects were murdered in Barcelona itself. The bad period in Barcelona seems to have begun late in July when the anarchists opened the prisons, and to have ended, temporarily at least, early in October when the Anarcho-Syndicalists, now represented in the new Council of Señor Terradellas, seemed to acquire a more responsible outlook. However, Mr. King anticipated more trouble when the main forces of the F.A.I. returned from before Saragossa.

(3) All reports from Catalonia insist that conditions in outlying districts are even worse than in Barcelona itself. At Lerida, so Mr. King reports, in 24 hours 83 corpses were taken to the morgue, a grim picture, which is confirmed by Mr. Navarro, H.M. Vice-Consul in Tarragona. At Villa-nueva, early in October, 32 members of the Right were executed by way of reprisal for three local men killed in action against the insurgents. In

4 Dolores Ibarruri, 'La Pasionaria', was a member of the directorate of the Spanish Communist Party.
5 See No. 120.

Tarragona the massacre of 60 alleged Fascists or Right sympathisers on September 27th in reprisal for alleged bomb explosions produced a panic.

(4) At Valencia H.M.S. *Anthony* reported executions by the F.A.I. in defiance of the Civil Governor, 250 civil guards and 40 reputed Fascists being shot on September 26th. Mr. Pack, Commercial Counsellor at the Embassy at Hendaye, found the anarchists in complete control at Valencia as at Barcelona.

(5) At Almeria, according to a message received from H.M.S. *Acasta* on October 5th, about 20 persons were being shot nightly.

(6) The Acting Consul at Malaga reports the shooting of a number of suspected Fascists as reprisals for air raids, but adds that at the time of writing, September 15th, the newly constituted Committee of *Salud Publica* was doing much to check these executions.

(7) From Seville comes [*sic*] stories of atrocities committed on adherents to the Right in the neighbouring villages. Mr. Formby, Acting British Consul, reports that at Arahal '17 persons, including one elderly lady, were burnt alive in an underground cell into which petrol was poured', while at Genil the number of murdered 'Rights' was given as over 200.

(8) No less grim accounts come from the north of the country. At Gijon Mr. Stevenson, H.M. Consul at Bilbao, learnt on the 24th September[6] from the Belgian Consul, whom he found hiding from persecution, that a large number of suspected Rights estimated at between 500 and 1,000 had been executed after a pretence at trial, and that another form of terror was being practiced by the F.A.I., members of which visited bourgeois homes at night, murdering individuals and in some cases whole families.

(9) H.M. Consul at Santander reports that there too a flying squad of the F.A.I. is engaged in nocturnal visits and executions.

(10) At Bilbao itself H.M. Consul reports that the F.A.I. has executed numerous members of wealthy families; these executions are generally accompanied by robbery. Sir H. Chilton reports that a number of hostages aboard the prison-ships were butchered by the mob, including women. The number of hostages at Bilbao has dwindled in an alarming manner, being estimated on the 9th October by the Captain D. 5th Destroyer Flotilla as 550, whereas at the end of September it was thought to be three times that number.

(11) At San Sebastian a British subject, Mr. R. de Satorre, was executed on suspicion of having fired at members of the *Frente Popular*.

The only authentic mention of executions by the rebels comes from H.M. Consul at Tetuan, which speaks of 63 persons shot at Larache, among them being civilians and officials, adding that the rebels at Larache prided themselves especially on the justice of their régime. The ruthlessness of the Moorish *regulares*, especially in the matter of reprisals, is mentioned, e.g. by H.M. Consul in Seville, but no details are at present available on this subject. Several witnesses agree that, whereas the rebels are content to shoot outright, the Government adherents often torture their victims as well.

6 See No. 247.

Mr. Eden to Sir G. Clerk (Paris)
No. 1726 [C 7206/4/18]

FOREIGN OFFICE, *October 13, 1936*

Sir,

With reference to my despatch No. 1670 of October 6th[1] enclosing a copy of despatch No. 106[1] from the United Kingdom delegate at Geneva regarding the cessation of the Belgian guarantee in the proposed Western Pact,[2] I have to inform Your Excellency that the French Ambassador called on Sir Robert Vansittart this morning and said that his Government would very much like to be in early possession of the views of His Majesty's Government in regard to the Belgian desire to be guaranteed under the new Locarno but to give no guarantee themselves.

2. The Ambassador expressed the strongest disapproval of this idea and repeated some of the many objections which the French Government see to it. M. Corbin expressed the hope that His Majesty's Government would agree with the French Government on a point to which the latter attached so much importance.

3. Sir Robert Vansittart replied that we had already received a memorandum[3] from M. Delbos on the subject and that he was well aware of the objections which had been raised by the French Government. These would of course receive full consideration, and he would do his best to ensure that the points were examined as early as possible by the competent departments here.

I am, &c.,
(For the Secretary of State)
R. F. WIGRAM

[1] Not printed.　　　[2] See No. 292 below.　　　[3] See *ibid.*, note 1.

No. 291

Mr. Eden to Sir E. Drummond (Rome)
No. 1140 [R 6128/226/22]

FOREIGN OFFICE, *October 13, 1936*

Sir,

Signor Grandi asked to see me this evening. At the outset I told him with what pleasure His Majesty's Government had learned that the reports of his leaving us to become Governor of Rhodes were unfounded. The Ambassador said that he too was very pleased to come back. There had been a period when he had been in considerable doubt. His health had not been good and for a week or so he had really toyed with the idea of Rhodes. Signor Mussolini had been very good to him in making this offer and in his reception of him. Eventually, however, Signor Grandi had felt that at forty-one he could not retire into a life of almost total inactivity and just read of the doings of others. He had therefore decided to come back to London and Signor Mussolini had warmly approved his decision. He only hoped that he could now be of service.

2. In this connexion, His Excellency went on, he wished to speak to me once again frankly about Anglo-Italian relations. It was difficult for us to reconstruct Italian mentality on this subject. Abyssinia had formed an important part, but still only a part, of the foreign policy of Great Britain: that issue, owing to its developments had, however, been for Italy a vital one. Despite all this Signor Mussolini himself was really anxious to let by-gones be by-gones and to cooperate with His Majesty's Government. He desired nothing more, Signor Grandi emphasised to me, than to return to a period of full cooperation with us such as existed before 1935. Signor Grandi had had several conversations with him and this had been Signor Mussolini's theme. At the same time the Ambassador stated that he had great difficulty in persuading people in Italy that we too desired to let by-gones be by-gones. What Signor Mussolini had frequently asked him was: 'What do your people really want?' Signor Grandi explained that there had been a number of events, such as The King's visit to the Mediterranean, the Yugoslav-Turkish attitude thereto, our re-armament in the Mediter-ranean and so forth, which made it very difficult for Italy to believe that we reciprocated her genuine desire for improved relations.[1] This had led the Ambassador to ask himself whether there was not some small gesture of good-will that we could make which would have a psychological effect on Italian opinion quite out of all proportion to its real importance. Could I not think of something of this kind? British policy was usually very wise in discovering such gestures.

3. I replied that I fully appreciated the state of Italian opinion as explained to me by Signor Grandi. At the same time I hardly thought that the Ambassador in enumerating the Italian Government's causes for apprehen-sion as to our attitude quite did justice to the balancing elements in the scale. In recent months, for instance, the Press of this country had been markedly free from any anti-Italian bias (the Ambassador admitted the truth of this). Moreover, when in the last days of the Session I had announced the bringing to an end of our assurances to certain Mediterranean Powers, His Majesty's Government had thereby taken a step not very easy to take at that time to reduce the tension in the Mediterranean.[2] I assured the Ambassador that we sincerely desired to work with the Italian Government in securing an improvement in the European situation.

4. In the course of further conversation which ensued it became evident that what the Ambassador had in mind most of all was some gesture in relation to Abyssinia about which Italian opinion was very sensitive. He instanced our withdrawal of His Majesty's Consul from Gore as having had

---

[1] Cf. Nos. 169 and 175.   [2] See No. 21.

h very good effect in Rome.[3] I said there was in this fact a lesson for us both in our mutual relations. I would be quite frank and tell him that Mr. Erskine's withdrawal from Gore was not carried out in order to give satisfaction to Italy, but because the main purpose for which, as a Consul, he had been at Gore—the protection of British lives and property—had been fulfilled as far as it was possible to fulfil it by the evacuation of British subjects. Mr. Erskine's task was not political, but no doubt because the Italian Government suspected that it might be their relief was the greater at his withdrawal.

5. The Ambassador went on to say that he had been considering whether it was possible for us to take any action in respect of recognition in Abyssinia. He thought that very likely it was too soon for this and he certainly had no instructions from his Government, but he would ask me earnestly to consider whether there were not some small gesture on a par with the withdrawal of the Consul from Gore which we could make and which would have a further good effect upon our mutual relations. I told His Excellency that he was not setting me an easy task, but I would certainly consider his suggestion, though for the moment I must confess that I could not think of any initiative that we could take. Since, however, we were speaking of our mutal relations, perhaps I might ask him if he had heard anything of an individual in Majorca called Rossi[4] whose activities had achieved a certain publicity. The Ambassador at once admitted Rossi's existence, but found it impossible to believe that his activities could in any way be anti-British. I replied that my information was rather contrary to that. I had the impression that I had read reports which indicated that Signor Rossi had even taken part in demonstrations which had a definite anti-British tinge. Signor Grandi again expressed surprise at this information and pointed out that if there was one thing about which England, France and Italy were all agreed on, it was that the Balearic islands should continue to belong to Spain. Not one of the three could afford to see anyone else established there. I did not ask Signor Grandi to make enquiries about Signor Rossi's activities, but I have the impression that he will say something to Rome.

6. Signor Grandi instanced as yet another cause of Italy's suspicions the British action in regard to the Spanish complaints against Italy, Germany and Portugal on the Non-Intervention Committee. I explained that our action in this instance so far from being hostile had been specially taken to avoid a more abrupt initiative from any other quarter.[5] Signor Grandi said that while he appreciated this it was less easy to explain to others why we and the Soviet Government appeared to be taking up the same complaints at the same time. He was afraid that the activities of the Soviet Government recently had been directed towards complicating relations in Europe.

[3] Following a deterioration in the situation in Western Abyssinia, Captain Erskine had been ordered to withdraw from Gore to Gambeila at the end of September, 1936. Cf. also Volume XVI, No. 334.
[4] See No. 266.   [5] Cf. No. 272.

7. Signor Grandi then spoke of the decision taken by the Assembly to admit the Abyssinian Delegation at Geneva.[6] I told him that in my view this decision was both right and unavoidable. After all, he must place himself in the position of the members of the League. The League and Italy had been at odds and at the outcome Italy had gained her objective. It was hardly acceptable that after that the League should be asked to refuse credentials to the Abyssinian Delegates in order to make room for Italy. In my view M. Avenol's visit to Rome[7] had not perhaps been altogether fortunate in its timing. Signor Grandi agreed and stated that the news of the League's decision had come as a complete surprise in Rome. He had been with Count Ciano at the moment when the message came through at 6.30 in the evening; they had looked at each other and Signor Grandi had said: 'Now I suppose in half an hour we shall announce our withdrawal from the League.' Count Ciano replied: 'Yes, a *communiqué* is already being prepared.' The *communiqué* had been taken to Signor Mussolini, but the latter had said 'No.' Signor Grandi said that he gave me this information in confidence because he thought it desirable that we should realise how much Signor Mussolini was sometimes misunderstood.

8. Finally Signor Grandi came to what appeared to be the main reason for his visit. He stated that he had received a telegram from Rome, I understood from Signor Mussolini himself, in which his attention was drawn to a report from Havas from Cairo to the effect that British troops in Egypt had been reinforced by two battalions totalling 3,000 men who were being stationed at Mersa Matruh. I understood that the message added that the barracks at Mersa Matruh were being prepared for their immediate occupation. The British authorities in Egypt, the Havas message continued, declined to give any explanation of this move. Signor Grandi said that he quite understood that other countries were willing to create suspicion between England and Italy, but this report had much disturbed Signor Mussolini who had withdrawn his troops from the Libyan border because we had withdrawn ours from Mersa Matruh. If it was accurate that we had made this sudden reinforcement then Signor Mussolini would have to take counter measures. The Ambassador stated that he would therefore be very grateful for any information that I could give him. I replied that this information was news to me and that on the face of it it seemed to me most unlikely. The number of our troops in Egypt, as the Ambassador would be aware, had been reduced owing to the troubles in Palestine but I would make enquiries and let him know the position as soon as possible. In the meanwhile I could only point out that the calculations of numbers in the Havas message was clearly incorrect—no two British battalions numbered 3,000 men. In the circumstances I thought it likely that the rest of the message was as incorrect as the calculations.

[6] At the fourth Plenary Meeting of the Assembly on September 23: see *L/N.O.J.*, *S.S. No. 155*, pp. 40–2.

[7] M. Avenol visited Rome from September 7 to 10 and had talks with Signor Mussolini and Count Ciano on the Italian attitude towards the League and the reform of the Covenant.

9. After making enquiries I have since caused His Excellency to be informed that there is no foundation for the report in question.

I am, etc.,
ANTHONY EDEN

No. 292

Sir E. Ovey (Brussels) to Mr. Eden (Received October 14)
No. 547 [C 7232/4/18]

Confidential   BRUSSELS, *October 13, 1936*

Sir,

I had occasion in my despatch No. 539 of October 9th[1] to report the view that the annoyance of the French with regard to Belgium's unwillingness to guarantee the eastern frontier of France was due to strategic and political conceptions no longer in consonance with the tendencies of the age.

2. I have since read in Sir Eric Phipps' despatch No. 1073 of October 5th[2] that this reluctance on the part of our Belgian friends is partly attributed to the concern felt in Belgium with regard to the possibility of France becoming definitely communist. This is undoubtedly true. There is a genuine fear in certain circles that France may become a country on which it would be useless to depend.

3. There are, however, several reasons why Belgium is unwilling to enter into any such commitments:

(i) the normal desire for peace and avoidance of entanglements;

(ii) the division of feeling between the Flemings (not necessarily unpatriotic) and the Walloons (patriotic and generally pro-French) with all that that involves in the difficult parliamentary situation;

(iii) the realisation that Belgium could be just as useful, if not more so, to Great Britain and France without guaranteeing either of the latter two Powers' territory. These reasons taken together put, I venture to suggest, any giving by the present National Government and *a fortiori* by another group Government, of such a guarantee out of the question.

4. If France, therefore, is not in a position to secure Belgium's guarantee, her continued insistence thereon becomes an irritant and the problem arises as to how the French Government's real interests can best be served without such guarantee. The principal French *desideratum* is security, military and political. The principal Belgian *desideratum* is also military and political security, but she wishes to play no part in the encirclement of Germany,

---

[1] Not printed. It referred briefly to a memorandum of October 2 which M. Delbos had communicated to Mr. Eden at Geneva, entitled 'Consequences from the Military Point of View of a change in the International Situation of Belgium as established by the Treaty of Locarno' (C 6944/4/18). This document, which emphasized the military disadvantages to France and Great Britain which might follow Belgium's ceasing to be a guarantor power, was a conflation of notes subsequently printed in *D.D.F., op. cit.*, No. 300. Sir E. Ovey thought that M. Delbos's arguments 'therein contained are militarily and politically fallacious'.

[2] Not printed.

has no offensive military spirit and has a cordial dislike of Communism in any form.

5. As regards political security, the guarantee of Belgian territory and *air* by Great Britain and France would obviously act as a deterrent to Germany, a deterrent so powerful as to render war unlikely except in the case in which Germany decides wantonly to attack the three Western Powers simultaneously.

6. There is, however, a school of thought to the effect that unless France does something soon to abate her unpopular demands Belgium may through fear of committing herself sink to mere 'neutrality'. Such 'neutrality' might degenerate into a state of unarmed servile acceptance of any fate which Germany might propose for Belgium; Belgium relying on its 'neutrality' might become powerless to oppose the slightest resistance to an invader by land or especially to react against a violation of its air. The conditions of 1914 might be reproduced. Even were England to intervene immediately it would be too late. The necessary staff contacts would be non-existent, and what is more, Belgium might even permit free passage to German aeroplanes and refuse Anglo-French assistance.

7. I do not entirely share this gloomy prognostication which is to my mind based on several false premises, but I admit that the danger exists. The false premises are:

(i) that neither the present Belgian Government nor the Belgian people at large show any immediate signs of wishing to sink so low or of losing the vivid memory of the horrors of 1914 which vitalizes the morale of the Army;

(ii) that the certainty of England's immediate intervention would be insufficient to deter Germany from such violation; and

(iii) that any new Locarno need leave any loophole for Belgium to evade her responsibilities.

8. Further, though I have not discussed the matter with the Prime Minister, I have no reason to believe that he has in any way given colour to the idea that he is not entirely 'sound'. His Government's military preparations are being pushed with commendable vigour in the face of strong opposition both from Flemish extremists and Socialists. This opposition will continue to grow so long as France by demanding that Little Belgium should guarantee Big France feeds its flames and any Belgian Government risks being split to its foundations.

9. The essence of a compromise would therefore seem to be one between the French demand for a guarantee, which Belgium will not give and which, if she did give it, would excite the worst suspicions of Germany,[3] and 'neutrality'. 'Neutrality' with its depressing aura should be warded off. Belgium need not be 'neutral'. Belgium, as a Member of the League of Nations, must shoulder its responsibilities under the Covenant. Such responsibilities are not necessarily very alarming, but such as they are

[3] A marginal comment by Mr. Sargent at this point reads: 'Why? it would be nothing new: only a continuation of Locarno.'

would form an incentive to military ardour capable of being referred to in public discourse without the speaker incurring any accusation of bellicosity. If France or Great Britain were unprovokedly attacked by Germany without violation of Belgium's land or air dominion, Belgium would only be bound to come to the support of those two countries—technically—as much as, say, Denmark or Finland. She could come to their aid or not according to her reading of the causes of the war and their bearing under her League obligations. If she decided that the *casus belli* under the Covenant did not arise and she remained neutral, her neutrality would provide the best wall of defence for France and Great Britain, leaving open on land only the Maginot line. If Belgian air or land were none the less violated, France and Great Britain would automatically come to her aid and France would acquire all the advantages so dear to the heart of the French military strategist.

10. The political situation in Belgium is such as to demand an early solution of this problem. A continuance of the present uncertainty gives the new Rexist party—now combined with the Flemish Nationals—unlimited opportunities for the creation of anti-French propaganda.

11. Monsieur van Zeeland is forced to bide his time. The Rexists are not. Were the Belgian Prime Minister in a position to declare that a new Locarno had been signed between Germany, France, Great Britain and Belgium by which all agree in their common pursuit of peace never to attack one another in any circumstances, and the first three to come automatically to Belgium's assistance if this agreement is broken as regards her, his hand would be immensely strengthened. He could reply to any accusation of subserviency to any Power that Belgium had undertaken no new obligation of any kind. Faithful to the Covenant she would take such action as the Covenant might prescribe, as Belgium was not a nonentity of whose paper 'neutrality' any aggressor could take wanton advantage, but an independent sovereign country, prepared to keep her powder dry so as to defend herself if attacked and to be in a position to cooperate with those who come to her aid.

12. Yet the French logical mind cannot see the matter except in the terms of the equation 'guarantor = guaranteed'. It has occurred to me that were neither the term 'guarantor' nor the term 'guaranteed' to be mentioned, France would get all the substance of her *desiderata*—with the loss of the alleged advantage of being able to use Belgium as a short cut to the Ruhr, offset as long as this disadvantage obtains by the protection afforded by a neutral Belgium defending by her neutrality half of France's frontier with the enemy.

13. I feel the matter is becoming urgent. The rift between France and Belgium is growing daily. The Belgian fear of Communism in France is not decreasing. The Flemings and the Rexists—daily more associated in public opinion with Nazi ideals—may by mistaken patriotism finally find themselves demanding 'neutrality'—a state of mind which might sink to an apathetic concurrence in a new German violation. We have here a

415

patriotic National Government—a patriotic single-minded King brought up in the traditions of his father, but the first might have to go or make concessions unworthy of its ideals, and the second might become a powerless figure pathetically prepared to lead another forlorn hope, but with no army and no national military enthusiasm behind him.[4]

I have, &c.,

ESMOND OVEY

[4] Minutes by Sir R. Vansittart and Mr. Eden were as follows. 'Sir E. Ovey takes a low view of Belgian possibilities, and if there is anything in this—there well may be—we must bear it in mind, & not rub the Belgian nose too much in their recent lapse. I agree that we may have to remind the French that we must take the world as we find it, lest worse befall. R. V. Oct. 18.' 'Yes, it was for reasons akin to those in this despatch, that I tried to persuade the French to be understanding of Belgian grievances when I was at Geneva. I am afraid I was not successful. The French were sensitive & "prickly". A. E. Oct. 20.' Cf. No. 297 below.

No. 293

Sir E. Phipps (Berlin) to Mr. Eden (Received October 15)
No. 284 Saving: Telegraphic [C 7254/4/18]

BERLIN, *October 14, 1936*

My immediately preceding saving telegram.[1]

Baron von Neurath told me spontaneously that Count Ciano was due in Berlin on October 20th. Count Ciano had tried to come here in August but had been put off by Baron von Neurath, who had tried, but in vain, to arrange that the visit should only last two or at most three days. Count Ciano, however, had insisted upon staying for four days, and upon bringing an enormous entourage with him (some twelve persons). The Chancellor, who is at Berchtesgaden, might come here for one day to see Count Ciano, or might possibly receive him down there. In any case, Baron von Neurath assured me the whole visit had been engineered by Count Ciano himself for purposes of self-glorification and advertisement, and nothing much would come of it.

I suggested some discussion of the Five Power Conference would take place and this Baron von Neurath admitted. It was for that reason, he added, that he had instructed Prince Bismarck to hand you the German reply today, and before Count Ciano's visit.

Baron von Neurath's spontaneous desire to reassure me (and I had expressed no alarm or even curiosity) was so marked as to inspire me with a certain vague and perhaps entirely unfounded suspicion.

[1] In this telegram, No. 283 Saving of October 14, Sir E. Phipps reported Baron von Neurath as saying that the German reply to the British memorandum of September 17 (Enclosure in No. 206) was about to be delivered. He professed to believe that an agreement might eventually be reached, and that the 'chief stumbling block would be the famous "exceptions"'. See No. 286, and No. 298 below.

No. 294

Letter from Lord Plymouth to M. Cahan
[W 13672/9549/41]

2, WHITEHALL GARDENS, S.W.I,[1] *October 14, 1936*

Sir,

I have the honour to acknowledge the receipt of your note of October 12th[2] in which, on instructions from your Government, you ask that I should convene the Committee on Non-Intervention in Spain forthwith to discuss the proposal which you make therein to provide for the immediate establishment of control over Portuguese ports with a view to preventing the alleged supply of arms through Portugal to the insurgent forces in Spain.

As you know, all the specific complaints, which have been brought against the Portuguese Government, of violations of the Agreement for Non-Intervention in Spain were submitted to and discussed by the Committee at the Meeting on October 9th[3] and the Portuguese Government have been requested, in accordance with the rules of procedure laid down by the Committee on September 21st, to supply, at as early a date as possible, 'such explanations as are necessary *to establish the facts.*' Since the reply of the Portuguese Government has not yet been received and since, moreover, your note of October 12th contains no additional evidence whatsoever to show that the Agreement is in fact being violated, I do not think it would be proper for me to summon a further meeting of the Committee at this stage to discuss this matter.

I am, &c.,
PLYMOUTH

[1] i.e. the address of the Secretariat of the N.I. Committee.　　[2] No. 287.
[3] See No. 278.

No. 295

Letter from Sir E. Phipps (Berlin) to Sir R. Vansittart
[C 7853/576/18]

BERLIN, *October 14, 1936*

Dear Van,

It may interest you to have a précis of the first interview which took place on the afternoon of September 4th between Mr. Lloyd George and the Chancellor as well as a summary of Lloyd George's talk with Hess two days later.[1] In addition to Ribbentrop—who never opened his mouth—the only persons present at this first interview were Herr Schmidt,[2] of the Ministry for Foreign Affairs, and Mr. Conwell Evans, who translated for Mr. Lloyd George. Both Herr Schmidt and his opposite number took notes which were

[1] Cf. No. 232, note 1, Mr. Lloyd George left Berchtesgaden for Stuttgart on September 7.
[2] Dr. Paul Schmidt, Counsellor and interpreter in the Personnel Department of the German Foreign Office: in his memoirs, *Statist auf diplomatischer Bühne 1923–45* (Bonn, 1949, pp. 336–40), he summarizes German impressions of Mr. Lloyd George during the visit, but says little about the discussions at Berchtesgaden.

subsequently found to tally on all important points. You have probably heard an account of the second interview at which several people, including Lord Dawson, were present.[3]

Ribbentrop had arranged a later date for the interview, but Lloyd George, alarmed by the possibility of French intervention in the Spanish civil war, asked Ribbentrop to fix an earlier date. Herr Hitler who was only too anxious to add Lloyd George to his trophies, agreed with alacrity and Ribbentrop's stock, which had been sagging, soared once more. Indeed I gather that Ribbentrop's delay in going to London is partly due to the fact that he is now so much in favour that he wishes to keep a leg in both camps and proposes to retain his organisation in Berlin and cross from London to Germany at short intervals. Baron von Neurath and Herr Dieckhoff are rather worried about the confusion to which this will give rise and view his London mission with foreboding, as he has no respect for established custom and no sense of time.

Lloyd George and his friend were fetched by Hitler's own car and escort—a most unusual proceeding—from the Grand Hotel Berchtesgaden to Herr Hitler's recently constructed villa overlooking Salzburg. The Chancellor came to the foot of the steps to meet his visitors and was clearly impressed by the importance of the occasion. Lloyd George on his side seemed equally impressed and, after a few complimentary remarks, the little party adjourned to a small drawing-room, where most of the conversation took place. After a few preliminary remarks Lloyd George expressed the hope that Germany would contribute to European appeasement by attending the Five Power Locarno Conference. France, as he had good reason to know, was in a very favourable state of mind, Great Britain was always ready to help, and the importance of Belgium was greater than people in Germany realised. The Chancellor agreed, but expressed the fear that a conference would not keep to the agenda, namely a new Locarno Treaty, but that it would tend to discuss extraneous matter. Efforts would be made to bring in Russia and Czechoslovakia and in the long run nothing would be achieved. Lloyd George answered that it was vital to keep the conference to the subject matter, namely a new agreement between the Western Powers. Germany could use the argument that as soon as the new treaty was concluded Germany

[3] In a letter of September 29 to Sir E. Phipps (C 6846/576/18), sending some information that he had obtained 'at second hand' about this interview, Sir M. Hankey said that Mr. Lloyd George asked Lord Dawson, his medical adviser, whether he saw any objection to the visit from a medical point of view; 'Dawson of Penn not only acquiesced but hinted that it would not be amiss if he were to join the party. L.G. was delighted; so it came about.' Sir M. Hankey also wrote: 'During his time in Germany L.G. saw every General or other important person he could who had been connected with the war. Fresh from writing his book [*War Memoirs*, 6 vols., 1933–6] he was able to confront them with exact situations and enquire why they did or did not do this or that. In the old fashion which I know so well, he was seeing these people at breakfast, lunch, tea and dinner, and pumping them, while the faithful Sylvester put it all down in shorthand notes.' Mr. A. J. Sylvester, Principal Secretary to Mr. Lloyd George, describes the visit in *The Real Lloyd George* (London, 1947), pp. 192–227. The fullest account is that of Mr. T. P. Conwell-Evans, printed in Martin Gilbert, *The Roots of Appeasement* (London, 1966), as Appendix 2.

would be prepared to discuss the Russian or any other question. For that matter, this and cognate questions could be discussed at the League of Nations. Hitler agreed and said that if a Western bloc could be formed it was quite likely that Czechoslovakia, Lithuania and other small Eastern States would come under the influence of the West.

Lloyd George then dilated on the advantages of an Air Pact, which he said would be warmly welcomed by British public opinion. Hitler was doubtful whether an Air Pact was feasible. Of course if the Western Powers had agreed to take up a common defensive attitude (*Abwehr Stellung*), presumably to Soviet Russia, such a pact could be concluded.

The talk then turned to conditions in Spain. Lloyd George expressed himself forcibly on the cruelties and barbarities on both sides. Though Hitler demurred, Lloyd George insisted that the insurgents were military reactionaries and that no good government could emerge from their victory. Lloyd George concluded his tirade by remarking that at all events Primo de Rivera had built motor roads on which one could travel in comfort and safety. This made Hitler smile. He asked Lloyd George how he had come from Munich and on learning that the new motor road had been used the Führer proceeded to give an enthusiastic account of his achievements and his intentions in the matter of motor roads. Lloyd George entered with equal enthusiasm into this discussion and remarked that he had tried in vain to get similar public works undertaken in England. He questioned Hitler as to his method of financing public works. Hitler replied that the average workman was entitled in any event to a dole of 60 marks per month. The State provided an additional 60 marks, or 120 marks per month. 37 per cent. of this total came back to the State in the form of taxes, etc., so that in reality the State obtained a workman for 25 marks plus the normal dole of 60 marks, or to put it another way, out of every 600,000 marks spent on roads 200,000 represented the increase in expenditure over the dole.

Hitler stated that taxation revenue had increased as the result of his measures year by year since he took office and the increase this year was about 20% over last year. The number of cars had increased by over 1 million since he abolished the car tax. The Government preferred to take revenue from petrol and lorries. These latter saved more than the tax by using the motor roads which shortened the distances, thus saving petrol and rubber. Furthermore the Government retained the ownership of all petrol stations on the new roads for itself.

This led the Chancellor on to the well worn theme of Germany's shortage of raw materials. He stated that no copper was used for rearmament purposes. All available supplies were handed over to the electrical industry. That was why Germany was so anxious to obtain colonies. Lloyd George who kept on interrupting the translator, missed this last point and apparently a misunderstanding occurred. Hitler assumed that Lloyd George deliberately evaded a discussion of the colonial question, whereas Lloyd George showed annoyance when he heard that Hitler had raised the subject.[4] The party

[4] Cf. No. 288.

419

then adjourned for coffee to the vast room with the immense plate glass window, dominating Salzburg and providing a panorama of the Alps on both sides of the valley.

When taking leave of Lloyd George the Chancellor made a little speech. 'It was you', he said, 'who galvanized the people of Great Britain into the will for victory. If any single individual won the war for the Allies it was you, and I am glad to be able to tell you so in person.' Lloyd George did not deny this soft impeachment. He was glad, he said, to receive this compliment from the greatest German of the age and the greatest since Bismarck's day. Whether Hitler appreciated this last limitation I have not been able to ascertain. Lloyd George then mentioned Ludendorff and Hitler remarked that he was now unapproachable. He had been a fanatical patriot, he was now ossified and was fanatical in his likes and dislikes.

The Chancellor again escorted his visitors down the steps to the car and Lloyd George received an ovation from the populace on the way back to Berchtesgaden.

On Monday September 6th Lloyd George saw Herr Hess. The conversation turned almost immediately to the question of raw materials. Asked what products Germany lacked, Hess replied that she was short of wool, copper, rubber, tungsten and fats. Lloyd George asked how many of these could be obtained from their former colonies and Hess replied that coffee and cocoa, as well as vegetable fats, were obtainable from Africa and potash from the South Seas. 'The South Seas', interposed Lloyd George, 'are held by the Japs. If you can get them back, I congratulate you.' Lloyd George then went on to say that the colonial question bristled with difficulties. It would be premature to raise it now, with the people of Great Britain. It would be wiser to delay it until a successful conference had taken place and the new Locarno Agreement signed.

Lloyd George went on to outline some scheme by which Germany could satisfy her immediate needs by paying in marks in her former colonies for such materials as she could get there, but Hess dissented and declared that the present state of affairs was untenable, namely the possession of colonial empires by small Powers. A *redistribution of colonies* was necessary.

Lloyd George replied that Winston Churchill felt strongly about the colonial question. Winston wanted to fight everybody at the same time, namely the Communists and Russia and Germany and some other people as well. Hess asked Lloyd George why the Conservatives were on the whole anti-German in England. 'The reason is obvious', said Lloyd George. 'It is the new German army, on which you have spent 800 million pounds I am told.' Hess did not dispute this figure, but rather defended it on the ground that Germany had to build up her army from scratch.

I shall report later on about Lloyd George's visits to factories,[5] provided of course there be anything of interest to repeat.

Yours ever,
ERIC PHIPPS

[5] No. 317 below.

No. 296

Letter from Sir F. Leith-Ross (Treasury) to Dr. Schacht

[*C 7391/99/18*]

TREASURY, *October 15, 1936*

Dear Dr. Schacht,

I have to thank you for your letter of the 1st October[1] enclosing the text of your recent statement in regard to the Three-Power Currency Declaration. I have read this carefully, and I am glad to note that you feel that the time has come nearer when something can be achieved to restore international co-operation. But it is clear that very delicate handling will be required if this objective which we all desire is to be realised, and I should like to have your views as to the procedure which should be adopted. I doubt if an international conference is likely to be of service: the situation of each country requires separate treatment, though all are interested in expanding trade. As I see it

(i) In the first instance, the countries which have maintained over-valued currencies by such measures as exchange controls, quotas and subsidies have to decide whether they want to readjust their internal economy to an international basis.

(ii) Given the *will* for readjustment, they should then approach the Three Powers (with as little publicity as possible) with a view to seeing whether the difficulties that exist on either side can be met by means of concerted action and mutual adjustment.

The Three-Power Declaration contains a general invitation to other countries to join in realising the programme there set out, but we cannot presume to judge what is in the best interests of Germany, and we must therefore leave you to take the next step, at your own time. But I hope that something may be done soon.[2]

With best regards, &c.,

F. W. LEITH-ROSS

[1] No. 256.

[2] The original draft of this letter was sent to the Foreign Office by Sir F. Leith-Ross for consideration on October 5. In a minute of October 6 Sir R. Vansittart deprecated some phrases in the latter part of the draft which might suggest that the British were taking the initiative in seeking an economic agreement. 'It wd be inadvisable for us to show *empressement* in taking the initiative, nor wd it be well for Sir F. Leith-Ross to find himself involved in some private but general negotiation with Dr. Schacht—for the latter, on present form, wd at once carry the subject-matter far beyond what Sir F. Leith-Ross wd or cd contemplate . . . R. V. Oct. 6.'

No. 297

Mr. Eden to Sir E. Ovey (Brussels)
No. 518 [C 7301/7284/4]

FOREIGN OFFICE, *October 15, 1936*

Sir,

The Belgian Ambassador came to see me this evening, when he read to me and left with me the attached communication from the Belgian Government.[1] I told his Excellency that I would not conceal from him that I had been considerably surprised and indeed perturbed by King Leopold's declaration. I could not help feeling that it was particularly unfortunate that the Belgian Government had not seen fit to inform us in advance or to consult with His Majesty's Government in any way. Indeed, the first that I had heard of the declaration was when I read it in the newspaper in the train on my way back from Sheffield that morning. If the Belgian Government had felt able to inform us in advance, it might have been possible to devise some means of meeting their difficulties in some other way.

2. The Ambassador seemed to feel unable to deny the force of this complaint, and could only say that he himself had received no prior information of the declaration, and that he could only imagine that the decision was taken suddenly. I must bear in mind that there were powerful motives of internal politics concerned. It was essential to improve the military defences of Belgium, and to do this a united national front was necessary. There was no doubt that the feeling of the Flemish section of the population towards France was by no means friendly. The Franco-Soviet Pact had been for many the last straw. Belgian opinion was fearful lest, as the outcome of that pact, France should become involved in hostilities with Germany, with the result that Belgium would be expected to come to the aid of France in a quarrel which was none of her concern.

3. I told his Excellency that in the circumstances which he described I thought that he was wrong in thinking that Belgium would be obliged to go

---

[1] Not printed. Addressing the Belgian Cabinet on October 14 on the subject of the new Defence Bill, King Leopold had stated that while the position of his country made it necessary for her to maintain an effective system of defence, which in itself contributed to the preservation of peace in Western Europe, Belgian commitments should extend no further. According to the translation of the speech transmitted in Sir E. Ovey's despatch No. 554 of October 15, received in the Foreign Office on October 16, King Leopold said that 'Any unilateral policy weakens our position abroad' and that an alliance 'even if purely defensive, does not fulfil our aim'; Belgian policy must 'aim resolutely at keeping us out of the quarrels of our neighbours'. The implications of this statement caused much unfavourable comment, especially in France, where the speech was regarded as an abrogation of Belgian obligations. The communication referred to, which Baron de Cartier handed to Mr. Eden on October 15, was intended to reassure His Majesty's Government that King Leopold's speech in no way affected Belgian commitments to the League of Nations or to 'engagements internationaux qu'il a contractés et qui le lient'. Cf. *D.D.B.*, *op. cit.*, No. 132: a similar communication was made to the French Government on October 16 (see *D.D.F.*, *op. cit.*, No. 363).

to the assistance of France. The Ambassador said that this might be so, but that the Belgian public could never understand it and that there was a strong feeling against being involved in the consequences of the Franco-Soviet Pact.

4. I then told his Excellency that, though I had not as yet received a full text from Brussels of the King's declaration (the Ambassador said that he was still without one, and complained of the inadequacy of the account at his disposal), there were certain points which I wished to put to the Belgian Government without delay, and I would be grateful if he would do so. Before doing so, I must, however, point out that His Majesty's declaration was all the more surprising in that we were already engaged in diplomatic exchanges in preparation for the Five-Power Conference. The communications which were now passing between us on this subject would clearly have to deal with the very issues to which His Majesty's declaration referred. It was all the more astonishing, therefore, that, whereas all the parties to the negotiations had agreed to keep them confidential, the Belgian Government should have made a public declaration which clearly concerned a most important aspect of these negotiations.

5. I then enumerated the points which I asked his Excellency to put to his Government. What, in the view of the Belgian Government, would be the effect of His Majesty's declaration on the remnants of the Locarno Treaty as it still exists between His Majesty's Government, Belgium and France? The Ambassador would remember that I stated in the House of Commons that we were still bound by the Locarno Treaty, even if Germany had denounced it. What would be the effect of the declaration upon this arrangement? His Excellency would remember that, under the old Locarno Treaty, Belgium did guarantee France, though she did not, of course, guarantee this country. It might even be open to the French Government to say, if they wished, that if Belgium ceased to guarantee France, then the old Locarno Treaty was no longer in force between them. What would then be the position of us three?

6. The second point as to which I wished to ask his Government was how His Majesty's declaration could be reconciled with the text of the proposals of the 19th March.[2] His Excellency would recall that the four Powers, Belgium, France, the United Kingdom and Italy, then undertook to work for 'obligations of mutual assistance between Belgium, France, the United Kingdom and Italy, or any of them.' Finally, I asked the Ambassador to point out to his Government that while it was quite true that we stated in our first preliminary note of the 17th September,[3] to which, incidentally, I reminded his Excellency that we had not yet received the Belgian reply, that we only asked for guarantees from France and Germany, and not from Belgium, we did not, however, say anything in that note about the Belgian guarantee to France. It might well be that such a guarantee would be judged to be necessary as part of the new western arrangement which we were contemplating making. Did His Majesty's declaration close the door to

[2] Volume XVI, No. 144.   [3] Enclosure in No. 206.

any such negotiation? If I understood the note which his Excellency had just left me aright, this would appear not to be so, but I feared that there was considerable danger of misunderstanding on this and other subjects. I pointed out to the Ambassador that His Majesty's declaration would be of the greatest service to isolationists in this country. Indeed, it was already being used for this purpose, and I showed his Excellency the headlines in the copy of the *Evening Standard* which had just reached me.

7. The Ambassador said that he would certainly transmit the points which I had made to him to his Government. He begged me, however, to believe that the last thing that the Belgian Government intended was to take any action which could arouse misgivings in this country. There was, however, a feeling in Belgium of some resentment against French policy.

I am, &c.,
ANTHONY EDEN

No. 298

Mr. Eden to Sir E. Phipps (Berlin)
No. 1148 [C 7325/4/18]

FOREIGN OFFICE, October 16, 1936

Sir,

The German Chargé d'Affaires called upon Sir Robert Vansittart on the 14th October and handed to him the German reply to His Majesty's Government's note in regard to the five-Power meeting.[1] The note was in German, and Sir Robert Vansittart said that until His Majesty's Government had had time to study it, Prince Bismarck would not expect him to make any comment.

2. Prince Bismarck said that he had only two observations to make. The first was that the German Government had not yet received the French reply to our note,[2] which they understood had been addressed to us some time ago, and when he had spoken to the Belgian counsellor on Friday it was apparent that the Belgians had not received it either.

3. Sir Robert Vansittart expressed surprise at this and said that we had understood from what had passed at Geneva that the French were communicating their reply direct to all the other parties concerned; otherwise we should have done so ourselves. We had been for the last week under the impression that the French note had in fact been circulated. Sir Robert Vansittart said that he would communicate with the French Embassy and say that as, no doubt owing to a mistake, we had found that the other parties concerned had not received the French document, we proposed to circulate it ourselves, and he would add that he thought that in future we should better be able to avoid these delays if the circulation was undertaken by a central agency, which should obviously be His Majesty's Government. (After

---

[1] No. 286. [2] See Enclosure in No. 263.

Prince Bismarck's departure Sir Robert Vansittart communicated in this sense with the French Embassy, and they promised to let him have a reply as soon as possible.)

4. Prince Bismarck said that as the French note had not been communicated to other Governments, the German Government did not wish theirs to be communicated either until we had received replies from all the Governments. The German Government had imagined that the reason why the French reply had not been communicated was that we were acting on the principle of waiting for all.

5. Sir Robert Vansittart said that His Majesty's Government would not circulate the German reply to any other Government without the permission of the German Government. At the same time he thought it would be a great mistake if their reply was withheld. We had, of course, been acting on no such principle as the German Government had imagined, for, as already explained, His Majesty's Government had thought that the French had already sent their document out. In any case it would be a great mistake for the various stages of the correspondence to be withheld from the other interested parties until every stage was complete. On the contrary, every document ought to be communicated all round as soon as it was received. Any other procedure could only result in infinite delays, and each Government must surely prefer to consider every document as it came in, although, as he thought was almost certain to be the case with His Majesty's Government, it might not be able to pronounce any definite opinion or formulate the next step until it had been able to appreciate the effect of all the replies as a whole. Sir Robert Vansittart asked Prince Bismarck to put this point of view to his Government, and he said that he would do so by telephone.

6. Prince Bismarck then said that since His Majesty's Government had not published the fact that the French had replied to them, the German Government did not wish the fact that we had now received their reply to become public knowledge either.

7. Sir Robert Vansittart said that here again he wondered if the German Government were wise in their own interests. There had already been much speculation in the press as to when, or indeed whether, the German Government would reply. We should certainly be questioned about this, and it would be difficult to tell an untruth about it to our press. What he thought ought to be done would be to let it become known that we had received both the French and the German replies, and that we hoped the outstanding ones would come to hand very shortly.

8. Sir Robert Vansittart asked Prince Bismarck to put this point of view also to his Government, and again he promised to do so.

9. Prince Bismarck later telephoned to say that his Government would agree to our communicating their note to the French when they had received the French note. They did not agree to its communication to the Belgian and Italian Governments except on a similar basis of reciprocity. As regards the fact of the note having been received, the German Government would

prefer that this was not published. Prince Bismarck agreed that the point was probably academic, since it would leak out—as in fact it has.

10. As a sequel to this conversation with Prince Bismarck, Sir Robert Vansittart saw M. Corbin on the 15th October and learned to his surprise that the French Government had communicated their note about the five-Power meeting to Belgium and Italy, but not to Germany.

11. M. Corbin explained that this latter omission had been due to the fact that the French Government thought that the German reply was about to be communicated, and that it would only cause this communication to be delayed if the French note were delivered.

12. Sir Robert Vansittart replied that, in any case, the omission seemed to him quite indefensible, and he urged that it should be rectified at once. M. Corbin subsequently telephoned to say that he had communicated with Paris, with the result that the French note would be communicated to the German Government, possibly on the same day, or at latest on the morning of the 16th October.

13. Sir Robert Vansittart told M. Corbin that, in accordance with an agreement come to at Geneva, we had not even told our press that we had received the French note. The Ambassador said that he thought this was due to a misunderstanding. Any such agreement was regarded as purely temporary, and the French Government did not wish to make a secret of the fact that they had communicated a note, although they naturally still wished secrecy to be kept about its contents.

14. On the 16th October Prince Bismarck telephoned to say that the German Government had now received a copy of the French note, and in consequence agreed to our communicating a copy of their note to the French Government. Sir Robert Vansittart accordingly handed a copy (in the original German) to the French Ambassador on the same day.

15. Subsequently Prince Bismarck telephoned to say that he had consulted his Government about the publication in the press of the fact that we had received the German note. The German Government would still prefer to say nothing about it, but if we felt that it was necessary to say something they agreed that we should say (1) that the French and German notes had been received in the last few days; (2) that press reports of the contents of these notes should be regarded as speculation.

16. Sir Robert Vansittart asked if the German Government would agree to our saying that the French note had been handed to the German Government and vice versa. Prince Bismarck replied that he thought his Government would not wish this, but that we should confine ourselves to the two points mentioned in paragraph 15 above.

I am, &c.,
ANTHONY EDEN

Mr. Eden to Sir E. Drummond (Rome)
No. 383 Telegraphic [C 7145/4/18]

FOREIGN OFFICE, *October 17, 1936, 3.10 p.m.*

Your despatch No. 1097.[1]

The following observations may assist you in further discussion of this subject with Italian Minister for Foreign Affairs.

You were right to tell Count Ciano that mere fact that Italy is not mentioned in paragraph 5 of our memorandum of September 17th[2] in no way implies any desire on our part to exclude her from the new Treaty. Our intention is, of course, quite the contrary and should be clear from paragraph 6 of our memorandum in which we specifically asked for Italian observations.

I do not share Signor Vitetti's view that fact that new Treaty would provide for guarantees to United Kingdom and Italy as well as to Germany, Belgium and France would necessitate three different instruments. Though our views are at present provisional only, we have been thinking of but one instrument: see in this connexion discussion between ourselves and Italian Government in February 1935 concerning arrangements to avoid a United Kingdom guarantee to Italy and vice versa under Air Pact. On February 7th, 1935 (see F.O. despatch No. 173),[3] Italian Ambassador informed us of Signor Mussolini's view that there should be a single agreement embracing all five Locarno Powers but excluding United Kingdom guarantee to Italy and vice versa. On the basis of these discussions we had some ground for assuming that in new Western Treaty Italian Government would not expect a guarantee from us or vice versa.

I do not feel that we are called upon to explain reason why we have not asked that Belgium should guarantee Great Britain: suffice it to say that our adherence in this respect to the old Locarno system was due entirely to strategic and not to political considerations. For obvious reasons the important guarantees for us—that of Italy being excluded in the circumstances described above—were those of France and Germany.

The important fact which seems to emerge from your conversation is that the Italian Government now prefer the distinction between guarantors and guaranteed as laid down in the old Locarno Treaty to the more general system of guarantees proposed for the new Treaty. The arguments advanced for this preference do not appear as given in your despatch to be very convincing. Do you think that there is some ulterior reason for this unhelpful attitude—or rather change of attitude?

For instance, I do not follow Signor Vitetti's argument that if Italy and Great Britain were guaranteed by France, Germany would attack Great Britain and Italy sooner than France because in such circumstances she would be opposed by only two Powers instead of three. Surely this danger (insofar as it exists at all) is still greater under the Locarno system where

[1] No. 275.   [2] See Enclosure in No. 206.   [3] Volume XII, No. 429.

Great Britain and Italy are guarantor but not guaranteed States? Being guarantors Germany would have the same inducement to attack one or other of them in the circumstances contemplated, and could moreover do so with greater chance of impunity since, if she did so attack either of them, she would not necessarily be opposed by any of the other parties to the Treaty, for none of them would be bound by any guarantee given to the victim of the aggression.

Again the argument that while under the old Locarno Treaty France would not take action in Central and Eastern Europe unless she had the consent of her two guarantors, that condition disappears under the new Treaty, does not seem to be altogether clear (paragraph 3 of your despatch).

I should be grateful for anything you can do to clear up the above points. In any case you should ask the Italian Government to be good enough to give us their views in writing as soon as possible, as in that form it will be easier to collate them with those of the other Governments concerned. Written replies have now been received from France[4] and Germany,[5] and Belgium is being asked to expedite hers.[6]

Another reason for hastening the written replies still outstanding is that the German Government have intimated that they do not wish their written reply to be communicated to those Governments who, for their part, have not yet furnished written replies.[7]

[4] Enclosure in No. 263.   [5] No. 286.   [6] See No. 297.   [7] See No. 298.

No. 300

Sir E. Phipps (Berlin) to Mr. Eden (Received October 20)
No. 291 Saving: Telegraphic [C 7411/97/18]

Confidential   BERLIN, *October 19, 1936*

My telegram No. 322[1] paragraph 2.

I learn from a very reliable source that term 'redistribution of colonies' represents the latest authoritative German standpoint. The shortage of raw materials, and scarcity of currency are causing serious embarrassment to the Nazi leaders, and making Dr. Schacht's position very difficult.

He is therefore so anxious for immediate help, that he, the Chancellor, Herr Hess, General von Epp and other moderate leaders profess that they would now accept as a final and comprehensive settlement the restoration of the Cameroons and Togoland, provided the other Colonial countries who possess far more than their share, viz. Belgium, Holland, Portugal and Australia also contribute to the pool.

If Dr. Schacht is to be believed Monsieur Blum practically undertook to urge his colleagues to restore French portion of the Cameroons and Togoland provided we surrendered our share of these two colonies.

According to my informant German Government would make no

[1] No. 288.

difficulty about military training or treatment of natives. Germany would accept principles laid down by British Government. Chancellor fully realises that presence of Italy in Abyssinia makes restoration of German East Africa almost impossible for us whilst South Africa would only yield up South-West to force.[2]

[2] In a further telegram, No. 292 Saving of October 20, Sir E. Phipps referred to telegram No. 291 and questioned 'Herr Hitler's readiness to accept even this settlement as final'. Sir R. Vansittart remarked that this telegram 'is confirmed by a letter I have had from Baron von Stumm [of October 21: C 7565/97/18] who came over here to propagand about the colonies. R. V. Oct. 23.'

No. 301

Sir E. Drummond (Rome) to Mr. Eden (Received October 22)
No. 1143 [C 7469/4/18]

ROME, *October 19, 1936*

Sir,

With reference to my telegram No. 654[1] of to-day's date, I have the honour to transmit to you herewith a translation of a letter,[2] dated the 18th October, which I received this morning from the Italian Minister for Foreign Affairs, enclosing the reply of the Italian Government to our memorandum of the 17th September[3] regarding the scope of the discussions which it is hoped to initiate in London shortly between the five Locarno Powers.

I have, &c.,
ERIC DRUMMOND

ENCLOSURE IN No. 301

Translation of a Memorandum communicated by Count Ciano

ROME [*October 18, 1936, XIV*]

The Fascist Government has carefully examined the suggestions put forward by the British Government in their memorandum of the 17th September last, in connexion with the diplomatic preparation of the conference of the five Locarno Powers, which it is the common wish of the two Governments to see held as soon as possible.

2. The Fascist Government have noted with satisfaction that the British Government share their point of view regarding the necessity for an exact and thorough diplomatic preparation of the conference and of the usefulness of discussion between the five interested Governments, before the conference begins, of the principal questions regarding the character and scope of the agreement which is to replace the Locarno Treaty. Among such questions, those mentioned by the British Government appear to the Fascist Govern-

[1] Not printed: it summarized the Enclosure to this despatch.
[2] Not printed. It said that copies of the document, which was not intended for publication, were being transmitted to the German, French, and Belgian Governments.
[3] Enclosure in No. 206.

ment to be of essential importance, but, before entering into a detailed examination of them, the Fascist Government is of the opinion that it should be clearly understood between the five Powers who are to take part in the conference what should be the general bases of the new agreement which is to be negotiated between them.

3. To the Fascist Government it seems that the most practical manner of proceeding to an exchange of ideas on this question would be to take as a starting point for the discussions the Treaty of Locarno itself, as it now is; and, instead of discussing *de novo* all the factors which led to its conclusion, to re-examine in common accord the structure of the treaty, in order to adapt it to those circumstances which in the meantime have been subjected to change without, however, altering either its general plan or its essential characteristics.

4. The Treaty of Locarno—fruit of long diplomatic elaboration—remains one of the most organic and best conceived instruments for the creation in Western Europe of those conditions of security to which our efforts are directed; and in the opinion of the Italian Government the new pact should retain its fundamental principles.

5. These principles consist in essence of: (*a*) The specific undertaking of France, Belgium and Germany not to have recourse to war in any question which may arise between them; (*b*) the joint guarantee by Italy and England of the non-aggression agreements between France, Belgium and Germany which form the foundation of the Locarno Treaty.

6. These two principles are, moreover, those to which the British Government rightly refer in the first paragraph of their memorandum.

7. The question of the guarantee is certainly the one which most especially interests England and Italy, and on this point the Fascist Government think a more precise exchange of ideas necessary.

8. From an examination of the British memorandum, the Fascist Government have gathered that it is the intention of the British Government to introduce into the guarantee system a new principle, that is to say, the principle of reciprocity. It seems to emerge from the British memorandum that the British Government would be ready to renew the Locarno guarantees, so far as concerns the non-aggression agreements between Germany, France and Belgium, in exchange for similar guarantees in favour of Great Britain on the part of Germany against France and on the part of France against Germany. That which in the *communiqué* of the 3rd February, 1935[4] was the principle on which the Air Pact was to be based would thus come to be used as the organic foundation for the entire system of guarantees in the new treaty.

9. This innovation seems to the Fascist Government to be of the greatest importance, and the Fascist Government would wish to call the attention of the British Government to what would, in their opinion, be its practical consequences.

10. To begin with, the Fascist Government have always regarded the

<hr>

[4] See Volume XII, No. 400, note 4.

Locarno guarantee as a joint Italo-British guarantee and have always considered that the real strength of the Locarno Treaty lay in the fact that the aggressor would in every case have found himself faced by the united forces of the Power attacked and of the two guarantors. The joint character of the Italo-British guarantee, and this union of the forces of the guarantors and the Power attacked, constituted the fundamental unity—for all practical purposes—of the Locarno Treaty.

11. Confronted with the suggestions contained in the British memorandum, the Fascist Government wonder whether this fundamental unity would be effectively maintained in a régime of reciprocal separate guarantees, or whether the Treaty of Locarno would not become split into two tripartite systems, which would fundamentally alter the position of the guarantors, do away with the joint character of the guarantee and, for all practical purposes, transform the Locarno Treaty into two separate pacts of mutual assistance: one Franco-Anglo-German and one Italo-Franco-German, only formally linked together in the common framework of a general pact. In the opinion of the Fascist Government, this would represent a general weakening of the Locarno system, which it is certainly not the intention of any of the five Governments to bring about.

12. It is perhaps unnecessary for the Fascist Government to call the attention of the British Government to the fact that, once the joint character of the Locarno guarantee is weakened, the Treaty of Locarno would come to lose not only one of its fundamental characteristics, but also a function to which an essential importance has always, and rightly, been attributed.

13. In proceeding to the examination of the other questions alluded to in the British memorandum, in regard to which the Fascist Government will not fail to make their own position clear, it seems to the Fascist Government to be necessary that the States signatories of the Locarno Treaty should be in agreement as to the character of the new treaty and should settle whether or not it is their intention to reconstruct the Locarno Treaty on its original foundations.

No. 302

Letter from Mr. G. H. S. Pinsent[1] *(Berlin) to Sir F. Leith-Ross (Treasury)*
[C 7637/99/18]

BERLIN, *October 19, 1936*

My dear Leithers,

I delivered your letter[2] personally to Schacht on Saturday October 17. He opened it and spent about ten minutes discussing its contents and other things in his usual rather challenging manner. It is not necessary to go in detail into what he said ('We cannot be forced to take any decision which

---

[1] Mr. Pinsent was Financial Adviser in the British Embassy at Berlin. A copy of this letter was sent by Sir F. Leith-Ross to Mr. H. M. G. Jebb on October 27.
[2] No. 296.

we do not wish to'—'There will be no peace so long as England tries to hold the world at her mercy'). But he did not think that your letter took things much further (this after explaining carefully that his letter to you made no enquiries, but only the suggestion of personal discussion). His main reaction seemed indeed to be disappointment at finding nothing in your letter about such a discussion. I could not of course tell him that the possibility of your paying a visit to Berlin had been seriously considered, but when a little later he made some hopeful remarks about the forthcoming Locarno Conference, I suggested that that Conference might afford an opportunity for some progress in the direction contemplated in your letter.

He pounced on the suggestion on page 2 of your letter that any country desiring to adjust its internal economy should approach the *three* Powers. To mollify him I suggested that you had put it this way as a matter of form and that you probably did not in fact expect Germany to approach all three.

He emphasized in the course of the conversation the fact that a devaluation would not make it possible for Germany to abolish her exchange restrictions immediately.

As he seemed to hesitate between sending you an immediate reply and postponing it, I suggested that he should choose his own time.

I hope very much that there will be some opportunity before long for you to meet Schacht. I have been hoping for this ever since you came back, as I think it might both knock some of the nonsense out of Schacht's head and perhaps help to strengthen his hand here—at least if he behaves properly and does not play his eternal game of fishing for commitments from the other side without offering any himself.

Yours ever,

G. H. S. Pinsent

No. 303

Sir E. Drummond (Rome) to Mr. Eden (Received October 20, 9.30 a.m.)
No. 658 Telegraphic [C 7443/4/18]

ROME, *October 20, 1936, 1.15 a.m.*

Your telegram No. 383.[1]

I saw Count Ciano this afternoon two hours before he left for Berlin[2] and said that I had received this morning Italian reply to our memorandum of September 17th.[3] I had been glad to receive this document as my Government had instructed me to press for it and I was transmitting it to London at once. I then informed him of the position regarding written replies and that we were endeavouring to expedite the only outstanding one, namely Belgian.

---

[1] No. 299.   [2] Cf. No. 293.   [3] See No. 301.

2. Meanwhile I went on that I had reported to you my last conversation with him and Signor Vitetti[4] and had received instructions on certain points. My former statement regarding intention of His Majesty's Government that Italy should be fully included in new Treaty was perfectly correct. I hoped our earlier conversation had helped to clear up any misunderstanding on this point and I was glad to see that Italian reply recognised that this was our desire. My Government had not yet decided as to what form the new proposed agreement should take. We were inclined, however, to one agreement and not to two or three separate ones as Italian Government seemed to fear. I rather assumed what was in the mind of His Majesty's Government was something on the lines of proposed Air Pact of 1935, lines of which Signor Mussolini had advocated; he would remember, no doubt, that arrangement envisaged one general protocol between all the Powers concerned and a special protocol between the United Kingdom and Italy by which neither of these two countries would expect mutual assistance.

3. I then dealt with the first of the two arguments which Signor Vitetti had put forward on the lines of paragraph 5 of your telegram under reference. Count Ciano quickly took this point and appreciated it. As regards the second argument, see paragraph 6 of your telegram, I said that if under the old Locarno system Italy and the United Kingdom could if they thought fit veto in practice France going to the aid of Russia under Franco-Soviet Pact by attacking Germany the situation would so far as I could see remain unchanged under the new Locarno arrangements now being suggested by His Majesty's Government. Count Ciano did not endeavour to refute this argument but explained that these were no more than points that had arisen in the course of conversation.

4. Turning again to general position I said that it seemed to be today very difficult to distinguish between air, land and sea warfare. Count Ciano immediately agreed and said that an attack by air obviously implied war both by sea and by land. I remarked this being so it seemed to me that our present proposals were a perfectly logical extension of the position of 1935 according to which the old Locarno Pact existed but was to be supplemented by a separate Air Convention. To this Signor Mussolini had agreed. Was there not therefore some change in Italian attitude? Might I ask him a question on my own initiative which I thought however might considerably help my Government to clarify the position? Supposing a return were made to the old Locarno Pact would Italy be ready simultaneously to conclude Air Convention on the lines laid down in 1935? Minister for Foreign Affairs seemed rather taken aback by this question and said that he could not answer it at once. He observed that much had happened since 1935 though he admitted the position of Italian Government had then been as I had set it out; but there was now a new situation as regards Belgium. There were also French and German replies to our memorandum. He characterized the French reply[5] as being complicated and full of reserves. He gave me

4 See No. 275.   5 No. 263, Enclosure.

the impression that he was restraining his language and clearly he greatly disliked French answer. He then spoke of German reply thus showing that copy had already been communicated to the Italian Government.[6] He mentioned that while French answer required full and complete application of Covenant and of Article 16, German answer declared that a new Locarno arrangement must have no reference whatever to Article 16 or to Covenant. There was therefore complete opposition of views; for all these reasons he would have to think over the question I had put to him about Air Pact. He would do so and would give me an answer on his return from Germany when he would not only record to me what had passed during his visit but would resume the present discussion.

5. At the end of paragraph 4 of your telegram under reference you ask whether there may be some ulterior reason for Italian Government's change of attitude. This point will be dealt with fully in a telegram tomorrow.[7]

[6] Sir R. Vansittart thought it a little difficult 'to understand why Italy shd have received direct from Germany a copy of the paper that Germany wd not let *us* give Italy ... R. V. Oct. 21'.

[7] No. 312 below.

No. 304

Mr. F. G. Coultas (Seville) to Mr. Eden (Received October 21, 9.30 a.m.)
No. 18 Telegraphic [W 14062/62/41]

SEVILLE, *October 20, 1936, 8.45 p.m.*

Your telegram No. 29.[1]

General situation has been marked by rapid return to normal life and resumption of work in areas held by insurgents. Enactments have been confined to securing functioning of administrative units normally depending on Madrid and control of foreign exchange.

Franco on (? August 10th)[2] as head of military Government broadcast following statement of policy in which his care for working and middle classes was forcibly emphasised. New State is to be totalitarian and authoritarian. Regional aspirations will be respected within national unity. Historic place of Municipality in public life will be strengthened. Popular suffrage is to be replaced by technical corporations representative of national activities. Welfare of the country's populations is to receive preferential attention and pending participation of working class in profits of production, within an organisation excluding class conflict, their present gains will be safeguarded unless at variance with national interests. Commercial policy

[1] This Foreign Office telegram of October 16 referred to a Foreign Office request of October 1 for a general report on 'qualities and aims of rebel leaders and of General Franco in particular' and pointed out that no general report had been received from Mr. Coultas, H.M. Consul in Seville, since August 5.

[2] Presumably at the beginning of October: cf. No. 267.

434

will be based on preferential racial and political affinities with due regard to traditional connexions of reciprocal benefit. State though secular will work in harmony with the church each respecting the liberty of the other within their respective spheres. Outstanding feature of present crisis is phenomenal growth of national syndicalist youth movement known as *Falange Español.* Recruited from all classes not excluding known extremists it supports army policy of corporative State but with more violent emphasis on rights of labouring classes. As its members are largely responsible for policing of the country naturally opportunities for propaganda are unlimited and make a much wider appeal than Carlist *Requetes* though individually inferior in quality. Former's political pretensions if backed by outstanding leader, at present apparently lacking, might provide seeds for future conflict with military leaders who are already taking precautions to clip the wings of both groups. Franco who was previously inactive politically gained military experience in Morocco; reticent, serious and devoted to his profession; one of the organisers of the foreign legion, inspired suppression of 1934 revolt and reorganisation of army commenced by Gil Robles. Voiced army and popular discontent in a letter to Madrid Cabinet some weeks previous to present outbreak. Cabanellas,[3] lifelong republican, is merely venerable figurehead. Mola,[4] professional soldier with no marked political affiliation. Queipo,[5] stormy petrel, exiled to France during the last dictatorship, attached as military adviser to the first President of the Republic, capable, courageous soldier and clever propagandist. Return of monarchy does not appear to be an immediate issue.

[3] General Miguel Cabanellas y Ferrer (1862–1938), appointed Inspector-General of the National army on October 2, 1936.   [4] General Emilio Mola Vidal (1887–1937).
[5] General Gonzalo Queipo de Llano y Serra (1875–1951).

No. 305

Mr. Eden to Mr. Ogilvie-Forbes (*Madrid*)
No. 195 Telegraphic [*W 13885/62/41*]

FOREIGN OFFICE, *October 20, 1936, 10 p.m.*

While appreciating what you have hitherto done[1] with the full approval of His Majesty's Government to mitigate dangers to or sufferings of non-combatants, I feel impelled to draw your attention to the following important and urgent matter.

[1] In his telegram No. 376 of October 18 Mr. Ogilvie-Forbes referred to earlier telegrams (see No. 268, notes 1, 3) about the possibility of a general massacre after the fall of Madrid, and said: 'I am searching my conscience as to what more I can do for the prisoners.' He thought that Mr. Eden 'might now have Franco informed of this very grave danger and/or issue public warning indicated in your telegram under reference without, if possible, compromising me'. A note on the filed copy of telegram No. 376 read: 'It was decided by the S. of S. this morning that an appeal shd be sent to both sides to agree upon an exchange of hostages & an offer of "good offices" be made by H.M.G.' Telegrams in this sense were to be sent to Sir H. Chilton and Mr. Ogilvie-Forbes. Cf. *The Times*, October 21, p. 14.

It has become a matter of common knowledge that in the course of the present troubles in Spain large numbers of hostages have been taken and held.

This applies more especially to the capital where so large a population is concentrated.

There would appear to be most serious reason to fear that, in the absence of sufficiently reliable means of ensuring the safety of these persons, a situation might arise when they would be in danger of attack or even of a wholesale massacre.

In the face of such a possibility and of the further terrible consequences which might ensue His Majesty's Government feel impelled to make an urgent appeal on purely humanitarian grounds to the authorities on both sides to come to an agreement for an exchange of all such hostages and more especially for the release and removal into some place of safety of any woman who may have been included among these hostages.

To this end His Majesty's Government would be ready to give their own good offices in any way which may be acceptable to both parties and they would gladly offer the services of the British navy in any cases where transport by sea might be required.

You should make an immediate communication in the above sense to the Spanish Government and inform them that His Majesty's Government trust they will give this suggestion all possible consideration and let you have an early reply.

You should keep naval authorities closely in touch with developments and arrange details of any evacuation with them direct.

Similar telegram[2] has been sent to His Majesty's Ambassador, Hendaye, with reference to work done by Dr. Junod.[3]

[2] No. 207 of October 20 to Sir H. Chilton.

[3] Dr. M. Junod, Swiss Representative of the Red Cross, had been active since the beginning of the civil war in arranging for the exchange of hostages and political prisoners. He described his experiences in *War without weapons* (London, 1951). Foreign Office telegram No. 196 of October 21 to Mr. Ogilvie-Forbes instructed him to substitute the following for the final sentence of telegram No. 195: 'Similar instructions containing also appreciative reference to work done by Dr. Junod have been sent to H.M. Ambassador Hendaye.' The British note was presented to representatives of the government and insurgent authorities on October 21.

Mr. Ogilvie-Forbes's telegram No. 406 of October 24 gave the text of a long reply from Señor del Vayo of that date. It denied that there were any political hostages in the capital, said that political prisoners held were detained because of direct rebellion or activities hostile to the Republic, and expressed surprise at references to a possible general massacre. Although the 'Spanish Nation' was exasperated by the one-sided application of the Non-Intervention Agreement, the authorities were confident that 'no regrettable incidents' would occur.

Sir H. Chilton's telegram No. 257 of October 30 gave the text of the Marquis Merry del Val's reply of that date. The communication was headed 'Pro memoria' and unsigned. It stated that the British Government's alarm was 'evident and justifiable' with regard to 'persons detained by the Reds' but not with regard to 'the zone occupied by the national army' where there was 'an authority responsible for lives and good treatment of those detained'.

No. 306

Sir E. Phipps (Berlin) to Mr. Eden (Received October 21)
No. 295 Saving: Telegraphic [C 7460/5740/18]

BERLIN, *October 20, 1936*

Dr. Schacht had a long conversation yesterday with a German friend the substance of which has been repeated to a member of my staff. He gave a full account of his discussions in Paris[1] and showed his friend report which he had prepared for Chancellor regarding his conversations with M. Blum and other French Ministers and also showed him subsequent correspondence which he has had with M. Blum.[2]

According to Dr. Schacht's account M. Blum expressed a strong desire to get rid of his association with French Communist party and stated that if an agreement could be reached between France and Germany he would be prepared to abandon Franco-Russian Pact as unnecessary.

My French colleague has also prophesied that within a measurable time a fresh French Government will have to be formed without communists.

[1] See Nos. 141, 145, and 210.   [2] Cf. Nos. 223, 228, 261, 300, and 302.

No. 307

Sir E. Phipps (Berlin) to Mr. Eden (Received October 21, 3 p.m.)
No. 296 Saving: Telegraphic [C 7461/97/18]

BERLIN, *October 20, 1936*

My telegrams Nos. 291[1] and 292[2] Saving and my immediately preceding Saving telegram.[3]

In conversation with the same German friend Dr. Schacht dealt at length with colonial question. He said that both in conversation and in writing to Dr. Schacht Blum had spoken of 'initiative' which he was taking with regard to colonial question. Dr. Schacht did not, however, inform his friend whether Blum had mentioned any particular territories as open to discussion.

According to Dr. Schacht the Chancellor has now entrusted him with colonial question which is to be treated in the main as an economic matter. Dr. Schacht agreed with postponement of Breslau meeting[4] on the ground that agitation of this kind was not the right approach to the matter. Dr. Schacht would accept transfer of a colony on terms that there should be German currency and German administration and no recruitment of natives. He considers the transfer of a colony would immediately solve difficulties in supplying two important commodities, viz. fats and timber.

In repeating this conversation to a member of my staff Dr. Schacht's friend found it extremely difficult to give an opinion whether (a) some

[1] No. 300.   [2] *Ibid.*, note 2.   [3] No. 306.   [4] Cf. No. 288.

concession or [?on] colonial questions would really increase Dr. Schacht's credit so much as to enable him to ensure the adoption of a more liberal economic policy in Germany or (b) the German Government were really in a position to accept as a final and comprehensive settlement the solution suggested in first paragraph of my telegram No. 291 Saving. It is evident however that Dr. Schacht's proposed terms are incompatible with 'open door' in transferred colony.

The same informant had previously had a conversation yesterday with German Minister for Foreign Affairs in which the latter declared that he was opposed to Germany's colonial demands except for the fact that they formed a useful instrument of pressure on His Majesty's Government.

No. 308

List[1] of probable infractions of the Agreement regarding Non-Intervention in Spain based upon evidence supplied by British official sources

[*W 14097/9549/41*]

FOREIGN OFFICE, *October 20, 1936*

It should be noted that His Majesty's Consular Officers have not been instructed to seek out information of this nature, the opinion being held that the sole duty of His Majesty's Government in the first instance was to see to the application of the Agreement in the United Kingdom rather than to seek evidence of infractions by other countries.

For this reason the information at our disposal as voluntarily supplied by His Majesty's Ships and Consular Officers is somewhat meagre.

No information containing sufficient evidence to warrant a charge being made is available in regard to Germany, France or Portugal.

Italy

(1) On September 7th the Italian s.s. *Nereide* discharged a cargo at Palma which, from observations made by His Majesty's Ship *Galatea* was seen to

---

[1] A minute by Sir G. Mounsey of October 16 said that Mr. Eden had seen recent papers 'relating to Soviet activities in contravention of the non-intervention agreement and is impressed with the evidence which they supply'. He thought, however, 'that the question of whether we should produce this, either alone or with other available evidence against other countries, to the Committee must be subordinated to the decisions which must be arrived at, immediately, as to the prospects of continuing the agreement in being and as to the policy of H.M.G. in the event of its prospective or actual collapse'. Mr. Eden asked that Lord Plymouth should send a reminder on Monday, October 19, to the German, Italian, and Portuguese Governments asking for immediate replies to the charges made against them in time for a meeting of the N.I. Committee on October 23. Commenting on this note on October 21, Sir R. Vansittart wrote: 'I think it is clear from this that our eye-witness evidence against Russia is clearer, more detailed and more recent than against Italy. And the quantities are greater too . . . I therefore think we could well go ahead in regard to Russia. Since no case can be made out against Germany, France or Portugal I wd be averse to indicting Italy alone again.'

include 6 fighters and an unknown quantity of bombs, shells, rifles and ammunition. On the same day 3 Italian bombers arrived.

(2) His Majesty's Vice-Consul at Palma reported that on September 23rd cargo was transferred from the Italian s.s. *Sicilia* to the Italian destroyer *Malocello* which landed the cargo on September 23–24. The cargo was believed to contain ammunition and bombs but this could not be confirmed.

(3) His Majesty's Vice-Consul at Palma reported that on September 25th the unloading of cargo from an Italian steamer at Palma on to the Italian cruiser *Polar* took place all day.

(4) On October 3rd His Majesty's Vice-Consul at Palma reported that the landing of arms which had been transferred from Italian merchant ships to Italian men-of-war was still continuing and was being observed by our men-of-war.

Soviet Russia

(1) His Majesty's Ship *Active*, Cartagena October 10th. Spanish hull *Campeche* unloading 4″ guns, trench mortars, hand grenades and large quantity of rifles and ammunition all from Russia. Russian Senior Air Officer Commanding reported to have arrived.

(2) His Majesty's Ship *Arrow*, Cartagena October 15th. Most reliable information that Russian steamer *Komcomon* disembarked 49 tanks, 80 military 3-ton lorries with Russian crew of two or three men each—total 300 men who are reported to be trained in aviation.

(3) His Majesty's Ship *Grafton*, Cartagena October 15th. Russian steamer *Stari Bolshevik* arrived from Odessa October 15th with military lorries and tanks. Reported on 19th October by His Majesty's Ship *Grafton* to have unloaded:

> 20–25 cases as for aircraft, containing dismantled
> machines painted green.
> 18 3-engine machines.
> 15 large tanks.
> 320 cases of bombs.
> Large quantity of ammunition and aviation spirit.[2]

[2] Copies of this document were circulated to the Cabinet at its meeting on October 21. The Cabinet agreed that Mr. Eden should prepare a memorandum embodying the particulars, in the light of the Cabinet discussion, for consideration by the N.I. Committee.

No. 309

Mr. Eden to Mr. Lloyd Thomas (Paris)
No. 1774 [C 7464/4/18]

FOREIGN OFFICE, *October 20, 1936*

Sir,

Sir Robert Vansittart asked the French Ambassador to come and see him today and took the occasion to ask him what exactly was meant by the reference to a guarantee of 'possessions and dependencies' in paragraph 5 of the French Government's reply to His Majesty's Government's memorandum of September 17th.[1]

2. M. Corbin admitted that he did not know exactly what was meant. He suggested one or two hypotheses but said that he would prefer not to record them and to obtain an authentic explanation from his Government. Sir Robert Vansittart said that he would be grateful if he would do so, for although he was only enquiring unofficially, the point would certainly be raised in any close examination of the French Government's reply.

3. The Ambassador then referred to the recent speech of the King of the Belgians.[2] He said that the French Government had received various communications from the Belgian Government which did not, however, entirely clear up the situation, and he did not think that it would be cleared up until either M. van Zeeland or M. Spaak, or perhaps both of them, came to Paris, as he believed that they were likely to do in the course of this week. M. Corbin added that the discussions which the French Government would have with them would not be in any way summary, and that the Belgian Government would be handled with all due care and tact. He himself was convinced that time and patience would be necessary to arrive at the solution of the present difficulty.

4. Sir Robert Vansittart replied that he was glad to hear that these were the intentions of the French Government, for he had always hoped that they would take the line of patience and not of precipitation. He reminded the Ambassador that there was a school of thought in Belgium, though no doubt at present not an important one, which favoured a much more negative and inglorious form of neutrality than anything contemplated by the present Belgian Government. He said that he thought it quite likely that unless the present Belgian Government were handled with due care and consideration the result might be to strengthen that school of thought.

> I am, etc.,
> (For the Secretary of State)
> R. F. WIGRAM

---

[1] Enclosure in No. 263.   [2] See No. 297.

No. 310

Sir H. Kennard (Warsaw) to Mr. Eden (Received October 23)
No. 449 [C 7552/6703/55]

WARSAW, *October 20, 1936*

Sir,

I have the honour to report that at my first interview with the Minister for Foreign Affairs since his return from one month's absence I expressed

440

my surprise that the Polish delegation at Geneva and the press here had taken up the question of Polish colonial aspirations with such vigour recently, more especially in view of the fact that his Excellency had a year ago told me not to take this campaign too seriously as his Government fully realised the difficulties involved.[1]

2. M. Beck drew my attention to Poland's present position, both as regards raw materials and emigration. It was becoming increasingly difficult for Poland to purchase raw materials in foreign currency unless she obtained some compensation in the export of manufactured articles or facilities for emigration. At the present moment Polish emigration was considerably less than it had been before the war, despite the great increase in population since that period. The situation had been further aggravated by the Jewish problem. The Polish Jews had in the past gained a livelihood as retailers in the small towns and villages, but were now rapidly losing this business owing to the growth of the co-operative movement and larger concerns having greater facilities of distribution. The peasant also, both in a cultural and material sense, was improving his outlook and becoming more restive in regard to the Jewish monopoly of this business. While he hoped that Jewish emigration to Palestine might be resumed on a larger scale at some future date, he felt that this was not sufficient for Jewish requirements and that some other outlets must be found for them.

3. In these circumstances, while he did not suggest that some colony should be presented to Poland as a gift, he felt that, in view of the references by Sir Samuel Hoare to the question of raw materials[2] and to the general discussion which had been taking place lately on this question[3] and that of emigration, it was Poland's duty to draw attention to her special needs in this sphere in order that they might be kept in mind in the event of any general consideration of the question. He did not attach any political importance to the matter, as for Poland it was largely an economic question, and he intended to warn those who were conducting this propaganda here

[1] At the second meeting of the 93rd session of the League Council on September 19 M. Beck had expressed the hope that the composition of the Permanent Mandates Commission might be reconsidered with a view to the inclusion of representatives of other countries 'which for one reason or another were keenly interested in certain of the problems which the Mandates Commission had to discuss' (*L/N.O.J.*, July–Dec. 1936, pp. 1143–4). In his telegram No. 38 Saving of September 23 Sir H. Kennard said that according to Polish press comment this statement marked 'the opening of a campaign to secure for Poland possibilities of colonial expansion'. The Polish case was also presented before the Second Committee of the Assembly at its 6th meeting on October 5 by M. Rose (*L/N.O.J.*, *S.S. No. 157*, pp. 45–6) and before the Sixth Committee at its 5th meeting on October 6 by M. Komarnicki (*L/N.O.J.*, *S.S. No. 161*, pp. 32–3).

[2] In his speech of September 11, 1935, to the League Assembly: see Volume XIV, Appendix IV.

[3] At the 6th meeting of the Second Committee of the Assembly on October 5 Mr. W. Morrison, the United Kingdom representative, proposed a resolution for setting up an enquiry into the question of commercial access to raw materials: see *L/N.O.J.*, *S.S. No. 157*, pp. 38–43. The resolution was adopted by the Assembly on October 10 to ask the Council to appoint such a committee: see *L/N.O.J.*, *S.S. No. 155*, pp. 141–2.

that they should be careful not to lend it an exaggerated importance and to observe more discretion in what they said or wrote in this respect.[4]

I have, &c.,

H. W. KENNARD

[4] In a minute of September 29 on Sir H. Kennard's telegram No. 38 Saving (see note 1 above) Sir R. Vansittart commented: 'The Polish claim to colonies is abracadabrante [*sic*] but it is as good as the German, which I myself favour—eventually. But the only, & very unjust & very real & quite sensible, reason why we prefer the German to the Polish claim is that the Germans are stronger. I hope that we shall not sell colonial retrocession to the Germans except at a whacking price.'

No. 311

Mr. MacKillop (Moscow) to Mr. Eden (Received October 24)
No. 604 [W 14276/9549/41]

MOSCOW, *October 20, 1936*

Sir,

With reference to my telegram No. 164 of the 17th October[1] and connected correspondence relative to the attitude of the Soviet Government towards events in Spain, I have the honour to inform you that the press continues to devote considerable space to the question and there seem to be reasonably clear indications of the intention of the Soviet Government to take further definite steps to give concrete proof of their dissatisfaction with the present situation and particularly with the work of the London Committee on non-intervention.

2. 'Izvestiya', in a leading article dated the 18th October, says no more than the truth when it declares that the Soviet Government never considered the non-intervention agreement to be a just one. 'An agreement which placed a legal Government on the same plane as rebels contradicted the elementary principles of justice and of international law. The Soviet Government only signed the agreement at the insistence of England and France and on the assumption that they would seriously endeavour to ensure its fulfilment. We are entitled to expect an answer from England and France as to whether it is possible to leave in force an agreement which is being violated every hour.'

3. The leading article in 'Pravda' on the same day is in a similar strain, declaring that the *mise en demeure* of the Soviet representative in London is forcing the London Committee into the dilemma of having either to refrain from encouraging intervention by the Fascist States and seriously to attempt to secure the fulfilment of the non-intervention agreement by all its signatories, or alternatively of having to recognize that the agreement and the activities of the Committee only serve to mask the military assistance which the rebels are receiving from Germany, Italy and Portugal. 'Pravda' concludes that the non-intervention agreement, while it has not prevented

[1] Not printed.

the rebels from receiving arms, has created a blockade of the legal government. 'Such a state of things can no longer be tolerated'.

4. These seem clear enough indications that the Soviet Government no longer consider themselves to be really bound by an agreement into which they entered reluctantly and in which, as has been recorded in earlier reports, they have for some time past been but restive participants. Moreover, almost throughout its currency they have continued (expressing their action in the most uncontroversial terms possible) regularly to permit the collection of funds for the partisans of the Spanish Government and the despatch of supplies of provisions and clothing, while being fully aware that other participants in the non-intervention agreement took exception to such action. Moreover, it is not easy to see how they could radically alter the nature of their assistance to the partisans of the Spanish Government even if they were to free themselves, as they well might at any moment, from the theoretical restraint which is placed on them by participation in membership of the London Committee. The despatch of arms to the supporters of the Spanish Government would, of course, be such a radical departure, but it is doubtful whether, on the criterion of material practicability as well as on that of even relatively sane policy, such action would not fall outside the limits of the assistance *within their power*,[2] to which M. Stalin has been careful to restrict the recognized duty of the toilers of the Soviet Union towards the revolutionary masses of Spain. A Soviet ship known or even suspected to be carrying arms for the government supporters, and lacking any sort of effective armed convoy, would seem a singularly vulnerable object for the hostile watchfulness of ships of war as it neared its destination.

5. Even if the action of the Soviet Government has in fact, as would certainly appear at the moment, more of a tactical than of a practical bearing, which would not be radically altered by mere withdrawal from the London Committee, it is none the less far from being unimportant. Gestures of class and political solidarity with sections of foreign opinion have, as characteristics of Soviet policy, been latterly out of favour and have in general been subordinated to national policy, to the practice of treating international questions as between responsible governments, and to the necessity of making sacrifices to ensure, or at least to render possible, collaboration between the government of this country and the governments of certain others which it was hoped, as the result of that collaboration, might be induced to bear part of the burden of safeguarding the integrity of the Soviet Union. It is true that the sympathies of the Soviet Government lie in this case on the side of a government recognized by other foreign States as well as by themselves, but that fact seems of considerably less importance than the return of M. Stalin himself to the international arena, in the exchanges reported in my telegram No. 162,[1] in the character of the spokesman of communism.[3]

---

[2] A marginal note at this point by Mr. Roberts read: 'The Madrid Govt. have already expressed their thanks to Moscow for arms received, of which we have ample evidence.'

[3] Cf. No. 333, note 5, below. Commenting on this passage Mr. L. Collier, Head of the

6. It is of course common ground that the Soviet Union are anxious to win back some of the sympathy which they normally enjoy in advanced political circles (not exclusively Marxian) in other countries—a feeling which they have steadily sought to exploit and to capitalize in their own material interest, and which they have in an appreciable measure lost of late, whether in alienating academic Marxians by too national and too empirical a policy or in estranging liberal admirers by the rigours of the Trotskist trials. The tactics adopted by Soviet leaders in relation to the affairs of Spain, apart from the single step of original participation in the non-intervention agreement, have consistently tended in the direction of attempting to regain this lost ground.

7. Nevertheless the opportunity offered by the Spanish imbroglio must have been equally apparent at the time when the Soviet Government, however reluctantly, did in fact put their hands to that agreement, the Italian reservation on indirect intervention as well known, the limited scope and functions of the London Committee—an organism which never in fact enjoyed, as the Soviet criticisms apparently assume that it did, equal authority with the League Assembly—as clearly understood. Yet at first, policy, in the sense of a recognized over-riding interest in collaboration with France and Great Britain, conquered an instinctive aversion from the individual step which that policy dictated. If instinct now has its turn one is inclined to ascribe that fact (though of course no conclusive evidence is available) to a growing sentiment on the part of the Soviet leaders that policy is failing to produce the hoped-for results and that there is consequently less reason to allow it to inhibit doctrinal or class sympathies. The Litvinov fabric, that product of much patient skill and industry, shows more than one crack in its once imposing façade. The hope of British participation in a collective system excluding Germany is now but a faint one: a general agreement including Eastern Europe must wait on the conclusion of a Western pact, while the latter itself must by all appearance wait for some little time yet: France is on better terms with Poland, and more and more evidence is accumulating that dissatisfaction with the Franco-Soviet pact and its implications exists to a very appreciable extent in Western Europe— not only in Great Britain and in Belgium, but in France itself.

8. What is happening in Western Europe at the present time is thus of decisive importance for this country. The Franco-Soviet pact is the corner-stone of Soviet foreign policy and if it can take the strain the fabric is not irrevocably doomed to collapse. If on the other hand the various forces which are working within and without France finally succeed in breaking this connexion between the West and the East, the Soviet Union will of

Northern Department, remarked in a minute of November 6: 'I venture to think that it is not necessary to assume that the Soviet Government's action in the Spanish question denotes any fundamental change in their recent foreign policy. It is more likely, in my opinion, that . . . the Soviet Govt. will always seek to reinsure themselves in other quarters, so long as they suspect H.M. Govt. and/or the French Government of being ready to leave them to face Hitler unaided.'

course find itself forced into an attitude of defensive and anxious isolation in respect of a hostile Germany, but in addition to this obvious consequence it will be freed from those special inhibitions of specific eccentricities in foreign relations to which it consciously submitted while still of the opinion that national ends could be served by a mainly orthodox foreign policy. Material inhibitions would of course remain, indeed the opinion might be hazarded that preoccupation with the unprecedented task of planned development of a sixth part of the earth's surface, and with the rival development of Germany, would necessarily obscure Soviet perceptiveness in regard to the internal as well as the external policies of the nations of Western Europe. But it would be unprofitable to pursue these premature speculations and it must be left to the future to determine whether M. Litvinov did in fact receive his Order of Lenin in the very nick of time.[4]

I have, &c.,
D. MacKillop

[4] In a minute on this despatch Sir G. Mounsey remarked: 'The Spanish situation is producing a new and unexpected rift in the Franco-Soviet agreement. G. M. 4.10.36.'

No. 312

Sir E. Drummond (Rome) to Mr. Eden (Received October 21, 9.30 a.m.)
No. 660 Telegraphic [C 7457/4/18]

ROME, *October 21, 1936, 12.45 a.m.*

In your telegram No. 383[1] you asked me whether Italy had any ulterior motives for her present attitude towards Locarno discussions. I think she has, but the question is not an easy one.

2. When I had my conversation with Count Ciano and Signor Vitetti—see my despatch No. 1097[2]—I derived the impression that they feared that if there were arrangements by which the United Kingdom was guaranteed by France and Germany, Italy would be rather left in the cold even if similar arrangements existed under which Italy would be guaranteed by France and Germany; Italians seem to think the former arrangement would inevitably be of more importance than the latter. Incidentally I doubt whether Italy really wishes to be guaranteed by France and Germany and to avoid the problem being posed they would prefer that the United Kingdom should not receive any guarantee. It is an example of the rather devious ways of Italian thought. Secondly the Italian Government undoubtedly appreciated the old Locarno system for reasons of prestige and because it implied cooperation and consultation between Italy and the United Kingdom as two guarantor States who were to some extent *au dessus de la mêlée*.

3. Meanwhile as you will have realised Italy is playing up to Germany

[1] No. 299.　　　[2] No. 275.

as hard as she can—visit of Count Ciano, exchange of missions, etc. This rapprochement is no doubt due in its essence to similarity of the two régimes and particularly at this juncture to a common detestation of Bolshevism and a fear of the spread of communist doctrines. Enforcing this 'parallelism' is also useful to Italy because (a) it increases her importance and nuisance value present and potential, (b) it is in design a form of pressure on us in particular though in fact the effect on France may be greater.

4. It is a form of pressure on us because in my view few things would give Italian Government at the present moment greater pleasure than to return to really friendly relations with His Majesty's Government. No doubt Italy still hankers after the idea of a four or five power pact on a consultative basis to take the place if not the form at least in practice of the Council of the League. Amongst other results this would keep Russia away from the inner circle of European affairs and settlements. But if Italy cannot obtain such a consultative pact she would rather be on special terms with us than with either France or Germany. If however we show no visible signs of an advance on our present attitude Italy may soon think that a choice is being forced on her between France and Germany, in which case she will certainly prefer to choose the latter. Any concrete sign from us that we are ready to go back to a pre-Abyssinian world would at present be most welcome to Italy; if no such sign is forthcoming she may well think we are not interested (she will interpret our attitude as 'holding on to our grudge too long') and in these circumstances there is I believe real danger of her running out of the course and coming to some definite political arrangement with Germany.

5. It may therefore be worth while considering what the Italians mean by being once more on really friendly terms with ourselves. My views on this point are contained in a later telegram.[3]

[3] No. 314 below.

No. 313

Sir C. Wingfield (Lisbon) to Mr. Eden (Received October 22, 9.30 a.m.)
No. 202 Telegraphic [W 14119/9549/41]

Important   LISBON, *October 21, 1936, 11 p.m.*

Your telegram No. 146.[1]

Yes. I still have no evidence that Portugal is committing breaches of agreement. I have of course no means of making investigations if anything is being sent secretly but I do not believe that war material is being sent to Spain on any considerable scale since Portugal has little if any to spare and would be foolish to break her engagements respecting transit when insurgent ports are open for direct traffic.

[1] This Foreign Office telegram of October 21 referred to Sir C. Wingfield's telegram No. 185 of September 17 (No. 199) and said that it was presumed 'that your general opinion remains the same'.

Accusations in the press and those that reach me anonymously seem generally to be based on the assumption that as Portugal favours the insurgents and the latter maintain agents for forwarding supplies from Lisbon all kinds of supplies are furnished to them. But when specific cases are mentioned they generally either occurred before agreement came into force or else concern supply of petrol or other goods which are not prohibited.

The Minister for Foreign Affairs told me today that he hoped to send his answer to Spanish and Russian accusations[2] by Air Mail Saturday. He had sat up most of last night finishing it and it was being translated as quickly as possible.

[2] See Nos. 215, 265, 270, and 287.

No. 314

Sir E. Drummond (Rome) to Mr. Eden (Received October 22, 9.30 a.m.)
No. 662 Telegraphic [R 6249/294/67]

ROME, *October 21, 1936, 11.40 p.m.*

My telegram No. 660.[1]

What does Italy's desire to be on really friendly terms with ourselves imply? Reduction in the near future of legation in Addis Ababa to a consulate-general and withdrawal of legation guard[2] would I believe help but it is not recognition and would only be a beginning. The real crux of the problem lies in the Mediterranean including its exits and in particular the Suez Canal.

Position at present is that Italy remains deeply suspicious of our motives in the Mediterranean and this in spite of assurances which have been offered both in Rome and in London that we wish for nothing better than to be on friendly terms with Italy, and in spite of explanations given respecting the King's recent holiday tour, First Lord of the Admiralty's visits, and invitation to Turkish fleet to visit Malta.[3] It is hard to say whether these suspicions are actively present in the mind of Signor Mussolini himself and that of course is what chiefly matters; but they are certainly present in the minds of many of his advisers though not perhaps to the same extent in those of Ministry of Foreign Affairs officials. Nevertheless suspicions are present (compare discussions of University Institute of International Affairs at Milan)[4] and must sooner or later be dealt with and dealt with in a manner which can ultimately be made known to public opinion in Italy; in my view sooner would be better than later.

To return to Italian desiderata. As regards the Suez Canal she would no doubt like assurances that this will never be closed to her now that she

[1] No. 312.   [2] Cf. Volume XVI, No. 486, note 2.   [3] See No. 169.
[4] Presumably a reference to the three-day national congress for the study of foreign affairs in the Ducal Castle at Milan which had been opened by a speech from Count Ciano on October 15: see *The Times*, October 17, p. 11.

is in possession of Abyssinia. As regards the Mediterranean in general, the impression that I and members of my staff have derived from various conversations—though no concrete evidence can be adduced—is that Italy would wish in the first instance to discuss this subject direct with us. No doubt in any event she would desire to *keep* Germany out of Mediterranean affairs. To assess the actual line on which Italy would desire to see the Mediterranean problem solved is difficult since I have received no first hand indication of any kind on this subject. It seems probable however that she has chiefly in mind some mutual limitation (a) of naval forces and (b) in development of defence measures. I assume that we should not be prepared to discuss any suggestions of this kind although the Italian proposals might be found to be less unreasonable than is generally supposed. Short of this Italy might be interested in conversations designed to provide mutual non-aggression coupled perhaps with an exchange of declarations as to our respective policies in the Mediterranean viz. on our side freedom for our Imperial communications and on their's [*sic*] security for their vital interests. As has often been pointed out these respective policies seem far from being incompatible. The question of mutual assurance regarding territorial status quo in the Mediterranean may be also worth consideration.

How far we should be prepared to consider discussions with Italy on such lines and how far it would be possible to do so without prior consultation with France and possibly other Mediterranean Powers are matters of high policy with which I am not competent to deal. I have not of course broached the subject in any way here with Italian authorities.

If, however, a decision were reached in principle that some understanding with Italy over the Mediterranean were possible—although impracticable for the moment until negotiations for a Western pact are disposed of—there would in my view be great advantage in letting the Italians know this. What is necessary in order to dispel the present Italian suspicions is some definite and early indication that we are ready to discuss the Mediterranean with them within a reasonable time. A hint, if conveyed in the right quarter and in the right way, might prove sufficient.

It would of course be possible and may indeed be preferable to raise questions of possible conversations between ourselves and Italy over the Mediterranean by way of a purely personal suggestion on my part in which I would state that I was speaking entirely without instructions: in this way His Majesty's Government would be in no way committed. I might thus be able to obtain some definite indication of what the Italian Government have in mind.

No. 315

Mr. Eden to Mr. Lloyd Thomas (Paris)
No. 1779 [W 14115/9549/41]

FOREIGN OFFICE, *October 21, 1936*

Sir,

At the end of a conversation with the French Ambassador today we spoke of the meeting of the Committee of Non-Intervention. In reply to a question the Ambassador stated that his Government were willing that the Committee should meet on Friday,[1] but that they did not themselves propose to put forward any complaints of infractions against other Governments. They were in a specially difficult position, and did not wish to provoke counter charges.

I am, &c.,
(For the Secretary of State)
D. F. HOWARD

[1] October 23.

No. 316

Mr. Eden to Sir E. Drummond (Rome)
No. 1165 [W 14134/9549/41]

FOREIGN OFFICE, *October 21, 1936*

Sir,

I asked the Italian Ambassador to come and see me this evening. I told Signor Grandi that the Non-Intervention Committee would be meeting on Friday afternoon. We had already received the German reply to the charges which had been made,[1] and I very much hoped that the Italian Government would also be able to let us have a reply by Friday, so that the Committee could get to work again.

2. After some discussion Signor Grandi said that he would get into touch with Rome and do his best to let me have at least an interim reply. His difficulty was that not only Count Ciano, but also two of the senior officials of the Italian Foreign Office, were now in Berlin, so that it was difficult to find anybody to consult.[2] He promised, however, to consider what he could do.

3. Signor Grandi then asked me whether I had considered what was to be the next step. He understood that the German reply would contain charges against the Soviet Government, and he himself had made charges against them at the last meeting. Were we to continue to make charges one against the other? That seemed to him hardly a profitable procedure.

[1] The German Government's note of October 21 is not printed in *D.G.F.P.*, Series D, vol. iii. A translation of the note is filed at W 15189/11115/41; see also *The Times*, October 22, 1936, p. 15. [2] Cf. No. 293.

He wondered whether I had considered the possibility of a Commission of investigation on the spot. He made this purely as a personal suggestion. Much must depend upon the Portuguese attitude, but if they were willing he felt fairly confident that his Government would make no difficulty.

4. I replied that I would certainly think over this suggestion, which seemed to me a useful one, and as such it might well be considered by the Committee. At the same time I thought that the attitude which was being adopted towards information which might be laid before the Committee was all wrong. There ought to be no question of national sensitiveness in a matter of this kind. We ought all to want the Committee to work, in which case there was no reason why we should resent any information which anyone might bring to it. His Majesty's Government for instance would feel no ill will whatever against any country which might bring charges against us. On the other hand if we wanted the Committee to be effective we ought to be grateful for the information. Signor Grandi did not dissent from this. He added, however, that the situation was complicated by what I had described in a previous conversation, as the religious fervour which some Governments felt on one side or the other.

I am, &c.,
ANTHONY EDEN

No. 317

Letter from Sir E. Phipps (Berlin) to Mr. Eden
[C 7853/576/18]

Private   BERLIN, *October 21, 1936*

My dear Anthony,

My letter to Van of October 14th.[1]

I learn from Hitler's entourage that he was tremendously impressed by Lloyd George. He had never realised what a dynamic personality and inexhaustible energy the former Prime Minister possessed. Hitler remarked that he had never met any German aged fifty with the energy of this Englishman of seventy-three. It was no wonder, he said, if Clemenceau were equally active, that the Allies won the war.

He was greatly relieved that Lloyd George had not raised the Jewish question with him. At neither interview, it seems, was the Jewish or the Church question raised. No foreign visitor has apparently made anything approaching the same impression on Hitler, and he hopes to induce Lloyd George to come to Berlin some day.

Both Goering and Goebbels are greatly disappointed because Lloyd George refused to meet them. It seems that Goebbels was most anxious that Lloyd George should come to Berlin, but Lloyd George on his side was equally determined that though he would like to see Berlin, he would not like to see Goebbels. Goering telephoned to say that he could receive

[1] No. 295.

Mr. Lloyd George on such and such a day, but Lloyd George ignored the hint. Finally Goering telephoned that he was coming to one of his shooting boxes near Augsburg, and would await Lloyd George there. To which Lloyd George replied that he was going to the Hook and Goering could go to the devil. The unfortunate Nazis who had to convey these refusals did not relish their task. Never before, since the Nazis came into power, had anyone, German or foreign, flouted the invitations of their leaders in this fashion.

The German Government, it seems, sent a special coach to receive Lloyd George and his party at the Hook, so that they travelled in great comfort to Munich. No carriage was provided for the return journey, possibly because of Lloyd George's cavalier treatment of the 'Berlin Bonzen'.

To give him his due, Lloyd George must have been a sore trial to his hosts. Except at the interviews with the Führer he rode the high horse, and flatly refused to keep to the programme or play up to the local bigwigs.

He visited the Daimler works at Stuttgart, and listened absorbed to an account of the Nazi method of dealing with labour disputes—which, as you know, is to all intents and purposes the system introduced by the despised Brüning Government, viz. compulsory arbitration, no strikes or other stoppage of work, etc. When the Nazis thought they had completely won him over they trotted out their *pièce de résistance*, namely the Nazi law which forbids industrial companies to pay a dividend of more than 6%. Lloyd George turned immediately to Dr. Manthey, who was in charge of the proceedings, and began to cross-question him. He himself, he said, had attempted to tax the excess profits of armament firms during the war, but the profiteers were as wily as professional boxers; they diddled him at every turn. They began, he said, by distributing bonus shares or watering their capital, or establishing subsidiaries, or buying land, and the more he went after them, the more ingenious they became in evading him. He demanded a full account there and then of all the German legislation dealing with this point. Needless to say nobody could provide an answer and I gather that the Nazis got out of it with the usual promise to send full information to Churt.

On another occasion, during a visit to some educational institute, Lloyd George announced in a loud voice that all this was pure propaganda, to which he was not prepared to listen, and then, to the horror of his bear-leaders, walked straight out of the place.

Lloyd George expressed the opinion to his entourage that Ribbentrop was a poor creature to send to London as Ambassador. 'That man', he said contemptuously, 'could never hold his own in a political conversation and as for representing his country at an international conference, he would be quite out of his element and at the mercy of any intelligent opponent.' When one of the bystanders remarked that Ribbentrop had success-fully concluded the Naval Agreement with England, Lloyd George merely remarked 'Any fool can give cream to a cat.'

Hitler had evidently been misled by Ribbentrop as to Lloyd George's influence in England. He has since remarked to his entourage that despite Lloyd George's encomiums in the 'News Chronicle'[2] and despite the cordiality evinced by other British visitors, especially during the Olympic Games, British public opinion remains obdurately anti-German. He also remarked that we are an incalculable people. During the Abyssinian campaign we seemed incapable of taking any decision on anything. Yet a few weeks later we took prompt military measures in a situation where other countries would have havered for months, namely in Palestine. We had also signed a treaty with Egypt showing that our capacity for reaching a decision on very big issues was in no way impaired.[3] Our prestige, which had fallen, has, in his opinion, now been restored in the world.

To return to Ribbentrop, whom we had to a farewell dinner here last night, I hear that it is his intention to come back to Berlin very frequently. (He will even return for a fortnight in November.) He will keep on his offices here, a thoroughly unpractical arrangement, but which will give him a good pretext for coming over; this he is anxious to do both for political and personal (cherchez la femme) reasons. He has chosen two excellent subordinates from the Ministry for Foreign Affairs (Woehrmann[4] and Kordt[5]) who will do all the hard work in London, and who look forward with much misgiving to their task of keeping their master straight. The fact is he is a lightweight (I place him near the bottom of the handicap), irritating, ignorant and boundlessly conceited. He will also take with him a couple of S.S. toughs to act as A.D.C.s to himself, and incidentally perhaps as Nazi spies on the diplomatic staff of the Embassy.

Ribbentrop arrived rather late, dazed and deaf at our dinner, having flown to and from the Führer at Berchtesgaden since breakfast! He told Frances[6] that on the whole he did not really know whether Tom Mosley[7] sprang from the soul of the English people. Frances replied that he undoubtedly did not. Mosley was here incognito the other day and did not make a favourable impression.[8] After dinner I had some talk with Ribbentrop, or rather he talked at me. It was mostly on Communism and the terrible danger that not only France but also Great Britain ran of being submerged by it. The Nazi is of course unable to see how Communists can possibly be defeated except by putting them in camps, beating them 'up' and making them into slaves.

Very Confidential. Hitler has promised Ribbentrop he shall be Minister for Foreign Affairs if his London mission is successful (in other words, I

[2] See No. 232, note 1.   [3] See Volume XVI, Appendix V.

[4] Herr Ernst Woermann, formerly head of the European section of the Political Department of the German Foreign Office.

[5] Herr Erich Kordt became a Counsellor of the German Embassy in London on Herr von Ribbentrop's staff.   [6] Lady Phipps.

[7] i.e. Sir Oswald Mosley, founder in 1932 of the British Union of Fascists.

[8] It was reported in *The Times*, October 17, 1936, p. 12, that Sir Oswald Mosley had paid an 'unobtrusive visit to Berlin last week, during which he is understood to have had a talk with Dr. Goebbels'. The purpose of his visit was in fact his marriage to Lady Diana Mosley: see Sir Oswald Mosley, *My Life* (London, 1968), pp. 362–4.

suppose, if he brings back colonies and credits in his suit-case). If Neurath ever finds this out he will be more than ever anxious to stab Ribbentrop in the back.

One last word to this already too long letter: I hear Hitler much regrets having sent us his reply on the Five-Power Conference before King Leopold's bombshell.[9] If he had waited till the bursting of the latter his answer would have been wonderfully withering. Ribbentrop, it appears, would in that case have suggested to Hitler to propose to us a joint Anglo-German guarantee of Belgium!

Yours ever,
ERIC PHIPPS

[9] See No. 297.

No. 318

Sir E. Phipps (Berlin) to Mr. Eden (Received October 23)
No. 300 Saving: Telegraphic [C 7500/97/18]

Confidential   BERLIN, *October 22, 1936*

My recent telegrams will have shown that Germany's colonial appetite is growing as quickly as I apprehended in my telegram No. 133 of March 28th.[1]

When Dr. Schacht boasted to me in December last (my telegram No. 287 Saving of 5th December),[2] that he had converted the Führer to the colonial thesis I told him that I did not consider he was to be congratulated upon that conversion, (which means that Germany will not be satisfied even by the fulfilment of the alarmingly ample demands set forth in 'Mein Kampf').

Herr Hitler in that work makes a slashing attack on Germany's pre-war foreign policy and criticises amongst other things the importance attached to colonial expansion. 'And so', he concludes (p. 742),[3] 'we National Socialists deliberately draw a line under the aims of the foreign policy of our pre-war period. We take up the thread broken six hundred years ago. We stop the never-ending Germanic migration to the South and West and turn our eyes to the land in the East. We at last finish with the colonial and mercantile policy of the pre-war time and go over to the territorial policy of the future'.

There is no reason to believe that Herr Hitler is now prepared to revise this dictum, to abandon his aspirations in Europe and to be satisfied, even for a measurable period, with colonies. On the contrary, assuming that

[1] Volume XVI, No. 177.

[2] Not printed (C 8047/21/18/1935). In this telegram Sir E. Phipps gave an account of a conversation of December 2, 1935, with Dr. Schacht, who said that Germany must have colonies in order to overcome her economic difficulties, and claimed to have converted Herr Hitler to the idea of colonial expansion as against that of expansion towards the East.

[3] The reference is to p. 742 of the standard German edition of *Mein Kampf*, from which the passage quoted in this paragraph has been translated.

the return or acquisition of some colonies will, as Dr. Schacht claims, patch up the sole weak chink in his armour, the effect of our surrender would probably only be to accelerate or at any rate to facilitate, the execution of the programme for Eastern expansion laid down in 'Mein Kampf'. But the German colonial programme now advocated, viz. a redistribution of the Belgian, Portuguese, Dutch and possibly Australian possessions would not be mere surrender on our part, it would also be a betrayal by Great Britain and France (not to mention the League) of the small States concerned. The unscrupulous Dr. Schacht doubtless thinks that His Majesty's Government, rather than give up British or Dominions mandated territory, would be ready to connive at the blackmailing by Germany of these small States, whose possessions, moreover, would be more valuable to her than the former German Colonial Empire, the return of which to Germany would, I have always felt, only constitute an appetising 'hors d'œuvre' for a really square Teutonic meal later on.

To attempt to assess the danger to the British Empire by the establishment overseas of German air and submarine bases or by added facilities for long-distance flying would clearly be outside my province. I may be permitted, however, to express grave doubts, despite Herr Hitler's assurances to the contrary, whether Germany would not eventually declare herself to be compelled to violate the Anglo-German Naval Agreement in order efficiently to protect a colonial Empire of which, at the time of its signature, she was not yet possessed.

Further, it might be well to remember Dr. Schacht's admission to me last December that Nazi extremists would be got rid of by being sent to any future German colonies. These gentry would not be very agreeable neighbours, nor would they be likely to be over squeamish in their treatment of the unfortunate natives.

Monsieur Blum has shown himself to be short-sighted if he encouraged Dr. Schacht over the Cameroons and Togoland as much as that gentleman pretends.[4] Fear, as the French saying goes, is a bad counsellor, but fear has often counselled the French of recent years. It is my firm conviction that to encourage even a beginning of German colonial expansion is merely to whet the German appetite, increase German prestige and strength and ultimately to render more probable an Anglo-German conflict.

Should any further colonial overtures be made by Dr. Schacht or others the British or French interlocutors concerned might quote 'Mein Kampf', and might point out politely but firmly that Great Britain and France are not prepared to discuss the already Gargantuan menu set forth for Germany in her bible—*plus* the substantial repast that contributed to the undoing of the Hohenzollerns. But Monsieur Blum's imprudence in receiving, and subsequently corresponding direct with, Dr. Schacht has already raised dangerous hopes in Germany, and the accusation is beginning to be made in private conversations that it is now Great Britain and not France who is holding up a reasonable settlement.

[4] Cf. No. 300.

No. 319

Sir E. Phipps (Berlin) to Mr. Eden (Received October 23, 11 a.m.)
No. 301 Saving: Telegraphic [C 7501/97/18]

BERLIN, *October 22, 1936*

My immediately preceding Saving telegram.[1]

I gather from reliable sources that the following represent Germany's present minimum colonial requirements.

1. The Cameroons and Togoland.
2. A small portion of the Belgian Congo, with a portion of Angola to round it off.
3. Ex-German New Guinea.
4. The Japanese would be expected to give a guarantee of neutrality in respect of the Dutch colonial possessions, while the Dutch would be expected to make some contribution to the pool.[2]

[1] No. 318.
[2] In a later telegram, No. 312 Saving of October 28, Sir E. Phipps referred to paragraphs 3 and 4 of the above telegram, and said that he had since ascertained from the same source that Germany would not be content with less than the whole of New Guinea, excluding the portion which was British before the war, namely Papua. This would represent the Australian and Dutch contributions. He gathered that Dr. Schacht, impressed by figures showing that Germany could not get large quantities of raw materials from all her former colonies, had decided to alter the basis of Germany's colonial claim, and to ask, not for colonial restoration, but for raw material areas. To this Herr Hitler was said to agree.

No. 320

Sir C. Wingfield (Lisbon) to Mr. Eden (Received October 23, 2 p.m.)
No. 208 Telegraphic [W 14221/9549/41]

Important   Confidential   LISBON, *October 23, 1936, 12.30 p.m.*

My immediately preceding telegram.[1]

French Minister who returned yesterday evening from two days excursion agrees that war material has not been going to Spain from Portugal since the agreement . . . [2] for he might certainly have heard of it had any considerable quantity been sent. He saw no lorries on the road between Badajos and Lisbon which is natural route for supplies to take.

He feared there is the danger that British and French Governments may support the Soviet suggestion to send commission of enquiry to Portugal. He is telegraphing to point out the deplorable repercussions of such an attitude on our relations with Portugal which would be thrown into the arms of Italy and Germany, would leave the London Committee[3] and would refuse to receive the proposed Commission in Portugal.

Internal situation here would also be very adversely affected which would not be to our interests.

[1] A note on this file by Mr. Shuckburgh stated that this telegram should refer to Lisbon telegram No. 202 (No. 313).
[2] The text was here uncertain.   [3] i.e. the N.I. Committee.

No. 321

Memorandum[1] by Mr. Eden on preparations for the Five-Power Conference

[C 7719/4/18]

FOREIGN OFFICE, *October 23, 1936*

I circulate to my colleagues herewith a statement[2] comparing the views of the different Governments concerned, on the preparations for the Five-Power Conference.

2. The vital difference seems to concern the point dealt with in paragraph 5[3] of the statement, i.e., the question whether the non-aggression arrangements shall be subject to exceptions, such, particularly, as those laid down in Article 2 of the Treaty of Locarno concerning action under the Covenant of the League of Nations. If there are no exceptions at all, this would mean that no party subscribing to the proposed non-aggression arrangements could come to the assistance of a non-signatory Power if attacked by a party to those arrangements. Thus, France could not in such circumstances assist Russia, Czechoslovakia or Poland if attacked by Germany, nor could Great Britain—on the assumption that she became a party to a non-aggression arrangement—assist Egypt or Iraq if attacked by another party to such an arrangement. Further, a State in this position could not go to the assistance of a State attacked in violation of the Covenant. This would be incompatible with our obligations under the Covenant.

3. A second difference concerns the question of the manner in which a decision is to be reached as to whether a non-aggression undertaking has been violated, i.e., is, or is not, the League of Nations to be the deciding body? We have known since the 31st March that Germany would not accept the decision of the Council in this matter, for in their note of that date[4] the German Government suggested the constitution of an international court of arbitration for the purpose. Now they seem to have abandoned even this proposal and to be anxious to leave the decision to the parties to the Treaty. This proposal is certainly just as practicable as that of the court; but it is scarcely conceivable that we could agree to the League Council being deposed in this fashion.

4. Another difficulty is likely to arise owing to the general German reservation regarding the approach to an Eastern and Central European settlement. The Germans maintain that the Western Treaty must be concluded before anything else can be discussed, and even then they reserve their attitude (see paragraph 9(1) of the statement). There would probably be no obstacle to the completion of the Western Treaty first; but *if*

---

[1] Circulated to the Cabinet at its meeting on October 28 as C.P. 278(36): see No. 349, note 1 below.

[2] Not printed: it was a preliminary draft of No. 349 below and its points are sufficiently indicated by the present memorandum.

[3] Paragraph 4 (ii) in No. 349 below.   [4] See Volume XVI, No. 193, note 2.

the western negotiations were successful there must be no doubt that there will be a sequel. At present Germany seems to be unwilling to admit this. Russia and France's clients of the Little Entente would not allow her to conclude a purely Western Treaty if all sequel to it were specifically ruled out.

5. Three differences have developed on the question of guarantees (see paragraphs 4 and 7 of the statement). The first concerns the guarantees for which we have asked from France and Germany, supposing that Italy would require the same for herself. The French are prepared to support our view; but the Germans and Italians seem to be opposed to any extension of the guarantee system as it existed under the Locarno Treaty. The Chiefs of Staff are being consulted; but there seems *prima facie* to be no reason why we should not have reciprocity, which would make the Treaty more acceptable at home. We should not, therefore, abandon our request for guarantees at least unless and until all the other points are reasonably settled.

6. The second difference arising out of the question of guarantees concerns Belgium. She is now unwilling to give any guarantees at all, even to France, though she promises 'scrupulous fidelity' to her obligations under the Covenant. We do not want a guarantee from Belgium; but the French do. If there were no guarantee from her, it would have to be clearly understood that Belgium, if she only undertook to defend her own territory, would not tacitly allow foreign aircraft to cross her territory to attack a third Power. The Chiefs of Staff are being consulted on the value of the Belgian guarantee to France.[5]

7. There is a further difference—though not perhaps a serious one—which seems likely to develop in respect of the guarantees (paragraph 4 of the statement). This arises out of the French suggestion that not only the metropolitan frontiers of the parties to the Treaty should be guaranteed, but also those of their possessions and dependencies. This might suggest (an enquiry has already been addressed to the French Ambassador on the point) that the French would like to see the Treaty extended to cover colonial possessions—an additional obligation for us and without any counter-advantage if we obtain no guarantee for ourselves. On the other hand, even if we did obtain a guarantee, the effect would be to convert a pact limited to certain European frontiers of vital importance to us into one which would involve us in responsibilities in parts of the world of no special importance to us. Incidentally, this proposal would almost certainly be strongly opposed by Germany and Italy, the latter of whom would see in it an attempt to extend the Treaty to the Mediterranean. It is probable that the French could be brought to drop this point without much difficulty.

8. There is a difference between the French and Germans over the question of the demilitarised zone (paragraph 9(2) of the statement). It is, however, not believed that the French would press seriously for the restriction of the right of fortification on the German side of the frontier; and it seems doubtful whether this point is really one which, with agreement reached on the other matters, would ultimately hold up the settlement.

[5] See No. 332 below.

9. On one other point mentioned in paragraph 9 of the statement are serious difficulties to be anticipated; and that concerns the French proposal for staff conversations. We are committed to these under article VII of the Text of Proposals of the 19th March, 1936,[6] provided they are open to all Five Powers.

A. E.

[6] Volume XVI, No. 144.

No. 322

Mr. Eden to Mr. Lloyd Thomas (Paris)

No. 1800 [W 14308/9549/41]

FOREIGN OFFICE, *October 23, 1936*

Sir,

The French Ambassador asked to see me this morning about the meeting of the Non-Intervention Committee, and I asked Lord Plymouth to be present also. M. Corbin indicated his anxiety as to the future work of the Committee. In answer to questions he made it plain that it was the desire of the French Government that the Committee should go on and that in their view the non-Intervention Agreement had benefitted [*sic*] the Government rather than the rebels.

2. After some discussion as to the procedure of the Committee the Ambassador stated that he had been considering what line could be most usefully pursued, and had come to the conclusion that the Committee might consider a proposal for supervision on the spot. I understood that His Excellency had even submitted this suggestion to his Government. In M. Corbin's view if this supervision was to be effective it would require the approval of both belligerents in Spain. He himself doubted whether the Spanish Government would be willing to give it. After further discussion we agreed that it might be advantageous if the Committee this afternoon were to instruct a sub-committee to examine proposals for making the non-Intervention Agreement more effective. The suggestion of M. Corbin, which had previously been made by Signor Grandi,[1] might then be considered.

3. Finally I asked the Ambassador whether his Government had considered what their attitude would be if and when the insurgents reached Madrid. Were they going to withdraw their representative or were they going to leave him there, and if so did they propose to accord the insurgents any form of recognition? M. Corbin stated that he did not think his Government had come to any conclusion on this difficult matter, but that at one time they had considered withdrawing their representative. What was our attitude likely to be? I replied that while Mr. Ogilvie-Forbes had authority to leave Madrid at any time should he consider it necessary, I did not anticipate

[1] See No. 316.

that he would do so.[2] And indeed there would be considerable difficulty in ignoring altogether the existence of the authority which was in possession of the Spanish capital. On the whole my mind at present inclined to recognising the insurgents as belligerents if and when they took Madrid. This procedure would no doubt have been followed at an earlier stage, but for the non-Intervention Agreement. I would be grateful if the Ambassador would indicate to his Government that this was our present intention, and ask whether they concurred, or if not what alternative policy they suggested we should pursue. The Ambassador replied that he would certainly do so, but that his own impression was that his Government might see some difficulty in recognising the insurgents as belligerents because of the rights which they must in consequence enjoy.[3]

I am, &c.,
ANTHONY EDEN

[2] Cf. No. 236.
[3] Sir G. Mounsey pointed out on October 26 that Mr. Eden's statement above, that his present inclination was to recognize the insurgents as belligerents, was 'not quite the same thing as the action approved on W 12501/62/41' (see No. 243, note 2). In a minute of October 27 Mr. Eden remarked 'I did it wrongly (I am sorry)'. A copy of the draft declaration was given by Sir G. Mounsey to M. Cambon on October 29: see No. 344 below.

No. 323

Mr. Eden to Sir E. Ovey (Brussels)

No. 541 [*C 7571/4/18*]

FOREIGN OFFICE, *October 23, 1936*

Sir,

The Belgian Ambassador came to see me this morning, when he left with me the attached note[1] in reply to the British memorandum of September 17th.[2] His Excellency went on to give me some account of the circumstances in which the Belgian declaration was made.[3] He stated that he was in a position to do this, since he had been over to Brussels in the last day or two, and in the course of his visit had had a conversation with King Leopold, as well as with M. van Zeeland, M. Spaak and others. From these conversations it appeared that the King's declaration had been a draft of His Majesty's own composition and that he had read it at a meeting of the Council of Ministers over which, contrary to the normal procedure he had himself presided. At the conclusion of the reading of the memorandum M. Vandervelde[4] had jumped up and had declared that it was so good that it must at once be made public. The Ministers had agreed to this without apparently appreciating the full international consequences of their decision. The objectives which they had in mind in so doing were limited to domestic political fields.

2. Baron Cartier went on to explain the depth of anti-French feeling now existing in Belgium. The attitude of the French press, the speeches of some

[1] See Enclosure below. [2] Enclosure in No. 206. [3] See No. 297.
[4] Belgian Minister of Public Health.

of the French Deputies, one of whom had spoken of King Albert[5] as having been glad to fly to Havre during the war, had aroused keen resentment among all sections of Belgian opinion, Walloon as well as Fleming. Moreover, the French suggestion published in their press that M. Spaak should come to Paris 'or rather to Canossa' to explain the Belgian statement, had aroused indignation. France was altogether too indifferent to the feelings of Belgium. The Ambassador was more worked up on this subject than I have ever seen him.

3. In reply I told the Ambassador that whatever any of our feelings might be about our treatment by the French nation, or any other nation, we had to be careful not to allow this to influence our political judgment, since the realities of the international situation were not affected thereby. I therefore hoped that the Belgian Government would, in a communication which I understood they were sending to the French Government,[6] do all in their power to meet the apprehensions of the latter. These, I understood, related more especially to Article 16 and to the position of Belgium under the old and still existing Locarno Treaty.

4. The Ambassador undertook to tell the Belgian Government what I had said.

5. His Excellency emphasised that if Belgian feeling against France was strong, there was both sympathy for and support of the policy of His Majesty's Government. The Belgian Government were most anxious to help us in any way that they could.

6. I replied that we fully appreciated this, and were grateful for it. At the same time I felt I must point out to the Ambassador that the satisfaction with which the Belgian Government in their note greeted the fact that His Majesty's Government did not ask for a guarantee from Belgium in the projected new Locarno, did not seem to me by itself fully to justify their claim that they should not guarantee the French Government either. The two guarantees were not on all-fours. In the old Locarno Belgium did guarantee France, though she had never guaranteed this country. I therefore repeated my hope that His Excellency would make clear to his Government our point of view, as I had expressed it to him.[7]

I am, etc.,
ANTHONY EDEN

ENCLOSURE IN No. 323

Memorandum[8] *en réponse à la Note anglaise du 17 septembre 1936*

BRUXELLES, *le 22 octobre 1936*

Par son memorandum en date du 17 septembre, le Gouvernement britannique a bien voulu communiquer au Gouvernement belge ses suggestions

[5] King Leopold's father, who died on February 17, 1934.

[6] Cf. *D.D.B., op. cit.*, Nos. 142, 157, 160, and 161.

[7] Baron Cartier gave a somewhat fuller account of this interview in *D.D.B., ibid.*, No. 156.   [8] See also *ibid.*, No. 152.

concerning l'object de la discussion que l'on espère ouvrir à Londres entre les cinq Puissances signataires du Traité de Locarno. Il a, en même temps, exprimé le désir de recevoir, soit par écrit, soit verbalement, les observations du Gouvernement belge.

2. Aux termes du *communiqué* adopté à Londres le 23 juillet 1936,[9] 'la première tâche à remplir devra être de négocier un nouvel accord destiné à se substituer au Pacte rhénan de Locarno, et de régler par la collaboration de tous les intéressés, la situation créée par l'initiative allemande du 7 mars.' La note britannique du 17 septembre énumère un certain nombre de questions qui, à cet effet, pourraient utilement retenir dès maintenant l'attention des Gouvernements intéressés. Le Gouvernement belge marque volontiers son accord sur le programme ainsi défini.

3. Dans son memorandum, le Gouvernement britannique a bien voulu exposer quelle est, provisoirement et d'une manière générale, son opinion sur les différents points ainsi énoncés.

En réponse à l'invitation qui lui a été adressée, le Gouvernement belge a l'honneur de confirmer par écrit sa propre manière de voir.

4. En ce qui concerne la portée du nouvel accord destiné à remplacer le Traité de Locarno, le Gouvernement belge estime que cet accord devrait prévoir des engagements de non-agression entre les Puissances intéressées.

5. Quant aux clauses qui garantiraient l'observation de ces engagements, le Gouvernement du Roi a été particulièrement heureux de constater que, comme par le passé, le Gouvernement de Sa Majesté britannique est disposé à maintenir à la Belgique le bénéfice de sa garantie, qui est d'une grande importance pour la paix de l'Europe.

Le Gouvernement belge a, de même, constaté avec satisfaction que le Gouvernement britannique ne subordonne pas sa garantie prévue en faveur de la Belgique à la prestation d'une garantie réciproque. Le Gouvernement belge estime que cette question devrait, en ce qui le concerne, se poser dans les mêmes termes à l'égard des autres États qui seraient parties à l'accord et il croit utile d'en préciser les motifs.

6. En raison de la situation géographique de la Belgique, toute agression dont celle-ci serait la victime constituerait une menace directe contre d'autres Puissances. En défendant l'accès de son propre territoire, la Belgique contribue de la manière la plus efficace à la sécurité des États qui l'environnent. L'accomplissement de cette mission est de nature à exiger d'importants sacrifices et un très grand effort.

Consciente de ses devoirs envers les autres nations comme envers elle-même, la Belgique y est résolue. Elle se crée par là un droit à une aide éventuelle que les Puissances menacées à travers son territoire auraient un intérêt vital à lui prêter.

Elle croit ainsi remplir jusqu'à la limite de ses forces la fonction qui lui revient dans cette région de l'Europe qui fut si souvent exposée aux ravages de la guerre.

La Belgique ne bornera cependant pas là sa contribution à l'œuvre de la

[9] See No. 14, note 3.

sécurité collective. Elle conservera aux obligations inscrites dans le Covenant la scrupuleuse fidélité dont elle a toujours fait preuve dans le passé.

7. En ce qui concerne les dispositions spéciales à prévoir en cas d'une attaque aérienne, le Gouvernement belge a marqué depuis plus d'un an l'intérêt qu'il portait à semblables suggestions.

8. Enfin, le Gouvernement du Roi est d'avis que le nouvel accord pourrait utilement, comme le Traité de Locarno, contenir des clauses d'arbitrage et de conciliation.

Il considère que le règlement des problèmes posés par la sécurité occidentale contribuerait puissamment à assurer la paix en Europe. Il est prêt à apporter, en vue de la conclusion d'un tel accord, tout le concours en son pouvoir.

No. 324

Mr. Eden to Sir C. Wingfield (Lisbon)
No. 422 [W 14309/62/41]

FOREIGN OFFICE, *October 23, 1936*

Sir,

The Portuguese Chargé d'Affaires asked to see Sir R. Vansittart this morning, when he left with him the attached memorandum giving the reasons for which the Portuguese Government proposed to 'suspend their recognition of the Spanish Government'.[1] Sir Robert replied that he would at once report this conversation to me, but that he felt sure that His Majesty's Government would much regret to hear of this Portuguese decision. The Chargé d'Affaires, however, explained that the decision had already been taken, and was to be given effect to today.

2. I sent for the Portuguese Chargé d'Affaires later in the morning, and in the presence of Sir R. Vansittart further discussed with him the Portuguese initiative. I told him that Sir Robert had correctly interpreted the sentiments of His Majesty's Government, and stated that we would deeply regret such a step as the Portuguese Government envisaged. I asked him to get in touch with his Government forthwith and to ask them urgently to refrain from taking any such action until there had been an opportunity for further consultation with us.

3. M. de Calheiros e Menezes undertook to do this, but pointed out that since unhappily there was no telephonic communication with Lisbon he feared that my message might not reach Lisbon until action had already been taken.

4. I replied that if that was so I could only ask the Chargé d'Affaires to report the circumstances to me, when we would have to consider the position. If, however, action had not actually been taken at Madrid, which was the important point, then I would ask the Government to refrain from doing

[1] Sir C. Wingfield's telegram No. 209 of October 23 said that 'Portuguese Government have today handed note to Spanish Ambassador breaking off relations. He is to leave Lisbon on Monday [October 26].'

so until further consultation had taken place. The Portuguese Chargé d'Affaires undertook to telegraph at once, and in the meantime explained that para. 2 of the enclosed memorandum related to Alicante, and para. 4 to Madrid. It was, however, to para. 5 that the Portuguese Government attached most importance. They had sent a number of Left-Wing Spanish refugees back to their own country. On arrival at a Spanish port the Spanish local authorities maintained that all the refugees had not been delivered, and that there were still others on board. They had even attempted to force their way into the Portuguese warship, despite the most specific assurances from the Portuguese Captain that he had delivered everybody up. Eventually it was only on the threat of the Portuguese Commander of the ship that he would fire that the Spaniards desisted from their efforts. Such conduct was really intolerable. We pointed out, however, that however grave a view the Portuguese Government took of this incident it was surely one to call rather for representations than for a suspension of negotiations. This term 'suspension' was entirely new to us, and we were by no means clear as to what it entailed. The Chargé d'Affaires explained that in his understanding it would involve the withdrawal of the Portuguese Chargé d'Affaires from Alicante. There was, I understood, no longer any Portuguese representative in Madrid itself.[2]

I am, etc.,
ANTHONY EDEN

ENCLOSURE IN NO. 324

List of Reasons for proposed Suspension of Recognition of Spanish Government by Portuguese Government

The attitude of the Government of Madrid

1. In giving wide publicity to the grave and unfounded accusations which they made against the Portuguese Government before the latter had given any reply;
2. In violating the correspondence addressed to the Portuguese Chargé d'Affaires and abusively retaining it;
3. In humiliating the diplomatic agents of the Portuguese Government;
4. In ordering the public search of their offices;
5. In attempting to attack a vessel flying the pennant of the Portuguese navy;
6. In pretending to believe that the Spanish Ambassador is deprived of his liberty in Lisbon.

[2] The Portuguese Chargé d'Affaires told Sir G. Mounsey on October 24 that after his conversation with Mr. Eden on the 23rd he had telegraphed urgently at 1 p.m. to Lisbon. The reply had come that it was now too late to delay action about withdrawing Portuguese diplomatic representation from Spain. Sir R. Vansittart minuted on October 24: 'I don't think we can do any more for the present; but we might review the situation when or if Madrid falls . . . But it is at present no further use to touch this iron while it is so hot. A little cooling will be helpful.' Cf. *D.A.P.E.*, *op. cit.*, Nos. 526, 527, 531, 532, 533.

No. 325

Mr. MacKillop (Moscow) to Mr. Eden (Received October 24, 3.20 p.m.)
No. 174 Telegraphic [W 14352/9549/41]

MOSCOW, *October 24, 1936, 3.20 p.m. [sic]*

My immediately preceding telegram, last sentence.[1]

Soviet Ambassador's communication seems clear indication that Soviet Government consider their formal (? acceptance of) obligations in respect of intervention in Spanish affairs to have lapsed and in particular that they now hold themselves free to send arms for use of Spanish Government. There is however no indication whether they intend merely to make use of this theoretical freedom as purely tactical element for political purposes or alternatively to seek to give it practical effect.

[1] Telegram No. 173 of October 24 said that the text of M. Maisky's statement of October 23 to the N.I. Committee (see No. 328, note 4, below) and what purported to be details of the seventh sitting of the Committee had been published in that day's Soviet press. After a summary of press comment the last sentence of the telegram read: '*Izvestia* has similar leading article, conclusion being that the Soviet Union have defined their position with absolute clarity; decision now depends on other participants in the Agreement.'

No. 326

Mr. Eden to Sir G. Clerk (Paris)
No. 1803 [C 7599/4/18]

FOREIGN OFFICE, *October 24, 1936*

Sir,

The French Ambassador came to see me this morning, when he said that he wished to hand me the attached aide-mémoire from his Government.[1] M. Corbin emphasised that this document was not a note in the official sense at all. He asked me to treat it as a recorded conversation. The object that the French Government had in mind in giving me this information just now was in order that we might know something of their reactions to the German note in reply to our memorandum of the 17th September. M. Corbin said that he imagined that I would now be examining all the replies with a view to making further approaches to the Governments concerned in this

[1] Not printed here: it was based on instructions sent to M. Corbin and printed in *D.D.F.*, *op. cit.*, No. 389. The French Government were commenting on the German communication of October 14 (No. 286), which they considered gave no grounds for optimism. They thought that a time limit for the negotiations should be fixed, expressed the hope that the British Government would maintain their request for a guarantee, and asked for British support for their own formula with regard to the problem of 'exceptions', as set out in paragraph 10 of their memorandum of September 30 (No. 263).

connexion. It was in order that we might have the French point of view in mind that he was leaving me this aide-mémoire.[2]

I am, &c.,

ANTHONY EDEN

[2] Minutes on this file were extensive. It was not thought that the fixing of a time limit would be practicable or desirable. It was agreed that the British Government should stand by their request for a guarantee: Sir R. Vansittart thought that 'it wd make the new treaty—if any—more acceptable to our public'. He asked Sir W. Malkin and Mr. Sargent (October 30) to try their hand at a draft proposal for dealing with the 'exceptions' difficulty.

No. 327

Mr. Eden to Sir G. Clerk (Paris)

No. 1804 [W 14390/9549/41]

FOREIGN OFFICE, *October 24, 1936*

Sir,

I had a brief conversation with the French Ambassador at the conclusion of the Non-Intervention Committee meeting this morning.[1] M. Corbin stated that the Soviet Ambassador had undertaken to consult his Government on the meaning of their Note.[2] The Ambassador agreed that the Soviet Government had placed themselves in a very false position by their action. We also agreed that our two Governments should remain in close contact on this subject during the next few days and that our purpose must continue to be to do all in our power to keep the Committee going and to make the Non-Intervention Agreement effective. We must make it clear to the world that we were being active with this object in view.

I am, &c.,

ANTHONY EDEN

[1] The reference is presumably to the sixth meeting of the Chairman's Sub-Committee, held at the Foreign Office at 10.30 a.m. on October 24.
[2] See No. 328, note 4 below: cf. No. 325.

No. 328

Mr. Eden to Mr. Ogilvie-Forbes (Madrid)

No. 210 Telegraphic [W 14372/9549/41]

FOREIGN OFFICE, *October 25, 1936, 6 p.m.*

Following is text of communication made by His Majesty's Government to the Non-Intervention Committee on October 23rd.[1]

From the outset of the civil war in Spain, the chief concern of His Majesty's

[1] Lord Plymouth made this communication at the beginning of the seventh meeting of the N.I. Committee, in accordance with the Cabinet Conclusions of October 21: see No. 308, note 2.

Government in the United Kingdom in supporting the policy of non-intervention and in consenting to the establishment in London of a Committee for the application of the Agreement to which the European Governments had voluntarily subscribed, was to prevent the civil war from spreading beyond the Spanish frontiers and to secure a measure of co-operation amongst the Powers in what threatened to become a most dangerous international situation.

2. The purpose of the Committee is to ensure as far as possible the effective application of the Agreement. It was naturally to be expected that the maintenance in being of the Committee would prove a factor of importance in itself by acting as a deterrent to the supply of arms to Spain. At the same time it is clear that the Committee's task must inevitably include the examination of any important evidence which may be brought forward showing that the Agreement is not being strictly enforced.

3. This constructive purpose can only be achieved by frank co-operation between the participating Governments, and in the view of His Majesty's Government it follows that each Government should contribute its share by keeping the other Governments supplied with all reliable information bearing on the application of the Agreement which may be in their possession, and which in their view requires common investigation.

4. His Majesty's Government for their part are at all times ready to examine attentively any reports received by the Committee from other Governments which may show that the Agreement is not being carried out in the territories for which they are responsible. It is in this spirit that they are making careful enquiries regarding the incident of the steamship *Bramhill*.[2] His Majesty's Government believe that the Committee will best fulfil its difficult task if its members are willing to examine all similar information in an impartial spirit, and with the firm intention of excluding political considerations which may endanger the realisation of the common aim.

5. Since the last meeting of the Committee His Majesty's Government have given careful study to the information in their possession in order to see to what extent it provides evidence that serious infringements of the Agreement are taking place. They feel that for the reasons stated above it is their duty to furnish the Committee with certain information based on reliable first-hand evidence, which tends to show that some infractions have in fact occurred. It will be for the Committee to take such action in regard to this information as seems fit.

(1)[3] The Spanish oiler *Campeche* was seen on October 10th to be unloading at Cartagena 4-inch guns, trench mortars, hand grenades and large quantity of rifles and rifle ammunition of Russian origin.

[2] See No. 273.

[3] The particulars in the four paragraphs that follow were not included in the statement by Lord Plymouth printed in the minutes of the meeting, which state at this point that the information which His Majesty's Government wished to communicate would be 'available for circulation to the members of the Committee before the termination of the meeting'.

(2) On October 15th the Russian steamer *Stari Bolshevik*, port of registry Odessa, arrived at Cartagena and it is reported that after unloading a certain quantity of foodstuffs, *Stari Bolshevik* then proceeded to land cases containing component parts of eighteen 3-engine aircraft and other stores including fifteen large tanks, 320 cases of bombs, and a large quantity of ammunition.

(3) On October 19th, the Russian steamship *Chrushchev* which had previously called at Cartagena, arrived at Alicante and on the following day landed 85 military lorries of approximately 3-ton type, which were handed over to the 'Transportes Militares'. The only permanent markings visible on these lorries were on the tyres and were in Russian letters.

(4) His Majesty's Government also have reliable information to the effect that on the 7th September the Italian steamer *Nereide* discharged at Palma, Majorca, a cargo which was seen to include six fighting aeroplanes and a quantity of bombs, shells, rifles and ammunition. On the same day three Italian bombing planes arrived at Palma.[4]

Repeated to Moscow and Rome Nos. 134 and 400.

Repeated Saving, en clair by post, to Paris No. 111, Berlin No. 51 and Hendaye No. 21.

[4] During the remainder of this meeting there were references to further charges and counter-charges, which were for the most part left over for discussion at a future meeting of the main committee or of the Chairman's Sub-Committee. Lord Plymouth read a letter which he had received at 1 p.m. that day from M. Maisky (see *D.V.P.S.*, *op. cit.*, No. 327, and Nos. 329 and 330). After complaining that systematic violation of the non-intervention agreement had created 'a privileged situation for the Rebels' and that 'the Agreement has turned out to be an empty torn scrap of paper' it proposed as the only way out of the situation the 'return to the Spanish Government [of] the right and facilities to purchase arms outside of Spain, which right and facilities are enjoyed at present by the Governments of the world, and to extend to the participants of the Agreement the right to sell or not to sell arms to Spain'. The letter went on to say that in any case the Soviet Government was compelled to declare that it could not 'consider itself bound by the Agreement for Non-Intervention to any greater extent than any of the remaining participants of the Agreement'. The letter also stated that Portugal had become the main base of supply for the rebels. This letter was referred to the Chairman's Sub-Committee for elucidation of certain aspects of M. Maisky's statement. The Portuguese representative said that the reply of his government had just been received and would be submitted to the Committee forthwith. The Committee also considered the German Government's reply of October 21 (see No. 316, note 2) concerning breaches of the agreement placed before the fifth meeting of the Committee by the British Government on October 9 (cf. No. 272). Lord Plymouth considered that the German reply had dealt satisfactorily with all except two of the points raised, and he asked for further elucidation of these. It was agreed that the Soviet proposal of October 12 for the establishment of Anglo-French control of Portuguese ports could not be dealt with until the Portuguese Government's reply had been considered.

No. 329

Mr. Lloyd Thomas (Paris) to Mr. Eden (Received October 27, 8.30 a.m.)
No. 431 Saving: Telegraphic [W 14430/9549/41]

PARIS, *October 26, 1936*

The Minister for Foreign Affairs who returned from Biarritz on Saturday night told M. Léger yesterday that he was delighted with the result of the Radical Congress.[1] The unanimity and enthusiasm of the party had exceeded his fondest hopes, and his own position, as well as that of MM. Daladier[2] and Chautemps, had been greatly strengthened. One important result was that the Government were now sure of being able to resist the demands of Moscow and of their own extremists for intervention in Spain. Whatever the German, Italian or Russian Governments decided to do, the French Government were determined that nothing should now provoke them to intervene. They would conform their attitude to that of His Majesty's Government and would continue to facilitate the work of the London Committee, even to the point of accepting a control commission on the Franco-Spanish frontier, provided that a similar commission were despatched to the frontier between Portugal and Spain.

[1] The Annual Congress of the Socialist Radical party opened in Biarritz on October 22: see *The Times*, October 22, 1936, p. 15.
[2] Minister of National Defence and War, Vice President of the Council, and Chairman of the Socialist Radical party.

No. 330

Mr. Lloyd Thomas (Paris) to Mr. Eden (Received October 27)
No. 438 Saving: Telegraphic [C 7626/5740/18]

PARIS, *October 26, 1936*

Sir E. Phipps' telegram No. 295.[1]

1. As regards Doctor Schacht's statement that, in conversation with him last August, Monsieur Blum expressed a strong desire to get rid of his association with the Communist party, Monsieur Blum himself has publicly indicated more than once since then that he is not prepared to drop the Communists of his own accord but that if the Communists withdraw their support from him, and thus bring about the disintegration of the *Front Populaire*, he will not attempt to continue in office with the support of another majority in the existing Chamber. I have no reason to suppose that Monsieur Blum does not mean what he has said. He may, indeed, find the Communists somewhat embarrassing partners, and no one can say what political constellation might achieve power after an eventual disintegration of the existing *Front Populaire* and the general election which, as Monsieur Blum and Monsieur Chautemps have both warned the public,

[1] No. 306.

would be the consequence of any such disintegration. All the information at my disposal serves to emphasise Monsieur Blum's essential loyalty to his partners in the existing *Front Populaire* so long as they remain in that *Front,* and it seems hard to believe that he would have talked on the subject of his internal difficulties or referred in a disparaging way to his own political supporters in conversation with a German Cabinet Minister on an official visit to Paris.

2. As regards Doctor Schacht's statement that Monsieur Blum declared that if an agreement could be reached between France and Germany, he would be prepared to abandon the Franco-Soviet Pact as unnecessary, it is not unlikely that Monsieur Blum, in common with other intelligent Frenchmen, may believe that were a firm and satisfactory agreement to be reached between France and Germany the main raison d'être for the Franco-Russian pact would cease to exist and that it could accordingly be allowed to lapse. On the other hand, Monsieur Blum may have considerable doubts as to whether any such Franco-German agreement is possible. It is conceivable that the phrase quoted in Sir E. Phipps' telegram under reference, so far from being one actually used by Monsieur Blum, was one of Doctor Schacht's own statements, namely that without the abandonment by the French of the Franco-Russian Pact there could be no Franco-German agreement turned round and put into the mouth of the French *Président du Conseil.*

3. As regards 'the subsequent correspondence with Monsieur Blum', I have it on the assurance of Monsieur Léger that this correspondence was limited to a letter in which Monsieur Blum gave Doctor Schacht a faithful account of his conversation with you, and gave it as his opinion that no further progress could be made until you had expressed the views of His Majesty's Government: and to Doctor Schacht's acknowledgment of Monsieur Blum's communication.

4. Monsieur Léger said that he deprecated and discouraged conversations of this nature with Doctor Schacht who tried to induce the *Président du Conseil* and the Minister for Foreign Affairs to put their cards on the table without at the same time committing the German Government in any way.

Copy Berlin by bag.

No. 331

Record by Mr. Sargent of a conversation with M. Cambon
[*C 7612/4/18*]

FOREIGN OFFICE, *October 26, 1936*

With reference to Sir R. Vansittart's recent conversation with the French Ambassador,[1] M. Cambon showed me to-day a telegram from the Quai

[1] No. 309.

d'Orsay explaining the reasons why the French Government had, in their Note[2] replying to our memorandum of September 17th,[3] suggested that the guarantees under the new treaty should apply in the case of acts of aggression against 'possessions et dépendances'.

Briefly, the Quai d'Orsay's argument was that it might easily happen that an aggressor, having decided on a war, might find it convenient to launch his aggression not against France's guaranteed frontier in Europe, but by attacking, for instance, her lines of communication between Morocco and France. As an instance of this possibility reference was made to the fact that in 1914 the 'Goeben' bombarded Algiers before the French frontier had been violated.

I told M. Cambon that while the argument might technically be quite convincing, it was incomplete in so far as it did not take into account the political and psychological effect of the French proposal. The extension of the Locarno guarantees was bound to arouse the suspicions of all sorts of people, particularly the Italians, while British public opinion, which had been gradually realising that the defence of the Franco-German frontier was a vital British interest, would certainly not understand why this country was now to be asked to guarantee French frontiers all over the world. No doubt the French proposal would make the guarantee more watertight, but during the last eleven years none of us had worried about the gap which the French had now discovered. However much one tried to provide for every sort of contingency, some such gaps would always be bound to exist, and the problem of filling them ought to be treated as a question of political expediency rather than of technical drafting. As regards the present French proposal I felt sure it was a case of 'le mieux est l'ennemi du bien'.

M. Cambon seemed to agree with this view, and said that it would be useful if these considerations could be put to his Government. I suggested that this could probably best be done as the result of a further conversation between the French Ambassador and Sir R. Vansittart.[4]

O. G. SARGENT

[2] Enclosure in No. 263.   [3] Enclosure in No. 206.

[4] With Mr. Eden's agreement, Sir R. Vansittart proposed on October 27 'to dissuade M. Corbin from this proposal when I next see him'. He wrote later: 'I have told M. Corbin that I think his Govt. wd. be wise to let this drop, anyhow for the present. We have more important fish to fry; and it is still doubtful whether we shall be able to find the requisite frying pan. R. V. Nov. 16.'

No. 332

Report[1] *by the Chiefs of Staff Sub-Committee on the position of Belgium in the proposed Five-Power Conference*

[*C 7631/4/18*]

2, WHITEHALL GARDENS, S.W.1, *October 26, 1936*

Introductory

In our Report on the preparations for the Five-Power Conference, the conclusions that we recorded on the question as to whether

'Belgium should be relieved of giving any guarantee, and her commitments limited to an understanding to defend her own territory,'

were as follows:

'(i) An effective Belgian neutrality would be greatly to our advantage and should not deliberately be rendered impossible, even though the chances of its being maintained throughout a Western European war are remote.

(ii) We should, therefore, welcome a request by Belgium that she should not be a guarantor Power, but should merely give an undertaking to defend her own territory.'[2]

2. Since then, Belgium has made a public declaration of her policy.[3] For the future she is determined to ensure the protection of her own frontiers, but she intends to have no obligations as a guarantor Power. In other words, Belgium has adopted the precise attitude which we hoped, from the military point of view, that she would adopt.

3. We have been informed by the Foreign Office that the French Government feel strongly on the subject of this declaration of Belgian policy, and that their Ambassador has indeed expressed the hope that His Majesty's Government would support the French Government in urging the Belgian Government to remain a guarantor State.

4. We have, therefore, been requested[4] (see Appendix) to re-examine the conclusions summarised in paragraph 1 above, in the light of the arguments adduced by the Belgians and France, in the notes which are annexed to the Appendix to this Report. (Enclosures Nos. 1[5] and 2[6] respectively.)

Belgian Arguments

5. It would appear that Belgium has two principal reasons for her unwillingness to be a guarantor Power. In the first place, she desires to avoid

---

[1] Circulated as C.I.D. Paper 1269–B (C.O.S. 518).

[2] C.I.D. Paper 1260–B (C.O.S. 511), paragraph 45: see No. 156.

[3] See No. 297.

[4] In a letter of October 16 from the Foreign Office to the Secretary of the C.I.D., not printed.

[5] Not printed: it was the same as No. 249.

[6] Not printed. It gave the text of Geneva despatch No. 106 of October 2 enclosing a memorandum of that date given by M. Delbos to Mr. Eden: see No. 292, note 1.

the risk of being drawn into war as a result of French commitments in Central and Eastern Europe, and particularly as a result of the Franco-Soviet Pact. With this desire we have every sympathy, the more so since we recently emphasised in our Report on the preparations for the Five-Power Conference, the importance, from our own point of view, of taking 'steps to ensure that any guarantee we give will not automatically draw us into a war which has as its origin the rectification of Germany's Eastern frontier.' (Enclosure to C.I.D. Paper No. 1260–B, paragraph 48.) In the same Report[7] we stressed the necessity, from the military point of view, for limiting our commitments in Europe, and for undertaking no liability to engage in any war in which our vital interests are not affected. It may be that in any case Belgium's chance of maintaining an effective neutrality throughout a Western war is small; but in our opinion the chance will be very much greater if she is relieved of any guarantees and if her only commitment is an understanding to defend her own territory.

Moreover, the greater her chance of maintaining her neutrality effectively the less is the likelihood of our being dragged in; consequently we ought to support her in gaining this end by relieving her of any guarantees.

6. Secondly, it seems that the Belgian Government desire to promote national unity in support of a national foreign policy, and thereby, to obtain the support of the Belgian people for the strengthening of their military forces and defences. As to this, it is clear that any action which renders Belgium the more able to defend her own territory, is to our advantage from the military point of view. If, therefore, the giving of a guarantee to France would, as we believe to be the case, wreck the hope of Belgian national unity in the field of foreign policy, and thereby prejudice the military preparations which, we learn, are being undertaken by the Belgian Government with commendable vigour in the face of strong Parliamentary opposition, it would be unwise on our part to use our influence in support of the French demand for any such guarantee.

French Arguments

7. Turning now to the French objections to the declared policy of the Belgian Government (see Enclosure No. 2 to Appendix), they draw attention in the first place to its implications from the Belgian point of view. They argue that the close collaboration in the preparation of concerted defence plans that has hitherto existed between the French and Belgian General Staffs will no longer be possible. As a result, there will be inevitable delay in the assistance that can be given by the French Army, and a risk that Belgium may be overrun before such assistance can become effective.

8. There is, of course, some force in this argument. We would observe, however, that we have been informed by the Chief of the Imperial General Staff that General Gamelin, the Chief of the French General Staff, informed our Military Attaché in Paris, as recently as last March, that the

---

[7] *Note in original*: Enclosure to C.I.D. Paper No. 1260–B, paragraphs 4 and 5.

French were prepared to support Belgium, only if it was known for certain that the British Field Force was on its way to Belgium. It seems probable that this threat to leave Belgium to her fate was intended to force us into a definite commitment to send the Field Force to Belgium at the outset of the war, and to undertake, in time of peace, the detailed military conversations that this commitment would involve. In these circumstances we are left with the strong impression that what the French most fear from the Belgian declaration—although they do not admit it—is that the termination of the existing close liaison between the French and Belgian General Staffs will automatically put an end to any hope of the Franco-British military conversations.

9. As to this, it is our opinion that mutual assistance pacts on a multilateral basis have no more military value than the Covenant of the League. Any multilateral agreement, as we have previously pointed out,[8] precludes the possibility of effective staff conversations between the parties thereto, since it is clearly impracticable to concert plans with A for war against B and, at the same time, with B for war against A. We have also expressed the view[9] that bilateral staff conversations or conversations between a limited number of the parties to a multilateral agreement would be invidious, and would, moreover, tend to involve us in military commitments which would fetter our freedom of action as to the form that our intervention might take when the occasion arose. Therefore, we again wish to emphasise that, whatever the position of Belgium in any new treaty that may be negotiated, other of course than a definite alliance, we should not be committed to military conversations, either with France or with Belgium. It might be thought right to make a definite statement to this effect to the French Government.

10. Turning again to the French objections, they argue that the recent Belgium [*sic*] declaration involves grave consequences to French and British interests. In the first place, the concentration of the French and British forces would, they consider, be prejudiced by the fact that, in the absence of a pre-concerted plan, the distant Franco-Belgian cover, which is at present contemplated, would not be available in time. This argument assumes, without justification, that we are committed to despatching the Field Force to France at the outset of hostilities.

11. Apart from this, the French contend that the most serious consequences of Belgian neutrality would arise in connection with aerial warfare (see Annex to Enclosure No. 2, Section II). They point out, in particular, that both France and Great Britain would, under the new Belgian policy, be deprived of the Belgian anti-aircraft observation service and anti-aircraft defences, and of the use of Belgian aerodromes. Great Britain would thus 'find it impossible to operate on the vital zone of the Ruhr, and the German bases in Westphalia,' whilst the French air forces would be unable, without inevitable difficulties, to reach these objectives, for to do so they would have to make long flights over German territory. Germany, on the

---

[8] *Note in original*: Enclosure to C.I.D. Paper No. 1260–B, paragraphs 59 to 62.
[9] *Note in original*: Enclosure to C.I.D. Paper No. 1260–B, paragraphs 59 to 62.

other hand, would be able to attack London from bases on the North Sea, whereas 'Great Britain would have no chance of attacking, by way of reprisal, German objectives of comparable importance['].

12. It is our view that recent technical developments have reduced the potential value to us of the Belgian observation service and anti-aircraft defences, and it is an over-statement to suggest that it would be impossible for us to operate against the Ruhr without the use of Belgian aerodromes. We could clearly do so by operating from bases in N.E. France, and the tactical difficulties in doing so would be largely offset by the greater certainty of occupying them and the added security and convenience of such bases and their lines of communication as compared to those in Belgium. Though we agree generally with the French thesis that a neutral Belgium would enable German Air Forces to attack our vital areas in greater strength than we could attack theirs, it must be observed that even if Belgium were not neutral, the Germans would still have the advantage due to the far greater importance and vulnerability of London than any comparable objective in Germany.

13. We have, however, seen a Record[10] of a conversation between Mr. Strang and M. Massigli in which the latter 'admitted that there might be ways of getting round these difficulties, even if Belgium gave no express guarantee. She might, for example, consent to the passage of French or British forces, through or over her territory, in circumstances to be defined in the new treaty, and indeed, she was bound to do so under Article XVI(3), of the Covenant, if France and Great Britain were acting under that article.' The possibilities of the case clearly call for the most careful examination.

CONCLUSION

14. The foregoing examination of the arguments adduced by the Belgians and French has led us to the conclusion that, from the military point of view, the balance of advantage is to be derived from adhering to the recommendations quoted in paragraph 1 above.

15. Accordingly, our answers to the specific questions put to us by the Foreign Office, are as follows:

(i) From the military point of view, His Majesty's Government should *not* ask that in the new Treaty Belgium should guarantee the United Kingdom; and

(ii) From the military point of view, His Majesty's Government should *not* support the view of the French Government that in the new Treaty Belgium should guarantee France (and Germany).[11]

ERNLE CHATFIELD
E. L. ELLINGTON
C. J. DEVERELL

[10] *Note in original*: Enclosure to Paper No. C.O.S. 516 [not printed].

[11] The conclusions in paragraph 15 were approved by the Committee of Imperial Defence at its meeting on October 29, and by the Cabinet at a meeting held on November 4.

No. 333

Letter from Mr. Lloyd Thomas (Paris) to Sir R. Vansittart
[*W 14793/9549/41*]

Private & Secret   PARIS, *October 26, 1936*

My dear Van,

Léger told me in confidence this morning that he had on Saturday sent for the Russian Chargé d'Affaires, in the absence of Potemkin,¹ and talked to him very seriously about the action of the Russian representative on the Non-Intervention Committee. He had pointed out to M. Hirschfeld that this was the first occasion of a serious divergence between French and Russian policy since M. Barthou's visit to Moscow,² and that this was not only a grave divergence but one which would inevitably be published before the whole world. The principal object of the Franco-Soviet Pact³ and of the collaboration between the two Governments had always been the maintenance of peace, and the present policy of the U.S.S.R. would, in the opinion of the French Government, lead to war. The French Government, he told M. Hirschfeld, had reliable information that four or five Russian cargo boats had recently left the Black Sea for Spanish ports with cargoes of arms on board. Before they arrived at their destination there was every possibility that they might be intercepted and that an open conflict with Italy and Germany might ensue. He did not understand, in the circumstances, how the Russian representative could properly continue to attend the meetings of the London Committee, and, in any case, his presence at those meetings would not conceal Russian acts of intervention or prevent the ultimate conflict with other European Powers. The Russian Chargé d'Affaires agreed with Léger's statement of the case, but not with the conclusions he drew, for he professed to deny that the action of the Russian Government would lead to war and was confident that they would be able to find some way of avoiding a serious incident. Whatever happened however, he said, the Russian Government were now prepared to go to any lengths to help the Government of Madrid. They had come to the conclusion that they could not afford to see the proletarian régime in Spain suppressed, and though they might already be too late they were going to do everything in their power to enable them to resist General Franco and to prevent the establishment of another Fascist régime. Léger told him that the French Government would regard this as a very serious statement and he begged him to warn the Government of Moscow accordingly and at the same time to tell them that the French Government would not follow the U.S.S.R. in this policy for they were determined in no circumstances whatever to intervene on either side in the Spanish civil war. Léger said that he was somewhat puzzled by

¹ M. Vladimir Potemkine was Soviet Ambassador at Paris.
² As French Foreign Minister in 1934 M. Louis Barthou is recorded as visiting Warsaw, Belgrade, Bucharest, and London, but not Moscow. The reference should presumably be to M. Laval, who visited Moscow in May 1935.
³ Signed in Paris, May 2, 1935; see Volume XIII, No. 156.

this sudden change in Russian policy. Stalin had no ideals; he was a realist and an opportunist and he had been prepared to cooperate for a few years with the bourgeois Governments of Europe with a view to avoiding war in this continent until Russia was armed once more and free from the menace of war in the Far East. France had been anxious to deny Russia to Germany, and the Soviet Pact had consequently been concluded with no illusions on either side. He could not, however, see what reason had now decided Stalin to depart from his former policy and to risk war with Germany. He could only imagine that the idealists in Russia, the followers of Lenin and Trotsky and the advocates of world war and revolution, had proved too strong for him in spite of Stalin's savage repression and the tragic example of Zinoviev and Co.[4] Stalin, he supposed, had made up his mind that he must be prepared to take the risk of intervention in Spain if he was to hold his own against the growing opposition of the ideologists of the Russian Revolution. In any case, he took a serious view of the present situation. This disagreement on a major issue of policy might well affect the whole future of relations between France and Russia and of the working of the Franco-Soviet Pact. He told me that he had begged the Russian Chargé d'Affaires to convey a warning in this sense to his Government.[5]

Yours ever,
HUGH

[4] Cf. Nos. 129 and 130.
[5] Commenting on this letter in the course of a minute to Mr. Eden, Sir R. Vansittart remarked that if the letter were to be taken at its face value 'it would seem that the Russians were prepared to go the limit. Without going quite so far, I think they are probably prepared to go to great lengths . . . It is rather a surprising development seeing that the growth of the German danger in Europe had, since 1933, been until this summer steadily tending to cause Russia to make friends so far as possible with the western democracies and to go slower on the revolutionary doctrines. Now not only has the slowing down been changed, but an enormously increased tempo has been adopted . . . R. V. 27th October, 1936.' A note by Mr. Hoyer Millar of 29 October read: 'The S. of S. mentioned this at yesterday's Cabinet.'

No. 334

Sir E. Drummond (Rome) to Mr. Eden (Received October 27, 5.15 p.m.)
No. 667 Telegraphic [C 7655/4/18]

ROME, *October 27, 1936, 4 p.m.*

My telegram No. 658 last sentence of paragraph 4.[1]

Count Ciano has not yet asked me to come to see him in order to give me an account of his visit to Berlin[2] and to renew our conversation about the

[1] See No. 303.
[2] On this visit, which laid the foundations of the Rome–Berlin Axis, Count Ciano arrived in Berlin late on October 20, and had conversations with Baron von Neurath on October 21, 22, and 23. A draft protocol relating to points of interest to both countries had been drawn up before the visit, and after discussion was signed by the two as the Italo-German

Locarno Pact and he may expect me to take the initiative. If this proves to be so, it would be pleasant if I could start the conversation by informing him of your decision to withdraw the Legation guard at Addis Ababa[3] and unless you see objection I propose to wait until I receive your instructions on this subject.

Meanwhile the press here implies that the two governments intend to reject the idea which they accepted in 1935 of an Air Pact see . . . [4] paragraph 2 of my telegram No. 666.[5] If Italy bases her rejection on recent Belgian action might I say that it is by no means certain that Belgium will refuse to consider such a separate arrangement regarding air guarantees? I should naturally be grateful for any indications you may feel able to give me as to line I should adopt in discussing new Locarno proposals with the Minister for Foreign Affairs.

Protocol of October 23 (*D.G.F.P.*, vol. v, No. 624; cf. Nos. 618, 620, 621, 622, and editorial note, pp. 1122–4); *Ciano's Diplomatic Papers* (London, 1948), pp. 51–55. Count Ciano had an interview with Herr Hitler at Berchtesgaden on October 24, of which his own account (*ibid.*, pp. 56–60) has survived. No record of the conversation has been found in the German Foreign Ministry archives (*D.G.F.P.*, *op. cit.*, p. 1141).

[3] Cf. Volume XVI, No. 486, note 2.

[4] The text was here uncertain.

[5] This telegram of October 26 summarized an article in *Giornale d'Italia* in which Dr. Gayda listed points of agreement reached by Italy and Germany during Count Ciano's visit to Berlin. Paragraph 2 stated that the two powers were agreed that the problem of western and central Europe should be dealt with separately without the addition of other pacts 'such as a partial northern air pact'; the 'new Locarno' should be on the basis of the old.

No. 335

Mr. Eden to Mr. Ogilvie-Forbes (Madrid)
No. 214 Telegraphic [W 14466/62/41]

FOREIGN OFFICE, *October 27, 1936, 5 p.m.*

Your telegram No. 406.[1]

I took an opportunity today[2] of telling the Spanish Ambassador I was extremely disappointed in the Minister of State's reply to your note.[3]

[1] See No. 305, note 3.

[2] During a conversation with Señor Azcárate on the morning of October 26, recorded in Mr. Eden's despatch No. 632 to Sir H. Chilton of even date. In addition to the points mentioned in the present telegram, Mr. Eden recorded an unofficial enquiry by the Ambassador as to whether the British Government would take charge of Spanish interests in Lisbon following the Portuguese decision to sever relations with the Spanish Government (cf. No. 324). The Ambassador also complained of difficulties encountered by a Spanish ship, *Cristóbal Colón*, at Bermuda on its way to Mexico, and of the fact that certain Spaniards intending to visit England had been turned back. Mr. Eden promised to have these complaints looked into. It was decided on October 28 that His Majesty's Government could not undertake the representation of Spanish interests in Portugal.

[3] See No. 305, note 3.

The Ambassador maintained that his Government had particularly resented our reference to hostages who were really prisoners. I said that the label was unimportant, and expressed regret at the Spanish Government's description of the women prisoners as being worse than the men.[4] I urged His Excellency to inform his Government of my views and of my anxiety to discuss urgently with them whether the women at least could not be removed into some safe place to be agreed on. This the Ambassador eventually said he would do.

2. His Excellency said that he realized His Majesty's Government could not now cancel the policy of non-intervention but he begged that we would not make unnecessary difficulties if others by their action were to bring it to an end.

Repeated to Hendaye No. 213.

[4] In his telegram No. 405 of October 24 Mr. Ogilvie-Forbes said that after receiving Señor del Vayo's reply to the note of October 21 he 'particularly asked Minister of State whether his note covered the women as well as men prisoners. He said that it did and Secretary General subsequently informed me that Government considered the women they had arrested worse enemies than the men.'

No. 336

Mr. Eden to Mr. Ogilvie-Forbes (Madrid)
No. 218 Telegraphic [W 14342/62/41]

FOREIGN OFFICE, *October 27, 1936, 10 p.m.*

My telegram No. 214[1] and your telegram No. 412.[2]

You may if you wish use similar language in speaking to the Minister of State.

Unless, which seems improbable, Spanish Government reconsider their attitude, I do not propose to pursue matter further with them. You should bear in mind, however, that our offer[3] remains open in event of fresh occasion arising for reverting to it.

Repeated to Hendaye.

[1] No. 335.
[2] In this telegram of October 26 Mr. Ogilvie-Forbes reported that as a result 'of correspondence about prisoners we are in a squall which I hope will pass but I must for the present go slow with such enquiries'. He added that three days before he had been refused 'admission to a certain prison, the first time this has happened'.
[3] Cf. No. 305.

No. 337

Mr. Eden to Sir E. Phipps (Berlin)
No. 1201 [C 7646/3727/18]

FOREIGN OFFICE, *October 27, 1936*

Sir,

Herr von Ribbentrop came to see me this morning to pay a formal visit on his appointment as German Ambassador. In the course of the conversation His Excellency remarked that he would like to tell me for my private information that not only was he glad to come to London, but that his appointment was the outcome of his own suggestion. Other arrangements had been made, when he spoke to the Chancellor at Bayreuth and asked him to let him undertake this work. Herr von Ribbentrop had done so because he was convinced that nothing was so important in Europe today as the improvement of Anglo-German relations. He was sure that this improvement could be brought about. At any rate he himself was prepared to work to the utmost for that objective. If he succeeded he was sure that he would thus be making the greatest possible contribution to the peace of Europe. If he failed the disappointment would be grievous also.

2. I thanked the Ambassador for this communication, and said that we could not but be gratified at the preference which he had himself expressed to serve in London. We would do our utmost to facilitate his task. At the same time he would realise that Anglo-German relations were not a problem for our two countries alone. There were other pieces on the European chess-board. Herr von Ribbentrop replied that he fully appreciated that there were many difficulties ahead. To the Chancellor, however, nothing seemed so important as the peril of communism. He had seen Herr Hitler within the last 48 hours, and that had been once more the Chancellor's definite opinion. He fully realised that we did not altogether share this view. Herr von Ribbentrop then spoke at some length in familiar terms about the German view of the communist peril.[1]

I am, etc.,
ANTHONY EDEN

[1] Cf. J. von Ribbentrop, *Zwischen London und Moskau*, pp. 90–3.

No. 338

Letter from Mr. W. Roberts to Mr. F. Hemming
[W 14335/9549/41]

FOREIGN OFFICE, *October 27, 1936*

Sir,

At the 6th meeting of the Sub-Committee of the International Committee for the Application of the Agreement regarding Non-Intervention in Spain held on Saturday, 24th October, the delegates present agreed to consult their respective governments with a view to ascertaining what would be their attitude, if the Non-Intervention Agreement is maintained on its present basis, to a proposal for the establishment, subject to the concurrence of the two parties in Spain, of an impartial body of persons, stationed on Spanish soil at the principal points of entry by sea and by land, for the purpose of reporting, when called upon to do so by the Committee, on any specific case in which a breach of the Agreement might be alleged to have taken place.

2. I am directed by Mr. Secretary Eden to inform you that His Majesty's Government in the United Kingdom would be prepared to cooperate with other governments in any scheme of this nature which might prove possible on practical grounds, provided that the two parties in Spain agree to it.[1]

I am, &c.,

WALTER ROBERTS

[1] Foreign Office commentators seem generally to have agreed with Mr. Shuckburgh's view that the 'whole proposal in fact seems to be a very dubious one and our reason for putting it forward must be rather the need for keeping the Non-Intervention Agreement in being than any idea that it will be of practical effect'. Difficulties that he indicated in a minute of October 26 included the unwillingness of either side to give full facilities, the fact that the Madrid Government would consider supervision ineffective in the case of aircraft flown (to insurgent destinations) under their own power, the probable lack of independent inspectors, and the provision of adequate protection for them in view of the dangerous situation at most Spanish ports. Lord Plymouth wrote: 'It is obvious that the difficulties in the way of this proposal are formidable. It is, however, extremely unlikely, as has already been pointed out, that we shall be called upon to put it into practice, since I cannot believe that either the Spanish Govt or the insurgents will agree to it. The point about aircraft is one that may be taken up by the U.S.S.R., but we must risk that ... P. 27.10.36.'

No. 339

Mr. MacKillop (Moscow) to Mr. Eden (Received October 28, 1.50 p.m.)
No. 179 Telegraphic [W 14548/9549/41]

MOSCOW, *October 28, 1936, 2.25 p.m.* [*sic*]

Your telegram No. 134.[1]

I take it that allegations of despatch of arms to Spain by Soviet Government may be considered for the moment as sub judice and that they will be held to be either proved or disproved on the basis of evidence available, or to be made available, of actual unloading of cargoes of munitions at Spanish ports.

No reliable evidence of despatch from the U.S.S.R. of such cargoes is or will be obtainable by the Embassy. The only contribution which we can therefore make is in the form of a summary of the material possibilities of the U.S.S.R., as regards exports of munitions.

On this point Military Attaché considers Soviet Government would find little difficulty in supplying sufficient tanks, field-guns, anti-aircraft guns,

[1] A repetition of No. 328.

and rifles with appropriate ammunition, also lorries to form an important addition to Spanish Government's forces without such a gift proving at all a serious disadvantage to the Red Army.

The Air Attaché advises me that the output of military air-frames in the U.S.S.R. today can hardly be less than 4,000 per annum and that this output is now more than is necessary for the supply of Soviet Air Force at its present strength. It seems therefore that the Soviet factories in 1937 would be in a position to make good any deficiency of stocks which might be brought about by despatch of aircraft in reasonable numbers to Spain this winter. The stocks of aircraft fit for the purpose are probably immediately available from factory and Central reserves.[2]

[2] There was some clarification of the Soviet Government's intentions at the eighth meeting of the N.I. Committee on October 28, when consideration of M. Maisky's letter of October 23 was resumed (cf. No. 328, note 4). M. Maisky made a further statement to the effect that until guarantees against further supplies of war materials to the rebel generals had been created, the Soviet Government were 'morally entitled not to consider themselves more bound by the Agreement than those Governments which supply the rebels in contravention of the Agreement'. He also mentioned the proposal for control over Portuguese ports, and stated the willingness of his government to agree to the establishment of control over Spanish ports and along the Spanish frontier, including those portions not occupied by the rebels, subject to the 'consent of the legitimate Spanish Government'. This question was referred to the Chairman's Sub-Committee. The meeting after considering complaints of alleged breaches of the Agreement by Italy (cf. No. 272, note 3), which Signor Grandi comprehensively rejected, agreed (M. Maisky dissenting) to Lord Plymouth's view that 'the Committee had received no proof of a breach of the Agreement by the Italian Government'. The Committee then examined in detail the various complaints against the Portuguese Government, and agreed (M. Maisky scornfully dissenting) to Lord Plymouth's view that, under the rules of procedure adopted by the N.I. Committee, there was in this case too no proof of a breach of the Agreement. M. Maisky's report to Moscow of this meeting is printed in D.V.P.S., op. cit., No. 337.

No. 340

Record by Sir G. Mounsey of a conversation with M. Corbin
[W 15084/9549/41]

FOREIGN OFFICE, *October 28, 1936*

The French Ambassador asked to see me before the meeting of the Non-Intervention Committee this afternoon, and inquired in particular whether we had any confirmation of Portugal's reported action in recognising General Franco's régime.

I gave His Excellency the substance of Sir C. Wingfield's annexed telegram[1] and reminded him that, as I had previously told him, we have repeatedly

[1] In telegram No. 211 of October 27 (received October 28, 9.30 a.m.) Sir C. Wingfield reported a conversation with Senhor Vasconcellos, Portuguese representative at the League of Nations, who denied reports from London through Havas that the Portuguese Government had recognized the Burgos Government. 'He added that he personally did not believe Portuguese Government would do so immediately.'

expressed our hope that the Portuguese Government would consult or warn us before taking such a step. They were of course not committed to do so, but we lost no opportunity of reiterating our hopes.

M. Corbin seemed somewhat relieved, but was inclined to connect this question with the proposed instructions we have submitted to him for Mr. Forbes' attitude when General Franco takes Madrid.[2]

His hesitation, I discovered, was based on the fear that General Franco might, after we had entered into *de facto* relations with him, perpetrate retaliatory or other excessive military measures of which neither of our Governments could approve.

I suggested that, should this occur, we would be in some ways on much stronger ground, having entered into *de facto* relations with him, in taking him to task for any such excesses on his part. M. Corbin was rather impressed with this argument.

As he was leaving, rather late for the committee meeting, M. Corbin mentioned that he had had a long talk with his Soviet colleague yesterday. He found that M. Maisky takes quite a different view from ourselves of the uses of the Committee to which he apparently attaches no importance at all.

I asked M. Corbin whether it was his impression that the Soviet Government intended to leave or break up the Committee. He was categorically of opinion that they had no such intention.

I said I thought this was rather an important point for us all. I gathered the Germans and Italians were also not disposed to break up the Committee or the non-intervention agreement, and if this was the case we had a perfect reply to all the critics of the agreement in the patent fact that, whatever difficulties were being encountered and whatever charges were being made and rebutted on various sides, none of the Powers who had agreed to come into the non-intervention agreement were really willing to break it. This must afford the best proof of its utility and of the absence of any other practical policy.

M. Corbin seemed to accept this argument also with some approval.[3]

[2] Cf. No. 322, and No. 344 below.

[3] Minutes by Sir R. Vansittart and Mr. O. C. Harvey read: 'Interesting and useful. R. V. Oct. 28.' 'Seen by S. of S. O. C. H. 28/x.'

No. 341

Sir C. Wingfield (Lisbon) to Mr. Eden (Received October 30, 5 p.m.)
No. 214 Telegraphic [W 14763/9549/41]

LISBON, *October 30, 1936, 3.25 p.m.*

My telegram No. 212.[1]

Today's Press publishes Portuguese Note of October 22nd to Non-Intervention Committee in reply to Spanish accusations.[2]

[1] Of October 29, not printed (W 14656/9549/41).

[2] The full text, with an English translation, is printed in *D.A.P.E., op. cit.*, No. 520.

Summaries of your speech in the House of Commons yesterday[3] are also published with greatest satisfaction. Passages criticising Russian attacks on Portugal stating that information received by His Majesty's Government is to the effect that Portugal has not violated the agreement are quoted,[4] and 'Diario de Noticias' declares that for many years Europe has not been reminded of the alliance with such firmness.

[3] In this speech of October 29 Mr. Eden reviewed the development of non-intervention since the beginning of the war in Spain, affirmed the belief of His Majesty's Government that non-intervention was the only possible policy to pursue, and, rejecting Soviet criticism, defended the work of the N.I. Committee: see 316 H.C. Deb. 5 s., cols. 39–51.

[4] Mr. Eden stated that 'there is no first-hand evidence available that the Portuguese Government are breaking the agreement' and referred to Portugal as 'the smallest of these Governments, and the one singled out by Soviet Russia': see ibid., col. 47.

No. 342

Sir E. Phipps (Berlin) to Mr. Eden (Received October 31)
No. 317 Saving: Telegraphic [C 7742/97/18]

BERLIN, *October 30, 1936*

After a luncheon party yesterday Dr. Schacht drew me aside and tackled me on the colonial question.

He said that he could not understand Great Britain's attitude in declining even to discuss this matter, which was the only obstacle to a satisfactory arrangement between our two countries.

I repeated to him the arguments which I have already used to him and to Dr. Goebbels and which I reported at the time. I laid stress on the practical unanimity of public opinion in Great Britain against any return of the mandated territories, etc., and I drew Dr. Schacht's attention to the resolution of the Margate Conference.[1] He replied that British public opinion would have to be altered, but that he welcomed one of the Margate resolutions which opposed the return of the colonies chiefly on the ground that they might serve as military, naval or air bases and as recruiting grounds for black troops for Germany. The Chancellor, he declared, would be quite ready to give the most positive and far-reaching assurances on these points. I replied that this would seem to infringe the meaning of that blessed word 'Gleichberechtigung', but he vowed that that would never be invoked in this respect.

Dr. Schacht, finding no response from me, angrily remarked that during his recent visit to Paris he had found M. Blum and other Frenchmen more reasonable than us, and he quoted Madame Tabouis in the 'Oeuvre' of the day before yesterday. It was not, he said a question of prestige but of pure economics and raw material. He even indicated that the question of 'sovereignty' might be waived. (This presumably meant a return to the old and unpractical idea of chartered companies, but I did not inquire, as

[1] Cf. No. 261, note 1.

483

my last wish was to give Dr. Schacht an excuse for pretending that we were in any way 'negotiating'). In the course of our talk he only specifically referred to the Cameroons and to New Guinea.

Dr. Schacht alternately wheedled and blustered. When he found both methods left me cold he said that the popular enthusiasm at General Goering's speech the night before last was boundless and that if General Goering had asked his audience to applaud a decision to make war they would have done so unanimously.[2] He then brought the conversation to an end by saying that if Germany found it impossible to reach an agreement with us she might still turn to . . . . . [3] Russia.[4]

[2] In this speech of October 28 General Goering referred to the shortages in Germany of food and raw materials as due to absence of colonies. In a minute of October 30 Mr. Wigram said that there were two criticisms to be made of the speech. 'The first—the less important perhaps—is that in making his case General Göring deliberately travesties the facts . . . The second and much more serious criticsm . . . is his attempt to throw on this country—with which he and Herr Hitler and all the German Ministers and the new Ambassador here lose no opportunity of saying that they desire the friendliest relations—all the blame for Germany's economic difficulties . . .' Mr. Sargent, Sir A. Cadogan, and Sir R. Vansittart agreed that such misrepresentations should no longer be submitted to 'without some sort of protest'. Mr. Eden likewise agreed (November 1).

[3] Punctuation as in the original.

[4] A minute by Sir R. Vansittart read: 'This is an ominous interview. The admission, or rather the aspiration, at the end is another justification of the Franco-Soviet pact. R. V. Oct. 31.'

No. 343

Mr. Eden to Mr. Lloyd Thomas (Paris)
No. 1838 [C 7740/4/18]

FOREIGN OFFICE, *October 30, 1936*

Sir,

During the course of a conversation today with the French Ambassador, His Excellency asked me whether I had yet received from Sir E. Drummond an account of any interview he might have had on Count Ciano's return from Berlin.[1] I replied that so far as I was aware no such interview had yet taken place. M. Corbin then gave me a summary of the outcome of Count Ciano's interview with the French Ambassador.[2] It was far from satisfactory. The Italian Foreign Minister had stated that the Italian and German Governments were in 100 per cent agreement about Locarno; were no less in agreement in their policy towards Spain, and intended to recognise General Franco soon, perhaps even before he reached Madrid; had arrived at an understanding to respect the integrity of Austria; and had undertaken to try to come to an agreement about their respective trade positions in the Danubian countries. As to the League of Nations, Count Ciano thought it unlikely that Germany would return. Italy was still waiting for it to be

[1] Cf. No. 334.   [2] Cf. *D.D.F.*, *op. cit.*, No. 410.

made possible for her to co-operate. She would not expect to be asked to wait too long. The Ambassador indicated that Count Ciano's report had created a bad impression in Paris, where it had not been expected that the Italian Foreign Minister would have gone so far to meet the German view. Nor, M. Corbin understood, had the German Government given us the impression that there was anything like such a complete accord. It did not seem therefore that Germany and Italy were playing a straightforward game. We had frequently emphasised in this country our desire to avoid blocs, and the French Government shared that view, but now it was clear that the Italian and German Governments were in fact forming such a bloc and gaining the consequent advantage. If this was so was it not important that we and the French Government should consult together soon about the future of the Locarno negotiations? His Government had sent us notes on the 16th[3] and 30th September[4] to which as yet they had received no answers.

2. In reply I expressed some surprise at the account which the Ambassador had given me of Count Ciano's interview with the French Ambassador in Rome, and agreed that it appeared to be plain that the results of Count Ciano's visit were in excess of those which had previously been reported to us from Berlin. If it were true that the Germans and the Italians were creating this bloc, I was not sure in the long run that they would benefit from such a policy. At the same time it was clearly desirable that if this were happening our own two Governments should keep in close contact. I then gave His Excellency an account of the procedure which we proposed to follow in respect of the Locarno negotiations. M. Corbin said that he would report to his Government.

I am, &c.,
Anthony Eden

[3] See No. 202.   [4] Enclosure in No. 263.

No. 344

Mr. Eden to Mr. Lloyd Thomas (Paris)
No. 1840 [W 14762/62/41]

FOREIGN OFFICE, *October 30, 1936*

Sir,

The French Ambassador asked to see me this morning when he said there were two or three matters about which he wished to speak to me. The first was the action to be taken by His Majesty's Government if and when the insurgent forces reached Madrid. The French Government saw objections to admitting that the insurgents were entitled to belligerent rights. They feared that to do this would result in incidents at sea which would be very embarrassing.

2. I replied that in this connexion I could give the Ambassador some comfort, as I understood our projected declaration, of which His Excellency had

received a copy[1] from Sir G. Mounsey, would not necessarily have the effect of granting the Spanish Government belligerent rights. Indeed, it would even be open to us to argue on that text against the granting of such facilities.

3. M. Corbin replied that this would certainly be a relief to his Government, but there remained other divergences of view between us. They did not like, for instance, our reference in the text to 'provisional' Government. More important than this, however, was the present difference in our intentions as to our representation in Madrid should the insurgents enter. The French Government's present plan was to withdraw all diplomatic representation and to leave their interests in the charge of a Consul. They thought there were numerous advantages in this course. If at a later date the time came to recognise in some form or other the insurgent Government, then the act of that recognition could be used as a bargaining point. Moreover, who could tell what would happen when the insurgents entered Madrid? Maybe there would be massacres. If so the French Government would be in a position of grave embarrassment if they had left their representative in Madrid. They might even be charged with having thereby lent a measure of approval to such proceedings.

4. In reply I told the Ambassador that we were most anxious to work closely with the French Government in all matters connected with this troublesome situation, and if their anxiety would be relieved by some modification in the text of our declaration, I was prepared to consider any suggestion which the French Government might have to make. On the other hand I did see considerable disadvantage in removing all diplomatic representation from Madrid at the present time. After all the interests which our representatives were now defending in Madrid would require their activities no less if the insurgents were to enter the city. There were, moreover, I understood, certain commercial problems. We had a trade agreement with Spain and its working had of course been greatly complicated by recent happenings.[2]

5. The Ambassador replied that he understood the French had no such agreement at the present time, and reiterated the difficulty which the French Government would find in leaving a representative in Madrid. He admitted that the relations of the French Government with the insurgents must in any event be difficult for some time to come. No doubt they would be to a considerable extent under the influence of Germany and Italy. I said that this might well be so, but was it really a good argument for withdrawing our representatives from Madrid? There might well be some advantage in our not refusing all contact with General Franco. Our Consul at Vigo, for instance, had found his position difficult owing to the fact that the local Spanish authorities felt that we had treated them coldly.

I am, &c.,
ANTHONY EDEN

[1] See Appendix to this document.   [2] See No. 1, note 12.

*Draft public statement on the attitude of His Majesty's Government
in the United Kingdom towards the present situation in Spain*

His Majesty's Government in the United Kingdom have had constantly under consideration the course of events in Spain ever since the month of July when the Government in power were faced with a military revolt of a most serious character.

2. This revolt has not been suppressed; the forces of the insurgents are now in effective occupation of large areas, including many provinces in the North, West and South-West parts of the country, as well as the Spanish zone of Morocco and Spanish overseas territories.

3. The insurgents have set up a provisional government, known as the Council of National Defence, under the leadership of General Franco. While His Majesty's Government do not consider that the present situation justifies their recognising this Government as the Government of Spain, they are nevertheless bound to take cognisance of the fact that large areas are now under the effective control of the insurgents. The responsibility of His Majesty's Government for the protection of British interests extends throughout the whole of Spain and in carrying out this duty they are bound to take account of these developments. They accordingly propose to enter into such *de facto* relations with the Provisional Government, in the areas which the latter effectively controls, as may be necessary for the proper protection of British interests.

4. The attitude of His Majesty's Government towards the contending parties has been and is governed by the International Agreement for Non-Intervention between the countries concerned, and this agreement has rendered it unnecessary for any further definition of the attitude of His Majesty's Government (such as a formal proclamation of neutrality) to be issued. The decision which His Majesty's Government have now reached, as explained above, is not only consistent with, but involves, the continuance by them of this policy of non-intervention.

No. 345

Sir E. Drummond (Rome) to Mr. Eden (Received November 2)
No. 1183 [C 7787/4/18]

ROME, *October 30, 1936*

Sir,

In amplification of my telegram No. 671 of to-day's date,[1] I have the honour to inform you that I went to see Count Ciano this morning to learn from him the results of his visit to Berlin, which he had promised to impart to me on his return.

---

[1] Not printed.

2. I asked him whether he was satisfied with this visit.[2] He replied that he was and that he thought good work had been done for European co-operation. I remarked that it seemed to me that the test of this would be future negotiations over the Locarno Pact. What did he think were the prospects of a successful issue to these negotiations? Count Ciano replied that he was fairly optimistic, even though the five replies were very divergent. He had been wondering what the next step would be. I answered that I presumed that the next step would be that my Government, having collated the replies, would address a further communication to the Powers in question; but did he not think that the German point over 'exceptions' was likely to cause great difficulty? I would take a purely hypothetical case: if the German thesis were accepted, Germany could, for instance, attack Poland, and neither France nor Great Britain nor Italy could attack Germany owing to the new Locarno agreement. Count Ciano stated that he thought I was going rather far. Germany had not definitely refused to make any exceptions but said that proposals for exceptions must be put forward by a third Power and she would then consider them. I admitted that this was so but pointed out that the German desire was for no exceptions whatever.

3. Count Ciano said that the satisfactory point in all the replies—in fact, the only one that was common to all five—was the wish for a new Locarno. He considered that some agreement of this nature was of the greatest importance and the Italian Government were most anxious to reach a settlement. Something must be done to bring the four Powers together. It will be seen that Count Ciano took a more optimistic view of the German attitude than that revealed by Sir Eric Phipps's account of his recent conversation with Baron von Neurath (see Berlin telegram No. 327).[3]

4. I then asked His Excellency whether he could now give me an answer to the point I had made in a previous interview, viz: whether the Italian Government would be ready to accept a new Locarno on the same basis as the old plus an air pact. Count Ciano remarked that he did not see how air warfare could be separated from war on land and sea, and I knew his views about separate guarantees of this general character. I replied that in 1935 such a separation had been proposed and the Italian Government had agreed, at any rate in principle. In fact, Signor Mussolini himself had accepted a method for the application of such a pact, namely a general pact with a separate protocol excepting mutal assistance as between our two respective countries.[4] Count Ciano said that this might be so but he was still sceptical. I remarked that in that case Italian policy had changed and I wondered what the reasons for such a change were. Count Ciano answered that everything in life changed, but he added that he was not

---

[2] Cf. No. 343.

[3] In this telegram of October 27 Sir E. Phipps reported that according to Baron von Neurath 'Count Ciano's visit was of no particular importance and had had no hidden motives', although it might be 'useful to the cause of peace', but he declared himself 'very doubtful' as to the possibility of concluding a Western pact.

[4] Cf. Volume XIII, Nos. 182 and 205.

fully cognisant of what had happened in 1935. He had been too busy lately to go into the point I had raised but he would now look it up and let me have a definite opinion later.

5. From this we passed again to his Berlin visit. He stated that he really had nothing more to tell me than had already appeared in the interviews which he had given to journalists.[5] Nothing had been done at Berlin which had been directed against any third Power. The most important point had been, in his view, the common policy of the two Powers about Bolshevism. I observed that surely Communism hardly existed in Italy. Count Ciano said that this was so. In fact, during the Spanish troubles the authorities had been specially on the lookout for signs of Communist activity but during the last three months had only arrested seven Communists in Italy. The position was not, however, the same in Germany. The Nazi Government had had only three years of power and in the big towns there was certainly still a Communist nucleus, though he thought it was diminishing. Germany was, however, really frightened of the advance of Communism in other countries, as the danger of contamination was very strong. Events in Spain afforded proof of this. He considered that General Franco would very shortly be in possession of Madrid. I observed that this was not the final victory and I thought that he would have great trouble in Catalonia. Count Ciano replied that he doubted whether this would be so unless the French supported the idea of Catalan independence. He believed that if France did so she would be making a great mistake as there were a large number of Catalans living on the French side of the frontier and an independent Catalonia would be a nucleus for irredentism. If France did not give any such

[5] A point in these discussions which was not given to the journalists was the communication by Count Ciano to Herr Hitler on October 24 of the memorandum by Mr. Eden on 'The German Danger' which with accompanying documents had been circulated to the British Cabinet on January 17, 1936, and of which a copy had come into Count Grandi's hands sometime before the following September 3: see Volume XV, No. 460, note 4. Count Ciano, in *L'Europa verso la Catastrofe* (Milan, 1948), p. 94, makes it clear that the Führer, although reacting violently on reading the documents, continued to show some uncertainty on the subject of 'English encirclement' being still, it was thought, influenced by the anglophil optimism of Herr von Ribbentrop. According to a report from French journalistic sources which reached the Foreign Office in a letter of November 4 from the Industrial Intelligence Centre (C 7854/4/18), Count Ciano had first proposed to Herr Hitler a four-power guarantee of frontiers with France and England, outside the framework of the League. If, as he anticipated, the British Government refused to exclude from consideration Eastern Europe and the U.S.S.R., he proposed a three-power guarantee between Germany, Italy, and France. Herr Hitler liked the first but would have nothing to do with the second proposal on the ground that in a war Great Britain would suffer early setbacks but no one could defeat her (and a good deal more to the same effect). Commenting on this report on November 16, Mr. Sargent wrote: 'There seems nothing inherently improbable in this story, and Hitler's alleged attitude is what one might expect . . . But unfortunately that is not the whole of the picture, and it would be highly dangerous to estimate Germany's future course solely on the strength of Hitler's own views and without taking into account the force which is being created by economic pressure and by mass propaganda in Germany. It is this force which may well get beyond Hitler's control one of these days and drive him to action which he would otherwise avoid.' Commenting on the last sentence, Sir R. Vansittart wrote: 'Yes, this is leaving out of account Goering & the lunatics. R. V.'

support, then he believed that General Franco's difficulties would not be so great, particularly as he would be in possession of the Balearic Islands. I observed that according to the press reports Italy was in fact in possession of these islands. Count Ciano answered smilingly that, as I knew, this was entirely untrue, and quoted to me the part of the Berlin declaration, for which he himself had pressed, to the effect that full Spanish integrity, covering both the mother country and her colonial possessions, would be assured. He said that there was in Majorca an Italian, namely Rossi, but he wore a Spanish uniform and Italy had no designs whatever on the islands.[6] Count Ciano then assured me that neither he nor his Government had had any dealings with General Franco before the revolution broke out: in fact he had not even known his name. Later, of course, there had been certain contacts. He repeated this point two or three times, I think in order to endeavour to convince me that Italy had had no part in promoting the revolution.

6. His Excellency then gave me some account of his impressions of German personalities. He said that Herr Hitler was adopting more and more an Olympic[7] attitude, and that nothing now in Germany was done except under the authority of General Goering, who was definitely the second most important personality. In fact he would rank them: first Hitler, then Goering and after these two the rest. General Goering represented the old Prussian type. He did not think he was a clever man but he had certain definite and ingrained ideas and great will to carry them through. As a soldier he saw everything from the point of view of national defence, and all his economic policy would be devoted to military exigencies. I asked Count Ciano if he had read General Goering's most recent speech about colonies.[8] He said that he had only seen press reports but had not yet had the text, and he wondered what my reaction to it was. I replied that all I could say for the moment was that it did not seem to me likely to facilitate matters generally, and in particular such a speech, made immediately after Herr von Ribbentrop's arrival in England, could not but render the latter's task far more difficult. Count Ciano agreed and said that he thought it must have been a very disagreeable shock to Herr von Ribbentrop. He himself had no knowledge that any such speech would be made.

7. In conclusion Count Ciano told me that he was going up to Milan for his father-in-law's speech there which he said would be of great importance as he was making a *tour de l'horizon* and would refer specially to international affairs.[9]

[6] Cf. No. 266.

[7] It was suggested on the filed copy that this should read 'Olympian'.

[8] See No. 342, note 2.

[9] In this comprehensive speech to Blackshirts on Sunday, November 1, in the Piazza del Duomo, Signor Mussolini, after glorifying Italy's demolition of Abyssinia, the League, the 'illusion of disarmament', and the 'commonplace' of 'indivisible peace', announced the formation of a German–Italian axis: 'The meeting at Berlin resulted in an Agreement between the two countries on certain questions, some of which are particularly interesting in these days. But these Agreements, which have been included in special statements and

8. I have sent a copy of this despatch to His Majesty's Ambassador at Berlin.

I have, &c.,
ERIC DRUMMOND

duly signed—this vertical line between Rome and Berlin is not a partition, but rather an axis around which all the European States animated by the will to collaboration and peace can also collaborate.' Speaking of relations with Great Britain he remarked that if 'for others the Mediterranean is a route, for us Italians it is life' but went on to say that, between the two countries, a 'bilateral clash is not to be thought of, and much less a clash that, from being bilateral, would immediately become European. Consequently there is only one solution: a sincere, rapid, and complete agreement based on the recognition of reciprocal interests . . .' These extracts are taken from an authorized Italian translation of the speech, printed in *Documents on International Affairs 1936* (London, 1937), pp. 343–9.

No. 346

Mr. Ogilvie-Forbes (Madrid) to Mr. Eden (Received November 1, 10 a.m.)
No. 437 Telegraphic [W 14828/62/41]

MADRID, *October 31, 1936, 9.50 p.m.*

My telegram No. 430.[1]

Secretary General of the Ministry of State after an appreciative reference to my call at the Ministry last night to convey your thanks for the release of the Legal Adviser to the Embassy[2] and to my personal condolences for yesterday's bombing outrage on children, spoke to me privately but seriously on the deterioration of the relations between Great Britain and Spain which he considered to have become decidedly cold as a result of our policy of non-intervention in general and our alleged unfair treatment of Spanish complaints lodged with Non-Intervention Committee. He said that Great Britain was treating Spain like Abyssinia by insisting on a policy of non-intervention which denied arms to the Spanish Government and yet did nothing to prevent the rebels from obtaining war material. He felt that the members of his (?Majesty's) Government and of the Committee were instinctively hostile. He also complained that business and especially banking circles were unfriendly and unnecessarily denied credits and other facilities. He added that this was the opinion of the man in the street.

2. I replied that our policy of non-intervention was intended to prevent a European war and to restrict as much as possible the sufferings of the people of Spain, for free traffic in arms would on balance benefit the rebels. I added that if there was any additional coldness in Anglo-Spanish relations I was certain it was due to the painful impression caused on British people by

---

[1] In this telegram of October 30 Mr. Ogilvie-Forbes referred to the bombing of Madrid by the rebels that afternoon. 'In Getafe about thirty small children were killed or horribly maimed . . .'

[2] See No. 252.

491

all the private murdering of men and women which had taken place and by the clumsiness of censorship which had made the newspaper readers assume the worst. Señor Urena admitted the murders and could but point to Badajos and Toledo hospital.

3. There is no doubt that at the present moment we are unpopular with both sides. This is inevitable.

CHAPTER VI

British memorandum of November 19 on Five Power Conference: search for Anglo-Italian rapprochement: plans for supervision of Spanish imports

November 2–30, 1936

No. 347

Conclusions[1] *of the eighth meeting of the Chairman's Sub-Committee of the N.I. Committee held in the Foreign Office on Monday, November 2, 1936, at 3.30 p.m.*

[*W 15137/11115/41*]

Present: UNITED KINGDOM: The Earl of Plymouth, *Chairman*;
    BELGIUM: Baron de Cartier de Marchienne;
    CZECHOSLOVAKIA: M. Vilém Černý;[2]
    FRANCE: M. Charles Corbin;
    GERMANY: Prince von Bismarck;
    ITALY: Signor Guido Crolla;[3]
    PORTUGAL: Senhor Francisco de Calheiros e Menezes;
    SWEDEN: Baron E. K. Palmstierna;
    U.S.S.R.: M. Jean Maisky;
    Mr. Francis Hemming, Secretary to the Sub-Committee.

1. As arranged at the last plenary session of the Committee, held on Wednesday, 28th October, 1936,[4] the Sub-Committee resumed the consideration, begun at their meeting held on 24th October, 1936 (N.I.S.(C)(36) 6th meeting, conclusion 3), of a proposal for the establishment of a system of supervision designed to secure the execution of the Agreement.[5]

At the conclusion of the discussion, all the members of the Sub-Committee agreed, at the request of the Chairman:

(1) to obtain the instructions of their respective Governments on the following elaboration of the scheme put forward at their meeting held on 24th October, 1936, prepared by the Secretary to the Committee in the light of the discussion at this meeting:

the establishment of two impartial bodies of persons, stationed in

---

[1] Circulated to the N.I. Committee as N.I.S.(36)129.
[2] Czechoslovak Chargé d'Affaires in London.
[3] Counsellor to the Italian Embassy in London.
[4] Cf. No. 339, note 2.   [5] See No. 338.

Spain and the Spanish Dependencies, at the principal points of entry (by land and by sea), it being understood:

(a) that the proposed bodies should only be appointed with the consent of both the parties in Spain, and therefore that Spanish Sovereignty would in no way be infringed by their appointment;
(b) that one body should be stationed in those parts of Spain under the control of each of the parties respectively;
(c) that, in order to secure the strictly neutral character of both bodies, the personnel of those bodies should be appointed at a plenary session of the International Committee for the Application of the Agreement regarding Non-Intervention in Spain.
(d) that full facilities would be given by both parties in Spain to enable the proposed bodies to satisfy themselves by all appropriate methods that no imports, contrary to the Agreement, were taking place;
(e) that the functions of the proposed bodies should be:

> EITHER   (i) to submit reports on their own initiative to the International Committee on any case where it appeared to them that a breach of the Agreement was taking place;
> OR   (ii) to furnish reports to the International Committee only on particular cases, when called upon to do so by that body.

(2) to ask their respective Governments to state whether they would agree to an approach being made to the two parties in Spain at the earliest possible date after the terms of that approach (discussed in conclusion (1) above) had been finally settled.

2. The Sub-Committee agreed:

(1) to invite the members of the Main Committee to obtain the instructions of their respective Governments on the two questions set out in conclusion (1) above;
(2) to instruct the Secretary to the Committee to write letters immediately to the members of the Main Committee, drawing attention to the two questions discussed in conclusion (1) above, and requesting them to obtain the instructions of their respective Governments thereon.

3. At the conclusion of the meeting, the Sub-Committee agreed:

that the News Department of the Foreign Office should issue to the Press the *communiqué* set out in Annex A[6] to these minutes. (For the French text of this *communiqué*, see Annex B.)[7]

[6] Not printed: it appears in *The Times* of November 3, 1936, p. 15.
[7] Not preserved in the Foreign Office archives.

No. 348

Mr. Eden to Viscount Chilston (Moscow)
No. 569 [W 15074/9549/41]

FOREIGN OFFICE, *November 3, 1936*

Sir,

The Soviet Ambassador asked to see me this evening when he stated that he had not seen me for some months. He wished to speak to me of the international situation as it was viewed by his Government at this time.

2. M. Maisky began by asking me what progress was being made with the Locarno conversations. I told him that we had received answers from everybody and were collating the replies and hoped soon to be in a position to address another note to the parties concerned. I gave M. Maisky no indication of the different points of view taken up in the negotiations beyond saying that there had been no surprise developments so far.

3. With reference to the League of Nations, the Ambassador said that despite all difficulties the Soviet Government were determined to make one more effort to make the League work. In that connexion His Excellency invited my attention to certain proposals made by M. Litvinov at Geneva.[1]

4. The Ambassador then proceeded to speak at some length of the Soviet Government's attitude towards the Spanish conflict. He began by saying that he hoped that we should not take the occasion of our differences of opinion on this subject for unduly magnifying them and he hoped the words of the *communiqué* agreed in Moscow between us on the occasion of my visit still stood, i.e. 'there is at present no conflict of interest between the two Governments on any of the main issues of international policy'.[2] The Soviet Government were certainly not anxious to magnify any differences and they hoped we would pursue the same attitude.

[5.] His Excellency went on to give what he described as an exposition of the motives which had actuated the Soviet Government in the Spanish conflict. He was emphatic that the Soviet Government's admitted sympathy with the Government in Spain was not due to their desire to set up a Communist régime in that country. I remarked that the Ambassador could hardly be surprised if other people thought differently in view of the declared objective of the upholders of Communism to make their method of Government universal. The Ambassador replied that it was quite true that this was their ultimate objective but it was a very distant one—nobody [in] Russia today thought that it could be achieved for instance in our lifetime—and the Soviet Government's purpose in attempting to assist the Spanish Government was far more immediate than that. They saw the Spanish Government as a friend of peace. If the Government triumphed there might be a Government that was far to the Left in that country but it would not be a Government that would wish to create any disturbances outside its own borders.

---

[1] Presumably a reference to M. Litvinov's participation in the Special Main Committee of the League on the application of the Covenant: see *L/N.O.J.*, *S.S. No. 154* and *No. 162*, *passim*.　　　　　[2] See Volume XII, No. 673, note 32.

It would pursue a peaceful policy. It would not, for instance, seek to disturb us at Gibraltar. On the other hand, if General Franco were to win the result would be acclaimed by both Germany and Italy as a great victory for them; their prestige and influence would be greater still and General Franco would be virtually under their control. The Ambassador confessed that he really could not understand our attitude in this matter—surely we could not wish to see another Fascist Government in the Mediterranean. Perhaps we thought that we could influence General Franco—and to some extent no doubt this belief was justified—but we could scarcely expect our influence to be as great as that of the German or Italian Governments who had given him active help. The Soviet Government were convinced that if General Franco were to win the encouragement given to Germany and Italy would be such as to bring nearer the day when another active aggression would be committed—this time perhaps in Central or Eastern Europe. That was a state of affairs that Russia wished at all costs to avoid and that was her main reason for wishing the Spanish Government to win in this civil strife.

6. I repeated to the Ambassador our reasons for supporting the non-intervention policy in Spain. I told him that the rest of his arguments seemed to me to be based on the contention that we could not have good relations except with Governments of our own political complexion. I did not take that view. We had had very good relations with Italy for many years while she was a Fascist State, maybe such relations would one day be restored. Our relations with Portugal today were excellent, and I did not think that the Ambassador would say that our relations with the Soviet Government were very bad. The policy which we had pursued in the Spanish conflict was the one which we believed most calculated to preserve the peace of Europe, though admittedly there might be differences of opinion on that score.[3]

I am, etc.,

ANTHONY EDEN

[3] A minute by Mr. Collier read: 'I think M. Maisky's account of his govt.'s motives is substantially accurate. L. C. Nov. 10th.' M. Maisky's account of this conversation is printed in *D.V.P.S.*, *op. cit.*, No. 344.

No. 349

Memorandum[1] by His Majesty's Government in the United Kingdom regarding the Agenda of the Five-Power Conference, communicated to the Belgian, French, German, and Italian Ambassadors by Sir R. Vansittart on November 4, 1936

[C 7713/4/18]

FOREIGN OFFICE, November 4, 1936

In order to prepare the way for the negotiation of a new treaty to take the place of the Treaty of Locarno, His Majesty's Government in the United

[1] Mr. Eden circulated the memorandum C.P. 278(36) (No. 321) to the Cabinet at its

Kingdom in their memorandum of the 17th September[2] enumerated certain points to which it was felt the attention of the five Governments might well be directed, and which might profitably be discussed by them through the diplomatic channel in advance of any meeting. The list submitted by His Majesty's Government was not to be considered in any way as exhaustive.

2. The communications in reply to this memorandum have now been received by His Majesty's Government from the other four Governments.

3. A comparison of the views of the five Governments as expressed in these communications reveals not unnaturally a variety of opinions on certain points. His Majesty's Government would not propose to discuss at the present stage every point on which differing views are held; but they would suggest to the other Governments concerned that it would be useful to examine further some of these matters where they involve fundamental issues, in order to see whether, as a result of further elucidation and discussion, the various views expressed could not be reconciled in such a way as to enable the Governments to agree on certain fundamental principles as a basis for the conference which they have in view.

4. The subjects which His Majesty's Government would thus invite the Belgian, French, German and Italian Governments to consider further, in the light of the views which have now been expressed, are as follows.

(i) *What is to be the form of the new agreement?*

His Majesty's Government state, in their memorandum of the 17th September, that they 'assume that the new agreement will include certain non-aggression arrangements, whereby the participants would agree in no case to attack or invade each other by land, sea or air, or to resort to war against each other. (For His Majesty's Government's views on "exceptions" see point (ii) below.) ... His Majesty's Government would be ready to guarantee the observance of such arrangements as between Germany, on the one hand, and France and Belgium, on the other, in return for similar guarantees for the United Kingdom from France against Germany and from Germany against France.'

The *French Government* state, in their memorandum of the 30th September, that they 'consider that the provisions of the Treaty of Locarno should be

meeting on October 28, and said that he intended to send a note to the other Locarno powers indicating the results of the Foreign Office's collation of their replies (see Nos. 263, 286, 301, and 323) to the British memorandum of September 17 (No. 206). In doing so he proposed to limit himself to the points mentioned in paragraphs 2–6 of C.P. 278(36). The Cabinet showed some doubts as to whether the point raised in paragraph 4 of C.P. 278(36) should be treated as a matter of major divergence between the French and German points of view or be referred to in a different part of the note. Mr. Eden said that the matter was bound to be raised by some other Government if it was not included in his note, but he undertook to consider the matter further. In a minute of October 29 Sir R. Vansittart commented: 'Nobody is thinking of an *Eastern* Pact any more. It is the question of a settlement in *Central* Europe that is important—not necessarily a Central *Pact*, but at least a Central *appeasement*. And we shall not get away on less, nor should we hope to do so.' See paragraph 5 below.　　　　　　　　　　　　　　　　　　　　　[2] No. 206.

maintained subject to the inclusion of the modifications and additions rendered necessary by present circumstances or which experience seems to render desirable. Just as the Treaty of Locarno is based upon a guarantee of the territorial status quo resulting from the frontiers between Germany and Belgium and between Germany and France, and a guarantee of the inviolability of these frontiers, the new agreement should be based upon the recognition of the fact that there does not exist between the contracting parties any territorial dispute, and, consequently, in their mutual relations, upon an individual and collective guarantee of the territorial status quo as well as of the inviolability of the frontiers of their possessions and dependencies. Each signatory would undertake vis-à-vis each of the other signatories not to proceed to any attack or invasion by land, sea or air, and not to resort in any event to force. (For French Government's views on "exceptions" see point (ii) below.) In case of failure to observe the obligation of non-aggression, assistance (the obligation to render which must not be less extensive than that resulting from the Treaty of Locarno) should be rendered by the other signatory Powers to the Power attacked. . . The French Government wish to declare at once that, subject to reciprocity, they are ready to contract the obligations of guarantee and assistance referred to above towards each of the Powers parties to the new agreement.'

The *German Government* state, in their memorandum of the 12th October, that they, 'as already proposed in their peace plan of the 31st March last, regard obligations for non-aggression between Germany, on the one hand, and Belgium and France, on the other, and the guaranteeing of these obligations by Great Britain and Italy, as the essential elements of the pact. The answer to the question whether these elements in the treaty should further be supplemented by non-aggression and guarantee obligations between other treaty partners will have to depend on whether such an extension of the system of the Locarno Treaty is in the general interests of peace and whether it can be introduced without upsetting the necessary balance of the treaty system. The German Government will only be able to form their final judgment on this point when they have learned the views of the other Governments concerned.'

The *Italian Government* state, in their memorandum of the 18th October, that in their opinion 'the new pact should retain the fundamental principles of the Treaty of Locarno. These principles consist in essence of: (a) the specific undertaking of France, Belgium and Germany not to have recourse to war in any question which may arise between them; (b) the joint guarantee by Italy and England of the non-aggression agreements between France, Belgium and Germany which form the foundation of the Locarno Treaty. . . The Italian Government have gathered that it is the intention of the British Government to introduce into the guarantee system a new principle: that of reciprocity. It seems to emerge from the British memorandum that the British Government would be ready to renew the Locarno guarantees, so far as concerns the non-aggression agreements between Germany, France and Belgium, in exchange for similar guarantees in favour of Great Britain on the part of Germany against France and on the part of France against Germany. That which in the *communiqué* of the 3rd February, 1935,[3] was the principle on which the Air Pact was to be based would thus come to be used as the organic foundation for the entire system of guarantees in the new treaty.

This innovation seems to the Italian Government to be of the greatest importance, and the Italian Government would wish to call the attention of the British Government to what would, in their opinion, be its practical consequences. To begin with, the Italian Government has always regarded the Locarno guarantee as a joint Italo-British guarantee, and has always considered that the real strength of the Locarno Treaty lay in the fact that the aggressor would in every case have found himself faced by the united forces of the Power attacked and of the two guarantors. The joint character of the Italo-British guarantee, and this union of the forces of the guarantors and the Power attacked, constituted the fundamental unity—for all practical purposes—of the Locarno Treaty. Confronted with the suggestions contained in the British memorandum, the Italian Government wonders whether this fundamental unity would be effectively maintained in a régime of reciprocal separate guarantees, or whether the Treaty of Locarno would not become split into two tripartite systems, which would fundamentally alter the position of the guarantors, do away with the joint character of the guarantee and, for all practical purposes, transform the Locarno Treaty into two separate pacts of mutual assistance: one Franco-Anglo-German and one Italo-Franco-German, only formally linked together in the common framework of a general pact. In the opinion of the Italian Government, this would represent a general weakening of the Locarno system, which it is certainly not the intention of any of the five Governments to bring about. It is perhaps unnecessary for the Italian Government to call the attention of the British Government to the fact that, once the joint character of the Locarno guarantee is weakened, the Treaty of Locarno would come to lose not only one of its fundamental characteristics, but also a function to which an essential importance has always, and rightly, been attributed.'

The *Belgian Government* state, in their memorandum of the 22nd October, that they 'consider that the agreement must provide for undertakings of non-aggression between the interested Powers... The Belgian Government note with satisfaction that the British Government do not subordinate the guarantee which they are disposed to give to Belgium to the receipt of a reciprocal guarantee. The Belgian Government consider that this question must, so far as they are concerned, be viewed in the same manner by the other signatory States, and they think it desirable to explain the reasons. As a result of the geographical situation of Belgium, any aggression of which she might be the victim would be a direct menace to other Powers. By defending the access to her own territory Belgium contributes in the most effective manner to the security of the States which surround her. The accomplishment of this task demands important sacrifices and a very considerable effort. Conscious

---

[3] See Volume XII, Annex to No. 400.

of her duties towards the other nations as towards herself, Belgium is resolved to undertake it. By so doing she creates for herself a right in given circumstances to assistance which the Powers threatened across her territory would have a vital interest to give her. She considers that she will by these means fulfil to the limit of her powers the duty which is hers in this region of Europe which has so often been exposed to the ravages of war. Belgium will not, however, confine to this her contribution to the work of collective security. She will continue to observe in respect of the obligations of the Covenant the scrupulous fidelity which she has always shown in the past.'

(ii) *Would these non-aggression arrangements be subject to exceptions on the lines laid down in article 2 of the Treaty of Locarno?*

His Majesty's Government stated, in their memorandum of the 17th September, that, in their view, the non-aggression agreements should be 'subject to certain exceptions on the lines which were laid down in article 2 of the Treaty of Locarno.'

The *French Government* state that the obligation of non-aggression should not impede 'the exercise by one of the signatory Powers of the right of legitimate defence, that is, of the right to oppose the violation of the obligation defined above . . . It shall not be possible for the benefits of this new treaty (and, in particular, the obligation to render assistance which results from it) to be invoked by a signatory Power which fails to observe the obligations laid down in it, or which shall undertake in Europe something contrary to the territorial integrity or political independence of another Power, in particular by launching against the latter an unprovoked attack. Consequently, the principle of assistance could not be brought into force against a signatory State which, in accordance with the principles of the Covenant of the League of Nations, resists an act of aggression by one of the contracting parties against a State which is not a contracting party. In laying down this principle, the Government of the Republic have in mind the provisions of article 2 of the Treaty of Locarno.'

The *German Government*, 'in their peace plan of the 31st March, have already declared themselves prepared for a renunciation of aggression vis-à-vis Belgium and France unrestricted by any exceptions. From their standpoint they have no motive for weakening the security for peace which lies in the conclusion of such an agreement for the renunciation of aggression by demanding exceptions of any kind whatever. In case the other Governments concerned should think it necessary to insist on making exceptions of this kind, it would be for them to put forward proposals to this end. Meanwhile, however, the German Government must indicate at once that they do not consider the method proposed by His Majesty's Government in their memorandum of the 17th September to be practicable. In article 2 of the Locarno Treaty, to which the memorandum refers, the important exceptions in practice to the provisions for the renunciation of aggression are laid down with reference to the provisions of the Covenant of the League of Nations, and in particular to article 16 thereof. The repetition of the use of this method is, in the view of the German Government, precluded by the fact that the interpretation of article 16 has led to the well-known differences of opinion between Germany and the other Locarno Powers, and, furthermore, by the fact that the discussion regarding the future of article 16 and other provisions of the Covenant of the League of Nations is at present still quite open.'

The *Italian Government* do not discuss this question pending a decision on question (i).

The *Belgian Government* express no view.

(iii) *How shall a decision be reached as to whether the non-aggression undertaking has been violated?*

His Majesty's Government expressed the view that 'the question whether the non-aggression undertaking has been violated should be submitted to the Council of the League of Nations. In the case of a flagrant violation of a frontier, the guarantees might operate immediately, as in the Treaty of Locarno, pending a final pronouncement by the Council.'

The *French Government* state that 'at least the mechanism contemplated by the Treaty of Locarno (article 4), which comprises, on the one hand, the recognition by the Council of the League of Nations of the fact that an act of aggression has taken place, and, on the other, in the event of a flagrant violation of the above-mentioned obligation, the immediate application of the guarantees pending a definite decision of the Council, should be maintained with the necessary addition to forestall the danger of sudden air attack.'

The *German Government* 'do not consider it either necessary or appropriate to submit to the Council of the League of Nations the question of deciding whether an infringement of the obligation of non-aggression has taken place, and consequently whether the guarantee obligation has entered into force. It would be necessary to examine whether such decisions should not be reached by a common decision of the parties to the treaty who are not in a given case directly parties to the conflict. A distinction between flagrant breaches of the treaty and other kinds of breaches of the treaty, such as was laid down in the old Rhine Pact, will no longer come into consideration in the new pact.'

The *Italian Government* express no view, in the circumstances described above.

The *Belgian Government* express no view.

5. A further point on which a certain divergence of view seems to exist concerns that passage in the London *communiqué* of the 23rd July,[4] which was quoted in His Majesty's Government's memorandum, and which reads:

'If progress could be made at the five-Power meeting, other matters affecting European peace would necessarily come under discussion. In these circumstances, it would be natural to look forward to the widening

[4] See Volume XVI, No. 476.

of the area of discussion in such a manner as to facilitate, with the collaboration of the other interested Powers, the settlement of those problems the solution of which is essential to the peace of Europe.'

On this point the *French Government* state that their memorandum 'does not take into account all the questions which will arise in the course of the forthcoming conference for the solution of which the collaboration of other countries will be indispensable. It has been purposely limited to the principal problems connected directly with the negotiation of the treaty to be substituted for the Treaty of Locarno, and which, for this reason, and subject to the eventual participation of the Netherlands in the negotiations does not call for the participation of other Powers than the signatories of the last-named treaty. The Government of the Republic wishes to point out that, in accordance with the spirit of the arrangement of the 19th March, 1936,[5] and of the London *Communiqué* of the 23rd July, this negotiation should be the prelude to a wider negotiation which implies the collaboration of the interested Powers.'

The *German Government* 'assume from the terms of the invitation conveyed to them on the basis of the London *Communiqué* of the 23rd July last and their reply thereto, that the subject to be dealt with by the conference will be the replacement of the old Rhine Pact of Locarno by a new pact between Germany, Belgium, France, Great Britain and Italy. If the *communiqué* in question contemplates the discussion later on of other problems connected with the securing of European peace, a decision with regard to these problems (as, indeed, the *communiqué* itself indicates) can only be reached when the result of the conference of the Five Powers, with respect to the subject to be dealt with at that conference, has been arrived at. The German Government must therefore reserve till then their attitude with regard to the question whether, and if so which, other problems in given circumstances might later be discussed.'

The *Italian Government* do not deal with this point.

The *Belgian Government* express no view.

6. His Majesty's Government desire to invite the views of the French[6] Government as to how this variety of opinion can best be reconciled. It is the intention of His Majesty's Government to make at an early date a further communication to the French[6] Government, giving their own views on these matters.

7. As regards subsequent procedure, they would be glad also to be informed whether, in the view of the French[6] Government, the best method of procedure would be the diplomatic channel, or whether a meeting of the representatives of the Five Powers should be convened.

8. A similar memorandum has been addressed to the Belgian, German and Italian Governments.[7]

---

[5] See Volume XVI, No. 144.

[6] *Note in original*: Also Belgian, German and Italian Governments.

[7] *Note in original*: Mutatis mutandis.

No. 350

Sir E. Phipps (Berlin) to Mr. Eden
(Received November 6)

No. 1179E [C 7901/99/18]

Confidential   BERLIN, *November 4, 1936*

Sir,

The launching of the Four Year Plan marks, if not a new departure, at all events a new stage in Germany's economic development. It is therefore a suitable moment to attempt the task of appreciating the position to-day, in so far as it can be done.

2. The seeds of the present difficulties were sown many years ago. In particular two vital decisions were taken by Germany before even the Nazi Government came into power. One was the introduction of exchange restrictions in 1931 by Dr. Brüning and Dr. Luther, intended as a defence against the spectre of inflation; the other was the reversal by Herr von Papen in 1932 of the Brüning deflationary policy and the invention of a mechanism for financing public works (which were begun on a small scale only).

3. On these two bases—to which must be added a third vital factor, namely the decision to prevent any rise in wages—the Nazi Government has founded a policy which eclipses both in degree and in kind all the notions of its predecessors. By fresh Government borrowing, which may be estimated to be of the order of magnitude of RM 25 milliard (as compared with an initial debt of RM 12 milliard at the end of 1932) it has carried out a programme of public works and rearmament which has raised production in general to the neighbourhood of the boom level of 1928/29, and has reduced unemployment from 6 million to 2½ million at the winter peak, or from 5 million to 1 million at the summer trough of the curve. The unemployment figures are perhaps doctored to the tune of half a million or so, and it must be remembered that nearly a million men have been absorbed into military or para-military service, but the Government has for all practical purposes fulfilled its promise of reducing unemployment to bedrock level.

4. The various pieces in the picture fit closely together. The surplus energies of the population, as evidenced by the unemployment of 1932/33, have been set to work mainly for the production of capital goods in the form of armaments and armament factories, roads, etc., while the increase in the production of consumption goods has been relatively small and probably hardly enough to maintain the scale of consumption of a man in full employment, although it has provided for the increased consumption of those who were formerly unemployed. The larger incomes have been severely cut, the profits of manufacturers and retailers squeezed, and the element of increased prosperity is strictly limited to the provision of work for the unemployed. The maintenance of the wage level has been accompanied by the endeavour to keep prices from rising. It has been essential thus to prevent the stimulus given by the Government's investment from petering out in price rises or

503

increased individual consumption, for this has produced the maximum effect in the direction in which the Government desired, viz. the reduction of unemployment.

5. The exchange restrictions on the other side have been equally important in one respect which was not contemplated by their original authors, viz. they have prevented capital from leaving the country, which it would otherwise have done as a result of the Government's persecution of the Jews and of its political opponents, and generally as a result of the desire to spread risks. Thus capital resources have been retained within the country, and have in fact been practically monopolised by the Government.

6. A public debt in the neighbourhood of RM 40 milliard cannot, however, be regarded as dangerous. It represents only the Central Government's tax revenue for 5–6 years at the present rate, as compared with a public debt equivalent to over 10 years' tax revenue in the United Kingdom or France. Nor has the Government's policy had any untoward effects so far on the money and capital markets. On the contrary it has caused long term interest rates to fall and the money market to be extremely liquid—though there are slight signs now of a coming stiffening of interest rates. It is true that of the Government borrowings only a little over RM 3 milliard have been hitherto consolidated. For the rest, in the first stage, they have been effected mainly by the substitution of Government debt for other debt, with only a relatively moderate rise in the total volume of bank credit. The process of substituting Government paper for commercial paper in the banks' holdings seems to have been nearly completed this year (the manager of a large provincial bank told me that his bank holds only RM 15 million of genuine commercial paper among total liquid assets of RM 200 million), and the Government has recently had to effect its borrowing more directly from industry itself. Since, however, industry is kept liquid by the constant stream of Government orders, there seems to be no difficulty for the time in continuing this process. But it must some time be brought to an end, and it is significant that Dr. Schacht is reported to be pressing more urgently than before for a real balancing of the budget, so far as necessary by increased taxation. His only success so far is the recent increase in the Corporation Tax, to bring in a relatively small additional revenue of less than RM 500 million per annum.

7. The main difficulties in the whole position have appeared from the start on the exchange side. The maintenance of the nominal value of the Reichsmark, after the crisis of 1931 and the British and American devaluations, kept the German price level so much above the outside level that export trade on a straightforward basis became progressively more difficult. It has been kept going by a series of acrobatic feats in the subsidising of exports, trading in depreciated Marks with individual countries or in individual transactions, the forcing of German exports by means of clearings on the smaller raw-material-producing countries etc. These measures have in many cases raised the cost of imports; but, in combination with the reduction of the cash transfers in respect of the service of Germany's external

debt in the last year or two to a nominal amount of less than $1\frac{1}{2}\%$ interest with no redemption, they have just, though only just, enabled Germany to maintain her essential supplies of raw materials from abroad. These supplies have been eked out by rationing and by every kind of internal control, including the prohibition of new investments in a number of the less essential trades. In the last year Germany has even succeeded in restoring to outward appearance an export surplus, though it does not appear that this surplus was realisable in foreign exchange. At the same time she has made the greatest effort to maintain and increase her agricultural production by raising internal prices. According to Herr Hess' speech on October 12th,[1] Germany is now wholly independent of imports of flour, meal, potatoes, sugar and drinking milk; vegetables and meat have only to be imported in small quantities. Her only vulnerable point is her dependence on foreign fats and fodder. Nevertheless the enormous requirements of the rearmament programme have kept the German nation perpetually on the verge of serious shortages, which in the last two years have practically become endemic. First eggs are short, then butter, then meat, then rubber; and the Government has to take steps to meet each occasion. Last winter was bad, and the coming winter seems likely to be in reality worse, although the Government is sufficiently warned of the dangers to be ready to prevent any too startling or acute shortages in the food supply.

8. Meanwhile industry, under the stimulus of the rearmament and public works programmes, continues to flourish. The index of industrial production, taking the 1928 index figure as 100, has risen from the low figure of 56 at the end of 1932 to 99 in June of this year. The output of the motor car industry during the first six months of 1936 was 25% higher than during the same period of 1935. Price reductions on the home market were announced by a number of motor car firms and preparations are fairly well advanced for the production, in accordance with Herr Hitler's instructions of a 'Peoples' Car', which is to be sold for less than a thousand marks (£50 at par). Banks have paid dividends, shipping concerns have been reorganised and many large concerns have emerged from the trough of the 1931 crisis. In several industries new buildings are being erected and works extended, sometimes with financial assistance from the Government, but more often out of the profits of the firm.

9. 'Capital,' says the photographer, 'will you now hold the position'. This is in effect the problem, into which a new, unexpected and disconcerting factor has been introduced, namely the recent currency devaluation.[2] To what extent Germany's foreign exchange position may be affected by a serious loss of markets in the countries which have recently devalued is shown in the [table on the following page].

10. Germany's active balance on the whole of her world trade only amounted to 111 million RM. in 1935, and while she had an active balance of RM. 320 million for the first nine months of this year, it is clear that if her export surplus in the above countries were reduced by a third, the effect on

[1] See *The Times*, October 13, 1936, p. 15.   [2] See No. 248, note 4.

1935

	Imports	Exports	Export Surplus
	Value in million RM.		
France	154·2	252·8	98·6
Switzerland	114·4	256·9	142·5
Netherlands	196·1	404·2	208·1
Italy	187·5	278·3	90·8
Czechoslovakia	121·4	130·0	8·6
			448·6 [sic]

the currency situation would be serious. In addition to difficulties in the markets of the devaluated countries themselves, Germany will have to meet increased competition from these countries in other markets. The news of the agreement between France, Great Britain and the United States was received here with consternation both for its political and economic implications. As regards the economic aspect, the Ministry for Foreign Affairs prepared a memorandum pointing out that at all events at first a serious restriction of Germany's exports was to be expected but that the evil would be kept within measurable bounds if Italy did not follow suit. The subsequent Italian devaluation was a further blow which plunged the Economic Department of the Ministry for Foreign Affairs into deep pessimism. The department is now, under instructions, somewhat hopelessly examining the practicability of putting German counter measures in force.

11. The fact that the currency agreement was concluded so quickly and secretly by 'democratic chatterboxes' came as a shock to German ministers. When, in addition, they are told by their experts that the result will be an aggravation of the already difficult situation here, the old bogey of encirclement rises before their eyes. Hence the extremely bitter tone of the recent official utterances on economic matters.

12. The Four Year Plan now announced is but the logical development of the policy adopted during the last few years. On military as well as economic grounds the German Government has decided to make the country as independent as possible of foreign resources. Both Herr Hitler and the General Staff attach the greatest importance to the rôle played by the economic factor in the last war and they are determined that the history of Germany's collapse under economic pressure shall not repeat itself. As I reported at the time, the experience of Italy under the régime of sanctions drove this lesson home.

13. General Göring's speech, reported in my despatch No. 1159E of October 29,[3] threw little light on the technical details of the plan. As he himself said, he was speaking not as an expert or as an economist, but as a plain man determined to push the thing through. Nevertheless it is clear that the plan has two objects in view, the maintenance of prices at their

[3] Not printed: see No. 342, note 2.

present level and the restriction of imports through the production of substitute raw materials.

14. The recent rise in prices is not reflected in official statistics and accurate information is therefore not available. Reports from Chambers of Commerce, however, in different parts of the country show that rises have taken place in cloth, woollen goods in the furnishing trade, leather, packing paper, grease paper and rubber tyres. Foodstuffs, especially meat and cheese, have also risen. I annex a table[4] compiled from actual experience, showing the retail prices in force in September 1936 compared with those of a year ago.

15. It is not denied in official utterances that rises have taken place. Indeed the measures taken and threatened against the so-called profiteers constitute an admission of what is common knowledge. In the last few weeks the press has prominently reported proceedings against farmers and butchers for charging excessive prices or for unauthorised slaughtering. Herr Wagner, the Gauleiter of Silesia, has been appointed Price Controller with wide powers. Severe penalties, including penal servitude, may be imposed for hoarding or profiteering. In my despatch No. 1109 of October 16[4] I reported that a chain store on being fined for charging excessive prices had declined to stock the goods in question. This expedient is now expressly prohibited under the new regulations. A retail dealer's lot this winter will not be an enviable one. What with prices cut to the bone on one hand, and on the other high taxation coupled with voluntary contributions, it will be hard to make both ends meet. It may be remarked in passing that the Nazi Party came into power largely on the shoulders of the small shopkeeping class.

15. [sic] On what may be described as the industrial side the Four Year Plan is little more than an intensified continuation of developments which were already in progress aiming at the expansion of the production of synthetic petrol, rubber and textile materials, the use of inferior home iron ores, etc. The Plan, together if necessary with a new housing programme, will no doubt be pushed forward to maintain employment as the demand for armament supplies passes the peak.

16. No indications are yet available as to the total financial cost of the new Four Year Plan; probably nothing like complete plans have yet been worked out. It appears probable, however, that the Government will not itself provide finance for the new factories, but will oblige existing industrial companies to furnish a part of the necessary funds themselves out of their reserves and to borrow the rest from the banks. One article in the press mentions as typical a new staple fibre factory which has a capital of RM 4 million and a long-term bank credit of RM 8 million guaranteed by the Reich, bearing interest at $5\frac{1}{2}\%$ and redeemable at the rate of 9% per annum. Whether Government guarantees will always be given will no doubt depend on the nature of the case. In the case of staple fibre, the cost of production is greater, though not very much greater, than that of cotton, but the shortage of cotton is such that the demand for staple fibre even at the present price cannot be satisfied for a long time. Even in these favourable conditions,

4 Not printed.

however, it seems that Government guarantees are necessary. In the case of petrol I hear from one source that the cost of production has now been brought down to about three times the cost of imported petrol; and if this is correct, and if the sale price to the public is maintained at its present level (which of course in the case of imported petrol covers import duty as well as distribution costs), the manufacture of synthetic petrol will be assured of a good profit. From another source, however, I learn that the real cost of production is a matter of great uncertainty owing to doubts about the necessary allowance for amortisation. The Dye Trust's Leuna factory, the first producer of synthetic petrol, which only started work a few years ago has already been reconstructed twice to take account of technical advances; and I am told that the Dye Trust is inclined to the view that for further synthetic petrol factories the very short period of five years ought to be allowed for the amortisation of the capital.

17. Mention must here be made of the campaign to diminish the consumption of petrol by the increased use of Diesel Engines in heavy lorries and the use of coal and other gas as a motive fuel for omnibuses and lorries. Altogether the plan will not come into being without the exercise of an enormous amount of Government control and supervision, in which the interests of the industrialists would be the last to be considered. The 'Schwarze Korps' has even gone so far as to warn industrialists that this is perhaps the last opportunity they will have of demonstrating their famous private initiative; and that, if the capitalist system fails to prove its merits on this occasion, it may well be done away with.

18. All the home-produced raw materials comprised in the plan are more expensive, or cost more to work, than the imported products (just as the cost of home-produced foodstuffs is in many cases three or four times that of imported articles). As the plan proceeds it will raise the cost of certain finished goods and will thus in its turn have a deleterious effect on the export trade, which will partly set off the saving on imports of the natural products. It can further only impoverish the country to use synthetic petrol costing three times as much as imported petrol, instead of manufacturing export goods which could be exchanged for imported petrol. The whole tendency is thus towards a further lowering of the standard of living, which would only be avoided if the cost of manufacturing the synthetic products could be considerably reduced. Again, if at some stage Germany re-establishes her commercial relations with the outside world, she will presumably be unwilling to sacrifice her agriculture or the factories she has built for the production of synthetic industrial materials; she may even go further and complete on defence grounds her plans for the erection of further factories of this kind. To this extent her commercial relations with the outside world cannot be restored, and her own economic position may be adversely affected, until there is a complete reversal of policy.

19. There is little doubt that the German expansion has been carried out to some extent by drawing on reserves. The maintenance and the keeping up to date of industrial equipment has been partly neglected, where

or example export markets have fallen off, and a revival of exports would require either fresh capital expenditure in bringing this equipment back into use or else would be dependent on finding markets for fresh products such as armaments. But Germany's economic reserves are enormous, and neither this feature nor the expansion of the public debt seems likely to set a limit within measurable time to her present activities. On the other hand it is becoming progressively difficult, though not necessarily impossible, to maintain raw material supplies and it may become more difficult as the result of the recent devaluations in other countries. Although Germany refused not only in 1931 and 1933, but again in October 1936, to adjust her price level by an official devaluation of the Mark (instead of by the fantastic complication of subsidies and special marks), the question is very much alive. It is realised on the one hand that Germany's task in securing raw materials would be considerably easier if her price level were adjusted and if the movement towards the reduction of trade barriers generally makes effective progress. Dr. Schacht has almost gone so far as to hint that he might contemplate such an adjustment if 'some remainders of the past' could be liquidated; he is referring presumably to a settlement regarding Germany's foreign debt (on which he is still hesitating to put forward any specific proposal) and to a return of colonies (for which his infatuation seems as great as ever.) On the other hand a devaluation of the Mark would not make it possible to abolish the exchange restrictions, since it would still be essential to prevent capital, whether Jewish or other, from leaving the country. Devaluation would only make it possible immediately to modify or abolish export subsidies, to exercise a lighter control on trade transactions, to reduce the number of different kinds of blocked Marks, and perhaps to hope in the near future for some increase in foreign credit of a strictly commercial character. On the other hand there are Party circles who regard Germany's economic isolation as desirable in itself; the highly important and influential *Wehrwirtschaftstab* (Military—Economic Staff) of the War Ministry favour it on military grounds. More moderate opinion seems to have serious fears of the political consequences of the rise in prices which would no doubt follow a devaluation, and the possible necessity of a rise in wages; but in these quarters there has lately appeared a new effort in terminology, 'the parallel development of wages and prices'—perhaps as a result of the fact that the prices of many kinds of goods are willy nilly rising. The question of a devaluation thus remains in the balance, although it may be only a matter of months before the balance tips to one side or the other.

20. There used to be a joke to the effect that the economic situation of Germany was serious, but not hopeless, whilst the Austrian situation was hopeless but not serious. General Göring's diagnosis at the *Sportpalast* was that Germany's situation was bad and would get worse, but that it was hopeful. Although it may be difficult to share General Göring's robust optimism, it cannot be said that anything in the form of an economic breakdown is in sight. The very expression 'economic breakdown' sometimes covers a lack

of clear thinking; the only kind of breakdown that could really occur in the near future would be psychological, a loss of confidence in the present régime and its methods. Of this there is no present sign. A well known banker wryly remarked to a member of my staff that there was at all events one thing to be said in favour of totalitarian régimes, namely that lack of confidence was forbidden. There seemed, therefore, no reason why the swindle should not go on and the 'inevitable' day of reckoning postponed till the Greek Kalends.

21. A factor which gives confidence to the man in the street and to many well informed Germans as well is the continued presence of Dr. Schacht in the Cabinet. His disappe[a]rance would provoke widespread anxiety, a fact of which Herr Hitler is aware. His attitude towards recent developments and his future prospects are therefore matters of great importance.

22. Dr. Schacht's position in the National Socialist Government is a peculiar one. He is not, and never was, a National Socialist. He does not believe, and never did believe, in autarchy, anti-Semitism, the racial theory, *Blut und Boden* or the other fundamentals of the Nazi creed. He is a democrat, but a soured democrat, thanks to his experiences at the hands of the western democracies in connection with the protracted tragedy of German Reparations. He joined the Hitler Government because he had been dismissed by a Weimar Government in much the same frame of mind as Herr von Papen and Herr Hugenberg. He knew very little about the Nazi movement and imagined that the newcomers could be tamed and influenced by wise counsels and that a semi-autocratic but essentially sensible Government, in which he would be economic and financial dictator, would emerge from the revolutionary movement. He discovered in a very short time that he had made a profound mistake. He found himself dealing with fanatics, gangsters and idealists, as typified by Goebbels, Röhm and Hitler, of a kind that he had never before encountered in Germany. One might compare Dr. Schacht's position to that of a skilled navigator who in a moment of pique joined a pirate vessel, confident that he would reform the pirate captain and his crew. He has found himself compelled to engage in piracy and to steer most dangerous and unorthodox courses, despite his protestations. If the craft is wrecked he knows that he will be the first to drown and he finds that it takes all his skill in navigation to avoid shipwreck. His fate is bound up with that of the pirates and though he disapproves of their piracy he must abet it in his own interest, though there are moments when his soul revolts.

23. Luckily for Dr. Schacht Herr Hitler had no knowledge of currency or finance and he was, and is still, sufficiently intelligent to disregard the advice of his Party friends. He will retain Dr. Schacht so long as the ship of State remains afloat. If it threatens to founder he may have no choice but to pitch him overboard.

24. Dr. Schacht is therefore faced with a difficult task. He has to find a compromise between political expediency and the dictates of financial common sense. He has succeeded in providing the funds for rearming

Germany and the funds for the Nazi unemployment campaign. He has succeeded in warding off the worst attacks of the Nazi extremists. There has been no general confiscation of Jewish or other property and, though dividends are limited to 6 or 8 per cent. and there is considerable interference with private enterprise, the foundations of the capitalist system have not been undermined in Germany. He is, moreover, in the strong position of being able to say, 'I told you so' when the German Government finds itself short of currency, of raw materials, and finally of internal food supplies.

25. Within the Government he is more or less the leader of the moderate party. He has the support of Baron von Neurath, the German Army and the Civil Service. He finds very helpful points of contact with General Goering, who is an old army officer with few Nazi proclivities in his saner moments.

26. In demanding the restoration of Germany's colonies Dr. Schacht is actuated by several motives—self-protection, natural inclination, and patriotism. He is alarmed by the shrinkage of world trade. Even if this is stemmed he realises that Germany's share in it is insufficient as a basis for her economy and her ambition as a Great Power. He foresees a progressive deterioration which will either bring about his own downfall or an international explosion. Both consummations would be highly undesirable, for Dr. Schacht, despite his bluster, is not in his heart of hearts a believer in aggression. As a way out he can only think of colonial restoration. He is no believer in the new Four Year Plan, but, to go back to the analogy of the pirate ship, he must help to work any pump which will save the craft from foundering, because he himself is on board.

27. Perhaps the strongest element in Dr. Schacht's position is the fact that there is no outstanding competitor for the presidency of the Reichsbank in the field. Furthermore, Herr Hitler is notoriously conservative in the matter of his lieutenants. He dislikes new faces and on principle he believes that a dictator should not admit that he has made a mistake. To dismiss a Minister is equivalent to admitting that an error of judgment was commited in appointing that Minister.

28. Several hearts beat in Dr. Schacht's breast, a Liberal Democratic one, a National Socialist one and an international one. At times one beats more strongly than the others. This accounts for his inconsistencies of speech and action. He was in office when Liberal Democratic Germany was denied the smallest concession. To-day he sees autocratic Nazi Germany freed by her own initiative from many of the fetters of Versailles and he reflects bitterly that the world is ruled by unreason, selfishness and force. He is glad, as a patriotic German, that Germany has recovered the Rhineland, but if Nazi Germany had been given twelve hours to quit the Rhineland, and if the Nazi leader had lost courage and given way, Dr. Schacht's 'Schadenfreude' would have been sincere. When he sent you a message recently to beware of the promises of the present German Government[5] he was writhing under Nazi attacks which he eventually overcame, with the aid of General Goering. I can well imagine Dr. Schacht, piqued by our

[5] Cf. No. 185, note 6.

refusal to give Germany colonies, urging General Goering to perfect such an air force as would bring London to reason. He would be equally sincere in both cases.

29. Dr. Schacht is a clever tactician. He has now scored a distinct success in his handling of the questions of the moment, the currency, food, and material shortage in Germany, for which he, in a sense, can be held by the uninformed German public to be responsible. He has induced the Nazis to take up the front line positions in the new campaign for the Four Year Plan. When General Goering addressed the Berlin populace at the *Sportpalast* on October 28th, Dr. Schacht was present merely as an expert. His name was mentioned by General Goering in the same breath as that of the unimportant Nazi 'Expert' Herr Keppler. As he told me next day he was distinctly relieved when the Führer agreed with him that an outstanding personality like General Goering should be entrusted with the noble task of rallying the country for the new campaign. If the campaign fails General Goering and the Nazi Party, and not Dr. Schacht, will be responsible.[6]

I have, &c.,

ERIC PHIPPS

[6] Sir E. Phipps was thanked in despatch No. 1283 of November 20 to Berlin for an admirable addition to the despatches on general conditions in Germany 'of which you have supplied so continuous a series during the last three years'. Extensive minutes included Mr. Wigram's observation on November 7 that if Germany found that she had not adequate foreign exchange to buy certain raw materials the difficulties were almost entirely of her own making and resulted from the rapidity and extent of her rearmament. He hoped that the arguments used in the despatch would be borne in mind 'should any new attempt be made by Mr. Norman [Governor of the Bank of England], and those who share his views, to prove that Dr. Schacht is a harmless person and that Germany ought to be assisted in her difficulties'.

Mr. Ashton-Gwatkin did not think that 'Mr. M. Norman is so anxious to assist the present German Govt.' He thought that Germany's 'economic weakness is such, that I cannot believe her military experts would counsel war; or that the German Govt. would go to war, unless they were quite desperate'. Mr. Sargent thought the despatch 'of extreme value in present circumstances', but agreed with Mr. Wigram's comment that its circulation beyond the Cabinet should be limited in view of the 'great disadvantage' to 'Sir E. Phipps' position' of any leakage. Sir R. Vansittart remarked on November 13: 'I hope we shall not be bluffed, by this talk of explosions in Germany, into any assistance without adequate return—for if we lend ourselves to that we shall never get any return at all . . .' Mr. Eden commented on this: 'I agree, most emphatically. A. E.'

Mr. Eden added the following minute. 'An admirable despatch for which we should certainly thank warmly. It is becoming increasingly clear that we shall have one more chance, perhaps a final one of coming to terms with Germany. If we are to have any chance of success, she must be given *nothing* except she change her political ways. To ease Germany's economic difficulties without political return is merely to facilitate her rearmament, & make it easier for her to carry on her politico-economic policies in Central & South Eastern Europe. In this connexion the complaints of Yugo-Slavia's trade representative now in this country are most important. Germany may be poor, but she can still buy foodstuffs from Jugo-Slavia at enhanced prices in order to obtain in return that greater share of Jugo-Slavia's trade she needs for political purposes . . . A. E. Nov. 16.'

No. 351

Letter[1] from M. Maisky to Lord Plymouth
[W 15575/9549/41]

Secret   SOVIET EMBASSY, *November 4, 1936*

Sir,

I beg to acknowledge receipt of Mr. Hemming's letter of the 23rd October.

The letter under reference was accompanied by a memorandum from the Foreign Office containing information alleging violations of the Non-Intervention Agreement by the U.S.S.R.[2]

This information has been submitted for investigation to the appropriate authorities in the U.S.S.R., and as a result I have the honour to state the following:

1. The Spanish tanker *Campechio* took on in Batum a cargo of oil products; no arms or munitions or any other goods covered by the embargo were loaded on the *Campechio* in the U.S.S.R.

2. The Soviet steamer *Stari Bolshevik* took from the U.S.S.R. to Spain a cargo of lorries, spare parts and tyres. No goods of a military nature, and more particularly none of those contained in point 2 of the Foreign Office memorandum, were among her cargo.

3. The Soviet steamer *Chrushchev* carried from the U.S.S.R. to Spain, a cargo of foodstuffs (sugar and lentils), lorries, spare parts and tyres.

In view of the above I reject most definitely the allegations contained in the Foreign Office Memorandum regarding the three ships mentioned above as absolutely unfounded.

Accept, Sir, the expression of my high consideration and esteem.

J. MAISKY

[1] This letter was addressed to Lord Plymouth as Chairman of the N.I. Committee and circulated to the Committee as document N.I.S.(36)131.

[2] Cf. No. 328.

No. 352

Minute[1] by Mr. Eden
[R 6646/226/22]

FOREIGN OFFICE, *November 5, 1936*

Does anybody in the Foreign Office really believe that Italy's foreign policy will at any time be other than opportunist? Any agreement with Italy

[1] These reflections were engendered by a memorandum of November 2 by Mr. Sargent, who noted that it should be read 'in the light of Rome telegrams 660 and 662' (Nos. 312 and 314). He remarked that for some time it had become 'increasingly evident that it is dangerous to leave Anglo-Italian relations any longer in their present unsatisfactory state'. As regarded the form of an agreement there seemed to be two alternatives: either a multi-lateral Mediterranean Pact, or a direct Anglo-Italian arrangement. The former 'would be

will be kept as long as it suits Italy. Surely nobody can now place any faith in her promises. All this is not argument against seeking to improve Anglo-Italian relations, but against placing an exaggerated valuation on any such improvement if and when we get it. The Chiefs of Staff speak naively about not having to develop Cyprus as a base if we improve relations with Italy, without apparently realising that if relations are improved it will be because that suits Italy for the moment, and that no amount of promises or understandings or renewed professions of friendships, or even humble crawlings on our part will affect Mussolini's course. On the other hand a little plain speaking may. We must be on our guard against increasing the dictator's prestige by our own excessive submissiveness.

We have said we mean to revive the League. If we intend that then all these policies should be looked at from that point of view. I should prefer the dep[artmen]t to consider action we can take to effect this.

In any event I have said my say in the House of Commons[2] and we will have no more approaches to Italy, official or unofficial, until we know, and have studied, Italy's reaction to my speech.

A. E.

unduly cumbrous, and even so might not itself be effective in improving Anglo-Italian relations'. He preferred the second. 'If there is goodwill some sort of agreement ought to emerge: if the goodwill is lacking we will find this out quietly and without attracting all the publicity which multilateral negotiations would necessarily involve.' The approach should, at least in the first instance, take the form of more or less unofficial soundings.

   [2] See No. 353, note 2 below.

No. 353

Record by Sir R. Vansittart of a conversation with Signor Grandi
[*R 6602/226/22*]

FOREIGN OFFICE, November 6, 1936

The Italian Ambassador came to see me this morning, and I told him of the step that we were about to take in withdrawing the Legation Guard at Addis Ababa.[1] I said that this, taken together with the friendly utterances of the Secretary of State in the House of Commons[2] and of Lord Halifax

   [1] See Volume XVI, No. 486, note 2.
   [2] In the course of a general survey of foreign policy in the Debate on the Address in the House of Commons on November 5, Mr. Eden said that there 'never has been, so far as concerns this country, an Anglo-Italian quarrel . . . The differences that have existed between us and Italy have been due to our differing—I regret to note, still differing—conceptions of the methods by which the world should order its international affairs.' He referred to Signor Mussolini's statement at Milan on November 1 (see No. 345, note 9) that the Mediterranean was for Great Britain only a route or short cut to her outlying territories. 'It will be as well that I should say at once that the implication that freedom to come and go in the Mediterranean is for this country a convenience rather than a vital interest is one which does not fully describe our interests. For us the Mediterranean is not a short cut but a main arterial road . . . Consequently we take note of, and welcome, the

in the House of Lords,[3] must be taken as a considerable advance on our part to the improvement of Anglo-Italian relations which had left so much to be desired of late and with so singularly little cause. I said that I should personally have expected that when sanctions were lifted in the summer there would have been an improvement and a cordial Italian response in the shape of a desire to let bygones be bygones, and to return as speedily as might be in an imperfect world to the old friendly basis of Anglo-Italian relations. Nothing of the sort had, however, happened, and a critical and carping note had almost immediately been manifest in the Italian Press, which had increased in vehemence until within the last few days we had actually found Dr. Gayda threatening us explicitly with war.[4] These, I said, were hot and high words and, addressed from one great nation to another, particularly when the Press in question was strictly controlled and inspired by its Government, were dangerous and provocative stuff. It would have been easy for us to have asked Signor Grandi to call and to have requested an explanation of what was meant by these heated and childish outbursts. We might anyhow have asked him if there were any Italians left with a sense of humour when Dr. Gayda reproached us with our warlike preparations and forgot to mention Signor Mussolini's own speech about 8,000,000 bayonets some of which had actually been blooded. But we had done none of these things. We had treated Dr. Gayda with the humour he deserved but did not possess, and then twenty-four hours later we had made two distinct but related gestures of friendliness towards Italy. I earnestly hoped the Italian Government would reciprocate this friendliness with the cordiality it deserved, and that in any case the Italian Government would not make again the same mistake that it had made in the summer of treating every measure that would alleviate grievances as merely a starting point for a lot more.

The Italian Ambassador said that he had shared this hope, and would do his best to promote it, but he was evidently very despondent and begged me

assurance that Signor Mussolini gives that Italy does not mean to threaten this route nor propose to interrupt it. Nor do we. Our position is the same . . . In these conditions it should, in our view, be possible for each country to continue to maintain its vital interests in the Mediterranean, not only without conflict . . . but even with mutual advantage' (317 *H.C. Deb. 5 s.*, cols. 282–3).

[3] Lord Halifax had spoken on Anglo-Italian relations in the House of Lords on November 3 in the debate on the Address. He said: 'So far as we are concerned, I see no reason why it should not be possible easily to reach complete understanding where misunderstanding has, in some quarters, existed . . . Although Italy and this country have great interests in the Mediterranean, it is in my view quite unprofitable to argue which of these interests are more important because, quite evidently, that is a subject on which argument might be indefinite; but the past history of those nations has shown these interests to be not divergent but complementary, and I venture to assert that the greatest of all these interests for both countries is that of peace' (103 *H.L. Deb. 5 s.*, col. 28).

[4] In Rome telegram No. 675 of November 3, Sir E. Drummond reported an article in *Giornale d'Italia* in which Dr. Gayda stated that 'England is clearly pursuing an anti-Italian policy': Italy's relations with England were 'dominated by dilemma of either a frank peace or an inevitable war in the Mediterranean'.

that this action might be duplicated at Rome, where it might possibly have some effect. I have never seen the Ambassador so cast-down or spiritless. He was evidently labouring under the stress of extreme anxiety. He found great difficulty in expressing himself, and repeated, as he had done on a previous occasion, that anything that he said was not to be quoted, for he had instructions to do nothing, and he could indeed do nothing but stand by and see Anglo-Italian relations deteriorate to the profit of Germany in a manner that filled him with gloom and nearly with despair. He accepted the gestures, which I had described, with friendliness and a sincere hope that they might be taken in Rome as the beginning of better days, but he had evidently no confidence in that or in the future of his country's foreign policy. It is clear that the Italian Ambassador thinks that the approach between Rome and Berlin has been practically, if not quite, completed, and although he evidently thinks at the same time that there is still room for some sensible endeavour on both our sides to redress the balance of his country's relations, he has no great confidence. On the contrary although, and perhaps because, the policy of his official lifetime has been built on intimate collaboration between Italy and England, it was clear to me that he considered his country engaged upon a course that would culminate in Anglo-Italian hostility to the profit of a third and ill-intentioned party. On all these points the Ambassador was not so explicit as I have here set down. Indeed as I have already indicated he was at times not very articulate, but the gist of his halting and embarrassed utterances made his real opinion quite clear. As at my last interview with him he repeated again and again: 'Lose no more time, no more time,' and having said so, he invariably hastily repeated that his instructions were to do nothing here. He did, however, say, and say very clearly, that he hoped that we should not endeavour to redress Anglo-Italian relations by too piece-meal methods. He pressed me strongly in the matter of reducing the Legations to Consulates, and said that he was of course well aware that we were already considering this, but had found the French a stumblingblock. (He did not say from what source he had obtained this information, which would be on the face of it unlikely to emanate from the Quai d'Orsay). He hoped that the withdrawal of the Guard might be speedily followed by the reduction of the Legation, and he said that on this point he was continually being pressed. He also made it quite clear that in his view Anglo-Italian relations would not resume their normal course until we had recognised the Italian conquest of Abyssinia, though he said that one great advantage of reducing the Legations to Consulates would be that the step might be interpreted in some Italian quarters as being a sort of indirect recognition (he said that of course it would not constitute a real recognition) and in this light it would be very useful as a temporary measure for giving satisfaction without commitment.

I spent a considerable time in endeavouring to revive the Ambassador's drooping spirits and to galvanise him into helpful action at Rome, but he gave me more and more the impression that he could make little contribution in this direction, and that any assurances and explanations from him would be suspect in Rome, and that if we had anything helpful to say on these topics, we should do well to say it ourselves and directly. Incidentally he asked me again for the third or fourth time, and again stressing the urgency of losing no more time, whether it would not be possible for me to find some occasion to spend a day or two in Rome and to explain personally to Mussolini the real state of mind in this country and the total absence of any desire for revenge. He felt strongly that the personal touch was what was indispensably needed with Mussolini and was all too clear that he did not feel able to apply that touch himself.[5]

R. V.

[5] In an undated note on this record Mr. Eden commented: 'I am told that Grandi shows no signs of "drooping spirits" at the non-intervention cttee. I sometimes wonder whether he is not merely a very good Ambassador, first class at raising his country's value? A. E.' Sir R. Vansittart replied: 'I don't think he has any cause to show signs of drooping spirits at the non-intervention Committee. He & Bismarck have worked together so closely that they are more than fulfilling the purpose of their governments; and between them they are so much too good for Maisky & his Govt—who have played their cards incredibly badly—that the non-intervention Committee is in Grandi's eyes a great success for Grandi—and Italy. R. V. Nov. 9.'

No. 354

Mr. Eden to Mr. Lloyd Thomas (Paris)

No. 1877 [*W 15281/62/41*]

FOREIGN OFFICE, *November 6, 1936*

Sir,

During the course of a conversation today with the French Ambassador, His Excellency spoke of the situation in Spain. He had seen M. Delbos, who was much pre-occupied that in our proposed declaration we intended to describe as a 'provisional Government' General Franco's administration after their occupation of Madrid.[1] I replied that I could give His Excellency some comfort on that score, since on further reflection I did not now intend to issue any proclamation, but simply to allow Mr. Ogilvie-Forbes to remain in Madrid where he would have such contacts with General Franco's administration as was necessary for practical purposes. If I had to make any explanation of Mr. Ogilvie-Forbes' position I would do so in a statement in the House of Commons. M. Corbin expressed himself as greatly relieved at this.

2. I then asked him to urge the French Government to reconsider their decision to leave only a Consul in Madrid. But M. Corbin replied that he was sure the French Government could not modify the view they had taken. He was inclined to belittle my comments on the risk of General Franco falling further into the hands of German and Italian advisers if he were completely tabooed by us even after he reached Madrid. According to the

[1] Cf. No. 344.

French Government's information, M. Corbin said, the Germans were already making themselves extremely unpopular in Spain, and at the present rate General Franco's own adherents would shortly be fighting their advisers.

3. Finally the Ambassador said that the position that would arise if the Spanish Government retired to Catalonia had been causing the French Government considerable anxiety. He thought that they would probably keep some sort of diplomatic contact with whatever survived of the present Spanish Government. I asked the Ambassador whether this meant that they intended to recognise Catalonia's independence. I hoped not. The Ambassador assured me that there was no intention of doing this, but intimated that with a confused situation in the Basque provinces as well as in Catalonia and Malaga the French Government would be very chary of giving General Franco any kind of recognition and would wish to keep some diplomatic contact with the Spanish Government, whether it took refuge in Valencia, Alicante or Barcelona.

I am, &c.,
ANTHONY EDEN

No. 355

Mr. Eden to Sir E. Drummond (Rome)

No. 1221 [W 15086/9549/41]

FOREIGN OFFICE, *November 6, 1936*

Sir,

I have to inform Your Excellency that Sir Robert Vansittart asked the Italian Ambassador to come and see him on the 24th October, and drew his attention to the activities of Signor Rossi in Majorca.[1]

2. Sir Robert said that he was well aware that the Italian Government would describe Signor Rossi as a volunteer. None the less he was an Italian subject, and no Italian subject would dare to indulge in the activities displayed by Signor Rossi in Majorca against the wishes of his Government, or indeed without their implied authority. Some time ago, Signor Rossi had taken part in a local banquet, and had made such an inflammatory and anti-British speech that it had resulted in something like an anti-British demonstration afterwards. His Majesty's Government would have been quite inclined at the time to protest to the Italian Government, but with marked restraint, they had contented themselves with just a sufficient mention of Signor Rossi's name to the Italian Government to show that they were not unaware of his activities. Now, however, Signor Rossi had added fuel to the fire. He had made another speech on the 17th October, saying that

---

[1] Cf. No. 266. An Admiralty telegram of October 23 (received 3.59 p.m.) from Palma referred to 'persistent infiltration of Italians increasing proportion of whom are officers' and said that in view of a speech by Signor Rossi reported on October 22, the vice-consul (Lt. Comm. A. Hillgarth) 'now considers possibility exists of attempted coup' (W 15289/9549/41).

the Italians were in Majorca for ever, that it belonged to them, no matter what happened in Spain, and that they would never be ejected. This was an outrageous performance, and in flagrant conflict with the assurances officially given to His Majesty's Government by the Italian Government on the subject of the Balearic Islands. Sir Robert feared that if the utterances of this irresponsible young man were to become known in this country (he could be classed as irresponsible, though it was difficult to believe that he was wholly discountenanced), there would certainly be some very adverse criticism which might even throw unjustifiable doubt on the value of the Italian assurances. His Majesty's Government had no such doubts, and it would be unfortunate if the continued presence of the youthful and over-eloquent Rossi in the Balearic Islands were to lend illegitimate colour to doubts. It was hoped therefore that the Italian Government would take early steps to see that this youthful volunteer returned to his native land, and that meanwhile he would take no further part in banquets, and would refrain from all red wine before he rose to his feet.

3. Sir Robert added that apart from this His Majesty's Government had information of the continued infiltration of Italian officers into the Balearic Islands. He expressed the hope that this also would be stopped. Even from the Italian point of view those islands were now safe from invasion by the forces of the Madrid Government, and there should be no further motive for the presence of this large additional personnel. Where no motive could be found, suspicions would always arise.

4. The Italian Ambassador took all this in good part, and said he would do what he could with his Government in the sense requested.

I am, etc.,
(For the Secretary of State)
D. F. HOWARD

No. 356

Mr. Eden to Sir E. Drummond (Rome)
No. 1225 [R 6580/226/22]

FOREIGN OFFICE, *November 6, 1936*

Sir,

The Italian Ambassador asked to see me this evening when we had a long conversation on Anglo-Italian relations. Signor Grandi had received no actual communication from Rome on the subject of my speech of yesterday,[1] but he clearly considered that his Government would be disappointed. They had hoped for something more, and Signor Grandi was urgent that the Italian conquest of Abyssinia should be recognised without delay. He

---

[1] See No. 353, note 2.

feared that it would seem to Signor Mussolini that Italy had made an advance and received a rebuff. He hoped his fears were unjustified, but he had asked to see me in order, if possible to send a message to Rome which would help to bring about the objective he desired so much.

2. I replied that I really did not think that His Excellency's description of Signor Mussolini's speech at Milan[2] could bear the interpretation that he had put upon it. If it were possible for a man from Mars to come to this earth and compare the texts of our two speeches I was convinced that he would not decide that Signor Mussolini's was the more forthcoming. The Ambassador knew England, and I asked him whether it was not true that nine out of ten English readers of Signor Mussolini's speech would not have regarded it as the gesture towards better relations with this country which I had shown by my speech in the House that I had accepted it as being. I asked the Ambassador to accept that my statement which had been carefully considered by the Government was definitely intended as an attempt to bring about a rapprochement between our two countries. We should like to let bygones be bygones. My assurances in respect of the Mediterranean were quite specific and it was hard to imagine what more we could be expected to say. After all if His Excellency would review the events of the past year he would realise that in effect Italy had succeeded against the League. There was no attempt to deny that. Our efforts as a member of the League had been in vain. In spite of all this there was no kind of rancour on our part, still less any thought of revenge. I hoped, however, we should not be asked now to recognise the conquest of the victim of aggression we had failed to protect as a price of improved relations with Italy. I was sure that this was the wrong way to go about it. If it were possible for the Italian Government to accept my declaration in the spirit in which it had been intended and in the spirit, I reminded the Ambassador, in which all sections of the French press, even the Right, and the German press had accepted it, then matters would be much easier for us to arrange in the future. If, however, Rome expressed dissatisfaction, then the task of improving relations would become more difficult, which was certainly the last thing we in this country desired.

3. The Ambassador stated that he fully appreciated these points, and he also acknowledged that the statement about Italy truly represented our national point of view. Unfortunately until there was recognition the Italian Government would be persuaded that we were harbouring some thought of revenge and intended to take some action in Africa in our Imperial interests against Italy. I replied that this was surely a very difficult reasoning to accept, since if we had any sinister motives, which we had not, our best method would certainly be to recognise, and then wait for our opportunity to take action. If we indeed cherished motives such as these the mere act of recognition could hardly be expected to check us. The Ambassador admitted the force of this, and said that he was grateful for our talk which would assist him in trying to put the position before his Government in the

[2] See No. 345, note 9.

most favourable light. He added that he wished that we could bargain over the matter of recognition. This might be the best method of settlement.

I am, &c.,

ANTHONY EDEN

No. 357

Mr. Ogilvie-Forbes (Madrid) to Mr. Eden
(Received November 7, 1 a.m.)

No. 460 Telegraphic: by wireless [W 15243/62/41]

Immediate   MADRID, *November 7, 1936*

My telegram No. 458.[1]

Minister of State visited me this evening[2] and said that he had come in compliance with promise made to you to [? inform] me beforehand when danger was imminent. He said that moment had now arrived and that Spanish Government would leave tomorrow morning for Valencia. A military Government would be established in Madrid to carry on the struggle. He spoke with emotion and was not able to give me any further information. I thanked him for his visit and expressed sincere hope that our pleasant personal relationship would one day be resumed.

Commander-in-Chief Mediterranean informed. Please inform His Majesty's Ambassador.[3]

[1] In this telegram of November 6 Mr. Ogilvie-Forbes reported on the progress of the rebel attack, and said that a determined effort had been made to remove the Embassy guard. 'I had to speak very firmly to the Minister of State in order to obtain reversal of this order which I understand is being carried out at all Embassies except United States and ourselves.'

[2] i.e. November 6.

[3] In a minute of November 9 Mr. Maclean noted that Señor del Vayo 'did not indicate that Mr. Forbes was expected to go to Valencia with the Govt.'

No. 358

Sir E. Drummond (Rome) to Mr. Eden
(Received November 7, 9.30 a.m.)

No. 681 Telegraphic [R 6585/226/22]

ROME, *November 7, 1936, 3.15 a.m.*

Having dealt with question of Legation Guard[1] I said to Count Ciano this evening that I hoped this action on the part of His Majesty's Government, coupled with statements made by yourself[2] and Lord Halifax[3] both in friendly reply to Signor Mussolini's recent speech,[4] would be regarded by

[1] See No. 378, note 8 below; cf. Volume XVI, No. 486, note 2.
[2] See No. 353, note 2.   [3] See *ibid.*, note 3.
[4] See No. 345, note 9.

Italian Government and the Press as a great step forward on the path of conciliation. If they were not so received I feared that the result would be to delay the process of restoration of relations on to old footing between our two countries for which His Majesty's Government and I personally, as he knew, were sincerely anxious. I recalled that he had welcomed assurances I had brought back from London on returning from leave although he had said he could not make public use of them;[5] now friendly statements had been made by the two Ministers in both Houses and Lord Halifax's statement showed that earliest possible opportunity had been taken by His Majesty's Government to reply to Milan speech.

2. After asking whether he might speak very frankly, which I said I hoped he would always do, His Excellency stated that while he had greatly appreciated Lord Halifax's statement he was not quite so happy about your own. He then referred to the final sentence of your statement into which, in the version published in Italian newspapers, a conditional has crept making it appear that you said 'if it were possible for the two nations to maintain their own vital interests in the Mediterranean not only without conflict but with reciprocal advantage'. He said always basing himself on Italian text that he wished speech could have constituted something more than an [? intention] and could have contained a wish. (Since my interview I have been glad to receive telegram containing actual text of your speech and have sent this text urgently to the Minister by hand to his Private Secretary with a personal letter pointing out that it should completely remove apprehensions he expressed.) As however exact text was not available at my interview I replied that I knew that your intentions in this speech were as conciliatory as possible. His Excellency must remember that though certain passages in Mussolini's speech were highly unpalatable to British public opinion, viz., those regarding future of the League and ridiculing the idea of collective security—here Count Ciano interjected that speech was very friendly to us—yet these passages had not been taken up either by yourself or Lord Halifax.

3. On His Excellency referring to the first part of your statement I rejoined that it was really most unfair that Italy should continue to accuse Great Britain for action which she had felt bound to take in accordance with her obligations under the Covenant. Indeed, Mussolini himself had once told me that he understood our point of view though he did not agree with it. Count Ciano then referred to our sending the Home Fleet into the Mediterranean[6]—an action unfriendly in itself and taken outside the framework of the Covenant; I replied, as I have replied before, that in view of the threats which had appeared in the Italian Press no British statesman could have taken any other action; and indeed when I had once asked Signor Mussolini if this would not have been his policy if he had been in our shoes he had nodded assent.

4. After this interchange we decided to leave the past and to concentrate on the future. I once more expressed sincere hope that he would do his

[5] Cf. No. 271. [6] i.e. in August, 1935: see Volume XIV, No. 501, note 3.

utmost to assure a warm welcome for the two speeches and for our action in withdrawing Legation Guard. This, I felt, was the first and necessary step to re-establish cordial relations. The Minister stated that he too was most anxious to attain this end and that he would at once see Head of Government and endeavour to persuade him to take the line I had indicated. He was grateful for the explanations I had given.

No. 359

Mr. Eden to Mr. Ogilvie-Forbes (Madrid)
No. 249 Telegraphic [W 15243/62/41]

Important FOREIGN OFFICE, *November 7, 1936, 7 p.m.*

Your telegram No. 460.[1]

His Majesty's Government feel that the moment is approaching when with a view to the proper protection of British interests in the territories under the control of the insurgents, closer contact is required between themselves and the Council of National Defence, than is possible under arrangements by which His Majesty's Ambassador at Hendaye is not in direct communication with General Franco.

2. You are accordingly authorised upon the entry into Madrid of the insurgent forces, to establish such *de facto* contacts with General Franco's administration as are practically necessary for the protection of British interests. There is, of course, no question at the present stage of recognising that government as the legal government of Spain.

3. I note from your telegram that Minister of State did not suggest that you should follow him to Valencia. If the Government of President Azaña should enquire whether His Majesty's Government intend to transfer His Majesty's Embassy from Madrid, you may inform them that you are remaining at Madrid to ensure the continued protection of British interests there. We are considering what arrangements may have to be made for maintaining contact with the Spanish Government at Valencia. In the meanwhile the presence of Señor de Azcárate in London ensures the maintenance of an alternative channel of communication with his Government.

Repeated to His Majesty's Ambassador, Hendaye, and His Majesty's Consul, Valencia.[2]

[1] No. 357.   [2] Mr. W. J. Sullivan.

No. 360

Sir C. Wingfield (Lisbon) to Mr. Eden
(Received November 7, 10.20 p.m.)
No. 221 Telegraphic [W 15306/62/41]

Important   LISBON, *November 7, 1936, 8.50 p.m.*

Portuguese Prime Minister[1] told me this afternoon that insurgents were already in Madrid. After the fall of that city it would be difficult to withhold recognition much longer, particularly for the Portuguese whose whole frontier ran along the territory occupied by them.

Secretary-General of Ministry of Foreign Affairs[2] has since explained that Portugal will act independently, not in agreement with any groups of Powers, unless all agree to act together at once. But Portuguese Government desire His Majesty's Government should be notified that Portugal may feel obliged to act at any moment.

I understand that insurgents [? will be] recognized as *de jure* government of Spain not merely as belligerents.

[1] Dr. Salazar, who also became Minister for Foreign Affairs on November 6, following the illness of Dr. Monteiro.
[2] Senhor Teixeira de Sampaio.

No. 361

Report[1] by the Chiefs of Staff Sub-Committee on German and Italian objections to a guarantee of the United Kingdom
[C 8049/4/18]

2 WHITEHALL GARDENS, S.W.1, *November 9, 1936*

In our Report[2] on the preparations for the proposed Five-Power Conference we expressed the view that, from the military point of view, we had, on balance, something definite to gain from receiving guarantees from France against Germany, and from Germany against France, in any new Agreement; and we therefore recommended that every endeavour should be made to obtain such guarantees.

2. The Secretary of State for Foreign Affairs had now asked the Committee of Imperial Defence[3] to consider this question in the light of the objections made by Germany and Italy to a guarantee to the United Kingdom, and to advise 'whether the military value of such a guarantee is sufficient to render it desirable that we should make the receipt by ourselves of such a guarantee a *sine qua non* in the negotiation of a new Five-Power Pact, or whether we should be prepared, if necessary, to withdraw our demand for a guarantee in order to facilitate the conclusion of a Five-Power Pact.'

[1] Circulated as C.O.S. 522.   [2] No. 156.
[3] In a letter of October 21 from Mr. Sargent (C 7387/4/18).

3. As the result of a careful re-examination of the problem, we see no military reason to modify the opinion quoted in paragraph 1 above.

4. On the other hand, as we have frequently emphasised in the recent past, we consider it vitally important at the present juncture that we should leave no stone unturned to lessen the chances of our being involved in war, at least until such time as our defensive preparations are much further advanced than we can expect them to be for some years. If, therefore, it is the view of the Foreign Office that a Five-Power Pact is likely to make a substantial contribution to the cause of peace, we ought to make any reasonable concession that will facilitate its conclusion.

5. There is another point. We have on more than one occasion invited attention to the importance, from a military point of view, of a resumption of our former friendly relations with Italy. It will be seen from Sir Eric Drummond's telegram[4] of the 19th October, that Italy is the nation that has the strongest objection to our receiving any guarantees. We feel that, apart from the much wider considerations indicated in the preceding paragraph, it would be a mistake to cling to yet another bone of contention with Italy for the sake of the advantage that we might hope to derive from such guarantees.

6. We therefore consider that in view of the considerations in paragraphs 4 and 5 above, it would be wiser, if necessary, to forgo the advantage that is to be gained by receiving guarantees from France and Germany.[5]

ERNLE CHATFIELD
E. L. ELLINGTON
C. J. DEVERELL

[4] See No. 301, note 1.

[5] Mr. Wigram was evidently dissatisfied with this report. Referring to paragraph 4 he confessed that he found it 'a little difficult to see how the Five-Power Pact is going to make that "substantial contribution" as against the present position'. With regard to paragraph 5 he thought 'that we are getting deeper and deeper into the realm of unreality if we are going to believe that the receipt for us of a guarantee from France against Germany (and, for what it is worth, a guarantee from Germany against France) can, with any justice whatsoever, be described as "another bone of contention with Italy" . . . R. F. Wigram. 9/11.'

No. 362

Mr. Eden to Sir H. Kennard (Warsaw)
No. 363 [C 8013/33/55]

FOREIGN OFFICE, *November 9, 1936*

Sir,

The Polish Minister for Foreign Affairs called on me this morning,[1] when we spoke of the situation in Danzig.[2] Colonel Beck did not disguise the

[1] M. Beck was in London from November 8–12: cf. No. 144.

[2] Since the League Council meeting on October 5 (see No. 242, note 2) a rigorous programme of political repression had been pursued by the Nazi Government in Danzig: the Social Democratic Party was dissolved on October 14 and a number of its members arrested,

fact that the situation which had confronted him on his return to Warsaw had caused him considerable preoccupation. He had begun even to ask himself whether the dynamic energy of the Nazi State was to be felt with really serious consequences in the Free City of Danzig. Colonel Beck then described to me the exchanges which he had had with the German Government and with the Senate of Danzig. He stated that he had received the most categoric assurances from the German Government that they had no intention either to create an international issue out of the Danzig situation or to seek to challenge the connexion of the League with Danzig. Within the last forty-eight hours M. Beck added he had had further assurances to the same effect. There remained, however, the difficult local position, and in this respect he had thought it necessary to react somewhat violently against the Nazi policy of *fait accompli*. He had made it clear to the Senate that the Polish Government were not prepared to contemplate a situation where changes were effected by violence.

2. At a later stage in the conversation, M. Beck, in summing up the situation, stated that he thought in certain respects it might be argued that the Constitution was not very satisfactory. At least it did not take account of what was the present-day state of affairs in a large part of Eastern Europe. On the other hand, he admitted that it was quite impossible for the League to be associated with a condition of affairs where those who disagreed with the Government of the day were subjected to violent treatment. What he thought was required was a state of things under the ægis of the League, in which those who had opposition views should be allowed, if not to make those views prevail, at least to hold them without unpleasant physical consequences.

3. M. Beck divided the Danzig problem into three sections. The first concerned the general position of the League in Danzig and the recognition of its connexion with the Free City. In so far as this was concerned, he was fully satisfied with the assurances of the German Government. The second concerned Polish right both in respect of transit and of Polish commercial rights in the city. In respect of this also M. Beck was convinced that a satisfactory solution could be found. The third and the most difficult problem was the Constitution. The Nazis had not a two-thirds majority in the Free City, and he was doubtful if they could get it. He estimated their strength at about 60 per cent. On the other hand, the Constitution made revision impossible unless a two-thirds majority desired it. Here then was the *impasse*. He had been considering whether there were any concessions of procedure that could be made to the Danzig Senate without infringing the Constitution, in return for which the Senate should be compelled to under-

and other opposition parties threatened with the same fate. Herr Greiser, President of the Danzig Senate, and Herr Forster, Nazi *Gauleiter* for Danzig, led the campaign for the rejection of all interference in Danzig affairs, from either the League or the Polish Government. Alarm was expressed in the Foreign Office at this direction of events and on October 20 Mr. Eden had asked the Polish Ambassador to urge his government to treat the problem seriously and carry out the mandate entrusted to them by the League.

take to modify their attitude towards the League. In the last resort much depended on how firm an attitude the League was prepared to take towards the Free City.

4. Herr Greiser was at present away undergoing a cure. His illness was real and not diplomatic. M. Beck indicated that he had some hopes and indeed some reason for believing that Herr Greiser might soon have a successor, and possibly Herr Forster also. In any event he proposed himself to ask the President of the Danzig Senate to come and see him in Warsaw. These conversations will begin about the 15th November. At the outset M. Beck would make it plain to the President of the Senate that if the Council had so far shown a certain tolerance in its attitude to the Free City this must not be misunderstood. If the Senate were prepared to co-operate with the League, to accept the Statute and to acknowledge the Constitution subject to some small amendments in procedure which might be agreed upon, then well and good. If not, then a position of the greatest gravity affecting the whole of Eastern Europe would be created. M. Beck hoped that as an outcome of this interview he would be in a better position to judge what were the chances of his conversation having a fruitful outcome. There was no doubt that the sharp tone in which the Danzig Senate had been spoken to by the Polish Commissioner-General had had a salutary effect and had even come as something of a shock. M. Beck mentioned that he was going to replace M. Papée by a stronger man. He had nothing against his Commissioner, but after five years in as exacting a post as Danzig he deserved a rest. M. Beck said that he was putting in his place the best man he could find.

5. Speaking of the general situation, I told M. Beck that my attitude, and I thought that of the other members of the Committee of Three, was as follows: We had no desire to make of Danzig a great international question if this could be avoided. That was why we had not called a meeting of the Committee of Three, because we did not wish to complicate the Polish Government's negotiations. At the same time it was really impossible for us, as members of the Council, to countenance a state of affairs in Danzig where members of the Opposition were subjected to violent treatment. What seemed to me so intolerable in the present situation was not only the fact of the situation in Danzig, but also the whole attitude of the Danzig Senate towards the League. Not only the matter but the manner were thoroughly unsatisfactory. M. Beck agreed with this and remarked that a grave weakness in the League's position in Danzig was that when the Constitution had been drawn up no provision had been made for the necessary authority to enforce it. It was quite true that Polish troops were available in the last resort, but this obviously referred to some grave crisis and not to the ordinary day to day administration of the City. If there had been an international force as there was in the Saar the position would have been very different, but the League had no force in Danzig to give effect to its decisions.

6. So far as I was concerned as *rapporteur*, I continued, M. Beck could count upon me to give him all possible support. I had not sought to intervene either at Berlin or elsewhere, because I did not want to handicap him in his

efforts. At the same time, if he wished to make it clear to the representative of Danzig, whom he was to see at Warsaw next week, that the *rapporteur* was watching this position closely and was not prepared to accept an arrangement seriously detrimental to the authority of the League, then he was certainly at liberty to do so.

7. M. Beck replied that he fully understood the position. Great though the difficulties were, he was going to persist at his attempt at negotiations. If he succeeded he would report the result of his efforts to the Committee of Three, and it would be for us to say whether we could accept them or not. If he failed he would likewise come to us and we could discuss what action was to be taken. In the meanwhile he thought it was desirable to go on with consideration of the appointment of a new High Commissioner. The Polish Government were ready to accept some neutral for this post, and the assurances he had received from Berlin showed that the German Government were in a like position. In the circumstances, he thought that it would have a reassuring effect if, in any statement that was made about M. Beck's visit to London, it could be indicated that we had discussed the Danzig question, and that we were already consulting about the name of a new High Commissioner to take Mr. Lester's place. M. Beck added that the mere fact of his coming to London had had a salutary effect in Germany. He had given it out in Warsaw that Danzig would be one of the matters we should discuss.

I am, &c.,

ANTHONY EDEN

No. 363

Sir E. Drummond (Rome) to Mr. Eden
(Received November 10, 9.30 a.m.)
No. 685 Telegraphic [*R 6679/226/22*]

ROME, *November 10, 1936, 12.35* [*a.*]*m.*

Your telegrams Nos. 415[1] and 416.[2]

I feel it would be a mistake for me to say anything more to the Foreign Minister at present. In any case he is, as you know, away from Rome for some days. Withdrawal of Legation guard, signing of commercial arrangements and speeches of Lord Halifax and yourself have all had a considerable effect and I am inclined to believe the first stage of a rapprochement is well under way. Many of my colleagues are astonished and generally happy at evident desire of Italian authorities to welcome these three factors as evidence of a renewal of friendly relations. I think therefore that it would be wiser to lie low for a little on general questions though I intend to take up the

---

[1] This telegram of November 7 is not preserved in the Foreign Office archives: it summarized No. 356.

[2] Of November 7, not printed: it instructed Sir E. Drummond to speak to Count Ciano on the lines of No. 353.

attitude of certain Italian press correspondents in London. (See my letter to Sir R. Vansittart of November 7th).[3] If within ten days or a fortnight we can announce reduction of legation to a consulate-general the effect will certainly be excellent; though I feel bound to add that in many Italian and even diplomatic circles here it will be regarded in the sense of a *de facto* recognition of annexation. I trust, however, that we shall not allow this consideration to stand in our way. See in this connexion Mr. Ingram's telegram No. 521 of July 30th.[4]

As to the Mediterranean Signor Mussolini and Count Ciano are both openly speaking of a 'Gentleman's Agreement' as opposed to any formal Pact. I do not yet know what is really in their minds as to the substance of such an agreement but I am still inclined to think it may be a recorded exchange of views or declarations about our respective policies on recent German-Italian model. I have a suspicion that what Count Ciano is aiming at is a visit to London where such an exchange could take place. This would be in accordance with his character and Signor Mussolini is anxious at present to push him forward as much as possible. The point is worth bearing in mind though I appreciate that such a visit is unlikely to be a practical proposition in existing circumstances.

I have not used the argument about Italian ingratitude at the raising of sanctions here because any reference to the latter rouses great resentment and recalls the past controversies.

You will by now have received my despatch No. 1199[5] giving full account of what I have been able to learn of results of Count Ciano's visit to Berlin. It is, I fear, clear that entente established between Berlin and Rome is close but Signor Mussolini and Count Ciano are still telling everyone, not only British listeners that what they really desire is friendship with us and I believe that their assertions are genuine. Signor Mussolini apparently still has in mind some four Power agreement or perhaps with Poland five in which we shall exercise pressure on France and he on Germany to be reasonable; and execution of any such plan presupposes close contact between Rome and London.

[3] Not traced in the Foreign Office archives.

[4] In this telegram Mr. Ingram reported a conversation in which Count Ciano urged unofficially the advantages for the British Government of reducing the Legation in Addis Ababa to a Consulate-General, and said that the Italian Government would not regard this as a recognition of Italian sovereignty.

[5] Of November 4, not printed: it was a fuller version of No. 345.

Mr. Eden to Sir H. Kennard (Warsaw)
No. 368 [*C 8046/7996/55*]

FOREIGN OFFICE, *November 10, 1936*

Sir,

During the course of my conversation with M. Beck this morning, I gave his Excellency some account of the progress of our Locarno negotiations. I also referred to the recent declaration of policy by the Belgian Government.[1] M. Beck mentioned in this connexion that he had recently been on a visit to Brussels, and when there had noticed certain symptoms of uneasiness among the Belgian public. This was due in the first place to their suspicion of the Franco-Soviet Pact and of their fear of being drawn into any European trouble as a result of it, and in the second instance to anxiety as to the League's future. As regards the negotiation of a new Western Agreement, M. Beck again expressed the importance to his country of an arrangement which would not close the door to the working of the Franco-Polish Pact. This pact was of the greatest importance to Poland, and he ventured to think of some importance to His Majesty's Government also. After all, if Germany were ever to attack France, it would be surely of some help to us to know that Poland would then come to France's assistance. Though he did not pretend that Poland's resources were comparable to our own, still he thought that their assistance on land would be of some account. Poland, however, could not practise charity, and her readiness to come to the help of France, in the event of that country being attacked, which was unchanged, and which had been reaffirmed to the French Government at the time of the Rhineland incident in March, was dependent on France being able to come to the help of Poland. It was, therefore, important that her engagements should allow her to do this.

2. I replied that I fully appreciated the significance of the observations which M. Beck had made, and that there was no intention in the mind of His Majesty's Government to make an agreement among the Western Powers at the expense of anybody else. This had been made clear in the *communiqué* which had been issued at the conclusion of the Three-Power Conference at the end of July.[2]

3. M. Beck then said that with this consideration in mind he had been attempting to draft a *communiqué* which might form a fitting conclusion to our exchanges of view. He was quite prepared for one of two types of *communiqué* —either a completely anodyne document which said scarcely anything at all, or a more serious attempt to show the identity of our points of view. If the latter course were pursued, however, then it would be necessary to show that some account had been taken of Poland's legitimate rights. M. Beck then produced a copy of a proposed *communiqué*,[3] which, after comparison

[1] See No. 297.   [2] See Volume XVI, Annex to No. 476.
[3] Not printed. The text of the *communiqué* issued to the press on November 11 at the conclusion of M. Beck's visit is printed in *The Times*, November 12, 1936, p. 14.

with my own draft, we decided should be further discussed between members of his own staff and the Foreign Office.

I am, &c.,

ANTHONY EDEN

No. 365

Letter from Sir E. Phipps (Berlin) to Mr. Eden
[*C 8168/576/18*]

Private and Personal   BERLIN, *November 10, 1936*

My dear Anthony,

You will probably have heard at first hand the impressions of Lord and Lady Londonderry,[1] Lady Maureen[2] (to whom Goering appears to have made an 'expansionist' confession), and Castlereagh.[3] It seems that the next distinguished visitor to Germany may be Lord Derby, accompanied by Charlie Montagu.[4]

Goering, as you know, entertains his English guests in a lavish and generous manner, but so far they have been unable to give him anything in return (not even a colony). I fear the result of all this one-sided hospitality may well be an attempt on Goering's part, which it will be difficult to resist, and perhaps still more difficult to satisfy, to come to England (possibly as Hitler's representative at the Coronation). If we resist we may incur Goering's undying hostility and if we let him come we run quite a good risk of his being shot in England. Neither of these alternatives would be likely permanently to improve Anglo-German relations. (Incidentally I hear from a first-class source that Blomberg also is very keen to be the chief German representative at the Coronation. He, of course, would be far more suitable from our point of view, and I only hope he may eventually be chosen).

I often wonder what is the object of all these visits, apart of course from the very natural wish of the visitors to see so strange a being as Goering at close quarters. I realise that in our free country the Government cannot always prevent Mayfair from rushing Hitlerwards, but if some of the visitors could be choked off I think it would be a good thing. So far as I can see they only raise false hopes here and will eventually arouse more resentment in the German breast than even that curmudgeon—the British Ambassador —who has always obstinately declined to give Goebbels, Schacht and Co. the slightest hope of obtaining the smallest colony. Now it is well-nigh

[1] Lord Londonderry, former Secretary of State for Air and Lord Privy Seal, and Lady Londonderry had visited Germany on the way back from a visit to Roumania, and after being the guests of Herr Goering they were received by Herr Hitler in Berlin on October 30, 1936: see *The Times*, October 31, 1936, p. 11.

[2] Lady Maureen Stanley, wife of the Rt. Hon. Oliver Stanley, President of the Board of Education and son of Lord Derby.

[3] Eldest son of Lord Londonderry.

[4] Lord Derby, former Cabinet Minister and Ambassador to Paris from 1918 to 1920, was married to Lady Alice Montagu, sister of the stockbroker Lord Charles Montagu.

impossible, with the best will in the world, for the gallant General's guests whilst actually partaking of his Gargantuan repasts, to adopt this attitude of reserve. Yet is not reserve the only prudent attitude unless and until we definitely decide to grant the German demands? Meanwhile, of course diplomacy stinks in the Nazi nostrils. I believe Goebbels suggested to Lady Maureen that 'somebody' should come here to discuss matters with the powers that be, but that 'somebody' was on no account to be a diplomat!

Now Schacht, finding that Leith-Ross will not come here, is again itching to go to London.[5] He hopes, doubtless, to complete there his good work with Blum in Paris.[6] The fact is Blum, whatever he may pretend, must have been imprudent with that wily and unscrupulous man. In any case he evidently passed on the awkward colonial baby to us by saying that he would consult his English friends in the matter. What he should have said was that the matter was far too important to discuss off-hand without consulting his own Cabinet. Meanwhile he should have carefully refrained from giving Schacht any hopes whatever. I earnestly trust that if Schacht does go to London he may be told the same thing by all in authority, viz. that if Germany prefers guns to butter, as she openly boasts, she is quite welcome, but that Great Britain firmly declines to supply the butter so long as German policy continues on its present course. I hope all concerned will be quite frank, and if necessary brutal, with Schacht, who, besides being a prize liar, is a bully, and mistakes politeness for weakness. Certain City circles seem to be far too much under his spell; but that is perhaps only due to their hope of thawing certain frozen credits. It must be remembered that if he does come to London, he will certainly make use of his visit and advertise it afterwards in whatever way he thinks best suited to his own interests.

The general public here is in complete ignorance of the fact that I made representations regarding Goering's and Goebbels' speeches. Only the few who read the foreign press are aware of it. Incidentally, it is only another instance of Goering's old-world tact and courtesy that he should, in the presence of his guest (Lord Londonderry), have sneered at the 'superior intelligence of the English', thereby making the whole Sportpalast rock with laughter.[7]

I sometimes fear you must think me too prone to pessimism, but frankly the longer I stay here the less cause I find for rejoicing. I believe the Nazi extremists, who, as you know, opposed Ribbentrop's appointment to London, are now ready to wait and see what success attends that worthy's attempts to woo Great Britain. If he fails the 'Party' will give up playing what the French call 'la carte anglaise' and will strain every nerve to isolate us, and then 'Gott strafe England' will be their motto. To attain that object they hope (1) that France will go Communist and fall a prey to civil war 'à l'Espagnol', or (2) that France will go Fascist and come to a separate arrangement with Germany. Here perhaps the German medicine men of the

[5] Cf. Nos. 135, 256, and 302.   [6] See Nos. 141 and 145.
[7] Cf. No. 342, note 2.

532

mind may make a wrong diagnosis, for it seems by no means certain that a Fascist France need necessarily turn her back on us or throw in her lot with Frau Germania. But in any case it seems absolutely essential for us that (1) a strong Government, capable of restoring and preserving order, should soon emerge in France, and (2) that we should continue to work in as close collaboration with France as possible. I hardly dare to advocate a (3), but at the risk of shocking you I will set it down as an eventuality so blissful for a British dweller in the Wilhelmstrasse to contemplate as to savour of Paradise—a re-establishment of our traditionally friendly and cordial relations with Italy. *Then*, with an admittedly well-disposed Roosevelt America in the background, we could pursue the even tenor of our re-armament course without worrying too much over the German gangsters' hot air and breath.

Yours ever,
ERIC PHIPPS

No. 366

Sir E. Drummond (Rome) to Mr. Eden
(Received November 11, 9.30 a.m.)
No. 687 Telegraphic [R 6693/226/22]

ROME, *November 11, 1936, 12.30 a.m.*

My telegram No. 685.[1]

Marquis Theodoli[2] who has been in touch with Signor Mussolini and Count Ciano within the last few days has, on instructions resumed his contacts with the Embassy and in a long conversation yesterday I asked him his views on possible contents of Gentlemen's Agreement recently adumbrated by the head of the government. He replied and I gather he was basing himself on Signor Mussolini's own views that speeches exchanged between Duce on the one hand and Prime Minister, yourself and Lord Halifax on the other would provide basis for a formula. Signor Mussolini agreed that there was no point in discussing whose interests were greatest in the Mediterranean as each admitted the other's interests were vital. When asked whether agreement would necessarily be a written one, Theodoli pleaded ignorance but quoted the Salisbury-de-Robilant agreement which had had a valid[it]y of 40 years though it was not to be found in any diplomatic archives.[3]

[1] No. 363.
[2] Italian Senator, and Chairman of the League of Nations Permanent Mandates Commission.
[3] The reference is evidently to the Anglo-Italian agreements of 1887, which are usually considered to have lost most of their meaning by 1896. There is an extended note on these agreements in Volume XVI of this series (No. 361, note 5). Marquis Theodoli may have had in mind the fact that reasonably good relations between Italy and the United Kingdom had continued from 1887 until the exchange of notes by the British and Italian Governments on 14 and 20 December 1925 with regard to their interests in Ethiopia (cf. Volume XIV, pp. 1–2).

(I am endeavouring to run this agreement to earth but I should be grateful for any details you can give me).[4] That was an example of mutual trust. He added further that head of government was willing to give every possible assurance regarding Lake Tsana and to conclude necessary arrangements regarding Sudan boundaries and Gambeila enclave. I pointed out how important it was that Gentlemen's Agreement if reached should not have the appearance of being directed against France or of detaching us from France. Such a possibility in Theodoli's opinion was out of the question since in essence the agreement would merely state that our interests did not conflict but that we would each take steps to safeguard them. You will notice that if Theodoli's description is correct that there is no suggestion of limitation of naval forces or defensive fortification in the Mediterranean.

2. Theodoli then assured me that Signor Mussolini was not committed to Germans on general policy. A time might come in Duce's opinion when Italian-German interests might conflict but Italian-British interests were necessarily similar. Speaking of Franco-Soviet Pact Theodoli suggested that it need not be annulled but that it should be allowed to lapse as had the Treaty of Rapallo. In this case I enquired would Germany agree to a new Locarno? His Excellency shrugged his shoulders and said this was precisely a case where Italy could be exceedingly useful since Germany would not wish to find herself isolated.

3. Speaking of Russia His Excellency asked me to note skilful manner in which Signor Mussolini had dealt at Milan[5] with the question of communism as such (compare results of Berlin meeting) he had said nothing specifically hostile to the Soviet Government. Signor Mussolini's view was that communism was not an article for export and must be combated abroad but that he could not object to it as an internal doctrine in Russia itself. The Marquis then made some observations of great interest. He said that idea of a Four Power Pact must be abandoned, since such a pact was impossible without the participation of Poland. If however the Four became a Five Power Pact it would give the impression of being directed against and designed to encircle Russia; it was not therefore a possibility. In fact the position of Poland had killed the Four Power Pact. This made the conclusion of a new Locarno agreement all the more necessary. I could not be certain whether my interlocutor was giving rein to his own thoughts on this subject or those he had been authorised to express but I do not believe that he would hold such language unless it had been inspired either by Signor Mussolini himself or less probably by the Palazzo Chigi.

4. This language is un-apparent [sic] contradiction to my past reports regarding Signor Mussolini's anxiety for a Four or Five Power Pact; nevertheless I do not think that he has changed his views on the essence of the

[4] In a letter of November 13 to the Chancery of the British Embassy in Rome, the Southern Department forwarded copies of memoranda written by Sir T. H. Sanderson in 1902 and 1903 about the Mediterranean agreement; he thought that their validity had lapsed in 1892 when Lord Rosebery became Foreign Secretary.

[5] See No. 345, note 9.

matter. He still desires some arrangement in virtue of which the Four Powers will co-operate in European affairs but he may now tend to the view that such co-operation can best be effected or at any rate initiated through the conclusion of a new Locarno Treaty.

5. Marquis Theodoli touched on other subjects of interest and I am reporting fully by despatch.[6]

[6] No. 1223 of November 13 (R 6878/3928/22), not printed.

No. 367

Mr. Ogilvie-Forbes (Madrid) to Mr. Eden
(Received November 12, 11 a.m.)
No. 488 Telegraphic: by wireless [W 15611/62/41]

MADRID, *November 11, 1936*

My telegram No. 478.[1]
Present position appears to be a stalemate. Yesterday insurgents who had established themselves on western bank of Manzanares opposite the Royal Palace were driven back by international brigade towards the western side of Casa del Campo where they remain. Government this morning still held the road to Escorial although it was under insurgent fire from Pozuelo.

Bombardment of the City continues. Total casualties 9th November and November 10th among civilians 6 killed and 140 injured.

About 190 people now in the Embassy.[2]

[1] Not preserved in the Foreign Office archives.
[2] Replying to telegram No. 488 in Foreign Office telegram No. 270 of November 14, Mr. Eden said: 'I wish to remind you that you have my permission to withdraw from Madrid if and when you consider it necessary to do so.' He asked for Mr. Ogilvie-Forbes's 'views on the probability of such an eventuality'.

No. 368

Mr. King (Barcelona) to Mr. Eden
(Received[1] November 12)
No. 214 Telegraphic [W 15616/9549/41]

BARCELONA, *November 11, 1936*

Russian ship *Kurck* [*Kursk*] arrived here a few days ago and another small craft without name but bearing a Catalan flag. Cargoes of these vessels are not being passed through the customs and secrecy surrounding their unloading leaves no doubt that cargo was war material.

British subject named Patrick Smythe arrived in Spanish ship *Ciudad de*

[1] Via Captain (D)1 and the Admiralty.

Mallorca early October from Marseilles. Vessel brought about five or six aircraft assembled, the (? engines) being mostly old ones. Smythe who was employed as a local escort and is leaving country reports an air base is being constructed at Albacete.

About 2215 yesterday 10th November six salvoes were fired from some vessel at sea. The shells did not fall in the town.

No. 369

Note[1] by Mr. D. D. Maclean on alleged Soviet infringements of the Non-Intervention Agreement

[*W 15174/9549/41*]

FOREIGN OFFICE, *November 11, 1936*

Since the last summary of evidence of Soviet infringements of the Non-Intervention Agreement was compiled (most of which was laid before the Committee), the following details of further alleged breaches by the U.S.S.R. have been communicated to the Foreign Office.

1. H.M.[S.] *Resource* states that the Russian steamer *Georgio Dimitrov* arrived at Alicante on the 23rd October and unloaded 50 3-ton lorries which were labelled 'Transportes Militares'.

2. On the 24th October it was reported by Mr. McMean of the *Sociedad Espanole de Construccion Naval* that the Soviet Union ships *Neva* and *Volgoles* had landed 150 large Russian aeroplanes in the arsenal at Cartagena. As the result of enquiries through the Admiralty Mr. McMean subsequently obtained a second confirmation of this statement from his source in the Arsenal, whose reliability he vouched for.

H.M.S. *Grafton* subsequently confirmed from a 'completely reliable source' that there were on November 2nd in Cartagena at least 50 Russian aircraft in various stages of assembly at the aerodrome at Alcazares. Part of the aerodrome had been taken over by Russians and all Spanish personnel excluded. Russian machines and crews had carried out the air raids on Navalperal and Granada on evening of October 29th.

3. The Soviet Union ship *Ingul* arrived at Alicante from Cartagena on the 26th October and discharged 70 lorries on the 28th October.

4. The Soviet Union ship *Transbalt* sailed from Cartagena on 29th October without discharging deck cargo of lorries. She arrived at Alicante and disembarked at least 80 lorries.

5. H.M.S. *Grafton* reports on November 1st that it is definitely established that the Soviet Union ship *Karl Lepin* was observed unloading at Cartagena armoured cars of two sizes, complete with crew: 'over 20 were actually counted'.

[1] In a covering minute Mr. Maclean wrote: '. . . We have received a considerable amount of evidence since H.M.G. submitted a case against Russia [see No. 328], and I attach a note on the most striking instances. D. D. Maclean 11/11.'

6. His Majesty's Consul, Bilbao, reported from personal observation that aircraft and other war materials were landed at Bilbao on 4th November from a Russian steamship whose name was unascertainable.

7. H.M.S. *Grafton* reports: the Russian steamer *Blagdev* which arrived at Cartagena on the 4th November discharged at least 18 Fighter Aircraft.

I understand that the question whether the export of military lorries to Spain is a breach of the Agreement has been and is under consideration by the Committee: probably nothing useful could therefore be done with items 1, 3 and 4 above.[2]

The strongest evidence appears to be that against the *Karl Lepin* and the *Blagdev* (Items 5 and 7), while the evidence against the *Neva* and the *Volgoles* (Item 2), though second or third hand, is fairly substantial.[3]

[2] Mr. Shuckburgh agreed on November 13 that 'nothing useful can be done with the "lorries"'; he thought that 'Cases 5 & 7 are quite good', but was not sure 'whether Lord Plymouth wants to put in any more evidence to the Cttee'.

[3] Sir G. Mounsey remarked on November 14 that as so little headway could be made 'by putting in evidence to the Committee here' it would seem preferable 'to concentrate their attention more upon the organisation of control on the spot'. Lord Plymouth wrote: 'I agree with Sir G. Mounsey. I can see no object in—indeed there are many objections to—putting forward any further complaints at this stage. We can produce these cases, if necessary, later on. P. 16/11/36.'

No. 370

Note[1] by Mr. Hemming on financial aspects of the proposal to establish a system of supervision in Spain[2]

[*W 15624/9549/41*]

Most secret   2 WHITEHALL GARDENS, S.W.1, *November 11, 1936*

I. *The Cost of the Scheme*

In accordance with the instructions given to me at yesterday's meeting of the Chairman's Sub-Committee, I conferred yesterday afternoon with the United Kingdom Customs Department, the Foreign Office and other Departments, with a view to preparing a provisional estimate of the numbers of persons who would be required to be employed if the scheme of supervision were put into operation, and what would be the cost of that scheme.

2. The estimate now submitted in Annex A[3] has been prepared on the assumption that Supervision Posts will be established at 40 selected places in Spain, these places being either ports or railway stations on the Spanish

[1] Circulated to the N.I. Committee as N.I.S.(36)147.

[2] See No. 338. At the tenth meeting of the N.I. Committee on November 4 the members were asked to take note of the scheme as proposed to the Chairman's Sub-Committee on November 2 (No. 347) and to obtain the instructions of their respective governments thereon. At the meeting of the Chairman's Sub-Committee on November 10 it was agreed to recommend to the main committee that the proposals should be communicated to the two contending parties in Spain.   [3] Not printed.

side of the land frontiers. The places at which it is suggested that Supervision Posts should be established are enumerated in Annex B[3] attached hereto.

3. The staff suggested for each Supervision Post consists of one Agent, one Chief Supervising Officer (who would act as his deputy) and 15 Supervising Officers and Assistant Supervising Officers.[4] Of the 15 Supervising Officers, 10 would be required to provide a continuous watch throughout the twenty-four hours at one point within the area covered by the Supervision Post. The remaining 5 Supervising Officers would be engaged in watching the discharge, or transfer, of cargoes and in calling for the opening of suspicious packages. Obviously, it must be anticipated that arms, etc., would often be disguised as other forms of merchandise.

The staff outlined above for each Supervision Post would require to be considerably increased in the case of Supervision Posts established at large ports such as Barcelona.

4. I must make it clear that the Customs Department consider that the information available is not sufficient to enable detailed estimates to be prepared. In the opinion of that Department, however, a staff on the scale indicated above represents the absolute minimum required. Provision has been made in the estimate for a small margin to deal with sickness, leave, etc. In order to secure an effective supervision of the ports (large and small) and the various road entries into Spain, a very much larger number of Supervision Posts would require to be established, and the total staff involved would be not less than ten times as much as that now proposed. No genuine attempt to supervise, even in the most general way, 40 places in Spain could be made with a smaller staff than that suggested above.

5. It should be pointed out that the effect of establishing Supervision Posts at a number of selected places in Spain will inevitably cause illicit traffic to be diverted to routes not at present used. Moreover, the scheme proposed does not provide for the supervision of the Spanish coast-line and land frontiers as a whole.

6. The scheme prepared by the Chairman's Sub-Committee contemplates that full facilities will be given by the Spanish authorities to the proposed staff to carry out their duties. In the existing circumstances it is, however, unlikely that whole-hearted support would be forthcoming, and it is necessary to face the possibility that, if the scheme were once launched, it might be necessary almost at once to increase considerably the numbers of the Supervising staff and also to provide in some appropriate manner for their protection.[5] In any case, it will certainly be necessary to provide special life insurance policies for the personnel engaged. Moreover, the salaries proposed are rather higher than would normally be paid to officers of comparable rank. This is essential, in view of the dangerous character of the work and

[4] This document was read and heavily under-scored by Sir R. Vansittart, who placed an exclamation mark in the margin against this sentence.
[5] The last part of this sentence was underlined by Sir R. Vansittart, with the marginal comment, 'Yes indeed! RV.'

the unpleasant conditions under which it will be carried out. Lodging allowances are proposed, in view of the inevitable difficulty which will be experienced in obtaining suitable accommodation.

7. It is essential that provision of not less than 25% should be made for 'contingencies', as it must be anticipated that substantial demands for extra staff will be made by the Agents directly the scheme comes into force.

8. It will be seen from the table given in Annex A that in addition to the Agents in charge of the Supervision Posts, a total staff of nearly 1,000 officers would be required in Spain. Of these, the majority must necessarily be trained Customs Officers.

9. It is proposed to provide one interpreter at each Supervision Post for the purpose of enabling the Agent in charge to communicate with the local Spanish Authorities. Quite apart from this, however, the language question will inevitably make the internal working of the Supervision Service very difficult. In the estimate now submitted, it has been assumed that at any given Supervision Post, the whole of the staff would belong to one nationality. For example, if the Agent at Vigo were a Finnish subject, then all the Supervising Officers working under him at Vigo would also be of Finnish nationality. If an arrangement on these lines were not adopted the scheme would be even more difficult to work than it inevitably will be; the numbers of the staff would require to be increased; and the cost of the scheme would be proportionately raised.

10. The scheme in its present form does not provide for the supervision of the arrival of aircraft into Spain by air. If, however, a scheme of this kind were adopted in addition, as is contemplated by the Chairman's Sub-Committee, I am advised that the additional expenditure involved in supervising 40 airports would probably be equal to about one-third of the total expenditure shown in Annex A attached hereto, that is to say £265,000. In this connection it should be observed that the number of airports in Spain is much larger than 40, and moreover, that landing grounds can be readily improvised. In addition, there is the possibility that aircraft entering Spain illicitly might fly direct to military aerodromes.

II. *The allocation of the cost of the scheme*

11. The cost of the scheme of supervision might be allocated between the various countries concerned, on the basis of the value of the imports by those countries into Spain. An examination of the available statistics shows (*a*) that separate figures are not available for a considerable number of the countries concerned and (*b*) that some of the countries most concerned would be called upon to pay a disproportionately small contribution, while some of the countries which have practically no interest in the Spanish question would be called upon to pay much larger contributions than there is any reason to suppose that they would be willing to accept. This basis of allocation must therefore, I think, be abandoned as unworkable.

12. An allocation based upon the contributions made by the various

countries towards the cost of the League of Nations would produce inequitable results of a similar but less marked character, quite apart from the fact that Germany is not a member of the League. It is worth noting, however, that the combined contributions to the League by the United Kingdom, France, Italy and the U.S.S.R., together with a hypothetical contribution by Germany (assumed for the present purpose as being equal to that of the U.S.S.R.) would amount to 63 per cent of the total contributions involved.

13. As will be seen from Annex A the total cost of the scheme if it were in operation *for a full year* would amount to approximately £1,000,000. It seems unreasonable to anticipate that the smallest countries represented on the Committee would be willing to contribute more than £1,000 per annum towards the cost of the scheme. In other words, it seems that it would be a necessary part of any basis of allocation likely to be accepted by the countries concerned that contribution of the smallest and least interested country should not exceed one-tenth of one per cent of the total cost of the scheme.

14. The only basis of allocation that I have been able to think of which pays regard to the considerations set out in paragraphs 12 and 13 above is the following:

(a) 80% of the cost to be defrayed in equal shares by the United Kingdom, France, Germany, Italy, and the U.S.S.R., the contributions of each of these countries amounting to 16% of the total cost of the scheme.

(b) The remaining 20% of the cost to be defrayed by the other 22 countries represented on the International Committee, their contributions being calculated in proportion to the contributions which they make towards the cost of the League of Nations.

15. If it is assumed for the present purpose that the total cost of the scheme on *an annual basis* would amount to £1,000,000, the maximum contribution (i.e. that to be paid by the five countries referred to in paragraph 14(a) above) would amount to £16,000 per annum, while the contribution of the smallest countries (e.g. Luxemburg and Albania) would amount to £1,000.

16. The percentage contributions by each country represented on the International Committee under the scheme put forward above and their sterling equivalents on the assumption that the annual cost of the scheme is £1,000,000 are shown in Annex C attached hereto.[6]

FRANCIS HEMMING

[6] Not printed. In a minute of November 16 Mr. Shuckburgh remarked that as the scheme involved very large expenditure by H.M. Government, Mr. Eden would wish to consult the Cabinet (on November 18) before agreeing to it. He then referred to the many objections to the plan. 'It is expensive and cumbersome; it will take a great deal of time to put into effect; it will doubtless cause considerable friction between the participating governments and will raise a number of difficult problems in its execution; and, in the remote eventuality of its being accepted by the two parties in Spain, it is not very likely to prove effective.' He admitted however that it was 'put up originally because the consideration of such a scheme appeared to be the only thing the Committee could do to show that it genuinely

desired to make the Non-Intervention Agreement effective'. He asked, 'Have we got to acquiesce in being thus involved in the events in Spain in order to keep the Committee and the Agreement in being?' He noted that M. Corbin was very shocked at the sums mentioned, and had suggested 'that the Committee ought to content itself with a much less ambitious (and admittedly practically ineffective) scheme for sending a small body of inspectors to travel from port to port in pursuit of the large infractions'.

Sir G. Mounsey suggested, and Lord Plymouth agreed (November 17) that H.M.G. could postpone a decision pending the reply of the two parties in Spain. Lord Plymouth thought that M. Maisky would not accept Mr. Shuckburgh's suggestion for a modified scheme, and would blame the British Government if control broke down for failure to support an effective scheme. He added that he himself had 'always taken the line that the scheme should be made as effective as possible'.

Sir R. Vansittart thought the plan 'quite fantastic . . . It has no doubt been useful to gain time by toying with these ideas, but I hope that we shall sponsor nothing of this kind— though I wd not necessarily reject Mr. Shuckburgh's idea of something less ambitious . . . R.V. Nov. 17.' The Cabinet on November 18, after listening to Mr. Eden's description of the work of the N.I. Committee, recognized that the 'object of the Agreement had been to prevent the Spanish Civil War from spreading into the rest of Europe, and for this purpose it was still effective. The general view of the Cabinet, therefore, was that it was desirable to keep the Non-Intervention Committee in existence at present. As the British scheme for making it effective had been heavily criticised on the ground of its cost, it was suggested that advantage might be taken of a French suggestion to draw up a more economical scheme, which could then be considered by the Committee.'

No. 371

Mr. Eden to Sir C. Wingfield (Lisbon)
No. 151 Telegraphic [W 15306/62/41]

FOREIGN OFFICE, *November 12, 1936, 12.20 p.m.*

Your telegram No. 221.[1]

Please thank Portuguese Prime Minister for informing us beforehand of the intentions of his government in this matter.

As regards our own position you may tell him for his confidential information that His Majesty's Chargé d'Affaires at Madrid has been authorised upon the occupation of the capital by the insurgent army to establish such *de facto* contacts with the new administration as are practically necessary for the protection of British interests.[2] You should add that His Majesty's Government do not consider that the present situation justifies their recognising that administration as the Government of Spain.[3]

[1] No. 360.   [2] See No. 359.
[3] Sir G. Mounsey had suggested the addition to this telegram of a statement that His Majesty's Government 'would be glad to learn whether it is not still possible for the Portuguese Government to act in concert with them in limiting the degree of recognition which they will at first accord to General Franco's régime to that of *de facto* relations'. Mr. Eden, however, agreed to the omission of this passage following Sir R. Vansittart's objection. 'I am doubtful about this. We shd probably fail to restrain the Portuguese Govt—who will probably act anyhow as they foreshadow & with the German & Italian govts—& they wd certainly give away our attempt to Genl. Franco. If the Germans & Italians recognise anyhow, it *really* isn't worth trying to stop the Portuguese. They won't really add much to our embarrassments. R. V.'

No. 372

Note by Mr. Shuckburgh for Lord Plymouth
[W 15884/9549/41]

FOREIGN OFFICE, *November 12, 1936*

As you know, the Soviet Government, in reply to our three accusations against them, have entered a simple denial of all the facts which we have alleged.[1] Although this question is not on the agenda for this afternoon's meeting[2] you may wish to make some statement re-affirming the soundness of the evidence on which we based our accusations. Even if you do not do this this afternoon, we ought presumably to make some reply to the Russian note which is almost insulting in its abruptness.

I have consulted the Admiralty and they agree to your stating, if necessary, that these cases were based on evidence supplied by H[is] M[ajesty's] Ships. I assured the Admiralty that it is not your intention to mention specifically the names of any ships or of any officers, and that there is, of course, no question of the officers themselves being called upon to supply confirmation of their statements or in any way being dragged forward into the limelight. The Admiralty gave their consent 'on the understanding that if the Russians continue to deny the accusations, the matter (that is the question of the authenticity of the sources) cannot be carried any further but must be allowed to drop'.[3]

C. A. E. SHUCKBURGH

[1] No. 351.　　　　　　　　　　　　　　[2] i.e. the eleventh meeting of the N.I. Committee.
[3] M. Maisky's letter was, in fact, not discussed further. In a minute on another file (W 15880/9549/41) Mr. Shuckburgh wrote: 'Lord Plymouth has told me that he does not wish to place any more evidence of breaches before the Committee at present. We are, however, keeping a file of all this evidence, grouped according to the country responsible, in case it is wanted at a later date. C. A. E. Shuckburgh, 18/11.' Cf. No. 369, note 3, and see *D.V.P.S., op. cit.*, No. 360.

No. 373

Letter from Mr. W. Roberts to Mr. F. Hemming
[W 15497/9549/41]

Immediate　　　　　　　　　　　　　　FOREIGN OFFICE, *November 12, 1936*
Sir,

In the course of the work of the International Committee for the Application of the Agreement regarding non-intervention in Spain mention has been made of a consignment of arms having been delivered to Spain by the British S.S. *Bramhill*.[1] His Majesty's Government in the United Kingdom have made careful enquiries into this matter and I am directed by Mr. Secretary Eden to communicate to you the following information which they desire to submit to the Committee.

[1] See No. 273.

2. The S.S. *Bramhill* left London in ballast for Hamburg in the early part of September, with orders to pick up a general cargo for Spain. The master had no written information about the cargo with the exception of a letter from the Company's shipping agents which stated 'your agents in Hamburg will be Lassen and Company, Aktiongesellshaft'. He had no instructions regarding the voyage.

3. On arrival at Hamburg the master was disconcerted to find that his cargo was to contain arms. Since however the freightage had been paid in advance he had no alternative but to proceed. The ship was accordingly loaded and the arms were delivered at Alicante.

4. So far as the master has been able to recollect the cargo consisted of ten cases of machine guns, approximately 600 tons of small arms ammunition in boxes, and approximately 300 tons of rifles and revolvers in boxes. The boxes bore the marking 'Handfeuerwaffen: Ib. Munition'. His Majesty's Government have made such enquiries as were possible regarding the origin of these goods but have not yet been able to establish any satisfactory evidence on this point.

5. It will be evident to the Committee that this case does not involve a breach of the Agreement on Non-Intervention by His Majesty's Government since none of the arms carried by the *Bramhill* originated in or passed in transit through the United Kingdom. This incident does, however, raise an important matter which I am to suggest should be considered by the Committee.

6. It will be recalled that the German Delegate, in a communication to the Committee dated the 1st October (N.I.S.(36)68) stated that the arms embargo regulations of the German Government apply only within the sphere of the German internal customs area, but not in the parts of Germany which, as areas excluded from customs, or free zones, lie outside the internal customs area and consequently are counted as external territory for customs purposes . . . [2] Vessels which moor in harbours of the areas excluded from customs, or of the free zone, are not dealt with by customs officials . . . [2]

7. As examples of these free areas the German representative referred particularly to the Hamburg free port customs exempted zone, and the Hamburg–Waltershof customs exempted zone. It therefore appears that there exists at Hamburg, as well as at the other free ports mentioned by the German representative, the possibility of serious leakages in the system of non-intervention, such as would explain the occurrence of cases like that of the S.S. *Bramhill*. I am to suggest that the Committee should examine at an early date what possibilities exist for filling this gap in the non-intervention system.

I am, &c.,
WALTER ROBERTS

---

[2] Punctuation as in the original.

No. 374

Mr. Eden to Sir E. Phipps (Berlin)
No. 1254 [C 8096/4/18]

FOREIGN OFFICE, *November 12, 1936*

Sir,

The Counsellor of the German Embassy asked to see me this morning, when he began by thanking me for receiving him. He knew that this procedure was unusual, but since Herr von Ribbentrop was ill and there were certain matters about which the German Government desired to receive information, he had been specially anxious to see me. The German Embassy had stated on the telephone that the purpose of the visit was to make certain communications about the proposed Five-Power Conference. It soon emerged from the conversation, however, that their real anxiety was with reference to my conversations with M. Beck[1] about which Herr Woermann plied me with questions.

2. Our *communiqué*[2] referred to certain Polish interests in the Western Pact. Could I explain exactly what this referred to? I replied that these Polish interests were those which had already been allowed for in the previous Locarno Treaty. It was natural that Poland should desire that a like allowance should be made for her special position in any new arrangement. Moreover, I could not imagine that this could offer any difficulty for the German Government, since they had taken cognisance of the Franco-Polish Pact in their own non-aggression treaty with Poland. Herr Woermann admitted that this had been so at the time, though he was not sure what the German position would be in relation to this in any new arrangement that might be come to. Did he understand that I had agreed with the Polish Government's view on this question? I replied that it certainly was our view that account must be taken of the Polish Government's position as had been done in the past.

3. The Counsellor then asked whether I had any information to give him about Danzig, since he presumed this had formed a topic of the conversation between us. I replied that we had certainly discussed the matter, but that Herr Woermann would realise the particular position of Danzig and that though I was quite willing to discuss the matter unofficially with him, the German Government had no direct status in the matter. The Counsellor agreed. Continuing, I told Herr Woermann that the Polish Government had been charged by the Council with endeavouring to secure an improvement in the situation in Danzig,[3] and we hoped that they would be successful. The last thing I wanted as Rapporteur in the matter was that Danzig should become a grave international issue. At the same time it was impossible for matters to continue as they had been doing recently. If a reasonable and respectable arrangement could be come to well and good, but nobody could regard the present condition as satisfactory, nor was it

---

[1] See Nos. 362 and 364.   [2] See No. 364, note 3.   [3] See No. 242, note 2.

one which the League Council could be expected to tolerate. It might be that the German Government could contribute by giving prudent counsel locally. The Counsellor replied that he felt sure that the German Government also were anxious to avoid difficulty over Danzig. They would like to make some arrangement direct with Poland. There was, however, the difficulty of the Constitution. I replied that the Constitution was a part of the Statute, which was in itself an indivisible whole. I fully realised the local difficulties of the situation.

4. Herr Woermann then asked whether any decision had been reached as to the appointment of a new High Commissioner.[4] I replied that no decision had been taken, nor would one be taken before the Danzig Senate was given full information. At the same time, both M. Beck and I had a number of names in mind, and we hoped that a decision might be reached before the end of the year.

5. Herr Woermann went on to say that Herr von Ribbentrop's attention had been drawn to a statement in the 'Daily Telegraph' that the German Government had intimated in Rome that they would regard an Anglo-Italian arrangement as a breach of the arrangement arrived at with Count Ciano in Berlin. Though the Ambassador was convinced that this was not true, Herr Woermann had, on his instructions, telephoned to Berlin this morning, and received a definite assurance that there was no foundation in this report.

6. Herr Woermann then asked me whether I could tell him whether there was any foundation for the reports appearing in the press about Anglo-Italian conversations. I replied that I had nothing to add to the public statements which had been made, in the first instance by Signor Mussolini at Milan,[5] then by myself in the House of Commons,[6] and the Prime Minister at the Guildhall.[7]

7. Herr Woermann said that he had a message from his Government on the subject of the negotiations for the projected Five-Power Conference. In view of the fact that the German Government understood that we should shortly be expressing our own views about these negotiations, the German Government did not propose to make any further comments themselves until they had an opportunity of studying our suggestions. Our last note[8] had, however, asked whether the German Government preferred the negotiations to continue through the diplomatic channel; this was the view of the German Government. I asked Herr Woermann if he could tell me what were the Ambassador's views as to the possibilities of the meeting of the Conference. The Counsellor replied that while diffident to express an opinion

---

[4] See *ibid.*   [5] See No. 345, note 9.   [6] See No. 353, note 2.

[7] During a general review of British foreign policy in his speech at the Lord Mayor's Banquet on November 9, Mr. Baldwin stated that he was 'glad to note the manner in which opinion in that country [Italy] appears to have received the assurance of my right hon. friend, the Foreign Secretary, that the relations of this country and Italy in the Mediterranean are not divergent, but complementary': see *The Times*, November 10, 1936, p. 21.   [8] No. 349.

without consulting the Ambassador, his own view was that his Government still hoped for the meeting, though they realised that the main difficulty would arise from the connexion of this proposed Western Pact with Eastern Europe. The German Government could not really be expected to recognise the Franco-Soviet Pact.[9]

I am, &c.,
ANTHONY EDEN

[9] In a minute of November 17 on this despatch Mr. Baxter wrote: 'As regards para. 3, a draft tel. to Warsaw [No. 84 of November 17, not printed] has been submitted on the S. of S.'s instruction, asking Sir H. Kennard to inform M. Beck of the position, and enquire whether he would like us to speak similarly at Berlin. As regards para. 4 I spoke to Dr. Woermann on Nov. 14, and told him that the appointment of League High Commissioner at Danzig was one made by the League Council; that the matter would probably therefore be dealt with in January at Geneva; that on previous occasions the Polish and Danzig representatives at Geneva had been kept informed before the appointment was made, and that I presumed the procedure would be the same in the present case.'

No. 375

Viscount Chilston (Moscow) to Mr. Eden (Received November 21)
No. 635 [W 16235/9549/41]

MOSCOW, *November 13, 1936*

Sir,

In paying my visit a few days ago to M. Litvinov on my return from leave, we had a general conversation on various matters of political interest, in the course of which, in regard to Spain, I asked him whether in view of the refutation by M. Maiski [*sic*] of some charges recently brought before the Non-Intervention Committee of supply of war material,[1] it was to be believed that no Soviet war material was going into Spain and that the presence, for instance, of Russian officers and of tanks, as had been reported by press correspondents in Spain was not to be credited.

2. M. Litvinov, of course, was too clever to make a definite denial: he only implied that naturally charges had been brought against each party of those who were supposed to be aiding the one side or the other in this rebellion against the Spanish Government. Nothing submitted to the Committee, however, was capable of being proved unless actual eye-witnesses were called and the only practical way was to establish a system of control by neutral agents at all points of entry, including Portugal. Any decision of the Committee to this effect would have to be taken unanimously; and moreover of course it would be necessary that General Franco should agree to a control also in the territory and ports occupied by his forces. M. Litvinov said that as a matter of fact he had received the proposals of the Committee on this matter[2] and had already replied with certain counter-suggestions, all of which except one appeared to have been agreed.

[1] See No. 351.   [2] Cf. No. 370.

He added that if such procedure of control could be now enforced properly it would hardly be necessary to continue disputes about alleged interventions up to the present: in fact, as he somewhat naively put it, the past could be washed out.

3. I may mention that on my remarking to him that it seemed to me that anything but neutrality was most dangerous, M. Litvinov said he did not see why intervention, in the sense of aiding the Spanish Government against rebels while others were aiding the latter, need necessarily lead to collisions or danger of war.[3]

I have, &c.,
CHILSTON

---

[3] In a minute of December 2 Mr. Collier remarked: 'M. Litvinov knows, of course, that German and Italian intervention will go on whatever the Committee does; so he does not feel called upon to take non-intervention seriously.'

No. 376

Mr. Eden to Sir E. Drummond (Rome)
No. 428 Telegraphic [R 6693/226/22]

Immediate   FOREIGN OFFICE, *November 14, 1936, 4 p.m.*

Your telegrams Nos. 682[1] and 687.[2]

His Majesty's Government have considered from every point of view the desirability of responding to friendly advances made by Signor Mussolini indirectly through Mr. Ward Price and the Marquis Theodoli. They are relieved to find that what he has in mind is not so much negotiation of formal treaty as declarations of policy, elaborating the proposition that British and Italian interests in the Mediterranean are not conflicting but complementary. Such parallel declarations containing mutual assurances on points of interest to both countries would probably be the most advantageous and least difficult form to follow.

---

[1] In this telegram of November 8, Sir E. Drummond reported that on November 5 Mr. Ward Price of the *Daily Mail* had had an interview with Signor Mussolini, which was to be published in the *Daily Mail* on November 9. Referring to the invitation to England in his Milan speech of November 1, Signor Mussolini said that what he had in mind was a 'gentleman's agreement' (his own words); he felt that a renewal of Anglo-Italian friendship and collaboration was necessary, but did not wish to add another 'pact' to the long list already existing. Replying to a question as to rumours of Italian designs upon Mallorca and a deal with General Franco and the Spanish nationalists, he 'flung his arms out and said that the idea had never entered his head'.

[2] No. 366. In a note dated November 10, Mr. Sargent referred to Mr. Eden's minute of November 5 (No. 352) which had directed that there were to be no more approaches to Italy, official or unofficial, until Italy's reaction to Mr. Eden's speech of that day (No. 353, note 2) was known. He remarked that for the first time Signor Mussolini had put forward a concrete proposal, that it suited British policy that he should deprecate a signed pact, and that simply to ignore the Ward Price interview while waiting for more direct diplomatic approaches might be taken in Rome as a rebuff. Telegram No. 428 was the result of further discussion in the Foreign Office on the basis of this minute.

2. Whilst it is difficult, without knowing more of what is in Signor Mussolini's mind, for me to judge what would be the best line of approach or to decide what would be the most promising subject with which to open the discussion, it is essential that you should know from the very start, for your own information, with what reservations and desiderata any discussions could be conducted.

3. We would want the Italian Government to make at least the following contributions towards the proposed *détente*:

(*a*) Acceptance without qualification of the territorial status quo in the Mediterranean.

(*b*) Renunciation of anti-British intrigue and propaganda in the Near East.[3]

(*c*) Italian adhesion to the Montreux Convention.[4]

(*d*) Italian adhesion to the London Naval Treaty of 1935.[5]

(*e*) We should of course also aim at securing Italy's effectual return to the League. The stages at which these points could most advantageously be broached would require careful consideration; (*b*) for instance would be particularly delicate. On the other hand some of these, i.e. (*c*) and (*d*) are of course in Italy's own interest.

4. Against this you will understand that we for our part are not prepared:

(1) To enter into fresh commitments in the Mediterranean.

(2) To take any course liable to arouse the fears and suspicions of any other Mediterranean country.

(3) To agree to limit the size and location of our military and naval forces or establishments in the Mediterranean or Red Sea basins.

(4) To recognise for the present the Italian conquest of Abyssinia.

5. Do you consider that with these limitations and desiderata in mind there is a good prospect of carrying a step further the recent *détente* with Italy by means of direct conversations with Signor Mussolini on the subject of Anglo-Italian relations generally? You would no doubt open any such conversations by expressing our satisfaction with the recent improvement of relations signalised by the public pronouncements on both sides, the conclusion of the commercial agreement, the withdrawal of the Legation Guard from Addis Ababa etc., and would endeavour to elicit Signor Mussolini's views on the gentleman's agreement which he proposed in his interview with Mr. Ward Price. You would have to judge at what stage to introduce our desiderata. Of these only (*a*) could conveniently figure in a public declaration of policy. I should however desire that definite assurances in some form or other as regards the other four should be given simultaneously with the publication of any declarations of general goodwill and mutual understanding, of which they would be concrete evidence. Do you think

[3] Cf. No. 274.   [4] See Volume XVI, No. 540.
[5] See Volume XIII, No. 718: the treaty was in fact signed on March 25, 1936.

that Signor Mussolini would in that case ask for corresponding contributions from us? If so, what would they be likely to be? You would have to make it clear if he raised any of the subjects enumerated in paragraph 4 that you could not discuss it.

6. As regards the recognition of Abyssinia I do not wish at any stage to make it the subject of a bargain with Italy. In any case the question is not yet ripe. The reduction of the status of the Legation at Addis Ababa to that of a Consulate-General falls into a somewhat different category. There would be local advantages in making such a reduction immediately, and it may in any case be necessary to take this step before long. But I do not consider that it could form part of an Anglo-Italian agreement any more than the question of recognition. This particular subject should be kept outside the range of any conversations with Signor Mussolini for a general *détente*, not because we intend to refuse to make this change, but because we wish to make it spontaneously and not as part of any bilateral arrangement.

7. It would be of great assistance to me to have your personal views on this telegram before taking any further decision. You will realise that it is essential at this stage to observe secrecy and consequently it will not be possible for you to consult any Italian opinion.

No. 377

Mr. Eden to Sir E. Drummond (Rome)
No. 429 Telegraphic [R 6813/226/22]

FOREIGN OFFICE, *November 14, 1936, 5.15 p.m.*

At my request the Italian Ambassador came to see me on the 13th November before leaving to-day for Rome to attend the meeting of the Fascist Grand Council.

I began by telling Signor Grandi how much the courtesy and consideration shown by Marshal Graziani to His Majesty's Chargé d'Affaires at Addis Ababa in connexion with the departure of the Legation guard (see my telegram No. 425)[1] had been appreciated here.

Signor Grandi heard this with obvious pleasure, and remarked that this was one more sign of improved relations which had been effected at a greater speed than he would have dared to hope. He remarked that my comment that the Mediterranean was not a short cut but a main arterial road had been fully understood in Rome.[2] I replied that it was all the more satisfactory since this was surely a definition that could be acceptable to us both: there was plenty of room for two cars and even more abreast on a main arterial road, whereas a short cut might become uncomfortably congested.

His Excellency then said that as he was certain to see Signor Mussolini within the next 48 hours, he would be very grateful for any guidance that

---

[1] Not printed: cf. Volume XVI, No. 486, note 2.   [2] Cf. No. 353, note 2.

I could give him as to what he should say as to His Majesty's Government's attitude in respect of Anglo-Italian relations. He felt sure that we had been gratified, as he had been, by recent events. He had himself in the last day or two received many indications, not in themselves important but symptomatic, of the extent of the satisfaction felt in Rome and of the reality of the Italian Government's desire to better their relations with this country. Had I, for instance, seen Signor Mussolini's article in 'The Daily Mail' and his suggestion of a 'gentleman's agreement'?[3] The question was how this better atmosphere was to be used.

I replied that Signor Grandi would have seen from the Prime Minister's declaration at the Guildhall that we too were gratified at this improved atmosphere.[4] Moreover, as I understood the position, Signor Mussolini was anxious to carry matters a stage further. We were quite ready to do this. But, speaking frankly, I did not know what Signor Mussolini had in mind in his reference to a 'gentleman's agreement'. I thought it probable that he did not intend anything in the nature of a pact. Personally I hoped this was so for a variety of reasons. Signor Grandi at once remarked that he felt confident that Signor Mussolini had not a pact in mind. Maybe, I continued, that something in the nature of an exchange of declarations was what was intended. With this suggestion also Signor Grandi concurred. I made it clear that His Majesty's Government had not yet fully considered what further step might be possible, but that they appreciated the desire on the Italian side that this improvement should be followed up and were willing to co-operate for that purpose.

We then spoke of the situation in Abyssinia. I told Signor Grandi that I hoped that as an outcome of his conversation with Signor Mussolini in Rome the question of recognition would not be coupled with any suggestion that might be made for an exchange of assurances or whatever it might be. It seemed to me much better to treat this Abyssinian problem separately. Had we, for instance, attempted to bargain about the question of the Legation guard, I was confident that the salutary effect upon Anglo-Italian relations would have been destroyed. The Ambassador said he fully appreciated the position, and clearly thought that there were advantages in the method which I suggested, and indeed that Signor Mussolini would appreciate our attitude. He added that the Quai d'Orsay were always trying to bargain over the Abyssinian situation.

Finally the Ambassador left in very good spirits and said that he returned to Rome in very different heart from that which he experienced at this time last year. The truth was that seven months of bad relations between our two countries was not enough to destroy the traditional friendship.[5]

---

[3] No. 376, note 1. [4] See No. 374, note 7.

[5] Signor Grandi's departure was, in fact, postponed. He saw Sir R. Vansittart on the morning of November 17 and said that he was departing for Rome that afternoon; the Grand Council would meet in Rome on the 18th. He had told Signor Mussolini that Mr. Eden was reflecting on the form and content of an Anglo-Italian gentleman's agreement, and Signor Mussolini had said that he was doing the same and hoped to give the Ambassa-

dor his instructions when he saw him. He was relieved to hear that the British government favoured an agreement in the simplest possible form; the French were understood to favour a more elaborate pact, but this did not find favour in Italian eyes. Mr. Eden gave an account of these discussions to the Cabinet on November 18. The Cabinet agreed to 'authorise the Secretary of State for Foreign Affairs to continue his negotiations with a view to improving relations with the Italian Government'.

No. 378

Sir E. Drummond (Rome) to Mr. Eden (Received November 17)
No. 1240 [J 8564/3957/1]

Confidential   ROME, November 15, 1936

Sir,

In your confidential despatch No. 1226 (J 8375/3957/1) of November 9th,[1] you asked for an expression of my personal views as to whether the assurances received during the last eighteen months, concerning the intention of the Italian Government to respect British rights in Ethiopia, must now be regarded as a dead letter. It is by no means easy to answer this question or to express hard and fast opinions on the various other points raised in your despatch. You will however have received by the last bag my despatch No. 1220 of November 12th[1] reporting a conversation on November 10th with the Head of the African Department of the Ministry of Foreign Affairs, which throws some additional light on the questions at issue, while a semi-official letter of November 13th[1] addressed to your department gives a detailed account of that part of a recent conversation between a member of this Embassy and the Marquis Theodoli which dealt with Signor Mussolini's views on the importance of collaboration in East Africa.

2. My own personal view is that the problem of the settlement of questions outstanding between Italy and Great Britain relating to Abyssinia forms part of the wider question of a general settlement between the two countries. Signor Mussolini has expressed the desire to reach an arrangement with us over the Mediterranean. He regards the Mediterranean as the nodal point in the relations between the two countries, and he feels that if this is once cleared away it will be possible to resume the traditional friendship which I continue to believe he genuinely desires. In my view, an understanding over the Mediterranean will be found to be in Signor Mussolini's opinion a *sine qua non* of any general settlement.

3. In a recent despatch (No. 1223 paragraph 4 of November 13th)[1] I suggested that if His Majesty's Government were likely to subscribe to some comparatively simple formula regarding our respective rights in the Mediterranean and if they were interested in a general settlement with Italy, then the opportunity of the conversations about the Mediterranean should be taken to consider various other questions in which we are particularly interested, and I mentioned in particular questions relating to East Africa

---

[1] Not printed.

and Arabia. A satisfactory solution of the latter questions would clearly be greatly facilitated if they could be embraced in negotiations for a general settlement, but at this point in the argument the question of the formal recognition of the Italian conquest of Abyssinia begins to play an important part. If we were to attempt a simultaneous settlement of questions outstanding between His Majesty's Government and the Italian Government, to include the Mediterranean, East African and other points (our rights and interests in Ethiopia require some form of confirmation), it seems certain that the Italian Government, holding that a request for confirmation was tantamount to a *de facto* recognition of Italian claims there, would maintain that such recognition was a prerequisite to giving the required assurances. This would not, of course, apply to an attempt on our part to obtain from the Italians, for example, a re-affirmation of the undertakings regarding the Arabian coast recorded in the 1927 Rome conversations.[2] To open conversations however on our rights and interests, for example, in Lake Tsana, in Western Abyssinia and in regard to pasturage rights on the Somaliland border, would certainly be regarded by the Italian public at large, whatever the Italian Government might themselves say, as amounting to *de facto* recognition; and I presume the effect of such action on the other members of the League would have to be taken into consideration. Moreover, I assume—but this is not a point on which the Embassy's opinion is of any value—that any arrangements we might make with the Italians regarding our rights and interests in Abyssinia could only be of the nature of a modus vivendi, and that arrangements carrying the full implication of treaty rights could not be negotiated before formal recognition had been accorded. If this is so, and if His Majesty's Government would regard with some hesitation a course of action which might be held by other members of the League to be at variance with League doctrines in general—namely for a third country to reach an agreement with an aggressor Power on points of interest to that third Power in the territory of the aggressed before the guilt attaching to the aggressor country had been generally condoned and the resulting situation regularised—then we must consider whether a second line of policy exists.

4. Always assuming, as I think we must, that the Italian Government will not be ready to discuss points of mutual interest in Abyssinia until we have given them some form of tangible satisfaction over the Mediterranean, might it not be possible to obtain them, in exchange for a Mediterranean understanding, an undertaking, in some form or other, to respect all the assurances they have given us during the last eighteen months or two years regarding our rights and interests in the former Ethiopian Empire; in other words, to place in cold storage, so to speak, the safeguarding of our rights and interests until such time as we could negotiate with Italy new understandings, which could be registered at the League since they would have been negotiated after formal recognition? I cannot say with any certainty

---

[2] See Series IA, Volume II, No. 469.

whether the Italian Government would be prepared to consider such a suggestion; but I believe that Signor Mussolini's desire for some formal Mediterranean agreement is so strong that he might well be prepared to give us the desired undertaking, the more so perhaps as our offer would show clearly enough that *de jure* recognition was unlikely to be long delayed.

5. The third alternative is less pleasant to contemplate. If His Majesty's Government were to show that, in spite of the conciliatory pronouncements by yourself, by Lord Halifax and by other Ministers of the Crown, we were not in fact prepared to reach any formal understanding over mutual interests in the Mediterranean, then I fear that within a comparatively short time relations between the two countries cannot but deteriorate, and that should this happen, the many assurances which the Italian Government have offered during the past two years regarding their intentions to respect our rights and interests in Abyssinia would have to be regarded as of uncertain value. In such circumstances they would be only too likely to make use of the arguments outlined in paragraph 3 of your despatch under reference, although I would not wish to exclude the possibility that they might, even in these circumstances, respect such pledges as they have already given regarding Lake Tsana.[3] If the Italian Government were determined to take this course, no consideration of international usage would, I feel, restrain them; more particularly as the principles of international law on the points involved seem to be far from well defined.

6. I have spoken about a formal understanding with the Italian Government over our mutual interests in the Mediterranean, and I should perhaps explain a little further what I understand by this phrase, or rather what might constitute the minimum requirements of the Italians justifying the expression 'formal'. You will have noticed the very great change for the better which has occurred in Anglo-Italian relations as the result of (*a*) your speech and that of Lord Halifax in Parliament,[4] (*b*) the withdrawal of the guard from the Legation at Addis Ababa,[5] and (*c*) the signing of the recent clearing and commercial agreements.[6] The reception accorded in particular to the withdrawal of the Legation guard leads me to believe that the reduction of the Legation to a Consulate would have a very great effect. Further, the fact that when I asked the Marquis Theodoli the other day[7] whether a Gentleman's Agreement over the Mediterranean would need to be put in writing he was unable to give me an answer, but referred me to the Salisbury–de Robilant Agreement, seems to show that the agreement in the Mediterranean need not be excessively formal.

7. As I have endeavoured to show, it is in my opinion, not beyond the bounds of possibility that the conclusion of a Mediterranean agreement would

---

[3] See Volume XVI, No. 493, note 3.   [4] See No. 353, notes 2 and 3.

[5] See Volume XVI, No. 486, note 2.

[6] A Commercial Agreement and Exchange of Notes, and an Agreement regarding Commercial Exchanges and Payments, were signed in Rome by British and Italian representatives on November 6, 1936: see *L/N Treaty Series*, Volume 177, pp. 170–219.

[7] See No. 366.

have the effect of ensuring respect of our interests in Abyssinia until such time as *de jure* recognition would enable them to form the subject of definite negotiations. We should therefore utilise any conclusion of a Mediterranean understanding to secure Italian acquiescence in leaving our rights and interests in Abyssinia unimpaired until the appropriate moment for recognition arrives; and I do not consider such an aim to be beyond the scope of realisation. The time and atmosphere factors are however all important. I do not think that the time available is indefinite, but a Mediterranean agreement would create an atmosphere that would greatly diminish the risks of delay, and the reduction of the Legation to a Consulate would be considered here as an earnest of our intentions in a future not too distant.[8]

I have, &c.,

ERIC DRUMMOND

P.S. This despatch was written before the receipt of your telegram No. 428[9] on which I will telegraph my observations as soon as possible.

[8] This despatch provoked extensive minuting in the Foreign Office. Mr. G. H. Thompson, a First Secretary in the Abyssinian Department, in minutes of November 18 and 26 and Mr. Strang (November 26) urged an early decision to reduce the Legation at Addis Ababa to a Consulate General: Mr. Thompson said that in his opinion 'a settlement of the Legation question will be an effective step towards a liquidation of the Abyssinian problem, which is a necessary preliminary to giving effect to the Cabinet decision for the restoration of normal relations with Italy'. In a minute of November 27, however, Sir R. Vansittart expressed the view that there should be 'some marked progress towards the Anglo-Italian agreement . . . before we actually *take* the next step forward', and Mr. Eden minuted his agreement with this on November 29. Telegram No. 136 Saving of December 2 to Paris instructed Sir G. Clerk to broach the subject with M. Delbos of an Anglo-French *démarche* regarding the status of British and French representation in Addis Ababa, to be made around the middle of December, and the *démarche* was finally made in Rome on December 21: see Volume XVI, No. 486, note 2.

[9] No. 376.

No. 379

Mr. Eden to Sir E. Drummond (Rome)

No. 430 Telegraphic [W 15837/9549/41]

FOREIGN OFFICE, *November 16, 1936, 7 p.m.*

On the 13th November Sir Robert Vansittart told the Italian Ambassador that he had noticed that Signor Mussolini in his interview with Mr. Ward Price[1] had made the most satisfactory and ample declarations as to the absence of any Italian intentions in regard to the Balearic Islands. As Signor Mussolini had often made important declarations in this way, Sir Robert felt that these pronouncements had the force of official pronouncements, and presumed that his view was correct.

Signor Grandi said that this view was of course correct. Had he not

[1] See No. 376, note 1.

himself on three occasions[2] given His Majesty's Government the most explicit assurances on behalf of his Government in this respect?

Sir Robert replied that he was by no means underrating these assurances or casting the least doubt upon them; here, however, were the *ipsissima verba* of the Duce himself and Sir Robert only wanted to be in a position to say the right thing from the Italian point of view in case any question as to their exact value in the 'interview' form were raised. In view, therefore, of what Signor Grandi had said to him, he would propose to meet any such question merely by saying that of course Signor Mussolini's words must be taken as a full and sufficient official assurance, but that indeed this was almost unnecessary seeing that the Italian Ambassador had already spontaneously and on several occasions considerably prior to Signor Mussolini's declaration given the same assurances to His Majesty's Government.

Signor Grandi replied that he hoped that this reply would be returned to any question and indeed he expressed the hope that the occasion for giving it would be found.

The Ambassador said that he was returning to Rome in a very optimistic frame of mind, prepared to carry on the good work steadily and without undue haste.

On the 16th November Signor Grandi told Sir Robert that he had been instructed by Signor Mussolini to express to His Majesty's Government the great gratification which he, Signor Mussolini, had had in reading Signor Grandi's account of his conversation with me on November 13th (see my telegram No. 429[3] of November 14th and my despatch No. 1252 of November 13th).[4]

Despatch follows.[5]

2 Cf. Nos. 103, 188, and 291. 3 No. 377. 4 Not printed.
5 No. 1263 of November 16, not printed.

No. 380

Sir E. Drummond (Rome) to Mr. Eden
(Received November 17, 9.30 a.m.)
No. 695 Telegraphic [R 6867/226/22]

ROME, *November 17, 1936, 12.40 a.m.*

Your telegram No. 428.[1]

As His Majesty's Ambassador in Rome I am greatly encouraged to know that His Majesty's Government are prepared to pursue further the proposal made by Signor Mussolini for a 'gentleman's agreement'.

I propose first to deal with the points raised in paragraph 4 of your telegram.

Point 1. I do not believe that Signor Mussolini has any intention of asking us to assume fresh commitments in the Mediterranean.

1 No. 376.

Point 2. He would not wish an Italo-British understanding to have even the appearance of being directed against any other Mediterranean country.

Point 3. I do not think he has this point in mind, though unhappily it has been indicated by some of our own newspapers. Should he raise it, arguments drawn from his own speeches are so overwhelming and the fact that he could hardly ask for limitation on our side without exposing himself to a request for limitation of Italian air forces etc., make me feel that even if he does indicate some such wish he could be led to abandon it without overmuch difficulty. It could further be pointed out to him that as the object of the understanding is to dispel all suspicion and friction between the two countries, to press this question is evidence on his side of suspicion about our ulterior aims. I therefore think that though he may make a tentative suggestion on the subject, the point is not likely to constitute a definite stumbling-block to an agreement.

Point 4. If we make clear our position as outlined in paragraph 6 of your telegram, I do not consider that he would regard this point as requisite to an understanding, please see in this connexion my despatch No. 1240[2] of November 15th, replying to your despatch No. 1227[3] of November 9th, which I am sending by special messenger to Paris today.

I now turn to the desiderata set forth in the third paragraph of your telegram under reference.

A. No general difficulty, but how would this affect or be affected by possible developments in Syria?

B. We can probably secure assurance from Signor Mussolini of a general character. How far it will be kept is difficult to say, though there might well be a temporary amelioration. As you will remember, see my despatch No. 1096,[4] when I taxed the Minister for Foreign Affairs with such propaganda he professed complete ignorance of it. If we were able to produce concrete evidence of intrigue, it would greatly help.

C. I think this is possible though more difficult, because in Italian eyes a question of prestige is involved and I understand Signor Mussolini himself has in the past been the main obstacle to Italian adhesion. He is irritated at the thought that such an important agreement could be reached without Italian participation, and Count Ciano is said once to have muttered 'some day we shall destroy the Montreux Convention'. Further, is it not possible that German influence will be brought to bear against Italian adhesion? Nevertheless I do not believe this adhesion to be unobtainable and the item might perhaps be in some way absorbed under A.

D. More difficult still to combine with an Italian agreement. Apart from certain Italian technical objections, of which you are aware, we have I think always treated the Naval Agreement solely on its merits and as a thing apart from political consideration. Moreover to press Italy on a matter of this kind in connexion with a Mediterranean understanding is, I fear,

---

[2] No. 378.

[3] A marginal note here reads: 'A printed form forwarding copies of Confidential Print'.

[4] No. 274.

likely to lead by analogy, however false, to requests by Signor Mussolini for limitation of our forces in that sea. I trust therefore that you may see your way to waiving this question in the hope that Italy will before long realize that it is in her own interests to adhere to the 1935 Naval Treaty. Friendly relations between the two countries which will result from the conclusion of a Mediterranean understanding are more likely to bring about Italy's adhesion to the Treaty than an attempt to force adhesion as part of the price of the understanding.

E. Though naturally I completely appreciate and understand the importance of this subject, I would earnestly request you to take the following points into consideration:

To urge Signor Mussolini to resume effectual work with the League at the present time is to ask him to throw over completely the statements he made in his Milan speech about the League and collective security. In my opinion he neither can nor will do so nor would he consider such resumption until the majority of the States forming the League have recognised the Italian conquest of Abyssinia. Further, if my information is correct (see in this connexion my despatch No. 1199,[5] paragraph 5) agreement was reached at Berlin that neither Germany nor Italy would move in the revision of the League without previous mutual consultation. If in such circumstances we urge full resumption by Italy of League activities, Signor Mussolini would at once suspect that one of our objects is to undermine his present understanding with Germany—there have already been strong press reactions to suggestions from London that an Anglo-Italian agreement would weaken the Italo-German entente, and he would in my opinion refuse to proceed with the conversations should we insist on the point.

I have not abandoned hope of his ultimate return to League co-operation, but it will only be by a process of time and under our gradual influence. The question of League reform is also likely to loom large in his eyes. To try to hasten matters now would to my mind prove fatal. I therefore venture to urge with all the emphasis I can command that we should not make this an essential point for an understanding. Indeed I should greatly prefer that it should not be raised at all beyond perhaps the expression of a hope that once understanding is reached Italy's full co-operation with the League will be facilitated when the Abyssinian question is finally settled.

To sum up.

I believe we can reach the desired and desirable understanding if we were prepared to limit our desiderata to Points A, B and C. I regard D as extremely difficult and as likely to raise unwelcome counter-proposals. Insistence on E is I fear likely to wreck the conversations.

I do not consider that Signor Mussolini will initiate any of the forbidden subjects under 1, 2 or 4. If he raises 3, I feel that we can probably induce him to abandon it.

You further ask me in paragraph 5 whether Signor Mussolini is likely

<hr>

5 See No. 363, note 5.

to ask for corresponding concessions in return for acceding to our desiderata. If our . . . 6 are limited to A, B and C, I doubt whether he will do so, and I can at the moment think of nothing which he is likely to put forward. It is essentially a Mediterranean understanding which he desires. On the other hand if we insist on D and above all E, the whole scope of the conversations will be altered, and we shall enter the highly controversial sphere of general European politics.

Final method of approach.

This is delicate ground bearing in mind Count Ciano's position. In view however of the fact that the matter is of first class importance and arises directly out of Signor Mussolini's Milan speech and his interview with Ward Price, I feel I should be justified in asking Count Ciano to arrange for an interview à trois, starting the conversation in the way you suggest, provided that I can state that you are anxious to follow up Signor Mussolini's suggestion for a 'gentleman's agreement'.

It would then be possible for me to continue discussions here in the light of the interview. There is unlikely alternative which I feel bound to put before you. I do not know what view you take of a possible invitation to Count Ciano to visit London for the conversations, but if this were practical proposition then I think we should find the path considerably smoothed since the Minister for Foreign Affairs would be so delighted at such an invitation that he would do his utmost to return with an understanding in his pocket in the form of a signed *procès verbal* or even an agreed *communiqué*. I realise of course that an invitation of this nature could in [*sic*] any way only be issued after exploration through the preliminary talks here of what is in Signor Mussolini's mind.7

6 The text was here uncertain.

7 In Foreign Office telegram No. 438 of November 19 to Rome, Mr. Eden thanked Sir E. Drummond for his considered advice, by which he was 'inclined, provisionally, towards working in the first instance for an exchange of purely general declarations, in the expectation that this may be accompanied or closely followed on Italian side by spontaneous acts calculated to produce confidence and goodwill all round'. He thought it best to await Signor Grandi's return before carrying the conversations further, and suggested that confusion might result if Sir E. Drummond were to make a definite approach to the Italian Government in Rome.

No. 381

Sir H. Chilton (Hendaye) to Mr. Eden
(Received November 17, 3.20 p.m.)
No. 282 Telegraphic [W 15914/9549/41]

Immediate   HENDAYE, *November 17, 1936, 1.45 p.m.*

Burgos Government have requested me to convey to you communication date November 15th of which the following is a translation.

'The scandalous traffic in arms, ammunition, tanks, aeroplanes and even toxic gasses [*sic*] which is being carried on through the port of Barcelona is well known. All this material is being transported to this port in ships flying different flags whose real nationality in its greater part is Russian or Spanish.

The National Government being resolved to prevent this traffic with every means of war at its disposal will even go so far if this were necessary as to destroy that port and therefore it warns all foreign ships anchored in that harbour of the desirability of abandoning it in a very short time to avoid consequences or damage which unintentionally might be caused to them on the occasion of military action referred to of which no further warning will be given. Foreigners and non-combatants residing in Barcelona are likewise advised to leave that town and particularly the areas near the port in order not to suffer any damage to themselves which we wish to prevent.'[1]

[1] On November 17 Rear-Admiral Troup, the Director of Naval Intelligence, Admiralty, told Mr. Roberts that he felt sure that H.M.G. had the right to demand a safe anchorage at Barcelona. Mr. Roberts pointed out that no information pointing to immediate operations against Barcelona had been received, but agreed to send a telegram to Sir H. Chilton asking for assurances (see No. 382 below). On November 18 Sir R. Vansittart minuted that he wondered 'if we are not taking this threat a little too seriously. General Franco is not yet in a position to destroy Barcelona.' On November 20, in reply to a question by Mr. Attlee, Mr. Eden read to the House of Commons the text of General Franco's communication of November 15, and explained the steps subsequently taken by the Foreign Office: see 317 *H.C. Deb.* 5 *s.*, cols. 2073–4.

No. 382

Mr. Eden to Sir H. Chilton (Hendaye)

No. 239 Telegraphic [*W 15914/9549/41*]

FOREIGN OFFICE, *November 17, 1936, 11.30 p.m.*

Your telegram No. 282.[1]

On November 14th Military Governor of Palma on behalf of General Franco's Government warned the Rear Admiral Commanding Third Cruiser Squadron of possibility of military operations against Ports of Tarrogona, Valencia, Alicante and Cartegena and asked him to inform all foreign warships as security could only be guaranteed in certain recommended anchorages. No mention was made of Barcelona.

In view of warning transmitted in your telegram under reference Admiralty feel that we are entitled to request similar guarantee in respect of Barcelona.

Please address immediate request to authorities at Burgos in the above sense asking for particulars of recommended anchorages.

You should add that His Majesty's Government feel obliged to request that before operations are commenced proper time shall be allowed for evacuation of British residents.

Repeated to Barcelona No. 162.

[1] No. 381.

No. 383

Mr. Ogilvie-Forbes (Madrid) to Mr. Eden
(Received November 18, 9.30 a.m.)

No. 511 Telegraphic: by wireless [W 15979/62/41]

Immediate   MADRID, November 18, 1936

Your telegram No. 270.[1]
Please see my telegrams Nos. 332,[2] 245,[3] 158[4] and 140.[5]
I will now examine reasons for and against withdrawal of the Embassy and Consulate from Madrid in the light of the present situation.

A. *For*:
1. Safety of life.
2. Avoidance of incidents.
3. Departure of the Government.

B. *Against*:
1. Preservation of life of British subjects and of Spanish employees.
2. Protection for what it is worth in the present anarchy of British interests.
3. Deplorable political effect and loss of prestige especially if other Missions stay.
4. Absence of means of transport and of accommodation en route to the coast for people we are morally bound to protect.
5. Fact that while presence of the Embassy cannot guarantee their lives it may make all the difference.

Before commenting and drawing conclusions on the above it should be noticed:
(i) That British subjects who could and should have gone do not deserve my special consideration.
(ii) That with the exception of Mr. Scott and myself all the Embassy and Consulate Staff are volunteers at their own risk and always with perfect liberty to leave.
(iii) That the present refugees are of different class and circumstances from the last batch.
Comments:
(A)(1). By withdrawing staff their own lives would be saved but all others, mainly innocent humble people driven out of their houses either by the bombardment or enemies on this side would be left in the lurch.
(2). Incidents would not be avoided. Embassy would be more easily plundered if vacated or tenanted only by Spaniards.

[1] See No. 367, note 2.
[2] In this telegram of October 9 (W 13308/62/41) Mr. Ogilvie-Forbes reported that he had told his French colleague that he was determined to stay in Madrid.
[3] No. 236.
[4] This telegram of September 8 (W 10883/62/41) gave an account of the general situation in Madrid and arrangements for guarding the Embassy.
[5] See No. 176, note 2.

(3). It is true that prior departure of Spanish Government takes much of the political sting out of evacuation of Embassy but it would cause consternation both in foreign and in Anglo-Spanish circles.

(B)(1). Our presence will help to save lives of British subjects indicated in A.(1). We cannot guarantee them from bombs or shells or even raids, but they are much safer here than at home.

(2). Comment unnecessary.

(3). Chilean Ambassador now with 600 Spanish refugees, Mexican with 400 and Argentine Chargé d'Affaires with 150, all intend to stay until the bitter end because they fear their inmates would otherwise be murdered. Other Missions will, I understand, follow suit and many European representatives who have departed, such as Norwegian, Dutch, Danish, Belgian, French, Finnish and Yugoslav have left behind some kind of representative in charge of their interests and many of them have Spanish refugees. Surely Great Britain should not shirk what others are enduring.

(4). Is a very practical and indeed paramount consideration. There is neither transport nor housing nor arrangements for future maintenance for all the people we would have to take on 200 miles of road to the sea who range from 17 days to 71 years.

My conclusion is that we must stay here and stick it out as best we can. Everything possible is being done to protect British subjects here and my conscience is clear whatever may happen. I feel we are in honour bound to stand by the unfortunate people who, relying on our presence here, have come in for protection.

If the worst occurs what better end than that of Cavagnari[6] in the execution of duty.

I much appreciate the helpful and sympathetic way in which your instructions to me are always couched.

Repeated to Hendaye No. 71.

[6] Major Pierre Louis Napoleon Cavagnari (1841–79), later Sir Louis, negotiated the treaty of Gandamak of May 26, 1879, at the conclusion of the second Afghan war, and was then appointed British envoy to the Amir of Afghanistan, Yakub Khan. He took up his appointment at Kabul on July 24, 1879, and was massacred there with his staff by riotous Afghan troops on September 3.

No. 384

Mr. King (Barcelona) to Mr. Eden
(Received November 19, 9.30 a.m.)
No. 223 Telegraphic [W 16083/9549/41]

BARCELONA, *November 18, 1936, 10 p.m.*

Your telegram No. 160 of November 17th.[1]

I consider statement regarding traffic in war material in Barcelona greatly exaggerated. Information is very difficult to obtain but I believe

[1] Not printed: it repeated to Barcelona Sir H. Chilton's telegram No. 282 (No. 381). Foreign Office telegram No. 161 of November 17 asked for Mr. King's comments.

only two Russian steamships have arrived of which one the *Kursk*[2] almost certainly brought munitions. Mexican ship *America* also brought munitions I believe and Norwegian steamship *Columbia* brought toluol and various acids which latter *might* be intended for commercial products.

My Italian colleague who has seen the text of the Burgos telegram agrees with me that it exaggerates.

French Consul however thought that there had been formidable importation of munitions here and in the northern ports of Catalonia. This I doubt.

It is possible that insurgent threat to bombard Barcelona may be regarded as a bluff for the present but I think preparations should be made to evacuate this place at very short notice and I am warning the Colony accordingly.

What most people here fear, foreigners as well as Spaniards, is less the bombardment than attack from Reds on all except the proletariat if Madrid falls. German and Italian Consuls have received instructions to evacuate all possible remaining nationals and to leave themselves with staffs, closing the Consulates. Both embarked this afternoon but Italian remaining for the present on ship at Barcelona.

In reply to their report of Consular meeting here of 2nd November, see my despatch 243 of November 3rd,[3] they were told to remain even if separate Catalan State should be established. New instructions therefore may indicate that Berlin and Rome are about to recognise Burgos Government.

French Consul is very anxious for London and Paris to follow common policy and he is asking for instructions to follow my lead here.

[2] See No. 368.   [3] Not printed.

No. 385

Record by Sir R. Vansittart of a conversation with the German Ambassador
[*W 16283/62/41*]

FOREIGN OFFICE, *November 18, 1936*

The German Ambassador called upon me this afternoon and said that although he had no instructions from his Government he thought it was not only a courtesy but his duty to let us know that the German Government were recognising the Franco Government in Spain in the course of the evening.

Herr von Ribbentrop said that the German Government had reached this decision because they considered that General Franco's régime offered the only prospect of stable government in Spain. Herr von Ribbentrop also dwelt on the extent to which German interests in Spain had already suffered at the hands of the Left. He added that he would shortly be in possession of photographic evidence of the most appalling atrocities committed by the communists and anarchists in Spain, so appalling indeed that he preferred not to dwell on it.[1]

[1] The German and Italian Governments announced in identical terms in Berlin and Rome on the evening of November 18 that they had officially recognized the Spanish Government of General Franco, and had recalled their respective diplomatic missions from Alicante and Madrid. The text of the German announcement was printed in *The Times* of November 19, p. 14. Cf. *D.G.F.P.*, Series D, vol. iii, Nos. 123, 124.

No. 386

Memorandum by the Central Department on German air strength[1]

[*C 8249/3928/18*]

Secret   FOREIGN OFFICE, *November 18, 1936*

On November 10th the Minister of Defence stated in the House that the British metropolitan strength was 80 squadrons, including 16 auxiliary squadrons but excluding the Fleet air arm (102 machines at home and 113 overseas) and of course the 25 regular squadrons overseas and in India (268 machines).[2]

2. Mr. Churchill stated in the House on November 12th that our 80 12-machine squadrons gave us a total of 960 first-line home defence aircraft; but, as Sir T. Inskip had included auxiliary squadrons, he considered that the comparable German strength was 1,500 first-line aeroplanes comprised in not less than 130 or 140 squadrons, including auxiliary squadrons.[3] By auxiliary squadrons it must be supposed that Mr. Churchill meant training squadrons and did not refer to the machines of the German Air Sport Organisation, which are not yet formed into squadrons.

3. The Prime Minister stated at a later stage in the debate on November 12th that Mr. Churchill's estimate of the German metropolitan first-line air strength (there is, of course, no non-metropolitan German air force) 'is

[1] In this memorandum, produced under his direction, and in No. 390 below, Mr. Wigram was endeavouring to drive home some points about Britain's air defences which were being adumbrated by Mr. Churchill at this period. It is now well known that Mr. Wigram had been in close touch with Mr. Churchill since the spring of 1935 and had supplied him with confidential information, mainly it would appear in the shape of Foreign Office reports from Germany. The impropriety of such action is lessened by Mr. Churchill's unique standing, the fact that more than twenty other civil servants and Government officials also took this course, the willingness of Cabinet ministers to keep him informed (in the hope of convincing him of the fallaciousness of his estimates), and his access to French secret information supplied by MM. Flandin and Blum. The subject is judiciously examined in Gilbert, *op. cit.*, especially pp. xxi, 712–13, 717–18, 738, 749, 757. In spite of an element of hero-worship in Wigram's attitude he differed from Churchill on important points of policy, such as the Anglo-German naval agreement and the German militarization of the Rhineland. (Cf. Volume XV, No. 455.)
[2] 317 *H.C. Deb. 5 s.*, col. 742, November 10, 1936.
[3] *Ibid.*, cols. 1114–15, November 12.

definitely too high';[4] and to-day he recalls his statement of 1934 that the Government intended to increase the Air Force so that it should be equal in strength to that of any country within striking distance of our shores.[5]

4. It is important to understand these differences. *First, there is no real difference between Mr. Churchill and the Air Staff as to the number of formed German squadrons.* From a statement by the German Air Ministry and our own Air Staff estimate we know that the Germans had 88 squadrons on October 1st last plus, according to our Air Ministry estimate, 11 coastal command squadrons: total 99 squadrons. The Air Ministry hold that these are 9-machine squadrons, each with 3 machines in immediate reserve in the sheds. Thus, the Air Ministry give the total strength of these squadrons as 890 machines; but Mr. Churchill and the French Air Staff count in the three machines in immediate reserve in the sheds, which gives a total strength of 1188.

5. In addition to these regular squadrons, Mr. Churchill allows for 30–40 additional squadrons, which he apparently describes as auxiliary squadrons. The Air Ministry admit the existence of these 30–40 additional squadrons (they incline to the figure of 30), but describe them as training or embryo squadrons about to be thrown off from the parent squadrons as additional regular squadrons. As 9-machine squadrons their total strength is approximately 270 machines which, with the 890 machines of the regular squadrons, gives the total of some 1160 machines admitted by the German Air Ministry and estimated by our own Air Ministry on October 1st last. Mr. Churchill, on the other hand, describes these 30 additional squadrons as 12-machine squadrons; and the total of some 360 machines thus obtained added to his estimate of 1188 machines for the regular squadrons gives his total of 1500 machines.

6. Thus, whilst there is no real difference between Mr. Churchill and the Air Ministry as regards the number of squadrons, there is a difference of

[4] 317 *H.C. Deb. 5 s.*, col. 1150, November 12. It was in this debate on the Address that Mr. Baldwin (*ibid.*, cols. 1144–5) referred to the East Fulham by-election of October 26, 1933 'when a seat which the National Government held was lost by about 7,000 votes on no issue but the pacifist . . . Supposing I had gone to the country and said that Germany was rearming and that we must rearm, does anybody think that this pacific democracy would have rallied to that cry at that moment? I cannot think of anything that would have made the loss of the election from my point of view more certain.' He went on to point out that by biding his time he later won a general election with a large majority and a mandate for rearmament, 'a mandate for doing a thing that no one, 12 months before, would have believed possible'. Sir Winston Churchill in *The Second World War* (London, 1948), vol. i, pp. 169–70, thought that this statement 'carried naked truth about his motives into indecency', but added that 'Mr. Baldwin was of course not moved by any ignoble wish to remain in office . . . His policy was dictated by the fear that if the Socialists came into power, even less would be done than his Government intended.' Mr. N. Chamberlain is reported by his biographer as saying that 'S.B. had forgotten, or did not choose to mention, the long period occupied in examining the deficiencies and drawing up a new programme, which in turn had to be reviewed and revised (mostly by me!)': K. Feiling, *Life of Neville Chamberlain* (London, 1946), pp. 312–13.

[5] In a speech to Scottish Conservatives at Glasgow on November 18; *The Times*, November 19, 1936, p. 16.

some 320 machines; and these machines are the machines which the Air Ministry describe as in immediate reserve in the sheds. Were we to add to the United Kingdom grand total of 960 machines on November 1st the machines in immediate reserve in the sheds, the addition would amount to 480 machines, as each of our 12-machine squadrons has 6 machines in immediate reserve in the sheds. On this showing we should have a total of 1440 machines in our home regular and auxiliary squadrons as against the German total of 1500. On the other hand, no one has made any allowance for the machines of the German Air Sport Organisation which will presumably be forming into auxiliary squadrons before many months are past.

7. From the foregoing it will be seen that the real comparison is either between 960 British regular and auxiliary machines in 80 squadrons (on November 1st, 1936) as against 1160 German machines in 99 squadrons (on October 1st, 1936), *or* between 1440 British machines in 80 squadrons including the immediate reserve in the sheds as against some 1500 German machines in 99 squadrons including the immediate reserve in the sheds.

8. Neither comparison seems to be particularly reassuring and it is very much less reassuring when the following additional factors are taken into account:

(1) The approaching development of the German Air Sport Organisation corresponding generally to our auxiliary air force;

(2) the fact that the range of our aircraft is at present admittedly considerably inferior to, and cannot before 1938 or 1939 equal that of the German machines; even the very comparative parity, which we now enjoy with Germany, is deceptive in that the performance and number of our bombers is inferior to theirs, and, under existing plans of development, will remain inferior. (N.B. Yet no one disputes the fact that we are more vulnerable than Germany so that it might have been thought that parity, if not superiority, in bombers would be essential.[)]

(3) The fact that the Germans are at the moment producing some 320 aircraft a month, of which 200 are military, against a smaller production in this country (it is believed about 170 military machines a month). We shall not reach the German figure of production for at least nine months and, at the present rate, it will not be before 1938 or even 1939 that we shall be producing 'en masse' bombers equal to the German ones.

(4) The fact that while there is now little doubt that the Germans have a further stage of development subsequent to the 1500 first line machines of April next, and will probably be working to 2500 first-line machines in March 1939, we have, so far as is known, not yet thought out any stage subsequent to next April: yet experience shows that plans of this kind cannot be improvised.[6]

[6] For the background of these discussions see N. H. Gibbs, *Grand Strategy* (London, 1976), vol. i, pp. 532–53 and *passim*.

No. 387

Sir C. Wingfield (Lisbon) to Mr. Eden
(Received November 19, 8 p.m.)

No. 224 Telegraphic [W 16187/9549/41]

LISBON, *November 19, 1936, 6.42 p.m.*

Your telegram 151.[1]

Today's 'Diario de Noticias' welcomes Italian-German recognition of Burgos Government[2] as putting an end to intolerable situation involving discussions of non-intervention with a State that does not keep its engagements and resulting in subterfuges of dilatory diplomacy which tolerates plots of Moscow against western civilisation. Discredited and ineffectual London Committee has sustained a mortal blow since the Governments that have recognised the insurgents cannot now treat with Soviet Government otherwise than organiser of war against legitimate Spanish Government. The farce of Russian Ambassador 'exchanging smiles with Lord Plymouth' must end. No one can hesitate between the attitude of Germany and Italy and subversive activities of Russia.

In view of censorship this article may be a sign of intention of the Portuguese to withdraw from the Committee but nothing has been said to me on the subject.[3]

[1] No. 371.   [2] See No. 385, note 1.   [3] Cf. *D.A.P.E.*, *op. cit.*, Nos. 600–8.

No. 388

Mr. Eden to Mr. Ogilvie-Forbes (Madrid)

No. 279 Telegraphic [W 15979/62/41]

FOREIGN OFFICE, *November 19, 1936, 11 p.m.*

Your telegram No. 511.[1]

I greatly appreciate the spirit in which you have put before me the considerations governing your decision to remain in Madrid.

You may be assured of my support in the decision you have taken and of my earnest hope that no harm may befall you or those under your protection during the ordeal through which you are passing.

[1] No. 383.

No. 389

Memorandum[1] by His Majesty's Government in the United Kingdom regarding the Agenda of the Five-Power Conference, communicated to the Belgian, French, German, and Italian Ambassadors on November 19, 1936

[*C 8265/4/18*]

FOREIGN OFFICE, *November 19, 1936*

In their memorandum of the 4th November[2] His Majesty's Government in the United Kingdom had the honour to invite the Belgian, French, German and Italian Governments to consider further a number of matters in order to see whether the various views expressed by the five Governments thereon could be reconciled. In that event it would be possible to agree on certain fundamental principles as a basis for the proposed conference. His Majesty's Government added that it was their intention to make known at an early date their own views on these matters.

2. The first of these matters concerns the guarantees to be provided in the new treaty, and in this memorandum His Majesty's Government wish, for their part, to deal with the questions of a guarantee to this country by France and Germany.

3. On this subject the German Government have suspended a final expression of their views until they have learned those of the other Governments, and the Italian Government have given reasons why they doubt the desirability of extending the non-aggression and guarantee obligations of the new treaty beyond the limits of the Treaty of Locarno.

---

[1] The first draft of this memorandum was prepared in the Foreign Office by Mr. Sargent, Sir W. Malkin, and the Central Department. Sir R. Vansittart described it on November 10 as 'a brilliant paper', and in particular praised the handling of the problem of mutual assistance in paragraph 5 (paragraph 6 of the final version here printed). The draft, after some further polishing up in the Foreign Office, was considered by the Cabinet on November 13: Sir R. Vansittart described the concluding portion of the record of this meeting as 'deplorable'. The Cabinet decided to omit altogether the original paragraph 5 relating to Belgium's position as to the guarantees, and felt that references to the League of Nations should be less categorical. Among other changes they preferred 'hope' instead of 'assume' in the last sentence of paragraph 15. It was also proposed in the same paragraph to substitute, for a statement in the Foreign Office draft that a successful outcome of the five-power conference was 'intended to lead to the solution' of other European questions, the more cautious phrase: 'might be expected to make approach possible to.' This sentence was, however, omitted altogether from the final draft. The process of drafting, and the outspoken criticism inside the Foreign Office of the Cabinet's attitude, can be followed in files C 8112, C 8171, and C 8265 (4/18). Sir R. Vansittart minuted on November 14: 'The Cabinet are already beginning to run away from the London *communiqué* [Volume XVI, No. 476] which was a minimum. I think they will get into trouble if they do. The *fons et origo* of this lies in the view that "the essential object is to get into conversations with the Germans". That is a perversion. The essential object is to get a good, durable, defensible treaty with the Germans. And we shall only get that by firmness. There is nothing of that in all the watery amendments suggested. R.V. Nov. 14.' The final text of the document was agreed at a further Cabinet meeting on November 18.

[2] No. 349.

4. His Majesty's Government see no reason to abandon their view that the United Kingdom should receive guarantees from France and Germany, but they would appreciate a further exposition of the views of the German and Italian Governments on this point. In this connexion His Majesty's Government would recall that in the discussions on the subject of the proposed Air Pact between the five Powers in the spring of 1935 it was proposed that the guarantees to be given should include one to Great Britain by Germany and France; and His Majesty's Government were then under the impression that this proposal was agreeable to Germany and Italy. It is true that on that occasion only air attack was under consideration; but it is difficult to contemplate an air attack which will not involve the other arms.

5. The second question which it is necessary to consider is whether the proposed non-aggression arrangements should be subject to exceptions, and, if so, what the nature of these exceptions should be. On this point there is a difference of opinion between the views expressed by His Majesty's Government and the French Government on the one hand and the German Government on the other. While the two former Governments considered that certain exceptions would be necessary, the German Government 'have no motive for weakening the security for peace which lies in the conclusion of such an agreement for the renunciation of aggression by demanding exceptions of any kind whatever. In case the other Governments concerned should think it necessary to insist on making exceptions of this kind, it would be for them to put forward proposals to this end.'

6. His Majesty's Government fully appreciate that the position of the German Government may in this respect differ from that of other signatories to the proposed treaty. Germany is not at present a member of the League of Nations, and is not, so far as His Majesty's Government are aware, a party to any special arrangements for the rendering of mutual assistance against aggression. The other signatories to the proposed treaty, however, are all bound by the provisions of the Covenant of the League of Nations, and some of them have, in addition, arrangements for mutual assistance in certain circumstances with States who would not be signatories to the new treaty. It is obvious that the treaty must not be inconsistent with the obligations resulting from the instruments referred to; it would, for instance, be impossible for His Majesty's Government to become a party to arrangements which might be incompatible with the provisions of their treaties with Iraq and Egypt.

7. It appears, therefore, to His Majesty's Government to be inevitable that the proposed non-aggression arrangements should be subject to such exceptions as may be necessary to make them acceptable by those signatories whose position is as indicated above. If so, the question arises as to what the basis of such exceptions should be. In their memorandum of the 17th September[3] His Majesty's Government expressed the view that they should

---

[3] No. 206, Enclosure.

be on the lines which were laid down in article 2 of the Treaty of Locarno. The German Government, in their note of the 12th October,[4] point out that in article 2 of the treaty the important exceptions are laid down with reference to the Covenant, and in particular to article 16 thereof, and they give reasons which in their view preclude the repetition of the use of this method.

8. In these circumstances His Majesty's Government desire to suggest for the consideration of the other Governments concerned the possibility of taking as the basis of the exceptions (apart from the case of legitimate self-defence) an act of aggression by a signatory to the new treaty against a non-signatory which constitutes a violation of some instrument by which the signatory in question is bound. All the proposed signatories to the new treaty are bound by the Pact of Paris, to which almost all the nations of the world are also parties; all of them, except at present Germany, are bound by the provisions of the Covenant of the League of Nations; and any of them may also be parties to non-aggression arrangements with particular countries. It seems to His Majesty's Government entirely legitimate, and indeed necessary, that an attack by a signatory to the new treaty upon a non-signatory, in violation of an obligation resulting from any of the instruments mentioned above, should entitle any of the other signatories to come to the assistance of the victim of aggression without thereby violating its non-aggression undertakings towards the signatory concerned. This appears to His Majesty's Government to be the scheme of the German-Polish declaration of the 26th January, 1934,[5] since it is there stated that the two Governments have decided to base their mutual relations on the principles of the Pact of Paris. If this scheme were adopted, the rendering of assistance in such circumstances to a non-signatory would not bring into operation, on one side or the other, the guarantees to be provided in the new treaty. It appears to His Majesty's Government that an exception on this basis would cover all the cases for which it is proper that provision should be made, and they desire to commend this suggestion to the consideration of the other Governments concerned.

9. The next and third question which arises is how a decision should be reached as to whether the non-aggression arrangements in the new treaty have been violated. If these are to contain exceptions such as those suggested above, this question assumes particular importance, for in order to determine whether the non-aggression arrangements have been violated it might be necessary to determine whether a signatory had attacked a non-signatory in breach of an instrument which was binding between them. It appears accordingly to His Majesty's Government to be of particular importance to provide a method of determining this question which should be efficacious, rapid in its action and such as to command the confidence of the Governments concerned and of their peoples.

10. In their memorandum of the 17th September His Majesty's Government expressed the opinion that the best method of determining this question

4 No. 286.   5 See Volume VI, No. 219.

would be to confide the decision to the Council of the League of Nations. In their view the Council, both as regards its composition and the conditions in which it works, would be a more effective body for the purpose in question than any other. In this connexion the following considerations are, in the opinion of His Majesty's Government, relevant. Whatever changes may be introduced in the working of the League, it appears probable, and it is certainly the view of His Majesty's Government in the United Kingdom, that the peace-preserving functions of the Council will become even more important than in the past. It is therefore probable, to say the least, that in the event of its being necessary to determine whether a breach of the non-aggression arrangements had occurred, the Council would have been dealing with the case practically from the outset and would be in full possession of the facts; and therefore, from the point of view both of the authority which its decision would carry and the rapidity with which such a decision could be given, the Council would be a more effective instrument than any other extraneous body.

11. The German memorandum of the 31st March, 1936,[6] proposed such an extraneous body in the institution of an international court of arbitration which would have competence in respect of the observance of the various agreements concluded. This proposal is not repeated in the German memorandum of the 12th October, but His Majesty's Government desire to say that for the purposes of deciding the question now under consideration such a court, which is apparently intended to be an *ad hoc* tribunal and might well be meeting for the first time when it had to decide whether an infraction of the non-aggression arrangements had taken place, would not in their opinion present, from the point of view either of rapidity of decision, full acquaintance with the facts or the authority which its decision would carry, the same advantages as would the Council of the League.

12. The German Government now suggest that the decision should be reached by a common decision of the signatories to the treaty who are, in a given case, not directly parties to the conflict. His Majesty's Government do not see that this solution would present any advantages over the course of leaving each guarantor to decide for itself, and in their opinion it would possess distinct disadvantages as compared with the system of reference to the Council, which the Treaty of Locarno provided for use in the case of both flagrant and non-flagrant violations.

13. In their observations on this question the French Government, the German Government and His Majesty's Government all mention the case, which was dealt with in article 4(3) of the Treaty of Locarno, of immediate action by the guarantors pending a subsequent decision as to whether a violation of the non-aggression arrangements had taken place. His Majesty's Government note that in the German Government's view 'a distinction between flagrant breaches of the treaty and other kinds of breaches of the treaty such as was laid down in the old Rhine Pact will no longer come into consideration in the new pact.' In the view of His Majesty's Government,

[6] See Volume XVI, No. 193, note 2.

however (and this view is confirmed by the discussion of the proposed air pact which took place last year), it is no less necessary now than it was previously to make provision for cases where a sudden and unprovoked attack (such, for instance, as an air attack) is made in violation of the non-aggression arrangements. In such circumstances immediate action by the guarantors may be essential, and it would not be possible to await a decision of the competent body. It appears, however, to His Majesty's Government to be highly desirable[7] to provide, as was done in the Treaty of Locarno, that the guarantors, in deciding to intervene, should know that their decision is subject to a subsequent pronouncement by some appropriate body, so as to ensure that action without a previous finding by that body would not be taken except in cases where no reasonable doubt could exist. If it is decided to adopt the Council of the League as the body to decide whether an infraction of the non-aggression arrangements has taken place, there would be no difficulty in reproducing the scheme of the Treaty of Locarno in this respect.

14. His Majesty's Government fully appreciate the importance and difficulty of this question as to how a decision should be reached whether the non-aggression arrangements in the new treaty have been violated, and they would not wish, so far as they are concerned, to exclude from consideration any proposal which may be made for dealing with it. But for the reasons stated above they are still of the opinion that the best course would be to entrust the decision to the Council of the League.

15. Lastly, there remains the further point raised in His Majesty's Government's memorandum of the 4th November, namely, the point that other matters affecting European peace would, in the words of the *communiqué* of the 23rd July, necessarily come under discussion if progress could be made at the Five-Power Conference. The German Government, in their memorandum of the 12th October, state that they must reserve, until the result of the Five-Power Conference has been reached, their attitude with regard to the question whether, and if so, which, other problems might later be discussed. His Majesty's Government feel obliged to make it clear that the importance which they attach to the successful outcome of the conference of the five Powers is due not only to their wish to see a new treaty take the place of the Treaty of Locarno, but also because they continue to assume that if progress can be made at this meeting, other matters affecting European peace will necessarily come under discussion.

16. His Majesty's Government in the United Kingdom hope that they may receive the views of the Belgian[8] Government on the questions dealt with in this memorandum at as early a date as possible.

17. A similar memorandum has been communicated to the French, German and Italian Governments.[9]

---

[7] The Cabinet agreed on November 18 to substitute 'desirable' for the word 'essential' given in the first draft.

[8] *Note in original*: Also French, German and Italian Governments.

[9] *Note in original*: Mutatis mutandis.

Letter from Sir R. Vansittart to the French Ambassador

FOREIGN OFFICE, *November 19, 1936*

My dear Ambassador,

When handing you this afternoon the memorandum containing our views on the proposed new Western Treaty, I forgot to call your attention to the fact that we had intentionally omitted any reference to Belgium's proposal not to be a guarantor Power in the new treaty. We did this because we considered that this question was so delicate and affects our two Governments so directly that it would be preferable that the matter should be reserved for the present for oral discussion.

We hope, therefore, that you will adopt the same reticence and not mention this matter in your memorandum.

R. VANSITTART

No. 390

Minute¹ by Mr. Wigram on the comparison of British and German air strengths

[*C 8249/3928/18*]

FOREIGN OFFICE, *November 19, 1936*

In March 1935 Herr Hitler told Sir J. Simon in Berlin that Germany had attained parity with Britain in the air.² He was proceeding on the basis that in a statement in Parliament the Air Minister had said that we had some 800 first-line machines. Subsequently, this statement of the British Air Minister was itself shown to be an exaggerated description of the strength of our metropolitan air force, which was shown to have a first-line strength (but with full reserves) not exceeding 600 machines. The balance which had been counted in to the 800 strength was the Fleet air arm which cannot be relied upon to be available in this country at any given moment, and the regular squadrons overseas.

But Herr Hitler himself was also grossly exaggerating at that time for he had no reserves whatever, his 800 machines including, in fact, practically every military machine which could fly in Germany.

However, it was already recognised—and the Foreign Office were well aware, as the correspondence of the time shows—that the important matter was not at that moment comparative first-line strengths but the potential of manufacture; and if the records are consulted it will be seen that there was a strong feeling in this office (which was based on talks with the Air

¹ In this minute Mr. Wigram was commenting on the memorandum of November 18 (No. 386) produced by the Central Department under his direction. An opening sentence, here omitted, called attention to paragraphs 7 and 8 of No. 386.
² See Volume XII, No. 651.

Staff) that the air industry ought to be organised in order to enable us to compete with Germany in the future. It was decided otherwise.

It is legitimate in November 1936 to recall these views of the Foreign Office just 20 months ago. At that date we still had a considerable superiority over Germany. To-day, owing no doubt almost entirely to the better organisation of the German industry, that superiority (as the memorandum within[3] shows) has completely disappeared and the Germans are, in fact, superior, although only yesterday the Prime Minister recalled his statement of 1934 that we would never be inferior to any Power within striking distance of our shores.[4]

Within four or five months the present stage of development of the German Air Force will be complete (1,500 first-line machines with full reserves). We know—and the Air Staff have admitted—that a new stage is in preparation in Germany, a stage which, on a conservative estimate, is likely to aim at a figure of 2,500 machines in the first line, with full reserves, probably by the spring of 1939.

What steps are we taking to prepare a further stage of development corresponding to that already in preparation in Germany? None whatever, so far as is known.[5] What steps further are we taking to ensure that we can catch up—for it is now a matter of catching up—Germany in the matter of production? We talk a lot about the shadow industry; but one thing is certain and that is that in the organisation of the industry we are not taking steps comparable to those being taken by Germany.

It is said that action of that kind would be too expensive, and would imply too much interference with the industry, etc. But it is legitimate to ask, and those who in the Foreign Office see the extensive information which is available as to the political intentions of Germany cannot help asking, whether further delay and a continuance of what look very like inadequate measures in matters so vital to us will not expose us in quite a near future to the most terrible demands which we shall not be strong enough to resist.[6]

R. F. WIGRAM

N.B. Please see also the 'Sunday Times' article annexed: and note the success of the German propaganda—*950 machines, they tell the British public, is their first line strength: they have admitted to our Air Ministry that it is 1150!*[7]

---

[3] i.e. No. 386. [4] See *ibid.*, note 5.

[5] Sir A. Cadogan queried this statement. The British rearmament plans have been described in M. M. Postan, *British War Production* (London, 1952), Chapter II, and other works. An important article by Dr. R. J. Overy, 'The German pre-war aircraft production plans: November 1936–April 1939' (*E.H.R.* October 1975, No. CCCLVII), an up-to-date survey based on published sources and unpublished German documentation, analyses the German aircraft production figures, and shows that there were obstacles to the fulfilment of the German plans which the pessimistic British officials tended to ignore.

[6] A second Parliamentary deputation (see No. 36, note 7) called on Mr. Baldwin on November 23 to discuss the state of British defences. Mr. Churchill gave the meeting the 'latest' French figures of German air strength, which he had received from M. Blum. See Gilbert, *op. cit.*, pp. 800–7.

[7] Commenting on this remark, Sir R. Vansittart wrote: 'Mr. Leeper [Head of the News

Department] shd. call the attention of the "Sunday Times" to this, unless we are tied into knots by any pledge of secrecy. In that case he shd. merely let not only the "Sunday Times" but the rest of the press know, discreetly & at intervals, that 950 is an understatement. I will tell a few of the proprietors myself, beginning with Lord Camrose. It is impossible to let our public go on being fooled by this spate of propaganda.

As to the rest of Mr. Wigram's very useful & cogent memorandum & minute, this is probably the most important aspect of a situation is [sic] that is *really* dangerous for us in so many ways. I think he is right in saying that we have as yet no plan with which to meet the impending fresh German expansion [a marginal comment by Mr. Eden here reads: "I do not think so. A.E."]: we are having difficulties enough with our *present* programme, presumably because our basis has not yet been broadened enough . . . Meanwhile the S. of S. shd. undoubtedly see this, and I will discuss it with him, when he has leisure. I have some additional comment to make. R.V. Nov. 25.' These papers were marked as having been seen by Mr. Eden on December 7, and by Lord Plymouth on December 8.

No. 391

Mr. Eden to Sir G. Clerk (Paris)

No. 1952 [R 6942/6799/96]

FOREIGN OFFICE, *November 19, 1936*

Sir,

The French Ambassador asked to see me last night, when he stated that his Government would be glad to know how we viewed their suggestion that there should be a joint protest in Berlin in connexion with the German Government's action in denouncing the 'rivers' clause of the Treaty of Versailles.[1] The Ambassador added that he knew there had often been differences of opinion on this subject of protest in the past, the French Government thinking it necessary to put themselves on record as disapproving, while we were inclined to regard protests not followed by action as a somewhat useless proceeding.

2. I replied that the Ambassador had rightly diagnosed our usual attitude, and though I had not come to a final decision in the matter my present inclination was to rest content with the statement which I had made in the House of Commons, which was probably a more effective statement of our point of view than any protest could be.[2] I appreciated, however,

[1] On November 14 1936 the German Government had declared that they no longer considered themselves bound by the Articles of the Treaty of Versailles relating to international rivers in German territory, i.e. the Elbe, Oder, Rhine, and Danube, denounced the Rhine Agreement of May 1936 and withdrew their representative from the International River Commissions. For the German Note of November 14 and the events leading up to its presentation see *D.G.F.P.*,forthcoming volume in Series C, vol. vi, Nos. 18 and 25, and editorial notes pp. 37–43 and 51–3.

[2] In reply to a question from Mr. Attlee on November 16 Mr. Eden had stated that it was a matter of regret that the German Government 'should once again have abandoned procedure by negotiation in favour of unilateral action. These regrets are not due to fear that any important British trading interests have been jeopardised by the German Government's decision, but to the fact that action of this character must render more difficult the conduct of international relations': 317 *H.C. Deb. 5 s.*, cols. 1334–5.

that the French Government had made no like statement. The Ambassador said that this was so and that the French Government were in touch with a number of Governments with a view to a joint statement being made. He understood that both Belgium and Poland were favourable to this course, whereas Italy had refused. In the circumstances much would, of course, depend upon the attitude of His Majesty's Government.

3. I replied that Mr. Keane, our representative on the International River Commissions, was at present making a report. I would study it as rapidly as possible and give his Excellency our considered views on this subject on Friday.[3]

I am, &c.,
ANTHONY EDEN

[3] Mr. Keane's report is filed at R 6973/6799/96. No record has been found of a further conversation on this subject between M. Corbin and Mr. Eden on Friday November 20. On November 21 an aide-mémoire was communicated to the Foreign Office from the French Embassy which said that the French Government had instructed their representatives to enquire of interested governments their attitude towards a joint protest against the German action. A further note of November 24, however, stated that the French Government, having received replies to their enquiry, had now come to agree with His Majesty's Government that the best plan was for each government to make an individual protest to the German Government. Mr. Eden's note of December 2 to Herr von Ribbentrop concerning the German denunciation of the 'rivers clause' is printed as No. 428 below.

No. 392

Mr. Eden to Sir G. Clerk (Paris)
No. 1953 [W 16115/9549/41]

FOREIGN OFFICE, *November 19, 1936*

Sir,

During the course of a conversation with the French Ambassador last night we spoke of the work of the non-intervention committee which is dealing with the traffic in arms to Spain.[1] I remarked that the scheme which appeared to have been worked up by our experts seemed to me an extremely elaborate one, and to this the Ambassador assented. In the circumstances could not M. Corbin approach his Government and ask them whether they could not work out something on similar lines. M. Corbin replied that he had already communicated with his Government on this subject and so far received no answer.[2] He would certainly give further consideration to my suggestion.

I am, &c.,
ANTHONY EDEN

[1] See No. 351: cf. No. 370.   [2] Cf. No. 370, note 5.

No. 393

Sir E. Drummond (Rome) to Mr. Eden
(Received November 20, 9.30 a.m.)
No. 703 Telegraphic [R 6962/226/22]

ROME, *November 20, 1936, 5 a.m.*

I asked Minister for Foreign Affairs this afternoon[1] if he had seen Signor Grandi and if he was satisfied with what the latter had said.[2] He replied that they had had a long talk and that things seemed quite satisfactory. I remarked that I was particularly glad of this as I had feared that a rather foolish passage in the 'Times' might have aroused some resentment. I felt sure, speaking personally, that this passage would not have met with approval of my Government.[3] To this Count Ciano answered that I would have noticed perhaps that Press references to remarks I had in mind had been practically nil: only one or two small papers had reproduced passage in question. He had not been much disturbed by it.

2. I then said that I should like to consult him purely personally and not as Ambassador on a question which had occurred to me. It might or might not happen—I wanted to be very careful—that I should receive instructions to go and see the Head of the Government. What would be his feelings? How did he think this could best be arranged? Of course if I got such instructions I should have to see him first and talk them over and then perhaps we might together go to see Signor Mussolini.

3. Count Ciano observed that he had no objection whatever in principle either to my seeing Signor Mussolini alone or—and he thought this might be preferable—that we should see him together. But I must bear in mind that if I did so the whole Press would be full of it. He therefore was inclined to think it would be a mistake for such an interview to take place unless and until we were comparatively certain that we could reach agreement. If I saw Signor Mussolini and things went wrong result would be worse than before.

4. I said that I appreciated this but there were certain explanations of things which Signor Mussolini had said for which I might have to ask. For instance what was in his mind when he spoke of a Gentleman's Agreement? To this Count Ciano replied that he did not think it meant more

---

[1] November 19.   [2] See No. 377.

[3] Commenting on reports of German–Italian–Japanese *rapprochement*, *The Times* in a leader of November 18 wrote: 'As for Italy, she is to approve publicly of Japan's violation of her international obligations while Japan does the same by her. If there is not honour there is at least mutual admiration among thieves. The gesture is charming but completely empty . . .' A minute by Mr. W. R. C. Green of November 19 called the article 'a masterpiece of unctuous priggishness'. Sir E. Drummond was instructed in Foreign Office telegram No. 437 of November 19 to inform the Italian Government, 'in whatever informal manner you think best that "Times" article, which I regard as most unfortunate, was in no way inspired'.

than declarations of policy on the lines already made—certainly not any formal pact.

5. I did not think it wise to pursue the matter further and emphasized that my question had been purely hypothetical as it might well be that my Government would prefer to pursue conversations through Signor Grandi in London and Minister for Foreign Affairs said that of course this was possible but he thought it far better that conversations should take place here since contact with Signor Mussolini would be much easier.[4] He added that in his opinion there was no pressing hurry. Relations were now quite friendly; we could therefore consider matter calmly.

[4] In a marginal comment on the words 'would be much easier' Mr. Sargent wrote: 'It does not seem to be at all easy to judge by §3 of this tel!'

No. 394

Sir E. Drummond (Rome) to Mr. Eden
(Received November 20, 9.30 a.m.)
No. 704 Telegraphic [W 16191/9549/41]

ROME, *November 20, 1936, 5 a.m.*

When I saw Minister for Foreign Affairs this evening I took the opportunity of saying to him that I had found many of my colleagues were greatly disturbed by the recognition by Italy of General Franco's government,[1] because they thought that it signified the end of non-intervention agreement and the committee. Count Ciano said that this was by no means the case; Italian Government intended to go on in the non-intervention committee which was devoted solely to questions relating to supply of munitions to both parties. Therefore recognition did not in any way change the position. It had been brought about somewhat earlier than had been intended namely before the fall of Madrid owing to a note which he thought we must also have received from Caballero government about bloc[k]ade.[2] This seemed to raise somewhat complicated question and was couched in an arrogant tone. Italian Government had thought it much better to have a clear situation

[1] See No. 385, note 1.
[2] This note was dated November 13, according to No. 397 below. It was apparently the same as a note referred to by Mr. Ogilvie-Forbes in his telegram No. 519 of November 18, but this telegram has not been preserved in the Foreign Office archives. A summary which has survived reads as follows. 'Has received note from Spanish Government stating that all ports of Spanish peninsular, [sic] sovereign southern [sic] Government territory, Spanish [text uncertain] Moroccan protectorate and colonies Rio de Oro, Ifni and Guinea both continent and insular having been declared war zones Government of Republic has given orders that no ship shall enter these ports or Spanish territorial waters without first obtaining its permission. This measure, the note continues, affects national and foreign vessels alike and aims at reducing, so far as possible, risks to them from military operations. Spanish Government consider[s] itself exempt from all responsibility for damage arising from the military operations until the end of the present military insurrection.'

as far as they were concerned and had accordingly proceeded to recognise. But the question of supply of arms and ammunition and that of recognition were totally distinct.

No. 395

Viscount Chilston (Moscow) to Mr. Eden
(Received November 20, 3.45 p.m.)
No. 195 Telegraphic [W 16215/62/41]

MOSCOW, *November 20, 1936, 5.2 p.m.* [*sic*]

Your statements in the House of Commons in reply to questions regarding recognition of insurgents by Germany and Italy[1] are sharply criticised in today's press. Reference to 'other countries more responsible than Germany or Italy' for contravention of non-intervention agreement must be classed definitely, says *Izvestia*, amongst those acts which are convincing German and Italian Fascists that England's attitude towards General Franco is identical with that of Germany and Italy. In view of such an assertion which is 'contrary to all known facts' and is clearly designed to absolve Germany and Italy from their self-evident responsibility, it is not surprising that these countries should evince growing belief that they can do anything with impunity. If British and French leading newspapers regard recognition of Franco's gang as an event which increases difficulties and dangers of international situation they should blame for this those who like Mr. Eden by their activities or declarations are simply encouraging the incendaries [*sic*] of war.

Pravda attacks also your statement that there is a difference between recognition of a belligerent and recognition of either side as Government of Spain. Such a statement at a moment when German and Italian bombers are destroying defenceless population of Madrid and reducing city to ruins amounts in fact to support and encouragement of their criminal activities. Your insinuations against an unknown third Power show up all hyprocricy [*sic*] of 'humanitarians' of London Committee and will help interventionists in their task of stultifying any attempt to render that committee effective. Such acts are scarcely calculated to lessen extreme tension of European situation.

[1] In the House of Commons on November 19 (317 *H.C. Deb. 5 s.*, col. 1923) Mr. W. Gallacher asked whether the declaration by the German and Italian Governments of recognition of General Franco's Government was not 'an open and deliberate breach of non-intervention' and whether the British Government proposed 'to meet this new aggression by their policy of "do nothing"?'

Mr. Eden replied: 'Certainly not. It is quite possible to pursue a policy of non-intervention in respect of the supply of arms while recognising a Government of one side or the other. This is, in fact, what most nations have been doing hitherto, because they have recognised the Government of Spain but have pursued a policy of non-intervention. So far as breaches are concerned, I wish to state categorically that I think there are other Governments more to blame than those of Germany or Italy.'

No. 396

Sir E. Drummond (Rome) to Mr. Eden
(Received November 20, 7.40 p.m.)
No. 708 Telegraphic [R 6976/226/22]

ROME, *November 20, 1936, 7.45 p.m.* [*sic*]

Your telegram No. 438.[1]

I understand that the line that you are inclined to follow is to negotiate an early exchange of political declarations about the mutual interests in the Mediterranean bringing in point A as set forth in 3rd paragraph of your telegram No. 428[2] namely territorial status quo and point 2 paragraph 4 namely intervention directed against any third Power. Adhesion by Italy to Montreux Convention, and to 1936 Naval Treaty would be dealt with separately and you hope that such adhesion would through spontaneous Italian action at least closely follow conclusion of Mediterranean understanding. No doubt you would inform Italian Government of your expectations.

If these assumptions are correct I entirely agree.

I do not consider that any harm will ensue by waiting for Signor Grandi's return, in fact it would be an advantage as he will have had opportunities for full discussions with Signor Mussolini and will be able to tell you better than I can or ascertain what is in the latter's mind. I feel, however, particularly after my conversation yesterday[3] with the Minister for Foreign Affairs that it would probably be best for negotiation on texts of declarations to be carried out here. Count Ciano would clearly like to secure the honour of concluding understanding and I believe that we can more easily persuade him should it be necessary to adopt our point of view on any given question than if Signor Grandi were main channel of communication to Italian Government.

[1] See No. 380, note 7.　　　[2] No. 376.　　　[3] See No. 393.

No. 397

Sir E. Drummond (Rome) to Mr. Eden (Received November 24)
No. 249 Saving: Telegraphic [W 16479/62/41]

ROME, *November 20, 1936*

My telegram No. 704.[1]

Today's press publishes articles explaining that the Italian and German recognition of General Franco's government had been 'accelerated' by Largo Caballero's note of November 13th proclaiming all Spanish ports as war zones. The note is published this evening, and Gayda ridicules its pretensions in a long article in the 'Giornale d'Italia'. He argues that Caballero's government is not only incapable of making a blockade effective,

[1] No. 394.

579

but is also incapable of exercising any effective control over the territory it claims to govern. The president of the Spanish Republic had fled to Barcelona, where a Basque government had been constituted which had nothing in common with the government which had fled from Madrid but its 'red fanatisism [*sic*]'. But another motive power behind the act of Italy and Germany was 'the open intervention of Communist Russia in Spanish affairs', with the definite object of securing a fresh means of European revolution. This had imposed a definite reaction upon the nations who were courageous and far-sighted and sound internally. Gayda continues: 'It must be clearly said, without any useless periphrasis, that Italy does not intend to see planted on the shores of the Mediterranean, on Spanish soil, a new centre of Red revolution, a new base of political and military operations for communism.' If certain great Powers had thought fit at Montreux[2] to open the doors of the Mediterranean to Soviet ships of war, loaded with arms and munitions at the service of world revolution, Italy and other powerful nations of Europe were determined to be good watchdogs and prevent 'the grave mistake' from becoming 'the beginning of more irreparable destruction of European order'. 'With this task', Gayda goes on, 'the defence against communism by Italy and Germany in Europe, as by Japan in Asia, will not only be passive, but will take those reactive, not offensive, forms, which the aggressive initiative of the Soviets and their communist committees will impose.'

This is the second time Gayda has given it to be understood that the Montreux agreements gave a new liberty to the movement of Russian warships.

[2] Cf. Volume XVI, Chapter VI.

No. 398

Sir E. Phipps (Berlin) to Mr. Eden (Received November 23)
No. 369 Saving: Telegraphic [W 16376/9549/41]

BERLIN, November 21, 1936

At a reception last night at the Austrian Legation I told Baron von Neurath that I hoped the recognition by Germany of General Franco[1] did not imply that German participation in the London non-intervention Committee would cease.

His Excellency replied that it would not, but he added smilingly that 'non-intervention' in Spain had for some time past been a farce.

I hear from another source that the Chancellor[2] has been apprehensive of late lest a Russian submarine should attack a German merchant-ship in the Mediterranean. He has in this connection been inquiring of his experts as to the radius of such a submarine's action.[3]

[1] See No. 385, note 1.   [2] Herr Hitler.
[3] A minute by Mr. Shuckburgh read: 'The Chancellor presumably will not be unduly worried by a German submarine sinking a Spanish warship. C.A.E.S. 24/11.'

No. 399

Mr. Eden to Sir H. Chilton (Hendaye)
No. 246 Telegraphic [W 16392/62/41]

Immediate   FOREIGN OFFICE, *November 22, 1936, 9 p.m.*

Please take immediate steps to get into touch with General Franco and give him the following information, which I am anxious should reach him if possible before I make public announcement in House of Commons to-morrow afternoon.[1]

His Majesty's Government have been considering further the importation of arms into Spain by sea. His Majesty's Government intend to continue not to accord belligerent rights at sea to either side in the Spanish struggle. Their policy is to take no part in the conflict on either side. In pursuance of this policy it is the intention of His Majesty's Government that British shipping should not carry war material to any port in Spain. Therefore in addition to the action which His Majesty's Government have already taken to prevent the export of arms from this country to Spain they are considering what further action they themselves can take to prevent transport of arms by British ships to Spain.[2]

A similar communication is being made to the Spanish Government.

---

[1] Following the communication of November 15 from General Franco's Government threatening the safety of foreign ships in Spanish ports (No. 381) the question of whether to accord belligerent rights to the parties in the Spanish struggle had been debated both in the Foreign Office and amongst members of the Cabinet. A meeting of ministers at the House of Commons on November 22 decided that 'The general policy of the Government is one of a continuance of Non-Intervention, that is to say to take no part in the conflict on either side', and that therefore it was 'the intention of His Majesty's Government that British shipping should not carry war material to any port in Spain. The best method of securing this is to legislate so as to ensure that British ships do not carry arms and ammunition to any Spanish port.' They agreed that Mr. Eden should send messages accordingly to the Spanish Government and General Franco's Government, and that after consulting the Board of Trade as to the feasibility of the proposed legislation, he should make a statement of policy in the House of Commons, which he did on November 23: see 318 *H.C. Deb. 5 s.*, col. 7.

[2] The conclusions reached by the Ministers' meeting on November 22, and a draft Merchant Shipping Bill framed to secure the suggested legislation, were discussed at the Cabinet meeting of November 25. Mr. Eden said that 'it would be necessary to watch for a favourable opportunity to confer belligerent rights on both parties in the Spanish struggle', which might occur with the fall of Madrid. Sir S. Hoare argued against delay in the recognition of belligerent rights, but the Cabinet finally agreed to approve the policy adopted at the Ministers' meeting, and to the introduction of the Merchant Shipping (Carriage of Munitions to Spain) Bill which would enable ships of H.M. Navy to prevent United Kingdom vessels from carrying arms to Spain. The Bill became law on December 3, 1936.

Sir G. Clerk (Paris) to Mr. Eden (Received November 23)
No. 504 Saving: Telegraphic [C 8347/4/18]

PARIS, *November 22, 1936*

The speech which you delivered at Leamington on Friday has been given the widest publicity over the week-end in the French press, which in general welcomes it enthusiastically.[1] Particular attention has naturally been paid in the first place to your statement that, in accordance with the existing obligations of His Majesty's Government, British arms might and would, if occasion arose, be used in the defence of France and Belgium against unprovoked aggression. It is claimed by many commentators that these are the words which should have been spoken by Sir E. Grey in 1914 and that if so clear and precise a definition of British policy had then been given war might have been averted. While this part of your speech has been received with the deepest interest and sympathy, great attention has also been paid to the remainder and in particular to your statement that British arms might and would, if a new western European settlement could be reached, also be used in defence of Germany in the case of unprovoked aggression against that country. The only discordant note in the welcome which your speech is given is provided by the 'Humanité' (Communist) which finds nothing remarkable or sensational in it and is extremely critical of your recent statements in the House of Commons with regard to the Spanish question.[2]

The 'Populaire' (Socialist) as yet contains no comment on your speech, but Radical Socialist papers are full of praise. Thus Madame Tabouis in this morning's 'Oeuvre' (Radical Socialist) while declaring that the reception accorded to your speech in Germany has not been favourable, states that in the opinion of responsible French circles no better speech has been made by a British Minister for Foreign Affairs since the Treaty of Versailles was signed. For years and years France had never been able to obtain from

[1] A full report of this major speech on international affairs by Mr. Eden to his constituents at Leamington on Friday, November 20, was printed in *The Times*, November 21 (p. 14). The speech is not mentioned in his memoirs. It included the following passage. 'There can be no doubt that attempts to uphold international law have not benefited from the comparative decline of British strength in arms which has existed in recent years. The equilibrium is now being restored—nobody but a would-be aggressor will complain. But, it may be asked, for what purpose will these arms be used? Let me once again make the position in this respect perfectly clear. These arms will never be used in a war of aggression. They will never be used for a purpose inconsistent with the Covenant of the League or the Pact of Paris. They may, and if the occasion arose they would, be used in our own defence and in defence of the territories of the British Commonwealth of Nations. They may, and if the occasion arose they would, be used in the defence of France and Belgium against unprovoked aggression in accordance with our existing obligations. They may, and, if a new Western European settlement can be reached, they would, be used in defence of Germany were she the victim of unprovoked aggression by any of the other signatories of such a settlement . . .'   [2] Cf. No. 395 and No. 399, note 1.

England anything but vague promises of collaboration, but now it had been put down in black and white that Great Britain would defend France and Belgium in the event of unprovoked aggression. After reflexion, your speech was interpreted in responsible French circles as a public commentary on the British Locarno note handed yesterday to all the Locarno Powers.[3] This commentary, containing as it did at the same time an affirmation of alliance with France, an offer to Germany and a threat to the latter that the Franco-British alliance might stand alone, was likely to have a considerable influence on the Locarno negotiations and for the maintenance of peace. An editorial in this morning's 'Ere Nouvelle' (Herriotist) sees in your speech a pledge of Great Britain's adherence to the policy of collective security. This, however, imposes certain obligations of wisdom and prudence on France and the editorial concludes with a warning to France not to get involved in the Spanish conflict but to stick to its policy of non-intervention. The 'République' (Radical) and the 'Petit Journal' (Left Centre) are pleased that the defence of France and Belgium is definitely included among the vital interests of Great Britain.

As for the press of the Right, Wladimir d'Ormesson, writing in the 'Figaro' (Right) this morning, maintains that your statement of His Majesty's Government's obligations towards the defence of France, Belgium and Germany contains nothing new but is nevertheless welcome. He thinks that your motive was firstly to emphasise Franco-British solidarity and secondly to exercise pressure on Germany to negotiate a new Locarno Pact. In this morning's 'Echo de Paris' (Right) Henry de Kerillis states that it is because all parties in England are now alive to the German menace that you have been able to utter such decisive words and ones so contrary to England's preferences, habits and traditions. France was in miraculous fashion restored to a favourable situation and it was to be hoped that she would profit by it by putting a stop to partisan policy and effecting the union and reconciliation of all Frenchmen in the face of external danger.

A leading article in yesterday's 'Temps' stated that you had defined Great Britain's position in a manner so formal and categoric that there could be no misunderstanding with regard to an attitude which had hitherto given rise to contradictory interpretations. Last night's 'Paris Soir' printed brief statements in commendation of your speech by MM. Mistler and Grumbach, the President and Vice-President respectively of the Foreign Affairs Commission of the Chamber, and by MM. Georges Bonnet and Paul Reynaud, the ex-Cabinet Ministers.

[3] No. 389.

No. 401

Sir H. Chilton (Hendaye) to Mr. Eden
(Received November 23, 2.45 p.m.)

No. 299 Telegraphic [W 16387/62/41]

HENDAYE, November 23, 1936, 12.50 p.m.

My telegram No. 298.[1]

I have shown Burgos communication to French Ambassador and rubbed in the last sentence.[2] He said that in view of information contained in your telegram No. 246[3] he would take up with his Government the question of infiltration into Spain across the French frontier of recruits for the Red Army.

[1] This telegram of November 22 gave the reply of the Burgos Government to an urgent joint appeal of November 21 from the British and French Ambassadors to take the greatest care to restrict any military operations at Madrid to purely military objectives. Sir H. Chilton had been instructed to take this step following an urgent message from the French Government to the Foreign Office to the effect that leaflets had been dropped in Madrid giving notice that unless the city surrendered at once it would be destroyed 'to-night' (apparently November 20). The reply denied that any such threat had been issued, and regretted that the situation necessitated bombardment of tactical objectives in street fighting.

[2] This sentence read: 'Madrid is not defended by Spaniards but in great majority by foreigners who pass in thousands without difficulty across the French frontier.'

[3] No. 399.

No. 402

Mr. Eden to Sir H. Chilton (Hendaye)

No. 249 Telegraphic [W 16528/62/41]

FOREIGN OFFICE, November 23, 1936, 10 p.m.

My telegram No. 248 of today.[1]

You should make the following additional communication to the Burgos authorities.

The Legislation which is being obtained will confer powers on H.M. ships to take any British ship which has been ascertained to be carrying war material to Spain into a British port.

Similarly any British ship suspected of carrying war material to Spain will be taken to a British port for examination.

Instructions are being issued to H.M. ships accordingly.

His Majesty's Government trust that the above information, together with that contained in my telegram referred to above, will be brought to the notice of all Commanders of warships under the orders of General Franco.

[1] The telegram, despatched at 4.45 p.m., instructed Sir H. Chilton to inform the Burgos Government that 'it is not anticipated that after our legislation has been passed [see No. 399, note 2] any British ships will attempt to take arms to Spain' but that His Majesty's Government would give their 'immediate and careful attention' to any 'reliable evidence pointing to any such attempts being made'.

No. 403

Mr. Eden to Sir G. Clerk (Paris)
No. 1985 [C 8403/4/18]

FOREIGN OFFICE, *November 23, 1936*

Sir,

The French Ambassador asked to see me this morning, when he began by expressing his Government's satisfaction with the note[1] which we had addressed to the other signatories of the Locarno Treaty. While the French Government were not in agreement with our note in all points of detail, they did approve its general lines, and the Ambassador understood that the French Government would be addressing us a communication very shortly in order to make this clear.

2. The French Government, the Ambassador continued, still felt some anxiety about the Belgian position, and greatly hoped that I would be able to advance matters during my conversations with M. van Zeeland this week.[2] The Belgian Government had moved very far since the conversations of last March, and the French Government fully appreciated Belgium's internal difficulties. At the same time they did wish to know where they stood, and it was really imperative to be certain that Belgium stood by the Covenant and by Article 16. The French Government felt that we were better placed than anyone else to secure this clarification in the Belgian position.

I am, &c.,
ANTHONY EDEN

[1] No. 389.
[2] M. van Zeeland visited London on November 27 and 28: see No. 430 below.

No. 404

Mr. Eden to Sir G. Clerk (Paris)
No. 1986 [R 7063/226/22]

FOREIGN OFFICE, *November 23, 1936*

Sir,

At the conclusion of a conversation with the French Ambassador this morning[1] His Excellency spoke to me of our negotiations with Italy. These, he stated, were causing the French Government very considerable anxiety. It might be extremely embarrassing for them were certain forms of Anglo-Italian arrangement come to in respect of the Mediterranean. They felt the need of the greatest caution in order to ensure that whatever our intentions this understanding was not interpreted in certain quarters as being directed against France. There might be several motives in the Italian desire

[1] Cf. No. 403.

for rapprochement. Maybe it was just a genuine desire to ease the tension between the two countries, or possibly it was an attempt not ill regarded from Berlin to show that France could be left out of important negotiations.

2. For all these reasons the French Government were seriously apprehensive of the effect which the outcome of our negotiations with Italy might have upon French public opinion.

3. I told the French Ambassador that his fears seemed to me much exaggerated. As I had already told him there was no question of an alliance or even of a pact with Italy. I did not know what form the outcome of our negotiations would finally take. As he knew Signor Grandi had not yet even returned from Rome, and until he did we could not be aware what was in Signor Mussolini's mind. In any event, however, we should naturally be extremely careful not to agree to any action which could be interpreted as being directed against a third party, and, as I had previously told the Ambassador, I would keep him fully informed of all developments. Meanwhile I had taken the opportunity of Prince Paul's visit to this country[2] and of an interview I had had with the Turkish Ambassador[3] to speak to both these States in the sense in which I had already spoken to him. I was confident that they had complete faith in us and in what we were doing. This seemed somewhat to reassure the Ambassador, though it is clear that the French Government are very apprehensive.[4]

I am, &c.,

Anthony Eden

[2] Prince Paul, First Regent of Yugoslavia, arrived in England on November 11 on a visit to the Duke and Duchess of Kent.

[3] See No. 407 below.

[4] After this conversation with Mr. Eden, M. Corbin went to see Mr. Sargent, in order to explain the feelings and fears of the French Government in greater detail. Mr. Sargent endeavoured to persuade him, as Mr. Eden had done, that there was no danger that an Anglo-Italian détente would lead to French isolation, but he 'refused nevertheless to be comforted' (R 7303/226/22). Cf. D.D.F., Series 2, vol. iv, No. 30. In a minute of November 27 Sir R. Vansittart described the French fears as 'childish'. 'Anglo-French relations have never been better, & we will certainly do nothing to weaken them if the French don't do so by crying out when they are not only not being hurt but actually helped.'

No. 405

Mr. Eden to Sir G. Clerk (Paris)
No. 1987 [*W16529/62/41*]

FOREIGN OFFICE, *November 23, 1936*

Sir,
During the course of a conversation with the French Ambassador this morning His Excellency stated, in a reference to the situation in Spain, that I was at liberty to make it clear in the House that not only had the French Government not asked us to reconsider our attitude to non-

intervention, but they were definitely of the opinion that non-intervention should continue.

2. I then gave M. Corbin an account of the statement which I was to make on the Spanish situation at Question time in the House of Commons.[1] The Ambassador at once expressed his agreement with this statement, and said that he was particularly glad that we were not granting belligerent rights at this stage. To do so would certainly give the impression that we were going to facilitate General Franco's blockade. This in turn would have encouraged Italy to assist Franco to make his blockade effective, which he certainly could not do alone. By our clear statement we would check, if we did not actually stop, any Italian tendencies in this direction, and this was most important.[2]

I am, &c.,
ANTHONY EDEN

[1] Cf. No. 399, note 1.
[2] M. Corbin's account of this conversation is printed in *D.D.F.*, *op. cit.*, No. 21.

No. 406

Letter from Major C. S. Napier (War Office) to Mr. Roberts

[*W 16391/9549/41*]

Secret   WAR OFFICE, *November 23, 1936*

Dear Roberts,

Following our conversation on Friday[1] I enclose a note on the supply of arms to Spain. So far as aircraft are concerned this has been prepared in consultation with the Air Ministry. You will see that our evidence does not bear out Mr. Eden's statement in the House on the 19th of November that 'there are other Governments more to blame than those of Germany or Italy'.[2] I cannot help feeling afraid that this statement may be seized on by Germany or Italy to justify intervention, at least to their own nationals.[3]

You also asked me for my views on what evidence could safely and usefully be submitted to the Non-Intervention Committee by His Majesty's Government. I am dealing with this separately.

I do hope you will not hesitate to make use of our specialised experience of arms traffic. At the time of the Abyssinian crisis, when the then Foreign Secretary was particularly interested in the arms situation, I was asked if we could furnish weekly or fortnightly bulletins. We much prefer to make up our summaries (of the sort I have been supplying to you) at intervals

[1] November 20.   [2] See No. 395, note 1.
[3] In a minute of November 23 Mr. Roberts referred to this conversation with Major Napier, whom he had told that he felt sure that Mr. Eden 'had in reality no doubts as to the flagrant manner in which both Germany and Italy had disregarded the Agreement'. It was not easy, however, for the Department to collate and assess at their proper value the individual reports which continued to be received, and he accordingly asked Major Napier to prepare the note which appears as an enclosure to this document.

of a month because we then have an opportunity of weighing up our information in the light of confirmatory or conflicting reports; for you will realise that the grain needs to be sifted from the chaff. At need, however, I am always ready to advise you on such information as we have.

Yours sincerely,
C. S. NAPIER

ENCLOSURE IN No. 406

Note on the supply of arms to Spain in contravention of the Non-Intervention Agreement

1. The arms supplied to Spain from European countries fall into two categories, which need to be clearly distinguished:

A. Arms, the movement of which governments cannot, or do not, control. No blame, other than a charge of inefficiency, attaches to the governments of the countries of origin or transit. In certain countries the roots of the illicit trade in arms are so well established that it simply cannot be brought under control. Legislation does not constitute control.

The volume of this traffic is very considerable and the bulk of the material has gone to the Spanish Government: but it mainly comprises small arms and ammunition, grenades, powder and the like, which are unimportant in comparison with—

B. Modern weapons, e.g. aircraft, A.A. guns, tanks, bombs and gas, supplied by, or with the permission of, governments. These are the weapons with which the war will be won or lost.

These two categories constitute entirely different problems for the Non-Intervention Committee: the one is a police matter, the other a question of power-politics and their repercussions.

Three governments have supplied arms—Italy, Germany and Russia. There is no evidence on which to convict any other government of breaking its obligations.

2. *Arms from Italy*

Note. Our information of Italian action may not be complete but, such as it is, it is of unimpeachable authority.

Prior to her non-intervention declaration on 28th August Italy despatched 50–60 aircraft, with bombs, pilots and mechanics. Of these aircraft 20–24 were landed at Vigo on and after 28th August.

On the 1st September Franco asked Rome for armament for the cruiser *Canarias* and on 3rd September for another 24 aircraft. Rome promised to supply.

Since 28th August, and up to the second week of November, the following have been sent from Italy—

Aircraft at least 75.
Bombs, aircraft stores, pilots and mechanics in proportion.

Armament (guns and machine guns) for the Cruiser *Canarias*: several of Franco's transports have been armed at Spezia.

Tanks—number not known, but probably of the order of 100.

Gas—There are grounds for believing that a report (from a reliable commercial source) that gas cylinders from Spezia were unloaded at Seville on 13th November is correct.

This material supplied by Italy is either—

(*a*) Material in use by Italian units in Spain, which are co-operating with Franco, but remain under control of the Italian Government: or

(*b*) Material sold to Franco, partly for cash, partly on a barter basis for copper.

Italy's future intentions may be deduced from—

i. Mussolini's advice to Franco to reject the supervision scheme proposed in the Non-Intervention Committee as likely to hamper the supply of arms.

ii. The report to Franco from his representative in Rome, dated 16th November, that he 'has definitely been able to deduce that the Italian Foreign Office has made up its mind to give all necessary help'. The cooperation of Italian submarines has already been promised to Franco.

3. *Arms from Germany*

Note. Our information of German action is less full than in the case of Italy: much of it is entirely reliable but it cannot be regarded as in any way complete.

Prior to her non-intervention declaration on 24th August, Germany supplied 26 aircraft to Spain with bombs, pilots and mechanics. At the end of August at least three German vessels unloaded war material at Vigo and Seville, but these had been despatched before 24th August.

During September and October the following were sent from Germany—

Aircraft	at least 35
Incendiary bombs	at least 4,000
Aircraft machine gun ammunition	at least 500,000 rds

and other war material of which the details are not certainly known: it probably included tanks, A.A. guns, field guns and shell. On 1st November two German ships (known as having already taken war material to Spain) were reported by H.M. Consul at Hamburg as loading tanks and munitions.

Germany, like Italy, is taking copper in exchange for war material, and has also supplied trained personnel, of which a proportion are organised in German units. It is probable that the scale of German assistance is at least comparable to Italian: in terms of copper it is larger, but this copper may cover economic as well as military assistance.

4. Arms from Russia

Note. Our information of Russian action is very full and circumstantial in regard to the volume of traffic, but not as to exact details.

There is no evidence on which to convict Russia of having sent war material to Spain before the second half of September. The first supplies of Russian war material reached Spain about October 1st.

The volume of war material supplied since October 1st has been very large and by mid-November certainly compared well with the contributions of Italy and Germany. The bulk of this traffic is from the Black Sea. Arms are also reaching Spain from the Baltic, but in this region it is difficult to distinguish Russian from other illicit traffic.

Although almost every vessel engaged in carrying war material from Russia is known, it is extremely difficult to estimate quantities, because care is taken to supply provisions and lorries (which probably constitute no breach of the non-intervention agreement) at the same time. The following have been supplied:

> Aircraft   at least 75
> Tanks   probably 100 or more

and several thousand tons of other war material including bombs, guns and shell, mortars, small arms and ammunition. Trained Russian personnel have accompanied this material.

Reports that gas has been supplied come only from Italian sources and are, so far, unconvincing.[4]

[4] This report and Major Napier's letter led to some lengthy minuting. Mr. Collier wrote on November 24 that he too had been surprised by Mr. Eden's statement, since the papers which he had seen seemed to establish 'not only that the Italian and German Governments had begun to ship arms to General Franco before they joined the Non-intervention Agreement . . . but that, in the case of Italy at least, there was evidence that the Spanish revolt had originally been prepared' with Italian connivance if not instigation. He thought that the Soviet Government only began to supply arms when German and Italian non-observation of the Non-Intervention Agreement became apparent. What really perturbed him however was the growth of a belief in Liberal and Labour circles 'that the Government have been induced by people who I have heard described as "Conservatives first and Englishmen afterwards" to adopt a policy of conniving at Signor Mussolini's now avowed policy of spreading Fascism throughout the world as an antidote to Communism . . .' Mr. O'Malley on November 30 disagreed with the view that it was 'Signor Mussolini who started the trouble'; he thought that the Soviet Government or Third International had been asking for trouble, in Spain and elsewhere, for many years back. While 'refraining from arguing the question of whether the dictators or the communists are the more dangerous to ourselves' he said about Mr. Collier's reference to 'Conservatives first' that he was 'certainly not prepared to fit this party-coloured cap on my own head'. Sir G. Mounsey (December 1) said that he did not see 'that the Secretary of State's observation in the House was unfounded'. Sir R. Vansittart, also on December 1, did not comment on Mr. Eden's assertion, defended British policy on the ground that 'We simply have not the wherewithal to face the possibility of trouble on 3 fronts', and asked who exactly were the 'Conservatives first and Englishmen afterwards' and what exactly were they supposed to have done.

No. 407

Mr. Eden to Sir P. Loraine (Angora)
No. 156 Telegraphic [R 7026/226/22]

FOREIGN OFFICE, *November 24, 1936, 3 p.m.*

I told Turkish Ambassador[1] on November 23 that in view of certain press reports of Anglo-Italian negotiations, I was anxious to make present position clear to him. In entering upon these conversations there was no intention in our mind, nor, I felt confident, in that of Italian Government, of coming to any arrangement either at the expense of or affecting in any way our good relations with a third party. Our sole object, and in this also I thought Italian Government were in agreement, was to bring about a lessening of recent tension and a general improvement in our mutual relations. Neither side were [*sic*] contemplating an alliance or even a pact, but I felt sure Ambassador would agree that any conversations leading to an Anglo-Italian *détente* were to be welcomed.

2. His Excellency thanked me and felt sure this communication would be very welcome to his Government. They certainly had never suspected for a moment that we would take any action detrimental to our existing friendships, but they would nonetheless welcome any negotiations leading to an improvement in Anglo-Italian relations.

Repeated to Rome.

[1] H.E. Bay Fethi Okyar.

No. 408

Sir E. Phipps (Berlin) to Mr. Eden (Received November 26)
No. 382 Saving: Telegraphic [C 8427/4/18]

Confidential   BERLIN, *November 25, 1936*

Your speech at Leamington[1] with its reference to France and Belgium has not unduly disturbed the higher Nazi circles.[2] Their information, obtained from hosts of Nazi observers in England, is to the effect that the British public will not fight again for France or Belgium for at least a generation, and that the fighting spirit is so dormant in England that only an attack on the Empire would awaken it.[3]

[1] See No. 400, note 1.
[2] In an earlier telegram, No. 343 of November 21, Sir E. Phipps referred to comments on the speech in the German press. Herr Scheffer in the *Berliner Tageblatt* had remarked that if a new Western European settlement bringing in Germany were not achieved the result, in practice, would be an Anglo-French alliance.
[3] Commenting on this paragraph in a minute of November 26, Mr. Wigram wrote that it showed the rashness of a recent statement by the General Staff 'that it was now so well-known that England would defend Belgium that a German invasion was much less to be feared'.

In this connexion I learn from the same reliable source that Herr von Ribbentrop is busy perfecting the Nazi intelligence and propaganda service in England.[4] Germans abroad who refuse to do intelligence or propaganda work, if called upon, are either recalled to Germany or submitted to business pressure from this end.

[4] Mr. Wigram also referred to means of prohibiting the action of Nazi agents in Britain, and said that it was 'the view of the responsible technicians that were His Majesty's Government to take action of this kind, the Nazi organization would have to go underground, which would greatly hamper its activities'. Sir R. Vansittart also hoped that 'the Government will now take the firm course and tackle the question of these Nazi (& Communist) organisations in England . . . R.V. Nov. 28.' Mr. Eden, however, wrote: 'I am afraid that I am not clear how the action apparently proposed by Sir R. Vansittart is going to stop the Germans "perfecting the Nazi service". Maybe we shall know less about it, but is that an advantage? A. E. Dec. 1.'

No. 409

Sir E. Phipps (Berlin) to Mr. Eden
(Received November 26, 9 p.m.)
No. 385 Saving: Telegraphic [W 16751/62/41]

BERLIN, *November 25, 1936*

When I saw the Minister for Foreign Affairs[1] this morning I did not find any disposition in him to be unduly perturbed about Spain.

His Excellency thinks General Franco will win in the end, but that the war may drag on for a very long time. He said that German military experts thought the Reds had made a great mistake in sending so many men to the relief of Madrid, instead of forming a fresh force to outflank General Franco.

[1] Baron von Neurath.

No. 410

Mr. Eden to Sir E. Drummond (Rome)
No. 1300 [R 7117/226/22]

FOREIGN OFFICE, *November 25, 1936*

Sir,

The Italian Ambassador came to see me this evening, when he gave me some account of the conversations which he had had in Rome.[1] Speaking first of the background, which Signor Grandi said he wished to depict to me in order that I might more clearly understand the position, the Ambassador explained that he had at one time been a little anxious lest there should be too much optimism in Italy as to what could be achieved in the way of an agreement between us. In the minds of the public recognition of the conquest

[1] Cf. No. 377, note 5.

of Abyssinia loomed much too large, and the anticipation there seemed to be that we should soon get an agreement which would embody such recognition. The Ambassador hastened to add that this was not of course in Signor Mussolini's mind, nor in Count Ciano's. They fully understood our position in the matter, and the fact that we could not bargain. Indeed it suited them. They realised that at some time or other, and in our own way, we should probably take some action, and the date or form of recognition did not worry them.

2. As to the form which the 'Gentlemen's Agreement' was to take, Signor Mussolini had asked the Ambassador to say that there would be no difficulty whatever on the Italian side. Indeed I derived the impression that Signor Grandi was still vague as to both form and content. He suggested that the document might embody some reference to the complementary nature of our interests in the Mediterranean, and possibly (and I understood this was Signor Grandi's own suggestion) a declaration from each of us that we would consult together in the event of any matter arising which might be held to threaten our good relations. Signor Mussolini entirely shared our view that it would be much wiser to have no pact. There had been too many of these already and they were discredited, and his final instructions to Signor Grandi had been to see me and learn what my ideas were. This was not, the Ambassador begged me to believe, because Signor Mussolini wished to throw the ball back to us, but because he was genuinely prepared to consider our ideas in the matter.

3. I replied that we had not considered the matter in detail since the Ambassador's departure because I thought it better to await the result of his conversations with Signor Mussolini.[2] Now, however, I understood it was his Government's wish that we should turn our minds to the matter in detail. Signor Grandi said that this was so. He would be glad if we could let him have our suggestions as soon as was convenient. In his view it was necessary to make progress at a measured pace, not trying either to rush things unduly, nor allowing them to lag too long.

4. I then told the Ambassador that there was one aspect of this matter which I felt sure that we should both wish to keep before us throughout our conversations. It was important to do nothing to arouse even a mild form of anxiety among third parties. I had therefore taken upon myself to assure both the French Government[3] and the Yugoslav and Turkish[4] Governments that not only was it not in our mind to come to any arrangement which could in any way be construed as directed against a third party, but that I was convinced from what the Ambassador had told me that nothing of the kind was in Signor Mussolini's mind either. The Ambassador appeared gratified at this and said that this truly represented the situation.

5. Speaking of Italy's relations with France the Ambassador stated that the agreements reached in Rome between M. Laval and Signor Mussolini in 1935[5] still stood.

[2] Cf. No. 393.   [3] See No. 404.   [4] See No. 407.
[5] Signed in January, 1935: see Volume XIV, No. 90, note 3.

6. Signor Grandi went on to say that he had had one difficulty on the Fascist Grand Council which he wished to mention to me which showed how sensitive opinion in Italy still was. He had spoken for two hours on Anglo-Italian relations. Among the points which he had emphasised had been the satisfactory attitude of our press. He had been somewhat taken aback, however, when at the conclusion of his remarks he was asked how he explained the leading article in the 'Times' of the day before, which he had not seen, more particuarly the reference to Japan and Italy as the two thieves.[6] Signor Grandi knew, of course, that the British press was independent, and said so, but it was not easy to make a body like the Fascist Grand Council understand this. I then told His Excellency that the article in question had not in fact been in any way inspired from the Foreign Office and that on my instructions Sir E. Drummond had made this clear to Count Ciano.

7. Signor Grandi then spoke of the report which had appeared in the press this morning of some movement of our ships from Malta to Spain.[7] Here again I was able to tell the Ambassador that there was no truth in this report and to explain to him that the First Lord of the Admiralty had made this abundantly clear in a statement in the House of Commons an hour ago.[8] Signor Grandi was much relieved at this explanation which he said he would at once telegraph to Rome.

I am, &c.,

ANTHONY EDEN

[6] See No. 393, note 3.   [7] See *The Times*, November 25, 1936, p. 13.
[8] See 318 *H.C. Deb. 5 s.*, cols. 405–6.

No. 411

Mr. Eden to Sir E. Drummond (Rome)

No. 1302 [W 16668/62/41]

FOREIGN OFFICE, *November 25, 1936*

Sir,

During the course of a conversation today with the Italian Ambassador His Excellency referred to Spain (see last paragraph of my despatch No. 1300 of today's date[1]). I told Signor Grandi that since he had mentioned the Spanish troubles I would avail myself of the opportunity to tell him of our increasing anxieties in relation to certain developments there. I understood of course the reasons for the rival desires of Germany and Italy on the one hand and Russia on the other in Spain. At the same time we were inevitably apprehensive as to the effect this might have on European relations. In my view we ought all of us to be extremely careful in relation to our attitude to Spain. The Ambassador in reply admitted that unfortunately the civil war had not finished quickly. He begged me to believe that the

[1] No. 410.

Italian Government had genuinely wished to observe a non-intervention agreement. It was quite true that they had sent a lot of help to General Franco previous to the non-intervention agreement. But after that their eyes had been fixed on France. When they found that the French Government had faithfully observed the agreement, they had been the more determined to do the same themselves. Then there had come the Russian attitude and the help they had given to the Spanish Government to an extent which it was impossible to ignore. Why had Russia to butt into this business at all? France, who had a Socialist Government and who was a neighbour of Spain was behaving perfectly correctly. There could only be one reason for the Soviet intervention: their desire to create a Communist State in Spain next door to France. The Ambassador emphasised to me that he had been surprised at the extent of the anti-Communist feeling in Italy. The Russians professed that this was due to a rapprochement between Germany and Italy. This was far from being the truth. The real cause was the spectacle of Russia taking a hand in Mediterranean affairs which made Italians of all classes apprehensive and which had aroused among the Fascists a feeling somewhat similar to that of the old party days of strife with the Communists in Italy itself.

2. The Ambassador mentioned that he had been very glad to see in the press reference made to the assurances which he had given us about the Italian Government's attitude towards the Balearic Islands.[2] He wished once again to make it absolutely clear that Italy had no desire or intention to see any part of Spain's territories whether colonial or otherwise, pass out of her hands. Indeed Italy's policy in this respect was the same as ours, i.e. she wished to see Spain continue as she had been up to the present—a neutral Power.[3]

I am, &c.,

ANTHONY EDEN

[2] See Nos. 103, 188, 291, and cf. No. 379. See also *The Times*, November 25, 1936, p. 14.
[3] A secret treaty between the Italian and Spanish Nationalist governments, negotiated by General Franco and Count Ciano's secretary, Signor Filippo Anfuso, was signed on November 28, 1936. It contained six clauses, the effect of which on the Italian side was to pledge support to ensure the success of the Nationalist cause. The two powers promised each other neutrality in the event of one of the contracting parties finding itself in conflict with one or more powers, with the use of ports, airlines, railways, and roads. On the other hand, the first clause contained an Italian assurance as to the conservation of the independence and integrity of Spain, 'including both metropolitan territory and colonies'. Although ostensibly directed against third parties, that amounted to an Italian pledge to respect Spanish territory, including the Balearic Islands. See on this point Coverdale, *op. cit.*, pp. 153–6. The text of the agreement was printed in *Ciano's Diplomatic Papers*, pp. 76–7, and is reproduced in Coverdale, pp. 413–14.

No. 412

Sir E. Phipps (Berlin) to Mr. Eden
(Received November 28, 11.50 a.m.)
No. 391 Saving: Telegraphic [C 8513/33/55]

BERLIN, *November 26, 1936*

Following from Prague. Begins.

A responsible and usually reliable émigré gives us the following information said to be supplied by a Danzig German in close touch with Forster.

Danzig is to be occupied in December by units of German Navy; the inhabitants at the same time declaring their wish to be re-incorporated with Germany.[1] German Government reckons on British acquiescence and Polish weakness coupled with concessions for Gdynia.

Would you inform Foreign Office if you think that worth while.[2] Ends.

Repeated to Warsaw No. 11 Saving.

[1] Cf. No. 139.

[2] In telegram No. 394 Saving of November 28 Sir E. Phipps said that he thought it 'highly improbable' that Herr Hitler would take any action to alienate Poland at the present moment, and that he therefore doubted the authenticity of the report from Prague. Sir R. Vansittart, however, in a minute of December 1 said that he did 'not think it quite so improbable as Sir E. Phipps does. The German F.O. and the Reichswehr wd. naturally be against this adventure, but some of "the Party" think—and talk—otherwise'. Telegram No. 89 to Warsaw of December 2 instructed Sir H. Kennard to inform M. Beck privately of the contents of telegram No. 391. Cf. No. 425 below.

No. 413

Minute by Sir A. Cadogan on a proposed system for the supervision of aircraft entering Spain by air

[W 16559/9549/41]

FOREIGN OFFICE, *November 26, 1936*

I can't help saying that the Air Scheme[1] seems to me the purest fantasy—and costly fantasy at that. But of course we must not be caught killing it.

It depends, for its operation, on the consent of both sides, and I understand from Mr. Roberts that we have reason to know that this will not be forth-

[1] The Chairman's Sub-Committee of the N.I. Committee appointed on November 12, 1936, a Technical Advisory Sub-Committee consisting of service attachés of the countries represented on the Chairman's Sub-Committee. This body prepared a report (N.I.S.(36) 167) with a plan for the establishment of a system of supervision of aircraft entering Spain by air, as distinct from land and sea routes. Mr. Hemming on November 23 circulated a note on the estimated cost of the plan. In a minute, also of November 23, Mr. Shuckburgh summarized the plan in the following terms. 'This scheme, like that for sending 1,000 officials to Spain, was conceived in a mood of fantasy. We are to appoint 20 air agents, 61 assistant air agents, 29 clerical officers, 29 interpreters and 29 typists, to be scattered about in all countries lying within 1500 miles of Spain. This includes all the countries of Europe.' Mr. Hemming estimated the cost in a full year as £170,000.

coming.[2] In these circumstances I most reluctantly submit that we should disingenuously give it our (mildest possible) blessing in principle. This might perhaps be in the form that though we are not satisfied with the scheme, we are unable to suggest a better alternative, and we agree that the Madrid Government and the Insurgent authorities be sounded as to their acquiescence.

I sincerely hope they will reject it as, if they do not, we shall be committed to considerable expenditure and to the application of a scheme which in point of efficacy can be compared only to that under discussion between the Walrus and the Carpenter.[3]

[2] Mr. Roberts also pointed out, in a minute of November 25, that the scheme did not apply to military aerodromes, and it would, therefore, he concluded, be quite ineffective in Germany, Italy, and the Soviet Union. 'It is not surprising then that their representatives on the sub-committee have raised no objection to it or that the German rep[resentative] has expressed himself as heartily in favour of it.'

[3] Late on November 26 Sir G. Mounsey addressed the following minute to Lord Plymouth. 'The Secretary of State spoke to me about this paper this evening, and asked me to let you know his views which are as follows.

1. As regards this paper, H.M. Govt. cannot express an opinion on its merits without further time for reflection.

2. They would welcome the production by the French Government of their views on the land scheme, which has been criticised on the grounds of its elaborateness and expense. It was understood that the French Govt. have something simpler in mind and their suggestions would be welcomed.

3. H.M. Govt. maintain their view that before any of these schemes can be usefully pursued further in any detail, it is essential to ascertain whether the authorities in Spain would permit, welcome or co-operate with the Committee's representatives in formulating means of control and observations on the spot. G. M. 26.11.36.'

The schemes for both land and air control in Spain (cf. Nos. 338, 370, 392, and 399) had been discussed at a meeting of the Cabinet on November 25, at which Lord Plymouth reported on the proceedings of the N.I. Committee and said that he 'could not postpone making a statement of the Government's policy much longer' with regard to the land scheme. The Cabinet agreed that Lord Plymouth should inform the Committee that 'His Majesty's Government would agree in principle to the scheme for making non-intervention effective in Spain'; that Mr. Eden should 'give a sharp reminder to certain Governments that notoriously were supplying war material to one side or the other that this arrangement would be unnecessary if they would take steps to stop the exportation of arms to Spain'; and that there was no objection in principle to the Foreign Office acting as a channel of communication to the two parties in the Spanish struggle. See No. 427 below.

No. 414

Mr. Eden to Sir H. Chilton (Hendaye)

No. 254[1] Telegraphic [W 15998/62/41]

FOREIGN OFFICE, November 27, 1936, 2.15 p.m.

It is proposed to give Mr. Consul Sullivan[2] temporary local rank of First Secretary in order that he may be in a better position to act as channel

[1] No. 300 to Mr. Ogilvie-Forbes, Madrid. [2] Cf. No. 359.

of communication with Spanish Government now at Valencia. Do you see any objection?[3]

[3] Sir H. Chilton replied in telegram No. 305 of November 27 that he had no objection. Mr. Sullivan was given the temporary local rank of First Secretary on December 19, 1936.

No. 415

Sir E. Drummond (Rome) to Mr. Eden (Received November 27, 3.20 p.m.)
No. 717 Telegraphic: by telephone [R 7187/226/22]

Important ROME, *November 27, 1936*

After a dinner at the Palace last night given in honour of Admiral Horthy,[1] Minister for Foreign Affairs asked me when I was likely to come and see him and discuss the possibilities of a gentleman's agreement. I said that I had heard nothing further as yet from my government (your telegram No. 444[2] arrived this morning) but that I knew that they had thought it best and more courteous to await the return of Signor Grandi to London, particularly as the latter had no doubt had conversations with Signor Mussolini on the subject. Count Ciano appeared slightly irritated by this answer and said 'I know exactly what the Duce has in mind far better than Signor Grandi; although he has some general idea, my knowledge is much more complete'. What was in Signor Mussolini's mind, he went on, was something very simple—just a few lines. Count Ciano thought it would be a great mistake to go into any details and in particular into questions of limitation of forces of which mention had been made in the British press; on this point I immediately agreed with him. He said perhaps the best method of procedure would be to eliminate the things we neither of us wanted, thus arriving at what we actually did want. When I replied that of course one of the things we should not want was that the understanding could be thought to be directed against anyone else, Count Ciano said he entirely agreed. He suggested the sort of thing that was desirable was an agreement to respect each other's mutual interests in the Mediterranean and consult each other if these interests were threatened. As this might have implied idea of a consultative pact I suggested as a variant that we should respect each other's mutual interests in the Mediterranean and take no action to the contrary to such interests. Count Ciano observed that if we respected each other's interests we should certainly take no action contrary to them. On my suggesting that we might also propose existing territorial status quo in the Mediterranean should be respected by us both I gathered from what Count Ciano said that he would see no difficulty on this point.

2. His Excellency then mentioned Abyssinian question and stated that while he fully understood our position and did not expect any immediate recognition he would like to clarify the position. I answered that I did not think it would be possible to deal with these two matters together—we

[1] Regent of Hungary.   [2] A telegraphic version of despatch No. 1300 (No. 410).

wanted to keep liberty of spontaneous action over Abyssinia. Count Ciano answered that he understood our attitude but that he would like to make with me a general 'tour of the horizon' which would include Ethiopia. He told me that he had spoken to Signor Mussolini about my suggested meeting with the latter[3] and Signor Mussolini had agreed that such an interview would be a mistake until matters were sufficiently far-advanced to make success certain. Once I saw the head of Government the press would expect immediate results.

3. It was clear from my conversation which was conducted in circumstances of considerable difficulty since there were continual interruptions, that Count Ciano is extremely anxious to carry on conversations here and himself to sign the agreement or at any rate to be the main responsibility for its conclusion. He clearly does not wish that this role should be reserved for Signor Grandi. Personally, I feel that it would be wise to make a tour of the 'horizon' which he suggested. It would enable me to raise such questions as Montreux treaty, naval treaty of 1936 and even League questions in a perfectly friendly and non-committal fashion. Nor do I see any objection in listening to what he has to say about Abyssinia. I shall of course be most careful not to commit myself in any way.

4. In the course of our discussions Count Ciano suggested that I should come and see him and have a quiet talk early next week—he even suggested the end of this. I think therefore that I should suggest Tuesday, December 1st, and I should be grateful if you found it possible to supply me before that date with a tentative formula regarding our interests in the Mediterranean.

[3] Cf. No. 393.

No. 416

Sir E. Phipps (Berlin) to Mr. Eden (Received November 28, 8.30 p.m.)
No. 393 Saving: Telegraphic [C 8512/99/18]

BERLIN, *November 27, 1936*

I learn that Propaganda Minister has summoned provincial Nazi leaders in order to institute a campaign against rumours of war.

It appears that the four years plan has aroused grave misgivings and that the peasantry believe *raison d'être* of economic independence is merely a prelude to war. The recognition of General Franco and German-Japanese agreement[1] have intensified these rumours so much that counter action has become necessary. Doctor Goebbels is informing local leaders that nothing is further from Chancellor's mind than war, that intervention in Spain is out of the question and that the populace must be convinced without undue publicity that this is the case.[2]

[1] See No. 421, note 3 below.
[2] Minutes by Mr. Wigram, Mr. Sargent, and Sir R. Vansittart included the following comments. 'We must not forget that the German leaders have constantly emphasized the

pacific intentions of Germany and of Herr Hitler himself . . . Some little time ago the Embassy told us that if war came, every German would believe his country was guiltless. Therefore this action on the part of Dr. Goebbels need not surprise us. It is accompanied, as we know, by wholesale preparations for war and in particular, by the extraordinary campaign for "Wehrfreudigkeit" one stage of which (now presumably almost complete) teaches the terrible war preparations of Germany's enemies . . . and the second step of which (which is only just beginning now that the German "counter" armaments have made sufficient progress) teaches the wretched physique and lack of courage etc of these same enemies. R. F. Wigram. 30/11.' Mr. Sargent (November 30) thought the fact 'that the German people should be reacting against a fear of war is quite a new phenomenon, and it will be extremely interesting to see whether it develops'. To this Sir R. Vansittart replied: 'I expect this is only a temporary relaxation of temperature. The need for that is bound to come from time to time.'

No. 417

Mr. Eden to Sir G. Clerk (Paris)

No. 2012 [W 16840/62/41]

FOREIGN OFFICE, *November 27, 1936*

Sir,

I asked the French Ambassador to come and see me this evening when I told him that I had read with interest the record of his conversation with Lord Plymouth this morning,[1] and I wished to discuss the matters to which he had then referred a little further in order that I might learn as completely as possible what was in the mind of the French Government.

2. We spoke first of the League Council, when the Ambassador said that M. Delbos was much preoccupied at the prospect of this meeting which he regarded as in every way unfortunate. It was difficult to see how it could achieve anything and it would have the effect of driving Italy further from the League. On the other hand, it had to be admitted apparently that the Spanish Government had a right to ask for a meeting. If we shared these preoccupations, was there anything we thought could be done? I replied that I entirely agreed with M. Corbin's analysis of the difficulties. Unhappily I did not see any way out. I had been asked by the Chilean Ambassador, who was, I understood, now President of the Council whether I had any views as to a date and had replied that I certainly could not make any suggestions without further reflection. Perhaps the first step might be for each of us to see the Spanish Ambassadors accredited to our capitals and try and find out what was in their minds and what they hoped to gain by a meeting of the Council. I was apprehensive that among the difficulties which might conceivably be raised might even be the authority of the Spanish Government itself. In this connexion I did not know what view the

[1] Not printed. Most of the points raised were re-examined in Mr. Eden's conversation with M. Corbin, who did, however, begin by telling Lord Plymouth that M. Litvinov had spoken to the Spanish representative in Moscow about his government's plan to bring the affairs of Spain before the League Council and had said that he considered this course to be 'most inadvisable'.

South American States, for instance, took. Some of them were, I believed, sympathetic to General Franco even though they had not recognised him.

3. The Ambassador then spoke of the possibility of some international initiative being taken in an attempt to put an end to the fighting in Spain.[2] At first sight the Ambassador admitted that the chances seemed poor indeed. On further reflection, however, there were certain considerations which should be taken into account. Matters were not going well with General Franco and the Portuguese representative on the Non-Intervention Committee had been quite frank on the subject to the Ambassador only today. In the circumstances, Germany and Italy might wish to extricate themselves from a very difficult position and might accordingly be more willing to listen than they would otherwise have been. On the other hand, the Ambassador was by no means sure that the Spanish Government would look favourably on this initiative. In any event, there was much to be said for a joint endeavour by our two countries to put a stop to this appalling state of affairs which was a reflection on modern European civilisation. The Ambassador thought it just conceivable that we might get the agreement of Germany, Italy, Russia and Portugal to make the attempt. But he was not sanguine that the attempt would succeed at this stage. Even if it did not, however, it would have its psychological effect in Spain itself as well as outside of it. It was the intention of the French Government that as a stage of this initiative the six powers should reaffirm their adherence to the policy of non-intervention. This would be an indication, as it were, that some of them at least were turning over a new leaf in their conduct in [t]his respect at the same time as they took the initiative to bring the fighting to an end.

4. I remarked that the difficulties would be as apparent to the Ambassador as they were to me, and I should like a little more time in which to reflect on the suggestion. At the same time it was clear there were difficulties in any step and I thought there was some force in his analysis of the present attitude of Germany and Italy towards the Spanish situation. Furthermore, if some initiative of this kind were under way, then it might be reason for delaying for a while at least the actual meeting of the Council. Finally I undertook to see the Ambassador again in the matter as soon as possible.

I am, &c.,

ANTHONY EDEN

[2] In making this proposal, M. Corbin was following instructions from M. Delbos telegraphed to him late on November 26: *D.D.F.*, *op. cit.*, No. 39.

No. 418

Mr. Eden to Sir G. Clerk (Paris)
No. 2016 [W 16890/9549/41]

FOREIGN OFFICE, *November 27, 1936*

Sir,

During the course of a conversation with the French Ambassador today[1] His Excellency referred to the situation in the Balearic Islands, which, he said, was giving his Government cause for grave anxiety. The activities of Italians in Majorca were of a character which it was difficult to reconcile with any policy except an intention to attempt to secure a dominating position on the Island. The Ambassador referred to the activities of Signor Rossi and Signor Margottini. The latter, he said, had been an Italian Delegate to the Naval Conference. These activities indicated an attempt by the Italians to secure commercial control of the Islands. The Ambassador gave as an example that whereas the French air line which had been accustomed to use Majorca as a landing place previous to the Civil War had not been allowed to resume operations, an Italian commercial air line had been opened. Similarly he understood that an Italian shipping line was now calling at Majorca. A Foreign Legion was being raised in the Island which was open to enlistment by Italians, and which, he understood, consisted for the most part of Italians. It was quite true that assurances had been given by the Italian Government to us,[2] at the same time the facts as they were now known to the French Government seemed hard to reconcile with these assurances.

2. In the circumstances the French Government thought it desirable to indicate that they were keeping what was happening under observation. With a view to emphasising this they were considering instructing their Admiralty to send a ship to Palma.

3. I replied that we fully agreed as to the desirability of watchfulness over what was going on in the Balearic Islands. Indeed I thought we had more than once suggested that the French Government should themselves approach the Italian Government in order that they might receive assurances similar to those that had been given to us. Moreover, we thought that the more watchful the French Government were the better. After all, the future of the Balearic Islands, though it was a matter of interest to us both, was of more vital concern to the French Government than it was to us. So far as a ship was concerned, I thought it a good plan on the part of the French Government to send one. We had in fact had a ship at Palma almost continuously since the Civil War began.

4. The Ambassador seemed surprised and somewhat comforted at what I said about a British ship and asked whether we could not perhaps send one more, when the French Government might send two.[3]

---

[1] Cf. No. 417.   [2] See No. 411, note 2.

[3] In reply to a query on the file as to whether it was desired that the Admiralty should

5. Finally he remarked that he thought it likely that M. Delbos might make clear the attitude of the French Government on the matter of the Balearic Islands in the course of the debate which was to take place in the French Chamber next week.[4]

I am, &c.,
ANTHONY EDEN

be asked to keep a second ship permanently at Palma, Sir G. Mounsey wrote: 'I hardly think we need send another ship to the Balearic Isles just after receiving renewed Italian assurances. It would look very distrustful. G. M. 3.12.36.' Sir R. Vansittart replied: 'We had better leave this to the Admiralty. R.V. Dec. 4.' However, the matter was discussed by the Cabinet on December 9. It approved in principle Mr. Eden's proposal 'that a second British ship should be stationed in the Balearic Islands subject to its proving practicable'.

[4] Cf. *D.D.F.*, *op. cit.*, No. 53 for M. Corbin's account of this conversation.

No. 419

Mr. Ogilvie-Forbes (Madrid) to Mr. Eden
(Received November 29, 10 a.m.)
No. 557 Telegraphic: by wireless [*W 16842/62/41*]

MADRID, *November 28, 1936*

Minister of State on November 27 appealed to the Council of the League of Nations under Article 11 to examine as soon as possible complaints of the Spanish Government regarding intervention of Germany and Italy in the civil war and their recognition of Burgos Government.[1]

[1] Cf. No. 417. Señor del Vayo's telegram to the Secretary-General is printed in *L/N.O.J.*, *January–June 1937*, p. 35. Mr. Strang recorded (W 17238/62/41) a telephone conversation of November 28 with M. Avenol, who was at that time in Paris. M. Avenol referred to the Soviet Government as being unenthusiastic about such a meeting but apparently reconciled to it as unavoidable. The French were conscious of the embarrassment to which the appeal might give rise: this feeling was stronger among the officials than among the ministers. Mr. Strang, on Mr. Eden's instructions, then indicated to M. Avenol the British attitude, which was one of grave doubt as to the wisdom of calling an extraordinary session of the Council in response to the Spanish appeal. On the other hand, there was seen to be 'the greatest difficulty in the members of the Council refusing to accede to the Spanish request'. M. Avenol said that if the Members of the Council agreed that the meeting should take place he would propose to the President a meeting on December 7. After reporting this conversation to Mr. Eden, Mr. Strang telephoned Mr. Eden's agreement, adding that this 'did not necessarily mean that we were committed to accepting that particular date'. The Chilean representative, Señor Edwards, wrote on November 29 to M. Avenol saying that his Government considered that an early meeting was undesirable but that if the meeting was inevitable it should take place on December 14 rather than an earlier date. It was finally agreed that the Council should meet for the Ninety-fifth (Extraordinary) session on December 10 (*L/N.O.J.*, *ibid.*, pp. 6 and 35).

No. 420

Sir E. Drummond (Rome) to Mr. Eden (Received December 3)
No. 1288 [C 8701/4/18]

ROME, *November 28, 1936*

Sir,

I have the honour to inform you that Signor Attolico, the Italian Ambassador in Berlin whom I have known for a long time past as he worked with me for fully five years in Geneva, called to see me for a few minutes yesterday evening. After some general conversation he began to criticise our latest note to the Locarno Powers.[1] He observed that by that note we were in fact extending the 'exceptions' in the old Locarno Treaty by our reference to the Pact of Paris. I remarked that I did not quite see how he maintained this view, because it was clear under the old Treaty that the Covenant of the League prevailed over Locarno arrangements and that therefore if a State signatory of the Locarno Treaty attacked a League State, the other signatories would be free from their Locarno obligations and would be allowed to assist the attacked State. Signor Attolico admitted that this might be so in theory but added that it was useless for us to expect that Italy and Germany would accept our present proposals. Indeed if we pressed them the impression would be created that we did not really wish for a new Locarno. I strongly demurred to this point of view.

2. His Excellency indicated quite clearly that the real objection of Italy and Germany was to the Franco–Soviet and Czechoslovak–Soviet Pacts. Apart from these, he saw no difficulty in other exceptions such as the Franco–Polish pact. We could, he said, obtain eighty per cent of the old Locarno if we wanted it, but neither Germany nor Italy could possibly accept today any European arrangements which admitted Russia to even an indirect participation in Western European affairs. This was entirely due to happenings in Spain. The truth was that fifty-one per cent of the agreement between Germany and Italy (he told me that the actual terms of the agreement had been all settled before Count Ciano's visit to Berlin) was due to the Spanish crisis.[2] The Fascist and Nazi authorities had seen in developments in Spain a potential threat to their régimes and when there was any question of the régime being in danger no political considerations of any other kind were allowed to stand in the way. I would draw your attention to this last observation which seems to me to be of considerable interest.

3. Lastly, Signor Attolico endeavoured to persuade me that much harm was being done by what he called our hesitant policy. We ought to recognise facts and General Franco's government. I observed that I thought that much harm was being done by precipitancy and that I doubted whether the recognition of General Franco's government was, as yet at any rate, justified.[3]

[1] No. 389.　　　　　　　　　　　　　　　　　　　　　[2] No. 334, note 2.
[3] Mr. Wigram on December 7 noted this as 'the first indication we have of the German

604

4. I am sending a copy of this despatch to His Majesty's Representative at Berlin.

I have, &c.,
ERIC DRUMMOND

and Italian attitude to our latest memorandum'. Sir R. Vansittart wrote: 'This is dishonest stuff, but it is what we shall meet with from Germany & Italy jointly. It is also impracticable stuff—and they know it—because nothing will induce France to give up her existing agreements. Nor is there any valid reason on earth for discriminating between her agreements with Czechoslovakia & Poland, except that the former is destined for aggression at some not very distant date. We can obviously count no more on a "Western Pact", & this mood would not enhance its value even if we got it. R. V. Dec. 10.' Mr. Eden wrote: 'Interesting, but there is nothing unexpected in this. It is worth noting that this is the second occasion on which it has been suggested that we do not want a western agreement. A. E. Dec. 15.'

No. 421

Record by Sir R. Vansittart of a conversation with the Japanese Ambassador[1]

[W 17163/62/41]

FOREIGN OFFICE, *November 30, 1936*

The Japanese Ambassador came to see me this afternoon to ask if I could give him any information as to the intentions of His Majesty's Government in regard to the recognition of General Franco.

I replied that all that I could tell him had already appeared in the press, which was the legislation prohibiting the carriage on British vessels of munitions of war to Spain.[2] Further than that there was nothing in contemplation.

The Ambassador then said that he would like to ask me a frank question. If his Government were to follow the lead of the German and Italian Governments in recognising General Franco, would that tend to make people in this country think that Japan was acting under German influence as the result of the recent agreement?[3]

I said that a frank question deserved a frank answer. I should say that on public opinion here the effect would be exactly as he had anticipated. Indeed I did not see what other conclusion public opinion could be expected to draw. The agreement itself in the eyes of the man in the street had been ill-staged. The ordinary man could not quite understand why the countries that had least to fear from Communism were so anxiously and somewhat theatrically combining against it. Incidentally these dramatic combinations

---

[1] H.E. Shigeru Yoshida, K.C.V.O.   [2] See No. 399.
[3] Cf. No. 393, note 3: a German–Japanese agreement against the Communist International, the so-called Anti-Comintern Pact, and supplementary secret agreements had been initialled in Berlin on October 23 by Herr von Ribbentrop and the Japanese Ambassador in Berlin, M. Mushakoji. These agreements were signed on November 25, 1936: see *D.G.F.P.*, Series C, vol. v, pp. 1138–40, and vol. vi, No. 57.

were not exactly in accord with the view generally held in this country that the promotion of ideological blocs was undesirable. However, there it was. The agreement had been concluded with a roll of drums, and the result had been presented to the world with something of a flourish. After so much publicity the results had on examination seemed to the average eye a little tenuous. Sometimes, indeed, it had seemed to the man in the street even a little ridiculous. Judging by these not very impressive or wise results, the man in the street, or anyhow the man in Fleet Street, who had come to the conclusion that this dramatic affair was due to German rather than to Japanese inspiration, had begun to speculate as to whether after so much commotion there must not be something more in existence than met the eye. And whatever the truth about that, no surer way of stimulating speculation could have been adopted than the method which had been actually followed. If now on top of that, the Japanese proceeded to follow the German example in recognition, the man in Fleet Street would almost certainly indulge in further speculations, for he already thought that the German-Italian recognition had been premature, seeing it was now by no means certain who would win, and when, and how. The whole situation in Spain was in fact so doubtful that it was well to be cautious lest one should look a little silly. That at least was the attitude of the average man of common sense, and I thought it would be a principle from which it was generally unwise to depart widely.

The Japanese Ambassador said that this in fact was what he himself had felt also. He did not of course feel able to discuss the German–Japanese Agreement, and I said that I was equally disinclined to do so but that he himself had brought it up in the plainest fashion (I could see however that though somewhat ill at ease, he made no motion of dissent when I was pricking the agreement with mild ridicule. Indeed he evidently shared these criticisms himself).

He asked me in departing whether he might enquire again as to our intentions in regard to recognition, for he would like to advise his Government to keep in line with ours. I said that he might certainly do so and that I would keep him informed so far as was possible, but that at present there was really nothing to tell him beyond what I had already said.[4]

R. V.

[4] This record was initialled by Mr. Eden.

No. 422

Mr. Eden to Sir G. Clerk (Paris)
No. 2028 [W 17094/62/41]

FOREIGN OFFICE, *November 30, 1936*

Sir,

I asked the French Ambassador to come and see me this afternoon, when we discussed the Spanish situation. I told M. Corbin that I had received during the weekend a message from M. Léger stressing the importance the French Government attached to an early reply to their suggestion that a joint Anglo-French initiative should now be taken in favour of mediation in the conflict in Spain. I further understood the view of the French Government to be that it was important that this mediation should be set going before the meeting of the Council.[1] We were prepared to take part in this attempt to put a stop to the fighting, though I understood the French Government's conception to be that we should jointly approach Germany, Italy, Soviet Russia and Portugal in this initiative.

2. The Ambassador said that this was so. I suggested that it might also be valuable if we were at the same time to inform the United States Government of our intention and ask for their sympathy and approval.

3. M. Corbin then explained that it was his Government's intention that as a part of this attempted mediation we should all redeclare our adherence to the policy of non-intervention. I told him of my anxiety that such a declaration might not be taken very seriously in the world in view of the actual conduct of some of the present members of the Non-Intervention Committee. M. Corbin persisted, however, in believing that some such declaration would be necessary, if only as an indication that if mediation failed we should not all regard ourselves as free to intervene as much as we liked. Moreover, he hoped that it would be possible so to phrase the declaration as to make it clear that some of us at least would be turning over a new leaf.

4. At my request M. Corbin stated that he would ask the French Government further to clarify their view as to the procedure in mediation, and undertook to see me again in the matter tomorrow. We then discussed the question of publicity in connexion with our attempt at mediation. We agreed that it was undesirable that anything should be made public until the other Governments concerned had all been approached. After that what the Ambassador described as the leakages which inevitably occurred would matter much less.

5. We then spoke of the meeting of the Council and I told the Ambassador that I had a suggestion I wished to put to him. Did he think it at all possible that the French Government would consider inviting the members of the Council to meet in Paris this time? He would recollect that the last extraordinary session of the Council had been held in London,[2] and there was, I thought, much to be said for holding these exceptional meetings outside Geneva. It was important to show that the Council's action in this case was realist, and this might be most usefully effected by meeting in one of the great European capitals at a time when the French Government and ourselves were actively engaged in mediation. M. Corbin admitted that there was force in these arguments, but added that he had not of course any idea what the views of his Government would be. He would consult them and let me know as soon as possible. It was always something gained to know that

---

[1] Cf. No. 419, note 1.   [2] See Volume XVI, Chapter II.

we would be willing for our part to accept an invitation to Paris for a meeting of the Council were the French Government prepared to invite us.[3]

6. Reverting to the Spanish conflict the Ambassador remarked that in the view of his Government this was the right moment to make an attempt at mediation. The fact that General Franco's position was no longer promising might incline Germany and Italy to be willing to join. Moreover, the French Government had recently received an interesting account of a conversation between their Ambassador in Moscow and M. Litvinoff. From this it appeared that the Soviet Government were by no means averse to an attempt at mediation at this time. M. Corbin read to me the record of this conversation from which it appeared that the French Ambassador had spoken strongly as to the risks to the Soviet Government itself from the policy of intervention in Spain as well as from the activities of the Comintern in general.

I am, &c.,
ANTHONY EDEN

[3] According to M. Corbin's account of this conversation Mr. Eden merely suggested a meeting in either Paris or London rather than in Geneva: *D.D.F., op. cit.,* No. 62.

No. 423

Mr. Eden to Sir H. Chilton (Hendaye)
No. 796 [W 17095/62/41]

FOREIGN OFFICE, *November 30, 1936*

Sir,

The Spanish Ambassador asked to see me this morning when he stated that he had been instructed by his Government to explain to me their motives for asking for a meeting of the Council at this stage.[1] They had no intention of using this occasion for indulging in propaganda of any kind. He would undertake that their statement would be moderate. The Spanish Government were, however, seriously preoccupied as to the possible effect of incidents at sea which in view of the attempt of General Franco to impose a blockade now seemed much more probable. They were concerned from the point of view of the general international situation, which they had neither the desire nor the intention to complicate. The Spanish Government did not expect the Council to take decisions to meet this or that difficulty of the Spanish Government, but they did think it their duty to bring to the Council's attention certain international aspects of the Spanish problem. M. Azcárate added that he thought the Council might do some useful work and he mentioned the possibility that the Spanish Government might choose the meeting of the Council for expressing their approval of the Non-

[1] See No. 419.

Intervention Committee's plan for a measure of supervision in Spanish ports.

2. Finally the Ambassador said he wished to refer to the position in Valencia. His Government were somewhat perturbed at the fact that we were having contacts with the rebel authorities. He fully appreciated that these were for practical purposes and constituted no recognition. Nonetheless it remained a fact that our Ambassador at Hendaye was being used for communication with General Franco, while we had no diplomat at Valencia where the Spanish Government's headquarters now were.

3. I replied that insofar as concerned the latter place I was already making arrangements for our Consul in Valencia, who was a man of exceptional ability, to be given the local rank of First Secretary in order that he might be in close contact with the Spanish Government.[2] The Ambassador would appreciate that I did not wish to ask Mr. Ogilvie-Forbes or Mr. Scott to leave Madrid at this moment, but I was prepared to consider whether it were possible for us to arrange for a member of the Diplomatic Service to be available at Valencia a little later on. M. Azcárate expressed himself as gratified at my reply and once more repeated that any small attention of this kind that could be paid to the Spanish Government would be very much appreciated.[3]

I am, &c.,
ANTHONY EDEN

[2] See No. 414.

[3] In a minute of December 4 Mr. Shuckburgh wrote: 'It is sincerely to be hoped that the Council will not take up the Non-Intervention Committee's "supervision" schemes. An acceptance of these schemes by the Spanish Govt would be a pure piece of bluff, & it looks from this as if they intended to try it on . . .' Comments by Sir R. Vansittart and Mr. Eden were as follows. 'I think the Valencia govt. are probably going to accept the supervision scheme. The Ambassador has been saying so anyhow. The scheme is of course not really practical politics. R. V. Dec. 5.' 'If both parties in Spain accept the scheme we shall have to attempt to work it. A. E. Dec. 6.' Cf. No. 413.

CHAPTER VII

Western Pact proposals hang fire: conclusion of Anglo-Italian Gentleman's Agreement: discussion of supervisory schemes for Spain

December 1, 1936–January 2, 1937

No. 424

Viscount Chilston (Moscow) to Mr. Eden
(Received December 1, 9 p.m.)
No. 205 Telegraphic [W 17099/62/41]

MOSCOW, *December 1, 1936, 9.14 p.m.* [*sic*]

In my conversation with Monsieur Litvinov today a reference was made to the coming meeting of the Council of the League which the Spanish Government had requested.[1] Monsieur Litvinov said that far from encouraging it, or even insisting upon it as some press reports had pretended, he had urgently discouraged the Spanish Government from such a . . . [2] and he would like you to know this. He was convinced that it could have no good result either for Spain or for anyone; and the League would merely suffer a further discredit (to the profit of Germany and Italy).[3] He wished that His Majesty's Government could also have strongly deprecated the affair. He doubted whether he himself would attend the meeting. Support which he naturally would give to Spanish case would serve no useful purpose.[4]

[1] See No. 419.   [2] The text was here uncertain.   [3] Cf. No. 417, note 1.
[4] M. Litvinov's account of this conversation is printed in *D.V.P.S., op. cit.*, No. 390.

No. 425

Sir H. Kennard (Warsaw) to Mr. Eden (Received December 4)
No. 511 [C 8677/33/55]

WARSAW, *December 1, 1936*

Sir,

With reference to Berlin telegrams Nos. 391[1] and 394,[2] Saving, I have the honour to transmit herewith an interesting despatch[3] which I have received

[1] No. 412.   [2] See *ibid.*, note 2.   [3] Not printed.

from Lieutenant-Colonel Godfrey, military attaché at this Embassy, regarding the attitude which the Polish military authorities would adopt in the event of a National Socialist 'Putsch' in Danzig. You will see that it seems probable that the Polish authorities would prefer to face the risks of taking strong counter-measures from the very outset. The views expressed to Lieutenant-Colonel Godfrey are interesting, and in this connexion it will be remembered that Marshal Smigly-Rydz[4] has told the French Ambassador that if the Germans attempted to seize Danzig by force it was the definite decision of the Polish Government to employ all their military resources to resist such action (see Mr. Aveling's letter to Mr. Wigram of the 15th July last).[3]

2. I am sending a copy of this despatch to His Majesty's Ambassador in Berlin.

I have, &c.,
H. W. KENNARD

[4] General Rydz-Smigly had been made a Marshal of Poland on November 10, 1936, and had changed his name to Smigly-Rydz at the same time.

No. 426

Mr. Eden to Sir E. Drummond (Rome)
No. 451 Telegraphic [R 7189/226/22]

FOREIGN OFFICE, December 2, 1936, 4 p.m.

Your despatch No. 1223[1] and your telegrams Nos. 708[2] and 717.[3]

Having discussed the situation with the Italian Ambassador since his return (see my telegram No. 444),[4] I agree that the time has come for you to accept Count Ciano's proposal to have a general conversation on Anglo-Italian relations. In entering on these conversations you will constantly bear in mind the following considerations:

(1) It is the Italians and not we who have asked for a clarification of the present situation in the Mediterranean with a view to improving Anglo-Italian relations generally. In return for this clarification, therefore, it is for the Italians to contribute where necessary towards the improvement of Anglo-Italian relations which both parties desire.

(2) Both we and the Italians must use every means to reassure the French that nothing is being done to their detriment, and if possible they ought to be associated in any declarations on subjects of interest to France.

(3) Care must be taken not to give any legitimate umbrage to any other Mediterranean Powers, especially Turkey, Yugoslavia, Greece, and Egypt.

Subject to these over-riding considerations, the immediate object of your conversations will be to formulate a draft declaration regarding our common interests in the Mediterranean. It is natural that this declaration

[1] Of November 13, not printed: cf. No. 378.   [2] No. 396.   [3] No. 415.
[4] See *ibid.*, note 2.

should be accompanied or followed by further understandings for the removal of causes of friction in various spheres where Anglo-Italian relations do not necessarily coincide.

The actual Mediterranean declaration should be in as general terms as possible. It would probably be found most convenient that it should take the form of an exchange of notes between you and Count Ciano, which will be subsequently published. Each note would state the view and attitude of the Government of the writer and they would of course in effect have to be identical. For instance, our note would follow the lines of my declaration in the House of Commons on the 5th November,[5] i.e. the freedom of entry into and transit through the Mediterranean is a vital interest to the British Commonwealth of Nations; we do not consider our British interests in the Mediterranean to be in any way divergent from those of Italy but on the contrary to be complementary, and we desire that this shall be the case in practice in the future as it has been in the past. Since we have no desire to threaten or to attack the interests of Italy or any other Power in the Mediterranean, we are convinced that it is possible for Great Britain and Italy to continue to maintain their vital interests in the Mediterranean not only without conflict with each other or any other Mediterranean Power, but even with mutual advantage. Also the two Governments should declare that they desire to see respected the present territorial status quo in the Mediterranean.

You will realise that in these declarations it will be particularly important to find a form of words which will not offend the susceptibilities of the French, whose interests in the Mediterranean are also vital and far-reaching like those of Great Britain and Italy.[6]

As regards the *tour d'horizon* now proposed by Count Ciano,[7] from our point of view the object of such a general review would be to define cases where the Italian Government could afford us concrete evidence of their change of policy and of their desire to cooperate with His Majesty's Government in the future. As far as I can judge at present, this field presents no scope for concessions to Italy, and it would be well therefore from the outset to discourage any hopes which Count Ciano may cherish on this head—if indeed he does so. As to the actual topics which may come up for discussion in the course of this review, I can only at this stage deal with the most

[5] See No. 353, note 2.

[6] In the first draft of this telegram the following passage appeared at this point. 'In fact, the ideal solution would be that similar declarations should be exchanged simultaneously with France. I am not sure how far either the French or the Italian Government would be ready for such an extension of the present conversations. I must leave it to you to judge whether you think it desirable to put forward such a suggestion. Even if you have reason to think that the Italian Government would be agreeable, it would be fatal to put forward the idea without first assuring ourselves of a favourable French response.' This was deleted in view of Sir R. Vansittart's comment. 'I would not cumber the ground with this now. It will make our own negotiation so slow and difficult that we shall lose a great deal of time; and time is highly important. R. V.'

[7] Cf. No. 415.

obvious and give you with regard to them a general indication of the attitude you should adopt. While sharing—as the following paragraphs will show—your views about the danger of 'opening our mouths too wide' I do not of course wish to restrict you in any way from taking advantage of any other opening that may present itself. This I leave to your discretion, and you may of course have to reserve your views on specific points pending reference to me. Some of these topics are bound to raise questions of considerable delicacy (you have mentioned some of these in your telegram No. 695)[8] which I realise could only be treated successfully if the atmosphere were found to be particularly favourable. In the absence of such atmosphere I do not want you to press matters to the point where, by raising contentious issues prematurely, you might get involved in acrimonious discussions or be faced with flat refusals and so prejudice at the outset the prospects of a progressive *détente*.

Montreux Convention

On further reflection I do not wish you to take the initiative in inviting Italy to accede to this Convention.[9] As far as we are concerned Italy's abstention does not trouble us, and although it might give satisfaction to Turkey if Italy's accession were to result from our conversations with Italy, this consideration is not of sufficient importance to warrant our raising the suspicions of the Italians by showing too keen an interest in getting them to accede (especially at the present time when the situation is further complicated by the passage of Russian munitions to Spain through the Dardanelles). On the other hand, if Count Ciano raises the question of Italy's accession to Montreux you should of course encourage the idea.

London Naval Agreement

I concur in your observations under (D) of your telegram No. 695. In the general survey which you propose to make with Italian Minister for Foreign Affairs, you should leave no doubt in his mind that we should expect Italian adhesion to this Treaty to follow as a natural result of an improvement in the political relations between our two countries. In doing so, you can, if you think fit, remind Count Ciano that, with the general assent of all the Powers concerned, including Italy, we took a leading part in convening the London Naval Conference of 1935, after satisfactory preliminary talks had taken place with representatives of the Italian Government. The Italian Delegation cooperated most effectively in the negotiation of the Treaty up to the eleventh hour and the subsequent decision not to sign the Treaty was, in reality, dicatated by motives quite extraneous to the Conference itself.[10] In the circumstances, we should find it very difficult to understand any continued Italian refusal to co-operate in this work of preventing a race between all the naval Powers in the types and sizes of vessels and guns.

[8] No. 380.   [9] See Volume XVI, No. 540.
[10] Cf. Volume XIII, Nos. 681 and 701.

Italy's renewed co-operation in the work of the League

I agree generally with what you say in your telegram No. 695. You need not therefore mention the question of the League at all; but if Count Ciano does so you should confine yourself to a general expression of the hope that Italy will soon be able to resume full collaboration. You had better not link this up in any way with the further developments of the Abyssinian question at Geneva.

Propaganda

Another question on which it will be essential eventually to reach some kind of understanding is that of anti-British Italian propaganda in the Middle East.[11] While His Majesty's Government naturally have no complaint against such Italian propaganda as is purely pro-Italian and not designed to undermine British position or prestige, fact remains that Italy has recently carried on e.g. by means of Bari broadcasts, campaign which is clearly anti-British in intention. Moreover His Majesty's Government are satisfied that large sums from Italian sources have reached such notorious anti-British agitators as Shekib Arslan and Ihsan el Jabri, as well as other persons in Arabia, Palestine and other Middle Eastern countries whom they do not with to mention by name but who are known to have received subsidies from Italian sources. If there is to be any true rapprochement between this country and Italy and Anglo-Italian relations in the Mediterranean and the Middle East are to enter into a new phase, His Majesty's Government would clearly need some guarantee that these activities should cease. The point at which this topic should be introduced I leave to your discretion.

Abyssinia

Although the question of Italian sovereignty over Abyssinia is excluded from the scope of your conversations, it will certainly be no obstacle to their success if Count Ciano renews the assurances which have been given on a variety of occasions by the Italian Government concerning their determination to respect British rights and interests in Abyssinia as specified in the Tripartite Treaty of 1906 and the Anglo-Italian Exchange of Notes of 1925. You should also report to me any observations which the Minister of Foreign Affairs may make concerning border and other problems affecting British Somaliland, Kenya and the Sudan.

You should not yourself volunteer any remarks concerning the status of British representation in occupied Abyssinia. If, however, Count Ciano should refer to this subject you should remind him that we do not wish the question of Italy's position in Abyssinia to be a matter of bargaining and would prefer therefore to deal with this particular aspect of it separately from the present conversations.

In the above connexion I should explain, for your personal and confidential information, that consultations are taking place with the French Government on this matter.[12] While it may be necessary, should the latter persist in their

11 Cf. No. 274.   12 See No. 378, note 8.

present disinclination to act, for His Majesty's Government to take the initiative, it is not intended to proceed until the French Government have been given due notice.

Arabia

You raise the question of the Rome Understanding of 1927[13] in paragraph 4 of your despatch No. 1223, but until it is seen how the general talk between you and Count Ciano develops, it would, in my opinion, be preferable not to pursue the question of Arabia.

Egypt

I deal in my immediately following telegram[14] with various questions affecting Egypt, in case they are raised in the course of your conversations with Count Ciano; but you should not raise them yourself.

[13] See *ibid.*, note 2.   [14] Not printed.

No. 427

Stenographic Notes of the Twelfth Meeting of the Non-Intervention Committee, held in the Locarno Room, Foreign Office, on Wednesday, December 2, 1936, at 10.30 a.m.

[W 169/169/41]*

Lord Plymouth (*Chairman*):[1] Your Excellencies and Gentlemen, my object in calling this meeting at the request of the Sub-Committee was to consider with the least possible delay the three questions formulated by them last week. The texts of these questions were circulated in Paper No. 170[2] to

[1] Representatives of twenty-six European countries, in addition to Lord Plymouth representing the United Kingdom, attended this meeting.

[2] Not printed. The questions in this paper referred to here are indicated in the following passage of the minutes of the Chairman's Sub-Committee of November 27. It stated that the sub-committee agreed

'to inform the members of the Main Committee that they hoped that before the next plenary session of the Committee, each member would obtain from his Government instructions to enable him to state at that meeting

(i) whether they agree in principle with the scheme for the supervision of aircraft entering Spain by air, prepared by the Technical Advisory Sub-Committee (Committee Paper N.I.S.(36)167).

(ii) whether they agree to the immediate despatch to the two parties in Spain of the plan for the supervision of the importation of arms and war material into Spain at the principal points of entry by land and by sea, which was approved in principle at the eleventh meeting of the Committee, held on 12th November, 1936 (Committee Paper N.I.S.(36)164).

(iii) whether they agree to the action outlined in sub-section (ii) above, being taken forthwith, even if it is not possible immediately to secure agreement on the plan for the supervision of aircraft . . .'

all members of the Committee on Friday last with the request that they would obtain instructions from their respective Governments thereon.

I would remind the Committee that they have already, subject to reference to their respective Governments, given their approval in principle to the scheme for supervision by land and sea, and, speaking for the United Kingdom Government, I am now in a position to state that they agree to the scheme as outlined in Paper No. 164[3] being sent to the two parties in Spain, and also that they are prepared, provided that the other Governments represented here also agree, to co-operate in a scheme for the supervision of aircraft based on the principle of that set out in paragraphs 1(*a*) and 1(*b*) on page 13 of Paper No. 167.[4]

Our principal task to-day is to decide whether we are now in a position to communicate the scheme for supervision by land and sea to the two parties in Spain. I would like at this stage to remind the Committee that the document which we propose to communicate to the two parties does no more than sketch in broad outline the basis on which any actual system of supervision would be based; I think that it is important to bear in mind that by forwarding it for acceptance by the Spanish parties we are in no way committing our Governments in regard either to the total cost of the scheme, or to the method of apportioning that cost among the Governments of the countries concerned, or to other matters of detail; we should, in fact, only be affirming the willingness of our Governments to co-operate in the working out and the application of some scheme on the lines indicated, provided, of course, that the replies from both the Spanish parties are favourable.

From what I have already said, I hope I have made it clear that the view of the United Kingdom Government is that nothing should be allowed to interfere with the immediate task of communicating the plan to the two parties, and that a preliminary agreement on the air scheme, though desirable in itself, is not essential.

As recorded in the minutes of the last meeting of the Sub-Committee, that body agreed that the most convenient method of conveying the document to the Spanish parties was through the United Kingdom Government. My Government are willing to take the necessary action, and, if the Committee are able to reach agreement on the lines I have suggested, I shall be glad to have their views on the draft letter contained in Annex A of Paper No. 170.

I should be glad if Representatives of other Governments are now prepared to make statements on the points that I have raised.

His Excellency S. Dino Grandi (Italy): The Italian Government are taking into the most careful consideration the scheme for the supervision

---

[3] This paper (W 16515/9549/41) gave the text of the plan adopted at the eleventh meeting of the N.I. Committee, based on the scheme put forward at the eighth meeting of the Chairman's Sub-Committee (No. 347), for supervision in Spain to secure the application of the non-intervention agreement, together with Mr. Hemming's Note, N.I.S.(36)147, on the financial aspects of the scheme (No. 370).

[4] See No. 413, note 1: this paper is filed at W 16427/9549/41.

of aircraft entering Spain by air, prepared by the Technical Advisory Sub-Committee, and they will not fail to inform the Committee of their conclusions in the matter. The Italian Government have agreed to the immediate despatch to the two parties in Spain of the plan for the supervision of importation of arms and material into Spain at the principal points of entry by land and sea, which was in principle approved at the eleventh meeting of the Committee. The Italian Government agreed to the action outlined in the above paragraph, No. 2, being taken forthwith, even if it is not possible immediately to secure agreement on the plan for the supervision of aircraft. The Italian Government take note, as has been repeatedly stated by the Chairman and different members of the Sub-Committee, that the scheme for the supervision of aircraft and war material entering Spain by air and the scheme for the supervision of the importation of arms and war material into Spain at the principal points of entry by land and sea, are absolutely inter-connected and must be considered as a whole.

HIS EXCELLENCY M. CHARLES CORBIN (France): M. le Président, mon Gouvernement a eu à différentes reprises l'occasion d'indiquer quelle est sa position sur les différentes questions qui sont à l'ordre du jour de cette séance. Le principe de la surveillance à organiser sur le territoire espagnol, en ce qui concerne les importations d'armes et de matériel de guerre par terre et par mer, a déjà reçu son approbation. D'autre part, mon Gouvernement est prêt, ainsi que je l'ai indiqué précédemment, à collaborer à un système de surveillance destiné à assurer le contrôle des avions qui pourraient être expédiés en Espagne par la voie des airs.

Aujourd'hui il considère comme nécessaire de communiquer sans retard aux deux partis actuellement aux prises en Espagne les lignes générales du plan qui ont été élaborées et acceptées par le Sous-Comité.

Enfin, pour la transmission de ce plan, il ne voit que des avantages à ce que nous fassions appel à l'intermédiaire du Gouvernement britannique.

DR. WOERMANN (Germany): Le Gouvernement allemand est d'accord que la lettre soit transmise par l'intermédiaire du Gouvernement britannique aux deux partis en Espagne, pour ce qui concerne le contrôle par terre et par mer.

Je crois qu'il n'est pas nécessaire de faire en ce moment des réserves au sujet des détails, étant donné que le Président a fait observer qu'il s'agit actuellement seulement des grandes lignes du plan. D'autre part, je fais une réserve au sujet de l'indivisibilité des deux plans—celui destiné à assurer une surveillance par terre et par mer, et celui concernant la surveillance des avions, mais ces réserves n'empêchent pas l'expédition de la lettre.

Une autre réserve que je dois faire se réfère à la question du coût des plans, notamment en ce qui concerne les monnaies étrangères.

SENHOR FRANCISCO DE CALHEIROS (Portugal): D'accord avec les déclarations que j'ai faites à plusieurs reprises au sein du Sous-Comité, je dois déclarer maintenant que je m'abstiens de voter l'envoi de la lettre proposée aux deux partis en Espagne.

HIS EXCELLENCY COUNT EDWARD RACZYNSKI (Poland): I would like to say that my Government also agrees to the sending, as suggested by the Sub-Committee, of the letter asking the two parties for their consent to the measures proposed for the application of the Non-Intervention scheme as regards sea and land. At the same time I must point out that the details of the plan, as has been already explained by the Chairman, have not been discussed by the Committee, and I have not yet received any detailed instructions as regards the acceptance by my Government of the technical application of the plan, the apportioning of the expense and other questions of that sort, but I was instructed to express our willingness to accede to the proposal for sending the letter.

His Excellency M. Jean Maisky (U.S.S.R.): An ideal scheme of control would cover land, sea, and air. The scheme for land and sea is elaborated in considerable detail already, and is ready for submission to the Spanish Government and its opponents. The scheme of aerial control, on the other hand, is still in the preliminary stage. We have had the report of the experts, a very painstaking and detailed report, although somewhat complex, and it is obvious that the consideration of this report by the various Governments is not the task of a moment. From a number of Representatives we have had replies giving the attitude of their Governments in principle, but before the scheme of aerial control can be considered complete and brought more or less to a stage parallel with that for land and sea control, it is obvious that time will be needed in which to overcome certain difficulties. This probably means that with the best will in the world we shall have some time to wait before this aerial scheme can be submitted to the Spanish Government and its opponents. In view of this, a number of Representatives have suggested that, in order to lose no time, the Committee should immediately approach both combatants in Spain with the scheme for control on land and sea, while the presentation of the aerial scheme should be deferred until a later date. On behalf of the Soviet Government I support this proposal. I know that complete control is better than partial control, but partial control is a great deal better than no control whatsoever. Therefore I am strongly of the opinion that the Committee should immediately ask the Chairman to take the necessary steps for approaching the Spanish Government and its opponents with a view to ascertaining whether or not they agree, in principle, to the scheme of control on land and sea as put forward by the Committee. If both parties agree, then the necessary steps should be taken for arranging the application of this scheme. It must be made clear from the very beginning, of course, that a scheme for aerial control may follow at a later date. If it is thought advisable, in the opinion of the Committee, to proceed in the present circumstances, I have to state also on behalf of my Government that we accept the British Government as the intermediary in these conversations with the Spanish Government and its opponents, and we accept also the draft letter which was elaborated at the last Sub-Committee meeting.

Bay Sedat Zeki Örs (Turkey): May I express, on behalf of my Government, their approval of the scheme put forward by Lord Plymouth. They accept also with pleasure the proposal that the British Government should forward the scheme to the parties in conflict in Spain.

M. Jan Masaryk (Czechoslovakia): I am of the opinion that the plan for supervision of the importation of arms and war material should be sent to the two parties in Spain as soon as possible in the manner suggested by our Chairman. As far as the plan for air supervision is concerned, my Government is ready to co-operate in a system of supervision, the details of the application, of course, to be subject to further consideration as suggested by Lord Plymouth to-day.

Herr Georg Franckenstein (Austria): My Government agrees to the letter being sent by the good offices of the British Government. We make reservations with regard to the details of the scheme and with regard to the cost of the scheme.

Lord Plymouth (*Chairman*): Does any other Representative wish to express an opinion. I should be very glad to feel we have the unanimous support of the Committee for this proposal.

M. le Vicomte de Lantsheere (Belgium): Le Gouvernement belge a déjà indiqué son attitude dans cette question. Il a fait connaître ses opinions au Comité. Il est prêt à [s]e rallier à toutes propositions de surveillance des importations de matériel de guerre en Espagne qui réuniraient la majorité des voix du Comité et présenteraient un caractère impartial envers les deux partis en Espagne.

En ce qui concerne le projet de surveillance des importations par la voie aérienne, le Gouvernement belge ne voit pas d'objection de principe au système de surveillance qui a été élaboré; il serait disposé à y collaborer éventuellement.

M. Erik Colban (Norway): In view of the statement of the Chairman that the despatch of the letter does not commit the different Governments as to the details of the scheme, and, in particular, with regard to the way in which the scheme should be financed, I have no objection to the sending of the letter.

Jonkheer R. de Marees van Swinderen (Netherlands): Mr. President, the Netherlands Government has no objection at all to the sending of the letter, again with the same explicit reserve as the Norwegian Minister has made for his Government, that it would in no way anticipate our agreeing or not agreeing with the details of the reports.

Count Ahlefeldt Laurvig (Denmark): I am empowered to state, with reference to the three points enumerated in conclusion 1(*a*) of the thirteenth meeting of the Chairman's Sub-Committee held on Friday, the 27th November, at 10.30,

> 'that the Spanish [? Danish] Government have no objection to the immediate dispatch to the two parties in Spain of the plan for the supervision of the importation of arms and war material into Spain, but, at the same time, you must point out that the Danish Government have not yet come to any decision as to the expenses arising out of this plan,

nor to the question of the scheme for the supervision of aircraft entering Spain by air.'

Mr. C. J. O'Donovan (Irish Free State): I am very sorry, Mr. Chairman, that I have not yet had the decision of the Free State Government on this question. Mr. Dulanty is at present in Dublin, but I had hoped to hear from him this morning. As I have not yet heard I presume no decision has yet been made.

Lord Plymouth (Chairman): When do you think it will arrive?

Mr. C. J. O'Donovan (Irish Free State): I hope to be able to let the Secretary have it in the course of the day, if that will do.

Lord Plymouth (Chairman): You do not anticipate that there will be any objection?

Mr. C. J. O'Donovan (Irish Free State): No, my personal idea, if that is of any value, is that the reply would be something on the lines that the Norwegian Minister has outlined this morning.

Lord Plymouth (Chairman): Would the Representative of any other Government wish to make a statement, or may I assume now that the Representatives are agreed?

M. Bernard Clasen (Luxemburg): On behalf of the Luxemburg Government, I agree with the proposal which your Lordship has made. I should also like to make the necessary reservation with regard to the participation in the cost of the scheme, as that would necessarily involve special legislation in the Grand Duchy. With regard to the air scheme, I would like to point out that there is no aircraft industry in the Grand Duchy, that we have no airports and that the Assistant Air Agent, who is provided for under the scheme for Luxemburg, could probably be much more usefully employed in other quarters.

M. Simeon Radeff (Bulgaria): Le Gouvernement bulgare est d'accord pour l'envoi immédiat de la lettre qui se trouve à l'Annexe A du document N.I.S.(36)170.[5] Je fais cependant toute réserve au sujet des frais qu'entraînera ce plan.

---

[5] The text of this draft letter, as approved by the Chairman's Sub-Committee on November 27, was as follows: 'I have the honour to inform you that the International Committee have had under consideration the question of what steps could be taken by the Governments represented thereon to render more effective the Agreement for Non-Intervention.

2. The Committee have accordingly prepared the broad outlines of a scheme designed to secure this end. The document, a copy of which I have the honour at their request to enclose herewith [sic], embodies the principles upon which the Committee consider that a system of supervision could best be established.

3. The Committee have authorised me as their Chairman to express the hope that His Majesty's Government in the United Kingdom will communicate copies of this document to the two parties in Spain with a request that they will be so good as to state at as early a date as possible whether they are prepared to co-operate in the execution of such a scheme.

4. The Committee have also expressed the hope that, should His Majesty's Government be prepared to submit this document in the manner proposed, they will at the same time explain to the two parties in Spain that the plan now submitted deals only with the establishment of a system for the supervision of the possible entry into Spain in contravention of

Lord Plymouth (*Chairman*): Well, may I assume that other Representatives here adopt the same position as has been adopted by a number of other countries, namely, that they agree to this letter going forward to the two parties in Spain with reservations with regard to cost and matters of detail? Does the Roumanian Representative want to say anything?

M. C. M. Laptew (Roumania): I am in agreement with you, Sir.

M. August Schmidt (Estonia) and M. Georg Gripenberg (Finland) indicated their assent also.

M. Charlambos Simopoulos (Greece): Je suis d'accord aussi avec les mêmes réserves.

M. Constantine de Masirevich (Hungary): Et moi aussi.

Lord Plymouth (*Chairman*): I take it that is agreed. There is one point that I should like to clear up. I am a little puzzled by the statement of the Portuguese Representative. I do not quite know what it is meant to indicate. It is not meant to indicate any objection to our course?

Senhor M. Francisco de Calheiros e Menezes (Portugal): Abstention simplement.

Lord Plymouth (*Chairman*): Thank you very much. The next thing we have to do is to go through the draft of the letter which I hope you will now authorise me as Chairman of this Committee to send to the Secretary of State for Foreign Affairs. The text is given in Annex A of the same paper. I think the simplest way to do that is to take it paragraph by paragraph.

Paragraph 1. Any observations?

(No observations.)

Paragraph 2. There is just one small alteration here. I think that on line four, paragraph 2, 'herein' is better than 'herewith.' Are there any further observations on paragraph 2?

(No observations.)

Paragraph 3. Any observations?

(No observations.)

Paragraph 4. I have just one alteration, not really of substance at all, but just the wording. I suggest that in line five the words, 'the establishment of a system for' be left out, and equally in lines six and seven the words 'in contravention of the Non-Intervention Agreement' be left out, and that paragraph 5 should be run into paragraph 4. They would be joined together by the words 'but that,' and the paragraph as amended would read as follows:

'The Committee have also expressed the hope that, should His Majesty's Government be prepared to submit this document in the manner proposed,

the Non-Intervention Agreement of arms and war material at the principal points of entry by land and by sea.

5. The Committee attach great importance also to the question of securing an effective supervision of any aircraft which may attempt to enter Spain by air in contravention of the Agreement. They are at present engaged in the consideration of a scheme to deal with this aspect of the question.'

they will at the same time explain to the two parties in Spain that the plan now submitted deals only with the supervision of the possible entry into Spain of arms and war materials at the principal points of entry by land and by sea, but that the Committee attach great importance also to the question of securing an effective supervision of any aircraft which may attempt to enter Spain by air in contravention of the Agreement. They are at present engaged in the consideration of a scheme to deal with this aspect of the question.'

Is that amendment agreed to?

(Agreed.)

I take it that that letter is agreed to and that you authorise me to sign it and send it to the Secretary of State.

Is that agreed?

(Agreed.)

There is actually nothing further on the Agenda, but there is another short statement which I should like to make, with the permission of the Committee, on the general work of the Committee. I am authorised to say that the United Kingdom Government are not happy at the way the Agreement is working at the present time. They are confident that it is in the interests of Europe, and therefore of all our countries, that the Agreement should be scrupulously observed. Members of the Committee have observed that the United Kingdom Government are now taking steps themselves to prohibit the carriage of munitions to Spain in British ships from foreign ports, and I would express the hope that other Governments would look into this matter and consider, those of them at least who have not taken steps in this direction already, whether they could take similar action.

His Majesty's Government are worried on one point, and that is the reports that we see of the increasing arrival of foreign volunteers in Spain to take part in the Civil War there. I have taken it upon myself, and I hope the Committee will support me in what I have done, to call together a meeting of our Sub-Committee on Friday morning next in order to examine this question. It is a matter that was touched upon earlier on in our discussions, though we had not the time or the opportunity to go into it at all carefully then, and although it is agreed that the question of volunteers is outside the scope of the Agreement as it at present stands, we feel that it is one which calls for further examination on the part of the Sub-Committee. I hope that if the Committee see no objection, our examination will begin on Friday next, and that we may be in a position to make some report to the Main Committee at as early an opportunity as possible. Does anybody wish to make any remarks on my observations? The Swedish Minister?

BARON E. K. PALMSTIERNA (Sweden): This suggestion from the Chairman is naturally of great importance, and to my mind ought to be facilitated; but I should like to know first from the Secretary whether we have in response to earlier inquiries got full information available for the work of the

Sub-Committee; that is to say, whether all the countries have informed us if conscripts and reservists and people on active service always have to inform their Governments or have it noted on their passports, &c., when they are leaving the country, or not. That is naturally one of the main points for the work of the Sub-Committee. Some have done it—we have done it—but I do not know whether all the countries have submitted the information in this respect.

MR. FRANCIS HEMMING (*Secretary to the Committee*): In answer to the point raised by the Swedish Representative, this particular question originally came before the Sub-Committee under the heading of 'indirect intervention,' and a certain number of Governments, all those Governments on the Chairman's Sub-Committee, were asked to furnish that body with a statement of the views of their Governments on the points raised originally in a memorandum submitted by the Italian Government. The members of the Main Committee have never been asked to obtain the views of their Governments on this matter.

LORD PLYMOUTH (*Chairman*): I think that this is a matter which we shall, of course, discuss at once in the Sub-Committee. It will be easier for us then to form a judgment as to what the next step ought to be.

BARON E. K. PALMSTIERNA (Sweden): I only wished to mention the matter in case the Chairman liked those who have not answered on this point to give us more information. That was my whole point.

LORD PLYMOUTH (*Chairman*): I perfectly well follow the point of the Swedish Minister. It seems to me that there are a number of aspects of the question on which we should like information. The simplest course would be that we should discuss the matter in the Sub-Committee, and then perhaps formulate the questions with regard to which we should like the various Governments to provide us with information.[6] If there are no more observations, I think we will proceed to the drafting of our *communiqué*. I do not think there is really any need for an adjournment to-day; I think we can proceed straightaway to the consideration of our *communiqué*.

MR. FRANCIS HEMMING (*Secretary to the Committee*): The first paragraph will be formal, and will state that the Committee met this morning at the Foreign Office at 10.30. Then, I suggest that perhaps the most convenient course would be for the next paragraph to contain a fairly full summary of the opening statement by the Chairman, which gives a general picture of the position not only of the United Kingdom Government, but also of the other Governments, in regard to the reserves which they wish to make with regard to the cost of the scheme and its details. I suggest that it might read:

'The Chairman said that his object in calling the meeting, at the request of the Sub-Committee, was to consider with the least possible delay the questions formulated by them last week in regard to the plan for supervision in Spain, on which all members of the Committee had been requested to obtain the instructions of their respective Governments.

[6] See No. 449 below.

2. Lord Plymouth reminded the Committee that, subject to reference to their respective Governments, they had already given their approval in principle to the scheme for supervision by land and sea. Speaking for the United Kingdom Government, he was now in a position to state that they agreed to that scheme being sent to the two parties in Spain. They were prepared also, provided that the other Governments represented also agreed, to co-operate in a scheme for the supervision of aircraft based on the principles of the plan which had been submitted to the Committee. The principal task of the Committee to-day was to decide whether they were now in a position to communicate the scheme for supervision by land and sea to the two parties in Spain. He reminded the Committee that the document which it was proposed should be communicated to the two parties did no more than sketch in broad outline the basis on which any actual system of supervision would be based. He thought that it was important that the Committee should bear in mind that by forwarding it for acceptance by the Spanish parties they would in no way be committing their Governments in regard either to the total cost of the scheme, or to the method of apportioning the cost among the Governments of the countries concerned; or to other matters of detail. All that the Committee would, in fact, be doing would be to affirm the willingness of their Governments to co-operate in the working out and the application of some scheme on the lines indicated, provided, of course, that the replies from both the Spanish parties were favourable.

Lord Plymouth added that, at their last meeting, the Sub-Committee had agreed that the most convenient method of conveying the document to the Spanish parties would be through the United Kingdom Government. He was authorised to state that the United Kingdom Government were willing to act in this manner, should the Committee so desire.'

I think it would probably not be necessary even to summarise the statements of the various Representatives, as they are all very much in the same sense. We might have a new paragraph saying:

'After a full exchange of views, the Committee agreed to the immediate despatch to the two parties in Spain of the plan for the supervision of the importation of arms and war material into Spain at the principal points of entry by land and sea which they had already approved in principle at a previous meeting. The various Representatives entered reservations on behalf of their respective Governments in regard to the details of the scheme and to the apportionment of the cost.'

Then perhaps we might go on:

'The Committee further agreed to ask the United Kingdom Government to transmit the scheme to the two parties in Spain on their behalf; and for this purpose they agreed upon the terms of a letter to be addressed in this sense by the Chairman of the Committee to the Secretary of State for Foreign Affairs.'

Senhor Francisco de Calheiros e Menezes (Portugal): I would like you to put in Portugal abstaining.

Lord Plymouth (*Chairman*): I think that from every point of view it is of great importance that we should make it clear that the Portuguese Government did not oppose the proposal to send the scheme forward to Spain, because I think that that would have a very unfortunate effect.

Mr. Francis Hemming (*Secretary to the Committee*): In view of the fact that this *communiqué* will be issued directly after this meeting, and before the Irish Free State come to a decision, does the Irish Free State Representative desire the insertion of some words about his Government's position?

Mr. C. J. O'Donovan (Irish Free State): I do not think it is necessary.

Mr. Francis Hemming (*Secretary to the Committee*): Would it meet the point raised by the Portuguese Representative if we put in a new sentence immediately after the sentence in which it states that the Committee agree as follows:

'The Portuguese Representative declared that while the Portuguese Government did not oppose this proposal he was instructed to abstain from voting upon it.'

Senhor Francisco de Calheiros (Portugal): Après les mots 'The Committee agreed,' je voudrais qu'on mette 'avec l'abstention du Portugal.'

Est-ce qu'il ne serait pas plus simple de mettre tout de suite 'avec l'abstention du Portugal,' sans faire un nouveau paragraphe?

Lord Plymouth (*Chairman*): But that surely might create the impression that you oppose the proposal?

Senhor Francisco de Calheiros (Portugal): Abstenir ce n'est pas s'opposer — c'est prendre une attitude ni en faveur ni contre.

Je voudrais m'abstenir simplement. Je ne suis pas sûr comment on pourrait le dire en anglais, mais je pense que si on mettait: 'Le Comité est d'accord, abstention faite du Portugal, . . .'

Mr. Francis Hemming (*Secretary to the Committee*): Would not the words which I have already suggested meet the case:

'The Portuguese Representative declared that, while the Portuguese Government did not oppose this proposal, he was instructed by his Government to abstain from voting upon it.'

Senhor Francisco de Calheiros (Portugal): Cela me fait dire que j'ai fait la déclaration que je ne suis pas opposé; je ne voudrais dire qu'abstenir, pas une autre attitude.

Mr. Francis Hemming (*Secretary to the Committee*): I think that what the Portuguese Representative has said is perfectly clear: the only difficulty is to find some English words which give effect to that meaning. May I read the following words, which I do think represent what he has said:

'The Portuguese Representative declared that he was instructed by his Government to abstain from voting upon this proposal.'

Senhor Francisco de Calheiros (Portugal): D'accord.

Mr. Francis Hemming (*Secretary to the Committee*): Very well.

There remains only now the final paragraph dealing with the questions of the control of shipping and of foreign volunteers, raised by the Chairman, which might perhaps read as follows:

'3. The Chairman said that the United Kingdom Government were not satisfied with the working of the Non-Intervention Agreement. They were confident that it was in the interest of Europe and therefore of every country represented on the Committee that the Agreement should be scrupulously observed. He reminded the Committee that the United Kingdom Government were now taking steps to prohibit the carriage of arms and war material to Spain in British ships from foreign ports. He suggested that other Governments should consider the question of taking similar action, in so far as they had not done so already.

Lord Plymouth added that the United Kingdom Government were anxious also regarding the reports of the arrival, in increasing numbers, of foreign volunteers in Spain. As Chairman of the Committee, he had therefore asked the Chairman's Sub-committee to consider this question at a meeting to be held on Friday next. The question had been touched upon at earlier meetings of the Sub-Committee, but it had never been examined in detail. Though the United Kingdom Government agreed that the question of volunteers fell outside the scope of the Non-Intervention Agreement as at present defined, they felt that it was a matter which called for further examination in the manner suggested, with a view to the early submission by the Sub-Committee of a report for consideration by the Main Committee.'

Lord Plymouth (*Chairman*): Any observations?

(No observations.)

Mr. Francis Hemming (*Secretary to the Committee*): Then we might add that the Chairman's Sub-Committee will meet on Friday at 11 a.m.

Lord Plymouth (*Chairman*): I think that is all, thank you very much. I am much obliged for your co-operation in the most expeditious meeting that we have yet held.

(The proceedings then terminated.)

Note.—For the text of the Press *Communiqué* agreed upon in the foregoing discussion, see the appendices attached hereto.[7] The English text is given in Appendix 1, and a French translation of it in Appendix 2.

[7] Not printed. The substance of this press *communiqué* was published in *The Times*, December 3, 1936, p. 14.

No. 428

Note[1] from Mr. Eden to Herr von Ribbentrop
[*R 7061/6799/96*]

FOREIGN OFFICE, *December 2, 1936*

Your Excellency,

On the 14th November the German Embassy were good enough to communicate to this Department a note stating that the German Government no longer recognised as binding on themselves the provisions contained in the Treaty of Versailles respecting the waterways in German territory and the international river statutes which are based on the said provisions.[2] His Majesty's Government were all the more surprised to receive this communication, in view of the statement of the German Chancellor in the Reichstag on the 21st May, 1935,[3] after the denunciation of Part V of the Treaty of Versailles, to the effect that 'the German Government will unconditionally respect the remaining articles of the treaty regarding international relations, and will only carry out by means of peaceable understandings such revisions as will be inevitable in the course of time.' Baron von Neurath told His Majesty's Ambassador at Berlin on the 24th May, 1935,[4] that this statement related to certain further minor alterations which the German Government desired, such as international rivers and some restrictions connected with the Kiel Canal. Further, on the 31st May, 1935, the German Ministry for Foreign Affairs confirmed the Chancellor's statement in the Reichstag to Sir Eric Phipps.[5]

2. Your Excellency will recall that, in reply to a question in the House of Commons on the 16th November, I expressed His Majesty's Government's regret that the German Government should once again have abandoned procedure by negotiation in favour of unilateral action, and added that these regrets were not due to fear that any important British trading interests had been jeopardised by the German Government's decision, but to the fact that action of this character must render more difficult the conduct of international relations.[6]

3. His Majesty's Government are unable to admit that the International Rivers Régime, as set up by the peace treaties, was irreconcilable with German sovereign rights, but since the German Government had on many occasions since the signature of the Treaty of Versailles signified its dissatisfaction with numerous aspects of that régime, His Majesty's Government have always exerted themselves with a view to reconciling German desiderata with the interests of the other Powers concerned.

4. Indeed, the negotiations which had been proceeding over a considerable period, with a view to satisfying German claims, had recently been attended by a considerable measure of success. For instance, as regards the Rhine,

---

[1] Cf. No. 391, note 3.
[3] See Volume XIII, No. 222, note 1.
[5] See *ibid.*, No. 273.
[2] See *ibid.*, note 1.
[4] See *ibid.*, No. 242.
[6] See No. 391, note 2.

the other interested Governments had during the past year made such concessions to the German point of view, that the German plenipotentiary, acting presumably on instructions from his Government, was able in May last to initial a convention regulating navigation on that river along the general lines desired by the German Government. His Majesty's Government cannot accept the German thesis that the result of these negotiations was nullified by the refusal of the Netherlands Government to initial the convention, as the objections entertained by them were, as His Majesty's Government understand, on the point of being solved by means of discussions between the Belgian and Netherlands Governments. In any case the German plenipotentiary had signed a modus vivendi whereby the more important clauses of the draft convention were to be brought into force on the 1st January, 1937, between all the States represented on the Central Commission of the Rhine except the Netherlands.

5. As regards the Elbe, German desiderata were closely examined by members of the Elbe Commission during two sessions. As a result of these discussions it was found possible to give almost complete satisfaction to German demands, and on the suggestion of the German plenipotentiary a ten years' modus vivendi was initialled on the 5th October. On that date the German plenipotentiary asked that the agreement should be signed on the 24th November.

6. As regards the Oder, the reason that no solution acceptable both to Germany and to the other Powers concerned was ever reached must be put down to the fact that the German Government had consistently refused to take part in negotiations with this end in view. Had they agreed to negotiate, there is no doubt that they would have received a still larger measure of satisfaction than in the case of the Elbe.

7. As regards the Danube, the German desiderata, as set forth in the German note of the 29th May last, were receiving careful consideration, and His Majesty's Government cannot agree that the German Government had no prospect through the normal process of negotiation of receiving satisfaction with regard to them. His Majesty's Government themselves were, as the German Government are fully aware, in favour of meeting the German wishes in all essentials, and, in particular, had urged upon other members of the European Commission of the Danube the desirability of admitting Germany to that commission.

8. As regards the Kiel Canal, the German Government have on no occasion up to the 14th November last demanded a modification of the existing position. His Majesty's Government have thus never been given an opportunity of considering the alterations in the present régime which it now appears the German Government wish to effect.

9. While, in view of the considerations stated above, His Majesty's Government do not admit any justification for the step taken by the German Government, and while they make all reservations regarding the legal position thereby created, they will be glad to learn whether the German Government are still prepared to negotiate an international settlement for

regulating those waterways which must be considered as being of international interest.

I have, &c.,
ANTHONY EDEN

No. 429

Sir E. Phipps (Berlin) to Mr. Eden
(Received December 3, 1.50 p.m.)
No. 362 Telegraphic [*W 17231/9549/41*]

BERLIN, *December 3, 1936, 1.55 p.m.* [*sic*]

I learn from a reliable source that influx of Russian, Czech and French volunteers into Spain is causing the Chancellor intense irritation. During the last few days he has been telling his entourage that in his opinion Germany is perfectly entitled to send a German for every Russian and Czech in Spain. His military advisers are I believe perturbed at the prospect.[1]

[1] The United States Ambassador in Berlin, Mr. W. E. Dodd, recorded in his diary for December 5 a conversation with Herr Dieckhoff which gave him the impression 'that the Foreign Office officials were somewhat nervous about Hitler's intervention in Spain': *Ambassador Dodd's Diary 1933–1938* (London, 1941), pp. 372–4.

No. 430

Mr. Eden to Sir E. Ovey (Brussels)
No. 93 Telegraphic [*C 8592/7284/4*]

FOREIGN OFFICE, *December 3, 1936, 6.45 p.m.*

When recently in London on November 27th and 28th[1] the Belgian Prime Minister explained to me the attitude of his Government resulting from the situation created by Belgium's withdrawal of the guarantee she has hitherto given to France.[2]

He emphasised that he had not used the word 'neutrality' in describing Belgium's new position. He had no wish to see Belgium return to her position of before 1914. He stated definitely that his Government considered itself bound by all its existing obligations, that is, by the Covenant of the League, and by the arrangements of March 19th.[3]

As regards the Covenant, he did not deny that in certain circumstances Belgium was bound by paragraph 3, article 16 as regards the passage of troops across her territory. But he insisted that Belgium must be the judge of these circumstances; neither France nor any outside body must decide this question over Belgium's head.

M. van Zeeland stressed the fact that Belgium's obligations under the

[1] Cf. No. 403.   [2] Cf. No. 297.   [3] Volume XVI, No. 144.

arrangements of March 19th were of a provisional character. They must not become permanent obligations, and he warned me that the provisional period could not last much longer in view of the decreasing prospects of a new Locarno Pact. Should the present negotiations have to be abandoned, he proposed the following plan to take the place of this provisional régime.

France's obligations in the East were likely to upset negotiations for a new Locarno. They also made it hard for Belgium to assume commitments vis-à-vis France. But all parties agreed that Belgium's independence and integrity ought to be guaranteed, and he suggested this fact as a nucleus for a new treaty. Germany, Great Britain, France, Belgium and possibly also Italy should each agree to guarantee Belgium's independence and integrity. He thought moreover that the Netherlands might be ready to enter into such a treaty on the same terms as Belgium. Under such a treaty Belgium might perhaps furnish information to France and Great Britain to assure them of the continued efficacy of her defences, but she must be free to give similar information to Germany if the latter required it.

Such a treaty, he suggested, might be accompanied by an Anglo-French or possibly an Anglo-French-German treaty to guarantee the German-French frontier in the same way as it was guaranteed under Locarno, but Belgium would definitely not be a party to this second treaty.

He had been disappointed and surprised at French criticism of the King of the Belgian's speech.[4] It was pointed out to him that it was natural that France should be upset at being suddenly deprived of Belgium's guarantee after the assurances of mutual assistance exchanged last March, and that she should be anxious to preserve for the future some measure of technical cooperation with Belgium. M. van Zeeland replied that he was willing and indeed intended to initiate further conversations with French Ministers to reassure them of Belgium's policy and intentions. Despatch follows.[5]

[4] See No. 297, note 1.
[5] No. 608 of November 30, not printed. M. van Zeeland's accounts of his conversations with Mr. Eden are printed in *D.D.B.*, *op. cit.*, Nos. 174 and 176: cf. also No. 179. For the Foreign Office reactions to the proposals made by M. van Zeeland, see No. 433 below.

No. 431

Mr. Eden to Sir H. Chilton (Hendaye)
No. 263[1] *Telegraphic* [*W 17218/9549/41*]

FOREIGN OFFICE, *December 3, 1936, 10.30 p.m.*

International Non-Intervention Committee have requested[2] His Majesty's Government in United Kingdom to communicate to two parties in Spain for their approval document of which text is contained in my immediately following telegram.[3] This document embodies principles upon which Com-

[1] No. 314 to Mr. Ogilvie-Forbes (Madrid).   [2] See No. 427.
[3] No. 432 below.

mittee consider that a system supervising application of Non-Intervention Agreement could best be established.

Please communicate this text accordingly to Burgos authorities[4] on behalf of the Committee, with a request that they will be so good as to state as soon as possible whether they are prepared in principle to co-operate in the execution of such a scheme.

You should also explain that this scheme deals only with supervision of arms and war material entering Spain at principal points of entry by land and sea, but that Committee attach great importance also to question of securing effective supervision of any aircraft which may attempt to enter Spain by air in contravention of Agreement and are considering a further scheme to this end.[5]

His Majesty's Chargé d'Affaires at Madrid[6] is being instructed to make similar communication to Spanish Government[7] and I am also addressing note in similar sense to Spanish Ambassador here.

[4] 'Spanish Government' in No. 314.   [5] Cf. No. 413.
[6] 'His Majesty's Ambassador' in No. 314.   [7] 'Burgos authorities' in No. 314.

No. 432

Mr. Eden to Sir H. Chilton (Hendaye)
No. 264[1] Telegraphic [W 17218/9549/41]

FOREIGN OFFICE, *December 3, 1936, 11 p.m.*

Following is text referred to in my immediately preceding telegram:[2]

1. There shall be established by the International Committee two impartial groups of Agents, stationed in Spain and the Spanish Dependencies, at the principal points of entry by land and by sea.

2. The proposed groups of Agents will be appointed only with the consent of the respective parties in Spain.

3. The functions of the two groups of Agents will be to ascertain whether the Agreement for Non-Intervention is being strictly observed, and will include those enumerated in Sections 8 and 9 below, and such other functions as the respective parties in Spain and the International Committee may from time to time agree to assign to them.

4. One group of Agents will be stationed in those parts of Spain under the control of each of the parties respectively.

5. In order to secure the strict impartiality of these Agents, each Agent will be appointed by a unanimous vote at a plenary session of the International Committee.

6. The Agent of each group will act under the orders of a Chief Agent, who will maintain contact on behalf of the Agents of that group with the appropriate Spanish Authorities in the part of Spain in question.

[1] No. 315 to Mr. Ogilvie-Forbes (Madrid).   [2] No. 431.

7. The Chief Agents, and the Agents and their subordinates shall enjoy the immunities normally accorded to diplomatic officers, and the Chief Agents and the Agents shall have the right of free communication with the International Committee and its members and with one another. Further, the Chief Agents, and the Agents and their subordinates shall be granted by the respective parties in Spain full facilities to enable them to exercise the rights and to discharge the duties assigned to them and, in particular, those rights and duties enumerated in sections 8 and 9 below.

8. The facilities to be accorded by the respective parties in Spain to the Agents of the International Committee and their subordinates shall include:

(*a*) the right of free entry at any time into docks, railway establishments, and similar premises;

(*b*) the right of making such inspections as they may think proper in the premises referred to in (a) above, for the purpose of establishing whether any arms or war material are being imported into Spain in contravention of the Agreement for Non-Intervention.

(*c*) the right to call upon the responsible authorities for documents relating to the nature of particular consignments;

(*d*) the right to move freely from one place to another in the discharge of their duties within the portion of Spain in which they are stationed.

9. It shall be the duty of each Agent:

(*a*) when called upon by the International Committee, to investigate, and to report on, any particular case in respect of which a complaint has been submitted by a Government to the Committee;

(*b*) whenever, as the result of his own investigations, he has satisfied himself that a consignment of arms or war material (including aircraft) has been imported into Spain in contravention of the Agreement, to submit forthwith identical reports in regard thereto;

(i) to the Secretary to the International Committee;
(ii) to the Chief Agent under whom he is working;
(iii) to the Representative on the International Committee of the Government of the country from which such arms or war material have been imported, and, where appropriate, to the Representative or Representatives of the Government or Governments of any country or countries through whose territory such arms or war material have passed in transit.

10. The Chief Agents and the Agents working under them shall have the right at all times to communicate direct with the International Committee on any matter connected with the discharge of their duties.

No. 433

Memorandum[1] by Mr. Eden on the position of Belgium in the proposed Five-Power Conference

[*C 8744/270/4*]

FOREIGN OFFICE, *December 3, 1936*

I have read the report, No. C.O.S. 528, of the Chiefs of Staff Sub-Committee dated the 25th November, 1936, on the position of Belgium in the proposed Five-Power Conference.

2. This Report is based on the assumption that it is desirable that Belgium's commitments should be reduced to a minimum on the ground that there is reason to suppose that in that case it will be possible for her to keep out of any war launched by Germany against France and this country. This assumption raises a big political issue which I do not propose to deal with in this paper, since it will form the subject of a Report which I am making to the Cabinet as a result of my recent conversations with the Belgian Prime Minister. I would ask that meanwhile the Committee of Imperial Defence should take no decision on the Chiefs of Staff Report now before them. For my part, I will confine myself merely to inviting the Committee's attention to certain points of detail in the report which seem to me to call for comment and correction.

3. *Passage across Belgium in order to resist aggression.* Paragraph 4 of the report states 'that any suggestion that Belgium should allow British or French troops or air forces to move through or over her territory would

---

[1] This memorandum was drawn up in the Central Department as what Sir R. Vansittart called 'our answer to the new and impracticable policy suggested by the Chiefs of Staff' in the C.O.S. Sub-Committee Report of November 25 (C 8479/270/4) on the position of Belgium in the proposed Five Power Conference. A Foreign Office memorandum of November 20 had asked the Chiefs of Staff to consider two questions: whether it was considered important to press the Belgians for a formal undertaking not to allow Belgian territory to be used by an army attacking a third Power; and what importance His Majesty's Government should attach from a technical point of view to Anglo-French military co-operation with Belgium. The draft C.O.S. report was considered at a meeting on November 23 when Foreign Office representatives were present, although all reference to their presence was omitted in the final version and their views were not taken into account. The Report, couched in general political rather than technical terms, concluded that 'our policy should be so directed as to ensure the greatest possible chance of Belgian neutrality' and that therefore it was 'undesirable to add in any way to Belgium's existing or proposed commitments', and was received with great dissatisfaction in the Foreign Office. In a note of November 26 Mr. Sargent complained that the Foreign Office had 'been treated with scant courtesy and their views have been completely ignored', and that the Report contained 'inaccuracies, omissions and misstatements'. Mr. Wigram remarked on November 27 that 'we have not succeeded in getting a word of advice on these questions [those in the memorandum of November 20] from the military point of view'. The counter-report printed here, apparently drawn up by Messrs. Sargent and Wigram with Sir R. Vansittart's encouragement, was revised at Mr. Eden's request to consider the questions raised by M. van Zeeland (see No. 430), and was then circulated to the C.I.D. as paper 1288-B and used as a basis for a further memorandum for the Cabinet regarding Mr. Eden's conversations with M. van Zeeland (see note 4 below).

to that extent reduce the possibility of maintaining her neutrality.' Thus stated, the suggestion appears altogether too sweeping. In order to confine the question at issue within its proper limits the sentence quoted should be completed with the words 'in order to help resist an unprovoked aggression by Germany against either France or Great Britain.' While not wishing to question the view now expressed by the Chiefs of Staff, I would point out that in paragraph 13 of the report of the Chiefs of Staff dated the 26th October (C.O.S. 518)[2] it is stated that a most careful examination is called for as regards the possibilities of using paragraph 3 of Article 16 of the Covenant in order to reach some compromise between the French and Belgian Governments which will permit the passage of French (and British) forces across Belgian territory in certain circumstances.

4. *'Neutrality' of Belgium.* As regards the phrase 'maintaining her neutrality' which is used in the same paragraph of the Report of the Chiefs of Staff, I think the meaning would be clearer if the expression 'not becoming involved in hostilities' was used. The words 'neutrality' and 'neutralisation' are apt to lead to confusion in view of the terms of Article 16 of the Covenant of the League of Nations. Supposing the members of the League were, without any of them going to war with an aggressor, applying economic and financial measures to such an aggressor under Article 16, and possibly affording passage to troops under Article 16 (3), they would, according to the view which has so far prevailed, not be in the position of neutrals, as this term was understood in the past, though they would not be in the position of belligerents. It is perhaps therefore confusing to speak of 'maintaining Belgian neutrality.' Belgium has her obligations under Article 16, though there may well be room for doubt as to what exactly they amount to, and if she complies with these obligations it will mean that she cannot be 'neutral' in the old sense of the word. The question whether she should be relieved of her obligations under Article 16 is, of course, a very different one.

5. *Refusal by Belgium to allow an aggressor access to her territory.* I think there is a misconception in paragraph 5 of the report, at any rate if I am right in reading that paragraph as referring to the question in the Foreign Office memorandum of the 20th November (attached as an annex to the Report of the Chiefs of Staff) whether the Belgian Government should be called upon to define their undertakings so as to mean that they will resist not only a violation by the German army of Belgian territory, but also of Belgian air by German aircraft. But this question has nothing to do with Article 16 of the Covenant. Possibly the reference should have been to the considerations urged in the preceding paragraph 4. But if reference to Article 16 does not apply, have the Chiefs of Staff any other reason unstated in their Report for advising against the suggestion in the Foreign Office memorandum that Great Britain and France should call upon the Belgian Government to define their undertakings so as to mean that they will resist a violation of Belgian air by German aircraft? In the absence of very strong technical arguments a request for such a definition would, from the political point

[2] No. 332.

of view, seem to be eminently desirable and even necessary in present circumstances.

6. *Belgium's existing obligations.* Paragraph 7 of the Report states that 'it is undesirable that Belgium should make any addition to her present obligations.' But it is not proposed that she should do so. It is a question of the interpretation of her already existing obligations; and in this connexion the obligation undertaken by Belgium in Article VII of the London Agreement of the 19th March, 1936,[3] must not be lost from view. That undertaking was that the reinforcement of the security of Belgium, France, Italy and the United Kingdom, to be provided by the new proposed Western Treaty, 'will include, in particular, obligations of mutual assistance between Belgium, France, the United Kingdom and Italy, or any of them, with suitable provisions to ensure prompt action by the signatories in case of need as well as technical arrangements for the preparation of such measures as would ensure the effective execution of the obligations undertaken.'

7. *Technical co-operation between Belgium, France and Great Britain.* Paragraph 9 of the Report states that it is unacceptable that there should only be close co-operation between some of the parties to the agreement and impracticable that there should be such co-operation between all of them. I am not entirely convinced of the truth of this statement. There might be, did it ever become necessary, ways of getting over the difficulty; and there has, as is stated in paragraph 10 of the Report, been close co-operation between Belgium and France ever since 1925. I think, further, that the statement that, if France insists on conversations, there will be a breakdown of the negotiations for a multi-lateral pact is too sweeping. This is not certain; and there are other more serious differences of a purely political character between ourselves and Germany which are more likely to be the real cause of a breakdown, if, indeed, there is one.

8. *Nature of Chiefs of Staff conclusions.* Before completing my observations on details, I must point out that the Report of the Chiefs of Staff does not contain any comment *from the technical point* of view on the two questions put in the Foreign Office memorandum. The Report merely lays down that 'our policy should be so directed as to ensure the greatest possible chance of Belgian neutrality' and this 'is the principal object we have in view.' The questions put by the Foreign Office are then answered only from the standpoint of their bearing on this overriding political principle. They are not discussed at all from the technical or military standpoint.[4]

---

[3] Volume XVI, No. 144.

[4] The whole issue of the position of the Belgian Government and His Majesty's Government's future policy towards Belgium was reviewed in Mr. Eden's memorandum of December 5, C.P. 332(36) (C 8745/270/4). This paper took into consideration Mr. Eden's conversations with M. van Zeeland on November 27 and 28, and also M. van Zeeland's statement of foreign policy on December 2 in the Belgian Chamber during the debate on the Defence Bill, an extract from which was enclosed in Brussels despatch No. 643 of December 3 to the Foreign Office (C 8707/7284/4). The memorandum was submitted to the Cabinet on December 9. After some discussion the Cabinet agreed that M. van Zeeland's proposals for guarantees of Belgium and of the German–French frontier (see No. 430) contained

'serious difficulties' and that Mr. Eden should ask him not to pursue these proposals until it was found impossible to negotiate a new Locarno Treaty. Mr. Eden was authorized to advise the French Government to accept M. van Zeeland's assurance 'that he recognises Belgium's obligations under paragraph 3 of Article 16, provided that Belgium is alone judge of the circumstances when, and extent to which, she shall carry out these obligations'; Mr. Eden should ask the Belgian Government to 'define their undertaking to forbid access to their territory', and should make it clear to the French that he was 'not prepared to take part in any detailed discussions' of defence plans or the preparation of positions in Belgium for French troops.

Mr. Eden was also authorized to tell M. van Zeeland that he saw 'considerable advantage' in the Belgian Prime Minister holding unofficial conversations with the French Government. Apparently M. van Zeeland had already approached M. Blum with this intention, and may already have held the first of two secret meetings about which Mr. Eden knew nothing: on this point see D. Kieft, *Belgium's Return to Neutrality*, pp. 152–4 and 157.

No. 434

Mr. Eden to Sir E. Phipps (Berlin)
No. 232[1] Telegraphic [W 17138/62/41]

Important   FOREIGN OFFICE, *December 4, 1936, 3.20 p.m.*

You should, acting in concert with your French colleague, make a communication in the terms of my immediately following telegram[2] to the Government to which you are accredited.

In doing so you should emphasise the importance of reaching agreement on the proposed line of action as quickly as possible and request that the earliest consideration may be given to your joint proposals.

You should add that in order that their proposals may have the best possible chance of a favourable reception the two Governments do not intend to make any public statement on the subject until they feel assured from the replies received that their suggestions have been fully considered.

Repeated to Washington, No. 405.

[1] No. 146 to Viscount Chilston (Moscow), No. 457 to Sir E. Drummond (Rome), No. 158 to Sir C. Wingfield (Lisbon).
[2] No. 436 below.

No. 435

Mr. Eden to Sir R. Lindsay[1] (Washington)
No. 407 Telegraphic [W 17138/62/41]

Very Confidential   FOREIGN OFFICE, *December 4, 1936, 4 p.m.*
My telegram to Berlin No. 232.[2]

While we realise that the United States Government cannot be expected to take any action which might involve them in active steps connected with this proposal for mediation, we nevertheless attach the greatest possible

[1] H.M. Ambassador at Washington.   [2] No. 434.

importance to some public statement being made by the United States Government, at the appropriate moment, that they are in general sympathy with the step which it is proposed to take[3] and that any sincere effort to eliminate the dangers inherent in the conflict in Spain and diminish the sum of human suffering there will receive the moral support of the American people.

If meanwhile, and in addition to the above, the United States Government felt able to say a word in the capitals concerned in favour of their governments' participation in this mediatory effort, this would also be of the greatest possible value. But you should not, of course, urge the United States Government to do anything which they might consider embarrassing.

Please therefore, unless you have strong objection, see the Under Secretary of State at once[4] and, after informing him in the strictest confidence of the step which is being taken by United Kingdom and French Governments, enquire whether the United States Government would be prepared to issue such a statement at the appropriate moment and whether meanwhile they could give such assistance to the Mediatory Powers in the capitals concerned as they may find possible.[5]

[3] See No. 436 below.
[4] According to *F.R.U.S.*, *op. cit.*, p. 587, Sir R. Lindsay delivered Mr. Eden's message on the afternoon of December 4 to Mr. J. A. Dunn, Chief of the Division of Western European Affairs in the State Department. The Secretary of State, Mr. Cordell Hull, had left on November 7 to attend the Inter-American Conference for the Maintenance of Peace, which took place at Buenos Aires, December 1–23, 1936.
[5] Foreign Office telegram No. 408 to Washington of even date said that it had been suggested to the French Government that 'from the point of view of preserving secrecy it might be preferable that communication to United States Government should be made by you on behalf of the two Governments'.

No. 436

Mr. Eden to Sir E. Phipps (Berlin)
No. 233[1] Telegraphic [W 17138/62/41]

Important   FOREIGN OFFICE, *December 4, 1936, 4.5 p.m.*

1. The British and French Governments have exchanged views on the situation created by the prolongation of the civil war in Spain and have arrived at the following conclusions.[2]

[1] No. 147 to Viscount Chilston (Moscow), No. 458 to Sir E. Drummond (Rome), No. 159 to Sir C. Wingfield (Lisbon).
[2] See No. 422. M. Delbos followed up this approach by sending to M. Corbin on December 1 the draft of a joint communication to be addressed to the Soviet, German, and Italian Governments. The text of this draft is printed in *D.D.F.*, *op. cit.*, No. 69. On Mr. Eden's instruction the French draft was revised by Sir G. Mounsey, who commented on December 3: 'This draft eliminates the unessential parts of the French proposal, more especially their suggestions for re-affirmation of non-intervention, and concentrates on the idea of mediation. Paragraphs 1–4 and 6–7 of our draft follow the French draft, while paragraph 5

2. In the interests of peace, of the preservation of European civilisation and of humanity the Powers mainly concerned are bound to concert together with a view to saving Europe from the dangers involved in all forms of foreign political help in the internal struggle in Spain. To this end they must seek in common for further means of contributing more actively to the solution of the present crisis.

3. The two Governments note that the Governments of Germany, Italy, Portugal and the U.S.S.R. have like themselves by their adhesion to the principle of non-intervention and by their participation in the work of the London Committee affirmed their intention of subordinating all other political considerations to that of the supreme interest of the maintenance of peace.

4. Impressed by the great importance of maintaining and confirming this attitude before the world, the British and French Governments suggest that it is imperative that the other interested Governments should, with a view to the preservation of peace, join with them at once in declaring their absolute determination to renounce forthwith all direct or indirect action which might in any way be calculated to lead to foreign intervention in relation to the conflict in Spain.

5. The six Powers might also take this opportunity of announcing their intention of instructing their representatives on the London Committee to proceed at once to the consideration of immediate measures for establishing an effective control over all war-material destined for Spain.

6. In view of the considerations referred to in paragraph 2 above the two Governments further feel that a renewed effort should be made in the direction of relieving the troubled conditions prevailing in Spain.

7. To this end they are consequently moved to approach the other interested Governments with an invitation to join them in an endeavour to put an end to the armed conflict in Spain by means of an offer of mediation, with the object of enabling that country to give united expression to its national will.

8. If this proposal is accepted in principle, the six Governments would consider in further consultation together the form which their mediatory action would take.

Repeated to Washington, No. 406.

has been tentatively inserted by myself and Mr. Roberts in the hope of getting away from the doubtful political proposal on to a more practical economic and humanitarian line.' Mr. Eden presented the revised draft to M. Corbin on the morning of December 3, and it was accepted by the French Government on the same evening, subject to the addition to paragraph 7 after the word 'médiation' of the phrase, 'tendant à mettre l'ensemble du pays en mesure d'exprimer la volonté nationale'.

No. 437

Mr. Eden to Sir H. Chilton (Hendaye)
No. 810 [W 17428/62/41]

FOREIGN OFFICE, *December 4, 1936*

Sir,

The Spanish Ambassador asked to see me this evening when he stated that he was leaving for France within the next day or two to meet the Spanish Foreign Minister, Señor del Vayo, previous to his journey to Geneva. In the circumstances, the Ambassador wished to speak to me unofficially about the forthcoming Council meeting. It was Señor del Vayo's intention to use great moderation and reserve in the statement of the Spanish Government's case at Geneva.[1] The Ambassador himself would strongly urge this and he had the impression that this was the right method to pursue in the present international situation.

2. I replied that I was glad to hear what His Excellency had to tell me. I was convinced that the greater moderation and statesmanship the Spanish Government could show, however strong they might consider their provocation to have been, the better it would be not only for international understanding in Europe but also for the Spanish Government itself.

3. Señor Azcárate went on to say that, although he knew I had grave doubts as to the wisdom of the Council meeting, he still thought that there was useful work that might be done. It was conceivable, for instance, that the Council might pass a resolution supporting non-intervention together with some scheme of supervision. As I knew, his Government had not liked the policy of non-intervention, but he thought that if that policy were to be combined with a scheme of supervision, i.e. if it was to be made really effective, they might be in a position to support it at Geneva. I asked the Ambassador whether he thought his Government's support would extend to endorsing any efforts that might be made to prevent the influx of so-called volunteers to Spain. The present position was in our view extremely serious. It could not be in the interest of Spain herself that thousands of foreigners should pour into the country and make Spain their battle ground. Some day the present tragic chapter of Spanish history would have to be brought to a close. The presence of these foreigners fighting on both sides might then present a problem of the gravest character. It was therefore in Spain's interest as well as in ours to put a stop to this influx. The Ambassador agreed, and while inclined at first to argue that there was a difference between individual volunteers arriving on the Government side and actual military units from Germany, Señor Azcárate eventually seemed prepared to consider whether his Government might not endorse some such proposal at the Council.

4. The Ambassador expressed his anxiety at the situation which must exist in Spain for some time after the fighting came to an end. The country

---

[1] See No. 419, note 1.

would then require a measure of outside help to restore its national life. It would be difficult for Spain to accept the assistance of advisers of any particular nationality, even Englishmen and Americans, but if the help could be given under the auspices of the League it would appear under a different guise in Spanish opinion. In the circumstances he thought it might be useful if the Council could include in its resolution an offer of such technical help.

5. The Ambassador stated that another problem which was causing his Government keen anxiety was the naval aspect of the present civil war. He did not know whether the League could make any suggestions to help to meet this situation. In reply to a question the Ambassador added that his Government fully appreciated the position which His Majesty's Government had taken up in this matter of arms traffic.[2] They quite understood that, having taken up an attitude towards belligerent rights with which the Spanish Government were in full agreement, we had also to take certain steps to avoid incidents. So far from complaining of our attitude the Spanish Government fully endorsed it.

6. Finally the Ambassador said that he had heard rumours of late of the possibility of some effort being made at mediation by His Majesty's Government.[3] Naturally there was nothing he desired more than to see the present appalling state of affairs brought to an end. At the same time he thought he ought to warn me that mediation scarcely stood a chance if it was attempted while the attitude of the German and Italian Governments continued as it was at present. He thought that an indispensable first step was to approach the dictator Powers, including Russia, about their attitude.

I am, &c.,

ANTHONY EDEN

[2] See Nos. 399 and 402.   [3] Cf. No. 436.

No. 438

Sir E. Phipps (Berlin) to Mr. Eden (Received December 5, 12.30 p.m.)

No. 369 Telegraphic: by telephone [W 17437/62/41]

Immediate   BERLIN, *December 5, 1936*

My immediately preceding telegram.[1]

Before even reading our aide-mémoires Minister for Foreign Affairs reminded us that German Government had proposed on August 17th (see Berlin despatch No. 869)[2] that volunteers should not be allowed to proceed to Spain.

Baron von Neurath then and after we had given him an oral summary of the contents of our communication expressed himself sceptically as to the

[1] Not preserved in the Foreign Office archives. It reported the presentation to Baron von Neurath of the communication referred to in Nos. 434 and 436.

[2] Not printed: see No. 105.

possibility of inducing the Spaniards to cease fighting. I replied that it was quite possible that both sides might through exhaustion be ready to accept the mediation of the six Powers although they would probably decline that of a more restricted number of foreign States. I frankly stated that even though mediation should prove unavailing the mere fact of its attempt by the six Powers might certainly be considered as the beginning of better days in Europe. French Ambassador added 'and of the reforming of the concert of Europe'.

We all agreed that nothing whatever should for the present be said to the Press regarding our '*démarche*'.

No. 439

Note by Sir G. Mounsey of a conversation with the French Ambassador
[*W 17431/9549/41*]

FOREIGN OFFICE, *December 5, 1936*

The French Ambassador rang me up this morning to make the following enquiry in regard to the Soviet proposal for including the despatch of volunteers to Spain in the prohibitions under the Non-Intervention Agreement.[1]

Monsieur Corbin said that the Soviet proposal was to the effect that the Non-Intervention Agreement should be extended to the despatch of volunteers, and that the participating Governments should be asked to undertake to prevent the despatch or transit of volunteers to Spain.

Monsieur Corbin asked me what the attitude of His Majesty's Government was to this proposal, which he said would be, from the legislative point of view, difficult for the French Government to carry out.[2] It would, in fact, require fresh legislation, which it might take some time to pass, and he thought that the only way of expediting matters for his Government would be by the conclusion of an agreement to this effect among the Powers participating in the Non-Intervention Agreement. On the strength of such a fresh agreement, the French Government would be in a better position to press for speedy legislation to cover it in France.

I told Monsieur Corbin that I believed His Majesty's Government were entirely favourable to the conclusion of such an agreement, and that we had already powers under the Foreign Enlistment Act which would enable us to put it in force at very short notice.[3]

---

[1] Cf. No. 449, paragraph 3, below.   [2] On this point see *D.D.F.*, *op. cit.*, No. 95.

[3] Discussions on this issue (W 17160/9549/41) had also been stimulated by a message from the Dominions Office of November 30 which said that Mr. de Valera, President of the Irish Free State, wished to have urgently 'information as to the steps taken by the F.O. to prevent persons from this country going to Spain to fight either for the Government or the Insurgents'. The Foreign Office was not prepared to reply in writing, but had no objection to a telephone message, which was to the effect that no proclamation had been issued recognizing the parties in dispute in Spain as belligerents; that such a proclamation

I understood from recent discussions in the Secretary of State's room that we had contemplated issuing a warning notice to the British public in regard to their obligations under the Foreign Enlistment Act in the event of yesterday's discussions in the Non-Intervention Committee taking a favourable turn.

I do not know whether any decision has been taken on this question, and it was for this reason that I was not more definite in my reply to the French Ambassador.[4]

G. M.

would normally draw attention to certain clauses of the Foreign Enlistment Act and that it had not been thought desirable to make a statement unless the Non-Intervention Committee agreed to stop enlistment for service in Spain. The Law Officers were nevertheless of the opinion that even without a proclamation the Act was automatically in force so far as recruitment was concerned. Mr. J. P. Walshe, of the Foreign Ministry in Dublin, expressed himself as grateful for this information, and said that hitherto the Irish Free State had not attempted to stop persons going to France or Portugal, but that unless 'something was done a situation would soon arise in which Englishmen were fighting against Englishmen, Englishmen against Irishmen, and Irishmen against Irishmen'.

[4] Minutes by Mr. Shuckburgh and Mr. Roberts of December 3 had suggested that it might be advisable to issue a statement pointing out that under section 5 of the Foreign Enlistment Act it was an offence to quit the country or to go on board a ship with a view to quitting it to join the forces of either side. A draft statement to this effect was drawn up at a meeting in Sir W. Malkin's room on December 7. The Home Office and Dominions Office concurred in the issue of this statement. Mr. Eden, however, postponed a decision until he had had an opportunity to consult the Cabinet on December 16, after which it was decided to take no further action for the present (W 17160, 18567/9549/41). See also No. 481 below.

No. 440

Sir E. Drummond (Rome) to Mr. Eden (Received December 6, 10 a.m.)
No. 727 Telegraphic [R 7370/226/22]

ROME, *December 6, 1936, 2.30 a.m.*

Your telegrams Nos. 451[1] and 452.[2]

The Minister for Foreign Affairs was obviously delighted when I went to see him this evening[3] and told him that my Government had authorised me to accept his proposal for a general conversation on Anglo-Italian relations to deal in particular with suggested gentleman's agreement regarding the Mediterranean. I said that I would propose to deal with this understanding first and that I had brought with me a formula of a very general and preliminary character which might possibly form the basis for an exchange of notes on identic lines and I gave him that part of your declaration in the House of Commons on November 5th contained in your telegram under reference modifying very slightly the last sentence.

2. His Excellency after quickly reading through the draft said that in general he had little objection to make either to it or to the idea of an exchange of notes. He was however somewhat doubtful about suggestion respecting

[1] No. 426.   [2] *Ibid.*, note 14.   [3] i.e. December 5.

territorial status quo. There were many Mediterranean Powers interested in the status quo. Would it be either wise or possible for Italy and Great Britain to guarantee that status quo? I replied that no such engagement was envisaged; we merely stated that each country should declare its desire to see the status quo respected. Such a statement was of considerable importance since it would tend to destroy any suspicion that this understanding might otherwise arouse in the minds of smaller Mediterranean Powers. Minister for Foreign Affairs then said that if we were only dealing with a desire he was ready to accept this suggestion.

3. The only other criticism His Excellency made was directed to what he termed the vagueness of the terms of our draft particularly the sentence beginning 'since we have no desire'. Could not that sentence be strengthened? might we not leave out 'we are convinced that it is possible' and substitute something like 'Great Britain and Italy will continue to maintain'? Similarly 'since we have no desire to threaten' might be replaced by 'we will not threaten or attack etc.' His Excellency observed that these were only his preliminary observations and in general he gave me the impression that he would be very willing to meet our views on any doubtful point.

4. He told me that he had prepared for our discussion an informal and personal draft cast in the form of an agreement; ultimately he gave me a copy of it on the strict understanding that it should be considered as purely personal (translation of text is contained in my immediately following telegram).[4] You will see that the last sentence of the draft speaks of consultation and he asked me whether this sentence might not be added to our draft. I answered that I felt personally and I thought my Government would share this view that an agreement conveying the idea of a consultative pact was undesirable since it might appear to have an exclusive character. Count Ciano did not insist but asked me to refer the point to you. When he also pointed out that in his draft there was a statement to the effect that the understanding was not directed against any other Power I replied that our draft contained the same idea since we said we had no wish to threaten or attack the interests of Italy or any other Power.

5. My impression is that we need anticipate little difficulty in reaching an agreed form of words since the Minister for Foreign Affairs will not I believe be at all intransigent on drafting questions; in addition he seemed ready to acquiesce in my opinion that an exchange of notes containing a declaration of policy on the part of each Government was to be preferred to an agreement. Count Ciano on reaching this point in the interview summed up by saying that he considered an understanding on these lines most important from point of view of a goal in European situation and in the interest of peace.

6. I then said that there were two further points in connexion with exchange of notes on which I wished to speak. The first was that it was essential to make it clear that our mutual declarations were not directed against any other Mediterranean Power. Count Ciano fully agreed and

---

4 No. 441 below.

643

pointed out that his draft showed that he entirely concurred. Indeed he had inserted it because of what I had said to him on a previous occasion. My Government I went on felt it highly desirable that France who was a great Mediterranean Power and had vital interests in that Sea should be associated in some way with our declarations. This did not mean that we should have conversations *à trois* but it did mean that we should not wish that France should feel neglected. Would he consider the possibility, for instance, after we decided on text of our respective notes, of enquiry whether the French Government would be prepared to exchange identic notes with both of us. Alternatively it might be possible for His Majesty's Government to make similar communication to the French Government and obtain identic declaration from them in return. This was the only point in our conversation which seemed to disturb His Excellency considerably and he asked for time to think it over. Why he enquired should France be brought into a clarification of Anglo-Italian relations? Nothing we had in view was directed against France. Why therefore should she be considered? All that I could obtain from His Excellency at the moment was that if after our exchange of notes had taken place France desired to exchange similar notes with His Majesty's Government, Italy would see no objection; but even on this point he said he would prefer more time for consideration. In spite of all my efforts I could not get him to go further. It was obvious that he wished to limit the exchange of notes to Italy and the United Kingdom in the first instance. In reply to my question he said that he would be ready to take up the matter again any time after December 7th.

7. I next referred to his suggestion for a tour of the horizon. I had two points I should like to mention and no doubt he had others. On his inviting me to proceed I began with the question of anti-British propaganda and spoke to him most earnestly in the sense of paragraph on the subject in your telegram under reference. His Excellency by a gesture expressed complete ignorance and asked whether I could supply him with facts or names. I gave him the two names mentioned. Summing up I said that once friendly relations were completely established we should expect this inspired and paid anti-British agitation to cease.

8. I then turned to London Naval Agreement and stated that we sincerely hoped that Italy would as a result of agreement and improvement in relations which would follow accede to this instrument. After I had put forward all the obvious arguments Count Ciano expressed the belief that Treaty was still being examined by Italian experts, but did not think in principle there would be much difficulty in accession. But he wanted to ask me one question. Had treaty been ratified by the United States of America, France and ourselves? Until it had been Italian accession might be difficult. I replied that to the best of my knowledge the three Powers had ratified but that I would make sure of this point and let him know. These, I concluded, were the only two points outside the Mediterranean on which I wished to speak. What were his points?

9. His Excellency then said, 'let us close this chapter and begin chapter II.

What I want to talk about to you is Abyssinia. I quite realize from what you have said that you do not wish in any way to connect Abyssinia with present conversations but I feel bound to explain to you Italian point of view. It is all to the good and highly satisfactory if we can come to our Gentleman's agreement and I believe we shall be able to do so but its value will be greatly diminished in Italian eyes if British Government continue their "hard" attitude about Italian Empire. Things are moving. United States Minister has left or is shortly leaving Addis Ababa and a Consul is being sent to take his place.[5] I quite realize that you cannot give, and I do not ask for, *de jure* recognition, but if you could take some step to lessen the hardness to which I have referred if possible before conclusion of agreement it would have a most beneficial effect'.

10. In reply I begged him not to press me on this point. It was a matter on which we desired our hands quite free to take such spontaneous action as we thought fit, if and when the time came. I understood his point of view, I naturally would report it home, but I could do no more and I would beg him not to insist further. His Excellency said he was prepared to leave question in my hands.

11. I asked him if there was no other point he wished to raise as the horizon had seemed somewhat limited. He replied that this was the only point and again emphasized that he did not wish to connect the two questions in any way; the second, he thought had no connexion with the first but its effect on Italian public opinion would naturally be very great. My suggestions follow.[6]

[5] See *F.R.U.S.*, 1936, vol. iii, pp. 330–41.
[6] See No. 445 below. After the receipt of this telegram there was discussion in the Foreign Office as to the terms of the Anglo-Italian agreement. In a minute of December 8 Mr. O'Malley remarked that the 'idea of a *tour d'horizon* fizzled out pretty quickly'. Mr. Sargent in a long minute of December 9 pointed out that Count Ciano had 'shown no intention whatsoever of wishing to remove points of friction between Great Britain and Italy, without which the Gentlemen's Agreement regarding the Mediterranean will be of mighty little value if a general *détente* is what we want to bring about'. He 'evidently did not want to discuss anything but Abyssinia', whereas Great Britain was interested in the satisfaction of her border problems in British Somaliland, Kenya, and the Sudan, as well as in Italy's accession to the Montreux convention and the naval treaty, the diminution of anti-British propaganda and of Italian intrigues in Arabia, and in Italian co-operation with the League. He was in favour of an attempt to clear up all points of friction in the present phase of negotiations. Sir R. Vansittart remarked (December 9) that 'all' was a big word, and it appears that he would have preferred to postpone consideration of points other than 'propaganda' until the next round of discussion, and to proceed to the early signature of the agreement in the form of a draft which had been produced by Mr. O'Malley.

Mr. Eden, however, evidently wanted a fuller enunciation of British desiderata before the agreement was signed. He wrote: 'I agree emphatically with Mr. Sargent's minute. The Italians are at their old game of getting something for nothing. They are apprehensive of our growing strength in the Mediterranean and would no doubt greatly like to be reassured. But what do we get in return? Anti-British propaganda in the Near East, a redoubling of activity in Majorca and the most cavalier treatment of our representations or suggestions on any subject. This is not what we want. I trust therefore that the instructions which accompany to Sir E. Drummond the new, and admirable draft agreement, will make this clear. An agreement that only adds one more scrap of paper to the world, and changes nothing in fundamentals is not worth so much effort. A. E. Dec. 10.' See No. 482 below.

No. 441

Sir E. Drummond (Rome) to Mr. Eden (Received December 6, 10 a.m.)
No. 728 Telegraphic [R 7371/226/22]

ROME, *December 6, 1936, 2.30 a.m.*

Following is translation of Count Ciano's informal and personal draft referred to in my immediately preceding telegram.[1]

'The Fascist Government and British Government having proceeded to a friendly exchange of views as regards their own relations; recognizing that their interests in the Mediterranean are complementary, not divergent; animated by the desire to contribute increasingly to the betterment of relations between them and to the general cause of peace and security; have laid down the following points in common agreement: (1) the two governments undertake (literally "pledge themselves") to respect their reciprocal positions and they mutually assure to each other the freedom of communications in the Mediterranean and its accesses to the oceans together with freedom of their respective (seaborne) traffic (*nonche dei traffici rispettivi*). This undertaking is designed to further the ends of peace and is not directed against any other Power.

(2) The two Governments will proceed to friendly consultations should differences arise within the framework of the present agreement'.

[1] No. 440.

No. 442

Sir E. Drummond (Rome) to Mr. Eden (Received December 6, 10 a.m.)
No. 729 Telegraphic [W 17509/62/41]

ROME, *December 6,[1] 1936, 2.30 a.m.*

Your telegrams Nos. 457 and 458.[2]

French Chargé d'Affaires[3] received his instructions today[4] and we compared texts this morning. He saw Minister for Foreign Affairs just after I saw him this evening.

2. After disposing of Mediterranean agreement[5] I told Minister for Foreign Affairs that I wished to speak to him on a quite different subject, namely, Spain. I gave him *note verbale* in terms of your telegram No. 458 stating that these views had been concerted with French Government and I then spoke in the sense of your telegram No. 457.

3. I went on to say that the French Government, equally with His Majesty's Government, were much exercised about importation of war

[1] The date of despatch of this telegram was given as December 5, apparently in error.
[2] Nos. 434 and 436.
[3] M. Jules Blondel. M. de Saint Quentin had been appointed French Ambassador at Rome in succession to M. de Chambrun, who returned to Paris in November 1936, but could not take up his post as the French Government would not agree to refer to the King of Italy as 'Emperor of Abyssinia' in M. de Saint Quentin's credentials.
[4] i.e. December 5.
[5] See No. 440.

material and enrolment of volunteers for service in Spain and desired that an end should be put to these proceedings. I felt sure that Italy was as desirous of peace as we were; but as long as Spanish civil war continued there was always a danger to peace. His Excellency agreed. I then referred to possibility of mediation. His Excellency said that he must have time to consider the whole question but was not very hopeful. Italy had foreseen danger of enrolment of volunteers and had indeed put forward question in non-intervention Committee proposing that volunteers should be barred, but a large number of Russians were now in Spain and action we suggested, even if feasible, might come too late.

4. Speaking purely personally I then observed that war seemed rapidly developing into one between Russian, French and Extreme Left volunteers on one side and German, Italian and Extreme Right volunteers on the other and I quoted an American journalist who had just returned from Spain, to the effect that the bombers on General Franco's side were all German and flown by Germans and the fighting planes all of Italian make and flown by Italians. On the Government side both machines and airmen were all Russian. Conflict therefore was no longer Spanish.

5. Count Ciano was inclined to concur in this diagnosis but did not see what could be done. What did we intend by mediation? In his view there was no middle choice in Spain between an authoritarian government and communism; there was no room for a Kerensky government and even if one were established it would not last. General Franco who was making prima facie progress owing to disintegration on the Government side was ultimately sure of victory. We did not intend that Spain should be divided into two parts with Catalonia a communist republic and the rest of Spain under General Franco. Nor in his view was it to our interests that a communist republic should be set up in the Mediterranean. He would in any case think over our proposals; in reply to question he said he did not think he would be able to give me an answer for a day or two. He would, however, telephone to me when he was ready to talk. He emphasized that what he had said was only his first reaction to our proposals. I think it is certain that he intends to consult the German Government before returning any definitive reply.[6]

[6] Mr. Shuckburgh commented in a minute of December 12: 'The first reactions to our proposals in Berlin, Rome & Moscow are distinctly discouraging. The general opinion seems to be that they are not practical.' Cf. No. 438, and No. 444 below; *D.D.F.*, *op. cit.*, No. 104.

No. 443

Sir C. Wingfield (Lisbon) to Mr. Eden (Received December 6, 1.30 p.m.)
No. 230 Telegraphic [W 17446/62/41]

Important   LISBON, *December 6, 1936, 11.45 a.m.*
Your telegram No. 232 to Berlin.[1]
French Minister who does not return from Oporto till Monday[2] was informed by telephone yesterday that I was carrying out our instructions in

[1] No. 434.   [2] i.e. December 7.

anticipation of his return. I consequently left a memorandum with the Secretary-General of the Ministry of Foreign Affairs in the sense of your instructions asking him to inform the Prime Minister and the Acting Minister for Foreign Affairs[3] at once and explain that my French colleague had similar instructions.

From our conversation I gathered that his personal impression was that the proposals were not very practical. He enquired what would be the effect of a further declaration respecting non-intervention in Spain since the agreement to that effect was notoriously not being observed; and he asked whether there was any chance of mediation being accepted since the question as to which side was to rule Spain must at once arise.

I urged that our agreement despite breaches of it had so far prevented war from spreading to other countries. We were making one more effort to prevent the Powers from drifting into open participation in the civil war, the original parties to which might be getting near the end of their tether, and therefore be ready to accept mediation however difficult it was to suggest acceptable terms.

As the Prime Minister may receive me soon to discuss proposals I should be grateful to be furnished with any further arguments to recommend them to him.[4]

[3] Dr. Salazar.
[4] Foreign Office telegram No. 164 of December 10 instructed Sir C. Wingfield to refer, in his forthcoming discussion with Dr. Salazar, to the increasing danger of the arrival of fresh volunteers in Spain, and to point out 'that if this continues the present stage of apparent exhaustion will pass and possibility of mediation be indefinitely removed'. He was, however, apparently not invited at this stage to discuss the matter with Dr. Salazar. His telegram No. 232 of December 12, not preserved in the Foreign Office archives, referred only to a long Portuguese memorandum of December 11 giving the Portuguese reply. The full text of this memorandum is printed in *D.A.P.E.*, *op. cit.*, No. 669. A translation was forwarded to London by Sir C. Wingfield in his despatch No. 495 of December 15. A summary of the Portuguese position on mediation, written apparently by Mr. Shuckburgh on December 14, was as follows. 'The Portuguese Government are ready to join in affording help of all sorts to the suffering population of Spain on either side. They suggest that the Powers might later consider steps for the protection of the vanquished and for assisting the reconstruction of Spain. They are willing to consider the possibilities of mediation though they have no confidence in elections. They consider also that any plan for mediation must guarantee a "minimum liberty against terrorism" and "must take moral ideas into account". It is also necessary that both parties should agree.'

No. 444

Viscount Chilston (Moscow) to Mr. Eden (Received December 6, 1.15 p.m.)
No. 207 Telegraphic [W 17458/62/41]

MOSCOW, *December 6, 1936, 1.35 p.m.* [sic]

Your telegram No. 147.[1]
French Ambassador and I saw M. Litvinoff yesterday and made desired communication.

[1] No. 436.

M. Litvinoff said he would study proposals and consult his government and hoped to give a considered reply in two or three days. Meanwhile he could only say that anyhow first two proposals seemed at first sight impossible to be acceptable [*sic*]. As we knew he had always urged that control over imports of war material into Spain should be effectively imposed and he had agreed and co-operated in neutrality committee although Soviet Government had never shared view of our governments that the same attitude should be held towards both sides (the legal government in Spain and those in the rebellion against them).[2]

[2] Cf. *D.V.P.S.*, *op. cit.*, No. 401.

No. 445

Sir E. Drummond (Rome) to Mr. Eden (Received December 7, 9.30 a.m.)
No. 730 Telegraphic [R 7373/226/22]

ROME, *December 6, 1936, 9.55 p.m.*

My telegrams Nos. 727[1] and 728.[2]

Minister for Foreign Affairs is I feel quite ready to accept our suggested form for an understanding, viz. an exchange of notes, and will not press for his own draft which following Italian-German precedent he thought might be published as a signed *procès-verbal* or *communiqué*. Meanwhile there may be points in his proposals which you may consider acceptable and points on which our draft could be amended to meet his criticisms. If so and if you consider our conversation has been generally satisfactory I should be grateful if you felt able to send me a considered text for use at my next interview. I could of course draft a revised text here but in view of importance of phraseology and fact that I may be able to persuade Minister for Foreign Affairs to accept any form of words about which His Majesty's Government feel strongly you will probably think it preferable to prepare draft in London.

Your telegram to Paris No. 136 Saving[3] envisages a possible reduction of our Legation at Addis Ababa to a consulate by the middle of the month and it would be clearly advantageous if such a change of status could take place before and independently of gentlemen's agreement—a reversed procedure would lead to a wrong interpretation here. I should like however to be in a position to continue my conversations with Count Ciano towards the end of this week in order that they may be concluded if possible before the end of the year.

[1] No. 440.   [2] No. 441.   [3] See No. 378, note 8.

Mr. Eden to Sir R. Lindsay (Washington)
No. 412 Telegraphic [W 17447/62/41]

Important   FOREIGN OFFICE, *December 7, 1936, 1.50 p.m.*

Your telegram No. 322.[1]

I do not share the view of the Acting Secretary of State in regard to the utility of action by the United States Ambassadors at the capitals of the four Powers. It seems to me that for the advancement of the Anglo-French *démarche* it would in fact be of considerable assistance if the United States Ambassadors in the capitals concerned could be instructed to support the general principle of these representations.

Your Excellency will recall that the conversations now being conducted in those capitals are at present confidential in character.

On what basis, in these circumstances, is it proposed that an immediate statement by the President should be founded?

It would presumably have to be made quite spontaneously, without reference to any Anglo-French action and on some such ground as that of the apparent stalemate now reached at Madrid.

[1] In this telegram of December 5 Sir R. Lindsay referred to his conversation with Mr. Dunn at his home on the evening of December 4 (cf. No. 435, note 3) and said that for reasons 'which I think you would approve' he had asked the French Ambassador to make official representation on behalf of the two governments to the Acting Secretary of State (Mr. R. Walton Moore). Mr. Moore 'was averse from any *démarche* by the United States Ambassadors which he thought would lack authority but he was in favour of a statement by the President from his ship strongly supporting in general terms any action tending to limit (? duration) or scope of conflict in Spain'. Cf. *F.R.U.S.*, 1936, vol. ii, pp. 589–90; President Roosevelt was *en route* for Buenos Aires to attend the Inter-American Conference for the Maintenance of Peace.

In a further telegram of December 5, No. 323, Sir R. Lindsay said that he had left the approach to the French Ambassador because of a friendly warning from Mr. Moore 'to the effect that owing to fantastic rumours connected with the [abdication] crisis in England all the press were watching for any visit I might make to the Department [of State] and that my appearance there might produce undesirable publicity'.

No. 447

Sir E. Drummond (Rome) to Mr. Eden (Received December 7, 4.45 p.m.)
No. 732 Telegraphic [R 7376/226/22]

Important   ROME, *December 7, 1936, 3.25 p.m.*

My telegram No. 727,[1] paragraph 6 and my despatch No. 1276.[2]

Minister for Foreign Affairs asked me to go to see him this morning and told me that he had discussed with Signor Mussolini points raised in our

[1] No. 440.
[2] In this despatch of November 27 (R 7216/294/67) Sir E. Drummond referred to M. Corbin's concern at the prospect of his government's exclusion from any general

conversation of December 5th.[3] Head of Government had confirmed line that he, Count Ciano, had taken and there did not appear to be any difficulties; on one point however Signor Mussolini felt very strongly, namely, suggestion that France should be associated in some way with exchange of notes. Count Ciano then explained the purpose which Italian Government and he assumed His Majesty's Government had in mind was clarification of situation existing between them in Mediterranean, a clarification which was necessary as a result of certain recent events; no such clarification was necessary as between Italy and France. Moreover addition of France to exchange of notes would turn gentleman's agreement into a Mediterranean agreement which was something quite different from a clarification of Italian-British position. Further would not other Powers such as Turkey, Greece and Yugoslavia express wish to participate? How could they be refused?

I replied that I had rather feared that Head of Government might take this view but what objection would there be if after our notes had been published, French were to express wish to exchange similar notes, say with ourselves? Our point was that we did not wish in any way to neglect French interests.

His Excellency replied that as he had already explained there was no need for an exchange of notes between Italy and France and there hardly seemed any need for a clarification of policy as between France and the United Kingdom. He added however that if France wished to make a declaration about her policy in the Mediterranean no one of course could object.

Although the interview was most friendly I gained the impression from what Count Ciano let drop of his conversation with his father-in-law that if we insisted [on] associating France with exchange of notes Signor Mussolini would prefer to let the whole negotiation drop: he feels apparently most strongly on the subject. You will recall that I dealt with this possibility in my despatch under reference.

Anglo-Italian agreement concerning the Mediterranean: see No. 404. Sir E. Drummond believed that any attempt by the French Government to become a party to the Anglo-Italian conversations would be bitterly resented in Rome and would entail the collapse of the whole negotiation.
[3] See No. 440.

No. 448

Mr. Eden to Sir R. Lindsay (Washington)
No. 413 Telegraphic [W 17447/62/41]

Immediate   FOREIGN OFFICE, *December 7, 1936, 10 p.m.*
My telegram No. 412.[1]

It now appears that the French Government contemplate giving publicity to the Anglo-French *démarche* at the four capitals very shortly, possibly tomorrow.[2]

[1] No. 446.   [2] See No. 450 below.

They hold that considerable advantage is to be anticipated from securing the support of world opinion for this *démarche*; and they have already been approached by several South American Governments on the possibility of some form of mediation. They are accordingly proposing to notify the four Governments concerned that it is now their intention to make public the step taken by themselves in concert with His Majesty's Government in the United Kingdom at the four capitals.

In these circumstances you should inform the Acting Secretary of State that his suggestion of a statement by the President from his ship in the sense outlined would be most welcome to us, and that we think this statement could most effectively be made very soon after our own *démarche* has been made public here.

We will keep you informed of future developments in this direction as promptly as possible.

Repeated Paris, Berlin, Moscow, Rome, Lisbon.

No. 449

Report[1] of the Chairman's Sub-Committee of the N.I. Committee on the entry of foreign nationals into Spain for service in the civil war

[*W 18694/9549/41*]

December 7, 1936

I. *Introductory*

As arranged at the last plenary session of the Committee, held on Wednesday, the 2nd December, 1936,[2] we have had under consideration the question of the entry into Spain of increasing numbers of foreign nationals for the purpose of taking service in the civil war.

2. In the course of our consideration of this question, the United Kingdom Representative communicated to us the following message from the Secretary of State for Foreign Affairs in the name of the United Kingdom Government.

'Reports are reaching His Majesty's Government that nationals of foreign Powers are arriving in Spain in increasing numbers to take part in the Spanish Civil War on both sides. These reports are of such a nature that their evidence cannot be ignored. If this practice is allowed to continue it must have grave repercussions on international relations outside Spain, in addition to prolonging the conflict in that country.

In the view, therefore, of His Majesty's Government in the United Kingdom, it is their duty as a member of the International Committee on Non-Intervention to urge most strongly that the Committee should at once take this matter into consideration and agree decisions and measures to put a stop to this practice.'

[1] This was the second report of the Chairman's Sub-Committee; it was drawn up at the fifteenth meeting of the sub-committee on December 7, and circulated to the main committee as Committee Paper N.I.S.(36)177. For the first report see No. 204.

[2] See No. 427.

3. We also received from the U.S.S.R. Representative a communication, the text of which is given in Annex A attached hereto,[3] setting out the following proposals by the U.S.S.R. Government for dealing with the question of 'volunteers,' to which reference had been made in a letter addressed by the U.S.S.R. Representative to the Chairman of the Committee on the 11th November, 1936:

(1) To extend the obligations of the Non-Intervention Agreement to cover the sending of volunteers to Spain;

(2) That the Governments, parties to the Non-Intervention Agreements, shall undertake to prevent by every means the dispatch and transit of volunteers to Spain;

(3) That the Governments, parties to the Non-Intervention Agreement, shall be approached immediately, through their representatives on the Committee, with the object of obtaining their consent to the extension of the obligations of the Non-Intervention Agreement as proposed in paragraphs (1) and (2) above;

(4) That the Agents of the Non-Intervention Committee to be stationed at the principle [sic] points of entry by land and by sea in Spain should be entrusted with the additional duty of controlling the observance of the additional undertakings proposed above by all the parties concerned.

4. In this connection we have considered also certain proposals for dealing with the problem of indirect intervention as a whole, submitted to us by the Italian Representative in a memorandum dated the 18th September, 1936, a copy of which is attached hereto as Annex B.[4] The Italian Government have, in a communication orally conveyed to us, restated their original point of view on the question of indirect intervention, adding that they consider that this subject should not be examined in a partial or occasional manner.

5. Moreover, the question of indirect intervention, and in particular that of volunteers, had been raised by the German Government as early as the 17th August, 1936, when discussing with the French Government the question of adhering to the Non-Intervention Agreement.[5] Furthermore, the German Representative stressed, with reference to the letter addressed by the U.S.S.R. Representative to the Chairman of the Committee on the 4th December, 1936, the text of which is given in Annex A attached hereto, the fact that the problem arose from the presence in Spain of nationals of several countries.

II. *Conclusions*

6. We are all agreed upon the importance of dealing with all those forms of indirect intervention on which the Governments represented upon the Committee agree that practical steps can be taken. From our past discussions, one of these forms of intervention clearly appears to be the question of the

---

[3] Of December 4: not printed.   [4] Not printed.   [5] See No. 105.

entry into Spain of foreign nationals for the purpose of taking part in the civil war.

7. We consider it essential that an urgent examination of these questions should be undertaken by the Governments which are parties to the Non-Intervention Agreement. In view of the special urgency attached by certain Governments to the question of the entry of foreign nationals into Spain for the purpose of taking part in the civil war, we are agreed that the Governments should be asked whether they are prepared to accord special priority to the consideration of this particular aspect of the problem of indirect intervention.

III. *Action recommended by the Sub-Committee*

8. For the reasons set out in the preceding paragraphs, we recommend that the Representatives on the Committee should forward to their respective Governments the following communication on behalf of the Committee:

(*a*) The Committee, being of the opinion that all measures that may be practicable should be taken to deal with the question of indirect intervention, and in particular with the problem created by the departure for Spain, in increasing numbers, of foreign nationals for the purpose of taking service with one or other of the parties in conflict, desires to be informed whether the Governments which are parties to the Non-Intervention Agreement

  (i) agree in principle to the extension of the Agreement to cover indirect as well as direct intervention, so far as may be practicable, and whether they

  (ii) agree, as a first step, to the extension of the Agreement to cover the recruitment in, the despatch from or transit through, their respective countries of persons proposing to take part in the civil war in Spain.

   (Note. All the members of the Sub-Committee are in favour of course (i) above. With the exception of the German, Italian, and Portuguese Representatives, who are at present without instructions from their respective Governments, all the members of the Sub-Committee are in favour of course (ii) also. The assent of the Representative of the U.S.S.R. is conditional upon the acceptance of course (ii) as well as that of course (i).)

(*b*) The Committee hopes that the Governments concerned will furnish it as soon as possible with information showing the nature of the measures which are already in force in their respective countries, and setting out what further measures they would be prepared, in co-operation with the other Governments that are parties to the Non-Intervention Agreement, to introduce, in order to deal with

  (i) the entry into Spain of foreign nationals for the purpose of taking part in the civil war;

(ii) the entry into Spain of foreign nationals for the purpose of carrying out other activities which are in any way susceptible of prolonging or embittering the civil war;

(iii) the supply of financial aid to either of the parties in Spain;

(iv) any other aspects of the problem of indirect intervention which in their opinion should be considered by the Committee.

(c) The Committee take note of the fact that the United Kingdom Government, in drawing attention to the gravity and urgency of the questions raised by the entry into Spain of increasing numbers of foreign nationals for the purpose of taking part in the civil war, hope that the Governments concerned will give special priority to the consideration of the question of the recruitment, &c., in their respective countries, of persons proposing to take service with either of the parties in conflict. This view was supported by the Representatives of

(here insert names of countries)

in the name of their respective Governments, and also by the Representatives of the following countries in their personal capacity

(here insert names of countries)

Signed on behalf of the Sub-Committee:
PLYMOUTH, *Chairman*[6]

[6] The N.I. Committee at its thirteenth meeting on December 9 adopted the recommendations of this report, subject to a number of drafting amendments, and the representatives on the Committee agreed to forward the documents at once to their respective governments. The Chairman hoped that the governments would furnish their representatives with the desired information as soon as possible.

No. 450

Mr. Eden to Sir G. Clerk (Paris)
No. 2066 [*W 17547/62/41*]

FOREIGN OFFICE, *December 7, 1936*

Sir,

During the course of a conversation this afternoon with the French Ambassador[1] His Excellency asked me whether I had received any information as to the attitude of the various Governments concerned to our attempt at mediation. I replied that my information was fragmentary, but the German Government did not seem enthusiastic and had pointed out that they had favoured prohibition of the despatch of volunteers last August,[2] while M. Litvinoff had said that he could not agree to the first two proposals

[1] Cf. *D.D.F., op. cit.*, No. 110.   [2] See No. 438; cf. No. 105.

in our suggested programme.[3] Lisbon also appeared to see difficulties,[4] and I had as yet heard nothing from Rome.[5] All these answers were of course interim ones, and it was perhaps too early to form any definite view.

2. M. Corbin replied that his information was a little more encouraging. Rome had not refused, and had even indicated willingness to accept in principle, while stating that further information would probably be required on certain points. Moscow, the Ambassador understood, was distinctly sympathetic, though the reaction in Berlin was less good. In all the circumstances the French Government were considering whether the time had not arrived to make public the fact that we had taken this initiative in favour of mediation. We had stated that we would keep our proposals confidential until the Governments had had time to consider them. That time might now be held to be past and there was considerable advantage to be anticipated from securing the support of world public opinion for our endeavour.[6] Several South American Governments had already approached the French Government and there was also the position of the United States to be considered. I told the Ambassador that so far as the latter Government were concerned I understood that President Roosevelt was contemplating making some public statement of approval.[7] This would be an advantage if it could be done, but clearly it was difficult for the President to do so until our initiative was known. The Ambassador agreed and said this was precisely one of the reasons which made the French Government wish to make our initiative public as early as possible. After some further discussion we agreed that the French Government should inform the Governments whom we had approached of our intention to make our initiative known, and that M. Corbin should inform me further after this had been done. The French Government did not contemplate any publicity until tomorrow.[8]

I am, &c.,

ANTHONY EDEN

[3] See No. 444.   [4] Cf. No. 443.   [5] Cf. No. 442.

[6] Sir G. Clerk's despatch No. 1588 of December 6, reporting the foreign affairs debate in the French Chamber on December 4 and 5, concluded that all parties except the Communists favoured the government's policy of non-intervention and asked that it should be made more effective. A vote of confidence was passed by 350 votes to 171, the 72 Communists abstaining. In a minute of December 11 Mr. Howard commented: 'The French Communists do not want to intervene in the Spanish Civil War but at the same time they want to put an end to the Non-Intervention Agreement. The reasoning is difficult to understand.'

[7] Cf. Nos. 446 and 448.

[8] Particulars of the Anglo-French initiative were given to the press on the evening of December 9. See *The Times*, December 10, p. 14.

No. 451

Mr. Eden to Sir E. Drummond (Rome)
No. 466 Telegraphic: by telephone [R 7376/226/22]

Immediate   FOREIGN OFFICE, *December 8, 1936, 2.40 p.m.*

Your telegrams No. 727[1] and No. 732.[2]

When expressing the view that if possible France ought to be associated in any declarations on subjects of interest to France, I did not contemplate—especially in view of warning contained in your despatch No. 1276[3]—to ask that the proposed exchange of Notes regularising Anglo-Italian relations in the Mediterranean should be extended so as to include a similar exchange with France. Judging from the line which your conversation with Count Ciano took on December 6th[4] it does not seem that any special declarations or undertakings will be proposed, or that any points will be touched which would affect French interests in any concrete form.

As regards the general declaration on Anglo-Italian relations in the Mediterranean there is no need for you to press for French collaboration. It will be sufficient if you bear in mind, in discussing the text of the proposed Mediterranean declarations, my instructions in paragraph 4 of my telegram No. 451[5] to the effect that for the Mediterranean declarations a form of words must be found which will not offend the susceptibilities of the French or of other Mediterranean powers. We shall be sending you shortly a draft text for your use when you resume your conversation with Count Ciano.

Meanwhile you may make such use of the foregoing as you think advisable and in particular you should tell Count Ciano forthwith that you do not wish to insist on the idea that the French Government should be associated with the proposed Mediterranean declarations, which will be couched in general terms.

[1] No. 440.   [2] No. 447.   [3] See *ibid.*, note 2.
[4] The conversation was on December 5: see No. 440.   [5] No. 426.

No. 452

Mr. Eden to Sir N. Henderson[1] (Buenos Aires)
No. 114 Telegraphic [W 17543/62/41]

Immediate   FOREIGN OFFICE, *December 8, 1936, 10.30 p.m.*

The Argentine Ambassador[2] called at the Foreign Office on December 7 and on instructions from his Government made the following communication, which is understood to be sponsored by President Roosevelt.[3]

[1] H.M. Ambassador at Buenos Aires.   [2] H.E. Dr. Manuel R. Malbrán.
[3] President Roosevelt reached Buenos Aires on the cruiser *Indianapolis* on November 30, addressed the opening session of the Inter-American Conference on December 1, and left the next day.

The Argentine and other South American Governments were desirous of knowing whether His Majesty's Government in the United Kingdom and the French Government were considering the possibility of some means of bringing the present conflict in Spain to an early end, and whether they thought there was any way in which this object could be forwarded.

Before replying to this communication, Your Excellency should, if you have no objection, see Mr. Cordell Hull and inform him of the Ambassador's *démarche*.[4] You should tell Mr. Hull that, subject to any observations he may have to offer, you have been authorised to return a reply to the Argentine Government in the following sense.

His Majesty's Government in the United Kingdom greatly appreciate the inquiry which has been addressed to them. They have been in confidential consultation with the French Government and have, in concert with them, decided upon the action indicated in my telegrams Nos. 232 and 233 to Berlin[5] and 407 to Washington.[6]

This action having been taken at the four capitals, it is intended to publish very shortly the fact that this *démarche* has been made;[7] and His Majesty's Government would greatly welcome any support which the Argentine and other South American Governments feel that they could give to the step that they have taken.

It would further be suggested to the Argentine Government that the most effective and helpful support which they could give might perhaps take the form of some pronouncement, at an appropriate moment after the Anglo-French *démarche* has been made known, by the Pan-American Conference, such as an expression of its sympathy with and good-will for the success of the action taken.

If Mr. Hull is in agreement with this course, you should proceed to make a communication in the above sense to the Argentine Government, keeping in close touch with your French colleague.

[4] Cf. No. 435, note 3.   [5] Nos. 434 and 436.   [6] No. 435.   [7] Cf. No. 450.

No. 453

Record by Sir R. Vansittart of a conversation with M. Reynaud
[*C 8892/4/18*]

FOREIGN OFFICE, *December 8, 1936*

Monsieur Paul Reynaud[1] came to see me this afternoon and we had a long conversation which may be thus briefly resumed.

M. Paul Reynaud asked me if I had read his recent speech in the French Chamber,[2] in which he had advocated in effect that the Franco-Soviet Pact should be transformed at least to some extent into the reality which at present it is not.

[1] French Deputy and former Minister, member of the *Alliance républicaine de gauche*.
[2] On December 4: see *The Times*, December 5, 1936, p. 12.

I replied that I had read his speech and noticed this feature of it. He asked me what were my personal views on the point. I replied that though such action on the part of the French Government might be diversely received in the different political camps in this country, I thought that there was at present at least one general consideration which would be common to the majority of those camps. We were still engaged in an endeavour to reach a Five Power agreement. I did not over-rate the prospects of such an agreement; in fact at present they were undeniably poor. And they were poor because it seemed likely that the conditions which Germany would attach to any possibility of signature on her part would be of such a nature as to bar further progress. That was speculation or prophecy. What was certain however was that if the French Government proceeded at this moment to supplement the Franco-Soviet Pact by a military treaty or staff conversations, the Germans would immediately say that this had rendered all further progress impossible, and would allege that they would otherwise have been perfectly ready to come to a satisfactory agreement. They would in fact cause the entire blame for failure to be laid, with some plausibility, on French shoulders. My own personal view was, therefore, that it would be very bad tactics on the part of the French Government to expose themselves to this charge, particularly at a moment when I thought that public opinion in this country on the whole was rapidly increasing in their favour.

M. Paul Reynaud said that he quite saw the force of this reasoning. At the same time our military power was practically non-existent.[3] If France was involved in war on the Continent we should not at present be able to assist her with more than two divisions, and even those in nothing like the trim of 1914, and only after some delay. Meanwhile the French view of the situation was growing blacker. The French Embassy in Berlin in fact considered war likely in 1937.

I replied that I had long been aware of the views of the French Embassy in Berlin and had always considered them rather unduly pessimistic. (M. Paul Reynaud interjected that M. François-Poncet was by nature a pessimist.) There were no doubt many people here who thought that I myself was a pessimist, but I had never gone as far as the French Embassy in Berlin. And, that being so, it followed very naturally that I should think it unwise to formulate a policy on the basis of a pessimism with which I could not agree.

M. Paul Reynaud said that was all very well, but between discussing the possibility of supplementing the Franco-Soviet Pact and the actual turning of it into any kind of a reality, at least six months must elapse. M. Pierre Cot had told him this was so as regards the air, and six months was a long hiatus in present circumstances.

I replied that this however did not invalidate the reasoning with which I had begun our conversation and that I should still think it premature and unwise of France to consider the course that he had sketched, anyhow before

---

[3] A marginal note in Mr. Eden's handwriting here reads: 'What rubbish!'

we were surer of our ground, or of our lack of ground, as regards the Five Power pact. And I thought we should know more clearly where we stood early in 1937 and that it would only be then that true stock could be taken of the situation.

M. Reynaud again referred to the prognostications of evil in 1937, which were current not only in the French Embassy in Berlin but were very widespread in France itself.

I replied that although I was well aware of the seriousness of the European situation, I still thought that the French Embassy in Berlin and those who thought like them in France were painting it too black. There was always the possibility of an unpleasant surprise but I thought it probable that, on any normal showing, matters had not advanced as far as that.

M. Paul Reynaud concluded by repeating that he saw the force of my reasoning, and he indicated that he intended to be guided by it.[4]

R. V.

[4] Minutes on this record by Mr. Eden and Sir R. Vansittart were as follows. 'I am grateful to Sir R. Vansittart for his excellent advice to M. Reynaud. It is really invidious to say that our military power is "non-existent". We have by far the best navy in Europe (a *much* greater margin than 1914 over Germany). By next year we shall probably have a better air force than the French. It is only the army, which was never a formidable factor in British aid, which falls much short of 1914 standards. It might do the French good to be reminded of these things. A. E.' 'In justice to M. Paul Reynaud I ought to make it clear that he was *only* talking of the *army* at the point in question (*vide* his reference to "divisions"). As a matter of fact I did remind him of our great naval superiority and I painted a very favourable picture of our air force & its future. He not only accepted but fully shared *already* these two latter estimates. Since the advent of aviation it is always difficult to make it clear whether one uses "military" in the restrictive sense as opposed to "naval" as in days of yore, or whether it covers everything. It is as the latter that you have read it & as the former that he meant it. The instructive part is that this is of course a fresh sign—if any were needed—that the French count, & always will count, on us for a substantial supply of *ground-troops* even if not on the same scale as in 1914–1918. They don't go as far as that, but they do expect from us a "military" contribution in the narrower sense of the term. We shall not be able to keep on close terms with the French—and so shall drift towards isolation—unless we are able to make a real even though reduced "military" effort, as well as at sea & in the air—our next task at sea wd. *not* be very formidable or exacting. Nor do the French need our fleet quite so much as they did, for they are now 40% stronger than the Germans instead of being 40% weaker as in 1914. I have a strong feeling that many of your colleagues in the Cabinet do not grasp this when they talk of limiting the role of the army in future. R. V. Dec. 11.'

No. 454

Record by Sir H. W. Malkin of a conversation with Dr. E. Woermann
[C 8803/4/18]

FOREIGN OFFICE, *December 8, 1936*

The Counsellor of the German Embassy came, at his request, to see me yesterday[1] to obtain enlightenment on a point in our memorandum of

[1] Cf. No. 455, note 2, below.

November 19th about the Five-Power Conference.[2] At the end of our talk I suggested that it would be a good thing if he could put the precise enquiry on paper, though I explained to him that I was not sure that we should be able to give him a definite reply at this stage, because the matter was one which concerned other parties to the proposed pact more than us. He agreed to do this on a strictly personal basis, and has now sent me the attached letter.[3]

The point they are on relates, as was expected, to the position in relation to the proposed treaty of the Franco-Soviet Pact. In paragraph 13 of our memorandum we made it plain that in our view while we proposed that in the case where one party to the new treaty was alleged to have attacked another in violation of its terms, the Council of the League should (as was the case under Locarno) decide whether a breach of the treaty had been committed, so that the guarantee would operate, it was also necessary to retain the Locarno provision under which, if the guarantors were satisfied that there had been a breach and that immediate action was necessary, they could at once come to the assistance of the party attacked, subject to a subsequent reference to the Council. What Dr. Woermann wanted to know was our view as to the position where a party to the treaty had attacked a non-party, and another party wanted to come to the assistance of the State attacked; in other words, if Germany attacked Russia and France wanted to come to the assistance of the latter power, would she be entitled to do so without waiting for a reference to the Council of the League? It is, of course, the familiar point which arises on the Protocol to the Franco-Soviet Pact.

I explained to Dr. Woermann what I conceived to be the position in the circumstances postulated under Locarno when it was still operative as between the parties, i.e. that it was open to France to go to the assistance of Russia without there having been any previous decision by the Council, but that if she did so she ran the risk that if Germany considered that she had committed a breach of Locarno by her action, Germany would be entitled to bring this point before the Council of the League, and if the Council decided against France, the Locarno guarantee would operate against her. I think it is pretty clear, however, that an arrangement on these

[2] No. 389.
[3] The letter, dated December 7, enclosed a note in German with the following translation.

'In paragraph 13 of their Memorandum of November 19th, the British Government hold the view that special provision ought to be made in a future western pact for the case, where a sudden and unprovoked attack is made in violation of the non-aggression arrangements. In such circumstances immediate action of the guarantors may, in their view, be essential and it would not be possible to await a decision of the competent body.

The British Memorandum only mentions the case of an immediate action taken by the guarantors of the proposed treaty. Should a signatory A to the treaty, in the view of the British Government, be entitled to take immediate action against a signatory B without awaiting the decision of the competent body also in the case coming into conflict with the non-signatory power X and A taking the view that B had committed a flagrant attack against X?'

lines in the new treaty would not satisfy the Germans; the question whether under Article 16 of the Covenant France was entitled to come to the assistance of Russia without there having been a decision by the Council is of course the point on which the German view differed from that of the other signatories of Locarno in the discussions which took place last year.

Personally I have always thought that if we are to get a new treaty at all it will be necessary in some way to satisfy the Germans that the question whether France is entitled, without violating her non-aggression undertaking, to come to the assistance of Russia under the Franco-Soviet Pact will not be left to the decision of France herself; the Germans interpret the Franco-Soviet Pact as intended to produce this result, and though in our view they are wrong about it, it seems clear that they will make the receipt of adequate satisfaction on this point a condition of their participating in the proposed treaty. I think, therefore, that it is well worth while to consider whether it is possible to deal with the point in a manner which will give them adequate satisfaction, though it is difficult to see what we can say to them about it at this stage without previous consultation with the French.

I should add that Dr. Woermann explained that while he was assuming for the purposes of his enquiry (a) that there would be exceptions to the non-aggression undertakings, and (b) that the Council of the League would be the body to determine whether a breach of those undertakings had occurred, I must not assume that the German Government accepted either proposal. It seems to me nevertheless that if the German Government were intending to be entirely intransigeant [sic] on the question of exceptions, they would hardly have thought it worth while to make this enquiry at all, and if so, the fact that they have made it may perhaps be regarded as a rather hopeful sign; which would be another reason for considering seriously whether it is possible to meet them on the point which they have raised.[4]

H. W. M.

[4] Dr. Woermann's record of this conversation is printed in *D.G.F.P.*, Series C, vol. vi, No. 79.

No. 455

Mr. Eden to Sir E. Phipps (Berlin)
No. 1370 [C 8792/4/18]

FOREIGN OFFICE, *December 8, 1936*

Sir,

In the course of my conversation with Herr von Ribbentrop this evening His Excellency said that he wished to speak to me of the state of the Locarno negotiations. He would not conceal from me that our memorandum[1] had been a grievous disappointment to the Chancellor. He had himself seen Herr Hitler who had read it through and who, on the first and admittedly

[1] No. 389.

superficial reading, had been pessimistic of the prospect for the Conference. Our proposals seemed to the German Government to contain the same faults as had marred the old Locarno. The problem of eastern Europe was introduced again. The Ambassador maintained that he himself had been devoting a great amount of thought recently in an endeavour to solve this problem of the Eastern connexion with Locarno. He did not wish to be unduly pessimistic, but he feared that if it were not solved then no Locarno was possible.

2. In reply I agreed that this was, of course, the crux of the difficulty. We had always known it and the problem had existed in one form during the previous Locarno negotiations. Herr von Ribbentrop added that what Germany could never allow would be that France and Russia should be judges in their own case. That would be intolerable. I replied that this very difficulty had been present in our minds. Unfortunately Germany was not herself a member of the League any longer so that the protection which had existed in the past in a decision of the Council no longer presented the same security for her. We had considered whether some other body would serve the same purpose, but it was hard to see how this could be agreed. We did not pretend that our proposals were the last word; they were put forward to facilitate some progress. If the German Government would examine them in that spirit and point out their difficulties to us we would then see what could be done to meet them.

3. Herr von Ribbentrop replied that our memorandum was still being considered and in the meanwhile his Counsellor, Herr Woermann, had put several points to Sir William Malkin, the answers to which would, he hoped, clarify the situation.[2]

I am, &c.,
ANTHONY EDEN

[2] See No. 454. Mr. Wigram remarked in a minute of December 11 that the 'German Ambassador was not encouraging'; he thought that as likely as not 'Dr. Woermann's visit was simply intended to do what was possible to prevent the suspicion arising that Germany was not making every effort to secure the Treaty'.

No. 456

Mr. Eden to Sir E. Drummond (Rome)
No. 1348 [W 17729/62/41]

FOREIGN OFFICE, December 8, 1936

Sir,

I asked the Italian Ambassador to come and see me this evening when I told him that I wished to speak to him on the situation in Spain which was causing His Majesty's Government ever increasing concern. I then gave Signor Grandi a copy of my telegram to you No. 458 of December 4th[1] to read. The Ambassador asked whether you had yet seen Count Ciano in this matter.

[1] No. 436.

I said that you had, and read to the Ambassador portions of your telegram No. 729 of the 5th December.[2] Signor Grandi then explained that he thought it might be a little difficult for him to intervene now, since he had seen Sir R. Vansittart on Thursday[3] and asked him whether there was any truth in the reports then current of an Anglo-French initiative. On the strength of Sir Robert's denial he had telegraphed to Rome accordingly.[4] I explained to Signor Grandi that since Count Ciano had made it plain that the matter would take some days to consider I had asked him to come and see me in order that I might further impress upon him the keen desire which we felt to make an attempt to improve the present state of affairs. Unless some action were taken there was a real danger that Spain would become the battleground for a European conflict in miniature. This was surely not a state of affairs which any Government could contemplate with equanimity.

2. Signor Grandi replied that he would certainly report what I had said to his Government, and he felt sure that they also were preoccupied with the present situation and would very carefully consider our suggestion.[5]

3. I then told the Ambassador that I had received a communication from a Spaniard of international repute[6] well acquainted with Spanish conditions, which had confirmed our view and that of the French Government that the moment was now opportune to attempt mediation. In his judgment and ours those who thought that the alternatives were a Fascist Spain and a Communist Spain were probably mistaken. There might be other possibilities. To take one example: General Primo de Rivera's Government, though far from being a democracy in our sense of the word, could hardly be described as Fascist. Signor Grandi stated emphatically that it was not.[7]

I am, &c.,

ANTHONY EDEN

[2] No. 442.   [3] i.e. December 3.

[4] In a minute of December 9, referring to this sentence, Sir R. Vansittart wrote: 'What an odd man this is. See marked passage, which is completely untrue. So far from denying anything, I told him the truth when he put a point blank question to me. I said that the newspaper reports were true & that we *were* contemplating an "initiative", though it had not yet been taken. M. Corbin came to see me half an hour later . . . [He] agreed that I could have said nothing but what I did. It is odd that I shd have so immediate a witness to refute so patent an untruth. This must be recorded to Rome, since Signor Grandi has taken this line—in order to avoid action presumably. But—what a funny man. R. V. Dec. 9.' Mr. Eden wrote: 'I agree. Far from straight-forward. Dec. 10.' Mr. Eden's despatch No. 1390 to Rome of December 21 gave Sir R. Vansittart's version of this conversation, and remarked that Signor Grandi presumably 'took this disingenuous line in his conversation with me in order to avoid having to recommend the proposals to his Government'.

[5] In his account of the mediation negotiations to the Cabinet on December 9 Mr. Eden said that he had seen the Italian and German Ambassadors on the previous day, when the Italian Ambassador had 'been the more receptive of the two'.

[6] Presumably a reference to Señor de Madariaga: his review of the Spanish situation as given to Lord Cranborne on December 7 is filed at W 17694/62/41.

[7] The substance of this despatch was sent to Sir E. Drummond in telegram No. 473 of December 12, with the comment, 'I am anxious to do everything in our power to support this initiative for mediation, since the serious consequences of allowing present situation to continue become every day more apparent'.

No. 457

Sir R. Lindsay (Washington) to Mr. Eden
(Received December 9, 8.30 p.m.)
No. *330 Telegraphic* [W *17728/62/41*]

Immediate   WASHINGTON, *December 9, 1936, 1.45 p.m.*
My telegram No. 328.[1]

I learn from State Department that when news is published of Anglo-French *démarche* regarding Spain Acting Secretary of State will issue official statement expressing sympathy of United States Government and hopes that efforts towards pacification may succeed.

This is decision reached after communication to President and Secretary of State and is final.

[1] This telegram of December 8 referred to No. 448 and to Foreign Office telegram No. 414 of even date, in which Mr. Eden said that since publicity of the Anglo-French initiative was now expected within twenty-four hours, he much hoped that the United States statement would 'give us support and will specifically refer to our action'. Sir R. Lindsay said that he had acted as instructed 'last night' and had 'pressed the urgency of the case by telephone this morning'.

No. 458

Sir N. Henderson (Buenos Aires) to Mr. Eden
(Received December 9, 7.40 p.m.)
No. *130 Telegraphic* [W *17727/62/41*]

Immediate   BUENOS AIRES, *December 9, 1936, 3.37 p.m.*
Your telegram No. 114.[1]

I saw Mr. Hull this morning. He told me President Roosevelt had made no concrete proposal on the subject of Spain but had suggested in general terms when saying good-bye last week on board ship that situation should be watched and opportunity taken if possible by inter-American conference to give support to any action which His Majesty's Government and French Government might take with a view to terminating the conflict there.

Mr. Hull pointed out that position of conference was delicate one since whereas most South American countries were strongly in favour of the insurgents, others such as Mexico were equally strong on Spanish Government's side. Consequently any point which might give rise to acrimonious dispute within the conference needed careful handling lest it might tend to diminish that unity which it was one of the chief objects of the conference to display. Nevertheless as coming from the British Government he was not prepared to take any exception to the proposed reply to Argentine Government.

I told him that in these circumstances and realizing his difficulty I would,

[1] No. 452.

in making communication to Argentine Government and subject to any subsequent instructions I might receive from you (in which case I would inform him) omit therefrom the actual suggestion for a pronouncement by inter-American conference. Form of support would thus be left to initiative of conference itself. Mr. Hull agreed and said he would much prefer this.

I have acquainted French Ambassador with the above. He has so far received no instructions from his Government as to any communication to Argentine Government but will keep in touch with me.

I am accordingly addressing communication to Argentine Government as instructed by you but omitting suggestion in penultimate paragraph of your telegram under reply.[2]

[2] No further instructions on this matter were sent to Sir N. Henderson. Sir G. Mounsey minuted on December 14: 'The Conference is reported in the press to have adopted a draft protocol establishing non-intervention as a general principle. I think this is about as much as we could expect from it in the circumstances. G. M. 14.12.36.' Mr. Eden's initials follow (December 16). Mr. Hull omitted any reference to these communications in his memoirs, merely saying: 'The question of any action with regard to the civil war raging in Spain did not arise, despite the interest of all of us in the issues presented' (*The Memoirs of Cordell Hull*, London, 1948, 2 vols.), i, p. 501.

No. 459

Viscount Chilston (Moscow) to Mr. Eden
(Received December 9, 5.55 p.m.)
No. 209 Telegraphic [W 17767/62/41]

MOSCOW, *December 9, 1936, 7.35 p.m.* [*sic*]

My telegram No. 207.[1]

Reply received from Soviet Government states that they fully share the concern felt by His Majesty's Government in this matter and concur as to urgent desirability of taking concerted action to avert dangers resulting from intervention of individual Powers in Spanish internal affairs.

Note goes on to set forth as usual Soviet Government's views on justifiability of supplying a legal and recognized government with all forms of material including arms, their agreement nevertheless to join London committee on assumption that other members would act as loyally as themselves, their disillusionment, etc.

Soviet Government, note continues, are ready to declare afresh their willingness to abstain from direct or indirect actions which might lead to foreign intervention but they 'expect that full control will be ensured or guaranteed as regards corresponding abstention of other Powers'; fact that Soviet representative on London Committee has already pressed for establishment of effective control over importation of war material and also more recently for control over 'so-called volunteers'[2] provides in itself an answer to that part of the proposals.

[1] No. 444.   [2] Cf. Nos. 439 and 449.

Finally note states readiness of Soviet Government in principle to join in an attempt to put an end to armed conflict by an offer of mediation and to enter into conversations with other governments concerned with a view to discussing form which such mediation should take.

Full text[3] follows by air mail.

[3] Not printed, see *D.V.P.S.*, *op. cit.*, No. 403.

No. 460

Sir E. Drummond (Rome) to Mr. Eden
(Received December 9, 9.40 p.m.)
No. 736 Telegraphic [*R 7423/226/22*]

ROME, *December 9, 1936, 9 p.m.*

Your telegram No. 466.[1]

I saw Minister for Foreign Affairs this evening and told him you had no wish to insist that French Government should be associated with the proposed Mediterranean declarations. Count Ciano was obviously pleased and considerably relieved and said that message I had given him would make the matter much easier, in fact he did not foresee any further difficulties. He asked me however whether I could give him any information about his suggestion for consultation, see my telegrams Nos. 727[2] and 728.[3] I answered that I had not yet heard anything from you on this subject but I expected in the next few days to have some further general instructions and would then ask to see him. Minister observed that he felt sure that we should be able to find a common meeting ground about the point to which he had referred. My impression is that he will not insist at all vigorously on it.

[1] No. 451.   [2] No. 440.   [3] No. 441.

No. 461

Mr. Eden to Sir E. Drummond (Rome)
No. 468 Telegraphic [*R 7376/226/22*]

Personal   FOREIGN OFFICE, *December 9, 1936, 10.30 p.m.*

If there is any means of avoiding use of the expression 'Gentlemens' Agreement' [*sic*] in connexion with present proposed arrangement I should be very grateful. Exchange of assurances might be a better title and less likely to raise a smile, but I appreciate you may not be able to achieve this without causing offence which we must avoid.[1]

[1] In his telegram No. 737 of December 10, not preserved in the Foreign Office archives, Sir E. Drummond apparently held out some hopes that the use of this term could be avoided. Subsequently, however, it was evidently felt that as Signor Mussolini had chosen the term it would have to be retained.

No. 462

Mr. Eden to Sir G. Clerk (Paris)
No. 2071 [R 7303/226/22]

FOREIGN OFFICE, *December 9, 1936*

Sir,

With reference to my despatch No. 1986[1] of the 23rd November, I transmit to Your Excellency herewith a copy of a record of a conversation between the French Ambassador and a member of this Department[2] regarding recent developments in Anglo-Italian relations.

2. I shall be glad if you will repeat to the French Government the assurances given by me and by Mr. Sargent to the French Ambassador. You should emphasise that an improvement in Anglo-Italian relations is as much in the French interest as in our own, both because a potentially dangerous situation in the Mediterranean would thereby be eased and because the probability of the formation of a firm German-Italian bloc would thereby be lessened. In fact, His Majesty's Government would, for these reasons, be glad to see an effort by the French Government to bring about a similar improvement in their relations with Italy.

3. You should further point out to the French Government that Anglo-French relations have never been better than at present; that His Majesty's Government fully realise the magnitude of French interests in the Mediterranean, and that His Majesty's Government intend to keep the French Government fully informed of all developments arising from these conversations, though as a matter of fact there neither is nor will be any mystery about them, and the results will be made public. The French Government may, therefore, rest assured that throughout the conversations now in progress His Majesty's Government will do nothing to injure French interests or prestige and that so far as we are concerned close association with the French Government will be maintained.

I am, &c.,
ANTHONY EDEN

[1] No. 404.   [2] i.e. Mr. Sargent: see *ibid.*, note 4.

No. 463

Mr. Edmond (Geneva) to Mr. Eden
(Received December 10, 8.10 p.m.)
No. 164 L.N. Telegraphic [W 17839/62/41]

GENEVA, *December 10, 1936, 7.35 p.m.*

Following from Lord Cranborne.[1]

I had a long conversation with Señor del Vayo and Señor Azcárate this morning.

[1] United Kingdom representative at the ninety-fifth (extraordinary) session of the League of Nations Council.

At beginning Spanish Foreign Minister said that he would be glad if public meeting of Council could be postponed until tomorrow.[2] He had only last night seen Anglo-French *communiqué* with regard to mediation[3] and he had had no opportunity of considering it or consulting his Government. I said His Majesty's Government were very ready to fall in with his views on this point.

He then went into a lengthy disquisition with regard to misdeeds of rebel generals. Siege of Madrid had immensely embittered feeling. He had indeed definite information that Spanish rebel aviators were refusing to bomb civil population. This was now entirely done by Italians and Germans. In these circumstances though Spanish Government has not favoured policy of non-intervention they would not be opposed to anything which Council might say as to desirability of that policy being made effective. I replied that it was sincere wish of His Majesty's Government also that it should be made effective. In remarks which I made to Council at its public meeting I should make this clear. We recognised that there had most probably been breaches of agreement on both sides. We thought this contrary to interests of both Spain and of Europe.

I then went on to question of mediation. Present proposal arose from a French initiative but His Majesty's Government whole-heartedly co-operated in it both for humanitarian reasons and as means of furthering peace of Europe. Could Señor del Vayo give me any idea of attitude of Spanish Government to such proposals? He replied that he could give me no hope that they would be acceptable. A Spanish Government that even indicated that it was willing to consider negotiating with General Franco would in present embittered state of feeling in Spain be as good as finished. I urged him to reconsider this view. A blank refusal even to attempt to try to find a basis of settlement would have a most deplorable effect in England. Señor Azcárate seemed to share this view and said that under the circumstances would it not be better that subject should not be mentioned at all. I replied that this was quite impossible. To be frank, when Spanish Government had first proposed to bring Spanish situation before League His Majesty's Government had had great doubts as to utility of doing so. They had however agreed that a case seemed to be made out. But I would remind Señor del Vayo that by doing what they had the Spanish Government had recognised that Spanish civil war had international implications. Anglo-French initiative was natural corollary. If war threatened the peace of the world it should be brought to an end. This too was in the interests of Spain herself. If the war dragged on Spain would be reduced to a heap of ashes. Sooner or later a settlement must be reached. Why not try now? Señor del Vayo then pointed out that until replies had been received from Italy, Germany, Portugal and Russia the point would not be reached when it would be necessary for Spanish Government to express

---

[2] The first meeting (private) of the session took place on December 10 at 5 p.m.; the second (public) meeting on December 11 at 11 a.m.

[3] See No. 450, note 8.

an opinion. I said he might well put this to the Council. I should in any case mention the subject of mediation and I hoped that he would not express himself as definitely opposed. I hoped also that in anything he said he would be as moderate as possible.

I had the impression that Señor del Vayo did not favour mediation partly because he was convinced that if non-intervention could be made effective the Government would quickly win the war.

I finally raised question of a humanitarian initiative by some international body. Would such a suggestion be favourably received by Spanish Government? It would inevitably be of a preliminary character. Señor del Vayo said that in principle they would welcome such an initiative. In particular he expressed himself in favour of evacuation of civil population of Madrid if means could be made available.

Repeated to Madrid and Hendaye.

No. 464

Sir H. Kennard (Warsaw) to Mr. Eden
(Received December 11, 7.15 p.m.)
No. 63 Saving: Telegraphic [W 17926/62/41]

WARSAW, *December 11, 1936, 6.35 p.m.*

My telegram No. 59 Saving.[1]

French Ambassador has received instructions to collaborate with me in making identic communications to the Polish Government informing them of proposed offer of mediation in Spanish conflict by British, French, German, Italian, Portuguese and Soviet Governments.

I have informed him that I could take no action pending instructions from you. Meanwhile French Ambassador has acted alone.[2]

[1] This telegram of December 5 said that the Polish Council of Ministers was likely to issue a decree disclaiming the Polish Government's responsibility for Polish ships carrying arms to Spain.

[2] Two undated pencil comments by Mr. Eden on the filed copy of this telegram read: 'No harm in informing Poles also'; 'but French should have told us.' It appears that a telegram to Sir H. Kennard instructing him to act accordingly was drafted but not despatched. A subsequent minute by Mr. D. F. Howard said: 'I regret that owing to Mr. Shuckburgh's indisposition, this action has not been taken & I fear it is too late now. In any case the French Ambassador has acted alone. D. H. 21/12.'

No. 465

Letter[1] *from Mr. Eden to representatives of foreign governments in London*
[*T 17839/17825/379*]

FOREIGN OFFICE, *December 11, 1936*

Sir,

I have the honour to inform you that His Majesty King Edward VIII having executed an Instrument of Abdication, now carried into effect by an Act of Parliament to which His Majesty, as a final act of sovereignty, has given the Royal Assent, His Royal Highness the Duke of York, as the next in succession to the Throne, has this day succeeded thereto as provided by the said Act, and has been graciously pleased to signify that he will reign under the name of King George VI.

I feel confident that you will readily associate yourself with the earnest desire of the British people that the new reign may be a long and happy one.

I am, &c.,
ANTHONY EDEN

[1] See No. 282, note 3.

No. 466

Mr. Edmond (Geneva) to Mr. Eden
(*Received December 12, 7 p.m.*)
No. 165 Telegraphic: by telephone [*W 18001/62/41*]

GENEVA, *December 12, 1936*

Following from Lord Cranborne.

Following is text of resolution unanimously adopted by Council this evening.[1]

The Council, after hearing observations made before it and

I

Noting that it has been requested to examine a situation which, in terms

[1] The Spanish Government's appeal (No. 419) was considered at three public meetings of the League Council. The first, on December 11 at 11 a.m., was addressed by Señor del Vayo on the theme that the Spanish upheaval had been 'exploited, not to say, instigated, by European Fascist powers'. The government had accepted the non-intervention agreement, although profoundly convinced that it had every right to obtain what it needed to put down the rebellion, and despite cynical interventions on behalf of the rebels. 'The question now raised is how to . . . render the agreement effective.' The second public meeting, on December 11 at 5.30 p.m., was addressed by Lord Cranborne, who vindicated the policy of non-intervention, and hoped that the Council, 'in any resolution which it may decide to adopt with regard to the question before it, [will] show itself favourable to the strict enforcement of the non-intervention agreement'. A third public meeting on December 12, at 6.30 p.m., considered and adopted a draft resolution. The debate is fully reported in *L/N.O.J.*, *op. cit.*, pp. 7–21.

of article 11 of the Covenant, is such as to affect international relations and to threaten to disturb international peace or the good understanding between nations upon which peace depends,

considering that that good understanding ought to be maintained irrespective of the internal régimes of States,

bearing in mind that it is the duty of every State to respect the territorial integrity and political independence of other States, a duty which, for members of the League of Nations, has been recognised in the Covenant,

affirms that every State is under an obligation to refrain from intervening in the internal affairs of another State;

II

Considering that the setting up of a Committee of non-intervention and the undertakings entered into in that connexion arise out of the principles stated above,

having been informed that new attempts are being made in the Committee to make its action more effective, in particular by instituting measures of supervision, the necessity for which is becoming increasingly urgent,

recommends the members of the League represented on the London Committee to spare no pains to render the non-intervention undertakings as stringent as possible, and to take appropriate measures to ensure forthwith that the fulfilment of the said undertakings is effectively supervised:

III

Views with sympathy the action which has just been taken on the international plane by the United Kingdom and France with a view to avoiding the dangers which the prolongation of the present state of affairs in Spain is causing to peace and to good understanding between nations;

IV

Notes that there are problems of a humanitarian character in connexion with the present situation, in regard to which co-ordinated action of an international and humanitarian character is desirable as soon as possible,

recognises, further, that for the reconstruction which Spain may have to undertake international assistance may also be desirable,

and authorises Secretary General to make available the assistance of the technical services of the League of Nations should a suitable opportunity occur.[2]

---

[2] A minute by Mr. Strang read: 'The section of this resolution dealing with the humanitarian question should be read in conjunction with the declaration made by the Spanish Foreign Minister in the Council when accepting the resolution: viz that the resolution made clear that international action in this matter could, in conformity with the Council's constant practice, only be taken at the request of the Spanish Government.

Another point to note is that the Secretary General interprets the authority given to him as meaning that the assistance of the technical services of the League will be at the disposal, in a [?proper] case, of the Burgos as well as the Valencia Government. W. Strang. 21/2.'

No. 467

Translation of Memorandum communicated by the French Embassy on December 12

[*W 18208/9549/41*]

FRENCH EMBASSY, *December 12, 1936*

In the course of the recent discussion in the French Chamber on foreign policy M. Delbos spoke as follows:

'We are considering and shall continue to consider with vigilance the defence of our incontestable rights and of our permanent and vital interests in the Western Mediterranean, in Morocco, and in the strategic positions in the Ocean which dominate no less our lines of communication with Africa. Determined for our part to respect the status quo, we are no less determined to see that others do likewise, *de facto* as well as *de jure*.'

The French Chargé d'Affaires in Rome has been instructed, while making his *démarche* in the most friendly way possible, to explain to Count Ciano that if M. Delbos had refrained from alluding more precisely to a collection of facts which was, however, receiving his full attention, he was none the less concerned at the information which was reaching him on the situation in the Balearic Islands.

The activities of certain Italian agents unfortunately give the impression that these persons are anxious to exploit the Spanish affair for the purpose of ensuring Italian *de facto* control over the archipelago.

The establishment of any foreign authority over a position which dominates France's lines of communication with North Africa would affect French vital interests and create a situation which no French Government could regard with indifference.[1]

The French Government therefore hoped most sincerely that the Italian Government would see in the non-intervention undertakings sufficient guarantee for curbing spontaneous action on the part of agents in the Balearic Islands which run the risk of seriously damaging the cordiality of Franco-Italian relations.[2]

---

[1] A second memorandum of even date communicated by the French Embassy expressed anxiety about German activities at Tangier and in the Spanish zone of Morocco, drawing attention to the frequency of visits by German warships to the area, and the threat of German control over Spanish zone mining reserves. The note hinted at an Italo-German understanding regarding spheres of influence in the Mediterranean, a situation which 'merite de retenir l'attention la plus sérieuse de l'Angleterre aussi bien de la France'. A copy of this memorandum was sent to Mr. E. A. Keeling, H.M. Consul General at Tangier, in despatch No. 307 of December 22, asking him for a full report on German activity in Morocco. Mr. Keeling's reports will be printed in Volume XVIII.

[2] M. Corbin had been instructed to make this communication to Mr. Eden in a telegram of December 5 from M. Delbos: see *D.D.F., op. cit.*, No. 102.

No. 468

Sir G. Clerk (Paris) to Mr. Eden (Received December 16)
No. 1623 [W 18185/18040/41]

PARIS, *December 12, 1936*

Sir,

I asked the Minister for Foreign Affairs this morning what hopes, if any, he had as to the possibility of the suggested mediation in the Spanish civil war being accepted by the Powers most directly interested.[1]

2. M. Delbos said that he was by no means in despair. Soviet Russia, which Government he thought would not be sorry for an excuse to 'go into reverse', had accepted, while he had reason to believe that Germany and Italy would also accept in principle. Of course, he added, both those Powers would raise all sorts of difficulties and conditions, but he felt that the difficulties would not prove insuperable nor the conditions immutable, and that eventually a definite agreement might really be reached. He himself was making every effort to this end. He had sent a circular despatch to every French representative abroad to work in this sense on the governments and peoples where they lived, and he had addressed special messages to Dr. Saavedra Lamas and to the Pope. He hoped that Dr. Lamas, as President of the South American Congress now being held at Buenos Aires,[2] would be able to issue a suitable statement on behalf of all the States represented at the Congress. The Pope had replied that the Vatican would exert its influence diplomatically, but M. Delbos was continuing to urge that the issue of a Papal Bull would be far more effective. The Minister for Foreign Affairs added that he had discovered that the feelings of Poland as a Great Power had been somewhat ruffled by not being included in the original invitation.[3] He had therefore sent for the Polish Chargé d'Affaires and explained that the invitation had been addressed to Germany, Italy, Portugal and Soviet Russia as the Powers most notoriously concerned in the Spanish war, but that it was hoped that every civilised Power, and first and foremost Poland, would join in the effort to put an end to the horrors and dangers lurking in the Spanish situation. M. Delbos thought that the Polish ruffled feathers had thereby been successfully smoothed and that the support of Poland could be counted upon.

3. The Minister for Foreign Affairs ended by saying that what we must all seek for is to forbid the supply, not only of arms and munitions and aeroplanes and so on, but also of volunteers. The situation was appallingly dangerous. The fighting now was being conducted almost entirely by non-Spaniards—Frenchmen (on both sides), Germans, Italians, Czechoslovaks and others from Central Europe, a few Englishmen, and many Russians—curiously enough nothing like so many from Soviet Russia as was thought, but a great quantity of White Russians, fighting on the side of the Spanish Government.[4] M. Delbos said that no doubt this seemed as odd to me as it

[1] Cf. Nos. 434 and 436.   [2] See No. 435, note 4.   [3] Cf. No. 464.
[4] On this point see Thomas, *The Spanish Civil War*, Appendix 3.

had to him when he first heard of it, but it had been explained to him by a Russian with a great knowledge of Slav psychology. This man had said that the White Russians, though they hated the Bolsheviks, yet felt that they had deserted 'Mother Russia' and though they could not bring themselves to return to their country, this was their expiation, to risk death for Russia in a foreign country. As M. Delbos said, pure Dostoievsky. Meanwhile, the Spaniards proper were mostly occupied in 'executing' one another. Yesterday evening he happened to have met two reputable American journalists, one who had been with the Government forces, and one with the insurgents. He had not bothered to interrogate the one from Madrid, as he knew pretty well how things were there, but he had asked the one from the insurgent army why there had been such complete tranquillity behind the insurgent lines, and why there seemed to be no fear whatever of communications being cut or any of the other difficulties that might be expected. The journalist said that the answer was very simple. Anyone in the territory occupied by the insurgents who was even suspected of an unorthodox political opinion was killed out of hand.

4. I have ventured to record all this, not because it is necessarily true nor in itself of great importance, but because it accounted for and led up to the urgent appeal which M. Delbos finally made for your support and help in the attempt to bring about an end to the horrors of the Spanish civil war.[5]

5. I have sent copies of this despatch to His Majesty's Ambassador at Hendaye and to the British Delegation at Geneva.

I have, &c.,
GEORGE R. CLERK

[5] Minutes by Sir G. Mounsey and Sir R. Vansittart on this despatch included the following. 'M. Delbos' efforts to enlist world sympathy are no doubt very praiseworthy, but it would be more practical if he would himself consider what he means by mediation. We have been rushed by the French into this noble-sounding course,—mainly in the hopes of thereby saving the face of the League—but no one seems to have the remotest idea what form of mediation is contemplated. And everything goes to show that no form of mediation will be welcomed by either side in Spain . . . G. M. 23.12.36.' 'We shd. press the French Ambassador on this; but I don't suppose that the French have any really well-defined ideas. It wd. seem that there is nothing to choose between the Valencia & Burgos people as regards cold-blooded murder. I think we shd. give the press a hint of what goes on behind the insurgent lines as well as in Madrid. R. V. Dec. 23.'

Sir G. Mounsey then referred to a French Embassy note of December 24 'making vague suggestions on this question for our consideration'.

No. 469

Sir G. Clerk (Paris) to Mr. Eden (Received December 14)
No. 547 Saving: Telegraphic [W 17995/62/41]

PARIS, *December 13, 1936*

Satisfaction is expressed by the French press to-day with the terms of the resolution voted by the Council of the League regarding the affairs of Spain.[1]

[1] No. 466.

It is noted with approval that the resolution was voted unanimously and that it views with sympathy the Franco-British initiative for mediation. Newspapers of the Left praise the attitude of the Spanish representative at the Council meeting and emphasise that there was no attempt to question the legality of the Government now established at Valencia. There is considerable speculation as to the nature of the replies understood to have been despatched by the German, Italian and Portuguese Governments.

Repeated to Geneva by post.

No. 470

Sir E. Drummond (Rome) to Mr. Eden (Received December 16)
No. 258 Saving: Telegraphic [W 18232/18040/41]

ROME, *December 13, 1936*

Following is translation of Italian Government's reply dated the 12th December and referred to in my telegram No. 741.[1]

Begins.

In reply to the Note Verbale of the 5th ultimo from His Britannic Majesty's Embassy, regarding the situation in Spain,[2] the Italian Government has the honour to state the following:

(1) The Italian Government shares the desire expressed by the British and French Governments to subordinate any political considerations to the higher interest of civilisation and of peace, to eliminate any cause which may contribute to the extension of the dangers involved in the present crisis and, finally, to see normal conditions and order restored in Spain.

(2) So far as concerns the proposal of the two Governments for a new formal declaration of non-intervention in the affairs of Spain and a reinforcement of the measures to be taken for this purpose by the London Committee, the Italian Government particularly desires to recall that from the beginning it has maintained that the undertaking of non-intervention, to be efficacious, must be as complete as possible. That is to say it should comprise, in addition to the prohibition of the importation of warlike material into Spain, also the undertaking to prevent the despatch of volunteers and political agitators and the prohibition of money subscriptions and of any form of propaganda for or against either of the parties in the conflict. The Italian Government does not doubt that, if its way of thinking had been accepted from the beginning, the situation in Spain would today be very different. In fact it seems clear that the proposals today put forward by the two Governments would then have encountered in their realisation much less serious and grave difficulties than those which they will undoubtedly meet with in the present circumstances.

---

[1] Of December 13, not printed. It referred to Foreign Office telegram No. 458 (No. 436) and summarized the Italian Government's reply, which is translated in full in the present telegram.　　　　　[2] See No. 442.

However, the Italian Government would see no difficulty, even today, if all the other States agree, in examining in the London Committee all such measures as may appear most suited to ensuring a complete application and control of non-intervention, provided that these are contemporaneously accepted in their entirety.

(3) The British and French Governments put forward the idea of a mediatory action by the Powers principally interested, designed to put an end to the armed conflict which is bathing Spain in blood, in order to permit the country to express the national will. This idea naturally cannot but be received with favour by the Italian Government. The Italian Government asks itself, however, whether in the circumstances of today, the carrying out of an orderly plebiscite in Spain can fall within the scope of practical politics. Furthermore, the Italian Government must point out that—if the facts are objectively examined—it seems difficult to deny that the Spanish people have already sufficiently expressed their will in favour of the National Government, which has been able progressively to win for itself the approval of the greater part of the population and the possession of the greater part of the national territory. Nor can it any the less fail to point out that the reconciliation of the two parties in conflict appears today to be singularly difficult, both by reason of the anarchic tendency which indisputably predominates among the adversaries of the National Government and by reason of the acts of cruelty of which the latter have been guilty.

Nevertheless the Italian Government, desirous of not neglecting anything which may serve the higher aims of peace, is ready to examine in a spirit of friendly collaboration such proposals as the other Governments may feel able to formulate and to participate in their eventual realisation.

No. 471

Memorandum[1] by Mr. Eden on Spain and the Balearic Islands
[*W 18182/9549/41*]

FOREIGN OFFICE, *December 14, 1936*

1. My colleagues will recall that on the 19th August this year I circulated to them a paper (F.P.(36)10)[2] which, after outlining the general direction which the policy of Italy might be expected to take in the foreseeable future, drew particular attention to the advantages to itself which it might attempt to draw from the troubles in Spain. I said that the expedients open to Signor Mussolini for securing an advantage, initially political but ultimately strategic,

---

[1] Circulated as C.P.335(36) to the Cabinet for its meeting on December 16. The draft of the memorandum, written by Mr. O'Malley and extensively revised by Sir R. Vansittart, was sent to Mr. Eden on December 12. Mr. Eden commented on December 13: 'This is an excellent piece of work, produced with an amazing speed. I have made certain suggestions at [?as] to the later stages, in view of the French note now received, which should be added as an appendix [see note 8 below]. Our line should I think be, to give full support to the French in what is primarily though not exclusively a French interest. A. E. Dec. 13.' Mr. Eden added paragraph 12 to the draft.   [2] No. 115.

in the Western Mediterranean were numerous, that it was impossible at that time to foresee in what manner, at what point or by what stages the existing balance of power in the Western Mediterranean might be threatened. It was suggested that it would very possibly be brought about by the entry of Italy into some kind of special relationship with one of the two contending factions in Spain, as a consequence of which Italy would find herself in a position to influence in our disfavour the political and military action of the future Government of Spain or of some part of it. In view of these considerations and in order that His Majesty's Government might not again be reproached by the Italian Government, as has happened, with however little justification, in the Abyssinian case, for not having declared, sufficiently clearly or sufficiently early, the objections later discovered by the British Government to the action of the Italian Government, His Majesty's Chargé d'Affaires in Rome informed the Italian Minister for Foreign Affairs on the 12th September, on my instructions, that 'any alteration of the status quo in the Western Mediterranean would be a matter of the closest concern to His Majesty's Government.' In taking note of this communication Count Ciano assured Mr. Ingram that the Italian Government had not, either before or since the revolution in Spain, engaged in any negotiations with General Franco whereby the status quo of the Mediterranean would be altered, nor would they engage in any such negotiations in the future.[3] This assurance was subsequently re-affirmed spontaneously to the British Naval Attaché in Rome by the Italian Ministry of Marine, and the Italian Ambassador in London has on several occasions given me similar verbal assurances.[4]

2. It may be that in September and October last these statements represented the genuine intention of the Italian Government, but there is now the strongest indication that the development of events in Spain has placed such temptations in their way that they may have forgotten, or chosen to overlook, our warning. In any event, it is now clear that Signor Mussolini is doing that very thing which we feared, namely, attempting to enter into some kind of special relationship with the part of Spain, to wit the Balearic Islands, which he could presently turn to advantage in a number of ways. That contingency then having arisen which was contemplated in my earlier paper, it is necessary for me to ask my colleagues to consider seriously and urgently the precise nature of the British interests thus placed in jeopardy and the steps which it will be our duty to take in order to protect them.

3. The exact circumstances in which the Balearic Islands have become a focus of danger to British interests were not foreseen, indeed were hardly foreseeable. What was anticipated in August was the possibility that General Franco would make himself master of Spain largely as a consequence of help received from Italy, to whom he would thus in a sense have mortgaged the policy of his country. What, in fact, seems to have happened is that while something like a temporary stalemate has been reached in the civil war, the inhabitants of Majorca, traditionally indifferent to the course of political events on the mainland, and distressed and alarmed by the disturb-

[3] See Nos. 159 and 188.   [4] See Nos. 355, 379, and 411.

ance which this has recently introduced into their domestic life, have become disposed to welcome, or at least to tolerate, the prospect of the protection or suzerainty of a foreign Power which seemed to be both able and willing to assure them of the means of return to their normal and peaceful occupations and of protection from the menace of communism. It is not necessary for me here to describe in detail the events which have occurred in the Islands since the outbreak of the Spanish civil war, or the varying fortunes of the political groups into which the inhabitants of the Islands have from time to time been divided. It will perhaps be sufficient if I give a brief outline of the steps taken by Signor Mussolini to establish Italian leadership in them.

4. By the middle of November there were actually in operation in Majorca 17 new Italian aeroplanes actually in service, and in all probability 40 or 50 Italian machines in crates not yet assembled. To assist in the operation of these, about 50 Italians were available, of which 22 were pilots and the remainder engineers. These all belonged to the Spanish Foreign Legion and wore the uniform of that corps. Numerous cargoes of arms have been shipped to Majorca from Italy. Italian engineers were organising the construction of three additional aerodromes of modern design. In a general way Italy has already expended, and is continuing to expend, much more money in Majorca than would be consistent with an intention to withdraw altogether from the island after the termination of the Spanish revolution. Besides the aircraft numerated above, arms and materials have continued to enter the island to a value far in excess of anything the Majorcans could possibly hope to repay. Italian works in Majorca will, for many years, continue to provide a lucrative solution for unemployment, and the end of the Spanish revolution, whenever and however this occurs, will leave so much constructive work on new defences, barracks, roads, port works and improvements of all kinds half finished, that Italy must inevitably come then to be regarded as a welcome master or patron whose departure would be a matter of very great and serious loss to the prosperity of the inhabitants. It should be added that Italian is now taught as a compulsory subject in all schools in Majorca, and already the common people are beginning to make use of Italian phrases and to air with pride their knowledge of the Italian language.

5. Some parallel for these facts can no doubt be found on the mainland of Spain—although the Balearic Islands are now in no military danger or need of this excessive 'assistance'—but what is of specially sinister significance in the Islands is the position of an Italian subject, Count Rossi. Count Rossi's nominal title was, until recently, Chief of the Falange, a party which may roughly be described as the Fascists of Majorca, and in this capacity he has some 20,000 of the islanders under his direct control; but he is also the Head of the forces of Public Security (secret police) and for this purpose has some 200 Italian experts under his control who are employed in espionage, counter-espionage, administration, drill, supply, propaganda, instruction and military works. He is known to have been sent to the island with a direct personal mission from Signor Mussolini to organise the Fascist party,

but when representations on the subject were made to Count Ciano by His Majesty's Ambassador in Rome the former is reported 'to have laughed loudly and to have said that Rossi's proceedings were so ridiculous that he hoped we would pay no attention to them.' Count Ciano was informed that in a recent speech Count Rossi had said 'that Spain and Italy are brothers. We must possess the whole of the Mediterranean. It is ours.' Count Rossi had, moreover, on previous occasions made even more inflammatory speeches, of which we had to complain—in vain—to Signor Grandi. On this occasion Count Ciano replied—like the Italian Ambassador—that we should attach no importance to these youthful outbursts.[5] He, Count Ciano, had had no relations with him whatever, but in view of the popular feeling in Majorca it would be very difficult, if not impossible, to bring him back to Italy. The generally accepted opinion in Majorca is, however, that Count Rossi would become the first Italian Military Governor of the island. Since his return from Rome on the 11th November his title has been changed to 'Generalissimo di Majorca.'[6]

6. It is clear, then, from the situation thus depicted that what we may have to contemplate is the permanent hegemony by Italy of the Balearic Islands, introduced by an ostensibly spontaneous declaration of autonomy or by some other similar political manœuvre. The significance of such an event would be both strategic and political. The strategic aspect of things was considered in a report from the Chiefs of Staff (1259–B of the 24th August, 1936)[7] written before the full scope of Italian operations as described above could be foreseen. The relevant paragraph in this report is as follows:

13. An Italian occupation of any of the Balearic Islands would probably not be acceptable to the islanders themselves, but the possibilities of their having to submit to *force majeure* cannot be ruled out.

The naval facilities in these islands are at present as follows:

Majorca, 450 miles from Gibraltar, has no harbour entirely suitable for a naval base, since Palma and Pollenza Bay, although good in some ways, are too exposed. Minorca, which is still further from Gibraltar, has in Port Mahon a small, but heavily defended, naval base.

As regards air facilities, there are, so far as is known, no military air stations in the Balearic Islands at the present time; but there is no doubt that they could be established without great difficulty. It is understood that there is a satisfactory aerodrome site at Pollenza, and that civil seaplane services were operated at Port Mahon and Palma in 1932.

In view of the foregoing, an Italian occupation of any of the Balearic Islands would not vitally affect British strategical interests. At the same time it would give Italy a base for naval and air operations, 250 miles nearer Gibraltar than anything which she possesses at the present time. The menace to our control of the Straits and to Gibraltar itself would thus be increased.

[5] See No. 477, note 1 below. Sir E. Drummond's representations on the subject of Count Rossi on December 5 were reported in telegram No. 731 of December 6 (W17521/9549/41), not printed. [6] See No. 477 below regarding Count Rossi's recall. [7] No. 126.

The general conclusion is that Italian occupation of any of the Balearic Islands would not vitally affect British strategic interests, but this is based on the premise that, among other things, there were no military air stations in the islands. This premise is no longer valid, and the Chiefs of Staff may therefore wish for reconsideration of a position which may now lead them to a different conclusion. This, however, is not an aspect of things which I am qualified here to pursue. It is rather to the political implications of effective Italian control of the Balearic Islands to which I must draw attention. The perspective in which these should be viewed is, I hope, in part supplied by my paper of the 19th August, to which I invite reference. It is not, I think, disputed that the British position in the Mediterranean and Red Sea basins is largely maintained by that imponderable and contentious element called prestige, nor that the Abyssinian crisis, discovering as it did the inadequacy of British military preparations and a widespread reluctance in this country to employ a threat of armed resistance to a course on Italy's part which was diametrically opposed to the declared policy of England as of other members of the League of Nations, shook British prestige as nothing else had done since the conclusion of the war. It will also probably be agreed that the progress of British rearmament and the evidences of a powerful economic revival have done something to repair the damage and to secure the continued confidence and respect of foreign Powers in the Mediterranean and Red Sea basins in regard, first, to the general character of British foreign policy, and, secondly, to the determination of the United Kingdom Government to protect its own interests wherever these were called in question. But I do not like to contemplate how grave would be the risk to our position in the Mediterranean if Italy were permitted with impunity to make another move such as the establishment of Italian control in the Balearic Islands which would universally be recognised as a fresh and very important step towards a further propagation of her own constitutional theories and towards increased freedom of her military action in the Mediterranean. Nothing that we could say in explanation or justification of passivity or of merely ineffectual remonstrance would be credited. I doubt whether we could convince ourselves, I am certain that we could not convince others, that we had not from anxiety or timidity, or from a sense of our own weakness, been obliged to acquiesce in an Italian move which was, if not in immediate, at any rate in definite ulterior conflict with a vital British interest. I use the word 'vital' advisedly, for to permit, except under the sternest compulsion, the impairment of a vital interest would be for His Majesty's Government to abdicate the responsibilities of a Great Power. If we were to allow the suggestion that our action was of this character to reach all those listening ears on the coasts of the Mediterranean and Red Seas which have been assiduously taught by many agencies to expect premonitory crackings in the structure of the British Commonwealth of Nations and in the Colonial Empire, no man can foresee what disastrous modifications might not take place in the status of an Empire depending for its paramountcy not only upon armed strength, but upon opinions, nor what unexampled efforts in arms might not be exacted from us before the position could be re-established. These are grave words, too grave it may be thought to be applicable to what are, after all, speculative propositions; but to underestimate these might well be fatal.

7. Consideration of the courses open to us to meet the risks which I have summarily described reveals a simple but alarming prospect. I exclude the idea that we should publicly remonstrate with the Italian Government, unless we are prepared in the last resort for armed resistance to Italian designs. Nothing could be more futile or more provocative than public remonstrances which prove ineffectual. On the other hand, once the decision were taken that to prevent Italian domination of the Balearic Islands was a vital political interest for which the United Kingdom Government would fight, the way would be opened to many expedients, of which some would in my view suffice to restrain Italy from pursuing her plans in Majorca to a conclusion or from taking hostilities against this country. But all of these expedients would involve two essential things, one would be a demonstration of adequate military strength and the other would be a declaration in a wholly unambiguous form of the circumstances in which, and purposes for which, we were prepared to use that military strength. I need not at this stage develop these clearly indispensable pre-requisites; and I therefore turn briefly to the general considerations in the light of which the decision we may have to take one way or the other—to resist or to acquiesce—must be made.

8. The first of these is the position of France. The French interest is clearly safety of her African communications which is complementary to freedom of transit of British ships through the Mediterranean. There can hardly be any question that but a few short years ago the French would have joined whole-heartedly in combined resistance to Italy with ourselves based on a pre-ponderance of force which neither Italy nor Germany nor both together would be at all likely to have challenged. The progressive decrease in the relative military, naval and air strength of France, combined with the deterioration in the cohesion and resolution of the French people themselves and the mounting ambition and self-confidence of Germany and Italy, alter this picture. On the other hand, as the recent instructions sent by the French Government to their Ambassador at Rome show (see Annex),[8] they appear now to be fully alive to the dangers of a situation which is primarily, though not exclusively, a French interest.

9. The second general consideration relates, of course, to the use to which the German Government might turn a war in which England and France were engaged against Italy. While the intentions of the German Government are, in any given circumstances, very difficult to predict, prediction in this case is rendered all the more difficult by the fact that it is as yet impossible to postulate for a certainty the attitude of France. What can be said with some confidence is that Germany would not enter a war of the kind contemplated for the sake of rescuing Italy, and that, if she had recourse to arms for any purpose, it would more likely be for that of capturing and consolidating what in the development of power on the continent of Europe must be

[8] Printed as No. 467.

682

regarded as her first objectives, viz., for the purpose of ensuring predominance and free access to supply of all kinds on her Eastern and Southern borders. This prospect in itself is sufficiently alarming, but the possibility cannot be excluded that, in accordance with the teachings of a certain school of military strategy, she would employ the occasion to attack the strongest rather than the weakest section of the 'enemy front'; attack, that is, towards the Western rather than towards the South or the East. Moreover, Germany's relations with Italy are now very close and a large measure of Italo-German collaboration has undeniably been achieved of late. It might well be that the two dictators would stand together on this point also. The arguments which could be used in support of either the first or the second of these alternative suppositions, or in support of the view that Germany would prefer to go on building up her own strength while dog ate dog, are much too extensive to set out at length in this paper. I only mention them here in order to stress the fact that they fall inevitably to be considered before a wise decision can be reached on the question of how far we should assert ourselves in the Mediterranean and in order to record my own rather tentative conclusion that the probability of a considerable accession of strength to Germany resulting from war in which Great Britain and France were engaged against Italy is not unequally balanced by the probability that the relations with Germany could, for the future, be conducted with very much greater advantage to ourselves if we had demonstrated beyond all possibility of doubt that in the Mediterranean there is a point beyond which the United Kingdom cannot be driven by sapping and mining or by blusters and threats, and that where a vital interest is threatened, the English will be found, for all we speak so often and so smoothly of compromise and conciliation, not to be at heart a meek nor in action a timid people at all. On the other hand, it would of course be folly to contemplate the possibility of war with Italy without also having taken into account the possibility of Germany assisting her.

10. The problem is therefore a grave and far-reaching one, and I shall be glad if my colleagues will give to it their earnest and early consideration.

11. In view of the nature of the French representations in Rome, I consider that as a first step, while thanking the French Government for their communication, we should ask them to keep us informed of any reply they may receive. It is for consideration whether we should go further than this and give them any indication of our attitude in regard to any further steps they may contemplate.

12. As my colleagues are aware, His Majesty's Ambassador at Rome has recently had his first conversation with the Italian Minister for Foreign Affairs with a view to an eventual exchange of assurances regarding British and Italian interests in the Mediterranean.[9] I see no reason why these conversations should be delayed, owing to the present development in the Belearic [sic] Islands. On the contrary they will constitute a useful test of Italian bona fides, since the draft of the mutual assurances which Sir E.

[9] See Nos. 440 and 441.

Drummond is to be instructed to submit to Count Ciano will express the wish of both Governments to see maintained the territorial status quo in the Mediterranean.[10]

A. E.

[10] When this memorandum was discussed by the Cabinet on December 16 it was suggested that an Italian occupation of the islands was unlikely in view of the Italian Government's assurances, but that 'a rising in the Islands and the declaration of a republic' 'appeared more probable'. If General Franco won, the Italians would probably have an understanding with him allowing their use of the islands in an emergency; if the Spanish Government won a republic would still be declared in Majorca. If the Italians 'were to take Majorca we ought to take advantage of the situation to get ahead with the Gibraltar aerodrome'. Mr. Eden said that before taking any action in regard to Majorca he would like to know how seriously the Chiefs of Staff Sub-Committee regarded an Italian occupation from a strategical point of view.

No. 472

Letter from Viscount Chilston to Mr. Collier (Received December 19)

[*C 9043/4/18*]

MOSCOW, *December 15, 1936*

Dear Collier,

It may be worth mentioning that a secretary of the German Embassy who has just returned from Berlin told a member of my staff this morning that he had found the Wilhelmstrasse thoroughly depressed about all aspects of German foreign policy. The German-Japanese agreement[1] they thought a disaster: it would fatally compromise Ribbentrop's position in London (there seemed to be some professional jealousy here) without providing any compensating advantage for Germany: information about the development of communism in China and Japan was of no interest at all in Berlin!

If General Franco won, the Wilhelmstrasse thought, as stated in my despatch No. 707 of today,[2] that it would not help Germany: he would dislike the non-Catholic Nazis to whom he would owe a lot of money, and would at once make friends with England and France who could help him financially in the reconstruction of Spain better than Germany could. But in any case he was unlikely to win: there were 'only' three or four thousand German volunteers in Spain,[3] whereas there were 25,000 French volunteers, 'who were genuine volunteers', and were being organised into an efficient force by a 'pink' French general in Barcelona. The Italians had after all not sent any considerable forces, only specialists.[4]

Finally, as regards England German policy had been a complete failure: not only was there now an Anglo-French alliance in being but 'an English

[1] See No. 421, note 3.   [2] Not printed (W 18404/9549/1).
[3] A marginal note by Mr. Collier here read: 'There are at least 5,000 as we know.' Cf. *D.V.P.S., op. cit.*, No. 407.
[4] A marginal note by Mr. Wigram here read: 'They have now.'

official spokesman in the House of Commons' had actually stated that the integrity of Czechoslovakia was a British interest,[5] whereas a year ago we had been ostentatiously disassociating ourselves from that country's fate.

This is probably all stale news to you, but it struck me as an interesting indication of the state of mind in the German Ministry for Foreign Affairs at the moment and therefore, although rather outside my province, just worth reporting. The Secretary in question is unusually frank and even indiscreet, but we all like him and I hope nothing will be said which might suggest the source of this: his position is difficult enough as it is.

I am sending a copy of this letter to Phipps.[6]

Yours ever,
CHILSTON

[5] It is not clear to what this refers: cf. however No. 479, note 2, below.
[6] Mr. Eden minuted this letter as follows. 'Interesting. I wish that we could inject correspondingly better spirits into our own press which is still too defeatist. Mr. Leeper [head of News Department] should see this, though not of course for use. A. E. Dec. 31st.'

No. 473

Sir N. Charles (Brussels) to Mr. Eden
(Received December 16, 9.15 p.m.)
No. 83 Telegraphic [C 8982/4/18]

BRUSSELS, *December 16, 1936, 7.33 p.m.*

Your despatch No. 1370 to Berlin.[1]

Baron van Zuylen informed me privately today that German Minister has spoken to him recently regarding prospects of a new Locarno Treaty.

(2) Speaking of question of German Guarantee to Great Britain, German Minister said that German Government were averse to this. Baron van Zuylen enquired whether Germans would ever consider giving a guarantee to Italy [and] received an emphatic negative in reply.

(3) German Minister expressed great admiration for formula put forward in your memorandum of November 19th[2] in regard to non-aggression arrangements but when asked whether opinion he was giving was that of his government, he replied quickly that they were his own views. Baron van Zuylen had the impression that from the way the Minister had spoken Berlin was the source of his inspiration.

(4) German Minister however told Baron van Zuylen that it was most improbable that the German Government could ever allow Council of the League to be judge as to whether non-aggression arrangements envisaged in memorandum had been violated.

[1] No. 455.   [2] No. 389.

(5) The Baron said that he personally was pessimistic as to chances of a new Treaty. The Germans would not conclude any agreement so long as Franco-Soviet Pact existed and, in any case, he regretted that he had little faith in Germany's good intentions.

Repeated to Berlin.

No. 474

Mr. Eden to Sir E. Drummond (Rome)

No. 1379 [W 18258/18040/41]

FOREIGN OFFICE, *December 16, 1936*

Sir,

The Italian Ambassador asked to see me this evening, when he stated that in the course of our previous conversation,[1] when we had discussed ways and means of actually carrying out mediation, I had let fall a remark that it might be possible that actual mediation itself could be carried out by the three Mediterranean Powers.[2] He had put this to his Government and in their reply while he had been instructed to state that the Italian Government entirely shared our preoccupations as to the developments in the Spanish situation, they were doubtful whether mediation could be effectively carried out without the inclusion of Germany. The Ambassador thought that his Government had given exaggerated importance to a casual comment, but before explaining this to them he would like to make sure that he had understood me aright. I told the Ambassador that there certainly was no importance to be attached to my remark. He would perhaps remember that in our previous conversation he had pointed out the difficulties of mediation by a large number of Powers, when I had remarked that possibly at a later stage agreement might be reached to allow a few Powers to carry that actual work through, and I had suggested that these might even be the three Mediterranean Powers. But that suggestion (and it was no more) had referred to a later stage, for in order to set mediation on foot it was clearly indispensable that we should secure the co-operation of Germany and Russia in addition to the Mediterranean Powers. If his Government had any doubt as to my point of view in this respect I hoped he would clear the matter up.

2. The Ambassador said that he fully understood the position. He regretted if his report of our previous conversation had led to a slight misunderstanding in Rome, but he would clear the matter up.

I am, &c.,

ANTHONY EDEN

[1] Apparently that of December 8: see No. 456.

[2] This proposal is not mentioned in Mr. Eden's account of the earlier conversation, but there are further references to it in *D.G.F.P.*, Series D, vol. iii, Nos. 147, 149.

No. 475

Mr. Eden to Sir G. Clerk (Paris)
No. 2134 [W 18256/9549/41]

FOREIGN OFFICE, December 16, 1936

Sir,

The French Ambassador asked to see me yesterday, when he stated that his Government were anxious to consider with us what further steps we could take in connexion with our joint attempt to secure the enforcement of non-intervention and the practice of mediation in Spain. The Soviet Government's reply had been affirmative,[1] while those of Germany and Italy had not been wholly negative. They had in fact asked us to put up definite proposals. If we did so, they said, they would consider them. The Ambassador was anxious to know whether we had any views on this subject. He was sure that if we were to meet the dangerous complications that threatened us from the Spanish conflict it could only be done if we could secure some genuine system of control as quickly as possible. Had we received any answer from the two parties in Spain to the Committee's plan of control which we had submitted to them?

2. I said that we had received no answer as yet and I thought that both parties in Spain would probably be very reluctant to give one.[2] I fully shared His Excellency's desire for an effective scheme of control. The difficulty was, as he realised, to devise one. If all the nations concerned were really ready to observe an agreement then control would be largely superfluous. If they were not ready then I feared it would be very difficult to devise any form of control to meet such conditions. The plan which the Committee had had before them was a very costly one. I understood that the projected figure was somewhere near the rate of a million a year. This was an enormous figure. The Ambassador agreed, but added that if it was the price for averting a European war, that sum divided among the nations of Europe would not represent so formidable a total. Nonetheless he agreed that a less expensive scheme was desirable, and he was prepared to put one forward. The difficulty was that he did not wish to be accused of working for a less effective scheme than that which the Committee had already approved. He had understood from something which Signor Grandi had said to him a few days ago that the Italian Government might be willing to come into this scheme if it were not too elaborate or expensive.[3]

3. I suggested to the Ambassador that if this was so he could say to the Committee that he understood there was a desire for some simpler scheme and if so the French Government were willing to produce one. M. Corbin concurred and added that so far as land frontiers were concerned the French Government were willing to agree to supervision on their land frontier. The French Government were studying this very difficult control problem[4]

[1] Cf. No. 459.　　　　　　　[2] Cf. No. 463.　　　　　　　[3] Cf. No. 474.
[4] Cf. M. Massigli's long memorandum of December 16 on this subject: D.D.F., op. cit., No. 161.

687

and the Ambassador would be very grateful if we would do the same and if we could give the French Government the benefit of any conclusions we might arrive at.

4. Finally we spoke of the seriousness of the situation created for Europe by the attitude of certain Governments to the Spanish trouble, and the Ambassador remarked that it was time to make plain that if Europe wanted two blocs instead of solidarity then they could have it, but that those who wished for these blocs must not think that they would ultimately gain advantage therefrom.

I am, &c.,
ANTHONY EDEN

No. 476

Letter from Mr. Sargent to M. Roland de Margerie

[*C 8169/4/18*]

FOREIGN OFFICE, *December 16, 1936*

Dear de Margerie,

You will remember that you spoke to me on the 12th November and wrote to me on the following day about the French Government's proposal that in the new Western treaty the guarantees should be such as to cover aggression wherever it might take place, whether in Europe or in the possessions and dependencies of the States guaranteed, and that a suitable formula might be found to express this proposal.

I find that Vansittart subsquently spoke to M. Corbin on this subject[1] and suggested that, for the present at any rate, the French Government would do well not to press this proposal, since there were still so many more important problems to be solved in connexion with the Five Power negotiations.

I now write to confess that I have so far been quite unable to think of a suitable formula to meet the point made by your Government, and in the circumstances perhaps you will agree that it would be wiser not to try to pursue the matter any further at this stage.

Yours sincerely,
ORME SARGENT

[1] There does not appear to be any record of this conversation in *D.D.F.*

No. 477

Mr. Hillgarth (Palma) to Mr. Eden
(Received December 17, 1.36 a.m.)
No. 228 Telegraphic: via Admiralty [*W 18270/9549/41*]

PALMA, *December 17, 1936*

Reliably informed that Rossi is being recalled from Majorca permanently reason given his methods considered too conspicuous and his dealings with Military Governor inharmonious.[1] Believed he will be replaced by some form of Italian Military Mission. Reported also from usual(ly) reliable source insurgents have several foreign submarines, number believed to be ten, at their disposal for operations on Spanish Mediterranean coast.[2]

[1] Cf. No. 355. Sir E. Drummond had made a further complaint about Signor Rossi's conduct on December 5 (see No. 471, note 5). Count Ciano had replied that importance should not be attached 'to these youthful outbursts'. But he promised to send a warning to him to refrain from foolish public speeches 'which he hoped and believed would prove effective'.

[2] In a telegram via Admiralty wireless of December 23, Mr. Hillgarth reported: 'Rossi left for Italy this morning. I believe permanently. Atmosphere has improved slightly in consequence.'

No. 478

Mr. Eden to Mr. Ogilvie-Forbes (Madrid)
No. 356 Telegraphic [*W 18173/62/41*]

FOREIGN OFFICE, *December 17, 1936, 4.30 p.m.*

Your telegram No. 623.[1]

Question of supply of lorries is under consideration but as necessary arrangements will take time H.M.S. *Resource* is being instructed to leave Malta.[2]

In meantime I suggest you should inform Spanish Government of scheme pointing out that lorries would only be used for the Embassy, and ascertain if they would have any objection.

[1] In this telegram of December 15 Mr. Ogilvie-Forbes asked for a number of Army 30-cwt general service lorries to be placed at his disposal for the transport of food from the coast for the service of members of the British community in Madrid dependent on the British Embassy.

[2] Mr. Ogilvie-Forbes had suggested that H.M.S. *Resource* could help presumably by bringing the lorries from Malta. Minutes on this telegram show that the Admiralty did not like the proposal; the War Office thought it could find the lorries at Malta or Gibraltar, but would expect the Embassy to find drivers. In commenting on this on December 16 Sir G. Mounsey raised the question of Mr. Forbes's possible withdrawal. Sir R. Vansittart wrote: 'We shall have any amount of trouble if Mr. Ogilvie-Forbes stays on. And I'm not very clear what real good he will be able to do henceforth. We shd. at least therefore put the point to him. R. V. Dec. 16.' He approved the draft of telegram No. 356.

I am, however, again impressed by difficulties which you are encountering and which you will encounter in increasing measure in feeding community under your charge and should be glad to learn if you have had under reconsideration desirability of withdrawal from Madrid in view of changed military situation and of possibility of indefinite siege with its resulting difficulties and dangers to yourselves and colony.

No. 479

Mr. C. H. Bentinck[1] (Prague) to Mr. Eden
(Received December 19)
No. 42 Saving: Telegraphic [C 9062/4/18]

PRAGUE, December 17, 1936

Wide publicity has been given in the press to your speech at Bradford on December 14th[2] and to comments thereon in 'Morning Post'.[3] These comments are said to constitute an authentic interpretation of your words which have been heartily welcomed in Czechoslovakia.

Gist of press comments is to the effect that England is ready to assist States desirous of peace; that she recognises the position of Czechoslovakia in Europe and will not adopt an attitude of indifference in European affairs; that you had in mind the possibility of an attack by Germany on Czechoslovakia, which would be likely to embroil all Europe, including Great Britain. The clearer and more resolute the attitude of Great Britain, it is said, the more certain it is that peace will be maintained.

When I saw the Minister for Foreign Affairs on December 15th, he expressed considerable gratification at your remarks, as reported in the press.

[1] Mr. Bentinck had been British Minister and Consul-General at Prague since October 5, 1936.

[2] This speech was fully reported in *The Times* of December 15, p. 11. After an opening reference to the abdication crisis, Mr. Eden again spoke of Britain's interest in peace, its determination not to align itself with dictatorships of the right and left or with 'any group of states because they support the one or the other'. He was sure that his audience would have learned with 'the utmost satisfaction' of M. Delbos's statement in the Chamber of Deputies on December 4 that the forces of France, on land, on sea, and in the air, would be spontaneously and immediately used for the defence of Great Britain in the event of an unprovoked aggression, a declaration which applied also to Belgium. He referred to his similar affirmation with regard to France and Belgium in his Leamington speech on November 20, but reminded his audience that these declarations were not a new departure, but a reaffirmation of assurances given in the previous March after the Rhineland remilitarization. The speech also included the statement: 'If our vital interests are situated in certain clearly definable areas, our interest in peace is world-wide and there is a simple reason for this. The world has now become so small—and every day with the march of science it becomes smaller—that a spark in some sphere comparatively remote from our own interests may become a conflagration sweeping a continent or a hemisphere. We must therefore be watchful at all times and in all places.' There was no direct reference to Czechoslovakia.

[3] In a minute of December 22, Mr. V. J. Lawford remarked: 'I have been unable to trace any "Morning Post" article to which this might refer.'

No. 480

Letter from Sir H. W. Malkin to Dr. E. Woermann

[*C 8803/4/18*]

FOREIGN OFFICE, *December 17, 1936*

Dear Dr. Woermann,

I am much obliged to you for sending me the note enclosed in your letter of December 7th;[1] I am answering it in the same personal and private manner.

It seems to me that what underlies the enquiry in your note is an idea that if in the hypothetical circumstances there suggested signatory A took action against signatory B without awaiting the decision of the competent body, the legitimacy under the proposed pact of A's action would not be made the subject of a decision by the competent body at all, so that in fact A would be the sole judge of the legitimacy under the pact of his action. It is not our idea that this should be the position; we do not think that the question whether a signatory to the proposed pact has or has not violated the non-aggression undertaking should be determined by that signatory himself. Under Locarno, if the circumstances suggested in your note had occurred, and if signatory B considered that A's action was inconsistent with Article 2 of that treaty as not falling within any of the exceptions laid down in that article, B had the right (and was indeed bound) to bring the matter before the Council of the League under Article 4 (1), and if the Council held that A's action was not justifiable under Article 2, the guarantees provided by the treaty would have come into operation against A. Thus the legitimacy of A's action would have been determined not by A himself but by the Council of the League, and if A acted in advance of any finding by that body, he would run the risk that the guarantees would come into operation against himself if the Council decided against him.

It seems necessary that the proposed treaty should provide some corresponding method of ensuring that the legitimacy of *any* attack by one party to the non-aggression arrangements upon another party should, if challenged, be decided by the competent body. The exact method of producing this result is a matter to be discussed between all the proposed parties to the pact, and pending the receipt of the replies to our memorandum of November 19th,[2] it does not seem possible to say more than that I am sure that His Majesty's Government would be willing to give careful consideration to any suggestions which seem calculated to deal with the point in a satisfactory manner.

H. W. MALKIN

[1] See No. 454, note 3.   [2] No. 389.

No. 481

Letter from Mr. Howard to Mr. Hemming
[W 17818/9549/41]

FOREIGN OFFICE, *December 17, 1936*

Sir,

With reference to paper N.I.S.(36)179[1] I am directed by Mr. Secretary Eden to give you the following information regarding the attitude of His Majesty's Government in the United Kingdom towards the question of indirect intervention, with special reference to the problem of the entry into Spain of foreign nationals for the purpose of taking service in the civil war.

2. His Majesty's Government agree in principle to the extension of the Non-Intervention Agreement to cover indirect as well as direct intervention so far as may be practicable. They also agree as a first step to the extension of the Agreement to cover the recruitment in, the despatch from, or transit through their territory of persons proposing to take part in the civil war in Spain.

3. With regard to the measures in force in this country, I am to inform you that under the Foreign Enlistment Act, 1870, it is illegal for any British subject to accept or agree to accept any commission or engagement in the military, naval or air services of either party in the civil war or for any person in the United Kingdom to induce any other person to accept such an engagement. It is also an offence under the Act for any British subject to quit or go on board any ship with a view of quitting His Majesty's Dominions with intent to accept such an engagement, or for any person in the United Kingdom to persuade any other person to do so. Persons contravening this Act are liable to fine or imprisonment or both.

4. In addition to this the competent authorities of His Majesty's Government have refused to issue passports valid for Spain to any British subjects who are not able to give a satisfactory account of their reasons for wishing to visit that country, and passports are refused altogether to persons suspected of desiring to take service in the civil war.

5. With regard to paragraph (*b*)(ii) of the Committee's communication, I am to state that if it were brought to the notice of His Majesty's Government that any British subject desired to enter Spain for the purpose of carrying out activities susceptible of prolonging or embittering the civil war, the issue of a passport could be controlled in the same manner as in the case of persons volunteering for service in the armed forces of either side.

6. As regards the supply of financial aid to either of the parties in Spain, I am to draw attention to paragraph 3 of the letter W 13817/9549/41[2]

---

[1] See No. 449, note 6. N.I.S.(36)179 was a note by Mr. Hemming of December 9 calling the attention of the governments concerned to the recommendations in paragraph 8 of No. 449.

[2] This letter had followed some correspondence between Mr. Roberts and Mr. E. E. Bridges (an Assistant Secretary in the Treasury) as to the extent of the Treasury's power to prohibit public or private issues for Spanish clients.

which was addressed to you on the 10th November last setting out the attitude of His Majesty's Government in this matter. The relevant passage runs as follows:

As regards financial aid, His Majesty's Government have no knowledge of any proposals to raise money either by public issue or by private loans from financial institutions. If any such proposals did come before them, they would be prepared to consider what action could be taken by means of the existing arrangements relating to the issue of foreign loans in this market, or otherwise, with the object of preventing the transactions in question. There are, however, great difficulties in the way of imposing any effective control or prohibition of private subscriptions—though it should be noted that such appeals as have come to the notice of His Majesty's Government have been appeals for the relief of distress.

7. At the same time His Majesty's Government desire to make it clear that they are prepared to give favourable consideration to any proposals regarding the general problem of indirect intervention in Spain to which the other governments represented on the Committee may be willing to agree.

I am, &c.,

D. F. HOWARD

No. 482

Mr. Eden to Sir E. Drummond (Rome)
No. 481 Telegraphic [R 7373/226/22]

FOREIGN OFFICE, *December 18, 1936, 10 p.m.*

Your telegrams Nos. 727,[1] 728[2] and 730.[3]

I have carefully considered Count Ciano's criticisms of the outline of a possible declaration as given in paragraph 3 of my telegram No. 451[4] of December 2, and also the actual draft declaration now proposed by Count Ciano himself. Since I was only outlining in my telegram No. 451 the form which the proposed declaration might take, I do not wish to adhere to the actual wording used. I need not, therefore, discuss the points made by Count Ciano in paragraph 3 of your telegram No. 727. As regards Count Ciano's draft, however, I fear that the clause defining the attitude of the two Governments towards communications in the Mediterranean and towards freedom of its accesses would be altogether too precise for the object which we have in view, and might thus lead to misconceptions and misunderstandings. Also, I do not much like the suggestion of undertaking to consult together, since this action might be held to imply joint action to the detriment of other Powers. This, however, is now academic, since I see from your telegram No. 746[5] of December 15 that Count Ciano does not wish

[1] No. 440.   [2] No. 441.   [3] No. 445.   [4] No. 426.
[5] Not preserved in the Foreign Office archives.

to pursue the point. On the other hand, Count Ciano's draft omits all reference to the territorial situation in the Mediterranean. Since I attach capital importance to some such provision, I am rather disquieted to learn that Count Ciano was doubtful when you put this proposal to him, and I trust that after the explanations which you gave him in the matter, he will agree to a suitable provision being embodied in our proposed declarations.

In accordance with the suggestion contained in your telegram No. 730, I have prepared an alternative draft declaration which you should submit to Count Ciano at your next interview. The text is given in my immediately following telegram.[6] In this draft I have endeavoured to embody as much of Count Ciano's draft as possible. As regards the territorial question, you will observe that instead of providing for the maintenance of the status quo I propose that our declarations should speak of the 'national status of the territories in the Mediterranean area.' This wording, I feel, will be more appropriate to the circumstances and less open to subsequent misconstruction. Originally I had only contemplated a general provision on this subject, but in view of the unsatisfactory position with regard to the Balearic Islands, as explained in the last paragraph of this telegram, I now consider it essential that specific reference should be made in our declarations to the national status of Spanish territory.

While I recognise that the attitude of Count Ciano was reasonable in regard to the actual Mediterranean declaration, I have been somewhat disappointed at the unhelpful attitude he adopted towards the two extraneous questions which you raised with him (i.e., Italian accession to the naval treaty and the cessation of anti-British propaganda), and also at the absence of any suggestions on his part when it came to making the *tour d'horizon*, which he himself had proposed. In fact, the *tour d'horizon*, as far as I can see, reduced itself to nothing more than an attempt by Count Ciano to raise the Abyssinian question, although he knew that it was excluded from your present discussions.

In authorising you to enter upon these conversations with Count Ciano, I naturally supposed that the Italian Government, like ourselves, were anxious to reach a general *détente*, and, although I am quite prepared to agree with Count Ciano that the first step in this *détente* should be a clarification of our respective interests and policies in the Mediterranean, it is obvious that this in itself cannot bring about a *détente* until and unless other points of friction between our two countries are also progressively dealt with and removed. I had assumed that when Count Ciano proposed a *tour d'horizon* it was precisely this object which he had in view. The fact that I authorised you at the outset of your conversations to raise only two questions beyond the actual Mediterranean declaration was not intended to indicate that His Majesty's Government are completely satisfied with Anglo-Italian relations in all other respects. On the contrary, as you know, we have many causes for disquiet and complaint, and if I did not authorise you to refer to all of them at the outset it was because I did not want to rush matters or to introduce

6 No. 483 below.

at too early a stage awkward and delicate subjects which, if approached prematurely, might lead to undesirable recriminations. I hoped that if these could be dealt with progressively once the atmosphere had improved they might be susceptible of friendly and satisfactory solution. Indeed, if this is not the case, I am afraid that a mere declaration regarding the Mediterranean will not produce the *détente* which both Governments wish to bring about. Moreover, it must be borne in mind that we are discussing this Mediterranean declaration at the suggestion of the Italian Government, and, although we are naturally in favour of it, we look upon it not as an end in itself but as a means to a general rapprochement.

I had expected that Count Ciano's proposed *tour d'horizon* would offer us an opportunity of stating our views and expressing our wishes generally and not merely on the two points which you were instructed to raise on your own initiative. Since this has definitely not proved the case, you will appreciate the undesirability of leaving Count Ciano under the impression that if we obtain satisfaction on these two matters there are no other questions which are at present in an unsatisfactory state and which ought to be settled if the wished-for *détente* is to become a reality. I shall be glad, therefore, if at your next conversation with Count Ciano you will speak in the sense of my preceding paragraph and make it clear that we wish to use the present opportunity progressively to clear up all points of friction between our two countries. You should accordingly press for a real *tour d'horizon* permitting a review of all points of common interest. When this review has taken place, I shall be better able to consider which points you should merely mention as matters of interest to His Majesty's Government, and which in our opinion should form the subject of early discussion and agreement.

As regards specific questions, my views are set forth in my telegram No. 451, but the following supplementary comments may be of use to you.

British Interests in Abyssinia

Although Count Ciano insisted on discussing Abyssinia, he apparently gave no assurances regarding the respect of British interests and the amicable settlement of boundary questions which must inevitably arise before long. Compare hint given you by Marquis Theodoli as reported in your telegram No. 687.[7] Would it be possible to draw Count Ciano on these points?

Naval Treaty

It looks as though by raising the question of ratification Count Ciano hoped to evade the issue. I think you ought to bring him back to it. It would be well, therefore, for you to insist once more that, if Anglo-Italian relations are to derive that real benefit from the proposed declaration which we hope, it seems to us essential that Italy's accession to the naval treaty should follow very closely on the heels of the declaration itself. Otherwise, we shall be entirely at a loss to understand the Italian attitude on this question. In other words, while we do not want to make Italian accession a condition of the

7 No. 366.

conclusion of the declaration, we are entitled, I think, to have a precise statement of the grounds on which there is 'still much difficulty in accession.' The Italian technical grounds will not bear examination. They are altogether flimsy and are really mere pretexts. We can, therefore, only assume that there remains some political difficulty, and we are unable to conceive of any political difficulty which would not be at variance with the spirit which is to animate the conclusion of the declaration. As regards ratification, the position is that the treaty has been ratified by the United States, but not yet by France and ourselves. We have been waiting for the outcome of the naval negotiations now proceeding with Germany and Soviet Russia before reaching any final decision on the question of ratification. The probabilities are that it will now be possible for the treaty to be ratified before or shortly after the end of the present year.

Propaganda

This is, above all, a matter where the Italian Government can give tangible evidence of their goodwill and sincerity, but Count Ciano did not seem to think it necessary even to promise an investigation and apparently made no response to your statement that once friendly relations were completely established, we should expect the present inspired and paid anti-British agitation to cease. You should therefore revert to the question and insist that Count Ciano should give the matter his serious attention. In this connexion I would call your attention to the paragraph in my draft declaration regarding activities likely to impair good relations. This paragraph is intended to apply more particularly to unfriendly propaganda, and you can explain this to Count Ciano if you think it necessary. But I would not consider it satisfactory if this clause in the declaration was not at some stage supplemented by a direct assurance from Count Ciano and by some tangible evidence of a change of policy on the part of the Italian authorities. In this respect we must not, of course, be fobbed off by any request for a statement of our evidence. It would be for obvious reasons impossible to quote most of it. Nor by quoting specific instances should we wish to be laid open to the interpretation that those were all that we had to complain of or that other localities were not equally affected. The complaint is, in fact, general, and the propaganda would not, of course, be going on without official connivance and material support. The Italian Government must therefore necessarily know all about it.

Arabia

You should also mention Arabia, where I would like to see Anglo-Italian relations placed on a footing of complete friendliness. The matter is being studied here and it will, I think, suffice if you just mention the point, so that there will be no risk of our being accused at a later date of being indifferent thereto.

I do not wish to add to what I have already said in my telegram No. 451, but I should, of course, welcome any initiative by Count Ciano on either of these subjects.

Franco-Italian Relations

I have explained in my telegram No. 466[8] of 8 December that I do not wish to press for France to be associated with the proposed Mediterranean declaration, but this does not mean that I am not somewhat anxious as to the indirect effect that the strained relations which at present exist between France and Italy may have on the Anglo-Italian *détente* for which we are working. You should, if occasion arises, indicate this to Count Ciano.

Italo-Spanish Relations

You will recollect that in my telegram No. 456[9] of 4 December you were instructed to speak to the Minister for Foreign Affairs about the activities of Italians, and, in particular of M. Rossi, in the Balearic Isles. The account given in your telegram No. 731 of December 7[10] of your interview with Count Ciano, at which this matter was raised, has been carefully considered, and I can only say that His Majesty's Government are far from satisfied with the light-hearted manner in which his Excellency seems to have attempted to dispose of the question. It is useless for him to pretend that Rossi is an irresponsible supporter of the insurgents, since it is well-known that he was sent to Majorca with the knowledge and approval of the Italian Government. His activities and those of other Italian agents constitute a fresh development which cannot but cause His Majesty's Government grave concern, since they produce the impression that these persons are anxious to exploit the difficulties in which Spain is now involved for the purpose of ensuring *de facto* control by Italy over the islands. These activities, if not suspended, are bound to affect the future course of our relations with Italy and to deprive our proposed declarations of a great part of their value. Moreover, the publicity which this question of the Balearic Islands has thus acquired makes it necessary, in my opinion, that the assurances to be given regarding national status of Mediterranean territories in our proposed declaration should refer specifically to Spain.

[8] No. 451. [9] Not printed. [10] See No. 471, note 5.

No. 483

Mr. Eden to Sir E. Drummond (Rome)
No. 482 Telegraphic [R 7373/226/22]

FOREIGN OFFICE, *December 18, 1936, 10 p.m.*

My immediately preceding telegram.[1]

Following is text of proposed draft declaration.

His Majesty's Government in the United Kingdom and the Italian Government;

Animated by the desire to contribute increasingly, in the interests of the general cause of peace and security, to the betterment of relations between them and between all the Mediterranean Powers, and resolved to respect the rights and interests of those Powers;

Recognise that the freedom of entry into, and transit through, the Mediterranean is a vital interest both to the different parts of the British Empire and to Italy, and that these interests are in no way inconsistent with each other;

Disclaim any desire to modify, or, so far as they are concerned, to see modified, the national status of the territories in the Mediterranean area, particularly the territories of Spain;

Undertake to respect each other's rights and interests in the said area;

Agree to use their best endeavours to discourage any activities liable to impair the good relations which it is the object of the present declaration to establish.

This declaration is designed to further the ends of peace and is not directed against any other Power.

[1] No. 482.

No. 484

Mr. Eden to Sir E. Phipps (Berlin)
No. 1418 [R 7600/226/22]

FOREIGN OFFICE, *December 18, 1936*

Sir,

At the end of a long conversation with the German Ambassador yesterday Herr von Ribbentrop asked whether I could give him any information as to the progress of our conversations with Italy, more especially if there were any truth in the rumours that we might in due course be reducing the status of our Legation in Addis Ababa to a Consulate-General.[1]

2. In reply I told the Ambassador that our conversations were proceeding normally, though here too the task would be easier if non-intervention could be made effective and if the Spanish problem did not loom so large in all the international policies at this time. As regards the position of our Legation

[1] See No. 378, note 8, and Volume XVI, No. 486, note 2.

at Addis Ababa no instructions had as yet been sent to His Majesty's Ambassador in Rome. It was, however, clear that we could not indefinitely maintain a Legation at Addis Ababa in present conditions. In any event we had no intention of recognising Italy as the *de jure* Government of Abyssinia.

I am, &c.,

ANTHONY EDEN

No. 485

Mr. Eden to Sir E. Phipps (Berlin)

No. 1421 [C 9055/4/18]

FOREIGN OFFICE, *December 18, 1936*

Sir,

The German Ambassador asked to see me yesterday when we had a conversation of more than an hour's duration. Herr von Ribbentrop explained that he was shortly returning to Germany when he would have some conversations with the Chancellor and before doing so he wished to tell me frankly what was in his mind. He had read with care three speeches which I had made recently at Leamington,[1] at the Anglo-Belgian Luncheon[2] and at Bradford,[3] and he wished to put to me certain reflections which had occurred to him as a result.

2. These speeches which seemed to imply the possibility of German attack in the west, also contained certain new engagements. The assurance from France to ourselves given by M. Delbos[4] that France would come to our aid if we were attacked was certainly new. The Ambassador did not wish to dwell at length upon the German fear of Communism. It was, however, very real. This virus might conceivably infect France. He begged me to believe that that was the last thing he wished to see. His own friends were on the side of De La Rocque and Doriot in France and they regarded them as the most effective bulwark in that country against Communism. Nonetheless it was useless to deny that the danger existed. Supposing that at some later date there were to be a Communist France were not we by these exchanges of assurances showing something in the nature of benevolence towards possible attack by a Communist France on Germany?

3. In reply I explained to His Excellency that there was nothing new in the exchange of assurances which had passed between M. Delbos and myself. On the contrary these arose out of the arrangements which had been come to in London in March, which were themselves the outcome of the German reoccupation of the Rhineland. Still less of course was there the remotest

[1] See No. 400, note 1.
[2] The reference is to a speech made by Mr. Eden on November 27 at a lunch given in honour of M. van Zeeland's visit (see No. 430) by the British National Committee of the International Chamber of Commerce: see *The Times*, November 28, 1936, p. 14.
[3] See No. 479, note 2.
[4] A reference to M. Delbos's speech in the French Chamber on December 4: see No. 479, note 2, and *The Times*, December 5, 1936, p. 12.

idea in our mind of encouraging France thereby to any aggressive action. I was personally confident that there was not the least probability of France undertaking any such action. Her people were intensely pacifist. Moreover we did not desire, and the French Government had made it plain that they did not desire, any arrangement between ourselves alone. On the contrary, the whole purpose of our policy was to secure an agreement in which Germany would have her place. To this end a meeting of the three Powers had been held in London at the end of July[5] when an attempt had been made to secure a fresh start. All controversy about the re-occupation of the Rhineland was now virtually at an end. If a Western agreement were reached we should of course be fully ready to extend a guarantee to Germany similar to that given to France. This would fully meet the apprehensions His Excellency seemed to have.

4. The Ambassador agreed as to the need of securing some Western agreement. At the same time we were always faced with the same difficulty— the position of Soviet Russia and the Franco-Soviet Pact. He knew that we did not take the same view as the Germans did of this, since we were inclined to regard it more lightly. The German Government were quite clear in their own minds, however, that it did in fact constitute a military alliance. Otherwise why should the agreement have been reached? There was always a motive for all political action, and in his view the motive of this Pact was anti-German. The German Government could not be expected to come to an agreement which allowed for the operation of that Pact. When I remarked that our own information was that the Franco-Soviet Pact had no military agreement attached to it and that the French Government were not in fact prepared to enter into such an agreement, the Ambassador would have none of it. The German Government's information he maintained was quite different. For instance why were military officers continually passing to and fro across northern Germany from Russia to France unless for the purpose of military co-operation.

5. We then examined the relation of the Franco-Soviet Pact to a new Western Agreement and I gave the Ambassador a copy of Sir W. Malkin's letter to Herr Woermann of which a copy is attached, together with a copy of Herr Woermann's communication.[6] His Excellency read it and expressed some satisfaction at its terms. The two-fold difficulty, however, remained. Supposing at some future date Poland or Czechoslovakia were to be 'Red' and Germany was to be attacked by Russia from either of these countries, what guarantee could she have that France would not come to the assistance of Russia, claiming that Germany had attacked Russia, while Germany claimed that Russia had attacked her? We made the suggestion that there should be reference to some outside body. Germany could certainly never agree that France and Russia should be judges in their own courts, but who could be the outside body? How was it to be created? I pointed out to the Ambassador that under the Locarno Treaty the reference was to be to the

[5] See Volume XVI, Nos. 476 and 477.   [6] See Nos. 454 and 480.

Council of the League. This in our view had been one of the considerable advantages in the Locarno scheme of things. Now unhappily Germany was not a member of the League, and I admitted that this difficult problem of a body to whom reference should be made in consequence existed. It always seemed to us a little difficult to understand why the Franco-Soviet Pact could assume such formidable proportions, when in fact France had other similar arrangements in Eastern Europe, such as the Franco-Polish Pact, while Germany herself still had a pact with Russia. We could not help feeling that the political and still more the military importance of this pact were being exaggerated in Germany. The Ambassador replied that that depended upon the point of view. To Germany Communism seemed the enemy everywhere. Hence the arrangement which had been entered into with Japan[7] for dealing with that trouble at home. He deeply regretted that this country did not share Germany's point of view in this respect. He sincerely hoped we should never have Communism here, but for those who had once been under the direct menace of Communism the menace that that doctrine constituted would always be present.

6. After some further discussion I suggested to the Ambassador that he should study Sir W. Malkin's letter further with Herr Woermann which His Excellency undertook to do.

I am, &c.,

ANTHONY EDEN

[7] See No. 421, note 3.

No. 486

Mr. Eden to Sir E. Phipps (Berlin)

No. 1424 [W 18409/9549/41]

FOREIGN OFFICE, *December 18, 1936*

Sir,

During the course of a conversation yesterday with the German Ambassador we spoke of the situation in Spain. Herr von Ribbentrop said he would shortly be discussing this question with the Chancellor and he would like again to ask me whether I could give him any more details as to our view about mediation. I replied that in our view the first need was for all nations to stop sending arms or men to Spain. This we considered essential, and a duty which we all owed both to Spain and to Europe. If that first step could be taken it might then be possible to effect something in the way of mediation. It seemed to us that countries who were sending their nationals to Spain were assuming a terrible responsibility. I could hardly believe that Germany could really wish to engage any of her population in war in that country. Herr von Ribbentrop replied that certainly it was desirable to make non-intervention effective. The difficulty was how.

2. He had information that there were now something like 50,000 Russians in Spain, and that Communists from all over Europe were pouring into Spain from France. Germany did not want to see a Communist Spain, for she feared that such an outcome would result in France being infected also. Germany did not want a Communist neighbour on the West. How were we to avoid Spain being Communist? Did I see any hope of setting up a form of Government there that would not be Communist? How could that be achieved?

3. In reply I reaffirmed that the first step to be taken was to make non-intervention effective. Experience had shown that foreigners on Spanish soil had not been in the end welcome to Spaniards. History might well repeat itself. As civil wars progressed so the more extreme factions on either side were likely to obtain control and the result therefore of German or Italian aid sent to General Franco might be very different from what those Governments intended, and might in the end make a Communist Spain more, rather than less likely. After some further discussion on the subject the Ambassador undertook to repeat to the Chancellor the views of His Majesty's Government in respect of non-intervention.

I am, &c.,
ANTHONY EDEN

No. 487

Letter[1] from M. Maisky to Mr. Hemming
[W 18696/9549/41]

SOVIET EMBASSY, *December 18, 1936*

Sir,

I have transmitted to my Government the communication approved at the Committee's meeting on December 9th regarding the question of indirect intervention.[2] After due consideration of the communication my Government authorise me to state the following:

(A) The Government of the U.S.S.R. being desirous of collaborating with other Powers in bringing about the complete fulfilment of the obligations of the Non-Intervention Agreement and of making the control of the Committee over the fulfilment of same as effective as possible;

(I) Agrees in principle to the extension of the Agreement to cover indirect as well as direct intervention so far as may be practicable, and

(II) Agrees, as the first step, to the extension of the Agreement to cover the recruitment in, the dispatch from, or transit through the territories

---

[1] Circulated to the N.I. Committee as paper N.I.S.(36)190, with the title, 'The attitude of the U.S.S.R. Government towards the question of indirect intervention'. See also *D.V.P.S.*, *op. cit.*, No. 420.

[2] See No. 449, note 6.

of the contracting parties of persons proposing to take part in the civil war in Spain.

In connection with point (II) I beg to draw the attention of the Committee to the proposals made on behalf of my Government in my letter of December 4th[3] addressed to the Secretary of the Committee, and to suggest that these proposals be placed on the agenda of the Sub-Committee for discussion as soon as possible.

(B) As regards items I, II and III, I beg to state the following.

1. No recruitment for the purpose of taking part in the civil war (I) and or for any other purpose (II) is taking place in the U.S.S.R.
2. No loans or credits to the Spanish Government have been granted by any government or public body in the U.S.S.R. (III), and no request for such loans or credits has been made by the Spanish Government to the U.S.S.R. There is no prohibition at present of public subscriptions for funds intended for humanitarian purposes.

Measures in regard to items enumerated under point (B) could be introduced only after all the interested Governments undertook the requisite obligations in regard thereto.

The Government of the U.S.S.R. is fully prepared to discuss with all other members of the Committee measures to cover all forms of indirect intervention mentioned under items, I, II, III and IV of point (B) for the purpose of extending the Non-Intervention Agreement to cover such items.

(C) The Government of the U.S.S.R. fully shares the opinion of the United Kingdom Government as to the gravity and urgency of the questions raised by the entry into Spain of increasing numbers of foreign nationals for the purpose of taking part in the civil war, and therefore considers it essential and is prepared to give special priority to the consideration of the question of the recruitment etc., in the respective countries of persons proposing to take service with either of the parties in conflict.

Accept, Sir, the expression of my high consideration and esteem.

J. MAISKY

[3] See *ibid.*, note 3.

No. 488

Mr. Eden to Sir G. Clerk (Paris)
No. 305[1] *Telegraphic* [*C 8265/4/18*]

FOREIGN OFFICE, *December 19, 1936, 7.5 p.m.*

Please enquire whether French (German/Belgian/Italian) Government expect shortly to be able to reply to our memorandum of November 19th[2] regarding the Western European Pact negotiations.[3]

[1] No. 244 to Berlin, No. 94 to Brussels, No. 485 to Rome.   [2] No. 389.
[3] Mr. Eden on December 1 asked about the desirability of pressing the other governments

for a reply 'to our latest "Locarno" note'. Mr. Wigram suggested waiting for another week: 'Have we much to gain by expediting the German and Italian answers which may perhaps land us in an "impasse". R. F. W. 2/12.' Mr. Sargent thought it best to clear up the 'Belgian question' with the French and Belgians before pressing other governments. Sir R. Vansittart on December 7 agreed, and did not think there was much reason for haste. 'We are surely interested in gaining time—or not preventing others from wasting it —& I too fear that the next round of replies *may* bring us near to the end of a passage. If the Germans mean business they will reply without much pressure or will reply if the others do.' Mr. Eden, however, wrote: 'It must be remembered that we are "in charge" of these negotiations and have ourselves recently sent proposals to the other four powers. It is not good for our own position that these proposals should be ignored by all concerned, & therefore I favour a reminder all round next week. A. E. Dec. 8.'

No. 489

Sir E. Phipps (Berlin) to Mr. Eden
(Received December 21)
No. 442 Saving: Telegraphic [W 18547/62/41]

BERLIN, *December 19, 1936*

I hear that General Faupel[1] came here yesterday for one day to report to the Chancellor on Spanish situation and that he will return to Spain today. No mention has so far been made in the press of his visit nor did Minister for Foreign Affairs refer to it this morning when I asked his views on Spain. French Ambassador declares that General Faupel has brought a request from General Franco for two German Divisions but I cannot guarantee this.[2]

Baron von Neurath told me he had discussed the matter yesterday with General Franco's Chargé d'Affaires who had just arrived here and that General Franco was still hopeful of final victory in spite of present deadlock.

His Excellency maintains that there are very large numbers of French and Belgians fighting on the side of the Reds and he is having this pointed out in German press this evening. He remains sceptical as to possibility of bringing Spanish conflict to an end but agreed that we must try our best to limit it.[3]

[1] Lieutenant General Wilhelm Faupel was German Chargé d'Affaires in Spain, November 1936 to February 1937, and German Ambassador to the Spanish Nationalist Government, February–September 1937. He had arrived at Salamanca, which had become the headquarters of the Nationalist Government, by air on November 28, 1936.

[2] General Faupel's report of December 10 from Salamanca giving an estimate of the military situation in Spain said that General Franco, apparently on December 9, had asked for one German and one Italian division to be placed at his disposal. General Faupel 'explained to him that such a unit could, of course, only be under German command, which he understood'. *D.G.F.P.*, *op. cit.*, No. 148; cf. Nos. 144, 145.

[3] *Ibid.*, No. 155, shows that Herr von Neurath wrote to Field-Marshal von Blomberg on December 15 saying that he did not think it 'feasible to send a complete division . . . especially at the present time, when particularly strenuous attempts are being made by the Great Powers to limit the conflict and to bring about mediation'.

No. 490

Mr. Eden to Sir E. Phipps (Berlin)
No. 1427 [C 9087/4/18]

FOREIGN OFFICE, *December 19, 1936*

Sir,

The German Ambassador asked to see me today in order to clear up a point arising on Sir William Malkin's letter to Dr. Woermann, which I had shown him at our interview on December 17th, as recorded in my despatch No. 1421 of December 18th.[1] Dr. Woermann and Sir William Malkin were present at the conversation.

2. Herr von Ribbentrop explained that as the result of this letter he understood that it was our view that in the circumstances suggested in Dr. Woermann's letter the legitimacy of signatory A in taking action against signatory B would be the subject of a decision by the 'competent body'; but what he wanted to know was whether it was our view that the decision of the competent body would be given before or after signatory A had taken action, in other words whether signatory A would be bound, before taking action, to seek and obtain the authority of the competent body. He explained that in the view of the German Government the non-aggression undertaking to be embodied in the proposed western Pact should not contain any exceptions whatever, but that if there were to be any exceptions (a point on which he was, of course, not in a position to commit his Government) it would in his opinion be essential that action under them should not be taken until the competent body had decided that the circumstances would justify such action.

3. I explained to Herr von Ribbentrop that under the Locarno scheme the function of the 'competent body' was to decide whether there had been an attack by a signatory upon another signatory in violation of the provisions of that treaty, so that until an attack had taken place there was nothing for the competent body to decide, and that to confer upon the competent body the duty of deciding in advance whether the circumstances were such as to justify, under the treaty, an attack by one signatory upon another would therefore be to introduce quite a new idea. I pointed out however that in view of the risk which a signatory would have run under Locarno in taking action if there was any doubt as to whether such action would be regarded as justified under the treaty, it was inconceivable that a signatory would have so acted without previously taking all possible steps such as utilising the machinery of the Council (which, of course, was the competent body under Locarno), in order to ensure that such action, if taken, would not subsequently be held to involve a violation of the treaty.

4. I added that I now understood precisely what the German Government had in mind, and suggested that it would be of great assistance if they would indicate the procedure which they suggested might be adopted in the proposed

[1] No. 485.

treaty in order to ensure the result which they desired. If they would do this, we should be prepared to consider with the other parties to the proposed treaty whether it would be possible to find a solution on those lines. I further added that it would, in my opinion, be easier to deal with the point if all the countries concerned were Members of the League and the League machinery could be employed.

5. The German Ambassador is leaving today for Germany, where he will see Herr Hitler, and I hope therefore that a statement of the German Government's attitude on this point and their proposals for dealing with it may be forthcoming.

I am, &c.,
ANTHONY EDEN

No. 491

Sir H. Chilton (Hendaye) to Mr. Eden
(Received December 21, 7.5 p.m.)
No. 336 Telegraphic: by wireless [W 18608/9549/41]

HENDAYE, *December 21, 1936*

Your telegrams Nos. 263[1] and 264.[2] Control proposals.

Note[3] from Salamanca dated December 19th starts by expressing regret that His Majesty's Government which fulfils so high a mission in the defence of the vital principles of European civilisation does not seem to have grasped the greatness of the National Spanish movement and continues in the relations with the so called Government of Valencia whose Red and Anarchist hordes operate independently in the territory not yet occupied by the National Army.

Note then proceeds to ask for further details on the following questions.

(A). Which are the principle [*sic*] points of entry? Is it intended that secondary points such as many points on the Franco-Catalan frontier and small ports, anchorages and piers should be free from supervision?

(B). Are the non-intervention committee's agents to concern themselves only with the entry of war material into Spain or are they also to withdraw from the fronts the large stocks of arms bought with the gold stolen from the Bank of Spain and with the proceeds of other robberies from banks and private houses?

(C). Does the non-intervention committee intend to establish agents in French port towns such as Marseilles, Pe[r]pignan, Bordeaux, Bayonne and many others which are now centres of supply and recruitment for the various Red pseudo Governments and which nourish the anarchy that reigns in the territory not yet occupied by the National army?

[1] No. 431.   [2] No. 432.
[3] The full Spanish text of this note was forwarded to the Foreign Office by Sir H. Chilton in his despatch No. 809 of December 22 (W 18784/9549/41).

(D). It is notorious that in Red territory the so called Governments have no control over the masses. These Governments have not been able to secure the respect of Embassies and Legations or the personal safety of Consuls, as witness among other cases that have happened in Barcelona and Bilbao. Who then will guarantee the agents of control in the effective exercise of their functions?[4]

When information on these points has been received the National Government will continue its study of the non-intervention committee's communication.[5]

[4] In a minute of December 28 on despatch No. 809 (see note 3) Mr. Shuckburgh commented: 'These questions constitute the expected "delaying tactics" which we knew Burgos would adopt. It will be for the [N.I.] Committee to say whether any special explanations are necessary as a reply to them . . .'

[5] In a minute on this telegram Mr. Maclean wrote: 'We have sufficient evidence to show . . . that this reply has been made on the advice of the Italian and German Governments. D. D. Maclean. 23/12.'

No. 492

Mr. Ogilvie-Forbes (Madrid) to Mr. Eden
(Received December 21)

No. 642[1] Telegraphic: by wireless [W 18649/9549/41]

MADRID, December 21, 1936

Your telegram No. 365.[2]

Following is translated text of note which should reach you by bag on December 23rd.

Begins.

In acknowledging the receipt of the draft plan of control submitted for the consideration of the Spanish Government through the medium of Your Excellency,[3] I wish, in the very first place, to place clearly on record the following facts:

1. In Spain there are not two belligerents whose status allows of their being addressed in the same terms. There is, on one side, ours, a legitimate government, having its origin in the elections of the 16th February of this year, which elections are so recent that no one can even doubt the will of the country. And on the rebel side there is a handful of traitors to their own country, without any legal origin whatsoever, who have risen in arms precisely because they do not wish to respect the will of the country expressed so categorically on the 16th February, and behind them thousands of Moorish mercenaries brought in flocks from Morocco, and the military hordes of German and Italian fascists recently landed in Spain. To give to 'the authorities' of Burgos, authors of the wanton destruction of Madrid, steeped in

[1] Telegram No. 642 was received in the Foreign Office before telegram No. 640 (No. 493 below).
[2] Of December 21 (W 18281/9549/41), not printed.   [3] See No. 432, note 1.

dishonour and crime, international status, would be yet another sign of the depths to which international life has descended in our day.

2. For more than three months the Spanish Government has been denouncing to the Powers which signed the non-intervention agreement the flagrant violation of that agreement perpetrated by Germany, Italy and Portugal. Instead of during that time allowing the three above-mentioned Powers—who ignored the Committee of Non-intervention of London, and followed their usual tactics of presenting to the world 'on faits accomplis' [*sic*]—to continue to supply to the rebels aeroplanes and gases with which to murder the women and children of Madrid, it would have been possible, without the loss of a single day, to verify the facts denounced by the Spanish Government and stop the violations of the non-intervention agreement on the part of Germany, Italy, and Portugal, to whom must be attributed the continuation of the civil war in Spain, and who are responsible for the blood shed in the meantime.

3. It has always been the firm contention of the Spanish Government, and from this position it does not move one inch, that a legitimate government had and has full right to procure for itself in the light of day all the means and armament necessary to repress a rebellion in its own territory.

4. To arm the adversaries of the legitimate government from outside is a violation of all international principles, in addition to constituting a fresh form of aggression by means of armed assistance and contributing to an internal rebellion denounced by the representatives of Spain in the Assembly of the League of Nations. To give, on the contrary, to the legitimate government the means to maintain its authority in the country has been, until the case of Spain, the rule and practice to which international conduct has been in the habit of adjusting its life.

Each and every one of the facts mentioned would be sufficient to justify the Spanish Government in rejecting forthwith the draft plan of control detailed in Your Excellency's communication of the 4th December. Nevertheless, and without departing one millimetre from the position maintained up to the present, summarised in the foregoing paragraphs, and without proceeding for the moment to an examination of the plan, although a simple perusal of it shows that there are differences of such magnitude as that of not commencing by controlling the Portuguese ports, the channel through which the rebels have been obtaining supplies for so long, that Spanish Government, faithful to what it has hitherto maintained, that it places the supreme interest of the country above everything else, and in order that the non-intervention committee of London may not be able to allege at some future time that facilities have not been forthcoming to enable it to discover who it is that is violating the non-intervention agreement, agrees to accept in principle the draft plan of control, reserving fully the right to discuss it and oppose it in its entirety. Signed Francisco Largo Caballero.

Ends.

No. 493

Mr. Ogilvie-Forbes (Madrid) to Mr. Eden
(Received December 22, 9.30 a.m.)
No. 640 Telegraphic: by wireless [W 18613/62/41]

Important   MADRID, *December 21, 1936*

Your telegram No. 356.[1]

You mention community under my 'charge'. I suggest that this is a misconception, for if it were so, I would have cleared them out of Madrid long ago. 'Protection' is better term.

There is an important preliminary question. If the Embassy withdraws from Madrid,

1. Should it withdraw altogether from Spain or to Valencia or elsewhere? I learn that conditions are very bad, that it is overcrowded, liable to bombardment and to a possible further movement of Government. Would not transfer from Madrid to Valencia be from the frying pan to the fire?

2. To what extent should Spanish and foreign personnel be allowed to accompany us? Can they be left to their fate in these tragic circumstances? Embassy would of course be closed and caretaker if any would have no representative capacity.

In considering main question of withdrawal, interests of British subjects who refuse to leave now take a secondary place. I have nevertheless a distinct feeling that whatever you may decide about the staff it is my duty to stay here as long as it is physically possible. It is difficult to be precise about motives but they are roughly as follows:

1. Although unfortunately I cannot stop outrages committed by both sides my presence here and reports to you and a good position we have with the authorities are undoubtedly a deterrent.

2. You would have no channel with local experience for mediation and humanitarian work here of all kinds most urgently needed.

3. I am sure that local authorities and I think Valencia Government would not like Embassy to move and a representative upper class Spaniard admitted that he and his friends, despite any individual resentment at refusal of asylum, highly valued the presence of the Embassy and would deplore its departure as signal for attack on Missions harbouring refugees and for other outrages.

4. British property and interests would almost certainly be attacked and Embassy buildings probably looted for food and raided for refugees and valuables.

5. I place British persons last because most of these ought not to be here and are taking advantage of my presence.

There is however an argument against staying on, an argument of shame. Shame at staying on here with food supplies while surrounded by starving women and children. This is point on which I am sensitive.

[1] No. 478.

To sum up. I think that it is my duty to stay here until ordered out by you or by Spanish authorities for military reasons or bombed out or supplies exhausted and then to make the best of it. If we suffer casualties it cannot be helped as we are all volunteers.[2]

[2] This telegram produced a further bout of minuting in which the Foreign Office discussed the pros and cons of Mr. Ogilvie-Forbes's withdrawal. Mr. Howard (December 23) thought that he was weakening to a certain extent. Mr. Roberts (December 23) thought that Mr. Ogilvie-Forbes felt 'a personal call to continue as long as possible his work of mercy, and that he cannot leave without doing violence to his conscience'. Mr. Eden commented: 'I have no doubt this is true.' Sir G. Mounsey, however, in a long minute of December 23, summed up in favour of withdrawal; Sir R. Vansittart and Mr. Eden indicated their agreement.

No. 494

Mr. Eden to Mr. Lloyd Thomas (Paris)
No. 2174 [R 7650/226/22]

FOREIGN OFFICE, *December 21, 1936*

Sir,

During the course of a conversation with the French Ambassador today His Excellency spoke about the Anglo-Italian conversations in Rome. He stated that he had done his best while in Paris to bring it home to the French Government that a successful issue of these conversations was in their interest, and he thought that he had made some impression. But he wished to impress upon me how important it was that the publicity attendant on the conclusion of these conversations should be carefully handled. It would be of the greatest assistance to the French Government if they could be informed of the outcome of the conversations and of the terms of the agreement if possible 48 hours, or at least 24 hours before actual publication. The essential was that the French Government should be in a position to say 'Yes, we knew all about this and we warmly approve what has been done'. If they were placed in a position to take this line things would be very much easier for the French Government. I undertook to do my best to meet the French Government's wishes as to publication, and said that in any event it was our intention to keep the French Government informed, and also the other Governments principally interested in the Mediterranean.

2. I then gave M. Corbin a general account of the present state of our negotiations, pointing out that I had not yet received an account of the meeting between Sir E. Drummond and Count Ciano today.

3. The Ambassador thanked me and once again reminded me that there would be plenty of critics of the Government in France ready to say: 'You are always boasting of your good relations with the British, now see how they treat you. They make an arrangement with Italy and leave you high and

dry.' Such criticism could be met, but it was important not to underrate it, and to do everything possible to forestall it.[1]

I am, &c.,

ANTHONY EDEN

[1] A minute by Mr. Norton of December 29 included the following: 'Sir George Clerk telephoned this morning to emphasise the importance of letting the French Government know at least twenty-four hours before publication of the Anglo-Italian accord. He said that the withdrawal of Mr. Ogilvie-Forbes to Valencia [see No. 510 below] had perturbed the French considerably . . .'

No. 495

Mr. Eden to Mr. Lloyd Thomas (Paris)
No. 2176 [C 9106/4/18]

FOREIGN OFFICE, December 21, 1936

Sir,

The French Ambassador asked to see me this afternoon when he began by stating that he had been authorised by his Government to hand me the enclosed reply to our memorandum on the subject of the Locarno negotiations.[1] The French Government were anxious unless we saw any objection, to communicate their reply to Berlin and Rome. I told the Ambassador that far from seeing any objection to such a course I was inclined, as a first impression and before having read the French reply, to consider that there was every advantage in the French Government acting as they wished. We agreed that unless I saw any reason to modify this opinion within the next twenty-four hours, the French Government would act accordingly.

I am, &c.,

ANTHONY EDEN

[1] Cf. No. 389. The French reply, dated December 19, is printed in *D.D.F.*, *op. cit.*, as an *annexe* to No. 178. It was noted in the Foreign Office that the 'French Government are in general agreement with our views, as expressed in our memorandum of November 19th'. Sir R. Vansittart wrote on January 2, 1937: 'The French reply is satisfactory. If we have not already done so, we shd. let it be known that we have received it. This may hasten the others . . . It wd. be very dangerous to get representatives of the 5 powers round a table yet awhile. It might mean the premature end of negotiations. Anyhow I don't think the Germans wd. come.' Mr. Eden wrote: 'This is quite satisfactory. We must now await the other replies. A. E. Jan. 7.'

No. 496

Mr. Eden to Mr. Lloyd Thomas (Paris)
No. 2179 [W 18616/9549/41]

FOREIGN OFFICE, December 21, 1936

Sir,

When the French Ambassador came to see me this afternoon we spoke of the situation in Spain. The Ambassador explained that he had had conversations on this subject both with M. Delbos and with M. Blum. The latter's position was once again becoming very difficult—as difficult as it had been in August when there had been so much delay in the acceptance by Germany of non-intervention. He had been begged by French Ministers to impress upon His Majesty's Government the urgent need in their view for the acceptance of some scheme of control. If the Non-Intervention Committee were to meet on Wednesday[1] and then to adjourn until after the holiday with absolutely nothing done, he feared the effect of the *impasse* would be very serious indeed. The Committee now had a scheme which was much less ambitious than that originally proposed. Its cost, for instance, was little more than half of the original scheme, the total cost being at the rate of £600,000 a year. This when divided up among the European States was surely not too much to pay if it assisted to maintain peace. In any event he had been instructed to make his Government's position clear at the Committee on Wednesday. He would state that they favoured the scheme, that they wished it to be put into force at once, and that they were willing to pay their share of the expense. The French Government earnestly hoped that we would take up a similar attitude.

2. I replied that it seemed to me that even more important than a scheme of control was to attempt to secure agreement among all the Governments to stop their nationals going to fight in Spain. Surely it would be of the greatest assistance to the French Government if we could get a declaration from all the Powers concerned saying that they would take whatever legislative or administrative steps that might be necessary as from a certain date to stop their nationals leaving to take part in the Spanish War. The Ambassador replied that no doubt this would be helpful, but he was sceptical as to whether the other Powers would be willing to agree. Moreover even if they made promises, such promises would scarcely be believed after recent experience unless their sincerity could be checked. That was why the French Government attached such importance to a scheme of control, which even if not wholly effective would moderate the extent and number of the breaches.

3. I gave the Ambassador some account of my interview with M. Maisky[2] earlier in the day when His Excellency remarked that if Germany were really to send 50,000 men to Spain he really did not know how French opinion could be restrained.[3]

I am, &c.,
ANTHONY EDEN

[1] i.e. December 23.
[2] See No. 498 below.
[3] M. Corbin gives a somewhat fuller account (*D.D.F., op. cit.*, No. 189) of this interview. With regard to the control scheme Mr. Eden 'examinera s'il peut s'associer au projet de déclaration dont je communiquerai le texte à Lord Plymouth'. For his part M. Corbin promised, with regard to the problem of the volunteers, which Mr. Eden 'tient particulièrement à cœur', that the French Government 'le seconderait volontiers du moment qu'il s'agit d'un accord à établir entre toutes les puissances intéressées'. See No. 505 below.

No. 497

Mr. Eden to Sir N. Charles (Brussels)
No. 648[1] [C 9037/7284/4]

FOREIGN OFFICE, *December 21, 1936*

Sir,

With reference to my despatch No. 608 of the 30th November,[2] recording my conversation with M. van Zeeland regarding the attitude of the Belgian Government as a result of the situation created by the withdrawal by Belgium of the guarantee which she has hitherto given to France, I have to inform you that on the 17th December Mr. Sargent spoke to the Belgian Chargé d'Affaires on my instructions in the sense of the annexed aide-mémoire.

2. A copy of the aide-mémoire was at the same time given to the Belgian Chargé d'Affaires.

I am, &c.,
ANTHONY EDEN

ENCLOSURE IN No. 497

Aide-mémoire

FOREIGN OFFICE, *December 17, 1936*

There are certain points arising out of the recent conversation of the Secretary of State for Foreign Affairs with the Belgian Prime Minister which have now been further considered by Mr. Eden, as the latter undertook to do. It may be useful to set out the resultant comment at this stage.[3]

1. M. van Zeeland referred to article 3 of the text of proposals drawn up in London on the 19th March,[4] according to the relevant passage of which the parties to those proposals 'declare that nothing that has happened before or since the said breach of the Treaty of Locarno (i.e., the reoccupation of the Rhineland) can be considered as having freed the signatories of that treaty from any of their obligations or guarantees and that the latter subsist in their entirety.' In informing Mr. Eden that the Belgian Government consider themselves bound by this obligation, M. van Zeeland emphasised the fact that it was of a provisional character and that it could not be allowed to crystallise into a permanent obligation. He added that he considered that the provisional period could not last much longer in view of the decreasing prospects of a new Western treaty.

Mr. Eden does not suppose that the Belgian Government intend to raise the question of the continuance of this obligation until the exchanges of views at present proceeding between the five Powers are complete. He would, however, express the earnest hope that the Belgian Government will, while awaiting the conclusion of these exchanges, make no definite move in this

---

[1] No. 2168 to Paris, *mutatis mutandis.* [2] See No. 430, note 5.
[3] Cf. No. 433, note 4. [4] Volume XVI, No. 144.

matter without further discussion with His Majesty's Government in the United Kingdom.

2. M. van Zeeland seemed to suggest that in the event of the failure of the discussions now proceeding an attempt might be made to conclude a new treaty in which Germany, the United Kingdom, France, and possibly also Italy, would each agree to guarantee the independence and integrity of Belgium. He thought that the Netherlands might be ready to participate in such a treaty on the same terms as Belgium. He seemed also to think that such a treaty might be accompanied by another Anglo-French or Anglo-French-German treaty guaranteeing the frontier between France and Germany as it was guaranteed under the Treaty of Locarno, though Belgium would not be a party to this second treaty.

Mr. Eden feels bound to point out to M. van Zeeland that there seem to be serious difficulties in the way of this suggestion; and he would be grateful if, until the situation has further developed, the Belgian Government would refrain from putting it forward.

3. Mr. Eden has taken note of the Belgian Government's view that, while Belgium recognises herself to be bound by paragraph 3 of article 16 of the Covenant of the League of Nations as regards the passage of troops across her territory in certain circumstances, Belgium should in every case be the judge as to when and whether those circumstances had arisen.

4. Mr. Eden hopes that the steps which the recent declarations of King Leopold and M. van Zeeland have shown it to be the intention of the Belgian Government to take to prevent the passage of the forces of an aggressor State across Belgian territory apply not only to the passage of land but also to that of air forces. His Majesty's Government attach particular importance to this being the case.

5. Mr. Eden sees considerable advantage in M. van Zeeland acting on the indication which he gave to him in the course of his recent visit, that he will at an early date try to find a pretext for an unofficial visit to Paris to discuss the position with the French Government.

No. 498

Mr. Eden to Viscount Chilston (Moscow)
No. 651 [W 18617/9549/41]

FOREIGN OFFICE, *December 21, 1936*

Sir,

The Soviet Ambassador asked to see me this morning when he spoke to me about the situation in Spain. He said that he wished once more to emphasise the Soviet Government's desire was not to set up a communist administration in Spain. What they did desire was a set-back for the 'aggressor'. The Soviet Government's information was that the German Government was now considering the possibility of sending 60,000 men to Spain. The Reichswehr were opposed to such an adventure, but Herr Hitler and the Nazi Party were in favour of it and were using the argument that the Reichswehr's previous fears in respect of the occupation of the Rhineland had been unjustified. In view of Germany's present hesitation the Soviet Government considered that this was the psychological moment to attempt some action. What was His Majesty's Government's view?

2. I replied that we too were fully conscious of the dangers inherent in the situation in which several nations were allowing large numbers of their nationals to proceed to Spain. We had already expressed our view on this subject both through the diplomatic channel and in public.[1] I reminded the Ambassador that the Germans maintained that the Russians had the largest number of men in Spain at present. I did not know what the comparative figures were, but I had even heard the figure of 50,000 mentioned as the estimate for Russia.

3. The Ambassador immediately denied that the number of his country-men in any way approached that figure. In any event they had not sent regiments of soldiers, but only a small number of technical experts—I interjected 'And aviators'. The Ambassador did not specifically deny this.

4. M. Maisky went on to say that he wished to make it absolutely clear that his Government were prepared to join in any international action to stop the flow of volunteers to Spain. They were not prepared, however, to take any unilateral action and they hoped that neither we nor the French Government would do so or the only effect would be that Germany and Italy alone would be sending men to Spain.

5. On the Ambassador once again emphasising the seriousness of the situation created by the Spanish civil war and the attitude of the Italian and German Governments—more particularly the latter—towards that war, I asked the Ambassador what action the Soviet Government proposed to take. To this His Excellency replied that he thought it imperative to make it plain to Herr Hitler that we could not agree to the despatch of such a force as 60,000 Germans to Spain. After all, the despatch of such numbers as these amounted to an attack on Spain. So far as the attitude of the Soviet Government themselves was concerned, he thought that they would be willing to join us and the French Government in any action that we were prepared to take. He was, however, very sceptical as to anything definite emerging from the Non-Intervention Committee.[2]

I am, &c.,

ANTHONY EDEN

[1] Cf. Nos. 436, 442, 449, and 481.
[2] M. Maisky's report of this interview is printed in *D.V.P.S.*, *op. cit.*, No. 424.

No. 499

Sir E. Drummond (Rome) to Foreign Office[1]
(Received December 22, 9.30 a.m.)
No. 765 Telegraphic [R 7662/226/22]

ROME, *December 22, 1936, 2.45 a.m.*

PART I

Your telegrams Nos. 481[2] and 482.[3]

After dealing with reduction of status of Legation at Addis Ababa[4] I said to Minister for Foreign Affairs this morning that I had sent home the draft declaration containing his personal suggestions[5] and that my government had given it very careful consideration. They were now ready to adopt form which he had proposed, namely a draft declaration signed, I presumed, by the two of us rather than an exchange of notes. They had also endeavoured to embody a large part of his text in the new draft. I then gave him draft contained in your telegram No. 482 and he read it through.

2. When he reached the phrase 'particularly the territories of Spain' he stopped and said he regretted that he could not accept these words. He was ready to give us any formal assurances which we wished that as far as Italy was concerned there would be no modification whatever as regards status of these territories; they would remain Spanish. He had already given solemn assurances which had been made public on the point and he was ready to repeat them to us in whatever way we thought needful but he did not think it possible to accept the statement made in proposed declaration. His reason was that it would be unfair and do much damage if not indeed irreparable harm, to General Franco whose government Italy had recognised.[6] That such an expression should be used would imply that some doubt had existed as to whether General Franco had not intended to part with these territories and this would place him in an invidious position, particularly as one of his main appeals was to Spanish nationalism. He clearly felt strongly and genuinely on this point and said that it would be 'playing a low trick' on General Franco. He then observed that Rossi and his secretary were leaving the Balearic Islands tomorrow.[7] I said that I knew that their departure would be appreciated by my government but I trusted that activities of any other Italian agents who were in the Islands would be equally suspended. I said that I must lay stress on this point because the Balearic question loomed large in our public opinion. Count Ciano replied that as far as he was concerned he knew of no agents, and he again emphasised that if we wanted assurances about the future of the Islands he was prepared to give them to us. I said that I could only report his remarks on this point to my government.

[1] *The Times* announced on December 22 that Mr. Eden would leave London that day for Yorkshire, 'where he hopes to enjoy a fortnight's change of air'. He returned on January 4, 1937.

[2] No. 482.   [3] No. 483.   [4] Cf. Volume XVI, No. 486, note 2.
[5] No. 441.   [6] See No. 385, note 1.   [7] Cf. No. 477.

3. He then finished reading draft declaration and said that at first sight this was the only point to which he had objection to offer but of course he would require a little time to examine carefully the text.

4. Just before I left Count Ciano reverted again to the words in declaration 'the national status of territories in the Mediterranean area, particularly the territories of Spain'. He was not, he said, quite certain what the phrase 'the national status of territories' meant. Our previous text spoke of 'the territorial status quo'. Why had we changed it? He believed that our phrase had been chosen in order to facilitate the inclusion of the words 'particularly the territories of Spain'. I replied that I thought that the meaning was clear enough. Rhodes belonged to Italy; therefore national status of Rhodes was Italian and we disclaimed any desire to modify or to see modified that status. His Excellency said he understood but found translation of phrase into Italian very difficult. I gathered however that he was not likely to make difficulties on this particular point provided that we ultimately agreed to the omission of the words 'particularly the territories of Spain'. He repeated once more his readiness to give us any assurances we desired on this matter.

5. I proceeded to say that my government wanted to take this opportunity to clear up all points of possible friction and to improve our relations generally so that signing of declaration would not only cause a *détente* but would pave the way to a progressive and general rapprochement. Count Ciano concurred in this aim. I said this being so I should like to revert to certain questions which I had mentioned before and to make, as it were, the *tour d'horizon* for which he had himself asked on a previous occasion.

6. The first point was the naval treaty. I stated that although the United States had ratified this treaty neither we nor France had yet done so. We had been awaiting the results of our negotiations with Germany and with the Soviet Government. We hoped however to ratify early in the New Year[8] and we confidently expected that if and when we ratified Italy would quickly accede. This would constitute a most important point towards improvement of our relations. Count Ciano answered that, while he was not able to give me a definite assurance here and now, I could take it for granted that there would be no political difficulty about Italy's accession so soon as the three Powers had ratified. Italy could not accede thereby binding herself until these ratifications were completed. Treaty was now being examined from a technical point of view. I observed that I felt sure that from a technical point of view equally no difficulty would arise and I pressed him again. As a result he gave me to understand that once Mediterranean agreement had signed and ratifications were complete Italy would accede; he could undertake no formal engagement but invited me to leave the matter in his hands—adopting the same phraseology as I had myself used on a previous occasion when speaking to him about reduction of status of Legation at Addis Ababa. I feel convinced that we can rely on satisfactory action by Italy on this point.

[8] Cf. Volume XIII, No. 718.

7. I then spoke of anti-British propaganda in the Middle East and begged that he would give this matter his . . . [9] est possible attention since my government attached the greatest importance to it. To continue, I said, such propaganda would not be at all in accordance with friendly relations which we now hoped to induce. We heard from various sources that Italian propagandists were endeavouring to persuade Arabs generally that Italy treated and would treat them better than Great Britain, thus stirring up disaffection. His Excellency took note of the point and said that he would give it serious attention. He remarked however that he had been into the case of the two men whose names I had previously mentioned, namely Shekib Arslan and Ihsan El Jabi.[10] He had instituted a very careful enquiry which had resulted in statement being sent to the police that neither of these two men had been in Italy for the last year and a quarter. I said this was contrary to my information but he remarked that if he had not been convinced of the truth of what he said he would not have replied as he had done but would have left the matter in abeyance. He sent for the official who had been in charge of the enquiry in order that he should explain matters to me but unfortunately he was away for a day or two. In my view the main difficulty here lies in the fact that if Count Ciano gave us any assurance that propaganda would cease it would constitute admission on his part that it had existed, which so far he has denied. Nevertheless I think we can obtain in practice a change and a cessation at least to a considerable extent of these activities.

8. I then passed to Arabia and said that we wished our relations there to be placed on a footing of complete friendliness. Count Ciano replied that he was not aware of the situation in Arabia but certainly any questions which existed between us in those regions should be settled in most friendly fashion.

[9] The text was here uncertain.   [10] Cf. No. 426.

No. 500

Sir E. Drummond (Rome) to Foreign Office
(Received December 22, 9.30 a.m.)
No. 765 Telegraphic [R 7662/226/22]

ROME, *December 22, 1936, 2.45 a.m.*

PART II

9. I next raised the question of settlement of Franco-Italian relations. I said that we were not happy at the present state of relations between France and Italy and if they could be improved our *détente* would be all the more successful. Count Ciano replied that as a matter of fact there were no direct causes of friction between France and Italy. He explained the feeling against France over Abyssinian question had always been more bitter than against Great Britain. After Franco-Italian agreement of January 1935[1]

[1] See Volume XIV, No. 90, note 3.

718

Italy expected that France would refuse to apply Sanctions. Instead she had done so and this had led to the feeling that France had treated Italy unfairly and had caused special bitterness. When matters were beginning to improve the popular front Government came into power and the Spanish question arose. Italy was aware that France had furnished Spanish forces opposed to General Franco with very large quantities of aeroplanes and munitions and with numbers of men. Letter which had been published in French press recently afforded full confirmation of this point. I observed that letter had been ... [2] previous to non-intervention agreement but Count Ciano answered that this was all very well, but no government could so completely change its opinion in a day. Further the popular front government was always showing its hostility in small ways to Italy. He did not say that from Italian point of view Monsieur Blum's government might not be preferred to a Fascist government in France since aftermath would certainly cause Italy much trouble but this was beside the point. He further explained that relations between France and Italy had always been rather stormy. Violent love succeeded violent quarrels; he himself was optimistic about the future particularly if the Spanish question were once settled. France however had never made any generous gesture towards Italy. I remarked that French reduction of status of their Legation at Addis Ababa might be so regarded but I fear that Count Ciano from the look he gave me knows quite well that it was only owing to our persistence and to the fear of being left in the lurch that the French took this action.

10. I did not think it wise to mention the subject of the League at this interview though I was told yesterday[3] from a good source that when some outside person had spoken of the matter to Count Ciano he had replied, 'once we have made friends with the English we shall be able to inject new life into the League'.

11. Having thus exhausted all substantive points mentioned in my instructions I asked the Minister for Foreign Affairs whether he would now in his turn raise such subjects as he felt were likely to cause friction since we wished if possible to clear up everything outstanding between us. His Excellency answered that he could think of nothing for the moment and as the only questions which it occurred to me he was likely to raise were Egypt, Malta and Suez Canal I did not think it wise to press him any further although I observed that *tour d'horizon* had been distinctly of use.

12. Finally I remarked that speaking without instructions and quite apart from these questions I had heard that Turkish Ambassador had been to see him about Italy's accession to Montreux Convention. Could he tell me anything about this? I knew that my government would like to see Italy accede but they had prepared [? preferred] not to raise the point as they considered it a little delicate at present juncture. I could not however but observe that Italian press seemed singularly ill-informed about that convention since they talked as if owing to convention the Russian fleet could now pass through the Straits, which previously had been closed to them. He

[2] The text was here uncertain.   [3] December 20.

must know that this was not in accordance with the facts since by Treaty of Lausanne no difficulties had been placed in the way of exit. The Minister for Foreign Affairs answered that he had deliberately refrained up to a short time ago from any examination of Montreux Convention (I gathered that he had let his press write anything they chose on the subject whether accurate or not), but that he was now considering it and although Italy did not much like it he thought ultimately she would accede. Question had unfortunately been linked up with attitude of League of Nations and Italy had not therefore gone to Montreux.[4] Even though he did not altogether approve of the convention he had come to believe that its conclusion had been the only way out of a difficult situation. Finally he indicated that once our Mediterranean agreement was reached and relations between Italy and Turkey consequently became more friendly it was probable that Italy would accede to the convention.

13. Count Ciano enquired when I thought we should be able to sign agreement. I said that it might be well to allow a lapse of some days in order to show that there was no connexion between the action His Majesty's Government had taken with regard to Abyssinia and Mediterranean negotiations. I suggested if all went well that signature could perhaps take place towards the end of this month, say the 28th or 29th, but this of course must depend on views of my government.

[4] See Volume XVI, Chapter VI.

No. 501

Sir E. Phipps (Berlin) to Foreign Office
(Received December 23, 1.45 p.m.)
No. 387 Telegraphic [W 18765/62/41]

BERLIN, *December 23, 1936, 1.4 p.m.*

My telegram No. 442 Saving.[1]
Question of reinforcing General Franco is now in the foreground.
As reported in my telegram No. 448 Saving[2] the General Staff are against increased commitments in Spain. On the other hand the hotheads are urging that it will be disastrous for German prestige if General Franco is left in the lurch. Amongst the hotheads must be reckoned General Goering and the Air Ministry. A British subject who visited friends at the Air Ministry on December 21st found the atmosphere bellicose. He was assured that the German Government could not allow the Reds to win and that whatever German reinforcements were required to assure General Franco's victory would be sent out, cost what it might.
On previous occasions when it has come to a pinch Herr Hitler has overridden the prudent counsels of the General Staff.

[1] No. 489.   [2] Not printed.

No. 502

Sir E. Drummond (Rome) to Foreign Office
(Received December 23, 1.30 p.m.)

No. 770 Telegraphic: by telephone [R 7681/226/22]

Important   ROME, *December 23, 1936*

My telegram No. 765[1] and your telegram No. 482.[2]

Count Ciano told me this morning that he had been studying carefully the draft declaration I had given him.

He had consulted the Head of the Government regarding the phrase 'particularly the territories of Spain' and Signor Mussolini had completely confirmed the line he himself had taken with me. Italian Government could make no declaration which would have the appearance of reflecting on General Franco or on the policy of the Nationalist party.

Apart from this the Italian Government had only three modifications to suggest:

(*a*) The addition of the words 'exit from' to be inserted in paragraph 3 after words 'entry into', the phrase then reading 'entry into, exit from and transit through'.

(*b*) In paragraph 4 substitute for words 'national status of territories', the words 'the status quo of territories'. Count Ciano told me that he and his experts had been endeavouring to find a suitable Italian translation for 'national status' but had been unsuccessful. A literal translation would necessarily have reference to internal situation, laws etc. in the territories in question; they therefore hoped their modification would be adopted but were of course ready to consider any other form of words His Majesty's Government might care to propose.

(*c*) In penultimate paragraph substitute for word 'establishment' the word 'consolidation'. His Excellency thought this more closely represented the existing position.

[1] Nos. 499 and 500.   [2] No. 483.

No. 503

Sir E. Phipps (Berlin) to Foreign Office
(Received December 24)

No. 452 Saving: Telegraphic [C 9152/4/18]

BERLIN, *December 23, 1936*

The wise words of warning that you have recently uttered in public speeches and in the House of Commons have fallen unpleasantly on Nazi ears. It is unlikely therefore, nor do I wish it otherwise, that Herr von Ribbentrop is spending a very pleasant Yuletide with his master.

The German Ambassador's carefully laid English plans and opportunities for intrigue have, in certain important details, miscarried, and a review of his first official weeks in London can hardly have afforded either himself or Herr Hitler much cause for rejoicing.

Nazi Germany is beginning to realise that the brilliant period of bloodless victories by means of Treaty violations is over. I only trust that we shall continue to refrain from allowing ourselves to be bullied or coaxed into increasing its prestige and strength by weakening on the colonial question. Nazi Germany will not, I feel sure, venture to attack a rearmed Britain, merely because the latter declines to succumb to bluff.

No. 504

Letter from Sir F. W. Leith-Ross to Sir R. Vansittart
[C 156/37/18][1]

TREASURY CHAMBERS, *December 23, 1936*

My dear Vansittart,

I enclose herewith a record[2] of a talk which I had today with Lever[3] of the Prudential, who is the active head of the British Committee on German Long-Term Loans.

The first part of this note contains Lever's account of an interesting conversation which he had with Dr. Schacht on the 21st instant. Schacht stated that when he was in Paris he proposed to the French Government[4] a general settlement of outstanding questions, both political and financial; that in putting forward this proposal he had the Führer's authority and promise of full support; that he understood that the French Government would sound us on this proposal; and that he is gravely disappointed that we have taken no steps to examine it.[5] He added that he was ready to arrange a private visit here if that would help.

Schacht is such a curious fellow that he may have invented this picture and the account which he gives of his conversations in Paris does not correspond (if I remember aright) with the reports which we received of these conversations from the French side;[6] but it may be that Schacht did not explain himself very clearly to the French or that they on their side were not disposed to take him as seriously as he does himself. I think, however, that you ought to consider whether, in the light of this talk, it might not be a good thing to get Schacht over here and see whether he has any proposals which would help to break the present deadlock.

The second part of the conversation is primarily for the Treasury, but it may be of interest to you to see.

Yours sincerely,
F. W. LEITH-ROSS

---

[1] This file number refers to 1937.   [2] Not printed.
[3] Mr. E. H. Lever had been in Berlin to arrange for the renewal of funding of interest on non-Reich loans.   [4] See Nos. 141 and 145.
[5] Cf. Nos. 210, 228, and 229.   [6] See Nos. 145, 210, and 224: cf. No. 141, note 4.

No. 505

Foreign Office to Sir E. Phipps (Berlin)

No. 246[1] Telegraphic [W 18814/9549/41]

Important　　　　　　　　　FOREIGN OFFICE, *December 24, 1936, 7.30 p.m.*

For some time past His Majesty's Government in the United Kingdom have observed with growing concern the increasing number of foreigners entering Spain for the purpose of taking part in the civil war in that country. In their opinion this development constitutes a grave danger to the peace of Europe and they therefore consider that it is of the utmost importance that steps should be taken by the Governments represented on the Non-Intervention Committee to put an immediate stop to the departure from their respective countries of their nationals with a view to taking service with either of the parties in Spain.

At a meeting of the Non-Intervention Committee on December 4th,[2] the United Kingdom representative made an appeal in this sense, as a result of which all the representatives undertook on December 9th[3] to ask their respective Governments to agree to the extension of the Non-Intervention Agreement to cover indirect as well as direct intervention and as a first step that this extension should cover the question of 'volunteers'.

From the start the German, Italian and Portuguese Governments have taken the line that the question of 'volunteers' forms only a part of the more general one of indirect intervention and that all aspects of this latter question, especially the problem of financial assistance, should be dealt with together. It was, however, hoped that they might nevertheless agree to discuss the question of 'volunteers' first on the understanding that the other aspects of the problem would also be examined as soon as possible.

At a meeting held on December 22nd[4] Lord Plymouth again stressed the importance which His Majesty's Government attach to this question and the urgency with which they consider that it should be dealt with. He then proposed that in order to put a stop to the present situation, each Government should be asked to take itself the action necessary to prevent the departure of its nationals to take part in the war in Spain and that the date of the enforcement of the prohibition should be January 4th. In reply to this suggestion the representative of the U.S.S.R. said that he could not agree to any such prohibition until a system of control was actually in operation. This, as you will understand, would entail considerable further delay, and thus' defer the opportunity which this proposal offers to the participating Governments of giving fresh proof of their determination to make the operation of the Non-Intervention Agreement more effective.

[1] No. 497 to Sir E. Drummond (Rome), No. 168 to Sir C. Wingfield (Lisbon), No. 154 to Viscount Chilston (Moscow).

[2] The reference should be to the meeting of the Chairman's Sub-Committee on December 4: see No. 449, section I.

[3] See *ibid.*, note 6.

[4] This was the seventeenth meeting of the Chairman's Sub-Committee.

This step on the part of the Soviet representative made it possible for the German and Italian representatives to insist on the appointment of a technical sub-committee to examine the matter in further detail.

In these circumstances I have come to the conclusion that no further progress can be made in the Committee and I shall accordingly be glad if you will take the matter up immediately with the Government to which you are accredited.

You should stress once again the view already put forward by Lord Plymouth to the Committee that this question is by far the most important and urgent of all those arising out of the war in Spain with which the Governments are faced. The problem involved covers all forms of recruiting as well as volunteering for service in Spain whether by groups or individually. It is therefore in the opinion of His Majesty's Government vital, if serious international complications are to be avoided, that steps should be taken without further delay to put a stop to this increasing flow of foreign nationals to Spain. His Majesty's Government therefore earnestly hope that the German (Italian/Portuguese/Soviet) Government will agree to take such legislative or other appropriate action as may be necessary to prevent their nationals leaving their territory in order to take service with either party in Spain. You should add that His Majesty's Government are confident that the German (Italian/Portuguese/Soviet) Government will agree that such measures should be taken with the utmost possible speed and that they will be glad to learn whether the latter will be prepared to put the prohibition into effect on a date early in January to be fixed by agreement with the other participating Governments in order to ensure simultaneous action.

Your French colleague will receive similar instructions from his Government[5] and you should concert with him as to the time and manner of your representations.

Repeated to Paris No. 152 Saving.

[5] *D.D.F., op. cit.*, No. 205.

No. 506

Letter from Sir F. W. Leith-Ross to Sir R. Vansittart
[C 156/37/18]

Personal   TREASURY CHAMBERS, *December 24, 1936*

My dear Vansittart,

When I wrote to you yesterday[1] enclosing a record of my talk with Lever I had not seen the very secret telegrams giving the full details of Dr. Schacht's talk with M. Blum in August.[2] I have now received these and they appear

[1] See No. 504.

[2] In the first draft of a letter to Sir E. Phipps of January 7, 1937, Mr. Sargent wrote that following the receipt in the Foreign Office of No. 504 Sir F. W. Leith-Ross had been sent a copy of the memorandum of October 29 regarding Mr. Eden's talks with M. Blum (see

to confirm, in all the principal points, the statements which Schacht made to Lever.[3]

I can well understand that you don't like the method of procedure adopted, but one must take account of the internal situation in Germany, and surely it would be advisable to follow up Dr. Schacht's approaches to see if something can be made of them to relax the present tension. It might be that when it came down to brass tacks there would still be too wide a gap between us; but if Schacht talks like this to Lever, sooner or later his version will get into the Press and if the facts[4] were published here I am not at all sure that it would not provoke considerable criticism of our attitude.

No doubt you have this in mind, but personally I was so surprised at learning the full facts that I give you my reactions for what they are worth.[5]

Yours sincerely,
F. W. LEITH-ROSS

No. 230, note 5) and of Geneva telegram No. 81 Saving of October 2 (No. 261), in order to give him 'a picture of the position arising out of Schacht's conversations with Blum in Paris and in order to show him why we expected the next move to lie with Schacht'. It is not clear whether Sir F. W. Leith-Ross was also sent a copy of No. 210.

[3] Both letters from Sir F. W. Leith-Ross were sent on Sir R. Vansittart's instructions to Yorkshire for Mr. Eden, who made some marginal comments. At this point he wrote: 'I do not agree.'

[4] Mr. Eden here commented: 'I am not afraid of the facts which are not Schacht's version of them.'

[5] Mr. Eden returned Sir F. W. Leith-Ross's letters to the Foreign Office on December 29 with a note for Sir R. Vansittart which stated that 'We have never had any definite proposals of any kind from Schacht . . . I am always prepared to examine any offer from any quarter, but I am not prepared to make a concession in advance, and it is a concession to say that we will discuss the return of Germany's ex-colonies without knowing something of what I am to be offered in return'. Mr. Eden went on to say that he was very willing to discuss the question with Sir F. W. Leith-Ross, and asked if the matter could wait for his return to London. In a telephone conversation with Sir H. W. Malkin on December 28 he expressed a desire for Mr. N. Chamberlain to be present at the meeting as well, and in a minute of December 29 Sir R. Vansittart, noting receipt of a further letter from Sir F. W. Leith-Ross (No. 519 below) agreed with Sir H. W. Malkin's suggestion for a meeting between Mr. Chamberlain, Mr. Eden, and Sir F. W. Leith-Ross in the first week of January, stating that he himself would also like to be present. For Sir R. Vansittart's own reactions to this letter see No. 512 below.

No. 507

Sir E. Drummond (Rome) to Foreign Office
(Received December 26, 5.45 p.m.)
No. 775 Telegraphic [W 18827/9549/41]

ROME, *December 26, 1936, 5.25 p.m.*

Your telegram No. 497.[1]
French Chargé d'Affaires[2] and I saw Minister for Foreign Affairs in succession this morning but before doing so we compared our instructions

[1] No. 505.   [2] M. Jules Blondel.

and found them similar in substance though some difference was revealed in the method of presentation.

Count Ciano after reading my aide-mémoire observed that he had already informed French Chargé d'Affaires that we were now asking the Italian Government to act at the end of December on the proposals they themselves had made in July. I replied that this might be so but the situation was daily becoming more serious, and their original proposals had covered both volunteers and supply of money. In our view it was essential that volunteer question should be treated immediately; financial problem could be dealt with later. I told Count Ciano in reply to a question that a similar request was being made by the French Government and ourselves in Moscow. His Excellency then said that he must refer our proposals to the head of the Government who was absent from Rome; but that he hoped to let me have an answer very soon. I pressed for an answer if practicable by December 28th.

No. 508

Foreign Office to Sir E. Drummond (Rome)
No. 498 Telegraphic [R 7681/226/22]

FOREIGN OFFICE, *December 26, 1936, 6.30 p.m.*

Your telegrams Nos. 765,[1] 766[2] and 770.[3]

We agree to addition of words 'exit from' and substitution of 'consolidate' for 'establish', but do not like 'status quo', since word 'status' unqualified by word 'national' seems to us too wide; but we would accept either 'national status quo of the territories' or preferably 'status quo as regards the national sovereignty of the territories'.

I have carefully considered Count Ciano's objections to inclusion of words 'particularly the territories of Spain', and agree, albeit reluctantly, to their omission from published declaration. I shall however undoubtedly be pressed and reasonably pressed in Parliament with questions directed to ascertaining whether Italian assurances regarding integrity of Spanish territory hold good and it is essential that I should have most definite ground for replying to such questions satisfactorily. I therefore note with pleasure Count Ciano's offer 'to give us any formal assurances which we wished that as far as Italy was concerned there would be no modification whatever as regards status of territories of Spain. They would remain Spanish', and wish to avail myself of it. You should therefore ask him in whatever way you consider most judicious to hand to you on signature of declaration a note or letter confirming formally assurance quoted above, which I can publish if and when I think necessary.

---

[1] Nos. 499 and 500.
[2] Not preserved in the Foreign Office archives.
[3] No. 502.

My own view is that the best course of all would be that His Excellency should agree that this assurance in a note or letter should be published simultaneously with the declaration. This would obviate critical questions referred to above and give the best possible send off to the declaration.

The present opportunity should also be taken of confirming explicitly but orally various further assurances given to you by Count Ciano and reported in your telegram No. 765. Accordingly you should in the course of your next conversation tell him that I have learned with much satisfaction of his intentions in regard to Naval Treaty and Montreux Convention, and that I hope that promised Italian action will mature quickly once declaration has been signed; and I take note of Count Ciano's promise to discuss Arabian affairs in friendly spirit if this becomes necessary. I also desire to express confident hope that Italian Government will give serious consideration to our complaints of anti-British intrigue and propaganda in Middle East, and will, if and when these are found to be well-founded, bring such intrigue and propaganda to an end. His Majesty's Government feel that action on these lines will help to bring about that mutual friendship and confidence and co-operation which should be natural fruit of Joint Declaration, which, if it failed to produce this result, could only bring about recurrence in more acute form of the very anxieties which it is designed to remove.

His Majesty's Government will wish to notify French Government of substance but not text of public declaration as soon as it has been signed, and Your Excellency should stipulate that it shall not be made public until 48 hours after signature. You should tell Count Ciano that I assume his Government also will be glad to show this courtesy to the third great Mediterranean military power whose susceptibilities we must both be interested to take into account.

For your own information we shall also wish to convey similar notice to Egyptian Government, and a few hours' notice to representatives in London of Turkish, Yugoslav and Greek Governments.

No. 509

Foreign Office to Sir E. Drummond (Rome)
No. 499 Telegraphic [R 7681/226/22]

FOREIGN OFFICE, *December 26, 1936, 7 p.m.*

My telegram No. 498[1] paragraph 2.

You will appreciate that in fact, and from Italian point of view, it will make practically no difference whether I have in hand a communication for public use if necessary or whether there is publication simultaneously with declaration. For on the morning on which the declaration is published I shall of course be beset here with questions whether the declaration applies to Spain, and I shall surely and naturally have to say Yes. Any other course

---

[1] No. 508.

would be neither truthful nor fair to Italy. While therefore the two courses suggested come to the same in the end, the second would, being spontaneous, have obviously a better effect on Anglo-Italian relations and give the new declaration a much warmer send off.

You should make any use you think fit of the foregoing in discussion with Count Ciano.

No. 510

Foreign Office to Mr. Ogilvie-Forbes (Madrid)
No. 375 Telegraphic [W 18613/62/41]

FOREIGN OFFICE, *December 26, 1936, 10 p.m.*

Your telegrams Nos. 632[1] and 640.[2]

I have given full weight to the considerations which you have presented for and against the further maintenance of the Embassy at Madrid.

This question is, as I see it, governed by three main factors.

1. The political situation.

Madrid has been abandoned by the Spanish Government in favour of Valencia and is now enduring a siege which in your view as in ours has every appearance of bearing a prolonged character. There seems no prospect either of an early return of the Spanish Government or of an immediate entry of General Franco. In remaining in Madrid you are not likely therefore to be in close immediate contact with the important political authorities of either side.

2. The furtherance of humanitarian and relief work.

In reply to my inquiries, I have ascertained from the Spanish Ambassador here that the statement made by the Spanish Minister for Foreign Affairs at Geneva during the recent meeting of the Council[3] represents the considered attitude of his Government. Señor Azcárate informs me that the latter do not for the present desire the assistance of any organised international relief measures. They have asked the Secretariat General of the League for the names of experts on traffic organisation and from these names will select an adviser whose services they will engage. They will await the receipt of his reports before deciding on any relief measures on a large scale and intend to keep all such measures in their own hands.

So long as this continues to be the attitude of the Spanish Government His Majesty's Government in the United Kingdom cannot pursue their proposals for organised relief in Spain on any lines hitherto contemplated and must for the time being leave humanitarian and relief work in the hands of those voluntary organisations which are already at work in Spain and are allowed to continue their individual activities there.

---

[1] In this telegram of December 18 Mr. Ogilvie-Forbes commented on Spanish plans for food relief in, and evacuation from, Madrid.

[2] No. 493.

[3] See No. 466, note 1.

Should the attitude of the Spanish Government be modified at any time, the need for your closer contact with them and your presence at Valencia would become essential; while it would still no doubt be possible for you to visit Madrid from there for any humanitarian purpose.

3. The position of His Majesty's Embassy.

It is not to be expected that the British Embassy at Madrid should, in these conditions of siege, be able to act as a source of supply for extraneous bodies or persons. Every effort would of course be made by His Majesty's Government to cope with the difficulties of keeping the staff of the Embassy itself supplied with the necessary provisions, even, as a last resort, and if such can be arranged, by means of a special system of transport to the coast, associated with the help of His Majesty's Navy.

But there are serious objections of another kind to the establishment of such a system apart from the consideration which you have in mind, viz. the contrast between the adequately supplied Embassy and the increasing surrounding starvation. This measure would establish a precedent for your colleagues which might both be distasteful to the local Spanish authorities and liable to misinterpretation or abuse in other quarters. If on the other hand your example were not followed, you would be increasingly appealed to by your colleagues, charitable bodies, and, no doubt, Spanish persons, for urgent relief from imminent starvation. You could not possibly meet all these demands, and whether you endeavoured unsuccessfully to discriminate between them or rejected them all, your difficulties must be enhanced.

My conclusion is that on political and broader humanitarian grounds there is no call for your continued presence in Madrid, while for personal reasons your withdrawal is becoming daily more desirable.

The moment has therefore come when I must, however reluctantly, instruct you to make arrangements to close the Embassy in Madrid and to withdraw with your staff and the remaining British Subjects to the present seat of the Spanish Government viz. Valencia, where the problems of maintenance and supplies can be more easily dealt with in co-operation with His Majesty's ships.

In arranging for withdrawal, you should bear in mind primarily the needs of British interests and deserving British Subjects. I must leave to your discretion the exact details of the arrangements which you can make, but we shall of course be glad to assist you in any way we can.[4]

Repeated Hendaye, Valencia.

[4] An undated draft in Mr. Eden's handwriting of a private telegram to Mr. Ogilvie-Forbes, which was apparently despatched to Madrid as No. 376 of December 26, has been preserved in file W 18613/62/41. It reads: 'I am sure you will understand the reasons for which I have reluctantly come to this decision. I should like to take this opportunity to congratulate you very warmly on the skill and courage with which you have sustained British interests and prestige during the long trying and dangerous period that you have spent in Madrid. A. E.'

No. 511

Sir E. Phipps (Berlin) to Foreign Office (Received December 28)
No. 455 Saving: Telegraphic [W 18900/9549/41]

BERLIN, *December 26, 1936*

My despatch No. 1452 marked immediate of today.[1]

The French Ambassador has seen Dr. Gaus, who, in the absence of Baron von Neurath, Herr Dieckhoff and Herr von Weizsäcker, is in charge of the Ministry for Foreign Affairs until after the New Year.

Dr. Gaus, whilst pointing out that he could not of course commit his Government in any way, seemed to think that there was very little chance of the British and French proposals being accepted. He expressed regret that the German suggestion regarding volunteers had not been carried out last August.[2]

M. François-Poncet hinted that Germans, taken from the Army, were being sent to Spain in considerable numbers. Dr. Gaus did not take this remark in good part, and interjected that it was fortunate this accusation had not been made in writing.[3]

[1] Not printed. It enclosed a copy of the communication addressed by Sir E. Phipps that day to the German Government. This was identical, *mutatis mutandis*, with No. 505, and is printed in *D.G.F.P.*, *op. cit.*, No. 165. Also enclosed in the despatch was a copy of a similar communication made by the French Ambassador on December 26, based on his instructions printed in *D.D.F.*, *op. cit.*, No. 205.

[2] Cf. No. 105.

[3] M. François-Poncet gives a fuller account of this interview in *D.D.F.*, *ibid.*, No. 211. Fuller still is Dr. Gaus's account in *D.G.F.P.*, *op. cit.*, No. 167.

No. 512

Letter from Sir R. Vansittart to Sir F. W. Leith-Ross
[C 156/37/18]

DENHAM, *December 26, 1936*

My dear Leithers,

This is a minute which I have written on your letters.[1]

I have no papers with me here, but, with reference to Sir F. Leith-Ross's letters of December 23rd and December 24th I think that the facts, speaking from memory, are these. Dr. Schacht had conversations with the French in August, and they encouraged him to pursue and expect colonial cession. But His Majesty's Government had always pronounced against it,[2] and this opposition had been confirmed again at Margate.[3] In these circumstances it was not thought wise to *encourage* him to come here for a visit, which might result in some tactless pressure from him and a further negative by His Majesty's Government—thereby making matters worse. Nor if I remember rightly did we wish to discuss with Dr. Schacht the abortive

[1] Nos. 504 and 506.   [2] Cf. No. 210, note 2.   [3] See No. 261, note 1.

topic of disarmament at a moment so unfavourable to ourselves. (We have of late thought the French also rather tactless to dwell on this subject just now). Sir F. Leith-Ross therefore wrote to him a non-committal letter,[4] leaving the next move to him,—for we were reluctant to have the appearance of running after him, in view of what had occurred. But Dr. Schacht made no further move, so far as we know, except that now, instead of making the move toward Sir F. Leith-Ross he has been talking to Mr. Lever, again however without saying what exactly is in his mind. We have never wished to exclude any such conversations, if they are likely to get us further forward. That has been, and remains, our attitude. Since August, however, Dr. Schacht has made several further rather vehement speeches about colonies. It is likely therefore that this topic is included in his 'comprehensive settlement.' If so it will not be easily reached, so long as His Majesty's Government remain of their present mind. I therefore do not quite understand Sir F. Leith-Ross's second letter. All we wish to avoid is a meeting which, if fruitless, might increase tension. And that is why we preferred to leave the running to Dr. Schacht, in the hope that if he had anything helpful in mind he would come forward with it. As he still does not do so in any clear terms, would it be possible to elicit through Mr. Lever, even if not directly to Sir F. Leith-Ross—though this would surely be preferable—what precisely or approximately is in Dr. Schacht's mind, so as to be able to judge whether a meeting would be useful or merely bring about a collision of ideas. Perhaps Sir F. Leith-Ross would care to turn this over in his mind, and I will have a talk with him immediately the Christmas holidays are over,[5] when I shall have been able to refresh my memory with a glance at the previous papers, which are not with me in the country. Meanwhile he may rest assured that no one here wishes to be obstructive; but in dealing with Dr. Schacht it is advisable to be prudent, as illustrated by Sir E. Phipps' last experience of him, when Dr. Schacht rather basely misrepresented him in public after-wards.[6] We don't want anything of the kind to occur again, because *that* made matters rather worse instead of better. So, if as I understand from Sir F. Leith-Ross'[s] first letter, he would like to explore personally with Dr. Schacht, wouldn't some preliminary exploration be wise? I feel it probable that Sir E. Phipps would advise this if consulted. We must remember that Dr. Schacht's own position is so precarious that he is apt to be rather wild, and even tortuous, in his methods of defending it. But I repeat that we have no desire at all to be obstructive, only careful.

If there is to be a question of direct conversations with Dr. Schacht, our respective chiefs will of course have to be consulted and I expect they will want to consult Sir E. Phipps and possibly their colleagues. A visit by

---

[4] No. 296.   [5] Cf. No. 506, note 5.

[6] The reference is to a speech made by Dr. Schacht at Frankfurt on December 9 in which he criticized a suggestion by a foreign diplomat, ostensibly Sir E. Phipps, that Germany should reduce her birth-rate. In telegram No. 420 Saving of December 9 Sir E. Phipps said that Dr. Schacht's remark referred to a private conversation and contained 'two gross misstatements'.

Dr. Schacht would of course be likely to arouse considerable speculation and to have some political consequences.

Yours ever,
VAN

No. 513

Sir C. Wingfield (Lisbon) to Foreign Office
(Received December 27, 3.40 p.m.)
No. 242 Telegraphic [W 18825/9549/41]

LISBON, *December 27, 1936, 1.35 p.m.*

Your telegram No. 168.[1]

As I was confined to my bed with a chill and Secretary-General of Ministry of Foreign Affairs was away the French Minister obtained interview with the Prime Minister yesterday and made communication on behalf of both of us adding that I would confirm what he said later.[2]

The Prime Minister spoke of Portuguese reservations on this subject when they acceded to the agreement, of necessity of preventing other forms of intervention and of problem of Portuguese labourers who work in Spain.

My French colleague pointed out the urgency of the problem of 'volunteers' and ease with which normal frontier traffic can be controlled by a system of passes.

The Prime Minister promised to give the matter careful consideration.[3]

[1] No. 505.   [2] *D.A.P.E., op. cit.*, Nos. 695–8.   [3] See *D.D.F., op. cit.*, No. 214.

No. 514

Sir E. Drummond (Rome) to Foreign Office
(Received December 28, 9.30 a.m.)
No. 776 Telegraphic [R 7726/226/22]

Important   ROME, *December 27, 1936, 11.5 p.m.*

Your telegrams Nos. 498[1] and 499.[2]

Assurances as regards territories of Spain. I would propose to deal with this point as follows:

I would draft a note to Minister for Foreign Affairs rehearsing question put by Mr. Noel Baker and answer given by you in the House of Commons on December 16th[3] on the subject of assurances we have received from the Italian Government in regard to occupation of the Balearic Islands by Italian subjects. I would go on that 'His Majesty's Government deduce from these different assurances that so far as Italy is concerned there will be no modification whatever as regards status of territories of Spain, which will remain Spanish'. I would conclude by stating that His Majesty's Government would

[1] No. 508.   [2] No. 509.   [3] See 318 *H.C. Deb. 5 s.*, cols. 2434–5.

be grateful if His Excellency saw his way formally to confirm the correctness of this deduction. At my next meeting with Count Ciano I would show him the draft and enquire whether he would be prepared to give me a reply to it confirming and rehearsing in writing the accuracy of deduction put forward in my communication. I am hopeful that he will accept this suggestion and I shall do my best to obtain his agreement to simultaneous publication, if he will not agree to this then of course to publication as and when you think necessary. Point of this procedure is that owing to the wording of your answer in the House the suggested exchange of notes could not be interpreted in any way as damaging to General Franco. Do you approve?

2. *Propaganda.* I should much prefer not to use word 'intrigue' but to replace it by either 'anti-British activities' or 'anti-British agitation'. Do you agree?

3. *Montreux Convention.* I do not think I should be quite justified in placing Naval Treaty and Montreux Convention on the same footing (see paragraphs 6 and 12 of my telegram No. 765).[4] You will recall that as regards the former Count Ciano gave me to understand pretty definitely that once the Declaration had been signed and ratifications of Treaty were complete Italy would accede. As regards the latter he was by no means so definite though he indicated that once Declaration was signed and relations between Italy and Turkey consequently more friendly it was *probable* that Italy would accede. I hope therefore that you will give me discretion as to exact language I hold in regard to Montreux Convention.

4. May I assume that when communication is made to the French Government it will be definitely understood that no publication is to appear in French press until after publication here and in London?

4 Nos. 499 and 500.

No. 515

Mr. Ogilvie-Forbes (Madrid) to Foreign Office
(Received December 28, 9.30 a.m.)

No. 663 Telegraphic: by wireless [W 18845/62/41]

Immediate   MADRID, *December 27, 1936*
Your telegrams Nos. 375[1] and 376.[2]
Thank you, and your instructions will be carried out with all expedition.
On informing my staff of your decision His Majesty's Consul[3] has represented with some feeling that he wishes to remain in Madrid in order both to look after British subjects who remain and also for personal reasons. He has asked for an order in writing that he should leave.
I told him that I considered your instructions covered Consulate as well as Embassy and also that the good name of the Diplomatic Service and also

1 No. 510.   2 See *ibid.*, note 4.   3 i.e. Mr. J. H. Milanes.

733

of myself would be called into question if I went away and left Vice Consul at the post of danger but that I would nevertheless refer his request to you.

If therefore you wish that Vice Consul should remain I earnestly request you to make some public statement to vindicate my reputation as in future both the service and myself may be the object of very unjust and ill-informed criticism. That being so I am prepared to make the generous gesture of not opposing his request as his presence here might in certain circumstances save life of a British subject. I apologise for boring you with this subject but on consideration it is important. I would be grateful for a reply as soon as possible.[4]

Repeated to Hendaye No. 106.

[4] A telegram *en clair* of December 28 to Mr. Eden from the Committee of the British Chamber of Commerce in Madrid referred to British industrial and commercial interests and urgently requested that Mr. Milanes be permitted to remain 'as indispensable protection of these interests'. Foreign Office telegram No. 386 of December 29, despatched at 7.30 p.m., agreed Mr. Milanes should remain. It remarked that 'clear distinction can be drawn between necessity for withdrawing Embassy and question of leaving Consulate open for limited purpose indicated above' (i.e. by the Chamber of Commerce).

On January 1, 1937, 43 persons, of whom 30 were British, left the British Embassy for Valencia in two omnibuses provided by the Defence Junta. On January 3 Mr. Ogilvie-Forbes left with the remainder of the Embassy staff for Valencia, where four flats had been taken for them.

No. 516

Viscount Chilston (Moscow) to Foreign Office
(Received January 2, 1937)
No. 721 [C 51/3/18]

MOSCOW, *December 27, 1936*

Sir,

With reference to my despatch No. 710[1] of the 15th December, on the subject of Soviet hopes of an Anglo-French entente in place of the proposed new Locarno agreement, I have the honour to inform you that the 'Journal de Moscou' of the 22nd December devoted a leading article to a review of the results of Herr Hitler's foreign policy since he came to power. The chief interest of this article lies in the undisguised satisfaction with which the writer describes the growing isolation of Germany—a process which he attributes largely to recent changes in the attitude of His Majesty's Government. It is indeed in striking contrast to the grumbling pessimism and bitter complaints of British hesitancy which have characterised the Soviet press in recent months.

2. Herr Hitler, the 'Journal de Moscou' declares, has suffered defeat after defeat in the last few months. Having destroyed the Treaty of Locarno by remilitarising the Rhineland, he did all in his power to prevent the creation of any new agreement to take its place, his whole aim being to deprive France of British guarantees. With this end in view, Herr von Ribbentrop

[1] Not printed (C 9249/4/18).

even went so far as to propose an Anglo-German bilateral pact in place of Locarno. But the result was the exact opposite of what was intended: Locarno has in fact been replaced by an Anglo-French bilateral pact of mutual assistance, and it is Germany who finds herself deprived of British guarantees.

3. The writer, in his exuberance, goes on to propound the grotesque theory that the abdication of King Edward VIII represents another of the German Government's failures: the rôle of Mrs Simpson, 'stylée par ledit M. von Ribbentrop et son prédecesseur M. Hoesch', was to introduce Hitlerite influence into the English Court . . .[2] After reading such arrant nonsense, one's first instinct is to dismiss the whole article as worthless; but allowance should be made for the singular perversions of Soviet mentality where such questions are concerned—even M. Litvinov himself, as I have reported elsewhere, appears to suffer from similar hallucinations.

4. In France also, the writer continues, German diplomacy, which aimed at the disruption of the *Front Populaire* and the replacement of M. Blum by 'un leader radical connu pour son penchant pour l'Allemagne hitlérienne', has come to grief. (I may mention in this connection that the Soviet reader knows nothing of M. Blum's difficulties with the French Communists). As for Herr Hitler's trump card, the anti-Communist front, this also has turned out a complete failure: not a single other State has joined the German-Japanese treaty, not even Austria; the attitude of all countries uncontaminated by fascism has been markedly hostile; and Great Britain, which was to have been intimidated by the treaty, has reacted by proclaiming, in the series of announcements culminating in your speech at Bradford,[3] a policy diametrically opposed to that which Herr Hitler had wished to foist upon her. In Spain, despite the joint support of Germany and Italy, General Franco has failed to bring off a victory, and you have declared quite definitely that His Majesty's Government would not tolerate the expropriation, for the benefit of any Power, of the Spanish islands and possessions.[4] 'Cela signifie que l'Angleterre ne tolérera non plus l'asservissement économique de l'Espagne'.

5. Against all these failures Herr Hitler can show scarcely anything in the way of a positive achievement. As regards the Italo-German agreement he knows that M. Mussolini 'is getting out at the next station', and the struggle for the predominating influence at Budapest, at Sofia, and even at Burgos has already begun. Italy, moreover, is obliged for economic reasons to seek an understanding with Great Britain, and this in its turn will bring about a betterment of Franco-Italian relations. Belgium has been forced, notwithstanding the King's recent speech,[5] to proclaim her fidelity to the League of Nations and to the Anglo-French agreement. All that remains are M. Beck's pro-German activities, 'a few happy intrigues in Roumania and Yugoslavia', and perhaps also the election of the 'fascisant' M. Motta.[6]

[2] Punctuation as in the original.   [3] See No. 479, note 2.
[4] See No. 514, note 3.   [5] Cf. No. 297.
[6] M. Giuseppe Motta was elected President of the Swiss Federal Council for 1937 on December 17.

But the latter is an Italian rather than a German fascist, and M. Beck's game has been spoilt to a certain extent by the engagements entered into by Marshal Rydz-Smigly [*sic*] in exchange for French gold. As for Roumanian and Yugoslav hesitations, the Western Powers have only to show greater firmness towards Germany, and to tame Italy, for the smaller States to come down definitely on the right side of the fence.

6. Herr Hitler, the 'Journal de Moscou' concludes, is now reduced to attempting a futile bluff: he places the claim for colonies in the forefront of his demands, simultaneously moves up troops towards the Swiss and Czecho-slovak frontiers, and announces through the intermediary of Dr Schacht that if the claim is not met he will not answer for the consequences. But there is no reason to fear this threat, for in Germany's present state of economic and financial stringency any form of military adventure would be sheer suicide:

> 'Il suffit aux principales forces de l'Europe d'accueillir ces menaces avec courage et avec sang-froid et de manifester une tendance à l'union véritable, fût-ce de quelques-uns des principaux pays amis de la paix, pour que l'Allemagne baisse pavillon.
>
> Dans ce cas, l'Europe réussira, sinon à se libérer définitivement du cauchemar de l'hitlérisme, du moins à le dompter. Et le domptage de l'hitlérisme sera en même temps le domptage de l'agression, non seulement en Europe, mais dans les autres parties du monde.'

7. It is not long since the Soviet press were taking the commoner line that the danger of a German military adventure was increased by the present internal difficulties of the Third Reich; though it was of course never suggested here that anything should be done to assist in alleviating those difficulties.

8. The attitude of the People's Commissariat for Foreign Affairs, as revealed in this article, towards the Italian question, is of a certain interest. Although the Soviet press as a whole has reviled Italy with considerable venom during the last few months, the view has repeatedly been expressed that the Italo-German agreement is a hollow sham which will not long stand the strain of rivalry in Central Europe. The differences which appear to have arisen between Berlin and Rome regarding the methods of supporting General Franco have evidently encouraged the belief that Italy (as opposed to Poland) can yet be edged out of the German camp, and the 'Journal de Moscou' approves by implication the Anglo-Italian conversations. This has not, however, prevented the 'Pravda' of the 25th December from describing these conversations as a proof of Great Britain's weakness, and complaining that His Majesty's Government are still 'obstinately seeking salvation through agreements with the aggressors.' Probably the explanation is that the Soviet Government are still undecided whether or not to regard Italy as irreparably lost to the cause of encirclement. That they are still far from certain, not-withstanding their recent access of optimism, as to the position of His Majesty's Government, is shown clearly enough by the 'Pravda's' reaction

(reported in my telegram No. 34 saving of the 24th December)[7] to the leading article in the 'Times' of December 21st entitled 'The German Choice'.[8]

9. It might be thought that the increasing emphasis of the German Government on their need of colonies would be regarded by the Soviet Government with comparative complacence, as tending to direct the force of a German explosion away from themselves. But M. Lapinski, in the 'Izvestiya' of the 26th December, is at great pains to show that the German colonial claim, is not what it seems. 'What', he asks, 'is the hidden meaning, what are the strategy and tactics of all this colonial agitation? In British political circles the question has been asked more than once whether these German pretensions are to be taken literally or metaphorically. If literally, then "colonies" are really colonies. If metaphorically, the cry for colonies is merely one of the methods of demonstrating to the world that Germany is feeling constricted within her own borders and is obliged to secure some sort of an outlet—if not to colonies, then to somewhere in Europe itself. In this latter case "colonies" are merely a pseudonym for expansion of another kind, and an argument for the complete exclusion from future discussions and conferences of the problems of security in the East. Put in its crudest form, this would be tantamount to giving Great Britain the choice between nurturing Germany at her own expense and giving her blessing to a war in the East.' And M. Lapinski, who at the outset of his article laid stress on the extreme unlikelihood of any serious voluntary concessions on the part of the colonial Powers, is convinced that the question of internal prestige plays only a secondary rôle in the German claim. The predominant factor, he says, is undoubtedly the serious economic position of Germany to-day:

'Second-rate colonial acquisitions would of course not better this position. They could only help to hide from the eyes of the stupefied National-Socialist masses a bargain with the so-called democratic countries—a bargain the real object of which would be to terminate Germany's economic isolation and to secure the credits of which she stands so sorely in need'. . . .[2]

10. It would be utterly naive, however, in the opinion of M. Lapinski, to believe that 'with financial credits *plus* bananas and nuts from the Cameroons one could appease fascist Germany, satisfying the demands of the "moderate" National-Socialist groups. The programme of the "moderates" has so far served invariably as a bait or cloak, as a means of spreading false information and putting people off the scent, employed by those whose appetites are still very far from satiation point and who are ready to "muscle in" anywhere where there are pickings to be had. All those who have the cause of peace at heart must desire to remove a "focus of unrest"; but for this what is required is not illusions and sops, which merely whet the appetite, but firm intentions and an equally firm policy.'

11. M. Lapinski does not attempt to explain how firmness is to achieve

---

[7] Not printed.   [8] See *The Times*, December 21, 1936, p. 13.

this object; but the Soviet Government have never even attempted constructive criticism where Hitlerite Germany is concerned; being doubtless convinced that the 'focus of unrest' will only be removed with the removal of the Nazi régime itself. What is clear enough is that they do not entertain any illusions as to the ultimate effect of colonial and other concessions to Germany for which they themselves would not have to pay; they realize that the sum total of such concessions could never be sufficient to exorcise the demon, but would inevitably strengthen it, to their own ultimate detriment.[9]

12. I am sending a copy of this despatch to His Majesty's Ambassador at Berlin.

I have, &c.,
CHILSTON

[9] Mr. Torr marked the first two sentences of paragraph 9 and the last sentence of paragraph 10 and remarked: 'See marked passages . . . Moscow apparently is *not* inclined to favour an attempt to avert the Nazi danger by concessions at our expense. C. J. W. T. 5.1.' Mr. Collier commented: 'I agree that the marked passages are important. As regards para. 3, it is not only in Moscow that such a view of the constitutional crisis has been put forward! L. C. Jan. 8th.'

No. 517

Letter from Herr von Ribbentrop to Mr. Eden
[*C 147/1/18*]

WILHELMSTRASSE 63, BERLIN, W.8, *December 28, 1936*

My dear Mr. Eden,

Now that the Christmas festivities have passed and life is again returning to its ordinary course I am sorry to have to communicate with you in the following matter which has caused me some concern:

After my return to Berlin I have seen communications from Warsaw according to which a Polish news agency is publishing reports about the conversations which I was privileged of having with Your Excellency—the last in the presence of Sir William Malkin and Herr Woermann—before my departure for Berlin.[1] These reports, misrepresenting the actual situation, seem to give evidence of a knowledge of certain details of our conversations on the part of the London informant, that there has, apparently, been a leakage such as you will remember has been the case once before in another matter.[2] As on our side nobody but Herr Woermann and myself were informed about this matter, I wanted to draw your attention to this incident and to emphasize the inconvenience which must arise if such confidential conversations are published,[3] and how helpful it would be in our common endeavour for good relations between our two countries, if such occurrences could be avoided in future.

[1] See Nos. 484, 485, 486, and 490.
[2] A marginal comment by Mr. Eden here reads: 'I am aware of no such thing.'
[3] A marginal comment by Mr. Eden here reads: 'they were not published.'

Being absent from London and therefore not in a position to communicate with you personally, I have abstained from correcting these tendencious reports, which seem susceptible to give a wrong impression of the attitude of my Government to various points raised in our conversations, f[or] i[nstance] the Franco-Sovjet Pact. I am convinced that you will regret as much as myself such misleading communications, as I know you are aware that the whole object of the question communicated by Herr Woermann in writing to Sir William Malkin[4] was a request by my Government only for *supplementary information* as regards the British Memorandum dated the 19th of November.[5] The reply of the British Government to this request, as explained by yourself in our last conversation[6]—that a country being a party to a non-ag[g]ression arrangement under a new western pact would be entitled to take immediate action against another party in the contemplated case of a conflict of this party with a third power without awaiting the previous decision of the competent body—is an important element which I consider most regrettable and which must render the very idea of non-ag[g]ression illusory, as I already had the honour of pointing out during our last meeting. But there was nothing in our conversation which, as you will agree, could have implied in any way a change of the German attitude towards the Franco-Sovjet Pact, and all combinations to this effect are without any foundation.

I am certain that I am not asking you in vain kindly to contradict—should the occasion arise—such misleading reports, especially as I have had the privilege of pointing out to you that the British Memorandum has caused all but satisfaction on the part of my Government and that a reply is still pending.[7]

For the coming year 1937 I am sending you my very best wishes and the expression of my sincere hope for a good collaboration in the interest of both our countries

and remain,
my dear Mr. Eden,
Yours faithfully
J. RIBBENTROP

---

[4] See No. 454, note 3.   [5] No. 389.   [6] No. 490.
[7] This letter is printed in *D.G.F.P.*, Series C, vol. vi, No. 111. In minutes on this letter Mr. C. W. Baxter described it as 'a rude letter' (December 31) and noted that the News Department was satisfied that there had been no leakage in the British press. He drafted a reply. Sir H. W. Malkin wrote: 'Apparently what is troubling the Ambassador is the fear that he may be accused of not having made plain his government's attitude towards the Franco-Soviet Pact in relation to the negotiations, and it is true that both he and Dr. Woermann made it clear that the latter's enquiry must not be regarded as showing any modification of the German attitude in regard to such matters as the question of "exceptions". I have added a third paragraph to the draft reply with the idea that it might both serve to reassure him on this point and to show how ridiculous the idea is that any misdescription of the German attitude could have been given out from here; the question whether it is worth while adding the paragraph might perhaps be considered. H. W. M. 31st December, 1936.' Mr. R. A. Leeper wrote: 'Mr. Barker of the *Times* told me yesterday in confidence

that Litauer, representative in London of the Polish Telegraph Agency, had passed on to him this information which he had received either from Seibert of the *Völkischer Beobachter* or Hesse of the D.N.B. Barker took it for granted that this had been done with Ribbentrop's knowledge. Of that, however, I am not so certain. What matters is that the leakage *was* German. RAL. 2/1.' The letter of reply, signed by Mr. Eden and dated January 5, 1937, will be printed in Volume XVIII.

No. 518

Viscount Chilston (Moscow) to Foreign Office (Received January 1, 1937)
No. 725 [R 19/1/22]

MOSCOW, *December 28, 1936*

Sir,

With reference to paragraph 8 of my despatch No. 721[1] of the 27th December, I have the honour to transmit to you herewith[2] an extract, in translation, from an article by M. Kantorovich in the 'Izvestiya' of the 27th December on the present Anglo-Italian conversations. This seems to bear out the opinion I expressed in that despatch, that the Soviet Government do not yet know what to make of these conversations—whether to regard them as a deal with the enemy or as a praiseworthy attempt to drive a wedge into the Italo-German rapprochement. M. Kantorovich, though he does not believe in the possibility of re-establishing the Stresa front, is inclined to favour the latter hypothesis, but declares that the Anglo-Italian understanding must be judged by its practical effect on fascist intervention in Spain. The 'Izvestiya' reproduces on the same page various rumours from the foreign press regarding the alleged intention of Sr. Mussolini to withdraw Italian support from General Franco in the near future.

I have, &c.,
CHILSTON

[1] No. 516.   [2] Not printed.

No. 519

Letter from Sir F. W. Leith-Ross to Sir R. Vansittart
[C 156/37/18]

Secret and Personal   TREASURY CHAMBERS, *December 28, 1936*

My dear Van,

In reply to your letter of the 26th December,[1] your recollection is broadly correct. But when I wrote to Dr Schacht in October[2] saying that it was for him to take the next step, I was not aware that during his visit to Paris he had already taken the initiative and I should have hesitated to write as I did had I known the facts. For Schacht had proposed to the French Government that conversations should be undertaken 'soon and confidentially' between the French, German and British Governments 'with a view to an agreement being reached which would result in Germany taking her

[1] No. 512.   [2] No. 296.

part in giving guarantees for a European settlement and joining in an agreement for the reduction and limitation of armaments if in return she could obtain some satisfaction in the colonial sphere' (Paris Tel[egram] 335 Saving).[3] In addition Schacht indicated that Germany would give a guarantee to France and Britain that she would not attack Russia. Schacht's proposals were subsequently confirmed to the French Ambassador by Herr Hitler,[4] and it was stated that the 'German Government were waiting for an answer as to whether conversations could be followed up on this basis and they hoped for an answer both from the French Government and from His Majesty's Government.'

As I understood the position, you suggested a non-committal reply to Schacht in October[5] because you thought it unwise to embark on any economic discussions without getting satisfaction on political questions. But apparently Schacht had already suggested the discussion of a general political settlement; M. Blum, while disliking the method of procedure, expressed himself as 'very reluctant to allow such an opportunity of a European settlement, if it were one, to slip'; and yet no effort was made to ascertain whether or not a definite agreement could be worked out on the basis suggested by Schacht.[6] It is this failure to follow up Schacht's initiative in any way that seems to me quite capable of being turned into a rather damaging attack on our policy.

I should have thought it was worth exploring the possibilities, as secretly as possible, and it does not seem to me that such conversations, even if not immediately successful, could make matters worse. As regards the method of procedure, you have, I think, misunderstood my letter of the 24th[7] as suggesting that I would like to explore the possibilities personally with Dr. Schacht. What I suggested was that Schacht should be allowed to come over here on some pretext or other, e.g. a visit to the Bank of England, and you could then discuss matters with him yourself.[8] If you thought it desirable, I would of course be willing to go to Berlin, but this was not in my mind, and I should prefer not to do so, as the main difficulties are political rather than financial.[9]

I should be glad to come over and have a talk with you on the whole question when you get back, but I send you this line to clear up my intention.

Yours ever,

F. W. LEITH-ROSS

[3] No. 210.   [4] See *ibid.*, note 5.   [5] Cf. No. 296, note 2.

[6] Sir R. Vansittart commented at this point: 'I do not agree. Nothing precise has ever been offered by Schacht. If he had anything precise it was up to him to *offer* it, especially as he *wanted* something precise, the ex-German colonies.' Mr. Eden added: 'Yes. This is quite untrue. I am surprised that Sir F. L[eith] R[oss] should [?write] it.'

[7] No. 506.

[8] Sir R. Vansittart here commented: 'I wd. still [like to] know *approximately* beforehand what sort of thing he wd. be offering for the colonies!!'

[9] Sir R. Vansittart here commented: 'That is the whole point. We want a political settlement. The Germans show no such sign, & make no genuine offer. Now that they are in real difficulties of course they begin the vague barrage again. No valid reason however prevents them from being *precise*.'

No. 520

Viscount Chilston (Moscow) to Foreign Office
(Received December 29, 8.35 p.m.)
No. 226 Telegraphic [W 19015/9549/41]

Immediate   MOSCOW, *December 29, 1936, 8.40 p.m. [sic]*
My telegram No. 220.[1]

Monsieur Litvinov sent for me this evening and handed me written reply in the form of an aide-mémoire. The first part of this document states that Soviet Government share concern of British and French Governments at developments in Spain. There follows lengthy passage on overwhelmingly non-Spanish composition of insurgents' forces and impossibility of regarding German and Italian contingents as volunteers. Soviet Government are strongly in favour of arresting influx of foreigners into ranks of belligerents, witness their representatives' letter of December 4th to President of London Committee.[2] But example of declaration on prohibition of import of arms shows clearly that having regard to the attitude of certain members of London Committee to their international obligations any further agreements not accompanied by simultaneous establishment of control can only favour insurgents. Soviet Government are ready to associate themselves with Anglo-French proposals on the following conditions:

1. That parties to the agreement should declare their consent to the establishment of effective control of its execution.

2. That all measures of control should be taken as soon as possible regardless of attitude of insurgent generals.

3. That the parties should 'morally bind themselves' pending establishment of control to keep track of arrival of so-called volunteers 'through their official and unofficial agents on the spot' and that reports in such cases should be published for general information.

4. That as early a date as possible should be established for conclusion of agreement in order that in intervening period it should not be possible to increase existing despatch of so-called volunteers; and that point 3 should come into force immediately.

Note concludes that foregoing conditions are considered essential by Soviet Government for attainment of objective set forth in Anglo-French proposals.

Text by bag to-night.[3]

Monsieur Litvinov told me that he will have Soviet reply published 'as soon as the English newspapers publish *démarche* of His Majesty's Government.'

Repeated to Berlin, Paris, Rome.

[1] This telegram of December 27 referred to No. 505 and reported that M. Litvinov had promised a reply on the question of volunteers in Spain when he had consulted his government.
[2] See No. 449, note 3.
[3] Not printed; see *D.V.P.S., op. cit.*, No. 437.

No. 521

Minute by Mr. Sargent on likely developments in German foreign policy
[*C 9152/4/18*]

FOREIGN OFFICE, *December 29, 1936*

Unfortunately the closing of the brilliant period of bloodless victories is not the end of the matter.[1] In other circumstances the Nazis might have been content to rest on their laurels, but as the year closes these laurels are overlaid by three [*sic*] spectacular failures which cannot be ignored: the internal economic failure, which may lead to internal disaster; the failure of Hitler's anti-communist crusade, which represents a political victory for the Soviet Government; the failure to conquer Spain for Franco, which threatens to involve Hitler in a most dangerous military commitment; and, lastly, the failure to achieve the prestige of a colony. To these we may shortly be able to add the failure of Germany to hold Italy within her orbit. It is true that none of these failures is past remedy: they can all be either cured or liquidated, but only at the cost of humiliating reversals of policy, especially in the economic sphere and as regards the anti-Bolshevic [*sic*] campaign. At one time Lenin was faced with analogous failures and was strong enough to reverse the Bolshevist policy of the time, both at home and abroad. Will Hitler be equally strong: that is the question?

If he is, then we may look forward to a new Locarno Treaty; Germany's collaboration in clearing up the present economic and currency chaos in Europe; the limitation of armaments; the return of Germany to the League; the establishment of a real policy of non-intervention in Spain; and a *détente* with Russia and Czechoslovakia. Enumerated in this fashion such *volte face* sounds, alas, too good to be true or even possible.

I am afraid the converse is far more likely, in which case Hitler will decide to go on with his present policies with diminishing hope that one or other of them will lead to a success. For it is, I think, becoming alarmingly clear that he must have a success somewhere: he cannot continue to pursue his present increasingly dangerous (i.e. to the Nazi party) policies indefinitely under the shadow of the failures to which they have so far led.

What kind of successes can Hitler hope for? Does he still hope that his economic policy, or rather the political effects of his economic policy, will so frighten this country and France that he will be able to extort a colony by way of a palliative, but without giving any quid pro quo? This may still be possible, but his expectations must surely be beginning to fade.

As regards the anti-communist campaign, it is true that Hitler has already scored a little success with his Japanese treaty,[2] but it is a very fragile success and unless it is extended it looks as though the effect will soon wear off. Hitler must be said to have definitely failed in his original object, which was to pose as the saviour of European civilisation and to rally Europe round him. His anti-communist campaign is thus rapidly degenerating into the old

[1] This is a reference to No. 503, paragraph 3.   [2] See No. 421, note 3.

743

policy of expansion suitably disguised to reassure foreign opinion. At the present moment there would seem to be only two directions in which Hitler can still hope to achieve success with this discredited policy—either in Spain or in Czechoslovakia. But does he really think that the establishment of Franco's Government in Spain is going so to strengthen Germany politically and militarily as to make it worth while for him to run the risk of a Peninsular War without being able to protect communications between Germany and Spain? It seems almost incredible, and would indeed be entirely incredible if one had to deal with men of a normal make-up. But— and this I think is a point we would do well to bear in mind—if Hitler does abandon the Spanish venture as being altogether too dangerous, will he not be driven almost inevitably to seek the success he needs in Czechoslovakia, where the military conditions are considerably easier and where he may hope by the use of bluff and propaganda to isolate Czechoslovakia and prevent the intervention of Great Britain, France, or Italy?

I submit that the time has come when we ought carefully to consider our policy as regards Czechoslovakia and Central Europe, in view of the possibility of the storm centre shifting to that quarter in the near future.[3]

[3] Mr. Eden commented on this paper, which had evidently followed him to Yorkshire: 'I agree with this most interesting minute of Mr. Sargent's & particularly the last paragraph. Let us engage on this difficult task . . . I am sure [Sir R. Vansittart] will agree that a preliminary talk between us three in the dep[artmen]t (Sir R. V., Mr. Sargent & myself) is desirable as soon as I get back. A. E. Dec. 30th.' After Tuesday, January 5, had been suggested for this discussion, Sir R. Vansittart wrote: 'Yes, certainly, do let us have this meeting on Tuesday. I too agree with Mr. Sargent's diagnosis: it is contained in my recent long memorandum on the subject [Appendix II to this Volume]. R. V. Dec. 31.'

Mr. Wigram would also, no doubt, have been drawn into these discussions, but he died suddenly at his home at Seaford on December 31, 1936, at the age of 46. A personal tribute to him by Sir R. Vansittart appeared in *The Times* of January 2, 1937. He was succeeded as head of the Central Department by Mr. W. Strang, C.M.G.

No. 522

Foreign Office to Sir E. Drummond (Rome)
No. 502 Telegraphic [R 7726/226/22]

Immediate   FOREIGN OFFICE, *December 30, 1936, 4.30 p.m.*
Your telegram No. 776.[1]

(1) *Assurances as regards territories of Spain.* I agree to procedure you suggest but in place of formula you propose I should prefer if it is possible the following wording:

'In view of these assurances His Majesty's Government in the United Kingdom assume that so far as Italy is concerned the integrity of the present territories of Spain shall in all circumstances remain intact and unmodified.'

I have replaced the word 'deduce' by 'assume' because the previous assurances applied so particularly to Italy's relations with Franco that it

[1] No. 514.

744

seems difficult to 'deduce' therefrom a general undertaking which would apply equally to the case where the Valencia Government were able to re-establish itself throughout Continental Spain. The new wording of the formula is definitely intended to cover such an eventuality, and especially the case where the Balearic Islands might eventually remain the only territory subject to Franco's Government (i.e. the Spanish Government recognised by Italy), and might wish to place themselves under the protectorate of Italy.

(2) *Publication.* Although we shall not on signature communicate the text to the French Government, you will realise that it is impossible to ensure that tendentious versions of the text will not appear prematurely in the French press. It will be convenient if you can let me know beforehand when the signature of the declaration is fixed to take place.

(3) *Propaganda.* I have no objection to the proposed alteration in the wording.

(4) *Montreux Convention.* You have discretion as to the exact language to hold as regards Italy's accession to this Convention.

(5) *British interests in Abyssinia.* When in accordance with the instructions contained in paragraph 4 of my telegram No. 498,[2] you review again with Count Ciano the various subjects touched upon during your *tour d'horizon*, I would not wish you to omit all reference to British interests in Abyssinia, although your telegram No. 759[3] shows that this subject was discussed separately. On the other hand, in view of Count Ciano's reactions, as described in your above-mentioned telegram, to your reference to the Tripartite Treaty of 1906 and the Anglo-Italian exchange of notes of 1925, I do not wish to press him regarding British rights and interests in Abyssinia for an assurance which would specifically refer to those two instruments. I should be content with a renewal, for example, of the assurance which was given by the Italian Ambassador to Sir R. Vansittart on April 3rd last, to the effect that the Italian Government were more than ever conscious of their obligations towards His Majesty's Government and had no intention whatever of overlooking or repudiating them (see my despatch No. 406[4] of April 6th).

You should also take the opportunity to inform Count Ciano that His Majesty's Government have noted his statement to you on December 23rd regarding Gambeila (your telegram No. 772[5] third sentence) which equally represents the attitude of His Majesty's Government so far as British interests are concerned.

[2] No. 508.   [3] Of December 20, not printed (J 9109/9749/1).
[4] Not printed.   [5] Of December 23 (J 9146/4044/1), not printed.

No. 523

Sir E. Phipps (Berlin) to Foreign Office (Received December 31, 3 p.m.)
No. 389 Telegraphic [W 19162/9549/41]

BERLIN, *December 31, 1936, 2.53 p.m.*

My despatch No. 1452 of December 26th.[1]

Minister for Foreign Affairs who came to Berlin for funeral of General von Seeckt asked me to call on him to-day. He told me that we should receive German reply in writing in a few days. Italian and German Governments were consulting together. Meanwhile he could assure me that it would be of a . . .[2] nature.

German Government were most desirous of joining in general measures to prevent all foreign intervention in Spain. Their reply would propose closing Spanish land frontiers and a close international [? blockade of] Spanish ports. It would even declare desirability of forcing all foreigners now fighting in Spain to leave.

I pointed out that latter measure would be very difficult to enforce and that it therefore seemed more important to prevent fresh men from arriving than to withdraw those already in Spain. His Excellency agreed but said that it would be preferable if both measures could be enforced.

Baron von Neurath leaves Berlin again to-night.

Repeated to Paris, Moscow, Rome and Lisbon.

[1] See No. 511, note 1.   [2] The text was here uncertain.

No. 524

Sir E. Phipps (Berlin) to Foreign Office (Received December 31, 7 p.m.)
No. 391 Telegraphic [C 1/1/18]

BERLIN, *December 31, 1936, 6.45 p.m.*

Your despatch No. 1427 December 19th.[1]

I asked Minister for Foreign Affairs in the course of our conversation[2] when we might expect German reply to British memorandum of November 19th regarding Western Pact.[3] His Excellency said that Sir W. Malkin's letter of December 17th[4] had not made the matter any easier. In any case however the German Government felt that negotiations would be greatly facilitated once Spanish affair . . .[5] out of the way.

[1] No. 490.   [2] See No. 523.   [3] No. 389.   [4] No. 480.
[5] The text was here uncertain.

No. 525

Sir R. Campbell (Belgrade) to Foreign Office (Received January 7)
No. 46 Saving: Telegraphic [R 134/134/22]

Confidential   BELGRADE, *December 31, 1936*

The Infante Alfonso[1] who spent three days here recently as the guest of the Prince Regent, with whom he is intimate, gave His Royal Highness the following information.

The French Devoitine bombers in use in Spain were faster and generally superior to the Italian C.R. series. Notwithstanding that fact the Italians had brought down fifty-three French machines and the French only nine Italian ones. Reason of this was the great inferiority of the French pilots in comparison with the Italian whom the Infante considered the best in the world with the exception of the British. The Germans, he said, were having great difficulty with the training of pilots but their bombers were incomparably superior to any machine as yet in existence.

The Infante had been told by the Duke of Aosta, a great friend of his, that Signor Mussolini's programme was to have ten thousand fully trained pilots in three years' time. The Duke had also said that Signor Mussolini fully realised that Abyssinia could only absorb a small number of white colonists and that in three years' time Italy would have to look elsewhere for an outlet for her surplus population. On being pressed as to where that would be, the Duke, after some hesitation, had said Tunis.

In imparting this last detail Prince Regent claimed that it lent colour to the belief which he had so often voiced to me regarding Italian designs on Tunis. He also remarked that it was curious how the period of three years was always cropping up. It had done so again the other day when the German Minister here had told him that Count Ciano, who had been very frank in Berlin,[2] had said that there was no sentiment in Italian overtures to Yugoslavia but that these were due to the desire to have as many friends as possible when in three years' time Great Britain reached her maximum strength. Count Ciano, always according to German Minister, had also said that unlike that silly little man from Trieste, Suvich, who could not see beyond the Adriatic, he—Count Ciano—had a wider vision and vaster schemes.

---

[1] Eldest son of Alfonso XIII, King of Spain until the Republic was proclaimed in 1931. In a minute of January 25 Mr. Rumbold remarked that the Infante Alfonso was 'an expert on matters connected with aviation'.

[2] Cf. Nos. 334 and 345.

No. 526

Sir E. Drummond (Rome) to Foreign Office (Received January 1, 9.30 a.m.)
No. 779 Telegraphic [R 12/1/22]

Important   ROME, *January 1, 1937, 2.20 a.m.*

Your telegram No. 502.[1]

I handed to Minister for Foreign Affairs this afternoon[2] text of draft declaration relating to Mediterranean embodying amendments to which you agreed in your telegram No. 498,[3] including phrase 'status quo as regards national sovereignty of territories in Mediterranean area' (for final version of declaration see my immediately following telegram[4]). I pointed out that we had agreed to omit the words referring specifically to Spanish territory, but that I should be compelled to ask for some assurances in regard to Spain which could be published. After reading document Count Ciano agreed to it ad referendum, that is to say, subject to final consent of head of government; but he did not consider there would be any difficulty.

2. I next handed to Count Ciano drafts of exchange of notes concerning Spanish territories except that embodied in your new wording and added that my government held that some assurance from Italy on this point was essential. I explained that form we had chosen would seem to do no damage to General Franco and I then urged on him desirability of simultaneous publication or if he felt strongly on this point we could delay publication until the moment you considered it desirable.

3. Count Ciano said that he saw no objection to substance but did object to form of two drafts. Why should Italy be regarded as suspect in this matter? Why did we not ask for similar assurances from France? or he might ask for similar assurances from us. I replied that in latter case I felt sure that my government would be delighted to give them. His Excellency then said that he could and would give me a definite assurance similar to that he had already given Mr. Ingram namely that Italy had no political or territorial ambitions in Spain. In Italy's opinion it would be disastrous if a communist Spain emerged from present civil war; Italy had certainly given some help to General Franco not because she had territorial ambitions but because she entertained genuine feelings against communism. He feared it would be difficult to accept exchange of notes if these were to be published. They were in any case unnecessary since Spain was already clearly covered by Mediterranean declaration and he repeated that he could not understand why Italy alone should give these assurances to His Majesty's Government. If Parliament had been sitting he would have made a speech which you could have quoted in House of Commons but unfortunately Parliament had risen.

---

[1] No. 522.   [2] i.e. December 31.   [3] No. 508.

[4] No. 780 of January 1, 1937, not preserved in the Foreign Office archives. The text of the declaration is given in No. 530 below.

4. I did my best to calm him and pointed out that after all I was merely asking whether an interpretation based by His Majesty's Government on assurances already given by Italian Government was correct. This did not imply suspicion. If he wished and I saw he did wish, to dissociate exchange of notes from declaration I would suggest the two should be differently dated; exchange of notes could be dated today and we could sign declaration on January 2nd; but I felt bound to make it clear that my government considered this point about Spanish territories an essential one. His Excellency replied that he remained unconvinced but would (? sign) subject to Mussolini who he feared might take the same line as he himself had done.

5. I then turned to the other questions we had discussed during our past conversations and said that I should like to take this opportunity of endeavouring to summarise for the benefit of my government, our discussions on these points.

A. Naval treaty. I had told my government they could confidently assume that once ratifications were complete Italy would accede. Count Ciano answered that he thought I had overdotted the 'i's'. He had not gone as far as that; he had said 'leave the question to me' and he repeated that today. He was not pessimistic but he could not today give me a definite pledge. On this point my own view is that Italy will accede. If she did not I should feel Count Ciano had in fact committed a distinct breach of faith towards me.

B. Arabia. I stated that we had agreed and my government had noted Arabian affairs would be discussed between our two governments in a friendly spirit if this became necessary. Count Ciano confirmed this.

C. Anti-British activities and propaganda in Middle East. Before I could open on this question Minister for Foreign Affairs said he would like me to know that one of two individuals I had mentioned previously, Arslan, had come to Rome two days ago. He had refused to see him and he had taken care that he should receive no encouragement. I thanked him for the information but said that nevertheless I must ask that he should give this question of anti-British activities his serious attention; if he found that our complaints were justified would he see that activities and propaganda of which we complained ceased? He replied that he would again make enquiries and do his best; he would be however very grateful if we could give him chapter and verse to help him in these enquiries; up to the present we had been rather vague. Was it not possible he went on that my remarks concerning Arabs at our last interview were a reflection of very strong pro-Moslem policy adopted by Marshal Balbo in Libya? I replied that I was sure this could not be the case; and I added what might constitute legitimate pro-Italian propaganda in Libya might well be anti-British and illegitimate in countries such as Palestine and Egypt. My government I went on attached such importance to this point that if it was not met they felt that our Mediterranean agreement would lose a certain amount of its value. Minister for Foreign Affairs replied in his view Mediterranean agreement would show

749

Arabs and others that Italy and Great Britain were working together and therefore be helpful on the point under discussion.

D. Abyssinia. I quoted and gave him copy of assurance given by Signor Grandi to Sir R. Vansittart on April 3rd[5] and I asked His Excellency if he would confirm them. He replied that he would be glad to do so; he stood by all pledges given by Signor Grandi to His Majesty's Government.

E. Gambeila. I said that His Majesty's Government took the same line over Gambeila as did the Italian Government namely they agreed that ultimately there would have to be discussions between the two governments and meanwhile they equally reserved their rights. Count Ciano confirmed that this was also the Italian position. He added that he had been delighted to find the situation on the Sudan frontier between the Italian and British officials was now excellent. He had been a little worried when I first spoke to him on this subject since he feared that some young officers might be as he termed it six months out of date; he was very glad that no trouble had arisen on this score.

F. Montreux Convention. I said that I had understood once Mediterranean agreement was signed Italy would be prepared to give favourable consideration to question of accession to this convention. Count Ciano rather demurred to this statement and said that this was a matter which his government would obviously have to discuss with the Turkish Government; but Italy was now examining the treaty and so far as he could tell had no objection to it in principle.[6]

6. When I said that this ended my resumé His Excellency observed that we were in complete agreement except on one point of the exchange of notes. This point he must refer to Signor Mussolini and he was not too hopeful of result. I was just assuming a gloomy aspect when the telephone rang and His Excellency observed that that must be his father-in-law[7] and he would consult him at once on both points, viz. text of declaration and exchange of notes. In three minutes he returned exlaiming joyfully that all was well. After shaking hands we discussed dates and publications. We agreed that exchange of notes should be dated today, December 31st, and that declaration should be signed on January 2nd and published on morning of January 4th. Question of date of publication of exchange of notes is not definitely settled but I feel that Count Ciano will ask that in any event publication shall not take place till three or four days after publication of the declaration. In short he will leave it to you to decide when publication becomes necessary but he will I presume expect to have some twenty-four hours' notice. I also gave him the following draft *communiqué* for use on January 2nd.

'The British Ambassador and Count Ciano signed this morning on behalf of their respective governments a declaration concerning assurances with regard to the Mediterranean the text of which will be published in the immediate future', which he accepted. He observed that he understood that

[5] See No. 522, note 4.   [6] Cf. Volume XVI, No. 540.
[7] i.e. Signor Mussolini.

we wished for this forty-eight hours' delay in order to communicate text to the French; this of course was our own affair. I replied that it was our intention to communicate substance though not text to the French and I suggested that it might be courteous if Italian Government took similar action; but I added this was of course equally the affair of the Italian Government.

7. Count Ciano was clearly delighted that we had reached agreement.

8. I am telephoning this evening texts of notes to be exchanged.[8]

[8] These were contained in telegram No. 781, telephoned from Rome to the Foreign Office on December 31 at 9 p.m. and not printed here: the text of the notes is given in No. 530 below.

No. 527

Minute by Mr. Sargent on the Anglo-Italian conversations in Rome
[*R 12/1/22*]

FOREIGN OFFICE, *January 1, 1937*

We have obtained all our requirements, and what is particularly satisfactory is the acceptance without alteration of our formula regarding Spain.[1]

As regards the small points on which Count Ciano was inclined to make difficulties, i.e. the Naval Treaty, Propaganda in the Middle East, and Montreux, it will be easy to pursue these further if we want to in the still better atmosphere which we may expect after the publication of our Mediterranean Declaration.

It is instructive to note that Count Ciano demurred to the unilateral form of the assurances about Spain and to the subsequent publication of the exchange of notes. This shows clearly not merely that he felt that Italy was being asked to make a considerable concession, but—and this is still more important—it shows that Mussolini, by brushing these difficulties aside, is determined to take a long-sighted view and not be held up on points of prestige and *amour propre*. We ought, I feel sure, to do everything we can to encourage the continuance of this attitude on the part of Mussolini, and help him to realise that he has not made a mistake in giving this sudden turn to Italy's previous policy. The practical ways and means of doing this ought to be considered from now onwards, so that we lose no opportunity of reaping the practical benefits in the realm of international policy of the Anglo-Italian *détente* which we have now reached. In this respect one precaution will be very necessary, and that is that in all comments that we make or that the British press makes there should be no suggestion that our object in reaching this *détente* is to 'detach' Italy from Germany.

As regards publication, we can agree to the declarations being published in the morning papers of the 4th January (Monday) and had better tell Sir Eric Drummond that we propose to do so.[2]

As regards publication of the Spanish notes, the position seems to be that

[1] This minute was a commentary on No. 526.   [2] See No. 528 below.

751

we can fix a date so long as this date is three or four days subsequent to the publication of the declaration. I would suggest, therefore, that we should propose straight away that the exchange of notes should be published in the morning papers of the 7th.

I would suggest that we should at the same time congratulate Sir E. Drummond on the success of these negotiations and ask him to convey a suitable message from the Secretary of State on this occasion to Count Ciano and to Signor Mussolini.[3] If the Prime Minister would agree to send a similar message to Mussolini it would, I am sure, be highly appreciated and would be most useful in the circumstances.[4]

There remains the question of informing the French, Greeks, Yugoslavs and Turks.

We are pledged to tell the French 48 hours before publication, and therefore had better send for M. Corbin to-morrow and give him the 'substance' of the declarations, at the same time supplying Sir George Clerk with the necessary material to do likewise at the Quai d'Orsay.

Although we are under no similar pledge to the Greeks, Yugoslavs and Turks, I think it would be advisable to inform them on Saturday afternoon before they hear it from the French.

Although, as far as I know, we have never said anything to the French about the possibility of a special exchange of notes regarding Spain, the subject is one which interests them so closely that I think we ought to mention the matter to them at the same time as we tell them about the declaration. But since the notes are not going to be published until the 7th, the subject had better be mentioned in very general terms so as to avoid leakage, since any leakage on this subject is bound to be particularly irritating to Count Ciano. The subject need not be mentioned, I think, to the Greeks, Yugoslavs, and Turks.[5]

[3] Sir R. Vansittart agreed to the suggestions made in this and the preceding sentence.

[4] A marginal comment by Mr. Eden here read: 'I doubt the wisdom of this.'

[5] Concerning this sentence, Sir R. Vansittart wrote: 'I wouldn't do this till next week, if we are only publishing on the 7th. Let us minimise the leak. R. V.' Mr. Eden agreed. In a further minute Sir R. Vansittart wrote: 'I agree with everything in Mr. Sargent's minute. This is all most successful and gratifying. The Italians—in particular Mussolini—have behaved very well and accommodatingly. Let us be on the look out to follow up this success, for it is exploitable seeing that the Italians have certainly a good reason for their attitude. If we never *talk* of detaching them from Germany, but merely [a marginal comment by Mr. Eden here read: 'I agree. This is wise. A. E.'] exploit this success—bearing in mind that it has good reasons—we shall automatically loosen the Italo-German tie, & so have a more reasonable, or anyhow tamer, Germany to deal with. R. V. Jan. 1.' Mr. Eden wrote: 'I agree that this is very satisfactory, and I also agree generally with Mr. Sargent's minute. It is particularly satisfactory that we should have obtained our formula regarding Spain and I am glad that we were firm about this. I have only one criticism. From the point of view of reception in this country is there not much to be said for *simultaneous* publication of declaration & notes: a complete "clean up" between us? I should have thought this might have been put to Count Ciano. Finally let us bear in mind during our new relations with Italy that the latter has at least as much to gain from this better state of affairs as we. We shall lose nothing in Italian eyes by continuing to "nous faire valoir". A. E. Jan. 2.'

No. 528

Foreign Office to Sir E. Drummond (Rome)

No. 3 Telegraphic: by telephone [R 1/1/22]

Immediate   FOREIGN OFFICE, *January 2, 1937, 1.50 p.m.*

Your telegrams Nos. 778,[1] 779,[2] 780[3] and 781.[4]

I agree to publication of Mediterranean Declaration in morning papers on January 4th.[5]

As regards the exchange of Notes, I am convinced that the declaration would receive a much warmer and indeed unqualified reception in this country and would contribute still more effectively to our common object of removing all doubts and uncertainties which have recently clouded Anglo-Italian relations, if the Notes were to be published simultaneously with the Declaration. I wish you, therefore, while expressing my great pleasure at the happy outcome of the discussions, to impress upon Count Ciano most strongly that this apparently minor question of timing has a very real political importance, and that simultaneous publication would, in my opinion, for the reasons given above, be as advantageous to the Italian Government as to His Majesty's Government. If you fail to convince Count Ciano, I agree—though very reluctantly—to postpone publication of the exchange of Notes until the morning of January 7th.

You should take this opportunity to inform Count Ciano of the satisfaction I feel on the conclusion of this agreement between our two Governments, and express to him my hope that it may be the beginning of further co-operation between us in the cause of international appeasement and security.

Meanwhile I wish to express to Your Excellency my warm congratulations on the able and tactful manner in which you have conducted these negotiations to a successful issue.

[1] Not printed (R 7895/3928/22).   [2] No. 526.   [3] See *ibid.*, note 4.
[4] See *ibid.*, note 8.   [5] See minutes in No. 527.

No. 529

Sir E. Drummond (Rome) to Foreign Office

(Received January 2, 6.15 p.m.)

No. 3 Telegraphic: by telephone [R 31/1/22]

Immediate   ROME, *January 2, 1937*

Your telegram 3.[1]

Unless Signor Mussolini, to whom Count Ciano felt bound to refer the question, dissents, which latter thinks unlikely, Minister for Foreign Affairs has no objection to acceding to your desire for simultaneous publication of

[1] No. 528.

exchange of notes and of declaration on Monday morning—as at present advised he does not intend to publish notes here. He personally would have preferred different dates for publication, but has yielded to your views on the subject.

I gave him this evening your message of appreciation at conclusion of the agreement and I think this will be published here and a somewhat analogous message sent to Signor Grandhi [*sic*] for communication to you.

May I take the opportunity of thanking you for your congratulations and of expressing my gratitude for the consideration you have shown to the views I have ventured to put forward during the course of the negotiations.

No. 530

Texts of an Anglo-Italian Declaration with regard to the Mediterranean signed at Rome on January 2, 1937, and of an Exchange of Notes regarding the status quo in the Western Mediterranean published on the same date[1]

[*R 1/1/22*]

I. *Mediterranean Declaration*

His Majesty's Government in the United Kingdom and the Italian Government:

Animated by the desire to contribute increasingly, in the interests of the general cause of peace and security, to the betterment of relations between them and between all the Mediterranean Powers, and resolved to respect the rights and interests of those Powers;

Recognise that the freedom of entry into, exit from, and transit through, the Mediterranean is a vital interest both to the different parts of the British Empire and to Italy, and that these interests are in no way inconsistent with each other;

Disclaim any desire to modify or, so far as they are concerned, to see modified the status quo as regards national sovereignty of territories in the Mediterranean area;

Undertake to respect each other's rights and interests in the said area;

Agree to use their best endeavours to discourage any activities liable to impair the good relations which it is the object of the present declaration to consolidate.

This declaration is designed to further the ends of peace and is not directed against any other Power.

---

[1] Published as a British White Paper, *Italy* (*No. 1*) of 1937, Cmd. 5348. The texts of the three documents were printed in *The Times* of January 4, 1937, p. 12.

II. *Exchange of Notes*

His Majesty's Ambassador to Count Ciano

December 31, 1936

Your Excellency,

The Royal Italian Government may perhaps be aware that the Secretary of State for Foreign Affairs was asked in the House of Commons on 16th December[2] whether he would lay upon the table of the House the precise terms of the guarantee given to His Majesty's Government by the Government of Italy concerning occupation of Balearic Islands by Italian subjects.

To this question Mr. Eden replied that the assurances to which reference was made were given verbally. He proceeded to state that His Majesty's Chargé d'Affaires in Rome, acting on instructions, informed the Italian Minister for Foreign Affairs on 12th September that 'any alteration of the status quo in Western Mediterranean would be a matter of the closest concern to His Majesty's Government.' Mr. Eden continued that, taking note of this communication, Italian Minister for Foreign Affairs had assured Mr. Ingram that the Italian Government had not, either before or since the revolution in Spain, engaged in any negotiations with General Franco whereby the status quo in the Western Mediterranean would be altered, nor would they engage in any such negotiations in the future. This assurance, the Secretary of State added, was subsequently reaffirmed spontaneously to British naval attaché in Rome by Italian Ministry of Marine, and Italian Ambassador in London had on several occasions given to the Secretary of State similar verbal assurances.

In view of these assurances, His Majesty's Government in the United Kingdom assume that, so far as Italy is concerned, the integrity of the present territories of Spain shall in all circumstances remain intact and unmodified. They would, however, be grateful if your Excellency saw your way formally to confirm the accuracy of this assumption, and I have accordingly the honour to enquire whether your Excellency could supply me with such confirmation.

I avail myself of the opportunity to convey to your Excellency the expression of my highest consideration.

Count Ciano to His Majesty's Ambassador

Translation   *December 31, 1936*

Your Excellency,

I have the honour to acknowledge the receipt of your Excellency's note of to-day's date in which you draw my attention to a question asked in the House of Commons on 16th December last, and the reply given by Mr. Eden, on the subject of the assurances given verbally by the Royal Italian Government concerning the status quo in the Western Mediterranean. You reminded me that in taking note of the communication made by His Majesty's Chargé d'Affaires on 12th September I assured Mr. Ingram that

[2] See No. 514, note 3.

the Italian Government had not, either before or since the revolution in Spain, engaged in any negotiations with General Franco whereby the status quo in Western Mediterranean would be altered, nor would they engage in any such negotiations in the future.

I have consequently no difficulty, on behalf of the Royal Italian Government, in confirming the accuracy of His Majesty's Government's assumption, namely, that, so far as Italy is concerned, the integrity of the present territories of Spain shall in all circumstances remain intact and unmodified.

I avail myself of this opportunity to convey to your Excellency the expression of my highest consideration.

APPENDIX I

Account by Sir R. Vansittart of a visit to Germany in August 1936[1]

'A Busman's Holiday'*

Secret   September 10, 1936

These notes are put on paper to refresh my own memory. They are impressions—how should they be more at the end of a fortnight, however crowded?—of the undoctored record of the effect of personalities on a mind already familiar with the problem created by them. I have written in the personal form because I did not, and do not, think that my visit to Germany included any individual occurrence of sufficient importance for special notice or report; moreover, I adhered rather religiously to the limitation that I was in Berlin for pleasure and to establish contacts rather than to discuss any particular business. The *ensemble*, however, is perhaps worth recording.

I arrived in Berlin on the same day as the Italian Minister of Propaganda—a pleasant type of the hunted 'go-getter' that serves dictatorship. He lost no time in living up to his label; indeed, he set the pace of the political Olympiad a cracker, and no one who had witnessed this *ventre à terre* exhibition could be surprised at well-founded reports of 'parallelism' between Rome and Berlin. I was therefore in less hurry to see anyone except the Minister for Foreign Affairs as was my duty. Baron von Neurath is already well known to us, a comfortable squirearchic South German not always at ease with the present régime. He was most cordial, but remarked twice that he had never expected to see me in Berlin. His surprise typified the mind of many people in Berlin during the first days of my stay, when I amused myself by watching the eyes of those introduced to me. The tale of a hostile Foreign Office had evidently gone deep, and one cannot blame the German press when one has seen and suffered much of our own. This embarrassment, however, soon thawed, and was followed by a general rush of interest that turned to geniality.

Baron von Neurath, having accepted in general and rather 'hearty' terms the invitation to a Five-Power Conference—with the single but emphatic reservation that it could not take place before mid-October *at earliest*—showed little disposition to enter upon any detailed or preliminary discussion. When I said it was essential that if the meeting was to succeed—and failure would be disastrous—it would be essential that in the rather long interval an atmosphere of untroubled calm should be preserved, Baron von Neurath at once agreed. He said easily that on the German side nothing disturbing would be done—I wonder and doubt whether he had then heard of the impending increase in military service—and that he

[1] No copy of this paper seems to have survived in the Foreign Office archives. The copy printed here is from the private papers of Sir R. Vansittart and is reproduced by permission of Lady Vansittart and of Churchill College, Cambridge.

was confident of success in concluding a Western Pact. I said that was the first and easiest part of our task; we had left the sequel open and fluid in our *communiqué*;[2] but, although the essential thing was to make a beginning, and I hoped for a good start in October, we must not delude ourselves into thinking that we had cured a general disease by a local treatment—indeed, the original Locarno had some ramifications. And here at the beginning I should say something in explanation of much that follows. I felt early doubt, still not dissipated, whether in altered circumstances the Germans intend to act up to their own March offers respecting pacts with their neighbours in Central Europe, and, still more important, whether they truly mean business even as regards a fresh Locarno. As will be seen later, I think they can be won or held to their own doctrines and not much more; but even for that purpose considerable expatiation on the real necessity for these *minima* on the widest grounds was both timely and necessary.

But bluff, cheerful, Baron von Neurath prefers to cross bridges when he comes to them, or possibly even to keep away from all rivers but the Rhine, and so, as I approached difficult ground, turned south—to Spain, now clearly more on his mind than the troublesome details of a meeting yet distant. His lazy good nature tempts him humanly to turn his head from the worries of to-morrow, when those of to-day are loud in his ear. I met him on half-a-dozen subsequent occasions, and he spoke always of Spain—with a reasonable and balanced outlook and a disinclination for adventure not always shared in more belligerent quarters. Baron von Neurath is a likeable colleague, and if a *tour d'horizon* were ever to lead one up the garden path, the cause would be more a preference for smoothness than any less amiable motive.

A few days later followed an invitation for an interview with Herr Hitler, which had been arranged not by Herr von Neurath but by Herr von Ribbentrop. I understand that the Führer had given orders for the avoidance of rough passages and disputable corners. Bed-rock was to be avoided, partly perhaps to make a good impression, but more because, as I think, no details had been thought out. Moreover, an Olympic truce lay thick above the city, and had its effect on Herr Hitler's mood.

In the prevailing and remunerative lull he seemed an amiably simple, rather shy, rotundly ascetic, *bourgeois*, with the fine hair and thin skin that accompany extreme sensitiveness, a man of almost obvious *physical* integrity, very much in earnest, not humorous, not alarming, not magnetic, but convinced of a variable mission and able to impress himself so strongly that he impresses himself on those around him, perhaps I should say even on those constantly around him. They stand in tangible awe of him—and thereby, of course, hang many tales—although their ardently proclaimed affection is not therefore any the less sincere, on the contrary. Judged by the form of mid-August 1936—and no one would so judge— the rise and utter ascendancy of Herr Hitler would be puzzling, except to those who had seen him in action, not in an arm-chair, or listening rapt, after the grandiose dinner that he gave for us—with spinach and water for himself—to the best of German music in the resplendent new banqueting hall just completed to his own design. He has, particularly on such an occasion, a great natural dignity, or anyhow a dignity which is by now natural. His entourage reminded me that he is not only head of the Government like Signor Mussolini, but head of the State; he needs not reminder, but he has no airs, and unbends rather readily in private, even in public. He probably does so more easily toward a stranger, for

2 See Volume XVI, No. 476.

that is all in the day's work, than among his intimates; the very intensity of their admiration forbids it. He is not such an island surrounded by fluid yesmen as Signor Mussolini; Herr von Neurath probably likes an easy-chair too much to stand up to him, but both Dr. Goebbels and General Göring have got stuff of their own, and there is no Italian equivalent to them. Yet Herr Hitler's opportunities for either spiritual or physical intimacy would be clearly and sadly circumscribed, if he really needed them and particularly lacking when men most seek it, with women. The Führer is never *verführt*, and so he in turn circumscribes women and overrates them within those limitations. (The other school of unfamiliarity leads to the anti-feminism of Nietzsche, who, by the way, looks like being refloated off the rocks of his own shallows.) Those who succeed in politics are apt to get bridled as well as saddled with prestige, and would anyhow not be much good at kicking over traces.

This, then, was the August aspect. It underlined rather than effaced the other, which is known to history, the harder, more violent, mystically ambitious, hotly and coldly explosive traits, which flare capriciously and keep everyone not only in Europe but in Germany in such a state of nervous tension that I more than once heard the stadium compared with a crater. The Great Man—since we accept the incompatibility of epithet and noun—is a clear case of the chameleon; and it is well that he should be so, for in that the chief, if any, hope of the future lies.

The Führer certainly acted up to his *own* instructions, when I met him. Nothing could have been more friendly, but nothing could have been more general; and since as aforesaid I always sought to avoid any suggestion—particularly from other than German quarters—that I was in Berlin for purposes other than a friendly visit, I did not seek to push him far from the general to the particular.

Once started—Herr Hitler began by a slightly embarrassed and embarrassing pause, which I had to break—the conversation proceeded easily, and I was pleased to find it a real conversation, rather than the prophesied monologue. I naturally left the bulk of it to the Führer, but he can take interruption kindly. I spoke mostly in German with recourse to an interpreter when I thought advisable. Herr Hitler having with much frankness said, as he repeated on a subsequent occasion, that I had done well to come, I replied that I hoped my visit might at least serve to dispel some misconceptions, and to make understanding easier in the important months ahead. I thought such contacts as I hoped to establish in Berlin were important if we were to avoid undue and retarding suspicions on either side. It was practically impossible for a man in his position to make those contacts himself—the same held good for Signor Mussolini—and it was even difficult for persons of smaller note, yet employed at their own political headquarters, either to find time to travel or to do so often without exciting unwarranted comment. On the other hand, those who did travel were mostly lightweights or busybodies in search of sensations; they represented little in their own country, and often misrepresented much in order to ingratiate themselves with over-hospitable hosts. I hoped these might in future be treated with some caution, lest they hinder instead of helping us.

The Führer agreed, but passed quickly to an explanation and justification of what he had done in the past, both internally and externally, particularly the former. On this he spoke with volume and conviction, as on later occasions did Dr. Goebbels, General Göring and Herr Hess. They all said that they were misunderstood in England, and on this topic more listening than speaking is required. I found it necessary to say little here except that we were practical and reasonable people, who therefore looked more to the future than to the past. I began to develop this theme with reference to the prospects of the Five-Power Conference; but Herr Hitler preferred to consider the past with reference to Communism, and the future in the light of its manifestations in Spain and their repercussions on France.

I should here interpolate that this is the constant theme of every man and woman in Berlin; indeed, they can think and talk of little else. The obsession is in any case endemic, but Spanish events have reinforced their thesis, and one cannot be for a fortnight in Berlin without realising that Comintern complicity in Spain and activity in France has seriously prejudiced such chances as ever existed of obtaining a full European as opposed to a strictly Western settlement. Indeed, recent Communist performances in those countries and Brazil have left no prospect of bringing about any agreement between Germany and Russia, and any pressure on this point might wreck the chances of even a Western settlement and air pact without limitation—for what they may be worth. I sought, whenever occasion offered and in many interviews, to show on the lines set forth later the need of widening the area of appeasement as indicated in our London *communiqué*, but we shall have a stiff task to obtain any extension of a Western settlement at all. I always received careful but not responsive attention and sometimes even outward assent; and I am not entirely without hope of having produced some effect as regards Central Europe; but that will be the limit, and the Comintern has its own untimely manifestations to thank for a position which may be less welcome to wiser heads like M. Litvinov. The present Comintern drive in this country is probably a fresh illustration of the small importance of M. Litvinov compared with the real policy-merchants of Moscow.

It may also be opportune here to record my impressions as to the sincerity and extent of German fears of Communism and of Russia, which, seeing what is happening in Russia, is no longer necessarily the same thing. For it seems that Russia is gradually going national rather than doctrinal, and has, accordingly, two brands of Communism, one the old fiery stuff for export—people are shot for that now *in* Russia—and the other the mellower tonic for home consumption. I have always been one of those who found it hard to believe that Nazism had really saved Germany—let alone Europe—from Communism. The claim in regard to Europe is voided by what is actually happening there. In regard to Germany I did not, and do not, accept the claim because the middle-class is too efficient; because much that passed for Communism there was either of the radish variety or vaguely pinkish like 'a Radical' in the United States of America; and because many of the component atoms were volatile. But, just as pose becomes habit, so affirmation perseveringly applied becomes conviction, particularly when supported by much gratuitously supplied evidence. The policy and expenditure of the Comintern have therefore been successful from its own befogged standpoint[,] but surely the reverse on any longer view, *if* the ungainly and still incompetent giant is genuinely afraid of the fit, fifteen-stone Teuton—as I think he is, despite the contrary view sometimes held in the Baltic States and, in particular, by M. Munters. Incidentally the history of the last few months perhaps justifies ironically the allegation, oft opposed to *our* protests against propaganda, that the Soviet Government is distinct from and unable to control the Comintern. Be this as it may, every German of the present persuasion—and in a little while all the youth of the country will be of that persuasion—has an anti-Communist obsession. There is still much

Communism literally underground, for example in the Ruhr mines, but it has been stamped under for keeps, so far as one can see at present.

I drove with Herr Hess, unescorted, through the Communist quarters of Berlin without seeing a sour look, though there may have been many an averted one; and I doubt whether the ruling caste has much real fear of an internal recrudescence, which would be ruthlessly crushed. What it fears is an external convergence, that Communism will extend in Europe and round on, if not encircle, Germany. On this point the national mind seems made up owing, perhaps in equal parts, to reality, auto-suggestion and history, which 'is eaten cold.'

Moreover, in Germany, as in the United States of America, there is a vast provincialism not only of manners but of the spirit. One can make either Americans or Germans believe anything one wants—witness their text-books—provided *they* want it. And Germans do want it, for Nazism suits their character ten times better than Communism, even if the real differences between the systems are surely not ten-fold. It is, therefore, not only useless, but wrong, to argue with any German about the 'Red Peril,' and I did not, in general, attempt to do so; but I did attempt to distinguish between its categories. I admitted the spread of the doctrine, where the facts speak for themselves. I added, however, that the alleged military danger of Russia to Germany was barred by the existing map of Europe, which Germany, if really apprehensive, would accordingly be wise to keep in its present form. Moreover, national characteristics can be altered by new political systems but only to a limited extent; and even if Germany alarmed herself by exaggeration, no Englishman, who had fought *against* Germany for over four years, and *with* Russia for the worst part of three, could be brought to believe that the respective efficiencies of Russia and Germany—and surely everything depended henceforth on technical efficiency—were comparable, except to the overwhelming advantage of the latter. The compliment was unwelcome, but unanswerable, even on the strength of the Russian air-force and its alleged bases in Czechoslovakia.

This line I took not only with Herr Hitler but with most Germans of importance —Goebbels, Göring, Hess, Krosig, &c., bankers, industrials, the three most intelligent journalists, Scheffer, Kircher and Silex—and I will therefore in other respects also economise space by reporting these interviews as an *ensemble* where they covered the same ground (though of course I covered it with many variations of form, approach and detail).

Herr Hitler said that the argument of course did not reassure him (none of them wanted to be reassured). He thought the Left in Spain would eventually win. (This is in rather striking contrast with the assertion, often heard during my subsequent visit to France, that he would never allow the Right to lose.) If his prediction were verified, France would be infected dangerously, perhaps desperately, and the contagion would then spread to her associates, like Czechoslovakia where the seed was already sown. Germany would then be caught between two, if not three, fires, and must be prepared.

I replied that we should be slow to anticipate the jumping of other people's cats. The horrors of Spain might just as well have the effect of alarming as of infecting France, and cause her to step on the brake rather than on the gas. Herr Hitler readily and reasonably admitted this—some of my other interlocutors were less ready—and agreed that we must wait and see. I did not labour the point because of the certainty of further serious troubles before winter is out, perhaps before it is even in; but I added that the decisive factor for France was likely to be the economic difficulties of her own situation rather than the example of Spaniards, whom Frenchmen did not really rank with themselves. France would go her own gait. Spectators might label it Communism, but it would be at worst a sort of tricolour Communism, in which big industries might be nationalised and big fortunes expropriated, but the little man would be respected and national defence would be strengthened. Was this so very far from what some people had understood by National Socialism?

From this kind of material I made the most reassuring picture that I could, but I must admit some whistling to keep my courage up, and I might have whistled louder if my visit to France had come first instead of second. For I am by no means convinced of the accuracy of this picture. France will probably go further left, and further still in the event of a Communist victory in Spain, with all its violent consequences. Meanwhile, the Communists in France are already honeycombing the country with cells.

Anyhow, again none of them wanted to be reassured. To some the picture of increased strength—this is quite conceivable—was more unwelcome than the possibility of contagious chaos. Herr Hess said, with almost engaging naïveté, that this would indeed be the most distasteful solution of all. Germany would be framed, and on one side at least effectively, even if I was right about Slav inefficiency. Germany must therefore have not only weapons but friends, and, though she would sooner have England as a friend and associate than anyone else—*mutatis mutandis* the same was said to M. Laval, so M. Léger tells me—we must understand that she would have to choose those associates elsewhere if England would not play. General Göring made this point even more explicitly, and he added, with broad but slightly forbidding good humour, that beyond a certain point Germany could not and would not run after us. In particular, General Göring indicated that the British Empire was in as much danger from Communism as Germany—this sounded very like Herr von Ribbentrop's constant theme—and that the two countries should combine against it. I replied that we were a democratic country with room for such wide divisions of opinion that it could therefore not be combined or recruited in practice against any form of political doctrine. On the other hand, we were, of course, more than ready to be friends; the pressing need was to find a solid basis, and I hoped we should begin to lay that in the autumn. I was sure it would not be our fault if we failed. As to France, when I spoke of national defence I meant defence. There, as in England, the man in the street was perfectly pacific—this they all admitted—but would fight better for the coming France than under the old system, against which he had partially revolted. (I thought it well to insert this, for there may well be a dangerous tendency to write France off during her further and impending troubles.) Surely, however, it was unnecessary to go into this, since I assumed that not one of the three of us had any intention of making self-defence necessary. (It may be of interest here to note that both at our recent meeting with the French in London and during my visit to France I have derived from those in authority the impression that they at least still take it for granted that France would go to the assistance of Czechoslovakia if the latter were attacked by Germany.) I took this occasion to tell Herr Hitler and all his collaborators that, paradoxal as it might seem, he would find this French Government, despite the eighty-two Communist Deputies and the alleged disinclination of Moscow to facilitate any rapprochement between Paris and Berlin, more ready, within reason, to forget the past and look to the future than any of its predecessors.

I hoped that we might both be able to turn this goodwill to good account, lest it should fail and be succeeded by something more representative of, or subject to, the very influence that Germany professed to fear. This would increase the danger of a conflict of *Weltanschauungen*, a point which is dealt with later. Meanwhile, the reasonableness of the present French Government had been proved in London, and both England and Germany must surely be interested in not rendering M. Blum's task impossible, particularly on any German hypothesis that the fall of his Government might well betoken the end of one system and the beginning of another. As a matter of fact, the one thing really likely to produce full-blown Communism in France, and indeed everywhere, was another war. (During my subsequent stay in France I found it strongly held that the country could not politically survive a second world conflagration.) The possibility and advisability— on the preceding score—of coming to terms with France were not seriously disputed by any of those mentioned. Indeed, most of them recognised the broad and conciliatory tone of the London *communiqué*. Hitler himself certainly did so, though he naturally attributed the chief credit for this new tone to London, and I—equally naturally—did not contradict him. He went on to say, however, and so did most of his associates, that we were at a very critical period, and that we must not spoil the prospects of settlement by vaulting ambition; we ought to tackle what was immediately urgent *and possible*. This was exactly what I had expected; the German mind is not yet clear in detail, and is perhaps in no hurry to be so, but tends broadly to a limited Western settlement, if any. Whether the consequences or intentions of such a limitation have been thought out in full by the Führer, who is All, cannot yet be said with certainty or detail; but I should say that a good deal of thinking had been done around him. I said again that we were practical people, and would therefore agree that we ought to begin by the urgent and possible, but we must also consider another epithet—the necessary. Firstly, the average Englishman never could forget that the last war started in and about a corner of Europe which was almost unknown to him; and yet we had been drawn in, and the nation rightly thought it conceivable that the same thing might happen again. Indeed, we were not peculiar in that, for everyone assumed that, if anyone indulged in arson, the fire would spread. Secondly, Europe was suffering from a nervous disease in most of its members, and the eventual interest of *all* the doctors at the October bedside was a cure. But we should be bad doctors if we thought we could cure a disease by a cataplasm; and, if we muddled or scamped the cure, the nervous disease would become a nervous breakdown; a return to normality would become impossible, and there would be a further spread of the very discontent which afflicted and menaced *every* régime.

Herr Hitler replied by an eloquent description of his own hold on his own people. I found, indeed, that the whole dominant caste are completely confident on this score, thereby confirming my view as to the unreality of any German fear as to internal Communism, and this has been confirmed still further by Herr Hitler's speech at the Nuremburg Party Conference. I think I should feel equally confident if I were part of a system enforced not only by a man, but by a mass, a machine developed with the manifold and almost incalculable advantages of modern scientific technique, including not only the diffusion and control of all practical and spiritual communication, but the monopoly of 20th century poison-gas, aeroplanes and artillery. Nowadays the under-dog stays under. The less adroit Russians have thought or found it necessary to destroy vast quantities of 'doctrine-fodder'—sometimes by mock-trial, sometimes by frank massacre, sometimes by wholesale extermination as in the case of the kulaks—in order to drive home the impossibility of political resurrection. The Germans do not need to go so far; a nod is as good as a kick, though there are plenty of kicks going on—under the table. General Göring even offered to me a large bet that he would drive with me quite alone to the roughest spot I could find in Germany, that we should get out and stand there, and that nothing would happen. I replied that I had practically given up betting against certainties. Herr Hitler dilated confidently not only on the affection of his people, but on their stability. He had practically conquered unemployment, and meant to go further still. Times were admittedly hard, but no German was adding to his difficulties by asking for a rise of wages. He spoke in some detail on the labour situation, and went into some statistics which I need not reproduce. Briefly, his conclusion was that Germany now presented a solid front to the world-disease of discontent, and that in this respect her position was more impregnable than that of any other Power, owing to the strength of her political system.

If it came to that, I replied, we in turn might argue that we could hold out in the present rather senseless world longer than anyone else, because our economic and financial position was stronger than that of anyone else. We also had reduced unemployment, and should shortly be doing so even more by rapid increase of our armaments. Indeed, we could certainly outstay the world at rearmament, though we did not think the game would prove worth the candle. But this and other means of taking in our own washing would in our case, as in that of Germany, have a large element of unreality. The only real cure was a return to normality, and that was impossible without a return of confidence. What was happening, however, was that the tide of world-trade was falling year by year, leaving behind a wrack of decaying industries. It was always better to speak of concrete cases; so in several of my interviews I quoted, of deliberate purpose, the glass and textiles of the *Sudetendeutsche* districts. I mentioned these, I said, because I knew that Germany was interested in the difficulties of these people; and, as my interview with Herr Henlein betokened, so was I. But we all knew perfectly well that, even if the Czechoslovak Government were able to apply some palliatives, no cure was possible except as part of a 'far more world-wide' operation. What was needed everywhere, and particularly and notoriously in Germany herself was a restoration of export trade; that is what I meant by normality. So long, therefore, as this return to economic normality was barred by the absence of political confidence, so long as we all occupied ourselves with Appearance instead of Reality, we should achieve nothing, and, in the end, however strong; we should alike go over the dam. Some of us would last longer than others, but no system—not even the German— could endure in the remains of a world where discontent was endemic, because a normal man could not earn a normal living in a normal way. We should then indeed be within sight of *The Going Down of the West*,[3] whose distinguished German author, I noted with regret, had recently died.

It seemed to me that, if progress is to be made, German cocksureness must be partially shaken, or at least doubt suggested. This I thought more likely to be effected by an argument with a dash of *Weltanschauung* (and a German reference) especially among Germans who have a weakness for *Weltanschauungen* in general and easy, uncomfortable brands in particular. On nearly all the important Germans whom I met, including Herr Hitler, I accordingly tried part or all—as time permitted—of the following diagnosis of our common and fundamental troubles.

[3] *Der Untergang des Abendlandes*, by Oswald Spengler (1880–1936); Volume I was published in 1918 and Volume II in 1922.

I said that, to my mind, the root of our difficulty lay in the fact that a material and a spiritual crisis had come upon us simultaneously; both had been precipitated by the war, and would be rendered completely hopeless by another. The decline of faith was already visible before 1914, and the next four years had taken from men something more than their money or their lives. We were living at a sort of tea-time of belief; the incipient consequences had long been visible, and the conclusions to be drawn from them—and speedily drawn—were now of the highest importance. Curtly, the point that interested us both—and all—was this. In more credulous days it had been possible to still the murmurings of the mind with the suggestion that what men had lacked or suffered in this working world would be made good to them in some Beyond. Now this idea of supernatural compensation was paling; more, it made men angry. This was the reason why, like Verlaine, they saw 'la vie en rouge,' why the first step in getting out of hand, as in Russia or Spain, always comprised the destruction of churches and the slaughter of priests and even of nuns. One might explain the slaughter of priests by saying that they exercised a reactionary influence in politics, although I did not think that the Orthodox or Catholic Churches nowadays muscled into politics more than the Anglican and Nonconformist Churches. It was more difficult, however, to account for the dead-set against nuns and church-buildings except by the feeling of exasperation at having been so long lulled by the unrealisable, which they represented. Discontent, once called divine, was now definitely anti-divine. The supernatural was dropping out of economics beyond recall. If that sun were soon to be under our sea of troubles, it became only the more essential to render the average material life more endurable. And that was exactly where we were all failing—with ineluctable consequences. In the dual crisis material progress was nothing like enough to compensate for spiritual loss. Would man surmount, or even survive, the sadness of seeing the world go the way it *has* gone with dwindling hope of Direction? (Or does experience hit especially hard our own elder generation, which began at the end of Victorian optimism?)

Sometimes in these arguments I was met by the gambit that faith was *not* failing in Germany; in fact, that a religious revival was in train. To this I always retorted that what was happening in Germany was not revivalism, but the normal human spirit of contradiction. The churches in Germany considered themselves persecuted. Were this opinion and stimulus removed, it would shortly be seen that Germany offered no exception to the world phenomenon. I had heard talk of founding a substitute creed. Surely that was a hopeless quest. Any new religion would be either too vague for acceptance or concrete enough for further criticism—and anger. One might, of course, replace the imponderable by patriotism as a muscular or military code. But this merely amounted to the creation of a machine for making men efficient machines. If that was going to settle the spiritual side of the crisis, well and good. But it wouldn't; it would only lead, at immense cost, to more disappointment and wrath. On present form the human creature was as likely to be heading back toward the Tenth Century as forward to a millennium. Either it was too clever or not clever enough.

It came to this, then. The spiritual chaos probably was not, the material chaos probably—not certainly—was redeemable; and it was essential, if the situation was to be saved, that the redemption of the second should be on a scale to compensate for any failure in the first. Yet even the economic task would not be possible, unless it were preceded by a restoration of political confidence, which must be thorough and European. They mostly recognised that the political must precede the economic remedy. Somebody, I said, had to make a beginning, and beginning meant sacrifice. Without political confidence the man on the apparently safer side of the tariff wall would do nothing at his initial cost for the suspect on the other, and so, ultimately, for himself. As to the extent of the appeasement, I asked them all to note again that we had laid down nothing in advance. The first chapter was self-evident; to the sequel we had only pointed, and we must write it together. But a sequel there must be for the reasons which I had sketched. Moreover, there was a final point. In the last few months I had seen and heard a lot of talk everywhere about the danger of Europe splitting into hostile political *blocs*. This was possible and of course undesirable; but it was not the real and ultimate danger, because there was a greater one. Political *blocs* were always by their nature kaleidoscopic, superficial things. Who could doubt this if he considered the attitude of Italy during the last twenty-one years, and especially the last three of them. (I thought of the Italian Minister of Propaganda and hit him hard near, but I think above, the belt.) The true danger was that if we all drifted on, as we were at present doing, we should split not only Europe but the world—or the world would split itself—into irremediably opposed *Weltanschauungen*. That was a possibility not kaleidoscopic or superficial but profound and vital; the stage was already set for such a development, and some people were rash enough to desire it as a policy. But if it came to pass, the eventual explosion would be so lasting in its results that most of what we had so far labelled as Civilisation—for what it was worth—would be blown away like a cobweb. And as Germany's scheme of things would be certainly not the least menaced, it was in her interest, as it was in her power, to make a contribution in these literal years of grace to the prevention of the menace. Wherever we started, then, we always came back to the same three points: that a return to normality was essential, that an economic must be preceded by a political settlement, and that the area of appeasement must be as wide as possible.

I encountered surprisingly little opposition to either premises or conclusions, though I tried varying developments of them in every discussion, well knowing them to be unwelcome. There is, of course, a world of difference between tacit and explicit acceptance; but in one or two instances I came across recognisable echoes in second conversations. In any case I would urge most strongly that a Western agreement alone is not only unreal but dangerous in that it may produce a false sense of security; and that we should accordingly essay every argument for widening the area of settlement to a reasonable and proper extent. To the question of extent I will return later. Meanwhile the economic argument is a real lever in our hands, and we should not weaken it without goood value. It is evident from Dr. Schacht's conversations in Paris that not only he but Herr Hitler is genuinely concerned at the economic situation of Germany; indeed, those who understand these subjects—not numerous in the dominant caste—are probably a good deal less confident than they would at present care to admit. It will assuredly do them all no harm to be kept guessing for a while. We shall have a hard enough task anyhow to bring them to any effective settlement in Europe, and must therefore have made considerable progress past the obstacles on our political path, before we show any sign of parting with our one trump. (General Göring actually referred, though in passing, to a loan.) If we are prematurely accommodating we shall get nowhere, as is always the fate of those who put the cart before the horse. Economic causes are, of course, intertwined with our political troubles; but we cannot tell ourselves too often that Germany is not being ruled by men of economic mind—witness General Göring's appointment. They are talented and almost purely political adventurers; and for that reason we should not relax our grip on the accepted lever that the political must mainly precede the economic solution. There will, of course, be no absolute precedence, for the discussion of the one will bring about the discussion of the other. It is, however, important not to waver in our handling of the priorities; for it may well prove to be the case that Germany is not yet quite ripe for negotiation, and that she will need to feel both the pinch and our perseverance a little longer before we can hope to be successful.

I had several very friendly and useful conversations with Herr Dieckhoff, and am glad to have re-established such friendly contact with him. He was most anxious for closer relations between the two Foreign Offices. I said that I had made a contribution to that end by coming over despite my misleading reputation in Germany. I had thought it better to let them all have a good look at the *bête noire*, and to decide for themselves not only that it was not as black as it had been painted, but even that it was only a reasonable realist, more than ready to collaborate on any fair and sound basis. I spoke in this vein to many Germans, who, confidence being once established, were both frank in their past and friendly in their present views. I may fairly say that during my visit I succeeded in largely removing the idea that the British Foreign Office was peopled with professional anti-Germans. Herr Dieckhoff asked whether I would be able to come back in case of need (a similar suggestion was made by Herr Hitler to my wife). I replied that I would always make any contribution in my power to understanding, and that, if ever he and I failed to agree, he would henceforth know that it was because of honest conviction or political impossibility, and not because of any bias or ill-feeling. I should add that Herr Dieckhoff, like several other Germans who went out of their way to raise the point, was anxious that the meeting-place of the October Conference should be in London; and I found willing acquiescence in the suggestion that London was likely to, and should, develop into a kind of clearing-house for the exchanges preliminary to the meeting. In a word, I think Herr Dieckhoff will be as helpful as he is allowed to be, and perhaps his capacities for co-operation will be increased by the transfer to London of Herr von Ribbentrop, especially if the transfer involves the closing or disintegration of the rival office.

With this gentleman we shall have more trouble. I fear that he is shallow, self-seeking and not really friendly. No one who studies his mouth will be reassured. He was most markedly unenthusiastic about his appointment to London, of which I spoke to him many times with never a flicker of response. Our meetings throughout my stay were frequent and sometimes prolonged. To him one has to listen without much chance of interruption, when he really gets going on his set-pieces, for he is guided by his command of English. From these talks I always derived the impression of a divided mentality; perhaps he realised that it was well for him to get out of Berlin and impossible for him to refuse the post, but he was certainly reluctant to lose his personal contact with the Führer. His influence may be exaggerated by report for, as General Göring said frankly, the Führer alone decides policy; but all these men have views to air, and I suspect that Herr von Ribbentrop will continue to report direct to Herr Hitler as well as to the German Foreign Office, whom he has hitherto overridden but never served. We shall not suffer by his absence from Berlin, except in so far as we may find him a trial in London, for he himself will be on trial. It will be a case of our money or his life. The impossible will be expected of him, and it will be scored against him—heavily and with *Schadenfreude* among the party extremists, who hate him—if he fails to deliver the goods. German policy may well make those goods undeliverable; and in such case he may well turn ugly. Indeed he, and he alone, showed his hand, or perhaps I should say his teeth. He remarked on one occasion that 'if England didn't give Germany the possibility to live,' there would eventually be war between them, and one of them would be annihilated. I was careful not to enquire what was meant by 'the possibility to live,' for he would then have believed, or reported, himself to be in a negotiation. In any case the colonies would have cropped up, as they were often on the verge of doing; for Dr. Goebbels alluded to them with delicacy but clarity, and General Göring with clarity. I fear, therefore, that we shall not find the new Ambassador easy, because he will be uneasy himself. Frau von Ribbentrop, on the other hand, is genuinely delighted at their new appointment, perhaps with a tinge of relief at getting him away from Berlin. She will be popular in London, and will retain more value than some of her conquests.

This memorandum being mainly recorded for my own interest, I set down also a few further impressions of the men whom I met—characteristics without any pretence, on such short acquaintance, of being characters. In any event I am a little mistrustful of analysis, which usually means reading something into human nature.

The man with whom I got on best in Berlin was Dr. Goebbels. He seemed to me the deepest of them all. Report has him *capable de tout*; I found much charm in him—a limping, eloquent, slip of a Jacobin, 'quick as a whip,' and often, I doubt not, as cutting. One can imagine his influence, once in his stride, over audiences 'enslaved, illogical, elate,' as Kipling wrote of Americans fifty years ago; but he is a calculator and therefore a man with whom one might do business. More might be made of him if this kind of contact could be maintained; and, conversely, if it is not, he could become very damaging. My wife and I liked him and his wife at once; it is an obviously happy marriage, with attractive devotion on both sides. I mention this because tales have run riot on the morals of revived Germany. No doubt there are Ganymedes to minister to Olympians, and the appetites of new men come by feeding. Nothing, however, could be further from the truth in the case of the ruling clique; its domestic life seems irreproachable, witness the very pleasant Hess *ménage*, or even that of General Göring. I say 'even' because General Göring has been given a bad name in Europe, and though he doubtless has defects, this is not one of them. His really nice wife is a young lady of Riga, likely to keep her seat as well as the smile on the face of the tiger. The trouble about this bounding, primitive creature is that he has never grown up. General Göring enjoys everything, particulary his own parties, with the gusto of Smith minor suddenly possessed of unlimited tick at the school stores. The world is his oyster, and no damned nonsense about opening. These new men do not stint themselves or their guests. While money is no object—I can only guess what Dr. Schacht says—the taste of their entertainments is remarkable. Having seen their costliness, I am glad we waived our claim to the next Olympiad. The Japanese can have it, and welcome. Only once did discrimination falter—in the well-meant production of a Greek tragedy, perfectly staged and execrably acted: a good example of our persistent snobbery in pretending that the theatre of one age is compatible with another.

A propos of the Olympic games, in the past there has been controversy whether they were internationally beneficial or the reverse. I should say that they were at one time beneficial and that they are now the reverse, owing to the over-specialisation of athletics. What is applauded now is not the individual performance, but the national performer, often the product of a Government subsidy. The crowd was full of nationalism. There is a tendency toward competitive national advertisement, and the footsteps of Prestige can almost be heard on the track. One does not feel much amateur spirit in the air, but rather a jealously regarded professional demonstration. There is almost too much organisation all round; and from our own point of view the programme is greatly overburdened. It contains endless laughably unolympic items, which no Englishman will seriously practise; and, as these all count for crowns and medals, we shall always cut a poor figure in the total results. I was impressed by the fact that *our* Prestige was undoubtedly lowered by the relative failure of our team, although it was a really first-class amateur one. The other thing that struck me most at the Olympiad was the gymnastic display given in the arena by thousands of German youths and girls, the more striking in that, as Frau Göring informed me, they were in no sense picked, but came at random from the country. These tense, intense, people are going to make us look a C3 nation, if we elect to continue haphazard. And they will want to do something worth while with this stored energy. So it all depends on what they are being taught is worth while; and that brings me back to my old slogan about watching the text-books. They will give little comfort so far. I left Berlin with this impression, with many warm personal likings, and with gratitude for generous and universal hospitality.

The hospitality and the gratitude were both so genuine that one traces in oneself an instinctive hesitation in mentioning the reverse of the medal—a tribute to what must have been the general effect produced by the Olympiad. But the impression must be truthful and complete. The reverse of the medal was a thin, almost transparent, profile, with a high forehead and frightened eyes. Its name was, too appropriately, Israel. He came in by the back door of the Embassy plainly terrorised; indeed, he murmured—he never raised his voice above a murmur— that, were it known that he had come to see me, it would be the end of him. He mentioned a common friend, who had recently committed suicide, looked nervously over his shoulder, and asked if nothing could be done to alleviate the lot of his else doomed co-religionists. I had, in fact, been tempted to say something of this in Berlin while discussing Anglo-German relations; but the Ambassador was clear that, in the prevailing mood, any apparent 'intervention' would do far more harm than good to the victims. I replied accordingly; but I added that he should keep his heart up, for, if we all came to agreement in the autumn, the ensuing warmth might either tend to deter Germany from further persecution—Mr. Israel was very sure that another outbreak was on the way—or else make it more possible than now for a newly signed-up friend to put in a moderating word. With this perforce he had to be content, though it was little enough; and so departed, tremulous and dispirited, again by the back door. I did not relish this interview.

I had one or two others of some interest—with the French Ambassador and the Belgian and Czechoslovak Ministers, for example. With the two former I maintained frank contact, especially after hearing from the Foreign Office that my visit to Berlin had caused suspicion at the Quai d'Orsay.[4] 'There be many that say, who will show us any good.' I found all of them pessimists; all of them—and many others—expected some further unpleasant surprise after the Olympiad. The only difference of opinion was whether the surprise would be external, as the Diplomatic Body suspected, or whether it would be internal, as anticipated by Mr. Israel and the other body of opinion that anticipated serious party differences

---

4 See No. 60.

either before or during the Nüremberg rally. It has turned out to be the extension of military service, which nobody had prophesied just then; but the oracles will depict this as the prelude to some of the other seismic rumbles in the lap of time. There are, however, some less forbidding possibilities. The Czechoslovak Minister said that he thought an arrangement between Germany and Czechoslovakia possible on the same, possibly fallacious, lines as with Austria. I asked him how high he put the chances, and he replied that they were about even. This is not optimism, but it is worth remembering with our eye on October.

I also had two long talks with King Boris of Bulgaria, who had arrived in Berlin to increase the prospects of an heir through an operation on the Queen. He wished to see me before his incognito ceased and before he began seeing Germans. He suggested a meeting in a wood—I should add 'at midnight' if I were not being truthful. Happily this suggestion fell through, and we met at his hotel; but as we both—particularly he—suspected that there was a dictaphone about, our style was somewhat cramped. I mention this episode because it gives another aspect of the Berlin medal. King Boris was most friendly, but a little apprehensive lest his visit might be misinterpreted in Paris and London. He spoke of going from Berlin to these two capitals; but I told him that no one in London at least was thinking of misinterpretations, that he would find no one now in either London or Paris, and that if he were coming it would be better to come later. His troubles at home were not diminishing, he said, and he evidently needs encouragement.

I come back to the Germans and an assessment of my impressions. Those in authority would clearly like to come to an understanding, perhaps even something closer, with England—on their own terms. They would far sooner reach this relationship with us than with the sycophantic Italians, whom they still inwardly contemn and distrust. (Germans have tenacious memories, and though Lloyd George is obviously cultivating them, they have not forgotten his record, and say so.) The Italians are still above themselves and therefore still underrate us. The Germans do not make this tempting mistake, though they would like to do so; they have a lingering respect for our capacity to spring surprises, that is since we have begun rearming, though it would be quite unsafe to rely upon it without considerable reinforcement. The Germans would also sooner deal with us alone; but I doubt whether they retain any serious hope of dividing us from the French, unless France goes too far to the Left, and they realise that any agreement must begin with the Five Locarno Powers. I should, however, make it clear that there is no hope of any acceptable limitation of air forces. Russia is henceforth always going to be counted in and played up to the full; General Göring was explicit on this. In other words, Germany will claim, if this topic is raised at all, a great superiority over the Western Powers. That is her story and she will stick to it. It is a position that we cannot accept; so, if we wish to negotiate, we shall in this respect have to keep off the long grass of nature, and tread the lawns of artifice. But an air pact without air limitation is neither very convincing nor very valuable. There is also, as I have said, no prospect of inducing Germany to conclude any Convention with Russia; were we to continue our former pressure for an Eastern Pact, we should now either be told to mind our own business, or else we should risk the destruction of all possible negotiations. The ghost of M. Barthou would hardly recognise the Germany of 1936. A western agreement is attainable by itself; a paper settlement in Central Europe is also just possible, if we are tactful and determined enough—as I hope we shall be—though we shall have a hard struggle when once we run into the Polish and Czechoslovak appendages, where any attempt at a new Locarno will speedily land us. But that is the maximum in Europe, and we had better make up our minds to that before we start.

The Germans are, indeed, likely to attempt, as conditions of even a Western settlement, an illicit try-on in two further respects. Firstly, they will probably attempt to force a rupture between France and Russia; and there is a vast difference between that and a renunciation of any further pressure on Germany to conclude an Eastern Pact. In a word, the move would be inadmissible, and would have to be firmly rejected. Secondly, the Germans will probably try to get us to halt or call off our rearmament programme, now that the German Government have reaped the fruits of years of heavy over-expenditure on armaments. If we listen to any suggestion of this kind, we shall be committing eventual suicide, and meanwhile throwing away any chance of substantial understanding with them, not on a piece of paper marked with the meaningless figures 1936 or 1937, but in reality and over the years. Any understanding on armaments with the present Germany will only be safe and possible when the agreement of 1936, if reached, has worked securely for a number of years. On our firm grasp of this truth depends any prospect of making into an ultimate reality an agreement that will otherwise be eyewash. We are admittedly going to gamble—since the experience of the last five years has shown that no treaty nowadays has any reliable value *per se*—and the only justification for that course is to give oneself the best possible chance of eventual, not only immediate, success. The latter alone might well result in our going down to history as dupes despite many warnings. Our minimum conditions should, therefore, be the conclusion of a Western multilateral agreement—*without limitation*, which will be impossible unless we concede vast and undue superiority to Germany—with bilateral pacts of arbitration, non-aggression and non-interference in Central Europe, if we fail to work these into the frame of the new Locarno, for which we shall presumably first try. I say this should be our minimum because Herr Hitler offered them in the spring, though he may try to back out of them in autumn. He has already supplied a specimen in Austria, when it suited him. We must probably say good-bye to a multilateral pact in Central Europe, and certainly to an Eastern Pact, which will be a surmountable loss, if we can get geographically interposing agreements. That is a fair enough compromise—a great deal more up the German street than we should lately have thought admissible—and we shall be weak, indeed, if we are pulled beyond it. As it is, we shall have gone to the length of practically accepting Herr Hitler's March programme—a considerable diplomatic success for Germany, not for us. But on our side we must at least stand firm on two cardinal points: no denunciation of existing signatures, and no disarmament for several years, that is, until we have covered the needs of our absolute and quite independent national defence and guarded ourselves against ever being again in such a position as in 1935. Those are measures for cutting the coat according to the cloth, even if it turns out to be a cloak for German designs. What are those designs? Will the agreement hold, even when we have gone so far to get it? On present form, No; but it would be a counsel of despair to act on a negative. We shall have to perform an Act of Faith. After all, as Pascal argued, *autant croire*—if you can. It is possible, if not probable, that an agreement once on its legs will stand, and lead *all* its signatories into upright habits. We might succeed with Time, if we do not kill Time by premature disarmament. But what of the designs? Are they expansive? Yes. Where? In both Europe and Africa—but with no fixed or immediate priority. Let us consider for a minute what Big Boy Göring and the gentler Hess—and Ribbentrop with his 'possibilities of living' or war—really meant when they said that they would like, above all, to come to a firm understanding with us, but that, if we would not play, we must not be surprised if they took other partners. It plainly means, among other things, either that they expect of us complaisance in Europe or the colonies, or both. At present it means both. No one can play ostrich indefinitely with the colonial question; and as to Europe let us hear General Milch. He would like an alliance with England and Yugoslavia—not Italy—and he would like Roumania for a colony. These, and no doubt many other, tendencies and desiderata are in the air; but, if a treaty could become a habit instead of a manœuvre, we might succeed in modifying if not in eliminating them. If, however, we are going to give a serious run to the policy of *autant croire*—the right because the only one—are we giving it a full chance? Are we being consistent? That is more than doubtful. I am thinking, of course, of the stumbling-block of the colonies. By half-measures we shall certainly not succeed in the long run, and the play will have to run long, if it is going to run at all; or, rather, we might succeed by a half-measure, but certainly not by no measure of expansion at all. That is not cutting the coat according to the cloth, but ensuring that the seams will burst. Herr Hitler's speech at Nuremberg has surely made it clear that if we persist in refusing to return to Germany her former colonies, we shall either eventually have to fight for them, which I do not believe this country will readily do, or submit to the national humiliation of changing our tune later under pressure. We shall surely not be giving to our gamble its best chance, since we shall be undoing with one hand what we do with the other, thereby perforce limiting our success to the immediate—at utmost—and ignoring the eventual. This has always been my view, and I believe that the future will bear it out, even if inanimate. I suggest a little more reflection, if we really mean business. Would it not be possible—if it is necessary—to foreshadow colonial cessions, in the event of the autumn agreement, which I am postulating, working well and enduringly and of peace being maintained in Europe? This would tend to stabilise German ambitions for a while, during which the policy of *autant croire* would have a chance to strike root; and it would gain for us the time needed for our essential rearmament. And we should be facing Reality.

If we are going far in anything but self-deception, are we right in excluding the possibility of going far enough to make a real job of it? These people are the most formidable proposition that has ever been formulated; they are in strict training now, not for the Olympic games, but for breaking some other and emphatically unsporting world records, and perhaps the world as well. And yet there may be something to be made of them. In that respect I leave Berlin with better hopes than when I went. At present they are going wrong, are being taught wrong; this may be inevitable, but I prefer to think the contrary. For if as the French proverb has it, to talk of love is to make love, to talk of peace may be to make peace, if we can talk long enough. If we could hold them for a while by a combination of reasonableness and honest-to-God strength, we could still turn the corner. Sometime I should like to have another go at them, untrammelled by any sporting or festive façade, and therefore with licence to indulge in details and plain speaking instead of general disquisitions. For we shall have to come to that fairly soon, unless we are to come to less desirable grips; and we shall probably not be able to do so through Ribbentrop, who, being now compulsorily out for his own hand, will almost inevitably overplay it, and will quite inevitably lose his hold over the Führer unless he misrepresents us, like the itinerant British lightweights in Germany.

On my way from Berlin to Brittany I passed through Paris, and dined with M. Blum and M. Delbos, to whom I gave an account of my German impressions and the prospects of agreement in the autumn. As I had to catch a train at half-past 8, I had not time to speak to them as fully as I would have wished, but I had ample opportunity of making up for this curtailment by spending nearly a fortnight in Brittany in the same house as an old friend, my opposite number, M. Léger.[5] To him I spoke freely, and found him ready to agree with my ideas of the possible and impossible: a new Locarno, without limitation, that is a western pact with proper appendages or corollaries in Central Europe (I do not think he would be too particular as to the forms), and the abandonment of any Eastern Pact. He agreed in thinking the latter no longer practical or desirable politics, but he said that it would take M. Blum all his time to get the abandonment past his Left Wing supporters. (We have also received due notice from our own Opposition that they will resist any abandonment of an Eastern Pact.) This would make it more than ever impossible for this, or any, French Government to give up at German dictation any pacts already concluded. This includes not only Russia and Czechoslovakia, but the other countries of the Little *Entente* and Poland. As to Italy he said that pro-Italian feeling, a growth of 1935, was rapidly disappearing in France everywhere but in the south. I replied that I thought it would be most unreasonable of Herr Hitler to claim the abandonment of the existing, and that I did not believe he could seriously hope to induce France to isolate herself. On the other hand, I was relieved to find that he concurred in not asking the impossible of Germany; for English opinion wished to try out, with wide-open eyes, the policy of *autant croire*, and if France, at Russian instigation, blocked it, M. Blum would lose at the British swings more than he could win at the Russian roundabouts. I knew that M. Blum's chief profession and concern was collaboration with England; but M. Blum must remember, as I had told him in Paris, that the British Government was upheld by a very large Conservative majority, who were never prepared, and now probably less than ever, to make much sacrifice for red eyes. The Russian aspect of Spain could not fail to make a difference in these sections of English feeling. I begged M. Léger to repeat this to M. Blum, for I thought it would assist him in resisting undue Russian pressure or wrecking tactics; and there was something to be wrecked, for there was an undoubted possibility of limited progress. M. Léger agreed, and I am sure that we shall find him helpful; but he asked me what I thought an agreement, if obtained, would be worth. I replied that time alone could show, and that playing for time might therefore be a paying game. My known scepticism—and we had all learnt our lesson in regard to the signature of dictators—might lend weight to my advocacy of an attempt at faith. It might fail, but it would go hard with us, indeed, if we can find no faith at all even between mortals. M. Léger is ready to try the Act of Faith within reason. He does not want the attempt to be made in Switzerland, but would prefer London or Brussels as the scene, realising fully that no place on earth could be found where Herr Hitler and Signor Mussolini could be present in the flesh.

On one other point I felt bound to be truthful with the French. I had, as will be seen, preached as much as possible in Berlin the virtues and deserts of the present French régime. If that régime maintained its ground, international agreement was attainable, though with difficulty. If, however, France moved much further to the Left, we should probably find the Germans unmanageable. Moreover, I

[5] Cf. No. 85.

was by no means sure of the effect of such a development on my own countrymen. As the French Government well knew, there had been a strong wave of pro-German feeling in England for some time past; and it had only turned over since Germany had refused to reply to our questions. Opinion had come back into focus by the end of the summer; but I thought it more than probable that any further move by France in the direction of Communism would cancel the change favourable to France that had come about, and set all this wobbling body of opinion off again in the direction of Berlin. These anticipations, especially in regard to the effect on Germany, were sufficiently probable to make it well for the French Government to be aware of them. In some degree a fresh impetus might thus be given to that very conflict of *Weltanschauungen*, against which I had been preaching in Berlin. That was certainly the very last thing that would suit England.

M. Blum and M. Delbos both asked me to come and see them again on my return from Brittany, but I did not think it right to trouble them again, and came straight back to England. So ended a Busman's Holiday. I wonder why the *Daily Worker* thinks that I make a fortune out of the sufferings of busmen.

APPENDIX II

Memorandum by Sir R. Vansittart

'The World Situation and British Rearmament'*

[*C 8998/8998/18*]

Most Secret[1]   FOREIGN OFFICE, *December 31, 1936*

1. The moment is opportune to review the trend of world events in 1936, and to relate this background practically to our progress in national re-equipment. It is now also opportune, since we have entered upon the period of emergency, to check the studies and forecasts of the last half-dozen years in the light of the situation that has developed since the 'truce' of the Olympic games. The general trend has been almost uniformly unfavourable to our interests. To demonstrate this fact, it is only necessary to fill in the details. I have done so fully, but the situation is serious enough to warrant fullness, and I earnestly beg that both Memorandum and annexes may be comprehensively studied. It will be seen that the future should be considered without pessimism but with concern. The danger is much less that war may now be wittingly contemplated in serious quarters as 'an instrument of national policy' than that unreflecting currents are forcing themselves into shallow and turbulent courses likely to deepen into danger.

2. Time was when Japan was thought to be our chief danger. Foreshadowed events 'have changed all that' only too quickly, and, while Japan is now generally considered likely to await a war in Europe, Germany has become the recognised storm-centre of the earth. It is a thousand pities, for Germany presents the human animal at its most efficient and therefore—despite the envious self-pity of the Prussian character—at its most attractive for those who naturally prefer this quality to its shoddy opposites. Indeed, efficiency and self-pity, which invariably mean propaganda, combined with the patent and irritating errors of French post-war policy and with the real German grievances of the past—I think they still possess one real grievance in the colonial sphere—have to some extent obscured until recently the true course of events, and have anyhow powerfully and explicably influenced many people in this country. There are few who would not like, or even prefer, a German if he would let us, and the policy of His Majesty's Government has for long been directed to giving him every chance; but sentiments have nothing to do with facts, or with policy which has to follow facts. The only trouble—in theory—should be to ascertain them. Politically, however, it is always more normal for the mind to dwell in the immediate past than in its immediate successor—particularly when the past is more comfortable and leisurely—partly because accurate pictures take time to form and are not quickly supplied. It is

---

[1] The following note appeared on the first page of the printed copies of this memorandum: 'Much of the material used in the following memorandum is of so secret a nature, and any leakage might be so detrimental to some of the many sources from which it has been drawn, that I would ask for most particular care in the keeping of this paper. R. V.'

always the case, and it has been our own case, that impressions thus not only follow events but follow too far behind. Therein lie both a danger and a need for constant review. It is now of merely academic interest that the League in general and France in particular treated Germany in the past with too little generosity, and so stimulated 'self-help' in Germany to a highly dangerous degree now limited only by her strength. It is no longer the denial of her rights but of her desires that she regards as an injury. But it is unprofitable to dwell on the past or even too much in the present. It is the future that must be the subject of our preoccupations.

3. It may be convenient to begin this survey with the Far East. In 1932 there were strong indications of a desire on the part of the Japanese army for a trial of strength with Russia—a desire evanescent as Russian strength increased. This was followed by something like a *détente*, and there were even some symptoms of coming to terms. The Japanese have, indeed, now lost any stomach for armed adventure against Russia, save with iron companions and golden opportunity, though they have not yet reached the point of readiness for a non-aggression pact proffered in the past by a Russia grown indifferent. This state of deadlock suited our militarily unsubstantial position in the Far East, and any easement is to our loss. We can welcome nothing that might tend to drive Japanese expansionism south, and there is plenty of talk about that. Japan's financial weakness—she spends over 45 per cent. of the entire national budget on national defence—must be considered in the same light as Germany's, a factor which works both ways; up to an uncertain point it restrains; pushed beyond, it may produce external reck-lessness. The military, says Mr. Hall-Patch, do not take account of the economic consequences of the present military policy, and the officials and bankers offer no serious resistance to their demands. In both cases we are bound to reckon with this possibility of rash action in the future; and in such case, and in the altered circumstances described above, the aside of southward aggression may be as likely drama as an attack on bristling Russia, whatever the doctrinal mouthings of mid-stage. Japan still aims at hegemony, on which it is as overtly set in Asia as Germany in Europe.

4. Into this dubious situation the new German–Japanese Pact has been pro-jected, not unexpectedly; and it is significant that it has been negotiated not by the two Foreign Offices, but by Herr von Ribbentrop's rival office of amateurs and the equally short-sighted Japanese military.[2] Between the two general staffs there have been some previous symptoms of an intimacy which necessarily rouses suspicion as to the true substance of the agreement. We do not yet know the full contents, but we do know already that there is without question a secret agreement which may result in something like staff conversations. At present the *appearance* is that of co-operation against communism; but the appearance convinces no one, and the Russian Ambassador in Tokyo has not inaptly retorted, that the German and Japanese *police* cannot possibly need each other's assistance! What the agreement clearly does do, however—particularly in view of the conclusions of the preceding paragraph—is to introduce Japan into the orbit of European affairs at a particu-larly delicate and dangerous phase, and to increase the probability that, in given circumstances, Germany and Japan would now act together. The Japanese Ambassador in London has recently said that if we cannot find an alternative policy in which Japan could co-operate with us—and he is not helping us much to find it—those who favour an even closer relationship between Japan and Ger-many will have their way. He added that he regarded such tendencies as highly

[2] See No. 421, note 3.

dangerous for his own country. They are also dangerous for ours. The comment of the entourage of General Goering is also instructive. 'The ideological window-dressing of the published agreement might be politically necessary. The important thing, however, was not the *Weltanschauung*, but the fact that an agreement between the world's best soldiers had now been reached. It was particularly desirable that England's smug complacency should be shaken.' A high official in the confidence of Dr. Goebbels has added that an important reason for concluding the agreement was the desire 'to make sure of Japan. There had been an anxious time when it seemed probable that Japan, impressed by the Russian military preparations in the Far East, might come to an agreement with the Russians. This danger had been enhanced by the possibility of a renewal of Anglo-Japanese friendship; and it was believed that the British would even now work for a Russo-Japanese *détente*.' It will be noted how closely this information, obtained in mid-December, fits in with the account that I have given at the beginning of paragraph 3. The new development may have the effect of containing and paralysing Russia in the event of German aggression in Europe, and we know for a fact that the Japanese at least consider this to be in the German mind; on the other hand, it cannot be assumed that the arrangement is such as to preclude the prospect of any further *détente* between Russia and Japan. On this treacherous and speculative position we can but keep a close watch; and our only security will be the quick completion of the Singapore base and a strong fleet. One other significant feature must be quoted before we leave the Far East. We have heard much, and for years, of a Japanese desire for close friendship with this country. The words never materialised into deeds, because the Paper Dragon—as we were called—was not weighty enough. 'The military party in Japan are opposed to England,' said Mr. Sugimura recently. 'They respect Germany because of her force.' We have been patient, we do our best to keep up sentiment, to find a friendly modus vivendi; but the sentiments are apt to end in words for, as our greatest authority, Sir G. Sansom, puts it: 'a comprehensive arrangement is likely to be extremely difficult, because our interests are fundamentally opposed at almost every point.' And the only way to overcome that obstacle, respect begotten of strength, is lacking. We shall encounter the same phenomenon frequently in this review. It is difficult, for example, to extract from Japan with diplomatic forceps the ordinary courtesy of an apology for the Keelung incident. It is questionable how far her agreement with Germany has fortified or is likely to fortify her in this embarrassing ill-grace. The Chinese, for their part, fear that it will fortify Japan in designs or actions at their expense; and Japanese stimulation of the disruptive move in Suiyuan shows that both design and action are still in being. Our Ambassador at Peking comments that future developments seem to depend partly on 'how far the Japanese Government may be emboldened as a result of the German–Japanese agreement.' The situation is certainly deteriorating in China. On the other side may be set down that this flamboyant and over-dramatised diplomacy has been uncomfortably received in Japan; and the Japanese Minister for Foreign Affairs 'admitted *with regret* that the agreement would probably result in bringing the United States of America nearer to the Anglo-French point of view, *and away from Germany*.' The naïve candour of the italics repays reflection. The American press is, indeed, almost unanimous in taking a serious view of this agreement as a possible menace to peace. Some organs go further and treat it as 'the first step in a chain of events which might drag the United States into another world war through the back door of Asia.' The façade of the agreement is looked on with general scepticism, and there is a tendency to consider that Japan and Germany could have chosen no better means of turning the United States toward their former allies. These comments may be considered in conjunction with the anti-dictator feeling already prevalent in the United States of America.

5. In the Far East, therefore, we have to deal with one country, China, that is still chaotic and therefore a temptation; with another, Russia, that is still a merchant of 'dangerous thoughts,' and has a wholly uncertain future, seeing that events might really push her toward the hoity-toity, if not splendid, isolation with which at intervals she threatens the West; with a third country, Japan, that is strained, unscrupulous and definitely expansionist at alien cost—a necessary feature of expansion—joined now by a fourth to whom the same description applies, though the appetite is European and African instead of Asiatic. All this is cause for deep and urgent concern.

6. Turning to Europe, we find all the water that has passed under the broken bridges of this year equally turgid and rising toward flood. Little though we may like it, consistently though we have struggled against it, the Old Adam, of whose second coming I wrote in 1931,[3] has succeeded in re-creating once more a world where appetite is crudely territorial and where Force is measure and idol. It is the more unfortunate that the totalitarian States should be taut and esurient Have-nots, and that easy-going democracies should be the Haves; but the classification only renders more perilous the ideological antitheses, against which we are also struggling.

7. For what has happened? We should never make the mistake of lumping dictators together—even mentally—but Italy and Germany *have* come far to coalesce—a fact which 'dominates the whole situation along the Danube'—so far, indeed, that, as our Ambassador in Rome warns us, we should be unwise to betray any *overt* disposition to separate them—though of course we *must* separate them, if they do not separate themselves, as they well may. For the present Italy and Germany have a common policy, possibly in pressure upon this country, certainly in the disruption of the Little Entente, on which the agreement has already had its effect; and for the future we must trust to tact and time, and to the cultivation of ourselves as a counter-attraction, which can only be compassed among materialists by a rapid extension of our own material Force. So far the dictators are not impressed. The German Government is, on the contrary, inspiring a systematic belittlement of this country, and has infected an over-prone Italy. Count Ciano, no very solid, or perhaps too solid, a head, has testified to the contagion. The Italo-German agreement[4] is, in fact, causing both parties to feel unhealthily overweening, and the consequent belittlement of us is the basis of the anti-British drive that both countries (but particularly of course Italy) are conducting against us throughout the East, a drive that we shall be incapable of checking, if we do not extensively refurbish our own propaganda—a most important point—as well as our material re-equipment. This latter element is, however, the first, if not the only, antidote to Italian propaganda and to the effect of our Palestinian policy in the Near and Middle East. Meanwhile, we may, indeed should, attenuate our dangers in the Mediterranean by endeavouring to rebuild out of the wreck something of our old relationship with Italy. The first steps have been taken; the rest can be done, without humiliation or sacrifice, but we have not done it yet, nor shall we be able, without a continuous show and reality of strength, safely to inhabit the structure, even if re-erected. The policy of Italy, always opportunist

[3] Cf. Series Ia, Volume VII, Appendix.   [4] See No. 411, note 3.

and venial, has become more unblushingly so than ever—and more formidably, seeing that she has become a real, instead of an apparent, first-class power, incidentally with the Vatican, no mean ally, in her political pocket. If 'guns are better than butter,' they are also better than, or a guarantee of, any Italian undertaking. For us the most dangerous result of this conjuncture is that Count Ciano has promised Herr Hitler support in his colonial aspirations; and such promises between such partners usually have something hanging to them for the smaller one, possibly the Balearic Islands, judging by recent Italian action, which shows some intent to take root there, though perhaps in no grossly visible form. At present the position is that in the event of war Italy would certainly not be against Germany, and some further effort on our part will be necessary, if we are to ensure that she will not be against us. The youth of the Italian Army and of the Fascist Party have now a strong pro-German element. On the other hand the German army describe their relations with Italy as a 'love affair of convenience' but not a 'marriage.' The real differences remain; for, regardless of present tactics, the *Gleichschaltung* of Austria is a fundamental Nazi aim.[5] The German word of command is 'permeation, not conspiracy,' a change of method, not of aim. The *Gleichschaltung* is to be 'cold,' as they say, instead of hot. The Italians know this business of the Trojan Horse, and above all Signor Mussolini knows it and may keep the Hapsburgs up his sleeve to counteract, if necessary, the German drive in South-Eastern Europe, which may anyhow turn him our way again. Already indeed Italy is concerned to prevent the Danube basin and the Balkans from coming under German hegemony. Moreover, both countries are struggling for predominance in Hungary. Let us never disparage Mussolini, but pray on the contrary that he may endure, for he is our best hope hereabouts in a world whose imperfections may thus be measured. It has even been stated by one of his assistants—and it may be true—that he 'only accepted the German–Austrian agreement as a means of gaining time and guarding against some sudden German *tour de force*.' Opportunism again! In any event there is much leeway to make up; and if we cannot make it up with him we shall certainly not succeed with anyone else. It is the more advisable to succeed in that—apart from the past differences special to our two countries—Italy like Germany, though on a minor and even less practical scale, seems headed for autarky in preparation for a new war. In Italy's case the move cannot succeed, and must herald a slow economic decline. This in turn can only result in further adventure, in which we may be involved, or in an advance towards us with an eye to a loan or long-term credits.

8. Here again is something to our disadvantage. But there is more than that in the Mediterranean. The two dictator States are creating a third; and, by recognising General Franco's government before he is sure of winning, they have committed themselves irretrievably to making a success of his venture, thus limiting niceties as to means. This may well bring the dictators still closer together, anyhow for a while, though here again there are already signs that Italy is disquieted by the thoroughness of the German effort, and might conceivably be prised loose. It is true that the Soviet government, which seems lately bereft of statesmanship or

---

[5] *Note in original*: 'Any definite disagreement between Italy and Germany,' says Sir W. Selby, 'would leave the Austrian Government in no doubt as to which capital to look to for "marching orders" in the future. It would without question be Berlin. In Austrian eyes, however, a restoration of Anglo-Italian co-operation would materially alter the picture . . . The Austrian has not forgotten the lesson of the war.' This is probably one of the reasons behind the Italian desire for the façade of a Mediterranean agreement with us.

even card-sense, is largely responsible for making Spain the scene and cause of the bloodiest form of that very ideological struggle that we are seeking to prevent. The fact remains that the new totalitarian partners, who have been keeping their domains on a positive war-footing for the past few years, have cheerfully accepted the opportunity, and with their great quantities of surplus war material have turned ideological cannibalism into something even more concretely inimical to our interests. It is ironically true that, the crisis once precipitated, the victory of the Right would be no worse for us than the victory of the Left—a very extreme Left—which would spread a dividing and disintegrating contagion into France and from France to ourselves, and would so alter the European kaleidoscope as to present Germany with hegemony ready made. On the other hand, if Franco wins, the now combined weight of the two larger autocrats—unless natural causes and our own skill diminish their unity—will be too great for him, and he will be pulled more completely into their camp than his past proclivities and present interests render natural. We shall then be faced by at least a temporarily working combination of dictators, major, minor and minimus. And already I learn from a reliable German source that major's voluble henchmen—large appetite tends to loquacity—are anticipating the military uses of Spain in putting pressure upon us; while from an even surer source we are informed that Franco is already arranging with dictator minor to break Spain away from the League. We still hear German cries about encirclement, when it is clearly now not Germany but France that is being encircled, partly by her own doing. The latter indeed will probably soon have potential enemies on three frontiers, and a cooling friend on the fourth.

9. Another, but more contingent, Mediterranean anxiety must be taken into account. Italy for many years neglected her opportunities of winning Yougoslavia, the most promising young match in Europe. A rapidly growing Germany took her place in the courtship. Then came the Abyssinian adventure and the linking of dictators held apart at Stresa. Now *both* are heavy and conniving suitors; indeed, Germany is playing the matchmaker and urging Yougoslavia into a full alliance with Italy. Strange bed-fellows! If Germany is thinking chiefly of isolating Czechoslovakia, Italy is thinking of Yougoslav ports and of *us*. The Prince Regent and his Minister Stoyadinovitch are fortunately sound and suspicious; but a continuation of the unnatural union will not make it easy for them to resist increasing pressure, which again can only be offset and countered by the evident and welcome growth of our own strength. At present we are far from having enough to carry conviction here either. *It is the general opinion in Europe that we are moving too slowly for our own safety, let alone for anyone else's.* Yet the interest is ubiquitous, and will perhaps be more striking if I quote not France, or Belgium, or Russia or Czechoslovakia or Roumania, but a relatively disinterested country. 'I was struck in particular,' writes Sir W. Selby on the 16th November, 'by the almost exaggerated anxiety displayed by many of my Austrian friends, among them General Jansa, Chief of the Austrian General Staff, as to the intentions of England; and still more struck by their evident interest in the progress of British rearmament. Austria, dominated though she may feel herself to be by her two formidable neighbours, yet most ardently hopes that other forces may come in to maintain the balance, and prevent some untoward development, which would inevitably involve her, and as a result of which she feels certain she would once again be the major sufferer.' Yougoslavia feels this even more keenly: 'The bulk of the Yougoslav public,' says Sir R. Campbell, 'evinces great satisfaction that Great Britain is now seriously tackling her rearmament problem. It is to Great

Britain, if only she seemed a little less remote, that the majority of Yougoslavs would turn for guidance and support.'

10. The current both of events and opinions has thus lately been against us; and at this point we ought to face another important consideration. We still profess the League, and rightly, not only since no other principle of European salvation, however faint, is visible or existent, but also because on no other principle can this country be united in self-defence. The League is the new Sick Man of Europe—another point in our disfavour—and we have proclaimed our intention of setting him on his legs again. It can be done, indeed it *will* be done, naturally and almost automatically, if we allow the invalid to grow up again round a fully and recognisably rearmed England; for all the middle-weights and light-weights of Europe naturally prefer us and him to the new 'Rome–Berlin axis.' Even Hungary will keep off that if she can. Moreover, there is a growing irritation in Central Europe and the Balkans at Germany's commercial ruthlessness and 'debtor's penetration;' and the joint Anglo-Franco-American *communiqué* of the 26th September,[6] and its effect on the gold *bloc*, particularly on Italy, has had a profound political effect in all these regions. They, indeed all Europe, *can* therefore be further influenced politically, but only if we stimulate these States into self-preservation by our own more visibly marked example. For that, time presses, and presses hard. Unless we hasten, the Sick Man will be beyond cure or resurrection. He cannot linger for several years in his present anæmic condition. He has heard of a tonic, but he has not yet tasted it. Nothing else will serve.[7] The League stands for nothing consonant either spiritually or materially with the ambitions of expansionist States, whether in Europe or Asia. It clearly offers to them no concession in any way commensurate with their ambitions for territorial possession and domination; while conciliation, co-operation, collectivity are compatible with democratic individualism, but not with 'the heroic life' and the spirit of *Kampf*, as glorified in the Germany of to-day. It is therefore to be noted that the League has of late quite faded out of any German picture, and that the effective membership of Italy has ceased, at least temporarily—though pique may have something to do with this.

11. All things therefore point in the same direction, particularly in the last and most important case on our list. Germany requires more detailed consideration, for she is admittedly the cause of our rearmament, just as she is the focus of disquiet in Central Europe, which is now, in consequence, better disposed to, and less suspicious of, Italy. It will be well to start the review at the spot that we have already touched, her relations with Russia.

12. Germany has succeeded in impressing Russia with the apparent relentlessness of Herr Hitler's anti-Bolshevik campaign, which reached a new high-level at Nüremberg. The young Russian army, partially German-trained in the past (while Germany was secretly training its own experts in Russia, 1923–30), has still not got over 'the Tannenberg-complex,'—or 'the Indian sign,' as boxers would

---

[6] See No. 248, note 4.

[7] *Note in original*: It is admittedly doubtful whether in future we can count on the countries of Latin-America remaining members of the League, if it is to be used for any purposes other than discussion. They desire to keep out of European troubles, they are opposed to any further application of sanctions, and would pursue no policy in which Soviet Russia was playing a prominent part. On present indications they would probably not discriminate in selling to an aggressor, and we could not count on using their ports in time of war. But they are more likely to be held to the League if *we* have the strength to hold them.

call it—and there is probably much genuine fear of Germany in Russia, though some close observers in the Baltic States, such as M. Munters, deny this, and though there is a din of whistling to keep up self-confidence. The converse is only true to the extent that the average German has been so successfully bemused by the everlasting propaganda on the horrors of communism, that even secret opponents of the Nazi régime, found chiefly in the elder working-class and in Catholic circles, are prepared to accept it as a lesser evil. The real rulers of Germany, however, themselves in nowise share this inspired apprehension. The development of the anti-Russian campaign is one of the best-staged feints in history, and is recognised as such by all discriminating opinion in Central Europe, for the very good reason that it is largely designed as cover for German plans in Central and South-Eastern Europe. Our Intelligence Service is particularly insistent on this point, and adds, in confirmation of what I have just said, that 'the Bolshevik menace, saving civilisation and so on, is eye-wash; but the policy of establishing an international anti-Bolshevik front, under German leadership, is extremely realistic, as it is a specific vehicle for Eastern and South-Eastern expansion.' So realistic is it that Herr Rosenberg has recently contemplated a 'temporary *détente*' with the Catholic Church—involving no excessive sacrifice—in order to promote this front. It may be added that the campaign is also used for stirring up mud all round, for setting Right against Left and weakening the victim in the same way as Communism uses 'cells.' At present the outstanding example is Roumania, with the unchecked disease of The Iron Guard and four different 'shirts'. It is time that we ceased to be dupes of a cry that can be whipped up or cooled down at short notice. Let us not be fogged by the war of words, which are as bricks safely hurled by two calculating fishwives from behind the high and dividing fence of Poland, who anyhow will let neither of them into her back-garden for fear of the difficulty of eviction. 'It is safe to slang Russia when that country obviously would not go to war', said a Nazi at Nüremberg. The German and Russian publics will never be stampeded by any amount of shouting, for there are no publics to stampede. The dupes just shout too, till they are told to stop, and then tighten their belts for some Four or Five Years' Plan, though another leading Nazi remarked at Nüremberg that something different, and more tangible, would have to be staged next time to keep up popular enthusiasm. Slanging matches are, however, still useful on both sides of the fence. In Germany at least those in authority have not fear, but contempt, of Russia, and where this is not the case, the German is like a fifteen-stone man who has little real fire for pursuing an eternally receding Carnera in a limitless ring. When I was in Berlin I told all Germans whom I met that no member of a country that had fought *against* Germany and *with* Russia would ever believe that the former feared the latter militarily; and no one attempted to contest the compliment. Doctrinally I admitted of course that Communism had made progress, but not in Germany, where it is 'down and out' to all serious intents and purposes, though it can still raise its head feebly. This also was not contested. I drove round the former Communist quarters of Berlin with Herr Hess unescorted; and General Goering offered to stand about with me, equally unescorted, in any tough spot in Germany. They cannot have it both ways; nor do they really pretend to do so. General Goering, who is even more an officer than a Nazi—hence his present great superiority in popularity over Dr. Goebbels—belongs with other and more genuine generals to the party that would like to be on better terms with Russia, and would prefer her to Italy as an ally. Indeed, the bulk of the German army is of this persuasion;

and it is with the view of eventually substituting German for French influence that they are all concentrating on securing the rupture of the Franco-Soviet pact, an illustration that the French were not unwise in their policy of insurance. For the pact is no more than that, nor is it seriously regarded as more by any member of any continental General Staff. Militarily—unless far-reaching and not easily devisable measures can be found to transform it into reality—it is still a scarecrow stuffed with straw, but politically it offers scope for dark sayings on dark nights, and politically all Germans are determined to lynch it. This fact has been checked from many sources. I need here only quote Sir E. Phipps in October of this year: 'Were the two obstacles of Comintern propaganda and the Franco-Soviet Pact to be removed, it is not impossible that General Staff circles would be able to persuade Herr Hitler to come to terms with Russia.' To which the Military Attaché adds: 'The General Staff still hope that they may eliminate Herr Hitler's other advisers as they eliminated Captain Röhm. If and when this happens I feel confident that their objective is to come to an understanding with Russia. It is for this reason that they are so unanimous in joining National Socialist propaganda in trying to break down the Franco-Russian Pact, since this would be the first step towards taking France's place vis-à-vis of Russia.' The same tendency is shared by industrialists, and even by limited Party circles. The former have been particularly concerned by the loss of the supply of Russian manganese. Not that anyone of course thinks outstretched hands possible in any near future. Indeed, it might be well-nigh *im*possible, though there are strong contrary views, so long as Russia continues on her present course and Voroshilov keeps himself and his army out of the politics that he shows no sign of entering. Russia, in fact, is not at present tempted. The itch is in some German and not in Russian palms; but its presence in hands now loudest to applaud any hostile reference to the Franco-Soviet Pact measures the sincerity of the cry. Meanwhile we must from time to time remind ourselves that the Reichswehr secretly hopes that Stalin will execute some more Jews like Zinoviev and Kamenev, to facilitate the cry that Russia is purging itself of Semitic Marxism; and it hopes too for an eventual military dictatorship in Russia as in Germany, which alone would probably make practical politics of co-operation. We must also remember that on the one hand a new *bourgeoisie* is growing up in Russia, and that on the other hand the *Schwarze Korps*, the organ of the Nazi extremists, has threatened German capitalism with extermination, unless it makes a success of the Four-Year Plan. The complete suppression of the smallest spark of liberty is common to both. 'The mind of Germany has not merely been anaesthetised,' writes a German intellectual; 'I fear that it has been killed.' A letter from a former colleague and present businessman, discussing the possibility that the German economic machine might stop running and so bring Bolshevism, ends as follows: 'But how the Germans will distinguish Bolshevism from their present régime I do not know. No foreigner will notice the difference.' That indeed may become as difficult to define as the difference between a Republican and a Democrat in pre-Roosevelt days. It cannot, moreover, be soon forgotten how lightly in pre-Hitlerian days the human atoms flew from one horn to the other of the crescent or dilemma formed by Nazism and Communism. While therefore the doctrinal differences are still genuine, though far less profound than the innocent believe, there is little sincerity in the political or military campaign. 'The propaganda bureaux,' says a close observer, 'and the press in line behind them detect communism almost everywhere a workman in a foreign country demands a rise in wages. Apart from those suffering from auto-suggestion, there are few leaders who sincerely believe what they preach regarding the magnitude of the Communist menace to Europe.' (cf. Herr von Ribbentrop.) The German and Russian armies do not contemplate the geographical impossibility of attacking each other; but the bogey of Communism—designed to mesmerise countries or fractions of countries into the belief that association with the Nazi Government is the only antidote to disaster—is as inexhaustible as the claims of *Gleichberechtigung*, which includes much 'equality' not yet disclosed. The German–Japanese agreement accordingly professes hostility to the Comintern rather than to the Soviet Government; just as the German drive is directed against 'Semitic Marxism' and not against Russia, Soviet or otherwise. It would not take long to divert the campaign in another direction. Two months ago a German official spoke of the possibility that, 'under certain circumstances, the existing anti-Russian policy might be completely reversed.' When it was suggested that this would be a lot for the people to swallow, after all they had heard about Russia, he replied: 'Leave that to Goebbels.' Germany, then, lives under the régime of *Kriegswirtschaft* (a super-Dora condition) 'though Germany is in nowise threatened by its neighbours, and the Reichswehr General Staff admits openly that it has no reason to fear any attack by Russia.' This must surely cause every informed mind to ask itself at least one question.

13. What is the alternative direction? We have now had an indication of that. It has long been known that Dr. Goebbels has a strong strain of the old Tirpitz doctrine that this country is the ultimate enemy. At Nüremberg General Goering —who had previously remarked that the Jewish theme was becoming threadbare— joined him, and the consequence was made manifest in their two speeches on the Colonies, against which we protested. (Privately, General Goering goes further, and recently remarked in the presence of one of our most reliable sources that he would, when he could, present the Colonial demand, to which every German of importance is now publicly committed, 'on the point of a bayonet.') The intention of the move is to make us responsible for the sufferings of the German in the street during a winter of privation, from which we shall emerge with conveniently applicable odium, increased if the Four-Year Plan shows signs of failing. This was the deeper cause of our protest. None of this is surprising. Dr. Schacht has long harped on the urgent need of Colonial restitution, and on the 9th December he made in this connection a public and virulent attack on this country in general and our Ambassador in particular. Herr von Ribbentrop emphasised the need for colonial restitution in a speech at the Anglo-German Fellowship on the 15th December, which was praised by the German press. 'It would be a mutual deception if one were to evade the Colonial question,' writes Herr Silex. When I was in Berlin Dr. Goebbels practically asked for restitution, and in the case of General Goering we may omit the adverb. Both, moreover, said to me that Germany neither could nor would 'go on running after England.' That phrase is to be remembered, for it was one of the directions given to German journalists during Count Ciano's visit to Berlin. And on the morning of the 26th October a conference of the heads of the various Nazi press-departments was informed that '*the time is past when it seemed necessary to run after England*. German–Italian friendship would establish the authoritative system on the Continent on such a solid basis that England would be forced to come to terms.' (One of the reasons widely given to Nazis disappointed by the Austrian agreement was, and is, that it should gain the use of Mussolini as a means of pressure on Great Britain.) The connection with the Goering–Goebbels speeches is obvious. I may add that Herr

von Ribbentrop went even further in Berlin, and said to me verbatim that 'England must allow to Germany the means to live; else Germany and England would eventually come to war, in which one of them would be destroyed.' One can hardly expect language at once plainer and yet more ill-defined. It would, perhaps, be out of scale to compare Treitschke's words: 'Before every one of his wars Frederick the Great laid down with the utmost clearness what he hoped to attain. And how markedly Bismarck's grand frankness in large matters stands out. It was one of his most useful weapons, for when he stated plainly what he really meant, the lesser diplomatists always believed exactly the reverse.' By 'the means to live' Ribbentrop meant expansion both in Africa and Europe, but in easier quarters than Russia; and I have unimpeachable evidence that he believes in the necessity of war, though not with us. There are easier quarters in Danzig, or Memel, or Czechoslovakia, particularly in the mind of Bohle, the Leader of Germans Abroad, an important person—since Hitler is himself by origin a German Abroad[8]—to whom attention is not often enough directed. The leading Nazis, in particular Herr Goebbels and Herr Rosenberg, propound the belief that Germany must become paramount in South-Eastern Europe for the sake not only of Germany but of 'European Civilisation' (see paragraph 12); that Czechoslovakia is therefore the first obstacle, and therefore the obstacle must be removed. The break up of Czechoslovakia—which is more likely to be set afoot from within in the first instance—would clearly seal Austria's fate. In pursuance of 'this sorry scheme of things' the partly justifiable complaint as to Czech treatment of the German-Bohemians is being strengthened and duplicated by another—that Czechoslovakia is the outpost of Communist Russia in Central Europe. The *Völkischer Beobachter*—the chief Nazi newspaper—is continually on this line. Germany is accordingly trying to encircle Czechoslovakia, by approaching Roumania via Hungary. The idea is that Hungary and a totalitarian Roumania should come together under German auspices; and this necessitates Hungary being tactfully persuaded to moderate her revisionism vis-à-vis of Roumania. Germany is also working for a similar accommodation between Hungary and Yugoslavia. In these circumstances it seems locally incomprehensible that we should criticise anybody for seeking potential assistance where it can be got—even in the most suspect quarters. For it is common ground that the ultimate objective of *all* Nazis by one method or another—compare the similar aims and different methods of the military and the so-called moderates of Japan—is the Baltic–Adriatic–Black Sea block, where Germany is already far the largest commercial client, and wherein Roumania is the chief attraction, providing elbow-room and oil. Here it will be well to interject that, when schemes sound wild, we must not make the mistake of supposing Hitler to be surrounded by Yes-men like Mussolini. On the contrary the sub-leaders enjoy frankness and influence with a willing but sometimes slightly scared Führer, and play up cleverly to the fact that, of two persons

[8] *Note in original*: It is Hitler's ambition to unite into one organised 'Volksgenossenschaft' all persons of German blood. The Nazis have their own conception of 'nation' and 'people'. German citizens, subjects of the Reich, even if of foreign origin, are 'Deutsche Staatsangehörige,' whereas the term 'Volksgenosse' embraces all persons of German blood in the world. The creation of this universal Germanic community is one of the chief aims of the régime, though it does 'not necessarily' envisage the incorporation of *all* German minorities in the Greater Germany. The idea is that Germans everywhere should regard Hitler as their leader, and the Catholic Church is sometimes cited as a model rather than the British Empire.

in one god, the attractive *bourgeois* and the infallible demagogue, the latter is now predominant owing to Hitler's series of Successful Saturdays in foreign policy. His will is supreme. He remains incalculable even to his intimates, and is always liable to act, in his own words, 'with lightning-like rapidity' or 'intuition,' which sometimes means bad advice. 'When the time comes,' says one of our best sources, 'he will be capable of turning the terrific instrument of force and propaganda that he is forging in any direction at a moment's notice. Force, or the capacity to use force, is still the keynote, and Hitler has, in Goering, one who believes that *"by force alone will Germany ultimately get what she wants"*. He has not yet decided how Germany will move and when; but he is obsessed with the idea of expansion.'

14. To further and connect our understanding of the recent trend of events in Germany, it should be explained that Herr von Ribbentrop's *agrément* as Ambassador to this country was requested and obtained in July; yet during the whole of my stay in Berlin there raged a sharp struggle whether he should be appointed after all. 'The Party' do not like either the man or his policy. We need not here enter into the personal question, but the political side necessarily interests us. The thorough-paced party-man in Germany no longer greatly *desires* an arrangement with this country. He prefers—at present—the association of like with like— Italy. The army would prefer Russia, having neither confidence in nor respect for Italy. (And therein lies the opening for time and tact, to which I have referred.) The end of the struggle we know. Herr von Ribbentrop has been allowed to come here—on trial, like and with his policy. If he delivers the goods—loans and colonies—well and good; if not, he and the policy of 'running after England' may both be dropped, even if not overtly, in the alternative atmosphere which is in course of preparation. Meanwhile the German Embassy in London is being 'supervised,' and the Gestapo is established in Carlton House Terrace like the Ogpu in Soviet Embassies. Here then is the reverse of the medal. It may not necessarily be shown or applied, but that will depend on the toss of the coin. We must estimate the chances by every indication we can get, including history. German dislike and jealousy of this counrty became endemic during the quarter of a century preceding the Great War, and so manifested themselves constantly and inevitably, in particular during the Boer War. They flared out in full in 1914 and the Hymn of Hate period, when we were admittedly the chief enemy; and after the war they soon started again in lower strains (see Sir H. Rumbold's reports *passim*). Now they are going *sotto voce* and hand in hand with the campaign of belittlement, and the boost of Nazi propaganda is, of late, interwoven with Anglophobia even in mild and unlikely Austria. Already one of our most reliable sources reports that, 'of late, the theme of friendship with England has taken on rather a nasty tone, denoting asperity, impatience and malice.' Herr Darré, the Reich Peasant Leader, recently delivered a tirade against 'the shopkeepers' state of Carthage'—a curious expression. But *we* have long been described as a nation of shopkeepers, and we may also remember the Roman monomaniac's 'Carthage must be destroyed.' We need jump to no hasty or alarming conclusions on this, but we must rid our minds of the complacent assumption that the Germans are *necessarily* going—and staying—East. Again at a discussion early in December in Berlin between prominent Nazis 'the supporters of the pro-British policy did not have an easy time. It was agreed that British arrogance must be firmly dealt with' (cf. General Goering's entourage, in paragraph 4) 'and that England's governess attitude was insupportable. The tendency to look upon England as

a negligible quantity was distinctly noticeable—the military preparations of England could not have made much progress in a few months—and this attitude was partly due to the increase in confidence engendered by the German–Italian friendship.' (It will be seen how this confirms paragraph 7.)

15. We have, therefore, to be prepared for the possible development of the alternative policy, particularly since the attitude of His Majesty's Government in the past, and the Union of South Africa as lately as the 11th December with its pronouncement of an irrevocable mandate, have rendered it impossible for Herr von Ribbentrop to deliver his goods, either by way of colonies or of bringing the United Kingdom into the desired anti-Bolshevik front; and the Conservative party-meeting at Margate[9] has strengthened this impression among the Nazi party-leaders. Many of them look upon Great Britain as the greatest obstacle to German expansion and to the 'heroic conception' of life and German destiny. Vain efforts have been made, they say, to gain the friendship of this country, *but only as a benevolent neutral divorced from the League and anything in the nature of collective security.* It is recognised now in Berlin that our re-armament is in no small measure a reply to the ambitions of the Reich. General Goering reproached me with this in Berlin, and said several times that he did not see why German activities should cause us any disquiet. Since Nüremberg his attitude has changed, or rather it has developed inevitably. He has recently adopted the creed that 'England must be forced (*gezwungen*) by a display of power' (see paragraph 13). If either he or events cause his view to prevail, therefore, the policy to be applied on the failure of the Ribbentrop line might, at short notice, take the form that this country must be overawed into acquiescence in the expansionist policy of the Reich. For that purpose both Italy and Spain (see paragraphs 8 and 13) are to play their part, as well as the great development of German air-power. This, as General Goering also made plain to me, is to be pushed to parity at an inflated figure with Russia in any case, and to parity with Russia and France combined if possible. To me in August he put the figure at some 4,000. But, in an interview with Mr. Ward Price on the 19th November, the following dialogue occurs: 'I said that a Reuter message in the German papers reported that the aim of the British Air Ministry was to have 1,750 machines for home defence. What was the aim of the German Air Ministry?' General Goering said: '*Of course we can never be satisfied with so small a number of aeroplanes as England,* for our enemy is Russia, who has an enormous Air Force.' 'I asked his estimate of Russia's air strength. He said: '*Six to eight thousand machines.*' One of two conclusions may be drawn from a rise of between 2,000 and 4,000 machines in three months: megalomania or insincerity. (I see that German propaganda has given to Mr. Garvin[10] the figure of 6,000.) But all German armament is on this rapidly rising curve. I need not here go into details of the technical developments. Apart, however, from the great and continuous increases of material, including gas and bacteria, it is important to note that not only have the first and second army reserves now got instructions in the event of mobilisation, but—as reported by our Consuls and Military Attaché—doctors, nurses, motor-car drivers, all sorts and conditions of men and women down to charwomen. Women are being trained to take men's places in anti-air-raid precautions and in agriculture. The Hitler Youth is being made 'more directly an organisation for pre-military training,' with special formations for the mechanical branches of the fighting services. 'The General Staff is not merely concerned with the creation of combatants, but occupies itself with the preparation of the whole nation for war'—

[9] See Nos. 261 and 262.   [10] Editor of the *Observer*.

'total' war. The Minister of Labour has recently declared that the *Strength through Joy* movement is 'the mobilisation of the spiritual strength of the nation.' The meaning of these facts is clear, and they are as likely to serve the alternative policy as their ostensible purpose against the Red Bogey. In furtherance of the eventual policy of forcing this country through air-power, particular attention is being paid to the Rexists and Flemish nationalists, and M. Degrelle is in close touch with Herr Abetz, who belongs to the Berlin Bureau of Herr von Ribbentrop, and has spent a good deal of money without much result. 'The growth of Rexism in Belgium opens up possibilities in Western Europe,' a Nazi in close touch with Hitler remarked a week ago (and added that not only Degrelle but 'Tsankoff from Bulgaria and Mosley from England had come to Berlin for *co-ordination*'). It is for this reason that the new Belgian Minister has been treated with an affability in strong contrast with the 'incredible rudeness' which his predecessor reported to have been his lot; and the German advances culminated on the 20th November with the offer of a bilateral pact of non-aggression. Herr Abetz also operates in France, where I come across his traces from time to time, in the execution of orders to court, with a view to eventual detachment if possible, the Right, which has already shown itself last year to be pro-Italian and anti-British. (Ironically enough Franco-Italian relations have rarely been worse than *this* year.) The policy of *Mein Kampf* is to isolate France by dividing her from England; the new policy contemplates a similar but reversed process, which M. Blum's indiscretions in regard to the colonies have encouraged. These efforts, so far neither successful nor promising, are nevertheless being seriously pushed: by Goering through Freyberg to Chiappe, by Ribbentrop through Abetz to La Rocque, by Goebbels through Schmolz to Doriot. To be just, the majority of these loquacious policy-mongers do not think that all this need lead to war with the United Kingdom. They believe, on the contrary, that Germany will get her way everywhere by being irresistible, that we like others shall be *gezwungen* to terms, their terms, rather than face 'a futile war' (*einen aussichtslosen Krieg*); and this is the explanation of the above-mentioned campaign of belittlement of England, which has been started two months after the alternative policy was formulated with the object of assuring themselves and their prospective associates that there is nothing to fear.

16. Not everyone, however, takes the view that bluff will always be successful, and the theory is in itself most dangerous. Many, of course, like M. van Zeeland, consider 'Germany at present the most dangerous element to the peace of Europe,' and regard 'war as inevitable, unless the Great European Powers act together'— and unless, we might add, it were preceded and deferred by a new purge. M. van Zeeland's first dictum is correct, but his second is unduly pessimistic as yet. There have always been two prophylactics, collaboration and strength, one tried, the other untried. We have long been trying to secure that collaboration, but our trouble is that Germany prefers bilateralism—for multilateralism is unheroic— or even isolation. It makes, indeed, little sense for Dr. Schacht to complain of economic isolation when the army prefers autarky in preparation for another war. The Reichswehr would have preferred the Four-Year Plan to come earlier since, as indicated above, the first signs of failure may well mean external adventure on a scale which they would fain avoid for the present, though they consider it inevitable if the Nazi régime endures. And for that new Day of Destiny, openly announced by the German Commander-in-Chief on the 8th December,[11] the whole of

[11] See *The Times*, December 9, 1936, p. 13.

Germany, from childhood upward, is being braced and prepared. In memoranda of earlier years, I have pointed out that it would always be necessary to regard the education of the young as the most accurate signpost to the future. It has shown no sign of improvement. The German youth is being brought up on hard and aggressive militarism. *Wehrfreudigkeit* (or weapon-joy) 'the diversity of German efforts to make not only the army but the entire nation ready and willing to face war,' as Sir Eric Phipps defines it, is being taught all over Germany: the first stage proves the need for weapons in view of the terrible preparations of others; the second stage tells of the poor physique and lack of courage of others, and so fits in with the campaign of belittlement. There is a complete and still growing difference between our and their *Weltanschauung*, or conception of the world—their favourite word—and it is futile to blink that. (Indeed, Herr Seibert is now taking the line that understanding can only be founded on the admission of it.) 'Peace guaranteed by the victorious sword of a master-people' (see Annex C)—for which co-ordination on an anti-Bolshevik front might be the stalking-horse. The quoted words are Hitler's own. There is no escape from them, and none is desired, since 'the holy text of sword and gun' is what is being taught to young people all over Germany. One is reminded of Tacitus: *Solitudinem faciunt, pacem appellant*. It is indeed in the forming of the fast-coming generation that the gulf between the German soul and ours is being most disastrously widened. 'All young Germans are systematically imbued with the conviction that war, though a serious thing, remains an ever-recurring phenomenon and brings out the highest qualities of mankind.' Here again a volume could be written, but I will reduce it to the necessary minimum, with a recent quotation from the German press on the subject of a competition for school-children on the theme 'The People and Military Unity.' It runs thus: 'The most surprising factor is the number of war inventions put forward by the boys: many drawings and models deal with battles; tanks, shell-bursts, fighting-soldiers, are all represented—a particularly good example compared the natural camouflage of animals with the camouflage of troops in war.' If we compare this with the attitude of our own teachers toward recruiting and cadet corps, and add that German religion for youth—a youth Spartanly, fanatically, reared and inured from childhood to hardship and frightfulness—is being reduced to a sort of nebulous but fierce ancestor-worship—'there is too much Jewish ideology in Christian teaching,' says Herr Hitler—we have an illustration sufficient for this paper without labouring the point.[12] As a fair average specimen, however, I append (Annex D)[13] the programme of a *charity* concert given on the 16th December with a chorus of 2,000 Hitler youth. It speaks for itself.

17. How dangerous the situation is becoming may be gauged from Annex A.[14] These extracts have been drawn from a great body of material, and could easily and indefinitely be multiplied. I have, however, reduced them, for convenience

---

[12] *Note in original*: It is difficult to follow the anti-Christian policy of Nazi Germany, since she does not give the impression of being sure of it herself, and has not adopted the simply and comprehensibly negative policy of Russia. The verbiage is vague and immense, but the substitute creed would appear to reside in a god 'closely identified with the resurgence of Germany under the inspiration of Adolf Hitler.' God is certainly a German, as in Houston Stewart Chamberlain; and at times he appears to be just Germany. But the official scribes are not very sure of him or of themselves.   [13] Not printed.

[14] Not printed. This Annex contained extracts from reports from H.M. representatives in Germany regarding German intentions.

of reading, to the strict minimum necessary to give a clear impression of the whole; and I have chosen only those of recent date. *I would draw special attention to No. 18,* because it says at the end of 1936 what I have been saying for the last four years. There is not now a point in Europe which would not tell the same tale, particularly since Germany's internal armaments-programme and the way in which it has been financed have, in the eyes of the average Central European business man, brought her economic structure near to cracking—nearer than Italy's despite the inherent disparity of strength—with the possible consequences that might flow from the crack. ('Gold and foreign currency are exhausted: the credits from export balances abroad are such that they can no longer cover both the requirements of war-material and foodstuffs. Fats are already rationed according to the nature of the work performed. The shortage will extend to other categories early in 1937. Industrial experts have grave doubt whether a crisis can be avoided, and whether autarky can ever give sufficient employment to 70 millions of people within such limited boundaries where the Reichsmark is the currency.') Germany is everywhere admired with fear, and with good cause; and it is in the interest of the German people themselves, possessed of so much that is worth saving from a common wreck, that we should recognise the truth, and stem, before it is too late, the growing and misguided current (see paragraph 1) that is sweeping them away. In this we may find temporary and unwitting allies in the Reichswehr, which has no objection to war as such, but objects to any major war unless victory is assured from the start. That means no major war until the present position is corrected as regards the supply and training of officers and non-commissioned officers—say, eighteen months—and until suitable allies have been found. This is all to the good; and Hitler himself, except in cases of spontaneous combustion, is both wiser and more prudent than some of his entourage. Moreover, from the rank of Lieutenant-Colonel upwards, the Reichswehr officers are still mainly the nominees of Schleicher, who allowed none but his own men to turn the famous 'Major's Corner.' The result is twofold: they are men of sense, and they are indisposed to run undue risks for the murderers of their benefactor. They thus tend to act as a brake on the more irresponsible party-elements; and how irresponsible the men, and how necessary the brake, one fact will suffice to show. Three years ago, a German well acquainted with the New Men said to me that Goering was inwardly 'slapdash enough to bomb a German town to get a war started when he wanted one.' This year the general actually emitted the idea that bombs with Czechoslovak marks might be dropped on Nüremberg during the party rally. (This can be vouched for.) The Reichswehr scotched this particular absurdity, just as they have been resisting the very dangerous idea of sending two divisions to Spain, which has been ardently—and typically—sponsored by General Goering and the Air Ministry. There is evidence enough that the spirit of over-dramatic schoolboy conspirators is always in the wings of the theatre, and has an itch to be no mere scene-shifter, but to barge on to the stage with a speaking part. This element is always grotesque, but never negligible. There is no *immediate* danger from the Reichswehr, but there will soon be constant danger from the hot-heads, who may embark as lightly as Austria in 1914 on what they believe to be another Successful Saturday, and then find it turn into something far greater. Indeed 'our next Saturday surprise' is an all too lightly current expression. Moreover, the Army and Air Force are separate entities, and Goering as head of the latter can compromise and commit the former.

18. Politically we have been trying to meet and divert the coming crisis, first

by a comprehensive European settlement and, when that failed, by a Five-Power Agreement that should lead to a European settlement, less comprehensive, but none the less effective, by being confined to settlements first in Western and then in Central Europe, without the complication of any further agreement in Eastern Europe. This last would be unnecessary if Germany and Russia were kept apart by a barrier of treaties between Germany, Lithuania, Czechoslovakia, Austria and Poland, particularly as Germany and Russia do not really intend to attack each other. Our efforts need no description here. The two years of the first attempt have been described in a White Paper—which was travestied by Herr von Ribbentrop—and the second, which may soon equally be the subject of a White Paper, looks like failing too. We have done, and are still doing, a lot of patient and vain running after Germany, and the facts of this paper dispose of any cry about running after France. When I was in Germany, I tried hard to convince the German leaders (a) that a political settlement must be well under way before an economic remedy could effectually be applied or expected; (b) that failing an economic remedy even the strongest systems might go over the edge of the dam in the inevitable spiritual discontent; (c) that we should be wretched doctors if we supposed that the nervous disease, from which all Europe was suffering, could be cured by putting a plaster on one limb; (d) that we could never be content with anything less than a proper, and therefore general, cure, because we had never forgotten, nor could forget, that the last war started in a quarter then unknown to all men in British streets. They listened politely but unwillingly. For the fundamental reasons that I have already made clear, they do not really want the general cure; some of them do not even want the local plaster; and they are proving this so far by their conditions, which are of a nature to ensure fresh failure. In such an event Herr von Neurath has said that he will not break his heart, meaning that there are other ways of preserving peace. Nor need we break ours, not only for the same reason but for the following one. The number of treaties, or parts of treaties, torn up since 1931 by expansionist countries—Japan, Italy and Germany—now runs well into double figures; and since we are endeavouring to reach a new agreement with Germany, it will be opportune here to examine closely the value of the previous assurances of Herr Hitler. This record is set forth in Annex B,[13] and a study of it will inspire us with the needful watchfulness—indeed scepticism—*until an agreement, if obtained, has worked well in practice and over an adequate period*; and it will console us in the event of failure despite our efforts. It will be seen that the record is entirely consonant with Dr. Goebbels' speech in Berlin last January: 'If a Treaty has once become intolerable, there are higher laws than those written in ink.'[15] It may not only be consoling, it will always be vital, to bear this in mind: that no signature from Nazi Germany— nor for that matter from Italy or Japan—will be necessarily worth more than the paper on which it is written, unless and until that worth be proven by enduring observance. On all indications of the past and present, they will all keep a treaty so long as it suits them. Hitler's peace offer in March was treated with complete cynicism by menbers of his entourage, who regarded it as a propaganda appeal to foreign public opinion, particularly British and French, over the heads of the Governments. Moreover, 'at the time of the 25 years' peace-offer it became apparent that in concluding any pacts Hitler would have important mental reservations.' (Here again I quote our Intelligence Service.) 'He would not regard a pact as sacred if the other party were under 'international Marxist influence,' or if a

[15] See Volume XV, No. 464, note 2.

German minority were being ill-treated. He will be the judge in either respect. Even if there were a non-aggression pact with Czechoslovakia, a German invasion would not be an act of aggression, but a defensive measure against bolshevism (see paragraph 13). Hitler's assurances to Poland are regarded in the Nazi party as merely tactics.'

19. All that is not to say that we should not persevere in our efforts to obtain a treaty; on the contrary, we should do so, provided that we do not betray any over-anxiety for one, and provided that we maintain and intensify our rearmament, both before and after the attainment. I came back from Berlin with this feeling, and I see no reason to change it, though since then the sky has most visibly darkened. I still think that a treaty would be at best an Act of Faith which it would be justifiable to perform in default of any alternative; more especially since, *always with the second of the foregoing provisos*, we might just conceivably breed in Germany and her new colleagues—Germany appears to have done most of the running after Japan, while Italy has made the running after Germany—the spirit of treaty observance which has hitherto been lacking. And here we put our finger on the taproot of the evil. Contrariwise, they might become as unreliable in the new words pledged to each other as in the many words pledged to us. Until, however, we can be far surer of their morals than is possible on present showing, we must take them at their own valuation, which is disturbingly low; and we cannot allow ourselves or our public to suppose that any treaty will in any way dispense us from the duty of being fully equipped and on guard, whether in the North Sea, the Mediterranean or the Pacific. In all this there is nothing that should surprise and therefore shock us. We have had numerous and plain warnings from many sources spread over many years, though but lately heeded by this country, which long preferred comfortably to explain away the symptoms by diagnoses at variance with those of the professional advisers of His Majesty's Government. Therefore, in all amateur prescriptions during the vital years the one indispensable ingredient, strength, was always lacking; and for lack of it Germany was again inevitably infected with her endemic disease of the spirit, as we consistently predicted. The modern school in Germany is in strict accord with her classical policy; though modern Germany is being rearmed on a scale spiritually more ferocious and materially more formidable than anything ever seen before in this world. This continuity is illustrated by Annex C, which could, of course, be expanded to a book by examples of more persons and more literature from Frederick the Great onward. I have, however, confined it to the minimum necessary to establish the continuity. Nobody can grasp this reality without a full sense of the pity of it, the pity that so much of the world, including its most vital and virile parts, should have slid back into the pursuit of the worst form of the unreal. *Corruptio optimi pessima.* I have said before that others are also to blame for this; but that does not help us now.

20. One other great change has taken place to our detriment: the recent neutrality legislation in the United States. We scrambled through the last war by importing in its early stages some 500 million dollars' worth of American munitions. To-day, in the event of war, we can count on getting nothing. Our own supplies will therefore have to be more plentiful and *timely*.

21. Here is a strict account of the world in this year of grace—the grace is not yet over—where nothing but the verified has place in a catalogue of crazy materialism. It will be apparent how the puzzle fits when the pieces are taken all together. To this account I have therefore brought our information from all

sources, Embassy, Consulates, Secret Service, as well as other contacts that I was able to make during my visit to Berlin. Against them are to be set only some tourists and affable smatterers, for whom the Germans have a great contempt now, calling them the *Jein* men (a mixture of Ja and Nein) that is, men who say yes and no as required. The assembled facts must be faced, for it is only in their assembly that they speak; and it is improbable that this country has any real conception of their extent. We have to deal with the pathological as well as—indeed more than —the military. The cure is not hopeless, and it is clear which way it lies. The Nazi party is convinced that Power-Politics (*Machtpolitik*) will always win. Power-politics pervade all printed or declaimed words. Power-politics dominate the life of the whole State. It has yet to learn that power is no monopoly; and I think that the lesson can and must be amicably taught.

22. On the face of these facts we have begun the cure full late, and must pray for a grant in aid from fortune. What we have now to do is to decide whether, against this needful background, we are really doing all that our abilities permit and that the situation requires. There are, indeed, years that the locust hath eaten, and democracy moves more slowly than peremptory dictators. But are we reducing the handicap to the inevitable minimum? Are we satisfied with our own time-table in its relation to the described course of events? These are questions that we are now all bound to ask ourselves when we survey the world situation; *and I would suggest that we cannot feel satisfied in many enumerable respects*, although aware of all that is being done and of all the obstacles in doing more. We cannot now find a full remedy for German grievances, because the Germans cannot state them—their ambitions fly too high. Germany has indeed less a definite set of grievances than a sense of grievance, which Hitler maintains in a septic condition for his own purposes. There is no assigned bound to the Greater Germany of his ambitions, and he cannot say what he wants, because he does not know what, in a year or 18 months or two years, or more years, he will be strong enough to take, or feel pushed into trying to take. The injustices and 'inequalities' of the Treaty of Versailles have been progressively swept away; and, when people still gird at it, the inference must be that they have never known it well enough to realise how little remains, beyond the parts voluntarily and explicitly accepted. This is, as indicated, possibly one explanation of the anti-Communist campaign. The German people must be keyed up by emotion, and fear and hatred are the most powerful emotions. With so few grievances left under the Treaty of Versailles, Hitler uses Russia as the bogey. But that does not mean that action, when it comes, will be directed against Russia. Japan's anti-Communist clamour is equally artificial: Japan uses it as an excuse against China and possibly as an incitement against Russia; and Germany hopes to use Japan as an additional embarrassment to us in the Far East. In all this commotion we cannot know, because Germany does not yet know, when or where she will throw her ever-growing weight. We have therefore to be prepared for a date that is not ours.

23. This question of time is indeed everything, and it is the principal pre-occupation of the Foreign Office, since time is the very material commodity which the Foreign Office is expected to provide in the same way as other departments have to provide *other* war material. Now it may be generally said that the year 1939 is the first in which we shall be able to breathe with even comparative relief, although much will yet remain to be taken in hand. We shall not even then have reached safety. Germany is admittedly not yet ready for war on a considerable scale, either militarily, economically or politically. The Army wants time, must

have time, to create a better balance between the purely military preparations and the essential economic preparations—raw materials and food-supplies for the nation. These are facts of great import and comfort. But on any showing Germany will be ready for big mischief at least a year—and probably more—before we are ready to look after ourselves. To the Foreign Office therefore falls the task of holding the situation at least till 1939, and the foregoing account of the world shows that there is no certainty of our being able to do so, though we are doing our utmost by negotiating with Germany, endeavouring to regain lost ground with Italy, and reducing the demands on our still exiguous strength by a treaty with Egypt. Personally—and I think the fact is notorious—I have never been a Thirty-niner, if I may borrow a term from American history. I have never believed, and do not believe, that we can *count* on the European situation to hold so long; and, if it breaks, there is no present knowing how far the trouble will spread. The French, basing their view on the effects of a hard winter and with their eyes on the three powder-magazines, Czechoslovakia, Danzig and Spain, doubt even whether we can count on its holding through 1937. Even if the French take too dark a view—and they have done so before now—our preparations for defence may thus be based on the assumption of an optimistic date. *On the other hand, if, by the only devisable means, we can stabilise the position till 1939, we shall have more than a fair chance of turning the corner, and turning it for good.* On one condition it might be then not so much a question of being incipiently able to defend ourselves as of having averted the necessity. Those means can no longer be entirely or even mainly treaties; and that is why we are bound to pass beyond any one department to the consideration of the problem presented as a whole by European psychology and equipment. *The one condition will be a really impressive display of strength on our part*; and it would seem, in the light of what has already been recorded, that the display, to be efficacious, will have to be more impressive than the measures that we have as yet undertaken or contemplated. I recognise to the full the attendant difficulties, *but it may be cheaper to face them now*; for, as already pointed out, in such an event all peace-loving Europe would take heart of grace, and the League of Nations, on which we have consistently pinned our faith, might regain a spontaneous vitality that we can otherwise never again expect of it. Even if it did not, we should thereby shake the union of the two dictators, keep firm on our side and on the side of peace the two pivotal countries, Poland and Yougoslavia—all the more possible since Yougoslavia has lost confidence in and attachment to France— as well as the other members of the Little Entente and the Balkan States, who will otherwise all be drawn by self-preservation to the German band-waggon, much against their will and interests. In the contrary case, it is doubtful whether the Foreign Office will be able—*it certainly cannot undertake*—to manufacture the quota of Time assigned to it.

24. If, on the contrary, we utilise our assets, we have much in our favour. Friendship with this country is still the official German policy, and Hitler still puts colonial after European expansion. Indeed the colonial agitation, though widespread and tenacious, is largely artificial. Moreover, the Nazi party, if only it were wisely calculating, is not really in a position to embark on great adventure. Germany's economic weakness is notorious; nor is the present régime so firmly anchored in the hearts of the people that the present Government could lightly embark on any war that put the loyalty of the country to the acid test—though this may be different when the rising generation has supplanted its predecessor. The credit position too will bear no strain; the purchase of raw materials, of which

there is a shortage, offers great difficulty. There is considerable discontent in Germany—strikes and sabotage, repressed by executions, have occurred at the munition works of both Opel and Heinkel, in other armament factories, and even on board German warships; there has been an abortive revival of Communist activity—also quelled by executions—in the industrial areas and the ports. These outbreaks are not sufficient to imperil the régime; but impregnable solidity is unlikely where miners live on 23 marks a week. The armaments production for October was only 60 per cent. of the planned output owing to the lack of raw materials. Nourishment for heavy manual labour is already becoming too low. Harvests have been below estimate, and Herr Darré anticipates a six weeks' lack of essential foodstuffs, particularly fats, between now and March. Franco has also been a great disappointment to the General Staff, the adventure in support of him is unpopular in Germany, where the lengthening list of casualties is becoming known and causing alarm, which Dr. Goebbels has found it necessary to allay. The population share the fear of the Reichswehr about being drawn into a major war (though there is a time-limit to the fears of the soldiers). Mr. Eden's recent speeches, at Leamington,[16] at the lunch for M. van Zeeland,[17] and at Bradford,[18] though carefully bowdlerised and kept from the public with all else like them, have strengthened the hand of the Reichswehr, who do not want premature adventure, against the wilder Party—like Habakkuk 'capable de tout'—who have suffered a setback. *The stronger and more determined this country seems to Germany, the greater the deterrent to the hotheads,* and the more possible the end of the present régime. For if the Nazi system sees danger of exposure at home, its last resort might be war; but if it appeared 'a futile war' for *them,* the real generals would have more prospect of stopping that last resort. They disapprove at present of all this talk of movements against Czechoslovakia, Danzig, or even—cropping up again—the Corridor, for which, as of yore Lithuania would be the compensation. The Army, in a word, is not more *moderate* than the Party in its aims; but it is more *cautious.* That at least is something, and we ought to make use of it in the only way which the Army understands. It conceives of its *present* duty as the defence of German soil. It might not oppose, or be able to oppose, some incursion into Memel or Danzig, which would not be likely to bring about a general war; but it *would* oppose any premature adventure in Czechoslovakia, which *might* have that effect, just as it is already opposing adventure in Spain. Its weakness is the weakness of General Blomberg, who would not stand up to Hitler, if once the wild men had got at the Führer; and the real German Foreign Office, that might help, is largely shouldered out.

25. It has often been said that the misfortune of French policy since the War was to have been ruled by fear. That is now becoming the misfortune of all Europe. The shadow of M. van Zeeland's expressed dread overspreads the continent. Even Germans have said to me that they feel war to be somehow so certain that they would like to get away from the present mad management of their country, and come to England 'except that we don't think you'll get left out.' A member of the House of Commons writes to me: 'I have seen many Germans during the last months. They have all told me the same story: that the present German Government will only find one way out of their self-imposed problems, and that way is to provoke a war.' I have recently received expression of the same conviction—and desire to escape—from two further sources high in the Berlin hierarchy. One of them adds: 'We are powerless against this nonsense.' In an

[16] See No. 400, note 1.   [17] See No. 485, note 2.   [18] See No. 479, note 2.

intercepted document in my possession occurs the phrase: 'We must influence public opinion in England so that it forces the Government to keep out of *our next war.*' There is evidence that Hitler himself is now beginning to lend ear to the opponents of the Reichswehr who preach the despatch of large forces to Spain so as to wedge France between three totalitarian States in anticipation of this 'next war.' Nothing can cure this psychosis better—I believe that nothing else can cure it *at all* during the next critical few years—than *a marked display of our determination and abilities*—and nothing does greater disservice than the continual advertisement of our shortcomings. But these are in any case not hid, and some at least of the skeletons in our cupboard are familiar figures in foreign capitals. Our published recruiting figures are used for our daily disparagement abroad, with other damaging—and often accurate—insinuations or suspicions as to the rate of our general re-equipment. The under-rating of this country, one of the chief difficulties with which the Foreign Office has had to contend during the last decade, may now also become one of our chief dangers. There is a belief abroad that we are trying to solve our problems on the basis of 'business as usual,' and that, as before, we shall not be successful in the limitation. I would briefly add here one very weighty consideration. It is essential that Germany should no more under-rate France than this country. Of late Germany has been speculating on the disintegration of France, much as Italy used to do in the case of Yougoslavia. No policy could be more dangerous, and it should be regretted that France lends colour to it, as she continually does.

26. In conclusion, I venture to add a few words on the issue that seems most likely, at some future and undefined date, to involve us *directly*, the colonies. We must remember that now 'the return of all or most of the colonies is reckoned on with the utmost confidence;' indeed, many people in Germany have passed beyond the idea of a mere return to that of 'colonial redistribution.' I put forward a memorandum at the beginning of the year[19] advocating colonial restitution; and the findings of a full, fair and representative Committee were, for excellent reasons, against it.[20] The technical difficulties alone, I know, look well-nigh insuperable. But, knowing what we now do, is it coherent to maintain a refusal of even partial restitution *without accelerating our progress toward security*? Surely the trend of events points to one of two definite courses. I do not, of course, recommend that we should contemplate restoring even the Cameroons except in return for at least the showing of *full* European appeasement in an adequate treaty adequately observed over an adequate period. If it turned out to be worth nothing we could close down on any further conciliation. A stage has now been reached, however, when we might be well advised to keep this door ajar in the event of complete success, including, of course, a Central European settlement, if we are *not* going to hasten our steps. Admittedly such an intimation would not long satisfy Germany; indeed, the strongest argument against any elasticity on our part is the well-informed opinion that holds, with strong ground, Germany to be incapable of taking any concession except as an instalment of an indefinite bill (see paragraph 22). Yet a conditioned glimpse of an unpromised land would, if properly timed, attenuate what is still a plausible grievance, and remove a bone of contention that is barely worth a dog-fight or protracted snarls: for it would temporarily knock the bottom out of the Goering-Goebbels campaign to represent us as the obstacle to national expansion and the cause of individual suffering. Anyhow if we are never going to give back any colonies, we must state our case much more

[19] Volume XV, Appendix IV(*b*).   [20] Volume XVI, Appendix III.

clearly and publicly than we have yet done, for the benefit of Europe, *and still more of the United States. This last is a very important point,* if we desire, as we must, to count upon American sympathy in coming trouble.[21] 'People in Central and South-Eastern Europe,' writes a journalist with long experience of these countries, 'will never understand that British mentality which combined a horror of the status quo in Europe (an over-statement of course) with a determination not to surrender anything that Britain gained in the war.' If the Foreign Office is to produce the commodity of Time, we shall need help, and is it not safer to keep this door ajar than to strengthen Germany by loan or financial assistance, until we are both safer ourselves and surer of her intentions? Nobody who knows what is really going on in Germany can seriously believe that she can be kept quiet or satisfied by economic assistance alone. What she wants, and is preparing for, is expansion. Until that spirit and desire are checked, cured or sated, the danger will remain, unyielding to other sops. That method will not produce the anticipated effect on the rulers of Germany, who, with the exception of Dr. Schacht, are not economic-minded—Hitler, in particular, is quite at sea in economics—and if tried out to the full in advance of, or in the absence of, a reliable political settlement can only prove to be an illusion, *possibly an expensive one.* We need not, however, be narrow or dogmatic about this, for we have to keep a tiger sweet for two years, and we cannot wholly exclude any possibility of bettering his diet, if we wish him ultimately to change his appetite. What we must do is to avoid any dietary improvement of a dangerously strengthening nature. It is not in our interests that his food situation should remain 'catastrophic,' as it was recently described by a party leader. Palliatives, not remedies, might be our temporary watchword, for it is on the economic side above all that the German Army, though committed like the Nazi Party to a war economy, does not feel ready for war; and we must not altogether part with that asset, if the Foreign Office are really to make time. Accordingly, we might, for instance, reconsider some of the Ottawa duties with the idea of facilitating German trade to some extent, but mainly, of course, with the idea of contenting the United States of America. We might also consider the possibility of giving to Dr. Schacht some kind of an assurance not to *increase* our duties on German goods, even in the event of the devaluation of the mark; and we might also at least consider certain modifications of our tariff system, so as to permit of greater imports from *industrial Europe generally.* We shall have to be exceedingly careful, however, to keep within strict bounds for a while, partly on account of our own safety, and partly because any unwise assistance to potential men of prey would alienate Franklin Roosevelt the Second—who may be a person very different from Franklin Roosevelt the First—and so compromise any chance that we might have of finding a way round the disaster of the American neutrality legislation. We must not allow ourselves to be bluffed too far with the threat of an economic breakdown. We must also reckon on the possibility that, 'however

---

[21] *Note in original*: We have a good and improving position in the United States of America. The perennial question of the war-debt is still against us, we may find it hard to conclude a commercial agreement in any way adequate in American eyes, and there are the makings of trouble in the shipping dispute with the Government of New Zealand. But our prestige is still high, and the United States of America are generally and strongly opposed to dictatorships and therefore inclined towards our fellow-democracy. They might be further so inclined if Mr. Roosevelt carried out his vague idea of calling a 'World Peace Conference,' rendered abortive by the dictators. Such a step on his part might, indeed, help us in manufacturing Time.

much Schacht and the *Reichswirtschaft* Ministry may declare the contrary, there can be no sincere attempt at collaboration so long as a Nazi Government rules Germany. The Party must collapse if it were to relinquish its grip on the economy of the country. It has burned its boats, and, unable to retreat, must continue the pursuit of the fictitious conception, Autarchy.' This may be pessimism, but the source is a very high one. It is, indeed, not easy to see how collaboration is going [to be] easy. On the one side are countries that desire (1) a maximum degree of individual enterprise with a minimum of State control, and (2) ordered finances and balanced budgets. On the other side is a country that regards the first part of such a programme as a return to the despised liberalism that Nazism threw out. To change back to (1) would mean that the German Government must give up its greatest hold on its own people, a hold which makes every German as dependent on the Nazi Government as a Russian on the Soviet Government. The adoption of (2) would involve the removal of a vast number of Party posts and jobs that overlap those of State Bureaucracy. It would mean the end of the reckless spending of the present régime—both national and *personal*—and the end of the foreign propaganda expenditure of Goebbels, Ribbentrop and Bohle. It would mean the reduction of the armaments programme, the end of the 'heroic' life, and of 'heroic' education (see again Annex D). A return to normality would therefore mean such a humiliation for the present régime that, if they have their way, they would sooner—if they possibly can—go on as they are and chance the consequences, however dangerous. Economic independence is the ultimate goal of the Army, and can be relaxed to some extent at intervals. Germany has a way of attributing to outside pressure the things that she wishes to do for her own reasons. 'The assumption that every country other than Germany is to blame for Germany's economic difficulties is preached day in day out in Germany. Speeches such as Dr. Schacht's are bound to prepare the mind of the German people for adventures abroad, if conditions inside the country under its self-imposed siege become intolerable. It is clear, at any rate, that Germany's economic policy is to be summed up in terms of territory.' This is from the *Times* correspondent at Berlin, one of the best-informed men that I know. Meanwhile, the Army say that for the first time they are getting a Class A nation behind a Class A Army, and that you must not overfeed good hounds.[22] It is also to be considered that some tentative

[22] *Note in original*: 'The problem of German food-supply is expected to become little short of desperate as from February,' writes an equally well-informed and level-headed source in Germany. 'The Nazi régime cannot scramble through another winter on their present policy. There is apparently no illusion in high quarters on that score. They cannot get the people to continue indefinitely going without butter for guns. The greatest strain is likely to come before the new harvest is visible. A foreign diversion is therefore contemplated as a necessity in influential circles fanatically determined to continue the self-sufficing policy. Only if the carefully fostered belief in the disintegration of France and the aloofness of England is shaken is the policy likely to be abandoned.' This again is confirmed by probably the most authoritative source at my disposal as the year closes. 'Opposition to the Nazi régime is growing, due to low wages, food-shortage, the ban on individualism, unfulfilled promises, mistrust of foreign policy, unpopularity of the Spanish venture, fears of a European war. The Government's economic policy is viewed with widespread uneasiness, but in that direction the Government cannot back down. Nevertheless, if food-shortage should become really serious, as seems likely, one cannot exclude the possibility of some wild blow in order to involve the country in "war conditions," when all excuses for privation could be made convincing to the masses. The card will only be played as a last resort, but it is Realpolitik to people who have forced themselves into a desperate plight. There is, however, no proof that Germany will not pull through till next autumn.'

indication of colonial restitution would not strengthen Germany for some time, and without a loan she would probably be incapable of developing a colony: so much at least has been admitted by one of the German propagandists, who has lately been here for the dual purpose. I am aware of all the objections to this line, which have been so ably and fairly stated, that I need not recapitulate them; but, if the objections continue to hold the field, the case for the acceleration of our rearmament programme, in view of the warnings that we have received, is greatly strengthened. For if we are going neither to restore nor to rearm more quickly, we shall be heading eventually for the 'disagreeable surprise' promised by Dr. Schacht (Annex A, No. 19), or, as one of Dr. Goebbels' henchmen puts it: 'if England will not be reasonable now, we will ask for more later.' The least that will happen will be a long period of strained relations such as existed before 1914. Not that I overrate the strong element of bluff and bully in Dr. Schacht. Annex A, No. 18, is a far better-founded warning. If we ponder it in the light of the world situation and of our own position, we shall—in the words of a recent report of the Principal Supply Officers—'view the position with great apprehension.' An observer in a special position estimated in 1934 the breathing space at 5–10 years, an estimate with which of course I have never agreed. To-day he only feels justified in saying that 'the boiler is becoming steadily overheated, and the need for a safety-valve more urgent.' Could we come nearer to bridging that time-lag of at least a year in our preparations as compared with those of Germany, we could be confident of not having either to fight at a disadvantage, or alternatively to accept the humiliation of a forced, because too tardy, concession. And if that gap could be bridged, we should have come as near as is possible in the present world to having ensured general peace, and thus to getting within view of that limitation of armaments which has never yet been practical politics. We shall surely not get that view without turning the corner, of which I spoke in paragraph 23; and there seems only one sure road round that corner. It is to be trusted that means to take it might be devised without over-great damage to our export trade.

27. I had already written the foregoing when I received a communication from an impartial and judicious source, resident in Central Europe after long sojourn in Germany and newly returned from an extensive tour in the Balkans. In only one point does this source differ from my chronicle. He says: 'The Austro-German truce was simply the fruit of, and condition for, the Italo-German rapprochement. It does *not* just mean a change in German tactics with the aim of getting control of Austria in another way. This is a false interpretation which seems to have gained wide currency abroad.' And he adds: 'Austrian independence now only means self-government, unless Germany and Italy fall out.' In other words, he takes a more serious view of an agreement which I have not minimised. I would only comment that the Austrian Secretary of State has commented at the end of the year that an Anglo-Italian Agreement 'would entirely change the position of the Austrian Government.' In every other respect the ensuing estimate contains such striking confirmation of the contents of this memorandum that I make no apology for quoting from it as yet another concordant source.

'The fear of war—arising from the stupendous military strength, resolution, recklessness and incalculability of the bellicose dictatorships—is universal in these parts (see the end of paragraph 13), and dominates all other considerations. The statement that England is resolved to regain the lead in European affairs rouses some hope, but *the general feeling is that only a great increase in her armed strength could enable her to do that, whereas the general impression is that the gap between British and*

799

German armed strength, far from being reduced, is lengthening daily.' (See conclusion of paragraph 25.) 'The lesser States are scuttling desperately for cover. They want to keep out of a new war or be on the winning side. The recent attitude of two States so closely linked by tradition to British policy as Portugal and Belgium is significant of the state of mind in Danubian and Balkan Europe. Austria and Hungary are apparently tied to Italy and Germany so long as these countries march together. The Little Entente countries seem at their wits' end. Everybody, in fact, is thinking about and fearing war, but nobody knows what war.' (Cf. paragraphs 22 and 25.) 'The situation is now at the mercy of either of two dictators, or of some incident which will so far provoke their vanity as to make them commit themselves beyond repair. The apprehension is of some unexpected incident that may suddenly produce hostilities. Schuschnigg, Kanya[23] and Ciano all feel that events are moving inevitably towards war, but even they no longer foresee where or how. The kaleidoscopic changes in the situation are too bewildering.' (Cf. Italo-German rapprochement and Italy's courtship of Yugoslavia, paragraph 9, coupled with Italy's contradictory championship of revision and Germany's still more contradictory attempt to slow it down. See middle of paragraph 13.) 'The German propaganda against Czechoslovakia is one of the most virulent and mendacious things I have seen, and that is saying a lot.' (I regret that even the regular German Foreign Office have stoked it up, without really believing in the accounts of Russian aerodromes, and still less in the bolshevisation of a humdrum *bourgeois* republic.) 'Roumania and Yugoslavia are much worried by fear of the sequel. In the latter country the Germans and Italians are working hand in glove to ensure that Yugoslavia shall not again engage herself to fight with England against Italy in the Mediterranean.' (Cf. paragraph 9.) 'They are both so anxious to gain the good graces of these two countries that they have disclaimed sympathy with Hungary's revisionist aims so far as *these two* countries are concerned —a significant limitation. This strongly suggests that Germany and Italy are going for an early war, and are going to the limit to ensure Roumanian and Yugoslav neutrality. These two are bewildered by German propaganda, by the constantly growing strength of the dictators and the consequent ease with which they impose their will on Europe. If France and England show no ability to stop the rot, a landslide of the lesser States towards the dictators seems inevitable. The great majority of the seventy million people living between the Danube and the Balkans would till recently have rallied to a real British lead for humanity and against warmakers. *But the traditional instincts to turn to tried friends in the moment of danger are losing their potency through the weakness of the friends and the unprecedented military strength of the potential adversaries.*' The substance of this statement is generally correct, though a shade too highly coloured, and it bears out my diagnosis that the situation is one that calls not for pessimism but for serious concern.

28. I therefore sum up the world situation in relation to our interests at the end of 1936 as follows.

(a) The danger signals are manifold and universal. They present themselves with increasing urgency.

(b) Japan's attitude is still sufficiently treacherous and speculative to make the quick strengthening of our Naval position in the Far East imperative.

(c) But the *storm-centre* has moved with gathering momentum to *Germany*, where all dispassionate observers report *the systematic training, physically, materially*

[23] Hungarian Minister for Foreign Affairs.

and spiritually, of the whole German nation, from childhood upward, for war on a scale never before seen.

(d) Into this vortex have been, or are being, drawn the dissatisfied nations and elements, notably the Japanese, the Italians, and the Spanish insurgents.

(e) Germany is bent on creating an international anti-Bolshevik front under her own leadership, with a view to its serving as a specific vehicle for ultimate expansion. Czechoslovakia is under threat of disintegration, and plans are going forward to bring the Danubian countries and the Balkans under complete German domination. These may be steps toward 'Room for Existence' in the East; but no Russo-German conflict is really desired or contemplated in wiser German circles—anyhow for a long while to come.

(f) This campaign, while retaining its essential characteristics, can at will be *turned in an important new direction—against England*, as the chief obstacle in the way of Germany having 'means to live.'

(g) The above has related mainly to Europe, but there has been another change to our detriment—the neutrality law in the U.S.A., rendering us more than ever dependent on our own supplies.

(h) Politically we are working (a) to ensure a friendly Italy and (b) for a Five Power Agreement, on the basis of settlements first in Western and then in Central Europe, whereby Germany and Russia would be kept apart by intermediate barriers of treaties. But (b) is unlikely on present form to materialise, at least with any degree of sincerity.

(i) Anyhow the spirit of treaty observance is lacking, not only in Germany, but among her associates. Treaties can, at the best, be but acts of faith, and cannot alone preserve peace.

(j) *For the time being at least the only effective remedy will be the capacity to use the only argument in which Germany believes—that is, Force.*

(k) Time is vital, and we have started late. Time is the material commodity the Foreign Office has to provide. *Our aim must be to stabilise the position till 1939.* On present form we cannot be at all sure of doing so.

(l) We must act and state our case in such a way as to retain American sympathy at all times.

(m) With this object, and in order to enable us to turn the corner of 1939, the possibility of the cession of a colony should not be ruled out, as part of a political settlement.

(n) The risk would also be diminished by the adoption of some of the economic measures suggested in paragraph 26.

(o) But, still more, we must visibly quicken our pace in rearmament, for our present preparations are based on the assumption of a date that may not be justified by events.

(p) Finally, having taken account of all these facts, I would make a recommendation. We should act as suggested under (o), and, moreover, part with none of our leverage over Germany, economic, financial or colonial, without a full, tested and reliable return. On the other hand we should be careful to avoid any harsh action toward the German people that might rally the nation to a united front under the leaders of the Nazi régime. By this threefold recipe alone can moderates and moderation have any chance in Germany. If we firmly follow this threefold course, they may have a chance.